have the same inheritance rights as other children. The ruling was believed to be the first on the controversial issue by any state supreme court.

Also in January 2002, Marshall addressed the Massachusetts Bar Association Conference, where she called for "a revolution in the administration of justice" stating that the court system needed to improve its management system as well as its staffing and budget controls. In March
6
2002, her discussion of the court system's problems were amplified in a 52-page report that was published by a blue-ribbon panel appointed by Marshall.

THE GOVERNMENT [THAT THE FRAMERS OF THE CONSTITUTION] DEVISED REQUIRED SEVERAL AMENDMENTS, A CIVIL WAR, AND MOMENTOUS SOCIAL TRANSFORMATION TO ATTAIN THE SYSTEM OF CONSTITUTIONAL GOVERNMENT, AND ITS RESPECT FOR THE INDIVIDUAL FREEDOMS AND HUMAN RIGHTS, THAT WE HOLD AS FUNDAMENTAL TODAY.
THURGOOD MARSHALL

FURTHER READINGS

Teicher, Stacy A. 2000." A Subtle Revolution as Women Lead the Bench." *Christian Science Monitor* (January 5).

Lavoie, Denise. 2002. "Court Rules on Posthumous Conception." *Associated Press* (January 2)

MARSHALL PLAN

After WORLD WAR II, Europe was devastated and urgently needed an organized plan for reconstruction and economic and technical aid. The Marshall Plan was initiated in 1947 to meet this need.

The originator of the plan, U.S. Secretary of State George C. Marshall, introduced it in a speech at Harvard University on June 5, 1947. He pointed out two basic reasons for providing aid to Europe: the United States sought the reestablishment of the European countries as independent nations capable of conducting valuable trade with the United States; and the threat of a Communist takeover was more prevalent in countries that were suffering economic depression.

In 1947 a preliminary conference to discuss the terms of the program convened in Paris. The Soviet Union was invited to attend but subsequently withdrew from the program, as did other Soviet countries.

Sixteen European countries eventually participated, and, in July 1947, the Committee for European Economic Cooperation was established to allow representatives from member countries to draft a report that listed their requirements for food, supplies, and technical assistance for a four-year period.

The Committee for European Economic Cooperation subsequently became the Organization of European Economic Cooperation, an expanded and permanent organization that was responsible for submitting petitions for aid. In 1948, Congress passed the Economic Cooperation Act (62 Stat. 137), establishing funds for the Marshall Plan to be administered under the Economic Cooperation Administration, which was directed by Paul G. Hoffman.

Between 1948 and 1952, the sixteen-member countries received more than $13 billion dollars in aid under the Marshall Plan. The plan was generally regarded as a success that led to industrial and agricultural production, while stifling the Communist movement. The plan was not without its critics, however, and many Europeans believed the COLD WAR hostilities between the Soviet nations and the free world were aggravated by it.

♦ MARSHALL, THURGOOD 7

Thurgood Marshall, the first African American to serve on the U.S. Supreme Court, saw law as a catalyst for social change. For nearly 60 years, as both a lawyer and a jurist, Marshall worked to dismantle the system of SEGREGATION and improve the legal and social position of minorities.

Marshall was born July 2, 1908, in Baltimore, the son of a Pullman porter and a schoolteacher. He was a graduate of Lincoln University, a small, all-black college in Pennsylvania, and Howard University Law School in Washington, D.C. At Howard, Marshall excelled under the guidance of Vice Dean CHARLES HAMILTON HOUSTON, the first African American to win a case before the U.S. Supreme Court. Houston encouraged his students to become not just lawyers but "social engineers" who could use the legal system to improve society. Marshall graduated first in his law class in 1933.

Marshall's attendance at predominantly black Howard University illustrates the barriers faced by African Americans during the early twentieth century. Although Marshall wished to attend law school at the University of Maryland (a public institution in his home town of Baltimore), he was prohibited by law from doing so because of his race. This injustice helped set Marshall on a course of opposing all forms of official segregation that denied equal opportunities to African Americans.

After law school, Marshall set up a practice in Baltimore, representing indigent clients in civil rights cases. In 1936, his mentor Houston offered him a position with the National Association for the Advancement of Colored People (NAACP),

Thurgood Marshall.
LIBRARY OF CONGRESS

and in 1940, Marshall became director of the NAACP LEGAL DEFENSE AND EDUCATIONAL FUND, a position he held until 1961. Determined to eliminate segregation, Marshall coordinated a nationwide campaign to integrate higher education. He filed several successful lawsuits against public graduate and professional schools that refused to accept African-American students. These suits paved the way for similar cases at the high school and elementary school levels. Marshall also journeyed throughout the deep South, traveling fifty thousand miles a year to fight JIM CROW LAWS (a series of laws that provided for racial segregation in the South) and to represent criminal defendants.

Marshall argued 32 cases before the U.S. Supreme Court and won 29 of them. No doubt his most famous and far-reaching triumph before the High Court was BROWN V. BOARD OF EDUCATION OF TOPEKA, KANSAS, 347 U.S. 483, 74 S. Ct. 686, 98 L. Ed. 873 (1954). In that case, the father of African-American student Linda Brown sued the school board of Topeka, Kansas, over its segregation policy. Brown was required by law to attend an all African-American school several blocks from her home even though an all white public school was located in her own neighborhood. Under Kansas law, cities of more than 15,000 people, such as Topeka, could choose to operate segregated schools. Marshall argued that these segregated schools, defended by officials as "separate but equal," were unconstitutional.

8 The SEPARATE-BUT-EQUAL doctrine originated in PLESSY V. FERGUSON, 163 U.S. 537, 16 S. Ct. 1138, 41 L. Ed. 256 (1896), a case allowing segregated public accommodations for whites and blacks. In a plainspoken argument, Marshall dismissed as fallacy the notion that segregated schools offered the same educational experiences to black and white students. Sociological and psychological studies demonstrated that black children were in fact harmed by the policy of school segregation. The students' self-esteem was damaged and their future diminished when they were forced to accept inadequate facilities, equipment, and educational opportunities. Marshall argued that the only purpose segregation served was to perpetuate the myth of African-Americans' inferiority. A unanimous Court agreed and struck down the separate-but-equal doctrine, a

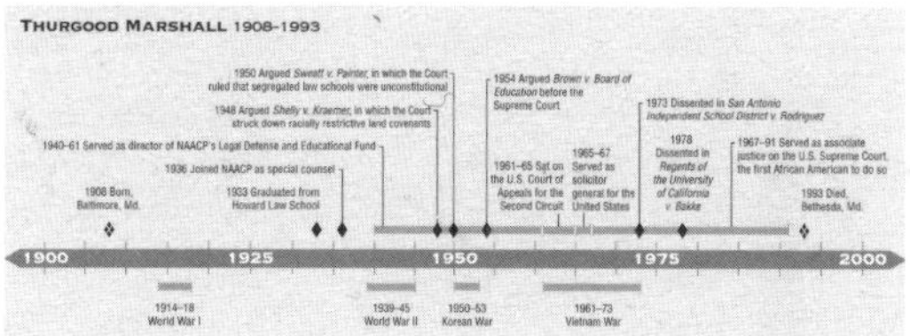

THURGOOD MARSHALL 1908–1993
1908 Born, Baltimore, Md.
1933 Graduated from Howard Law School
1936 Joined NAACP as special counsel
1940–61 Served as director of NAACP's Legal Defense and Educational Fund
1948 Argued Shelly v. Kraemer, in which the Court struck down racially restrictive land covenants
1950 Argued Sweatt v. Painter, in which the Court ruled that segregated law schools were unconstitutional
1954 Argued Brown v. Board of Education before the Supreme Court
1961–65 Sat on the U.S. Court of Appeals for the Second Circuit
1965–67 Served as solicitor general for the United States
1973 Dissented in San Antonio Independent School District v. Rodriguez
1978 Dissented in Regents of the University of California v. Bakke
1967–91 Served as associate justice on the U.S. Supreme Court, the first African American to do so
1993 Died, Bethesda, Md.
1900
1925
1950
1975
2000
1914–18 World War I
1939–45 World War II
1950–53 Korean War
1961–73 Vietnam War

THE FUTURE OF SOCIAL SECURITY

9 The payment of OLD-AGE, SURVIVORS, AND DISABILITY INSURANCE (OASDI) benefits has been a cornerstone of U.S. social welfare policy since the establishment of the SOCIAL SECURITY ADMINISTRATION in 1935. At the same time, the long-term financial stability of OASDI has been a constant worry. In the early years of the twenty-first century, concerns about Social Security mounted as policy makers assessed the impact of the retirement of the "Baby Boom" generation. Many younger people raised the issue of "generation equity." They express doubt that Social Security benefits will be available when they retire, and anger that they will be forced to pay, through payroll taxes, for the baby boomers' retirement benefits.

IN FOCUS

Reform of the Social Security system has always been a political hot potato. Retirees and those approaching retirement form a strong LOBBYING force, and they zealously protect their benefits. Employers and employees are equally vocal in their opposition to higher payroll taxes to fund OASDI. Thus, changes in Social Security required bipartisan support, which materialized in the face of an impending Social Security crisis. The 1982–83 National Commission on Social Security Reform successfully secured from Congress the short-term financing of OASDI. As a result, Congress passed a series of laws meant to accumulate surpluses as a hedge against future burdens. The Social Security surplus is the amount by which revenue from the federal payroll tax exceeds the amount of Social Security benefits paid out.

Shortly after these new laws went into effect, Social Security began running a surplus. Surplus Social Security revenue can be used to fund other government programs and to help retire the national debt. During the favorable economic climate of the late 1990s, Congress began to use the surplus to pay down the federal debt, hoping to better position the government to meet its obligations to future retirees. And, in 2000, the federal government generated enough revenue so that the entire Social Security surplus was available for paying off debt.

The state of Social Security became a major campaign issue in the 2000 elections, with both Republicans and Democrats attempting to appear as though they were guardians of Social Security assets. Candidates from both parties promised to create a "lockbox," meaning that the Social Security surplus would be spent entirely on debt retirement. With the advent of fiscally lean years in the early 2000s, the lockbox approach was largely disregarded by politicians who advanced other ideas about what to do with Social Security surpluses. These ideas included using the surplus to help offset decreases in revenues brought about by tax cuts and using the surplus to fund new or expanded spending initiatives.

Analysts argue that the real issue often is clouded. It is not how to spend the surplus now, but how to maintain the long-term solvency of the Social Security trust fund. Planners estimate that the income from the trust fund will exceed expenses each year until 2020. The trust fund balances will then start to decline as investments are redeemed to meet the increased expenses from a swelling retired workforce. Although it is estimated that 75 percent of the costs would continue to be met from current payroll and income taxes, in the absence of any changes, full benefits could not be paid beginning in 2030.

In its 1996 report, the Social Security Administration's Advisory Council looked at various long-term financing options for OASDI. The council could not reach consensus on a specific long-term plan, but it did suggest several types of financing that represent a marked departure from previous efforts to fund Social Security. The council noted that past efforts have generally featured cutting benefits and raising tax rates on a "pay-as-you-go" basis. The council agreed that this approach must be changed and offered three ways of restoring financial solvency.

One approach, called Maintenance of Benefits (MB), calls for an increase in income taxes on OASDI benefits, a redirection of some revenue from other trust funds, and, most importantly, the adoption of a plan allowing the federal government to invest a portion of the trust fund assets directly in common stocks. Rates of returns on stocks have historically exceeded those on federal government bonds, where all Social Security

A person who continues to work past the retirement age may lose some benefits because Social Security is designed to replace lost earnings. If earnings from employment do not exceed the amount specified by law, the person receives the full benefits. If earnings are greater than that amount, one dollar of benefit is withheld for every two dollars in wages earned above the exempt amount. Once a person reaches age 70, however, he does not have to report earnings to the SSA, and the benefit is not reduced.

Survivors' Benefits Survivors' benefits are paid to family members when a worker dies. Survivors can receive benefits if the deceased worker was employed and contributed to Social

momentous victory for Marshall, affecting public schools in twenty-one states.

Marshall was appointed to the U.S. Court of Appeals for the Second Circuit in 1961, and served there until 1965 when he was named SOLICITOR GENERAL for the United States. He was appointed to the U.S. Supreme Court in 1967 by President LYNDON B. JOHNSON and served as an associate justice for 24 years.

While on the Court, Marshall was known more for his impassioned dissents than for his majority opinions. In particular, as a staunch opponent of CAPITAL PUNISHMENT, he regularly voiced his disagreement with the majority in death penalty cases. He was also a firm backer of AFFIRMATIVE ACTION and contributed one of his most famous dissents in REGENTS OF THE UNIVERSITY OF CALIFORNIA V. BAKKE, 438 U.S. 265, 98 S. Ct. 2733, 57 L. Ed. 2d 750 (1978). In that case, Marshall criticized the high court's ruling that a public medical school's policy of reserving 16 of 100 spots for minority students was unconstitutional. Marshall also dissented in *San Antonio Independent School District v. Rodriguez*, 411 U.S. 1, 93 S. Ct. 1278, 36 L. Ed. 2d 16 (1973), disagreeing with the majority view that a Texas property tax system used to fund public education was acceptable, even though it allowed wealthier districts to provide a better school system for students in those districts than less wealthy districts could provide. Marshall objected strongly to the property tax arrangement, claiming that it deprived poor children of an equal education.

Marshall wrote the majority opinion in *Amalgamated Food Employees Union v. Logan Valley Plaza*, 391 U.S. 308, 88 S. Ct. 1601, 20 L. Ed. 2d 603 (1968), in which the Court declared that a shopping center was a public forum from which picketers could not be barred by private owners.

Marshall retired from the Court in 1991, but continued his criticism of government policies that were detrimental to African Americans or other disenfranchised groups.

Marshall died on January 24, 1993, in Bethesda, Maryland. Upon Marshall's death, nearly 20,000 mourners filed by his casket during the 12 hours it lay in state in the Great Hall of the U.S. Supreme Court.

FURTHER READINGS

Bland, Randall Walton. 2001. *Justice Thurgood Marshall: Crusader for Liberalism: His Judicial Biography (1908–1993)*. Bethesda, Md.: Academica Press.

Clemon, U.W., and Bryan K. Fair. 2003. "Lawyers, Civil Disobedience, and Equality in the Twenty-First Century: Lessons from Two American Heroes. *Alabama Law Review*, 54 (spring): 959–83.

Kennedy, Randall. 1999. "Thurgood's Coming": Long Before He Became the Nation's First Black Supreme Court Justice, Thurgood Marshall Was a Lawyer on the Razor's Edge of American Social Struggle. *American Lawyer* 21 (December): 94.

Maloy, Richard H.W. 1999. "Thurgood Marshall and the Holy Grail—the Due Process Jurisprudence of a Consummate Jurist." *Pepperdine Law Review* 26 (January): 289–352.

Tushnet, Mark V. 1997. *Making Constitutional Law: Thurgood Marshall and the Supreme Court, 1961–1991*. New York: Oxford Univ. Press.

Williams, Juan. *Thurgood Marshall: American Revolutionary*. 2000. New York: Times Books.

CROSS-REFERENCES 10

Civil Rights Movement; Integration; School Desegregation.

MARTIAL LAW

The exercise of government and control by military authorities over the civilian population of a designated territory.

Martial law is an extreme and rare measure used to control society during war or periods of civil unrest or chaos. According to the Supreme Court, the term *martial law* carries no precise meaning (*Duncan v. Kahanamoku*, 327 U.S. 304, 11
66 S. Ct. 606, 90 L. Ed. 688 [1946]). However, most declarations of martial law have some common features. Generally, the institution of martial law contemplates some use of military force. To a varying extent, depending on the martial law order, government military personnel have the authority to make and enforce civil and criminal laws. Certain civil liberties may be suspended, such as the right to be free from unreasonable SEARCHES AND SEIZURES, FREEDOM OF ASSOCIATION, and freedom of movement. And the writ of HABEAS CORPUS may be suspended (this writ allows persons who are unlawfully imprisoned to gain freedom through a court proceeding).

In the United States, martial law has been instituted on the national level only once, during the Civil War, and on a regional level only once, during WORLD WAR II. Otherwise, it has been limited to the states. Uprisings, political protests, labor strikes, and riots have, at various times, caused several state governors to declare some measure of martial law.

Martial law on the national level may be declared by Congress or the president. Under

WEST'S ENCYCLOPEDIA
of
AMERICAN LAW

2ND EDITION

WEST'S ENCYCLOPEDIA of AMERICAN LAW

2ND EDITION

VOLUME 3

COM TO DOR

THOMSON
★
™
GALE

Detroit • San Diego • San Francisco • New Haven, Conn. • Waterville, Maine • London • Munich

West's Encyclopedia of American Law, 2nd Edition

Project Editors
Jeffrey Lehman
Shirelle Phelps

Editorial
Andrew C. Claps, Pamela A. Dear, Jason M. Everett, Lynn U. Koch, John F. McCoy, Jeffrey Wilson, Jennifer M. York, Ralph Zerbonia

Research
Barbara McNeil

Editorial Support Services
Ryan Cartmill, Mark Hefner, Sue Petrus

Data Capture
Katrina Coach, Nikita Greene, Beverly Jendrowski, Elizabeth Pilette, Beth Richardson

Indexing Services
Lynne Maday

Permissions
Margaret A. Chamberlain

Imaging and Multimedia
Dean Dauphinais, Leitha Etheridge-Sims, Mary Grimes, Lezlie Light, Dan Newell, David G. Oblender, Chris O'Bryan

Product Design
Cynthia Baldwin, Kate Scheible

Composition and Electronic Capture
Evi Seoud, Mary Beth Trimper

Manufacturing
Rhonda Williams

© 2005 Thomson Gale, a part of The Thomson Corporation.

Thomson and Star Logo are trademarks and Gale is a registered trademark used herein under license.

For more information, contact
The Gale Group, Inc.
27500 Drake Rd.
Farmington Hills, MI 48331-3535
Or you can visit our Internet site at
http://www.gale.com

This publication is a creative work fully protected by all applicable copyright laws, as well as by misappropriation, trade secret, unfair condition, and other applicable laws. The authors and editors of this work have added value to the underlying factual material herein through one or more of the following: coordination, expression, arrangement, and classification of the information.

For permission to use material from this product, submit your request via Web at http://www.gale-edit.com/permission or you may download our Permissions Request form and submit your request by fax of mail to:

Permissions Department
The Gale Group, Inc.
27500 Drake Rd.
Farmington Hills, MI 48331-3535
Permissions Hotline:
248-699-8006 or 800-877-4253, ext. 8006
Fax: 248-699-8074 or 800-762-4058

Inside cover photograph reproduced by permission of the Library of Congress (Thurgood Marshall).

Since this page cannot legibly accommodate all copyright notices, the acknowledgments constitute an extension of the copyright notice.

While every effort has been made to ensure the reliability of the information presented in this publication, The Gale Group, Inc. does not guarantee the accuracy of the data contained herein. The Gale Group, Inc. accepts no payment for listing; and inclusion in the publication of any organization, agency, institution, publication service, or individual does not imply endorsement of the editors or publisher. Errors brought to the attention of the publisher and verified to the satisfaction of the publisher will be corrected in future editions.

Library of Congress Cataloging-in-Publication Data

West's encyclopedia of American law / Jeffrey Lehman, editor, Shirelle Phelps, editor.— 2nd ed.
  p. cm.
  Includes bibliographical references and index.
  ISBN 0-7876-6367-0 (hardcover set : alk. paper)
  1. Law—United States—Encyclopedias. 2. Law—United States—Popular works. I. Lehman, Jeffrey. II. Phelps, Shirelle.
  KF154.W47 2004
  349.73'03—dc22   2004004918

ISBN 0-7876-6367-0 (set), ISBN 0-7876-6368-9 (vol. 1), ISBN 0-7876-6369-7 (vol. 2), ISBN 0-7876-6370-0 (vol. 3), ISBN 0-7876-6371-9 (vol. 4), ISBN 0-7876-6372-7 (vol. 5), ISBN 0-7876-6373-5 (vol. 6), ISBN 0-7876-6374-3 (vol. 7), ISBN 0-7876-6375-1 (vol. 8), ISBN 0-7876-6376-X (vol. 9), ISBN 0-7876-6377-8 (vol. 10), ISBN 0-7876-6378-6 (vol. 11), ISBN 0-7876-6379-4 (vol. 12), ISBN 0-7876-9420-7 (vol. 13)

This title is also available as an e-book. ISBN 0-7876-9373-1 (set)
Contact your Gale sales representative for ordering information.

Printed in the United States of America
10 9 8 7 6 5 4 3 2

DEDICATION

West's Encyclopedia of American Law (WEAL) is dedicated to librarians and library patrons throughout the United States and beyond. Your interest in the American legal system helps to expand and fuel the framework of our Republic.

CONTENTS

The U.S. legal system is admired around the world for the freedoms it allows the individual and the fairness with which it attempts to treat all persons. On the surface, it may seem simple, yet those who have delved into it know that this system of federal and state constitutions, statutes, regulations, and common-law decisions is elaborate and complex. It derives from the English common law, but includes principles older than England, along with some principles from other lands. The U.S. legal system, like many others, has a language all its own, but too often it is an unfamiliar language: many concepts are still phrased in Latin. The second edition of *West's Encyclopedia of American Law (WEAL)* explains legal terms and concepts in everyday language, however. It covers a wide variety of persons, entities, and events that have shaped the U.S. legal system and influenced public perceptions of it.

MAIN FEATURES OF THIS SET

Entries

This encyclopedia contains nearly 5,000 entries devoted to terms, concepts, events, movements, cases, and persons significant to U.S. law. Entries on legal terms contain a definition of the term, followed by explanatory text if necessary. Entries are arranged alphabetically in standard encyclopedia format for ease of use. A wide variety of additional features, listed later in this preface, provide interesting background and supplemental information.

Definitions Every entry on a legal term is followed by a definition, which appears at the beginning of the entry and is italicized. The Dictionary and Indexes volume includes a glossary containing all the definitions from *WEAL*.

Further Readings To facilitate further research, a list of Further Readings is included at the end of a majority of the main entries.

Cross-References *WEAL* provides two types of cross-references, within and following entries. Within the entries, terms are set in small capital letters—for example, LIEN—to indicate that they have their own entry in the encyclopedia. At the end of the entries, related entries the reader may wish to explore are listed alphabetically by title.

Blind cross-reference entries are also included to direct the user to other entries throughout the set.

In Focus Essays

In Focus essays accompany related entries and provide additional facts, details, and arguments on particularly interesting, important, or controversial issues raised by those entries. The subjects covered include hotly contested issues, such as abortion, capital punishment, and gay rights; detailed processes, such as the Food and Drug Administration's approval process for new drugs; and important historical or social issues, such as debates over the formation of the U.S. Constitution.

Sidebars

Sidebars provide brief highlights of some interesting facet of accompanying entries. They complement regular entries and In Focus essays by adding informative details. Sidebar topics include the Million Man March and the branches of the U.S. armed services. Sidebars appear at the top of a text page and are set in a box.

Biographies

WEAL profiles a wide variety of interesting and influential people—including lawyers, judges, government and civic leaders, and historical and modern figures—who have played a part in creating or shaping U.S. law. Each biography includes a timeline, which shows important moments in the subject's life as well as important historical events of the period. Biographies appear alphabetically by the subject's last name.

ADDITIONAL FEATURES OF THIS SET

Enhancements Throughout *WEAL*, readers will find a broad array of photographs, charts, graphs, manuscripts, legal forms, and other visual aids enhancing the ideas presented in the text.

Indexes *WEAL* features a cases index and a cumulative index in a separate volume.

Appendixes

Three appendix volumes are included with *WEAL*, containing hundreds of pages of docu-

ments, laws, manuscripts, and forms fundamental to and characteristic of U.S. law.

Milestone Cases in the Law

A special Appendix volume entitled Milestones in the Law, allows readers to take a close look at landmark cases in U.S. law. Readers can explore the reasoning of the judges and the arguments of the attorneys that produced major decisions on important legal and social issues. Included in each Milestone are the opinions of the lower courts; the briefs presented by the parties to the U.S. Supreme Court; and the decision of the Supreme Court, including the majority opinion and all concurring and dissenting opinions for each case.

Primary Documents

There is also an Appendix volume containing more than 60 primary documents, such as the English Bill of Rights, Martin Luther King Jr.'s Letter from Brimingham Jail, and several presidential speeches.

Citations

Wherever possible, *WEAL* entries include citations for cases and statutes mentioned in the text. These allow readers wishing to do additional research to find the opinions and statutes cited. Two sample citations, with explanations of common citation terms, can be seen below and opposite.

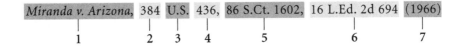

1. *Case title.* The title of the case is set in i and indicates the names of the parties. The suit in this sample citation was between Ernesto A. Miranda and the state of Arizona.
2. *Reporter volume number.* The number preceding the reporter name indicates the reporter volume containing the case. (The volume number appears on the spine of the reporter, along with the reporter name).
3. *Reporter name.* The reporter name is abbreviated. The suit in the sample citation is from the reporter, or series of books, called *U.S. Reports,* which contains cases from the U.S. Supreme Court. (Numerous reporters publish cases from the federal and state courts.)

4. *Reporter page.* The number following the reporter name indicates the reporter page on which the case begins.
5. *Additional reporter page.* Many cases may be found in more than one reporter. The suit in the sample citation also appears in volume 86 of the *Supreme Court Reporter,* beginning on page 1602.
6. *Additional reporter citation.* The suit in the sample citation is also reported in volume 16 of the *Lawyer's Edition,* second series, beginning on page 694.
7. *Year of decision.* The year the court issued its decision in the case appears in parentheses at the end of the cite.

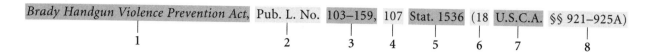

Brady Handgun Violence Prevention Act, Pub. L. No. 103–159, 107 Stat. 1536 (18 U.S.C.A. §§ 921–925A)

1   2   3 4 5 6 7 8

1. *Statute title.*
2. *Public law number.* In the sample citation, the number 103 indicates this law was passed by the 103d Congress, and the number 159 indicates it was the 159th law passed by that Congress.
3. *Reporter volume number.* The number preceding the reporter abbreviation indicates the reporter volume containing the statute.
4. *Reporter name.* The reporter name is abbreviated. The statute in the sample citation is from *Statutes at Large.*
5. *Reporter page.* The number following the reporter abbreviation indicates the reporter page on which the statute begins.

6. *Title number.* Federal laws are divided into major sections with specific titles. The number preceding a reference to the U.S. Code stands for the section called Crimes and Criminal Procedure.
7. *Additional reporter.* The statute in the sample citation may also be found in the *U.S. Code Annotated.*
8. *Section numbers.* The section numbers following a reference to the *U.S. Code Annotated* indicate where the statute appears in that reporter.

CONTRIBUTORS

Editorial Reviewers
Matthew C. Cordon
Frederick K. Grittner
Stephanie Schmitt
Linda Tashbook
M. Uri Toch

Contributing Authors
James Cahoy
Matthew C. Cordon
Richard J. Cretan
Mark Engsberg
Frederick K. Grittner
Lauri R. Harding
David R. Johnstone
Theresa J. Lippert
Frances T. Lynch
George A. Milite
Melodie Monahan
Kelle Sisung
Scott D. Slick

Contributors to Previous Edition
Richard Abowitz
Paul Bard
Joanne Bergum
Michael Bernard
Gregory A. Borchard
Susan Buie

Terry Carter
Sally Chatelaine
Joanne Smestad Claussen
Richard Cretan
Lynne Crist
Paul D. Daggett
Susan L. Dalhed
Lisa M. DelFiacco
Suzanne Paul Dell'Oro
Dan DeVoe
Joanne Engelking
Sharon Fischlowitz
Jonathan Flanders
Lisa Florey
Robert A. Frame
John E. Gisselquist
Russell L. Gray III
Frederick K. Grittner
Victoria L. Handler
Heidi L. Headlee
James Heidberg
Clifford P. Hooker
Marianne Ashley Jerpbak
Andrew Kass
Margaret Anderson Kelliher
Christopher J. Kennedy
Anne E. Kevlin
Ann T. Laughlin
Laura Ledsworth-Wang
Linda Lincoln

Gregory Luce
David Luiken
Jennifer Marsh
Sandra M. Olson
Anne Larsen Olstad
William Ostrem
Lauren Pacelli
Randolph C. Park
Gary Peter
Michele A. Potts
Reinhard Priester
Christy Rain
Brian Roberts
Debra J. Rosenthal
Mary Lahr Schier
Mary Scarbrough
Theresa L. Schulz
John Scobey
James Slavicek
Scott D. Slick
David Strom
Wendy Tien
Douglas Tueting
Richard F. Tyson
Christine Ver Ploeg
George E. Warner
Anne Welsbacher
Eric P. Wind
Lindy T. Yokanovich

CO-MAKER

One who becomes obligated, an obligor, under a negotiable instrument—such as a check or promissory note—by signing his or her name along with the name of the original obligor, thereby promising to pay on it in full.

A co-maker is a type of accommodation party, who is someone who has signed a COMMERCIAL PAPER to aid someone wishing to raise money on it. An accommodation party lends his or her name to another person and makes a promise to pay the bill or note when it is due if the other person defaults.

COMBINATION

In CRIMINAL LAW, an agreement between two or more people to act jointly for an unlawful purpose; a conspiracy. In patent law, the joining together of several separate inventions to produce a new invention.

An illegal combination in restraint of trade, defined under the SHERMAN ANTI-TRUST ACT, is one in which the conspirators agree expressly or impliedly to use devices such as price-fixing agreements to eliminate competition in a certain locality, e.g., when a group of furniture manufacturers refuse to deliver goods to stores that sell their goods for under a certain price.

In patent law a combination is distinguishable from an aggregation in that it is a joint operation of elements that produces a new result as opposed to a mere grouping together of old elements. This is important in determining whether or not something is patentable, since no valid patent can extend to an aggregation.

COMBINATION IN RESTRAINT OF TRADE

An illegal compact between two or more persons to unjustly restrict competition and monopolize commerce in goods or services by controlling their production, distribution, and price or through other unlawful means.

Such combinations—whether in the form of a contract, holding company, or other association—are prohibited by the provisions of the SHERMAN ANTI-TRUST ACT and other antitrust acts.

CROSS-REFERENCES

Monopoly.

COMITY

Courtesy; respect; a disposition to perform some official act out of goodwill and tradition rather than obligation or law. The acceptance or ADOPTION of decisions or laws by a court of another jurisdiction, either foreign or domestic, based on public policy rather than legal mandate.

In comity, an act is performed to promote uniformity, limit litigation, and, most important, to show courtesy and respect for other court decisions. It is not to be confused with FULL FAITH AND CREDIT, the constitutional pro-

Cargo ships docked in Newark, New Jersey. Commerce includes the transport of goods by sea.
AP/WIDE WORLD PHOTOS

vision that various states within the United States must recognize the laws, acts, and decisions of sister states.

Comity of nations is a recognition of fundamental legal concepts that nations share. It stems from mutual convenience as well as respect and is essential to the success of international relations. This body of rules does not form part of INTERNATIONAL LAW; however, it is important for public policy reasons.

Judicial comity is the granting of reciprocity to decisions or laws by one state or jurisdiction to another. Since it is based upon respect and deference rather than strict legal principles, it does not require that any state or jurisdiction adopt a law or decision by another state or jurisdiction that is in contradiction, or repugnant, to its own law.

Comity of states is the voluntary acceptance by courts of one state of the decision of a sister state on a similar issue or question.

COMMERCE

The exchange of goods, products, or any type of PERSONAL PROPERTY. Trade and traffic carried on between different peoples or states and its inhabitants, including not only the purchase, sale, and exchange of commodities but also the instrumentalities, agencies, and means by which business is accomplished. The transportation of persons and goods, by air, land, and sea. The exchange of merchandise on a large scale between different places or communities.

Although the terms *commerce* and *trade* are often used interchangeably, *commerce* refers to large-scale business activity, while *trade* describes commercial traffic within a state or a community.

COMMERCE CLAUSE

The provision of the U.S. Constitution that gives Congress exclusive power over trade activities among the states and with foreign countries and Indian tribes.

Article 1, Section 8, Clause 3, of the Constitution empowers Congress "to regulate Commerce with foreign Nations, and among several States, and with the Indian Tribes." The term *commerce* as used in the Constitution means business or commercial exchanges in any and all of its forms between citizens of different states, including purely social communications between citizens of different states by telegraph, telephone, or radio, and the mere passage of persons from one state to another for either business or pleasure.

Intrastate, or domestic, commerce is trade that occurs solely within the geographic borders of one state. As it does not move across state lines, intrastate commerce is subject to the exclusive control of the state.

Interstate commerce, or commerce among the several states, is the free exchange of commodities between citizens of different states across state lines. Commerce with foreign nations occurs between citizens of the United States and citizens or subjects of foreign governments and, either immediately or at some stage of its progress, is extraterritorial. Commerce with Indian tribes refers to traffic or commercial exchanges involving both the United States and American Indians.

The Commerce Clause was designed to eliminate an intense rivalry between the groups of those states that had tremendous commercial advantage as a result of their proximity to a major harbor, and those states that were not near a harbor. That disparity was the source of constant economic battles among the states. The exercise by Congress of its regulatory power has increased steadily with the growth and expansion of industry and means of transportation.

Power to Regulate

The Commerce Clause authorizes Congress to regulate commerce in order to ensure that the flow of interstate commerce is free from local restraints imposed by various states. When Congress deems an aspect of interstate commerce to be in need of supervision, it will enact legislation that must have some real and rational relation to the subject of regulation. Congress may constitutionally provide for the point at which subjects of interstate commerce become subjects of state law and, therefore, state regulation.

Although the U.S. Constitution places some limits on state power, the states enjoy guaranteed rights by virtue of their reserved powers pursuant to the TENTH AMENDMENT. A state has the inherent and reserved right to regulate its domestic commerce. However, that right must be exercised in a manner that does not interfere with, or place a burden on, interstate commerce, or else Congress may regulate that area of domestic commerce in order to protect interstate commerce from the unreasonable burden. Although a state may not directly regulate, prohibit, or burden interstate or foreign commerce, it may incidentally and indirectly affect it by a bona fide, legitimate, and reasonable exercise of its POLICE POWERS. States are powerless to regulate commerce with Indian tribes.

Although Congress has the exclusive power to regulate foreign and interstate commerce, the presence or absence of congressional action determines whether a state may act in a particular field. The nature of the subject of commerce must be examined in order to decide whether Congress has exclusive control over it. If the subject is national in character and importance, thereby requiring uniform regulation, the power of Congress to regulate it is plenary, or exclusive.

It is for the courts to decide the national or local character of the subject of regulation, by BALANCING the national interest against the STATE INTEREST in the subject. If the state interest is slight compared with the national interest, the courts will declare the state statute unconstitutional as an unreasonable burden on interstate commerce.

The U.S. Supreme Court, in the case of *Southern Pacific Co. v. Arizona,* 325 U.S. 761, 65 S. Ct. 1515, 89 L. Ed. 1915 (1945), held that an Arizona statute that prohibited railroads within the state from having more than 70 cars in a freight train, or 14 cars in a passenger train, was unconstitutional. The purpose of the legislation, deemed a safety measure, was to minimize accidents by reducing the lengths of trains passing through the state. Practically speaking, however, the statute created an unreasonable burden on interstate commerce, as trains entering and leaving the state had to stop at the borders to break

up a 100-car freight train into two trains and to put on additional crews, thus increasing their operating costs. The Court held that the means used to achieve safety was unrealistic and that the increase in the number of trains and train operators actually enhanced the likelihood of accidents. It balanced the national interest in the free flow of interstate commerce by a national railway system, against the state interest of a dubious safety measure. It decided that the value of the operation of a uniform, efficient railway system significantly outweighed that of a state law that has minimal effect.

However, where there is an obvious compelling state interest to protect, state regulations are constitutional. Restrictions on the width and weight of trucks passing through a state on its highways are valid, because the state, pursuant to its police power, has a legitimate interest in protecting its roads.

Where the subject is one in which Congress or the state may act, a state may legislate unless Congress does so. Thereafter, a valid federal regulation of the subject supersedes conflicting state legislative enactments and decisions and actions of state judicial or administrative bodies.

If Congress has clearly demonstrated its intent to regulate the entire field, then the state is powerless to enact subsequent legislation even if no conflict exists between state and federal law. This type of congressional action is known as federal PREEMPTION of the field. Extensive federal regulation in a particular area does not necessarily result in federal preemption of the field. In determining whether a state may regulate a given field, a court evaluates the purpose of the federal regulations and the obligations imposed, the history of state regulation in the field, and the LEGISLATIVE HISTORY of the state statute. If Congress has not preempted the field, then state law is valid, provided that it is consistent with, or supplements, the federal law.

State health, sanitary, and quarantine laws that interfere with foreign and interstate commerce no more than is necessary in the proper exercise of the state's police power are also valid as long as they do not conflict with federal regulations on the subject. Such laws must have some real relation to the objects named in them, in order to be upheld as valid exercises of the police power of the state. A state may not go beyond what is essential for self-protection by interfering with interstate transportation into or through its territory.

A state may not burden interstate commerce by discriminating against it or persons engaged in it or the citizens or property originating in another state. However, the regulation of interstate commerce need not be uniform throughout the United States. Congress may devise a national policy with due regard for varying and fluctuating interests of different regions.

Acts Constituting Commerce

Whether any transaction constitutes interstate or intrastate commerce depends on the essential character of what is done and the surrounding circumstances. The courts take a commonsense approach in examining the established course of business in order to distinguish where interstate commerce ends and local commerce begins. If activities that are intrastate in character have such a substantial effect on interstate commerce that their control is essential to protect commerce from being burdened, Congress may not be denied the power to exercise that control.

In 1995, for the first time in nearly 60 years, the U.S. Supreme Court held that Congress had exceeded its power to regulate interstate commerce. In *United States v. Lopez*, 514 U.S. 549, 115 S. Ct. 1624, 131 L. Ed. 2d 626 (1995), the Court ruled 5–4 that Congress had exceeded its Commerce Clause power in enacting the Gun-Free School Zones Act of 1990 (18 U.S.C.A. § 921), which prohibited the possession of firearms within 1,000 feet of a school.

In reaching its decision, the Court took the various tests used throughout the history of the Commerce Clause to determine whether a federal statute is constitutional, and incorporated them into a new standard that specifies three categories of activity that Congress may regulate under the clause: (1) the channels of interstate commerce, (2) persons or things in interstate commerce or instrumentalities of interstate commerce, and (3) activities that have "a substantial relation to interstate commerce . . . i.e., those activities that substantially affect interstate commerce." The Court then applied this new standard to the 1990 Gun-Free School Zones Act and found that the statute could be evaluated under the third category of legislation allowed by the Commerce Clause. But the Court noted that the act was a criminal statute that had nothing to do with commerce and that it did not establish any jurisdictional authority to distinguish it from similar state regulations. Because the statute did not "substantially affect interstate

commerce," according to the Court, it went beyond the scope of the Commerce Clause and was an unconstitutional exercise of Congress's legislative power.

The Court stressed that federal authority to regulate interstate commerce cannot be extended to the point that it obliterates the distinction between what is national and what is local and creates a completely centralized government. Although recognizing the great breadth of congressional regulatory authority, the Court in *Lopez* attempted to create a special protection for the states by providing for heightened scrutiny of federal legislation that regulates areas of traditional concern to the states.

In a novel application of the Commerce Clause, a federal court decided in *United States v. Bishop Processing Co.*, 287 F. Supp. 624 (D.C. Md. 1968), that the movement of AIR POLLUTION across state lines from Maryland to Delaware constituted interstate commerce that is subject to congressional regulation. The plaintiff, the United States, sought an INJUNCTION under the federal Clean Air Act (42 U.S.C.A. §§ 7401 et seq. [1955]) to prevent the operation of the Maryland Bishop Processing Company, a fat-rendering plant, until it installed devices to eliminate its emission of noxious odors. The defendant plant owners argued, among other contentions, that Congress was powerless to regulate their business because it was clearly an intrastate activity. The court disagreed. Foul-smelling air POLLUTION adversely affects business conditions, depresses property values, and impedes industrial development. These factors interfere with interstate commerce, thereby bringing the plant within the scope of the provisions of the federal air-pollution law.

The power of Congress to regulate commerce also extends to contracts that substantially relate to interstate commerce. For example, Congress may regulate the rights and liabilities of employers and employees, as labor disputes adversely affect the free flow of commerce. Otherwise, contracts that do not involve any property or activities that move in interstate commerce are not ordinarily part of interstate commerce.

Congress acts within its power when it regulates transportation across state lines. The essential nature of the transportation determines its character. Transportation that begins and ends within a single state is intrastate commerce and is generally not within the scope of the Commerce Clause. If part of the journey passes through an adjoining state, then the transportation is interstate commerce, as long as the travel across state lines is not done solely to avoid state regulation. Commerce begins with the physical transport of the product or person and ends when either reaches the destination. Every aspect of a continuous passage from a point in one state to a point in another state is a transaction of interstate commerce. A temporary pause in transportation does not automatically deprive a shipment of its interstate character. For a sale of goods to constitute interstate commerce, interstate transportation must be involved. Once goods have arrived in one state from another state, their local sale is not interstate commerce.

Interstate commerce also includes the transmission of intelligence and information—whether by telephone, telegraph, radio, television, or mail—across state lines. The transmission of a message between points within the same state is subject to state regulation.

Agencies and Instrumentalities of Commerce

Congress, acting pursuant to the Commerce Clause, has the exclusive power to regulate the agencies and instrumentalities of interstate and foreign commerce, such as private and common carriers. A bridge is an instrumentality of interstate commerce when it spans NAVIGABLE WATERS or is used by travelers and merchandise passing across state lines. Navigable waters are instrumentalities of commerce that are subject to the control of federal and state legislation. A bridge over a navigable stream located in a single state is also subject to concurrent control by the state.

An office used in an interstate business is an instrumentality of interstate commerce. Railroads and tracks, terminals, switches, cars, engines, appliances, equipment used as components of a system engaged in interstate traffic, and vessels (including ferries and tugs) are also subject to federal regulation. Warehouses, grain elevators, and other storage facilities also might be considered instrumentalities of interstate commerce. Although local in nature, wharves are related to commerce and are subject to control by Congress, or by the state if Congress has not acted.

The INTERSTATE COMMERCE ACT of 1887, which Congress enacted to promote and facilitate commerce by ensuring equitable interaction between carriers and the public, provided for the creation of the INTERSTATE COMMERCE COMMISSION. As designated by statute, the commission had jurisdiction and supervision of such carriers and modes of transportation as railroads, express-delivery companies, and sleeping-car companies. Concerning the transportation of persons and property, the commission had the power to enforce the statutory requirement that a certificate of public convenience and necessity be obtained before commencing or terminating a particular transportation service. The commission adopted reasonable and lawful rules and regulations to implement the policies of the law that it administered. The ICC was abolished by Congress in 1995 after Congress deregulated the trucking industry.

Business Affecting Commerce

Not every private enterprise that is carried on chiefly or in part by means of interstate shipments is necessarily so related to the interstate commerce as to come within the regulating power of Congress. The original construction of a factory building does not constitute interstate commerce, even though the factory is used after its construction for the manufacture of goods that are to be shipped in interstate commerce and even though a substantial part of the material used in the building was purchased in different states and transported in interstate commerce to the location of the plant.

Under some circumstances, however, businesses—such as advertising firms, hotels, restaurants, companies that engage in the leasing of PERSONAL PROPERTY, and companies in the entertainment and sports industries—may be regulated by the federal government. A business that operates primarily intrastate activities, such as local sporting or theatrical exhibits, but makes a substantial use of the channels of interstate trade, develops an interstate character, thereby bringing itself within the ambit of the Commerce Clause.

Discrimination as a Burden on Commerce

A state has the power to regulate intrastate commerce in a field where Congress has not chosen to legislate, as long as there is no injustice or unreasonable discrimination in favor of intrastate commerce as against interstate commerce. In a Colorado case, out-of-state students at the University of Colorado sued the state BOARD OF REGENTS to recover the higher costs of the tuition paid by them as compared to tuition paid by in-state residents. They contended that their classification as out-of-state students—which violated, among other things, the Commerce Clause—constituted unreasonable discrimination in favor of in-state students. The court held that the statutes that classified students who apply for admission to the state university into in-state and out-of-state students did not violate the Commerce Clause because the classification was reasonable. A state statute affecting interstate commerce is not upheld merely because it applies equally to, and does not discriminate between, residents and nonresidents of the state, as it can otherwise unduly burden interstate commerce.

Discrimination must be more than merely burdensome; it must be unduly or unreasonably burdensome. One state required a licensed foreign corporation with retail stores in the state to collect a state sales tax on the sales it made from its mail-order houses located outside the state to customers within the state. The corporation contended that this statute discriminated against its operations in interstate commerce. Other out-of-state mail-order houses that were not licensed as foreign corporations in the state did not have to collect tax on their sales within the state. The court decided that the state could impose this burden of tax collection on the corporation because the corporation was licensed to do business in the state and it enjoyed the benefits flowing from its state business. Such a measure was not an unreasonable burden on interstate commerce.

A state may not prohibit the entry of a foreign corporation into its territory for the purpose of engaging in foreign or interstate commerce, nor can it impose conditions or restrictions on the conduct of foreign or interstate business by such corporations. When intrastate business is involved, it may do so.

Similarly, a private person who conducts a business that has a significant effect on interstate commerce in a discriminatory manner is not beyond the reach of lawful congressional regulation.

RACIAL DISCRIMINATION in the operation of public accommodations, such as restaurants and lodgings, affects interstate commerce by impeding interstate travel and is prohibited by the CIVIL RIGHTS ACT OF 1964 (codified in scattered sections of 42 U.S.C.A.). In *Heart of Atlanta Motel v. United States,* 379 U.S. 241, 85 S. Ct. 348, 13 L. Ed. 2d 258 (1964), a local motel owner had refused to accept black guests. He argued that since his motel was a purely local operation, Congress exceeded its authority in legislating as to whom he should accept as guests. The U.S. Supreme Court held that the authority of Congress to promote interstate commerce encompasses the power to regulate local activities of interstate commerce, in both the state of origin and the state of destination, when those activities would otherwise have a substantial and harmful effect upon the interstate commerce. The Court concluded that in this case, the federal prohibition of racial discrimination by motels serving travelers was valid, as interstate travel by blacks was unduly burdened by the established discriminatory conduct.

State Taxation of Nondomiciliary Corporations

In February 2000, the U.S. Supreme Court added another layer to its sometimes complicated Commerce Clause JURISPRUDENCE when it held that the Commerce Clause forbids states from taxing income received by nondomiciliary corporations for unrelated business activities that constitute a discrete business enterprise. *Hunt-Wesson, Inc. v. Franchise Tax Bd. of Cal.,* 528 U.S. 458, 120 S.Ct. 1022, 145 L. Ed. 2d 974 (2000)

Hunt-Wesson Inc., a California-based corporation, was the successor in interest to the Beatrice Companies Inc., the original taxpayer in the case. During the years in question, Beatrice was domiciled in Illinois but was engaged in the food business in California and throughout the world. For the purposes of this lawsuit, Beatrice's *unitary* operations consisted only of those corporate family business units engaged in its global food business. From 1980 to 1982, Beatrice also owned foreign subsidiaries that were not part of its food operations, but that formed a discrete business enterprise. For the purposes of this lawsuit, the parties stipulated that these foreign subsidiaries were part of the company's *non-unitary* business operations.

These non-unitary foreign subsidiaries paid dividends to Beatrice of $27 million for 1980, $29 million for 1981, and $19 million for 1982, income that both parties agree was not subject to California tax under the Commerce Clause. In the operation of its unitary business, Beatrice took out loans and incurred interest expenses of $80 million for 1980, $55 million for 1981, and $137 million for 1982. None of those loans was related to borrowings of Beatrice's non-unitary subsidiaries that made the dividend payments to Beatrice.

On its franchise tax returns, Beatrice claimed deductions for its non-unitary interest expenses in calculating its net income apportioned to California. Following an audit, the California Franchise Tax Board applied the "interest offset" provision in California Revenue and Taxation Code Section 24344. Under that section, multistate corporations may take a deduction for interest expenses, but only to the extent that the expenses exceed their out-of-state income arising from the unrelated business activity of a discrete business enterprise; that is, the *non-unitary* income that the parties agree that California could not otherwise tax. The Section 24344 interest offset resulted in the tax board reducing Beatrice's interest-expenses deduction on a dollar-for-dollar basis by the amount of the constitutionally exempt dividend income that Beatrice received from its non-unitary subsidiaries.

Beatrice responded by filing suit in California state court to challenge the constitutionality of the law. The trial court struck down Section 24344 on the ground that it allowed the state to indirectly tax non-unitary business income that the Commerce Clause prohibits from being taxed directly. The California Court of Appeals reversed, and Hunt-Wesson, having intervened in the lawsuit as Beatrice's successor-in-interest, appealed.

In a unanimous opinion written by Justice STEPHEN BREYER, the U.S. Supreme Court struck down California Revenue and Taxation Code Section 24344. In reducing an out-of-state company's tax deduction for interest expenses by an amount that is equal to the interest and dividends that the company receives from the unrelated business activities of its foreign subsidiaries, Breyer wrote, Section 24344 enables California to circumvent the federal Constitution.

States may tax a proportionate share of the income of a nondomiciliary corporation that carries out a particular business both inside and outside the state, Breyer observed. But states may not, without violating the Commerce Clause, tax nondomiciliary corporations for income earned from unrelated business activities that constitute a discrete business enterprise. Thus, what California called a *deduction limitation* would amount to an impermissible tax under the Commerce Clause.

License and Privilege Tax

A state may not impose a tax for the privilege of engaging in, and carrying on, interstate commerce, but it might be permitted to require a license if doing so does not impose a burden on interstate commerce. A state tax on the use of an instrumentality of commerce is invalid, but a tax may be imposed on the use of goods that have traveled in interstate commerce, such as cigarettes. A state may not levy a direct tax on the gross receipts and earnings derived from interstate or foreign commerce, but it may tax receipts from intrastate business or use the gross receipts as the measurement of a legitimate tax that is within the state's authority to levy.

A state may tax the sale of gasoline or other motor fuels that were originally shipped from another state, after the interstate transaction has ceased. As long as the sale is made within the state, it is immaterial that the gasoline to fulfill the contract is subsequently acquired by the seller outside the state and shipped to the buyer. The state may tax the sale of this fuel to one who uses it in interstate commerce, as well as the storage or withdrawal from storage of imported motor fuel, even though it is to be used in interstate commerce.

Although radio and television broadcasting may not be burdened by state-privilege taxes as far as they involve interstate commerce, broadcasting involving intrastate activity may be subject to local taxation.

A state may impose a nondiscriminatory tax for the use of its highways by motor vehicles in interstate commerce if the charge bears a fair relation to the cost of the construction, maintenance, and regulation of its highways.

The Commerce Clause does not prohibit a state from imposing a tax on a natural resource that is produced within its borders and that is sold primarily to residents of other states. In *Commonwealth Edison Co. v. Montana,* 453 U.S. 609, 101 S. Ct. 2946, 69 L. Ed. 2d 884 (1981), the U.S. Supreme Court upheld a 30 percent severance tax levied by Montana on the production of coal, the bulk of which was exported for sale to other states. The amount of the tax was challenged as an unconstitutional burden on interstate commerce. The Court reasoned that the Commerce Clause does not give the residents of one state the right to obtain resources from another state at what they consider a reasonable price, for that right would enable one state to control the development and depletion of natural resources in another state. If that right were recognized, state and federal courts would be forced to formulate and to apply a test for determining what is a reasonable rate of taxation on legitimate subjects of taxation, tasks that rightfully belong to the legislature.

Crimes Involving Commerce

Congress may punish any conduct that interferes with, obstructs, or prevents interstate and foreign commerce, whether it occurs within one state or involves a number of states. The MANN ACT—which outlaws the transportation any woman or girl in interstate or foreign commerce for the purpose of prostitution, debauchery, or other immoral acts—is a constitutional exercise of the power of Congress to regulate commerce (18 U.S.C.A. §§ 2421–2424 [1910]). The counterfeiting of notes of foreign corporations and bills of lading is a crime against interstate commerce. Under federal statutes, the knowing use of a common carrier for the transportation of obscene matter in interstate or foreign commerce for the purpose of its sale or distribution is illegal. This prohibition applies to the importation of obscene matter even though it is for the importer's private, personal use and possession and not for commercial purposes.

The Anti-Racketeering Act (18 U.S.C.A. § 1951 [2000]) makes RACKETEERING by ROBBERY or personal violence that interferes with interstate commerce a federal offense. The provisions of the CONSUMER CREDIT PROTECTION ACT (15 U.S.C.A. § 1601 et seq. [2000]) prohibiting EXTORTION have been upheld, as extortion is deemed to impose an undue burden on interstate commerce. Anyone who transports stolen goods of the value of $5,000 or more in interstate or foreign commerce is subject to criminal prosecution pursuant to the National Stolen Property Act (18 U.S.C.A. § 2311 et seq. [2000]).

FURTHER READINGS

Cauthorn, Kim. 1995. "Supreme Court Interprets Scope of Congressional Authority under Interstate Commerce Clause." *Houston Lawyer* 33 (July–August).

McJohn, Stephen M. 1995. "The Impact of *United States v. Lopez:* The New Hybrid Commerce Clause." *Duquesne Law Review* 34.

Prentice, E. Parmalee and John G. Egan. 1981. *The Commerce Clause of the Federal Constitution.* Littleton, Colo.: F.B. Rothman.

Ramaswamy, M. 1948. *The Commerce Clause in the Constitution of the United States.* New York: Longmans, Green.

CROSS-REFERENCES

Civil Rights; Federalism; States' Rights; Telecommunications.

COMMERCE DEPARTMENT

The Department of Commerce (DOC) is an agency of the EXECUTIVE BRANCH of the federal government that promotes international trade, economic growth, and technological advancement. It performs many activities related to business, trade, and technology. Its numerous divisions work to foster business growth and to create jobs; to prevent UNFAIR COMPETITION in foreign trade; to distribute economic statistics and studies for use by businesses, the government, and the general public; to support and conduct scientific, engineering, and technological research and development; and to promote foreign trade and U.S. exports. As part of its broad mission, the DOC administers the Bureau of the Census, the Bureau of Economic Analysis, the National Oceanic and Atmospheric Administration, the National Weather Service, the U.S. PATENT AND TRADEMARK OFFICE, the National Institute of Standards and Technology, and several other major government agencies.

Originally part of the Department of Commerce and Labor, which was created in 1903, the Department of Commerce was established as a separate entity by law on March 4, 1913 (U.S.C.A. § 1501). The secretary of commerce sits on the president's cabinet along with the secretaries of the 13 other executive agencies of the federal government and other selected executive officials.

Although the activities of the Department of Commerce are not always prominent in the American consciousness, the department's efforts in administering economic programs have a major effect on the average citizen. Under the administration of President GEORGE H.W. BUSH, the Department of Commerce has administered a number of programs designed to enhance economic growth and to stimulate economic progress in the wake of a recession.

Economics and Statistics Administration

The Economics and Statistics Administration, supervised by the undersecretary for economic affairs, advises the president on economic developments and macroeconomic and microeconomic policy. It also makes economic forecasts and presents current economic data to the public through the National Trade Data Bank and the Economic Bulletin Board. The office oversees the Bureau of the Census and the Bureau of Economic Analysis.

Department of Commerce

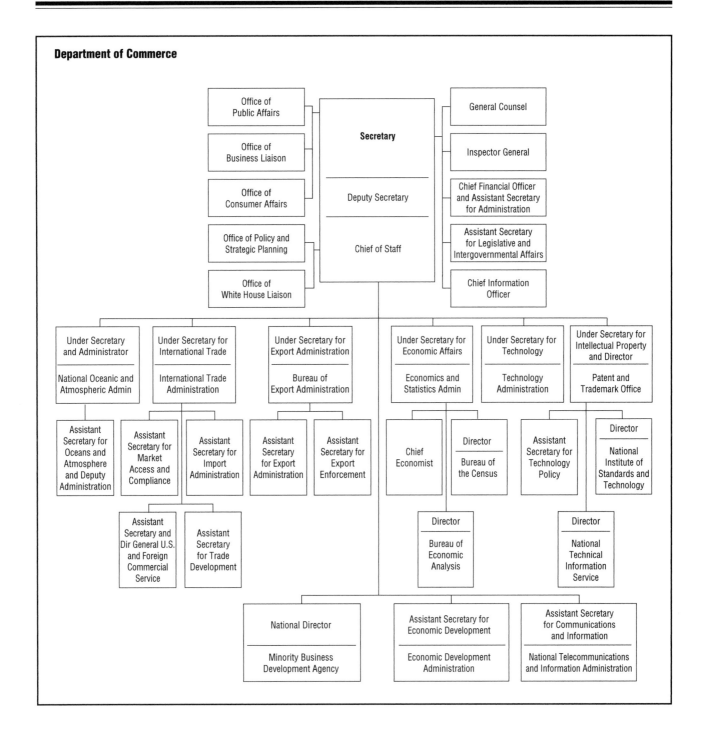

The Bureau of the Census was officially established as a permanent office on March 6, 1902 (32 Stat. 51). Its major duties are authorized by the Constitution (which requires that a census of the U.S. population be conducted every ten years) and by laws codified in Title 13 of the U.S. Code. By law, the census data collected from individuals must be kept confidential. However, statistics collected from the data are published for use by Congress, the executive branch, and the general public. The Bureau of the Census collects data on housing, agriculture, state and local governments, business, industry, and international trade. The bureau also publishes projections of future population trends. For a fee, the bureau will search records and furnish certificates to individuals who require evidence of age, relationship, or place of birth. The headquarters of the bureau is located in Suitland, Maryland, and the bureau operates 12 regional offices.

The Bureau of Economic Analysis, formerly the Office of Business Economics, was established on December 1, 1953. The bureau prepares and interprets statistics on the gross domestic product, personal income, foreign trade, and many other national accounts relating to commerce. It makes statistics available through numerous media and publications, including the monthly *Survey of Current Business.*

Bureau of Export Administration

The Bureau of Export Administration, with its offices of Export Administration and of Export Enforcement, directs the nation's export control policy, including the processing of export license applications. Export Administration oversees export licensing. It assesses whether export controls should be imposed upon specific products, with particular regard for the potential danger to U.S. national security that may result if the products are exported. This office works with U.S. allies to advocate for better ways of controlling strategic exports. Export Enforcement investigates violations of export-control laws, including possible diversions of exports to countries that are forbidden to receive particular products.

Economic Development Administration

The Economic Development Administration, established in 1965, works to generate economic and job growth in the United States, including developing the economies of distressed areas experiencing high unemployment; low income levels; or sudden, severe economic hardship. It funds public-works projects for public, private nonprofit, and American Indian groups, including industrial parks, roads, water and sewer lines, and airports. It also provides technical assistance and grants in order to promote business development.

International Trade Administration

Created in 1980, the International Trade Administration (ITA) works to improve the international trade position of the United States. The ITA oversees nonagricultural trade operations of the U.S. government and supports the efforts of the OFFICE OF THE U.S. TRADE REPRESENTATIVE. It includes the offices of International Economic Policy, Import Administration, and Trade Development, and the U.S. and Foreign Commercial Service. The last agency produces and markets services and products to promote U.S. exports, including seminars and conferences on international trade.

Minority Business Development Agency

Formerly the Office of Minority Business Enterprise, the Minority Business Development Agency was established in 1979. It helps to develop minority-owned businesses. The agency operates a network of six regional offices and four district offices that provide technical and managerial assistance to business owners and entrepreneurs.

National Oceanic and Atmospheric Administration

The National Oceanic and Atmospheric Administration (NOAA) was formed in 1970. It is authorized to explore and to map the global ocean and its living resources; to analyze and predict conditions of the atmosphere, ocean, sun, and space; to monitor and issue warnings regarding destructive natural events such as hurricanes, tsunamis, and tornadoes; and to assess the changing condition of the environment. Included in this wide mandate are such activities as protection of marine species; preparation of nautical and aeronautical charts and geodetic surveys; prediction of ocean tides and currents; satellite observation of the atmosphere and oceans; and management of ocean coastal zones. Offices of the NOAA include the National Weather Service; the National Marine Fisheries Service; the National Environmental Satellite, Data, and Information Service; the National Ocean Service; and the Office of Oceanic and Atmospheric Research.

National Telecommunications and Information Administration

The National Telecommunications and Information Administration (NTIA) was formed in 1978. It is responsible for advising the president on telecommunications policy; developing and presenting national plans at international communications conferences; managing federal use of the radio frequency spectrum; and administering the National Endowment for Children's Educational Television. Offices of the NTIA include the Public Telecommunication Facilities Program, which provides grants to extend delivery of public telecommunications services to as many citizens as possible, and the Institute for Telecommunication Sciences, which operates a research and engineering laboratory in Boulder, Colorado.

Patent and Trademark Office

The U.S. Patent and Trademark Office (PTO) awards PATENTS, which give inventors exclusive rights to their inventions, and registers TRADEMARKS, which provide businesses and organizations with rights to symbols and other features that distinguish their products or services. The PTO issues three types of patents: design patents, plant patents, and utility patents. A patent is valid for 20 years from the date when the application was filed. The PTO also participates in legal proceedings involving patents or trademarks; advocates for strengthening INTELLECTUAL PROPERTY protection worldwide; and maintains a roster of qualified patent agents and attorneys.

Technology Administration

The Technology Administration helps businesses to develop technology that will increase their competitiveness in the marketplace. It identifies and attempts to remove governmental barriers to the commercialization of U.S. science and technology; helps to identify priority technologies; monitors foreign competitors' progress in technology; advises the president on issues concerning commercial technology and related policy; and promotes joint efforts among business, government, educational institutions, and nonprofit organizations. The office also manages the National Medal of Technology Program, the president's highest technology award.

The Technology Administration operates the National Technical Information Service (NTIS), which collects and distributes scientific and technical information generated by the U.S. government and foreign sources. Its collection comprises over 2 million works. The NTIS Bibliographic Database is available on CD-ROM or online through commercial vendors. The Technology Administration produces the Federal Research in Progress Database, a summary listing of 140,000 federally funded research projects in progress. The NTIS also licenses government-owned inventions, operates the FedWorld computer system, and makes available a major Japanese on-line information system. The NTIS is a self-supporting agency, collecting its revenues through sales of its research products.

National Institute of Standards and Technology

The National Institute of Standards and Technology (NIST) was founded in 1901 as the National Bureau of Standards and was renamed in 1988. In addition to its traditional role as developer and protector of national standards of measurement, the institute has increasingly been called upon to help industry to use technology to improve product quality and reliability, improve manufacturing processes, and more rapidly bring to market products that use new scientific discoveries. The NIST administers the Malcolm Baldrige National Quality Award, first established in 1987, which recognizes outstanding quality achievement in business. The institute operates a world-class center in Boulder, Colorado, for science and engineering research, including research in the fields of chemistry, physics, electronics, materials science, computing, and mathematics. Its headquarters is located in Gaithersburg, Maryland.

U.S. Travel and Tourism Administration

Established in 1981, the U.S. Travel and Tourism Administration formulates and implements national policy relating to travel and tourism. It develops trade and statistical research programs to assist the tourism industry, and aids small- and medium-sized travel and tourist businesses. It operates regional offices in Amsterdam, Frankfurt, London, Mexico City, Milan, Paris, Sydney, Tokyo, and Toronto, as well as a Miami office that services South American markets.

Web site: http://www.commerce.gov/

FURTHER READINGS

U.S. Government Manual Web site. Available online at <www.gpoaccess.gov/gmanual> (accessed November 10, 2003).

COMMERCE, ELECTRONIC

Any sales transaction that takes place via computer or over the INTERNET.

In 1990, nobody would have predicted that by the end of the twentieth century people could conduct nearly all of their commercial transactions electronically. Today, a person with a simple Internet connection can purchase anything from clothing to books to jewelry to stereo equipment online. It is possible to purchase insurance, pay one's telephone bill, and buy groceries over the Internet. Banking transactions such as transfers from one account to another can be accomplished online quickly and efficiently. Although most commerce is still conducted in person, more than one-third of adults in the U.S. made at least one purchase online in 2002.

Electronic commerce (or e-commerce) has its origins in the 1960s, with the introduction of a computerized check-processing system called the Electronic Recording Machine—Accounting (ERMA). Banks used ERMA to process billions of checks each year, making it possible for nine employees to do the work of 50. During the 1970s, companies began using Electronic Data Interchange (EDI) to process purchase orders, invoices, and shipping notifications. Although EDI could save time and money, it was an expensive and somewhat cumbersome system, and small to mid-size businesses could not afford it.

The introduction of the Internet in the mid 1990s opened electronic processing up to companies of all sizes; anyone with a computer could connect to a global system that reached into countless businesses and homes.

The first major "virtual" company to appear on the Internet was Amazon.com, founded by Jeff Bezos in Seattle. Amazon.com began doing business in July 1995. Its premise was simple: People could purchase books online through Amazon.com for less money than the same books would cost at a local bookstore. Because Amazon.com had no actual retail stores (the books were stored in a warehouse), it could afford to keep prices lower than the competition. If Amazon.com had a buyer's order in stock in its warehouse, it could be delivered within two to three days. In some bookstores, a special order for an out-of-stock book could take weeks. (Today, Amazon.com sells a wide variety of products in addition to books.)

Not long afterward, in September 1995, Pierre Omidyar and Jeff Skoll founded eBay, an online auction service. Essentially, eBay allows sellers and potential buyers to deal online; as with a live auction, various buyers bid for an item, and the seller accepts the highest bid.

In the ensuing years, Amazon.com, eBay, and similar virtual companies cropped up on the Internet. Established "brick and mortar" companies also established an Internet presence. Today, the average person can find the local lawyer, doctor, dry cleaner, and baker on the Internet along with companies such as Amazon.com and eBay. Not every company offers online retail services; in truth, many smaller companies merely have one or two web pages on their site with a telephone number and a link to an E-MAIL address. For some companies, the Internet has proven to be a double-edged sword. On the one hand, a growing number of consumers expect that the businesses they deal with will have a web site. Even many self-employed indi-

viduals have web sites for precisely this reason. On the other hand, a web site that has nothing of substance to offer will simply drive potential customers away.

Why do people shop online? One compelling advantage is convenience. The idea of being able to sit in front of one's computer, look at different objects, compare prices, enter some data, press a button, and wait for a package to arrive two or three days later is attractive to many people, especially if they do not live close to major retail stores. (Or, for that matter, a person on the East Coast can make an online purchase from a West Coast store.) Speed is another factor. Most e-commerce retailers offer two- or three-day delivery (or next-day service for an additional fee. An online bookstore might be able to ship a hard-to-find book to the buyer in less time—and possibly for less money—than a small neighborhood bookstore that tries to track the book down.

In 2002, according to UCLA's third annual Internet Report (released February 2003), the percentage of adults using the Internet to make purchases actually dropped to 39.7 percent from a high of 50.9 percent the previous year. That figure does not necessarily reflect a loss of confidence or interest in online shopping, although some people may simply stop making online purchases once the novelty wears off. In fact, the average number of purchases made by those who still use the Internet for shopping nearly tripled between 2001 and 2002, from an average 0.8 to 28.32. The average dollar figure also rose between 2001 and 2002, from $70.21 to $100.70.

Even consumers who use the Internet on a regular basis do not necessarily see online shopping as a routine option. In fact, according to the UCLA report, many Internet buyers wait before they make their first online purchase (nearly half waited more than two years after their first Internet experience). By far the most common reason cited (32.4 percent) is fear of providing credit card information online. Other reasons include fear of deception, not knowing whether the online purchase would be cheaper than a "live" purchase, and uncertainty over what is available for sale online.

Thanks to improved technology that allows information to be encrypted when it is sent from one computer to another, it is extremely difficult for an unauthorized person to obtain one's credit card number or SOCIAL SECURITY number. (Proponents of e-commerce argue that it is no more dangerous to send one's credit card number over the Internet than it is to have it on a receipt that can be read by countless people.)

As for missing out on the experience of actually seeing and touching an object before purchasing it, many web sites now have detailed information as well as photographs of the merchandise being offered for sale. Even retailers that do not offer electronic purchases can do this. Lenscrafters, the large optical chain that is famous for its one-hour glasses service, clearly cannot sell its wares over the Internet. The Lenscrafters web site has pictures of many of its frames, as well as a guide to help visitors determine their facial shape and which frame would look best on them. (According to the UCLA study, many Internet shoppers browse through their local retail stores to examine a product, and after that they look on the computer to see whether they can order it for less online.)

A major breakthrough in safe electronic transactions came with the passage of the Electronic Signatures in Global and National Commerce Act. The statute, which was signed into law by President BILL CLINTON on June 30, 2000, had been passed 426 to 4 by the House and unanimously passed by the Senate. Better known as the E-Sign Act, it removes one of the most stubborn barriers to e-commerce by making it safe for people to transmit personal information over their computer.

The E-Sign Act authorizes legal recognition of electronic (digital) signatures, contracts, and records. It also provides a uniform framework for all of the states to follow. A number of states had enacted their own laws, which made interstate electronic commerce cumbersome at best. E-Sign can be quite useful for people who need to sign something by a deadline. A person who wishes to purchase HEALTH INSURANCE online, for example, can do so over the computer instead of having to fill out a form and mail it in and risk being presented with a rate increase that went into effect before the paperwork was received. With an electronic signature, the transaction is completed on the spot.

In June 1998, the U.S. DEPARTMENT OF COMMERCE issued a white paper that called for the creation of a not-for-profit corporation to help manage the Internet's infrastructure. This corporation became known as the Internet Corporation for Assigned Names and Numbers (ICANN). The best known function of ICANN is its coordination of the Domain Name Service

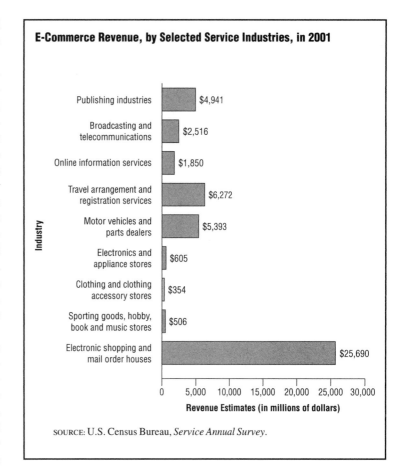

E-Commerce Revenue, by Selected Service Industries, in 2001

Industry	Revenue Estimates (in millions of dollars)
Publishing industries	$4,941
Broadcasting and telecommunications	$2,516
Online information services	$1,850
Travel arrangement and registration services	$6,272
Motor vehicles and parts dealers	$5,393
Electronics and appliance stores	$605
Clothing and clothing accessory stores	$354
Sporting goods, hobby, book and music stores	$506
Electronic shopping and mail order houses	$25,690

SOURCE: U.S. Census Bureau, *Service Annual Survey*.

(DNS). In other words, ICANN is responsible for overseeing the technology that allows Internet users to type in domain names (i.e., www.domainname.com) instead of long strings of numbers. This technology makes it easier for users to type in names of retail stores or online commerce sites. ICANN also oversees the Uniform Domain-Name Dispute Resolution Policy (URDP). This policy governs the methods by which corporate entities can choose and protect their domain names. All URDP cases are arbitrated through the World Intellectual Property Organization (WIPO), a group created in 1970 to safeguard intellectual property rights. Companies whose names are trademarked, or who are well-known organizations, are sometimes forced to contend with individuals who try to use a similar domain name. This practice is known as "cybersquatting." An example of a company that was the victim of cybersquatting is ABC Carpet Company, an established New York City-based retailer of rugs and other home accessories. In 1998, ABC registered the name "ABC Carpet & Home" (which it had begun using in 1995) with the U.S. PATENT AND TRADE-MARK OFFICE. Two separate individuals tried to use domain names with "ABC Carpet & Home" in them, and in both cases WIPO ordered that ownership of the domain names in question be transferred to the New York company. *ABC Carpet Co. v. Helen Gladstone*, WIPO Case No. D2001-0521; *ABC Carpet Co. v. Tom Boltz* and abccarpetandhome.com, WIPO Case No. D2001-0531.

One e-commerce question that has generated interest is whether states should be able to tax sales conducted over the Internet. Technically, Internet transactions are taxable, but a 1992 ruling by the U.S. Supreme Court held that states could only require sellers to collect taxes if they have a physical presence in the same state as the consumer. In 1998, Congress imposed a three-year MORATORIUM against any Internet taxes, which was renewed for two years in 2001. Meanwhile, the National Governors Association (NGA) introduced the Streamlined Sales Tax Project (SSTP) in 2000 to adopt uniform tax rates among the 50 states. The estimated date for SSTP's completion is late 2005.

FURTHER READINGS

Mark, Roy. 2003. "Bush Backs Internet Moratorium." *Boston Internet News* (May 16).

Secretariat on Electronic Commerce. 1997. *The Emerging Digital Economy*. Washington, D.C.: U.S. Department of Commerce.

UCLA Center for Communication Policy. 2003. *The UCLA Internet Report: Surveying the Digital Future*. Los Angeles: University of California Regents.

CROSS-REFERENCES

Justice Department; Internet; Taxation; Telecommunications.

COMMERCIAL CODE

A colloquial designation for the body of law known as the UNIFORM COMMERCIAL CODE *(UCC), which governs the various business transactions that are integral parts of the U.S. system of commerce. The UCC has been adopted in virtually all of the states.*

COMMERCIAL LAW

A broad concept that describes the SUBSTANTIVE LAW *that governs transactions between business entities, with the exception of maritime transportation of goods (regulated by* ADMIRALTY AND MARITIME LAW*). Commercial law includes all aspects of business, including advertising and*

marketing, collections and BANKRUPTCY, banking, contracts, negotiable instruments, SECURED TRANSACTIONS, *and trade in general. It covers both domestic and foreign trade; it also regulates trade between states.*

The term commercial law describes a wide body of laws that govern business transactions. The UNIFORM COMMERCIAL CODE (UCC), which has been adopted in part by every state in the United States, is the primary authority that governs commercial transactions. The UCC is divided into nine articles, covering a broad spectrum of issues that arise in commercial transactions. These articles govern the following: sales of goods, leases of goods, negotiable instruments, bank deposits, fund transfers, letters of credit, bulk sales, warehouse receipts, bills of lading, investment SECURITIES, and secured transactions.

A number of other laws also govern business transactions. For instance, although Article 4 of the UCC governs bank deposits, federal law in the form of statutes and regulations prescribe requirements for BANKS AND BANKING in general. Likewise, federal law governs such issues related to commercial law as bankruptcy and debt collection. Many of the federal laws related to commercial transactions are codified in title 15 of the U.S. Code.

Although the UCC controls most aspects of domestic commercial law, the COMMON LAW of contracts, as well as other state laws, still applies to some types of transactions that arise in business, such as contracts for services. INTERNATIONAL LAW is likewise an important component of this area. For instance, the United Nations Convention on Contracts for the International Sale of Goods has been ratified by approximately 62 nations, representing two-thirds of the world's trade.

Though the business world undergoes constant change, commercial laws generally have remained static. The COMMISSIONERS ON UNIFORM LAWS, in conjunction with the American Law Institute and other organizations, periodically revises the articles of the UCC. However, the revision process of the UCC is typically slow and deliberate. Recent revisions to Article 2 (governing the sale of goods) and Article 9 (governing secured transactions) took several years to complete. Thus, not only is commercial law substantially uniform throughout the United States, but also those who conduct business can proceed with commercial transactions with some degree of certainty as to the law that governs those transactions.

CROSS-REFERENCES

Banks and Banking; Check; Contracts; Mercantile; Merchantable; North American Free Trade Agreement; Promissory Note; Sales Law; Uniform Commercial Code; Warranty.

COMMERCIAL LAW LEAGUE OF AMERICA

The Commercial Law League of America (CLLA) was founded in 1895 to elevate standards and improve the practice of COMMERCIAL LAW, to encourage an honorable course of dealing among its members and among the profession at large, to promote uniformity of legislation in matters affecting commercial law, and to foster among its members a feeling of fraternity and mutual confidence. Its members are lawyers, commercial agencies, and law list publishers.

The league has been a pioneer in standardizing commercial practice. It continues to maintain and expand its program of activities in such areas as creditors' rights, commercial laws and legislation, and BANKRUPTCY and reorganization. In March 2003, the CLLA presented testimony and a formal position paper before a U.S. Congress subcommittee for meaningful bankruptcy reform, relative to the pending Bankruptcy Abuse Prevention and Consumer Protection Act of 2003, H.R. 975, 108th Cong., 1st Sess.

The CLLA maintains over 40 committees covering various areas of commercial law and other topics, such as world peace through law and world trade. Its activities include educational programs on legal issues of public interest and importance. Along with the American Bankruptcy Institute, it also sponsors the American Board of Certification (ABC), a non-profit organization that serves to improve and certify attorneys belonging to bankruptcy and creditors' rights bars.

The CLLA has sections on commercial collection agencies and young members; it also has committees on bankruptcy and the UNIFORM COMMERCIAL CODE. It publishes the *Commercial Law Journal* ten times a year and holds annual meetings, often combining national conferences with those of other prominent organizations, such as the National Association of Credit Management and the Finance, Credit and International Business Association (FCIB). In 1998, the CLLA began holding international credit conferences as well.

FURTHER READINGS

Commercial Law League of America. Available online at <www.cclla.org> (accessed June 2, 2003).

Commercial Law League of America. 2000. "League Business." *Commercial Law Bulletin* (November-December).

Miller, Judith Greenstone. 2003. "Bankruptcy Abuse Prevention and Consumer Protection Act of 2003." *FDCH Congressional Testimony* (March 4).

CROSS-REFERENCES

Bankruptcy; Uniform Commercial Code.

COMMERCIAL PAPER

A written instrument or document such as a check, draft, promissory note, or a certificate of deposit, that manifests the pledge or duty of one individual to pay money to another.

Commercial paper is ordinarily used in business transactions, since it is a reliable and expedient means of dealing with large sums of money and minimizes the risks inherent in using cash, such as the increased possibility of theft.

One of the most significant aspects of commercial paper is that it is negotiable, which means that it can be freely transferred from one party to another, either through endorsement or delivery. The terms *commercial paper* and *negotiable instrument* can be used interchangeably.

Since commercial paper constitutes PERSONAL PROPERTY, it is transferable by sale or gift and can be loaned, lost, stolen, and taxed. Commercial paper is a specific type of property primarily governed by article 3 of the UNIFORM COMMERCIAL CODE (UCC), which is in effect in all 50 states, the District of Columbia, and the Virgin Islands. Although Louisiana has not enacted all the articles of the UCC, it has adopted article 3.

Types of Commercial Paper

The UCC identifies four basic kinds of commercial paper: promissory notes, drafts, checks, and certificates of deposit. The most fundamental type of commercial paper is a promissory note, a written pledge to pay money. A promissory note is a two-party paper. The maker is the individual who promises to pay while the payee or holder is the person to whom payment is promised. The payee can be either a specifically named individual or merely the bearer of the

Checks are considered a type of commercial paper, as well as a specific kind of bank draft.
DENNIS DEGNAN/CORBIS

instrument who has it in his or her physical possession when he or she seeks to be paid according to its terms. A note payable to "bearer" can be paid to the person who presents it for remuneration. Such an instrument is said to be *bearer paper.*

A promissory note that is *payable on demand* can be redeemed by the payee at any time, whereas a *time note* has a date for payment on its face that establishes the date when the holder will have an enforceable right to receive payment under it. There is no obligation to pay a time note until the date designated on its face.

The ordinary purpose of a promissory note is to borrow money. Promissory notes should not be confused with credit or loan agreements, which are separate instruments that are usually signed at the same time as promissory notes, but which merely describe the terms of the transactions.

A promissory note serves as documentary evidence of a debt. It can be endorsed and sold at a discount to other parties, and each subsequent endorser becomes secondarily liable for the amount specified on the face of the instrument. A number of CONSUMER CREDIT dealings are funded through the use of promissory notes.

Certain types of promissory notes are sold at a discount, such as U.S. savings bonds and corporation bonds. Such an instrument is sold for an amount below its face value and can subsequently be redeemed on the due date or date of maturity for the entire face amount. The interest obtained by the holder of the instrument is the difference between the purchase price and the redemption price. In certain instances, bonds that are not redeemed immediately upon maturity accumulate interest following the due date and are ultimately worth more than their face value when redeemed at a later time. If such bonds are cashed in before maturity, the holder receives less than the face value.

A draft, also known as a bill of exchange, is a three-party paper ordering the payment of money. The drawer is the individual issuing the order to pay, while the drawee is the party to whom the order to pay is given. As in the case of a promissory note, the payee is either a specified individual or the bearer of the draft who is to receive payment according to its terms. The draft is made payable on demand or on a certain date. A common example of a draft is a cashier's check.

A draft is often used in business to obtain payment for items that must be shipped over long distances. Drafts are often the preferred method of payment for purchasers who want to examine goods prior to payment or who do not have the necessary funds available at the time of sale. The vendor might have reservations concerning the buyer's credit and desire payment as soon as possible. The procedure ordinarily followed in such instances is that upon shipment of the goods, the seller receives a bill of lading from the carrier. The bill of lading also serves as a certificate of title to the goods, which is ordinarily in the seller's name.

Upon shipment, the seller draws a draft against the buyer-drawee, who is required to pay the draft. The seller's bank is named as the payee. The seller endorses the bill of lading to the payee and attaches the bill to the draft. The seller can either negotiate these instruments to the payee at a discount or use them as security for a loan. Subsequently, the papers are endorsed by the seller's bank and delivered to a correspondent bank in the community where the buyer is located. The correspondent bank seeks payment of the draft from the buyer and when payment is made, the bank transfers ownership of the goods from seller to buyer by endorsing the bill of lading to the buyer. The buyer can then obtain the goods from the carrier upon presentation of the bill of lading, which demonstrates his or her title to the shipped goods.

A check is a specific kind of draft, which is drawn on a bank and payable on demand to a particular individual or to the bearer, in which case it can be written payable to "cash."

An individual who opens a checking account is engaged in a contractual relationship with a bank. The individual agrees to deposit money therein, while the bank agrees that it is indebted to the depositor for the amount in the account, in addition to promising to honor checks written for payment against the account when there are sufficient funds on hand to do so.

A certificate of deposit, frequently referred to as a CD, is a written recognition by a bank of the acquisition of a sum of money from a depositor for a designated period of time at a specified interest rate, coupled with a promise of repayment. The bank is both the maker and the drawee, and the individual making the deposit is the payee.

Ordinarily, certificates of deposit come in specific denominations that vary according to the length of the term that the bank will hold the funds and are available only for large sums of money. They are used mainly by corporations and individuals as savings devices since they generally bear higher interest rates than ordinary savings accounts. They must, however, be left on deposit for the designated time period. Ordinarily, a CD can be cashed in prior to the date of maturity, but some interest will be forfeited. Depending upon the provisions of the CD, however, a bank may have the legal right to refuse to close an account before the expiration of the designated date of maturity.

Negotiability

There are basic requirements for the negotiability of commercial paper. The instrument must be in writing and signed by either its maker or its drawer. In addition, it must be either an unconditional promise, as in the case of a promissory note, or an order to pay a specific amount of money, such as a draft. It must be payable either on demand or at a fixed time to order or to bearer.

The requirement that the instrument must be in writing can be met in various ways. The paper can be printed, typed, engraved, or written in longhand, either in ink, pencil, or both.

Ordinarily, specimens of commercial paper can be obtained from banks or stationery stores.

Similarly, there are a number of ways to comply with the signature requirement. The signature may legally be either handwritten, typed, printed, or stamped by a machine. Individuals who are unable to write their names can sign with a simple mark, such as an *X*. Also permissible are initials, a symbol, a business or TRADE NAME, or an assumed name.

The pledge or order for payment must be unconditional to insure certainty that the instrument will be paid, since it is used in place of money and as a means of obtaining credit.

When the paper includes an unconditional promise or order, supplementary facts can be mentioned that will not defeat its negotiability. For example, the paper can indicate the transaction was secured by a mortgage. It might mention a specific account or fund out of which payment is expected, although not required. Ordinarily, such a collateral statement is made for purposes of accounting and does not create a conditional promise or order to pay. Payment can, however, be limited to the total assets of a partnership, unincorporated association, or trust.

A promise to pay is conditional when it indicates that it is either subject to or governed by another agreement. When payment is conditional, negotiability is terminated and the instrument is not commercial paper. The holder of the paper cannot rely upon the face of the document to establish and fix his or her right to payment.

A paper does not qualify for treatment as a negotiable instrument if payment of it is to be made exclusively from a particular fund, unless such instrument is issued by a government or division thereof.

In dealing with a promissory note, practically any terms that state a definite promise will suffice to make the instrument legally enforceable. The phrase "I promise to pay" clearly demonstrates an unconditional pledge of payment; whereas an IOU is not deemed definite enough to warrant payment and, therefore, is not a negotiable instrument. There must be an order to pay in a check or a draft. A mere request, as in "I wish you would pay," is insufficient. Language used for courtesy, such as "please pay," does not, however, defeat the order. Suitable language to instruct payment would be "pay to the order of *X*."

The holder of the negotiable instrument must be able to ascertain the precise value of the paper by looking at its face. In certain instances, it might be necessary to compute interest, as in the case of a promissory note that bears a certain annual rate. A provision for interest does not impair the determination of the actual sum. In addition, certainty regarding the amount is not altered by the fact that the interest rate can differ before or after default or before or after a particular date.

The amount payable remains a fixed sum even in the event that it is paid in installments, or reduced by agreement of payment prior to a set time or increased following the date of payment. In addition, the certainty of the sum is not affected by a provision for collection of expenses and lawyer's fees.

The sum must be payable in money, which is a medium of exchange adopted by governments; otherwise, the document is not considered commercial paper.

An instrument must be payable either on demand or at a set time in order to have negotiability. Papers that are payable on demand are payable upon presentation, such as checks.

When a note or a draft is payable on, or prior to, a fixed date or for a set period thereafter, it is considered to be negotiable at a definite time. When an instrument is *payable on or before* a certain date, payment is required no later than the date indicated, although it can be made prior to that date. Similarly, a paper made payable at an established time *after sight* is payable at a definite time. After sight means that upon presentation of the instrument to the maker by the holder, payment will occur after the expiration of the time designated on the note. The payee of a note due one week after sight must be paid by the maker within a week of the date it is presented for payment. It need not be paid immediately upon presentation, since the terms of the note do not make it a demand instrument.

If the time provided for payment of an instrument is definite except for the presence of an acceleration clause, the time of payment of the instrument is still considered definite. That is, a note can provide that the time for payment will be accelerated if a certain event takes place or at the option of one of the parties to the agreement without destroying its negotiability. Also acceptable are extensions of the payment period, which can be made at the choice of the holder, maker, or acceptor, or immediately when a particular act occurs.

An instrument retains its negotiable quality even if it is undated, antedated, or postdated. An undated instrument takes effect immediately upon delivery to the payee. An antedated paper is given a date that has passed, and a postdated instrument is given a future date. In the event that an instrument is either antedated or postdated, the determination of the date on which it becomes legally operative is contingent upon the date that appears on its face and upon whether it is payable on demand or on a certain date. A postdated check cannot be cashed prior to the date appearing on its face, in spite of the fact that a check is ordinarily payable on demand.

An instrument is not negotiable if it is payable upon an occurrence of indefinite timing, even when the event is certain to happen, such as death.

The requirement that an instrument be made payable either to order or to bearer is met when the paper is made available to the bearer, or to an individual specifically designated, or to the order of that person, as in "X, or his order." An estate, trust, corporation, partnership, or unincorporated association may be designated as a payee of a commercial paper.

An instrument can be made payable to two or more people, either together or in the alternative. If the paper is made out to two parties together, as in "to X and Y," then both payees must endorse it before payment will be made. An instrument made out in the alternative, however, as in "To X or Y," requires endorsement by only one payee in order to be paid.

Checks and drafts are ordinarily written on printed forms, made payable both to order and bearer. An empty space is left between the words "pay to the order of" and "or bearer." When the name of the payee is inserted by the drawer, the paper is regarded as an order instrument in spite of the fact that the phrase "or bearer" is not deleted. In such instances, the presumption is that the drawer merely neglected to eliminate this language. An instrument is bearer paper, however, when it is made payable to a specific payee and the words "or bearer" are either typed or handwritten on the document as additions to it.

Bearer paper is made payable either to the holder, a specific individual, the bearer, or to cash. It is common for such an instrument to read "pay to the order of bearer." This occurs in the case where a printed form is used and the term *bearer* is written in following "pay to the order of." The word *bearer* serves to make the instrument bearer paper in such an instance.

Bearer instruments are tantamount to cash because they are freely transferrable from one person to another without requiring an endorsement. They are thereby not as secure as order instruments since if they are stolen, their terms permit payment to be made to whoever possesses them at the time they are presented for payment. Many banks require customers to endorse bearer paper prior to payment as a safety measure. This provides both the drawer and the bank with the name of the individual who is given payment.

Endorsements

An endorsement is the process of signing the back of a paper, thereby imparting the rights that the signer had in the paper to another person. The number of times an instrument may be endorsed is unlimited. There is no requirement that the word "order" be embodied in the endorsement. Four principal kinds of endorsements exist: special, blank, restrictive, and qualified.

An endorsement that clearly indicates the individual to whom the instrument is payable is a special endorsement.

A paper containing a blank endorsement is one that has the signature of the payee but no specific endorsee is designated. A check that is made payable to the order of X is endorsed in the blank when X signs it. Once endorsed, it becomes bearer paper and is negotiable by anyone who physically holds it. A blank endorsement is changed into a special endorsement if certain words are written above the endorsee's signature, such as "pay to the order of Y."

A qualified endorsement is one wherein liability is disclaimed by the endorser through inclusion of a phrase preceding his or her signature. Ordinarily, an unqualified endorser's liability may be either secondary, whereby the endorser is bound to pay if the individual expected to pay defaults and certain conditions are met or by WARRANTY, by which the endorser incurs liability upon ALTERATION OF THE INSTRUMENT. To disclaim secondary liability, the endorser can include the words "without recourse," thereby relieving himself or herself of any responsibility to pay it.

Attorneys who are the recipients of checks drawn in settlement of the claims of their clients commonly sign their clients' checks with qualified endorsements. This type of check is ordinarily made payable to the lawyer and client jointly. It is generally endorsed by the lawyer WITHOUT RECOURSE and given to the client. The attorney then is not liable if the client does not receive the money promised by the terms of the check.

A restrictive endorsement is conditional and attempts to prevent subsequent transfer of the document. The language of the endorsement indicates that the instrument is intended for limited use, such as "for deposit only," or specifies that the paper is meant for the benefit of the endorser or another individual, as in "Pay X in trust for Y." The condition imposed by a restrictive endorsement must be satisfied before payment can be properly made.

However, an endorsement that tries to prohibit further transfer of an instrument will not succeed. If a check says "Pay X only," it is still completely negotiable upon its endorsement by X.

Liability of Parties

An individual who signs an instrument is either primarily or secondarily liable for payment. Primary liability is extended to the person who is expected to pay first, and the individual who is legally responsible to pay upon the failure of the first party to do so is secondarily liable.

The maker of a promissory note is primarily liable, since that person is the individual who has originally promised to pay. He or she must meet this obligation when payment becomes due unless he or she has a valid defense or has been discharged of the debt.

The drawer of a check or draft is secondarily liable, since that individual does not make an unconditional promise to pay the instrument. He or she expects the bank to pay and promises to pay the amount of the instrument only upon notification of dishonor, a refusal by the drawee to accept the paper when properly presented for payment. This might occur, for example, if the bank refuses to pay a check due to insufficient funds in the drawer's checking account or because he or she has notified the drawee to stop payment.

The drawee of a draft or check has primary liability to the holder, an individual who has lawfully acquired possession and is entitled to payment, upon acceptance of the instrument by the drawee. A draft is accepted for payment when the acceptance is indicated by the drawee

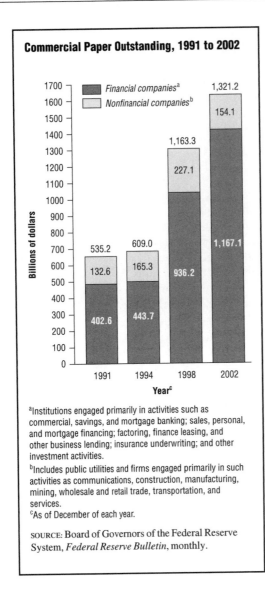

Commercial Paper Outstanding, 1991 to 2002

Financial companies[a]
Nonfinancial companies[b]

Year[c]	Nonfinancial	Financial	Total
1991	132.6	402.6	535.2
1994	165.3	443.7	609.0
1998	227.1	936.2	1,163.3
2002	154.1	1,167.1	1,321.2

Billions of dollars

[a]Institutions engaged primarily in activities such as commercial, savings, and mortgage banking; sales, personal, and mortgage financing; factoring, finance leasing, and other business lending; insurance underwriting; and other investment activities.
[b]Includes public utilities and firms engaged primarily in such activities as communications, construction, manufacturing, mining, wholesale and retail trade, transportation, and services.
[c]As of December of each year.

SOURCE: Board of Governors of the Federal Reserve System, *Federal Reserve Bulletin*, monthly.

on the face of the document. Certification of an instrument, such as a check, is its acceptance by a bank guaranteeing that payment will be forthcoming. A drawee is liable to the drawer if the drawee refuses to pay a draft or check that is properly drawn and presented because such action constitutes a noncompliance of the drawee's contractual obligation to the drawer.

Any person who places his or her unqualified endorsement on a commercial paper incurs secondary liability for its payment. Such liability occurs when the individual who has the primary duty to pay defaults on his or her obligation.

A maker or drawer is not relieved from payment of an instrument endorsed with the payee's name when an imposter manages to have a paper issued to himself or herself by the maker or drawer; when an individual signing on the behalf of the maker or drawer plans that the payee shall have no interest in the paper, for example, the case of a check being made out to a fictitious payee; and when the agent or employee of the maker or drawer designates the name of a payee with the intent that the named party will actually have no interest in the instrument. In the last two instances, the failure of the employer to use reasonable care in choosing and supervising employees makes the employer personally responsible for all losses that arise from his or her NEGLIGENCE. Many employers guard against such risks by taking out fidelity insurance policies to cover losses that might occur through employee misconduct.

Secondary Liability

Individuals who are secondarily liable on a negotiable instrument are not obliged to pay unless it has been presented for payment and dishonored. The commercial paper must first be given to the person who is primarily liable for payment. In the event that the instrument clearly notes the date of payment, the instrument must be presented on the date indicated. If payment is unjustifiably refused by the individual who has primary liability, the secondary party must be given notice of the dishonor and the presentation of the instrument for payment must be made within a reasonable period of time. What constitutes a reasonable time is contingent upon what type of instrument is involved. If the paper is a check, the drawer has primary liability for thirty days following the date on the check or the day it was given or sent to the payee, with the later date prevailing. An endorser is secondarily liable for seven days following his or her endorsement. When presentation does not occur within these time periods, either the drawer or the endorser may escape liability.

Individuals who are secondarily liable must receive notice of the dishonor of a commercial paper in order to be held liable for its payment. Such notice must be given by a bank prior to midnight on the date following the dishonor. Notice can be oral or in writing, as long as the language identifies the paper and indicates that it has been dishonored. If more than one person is eligible to obtain payment, only one of them need notify those parties who are secondarily liable.

Holders

A holder is an individual who is in possession of an instrument that is either payable to him or her as the payee, endorsed to him or her, or payable to the bearer. Those who obtain instruments after the payee are holders if such instrument is either payable to the bearer or endorsed properly to their order. The party in possession is not considered to be the holder in a case in which a necessary endorsement has been forged.

According to law, a holder may either be an ordinary holder or a holder in due course, who has preemptive rights to payment. An ordinary holder becomes a holder in due course upon taking an instrument subject to the reasonable belief that it will be paid and that there are no legal reasons why payment will not occur.

In more technical terms, to be a holder in due course, the party must take the paper for value, in GOOD FAITH, and absent the notice that it is overdue, has been dishonored, or is subject to an adverse claim. Such notice of problems affecting the validity of the instrument exists if the party either is specifically informed about something or otherwise has reason to believe in the existence of a problem.

A holder takes a paper for value when the holder has imparted something of value, such as property or services, in exchange for the value of the paper, as evidenced by its terms. In such a case, the individual becomes the holder for value.

If a paper is used in satisfaction of or as security for the repayment of a debt, even though the debt might not be due when the paper is taken, the instrument is taken for value. In addition, value is given when one commercial paper is traded for another.

A person who receives a check or other type of negotiable instrument as a gift is an ordinary holder as opposed to a holder in due course, since no consideration that is bargained-for value has been exchanged by the parties. A holder in due course has greater legal rights concerning protection for enforcement of the provisions for payment of a negotiable instrument than does an ordinary holder.

For an individual to be a holder in due course, the negotiable instrument must be taken in good faith that it represents a valuable legal right. There must be honesty in the transaction, but the determination of whether or not good faith is present is totally subjective.

Frequently, a due date is clearly specified on the face of the document. A holder is presumed to have knowledge of the terms appearing on the paper. If an individual is presented with a note on May 15 that is payable on May 1, he or she is regarded as having knowledge that it is overdue. A person is legally considered to have knowledge that a demand instrument is overdue if he or she accepts it after being informed that a demand for payment has previously been made and refused or if a reasonable period of time has elapsed since its issuance. Ordinarily, 30 days after the date on which a check was issued is a reasonable time period within which its presentation to a bank for payment should occur. An individual who accepts a check that is more than 30 days old is assumed to be doing so with the knowledge that it is overdue.

An instrument that has been dishonored ordinarily has that fact indicated on its face. For example, a check might be stamped "insufficient funds," "account closed," or "payment stopped." An individual who accepts such a document possessing knowledge of its dishonor cannot be a holder in due course. A person cannot be a holder in due course if he or she takes an instrument subject to his or her knowledge that a claim exists against it, such as when it has been stolen or transferred as a result of FRAUD.

Defenses

A holder of a negotiable instrument who has been refused payment when payment was due has a CAUSE OF ACTION against the party or parties liable for payment. Ordinarily, when an individual is sued on a negotiable paper, he or she will try to defend his or her right to refuse payment. Certain defenses, known as *real defenses,* are valid against ordinary holders as well as holders in due course, whereas *personal defenses* are only valid against ordinary holders.

Normally, any defense that can be asserted in an action concerning a contract may also be used in an action brought to enforce payment of a negotiable instrument. The legal incapacity of the maker, drawer, or endorser, a signature effected by duress, illegality, or fraud, and alteration of the instrument qualify as real defenses.

One of the most prevalent legal incapacity defenses asserted is infancy. The law affords protection to INFANTS by permitting them to evade their contractual obligations, even when, in some instances, they have reaped the benefits. A holder is usually excluded from receiving payment on a note from a minor.

Another incapacity defense is legal insanity or INCOMPETENCY. A party who has been legally declared insane or incompetent is not liable for any contractual obligations entered during that time so that if such a person signs or endorses a negotiable instrument, the transaction is nullified. Intoxication is not a valid defense to dishonor of a commercial paper.

Duress may be used as a defense in the event that the individual against whom a suit is brought can prove that he or she was subject to extreme pressure caused by another at the time of the execution of the paper. If the defendant signed the instrument subject to a threat of immediate physical violence or death, he or she is not legally bound to honor its terms since he or she had not freely entered into the transaction. Certain types of duress, such as a threat to report a wrongdoing to the police or to bring a civil lawsuit, are not valid against a holder in due course, although they can be used as valid personal defenses against an ordinary holder.

Certain jurisdictions deem a paper that has been negotiated to pay a usurious loan or gambling debt null and void. An individual can legally avoid payment to the holder in due course of such an instrument based on the illegal nature of the debt it was meant to pay.

Two basic types of fraud exist: *fraud in the essence* and *fraud in the inducement*. *Fraud in the essence* occurs when an individual is intentionally lied to about the nature of the instrument or its terms. It is a defense that is valid against both an ordinary holder and a holder in due course. *Fraud in the inducement* takes place when the party signing the paper is cognizant of its nature and terms but is misled into believing that the reasons for its creation have been satisfied when in actuality they have not. For example, an individual might be induced to issue a check for a certain amount to a mechanic who claims to have repaired a car. If the individual subsequently discovers that the car was not repaired, fraud may be used as a personal defense against the mechanic who has not performed his or her part of the contract to repair the car. Fraud in the inducement is only valid against an ordinary holder, not a holder in due course.

A *material alteration* is an addition or deletion of the language of an instrument, which changes the obligations of any party to it. A defendant may avoid liability for payment of a commercial paper if its terms have been materially altered. Examples of such alterations are a change in the date of payment or amount to be paid. When an individual's own negligence is a contributing factor to a material alteration, that negligence may not be asserted by him or her as a defense against someone who pays the instrument in good faith or against a holder in due course.

An alteration made by a holder that is both material and fraudulent can be used as a defense against enforcing the payment of the document by all those people whose agreements were changed. If these two conditions of materiality and fraud are not met, the instrument is ordinarily enforceable according to the way it was initially written, and none of those involved can use the alteration as a defense against payment.

When a holder in due course takes a paper following its fraudulent alteration by the previous holder, he or she is entitled to receive payment according to the original terms of the instrument prior to its alteration. None of the parties responsible for payment can use the alteration as a defense against a holder in due course, but it may be used against an ordinary holder.

Discharge from Liability

The most common way to be discharged from liability on a commercial paper is through payment. The intentional CANCELLATION OF AN INSTRUMENT by the holder by either marking the instrument paid or by destroying it discharges all liability.

The holder may also discharge an individual from liability for payment through renunciation. This can be accomplished when a document is signed and delivered by the holder or when a paper is relinquished to the party who is being discharged. A stop-payment order put on a check by its drawer has the effect of discharging the bank from liability for refusing to honor the check when presented for payment. It cannot, however, discharge the drawer from liability in cases where the drawer was contractually or otherwise obligated to pay the payee.

FURTHER READINGS

Bamford, Janet. 1992. *The Consumer Reports Money Book.* New York: Consumers Reports.

Blue, Ron. 1993. *Master Your Money: A Step-by-Step Plan for Financial Freedom.* Nashville, TN: Thomas Nelson.

Corley, Robert N., and William J. Robert. 1979. *Principles of Business Law.* Englewood Cliffs, NJ: Prentice-Hall.

Milling, Bryan E. 1993. *How to Get a Loan or Line of Credit for Your Business: A Banker Shows You Exactly What You Need to Do to Get a Loan.* Naperville, TN: Sourcebooks.

CROSS-REFERENCES

Bonds; Documentary Evidence.

COMMERCIAL SPEECH

See FIRST AMENDMENT; FREEDOM OF SPEECH.

COMMINGLING

Combining things into one body.

The term *commingling* is most often applied to funds or assets. When a fiduciary, a person entrusted with the management of funds other than his or her own in trust, mixes trust money with that of others, the fiduciary is commingling funds and thereby breaching his or her fiduciary duty.

A member of a corporation's board of directors commingles funds when he or she mixes personal funds with the funds of the corporation. An attorney who commingles his or her money with money belonging to a client is violating the ethics of the legal profession.

COMMISSION ON CIVIL RIGHTS

The federal Commission on Civil Rights evaluates CIVIL RIGHTS laws and policies of the U.S. government, follows legal developments regarding discrimination, investigates allegations that U.S. citizens are being denied their civil rights, and evaluates equal opportunity programs. It collects and monitors information on discrimination or the denial of EQUAL PROTECTION of the laws on the basis of race, color, religion, sex, age, handicap, or national origin. It also investigates equality of opportunity in voting, education, employment, transportation, housing, and the administration of justice.

The commission holds public hearings, publishes findings and reports, and maintains a toll-free phone line by which people may make complaints regarding civil rights. The commission disseminates the information it gathers but cannot enforce existing civil rights laws. It offers its findings and makes recommendations to the president and to Congress. Many of the commission's recommendations have been incorporated into laws, executive orders, and regulations. The commission also collects and stores civil rights information gathered from around the United States.

The Commission on Civil Rights was created by the CIVIL RIGHTS ACT of 1957, and it was later reestablished by the U.S. Commission on Civil Rights Act of 1983 (42 U.S.C.A. § 1975 et seq.). It maintains six regional offices and is headed by eight members, or commissioners, of whom no more than four shall come from any one political party. Members serve for three or six years. Four members of the commission are appointed by the president, two by the president pro tempore of the Senate, and two by the Speaker of the House of Representatives. The president designates a chairperson and vice chairperson from among the commission's members.

From the beginning, the Commission on Civil Rights has interjected itself in controversy. It has investigated activities ranging from discrimination to HATE CRIMES. Because appointments to the commission are political, its tone often swings from the right to the left, depending on who is president. During the 1980s, it issued opinions that were so conservative that some congressional Democrats wanted to shut it down. In contrast, during the 1990s, under the leadership of its outspoken chairwoman, Mary Frances Berry, it tilted toward the left.

The commissions most controversial recent action was its investigation into the 2000 presidential election in Florida. After a six-month investigation, the commission issued a report claiming that Florida's conduct of this election was marked by "injustice, ineptitude and inefficiency." The report claimed that minority voters were disenfranchised through unequal access to voting equipment and overzealous efforts to purge state voter lists of felons and other ineligible voters. It recommended that the JUSTICE DEPARTMENT initiate litigation to correct this discrimination.

The four commissioners who backed the report were all Democrats or otherwise considered liberal. Two Republican commissioners issued a dissenting report, stating that the Florida election problems were hampered by unintentional and unanticipated problems that were not motivated by racial bias and that did not disenfranchise minority voters. The dissent cited a study that low income and literacy rates were more likely than race to explain the number of ballots rejected in certain neighborhoods. In addition to the dissenters, Florida's Republican governor and SECRETARY OF STATE denounced the commission's findings.

Lost in the controversy over whether the commission's finding of bias in the Florida 2000 presidential election was itself biased were some non-controversial recommendations of the commission. These included better training for poll-workers, upgraded voting equipment that would be consistently used, and better resource allocation for voting education. Some of the commission's recommendations were later adopted by Florida for the 2002 election cycle.

The fact that appointees to the commission are political has meant that the appointment process to the commission itself has become political at times. For example, in 1993, Republicans refused to confirm a Democratic appointee for the chair of the commission. In 2002, a Republican appointee to the commission had to go to court before he could take his seat on the commission.

Nevertheless, the Commission had remained in existence for almost 50 years, and has made valuable contributions to America's civil rights debate in that period. Its web site, <www.usccr.gov>, gives important information on how to enforce federal civil rights laws, and different state civil rights organizations. As long as it exists, the commission will probably stir up controversy, but ideally it will continue to educate and enlighten about civil rights issues as well.

FURTHER READINGS

Carlson, Peter. 2002. "Uncivil Fights; The Commissioners Have a Job to Do. But First, They Have to Agree to Meet." *Washington Post* (October 30).

U.S. Government Manual Web site. Available online at <www.gpoaccess.gov/gmanual> (accessed November 10, 2003).

U.S. Commission on Civil Rights. 2001. *Voting Irregularities in Florida During the 2000 Presidential Election.* Available online at <www.usccr.gov/pubs/vote2000/report/main.htm>.

COMMISSIONER

A person charged with the management or direction of a board, a court, or a government agency.

A commissioner has the power and responsibility to administer laws or rules that relate to a specific subject matter over which he or she has authority. Generally, he or she is appointed specially, as in the case of a commissioner of court.

COMMISSIONERS ON UNIFORM LAWS

The United States has a central federal government, the authority of which is restricted to those powers given to it by the Constitution. Each state has its own system of legislative and judicial functions that operate in areas not within the exclusive control of the federal government.

Attempts have been made to provide an organized system of uniform legislation throughout the states. The Commissioners on Uniform Laws, properly known as the National Conference of Commissioners on Uniform States Laws and also referred to as the Uniform Law Commissioners, was established in 1890 to draft uniform and model laws on subjects where uniformity is desirable. The organization consists of more than 300 lawyers, judges, and law professors, each selected by the state governments. The acts approved by the organization do not become "law" in the states until they are adopted by legislatures of those states, and the Commissioners on Uniform Laws work with the legislatures to promote such enactments.

The organization has been most instrumental in persuading the states to adopt commercial laws approved by the commissioners, most notably the UNIFORM COMMERCIAL CODE (UCC). It has also drafted a number of laws relating in such areas as CHILD CUSTODY, business organizations, and consumer law. The commissioners often work in conjunction with such organizations as the AMERICAN BAR ASSOCIATION and the American Law Institute when drafting the uniform and model laws.

The web site of the Commissioners on Uniform Laws is located at http://www.nccusl.org.

COMMITMENT

Proceedings directing the confinement of a mentally ill or incompetent person for treatment.

Pursuant to statutory and case law, DUE PROCESS protections are afforded to persons who have been involuntarily committed, including periodic JUDICIAL REVIEW. Commitment has often raised difficult issues of BALANCING the civil liberties of the person who is subject to commitment against other competing interests, including the rights of society to be protected from individuals who might prove dangerous as a result of their mental illness or incompetence, and the community's interest in ensuring that these individuals receive proper treatment.

Each state has its own detailed statutory scheme providing for the involuntary commitment of individuals who might be mentally ill or incompetent. These statutes usually contain language defining the types of mental illnesses and conditions covered by the law, as well as certain conditions that are excluded from coverage—generally mental retardation, epilepsy, developmental disabilities, and drug or alcohol addiction. In addition, most state commitment statutes set forth specific criteria or standards that link these conditions to justifications for involuntary commitment.

Most jurisdictions have at least one criterion that is based on a person's dangerousness to himself or herself, or others. Some states require that other criteria that are closely related to dangerousness be met, such as the presence of a grave disability or an inability to provide for one's basic human needs, or that some medical or psychological treatment is essential to the person's welfare. Since the 1980s, some states have moved significantly away from a strict dangerousness standard for involuntary commitment. In Arizona, for example, a person who is "persistently or acutely disabled" because of mental illness may be subject to commitment (Ariz. Rev. Stat. Ann. § 36-540 (A) [1995]), and in Delaware, an individual who cannot make "responsible decisions" about inpatient care and treatment may be committed (Del. Code Ann. tit. 16, § 5001 [1995]). An even broader standard has been enacted in Iowa, where the law provides that a person may be committed if he or she is likely to inflict serious emotional injury on family or others who "lack reasonable opportunity" to avoid contact with that person (Iowa Code Ann. § 229.1 [West 1995]).

In most jurisdictions, commitment requires a showing that inpatient hospitalization is the least restrictive treatment alternative for the person, in addition to a showing of dangerousness. This requirement is based on the principle, established by the U.S. Supreme Court, that even though a government purpose might be legitimate and substantial, the purpose "cannot be pursued by means that broadly stifle fundamental personal liberties when the end can be more narrowly achieved" (*Shelton v. Tucker,* 364 U.S. 479, 81 S. Ct. 247, 5 L. Ed. 2d 231 [1960]). As a result, most states, through either statutes or case law, recognize a patient's right to be treated in the least restrictive setting.

Despite the difficult legal issues relating to the restriction of liberty that results from involuntary treatment, the U.S. Supreme Court has considered the constitutionality of civil commitment on relatively few occasions. In 1975, in perhaps its most significant decision on the issue, the Court held that a state "cannot constitutionally confine . . . a non-dangerous individual who is capable of surviving safely in freedom

by himself or with the help of willing and responsible family members or friends" (*O'Connor v. Donaldson,* 422 U.S. 563, 95 S. Ct. 2486, 45 L. Ed. 2d 396). The Court further stated that a "mere finding" of mental illness "cannot justify a state's locking a person up against his will and keeping him indefinitely in simple custodial confinement." Although the Court appeared to establish the right of a nondangerous individual not to be involuntarily committed, it left unresolved the issue of whether a mentally ill person has a constitutional right to treatment.

In a later decision, *Zinermon v. Burch,* 494 U.S. 113, 110 S. Ct. 975, 108 L. Ed. 2d 100 (1990), the Court further addressed dangerousness as a justification for civil commitment. It stated that involuntary commitment procedures "guard against the confinement of a person who, though mentally ill, is harmless and can live safely outside an institution." Confinement of such a person would be unconstitutional, the Court held.

The involuntary commitment of individuals who previously have been convicted of a crime has presented an entirely new set of constitutional considerations. The most significant issue has concerned whether a prisoner, following completion of her or his sentence, may be committed to a psychiatric facility without receiving the same due process protections afforded to other individuals who are subjected to civil commitment.

The high court addressed the issue in *Jones v. United States,* 463 U.S. 354, 103 S. Ct. 3043, 77 L. Ed. 2d 694 (1983). In *Jones,* the defendant was

Kenneth Donaldson, respondent in O'Connor v. Donaldson, displays the Supreme Court's opinion, which said that a state cannot hold a non-dangerous individual against his will if the person is capable of "surviving safely" on his own or with the help of friends or family.

AP/WIDE WORLD PHOTOS

acquitted of a crime by reason of insanity, but was confined to a psychiatric hospital for longer than his sentence would have been, had he been convicted. Michael Jones challenged the constitutionality of his commitment. A 5–4 majority of the U.S. Supreme Court affirmed the commitment. The Court reasoned that punishment of an insanity acquittee is inappropriate, and thus the length of the criminal sentence that would have been imposed, had the patient been found sane, was not relevant. Instead, the Court held, the duration of the commitment should depend on the patient's recovery. Thus, if the patient's condition warrants further treatment, the commitment could continue, regardless of the length of the sentence that otherwise would have been imposed.

The commitment of individuals who have been convicted of sex-related crimes has sparked even more intense debate. Courts in many states have had to address difficult questions involving so-called sexual predators: Should these individuals be allowed to re-enter society after they have served their prison terms? May a state detain them indefinitely without violating their constitutional rights?

These questions went before the U.S. Supreme Court in *Kansas v. Hendricks*, 521 U.S. 346, 117 S. Ct. 2072, 138 L. Ed. 2d 501 (1997). In that case, the Court reviewed the constitutionality of the Kansas Sexually Violent Predator Act, which establishes procedures for the civil commitment of persons who, due to a *mental abnormality* or a *personality disorder,* are likely to engage in *predatory acts of sexual violence.* Kan. Stat. §§ 59-29a01 et seq. Kansas invoked the act in committing an inmate who had a long history of sexually molesting children, and who was scheduled for release from prison shortly after the act became law.

In a 5-4 decision written by Associate Justice CLARENCE THOMAS, the Court rejected arguments that someone can be confined to a mental institution only if the person has been diagnosed with a *mental illness.* The Court also rejected arguments that the Kansas law violated the DOUBLE JEOPARDY provision of the FIFTH AMENDMENT to the U.S. Constitution, even though, under the law, persons who are first imprisoned for a sex crime may be institutionalized again when their criminal sentence has been served, based on some of the same evidence that had been used to convict them. The Kansas law created a *civil* commitment procedure that would result in confinement in a mental hospital, the Court said, and the protection against double jeopardy is only triggered by subsequent criminal punishments and prosecutions.

The U.S. Supreme Court's decision was hailed by Kansas and the 38 other states that had urged the justices to uphold the law. However, defense lawyers, civil libertarians, and mental health professionals warned that the decision might allow states to lock up convicts who are not truly dangerous to society. In effect, said several mental health experts, the ruling misuses mental hospitals for punishment purposes, singling out one category of violent criminal for unlimited incarceration without the safeguards afforded to criminal defendants in the BILL OF RIGHTS. Dissenting justices echoed these sentiments in *Hendricks,* writing that while they agreed in principle with idea that states may confine sexual predators who are deemed to be *mentally abnormal,* in this case it appeared that Kansas had not tried to treat the mental problems of the convict whose case was before the court. As a result, they wrote, his institutionalization functioned more like a punishment, and therefore it was unconstitutional.

Although 19 states now have laws authorizing civil commitment for sexual predators, courts in many of those states have been highly circumspect in applying them. For example, the Iowa Supreme Court ruled that the state could not commit a prisoner, who was serving a criminal sentence for operating a motor vehicle without the owner's consent, as a sexually violent predator, even though the prisoner had been convicted for sexually violent offenses in the past. *In re Detention of Gonzales,* 658 N.W.2d 103 (Iowa 2003). The prisoner was not confined for a sexually violent offense at the time that state filed its petition for commitment. Further, the state failed to prove, or even to allege, a recent OVERT ACT that met the statutory definition for being a *sexual predator.* The Iowa Supreme Court reasoned that it would not be just or reasonable "to allow the state to reach back in time, seize on a sexually violent offense for which a defendant was discharged, and couple this with a present confinement for a totally different offense—or, perhaps, a trivial one—and use the Sexually Violent Predator Act to confine the person."

FURTHER READINGS

Haycock, Joel, et al. 1994. "Mediating the Gap: Thinking about Alternatives to the Current Practice of Civil

Commitment." *New England Journal on Criminal and Civil Confinement* 20.

Parry, John. 1994. "Involuntary Civil Commitment in the Nineties: A Constitutional Perspective." *Mental and Physical Disability Law Reporter* 18.

Miller, Robert D. 1987. *Involuntary Civil Commitment of the Mentally Ill in the Post-Reform Era.* Springfield, Ill.: Thomas.

Winick, Bruce J. 1999. "Therapeutic Jurisprudence and the Civil Commitment Hearing." *The Journal of Contemporary Legal Issues* 10.

CROSS-REFERENCES

Patients' Rights.

COMMITMENT FEE

Compensation paid to a lender by a borrower for the lender's promise to give a mortgage at some future time.

A commitment fee, frequently employed in real estate transactions, is an expense separate from interest charged on the loan to be secured by the mortgage. The controversy surrounding nonrefundable commitment fees arises when a borrower decides not to proceed with the loan and then demands return of the fee on the premise that the lender has performed no services to earn it. The courts have consistently rejected this contention and held that the lender is entitled to the commitment fee either as LIQUIDATED DAMAGES for breach of contract or as compensation for earmarking the funds for loan to the borrower.

COMMITTEE

An individual or group of people to whom authority has been delegated by a larger group to perform a particular function or duty. A part of a legislative body made up of one or more individuals who have been assigned the task of investigating a certain issue and reporting their observations and recommendations to the legislature. The Senate has various committees, such as the Committee on Nuclear Energy. The name given to the person or group of people appointed by a court and charged with the responsibility of acting as the guardian of an incompetent person.

COMMODITY

A tangible item that may be bought or sold; something produced for commerce.

Commodities are defined as marketable goods or wares, such as raw or partially processed materials, farm products, or jewelry.

Intangibles, such as human labor, services, or advertising, are generally not considered to be commodities.

COMMODITY CREDIT CORPORATION

The Commodity Credit Corporation (CCC) is a federal agency that was established to stabilize and protect farm income and prices; to assist in the maintenance of balanced and sufficient supplies of useful or serviceable agricultural goods, especially articles of merchandise movable in trade; and to promote the orderly distribution of such products. It was organized on October 17, 1933, pursuant to an EXECUTIVE ORDER, as an agency of the United States.

From October 17, 1933, to July 1, 1939, the CCC was managed and operated in close affiliation with the Reconstruction Finance Corporation. On July 1, 1939, it was transferred to the AGRICULTURE DEPARTMENT under a presidential REORGANIZATION PLAN. Adoption by Congress of the Commodity Credit Corporation Charter Act on June 29, 1948, established the CCC as an agency and instrumentality of the United States under a permanent federal charter.

The CCC is managed by a board of directors and is subject to the general supervision and direction of the secretary of agriculture, who is an ex officio director and chairperson of the board. The board consists of seven members (in addition to the secretary of agriculture) who are appointed by the president of the United States by and with the advice and consent of the Senate.

In carrying out its principal operations the CCC utilizes the personnel and facilities of the Farm Service Agency (FSA) and, in certain foreign trade operations, the Foreign Agricultural Service. A commodity office in Kansas City, Missouri, has specific responsibilities concerned with the disposal (through donation, sale, or transfer) of designated commodities and products held by the Commodity Credit Corporation.

Commodity Stabilization

The CCC administers commodity loan programs, which are part of the "price support" system that has dominated U.S. agriculture since the 1930s. Farmers who agree to limit their production of specially designated crops can sell them to the CCC or borrow money at support prices. In 2003, the CCC managed loan programs for wheat, corn, rice, grain sorghum, barley, oats, oilseeds, tobacco, peanuts, cotton, and sugar.

Commodities acquired under the stabilization program are disposed of through domestic and export sales, transfers to other government agencies, and donations for domestic and foreign welfare use. The CCC is also authorized to exchange surplus agricultural commodities acquired by the CCC for strategic and other materials and services produced abroad.

Support Programs

Under Public Law 480, the Agricultural Trade Development and Assistance Act of 1954, as amended (7 U.S.C.A. 1691 et seq.), the CCC carries out other assigned activities. Along with providing domestic assistance to schools, hospitals, and nonprofit organizations, major emphasis is also directed toward meeting the needs of developing nations. Under the Food for Peace Act of 1966, which further amends the Agricultural Trade Act of 1954, agricultural commodities are procured and exported to combat hunger and malnutrition and to encourage economic improvement in developing countries.

The CCC is also involved in environmental issues. In 2000, the Agriculture Department implemented a two-year, $300 million incentive program designed to encourage increased production of biofuels (environmentally-friendly fuels) such as ethanol and soy-based biodiesel. As a result, the Commodity Credit Corporation provided cash incentives to bioenergy producers who increase their purchase of eligible agricultural commodities to expand production of ethanol, biodiesel, and other biofuels. Eligible commodities include barley, corn, grain sorghum, oats, rice, wheat, soybeans, and many seed crops.

FURTHER READINGS

Commodity Credit Corporation. Available online at <www.fsa.usda.gov/ccc/default.htm> (accessed May 29, 2003).

United States Department of Agriculture. Available online at <www.usda.gov> (accessed May 29, 2003).

CROSS-REFERENCES

Agricultural Law; Agriculture Subsidies.

COMMODITY FUTURES TRADING COMMISSION

The Commodity Futures Trading Commission (CFTC), the federal regulatory agency for futures trading, was established by the Com-modity Futures Trading Commission Act of 1974 (88 Stat. 1389; 7 U.S.C.A. 4a), approved October 23, 1974. The commission began operation in April 1975 and its authority to regulate futures trading was renewed by Congress in 1978. Its authority was again renewed with the Commodity Futures Modernization Act of 2000, which also mandated major reforms of the commission. The CFTC maintains a comprehensive web site at <http://www.cftc.gov>.

The CFTC consists of five commissioners who are appointed by the president with the advice and consent of the Senate. The commissioners serve staggered five-year terms and by law no more than three commissioners can belong to the same political party. One commissioner is designated by the president to serve as chairperson. The chair's staff includes the Office of the Inspector General and the Office of International Affairs.

To comply with the requirements of the Modernization Act, the commission underwent a restructuring in 2002. As a result, it consists of six major operating units: the Division of Clearing and Intermediary Oversight, the Division of Market Oversight, the Division of Enforcement, the Office of the Chief Economist, the Office of the General Counsel, and the Office of the Executive Director.

The CFTC regulates trading on the 11 U.S. futures exchanges, which offer numerous kinds of futures contracts. It also regulates the activities of some three thousand commodity exchange members, 360 public brokerage houses (futures commission merchants), about 38,000 commission-registered futures industry salespeople and associated persons, and 2,500 commodity trading advisers and commodity pool operators. Some off-exchange transactions involving instruments similar in nature to futures contracts also fall under CFTC jurisdiction.

The commission's regulatory and enforcement efforts are designed to ensure that the futures trading process is fair and that it protects both the rights of customers and the financial integrity of the marketplace. The CFTC approves the rules under which an exchange proposes to operate and monitors exchange enforcement of those rules. It reviews the terms of proposed futures contracts and registers companies and individuals who handle customer funds or give trading advice. The commission also protects the public by enforcing rules that require that customer funds be kept in bank accounts separate from accounts maintained by firms for their own use, and that such customer accounts be marked to present market value at the close of trading each day.

Futures contracts for agricultural commodities were traded in the United States for more than one hundred years before futures trading was diversified to include trading in contracts for precious metals, raw materials, foreign currencies, commercial interest rates, and U.S. government and mortgage SECURITIES. Contract diversification has grown in exchange trading volume, a growth not limited to the newer commodities.

The CFTC maintains large regional offices in Chicago and New York, cities in which eight of the nation's 11 futures exchanges are located. Smaller regional offices are located in Kansas City and San Francisco, and there is a suboffice of the Chicago regional office in Minneapolis.

FURTHER READINGS

Commodity Futures Trading Commision. *2002 Annual Report.* Available online at <www.cftc.gov/files/anr/anr2002.pdf> (accessed June 1, 2003).

COMMON

Belonging to or pertaining to the general public. Common lands, also known as public lands, are *those that are set aside for use by the community at large, such as parks and public recreation areas. Common also means habitual or recurring, such as offenses that are committed frequently or repeatedly. A* common thief *is one who has been repeatedly convicted of* LARCENY. *Something that is common is owned equally by two or more people, such as a piece of land. A* TENANCY IN COMMON *is an interest in land wherein at least two people share ownership.*

COMMON CARRIER

An individual or business that advertises to the public that it is available for hire to transport people or property in exchange for a fee.

A common carrier is legally bound to carry all passengers or freight as long as there is enough space, the fee is paid, and no reasonable grounds to refuse to do so exist. A common carrier that unjustifiably refuses to carry a particular person or cargo may be sued for damages.

The states regulate common carriers engaged in business within their borders. When interstate or foreign transportation is involved, the federal government, by virtue of the COMMERCE CLAUSE of the Constitution, regulates the activities of such carriers. A common carrier may establish reasonable regulations for the efficient operation and maintenance of its business.

A man hails a cab in New York's Times Square. A taxi is considered a common carrier, and, as such, is regulated by the state in which it operates.

AP/WIDE WORLD PHOTOS

COMMON COUNCIL

In English LEGAL HISTORY, *the name given to Parliament. In the U.S. legal system, the legislative body of a city or of a* MUNICIPAL CORPORATION.

COMMON COUNT

A traditional type of COMMON-LAW PLEADING *that is used in actions to recover a debt of money of the defendant based upon an express or implied promise to pay after performance had been rendered. In a common-count* PLEADING, *the plaintiff sets forth in account form the facts that constitute the basis of his or her claim, such as money had and received and goods sold and delivered.*

Common counts were once used to allege the grounds for actions of ASSUMPSIT, a common-law action for the recovery of money owed by a defendant to the plaintiff. The four classes of common counts were (1) the *indebitatus* count; (2) the QUANTUM MERUIT count; (3) the QUANTUM VALEBANT count; and (4) the ACCOUNT STATED count. The generalized nature of common counts enabled a plaintiff to take advantage of any ground of liability for which proof was available within the limits of the action of assumpsit. This is in contrast to special counts within which a plaintiff had to state a particular claim or be denied relief.

Common counts are no longer used for pleading purposes but have been replaced by complaints according to the Federal Rules of Civil Procedure and state codes of civil procedure.

COMMON DISASTER

A set of circumstances in which two individuals die apparently simultaneously.

In a common disaster there is no certainty of who died first, an important issue that frequently arises in the determination of the inheritance of property or the distribution of proceeds of a life insurance policy.

The *common disaster clause* found in insurance policies and wills is a provision that names an alternate beneficiary in the event that the testator and legatee or the insured and the beneficiary die simultaneously. SIMULTANEOUS DEATH acts are state laws that provide for the disposal of property in the event of a common disaster.

COMMON LANDS

An archaic designation of property set aside and regulated by the local, state, or federal government for the benefit of the public for recreational purposes.

Common lands established by the Federal government are known as public lands.

COMMON LAW

The ancient law of England based upon societal customs and recognized and enforced by the judgments and decrees of the courts. The general body of statutes and case law that governed England and the American colonies prior to the American Revolution.

The principles and rules of action, embodied in case law rather than legislative enactments, applicable to the government and protection of persons and property that derive their authority from the community customs and traditions that evolved over the centuries as interpreted by judicial tribunals.

A designation used to denote the opposite of statutory, equitable, or civil, for example, a common-law action.

The common-law system prevails in England, the United States, and other countries colonized by England. It is distinct from the civil-law system, which predominates in Europe and in areas colonized by France and Spain. The common-law system is used in all the states of the United States except Louisiana, where French CIVIL LAW combined with English CRIMINAL LAW to form a hybrid system. The common-law system is also used in Canada, except in the Province of Quebec, where the French civil-law system prevails.

Anglo-American common law traces its roots to the medieval idea that the law as handed down from the king's courts represented the common custom of the people. It evolved chiefly from three English Crown courts of the twelfth and thirteenth centuries: the Exchequer, the King's Bench, and the COMMON PLEAS. These courts eventually assumed jurisdiction over disputes previously decided by local or manorial courts, such as baronial, admiral's (maritime), guild, and forest courts, whose jurisdiction was limited to specific geographic or subject matter areas. EQUITY courts, which were instituted to provide relief to litigants in cases where common-law relief was unavailable, also merged with common-law courts. This consolidation of jurisdiction over most legal disputes into several courts was the framework for the modern Anglo-American judicial system.

Early common-law procedure was governed by a complex system of PLEADING, under which only the offenses specified in authorized writs could be litigated. Complainants were required to satisfy all the specifications of a writ before they were allowed access to a common-law court. This system was replaced in England and in the United States during the mid-1800s. A streamlined, simplified form of pleading, known as CODE PLEADING or notice pleading, was instituted. Code pleading requires only a plain, factual statement of the dispute by the parties and leaves the determination of issues to the court.

Common-law courts base their decisions on prior judicial pronouncements rather than on legislative enactments. Where a statute governs the dispute, judicial interpretation of that statute determines how the law applies. Common-law judges rely on their predecessors' decisions of actual controversies, rather than on abstract codes or texts, to guide them in applying the law. Common-law judges find the grounds for their decisions in law reports, which contain decisions of past controversies. Under the doctrine of STARE DECISIS, common-law judges are obliged to adhere to previously decided cases, or precedents, where the facts are substantially the same. A court's decision is binding authority for similar cases decided by the same court or by lower courts within the same jurisdiction. The decision is not binding on courts of higher rank within that jurisdiction or in other jurisdictions, but it may be considered as persuasive authority.

Because common-law decisions deal with everyday situations as they occur, social changes, inventions, and discoveries make it necessary for judges sometimes to look outside reported decisions for guidance in a CASE OF FIRST IMPRESSION (previously undetermined legal issue). The common-law system allows judges to look to other jurisdictions or to draw upon past or present judicial experience for analogies to help in making a decision. This flexibility allows common law to deal with changes that lead to unanticipated controversies. At the same time, stare decisis provides certainty, uniformity, and predictability and makes for a stable legal environment.

Under a common-law system, disputes are settled through an adversarial exchange of arguments and evidence. Both parties present their cases before a neutral fact finder, either a judge or a jury. The judge or jury evaluates the evidence, applies the appropriate law to the facts, and renders a judgment in favor of one of the parties. Following the decision, either party may appeal the decision to a higher court. Appellate courts in a common-law system may review only findings of law, not determinations of fact.

Under common law, all citizens, including the highest-ranking officials of the government, are subject to the same set of laws, and the exercise of government power is limited by those laws. The judiciary may review legislation, but only to determine whether it conforms to constitutional requirements.

FURTHER READINGS

Cantor, Norman F. 1997. *Imagining the Law: Common Law and the Foundations of the American Legal System.* New York: HarperCollins.

Kellogg, Frederic R. 2003. "Holmes, Common Law Theory, and Judicial Restraint." *John Marshall Law Review* 36 (winter): 457–505.

Pound, Roscoe. 1999. *The Spirit of the Common Law.* New Brunswick, N.J.: Transaction.

Strauss, David A. 2003. "Common Law, Common Ground, and Jefferson's Principle." *Yale Law Journal* 112 (May): 1717–55.

CROSS-REFERENCES

Adversary System; English Law.

COMMON-LAW ACTION

A lawsuit governed by the general principles of law derived from court decisions, as opposed to the provisions of statutes. Actions ex contractu, *arising out of a breach of contract, and actions ex* delicto, *based upon the commission of a* TORT, *are common-law actions.*

COMMON-LAW COURTS

The early royal courts in England that administered the law common to all.

For a time after the Norman Conquest of England in 1066, the king himself sat to hear cases involving royal interests and the court was called coram rege (Latin for "before the king"). When the king began delegating authority to administer justice, the tribunal he appointed was called Curia Regis, the King's Court. Out of the Curia Regis came the three royal common-law courts. The first offshoot was the Exchequer, which originally collected taxes and administered the king's finances, but by 1250 was exercising full powers as a court. Next to develop as a separate court was COMMON PLEAS, a court probably established by HENRY II during the latter half of the twelfth century to hear cases not involving the king's rights. The remaining part of the Curia Regis reviewed decisions of the Common Pleas by issuing writs of error. This court, later known as the King's Bench, also heard cases involving the king's interests, particularly criminal matters and cases involving high noblemen. For many years the work of the court was written as if proceedings before it were before the king himself. The common-law courts competed with the Chancery, which exercised EQUITY jurisdiction, and their struggles shifted the division of authority at various times. They were consolidated with the other high courts of England by the JUDICATURE ACTS in the late nineteenth century.

CROSS-REFERENCES

Law "Common-Law Courts" (Sidebar).

COMMON-LAW MARRIAGE

A union of two people not formalized in the customary manner as prescribed by law but created by an agreement to marry followed by COHABITATION.

A fundamental question in marriage is whether the union is legally recognized. This question is important because marriage affects property ownership, rights of survivorship, spousal benefits, and other marital amenities. With so much at stake, marriage has become a matter regulated by law.

In the United States, the law of marriage is reserved to the states and thus governed by state law. All states place restrictions on marriage, such as age requirements and the prohibition of intrafamilial marriage. Further, most states recognize marriage only upon completion of specified procedures. A typical statute requires a witnessed ceremony solemnized by a lawfully authorized person, submission to blood tests, and fulfillment of license requirements. However, in some states, the marital union of a man and a woman can still be achieved in the most simple, time-honored ways.

History

Marriage has evolved over the centuries, but some basic features have remained constant. In ancient Rome, it was accomplished by consent of the parties to live together. No forms were required, and no ceremony was necessary. This early Roman model of marriage was displaced when the Catholic Church declared in 1563 that marriages were not valid unless contracted in the presence of a priest and two witnesses. In England, under the Anglican Church, marriage by consent and cohabitation was valid until the passage of Lord Hardwicke's Act in 1753. This act instituted certain requirements for marriage, including the performance of a religious ceremony observed by witnesses.

The American colonies rejected the requirement of a religious ceremony but retained the custom of a ceremony, religious or otherwise. The ancient Roman concept of marriage by agreement and cohabitation was adopted by early American courts as valid under the COMMON LAW.

In the 1800s, state legislatures began to enact laws expressly to prohibit marriage without an observed ceremony and other requirements. Common-law marriage was prohibited in a majority of jurisdictions. However, the FULL FAITH AND CREDIT CLAUSE of the U.S. Constitution requires all states that prohibit it to nonetheless recognize a common-law marriage created in a jurisdiction that allows it. U.S. Const. art. IV, § 1. Laws in all states require a common-law spouse to obtain a DIVORCE before remarrying.

Common-law marriage is allowed in fourteen jurisdictions: Alabama, Colorado, Georgia, Idaho, Iowa, Kansas, Montana, Ohio, Oklahoma, Pennsylvania, Rhode Island, South Carolina, Texas, and the District of Columbia. The manner in which a state authorizes common-law marriage varies. Pennsylvania maintains a statute that declares that the statutory chapter covering licensed marriage does not affect the recognition of common-law marriage (23 Pa. Const. Stat. Ann. § 1103). In Georgia, the operative marriage statute simply states, "To constitute a valid marriage in this State there must be—1. Parties able to contract; 2. An actual contract; 3. Consummation according to law" (Ga. Code Ann. § 19-3-1).

Several reasons have been offered for recognizing common-law marriage. In some states, including Pennsylvania and Rhode Island, common-law marriage was originally permitted to allow for religious and social freedom. Some state legislatures have noted the private importance of marriage and assailed the insensitivity of governments purporting to regulate such a personal matter. Other states have been reluctant to require licensing and ceremony in consideration of the financial hardship such requirements impose on poor citizens.

Features

A common-law marriage has three basic features. When a common-law marriage is challenged, proof of the following elements is critical in most jurisdictions.

1. *A present agreement to be married.* The parties must announce to each other that they are married from that moment forward. Specific words are not mandated, but there must be evidence of an agreement to be married. Proof may consist of CIRCUMSTANTIAL EVIDENCE, including evidence that the partners have cohabitated and held themselves out to the public as being married. However, neither cohabitation nor a public holding out constitutes sufficient proof to establish the formation of a common-law marriage, either by themselves or taken together. An agreement to marry must be proved by the party asserting marriage.

2. *Cohabitation.* The parties must actually live together in order to support a claim of common-law marriage. Whether maintenance of a separate home by one of the parties will nullify a common-law marriage is a QUESTION OF FACT and depends on the circumstances of the particular case.

3. *Public representations of marriage.* The couple must consistently hold themselves out to the public as married. A married couple is expected to tell people that they are married. They should also file joint tax returns and declare their marriage on other documents, such as applications, leases, and birth certificates.

Legal Applications

A challenge to a common-law marriage can come from a variety of sources. For example, an insurance carrier or PENSION provider may contest a common-law marriage when one spouse claims benefits by virtue of the marriage. Often, it is one of the purported spouses who challenges the existence of a common-law marriage.

In *Flores v. Flores,* 847 S.W.2d 648 (Tex. App. Waco 1993), Peggy Ann Flores sought to prove that she had been married by common law to Albert Flores. Peggy and Albert were married in a ceremony on July 18, 1987, and divorced on March 9, 1989. They continued to live together until November 1990, when Albert moved away to live with his girlfriend, Lisa. Albert and Lisa were married on January 1, 1991.

Peggy filed for a second divorce from Albert on January 31, 1991. In the same proceeding, she applied for custody of their child, Joshua, and CHILD SUPPORT payments from Albert. The County Court, Brazos County, found that a common-law marriage had existed between Peggy and Albert following their 1989 divorce. The county court granted the second divorce and ordered custody and child support payments to Peggy. Albert appealed, arguing in part that there was insufficient evidence to support a finding both that Peggy and Albert had agreed to remarry and that Peggy and Albert had represented to others that they were married.

The Court of Appeals of Texas, Waco, agreed with Albert. The court of appeals opened its opinion by listing the important factual background. According to Peggy's testimony at the 1991 divorce proceeding, she had considered herself married to Albert after the 1989 divorce, and Albert had, on one occasion, introduced her as his wife after the 1989 divorce. Peggy's employer, Irma Ortega, testified that she did not know of the first divorce, that Albert sent gifts and affectionate notes to Peggy, and that Peggy kept a picture of Albert and Joshua at her workplace. Relatives of both Peggy and Albert testified that after the 1989 divorce, the relationship continued much as it had before.

Other testimony revealed that on a visit to a hospital after the divorce, Peggy told hospital personnel that she was single. Albert and Peggy signed a lease together that did not specify their relationship. Peggy used Albert's credit cards, and Albert paid the rent and other bills. They also maintained a joint bank account and carried on a sexual relationship.

Albert testified that Peggy had asked him to stay with her until she got "back on her feet." He also testified that he had moved in with Peggy after the 1989 divorce to help her and that he had informed Lisa that he was living with his former wife "and helping her out."

The court of appeals then addressed whether these facts sufficed to establish a common law marriage in Texas. The court said that while the facts must demonstrate cohabitation by the parties, public representations of marriage by the parties, and an agreement to be married, all three elements need not exist simultaneously for a common-law marriage to exist.

On the issue of whether the couple had agreed to be married again after the 1989 divorce, the court acknowledged that such an agreement can be inferred from cohabitation. However, the court warned that cohabitation is more common than it once was and that cohabitation evidence should be weighed more carefully than it has been in the past. After an examination of the record, the court concluded that there was no direct evidence of an agreement between Albert and Peggy to marry. The evidence showing that Albert and Peggy had lived together and shared resources did not compel a finding of an agreement to be married.

Nor did the evidence support a finding that Peggy and Albert had held themselves out as married. According to the court of appeals, one public representation of marriage did not constitute a public holding out. Other evidence offered by Peggy, such as the joint bank account, was insufficient to support public holding out, the court found. Thus, the court of appeals ultimately reversed the judgment of the county court and ordered that Peggy take nothing but child support payments from her suit.

Late Twentieth-Century Developments

During the last 15 years of the twentieth century a growing number of states, counties, and municipalities granted qualified legal recognition to unmarried "domestic partners." Known in some jurisdictions as "reciprocal beneficiaries," unmarried couples who receive legal recognition as domestic partners may be eligible for HEALTH INSURANCE benefits, life insurance benefits, and child VISITATION RIGHTS. Depending on the jurisdiction, domestic partners may also be entitled to hospital visitation rights.

However, in most jurisdictions domestic partners may only inherit from their partners or their partner's family if they are specifically named in the deceased's will. A few states allow domestic partners to inherit from each other or each other's family in the absence of a will, called intestate succession. By contrast, the law of all states that recognize common-law marriage allow both parties to the common-law marriage to inherit under state intestacy laws when either spouse dies without a will.

Also unlike common-law marriages, domestic partners may not typically ask courts to settle their post-relationship property disputes. Nor may domestic partners petition courts for ALIMONY awards, unless the partners entered a formal agreement for *palimony* prior to their cohabitation. *Marvin v. Marvin,* 18 Cal.3d 660, 557 P.2d 106, 134 Cal. Rptr. 815 (Cal. 1976). But if partners do enter a palimony agreement, they will generally be enforced, unless during the period of cohabitation the partners resided in Illinois, Georgia, and Tennessee, the three states that have expressly refused to recognize palimony agreements.

Every jurisdiction recognizing domestic partners as a legal entity has its own list of formal requirements that unmarried couples must satisfy before they will be formally recognized as domestic partners. The formal requirements in no two jurisdictions are identical. However, most jurisdictions do share many of the same core requirements.

These core requirements include that both partners must be older than 18 and unmarried, currently live together, apply together before a public official with authority to recognize them as domestic partners, and pay the related fees to be registered. To end a domestic partnership, most jurisdictions allow the couple simply to send a letter to the registrar of domestic partners. The letter must be dated and signed by both partners, and it must specifically request that the domestic partnership be terminated.

Laws in eight states and more than 100 municipalities now provide legal recognition for unmarried couples as domestic partners. This legislation often allows both opposite-sex and same-sex couples to form domestic partnerships, unlike the states that recognize common-law marriage, none of which expressly permits homosexual common-law marriages, and some of which expressly prohibit it. Pursuant to state and local domestic-partner legislation, 157 Fortune 500 companies, 3,960 private employers and unions, and 158 COLLEGES AND UNIVERSITIES were as of mid-2003 providing benefits to domestic partners. Although no nationwide statistics exist, the 2000 census revealed almost 10,000 domestic partners were registered in St. Louis, Missouri, alone, and more than 15,000 same-sex couples were registered as domestic partners in California.

FURTHER READINGS

Jasper, Margaret C. 1994. *Marriage and Divorce.* Dobbs Ferry, N.Y.: Oceana.

Wadlington, Walter J. 1990. *Domestic Relations Manual for Teachers: To Accompany Cases and Materials.* 2d. ed. Westbury, N.Y.: Foundation Press.

CROSS-REFERENCES

Circumstantial Evidence; Cohabitation; Domestic Partnership Law; Survivorship.

COMMON-LAW PLEADING

The system of rules and principles that governed the forms into which parties cast their claims or defenses in order to set an issue before the court.

The system prevailed in the common-law courts and in many U.S. states until it was replaced by statute with a procedure called CODE PLEADING in the nineteenth century. Those states that do not have systems of code pleading today follow the pleading procedures established by the rules of CIVIL PROCEDURE adopted for the federal district courts in 1938.

During the twelfth and thirteenth centuries a person with a grievance sought a writ from the king's chief minister, the chancellor. The writ ordered the defendant to submit to the plaintiff's demands or to appear and answer the charge made against him or her. Over a period of time, the format of the particular writs began to become standardized and were called FORMS OF ACTION. There were different writs for different types of actions.

The purpose of the writ was to assert the court's authority to hear the dispute and to demand the presence of the defendant. In this regard it corresponded to the modern summons. The plaintiff then had to state the claim against the defendant. For the pleading to be valid the plaintiff had to use exactly those words permitted by the form of action selected. Some forms of action, such as TRESPASS, became immensely popular because they allowed more variation in the facts pleaded than other forms. If a plaintiff selected a writ that did not fit the particular case the action was thrown out of court. If there were no writs for some kinds of actions and the chancellor refused to devise one then the aggrieved person could find no relief at all in the royal courts.

A defendant faced a similar array of established responses. The defendant could, for example, deny the plaintiff's right to legal relief even if the facts alleged were true. Such a response was known as a demurrer. A defendant could choose to enter a dilatory plea, which argued against the court's authority to hear that particular case rather than directly objecting to the plaintiff's claim. A third option was to enter a plea in bar which denied the plaintiff's right to maintain the action at all. An example of such a plea was a traverse, an assertion that some essential element of the plaintiff's case was lacking or untrue. Another plea in bar was confession and avoidance which stated that additional facts rendered the claim unenforceable, even if the plaintiff's facts were true.

Like the plaintiff, the defendant was limited to choosing a single position. The alternative responses were mutually exclusive even though they were not necessarily contradictory. For example, if the defendant pleaded a confession and avoidance he or she conceded the accuracy of the plaintiff's version of the facts and would not be allowed to contest those facts. The issue became the new facts that the defendant had asserted in order to avoid the effect of the plaintiff's allegation. The plaintiff had to argue against the newly introduced facts by entering a demurrer, a traverse, or another confession and avoidance.

Eventually the system of common-law pleading fell into an established order that proceeded alternatively from plaintiff to defendant and back to plaintiff. The plaintiff first stated the claim in a declaration and the defendant answered in a plea. The plaintiff was permitted to respond with a replication. Then came the defendant's rejoinder, the plaintiff's surrejoinder, the defendant's rebutter, and the plaintiff's surrebutter. No distinctive names were given to any pleadings used beyond that stage.

The system of common-law pleading eventually became so encrusted with requirements and risks that actions were won or lost on the fine points of pleading rather than on the merits of a party's case. The insistence on reducing every case to one claim and one answer created more problems than it solved. As a result, in 1948 many states began enacting code pleading, while other states eventually adopted rules of pleading patterned on the rules of federal civil procedure.

COMMON-LAW TRUST

More commonly known as a BUSINESS TRUST or a Massachusetts trust. A business organization for investment purposes by which trustees manage and control property for the benefit of beneficiaries who are protected against personal liability for any losses incurred.

COMMON PLEAS

Trial-level courts of general jurisdiction. One of the royal common-law courts in England existing since the beginning of the thirteenth century and developing from the Curia Regis, or the King's Court.

In the United States only Pennsylvania has courts of common pleas with the authority to hear all civil and criminal cases. In most states courts of common pleas have been abolished and their jurisdiction transferred to district, circuit, or superior courts.

For some time after the Norman Conquest of England in 1066, parties seeking justice from the king were greatly inconvenienced by the fact that the king was constantly on the move and frequently abroad. Scholars have speculated that the king was attempting to consolidate his power and that feeding and financing the royal household could be accomplished only by continually moving throughout the land. Parties could submit a dispute to a court held coram rege, before the king himself, only by pursuing the king in his travels. The barons finally forced the issue with King John in 1215 when they insisted on the following provision in the MAGNA CHARTA: "Common Pleas shall not follow our court but shall be held in some certain place." That certain place came to be Westminster, where some legal business was already being handled by the end of the twelfth century. There the Court of Common Pleas, also called Common Bench, heard all real actions and common pleas—actions between subjects that did not involve royal interests. It had no authority to hear criminal matters which were the special prerogative of the King's Bench. The Court of Common Pleas consisted of a chief justice and four (later five) associate justices. Appeals and their decisions were taken to the King's Bench but later to the Exchequer. The court was consolidated with the other high courts of England by the JUDICATURE ACTS in the late nineteenth century.

COMMON SCOLD

A person who frequently or habitually causes public disturbances or breaks the peace by brawling or quarreling.

Scolding, which was an indictable offense at COMMON LAW but is obsolete today, did not involve a single incident but rather the repeated creation of discord.

COMMON STOCK

Evidence of participation in the ownership of a corporation that takes the form of printed certificates.

Each share of common stock constitutes a contract between the shareholder and the corporation. The owner of a share of common stock is ordinarily entitled to participate in and to vote at stockholders' meetings. He or she participates in the profits through the receipt of dividends after the payment of dividends on preferred stock. Shares of common stock are the PERSONAL PROPERTY of their holder.

COMMUNIS ERROR FACIT JUS

[Latin, common error makes law.] Another expression for this idea is "common opinion," or communis opinio. *In ancient Rome, the phrase expressed the notion that a generally accepted opinion or belief about a legal issue makes that opinion or belief the law. Judges have pointed out that universal opinion may also be universal error. Until the error is discovered, however, the belief continues to be the law. The concept of* communis opinio *is not especially favored by contemporary U.S. courts.*

COMMUNISM

A system of social organization in which goods are held in common.

Communism in the United States is something of an anomaly. The basic principles of communism are, by design, at odds with the free enterprise foundation of U.S. capitalism. The freedom of individuals to privately own property, start a business, and own the means of production is a basic tenet of U.S. government, and communism opposes this arrangement. However, there have been, are, and probably always will be communists in the United States.

As early as the fourth century B.C., Plato addressed the problems surrounding private ownership of property in the *Republic*. Some early Christians supported communal principles, as did the German Anabaptists during the sixteenth-century religious Reformation in Europe.

The concept of common ownership of goods gained a measure of support in France during the nineteenth century. Shortly after the French Revolution of 1789, François-Noël ("Gracchus") Babeuf was arrested and executed for plotting the violent overthrow of the new French government by revolutionary communists. Etienne Cabet inspired many social explorers with his *Voyage en Icarie* (1840), which promoted peaceful, idealized communities. Cabet is often credited with the spate of communal settlements that appeared in mid-nineteenth-century North America. Louis-Auguste Blanqui offered a more strident version of communism by urging French workers during the 1830s to organize insurrections and establish a dictatorship for the purpose of reorganizing the government.

Communism received, however, its first comprehensive intellectual foundation in 1848, when Germans KARL MARX and Friedrich Engels published *The Communist Manifesto.* As technology increased and industry expanded in nineteenth-century Europe and America, it became clear that the GENERAL WELFARE of laborers was not improving. Although the new democratic governments gave new freedoms to workers, or "the proletariat," the capitalism that came with democracy had created different means of oppression. By drawing on existing theories of materialism, labor, and historical evolution, Marx and Engels were able to identify the reasons why, despite periodic drastic changes in government, common laborers had been doomed to abject poverty throughout recorded history.

In the first chapter of *The Communist Manifesto,* Marx and Engels argued that human history was best understood as a continuing struggle between a small exploiting class (the owners of the means of production) and a larger exploited class (laborers in factories and mills who often worked for starvation wages). At any point in time, the exploiting class controlled the means of production and profited by employing the labor of the masses. In the capitalism that developed alongside democracy, Marx and Engels saw a progressive concentration of the powers of production placed in the hands of a privileged few. Although society was producing more goods and services, the general welfare of the middle class, they believed, was declining. According to Marx and Engels, this disparity or internal contradiction in capitalistic societies predicted capitalism's doom. Over time, as the anticipated numbers of the middle class, or "bourgeoisie," began to decrease, the conflicts between laborers and capitalists would sharpen, and social revolution was inevitable. At the end of *The Communist Manifesto,* Marx and Engels wrote that the transfer of power from the few to the many could only take place by force. Marx later retreated from this position and wrote that it was possible for this radical change to take place peacefully.

The social revolution originally envisioned by Marx and Engels would begin with a proletariat dictatorship. Once in possession of the means of production, the dictatorship would devise the means for society to achieve the communal ownership of wealth. Once the transitional period had stabilized the state, the purest form of communism would take shape. Communism in its purest form would be a classless societal system in which property and wealth were distributed equally and without the need for a coercive government. This last stage of Marxian communism has as of the early 2000s never been realized in any government.

Russia

In October 1917, VLADIMIR LENIN and Leon Trotsky led the Bolshevik party in a bloody revolution against the Russian monarch, Czar Nicholas II. Lenin relied on violence and persistent aggression during his time as a Russian leader. Although he professed to being in the process of modernizing Marxist theory, Lenin stalled Marx's communism at its transitional phase and kept the proletariat dictatorship to himself.

Lenin's communist philosophy was designated by followers as Marxist-Leninist theory in 1928. Marxism-Leninism was characterized by the refusal to cooperate and compromise with capitalist countries. It also insisted upon severe restrictions on HUMAN RIGHTS and the extermination of actual and supposed political opponents. In these respects, Marxist-Leninist theory was unrecognizable to democratic socialists and other followers of Marxist doctrine, and the 1920s saw a gradual split between Russian communists and other European proponents of Marxian theory. The Bolshevik party, with Lenin at the helm, renamed itself the All-Russian Communist party, and Lenin presided over a totalitarian state until his death in 1924.

JOSEPH STALIN succeeded Lenin as the Communist party ruler. In 1924, Stalin established the Union of Soviet Socialist Republics (U.S.S.R.) by colonizing land surrounding Russia and placing the territories within the purview of the Soviet Union. The All-Russian Communist party became the All-Union Communist party, and Stalin sought to position the Soviet Union as the home base of a world revolution. In his quest for worldwide communism, Stalin sent political opponents such as Trotsky into exile, had thousands of political dissidents tortured and murdered, and imprisoned millions more.

HOUSE UN-AMERICAN ACTIVITIES COMMITTEE

Between 1938 and 1969, the House Un-American Activities Committee (HUAC) hunted political radicals. In hundreds of public hearings, this congressional panel set out to expose and punish citizens whom it deemed guilty of holding "un-American" views—fascism and communism. From government to labor, academia, and Hollywood, the committee aggressively pursued so-called subversives. It used Congress's subpoena power to force citizens to appear before it, holding them in CONTEMPT if they did not testify. HUAC's tactics of scandal, innuendo, and the threat of imprisonment disrupted lives and ruined careers. After years of mounting criticism, Congress renamed HUAC in 1969 and finally abolished it in 1975.

In the late 1930s, HUAC arose in a period of fear and suspicion. The United States was still devastated by the Great Depression, and fascism was on the rise in Europe. Washington, D.C., feared spies. In early May 1938, Representative Martin Dies (R-Tex.) called for a probe of fascism, communism, and other so-called un-American (meaning anti-patriotic) beliefs. The idea was popular with other lawmakers. Two weeks later, HUAC was established as a temporary committee, with Dies at its head.

Because Chairman Dies was in charge, the press referred to HUAC as the Dies Committee. The chairman had ambitious goals. At first, he set out to stop German and Italian propaganda. Early investigations focused on two pro-Nazi groups, the German-American Bund and the Silver Shirt Legion. But Dies had a partisan agenda as well. An outspoken critic of Roosevelt, he wanted to discredit the president's NEW DEAL programs. Contending that the Federal Writers' Project (a program to compile oral histories and travel guides) and Federal Theatre Project (employing out-of-work actors to help produce plays) were rife with Communists, HUAC urged the firing of thirty-eight hundred federal employees. In this atmosphere of conflict between the committee and the White House, the JUSTICE DEPARTMENT found the numbers grossly exaggerated; its own probe concluded that only thirty-six employees had been validly accused. The committee's first great smear ended with dismal results.

HUAC's limited success in its early years was largely due to its chairman's political mistakes. Besides alienating Roosevelt and the Justice Department, Dies made an even more powerful enemy in J. EDGAR HOOVER, director of the FEDERAL BUREAU OF INVESTIGATION (FBI). After Dies publicly criticized the director, Attorney General ROBERT H. JACKSON went on the attack, accusing HUAC of interfering with the FBI's proper role. Hoover himself saw to it that the turf battle was short-lived. In 1941 Dies was quietly informed that the FBI had evidence of his accepting a bribe. Although no charges were brought and Dies retained the title of chairman until 1944, he conspicuously avoided HUAC's hearings from that point on.

HUAC grew in both power and tenacity after WORLD WAR II, for several reasons. A deterioration in U.S.-Soviet relations started the COLD WAR, a decades-long battle of words—and, as in Korea and Vietnam, of bullets—in which Communism became identified as the United States' single greatest enemy. Both bodies of Congress, the White House, the FBI, and numerous conservative citizens' groups such as the John Birch Society rallied to the anti-Communist cause. Moreover, HUAC had new leadership. With Dies gone, Hoover was more than willing to assist with the committee's investigations, which was fortunate, since no congressional committee had the resources available to the FBI. When HUAC chairman J. Parnell Thomas announced in 1947 that the committee would root out Communists in Hollywood, he had nothing but HEARSAY to go on. No Hollywood investigation would have taken place if Hoover, responding to Thomas's plea, had not provided HUAC with lists of suspects and names of cooperative witnesses.

Thus began a pattern of FBI and HUAC cooperation that lasted for three decades. Hoover's testimony before HUAC in March 1947 illuminated their common interest in driving the enemy into the open:

> I feel that once public opinion is thoroughly aroused as it is today, the fight against Communism is well on its way. Victory will be assured once Communists are identified and exposed, because the public will take the first step

Stalin saw the Soviet Union through WORLD WAR II. Although it joined with the United States and other democratic countries in the fight against Nazism, the Soviet Union remained strongly opposed to capitalist principles. In the scramble for control of Europe after World War II, the Soviet Union gained power over several Eastern European countries it had helped liberate and placed them under communist rule. Bulgaria, Czechoslovakia, Hungary, East Germany, Poland, and Romania were forced to comply with the totalitarianism of Stalin's rule. North Korea was also supported and influenced by the Soviet Union. More independent communist

of quarantining them so they can do no harm. . . . This Committee renders a distinct service when it publicly reveals the diabolic machinations of sinister figures engaged in un-American activities.

The FBI director's prediction was right: quarantining of a sort did indeed follow.

The Hollywood probe marked a new height for HUAC. The committee investigated the film industry three times, in 1947, 1951–52, and 1953–55. The first hearing produced the so-called Hollywood Ten, a group of screenwriters and professionals who refused to answer questions about whether or not they were Communists. Despite invoking their FIRST AMENDMENT right to FREEDOM OF SPEECH, they were subsequently charged with contempt of Congress, tried, convicted, and jailed for between six months and one year. In later HUAC hearings, other film industry professionals invoked the Fifth Amendment—the constitutional protection against self-incrimination—and they too suffered. HUAC operated on the dubious premise that no innocent person would avoid answering its questions, and members of Congress frequently taunted witnesses who attempted to "hide," as they said, behind the FIFTH AMENDMENT. Not everyone subpoenaed was a Communist, but the committee usually wanted each person to name others who were, who associated with, or who sympathized with Communists. Intellectual sympathy for leftists was considered evil in itself; such "dupes," "commie symps," and "fellow travelers" were also condemned by HUAC.

These investigations had a tremendous effect. Hollywood executives, fearing the loss of profits, created a blacklist containing the names of hundreds of actors, directors, and screenwriters who were shut out of employment, thus ending their careers. In short time, television and radio did the same. For subpoenaed professionals, an order to appear before HUAC presented a no-win situation. If they named names, they betrayed themselves and others; if they did not cooperate, they risked their future. Some cooperated extensively: the writer Martin Berkeley coughed up 155 names. Some did so in order to keep working, but lived to regret it: the actor Sterling Hayden later described himself as a worm in his autobiography *Wanderer*. Others, like the playwright Lillian Hellman, remained true to their conscience and refused to cooperate. The HUAC-inspired blacklist caused a measurable disruption to employment as well as more than a dozen suicides.

HUAC's postwar efforts also transformed U.S. political life. In 1948, the committee launched a highly publicized investigation of ALGER HISS, a former high-ranking government official, on charges of spying for the Soviet Union. Hiss's subsequent conviction on perjury helped inspire the belief that other Communist spies must exist in federal government, leading to lavish, costly, and ultimately futile probes of the STATE DEPARTMENT by HUAC and Senator JOSEPH R. MCCARTHY. HUAC had laid the groundwork for the senator's own witch-hunt, a reign of unfounded accusation that came to be known as McCarthyism. By 1950, McCarthyism so influenced U.S. political life that HUAC sponsored the most sweeping anti-Communist law in history, the McCarren Act (50 U.S.C.A. § 781 et seq.), which sought to clamp down on the Communist party but stopped short of making membership illegal. The U.S. Supreme Court ultimately stripped it of any meaningful force.

HUAC came under fire in the late 1950s and early 1960s. After turning its attention on labor leaders, the committee at last provoked the U.S. Supreme Court: the Court's 1957 decision in *Watkins v. United States*, 354 U.S. 178, 77 S. Ct. 1173, 1 L. Ed. 2d 1273, overturned the contempt conviction of a man who refused to answer all of HUAC's questions, and, importantly, set broad limits on the power of congressional inquiry. Yet HUAC pressed on. In 1959 an effort to expose Communists in California schools resulted in teachers being fired and prompted some of the first public criticisms of the committee. By the late 1960s, as outrage over the VIETNAM WAR made public dissent not only feasible but widely popular, many lawmakers began to see HUAC as an anachronism. In 1969 the House renamed it the Internal Security Committee. The body continued on under this name until 1975, when it was abolished and the House Judiciary Committee took over its functions (with far less enthusiasm than its progenitors).

HUAC's legacy to U.S. law was a long, relentless campaign against personal liberty. Its members cared little for the constitutional freedoms of speech or association, let alone constitutional safeguards against SELF-INCRIMINATION. Much of its work would not have been possible without the steady assistance of the FBI, whose all-powerful director Hoover (1895–1972) died shortly after the committee's heyday had ended. HUAC is remembered today, along with Hoover and McCarthyism, as characterizing the worst abuses of federal power during the cold war.

governments emerged in Yugoslavia and Albania after World War II.

For nearly 50 years after the end of World War II, the Soviet Union and the United States engaged in a "cold war." So named for the absence of direct fighting between the two superpowers, the COLD WAR was, in reality, a bloody one. The Soviet Union and the United States fought each other through other countries in an effort to control the expansion of each other's influence.

When a country was thrown into civil war, the Soviet Union and the United States aligned themselves with the competing factions by pro-

viding financial and military support. They sometimes even supplied their own troops. The United States and Soviet Union engaged in war-by-proxy in many countries, including Korea, Vietnam, El Salvador, Nicaragua, Guatemala, and Angola.

Cuba officially adopted communism in 1965 after Fidel Castro led a band of rebels in an insurrection against the Cuban government in 1959. Despite intense opposition by the United States to communism in the Western Hemisphere, Cuba became communist with the help of the Soviet Union.

China

Communism was also established in China. In 1917, Chinese students and intellectuals, inspired by the Bolsheviks' October Revolution, began to study and promote Leninist Marxism. China had been mired in a century-long civil war, and many saw Lenin's brand of communism as the solution to China's internal problems. In 1919, at the end of WORLD WAR I, China received a disappointing settlement from Western countries at the Versailles Peace Conference. This outcome confirmed growing suspicion of capitalist values and strengthened the resolve of many Chinese to find an alternative basis for government.

On July 1, 1921, the Chinese Communist party (CCP) was established. Led by Chinese intellectuals and Russian advisers, the CCP ini-

tially embraced Russia's model of communism and relied on the organization of urban industrial laborers. By 1927, CCP membership had grown from fewer than 500 in 1923 to over 57,000. This increase was achieved in large part because the CCP had joined with another political party, the Kuomintang (KMT). KMT leader Chiang Kai-shek and KMT troops eventually became fearful of CCP control of the state, and in July 1927, the KMT purged communists from its ranks. CCP membership plummeted, and the party was forced to search for new ways to gain power.

Throughout the late 1920s and early 1930s, the CCP sought to change its strategies. The party was divided between urban, Russian-trained students and a wing made up of peasants led by Mao Tse-tung. At the same time, the CCP was engaged in battles with the KMT over control of various cities, and several CCP attempts to capture urban areas were unsuccessful.

Mao was instrumental in switching the concentration of CCP membership from the city to the country. In October 1934, the CCP escaped from threatening KMT forces in southern China. Led by Mao, CCP troops conducted the Long March to Yenan in the north, recruiting rural peasants and increasing its popularity en route. In 1935, Mao was elected chairman of the CCP.

Japan's invasion of China in 1937 spurred a resurgence in CCP popularity. The CCP fought Japanese troops until their surrender in 1945. The CCP then waged civil war against the KMT. With remarkable organization and brilliant military tactics, the CCP won widespread support throughout China's rural population and eventually its urban population as well. By 1949, the CCP had established Beijing as the capital of China and declared the People's Republic of China as the new government.

Chinese communism has been marked by a willingness to experiment. In 1957, Chairman Mao announced China's Great Leap Forward, an attempt to advance industry within rural communes. The program did not flourish, and within two years, Mao concluded that the Soviet Union's emphasis on industry was incompatible with communal principles. Mao launched an ideological campaign in 1966 called the Cultural Revolution, in which students were employed to convert opponents of communism. This campaign also failed, as too many students loyal to Mao carried out their mission with violent zeal.

After Chairman Mao died in 1976, powerful CCP operatives worked to eliminate Jiang Quing, Mao's widow, and three other party officials from the party. This Gang of Four was accused of undermining the strength of the party through adherence to Mao's traditional doctrines. The Chinese version of communism placed enormous emphasis on conformity and uniform enthusiasm for all CCP policies. With the conviction of the Gang of Four in 1981, the CCP sent a message to its members that it would not tolerate dissension within its ranks.

Also in 1981, the CCP Central Committee declared Mao's Cultural Revolution a mistake. Hu Yaobang was named chairman of the CCP, and Deng Xiaoping was named head of the military. These changes in leadership marked the beginning of CCP reformation. The idolization of Mao was scrapped, as was the ideal of continuous class struggle. The CCP began to incorporate into Chinese society technological advances and Western production management techniques. Signs of Western culture, such as blue jeans and rock and roll music, began to appear in China's cities.

In 1987, Hu Yaobang was removed as CCP chairman and replaced by Zhao Ziyang. Zhao's political philosophy was at odds with the increasing acceptance of Western culture and concepts of capitalism, and China's urban areas began to simmer with discontent. By May 1989, students and other reformists in China had organized and were regularly staging protests against Zhao's leadership. After massive demonstrations in Tiananmen Square in Beijing, the CCP military crushed the uprisings, executed dozens of radicals, and imprisoned thousands more.

Thus, the CCP maintained control of China's government. At the same time, it made attempts to participate in world politics and business.

The Demise of Communist States

In the late 1980s and early 1990s, several communist states transformed their governments to free-market economies. In 1985, Mikhail Gorbachev was named leader of the Soviet Union, and he immediately embarked on a program to liberalize and democratize the Soviet Union and its Communist party. By 1990, the campaign had won enough converts to unsettle the power of communism in the Soviet Union. In August 1991, opponents of Gorbachev

attempted to oust him from power by force, but many in the Soviet military supported Gorbachev, and the coup failed.

The Soviet Union was formally dissolved in December 1991. The republics previously controlled by the All-Union Communist party held democratic elections and moved toward participation in the world business market. Bulgaria, Czechoslovakia, Hungary, East Germany, and Poland also established their independence. Romania had conducted its own revolution by trying, convicting, and executing its communist dictator, Nicolae Ceausescu, at the end of 1989.

Communist control of governments may be dwindling, but communist parties still exist all over the world. China and Cuba have communist governments, and Spain and Italy have powerful Communist parties. In the United States, though, Communism has had a difficult time finding widespread support. The justice system in the United States has historically singled out Communists for especially harsh treatment. For example, JOSEPH MCCARTHY, a U.S. senator from Wisconsin, led an anti-Communist campaign from 1950 to 1954 that disrupted many lives in the United States.

Communism in the United States

Anti-Communist hysteria in the United States did not begin with Senator McCarthy's campaign in 1950. In *Whitney v. California*, 274 U.S. 357, 47 S. Ct. 641, 71 L. Ed. 1095 (1927), Charlotte Whitney was found guilty of violating the Criminal Syndicalism Act of California for

From 1950 to 1954, Senator Joseph McCarthy led highly publicized hearings that focused upon alleged Communist infiltration of the U.S. government and military.

AP/WIDE WORLD PHOTOS

organizing the Communist Labor Party of California. Criminal syndicalism was defined to include any action even remotely related to the teaching of violence or force as a means to effect political change.

Whitney argued against her conviction on several grounds: California's Criminal Syndicalism Act violated her DUE PROCESS rights because it was unclear; the act violated the EQUAL PROTECTION CLAUSE of the FOURTEENTH AMENDMENT because it did not penalize those who advocated force to maintain the current system of government; and the act violated Whitney's FIRST AMENDMENT rights to free speech, assembly, and association.

The Court rejected every argument presented by Whitney. Justices LOUIS D. BRANDEIS and OLIVER WENDELL HOLMES JR., concurred in the result. They disagreed with the majority that a conviction for mere association with a political party that advocated future revolt was not violative of the First Amendment. However, Whitney had failed to challenge the determination that there was a CLEAR AND PRESENT DANGER of serious evil, and, according to Brandeis and Holmes, this omission was fatal to her defense. Forty-two years later, the decision in Whitney's case was expressly overruled in *Brandenburg v. Ohio,* 395 U.S. 444, 89 S. Ct. 1827, 23 L. Ed. 2d 430 (1969).

The political and social protests of the 1960s led to an increased tolerance of unconventional political parties in the United States. However, this tolerance did not reach every state in the Union. In August 1972, the Indiana State Election Board denied the Communist party of Indiana a place on the 1972 general-election ballot. On the advice of the attorney general of Indiana, the board denied the party this right because its members had refused to submit to a LOYALTY OATH required by section 29-3812 of the Indiana Code. The oath consisted of a promise that the party's candidates did not "advocate the overthrow of local, state or National Government by force or violence" (*Communist Party v. Whitcomb,* 414 U.S. 441, 94 S. Ct. 656, 38 L. Ed. 2d 635 [1974]).

The Supreme Court, following its earlier *Brandenburg* decision, held that the loyalty oath violated the *First and Fourteenth Amendments.* In *Brandenburg,* the Court had held that a statute that fails to differentiate between teaching force in the abstract and preparing a group for imminent violent action runs contrary to the

constitutional rights of free speech and FREEDOM OF ASSOCIATION. Although the Communist party missed the deadline for entering its candidates in the 1972 general election, it succeeded in clearing the way for its participation in future elections.

In the twentieth century communism gained a hold among the world's enduring political ideologies and its popularity continues to ebb and flow with the shifting distribution of wealth and power within and between nations.

FURTHER READINGS

Bentley, Eric, ed. 2002. *Thirty Years of Treason: Excerpts from Hearings before the House Committee on Un-American Activities, 1938-1968.* New York: Thunder's Mouth Press/Nation Books.

Berlin, Isaiah. 1985. *Karl Marx: His Life and Environment.* New York: Oxford Univ. Press.

Gentry, Curt. 1991. *J. Edgar Hoover: The Man and the Secrets.* New York: Norton.

McLellan, David. 1979. *Marxism after Marx.* Boston: Houghton Mifflin.

Powers, Richard G. 1987. *Secrecy and Power: The Life of J. Edgar Hoover.* New York: Free Press.

Pozner, Vladimir. 1990. *Parting with Illusions.* New York: Atlantic Monthly.

Rosenn, Max. 1995. "Presumed Guilty." *University of Pittsburgh Law Review* (spring).

Solzhenitsyn, Alexander. 1973. *The Gulag Archipelago.* London: Collins/Fontana.

———. 1963. *One Day in the Life of Ivan Denisovich.* New York: Bantam.

CROSS-REFERENCES

Cuban Missile Crisis; *Dennis v. United States*; First Amendment; Fourteenth Amendment; Freedom of Association and Assembly; Freedom of Speech; Marx, Karl Heinrich; McCarran Internal Security Act; Smith Act; Socialism; Socialist Party of the United States of America; Vietnam War.

COMMUNIST PARTY CASES

The Communist Party Cases were a series of cases during the 1950s in which the federal government prosecuted Communist Party members for conspiring and organizing the party to advocate the overthrow of the U.S government by force and violence.

COMMUNISM became a central concern in U.S. law following WORLD WAR II, which ended with the Soviet Union occupying much of Central and Eastern Europe, after having liberated those areas from Nazi occupation. An ally of the United States for most of the war, Soviet President JOSEPH STALIN promised to hold democratic elections in the European countries he occupied. However, the governments in most of those countries were eventually converted into Soviet satellite regimes. Meanwhile, Soviet propaganda professed the goal of spreading communist revolution around the world, and Russian leaders remained publicly committed to this doctrine.

American leaders were concerned that talk of a global communist revolution was more than idle propaganda. In addition to the Iron Curtain of Soviet-style communism that had descended over much of Europe, China, another U.S. ally during World War II, was overtaken by communist revolution in 1949. That same year the Soviet Union announced that it had successfully detonated its first atomic bomb, ending a short-lived, U.S. nuclear monopoly. Shortly after this revelation, British scientist Klaus Fuchs and Americans JULIUS AND ETHEL ROSENBERG were implicated in an ESPIONAGE ring that was allegedly responsible for accelerating the Russian NUCLEAR WEAPONS program. In 1950 communist North Korea, aided by Chinese troops and Russian advisors, invaded South Korea, starting what would be a three year conflict.

Communist hysteria in the United States was ratcheted up another notch on February 9, 1950, when Senator JOSEPH MCCARTHY, a Republican senator from Wisconsin, ushered in the era of McCarthyism by delivering his famous speech at Wheeling, West Virginia, where he accused the U.S. STATE DEPARTMENT of harboring communists. The 1950s communist RED SCARE in the United States was marked by a series of freewheeling investigations conducted by several congressional committees, the most notorious of which was the House Committee on Un-American Activities (HUAC), which summoned before it thousands of Americans who were asked questions delving into personal beliefs, political affiliations, and loyalties.

The first Communist Party Case, *Dennis v. United States*, 341 U.S. 494, 71 S. Ct. 857, 95 L. Ed. 1137 (1951), was decided at the height of McCarthyism. Eugene Dennis was one of a number of persons convicted in federal district court for violation of the SMITH ACT, which proscribed teaching and advocating the violent and forcible overthrow of the U.S. government. 18 U.S.C.A. 2385. He and the others were alleged to have engaged in a conspiracy to form the Party of the United States in order to teach and advocate the overthrow of the United States government by force and violence. Such conduct was in direct contravention with the provisions of the

The criminal conviction of Eugene Dennis, under the Smith Act, was upheld by the Supreme Court in 1951.

AP/WIDE WORLD PHOTOS

Smith Act. Dennis unsuccessfully appealed his conviction and was granted certiorari by the Supreme Court.

In an opinion written by Chief Justice FREDERICK VINSON, the Court focused its review on two issues: whether the particular provisions of the Smith Act violated the FIRST AMENDMENT and the BILL OF RIGHTS and whether the sections in question were unconstitutional because they were indefinite in describing the nature of the proscribed conduct. The Court relied upon the determination of the Court of Appeals that the objective of the COMMUNIST PARTY OF THE UNITED STATES was to bring about the overthrow of its government by force and violence. From this perspective, it reasoned that Congress was empowered to enact the Smith Act, which was designed to safeguard the federal government against TERRORISM and violent revolution. Peaceable and lawful change was not proscribed, however. The power of Congress to so legislate was not in question, but the means it used to do so created constitutional problems.

The defendants argued that the statute inhibited a free and intelligent discussion of Marxism-Leninism, in violation of the defendants' rights to free speech and press. The Court countered that the Smith Act prohibits advocacy, not intellectual discussion, which is admittedly protected by the First Amendment. It continued, however, that the rights given by the First Amendment are not absolute and unqualified, but must occasionally yield to other concerns and values in society.

The Court decided that the CLEAR-AND-PRESENT-DANGER test, first formulated by the Supreme Court in 1919 in SCHENCK V. UNITED STATES, 249 U.S. 47, 39 S. Ct. 247, 63 L. Ed. 470, applied to the case and set out to explain its applicability. The forcible and violent overthrow of the government constituted a substantial enough interest to permit the government to limit speech that sought to cause it. The Court then reasoned that "If [the] Government is aware that a group aiming at its overthrow is attempting to indoctrinate its members and to commit them to a course whereby they will strike when the leaders feel the circumstances permit, action by the Government is required." The likelihood of success or success itself is not necessary, provided the words and proposed actions posed a clear and present danger to the government. The Court based its rationale upon the majority opinion in GITLOW V. NEW YORK, 268 U.S. 652, 45 S. Ct. 625, 69 L. Ed. 1138 (1925), "In each case [courts] must ask whether the gravity of the 'evil,' discounted by its improbability, justifies such invasion of free speech as is necessary to avoid the danger."

Concerning the issue of indefiniteness, the Court concluded that since the defendants were found by the jury to have intended the forcible overthrow of the government as soon as the circumstances permitted, there was no need to reverse their convictions because of the possibility that others might, in the future, be unaware of its proscriptions. When possible "borderline" cases arise, the Court would at that time strictly scrutinize the convictions.

The next major Communist Party case was *Yates v. United States*, 354 U.S. 298, 77 S. Ct. 1064, 1 L. Ed. 2d 1356 (1957), in which the Supreme Court reviewed the appeal of 14 Communist Party leaders who also had been convicted under the Smith Act. However, the Court in *Yates* reversed the convictions of all 14 defendants, distancing itself from *Dennis* on two grounds.

The *Yates* defendants were charged with conspiring to organize the Communist Party to teach members the duty of overthrowing the U.S government. The prosecution offered proof that the conspiracy had started in 1940, the year the Smith Act was enacted, and continued through 1951. The defendants had countered with evidence that the Communist Party had disbanded

after 1940 and was not reformed until 1945. Since the government offered no proof that the *Yates* defendants had helped reform the party in 1945, the defendants argued that prosecution had failed to prove the defendants were guilty of *organizing* the party. The Court found that the word *organize* was ambiguous and agreed with the defendants that under the Smith Act the word *organize* meant only the creation of a new organization and not the continuing participation in a party that disbands and later reforms.

Next the Court examined the portion of the indictment that charged the defendants with conspiring to advocate the duty and necessity of overthrowing the U.S. government by force and violence. The indictment was defective, the Court found, because it failed to distinguish between advocacy of forcible overthrow as an abstract doctrine and advocacy of immediate action to that end. The First Amendment protects the former type of speech, the Court emphasized, but not the latter. The government has the right to prohibit speech that advocates its forcible overthrow by a subversive political party that is *sufficient size and cohesiveness, is sufficiently oriented towards action, and other circumstances are such as reasonably to justify apprehension that action will occur*. The government had failed to prove that the Communist Party U.S.A. presented this type of threat, the Supreme Court concluded.

Several factors account for the Supreme Court's retreat from the *Dennis* opinion in *Yates*. Decided in 1957, *Yates* came at a time when both international and domestic tensions had subsided. The KOREAN WAR ended in 1953, the Senate had censured Joe McCarthy in 1954, President Eisenhower attended a cordial Geneva summit conference with new Soviet leadership in 1955, and HUAC investigations had precipitously tapered off. Time had also given Americans the opportunity to more accurately assess the minimal threat posed to national security by the Communist Party in the United States. Equally important, the Supreme Court was under new leadership. Chief Justice Vinson died in 1953 and was replaced EARL WARREN, a chief justice who began a legacy of greatly expanding the scope of civil liberties in the United States.

Twelve years after *Yates*, the WARREN COURT reiterated the First Amendment distinction between lawful subversive advocacy in the abstract and unlawful present incitement. In *Brandenburg v. Ohio*, 395 U.S. 444, 89 S. Ct.

1827, 23 L. Ed. 2d 430 (1969), the Court reversed the conviction of a KU KLUX KLAN leader under a state statute that prohibited advocacy of crime and violence as a necessary means to accomplish political reform. Ohio Rev. Code Ann. § 2923.13. The Court held that a state could not forbid advocacy of force or violence except where such advocacy is directed to producing imminent lawless action and is likely to incite or produce such action.

FURTHER READINGS

Belknap, Michal R. 1977. *Cold War Political Justice: The Smith Act, the Communist Party and American Civil Liberties.* Westport, Conn.: Greenwood.

Konvitz, Milton R. 1966. *Expanding Liberties: Freedom's Gains in Postwar America.* New York: Viking.

CROSS-REFERENCES

Freedom of the Press; Freedom of Speech.

COMMUNIST PARTY USA

Known officially as the Communist Party USA (CPUSA), the Communist party was formed in the United States in 1919, two years after the Russian Revolution had overthrown the monarchy and established the Soviet Union. Many American Communists had been members of the SOCIALIST PARTY OF AMERICA, but that party's socialist leadership opposed the Russian revolution and expelled those members who supported it. The Communists were even more left-wing than the Socialists and attracted a number of radicals and anarchists as well as Communists. By August 1919, only months after its founding, the Communist party had 60,000 members, while the Socialist party had only 40,000.

The administration of President WOODROW WILSON, fearful that American radicals might attempt to overthrow the U.S. government, began making mass arrests in the fall of 1919. Ultimately, 10,000 suspected subversives were arrested in what became known as the Palmer Raids (after U.S. Attorney General A. MITCHELL PALMER), with 249 deported to Russia. The Palmer Raids ended in May 1920, and the American Communists began to gain strength. In 1924, the party founded a newspaper, *The Daily Worker,* which, at its peak, had a circulation of 35,000. That same year, the party nominated labor activist William Z. Foster as its first candidate for U.S. president. Foster received 35,361 votes.

The death of VLADIMIR LENIN and the rise of JOSEPH STALIN caused dissent among the party in the United States, with some supporting Stalin and others supporting the views of Leon Trotsky. A number of Trotskyists formed the Communist League of America, and by 1920 the American Communist party had only 7,000 members. By then, the party was concentrating on helping to build LABOR UNIONS and improving workers' rights. They lobbied for higher wages, a national retirement program, and unemployment insurance. With so many Americans affected by the Great Depression, the Communist message sounded a note of hope to unemployed workers, and Foster received 102,991 votes in the 1932 presidential election. Still, many people were more comfortable with the less radical Socialist party, whose candidate, Norman Thomas, received 884,781 votes.

The Spanish Civil War created a renewed interest in the Communist party, with many of its members opposing the government of Francisco Franco. Many American Communists went to Spain to fight against Franco's forces. Once again, there was a mounting fear of COMMUNISM in the United States. The Communist candidate for president in 1940, Earl Browder, was forbidden to travel within the United States and had to conduct his entire campaign through written statements and recorded speeches.

During WORLD WAR II, the party had 75,000 members, and 15,000 registered Communists fought against Axis forces in Europe and Asia. The alliance with the Soviets did not survive beyond the war's end in 1945, and a wave of

In 1932 Communist Party presidential candidate William Z. Foster (left) received 102,991 votes. He is pictured with his running mate James W. Ford, the first African American to run for vice president.

BETTMANN/CORBIS

anti-communism swept the United States. Although the Communist party in the United States was arguably less radical than it had been in its early days (in 1948, the party endorsed the PROGRESSIVE PARTY candidate, former Vice President Henry A. Wallace, for President), the COLD WAR created a spirit of considerable distrust. In 1948, a dozen leaders of the party were arrested for violating the Alien Registration Act, which made it illegal to advocate or assist in trying to overthrow the government.

The House Un-American Activities Committee (HUAC) investigated individuals who were thought to have Communist ties, and Senator JOSEPH R. MCCARTHY (R-Wis.) claimed that Communists had infiltrated the federal government. Although many of these accused Communists had either never been party members or else had been involved briefly in the 1930s when the party was more active in organizing labor, invariably their lives were shattered. Membership in the Communist party dropped to about 10,000 by 1957, even though it was never illegal to be a member.

During the 1960s, the Communist party became involved in the CIVIL RIGHTS MOVEMENT and also the antiwar movement. Gus Hall, longtime general secretary of the party, ran for President in 1968 (the party had not run its own candidate since 1940) and received only 1,075 votes. He ran in subsequent years and in 1976 he received 58,992 votes. In 1988, instead of running, Hall pledged his support to JESSE JACKSON, who was seeking the Democratic nomination for president.

In the new millennium, the CPUSA maintains its commitment to the same political ideas that drove the Russian Revolution, but it embraces a more peaceful approach to creating change and social justice. Among the ideas it actively supports are socialized medicine, improved SOCIAL SECURITY benefits, stronger legislation to protect the environment, and full funding for education. The party also seeks greater cooperation with other political groups, believing that the best way to effect change is through the strength of broad-based coalitions.

FURTHER READINGS

Communist Party, USA. Available online at <www.cpusa.org> (accessed November 20, 2003).

Foster, William Z., 1952. *History of the Communist Party of the United States of America.* New York: International Publishers.

Jaffe, Philip J., 1975. *The Rise and Fall of American Communism.* New York: Horizon Press.

Klehr, Harvey, 1984. *The Heyday of American Communism: The Depression Decade.* New York: Basic Books.

CROSS-REFERENCES

Independent Parties; Socialist Party of the United States of America.

COMMUNITY-ORIENTED POLICING

A philosophy that combines traditional aspects of law enforcement with prevention measures, problem-solving, community engagement, and community partnerships.

From the 1930s to the 1960s, U.S. law enforcement relied on a professional policing model. This model was based on hierarchical structures, efficient response times, standardization, and the use of motorized patrol cars. Although this model improved efficiency, operations, and accountability, it proved inadequate when civil disturbances erupted in the late 1960s. Critics charged that police and the communities they served were alienated from each other, and a call came for community-oriented policing.

A first attempt was the team policing approach, which assigned responsibility for a certain geographic area to a team of police officers who would get to know the neighborhood, its people, and its problems. This harkened back to the early twentieth century when police walked a beat. The approach, however, proved ineffective because it placed more emphasis on long-term problem solving than on rapid response to crime incidents. Internally, team policing intruded on functional lines of authority, with patrol officers becoming involved in areas reserved to detectives and other specialists.

Community policing programs grew out of the failures of team policing. The goal of community policing is to bring the police and the public it serves closer together to identify and address crime issues. Instead of merely responding to emergency calls and arresting criminals, police officers in such programs get involved in finding out what causes crime and disorder, and attempt to creatively solve problems in their assigned communities. To do this police must develop a network of personal contacts both inside and outside their departments. This contact is fostered by foot, bike, or horse patrols—any effort that gets a police officer out of his or her squad car.

The community policing philosophy now dominates contemporary police work. The federal government promoted community policing through the passage of the VIOLENT CRIME CONTROL AND LAW ENFORCEMENT ACT OF 1994 (Violent Crime Control Act), Pub.L. 103-322, Sept. 13, 1994, 108 Stat. 1796. Title I of the Crime Act, the Public Safety Partnership and Community Policing Act, provided $8.8 billion to fund local law enforcement agencies as they developed and enhanced their community policing capabilities. To assist in this effort the JUSTICE DEPARTMENT created a new agency, the Office of Community Oriented Policing Services (the COPS Office), to develop, administer, and supervise new grant programs resulting from the act. By 2002, COPS had awarded grants to law enforcement agencies to hire over 116,000 community police officers, purchase crime fighting technology, and support innovations in policing. More than 12,000 law enforcement agencies have received COPS funding. COPS has also trained more than 130,000 law enforcement officers and community members through a network of Regional Community Policing Institutes and Community Policing Consortium.

A key element of community policing is an emphasis on crime prevention. The public has been encouraged to partner with the police in these efforts through the Neighborhood Watch Program. The National Sheriffs' Association (NSA) started the program in 1972 as a way to lower crime rates. The Neighborhood Watch has grown in popularity since the early 1980s and is now familiar to most people.

The Neighborhood Watch Program stresses education and common sense. It teaches residents how to help themselves by identifying and reporting suspicious activity in their neighborhoods. Most citizen groups concentrate on observation and awareness as the primary means of preventing crime. Some groups, however, look out for their neighborhood by actively patrolling on a regular basis. In addition, the Neighborhood Watch Program gives residents the opportunity to reinvigorate their communities. For example, some groups seek to address youth crime by creating activity programs, which range from athletic events such as "midnight basketball" leagues to tutoring and drug awareness programs.

One limitation of Neighborhood Watch Programs is that communities that need them the most are the ones that find them the hardest

to maintain. This is particularly the case in lower income neighborhoods where adults work multiple jobs with odd hours, thus making it more difficult to schedule meetings and organize events. It also makes it difficult for neighbors to get to know and care about one another in a way that makes them feel comfortable watching out for one another.

An effective Neighborhood Watch Program must follow certain steps to become an effective and ongoing crime prevention tool. The first step is to plan strategies that address the problems in the area. The second step is building a relationship and cooperation between law enforcement officers and residents. The third step is to assess the neighborhood needs and then to select and train volunteers. Finally, meaningful projects must be developed or else the group will lose interest.

The Neighborhood Watch Program has also been adapted for rural and sparsely-populated areas, and business districts. And, following the terrorist attacks of September 11, 2001, Attorney General JOHN ASHCROFT announced that Neighborhood Watch Programs would be furnished with information that will enable citizens to recognize and report signs of potential terrorist activities.

An emphasis on bringing police and the public closer together to identify and address crime issues is a mark of community policing. Such contact has been fostered by an increase of patrol methods, such as bicycle patrols, that get officers out of squad cars and into the community.

KELLY-MOONEY
PHOTOGRAPHY/CORBIS

FURTHER READINGS

COPS Office. Available online at <www.cops.usdoj.gov> (accessed June 3, 2003).

USAonwatch.org. National Sheriffs' Association: Neighborhood Watch. Available online at <www.usaonwatch .org> (accessed June 3, 2003).

COMMUNITY PROPERTY

The holdings and resources owned in common by a HUSBAND AND WIFE.

Community PROPERTY LAW concerns the distribution of property acquired by a couple during marriage in the event of the end of the marriage, whether by DIVORCE or death of one of the parties. In community property states all property accumulated by a husband and wife during their marriage becomes joint property even if it was originally acquired in the name of only one partner. The states that utilize a community property method of dividing resources were influenced by the CIVIL LAW system of France, Spain, and Mexico.

Laws vary among the states that recognize community property; however, the basic idea is that a husband and wife each acquire a one-half interest in what is labeled community property. A determining factor in the classification of a particular asset as community property is the time of acquisition. Community property is ordinarily defined as everything the couple owns that is acquired during the marriage with the exception of separate property owned by either of them individually. *Separate property* is that property that each individual brings into the marriage, in addition to anything that either spouse acquires by inheritance during the marriage.

Generally, four types of property acquired after marriage amount to community property: earnings, damages obtained from a personal injury suit, damages awarded in an industrial accident action, and rents and profits from separate property.

Divorce

In many community property law states, a husband and wife may enter into a PREMARITAL

AGREEMENT that there will be no community property. Divorce terminates the community relationship in all community property states; however, the manner in which the property is divided differs.

Upon the dissolution of a marriage, the source of property becomes important in determining whether an asset is community or separate property. Ordinarily, separate property includes that which is acquired through gift, DESCENT AND DISTRIBUTION, and devise or bequest. Each partner in a PROPERTY SETTLEMENT reacquires whatever he or she owned prior to the marriage.

In some states, community property is divided equally; in others, the division is based on the court's discretion. In certain jurisdictions, the guilt of a spouse in a divorce action can be a factor in reducing his or her share of the community property.

Inheritance Laws

Each spouse owns one-half of the couple's property in community property states, and, therefore, when a husband or wife dies only one-half of the marital property is inheritable since the surviving spouse owns in his or her own right one-half of the marital property.

COMMUNITY SERVICE

A sentencing option for persons convicted of crimes in which the court orders the defendant to perform a number of hours of unpaid work for the benefit of the public.

A person convicted of a criminal offense may be required to complete a sentence of community service directly or as an express condition of PROBATION. Typically, the community service will involve performance at a facility that has been authorized by the court or probation department. Community service is appropriate when it is reasonably designed to repair the harm caused by the offense.

COMMUNITY SERVICES, OFFICE OF

The Office of Community Services (OCS) was established within the HEALTH AND HUMAN SERVICES DEPARTMENT by section 676 of the Omnibus Budget Reconciliation Act of 1981 (95 Stat. 516; 42 U.S.C. 9905). Its mission, as stated on its website, is to "work in partnership with states, communities, and other agencies to provide a range of human and economic develop-

---

Community Property States, 2003

- Arizona
- California
- Idaho
- Louisiana
- Nevada
- New Mexico
- Texas
- Washington
- Wisconsin

SOURCE: *Tax Guide for Investors*, Fairmark Press, 1997–2003.

ment services and activities which ameliorate the causes and characteristics of poverty and otherwise assist persons in need." The goal of OCS services and programs is to help individuals and families become self-sufficient and to revitalize communities throughout the United States.

The OCS administers the Community Services block grant and discretionary grant programs established by section 672 (95 Stat. 511; 42 U.S.C. 9901) and 681 (95 Stat. 518; 42 U.S.C. 9910) of the Reconciliation Act. The office awards approximately $4 billion in block grants and $47 million in discretionary grants. It also provides grant money and technical assistance to the over three thousand Community Action Agencies and the Community Development Corporations that are locally based throughout the United States.

In 2002, the Office of Community Services implemented some of President GEORGE W. BUSH's faith-based initiatives. It awarded almost $25 million from its Compassion Capital Fund to 21 intermediary organizations; these organizations will provide technical assistance to help faith-based and community organizations access funding sources, operate and manage their programs, develop and train staff, expand the reach of programs into the community, and replicate promising programs. The office also awarded $850,000 in research grants to study how religious-based organizations provide social services and over $2 million to start a national clearinghouse of information to help faith-based organizations obtain government grants.

COMMUTATION

Modification, exchange, or substitution.

Commutation is the replacement of a greater amount by something lesser. To commute periodic payments means to substitute a single payment for a number of payments, or to come to a "lump sum" settlement.

In CRIMINAL LAW, commutation is the substitution of a lesser punishment for a greater one. Contrasted with clemency, which is an act of grace eliminating a sentence or punishment, commutation is the modification or reduction of a punishment.

The change from *consecutive prison sentences* to *concurrent sentences* is a commutation of punishment.

COMPACT

An agreement, treaty, or contract.

The term *compact* is most often applied to agreements among states or between nations on matters in which they have a common concern.

The Constitution contains the COMPACT CLAUSE, which prohibits one state from entering into a compact with another state without the consent of Congress.

COMPACT CLAUSE

A provision contained in Article I, Section 10, Clause 3, of the U.S. Constitution, which states, "No State shall, without the consent of Congress . . . enter into any Agreement or Compact with another State." Intended to curtail the increase of political power in the individual states that might interfere with the supremacy of the federal government or impose an unconstitutional burden on interstate commerce in violation of the COMMERCE CLAUSE.

COMPANY

An organization of individuals conducting a commercial or industrial enterprise. A corporation, partnership, association, or joint stock company.

COMPARABLE WORTH

The idea that men and women should receive equal pay when they perform work that involves comparable skills and responsibility or that is of comparable worth to the employer; also known as pay equity.

Many jobs are segregated by sex. For example, approximately 80 percent of all office secretaries are female, and approximately 99 percent of all construction workers are male. Both jobs demand valuable, if different, skills. However, the annual income of a secretary is only three-fifths that of a construction worker. Comparable worth seeks to remedy this and other sex-based wage inequities by identifying and eliminating sex as an element in wage setting.

The term *comparable worth* describes the notion that sex-segregated jobs should be reanalyzed to determine their worth to an employer. In practice, comparable worth consists of raising wages for traditionally female-dominated jobs to the level of those for comparable male-dominated jobs. Comparable worth should not be confused with equal pay for equal work. Rather, comparable worth policies promote equal pay for comparable work.

During World War II many women took jobs in what had traditionally been male fields of work. Ten years after the war ended, the Census Bureau released figures showing that women earned only 64 percent of what men earned.

FDR LIBRARY

Proponents of comparable worth argue that SEX DISCRIMINATION in wage setting has been built into society and has tainted the law of supply and demand. Women have endured centuries of devaluation, and the devaluation is reflected in the value attached to work traditionally performed by females. According to supporters, wages should be reset after comprehensive studies are made and statistical analyses undertaken to better reflect the true value produced by an employee.

Some critics of comparable worth maintain that wage fairness is achieved by allowing free-market forces to set the value of jobs. They argue that employers, not the courts or legislatures, should set wages and that sufficient legislation is already in place to prevent discrimination based on sex. They further argue that wage disparities are largely a result of innocent forces, such as differences in experience and education, the tendency of women to make educational choices that do not interfere with childbearing and child rearing, and the tendency of women to leave and reenter the job market more frequently than men.

Other critics of comparable worth, including some WOMEN'S RIGHTS advocates, argue that comparable worth efforts are well-intentioned but misplaced. According to these oppo-

nents, the best way for women to win wage equality is to integrate fully into all sectors of the economy. Comparable worth may work to the immediate benefit of those in traditionally "female" jobs, critics contend, but it fails to promote long-term advancement for women.

Generally, employees in a wage system based on comparable worth are paid according to job evaluations that concentrate on the differences between sex-segregated jobs. The job evaluations are conducted by vocational experts who examine the various characteristics of each job in the system, including the skill, education, and effort required; the level of independent decision making required; the working conditions; and accountability. The job evaluations yield a point total for each job, which is used to determine employee compensation.

In 1955, the U.S. CENSUS BUREAU published, for the first time, the ratio of women's to men's full-time, year-round, median annual earnings. The figures revealed that women were earning 64 percent of what men were earning. This imbalance persisted. In 1960, women aged 25 to 34 earned 65 percent of what men in the same age group earned. In 1980, the same women, now aged 45 to 54, were earning only 54 percent as much as men in the same age group. Census figures for 1980 also disclosed that full-time, year-round female professionals were earning less than semiskilled male blue-collar workers, and female college graduates were earning less than male high school graduates who had not attended college.

Women's pay became a national issue after the enormous contribution of women to the workforce in WORLD WAR II, and a simmering controversy shortly after the 1955 census report. The U.S. Congress took action by passing the EQUAL PAY ACT OF 1963 (29 U.S.C.A. § 206(d)) (EPA). The EPA mandates the same pay for all persons who do the same work, without regard to sex. This means that an employer may not discriminate between employees on the basis of sex by paying lower wages to women who perform the same work as men. In 1964, Congress enacted title VII of the Civil Rights Act of 1964 (42 U.S.C.A. § 2000e-2(a)), which provides that employers may not discriminate in employment practices on the basis of race, color, religion, national origin, or sex. Like the EPA, title VII prohibits employers from discriminating against women by paying them less than they pay males who perform the same work.

Women's rights advocates and LABOR UNION leaders were inspired by these bold federal acts and sought to extend them. In the fight against sex-based wage discrimination, women began to demand not only equal pay for equal work, but also equal pay for comparable work. States, cities, and towns began experimenting with the idea of wage restructuring based on comparable worth studies. In 1977, with the support of ELEANOR HOLMES NORTON (D-D.C.), then chair of the Equal Employment Opportunity Commission(EEOC), comparable worth came to national attention. Women's rights advocates adopted the slogan Fifty-nine Cents, which represented, according to Judy Goldsmith, past president of the NATIONAL ORGANIZATION FOR WOMEN (NOW), "the plain frightening fact that most women are paid just over half as much as men for the very same work." The comparable worth movement grew, but not without opposition. In 1985, President RONALD REAGAN described comparable worth as a "cockamamie idea."

The state of Washington was at the forefront of the comparable worth movement. In 1974, Washington began a study of sex-related differences for a selected group of sex-segregated positions in the state civil service. The study revealed that female employees in job classes requiring the same level of skill, effort, and responsibility earned 25 to 35 percent less than employees in comparable male-dominated positions. Despite these figures, the state legislature declined to implement comparable worth laws. Two more studies were conducted, in 1976 and 1980, and both corroborated the findings of the first study.

The Washington Legislature continued to reject comparable worth. In 1981, the EEOC refused to take action on charges filed with it against the state of Washington by the American Federation of State, County, and Municipal Employees (AFSCME) and the Washington Federation of State Employees (WFSE). On July 20, 1982, AFSCME and WFSE filed a CLASS ACTION suit against the state. The case was initiated by eight women and one man on behalf of all the male and female employees under the jurisdiction of the Washington Department of Personnel and the Washington Higher Education Personnel Board, who had worked or were working in positions that were 70 percent or more female. The government employees alleged that the state had discriminated against employees in female-dominated jobs by paying them lower wages than employees in comparable male-dominated jobs. This, according to the state employees, violated title VII of the CIVIL RIGHTS ACT of 1964. The District Court for the Western District of Washington agreed and awarded $400 million in back pay to female state employees.

The state of Washington appealed, and the U.S. Court of Appeals for the Ninth Circuit overturned the award (AFSCME, 770 F.2d 1401 [1985]). In its opinion, the Ninth Circuit court declared that an employer may set wages according to the prevailing market rate even if that market discriminates against women. According to the court, the value of a particular job is only one of several elements that influence the wages that the job commands. Another element, noted the court, is job availability. The court further recognized that the state in this case did not itself create any economic disparity. Although the state was free to institute a comparable worth policy, it could not be obliged "to eliminate an economic inequality that it did not create." Ultimately, the court held that, absent a discriminatory motive, it would not interfere with the state's decision to base wages on prevailing market standards.

After the appeals court decision, AFSCME, WFSE, and the state of Washington negotiated a comparable worth framework for state employees. The framework was based on the state's plan, which called for a gradual move to restructure its employees' wages on the basis of comparable worth. Washington now maintains a comparable worth statute, Revised Code of Washington, section 41.06.155, which mandates the achievement of comparable worth for all state government employees.

San Jose, California, was another early battleground for comparable worth proponents. In 1979, city government workers went on strike to protest wage disparities. After a nine-day strike, the city agreed to provide pay EQUITY adjustments and other salary adjustments to city workers. In 1983 and 1990, additional comparable worth adjustments were gained by the San Jose chapter of AFSCME.

Comparable worth has been won in numerous quarters through COLLECTIVE BARGAINING. Montgomery County, Maryland, workers negotiated pay equity increases in 1989, and in 1992, Montgomery County school employees received $484,000 in pay equity increases. In 1991, the

Best and Worst States in Earnings for Women

Five Best	Female Earnings per $1 Male	Five Worst	Female Earnings per $1 Male
Washington, D.C.	$0.90	West Virginia	$0.68
Hawaii	$0.80	Utah	$0.67
Florida	$0.79	Michigan	$0.67
California	$0.78	Louisiana	$0.66
Vermont	$0.78	Wyoming	$0.63

SOURCE: *Detroit Free Press*, "Michigan Among Worst in Equal Pay for Women," September 19, 2002.

Utility Workers of America negotiated a 15 percent pay equity increase for clerical workers in the Southern California Gas Company. In 1991 and 1992, clerical workers represented by the United Auto Workers (UAW) went on strike at Columbia University in New York. After a ten-month strike, an agreement was reached that included pay equity increases for both male and female workers.

Many courts are unwilling to order employers to enact comparable worth pay standards in the absence of legislation. Thus, comparable worth advocates have turned to the legislative process. Minnesota has been an enduring model for achieving comparable worth through legislation. In 1979, the Minnesota Department of Finance completed a study that included an evaluation of state and local government jobs. In 1981, the Council on the Economic Status of Women established the Task Force on Pay Equity to examine salary differences between comparable male and female jobs in state government. The task force report showed consistent inequities between comparable male- and female-dominated jobs, and the Minnesota state legislature passed the State Government Pay Equity Act in 1982 (1982 Minn. Laws c. 64, § 1 et seq.). In 1983, the legislature provided the funds for pay increases, and the Minnesota Department of Employee Relations (DOER) negotiated new contracts for state employees. These contracts included pay equity increases for underpaid female-dominated job classes and cost-of-living increases for all job classes.

In 1984, the Minnesota state legislature enacted the Local Government Pay Equity Act (Minn. Stat. Ann. §§ 471.991 et seq.), which mandated a comparable worth program for cities, counties, school districts, and other units of local government. In 1987 and 1988, the legislature passed laws that assessed fines for local government units that did not report according to provisions of the Local Government Pay Equity Act. In 1996, a DOER report revealed that 92 percent of local government units in Minnesota had achieved pay equity. Those not in compliance with reporting requirements were subject to penalties of up to five percent of state funding, or $100 a day.

Pay equity is a growing movement that builds on progress made in the 1980s. During that time, 20 states adjusted their payrolls to ameliorate sex or race inequities; seven of these states fully implemented broad-based comparable worth laws for their state government employees. States continue to lead in the area of pay equity. For example, New Hampshire has established reporting requirements and enforcement procedures to ensure fair pay; Vermont, West Virginia, and Wyoming have passed legislation requiring studies in comparable worth; and Maine's DEPARTMENT OF LABOR assists in enforcing existing pay equity laws in the state.

In the early twenty-first century, comparable worth legislation was introduced in over half the state legislatures. On the federal level, two newer pieces of legislation were introduced in 2003: the Fair Pay Act and the Paycheck Fairness Act. Representative Holmes Norton and Senator Tom Harkin (D-Iowa) introduced the Fair Pay Act in the U.S. House of Representatives and Senate respectively. The Fair Pay Act seeks to broaden the Equal Pay Act's protections against wage discrimination to workers in equivalent jobs with similar skills and responsibilities, even if the jobs are not identical. Senator Tom Daschle (D-S.D.) and representative from Connecticut Rosa DeLauro (D-New Haven) introduced the Paycheck Fairness Act in the Senate and House. The Paycheck Fairness Act is an attempt to provide better remedies to workers who are not being paid equal wages for doing equal work. Passage of the Paycheck Fairness Act would amend the Equal Pay Act and the Civil Rights Act of 1964.

FURTHER READINGS

Department of Labor, Bureau of Statistics. 2002. *Highlights of Women's Earnings in 2001.* (Report 960) Available online at <www.bls.gov/cps/cpswom2001.pdf> (accessed May 7, 2003)

National Committee on Pay Equity. Available online at <www.feminist.com/fairpay/index.htm> (accessed May 7, 2003).

CROSS-REFERENCES

Affirmative Action; Employment Law.

COMPARATIVE RECTITUDE

The principle by which a DIVORCE *is awarded to the party whose fault is less serious in cases where both spouses allege grounds that would justify a divorce.*

The idea of fault in divorce actions stemmed from the idea that a marriage remained alive until one partner's guilt destroyed it. This gave rise to problems such as people lying in court to obtain a divorce when both parties mutually wanted to end the marriage.

When a divorce based upon comparative rectitude occurs, the spouse with less fault might acquire rights denied to the other spouse, such as the right to remarry.

A divorce of this type, also called a *least-fault divorce,* is rarely granted. This is due to the increasing number of states that have adopted no-fault divorce laws, eliminating fault as a ground for divorce.

COMPELLING STATE INTEREST

See STRICT SCRUTINY.

COMPENSATION

A pecuniary remedy that is awarded to an individual who has sustained an injury in order to replace the loss caused by said injury, such as WORKERS' COMPENSATION. *Wages paid to an employee or, generally, fees, salaries, or allowances. The payment a landowner is given to make up for the injury suffered as a result of the seizure when his or her land is taken by the government through* EMINENT DOMAIN.

COMPENSATORY DAMAGES

A sum of money awarded in a civil action by a court to indemnify a person for the particular loss, detriment, or injury suffered as a result of the unlawful conduct of another.

Compensatory damages provide a plaintiff with the monetary amount necessary to replace what was lost, and nothing more. They differ from PUNITIVE DAMAGES, which punish a defendant for his or her conduct as a deterrent to the future commission of such acts. In order to be awarded compensatory damages, the plaintiff must prove that he or she has suffered a legally recognizable harm that is compensable by a certain amount of money that can be objectively determined by a judge or jury.

One of the more heated issues facing the U.S. legal system during the past quarter century has been the call for reform of states' TORT LAWS. HEALTH CARE providers and other organizations have sought to limit the amount of damages a plaintiff can receive for pain and suffering because they claim that large jury awards in MEDICAL MALPRACTICE cases cause premiums on medical insurance policies to rise, thus raising the overall costs of medical services. California took the lead in addressing concerns with rising medical costs when it enacted the Medical Injury Compensation Reform Act, Cal. Civ. Code § 3333.2 (1997). The act limits the recoverable amount for non-economic loss, such as pain and suffering, to $250,000 in actions based on professional NEGLIGENCE against certain health care providers. Although the statute has been the subject of numerous court challenges, it remains the primary example of a state's efforts to curb medical costs through tort reform.

Other states have sought to follow California's lead, though efforts to limit compensatory damages have met with considerable resistance. Opponents claim that because these limitations greatly restrict the ability of juries and courts to analyze the true damage that plaintiffs have suffered, defendants avoid paying an amount equal to the harm inflicted upon the plaintiffs. Medical organizations, such as the AMERICAN MEDICAL ASSOCIATION, continue to advocate for limitations on damages, however, and they have sought to encourage state legislatures to enact such provisions.

CROSS-REFERENCES

Damages.

COMPETENT

Possessing the necessary reasoning abilities or legal qualifications; qualified; capable; sufficient.

A court is competent if it has been given jurisdiction, by statute or constitution, to hear particular types of lawsuits.

A testator is competent to make a will if he or she understands what a will is and its effects, the nature and extent of the property involved, and the relationships with the people named in the will and those disinherited.

COMPETENT EVIDENCE

Information that proves a point at issue in a lawsuit.

Competent evidence is admissible evidence in contrast to incompetent or inadmissible evidence.

COMPLAINANT

A plaintiff; a person who commences a civil lawsuit against another, known as the defendant, in order to remedy an alleged wrong. An individual who files a written accusation with the police charging a suspect with the commission of a crime and providing facts to support the allegation and which results in the criminal prosecution of the suspect.

Once the suspect is indicted, the state becomes the complainant since the alleged wrong is considered a crime against the state.

COMPLAINT

The PLEADING *that initiates a civil action; in* CRIMINAL LAW, *the document that sets forth the basis upon which a person is to be charged with an offense.*

Civil Complaint

A civil complaint initiates a civil lawsuit by setting forth for the court a claim for relief from damages caused, or wrongful conduct engaged in, by the defendant. The complaint outlines all of the plaintiff's theories of relief, or causes of action (e.g., NEGLIGENCE, BATTERY, assault), and the facts supporting each CAUSE OF ACTION. The complaint also serves as notice to the defendant that legal action is underway. The Federal Rules of Civil Procedure govern construction of complaints filed in federal courts. Many state courts follow the same rules as the federal courts, or similar rules.

The caption opens the complaint and identifies the location of the action, the court, the docket or file number, and the title of the action. Each party to the lawsuit must be identified in the caption and must be a real party in interest, that is, either a person who has been injured or harmed in some way, or a person accused of causing the injury or harm. In addition, a party must have the capacity to sue or to be sued. If a party lacks capacity owing to mental incompetence, for example, the suit may be dismissed. Any number of parties may be named and joined in a single lawsuit as long as all meet the requirements of capacity and all are real parties in interest.

Courts of limited–subject matter jurisdiction, such as federal courts, require the complaint to demonstrate that the court has jurisdiction to hear the case. In general-jurisdiction courts, such as most state courts, a jurisdictional allegation is unnecessary.

The most critical part of the complaint is the claim, or cause of action. The claim is a concise and direct statement of the basis upon which the plaintiff seeks relief. It sets forth the RULE OF LAW that forms the basis of the lawsuit and recounts the facts that support the rule of law. Finally, the claim concludes that the defendant violated the rule of law, thereby causing the plaintiff's injuries or damages, and that the plaintiff is entitled to relief. For example: A negligence claim might begin with a statement that the defendant owed a duty of care to the plaintiff; that the defendant breached that duty; and that, as a result, the plaintiff suffered injuries or other damages. The conclusion then states that because the defendant's breach was the cause of the plaintiff's injuries, the plaintiff is entitled to compensation from the defendant.

The complaint may state separate claims or theories of relief in separate counts. For example, in a negligence case, count 1 might be for negligence, count 2 for breach of WARRANTY, and count 3 for FRAUD. Each count contains a separate statement of the rule of law, supporting facts, and conclusion. There is no limit to the number of counts a plaintiff may include in one complaint.

Federal courts and other jurisdictions that follow the Federal Rules of Civil Procedure require a brief, simple pleading known as a notice pleading. The notice pleading informs the defendant of the allegations and the basis for the claim. The rules require that the complaint contain "a short and plain statement of the claim showing that the pleader is entitled to relief" (Fed. R. Civil P. 8[a]). Rule 8(c)(1) states, "Each averment of a pleading shall be simple, concise, and direct."

Following the claim, the prayer for relief or demand for judgment appears. Commonly called the wherefore clause, the prayer for relief demands judgment for the plaintiff and relief in the form of the remedies the plaintiff requests. The plaintiff may demand relief in several forms. Money damages are compensation for injuries and loss. General money damages cover injuries directly related to the defendant's actions—such as pain and suffering, or emotional distress. Special money damages arise indirectly from the defendant's actions and may include lost wages or medical bills. The court

A sample complaint.

```
Letter of Complaint




                                                  Your Name

                                                  Address

                                                  Date


(Name/Address)



Dear _____ ,

On (specify date), I purchased a Sonic Dishwasher, style #1401B, from Bernard's Bargain Store in Tulsa, Oklahoma. It was installed by
employees from Bernard's store. The following day the appliance malfunctioned, causing a small electrical fire and damage to my utility
room wall. Based on written estimates, the approximate cost of repair to my home totals $972.50. In addition, I am seeking $488.89, which
represents the purchase price and/or replacement value of the dishwasher. Demand for this amount was made repeatedly to Mr. Victor
Tegeria, general manager of Bernard's Bargain Store, in person on (specify date), and (specify date); by telephone; and by two (2) certified
letters dated (specify date), and (specify date). To date, my requests for reimbursement have been ignored.




                                                  Sincerely yours,




                                                  Signature



--Send certified mail, return receipt requested.
```

awards exemplary or PUNITIVE DAMAGES when the defendant's actions are particularly egregious. The purpose of punitive damages is to punish the defendant and deter similar wrongdoing. Other types of damages are recovery of property, injunctions, and SPECIFIC PERFORMANCE of a contractual obligation. The plaintiff may demand alternative relief or several different types of relief, in the same complaint (Fed. R. Civ. P. 8[a]).

A demand for a jury trial may be included near the end of the complaint. The complaint must be signed by the plaintiff's attorney, indicating that the attorney has read the complaint; that it is grounded in fact, to the best of the attorney's knowledge, information, and belief; and that it is brought in GOOD FAITH.

Criminal Complaint

A criminal complaint charges the person named or an unknown person with a particular offense. For example, after the bombing of a federal building in Oklahoma City in 1995, authorities issued a JOHN DOE complaint, charging an unknown person or persons with the crime.

A criminal complaint must state the facts that constitute the offense and must be supported by PROBABLE CAUSE. It may be initiated by the victim, a police officer, the district attorney, or another interested party. After the complaint is filed, it is presented to a magistrate, who reviews it to determine whether sufficient cause exists to issue an arrest warrant. If the magistrate determines that the complaint does not state sufficient probable cause, the complaint is rejected and a warrant is not issued. In federal court, the complaint is presented under oath (Fed. R. Crim. P. 3).

FURTHER READINGS

Federal Employees News Digest, eds. 2000. *Whistleblowing: A Federal Employee's Guide to Charges, Procedures, and Penalties.* Reston, Va.: Federal Employees News Digest.

Kahan, Jeffrey B. 2001. "How to Prepare Response to Complaints." *Los Angeles Lawyer* 24 (April).

McCord, James W.H. "Drafting the Complaint: Defending and Testing the Lawsuit." *Practising Law Institute* 447.

CROSS-REFERENCES

Civil Procedure.

COMPLIANCE

Observance; conformity; obedience.

Compliance with the federal INCOME TAX laws is essential to avoid prosecution for TAX EVASION.

COMPOSITION WITH CREDITORS

A contract made by an insolvent or financially pressed debtor with two or more creditors in which the creditors agree to accept one specific partial payment of the total amount of their claims, which is to be divided pro rata among them in full satisfaction of their claims.

A composition with creditors is an agreement not only between the debtor and the creditors but also between the creditors themselves to accept less than what each is owed. It is a contract and such an arrangement is largely governed by contract law. There must be a meeting of the minds or mutual assent between the debtor and the creditors before a composition is created. A debtor must accept an offer by the creditors to accept partial payment of the amounts outstanding in order for the composition to be binding. The creditors themselves must also agree to the amount they will accept in satisfaction of their claims. They rely on mutual concessions of their rights to full payment in order to further the common purpose of securing their claims.

No standard form is required for a composition with creditors to be valid. A debtor can enter individual agreements with each creditor if it is clear that each follows a common purpose. All the creditors of a debtor do not have to agree to a composition. Those who do not participate are not bound by it.

Like any contract, a composition with creditors must be supported by consideration to be enforceable. Each creditor's promise to accept a pro rata share of the partial payment, as opposed to full payment of what is due, is consideration for the other creditors and the debtor. The surrender of debtor's right to file a petition for BANKRUPTCY is deemed consideration for the creditors.

Failure to obey the terms of a composition provides a basis for a lawsuit for breach of the agreement. The debtor is released from the duty of payment only after he or she has complied with the payment provisions. All the debts that are part of a composition are extinguished once a composition has been terminated.

Composition with Creditors

This agreement made on _____ [*date*], between _____

[*name of debtor*] ("Debtor") of _____ , _____ County,

_____ [*city, county, and state of debtor's residence or*

place of business], and _____ [*list names and addresses of the principal creditors*]
("Principal Creditors")

Debtor has been, and is now, engaged in the business of _____ . In the course of conducting business, Debtor has become indebted to the Principal Creditors in the several sums set opposite of their respective names in the schedule annexed hereto.

In consideration of the mutual covenants, promises, and conditions contained in this Agreement, it is agreed as follows:

1. **Schedule of Payments.** In exchange for the full satisfaction and discharge of the respective debts of the Principal Creditors, Debtor shall pay to each of the Principal Creditors _____ cents on the dollar on his, her, or its debt specified in the schedule annexed hereto.

2. **Release of the Debtor.** Each of the Principal Creditors hereby agrees to accept such composition in the full satisfaction of his, her, or its debt. When such compensation is duly paid to the Principal Creditors respectively, then the Debtor shall be released and discharged from the debts and liabilities that the Debtor now owes the Principal Creditors.

3. **Validity of Agreement.** This agreement shall become binding and effective although not executed by all of the creditors of the Debtor, and although all or any of the nonexecuting creditors may be paid in full. This agreement shall be void if the composition is not paid at the time and manner specified in this Agreement, or of the Debtor is adjudged bankrupt.

4. **Binding Effect.** This agreement shall legally bind the parties, and their respective legal representatives, successors, and assigns.

[*Signature of all parties*]

A sample composition with creditors.

Void Agreements

If one creditor is secretly paid more or given a preference, the other creditors can void the agreement because the law guards against the inequitable treatment of creditors. The preferred creditor cannot enforce or void the agreement. The debtor is entitled to recover payments made to such a creditor on the theory that a debtor is vulnerable to pressure by a creditor who has the power to force the debtor to file bankruptcy by refusing to enter into a composition.

Advantages

A composition with creditors usually benefits a debtor more than bankruptcy because it accomplishes the same end—discharge of all or most of a debtor's debts—without the stigma of bankruptcy. Unlike a bankruptcy discharge, a composition does not preclude future bankruptcy for six years. Creditors, however, are often reluctant to enter into a composition and those who refuse to do so are not affected by its terms.

Distinctions

A composition with creditors is not the same as an accord or an ASSIGNMENT FOR THE BENEFIT OF CREDITORS. Unlike an accord, which is an arrangement between a debtor and a single creditor for a discharge of an obligation by partial payment, a composition is an arrangement between a debtor and a number of creditors acting collectively for the liquidation of their claims.

A composition with creditors differs from an assignment for the benefit of creditors in a number of ways. It is created by contract, as opposed to COMMON LAW or statute. Only creditors who agree to it are bound, while an assignment discharges debts voluntarily released by creditors. The terms of the composition determine whether the debtor retains property. However, in most jurisdictions, the property of a debtor who has assigned it for his or her creditors' benefit is given to a third person with orders to sell it and distribute the proceeds to the creditors. Unlike an assignment, a composition is not a basis for an involuntary bankruptcy proceeding.

A sample form for composition with creditors can be found above.

COMPOUND INTEREST

Interest generated by the sum of the principal and any accrued interest.

Interest is normally compounded on a daily, quarterly, or yearly basis. The more often interest is compounded, the larger the principal will grow and the greater the interest the new principal will produce.

COMPOUNDING A FELONY

A criminal offense consisting of the acceptance of a reward or other consideration in exchange for an agreement not to prosecute or reveal a felony committed by another.

Compounding a felony is encompassed in statutes that make compounding offenses a crime.

COMPOUNDING OFFENSE

A criminal act in which a person agrees not to report the occurrence of a crime or not to prosecute a criminal offender in exchange for money or other consideration.

The offense is also committed when a person accepts remuneration for encouraging a witness to be absent from a trial or employs any unlawful tactics to delay a criminal proceeding.

Under the COMMON LAW and most modern statutes a compounding offense consists of three basic elements: (1) knowledge of the crime; (2) the agreement not to prosecute or inform; and (3) the receipt of consideration. The offense is complete when there is an agreement to either withhold evidence of the crime, conceal it, or fail to prosecute it. A crime is not compounded when a person merely reacquires property previously stolen from him or her; the crime would further require that the return of the stolen property was conditioned on an agreement not to report or prosecute the crime.

The individual compounding the crime must be aware of the previous offense although the person who committed it need not be tried or convicted. The fact that the person who committed the previous crime is not tried until after the prosecution for compounding occurs is irrelevant.

The consideration can consist of anything of value, such as money, property, or a promise of monetary gain. Only the recipient of the consideration can be guilty of compounding an offense. Although the person who offers the consideration is not considered guilty of compounding a crime, he or she might be guilty of BRIBERY.

At common law the compounding of any crime was an offense. Today many jurisdictions limit the offense to the compounding of felonies. The usual punishment is a fine, imprisonment, or both.

COMPRISE

To embrace, cover, or include; to confine within; to consist of.

In the law governing patents—grants of an exclusive right or privilege to make, use, or sell an invention or product for a term of years—the term *comprise* indicates inclusion rather than limitation. When a patent claim states that a particular product is comprised of certain elements, this means that other elements may also be present.

As used in the devise of land, comprise means to contain or embrace. A plot of land may be comprised of a certain number of acres.

COMPROMISE AND SETTLEMENT

Resolution of a dispute by mutual agreement to avoid a lawsuit.

Public policy favors the settlement of disputes to avoid lawsuits. Parties to conflicts that might otherwise end up in court are encouraged to resolve those conflicts by mutual agreement through their attorneys, through mediators, or even on their own. A compromise and settlement can be used for many types of disagreements including contract disputes, civil disputes, labor-management negotiations, criminal cases, and DIVORCE and custody problems.

The terms of a settlement agreement do not necessarily need to be equal. One party may give up more than originally intended. However, as long as the parties agree to the terms and the court views the compromise as fair, the settlement will be upheld by the court. A settlement is considered binding, and the court views it as final and conclusive. A compromise and settlement will be put aside only if there is evidence of bad faith or FRAUD.

A valid compromise and settlement can be in any form, written or verbal. A writing is not required unless specified by statute, court rule, or the terms set by the parties. When the agreement is written, it must clearly state the intentions of the parties.

A compromise and settlement must have the same elements as a contract: parties who have the capacity and authority to agree, an offer and

acceptance, and valuable consideration (consideration is something of value received or promised by one party to induce the other party to enter into an agreement).

Any party competent to enter into a contract can use compromise and settlement to resolve a conflict. There must be a meeting of minds in order to form a valid compromise; in other words, the parties must have the same understanding of the settlement. There must also be an offer of compromise and an acceptance of that offer. The offer can be made by either party. The terms of the offer must be clear and must show that the party making the offer intends to assume some obligation.

The offer can be made subject to certain conditions that must be satisfied for a valid compromise. For example, a creditor creates a conditional offer when he or she sends a promissory note for less than the full amount of a debt. If the debtor signs the note, he or she is agreeing to forgive part of the debt. If the debtor refuses to sign the note, the creditor's offer is rejected. The offer is conditioned on the debtor's signing the note.

An offer of compromise and settlement must be made within a reasonable time. Acceptance of an offer of compromise must likewise be made within a reasonable time, and on the terms offered. However, delay in acceptance is immaterial when the person making the offer is not prejudiced by it. Acceptance can be implied or expressed. If it is based on a condition that proves impossible to perform, no settlement is possible.

An offer of compromise can be withdrawn before acceptance, but not after. When an agreement is put in writing, either party may withdraw before signing. If court approval is necessary, one party can repudiate the agreement prior to the approval of the court.

Like any other contract, a valid compromise and settlement must be based on consideration. Anything of value exchanged by the parties, including money or property, is sufficient to support a compromise and settlement. If a debtor agrees to pay more than she or he thinks is owed, the additional amount is consideration in exchange for settlement of the debt. Resolution of family conflicts can also be considered valuable consideration. The adequacy of the consideration, however small or slight it might be, is usually not a matter for judicial scrutiny. Unless the consideration is so unfair as to shock the conscience, inadequacy of consideration does not justify setting aside a compromise and settlement.

Disputes involving family matters are frequently the subject of compromise and settlement. Increasingly, courts are encouraging, and sometimes mandating, that parties in divorce and custody matters seek settlement before pursuing an issue through trial. In a family setting, where issues are very personal and emotional, compromise and settlement provides a means of preserving some sense of the close relationship between the parties. Because the parties reach the final agreement together, family matters resolved through compromise and settlement tend to be more amicable than those resolved through litigation.

Compromise and settlement can also be used to settle disputes with the INTERNAL REVENUE SERVICE (IRS). A taxpayer who owes the IRS money may propose a compromise for the method or amount of its payment. When the government accepts this compromise offer, it becomes a binding contract (47B C.J.S. *Internal Revenue* § 1064 [1995]).

COMPROMISE OF 1850

The Compromise of 1850, also known as the Omnibus Bill, was a program of legislative measures enacted by Congress to reconcile the differences existing between the North and South concerning the issue of SLAVERY in newly formed TERRITORIES OF THE UNITED STATES.

The historical background of the enactment of the Compromise involved the increasingly hostile relationship between the northern and southern states of the Union over the existence of slavery. This hostility was partly due to the reluctant enforcement by northern states of the Fugitive Slave Act of 1793, which established procedures for the return of runaway slaves to their owners. The dissension was exacerbated in 1848 when the United States annexed Texas and gained new territories under the provisions of the Treaty of Guadalupe Hidalgo, which brought about the end of the Mexican American War. Abolitionists continued to favor the antislavery stance of the WILMOT PROVISO prohibiting slavery in the lands acquired from Mexico, which was proposed in 1846, but was never enacted into law. The South vehemently opposed the exclusion of slavery from the new territories.

In 1849 the request of California to join the Union as a free state resulted in heated debates on the floor of Congress. Many viewed the situation as a grave threat to the existence of the Union. HENRY CLAY returned to the Senate to propose measures, based upon the ideas of STEPHEN DOUGLAS, that would reconcile the

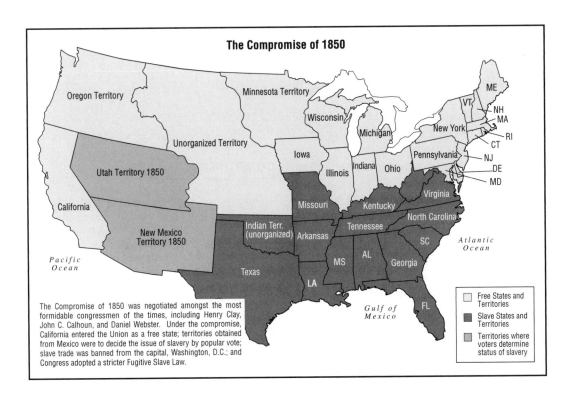

The Compromise of 1850

The Compromise of 1850 was negotiated amongst the most formidable congressmen of the times, including Henry Clay, John C. Calhoun, and Daniel Webster. Under the compromise, California entered the Union as a free state; territories obtained from Mexico were to decide the issue of slavery by popular vote; slave trade was banned from the capital, Washington, D.C.; and Congress adopted a stricter Fugitive Slave Law.

Free States and Territories

Slave States and Territories

Territories where voters determine status of slavery

ILLUSTRATION BY ERIC WISNIEWSKI. GALE GROUP

different positions of the North and South. The proposals included the admission of California into the Union as a free state, the right of the New Mexico and Utah territories to determine the slavery issue for themselves at the time of their admission to the Union, the outlawing of the slave trade in the District of Columbia, and the congressional enactment of the more stringent FUGITIVE SLAVE ACT OF 1850 (9 Stat. 462).

Due to the efforts of DANIEL WEBSTER and others, these controversial measures, which initially caused heated debate, were enacted by Congress in September 1850. Although labeled a compromise due to its position on slavery, the Compromise of 1850 had short-lived effect as a solution to the issue in light of the subsequent problems resulting in the enactment of the KANSAS-NEBRASKA ACT in 1854 (10 Stat. 277) and the onset of the Civil War less than ten years later.

CROSS-REFERENCES

"Compromise of 1850" (Appendix, Primary Document).

COMPTROLLER

An officer who conducts the fiscal affairs of a state or MUNICIPAL CORPORATION.

A comptroller, which is often synonymous with auditor, generally has specific duties including the supervision of revenue, the examination and certification of accounts, and the inspection, examination, or control of the accounts of other public officials.

A state comptroller's major function is the final auditing and settling of all claims arising against the state.

The chief financial officer of any private organization, such as a university or a corporation, is also called a comptroller.

Within the federal government, the office of the comptroller of the currency exists as part of the national banking system. The function of this office is to promulgate and execute rules and regulations that govern the national banks. The approval of the comptroller of currency is essential to the organization of new national banks, as well as the transformation of state-chartered banks into national banks and the consolidation and merger of banks.

The comptroller general of the United States is the leading official of the GENERAL ACCOUNTING OFFICE whose primary duty is to audit various governmental agencies.

COMPULSORY PROCESS

The method employed by which a person wanted as a witness, or for some other purpose, in a civil or criminal action is forced to appear before the court hearing the proceeding.

Compulsory process encompasses not only a subpoena, which is a command to appear at a particular time and location to provide testimony upon a certain matter, but also a bench warrant, which is a written order commanding a law enforcement officer to seize the person named and bring that person into court.

The SIXTH AMENDMENT to the Constitution provides that the accused in criminal prosecutions shall have the right "to have compulsory process for obtaining witnesses in his favor."

COMPURGATOR

In early legal practice, one of several character witnesses produced by someone accused of a crime or by a defendant in a civil suit to attest, in court, that he or she believed the defendant on his or her oath.

The process of compurgation, called WAGER OF LAW in England, was a type of absolution from a criminal or civil charge that enabled the defendant to come forward and swear to his or her innocence or nonliability. Through compurgation, the person on trial was able to conclusively contradict the charges and reinforce his or her position through others who testified under oath that they believed the defendant's testimony.

The use of character witnesses in a lawsuit by a party is derived from the old practice of summoning compurgators to buttress one's case.

COMPUTER-ASSISTED LEGAL RESEARCH

Technology that allows lawyers and judges to bypass the traditional law library and locate statutes, court cases, and other legal references in minutes using a personal computer, research software or the INTERNET, and an online connection.

The two largest computer-assisted legal research (CALR) services are WESTLAW, offered by Thomson Corporation's Eagan, Minnesota-based West unit, and LEXIS, offered by Reed Elsevier's Dayton, Ohio-based LexisNexis unit. Both services provide on-line access to the fundamental tools of the legal profession—court opinions, federal and state statutes, federal regulations, administrative law cases, and other law-related materials. Their extensive databases are updated frequently, providing attorneys with the most up-to-the-minute developments in U.S. law.

CALR systems contain thousands of databases. In addition to primary source materials, they offer access to business and economic journals, national newspapers, law reviews, federal tax abstracts, and financial data and materials. Specialized databases for narrower topics such as taxes, SECURITIES, labor, insurance, and BANKRUPTCY are also available.

When CALR was first developed in the 1970s, it borrowed Boolean search techniques from the field of computer programming. A Boolean search looks for a particular term or group of terms in a specific relationship to one another. CALR Boolean searches can include limits with respect to time: for example, court opinions are always dated, so an attorney can use a Boolean search to look for cases released in a given year or in a range of years.

CALR service providers have also created plain language search systems. Under the plain language approach, an attorney simply types in a search in the form of a question.

The following two samples demonstrate the difference between a Boolean search and a plain language search for the same issue: whether a successor corporation is liable for the cleanup of toxic waste left by a prior owner of the property. The two examples reflect WESTLAW notation; the notation for LEXIS would be similar.

Boolean search

(successor /5 corporation) /p (toxic or hazardous or chemical or dangerous /5 waste) /p clean! and da(aft 1/1/90)

Plain language search

is a successor corporation liable for the cleanup of hazardous (toxic) waste?

The sample Boolean search looks for the combination of *successor* within five words of *corporation,* in the same paragraph as the combination of *toxic* or *hazardous* or *chemical* or *dangerous* within five words of *waste,* within the same paragraph as *clean* or *cleanup* or *cleans* or *cleaned* or *cleaning* (the exclamation mark in *clean!* causes the computer to search for all words with *clean* as a root). Cases are limited to those dated after January 1, 1990.

Boolean search results usually are listed in reverse chronological order (the most recent case first). A plain language search ranks the first 20 documents that best match the search. The first ranked document is the one that most closely matches the terms in the search. A document will be ranked higher if the terms appear more often in that document.

Advances in computer technology have produced another innovation in automated research: voice recognition research. With this method, a search query is dictated either in plain language or by using Boolean terms and connectors. After the simple commands are spoken, the researcher's exact words appear on the computer screen and the requested documents are retrieved. The keyboard is not used at all during the search.

Legal researchers have the option of using CD-ROM (compact disc read-only memory) libraries, although these have become less popular in the early 2000s. A personal computer, CD-ROM drive, and specific software are required. Some CD-ROMs allow for access to a CALR online service (these require a modem).

Lawyers are also using the Internet, the public access electronic network. Because many statutes, court opinions, and LIBRARY OF CONGRESS materials are online, the Internet is becoming a valuable resource for business and legal research. It is also used for document transfers and client E-mail.

Recent Developments

Most judges, lawyers, and law librarians continue to rely on the traditional fee-based giants of online legal research—Lexis, Westlaw, and Loislaw (owned by New York-based Aspen Publishers, Inc., a subsidiary of Dutch publishing company Wolters Kluwer). However, more law-related professionals are turning to free Internet sites to conduct their legal research. A number of Web sites now provide free access to a variety of legal materials that include federal and state case law, codes and regulations, treatises, law reviews, scholarly articles, mainstream news stories, as well as legal forms, public records, and attorney directories.

Examples of Internet sites that provide free access to at least some of these legal resources are numerous, though the depth and breadth of coverage offered by each site varies. Among the myriad of such providers, FindLaw generally remains the benchmark for comprehensive quality. Many law school Internet sites also provide free access to a wide variety of information. One such example is the Legal Information Institute, a site maintained by Cornell Law

School (www.law.cornell.edu). This site provides a range of primary and secondary source materials, as well as directories to locate additional information on the Web.

FindLaw provides multiple channels to access information from its portal and caters the information to specific types of end users. These include channels for legal professionals, students, businesses, and the public. Material specific to these targeted audiences is made available as well as resources for all users, such as cases, codes, articles, and guides. Within each channel users can drill down to the area of law that interests them.

For example, students can look at outlines and examinations for a variety of legal courses, view employment opportunities, or learn about study skills. Business people can gain insights into starting a business, review different types of business organizations, and look into bankruptcy provisions. For the general public, topics include employment, immigration, personal injury, education, estate planning, and real estate law. FindLaw also continues to provide an excellent federal case law database that is searchable by title, citation, and full text. All cases from U.S. Reports from 1893 to the present are included.

While boatloads of legal information can now be obtained on the Internet free of charge, the information typically consists of unanalyzed, non-value-added material such as primary-source documents stripped of the editorial enhancements provided by pay services. Such enhancements include case synopses (editorially created summaries of the procedural history and holding of a case), case headnotes (editorially created snapshots of each court ruling in a case), statutory annotations (editorially created indices listing every case that has interpreted or applied a particular statute), and legal citators (editorially created reference guides telling users whether a legal authority may still be cited in court as good law), among others. Because these editorial enhancements can be so valuable in making legal research more efficient and successful, most law-related professionals remain willing to pay significant subscriber and user fees to access them.

FURTHER READINGS

Ebbinghouse, Carol. July 1, 2001. "Portals to the Future of Legal Information." *Searcher Magazine.*

Jatkevicius, James. March 1, 2003. "Free Lunch: Legal Resources from Plain to Polished.". *Online Magazine.*

The Lawyer's PC: A Newsletter for Lawyers Using Personal Computers. 1983– . Colorado Springs: Shepard's/ McGraw-Hill.

"A Show-Stopper from WESTLAW." 1992. *California Lawyer* (November).

"Three New Services for Lawyers on the World Wide Web." December 27, 2000. *Law Office Technology Review.*

CROSS-REFERENCES

Computer Law Association; Internet; Law Review.

COMPUTER CRIME

The use of a computer to take or alter data, or to gain unlawful use of computers or services.

Because of the versatility of the computer, drawing lines between criminal and noncriminal behavior regarding its use can be difficult. Behavior that companies and governments regard as unwanted can range from simple pranks, such as making funny messages appear on a computer's screen, to financial or data manipulation producing millions of dollars in losses. Early prosecution of computer crime was infrequent and usually concerned EMBEZZLE-MENT, a crime punishable under existing laws. The advent of more unique forms of abuse, such as computer worms and viruses and widespread computer hacking, has posed new challenges for government and the courts.

The first federal computer crime legislation was the Counterfeit Access Device and Computer Fraud and Abuse Act (18 U.S.C.A. § 1030), passed by Congress in 1984. The act safeguards certain classified government information and makes it a misdemeanor to obtain through a computer financial or credit information that federal laws protect. The act also criminalizes the use of computers to inflict damage to computer systems, including their hardware and software.

In the late 1980s, many states followed the federal government's lead in an effort to define and combat criminal computer activities. At least 20 states passed statutes with similar definitions of computer crimes. Some of those states might have been influenced by studies released in the late 1980s. One report, made available in 1987 by the accounting firm of Ernst and Whinney, estimated that computer abuse caused between $3 billion and $5 billion in losses in the United States annually. Moreover, some of those losses were attributable to newer, more complicated crimes that usually went unprosecuted.

The number of computer crimes continued to increase dramatically in the early 1990s. According to the Computer Emergency and

Response Team at Carnegie-Mellon University, the number of computer intrusions in the United States increased 498 percent between 1991 and 1994. During the same time period, the number of network sites affected by computer crimes increased by 702 percent. In 1991, Congress created the National Computer Crime Squad within the FEDERAL BUREAU OF INVESTIGATION (FBI). Between 1991 and 1997, the Squad reportedly investigated more than 200 individual cases involving computer hackers.

Congress addressed the dramatic rise in computer crimes with the enactment of the National Information Infrastructure Act of 1996 as title II of the Economic Espionage Act of 1996, Pub. L. No. 104-294, 110 Stat. 3488. That Act strengthened and clarified provisions of the original Computer Fraud and Abuse Act, although lawmakers and commentators have suggested that as technology develops, new legislation might be necessary to address new methods for committing computer crimes. The new statute also expanded the application of the original statute, making it a crime to obtain unauthorized information from networks of government agencies and departments, as well as data relating to national defense or foreign relations.

Notwithstanding the new legislation and law enforcement's efforts to curb computer crime, statistics regarding these offenses remain staggering. According to a survey in 2002 conducted by the Computer Security Institute, in conjunction with the San Francisco office of the FBI, 90 percent of those surveyed (which included mostly large corporations and government agencies) reported that they had detected computer-security breaches. Eighty percent of those surveyed acknowledged that they had suffered financial loss due to computer crime. Moreover, the 223 companies and agencies in the survey that were willing to divulge information about financial losses reported total losses of $455 million in 2002 alone.

Concerns about TERRORISM have also included the possibility that terrorist organizations could perform hostile acts in the form of computer crimes. In 2001, Congress enacted the Uniting and Strengthening America by Providing Appropriate Tools Required to Intercept and Obstruct Terrorism Act (USA PATRIOT ACT), Pub. L. No. 107-56, 115 Stat. 277, to provide law enforcement with the necessary tools to combat terrorism. The Act includes provisions that allow law enforcement greater latitude in hunting down criminals who use computers and other communication networks. The Homeland Security Act of 2002, Pub. L. No. 107-296, 116 Stat. 2135 also directed the UNITED STATES SENTENCING COMMISSION to review, and possibly to amend, the sentencing provisions that relate to computer crimes under 18 U.S.C.A. § 1030.

The Department of Justice's Computer Crime and Intellectual Property Section prosecutes dozens of computer-crime cases each year. Many of those cases involve instances of computer hacking and other unauthorized intrusions, as well as software PIRACY and computer fraud.

One set of especially destructive crimes—internal computer crimes—includes acts in which one computer's program interferes with another computer, thus hindering its use, damaging data or programs, or causing the other computer to crash (i.e., to become temporarily inoperable). Two common types of such programs are known in programming circles as "worms" and "viruses." Both cause damage to computer systems through the commands written by their authors. Worms are independent programs that create temporary files and replicate themselves to the point where computers grow heavy with data, become sluggish, and then crash. Viruses are dependent programs that reproduce themselves through a computer code attached to another program, attaching additional copies of their program to legitimate files each time the computer system is started or when some other triggering event occurs.

The dangers of computer worms and viruses gained popular recognition with one of the first cases prosecuted under the Computer Fraud and Abuse Act. In *United States v. Morris*, 928 F.2d 504 (2d Cir. 1991), Cornell University student Robert T. Morris was convicted of violating a provision of the act that punishes anyone who, without authorization, intentionally accesses a "federal interest computer" and damages or prevents authorized use of information in such a computer, causing losses of $1,000 or more. Morris, a doctoral candidate in computer science, had decided to demonstrate the weakness of security measures of computers on the INTERNET, a network linking university, government, and military computers around the United States. His plan was to insert a worm into as many computers as he could gain access to, but to ensure that the worm replicated itself slowly enough that it would not cause the computers to slow down or crash. However, Morris miscalculated how quickly the worm would replicate. By the time he released a message on how to kill the worm, it was too late: Some 6,000 computers had crashed or become "catatonic" at numerous institutions, with estimated damages of $200 to $53,000 for each institution. Morris was sentenced to three years' PROBATION and 400 hours of community service, and was fined $10,500. The U.S. Supreme Court declined to review the case (*Morris, cert. denied,* 502 U.S. 817, 112 S. Ct. 72, 116 L. Ed. 2d 46 [1991]).

Computer hackers often share Morris's goal of attempting to prove a point through the clever manipulation of other computers. Hackers, who, typically, are young, talented, amateur computer programmers, earn respect among their peers by gaining access to information through TELECOMMUNICATIONS systems. The information obtained ranges from other individuals' E-MAIL or credit histories to the Department of Defense's secrets.

A high-profile case in 1992 captured national headlines. In what federal investigators called a conspiracy, five young members of an underground New York City gang of hackers, the Masters of Deception (MOD), faced charges that they had illegally obtained computer passwords, possessed unauthorized access devices (long-distance calling-card numbers), and committed wire fraud in violation of the Computer Fraud and Abuse Act. Otto Obermaier, the U.S. attorney who prosecuted the youths, described their activities as "the crime of the future," and said that he intended to use the case to make a critical statement about computer crime. The indictment contained 11 counts, each punishable by at least five years in prison and individual fines of $250,000. Supporters of MOD's civil liberties questioned whether the gang members had done anything truly illegal.

MOD members Paul Stira and Eli Ladopoulos pleaded guilty to the charges against them. They confessed that they had broken the law but insisted that they had not done anything for personal profit. They were sentenced to six months in a federal penitentiary, followed by six months' home detention. John Lee and Julio Fernandez faced specific charges of illegally selling passwords for personal profit. Lee pleaded guilty and received a year behind bars, followed by 300 hours of community service. Fernandez bargained with prosecutors, offering them informa-

tion on MOD activities, and thus received no jail time. Gang leader Mark Abene, who was notorious in computer circles by his handle Phiber Optik, pleaded guilty to charges of fraud. A U.S. District Court judge sentenced Abene to a year in federal prison, hoping to send a message to other hackers. However, by the time Abene was released from prison in 1995, his notoriety had grown beyond the hacker underground. Many in the computer world hailed him as a martyr in the modern web of computer technology and criminal prosecution. Abene subsequently found employment as a computer technician at a New York-based on-line service.

Computer crime can become an obsession. Such was the case for Kevin Mitnick, a man federal prosecutors described prior to his arrest as the most wanted computer hacker in the world. In the early 1980s, as a teenager, Mitnick proved his mettle as a hacker by gaining access to a North American Air Defense terminal, an event that inspired the 1983 movie *War Games*. Like the MOD gang, Mitnick gained access to computer networks through telecommunications systems. In violation of federal law, he accessed private credit information, obtaining some 20,000 credit numbers and histories. Other break-ins by Mitnick caused an estimated $4 million in damage to the computer operations of the Digital Equipment Corporation. The company also claimed that Mitnick had stolen more than one million dollars in software.

Mitnick was convicted, sentenced to one year in a minimum-security prison, and then released into a treatment program for compulsive-behavior disorders. Federal investigators tried to keep close track of him during his probation, but in November 1992, he disappeared. Authorities caught up with his trail when Mitnick broke into the system of computer-security expert Tsutomu Shimomura at the San Diego Supercomputer Center—a move that was clearly intended as a challenge to another programming wizard. Shimomura joined forces with the Federal Bureau of Investigation to pursue their elusive quarry in cyberspace. Using a program designed to record activity in a particular database that they were sure that Mitnick was accessing, while monitoring phone activity, Shimomura and authorities narrowed their search to Raleigh, North Carolina. A special device detecting cellular-phone use ultimately led them to Mitnick's apartment. Mitnick was arrested and was charged on 23 federal counts. He plea-bargained with prosecutors, who agreed to drop 22 of the counts in exchange for Mitnick's guilty plea for illegally possessing phone numbers to gain access to a computer system. Mitnick was sentenced to eight months in jail.

Mitnick's case illustrates the difficulties that legislatures and courts face when defining and assigning penalties for computer crime. Using a computer to transfer funds illegally or to embezzle money is clearly a serious crime that merits serious punishment. Mitnick broke into numerous services and databases without permission and took sensitive information, in violation of federal laws; however, he never used that information for financial gain. This type of behavior typically has no counterpart outside of cyberspace—for example, people do not break into jewelry stores only to leave a note about weak security.

Some instances of computer crimes demonstrate the way in which small computer files that require relatively little effort on the part of the perpetrator can cause millions of dollars' worth of damage to computer networks. In March 1999, David L. Smith of New Jersey created a virus that lowered the security levels of certain word-processing programs and caused infected computers to send e-mail messages containing attachments with the virus to e-mail addresses contained in the infected computer's e-mail address book. The virus was activated on an infected computer when the user opened the word-processing program.

Smith posted a message on March 26, 1999, to an Internet newsgroup called "Alt.Sex." The message claimed that if a user opened an attachment, it would provide a list of passcodes to pornographic websites. The attachment contained the virus, which became known as the "Melissa" virus. Smith was arrested by New Jersey authorities on April 1, 1999, but not before the virus had infected an estimated 1.2 million computers and affected one-fifth of the country's largest businesses.

The total amount of damages was $80 million. Smith pleaded guilty in December 1999 to state and federal charges. He faced 20 months in a federal prison and a fine of approximately $5,000 for his crime. He faced additional time in state prison. According to U.S. Attorney Robert J. Cleary, "There is a segment in society that views the unleashing of computer viruses as a challenge, a game. Far from it; it is a serious crime. The penalties Mr. Smith faces—including

David L. Smith was arrested in April 1999 for creating and disseminating the "Melissa" virus, which infected an estimated 1.2 million computers and affected one-fifth of the country's largest businesses.

AP/WIDE WORLD PHOTOS

potentially five years in a federal prison—are no game, and others should heed his example."

Others have continued to commit such crimes. In February 2000, a computer hacker stunned the world by paralyzing the Internet's leading U.S. web sites. Three days of concentrated assaults upon major sites crippled businesses like Yahoo, eBay, and CNN for hours, leaving engineers virtually helpless to respond. When the dust had settled, serious doubts were raised about the safety of Internet commerce. An international hunt ensued, and web sites claimed losses in the hundreds of millions of dollars. After pursuing several false leads, investigators ultimately charged a Canadian teenager in March 2000 in one of the attacks.

On February 7, engineers at Yahoo, the popular portal web site, noticed traffic slowing to a crawl. Initially, suspecting faulty equipment that facilitates the thousands of connections to the site daily, they were surprised to discover that it was receiving many times the normal number of hits. Buckling under exorbitant demand, the servers—the computers that receive and transmit its Internet traffic—had to be shut down for several hours. Engineers then isolated the problem: Remote computers had been instructed to bombard Yahoo's servers with automated requests for service. Over the next two days, several other major web sites suffered the same fate. Hackers hit the auction site eBay, the bookseller Amazon.com, the computer journalism site ZDnet, stock brokerages E*Trade and Datek, the computer store Buy.com, the web portal Excite at Home, and the flagship site for news giant CNN. As each site ground to a halt or went offline, engineers tried in vain to determine where the digital bombardment had originated.

Experts expressed amazement at the attacks' simplicity as well as at the inherent vulnerabilities that they exposed in the Internet's architecture. Hackers had launched what quickly came to be known as a distributed Denial-of-Service (DOS) attack—essentially a remote-controlled strike using multiple computers. First, weeks or months in advance, they had surreptitiously installed commonly available hacking programs called "scripts" on 50 or more remote computers, including university systems chosen for their high-speed connections to the Internet. Later, they activated these scripts, turning the remote computers into virtual zombies that were ordered to send unfathomably large amounts of data—up to one gigabyte per second—continuously to their victims. These data asked the target web sites to respond, just as every legitimate connection to a web site does. The sheer multitudes of requests and responses overwhelmed the victim sites. To escape detection, the "zombies" forged their digital addresses.

Federal investigators were initially stymied. They had legal authority to act under 18 U.S.C.A. § 1030, which criminalizes "knowingly transmit(ting) a program information code or command" that "intentionally causes damage." Sleuthing was difficult, however. Not only had the hackers covered the trail well, but also the FBI had suffered numerous personnel losses to private industry. The bureau had to hire consultants and had to develop special software to assist in its manhunt. Moreover, as FBI official Ron Dick told reporters, the proliferation of common hacking tools meant that even a teenager could have orchestrated the crime.

In early March 2000, authorities arrested 17-year-old New Hampshire resident Dennis Moran, allegedly known online as "Coolio." The lead proved false. In mid-April, claiming to have found "Mafiaboy," Royal Canadian Mounted Police arrested a 15-year-old Montreal hacker. The youth, whose real name was not divulged, allegedly had boasted of his exploits online while trying to recruit helpers. Officials charged him with a misdemeanor for launching the attack upon CNN's website.

Although the DEPARTMENT OF JUSTICE continued its hunt, this denial-of-service attack was never completely resolved. Analysts have noted that DOS attacks have occurred for several years, although not to the extent as that of February 2000. In May 2001, for instance, the White House's web page was hit with a DOS attack that blocked access to the site for about two hours.

Based upon the sheer number of cases involving computer crime, commentators remain puzzled as to what is necessary to curb this type of activity. Clearly, technology for law enforcement needs to stay ahead of the technology used by the hackers, but this is not an easy task. A number of conferences have been held to address these issues, often attracting large corporations such as Microsoft and Visa International, but the general consensus is that the hackers still hold the upper hand, with solutions still elusive.

FURTHER READINGS

Cadoree, Michelle. 1994. *Computer Crime and Security.* Washington, D.C.: LC Science Tracer Bullet.

Gemignani, Michael C. 1993. *Computer Law.* New York: Clark Boardman Callaghan.

Irwin, Richard D. 1990. *Spectacular Computer Crimes.* Homewood, Ill.: Dow Jones–Irwin.

Mungo, Paul. 1992. *Approaching Zero.* New York: Random House.

Nugent, Hugh. 1991. *State Computer Crime Statutes.* Justice Department. National Institute of Justice.

Slatalla, Michelle, and Joshua Quittner. 1995. *Masters of Deception.* New York: HarperCollins.

Soma, John T. 1994. *Computer Technology and the Law.* Colorado Springs: Shepard's/McGraw-Hill.

CROSS-REFERENCES

E-Mail.

COMPUTER LAW ASSOCIATION

The Computer Law Association, Inc., was formed in 1973 to fill the need for mutual education by lawyers concerned with the unique legal considerations related to the evolution, production, marketing, acquisition, and use of computer communications technology. The association is committed to providing lawyers and law students concerned with the legal and practical aspects of computers, computer services, and computer communications with a forum for an exchange of ideas and an in-depth examination of related problems. The association's meetings are open to nonmembers for the purpose of fostering useful interdisciplinary dialogue.

Over the years, the association has sponsored a wide variety of programs, covering such areas as the use of the computer as a litigation tool; privacy issues related to data banks; competition in the computer and communications industries; contracting for computer technology; computer communications issues, particularly the Federal Communications Commission's second computer inquiry and the proposed legislation affecting TELECOMMUNICATIONS; the effect of the Copyright Act of 1976 (17 U.S.C.A. § 101 et seq.) on computer technology and the work of the National Commission on New Technological Uses of Copyrighted Works (CONTU); federal, state, local, and international taxation of computer-related properties, transactions, and activities; electronic funds transfer systems; liability for computer usage; computer technology in the next decade; contracting in the computer industry; marketing of software by nonsoftware specialists; negotiating contracts for custom software; and emerging national information systems, such as the national SECURITIES markets, E-MAIL, and CABLE TELEVISION.

The association holds semiannual conferences and publishes transcripts of the meetings. It amended and adopted new by–laws in 1995. Its members are lawyers and law students.

Web site: <www.cla.org>.

CROSS-REFERENCES

Computer Crime; Copyright.

❖ COMSTOCK, GEORGE FRANKLIN

George Franklin Comstock was born August 24, 1811, in Williamstown, New York. He graduated from Union College in 1834, was admitted to the New York bar in 1837, and received an honorary doctor of laws degree in 1858.

In 1847, Comstock began his service in the New York judiciary system as first reporter of the New York Court of Appeals, a position he held until 1851. From 1852 to 1853, he served as SOLICITOR GENERAL of the United States, then returned to the New York courts as justice of the New York Court of Appeals in 1855. He sat on the bench until 1861, becoming chief justice in 1860. In 1868, he was a representative at the New York Constitutional Convention.

Comstock pursued interests in the field of education in addition to his legal career. He was a trustee of Hobart College from 1870 to 1877 and of Syracuse University from 1870 to 1890. He established the St. John's School for Boys, which is located in Manilus, New York.

In the literary field, Comstock acted as editor for *Kent's Commentaries*.

Comstock died September 27, 1892, in Syracuse, New York.

COMSTOCK LAW OF 1873

The Comstock Law of 1873 was a federal law that made it a crime to sell or distribute materials that could be used for contraception or ABORTION, to send such materials or information about such materials through the federal mail system, or to import such materials from abroad. It was motivated by growing societal concerns over OBSCENITY, abortion, pre-marital and extra-marital sex, the institution of mar-

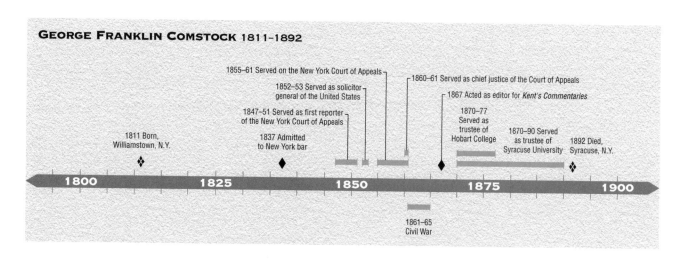

GEORGE FRANKLIN COMSTOCK 1811–1892

1855–61 Served on the New York Court of Appeals

1852–53 Served as solicitor general of the United States

1847–51 Served as first reporter of the New York Court of Appeals

1811 Born, Williamstown, N.Y.

1837 Admitted to New York bar

1860–61 Served as chief justice of the Court of Appeals

1867 Acted as editor for *Kent's Commentaries*

1870–77 Served as trustee of Hobart College

1870–90 Served as trustee of Syracuse University

1892 Died, Syracuse, N.Y.

1800   1825   1850   1875   1900

1861–65 Civil War

riage, the changing role of women in society, and increased procreation by the *lower classes*. Following the bloodbath of the Civil War and the emancipation of the slaves, many Americans sought a return to simpler times, while other Americans yearned for a nationwide spiritual and moral revival.

But the United States was undergoing rapid change during this period. The industrial revolution was making a large number of jobs available to members of both sexes, and women were taking advantage of this opportunity by entering the workforce in unprecedented numbers. The United States was also experiencing a significant wave of immigration. Some Americans complained that the new immigrants were tainting the moral fabric of the United States with their radical political beliefs and their permissive attitudes about sex. Members of the so-called *upper classes* grew worried that members of the *lower classes* were procreating at a faster rate, in part because better educated, more affluent women were postponing their childbearing years to lead lives of their own choosing, free from the dictates or needs of their fathers, husbands, or children.

The AMERICAN MEDICAL ASSOCIATION (AMA) voiced concern about abortion, not only because of the danger to women, but also because of the possibility of a woman *overlooking the duties imposed on her by the marriage contract*. The Catholic Church condemned abortion and BIRTH CONTROL as twin evils. States began enacting laws that made it more difficult to DIVORCE and gave single people greater incentive to marry.

In the middle of such local reform efforts in New York City was twenty-nine-year-old Anthony Comstock, head of the New York Society for the Suppression of Vice (NYSSV). Established in 1872, the NYSSV was financed by some of the wealthiest and most influential New York philanthropists. Comstock used their money to lobby the New York State Legislature for laws criminalizing pre-marital sex and ADULTERY, among other moral vices. He also used their money to lobby Congress for a law that would implement his overall agenda.

In 1873 Comstock got his wish, when Congress passed *An Act for the Suppression of Trade in, and Circulation of, Obscene Literature and Articles of Immoral Use*. March 3, 1873, ch. 258, § 2, 17 Stat. 599. Known popularly as the *Comstock Law*, the statute's avowed purpose was "to prevent the mails from being used to corrupt the public morals." The Comstock Law made it a crime to sell or distribute materials that could be used for contraception or abortion, to send such materials or information about such materials in the federal mail system, or to import such materials from abroad. Immediately after the law was enacted, Comstock was appointed special agent of the U.S. Post Office and given the express power to enforce the statute. Comstock held this position for the next 42 years.

Comstock claimed to have successfully prosecuted more than 3,600 defendants under the federal law and destroyed over 160 tons of obscene literature in his role as special agent. At first Comstock targeted what he considered to be easy prey, mail-order services and low-rent shops that sold cheaply produced photographs of nude women. Typically poor and uneducated, the defendants first prosecuted by Comstock often failed even to present a defense on their own behalf.

Comstock next targeted indecency in *high* culture, prosecuting prominent art gallery owners for selling European paintings containing partially clad women. But Comstock's attempted CENSORSHIP of traditional art triggered a groundswell of opposition. The *New York Times* criticized Comstock for overreaching. By 1887 many mainstream Americans who had originally supported the Comstock Law were now reconsidering that support in light of countervailing concerns over free speech. But Comstock was not deterred, continuing to prosecute alleged violators as they were made known to him.

At the turn of the century, 24 states had enacted their own versions of the Comstock Act, many of which were more stringent than the federal statute. The Comstock Law itself was recodified and reenacted several times in the twentieth century, and prosecutions for violations of the federal statute continued even as Americans became increasingly diverse and tolerant. As a result, several challenges were made to the constitutionality of the Comstock Law, most of them on FIRST AMENDMENT grounds. To the surprise of many observers, the U.S Supreme Court continued to uphold the Comstock Law into the 1960s. *United States v. Zuideveld*, 316 F.2d 873, 875-76, 881 (7th Cir. 1963).

The fate of the Comstock Law began to change, however, when the Supreme Court announced its decision in MILLER V. CALIFOR-NIA, 413 U.S. 15, 93 S. Ct. 2607, 37 L. Ed. 2d 419 (1973). In *Miller* the Supreme Court ruled that material is obscene if (1) the work, taken as a whole by an average person applying contemporary community standards, appeals to the prurient interest; (2) the work depicts sexual conduct in a patently offensive way; and (3) the work, when taken as a whole, lacks serious literary, artistic, political, or scientific value. Although the Comstock Law was never challenged on grounds that it violated the *Miller* standards for obscenity, the Supreme Court declared the law unconstitutional in 1983.

In *Bolger v. Youngs Drug Products Corp.*, 463 U.S. 60, 103 S. Ct. 2875, 77 L. Ed. 2d 469 (1983), the Supreme Court re-examined the reasons underlying the Comstock Law (then codified at 39 USCA § 3001) in light of the First Amendment standards governing commercial speech, which allow the government to regulate false, deceptive, and misleading advertisements if the regulation is supported by a substantial governmental interest. The Court concluded that the Comstock Law did not meet this burden. The government's interest in purging all mailboxes of advertisements for contraceptives is more than offset, the Court said, by the harm that results in denying the mailbox owners the right to receive truthful information bearing on their ability to practice birth control or start a family. "We have previously made clear," the Court emphasized, "that a restriction of this scope is more extensive than the Constitution permits, for the government may not reduce the adult population . . . to reading only what is fit for children."

CROSS-REFERENCES

Abortion; Adultery; American Medical Association; Birth Control; Censorship; First Amendment; Freedom of Speech.

CON

A prefix meaning with *or* together. *A slang abbreviation for* confidence, *as in* con man *or* con game. *To con someone is to deceive or take advantage of a person through* FRAUD *or trickery after winning the person's confidence.* Con *is also used as a slang abbreviation for* convict, *as in* ex-con *to mean someone previously incarcerated. An abbreviation for* contra, *which means* against. *To show the* pros *and* cons *of a particular issue means to present arguments or evidence on both sides.*

CONCEALMENT OF BIRTH OR DEATH

The crime of refusing to disclose the birth or death of a newborn child.

The offense is entirely statutory in nature, and state laws differ on its elements. In some jurisdictions the essence of the offense is the deliberate concealment of the birth; in others it is the willful concealment of the death. Intent to conceal the birth or death must be proven in order to obtain a conviction.

The concealment must be accomplished in such a manner as to prevent ascertainment of whether the child was stillborn or was born alive and died as a result of a HOMICIDE. There is no requirement that every other person be deprived of the knowledge of the birth or death of the child. The crime is still actionable when another person participates in withholding the information. Failure to provide notice of the birth of an infant who later dies does not constitute a concealment, however.

Evidence of stillbirth has been held to entitle an accused to an acquittal under some statutes. Under others it is essential to prove the live birth of the child. And in some states the offense can be committed regardless of whether there was stillbirth or live birth. ILLEGITIMACY is a necessary element of the offense in a majority of jurisdictions, based on the supposition that concealment is generally perpetrated only by those individuals wishing to conceal or destroy proof of the birth.

CONCILIATION

The process of adjusting or settling disputes in a friendly manner through extrajudicial means. Conciliation means bringing two opposing sides together to reach a compromise in an attempt to avoid taking a case to trial. ARBITRATION, *in contrast, is a contractual remedy used to settle disputes out of court. In arbitration the two parties in controversy agree in advance to abide by the decision made by a third party called in as a mediator, whereas conciliation is less structured.*

Conciliation is used in labor disputes before arbitration and may also take place in several areas of the law. A court of conciliation is one that suggests the manner in which two opposing parties may avoid trial by proposing mutually acceptable terms. In the past, some states have had bureaus of conciliation for use in DIVORCE proceedings.

The federal government has established the FEDERAL MEDIATION AND CONCILIATION SERVICE, an independent department devoted to settling labor disputes by conciliation and mediation, or settlement of disputes through the intervention of a neutral party.

CROSS-REFERENCES

Alternative Dispute Resolution.

CONCILIATION, INTERNATIONAL

A method by which the differences between nations may be settled by means of a commission employed to consider and report upon such differences.

When conciliation is used, a commission of inquiry is introduced to investigate and report on the facts surrounding a particular dispute. The report need not be in the form of an award, and the parties involved may freely decide whether or not they will give it any effect. Conciliation is distinguishable from ARBITRATION in that the terms of a conciliation settlement constitute mere proposals to the disputing powers, whereas an arbitration settlement is binding.

CONCLUSION OF LAW

The rule by which the rights of parties in a lawsuit are determined by a judge's application of relevant statutes or legal principles to the facts of the case that have been found to be true by the jury. The final judgment or decree rendered by a court based upon the verdict reached by the jury. Legal principles that provide the basis for the decision rendered by a judge in a case tried without a jury or with an ADVISORY JURY after certain facts have been established.

Under rules of federal CIVIL PROCEDURE, conclusions of law made in such cases must be stated separately from the findings of fact.

CONCLUSIVE

Determinative; beyond dispute or question. That which is conclusive is manifest, clear, or obvious. It is a legal inference made so peremptorily that it cannot be overthrown or contradicted.

A *conclusive* presumption cannot be refuted; no evidence can rebut it, as in the presumption that a child who is below a certain age has a fundamental inability to consent to sexual relations.

Conclusive evidence is evidence that is either unquestionable because it is so clear and convincing or because the law precludes its contradiction. A death certificate is considered conclusive evidence that a person has died.

CONCUR

To agree; coincide; act together. To concur is to evidence consent in an affirmative or concrete manner as opposed to merely acquiescing or silently submitting to a decision.

In appellate court practice, a judge may file a *concurring opinion,* which expresses accord with the conclusions of the majority opinion filed in the same lawsuit but at the same time separately states the judge's reason for reaching the same conclusions.

CONCURRENT

Simultaneous; converging; of equal or joint authority.

Concurrent estates is a term used in PROPERTY LAW to describe ownership of, or possessory interest in, a piece of property by two or more people jointly, such as a JOINT TENANCY or TENANCY IN COMMON.

Concurrent power is the authority of Congress and the state legislatures to make laws on the same subject matter while working independently of one another.

Concurrent negligence involves the negligent acts of at least two people that, although they might not have occurred at exactly the same moment, produce a single, indivisible injury.

Concurrent sentences are two or more prison terms to be served simultaneously, one of which might be longer than the others. The prisoner is entitled to be discharged after the longest of the terms is served.

CONCURRENT ESTATES

Ownership or possession of real property by two or more individuals simultaneously.

The three most common kinds of concurrent estates are JOINT TENANCY; TENANCY BY THE ENTIRETY; and TENANCY IN COMMON.

CONCURRENT JURISDICTION

The authority of several different courts, each of which is authorized to entertain and decide cases dealing with the same subject matter.

State and federal courts possess concurrent jurisdiction over particular civil lawsuits, such as an action to declare a state law unconstitutional. Federal courts have exclusive jurisdiction over other matters, such as cases involving PATENTS.

CONCURRENT RESOLUTION

An action of Congress passed in the form of an enactment of one house, with the other house in agreement, which expresses the ideas of Congress on a particular subject.

A concurrent resolution does not have the legal impact of a joint resolution, which has the force of official legislative action. It is more commonly employed as a method of expressing an opinion on some question. Commendations to victorious sports teams and statespersons and petitions from state legislatures to Congress or the president are examples of concurrent resolutions.

CONCURRENT WRITS

Court orders issued in duplicate originals; several orders issued at the same time for the same purpose.

A court could, for example, issue concurrent writs ordering the arrest of a person whose whereabouts were unknown, or it could issue concurrent writs for service on several defendants in a single lawsuit.

CONDEMN

To adjudge or find guilty of a crime and sentence. To declare a building or ship unsafe for use or occupancy. To decide that a navigable vessel is a prize or is unfit for service. To take privately owned land for public use in exchange for just compensation by virtue of the power of EMINENT DOMAIN.

CONDEMNATION

The process of implementing EMINENT DOMAIN, *whereby the government takes private property for public use.*

When land is condemned through eminent domain, owners must be paid just compensation and provided with notice and an opportunity to defend their rights.

CONDITION

A future and uncertain event upon the happening of which certain rights or obligations will be either enlarged, created, or destroyed.

A condition may be either express or implied. An *express condition* is clearly stated and embodied in specific, definite terms in a

A court may issue concurrent writs for the arrest of a person whose whereabouts are unknown.

UNDERWOOD & UNDERWOOD/CORBIS

contract, lease, or deed, such as the provision in an installment credit contract that, if the balance is paid before a certain date, the debtor's interest will be reduced.

An *implied condition* is presumed by law based upon the nature of a particular transaction and what would be reasonable to do if a particular event occurred. If a woman leases a hall for a wedding on a certain date, her ability to use the hall is based on its implied continued existence. If the hall burns down before that date, use of the hall is impossible due to fire; therefore, the law would imply a condition excusing the lessor from liability.

In the law of contracts, as well as estates and conveyancing, conditions *precedent* and *subsequent* may exist.

A *condition precedent* must occur before a right accrues. A woman may convey her house to her son based on the condition that the son marry by the age of twenty-five. If the son fails to marry by that age, he has lost his right to the house. Similarly, in contract law, if an agreement is signed by one party and sent to a second party with the intention that it will not become enforceable until the second party signs it, the second party's signature would be a condition precedent to its effectiveness.

A *condition subsequent* means that a right may be taken away from someone upon the occurrence of a specified event. An owner of property may convey land to a town on the condition that it be used only for church purposes. If the land conveyed is used to build a shopping mall, then ownership would revert to the original owner.

A condition subsequent may also affect a transaction involving a gift. In many states, an engagement ring is regarded as an inter vivos gift to which no conditions are attached. In some states, however, its ownership is considered to be conditioned upon the subsequent marriage of the couple involved; therefore, if a woman does not marry the man who gave her the engagement ring, ownership reverts to him and she must return it to him.

Concurrent conditions are conditions in the law of contracts that each party to the contract must simultaneously perform.

CONDITIONAL

Subject to change; dependent upon or granted based on the occurrence of a future, uncertain event.

A *conditional payment* is the payment of a debt or obligation contingent upon the performance of a certain specified act. The right to demand back payment if the condition fails is generally reserved.

CONDOMINIUM, INTERNATIONAL

A non-self-governing territory over which two states share administrative control. In this context the term coimperium *is sometimes used interchangeably with the term* condominium.

CONDOMINIUMS AND COOPERATIVES

Two common forms of multiple-unit dwellings, with independent owners or lessees of the individual units comprising the multiple-unit dwelling who share various costs and responsibilities of areas they use in common.

A *condominium* is a multiple-unit dwelling in which there is separate and distinct ownership of individual units and joint ownership of common areas. For example, in an apartment house, the individual owners would each own their own apartments while all the owners of the separate apartments would together own the parts of the building common to all of them, such as the entrances, laundry rooms, elevators, and hallways. The building is managed by the condominium association, either directly or through a professional manager. The owners of the individual units are jointly responsible for the costs of maintaining the building and common areas, but they are individually responsible for the maintenance expenses of their particular units.

A *cooperative* apartment house is usually owned and managed by a corporation, and the shareholders are tenants who lease their apartments from the corporation. The relative size of the apartment that a shareholder-tenant leases determines the proportion of the corporation's stock that that shareholder owns. Each shareholder-tenant pays a monthly assessment, based upon his or her proportionate share of the stock, to cover the principal and interest on the building mortgage, taxes, and maintenance costs.

History

The development of condominium and cooperative housing arrangements accelerated with increasing costs of real estate, inflation, increased urbanization, and population growth. Until the 1960s, the condominium as a separate form of ownership was relatively unknown in the United States. The development of condominiums was hastened when the FAIR HOUSING ACT OF 1968 (42 U.S.C.A. § 3601 et seq.) authorized the use of mortgage insurance, established under the National Housing Act (12 U.S.C.A. § 1701 et seq. [1934]), on one-family units in multiple-family structures.

Advantages

Some advantages of cooperative or condominium ownership are ownership interest in the premises; sharing high building site and maintenance costs; INCOME TAX deductions for the interest and taxes paid by individual owners; decreased risk of personal liability of the various members; and increased choice of location, since high real estate costs frequently preclude individual housing on expensive sites.

Condominium Ownership

An individual who purchases a unit in a condominium receives title to such unit in fee simple, owning it outright. The owner has all legal rights incident to ownership, including the right to sell, absent a RESTRICTIVE COVENANT limiting its use.

Title to a condominium also encompasses ownership of the land and common areas with the remaining unit owners. The individual owner has certain rights, such as use of the *common areas,* and certain obligations, such as paying his or her share of the expenses incurred for maintenance or improvements of the common areas, regardless of whether the individual owner approves of the upkeep or improvements. The size of the share of operating, maintaining, and improving costs of a building and common areas to be borne by an individual unit owner depends on the size of that owner's unit, usually measured by the number of rooms in the unit.

The three basic instruments used in the purchase of a condominium are a deed to the unit; a declaration of condominium; and the bylaws of the condominium association, the membership of which is comprised of the units' owners.

An individual buying a condominium receives a deed, which must be duly recorded in the appropriate county office. Such deed ordinarily describes the individual unit, the building in which the unit is located, and the property upon which the building is constructed. Generally it will also embody all limitations or restrictions imposed on the use of the unit and any other details agreed upon by the purchaser and

seller. The deed cannot contain any provision that is contrary to the rules of the condominium or declaration of condominium.

The declaration of condominium is the official record of the owner's rights and duties pursuant to receiving title to the condominium. It also states precisely what portions the owner of a unit owns and must maintain. State statute prescribes what must be included in the declaration of condominium. These requirements vary from one state to another, but a declaration of condominium must ordinarily contain the following: (a) a legal description of the land and buildings of the condominium, which is essentially the same information contained in the deed; (b) a description of each unit, including the address, size, number of rooms, and exact location within the building; (c) a description of the common areas and any restrictions upon the use thereof; (d) the pecuniary worth of each unit of the condominium and of the land under it, as well as the percentage of shares in the common areas assigned to each unit owner, usually based upon the number of rooms in his or her unit; (e) the number of votes assigned to each unit. The declaration of condominium must also state the procedure for making decisions concerning repairs, improvements, and similar costs, as well as provisions for amendment of the declaration or for ending the condominium arrangement. The number of votes assigned to each unit owner is in proportion to that owner's percentage share. A declaration must also provide the procedures for owners' payments of fees

A 1997 condominium development near Denver, Colorado. The condominium as a form of ownership agreement has grown rapidly in popularity since the 1960s.

AP/WIDE WORLD PHOTOS

and other costs and sanctions imposed for failure to pay them.

Condominium unit owners must adhere to the regulations set forth in the bylaws. The bylaws of a condominium—the rules and regulations by which the condominium association governs itself—are generally drafted by the developers of the condominium or the original purchasers of the individual units.

The bylaws ordinarily establish procedures for electing the officers or board members of the condominium association, conducting meetings, and handling routine building maintenance and insurance for the common areas. They prescribe any restrictions that may be imposed on the sale of individual units and penalties for violation of the rules.

A condominium unit may be purchased for cash; however, the more common procedure is for a mortgage to be obtained to help finance it. Since each unit is owned individually, if an owner defaults on mortgage payments or property taxes, no other unit owner is liable.

Cooperative Organization

A cooperative can be created in a number of ways:

1. *Corporate organization.* The most common type of cooperative organization is its corporate form. Three documents are required for the formation of a corporate cooperative: a corporate charter or certificate of incorporation; bylaws; and a proprietary lease or occupancy agreement. These three instruments together constitute the contract between the individual owners and the corporation. The relationship of the unit owners to the corporation is such that they are tenants as well as shareholders. Corporate financing is ordinarily accomplished by a single mortgage executed by the corporation, which covers the entire project. Since separate mortgages on the individual units are uncommon, occupants are dependent upon the financial stability of their fellow occupants.

2. *Co-ownership in joint tenancy.* In a JOINT TENANCY, title to the premises vests in all of the co-owners as joint tenants, which means that they have an undivided interest coupled with a RIGHT OF SURVIVORSHIP. Such an arrangement includes provisions for exclusive occupancy of individual units, vested in designated co-owners. This type of plan is not often practicable, since there must be

four unities in a joint tenancy: time, title, interest, and possession.

3. *Tenancy in common.* The occupants own the entire project collectively as tenants in common. Each tenant is given the right to occupy exclusively a specifically designated unit. A TENANCY IN COMMON differs from a joint tenancy in that each tenant owns an undivided portion; however, the portions are not necessarily equal. In addition, each tenant has the legal right to dispose of his or her undivided share or a portion thereof by deed or by will. Various covenants are employed to enforce the financial obligations in maintenance and operation by the co-tenants.

4. *Business trust.* In a BUSINESS TRUST or Massachusetts trust, title to the entire premises vests in the trustees of the trust. Certificates of beneficial interest are issued to the individual tenants, and each beneficial owner is assigned an exclusive right of occupancy of a specific unit under a proprietary lease.

Each tenant-shareholder may deduct on his or her federal income tax return a proportionate share of the interest that the cooperative corporation has paid upon its blanket mortgage, so long as the corporation does not obtain in excess of 20 percent of its gross income from sources apart from its tenant-shareholders.

FURTHER READINGS

Barton, Stephen E., and Carol J. Silverman, eds. 1994. *Common Interest Communities: Private Governments and the Public Interest.* Berkeley: Univ. of California Press.

Hyatt, Wayne S. 2000. *Condominium and Homeowner Association Practice: Community Association Law.* 3d ed. Philadelphia, Pa.: American Law Institute-American Bar Association, Committee on Continuing Professional Education.

Rohan, Patrick J. 1999. "Preparing Community Associations for the Twenty-First Century: Anticipating the Legal Problems and Possible Solutions." *St. John's Law Review* 73 (winter): 3–42.

Thomsett, Michael C. 1988. *How to Buy a House, Condo, or Co-Op.* Mount Vernon, N.Y.: Consumers Union.

Trigiani, Lucia Anna. 2002. *Reinventing the Rules: A Step-By-Step Guide for Being Reasonable.* Alexandria, Va.: Community Associations Press.

CROSS-REFERENCES

Community Property; Lease.

CONDONATION

In marriage, the voluntary pardoning by an innocent spouse of an offense committed by his or her partner conditioned upon the promise that it will not recur.

Condonation, which is used as a defense in DIVORCE actions based on fault grounds, is strongly supported by public policy. The institution of marriage and its preservation are considered essential for the stability of society, and therefore condonation is encouraged to promote the notion that marriages should not be lightly dissolved.

The elements of condonation are the resumption of normal marital relations after knowledge of the offense or offenses and the promise that the offense will not be repeated. Various cases have attempted to interpret whether or not condonation has actually taken place. If, for example, a wife commits ADULTERY and her husband, after discovering this, allows her to return to their home but does not resume normal marital relations with her, a full condonation has not taken place. Whether or not a marital relationship has been fully resumed is generally considered to be a QUESTION OF FACT in divorce cases.

Whether or not condonation has taken place is important in the area of maintenance or support obligations. In many states, remedies for nonsupport will be granted only when there is a showing that the husband has been guilty of a serious marital offense. If a husband who has committed such an offense can prove condonation, he can use this as a defense to his wife's claim of nonsupport. Similarly, condonation has important consequences in formulating the grounds for divorce. If a woman's husband has beaten her on a few occasions but she subsequently continued to cohabit with him, she might later be unable to sue for divorce on grounds of cruel and inhuman treatment.

Some offenses, such as mental cruelty, due to their ongoing, continuous nature, may not be eliminated by a showing of condonation.

CONFEDERACY

The association or banding together of two or more persons for the purpose of committing an act or furthering an enterprise that is forbidden by law, or that, though lawful in itself, becomes unlawful when made the object of the confederacy. More commonly called a conspiracy. *The union of two or more independent states for the purpose of common safety or a furtherance of their mutual goals.*

CONFEDERATE ATTORNEYS GENERAL

Following secession from the Union, the Southern states immediately began the process of establishing a separate government to guide their course. One of the first acts of the provisional congress of the Confederate States of America was to preserve the force and framework of existing law in the South by adopting the Constitution of the Confederate States, which closely mirrored the CONSTITUTION OF THE UNITED STATES OF AMERICA.

Though the Confederate constitution made provisions for the existence of a supreme judicial court, with powers like those of the SUPREME COURT OF THE UNITED STATES, the provisional congress refused to enact the legislation necessary to actually establish the national court. Therefore, the attorneys general of the Confederacy were often called on to act in place of a national tribunal and to render opinions interpreting the laws enacted by the Confederate congress. Accordingly their opinions were varied, covering both commonplace issues and constitutional questions.

From 1861 to 1865, the Confederacy was served by four full time attorneys general— Judah Philip Benjamin, Thomas Bragg, Thomas Hill Watts, and George Davis—and by Wade Keyes, who functioned at various times as assistant, acting, and *ad interim* (temporary) attorney general. As a group, they authored 218 opinions for Confederate president Jefferson Davis and members of his cabinet; most of the opinions were requested by the Departments of War, Treasury, and the Navy, and most were related to the fighting of, or financing of, the U.S. CIVIL WAR.

Judah Philip Benjamin

Judah Philip Benjamin (1811–84) was the Confederacy's first attorney general. Appointed by President Davis, Benjamin was confirmed on March 5, 1861, and served until November 21, 1861, when he was named secretary of war. As attorney general, he wrote 13 opinions on such matters as agricultural products tariffs, mail route contracts, and defense appropriations.

Wade Keyes Jr.

Wade Keyes Jr. (1821–79) was named assistant attorney general by Benjamin on May 6, 1861. He became a central figure in the Confederate Department of Justice, and he often assumed the responsibilities of the attorney general when the current appointee was absent or in times of transition.

Before taking the position of assistant attorney general under Benjamin, Keyes was a prominent Alabama lawyer who specialized in property cases. Born to wealth and privilege, he was educated at La Grange College and the University of Virginia. His parents financed an extended tour of Europe and, on his return to the United States, arranged for him to study law with several noted Southern attorneys.

Though Keyes directed his efforts to the PRACTICE OF LAW and generally avoided politics, he did hold public office for six years as chancellor of the Southern Division of Alabama. It was during his years in this office that Keyes was first noticed by Benjamin. Benjamin, impressed with Chancellor Keyes's administrative abilities, legal intellect, and writing skills, was instrumental in bringing Keyes into the newly formed Confederate Department of Justice.

In the course of Keyes's service to the Confederate president and cabinet, he authored 24 opinions—both for himself and for other attorneys general—on such diverse subjects as the duties of the attorney general; the treatment of prisoners of war; and, drawing on his former area of expertise, the appropriation of PERSONAL PROPERTY for the war effort. Following Watts's election as governor of Alabama and resignation as attorney general, Keyes stepped in and served as attorney general ad interim from October 2, 1863, to January 1, 1864, when George Davis was able to take the office.

Thomas Bragg

Thomas Bragg (1810–72) was named attorney general on November 21, 1861, when Benjamin became secretary of war. Bragg had been attorney general for only four months and had authored just seven opinions, when the escalating military conflict threatened his family and his personal interests. He resigned on March 18, 1862.

Bragg was born on November 9, 1810, in Warrenton, North Carolina, the son of Thomas Bragg and Margaret Crossland Bragg. He attended local schools in Warrenton and a military academy in Middletown, Connecticut, before studying law in Warrenton with John Hall, a North Carolina Supreme Court judge. Bragg was admitted to the bar and began the

practice of law in 1833 at the age of 23. On October 4, 1837, he married Isabella Cuthbert, the daughter of a locally prominent and politically active family.

Bragg continued to practice law for the next several years, and he began to take an interest in local politics. He was elected to the North Carolina legislature in 1844, and by 1854 he was governor of the state. After two highly successful terms as governor, he was sent to the U.S. Senate, where he served until the secession of North Carolina.

In spite of Bragg's brief service as attorney general, he remained a friend of, and adviser to, the Davis administration throughout the war. After the war, Bragg returned to practice in North Carolina and tried, without success, to restore the personal property and fortune he had lost during the war years. Bragg died on January 21, 1872, in Raleigh, North Carolina.

Thomas Hill Watts

On March 19, 1862, Thomas Hill Watts (1819–92) was named to succeed Bragg as attorney general. He served more than a year, and he wrote 99 opinions on MARTIAL LAW, reorganization of the military under CONSCRIPTION, pay allowances, rights of prisoners of war, treasonable offenses, and many other issues related to military service and the war.

At the outbreak of the Civil War, Watts had organized the Seventeenth Alabama Infantry Regiment and served as its colonel. He was commanding the regiment in Tennessee when he received the appointment as attorney general. Perhaps because of this background, he had a special affinity for the men on the front lines of the conflict and for men from his home state. He spent many hours visiting wounded Alabama soldiers at nearby field hospitals and camps.

Watts was born January 3, 1819, in Alabama Territory near the town of Greenville in present-day Butler County, Alabama. He was a middle son in a family of modest means. His parents, John Hughes Watts and Prudence Hill Watts, agreed to pay for his education at the University of Virginia if he agreed to forfeit any future claim to the family estate. He thought the bargain was a good one, and he graduated in 1839. He studied law locally and was admitted to the bar in 1840.

On January 10, 1842, he married Eliza Brown Allen. The Wattses had ten children.

While practicing law and providing for his growing family, Watts served several terms in the Alabama legislature in the 1840s. In 1850, he made an unsuccessful bid for a congressional seat.

As war approached, Watts was an outspoken opponent of ABRAHAM LINCOLN and a firm believer in the right of an individual state to determine its future. While serving as attorney general, Watts left the office in the hands of Keyes on several occasions in order to return home and tend to state business. During the course of those visits, he decided to make a bid for the Alabama governorship in 1863. He was successful. Following his election, he resigned his position as attorney general effective October 1, 1863.

Watts's term as governor of Alabama ended with the fall of the Confederacy. For his part in the rebellion, Watts lost his personal fortune in land and slaves, and, in 1865, he was sent to a Northern prison camp.

Three years later, he was pardoned by President ANDREW JOHNSON and permitted to return to Alabama to care for his ailing wife. She died in 1873. Following her death, Watts moved to Montgomery, Alabama, and resumed the practice of law. He remarried in September 1875. Watts died in Montgomery on September 16, 1892.

George Davis

George Davis (1820–96) took office as attorney general on January 2, 1864, and he served until the collapse of the Confederacy. He authored 75 opinions on issues such as the constitutionality of the conscription act, the legality of contracts for imports and exports, and the liability of the government for seized property and stored goods.

Davis was born March 1, 1820, at Porter's Neck, New Hanover (now Pender) County, North Carolina. His parents were Thomas Frederick Davis and Sarah Isabella Eagles Davis. He graduated first in the University of North Carolina class of 1838, and he was admitted to the bar in 1839.

He became a prominent and respected member of the local legal community, as well as a man of wealth and taste. He was married, on November 17, 1842, to Mary A. Polk, and they had a large family.

Davis had an early interest in politics, but as a WHIG PARTY member living in a DEMOCRATIC PARTY stronghold, he had little opportunity to serve. Finally, when North Carolina withdrew from the Union, Davis was sent to the provisional congress as a delegate from his state. The following year, he entered the Confederate Senate, where he generally supported the administration of the Confederate president. It was from his position in the Confederate Senate that Davis was tapped by the president and asked to take the office of attorney general after Watts resigned. Davis was unable to accept the office immediately, owing to the illness and subsequent death of his wife, so the position was temporarily filled by Keyes.

Davis's last act as attorney general was to advise the president and the cabinet to accept the terms of a presurrender agreement. The agreement was not accepted by the Union. After receiving word of General Robert E. Lee's surrender at Appomattox Courthouse, in Virginia, the attorney general resigned and became a fugitive.

Fleeing southward, Davis first sought to locate his children, who were staying with friends near Wilmington, North Carolina. He managed to elude federal forces for a while but was eventually captured at Key West, Florida. He was imprisoned and held until January 1, 1866.

After his release, Davis returned to Wilmington, North Carolina. Just six months after leaving prison, he married Monimia Fairfax, on May 9, 1866. He resumed his legal practice and found himself in demand as a regional speaker. In the mid-1870s, he was offered, and declined, the chief justiceship of the North Carolina Supreme Court. His last public appearance was to deliver the eulogy at the 1889 funeral of Jefferson Davis. George Davis died in Wilmington, North Carolina, on February 23, 1896.

FURTHER READINGS

Canfield, Cass. 1981. *The Iron Will of Jefferson Davis*. New York: Fairfax.

Catton, Bruce, and William Catton. 1971. *Two Roads to Sumter*. New York: McGraw-Hill.

Eaton, Clement. 1965. *A History of the Confederacy*. New York: Free Press.

The Opinions of the Confederate Attorneys General, 1861–1865. Buffalo: Dennis.

Sandburg, Carl. 1974. *Abraham Lincoln: The War Years*. New York: Dell.

CROSS-REFERENCES

U.S. Civil War.

CONFEDERATION

A union of states in which each member state retains some independent control over internal and external affairs. Thus, for international purposes, there are separate states, not just one state. A federation, in contrast, is a union of states in which external affairs are controlled by a unified, central government.

CONFERENCE OF CHIEF JUSTICES

Improving the state judicial system is the mission of the Conference of Chief Justices. Founded in 1949 as an association of chief justices of state supreme courts, the conference tackles organizational, administrative, and procedural issues at its biannual meetings and through standing and special committees. It is governed by a board of directors. Long regarded as an austere group with narrow concerns, the conference emerged in a broader role in the 1990s. Pressing concerns about a logjam of cases in state courts led it to open a new partnership with federal courts, resulting in the first-ever meeting between the highest judicial officers of both court systems in 1990. More dramatically, the conference broke its long-standing silence on politics: it entered a heated battle with the JUSTICE DEPARTMENT over ethics rules, made outspoken attacks on federal HEALTH CARE and crime legislation, and began earnestly LOBBYING Congress. This bolder identity caused ripples in the legal community as the conference announced its willingness to be a political player with the help of its research and lobbying arm, the National Center for State Courts (NCSC).

Traditionally, the Conference of Chief Justices tended to looked inward. Its membership includes, besides state supreme court justices, the highest judicial officers of the District of Columbia, Puerto Rico, and U.S. territories, and each jurisdiction has long faced similar concerns. State court systems are simple only in appearance: every system of trial, appellate, and supreme courts requires vast organizational resources. The conference was founded to share ideas, compare methods, and brainstorm new solutions to managing these behemoths. From the mid-1970s to the mid-1990s, meetings addressed matters ranging from the expanding role of the court administrator to the problems of caseload management and rules and methods of procedure. Not all these concerns were limited to the courts. The conference reacted in dismay to the ruling in the 1984 case of *Pulliam v.*

Allen, 466 U.S. 522, 104 S. Ct. 1970, 80 L. Ed. 2d 565 (1984), which overturned the historic doctrine of JUDICIAL IMMUNITY and permitted attorneys to collect awards against state judges, and it began an ongoing lobbying effort aimed at having Congress restore judicial immunity.

The conference's horizons started to broaden in the 1980s, as changes in federal policy began overloading state courts. The states have always handled the vast majority of civil and criminal cases, but the so-called war on drugs filled state court dockets with more cases than they could reasonably handle. By 1990, the conference's president, Chief Justice Vincent L. McKusick, of the Supreme Judicial Court of Maine, noted that Arizona's trial courts processed more drug cases annually than did all federal trial courts combined. The conference's response was to open a dialogue with the JUDICIAL CONFERENCE OF THE UNITED STATES, its federal partner. In September 1990, the highest officials of both systems met for the first time at the national level to address mutual concerns about drug and TORT cases. They formed the Federal-State Judicial Council to continue to seek solutions.

By 1994, the conference was taking bolder steps in a long-running dispute with the Justice Department. As far back as 1989, then attorney general RICHARD THORNBURGH had suggested changing the Justice Department's code of ethics to stop following Rule 4.2 of the American Bar Association's Model Rules of Professional Conduct. Upheld by the states and most federal courts, this rule governs the communication of lawyers in disputes: it specifically bars lawyers from communicating with a party who is represented by another lawyer, without that lawyer's consent. The Justice Department believed that the rule hampered federal prosecutors in their investigations, and in early 1994, Attorney General JANET RENO said the U.S. Constitution exempted federal prosecutors from the ethics rules of state bar associations. In August 1994, the conference passed a resolution blasting the Justice Department's position and advising state bars and supreme courts to enforce Rule 4.2. Conference members accused the department of blatant illegality, and legal observers expected the matter ultimately to end up before the U.S. Supreme Court.

Although the conference had traditionally refrained from taking overtly political positions, members decided in 1994 to enter the fray. Two issues troubled them: health care reform and the crime bill, both put forward by the administration of President BILL CLINTON. Using the research facilities of the NCSC, the conference claimed that health care reform would fill state courts with 90 million new claims. And in a strongly worded resolution, it lashed out at the original text of the crime bill for "indiscriminate federalization of crimes, the needless disruption of effective state and local law enforcement efforts, and the inefficient use of the special but limited resources of the federal courts." Going beyond harsh criticism, the conference directed the NCSC to lobby members of Congress in what became a partially successful effort at trimming the bill.

This departure from tradition excited the legal community. The *National Law Journal* spotted "new-found muscle and aggression" in the conference's activities, and other observers saw potential for the conference to become a major player in political debate. Not wishing to be viewed as a partisan organization, the conference itself vowed to limit its lobbying to issues that affected JUDICIAL ADMINISTRATION.

The conference maintained a lower profile since the mid-1990s and reaffirmed its commitment to improving the administration of justice. In 2002, it passed a resolution endorsing a report on public access to court information that seeks to bring uniform practices to the judiciary. In addition, the conference endorsed a resolution that seeks to make the system more accessible to self-represented litigants. With the precipitous decline in state government budgets in 2002 and 2003, the conference began to explore how far the judicial branch must go in sharing the financial burden with the other two branches of government.

FURTHER READINGS

"Chief Justices Meet, Grouse about Crime Bill." 1994. *National Law Journal* (February 28).

Conference of Chief Justices. Resolution 33. Endorsing and Supporting *Public Access to Court Records: Guidelines for Policy Development by State Courts* (2002). Available online at <www.ccj.ncsc.dni.us/resol33PublicAccess CourtRecords.html> (accessed May 21, 2003).

"Feds, State Judges in Showdown." 1994. *National Law Journal* (August 15).

National Center for State Courts. Available online at <www .ncsconline.org> (accessed May 21, 2003).

"Podium: Combining Resources." 1990. *National Law Journal* (November 19).

"State Court Chiefs Flex New Muscle—Chief Justices Conference Sheds Benign Image and Challenges Washington." 1994. *National Law Journal* (October 17).

CONFERENCE OF STATE COURT ADMINISTRATORS

Founded in 1955, the Conference of State Court Administrators is an association of the administrators of state courts and the courts of the District of Columbia, Puerto Rico, and Guam. According to the conference, its purpose is "to deal with problems of state court systems." Toward that end, the conference tries to

- encourage the formulation of fundamental policies, principles, and standards for state court administration.
- facilitate cooperation, consultation, and exchange of information by and among national, state, and local offices and organizations directly concerned with court administration.
- foster the utilization of the principles and techniques of modern management in the field of JUDICIAL ADMINISTRATION.
- improve administrative practices and procedures in and increase the efficiency and effectiveness of all courts in the several states.

The members of the conference are the principal court administrative officers of the several states, the Commonwealth of Puerto Rico, and any other jurisdiction that is elected as a full member of the CONFERENCE OF CHIEF JUSTICES. If any state or any other member jurisdiction of the Conference of Chief Justices does not have a duly appointed principal court administrative officer, the chief justice of that state or jurisdiction may designate an individual to take part in the activities of the Conference of State Court Administrators in an associate member status. An associate member is not eligible to vote or hold office. Serving as the secretariat is the National Center for State Courts. It publishes *State Judiciary News* and holds annual meetings.

CONFERENCE ON PERSONAL FINANCE LAW

The Conference on Personal Finance Law was founded in 1927 to encourage study, research, and education in the area of personal finance law. Its members are lawyers. The conference disseminates information on the history and current status of laws and regulations pertaining to personal finance, provides a forum for exchange of views on the subject among lawyers in the hope of stimulating improvement of legal procedures, and fosters sound development of consumer finance through education and publication. The conference stages an annual argument before the supreme court of the mythical state of Franklin in order to dramatize an important issue in the field of CONSUMER CREDIT.

The conference publishes *Quarterly Report* and programs and briefs related to the annual argument, which is staged during the AMERICAN BAR ASSOCIATION annual meeting.

CONFESSION

A statement by which an individual acknowledges his or her guilt in the commission of a crime.

One vital function of the U.S. judicial system is to determine the guilt or innocence of suspects who have been accused of crimes. Confessions can play a key role in making this determination. Courts in the U.S. have recognized the fallibility of inaccurate or involuntary confessions—such as those that have been obtained as the result of threats or trickery—and have developed a body of law to prevent untrustworthy confessions from jeopardizing a criminal defendant's CIVIL RIGHTS.

Confessions were always allowed as evidence in early English common-law trials, even when torture was used to elicit them. Not until the mid–eighteenth century did judges in England start to admit only confessions that they deemed trustworthy. To determine the trustworthiness of a confession, judges considered the circumstances surrounding it, whether a threat or promise coerced the suspect to confess, and whether the suspect confessed voluntarily.

The U.S. Supreme Court first addressed the issue of confessions in the 1884 case of *Hopt v. Utah,* 110 U.S. 574, 4 S. Ct. 202, 28 L. Ed. 262. Following the English common-law standard, the Court looked at whether the suspect had confessed voluntarily or as a result of a threat or promise. The Court first invoked the U.S. Constitution to support this voluntariness standard in the 1897 case of *Bram v. United States,* 168 U.S. 532, 18 S. Ct. 183, 42 L. Ed. 568.

In *Bram,* the Court applied the FIFTH AMENDMENT'S PRIVILEGE AGAINST SELF-INCRIMINATION to confessions in federal courts, observing that any amount of influence exerted to obtain a confession would render the confession involuntary and thus inadmissible. The *Bram* holding initially created a harsh standard of confession admissibility. Later decisions interpreting *Bram* lowered the standard by requiring that a confession be excluded from evidence only if the amount of influence that had been used to obtain it actually called into question the statement's reliability.

In 1936, the U.S. Supreme Court considered the issue of coerced confessions for actions in state court, rather than federal court, in *Brown v. Mississippi,* 297 U.S. 278, 56 S. Ct. 461, 80 L. Ed. 682. *Brown* involved three African-American defendants who had confessed to the murder of a white man only after being beaten and tortured by state police. The Court, this time, invoked the Fourteenth Amendment's DUE PROCESS guarantee in holding the confessions to be inadmissible because the police had obtained them in a way that violated basic liberty and justice principles. The Court in *Brown* announced a due process analysis to be employed by state courts on a case-by-case basis to determine whether, given the totality of the circumstances, a suspect had confessed voluntarily. The analysis was to include an assessment of the suspect's character and status as well as of the methods used by the police.

Case-by-case determination of the kind required by *Brown* proved to be unwieldy for state courts because the method was so fact-specific. Appellate courts had difficulty setting effective precedents because case outcomes depended solely on unique factual circumstances. As a result, the police were left with little guidance as to thew way to interrogate suspects properly and lawfully.

By the mid-1960s, the U.S. Supreme Court once again began to alter its approach to determining the admissibility of confessions. Starting with *Malloy v. Hogan,* 378 U.S. 1, 84 S. Ct. 1489, 12 L. Ed. 2d 653 (1964), the Court held that the Fifth Amendment privilege against SELF-INCRIMINATION, which previously had applied only to federal actions, now applied to state actions as well. Thus, the Court held, suspects in state court were entitled to the same standards governing confessions—initially set forth in the *Bram* opinion—as were suspects in federal court.

In MASSIAH V. UNITED STATES, 377 U.S. 201, 84 S. Ct. 1199, 12 L. Ed. 2d 246 (1964), the Court continued to move away from the FOURTEENTH AMENDMENT due process analysis that it had employed in its previous decisions. In *Massiah,* the Court held that the SIXTH AMENDMENT grants criminal defendants the RIGHT TO COUN-

SEL during post-indictment interrogations, and when this right is violated, confessions obtained are inadmissible. In ESCOBEDO V. ILLINOIS, 378 U.S. 478, 84 S. Ct. 1758, 12 L. Ed. 2d 977 (1964), the Court expanded this protection to pre-indictment confessions, holding that the right to counsel attaches when a police investigation becomes accusatory.

Two years later, the Court handed down the landmark decision MIRANDA V. ARIZONA, 384 U.S. 436, 86 S. Ct. 1602, 16 L. Ed. 2d 694 (1966), finding that police custody is inherently coercive, and therefore that criminal suspects in police custody must be informed expressly of their constitutional rights before interrogation begins. A suspect's *Miranda* rights include the right to remain silent and to have a lawyer present during questioning. Any statements made by the suspect may be used against him or her in a court of law. The Court held in *Miranda* that a suspect may waive any of these rights, but only if the waiver is made voluntarily, knowingly, and intelligently. But *Miranda* left these criteria essentially undefined, thus prompting a glut of litigation concerning the validity of *Miranda* waivers.

The Court attempted to clarify its position in *North Carolina v. Butler,* 441 U.S. 369, 99 S. Ct. 1755, 60 L. Ed. 286 (1979). Willie Thomas Butler had spoken with the police after they had advised him of his *Miranda* rights, then later sought to have the court exclude his incriminating statements because he had declined to sign a waiver agreement. In ruling against Butler, the high court adopted the "totality of the circumstances" approach for determining whether a waiver of *Miranda* rights is voluntary, knowing, and intelligent. Butler, the Court found, had implied a voluntary waiver through his words and actions, thus making an express written waiver unnecessary. *Butler* thus required courts to determine the voluntariness of a suspect's waiver case by case. *Butler* further instructed courts to invalidate seemingly voluntary waivers in instances of apparent coercion, deceit, or trickery on the part of police.

Another attempt at clarification came in *Moran v. Burbine,* 475 U.S. 412, 106 S. Ct. 1135, 89 L. Ed. 2d 410 (1986), in which the Court held that the suspect's confession had been voluntary and valid even though the police, after reciting *Miranda* rights, had failed to inform him that his attorney had been trying to contact him. The Court in *Burbine* found that although the police have a duty to convey *Miranda* rights, including the right to an attorney, there is no constitutional duty to inform a suspect when that suspect's attorney wants to confer. The Court further held that *Miranda* rights belong to the suspect, and therefore it was irrelevant that the police in *Burbine* had deceived the suspect's attorney by falsely stating that they would not interrogate the suspect. *Burbine* invoked a two-pronged test for courts to apply in determining waiver validity: (1) whether the suspect's choice to waive *Miranda* rights was free and uncoerced; and (2) whether the suspect fully understood the consequences of waiving those rights.

Nine months later, the Court refined *Burbine*'s first prong in *Colorado v. Connelly,* 479 U.S. 157, 107 S. Ct. 515, 93 L. Ed. 2d 473 (1986). Francis Barry Connelly, who was diagnosed as schizophrenic, made unsolicited murder confessions to the police while he was in a psychotic state. He continued to talk even after the police read him the *Miranda* rights. In attempting to exclude the confession at trial, Connelly's attorney argued that Connelly had no control over his psychotic delusions, and that the confession therefore had been involuntary.

Finding no POLICE MISCONDUCT, the high court ruled against Connelly, stating that "*Miranda* protects defendants against government coercion leading them to surrender rights protected by the Fifth Amendment; it goes no further than that." *Connelly* suggests that the voluntariness of a waiver depends on the conduct of the police, not the mental state of the suspect. Yet the mental state of the suspect may still play a role in *Burbine*'s second prong, which considers the suspect's awareness of *Miranda* rights and the consequences of waiving them.

Legal commentators have criticized *Miranda* and its subsequent line of decisions, stating that criminal suspects seldom truly understand the meaning or importance of the rights recited to them. Studies have indicated that the *Miranda* decision has had little effect on the numbers of confessions and requests for lawyers made by suspects in custody. What is more, critics of *Miranda* cite concerns that the police might fabricate waivers, as a suspect's waiver of *Miranda* rights need not be recorded or made to a neutral party. Proponents argue that *Miranda* protects criminal suspects and reduces needless litigation by providing the police with concrete guidelines for permissible interrogation.

Even though the idea behind *Miranda* rights is to protect suspects in custody from police coercion, the U.S. Supreme Court in 1991 held that coerced confessions nevertheless may be used in court if their use is harmless—in other words, if a jury would probably convict even without them (*Arizona v. Fulminante,* 499 U.S. 279, 111 S. Ct. 1246, 113 L. Ed. 2d 302). The police suspected that Oreste Fulminante had killed his 11-year-old stepdaughter, whose body was found in an Arizona desert two days after he had reported her missing. Before he was charged with the murder, Fulminante had received a prison sentence for an unrelated weapons-possession charge. While in prison on that charge, he confessed the murder to a fellow inmate, who actually was a paid federal informant. The informant had offered to protect Fulminante from other inmates in exchange for hearing the truth about the murder. Fulminante was subsequently indicted for the killing, and his confession was used at trial despite his objection. A jury found him guilty of murder and sentenced him to death. The U.S. Supreme Court applied the harmful error test and found that the jurors most likely would not have convicted Fulminante had they not heard his coerced confession, thus its use at trial was harmful. The Court ordered the case back for a new trial, this time without use of the confession.

Legal scholars have criticized the *Fulminante* decision for failing to follow decades of legal precedent holding that coerced confessions violate the due process rights of criminal suspects and that their use at trial necessitates automatic reversal, whether they are harmful or not. *Fulminante,* they argue, encourages the police to ignore the civil rights of suspects and to coerce confessions. Others argue that the decision is correct because it focuses on achieving an accurate determination of guilt or innocence regardless of whether constitutional rights are violated. Whatever its long-term effects, *Fulminante* will not be the final word in the progression of U.S. Supreme Court cases defining the law of confessions.

Recent Developments

In 1999, the U.S. Court of Appeals for the Fourth Circuit fueled long-standing speculation that *Miranda* would be overruled, when it held that the admissibility of confessions in federal court is governed not by *Miranda,* but by a federal statute enacted two years after that decision.

The statute, 18 U.S.C.A. Section 3501, provides that a confession is admissible if voluntarily given. Congress enacted the statute in order to overturn *Miranda,* the Fourth Circuit said, and Congress had the authority to do so pursuant to its authority to overrule judicially created RULES OF EVIDENCE that are not mandated by the U.S. Constitution. *United States. v. Dickerson,* 166 F.3d 667 (4th Cir. 1999).

The U.S. Supreme Court reversed. In an opinion authored by Chief Justice WILLIAM REHNQUIST, the Court said that, whether or not it agreed with *Miranda,* the principles of STARE DECISIS weigh heavily against overruling it now. While the Court has overruled its precedents when subsequent cases have undermined their doctrinal underpinnings, that has not happened to the *Miranda* decision, which the Court said "has become embedded in routine police practice to the point where the warnings have become part of our national culture." Although the Court acknowledged that a few guilty defendants might go free as the result of the application of the *Miranda* rule, "experience suggests that the totality-of-the-circumstances test which Section 3501 seeks to revive is more difficult than *Miranda* for law enforcement officers to conform to and for courts to apply in a consistent manner." *Dickerson v. United States,* 530 U.S. 428, 120 S. Ct. 2326, 147 L. Ed. 2d 405 (2000).

In another decision, the Court actually increased defendants' constitutional rights when it ruled that the protections provided by its decision in *Bruton v. United States,* 391 U.S. 123, 88 S. Ct. 1620, 20 L. Ed. 2d 476 (1968) (which held that the introduction of a non-testifying codefendant's confession incriminating both himself and the other defendant in a joint trial violated the other defendant's Sixth Amendment right to cross-examine witnesses) were applicable to a codefendant's confession that substituted blanks and the word *deleted* in place of the defendant's proper name. The Court said that redactions that simply replace the defendant's name with an obvious substitute, such as *deleted,* a blank space, a symbol, or other similarly obvious indications of alteration, result in statements that so closely resemble the unredacted statements in *Bruton* that the law must require the same result. The Court believed that juries will often react similarly to unredacted confessions and to poorly redacted confessions, as jurors often realize that a poorly redacted confession refers specifically to the defendant, even when the statement does not expressly link the defendant to the deleted name. Additionally, the Court stressed that by encouraging the jury to speculate about the removed name, the redaction might overemphasize the importance of the confession's accusation once the jurors figure out the redacted reference. *Gray v. Maryland,* 523 U.S. 185, 118 S. Ct. 1151, 140 L. Ed. 2d 294 (1998)

In *Martinez v. City of Oxnard,* 270 F.3d 852 (9th Cir. 2001), the U.S. Court of Appeals for the Ninth Circuit ruled that violating a defendant's rights against coerced confessions can give rise to a civil rights action against the police officer who attempted to coerce the confession. *Martinez* stemmed from a 45-minute emergency-room interrogation of a narcotics suspect who had been shot five times by a police officer while being subdued during the arrest. The suspect, who was rendered blind in one eye and paralyzed below the legs by the gunshot wounds, sued the officer who had conducted the interrogation. The officer interposed a defense of qualified IMMUNITY, claiming that he could not be sued for injuries suffered by the defendant while the officer was simply doing his job.

The district court rejected the officer's defense and granted SUMMARY JUDGMENT to the narcotics suspect on his civil rights claim under 42 U.S.C.A § 1983. In affirming the district court's decision, the Ninth Circuit ruled that a police officer may raise the defense of qualified immunity only when he or she could have reasonably believed that his or her conduct was lawful under settled law. In this case, the record revealed that the officer had doggedly tried to exact a confession from the suspect without first reading him the *Miranda* warnings, and that he then had proceeded to ignore the suspect's repeated requests for the officer to cease the interrogation until he was finished receiving medical treatment for his life-threatening injuries. No reasonable officer, the court concluded, could have believed that interrogating the suspect under those "extreme circumstances" comported with the Fifth Amendment's prohibitions against coerced confessions, and thus the officer was not entitled to assert qualified immunity as a defense. Accordingly, the district court's grant of summary judgment against the officer was affirmed. However, the U.S. Supreme Court granted the officer's petition for certiorari.

FURTHER READINGS

Chertoff, Michael. 1995. "Chopping *Miranda* Down to Size." *Michigan Law Review* 93.

Green, Jana. 1992. "*Arizona v. Fulminante:* The Harmful Extension of the Harmless Error Doctrine." *Oklahoma City University Law Review* 17.

Hourihan, Paul. 1995. "Earl Washington's Confession: Mental Retardation and the Law of Confessions." *Virginia Law Review* 81.

LaFave, Wayne R., and Fred L. Israel. 2001. *Criminal Procedure.* 6th ed. St. Paul, Minn.: West Group.

Stack, W. Brian. 1994. "Criminal Procedure—Confessions: Waiver of Privilege against Self-Incrimination Held Invalid Due to Police Failure to Inform Suspect of Attorney's Attempt to Contact Him—*State v. Reed.*" *Seton Hall Law Review* 25.

CROSS-REFERENCES

Criminal Law; Criminal Procedure; Custodial Interrogation.

CONFESSION AND AVOIDANCE

A form of plea that served as the formal answer to a plaintiff's complaint or declaration.

Under the old system of COMMON-LAW PLEADING, a defendant might choose to respond to the plaintiff's claim with a plea of confession and avoidance. By that, the defendant acknowledged the truth of the allegations in the plaintiff's declaration, either specifically or by implication, and then asserted that there were additional facts that neutralized the legal effect of the plaintiff's allegations.

CONFESSION OF JUDGMENT

A procedure whereby a defendant did not enter a plea, the usual response to a plaintiff's declaration in COMMON-LAW PLEADING, *but instead either confessed to the accuracy of the plaintiff's claim or withdrew a plea already entered.*

The result of a confession of judgment was that judgment was entered for the plaintiff on the confession alone without further proceedings being required.

A confession of judgment could also be accomplished if the plaintiff offered a *cognovit actionem,* a written confession made out earlier by the defendant. A creditor could demand that a borrower sign a cognovit note when the debtor first became indebted to the creditor. The cognovit note said in writing that the debtor owed a particular sum and voluntarily submitted himself or herself to the authority of the court. If the debtor later fell into arrears, the creditor could obtain a judgment against the debtor without even bothering to notify the debtor of the proceedings. A warrant of attorney served the same purpose as a cognovit note. The unfairness of the procedure has prompted most states to enact laws making agreements for the confession of judgment void.

CONFIDENTIAL COMMUNICATION

A form of PRIVILEGED COMMUNICATION *passed from one individual to another, intended to be heard only by the individual addressed.*

A confidential communication is ordinarily between two people who are affiliated in a confidential relation, such as an attorney and client, HUSBAND AND WIFE, or MASTER AND SERVANT.

If this type of communication is made in the presence of a third party, whose presence is not necessary for such communication, it is not considered privileged. In certain cases, the presence of a third party might be required, as where there is a language barrier such that one of the individuals engaged in the confidential communication needs an interpreter.

CROSS-REFERENCES

Attorney-Client Privilege; Marital Communications Privilege; Physician-Patient Privilege.

CONFIDENTIAL RELATION

Any connection between two individuals in which one of the parties has an obligation to act with extreme GOOD FAITH *for the benefit of the other party.*

Confidential relations, also known as fiduciary relations, are not confined to any specific

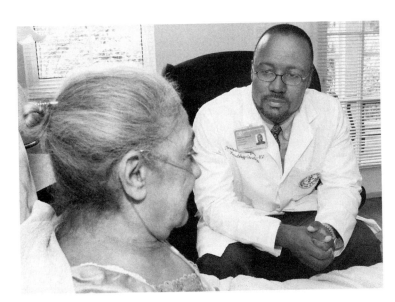

The relationship between doctor and patient is confidential: the doctor has a responsibility to act in good faith for the benefit of the patient.
AP/WIDE WORLD PHOTOS

relationships but refer to all those that are founded upon secrecy and trust. The duty of secrecy in such a relation is intended to prevent undue advantage that might stem from the unlimited confidence that one party places in the other. A confidential relation need not be a legal one, but rather may be moral, domestic, social, or personal. Kinship alone, however, is insufficient to give rise to a confidential relation.

Common examples of confidential relationships, which give rise to confidential communications, include attorney and client, HUSBAND AND WIFE, and physician and patient.

CONFISCATE

To expropriate private property for public use without compensating the owner under the authority of the POLICE POWER *of the government. To seize property.*

When property is confiscated it is transferred from private to public use, usually for reasons such as insurrection during a time of war or because the private property had been used in illegal activities. A person convicted of violating the INTERNAL REVENUE CODE by carrying untaxed cigarettes may suffer the penalty of confiscation of any property used in the crime—as, for example, a truck.

Confiscation differs from EMINENT DOMAIN and condemnation in that the person from whom private property is taken is not compensated for its value at the time of confiscation.

CONFISCATION

See EXPROPRIATION.

CONFLICT OF INTEREST

A term used to describe the situation in which a public official or fiduciary who, contrary to the obligation and absolute duty to act for the benefit of the public or a designated individual, exploits the relationship for personal benefit, typically pecuniary.

In certain relationships, individuals or the general public place their trust and confidence in someone to act in their best interests. When an individual has the responsibility to represent another person—whether as administrator, attorney, executor, government official, or trustee—a clash between professional obligations and personal interests arises if the individual tries to perform that duty while at the same time trying to achieve personal gain. The appearance of a conflict of interest is present if there is a potential for the personal interests of an individual to clash with fiduciary duties, such as when a client has his or her attorney commence an action against a company in which the attorney is the majority stockholder.

Incompatibility of professional duties and personal interests has led Congress and many state legislatures to enact statutes defining conduct that constitutes a conflict of interest and specifying the sanctions for violations. A member of a profession who has been involved in a conflict of interest might be subject to disciplinary proceedings before the body that granted permission to practice that profession.

CROSS-REFERENCES

Attorney Misconduct; Ethics, Legal.

CONFORMED COPY

A duplicate of a document that includes handwritten notations of items incapable of reproduction, such as a signature, which must be inscribed upon the duplicate with the explanation that it was placed there by the person whose signature appears on the original document.

Under the best evidence rule, a conformed copy is admissible as evidence in a lawsuit when the actual document is not available because it has been lost or destroyed. It is considered secondary evidence, while the original document is primary evidence. State and FEDERAL RULES OF EVIDENCE determine the admissibility of a conformed copy in their respective judicial proceedings.

CONFORMING USE

When land is employed in compliance with ZONING ordinances in a particular area.

All real property that is privately owned is subject to certain restrictions or LAND-USE CONTROL. Land that is not used in conformity with such controls is said to be of nonconforming use.

CONFRONTATION

A fundamental right of a defendant in a criminal action to come face-to-face with an adverse witness in the court's presence so the defendant has a fair chance to object to the testimony of the witness, and the opportunity to cross-examine him or her.

The BILL OF RIGHTS (the first ten amendments of the U.S. Constitution) specifies certain rights that are inherent to all individuals, in order to protect them from the ARBITRARY use of government power. Among these is the right to confront one's accusers in a criminal case, which derives from the SIXTH AMENDMENT: "In all criminal prosecutions, the accused shall enjoy the right . . . to be confronted with the witnesses against him." The Confrontation Clause, as this part of the Sixth Amendment is generally known, was understood traditionally to mean that criminal defendants had the right to be put in the presence of their accusers in open court, face-to-face, in front of the jury. This right was intended to give defendants the opportunity to cross-examine adverse witnesses, as well as to provide the jury with an opportunity to observe the demeanor of, and to make inferences regarding the reliability of, those witnesses. The substantive meaning of this right has been the subject of great debate, especially regarding the trying of CHILD ABUSE cases involving child witnesses. Does the Confrontation Clause provide the right to confront witnesses in open court, or does it simply convey a right to cross-examine witnesses?

Like most of the protections given criminal defendants in the Constitution, the right of confronting one's accusers has its origins in English COMMON LAW and in the experiences of the colonies before the American Revolution. Until the sixteenth century, the right of confronting one's accusers was nearly absent from the Anglo-American legal tradition. Then, with the introduction of the right to trial by an impartial jury and the firm establishment of the PRESUMPTION OF INNOCENCE, the right of confrontation came to be seen as an integral part of a proper defense of the rights of the accused. In the American colonies, the SALEM WITCH TRIALS in particular created an impetus for establishing the right of the accused to a face-to-face confrontation with the accusers—who, in those cases, were mostly children anonymously accusing their elders. Horrified by the widespread use of coerced and anonymous accusations in these trials, and by the executions that resulted, the Massachusetts Legislature established the right to confront one's accusers. Soon after, the colonial governor disbanded the special Salem court for witch trials; few accusers were willing to face their targets in open court.

The experience of the Salem witch trials made a great impression on the other colonies.

By the end of the sixteenth century, most of the colonies had established in their constitutions a right of confrontation that was similar to that recognized in Massachusetts. Thus, at the time of the writing of the Constitution, the right was so firmly entrenched that its inclusion in the Bill of Rights elicited no debate.

The Confrontation Clause gives criminal defendants two specific rights: the right to be present during all critical stages of trial, and the right to confront adverse witnesses. Each of these rights has certain limitations.

The right to be present during critical stages of trial allows defendants to participate actively in their defense by listening to the evidence against them and consulting with their attorneys. However, unruly, defiant, disrespectful, disorderly, and abusive defendants can be removed from the courtroom if the judge feels it is necessary, to maintain the decorum and respect of a judicial proceeding. If a defendant persists in DISORDERLY CONDUCT, yet demands to remain in the courtroom, the Sixth Amendment allows a trial court to have that defendant bound and gagged so that his or her presence does not disrupt the proceedings (*Tyars v. Finner*, 709 F.2d 1274 [9th Cir. 1983]).

The second prong of the Confrontation Clause guarantees defendants the right to face adverse witnesses in person and to subject them to cross-examination. Through cross-examination, defendants are allowed to test the reliability and credibility of witnesses by probing their recollection and exposing any underlying prejudices, biases, or motives that may cause the witness to distort the truth or to lie. However, the right of cross-examination also has limits. Courts may restrict defendants from delving into certain areas on cross-examination. For example, defendants may be denied the right to ask questions that are irrelevant, collateral, confusing, repetitive, or prejudicial. Defendants also may be prevented from pursuing a line of questioning that is meant solely for the purpose of harassment.

Under exceptional circumstances, defendants may be denied the right to confront their accusers face-to-face. In *Maryland v. Craig*, 497 U.S. 836, 110 S. Ct. 3157, 111 L. Ed. 2d 666 (1990), the U.S. Supreme Court upheld a statute that permitted a small child to testify via a one-way, closed-circuit television from a remote location outside the courtroom. In such situations, the Court ruled, the trial court must make a specific finding that keeping the witness out of the presence of the defendant is necessary to protect the witness from traumatic injury. The *Craig* decision has been the subject of some debate. VICTIMS' RIGHTS advocates and some prosecutors support the additional protection of witnesses, but defense attorneys have argued that shielding children from confrontation is risky, given that the reliability of children's testimony is often in dispute. Even when a witness is permitted to testify outside the presence of the accused, defendants maintain the right of cross-examination.

The importance of a defendant's right to confront and cross-examine his accusers face-to-face in open court was revisited by the U.S. Supreme Court in *Lilly v. Virginia*, 527 U.S. 116, 119 S. Ct. 1887, 144 L. Ed. 2d 117 (1999).

The case began when the state of Virginia charged Benjamin Lee Lilly with capital murder and called his brother Mark Lilly to testify against him during the trial. When Mark invoked his PRIVILEGE AGAINST SELF-INCRIMINATION, the prosecution sought to introduce a statement that Mark had made to the police in which he had admitted being with Benjamin on the night of the murder, and had told police that he saw Benjamin kill the victim.

The trial court admitted Mark's statement into evidence over Benjamin's objection that it violated the Confrontation Clause. In particular, Benjamin argued that the FIFTH AMENDMENT gave him the right to confront his brother face-to-face in open court, and that admitting his brother's out-of-court, HEARSAY statement without allowing him to cross-examine Mark violated that right.

The Virginia trial court overruled Benjamin's objection, finding that the statement fell within a "firmly rooted" hearsay exception. In Virginia, the trial court said, it is well settled that declarations against interest are a settled hearsay exception, and thus admissible against a criminal defendant without the declarant being subject to cross-examination.

A declaration against interest is an out-of-court hearsay statement made by a declarant who implicates himself in criminal activity or other wrongdoing, the trial court explained. Because such declarations are not considered to be self-serving, the trial court continued, they are deemed inherently trustworthy. In this case, the trial court noted that Mark Lilly had admitted committing a number of crimes that would have made him eligible for long prison terms if convicted.

Based in part on Mark's statement, the jury convicted the defendant of capital murder and sentenced him to death. The defendant appealed, and the Virginia Supreme Court affirmed. *Lilly v. Commonwealth*, 255 Va. 558, 499 S.E.2d 522 (Va. 1998). Although Virginia's high court recognized that Mark's statements were self-serving to the extent they shifted blame for the more serious crime of murder, from himself to his brother, it said that the self-serving nature of the statement went to the weight of the evidence, not its admissibility. The court also underscored the fact that prosecutors gave Mark no express promise of leniency in exchange for his statement.

The U.S. Supreme Court disagreed, reversing the Virginia Supreme Court's decision and remanding the case for further proceedings. Writing for a plurality of the justices, Justice JOHN PAUL STEVENS ruled that an accomplice's statements that tend to shift or spread the blame to a criminal defendant are presumptively unreliable, when that ACCOMPLICE has made himself or herself unavailable for cross-examination by invoking the privilege against SELF-INCRIMINATION.

The "absence of an express promise of leniency," Stevens wrote, does not ensure reliability because "police need not tell a person who is in custody that his statements may gain him leniency in order for the suspect to surmise that speaking up, and particularly placing blame on his cohorts," could be in his best interest. Stevens observed that while the presumptive unreliability of Mark's statement could be rebutted on remand to the trial court, any rebuttal evidence would need to take into account that the statement had been made in response to the government's leading questions.

On remand, the Virginia Supreme Court decided that the statement's presumptive unreliability could not be rebutted, and overturned the defendant's conviction. *Lilly v. Commonwealth*, 258 Va. 548, 523 S.E.2d 208 (Va. 1999).

FURTHER READINGS

Hall, Kermit L. 1992. *Oxford Companion to the Supreme Court of the United States.* New York & Oxford: Oxford University Press.

Hall, Kermit L. 2002. *Oxford Companion to American Law.* New York & Oxford: Oxford University Press.

CROSS-REFERENCES

Criminal Procedure.

CONFUSION

The combination or mixture of two things; the process of commingling.

Confusion has been used synonymously with merger, meaning a union of two separate entities that eliminates clear boundaries. *Confusion of rights,* for example, is a combination of the rights of debtor and creditor in the same individual. Similarly, a *confusion of titles* exists when two titles to the same property combine in the same person. A *confusion of debts* is a method of eliminating a debt or canceling it. This may occur, for example, upon the death of a creditor when the debtor is the creditor's heir.

CONFUSION OF GOODS

A blending together of property individually owned by two or more people so as to make it impossible to distinguish who owns what.

A confusion of goods results when the property belonging to two or more persons becomes so intermixed that it can only be identified as a large mass of goods. This might apply to such substances as oil or grain.

Generally, a wrongful, willful, or fraudulent intermingling of goods by an individual with the goods of another person results in FORFEITURE to the other person of all rights and interest in the resulting mixture.

CONGLOMERATE

A corporation operating in several different and unrelated enterprises, such as the movie industry, baking, and oil refining.

A *conglomerate merger* is one that brings together two firms with totally different product lines, economic relationships, and functions. Such a merger may violate antitrust acts inasmuch as it may have an adverse effect on competition.

CONGRESS OF THE UNITED STATES

The Congress of the United States is the highest lawmaking body in the United States and one of the oldest national legislatures in the world. Established under the terms of the U.S. Constitution in 1789, the House of Representatives and the Senate have for over 200 years created the federal laws governing the United States. Congress remains one of the few national assemblies that research and draft their own legislation rather than simply voting on bills created by the government in power. In addition to its legislative functions, the U.S. Congress is

Speaker of the House

As the presiding officer of the House of Representatives, the Speaker of the House holds one of the highest positions in Congress. The position is filled at the start of each two-year term in a vote by the full House membership. The selection of the Speaker is generally determined by the majority party, and thus the Speaker is always a leading member of that party. The Speaker's broad powers and privileges allow the majority to control the House's legislative agenda.

The significance of the office cannot be underestimated. The Speaker is in a position to set the rules of the House and to adjudicate when procedural conflicts arise. The Speaker's rulings can be challenged, but rarely are; traditionally, they are final. Behind the scenes, the office's power is even broader. This is because voting is a relatively small part of the House's business: its essential legislative work is done in committees. The Speaker plays a vital role in appointing committee chairs, influences the referral of bills to the committees, and effectively decides the timetables of the bills. Bills favored by the Speaker will leave committee more quickly and come to an early vote. The minority party's concerns will wait.

Outside Congress, the Speaker customarily enjoys high visibility in U.S. politics. The media frequently report the Speaker's opinions, transforming the office into a political bully pulpit much like that of the Senate majority leader, and the Speaker often campaigns for party loyalists in election years. Depending on which party occupies the White House, the Speaker can be either a strategically placed ally or powerful foe of the president. The relationship between the two branches of government does not end there: under the rules of succession, the Speaker is second in line after the vice president to assume the presidency.

Not every Speaker has been a high-profile individual. In 1999, the House elected J. Dennis Hastert (R-IL) to serve as Speaker, replacing **NEWTON GINGRICH**. Hastert served as a high school teacher for 16 years until he was elected to the Illinois House of Representatives, where he served for six years. He was elected to Congress in 1986.

Hastert has retained a relatively low profile in his two terms as Speaker, especially compared to that of his immediate predecessor. Gingrich was largely credited with leading Republican victories in Congress in 1994, when the GOP took control of both houses for the first time since 1954. He remained in the public spotlight for the next four years, including strong advocacy to fulfill the **CONTRACT WITH AMERICA** and other GOP programs. However, in 1997, he faced several charges for ethical violations stemming from alleged use of official House resources for unofficial purposes, and he was reprimanded and fined $300,000 by the House. Gingrich resigned suddenly in November 1998, almost exactly four years after the 1994 Republican victory.

FURTHER READINGS

Loomis, Burdett A. 2000. *The Contemporary Congress.* Boston: Bedford/St. Martin's.

Mayhew, David R. 2000. *America's Congress: Actions in the Public Sphere, James Madison through Newt Gingrich.* New Haven, Conn.: Yale Univ. Press.

empowered by the Constitution to ensure that the administration of government is carried out according to the laws it establishes, to conduct special investigations, and to exercise other special powers in relation to the executive and the judiciary.

History and Structure

Between 1774 and 1789, the CONTINENTAL CONGRESS served as the federal lawmaking body for the 13 American colonies and (after it passed the Declaration of Independence on July 4, 1776) the United States. The Continental Congress proved to be an ineffective national legislature, however, particularly after ratification of its founding constitution, the ARTICLES OF CONFEDERATION, in 1781. This congress lacked the authority to raise funds from the states and was not adept at the administration of federal government.

Senate Majority Leader

The Senate majority leader has somewhat less official power than the Speaker of the House. This is because the vice president is technically the Senate's presiding officer, a ceremonial position that calls chiefly for casting a vote in the event of a tie. The Senate majority leader's official duties include helping make committee appointments, helping establish a legislative timetable, and directing debate. Notably, in the Senate, these duties usually involve consultation with the leadership of the minority party. The comparatively diminished procedural powers of the majority leader hardly reduce the position's significance. As chief strategist and spokesperson for the majority party, the majority leader exercises considerable influence over political debate, and certain unique duties of the Senate itself lend extra influence to the role.

Differences between the House and Senate account for the contrasts in leadership duties. The House sends bills to the Senate, where they are debated extensively at a slower, more deliberate pace. For this reason, the majority leader is chosen from within the party's caucus less for the Senator's bureaucratic efficiency than for his or her knowledge, experience, and persuasive abilities. The Senate leader does not have the House Speaker's extensive authority over the legislative agenda: instead, bills are called up for debate depending on when the committees report them and on when both parties' leaders have agreed to schedule them. The majority leader can speed up the process for certain bills but requires the unanimous consent of the Senate to do so.

However, the majority leader exercises influence in important areas not open to the House Speaker. Only the Senate can approve treaties with foreign governments, and the Senate alone has the authority to confirm presidential nominations to the cabinet and federal courts. The majority leader, assisted by a lieutenant known as the majority whip, seeks to marshal the votes of the party's members on these matters. The responsiveness of the majority leader to the president's wishes thus plays a crucial role in shaping domestic and foreign policy as well as the composition of the federal judiciary.

The national importance of the majority leader was highlighted in December 2002 when Senator **TRENT LOTT** (R-MS) was engulfed in a firestorm of public criticism that forced him to give up his position as majority leader in the Congress beginning in January 2003. Lott, who had served as majority leader from 1996 until 2001, ignited the controversy at a 100th-birthday tribute to Sen. **STROM THURMOND** (R-SC). Lott said he was proud Mississippi had voted for Thurmond for president in 1948, when the South Carolinian ran on the segregationist "Dixiecrat" platform. Lott then said: "If the rest of the country had followed our lead, we wouldn't have had all these problems over the years."

Once this statement was picked up by the press, Lott tried several times to explain that his statement did not mean to imply he supported **SEGREGATION** or was a racist. President **GEORGE W. BUSH**, while supporting Lott in his leadership position, chastised his comments; within days commentators speculated how long Lott could hold on to his post. Three weeks after he made the comments, Lott resigned his leadership position. Senator Bill Frist (R-TN) succeeded Lott as majority leader. The episode made clear that Senate majority leaders have both an institutional role and a national leadership role in U.S. government.

FURTHER READINGS

Dinan, Stephen. 2002. "White House Turns Up the Heat When Lott Support Deteriorates." *The Washington Times* (December 21).

Redman, Eric, and Richard E. Neustadt. 2001. *The Dance of Legislation*. Seattle: Univer. of Washington Press.

The Framers of the Constitution, meeting in the Constitutional Convention of 1787, attempted to repair the shortcomings of the Continental Congress by creating a more effective federal legislature. The resulting Congress, made up of a House of Representatives and a Senate, first met with a quorum of members on April 1, 1789, in New York City, eventually

HOW A BILL BECOMES A LAW

Before a federal law can exist in the United States, it must first be introduced as a bill in Congress, and then pass through a series of steps. At any of these steps it may be effectively vetoed, or nullified, if it does not attract a majority of support. As a result, only a small percentage of all bills succeed in becoming laws. In the 103d Congress (1993–95), for example, 8,544 public bills and joint resolutions (generally the same as bills) were introduced, and only 465 became laws.

Introduction of bills Bills must be introduced, or sponsored, by a member of the House or Senate. Most bills are introduced simultaneously in both houses in order to speed their passage. Sponsored bills are placed in the "hopper," a mahogany box near the House Speaker's podium. A bill may be cosponsored by other members of Congress in order to earn wider political support. Bills receive special designation codes to identify their house of origin and the order in which they have been received. For example, the code H.R. 171 designates the 171st House bill of that congressional term, and S. 52 indicates the fifty-second Senate bill.

Ideas for bills may come from a variety of sources other than members of Congress, including the president, other government officials, interest groups, scholars, constituents, staff, and state and local officials. Although a member of Congress must sponsor a bill, anyone may draft a bill. Proposed bills are often drafted by executive agencies and special interest groups. Also, experts in the Senate and House offices of legislative

counsel help members of Congress draft bills.

Frequently, bills are grouped together into comprehensive bills, also called omnibus bills or package bills, to increase their chances of approval. This practice has become increasingly common, and as a result, Congress has enacted fewer but lengthier laws in recent decades.

Bills may be either private or public. Public bills include those authorizing spending for the federal government and those establishing the federal laws applicable to the general public, including criminal laws. Private bills deal with more specialized matters such as the claims of individuals regarding land titles and citizenship. If approved, these bills become private laws.

IN FOCUS

Although most laws originate as bills, some originate as joint resolutions, designated H.R.J. Res. or S.J. Res. Joint resolutions must pass through the same hurdles as bills, including required acceptance by both houses and the president, but generally deal with more limited matters. Constitutional amendments begin as joint resolutions, though they require ratification by three-fourths of the states instead of presidential approval.

Bills introduced in Congress must be approved by both houses in identical form during the congressional term in which they are introduced. (Each congressional term is two years; the 100th Congress, for example, officially began its term at noon on January 3, 1987, and ended it at noon on January 3, 1989.) Thus, a bill that is introduced during the 105th Congress must be passed before

the beginning of the 106th Congress. If it is not passed during that congressional term, it must be reintroduced in the next Congress.

Committee action After a bill has been introduced in the House or Senate, it is referred to an appropriate committee by the House Speaker or the presiding officer in the Senate. Committee referral can be a crucial determinant of a bill's success. If a bill is referred to a hostile or unreceptive committee, it may fail to be reported out of the committee, or be passed.

A committee assigns the bill to a subcommittee, which may hold hearings to consider the bill's merits. The subcommittee often amends the bill, in a procedure known as markup. After the subcommittee completes its work, the committee votes to approve and report the bill with amendments; to make further amendments; or to table the bill—that is, take no more action on it.

House Rules Committee House bills, unlike Senate bills, must pass through a rules committee before proceeding to the House floor. The House Rules Committee establishes the limits for debate and amendment of the bill, elements that can determine the bill's outcome. The Speaker of the House appoints all majority party members to the committee and exerts great influence over the committee and, as a result, the fate of legislation in the House.

Floor action Bills that are reported out of committee—including those that have passed through the House Rules Committee—proceed to the floor of the House and Senate.

reaching its full size at 65 representatives and 26 senators.

Article I of the Constitution sets forth the basic form and powers of Congress. As designed by the Constitution's Framers, the House is more responsive to public sentiment, and the

Senate is a more deliberate and stable body. JAMES MADISON, writing in *The Federalist,* no. 62, argued that members of the Senate should have a "tenure of considerable duration" and should be fewer in number in order to avoid the "intemperate and pernicious resolutions" often

The Speaker decides when the House will debate a bill. On the day that a bill is scheduled for debate, the House first votes on the rules of debate proposed by the Rules Committee. Once these have been approved, general debate begins. The typical length of general debate on the House floor is one to two hours, but for a controversial bill, debate may last four to ten hours. Each political party receives an equal amount of time to debate the bill.

After general debate, the bill proceeds to the amending phase. Here, House members engage in more lively debate as they attempt to win passage of the bill or kill it through the amendment process. Successful amendments can greatly alter proposed legislation, and even unsuccessful amendments can win significant publicity for a representative. During this process, House members vote on each amendment as it comes up for consideration.

Finally, after all amendments have been made, the House votes on the bill. Usually, this vote is recorded. Since 1973 the House has used an electronic voting system in which members insert a personalized card (roughly the size of a credit card) into one of more than forty voting stations on the House floor. They then press a button indicating whether their vote is Yea, Nay, or Present.

Because it is a much smaller body, the Senate maintains floor procedures that are much less formal than those of the House. The Senate allows each of its members more freedom to debate bills, and it allows the minority party to make more decisions than in the House.

Scheduling of bills in the Senate is determined jointly by the majority and minority party leadership, though the majority leader makes the final decisions. For most bills, the majority leader then obtains the unanimous consent of the Senate regarding the date a bill will be brought to the floor and the rules regarding its amendment and debate. Generally, senators are able to offer an unlimited number of floor amendments during debate. Debate is also theoretically unlimited; it does not end until all members are through talking. The Senate has a rule passed in 1917 called a cloture rule, which limits debate to thirty hours before a final vote is taken on a bill. The cloture rule is difficult to invoke because it requires the approval of sixty senators.

During floor debate, senators may engage in a practice called the filibuster, in which they speak on the floor for many hours in order to delay, defeat, or amend a bill. A senator may filibuster for as long as he or she can remain standing. Two senators may work together in a filibuster; when one tires, the other continues. In 1957 Senator STROM THURMOND, of South Carolina, then a Democrat, set the record for the longest solo filibuster in Senate history when he spoke for twenty-four hours and eighteen minutes in an attempt to defeat a CIVIL RIGHTS bill.

After debate is over, the Senate conducts a roll call vote to determine whether the bill passes or fails. In a roll call vote, each senator is asked to state aloud his or her vote on the bill.

Conference committee If the House and Senate versions of a bill differ, the two chambers form a conference committee to resolve the discrepancies. Roughly 10 to 15 percent of all bills—usually the most controversial ones—passed by Congress end up in a conference committee. Members of the conference committee are typically drawn from the committees that reported the bill. During the 1980s and 1990s, conference committees sometimes became quite large, involving as many as two hundred conferees when debating large budget measures. Party ratios on these committees reflect the ratios in Congress itself. Since 1975 conference meetings have been open to the public.

When the conference committee is done, a majority of conferees from each house sign the compromise bill and report it to Congress. The House and Senate then vote to approve the common bill. No amendments are allowed at this point. Because members have invested much time and effort in the bill by the time it has left a conference committee, it is nearly always approved.

Enactment into law Following approval by both houses of Congress, a bill is presented to the president for approval. Article I, Section 7, of the Constitution outlines the procedure for presidential judgment of legislation. The president has four options: sign the bill, which makes it law; VETO the bill and return it to Congress; refuse to take any action, in which case, after ten days, the bill becomes law without the president's signature; or, if less than ten days are left in the congressional term, "pocket veto" the bill by not signing it (because Congress has no time to take up the bill, the pocket veto kills the bill).

In the case of a normal veto, the bill must be approved again by Congress, this time by a two-thirds majority in each house. Because of this supermajority requirement, vetoes are difficult to override. No amendments can be made to a vetoed bill. Congress is not required to vote on a vetoed bill, and such bills are often simply referred to committee and tabled.

CROSS-REFERENCES

Joint Resolution.

passed by "single and numerous" legislative assemblies. Accordingly, the Constitution requires that senators serve six years in office, with one-third of them up for reelection every two years—whereas all House members, called representatives, go up for reelection every two years. In addition, the Constitution requires that senators be at least 30 years old to take office, whereas representatives must be a minimum of 25 years old. Moreover, senators were originally elected by state legislatures and representatives rather than the general population, but this pro-

Congressional Timeline: Nineteenth Century

SOURCE: *Congress and Its Members*, reprinted with the permission of the Congressional Quarterly, Inc.

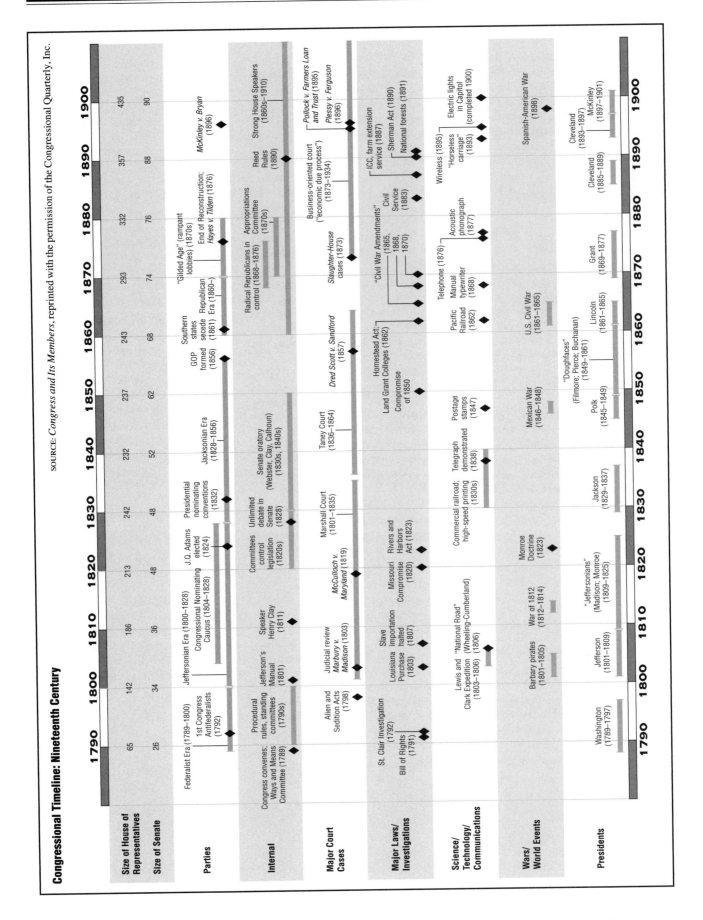

Congressional Timeline: Twentieth and Twenty-first Centuries

SOURCE: *Congress and Its Members*, reprinted with the permission of the Congressional Quarterly, Inc.

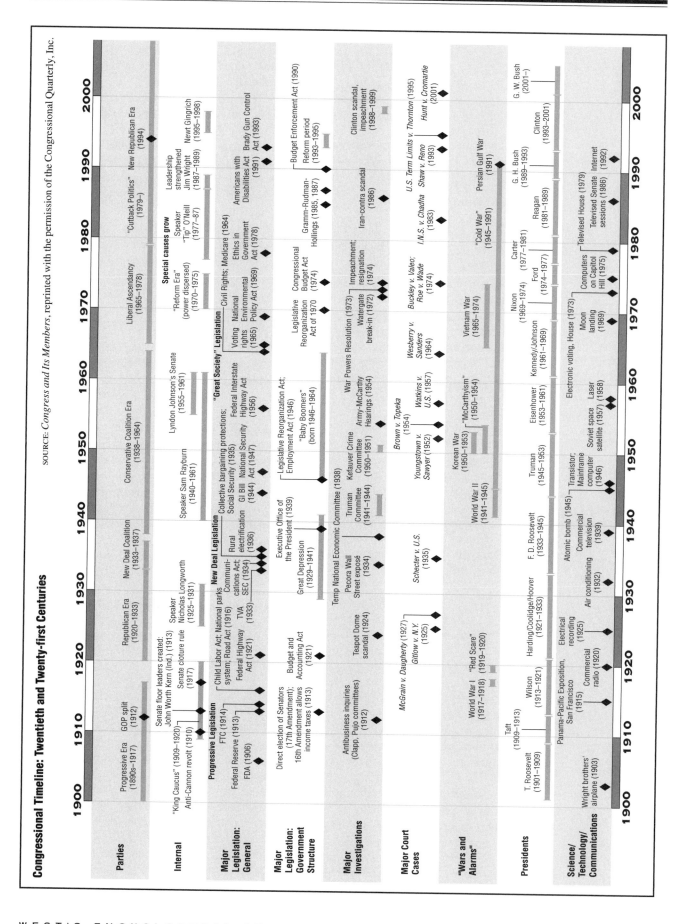

cedure was ended with the passage of the SEV-ENTEENTH AMENDMENT in 1913.

Congress has grown steadily in size as the nation has gained population and added states. The House reached its current size of 435 members in 1912, and the Permanent Apportionment Act of 1929 (46 Stat. 21, 26, 27) fixed its size at this number. The Senate reached 100 members after the admission of Hawaii as a state in 1959.

Powers of Congress

Article I, Section 8, of the Constitution defines the powers of Congress. These include the powers to assess and collect taxes; to regulate commerce, both interstate and with foreign nations; to coin money; to establish post offices and post roads; to establish federal courts inferior to the Supreme Court; to declare war; to establish rules for the government; and to raise and maintain an army and navy.

Article I, Section 8, also declares that "Congress shall have Power . . . To make all Laws which shall be necessary and proper for carrying into Execution the foregoing Powers, and all other Powers vested by this Constitution in the Government of the United States, or in any Department or Officer thereof." Called the NEC-ESSARY AND PROPER CLAUSE or the Implied Powers Clause, this part of the Constitution enables Congress to undertake activities not specifically enumerated by the Constitution but implied by its provisions. The Necessary and Proper Clause has been used to greatly expand congressional authority (MCCULLOCH V. MARY-LAND, 17 U.S. [4 Wheat.] 316, 4 L. Ed. 579 [1819]).

Another power vested in Congress is the right to propose amendments to the Constitution upon approval by two-thirds of both houses. Should two-thirds of the state legislatures demand changes in the Constitution, Congress must call a constitutional convention. Proposed amendments are valid as part of the Constitution when ratified by the legislatures or by conventions of three-fourths of the states. Either means of ratification may be proposed by Congress.

Congress retains a number of other special powers. It may act as a judicial body to impeach and try a president or other civil officer for misconduct; in such cases, the House impeaches, or charges, the official, and the Senate conducts the trial. Congress is also empowered to create and use administrative agencies and boards, such as the National Highway Traffic Safety Administration and the NATIONAL MEDIATION BOARD, to determine facts and to enforce its legislative policies and enactments.

The Constitution vests each house of Congress with distinct powers as well. The House, for example, has sole responsibility for originating all tax bills, and the Senate has power to approve treaties. The House also chooses the president and vice president if no candidate wins a majority of electoral votes in the presidential election.

Section 9 of Article I of the Constitution imposes prohibitions upon Congress. This section forbids Congress to suspend the privilege of HABEAS CORPUS, except in cases of rebellion; to pass EX POST FACTO, or retroactive, laws; to impose duties on exports; or to grant titles of nobility.

Apportionment

Seats in the Senate are apportioned, or distributed, evenly across the states, with each state receiving two. Seats in the House of Representatives are apportioned between the states on the basis of population, with the most populated states receiving the most representatives and no state receiving less than one. The Constitution requires that a census be conducted every ten years in order to determine the number of seats allotted to each state. An apportionment method called equal proportions is used so that no state will receive less than one member.

The Constitution does not mandate that states having more than one representative be divided into congressional districts, although a state legislature can make such a division. States cannot apportion congressional districts on a discriminatory or unreasonable basis.

Investigations

The Senate and the House of Representatives, acting together or independently, can authorize investigations, or hearings, to obtain information for use in connection with the exercise of their constitutional powers. Information gathered in congressional hearings helps lawmakers draft legislation and monitor the actions of government. It also informs the public about important issues confronting the nation. Noted congressional investigations have included the TEAPOT DOME inquiry in 1923, the 1973–74 Senate WATERGATE hearings, and the IRAN-CON-TRA investigation in 1987. Congress has also examined perceived threats to the government, as in the Army-McCarthy hearings of 1954 in which Senator JOSEPH R. MCCARTHY (R-WI) led an investigation into Communist influence in the U.S. government.

A congressional committee may conduct an appropriate investigation under the authority granted to it, but the methods used in the exercise of its investigative power must not violate the constitutional rights of those under investigation. The extent of the authority of a congressional committee must be determined at the time the particular information is sought and cannot be extended by later action of Congress.

Congressional investigations can be held to obtain information in connection with Congress's power to legislate and to appropriate funds, in addition to other express powers it possesses. Congress has wide discretion to determine the subject matter it studies as well as the scope and extent of its inquiry. An investigation must, however, be based on direct statements made to Congress, its members, or its committees. Congress or its committees may not indiscriminately examine private citizens in order to learn valuable information or to inhibit the exercise of constitutionally protected rights, such as FREEDOM OF SPEECH.

Individuals summoned in a proper manner, or subpoenaed, by Congress or a committee must comply and conform with the summoner's procedure. However, witnesses are legally entitled to refuse to answer questions that are beyond the power of the investigating body or that are irrelevant to the matter under inquiry. A witness who has not been given a grant of IMMUNITY can refuse to answer questions that tend to be incriminating under the protection afforded by the Self-Incrimination Clause of the FIFTH AMENDMENT to the Constitution.

Committees and Staff

The work of preparing and considering legislation is done largely by committees of both houses of Congress. The membership of the standing committees of each house is chosen by the political parties in Congress. Committee seats are generally distributed to members of different political parties in a ratio equivalent to party membership in the larger House or Senate. Thus, if a party has two-thirds of the seats in the House, it will have approximately two-thirds of the seats in each House committee.

Each bill and resolution is usually referred to the appropriate committee, which may report it

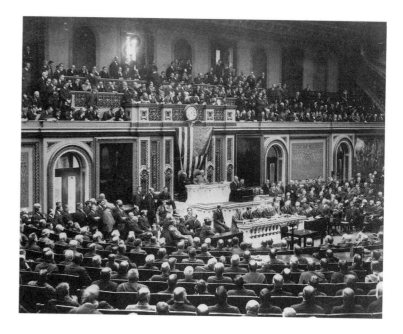

out (send it to the floor of the House or Senate) in its original form, favorably or unfavorably; recommend amendments; or allow it to die in committee without action.

A growing workload and the increasingly complex nature of the legislation it passes have caused Congress to hire an increasing number of staff. Thousands of staff workers support the Congressional members in their work.

President Woodrow Wilson addresses a joint session of the 64th Congress on February 26, 1917, with a request to arm U.S. merchant ships.
LIBRARY OF CONGRESS

FURTHER READINGS

Corwin, Edward S. 1978. *The Constitution and What It Means Today.* 14th ed. Rev. Harold W. Chase and Craig R. Ducat. Princeton, N.J.: Princeton Univ. Press.

Davidson, Roger H., and Walter J. Oleszek. 1981– . *Congress and Its Members.* Washington, D.C.: Congressional Quarterly.

Egan, Tracie. 2004. *How a Bill Becomes a Law.* New York: Rosen Pub. Group.

Felten, Eric. 1992. *The Ruling Class: Inside the Imperial Congress.* Washington, D.C.: Heritage Foundation.

"Gingrich Puts More Power into Speaker's Hands." 1995. *Congressional Quarterly Weekly Report* (October 7).

"Glossary of Congressional Terms." *Congressional Quarterly's Washington Alert* (February).

Hamilton, Alexander, James Madison, and John Jay. 1787–88. *The Federalist Papers.* Ed. Clinton Rossiter. Reprint, New York: New American Library of World Literature, 1961.

Harrigan, John J. 1984. *Politics and the American Future.* Reading, Mass.: Addison-Wesley.

"How a Bill Becomes Law." 1994. *Congressional Quarterly's Washington Alert.*

Jones, Gordon S., and John A. Marini, eds. 1989. *The Imperial Congress: Crisis in the Separation of Powers.* Mahwah, NJ: World Almanac Books.

Oleszek, Walter J. 1989. *Congressional Procedures and the Policy Process.* 3d ed. Washington, D.C.: Congressional Quarterly.

Riddick, Floyd M. 1985. *Majority and Minority Leaders of the Senate.* Washington, D.C.: U.S. Government Printing Office, April 3. S. Doc. 99-3.

CROSS-REFERENCES

Constitution of the United States.

CONGRESSIONAL BUDGET OFFICE

The Congressional Budget Office (CBO) is responsible for economic forecasting and fiscal policy analysis, scorekeeeping, cost projections, and an ANNUAL REPORT on the FEDERAL BUDGET. The office also underdakes special budget-related studies at the request of Congress. The CBO enables Congress to have an overview of the federal budget and to make overall decisions regarding spending, taxation levels, and any federal deficit or surplus. Congress is thus provided with a mechanism through which it can weigh the priorities for national resource allocation and explicitly address issues of fiscal policy.

The Congressional Budget Office provides Congress with basic budget data and with analyses of alternative fiscal, budgetary, and programmatic policy issues. The agency employs more than 200 full-time employees. Seventy percent of these employees hold advanced degrees in economics or public policy. CBO also retains a panel of economic advisors, including a number of scholars from top universities in the United States. It has specific responsibility for the following:

Economic Forecasting and Fiscal Policy Analysis

The federal budget both affects and is affected by the national economy. Congress considers the federal budget in the context of the current and projected state of the national economy. CBO provides periodic forecasts and analyses of economic trends and alternative fiscal policies.

Scorekeeping

Under the new budget process, Congress establishes, by concurrent resolution, targets (also known as ceilings) for overall expenditures for budget authority and budget outlays and for broad functional categories. It also establishes targets for the levels of revenues, the deficit, and the public debt. CBO "keeps score" for Congress by monitoring the results of congressional action on individual authorization, appropriation, and revenue bills against the targets that are specified in the concurrent resolutions.

Cost Projections

The Congressional Budget Office is required to develop five-year cost estimates for carrying out any public bill or resolution reported by congressional committees. At the start of each fiscal year, CBO also provides five-year projections on the costs of continuing current federal spending and taxation policies.

An Annual Report on the Budget

The Congressional Budget Office is responsible for furnishing the House and Senate Budget Committees (by April 1 of each year) with a report that includes a discussion of alternative spending and revenue levels and alternative allocations among major programs and functional categories, all in light of major national needs and the effect on the balanced growth and development of the United States.

Special Studies

The Congressional Budget Office undertakes studies that Congress requests on budget-related areas. As the establishing statute requires, such service is provided, in the following order of priority, to the House and Senate Budget Committees; the House and Senate Appropriations Committees; the Senate Finance and the House Ways and Means Committees; and all other congressional committees.

Web site: <www.cbo.gov>

CONGRESSIONAL-EXECUTIVE AGREEMENT

An accord made by joint authority of the Congress and the president covering areas of INTERNATIONAL LAW *that are not within the ambit of treaties.*

A congressional-executive agreement comes about in different ways. Congress may authorize the president to conclude a particular agreement already negotiated, as when a multilateral agreement establishes an international organization such as the INTERNATIONAL MONETARY FUND. Congress sometimes has approved presidential agreements by legislation or appropriation of funds to carry out its obligations.

It is now widely accepted that a congressional-executive agreement is a complete alternative to a treaty: the president can seek approval of any agreement by joint resolution of both Houses of Congress instead of by a two-thirds vote of the Senate alone. Like a treaty, such an agreement is the law of the land, superseding inconsistent state laws as well as inconsistent provisions in earlier treaties, other international agreements, or acts of Congress.

CONGRESSIONAL RECORD

A daily publication of the federal government that details the legislative proceedings of Congress.

The *Congressional Record* began in 1873 and, in 1947, a feature called The Daily Digest was added to briefly highlight the daily legislative activities of each House, committee, and subcommittee.

The text of the *Congressional Record* is not a verbatim transcript of the statements made on the floor of the Senate or the House of Representatives. After obtaining permission from their respective Houses to do so, members of Congress can revise their speeches prior to publication in the *Record* and are permitted to extend their comments to include remarks not made on the floor of Congress.

CONGRESSIONAL RESEARCH SERVICE

The Congressional Research Service (CRS) is a branch of the LIBRARY OF CONGRESS that provides objective, nonpartisan research, analysis, and information to assist Congress in its legislative, oversight, and representative functions. U.S. senators and representatives, and their staffs consult the CRS for timely and accurate information regarding major issues and policies. The CRS researches and advises on questions and concerns related to many subject areas. It is organized into six interdisciplinary research divisions: American Law; Domestic Social Policy; Foreign Affairs, Defense and Trade; Government and Finance; Information Research; and Resources, Science and Industry. Each division is organized into smaller sections, which focus on specific areas of public policy. The work of these divisions is supported by five offices: Congressional Affairs and Counselor to the Director; Finance and Administration; Information Resources Management; Legislative Information; and Workforce Development.

The CRS is made up of two reference divisions: the Congressional Reference Division and the Library Services Division. These provide reference, bibliographic, and other information

services using advanced methods of computerized searching.

The CRS conducts a host of other support activities for Congress. It develops specialized reading lists for members of Congress and their staffs. It operates the Library of Congress's automated legislative information systems, including digests of all public bills and briefing papers on major legislative issues. It also attempts to anticipate congressional research needs, and it develops seminars that allow members of Congress, their staffs, CRS researchers, and outside experts to exchange ideas on timely issues. The CRS has produced programs on the congressional CABLE TELEVISION system, and it provides language service support and translations for members of Congress.

The CRS is governed by a director, a deputy director, and a management team. The highest-level researchers are called senior specialists. They are often nationally and internationally recognized experts in their field of study. CRS offices include Special Programs, Operations, Policy, and Research Coordination.

The Congressional Research Service evolved from the Legislative Reference Service, which was created by the Legislative Reorganization Act of 1946 (codified as amended at Act of Aug. 2, 1946, ch. 753, 60 Stat. 812), and the Legislative Reorganization Act of 1970 (codified as amended at Act of Oct. 26, 1970, Pub. L. No. 91-510, 84 Stat. 1140). In the beginning of the twenty-first century, the CRS experienced tremendous growth as Congress sought to respond to the increasing scope and complexity of public policy issues. Specifically, the service expanded its website to enhance on-line research. In 2001, over 540,000 users accessed the CRS site to obtain reports and briefs. The CRS anticipates expanding web services as Congress demands 24-hour access to its research data.

FURTHER READINGS

Congressional Research Service. *2001 Annual Report.* Available online at <www.loc.gov/crsinfo/whatscrs.html#report> (accessed May 20, 2003).

CONJUGAL

Pertaining or relating to marriage; suitable or applicable to married people.

Conjugal rights are those that are considered to be part and parcel of the state of matrimony, such as love, sex, companionship, and support.

Loss of consortium is a loss of any or all conjugal rights.

❖ CONKLING, ROSCOE

Roscoe Conkling was for many years in the late nineteenth century the most powerful politician in the most powerful state in the Union, New York. Conkling served in both the U.S. House (1859–63 and 1865–67) and the U.S. Senate (1867–81). During his years in Congress, he became an influential Republican leader. Conkling was a close friend of President ULYSSES S. GRANT and an avowed enemy of other prominent Republicans of the day, namely, James G. Blaine, RUTHERFORD B. HAYES, and JAMES GARFIELD. Conkling twice turned down nominations to the U.S. Supreme Court, including a confirmed nomination in 1882. In the Senate, he fought ferociously for the continuation of political patronage—the system whereby elected officials appoint individuals to positions in the civil service and other areas of governments—and against the civil service reform efforts that would have ended it. His political machine in New York State was, according to his principal biographer, "one of the wonders of the age." Conkling himself, it might be said, was one of the wonders of the age—the Gilded Age, that is, the late-nineteenth-century era following the Civil War when business and moneymaking were the foremost concerns in the United States.

Conkling was born October 30, 1829, in Albany, New York. After attending Mount Washington Collegiate Institute, in New York City, he moved to Utica, New York, where he studied law with a local firm. He was admitted to the bar in 1850 and was immediately appointed district attorney of Albany. In subsequent years, and while still in his twenties, Conkling made a reputation for himself as an orator and aspiring politician at the Whig party's county and state conventions. In 1855, he married Julia Seymour—sister of Horatio Seymour, who was elected governor of New York in 1853 and 1863.

In 1858, Conkling was elected both mayor of Utica and representative to the U.S. Congress. He won the latter office as a Republican and served three terms. He became a Free-Soil Republican, strongly opposing the introduction of SLAVERY into the territories and new states of the U.S. West. After the Civil War was over in 1865, Conkling served on the Committee of Reconstruction, and on the Committee of Fifteen, where he helped draft the FOURTEENTH AMENDMENT.

At about the same time, one of the principal rivalries of Conkling's political career began to heat up. In 1866, while skirmishing over issues of Reconstruction in the House, fellow Republican Blaine, of Maine, in a famous speech before Congress, criticized Conkling's "haughty disdain, his grandiloquent swell, his majestic, supereminent, overpowering, turkey-gobbler strut"—words that became associated with Conkling for the rest of his career. Blaine became Speaker of the House from 1869 to 1875. Conkling never forgave him, and when Blaine ran for the Republican presidential nomination in 1876 and 1880, Conkling helped frustrate his candidacies. The rivalry between these two politicians was a defining feature of Republican politics in the 1870s and 1880s.

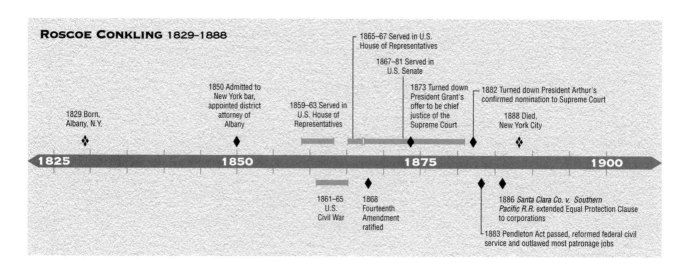

ROSCOE CONKLING 1829–1888

1865–67 Served in U.S. House of Representatives

1867–81 Served in U.S. Senate

1850 Admitted to New York bar, appointed district attorney of Albany

1859–63 Served in U.S. House of Representatives

1873 Turned down President Grant's offer to be chief justice of the Supreme Court

1882 Turned down President Arthur's confirmed nomination to Supreme Court

1829 Born, Albany, N.Y.

1888 Died, New York City

1825   1850   1875   1900

1861–65 U.S. Civil War

1868 Fourteenth Amendment ratified

1886 *Santa Clara Co. v. Southern Pacific R.R.* extended Equal Protection Clause to corporations

1883 Pendleton Act passed, reformed federal civil service and outlawed most patronage jobs

In 1866, Conkling was elected to the U.S. Senate from New York, winning a seat he would hold through two reelections, until his resignation in 1881. These were the years of Conkling's greatest political ascendancy, when he became the most powerful politician in New York. Most notoriously, Conkling gained control over appointments to the New York Custom House, the large administrative body that oversaw business at the nation's most important commercial hub. The Custom House's payroll was the plum of the patronage system, and Conkling appointed dozens of people to it. These people, in turn, became political allies, able to use their time and energy to aid the politician who gave them their jobs.

Conkling's power was solidified when Grant entered the office of president in 1869, a post he held to 1877. Conkling and Grant became strong political allies, and in 1873, Grant offered Conkling the position of chief justice of the Supreme Court, after Salmon P. Chase's death. Conkling refused the offer, believing his talents to be suited more to the role of politician than to that of judge.

In 1877 Conkling made important contributions to the electoral commission bill that resolved the contested election between presidential candidates SAMUEL J. TILDEN, a Democrat, and Hayes, a Republican. He also became a strong opponent of Hayes, who sought to end patronage by separating civil service officials from party control. Conkling asserted that a senator had the right to control the federal administration in his own state, and he opposed the idea that the president should make such appointments. In 1879, Hayes ousted many of Conkling's friends in the New York patronage system. However, in 1880, Conkling won reelection to the Senate, and his friend Thomas C. Platt was elected as a fellow U.S. senator from New York.

In the events surrounding the presidential election of 1880, Conkling became the leader of a group of Republicans known as the Stalwarts, who were fervent supporters of Grant. Opposed to the Stalwarts was the Half-Breed faction of the REPUBLICAN PARTY, which favored Blaine. At the Republican National Convention in the summer of 1880, Conkling made a desperate bid for the nomination of Grant as the presidential candidate. He failed, and his political machine quickly crumbled, though he did succeed in blocking the nomination of Blaine. Garfield and

Roscoe Conkling.
PHOTOGRAPH BY M. BRADY. LIBRARY OF CONGRESS

CHESTER A. ARTHUR, an ally of Conkling's, became the Republican nominees, and Conkling reluctantly supported them during the election. Conkling provided crucial campaign support to Garfield and believed that he would be rewarded for his help, but those hopes were dashed when Garfield nominated Conkling's enemy Blaine as SECRETARY OF STATE. Conkling opposed the Garfield administration after it assumed office, again over the issue of the right to control jobs in the New York Custom House. When he failed to prevent the confirmation of Garfield's appointees, Conkling resigned his Senate seat in disgust, on May 16, 1881, and persuaded Platt to join him. Conkling's defeat was an important gain for the presidency at a time when congressional powers were stronger than ever before or since.

Strangely enough, when the psychotic Charles Julius Guiteau assassinated President Garfield on July 2, 1881, he claimed to be a Stalwart who sought to remove Garfield and make way for Vice President Arthur. Much of the public outrage over Garfield's assassination was vented on Conkling, and, though Guiteau was only remotely associated with Conkling, many considered the assassin to be one of Conkling's followers.

After failing in an attempt to induce the New York Legislature to reelect him as senator after his resignation, Conkling retired from politics and began a successful and lucrative corporate law practice in New York City. He proved to be a highly effective trial lawyer. His clients included the financier Jay Gould and other notorious figures of the Gilded Age. On February 24, 1882, President Arthur, who had become Garfield's vice president through Conkling's help, attempted to repay his political debt when he nominated Conkling to take the seat of U.S. Supreme Court justice WARD HUNT, who was retiring. Conkling turned the nomination down, even after it had been confirmed by the Senate. Conkling was later upset that Arthur—whom Conkling sneeringly called His Accidency—had not decided to run a Stalwart-dominated administration. Indeed, in 1883, Arthur signed into law the Pendleton Act, also called the Civil Service Act (5 U.S.C.A. § 1101 et seq.), which was the first comprehensive act of Congress toward civil service reform, further dismantling the system whereby Conkling and others had amassed tremendous political power.

On December 19, 1882, Conkling appeared before the Court as a lawyer in *San Mateo County v. Southern Pacific R.R.*, 116 U.S. 138, 6 S. Ct. 317, 29 L. Ed. 589 (1885). Arguing on behalf of the railroad, Conkling sought to persuade the Court that a county tax violated the DUE PROCESS CLAUSE of the Fourteenth Amendment, which reads, " . . . nor shall any State deprive any person of life, liberty, or property, without due process of law." Previously, in the SLAUGHTER-HOUSE CASES, 83 U.S. (16 Wall.) 36, 21 L. Ed. 394 (1873), the Court had restricted application of the Due Process Clause to freed African Americans. Conkling, of course, had been involved in framing the Fourteenth Amendment, and now he argued that the clause was originally intended to protect corporations as well as persons. The Court did not make a decision regarding Conkling's claims, declaring the case moot after the railroad honored some of its tax requirements to the county.

In the 1886 case SANTA CLARA COUNTY V. SOUTHERN PACIFIC R.R., 118 U.S. 394, 6 S. Ct. 1132, 30 L. Ed. 118, the Court agreed with Conkling's claims that the term *person* as used in the EQUAL PROTECTION CLAUSE applies to corporations as well as natural persons. Conkling's arguments therefore influenced the later development of the doctrine of SUBSTANTIVE DUE PROCESS, which the Court used repeatedly to strike down state and federal regulation of business from the 1890s to the 1930s.

On April 18, 1888, Conkling died at age fifty-nine, in New York City, of complications surrounding a brain abscess. Despite his political stature, Conkling had sponsored relatively little significant legislation during his career. Though he did help create the Fourteenth Amendment, he played a fairly peripheral role in Reconstruction legislation. He was a politician motivated principally by personal rivalries rather than by ideas. He remains most well-known for his tremendous New York political machine and for his spirited political maneuvers that helped define the political atmosphere during the post–Civil War era in the United States.

FURTHER READINGS

Jordan, David M. 1971. *Roscoe Conkling of New York: Voice in the Senate.* Ithaca, N.Y.: Cornell Univ. Press.

CONNECTING UP DOCTRINE

A term relating to the admissibility of evidence which means that a fact may be admitted into evidence provided that its relevance will subsequently become apparent when it is linked to other facts presented later.

Proof that a witness was present at a certain time and place may be connected up with later evidence to show its significance to the case at bar.

CONNIVANCE

The furtive consent of one person to cooperate with another in the commission of an unlawful act or crime—such as an employer's agreement not to withhold taxes from the salary of an employee who wants to evade federal INCOME TAX. The false consent that a plaintiff gave to a defendant's past conduct during their marriage which the plaintiff presently alleges as a ground for DIVORCE.

Connivance has been used as a defense primarily in an action for divorce based upon ADULTERY. In situations where connivance is used, the facts must establish that the plaintiff either consented or knowingly acquiesced to the adulterous conduct of the spouse or created the opportunity for adultery by persuading someone to seduce the spouse. It is considered a logical extension of the equitable MAXIM of clean hands in that it would be unfair to permit a plaintiff to obtain judicial relief for a situation which he or she created. Practically speaking, however, connivance is rarely asserted as a defense. The modern trend in divorce laws is that there is little benefit to continuing a marital relationship between partners so indifferent to each other that they consent to a serious violation of their marital vows.

The defense of connivance cannot be asserted in an action based upon a state's no-fault divorce laws.

CONQUEST

A term used in feudal law to designate land acquisition by purchase; or any method other than descent or inheritance by which an individual obtains ownership of an estate. A term used in INTERNATIONAL LAW *for the process whereby a sovereign nation is, by force of arms, made to submit to another nation; the defeated country thus becomes part of the empire of the conqueror.*

CONSANGUINITY

Blood relationship; the relation of people who descend from the same ancestor.

Consanguinity is the basis of the laws that govern such matters as rules of DESCENT AND DISTRIBUTION of property, the degree of relation between which marriage is prohibited under the laws concerning INCEST, and a basis for the determination of who may serve as a witness.

Lineal consanguinity is the relation in a direct line—such as between parent, child, and grandparent. It may be determined either upward—as in the case of son, father, grandfather—or downward—as in son, grandson, great-grandson.

Collateral consanguinity is a more remote relationship describing people who are related by a common ancestor but do not descend from each other—such as cousins who have the same grandparents.

Consanguinity is not the same as affinity, which is a close relation based on marriage rather than on common ancestry.

CONSCIENTIOUS OBJECTOR

A person who, because of principles of religious training and moral belief, is opposed to all war regardless of its cause.

A conscientious objector may be released from the obligation to serve in the armed forces or to participate in SELECTIVE SERVICE registration. A conscientious objector must oppose war in any form, and not just a particular war, in order to avoid military service. He does not have to be a member of a religious congregation that forbids participation in war. Under the Military Selective Service Act (50 App. U.S.C.A. § 451 et seq. [1967]), a registrant needs only a conscientious scruple against war in all forms to obtain conscientious objector status. A conscientious scruple against war is an objection to war based on moral beliefs. A conviction that war is wrong, arrived at solely on intellectual and rational grounds, does not entitle one to exemption as a conscientious objector.

Under prior draft laws, conscientious objectors were divided into two classes. One class was composed of those who were opposed to all military service, regardless of whether it was combatant or noncombatant. This class was required to serve in civilian work that contributed to the national welfare, such as the Red Cross, but was exempt from military service. The other class was opposed to only combatant military service. These conscientious objectors were drafted into the ARMED SERVICES for noncombatant duty, such as in the medical corps.

Today there is no draft law; however, males are required to register for the Selective Service at the age of eighteen. Registrants can obtain a discharge, or a release, from the armed services on the ground of conscientious objection. A person who seeks a discharge on this basis must satisfy certain tests established by the federal courts. He must oppose all forms of war and object to any type of service in the armed forces. Total PACIFISM, however, is not required. Willingness to use force in SELF-DEFENSE to protect oneself and family does not defeat a claim of opposition to all war. Enlistment in the military service is also not inconsistent with a claim of conscientious objection.

The objection must be founded on deeply held moral, ethical, and religious convictions about right or wrong. Although this limits discharges to those persons who object to war for essentially religious reasons, which are individually held beliefs, it does not restrict discharges to only those who participate in organized religion. The test of a religious belief is not measured by traditional religious concepts but is based upon whether the belief is sincere and has an effect on the life of the nonconforming believer that is comparable with or parallel to traditional religious beliefs held by persons who believe in God. The objective or actual truth of the beliefs is not the standard used to measure the sincerity of the individual in his beliefs; the test is completely subjective, determined by what the individual actually believes. A military board's skepticism as to the sincerity of an objector's belief is not enough to deny a discharge; some objective evidence is required.

Conscientious objectors can be ordered to report for civilian duty in lieu of military service.

CROSS-REFERENCES

Selective Service System.

CONSCRIPTION

Compulsory enrollment and induction into the military service.

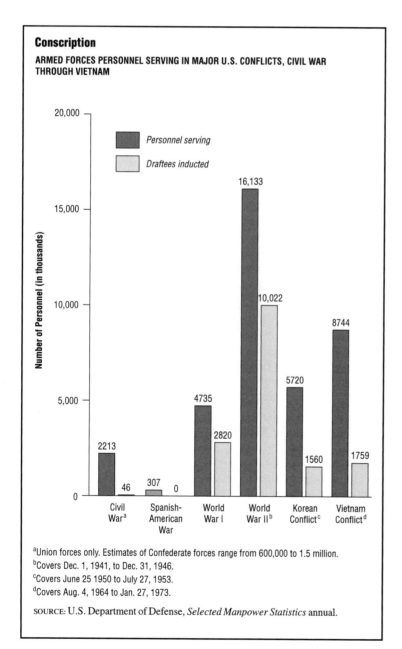

Conscription

ARMED FORCES PERSONNEL SERVING IN MAJOR U.S. CONFLICTS, CIVIL WAR THROUGH VIETNAM

[Bar chart with y-axis "Number of Personnel (in thousands)" ranging 0 to 20,000. Legend: dark = Personnel serving, light = Draftees inducted]

- Civil War[a]: Personnel serving 2213, Draftees inducted 46
- Spanish-American War: Personnel serving 307, Draftees inducted 0
- World War I: Personnel serving 4735, Draftees inducted 2820
- World War II[b]: Personnel serving 16,133, Draftees inducted 10,022
- Korean Conflict[c]: Personnel serving 5720, Draftees inducted 1560
- Vietnam Conflict[d]: Personnel serving 8744, Draftees inducted 1759

[a]Union forces only. Estimates of Confederate forces range from 600,000 to 1.5 million.
[b]Covers Dec. 1, 1941, to Dec. 31, 1946.
[c]Covers June 25 1950 to July 27, 1953.
[d]Covers Aug. 4, 1964 to Jan. 27, 1973.

SOURCE: U.S. Department of Defense, *Selected Manpower Statistics* annual.

Conscription is commonly known as the draft, but the concepts are not exactly the same. Conscription is the compulsory induction of individuals into the ARMED SERVICES, whereas the draft is the procedure by which individuals are chosen for conscription. Men within a certain age group must register with the Selective Service for possible conscription, but conscription itself was suspended in 1973.

Conscription first came into use as a legal term in France in 1798. It derives from the Latin *conscriptionem,* which refers to the gathering of troops by written orders, and *conscribere,* which means "to put a name on a list or roll, especially a list of soldiers." A person who becomes a member of the armed forces through the process of conscription is called a conscript.

Conscription typically involves individuals who are deemed fit for military service. At times, however, governments have instituted universal military service, in which all men or all people of a certain age are conscripted.

Most governments use conscription at some time, usually when the voluntary enlistment of soldiers fails to meet military needs. Conscription by national governments became widespread in Europe during the nineteenth century.

Some of the American colonies employed conscription. During the Revolutionary War, the American government used selective, temporary conscription to fill the ranks of its military.

The United States used conscription again briefly during the Civil War. The Union Enrollment Act of 1863 drafted all able-bodied men between twenty and forty-five years of age. The act provoked a hostile public response because it excused from military service those who were able to pay a fee of three hundred dollars. The law incited violent public disturbances, called the Draft Riots, in New York City between July 13 and 16, 1863. One thousand people were injured in the riots.

In 1917, one month after the entry of the United States into WORLD WAR I, Congress passed the Selective Draft Act (40 Stat. 76). The act created a government office to oversee conscription. It also authorized local draft boards to select eligible individuals for conscription. The following year, the Supreme Court upheld the constitutionality of conscription, noting that Article I of the Constitution gives Congress the power to "raise and support Armies" (*Selective*

Draft cases, 245 U.S. 366, 38 S. Ct. 159, 62 L. Ed. 349 [1918]).

Congress instituted the first peacetime use of conscription in 1940 when it passed the Selective Training and Service Act (54 Stat. 885). This act, which expired in 1947, enrolled those who served in U.S. armed forces during WORLD WAR II. In 1948, Congress passed the Selective Service Act (50 U.S.C.A. app. § 451 et seq.), which was used to induct individuals for service in the KOREAN WAR (1950–53) and the VIETNAM WAR (1954–75). Presidential authority to conscript individuals into the U.S. armed forces ended in 1973. No individual has been conscripted into the military since then.

In 1976, the SELECTIVE SERVICE SYSTEM was placed on a standby status, and local offices of the agency were closed. President JIMMY CARTER issued a proclamation in 1980 requiring all males who were born after January 1, 1960, and who had attained age eighteen to register with the Selective Service at their local post office or at a U.S. embassy or consulate outside the United States (Presidential Proclamation No. 4771, 3 C.F.R. 82 [1981]). Those who fail to register are subject to prosecution by the federal government.

In 1981, the Supreme Court upheld the constitutionality of requiring only men, and not women, to register with the Selective Service (ROSTKER V. GOLDBERG, 453 U.S. 57, 101 S. Ct. 2646, 69 L. Ed. 2d 478). The United States has never conscripted women into military service, nor has it ever instituted universal military service. It has conscripted only individuals meeting certain age, mental, and physical standards. Congress has allowed the deferral of conscription for certain individuals, including those who need to support dependents or are pursuing an education. Among those who have been declared exempt from service are sole surviving sons, conscientious objectors to war, and ministers of religion.

The U.S. government also has the power to conscript property in times of emergency.

FURTHER READINGS

Brophy, Alfred L. 2000. "'Necessity Knows No Law': Vested Rights and the Styles of Reasoning in the Confederate Conscription Cases." *Mississippi Law Journal* 69 (spring): 1123–80.

CROSS-REFERENCES

Involuntary Servitude; Solomon Amendment; Thirteenth Amendment.

CONSENSUAL ALTERATION

A change in a legal document agreed to by the parties and binding upon them.

Such consensual alteration is usually evidenced by the signing by each party of his or her initials and the date on which the agreement to the changes to the instrument is made.

CONSENT

Voluntary ACQUIESCENCE *to the proposal of another; the act or result of reaching an accord; a concurrence of minds; actual willingness that an act or an infringement of an interest shall occur.*

Consent is an act of reason and deliberation. A person who possesses and exercises sufficient mental capacity to make an intelligent decision demonstrates consent by performing an act recommended by another. Consent assumes a physical power to act and a reflective, determined, and unencumbered exertion of these powers. It is an act unaffected by FRAUD, duress, or sometimes even mistake when these factors are not the reason for the consent. Consent is implied in every agreement.

Parties who terminate litigation pursuant to a consent judgment agree to the terms of a decision that is entered into the court record subsequent to its approval by the court.

In the context of rape, submission due to apprehension or terror is not real consent. There must be a choice between resistance and acquiescence. If a woman resists to the point where additional resistance would be futile or until her resistance is forcibly overcome, submission thereafter is not consent.

CONSENT DECREE

A settlement of a lawsuit or criminal case in which a person or company agrees to take specific actions without admitting fault or guilt for the situation that led to the lawsuit.

A consent decree is a settlement that is contained in a court order. The court orders injunctive relief against the defendant and agrees to maintain jurisdiction over the case to ensure that the settlement is followed. (Injunctive relief is a remedy imposed by a court in which a party is instructed to do or not do something. Failure to obey the order may lead the court to find the party in CONTEMPT and to impose other penalties.) Plaintiffs in lawsuits generally prefer consent decrees because they have the power of the court behind the agreements; defendants who wish to avoid publicity also tend to prefer such agreements because they limit the exposure of damaging details. Critics of consent decrees argue that federal district courts assert too much power over the defendant. They also contend that federal courts have imposed conditions on state and local governments in CIVIL RIGHTS CASES that usurp the power of the states.

Most civil lawsuits are settled before going to trial and most settlements are private agreements between the parties. Typically, the plaintiff will file a motion to dismiss the case once the settlement agreement has been signed. The court then issues a dismissal order and the case is closed. However, if the defendant does not live up to the terms of the settlement agreement the plaintiff cannot reactivate the old lawsuit. This means filing a new lawsuit with the court and going to the end of the line in order to process the case.

In more complex civil lawsuits that involve the conduct of business or industry, and in actions by the government against businesses that have allegedly violated regulatory laws, consent decrees are regularly part of the settlement agreement. A court will maintain jurisdiction and oversight to make sure the terms of the agreement are executed. The threat of a contempt order may keep defendants from dragging their feet or seeking to evade the intent of the agreement. In addition, the terms of the settlement are public.

Certain types of lawsuits require a court to issue a consent decree. In CLASS ACTION settlements, Rule 23 of the Federal Rules of Procedure mandates that a federal district court must determine whether a proposed settlement is fair, adequate, and reasonable before approving it. Under the Antitrust Procedures and Penalties Act (the Tunney Act), 15 U.S.C.A. § 16(b)-(h), the court must review proposed consent decrees in antitrust suits filed by the JUSTICE DEPARTMENT. The statute directs the court to review certain items, including whether the decree advances the public interest.

The U.S. Supreme Court, in *Local No.93, Int'l Ass'n of Firefighters v. City of Cleveland*, 478 U.S. 501, 106 S.Ct. 3063, 92 L.Ed.2d 405 (1986), ruled that consent decrees "have attributes both of contracts and of judicial decrees." The division between contracts and judicial decrees suggests that consent decrees are contracts that resolve some issues through the consent of the parties. However, for some issues, the decree contains judicial acts rendered by the judge, not the parties. Commentators have noted that these dual attributes require a court to determine when it is appropriate to "rubber-stamp" a proposed settlement and when it is more appropriate for the court to treat the proposal as it would any judicial order.

The federal courts have been criticized for using consent decrees to reform prison systems, school systems, and other government agencies. Some courts have maintained oversight of agencies for many years and have imposed conditions that have cost state and local governments substantial amounts of money. Congress intervened in one litigation area when it passed the Prison Litigation Reform Act of 1995 (Pub.L. 104-134, 110 Stat. 1321). The law imposed strict limits on what federal courts could do in the future to improve prison conditions through the use of consent decrees. In addition, it gave government agencies the right to seek the termination of consent decrees, many of which had lasted for decades.

FURTHER READINGS

Kane, Mary Kay. 1996. *Civil Procedure in a Nutshell*. 4th ed. St. Paul, Minn.: West.

Mengler, Thomas M. 1988. "Consent Decree Paradigms: Models Without Meaning." *Boston College Law Review* 29.

CROSS-REFERENCES

Civil Action.

CONSEQUENTIAL DAMAGES

Injury or harm that does not ensue directly and immediately from the act of a party, but only from some of the results of such act, and that is compensable by a monetary award after a judgment has been rendered in a lawsuit. Detriment that arises from the interposition of special, unpredictable circumstances. Harm to a person or property directly resulting from any breach of WARRANTY *or from a false factual statement, concerning the quality or nature of goods sold, made by the seller to induce the sale and relied on by the buyer.*

In terms of the UNIFORM COMMERCIAL CODE (UCC)—a body of law governing commercial transactions adopted by every state except for a few articles that were not adopted in Louisiana—consequential damages are injuries that result from a seller's breach of contract.

Such damages include any loss from general or particular requirements and needs of the buyer that the seller at the time of contracting had reason to know and that could not reasonably be prevented by cover, the purchase of substitute goods or other alternatives.

CONSERVATOR OF THE PEACE

An officer of the government authorized by law to act in such a manner that will preserve and maintain the order and safety of the community and the general public.

The phrase *conservator of the peace* derives its meaning from its use in England during the Middle Ages. Until the reign of King Edward III, conservators of the peace were elected locally by the people. Subsequently they were appointed by the king. Among their duties were prevention of disturbances of the peace and arrest of individuals who did so. Around the year 1360, the duties of conservators of the peace were broadened by an act of Parliament to include the ARRAIGNMENT and trial of offenders. They, therefore, became known as justices of the peace.

In the U.S. legal system, a conservator of the peace is synonymous with a peace officer. A police officer, a CORONER, or a court officer may be considered a conservator of the peace.

CONSIDERATION

Something of value given by both parties to a contract that induces them to enter into the agreement to exchange mutual performances.

Consideration is an essential element for the formation of a contract. It may consist of a promise to perform a desired act or a promise to refrain from doing an act that one is legally entitled to do. In a bilateral contract—an agreement by which both parties exchange mutual promises—each promise is regarded as sufficient consideration for the other. In a unilateral contract, an agreement by which one party makes a promise in exchange for the other's performance, the performance is consideration for the promise, while the promise is consideration for the performance.

Consideration must have a value that can be objectively determined. A promise, for example, to make a gift or a promise of love or affection is not enforceable because of the subjective nature of the promise.

Traditionally, courts have distinguished between unilateral and bilateral contracts by determining whether one or both parties provided consideration and at what point they provided the consideration. Bilateral contracts were said to bind both parties the minute the parties exchanged promises, as each promise was deemed sufficient consideration in itself. Unilateral contracts were said to bind only the promisor and did not bind the promisee unless the promisee accepted by performing the obligations specified in the promisor's offer. Until the promisee performed, he or she had provided no consideration under the law.

For example, if someone offered to drive you to work on Mondays and Tuesdays in exchange for your promise to return the favor on Wednesdays and Thursdays, a BILATERAL CONTRACT would be formed binding both of you once you provided consideration by accepting those terms. But if that same person offered to pay you $10 each day you drove him to work, a unilateral contract would be formed, binding only upon the promisor until you provided consideration by driving him to work on a particular day.

Modern courts have de-emphasized the distinction between unilateral and bilateral contracts. These courts have found that an offer may be accepted either by a promise to perform or by actual performance. An increasing number of courts have concluded that the traditional distinction between unilateral and bilateral contracts fails to significantly advance legal analysis in a growing number of cases where performance is provided over an extended period of time.

Suppose you promise to pay someone $500.00 to paint your house. The promise sounds like an offer to enter a unilateral contract that binds only you until the promisee accepts by painting your house. But what constitutes lawful *performance* under these circumstances? The act of beginning to paint your house or completely finishing the job to your satisfaction?

Most courts would rule that the act of beginning performance under these circumstances converts a unilateral contract into a bilateral contract, requiring both parties to fulfill the obligations contemplated by the contract. However, other courts would analyze the facts of each case so as not to frustrate the reasonable expectations of the parties. In neither of these cases are the legal rights of the parties ultimately determined by courts by applying the concepts of *unilateral* and *bilateral* contracts.

In still other jurisdictions, courts have simply expressed a preference for interpreting contracts as creating bilateral obligations in all cases where no clear evidence suggests that a unilateral contract was intended. The rule has been stated that in case of doubt an offer will be presumed to invite the formation of a bilateral contract by a promise to perform what the offer requests, rather than the formation of a unilateral contract commencing at the time of actual performance. The bottom line across most jurisdictions is that as courts have been confronted by a growing variety of fact patterns involving complicated contract disputes, courts have turned away from rigidly applying the concepts of unilateral and bilateral contracts and moved towards a more ad hoc approach.

CROSS-REFERENCES

Contracts; Performance; Promise.

CONSIGNMENT

The delivery of goods to a carrier to be shipped to a designated person for sale. A BAILMENT *of goods for sale.*

A consignment is an arrangement resulting from a contract in which one person, the *consignor,* either ships or entrusts goods to another, the *consignee,* for sale. If the goods are transported by a carrier to the consignee, the name of the consignor appears on the bill of lading as the person from whom the goods have been received for shipment. The consignee's name appears on it as the person to whom delivery is to be made. The consignee acts as an agent on behalf of the consignor, a principal, in selling the goods and must take reasonable care of them while in his or her possession. The consignor does not give up ownership of the goods until their sale.

Under the terms of the consignment contract, the consignee agrees to pay the consignor a balance of the price received for any goods sold, which has been reduced by a fee, usually a small percentage of the sale price. Any goods that have not been sold must be returned to the consignor.

CROSS-REFERENCES

Shipping Law.

CONSORTIUM

The marital alliance between a HUSBAND AND WIFE *and their respective right to each other's support, cooperation, aid, and companionship.*

Loss of consortium is an actionable injury for which money damages may be awarded. The loss of the love, sexual relations, and services of a spouse are being considered tangible injuries to an increasing extent. An action for loss of consortium is based upon the inconvenience of having a spouse who has been injured. Such injury might result from MEDICAL MALPRACTICE, ASSAULT AND BATTERY, NEGLIGENCE, the sale of addictive drugs, WRONGFUL DEATH, or FALSE IMPRISONMENT. The key requirement is that the wrongful act has a debilitating effect upon the individual whose spouse is initiating the action.

Consortium encompasses services performed by a spouse. The COMMON LAW did not recognize a wife's right to services on her husband's part. Because she was viewed as a social and legal inferior, she could not demand that he work for her and, therefore, she had no remedy for loss of sexual relations, affection, or services. The wrongdoer was liable only to the husband directly.

A husband was considered to have suffered tangible damages for injury to his wife and, initially, had the sole right to bring an action for loss of consortium. The loss of services that had to be asserted included his wife's general usefulness, household services such as cooking and cleaning, industry, and frugality. Eventually, the assumption evolved that a man suffered these impairments upon injury to his wife, and damages were recoverable by him for any period in which he was divested of sex, fellowship, and affection, in spite of the fact that his wife might not be responsible for housekeeping.

Subsequently, the Married Women's Property Acts (29 Stat. 193 [1896]) emerged. Some states interpreted these acts to mean that a man could no longer sue for the loss of his wife's services, as she was a full legal person. Most states, however, interpreted the acts as extending to women the right to sue for loss of consortium. A plethora of recent cases indicate that either spouse may bring action for loss of consortium.

In 1950, the U. S. Court of Appeals for the District of Columbia in *Hitaffer v. Argonne Co.,* 183 F.2d 811 (D.C. Cir. 1950), held that women had a right to sue for loss of consortium. Many states directly repudiated its holding and adhered to the old rule, while others supported the change.

By the late 1970s, many courts revised their views and held that women may sue for loss of consortium. Other jurisdictions refuse to rule in favor of the change on the ground that it can be made only by the state legislatures.

Some states seek to prevent double recoveries by requiring that the spouse who is suing for loss of consortium assert that claim in the same action as the spouse who is suing for damages for injuries. When this might be inconvenient or impossible in some instances, other states require judicial supervision of the second action in order to ensure that the amount of damages awarded will not be excessive.

CONSORTIUM/ INTERGOVERNMENTAL CORPORATIONS AND CONSORTIUMS

Quasi-business associations formed to provide services, arrange financing, or operate certain enterprises.

The involvement of more than one state or institution can be advantageous in expanding the financial and administrative resources available to the entity and, in some cases, permitting services or products to be distributed on a larger and more efficient scale. Various banks, for example, may form a consortium with a government to finance a major development project that is too large for one bank to finance alone. The terms of the agreement forming the consortium or corporation will determine the reciprocal rights and duties of the members of the entity. While in practical terms there may be little difference between an intergovernmental consortium or corporation, the usual ad hoc nature of a consortium suggests its use for individual projects with a definite completion schedule. The widespread use of the corporate framework in other circumstances indicates that the corporate form works well when the entity must provide services over an indefinite period of time. The corporate structure, with its separate board of directors and management, can also protect the independence of the entity from direct political control and may help to facilitate access to private financial markets.

CONSPIRACY

An agreement between two or more persons to engage jointly in an unlawful or criminal act, or an act that is innocent in itself but becomes unlawful when done by the combination of actors.

Conspiracy is governed by statute in federal courts and most state courts. Before its CODIFICATION in state and federal statutes, the crime of conspiracy was simply an agreement to engage in an unlawful act with the intent to carry out the act. Federal statutes, and many state statutes, now require not only agreement and intent but also the commission of an OVERT ACT in furtherance of the agreement.

Conspiracy is a crime separate from the criminal act for which it is developed. For example, one who conspires with another to commit BURGLARY and in fact commits the burglary can be charged with both conspiracy to commit burglary and burglary.

Conspiracy is an inchoate, or preparatory, crime. It is similar to solicitation in that both crimes are committed by manifesting an intent to engage in a criminal act. It differs from solicitation in that conspiracy requires an agreement between two or more persons, whereas solicitation can be committed by one person alone.

Conspiracy also resembles attempt. However, attempt, like solicitation, can be committed by a single person. On another level, conspiracy requires less than attempt. A conspiracy may exist before a crime is actually attempted, whereas no attempt charge will succeed unless the requisite attempt is made.

The law seeks to punish conspiracy as a substantive crime separate from the intended crime because when two or more persons agree to commit a crime, the potential for criminal activity increases, and as a result, the danger to the public increases. Therefore, the very act of an agreement with criminal intent (along with an overt act, where required) is considered sufficiently dangerous to warrant charging conspiracy as an offense separate from the intended crime.

According to some criminal-law experts, the concept of conspiracy is too elastic, and the allegation of conspiracy is used by prosecutors as a superfluous criminal charge. Many criminal defense lawyers maintain that conspiracy is often expanded beyond reasonable interpretations. In any case, prosecutors and criminal defense attorneys alike agree that conspiracy cases are usually amorphous and complex.

The Elements of Conspiracy Agreement

The essence of conspiracy is the agreement between two or more persons. A single person acting alone cannot be guilty of conspiracy.

Quiz Show Conspiracies

In the 1950s, the new medium of television was fast becoming a staple in U.S. households, and quiz shows, with their low production costs and high-stakes drama, were enjoying immense popularity. Contestants on quiz shows played until they lost; some competed for months and won tens of thousands of dollars. The quiz show concept of rewarding intelligence with instant wealth appealed to the U.S. public and inspired many to seek an invitation to play.

In May 1958, Edward Hilgemeier was in the studio audience of the quiz show "Dotto" when he was approached by a "Dotto" producer. The producer asked if Hilgemeier would like to compete on the show. Hilgemeier, an aspiring actor, accepted the offer. On May 20, he went to the "Dotto" set as a standby contestant.

Marie Winn, a student at Columbia University, was the defending champion of "Dotto." A charming, animated native of Czechoslovakia, the twenty-one-year-old Winn had won "Dotto" on two consecutive nights. As Hilgemeier waited for his possible turn against Winn, he got the impression that studio personnel were unduly familiar with the woman.

Winn's first challenger that day was Yeffe Kimball Slatin. Hilgemeier watched as Winn defeated Slatin with ease; Winn seemed to have every answer at hand. After the contest between Winn and Slatin, Hilgemeier returned to the contestants' dressing room, where he discovered a notebook belonging to Winn that appeared to contain answers to "Dotto" questions. Hilgemeier notified Slatin, and the two returned to the dressing room, where one of them tore the apparent answer sheet out of Winn's notebook.

That night, after speaking to Slatin's lawyer, Hilgemeier and Slatin went to the "Dotto" offices, where they spoke with the show's producers. The "Dotto" producers promised compensation to both Hilgemeier and Slatin. Slatin agreed to stay quiet

about the affair for a nominal sum of money from "Dotto," but Hilgemeier, fearing for his reputation, refused. Hilgemeier took his information to Manhattan district attorney Frank Hogan and assistant district attorney Joseph Stone.

Initially, the Manhattan district attorney's office was skeptical of Hilgemeier's complaint. The rigging of quiz shows was, after all, not illegal. Shortly into the investigation, however, it became apparent to Hogan and Stone that a widespread conspiracy was in place to hide the truth from the public—and conspiracy to commit **FRAUD** *was* illegal.

The Manhattan district attorney's office convened **GRAND JURY** hearings, and a subcommittee of the U.S. House of Representatives held congressional hearings on the quiz shows' practices. Many producers and contestants lied to the grand jury and the congressional subcommittee about their role in quiz show trickery. On October 14, 1959, their elaborate web of deceit began to unravel when Charles Van Doren, a Columbia University professor, admitted to the subcommittee his involvement in a rigged quiz show, "Twenty-One." (This incident was the basis of Robert Redford's 1995 film *Quiz Show.*)

Quiz show producers and contestants eventually admitted their subterfuge to authorities. What emerged were stories of how favored quiz show contestants were coached to agonize and sweat over answers they already knew. On August 30, 1960, the U.S. Congress passed a bill that made giving or receiving assistance on a quiz show a federal crime. The bill was signed into law by President **DWIGHT D. EISENHOWER** two weeks later. Now, under 47 U.S.C.A. § 509, it is a federal crime to rig quiz shows with the intent to deceive the listening or viewing public. Under 18 U.S.C.A. § 371, a conspiracy to engage in prohibited practices regarding radio and television quiz shows is also a federal crime.

However, if a coconspirator dies prior to the indictment or trial, the surviving coconspirator may still be charged with conspiracy. A HUSBAND AND WIFE can be guilty of conspiracy. A corporation is considered a person for conspiracy purposes, so a corporation can be guilty of conspiracy, but it cannot conspire with itself. For example, if two or more employees within a corporation conspire to break the law and subsequently commit an act in furtherance of the conspiracy, the corporation itself is not criminally liable for conspiracy.

The agreement must be made voluntarily and with an intent to participate in furthering a common purpose. Mere knowledge or approval, in the absence of an actual agreement to cooperate, does not constitute conspiracy.

Once an agreement with criminal intent is made, the conspiracy is complete, unless the applicable statute requires the additional element of an overt act. The agreement need not be written or formal, and it may be proved by CIRCUMSTANTIAL EVIDENCE. A tacit understanding is sufficient to constitute agreement, even if no words are spoken that expressly communicate the conspiracy. Conspiracy exists if there is some form of mutual understanding between persons working together with a common unlawful end.

Intent Criminal intent is also necessary to create a conspiracy. This means that the parties must intend both to agree on and to engage in the unlawful act. Ignorance of the law is not usually a defense to a crime, but an unwitting conspirator may defend against conspiracy charges on grounds of ignorance. Ignorance will not be a defense if the person continues to participate in the common plan after learning of its illegality.

Either the purpose of the agreement or the means by which it is accomplished must be illegal to support criminal prosecution on conspiracy charges. If the purpose is unlawful, the offense is committed even if the means used to achieve the purpose are lawful. One illustration is where a noncustodial parent conspires with another person to KIDNAP the parent's child, and the child is abducted during a court-approved visit. Conspiracy also occurs if the purpose of the agreement is lawful but the means used to achieve it are illegal. For example, if a custodial parent chooses to retrieve a child who has been kidnapped by the noncustodial parent, an agreement to use unlawful force constitutes conspiracy.

Overt Act An overt act can be any step that indicates that the execution of the conspiracy has begun. This can be an innocuous act and need not be illegal unto itself. For example, if two persons agree to rob a bank, then purchase a ski mask, the act of buying the mask may constitute the overt act required to charge the two with conspiracy.

The overt act must follow the agreement and must be executed with an intent to carry out the purpose of the conspiracy. For example, if one of the potential bank robbers buys a ski mask after the agreement is made, the purchase may not constitute the overt act if the ski mask will not be worn to carry out the ROBBERY. An overt act need not be committed by each and every conspirator; an overt act by one conspirator solidifies the offense for all coconspirators. Thus, a conspirator who does not participate in the overt act can be charged with conspiracy.

If a conspirator completely and voluntarily renounces the criminal purpose to all conspirators, that person may withdraw from the conspiracy before the overt act is committed. Many jurisdictions require that the withdrawing conspirator also inform law enforcement officials or take measures to thwart the crime, in order to avoid criminal liability for the conspiracy.

Other Considerations

A conspiracy exists as long as measures are taken to conceal evidence of the crime. A person who did not participate in the original agreement can become a coconspirator after the actual criminal act if the person joins in the concealment of the conspiracy. Whether a coconspirator received personal benefit or profit is of no importance.

Generally, conspirators are liable for all crimes committed within the course or scope of the conspiracy. The application of this general rule varies from state to state. Ordinarily, an act is within the course or scope of the conspiracy if it is a foreseeable result of the agreement. In some states, a conspirator is not liable where he or she has no knowledge of the specific act and argues successfully that the act was beyond the scope of the conspiracy. Also, if the purpose of the agreement is later changed by coconspirators, a conspirator who did not participate in the alteration may not be held liable for the new conspiracy. A person is liable for conspiracy only in regard to the meaning of the agreement as he or she understands it.

In some jurisdictions, a person may be guilty of conspiracy even if a coconspirator is immune from prosecution. For example, if two persons conspire to commit murder and one is found to have been insane at the time of the killing, the other conspirator may not be exempt from prosecution for conspiracy.

One who provides services to conspirators will not be guilty of conspiracy if that person has not participated in the agreement and does not know that a conspiracy exists. There must be a willful participation in the conspiracy, as well as an intent to further the common purpose or design for conspiratorial liability. Therefore, aiding a conspiracy by selling material to further it does not make someone a conspirator if the person does not know of the conspiracy, even if that person knows the goods sold will be used for an unlawful purpose. However, if the circumstances indicate a conspiracy, one who cooperates and knowingly sells goods for illegal use may be guilty of conspiracy.

Generally, if a number of conspirators agree to carry out different functions in furtherance of the conspiracy, the agreement constitutes a single conspiracy. This is so even if the different functions amount to more than one unlawful purpose. In some states, however, the different functions may constitute multiple conspiracies if there is an agreement to commit more than one crime.

Punishment for the crime of conspiracy is ordinarily defined by statute and varies in accordance with the conspiracy's objective. For example, a conspiracy to commit a misdemeanor will not be subject to the same punishment as a conspiracy to commit a felony. Conspiracy may be alleged in a civil case if the plaintiff has suffered an injury as a result of the conspiracy. Civil conspiracy is ordinarily not a CAUSE OF ACTION, but the existence of a conspiracy may be used in determining the amount of damages in a civil action and the respective liabilities of civil codefendants for the payment of damages.

History of Conspiracy

Federal conspiracy statutes were first passed in 1909. Under 18 U.S.C.A. § 371, it is a crime to commit an offense against or to defraud the United States or any agency of the United States. If the crime actually committed is a felony, the punishment is a fine of not more than $10,000 or five years' imprisonment, or both. Under 18 U.S.C.A. § 372, it is a crime to conspire to impede or injure a federal law enforcement officer.

The U.S. Congress has made specific conspiracies illegal through a variety of statutes. For example, conspiracy to murder federal or foreign officials is prohibited by 18 U.S.C.A. § 1117, a freestanding statute. Conspiracy to kidnap is contained in subsection C of 18 U.S.C.A. § 1201, the federal kidnapping statute. Other federal statutes prohibit conspiracies to assassinate the president, the vice president, and their successors; assassinate the director or deputy director of the CENTRAL INTELLIGENCE AGENCY (CIA); assassinate or kidnap a Supreme Court justice; interfere with commerce and trade; violate computer laws; launder money; obstruct state or local regulation of gambling; injure property of the federal government; tamper with consumer products; gather, transmit, lose, remove, or destroy national defense information or materials; incite sailors to mutiny; engage in prohibited practices regarding radio broadcasts or game show contests; defraud the TENNESSEE VALLEY AUTHORITY; violate or interfere with VOTING RIGHTS; and sexually exploit children.

Conspiracy cases are often infamous for their ambition and breadth. The assassination of President ABRAHAM LINCOLN in 1865 by John Wilkes Booth was a product of a conspiracy between Booth and several supporters of the defunct Confederacy. In the early 1950s, the U.S. Congress conducted numerous hearings on Communist conspiracies against the United States. In the mid-1970s, several White House aides were indicted on charges of conspiracy in connection with the 1972 burglary of the offices of the Democratic National Committee in the Watergate Hotel, in Washington, D.C.

In November 1986, a Lebanese weekly, *Al-Shiraa*, reported that the U.S. government had secretly sold military weapons to so-called moderate factions in Iran. In exchange for the arms sales, according to *Al-Shiraa*, the moderate Iranians would work to secure the release of U.S. citizens held hostage in Lebanon. Thus began an investigation into a conspiracy that became popularly known as the IRAN-CONTRA AFFAIR.

Congressional investigations that followed the *Al-Shiraa* article revealed a covert "enterprise" connected with the arms sales. The operation, staffed by private citizens and funded by private monies, had diverted profits from the sale of the weapons to the Contras, a loosely knit military force in Honduras that sought to overthrow the socialist Sandinista government in Nicaragua.

Congressional investigations in the spring of 1987 revealed that the enterprise had been supervised by U.S. NATIONAL SECURITY COUNCIL (NSC) staff. The NSC, created by the National Security Act of 1947 (61 Stat. 496 [50 U.S.C.A. §§ 402]) and amended by the National Security Act Amendments of 1949 (63 Stat. 579 [50 U.S.C.A. § 401 et seq.]), existed to advise the president with respect to the INTEGRATION of domestic, foreign, and military policies relating to national security.

One of the many problems presented by the enterprise was its apparent violation of the Boland amendments to a series of appropriations bills. These bills were established in the early 1980s to prevent any "agency or entity of the United States involved in intelligence activities" from spending funds available to it "to support military or paramilitary operations in Nicaragua" (133 Cong. Rec. H4982-87 [daily ed. June 15, 1987]). The covert arms sales also violated procedural and substantive requirements of the Arms Export Control Act of 1976 (Pub. L. No. 90-629, 82 Stat. 1320 [22 U.S.C.A. §§ 2751–2796c (1989 Supp.)]). Moreover, the executive branch's failure to notify Congress of the covert arms sales flouted the reporting provisions of the 1980 Intelligence Oversight Act (Pub. L. No. 96-450, tit. IV, § 407(b)(1), 94 Stat. 1981 [50 U.S.C.A. § 413 (1982)]).

In 1987, Lawrence Walsh, a former AMERICAN BAR ASSOCIATION president and former federal judge, was assigned by the U.S. Court of Appeals for the District of Columbia Circuit, Independent Counsel Division, to investigate the Contra-funding scheme. In March 1988, Walsh charged Richard Secord, Albert Hakim, Oliver North, and John Poindexter with conspiracy to obstruct the U.S. government. North and Poindexter had worked for the NSC.

As in all conspiracy cases, an important goal of the prosecution was to determine who was involved in the agreement. A major issue in the Iran-Contra investigation was to determine precisely who in the EXECUTIVE BRANCH authorized or was aware of the arms diversions and, specifically, whether the president had knowledge of the unlawful activities.

In the legal battles that ensued over access to information in connection with the prosecutions, Walsh faced challenges by the RONALD REAGAN and GEORGE H. W. BUSH administrations, the JUSTICE DEPARTMENT, intelligence agencies, and lawyers for the accused. Ultimately, the White House refused to relinquish classified information crucial to the prosecutions, and Walsh was forced to drop all conspiracy charges. The Iran-Contra Affair resulted in criminal convictions of several persons directly connected with the Reagan administration, but Walsh was never able to link the president to a conspiracy to obstruct the U.S. government.

In another conspiracy case, Patricia Caldwell, a bookkeeper with the Northwest Community Exchange (NCE), was charged with conspiracy to defraud the United States because she refused to provide to the IRS certain account information it requested regarding NCE customers. The NCE was one of a number of warehouse banks, which promised their customers that they would not reveal account information to third parties, including the INTERNAL REVENUE SERVICE (IRS). As a result, the IRS shut down the warehouse banks, and it charged several customers and employees with conspiracy to defraud the United States. A jury convicted Caldwell of conspiring to defraud the United States, in violation of 18 U.S.C.A. § 371.

The Ninth Circuit Court of Appeals reversed Caldwell's conspiracy conviction (*United States v. Caldwell*, 989 F.2d 1056 [1993]). The government had argued that people have a duty to conduct their business affairs so as to not impair or impede the collection of revenue by the IRS. The majority opinion, written by Judge Alex Kozinski, rejected this interpretation of 18 U.S.C.A. § 371 and held that to defraud the government, a person had to act deceitfully or dishonestly. To allow otherwise would create an oppressive theory of criminal conspiracy. The court observed that under the government's theory, "a husband who asks his wife to buy him a radar detector would be a felon ... because their actions would obstruct the government function of catching speeders." According to the court, Congress did not intend to make a federal crime out of actions that merely make "the government's job more difficult."

The jury in Caldwell's case had not been instructed that it had to find that Caldwell agreed to obstruct the IRS's tax-collecting functions by deceitful or dishonest means. This failure to inform the jury about an essential element of conspiracy constituted reversible error, and Caldwell's conviction was overturned.

American Honda Conspiracy

The sheer size of a conspiracy can create distinct problems for prosecutors and defense attorneys alike. In 1993, U.S. attorneys in New Hampshire began to investigate employees of the American Honda Motor Company. By 1994, prosecutors had cobbled together an immense conspiracy-based commercial BRIBERY case.

The conspiracy prosecutions of American Honda executives and dealers began to develop in 1989, when Richard Nault, an automobile dealer in Nashua, New Hampshire, brought a civil suit against American Honda, claiming unfair treatment. In 1993, after testimony raised concerns of bribery, the judge in Nault's case recommended that federal authorities investigate the financial affairs at American Honda.

Investigations by the FEDERAL BUREAU OF INVESTIGATION (FBI) revealed a widespread pattern of illegal payoffs in which American Honda executives were given cash, jewelry, cars, and store ownership interests in return for the awarding of new Honda dealerships and favorable car allocations. According to the prosecutors, assistant U.S. attorneys Michael Connolly and Donald Feith, the alleged conspiracy involved twenty-two American Honda executives and dealers, encompassed thirty states, and was responsible for the misappropriation of approximately $50 million. In 1993 and 1994, prosecutors dangled various substantive and conspiracy charges before the executives and dealers.

By the end of 1994, only three of the alleged conspirators had refused to plead guilty: John Billmyer, an 18-year American Honda veteran and longtime vice president of auto field sales; Stanley Cardiges, another vice president of auto field sales and Billmyer's protégé; and Dennis Josleyn, whose last position was West Coast sales manager for Acura, American Honda's flagship automobile. In March 1994, Billmyer, Cardiges, and Josleyn were arrested at their homes, booked at local jails, and then released pending trial.

A federal GRAND JURY charged Billmyer with one count of conspiring with Cardiges and Josleyn to defraud American Honda, the United States, the TREASURY DEPARTMENT, and the IRS, in violation of 18 U.S.C.A. § 1341. Specifically, the indictment alleged that Billmyer, Josleyn, and Cardiges had conspired to receive money and gifts by secretly selling the valuable contract rights conferred on prospective dealers by American Honda.

Cardiges and Josleyn were charged with participating in the broad conspiracy with Billmyer and also conspiring to receive kickbacks in connection with an American Honda advertising campaign. Cardiges and Josleyn were further charged with violating the RACKETEER INFLUENCED AND CORRUPT ORGANIZATIONS ACT (18 U.S.C.A. § 1961 et seq.). In November 1993, Cardiges allegedly asked former American Honda zone manager Edward Temple to tell the FBI that payments the two had received from a hidden interest in a Conway, Arkansas, car dealership were actually loan payments.

American Honda was portrayed by prosecutors as a victim of the conspiracies. As the trial approached, lawyers for Cardiges and Josleyn prepared a defense that would further victimize the company. According to Cardiges's lawyer Philip Israels, any conspiracy case should have included the Japanese executives of Honda Motor Company International, the owner of American Honda. Israels maintained that the Japanese executives knew of, condoned, and even participated in the kickback schemes. Israels further charged that the federal government had information that suggested that Japanese executives knew of the kickbacks, and that the decision not to prosecute the Japanese executives was being used as a bargaining chip in trade negotiations between the United States and Japan.

Josleyn adopted a defense similar to that of Cardiges. Josleyn's attorneys, Paul Twomey and Mark Sisti, noted that the alleged conspiracy was so widespread that Japanese executives must have known of it. Josleyn would deny no specific facts. Rather, he would invert the meaning of the mountain of evidence uncovered by the prosecutors and the FBI, to show that the Japanese executives must have known about and approved of the kickback schemes. Such a showing would allow Josleyn's attorneys to argue that the alleged conspiracy was actually a lawful, routine business practice promoted by American Honda's parent company.

Billmyer had retired from American Honda in 1988. His lawyers, David Long and Kevin Sharkey, centered his defense on a variety of grounds. Their arguments included that the prosecution of Billmyer was barred by the five-year STATUTE OF LIMITATIONS on conspiracy charges because the indictment actually alleged multiple conspiracies, and any criminal liability for a conspiracy involving Billmyer expired in 1993; Billmyer had withdrawn from any alleged conspiracies by retiring in 1988; and New Hampshire was an improper venue because none of the acts Billmyer was alleged to have committed had any relation to New Hampshire.

In the months before trial, several motions to dismiss the case were denied by Judge Joseph DiClerico of the U.S. District Court for the District of New Hampshire. On January 22, 1994, after two years of maintaining his innocence and just one day before jury selection was scheduled to begin, Cardiges pleaded guilty to all charges. In exchange for lenient sentencing recommendations by the prosecutors, Cardiges agreed to testify against Billmyer and Josleyn. All the conspirators except Billmyer and Josleyn were prepared to testify to conspiracies to defraud.

The case proceeded to jury trial in February 1995 and was presided over by Judge DiClerico. In opening statements, assistant U.S. attorney Connolly submitted to the jury that the conspiracy was limited to a few rogue U.S. executives and dealers, and that the United States and American Honda had been conspired against and defrauded by them. Twomey declared that "the government is going to take you everywhere—north, south, east and west" to prove a conspiracy that was supposedly limited to U.S. executives and was completely unknown to Japanese executives. Long and Sharkey covered the litany of apparent infirmities in the government's conspiracy case against Billmyer.

A seemingly endless stream of witnesses then proceeded to testify against Billmyer and Josleyn. American Honda executives and dealers regaled the jury with descriptive accounts of opulence and excess. The kickback schemes resembled homage to the executives, a practice that Honda and Acura dealers called kissing the ring. Dealers and executives told of expensive offerings, including cash payments, free automobiles, Rolex watches, shopping sprees, swimming pools, and tuition payments for children. In several days on the witness stand, Cardiges alone testified to the receipt of approximately $5 million in kickbacks.

At the close of the government's case in chief, Long made a motion to dismiss, arguing that the suit was one of multiple conspiracies, that any conspiracy involving Billmyer supported by the evidence was barred by the statute of limitations, and that any payments or gifts received by Billmyer were unconnected to any conspiracy with Josleyn. The motion was denied, Billmyer called no witnesses, and Josleyn began his defense.

Throughout the presentation of the government's case, Josleyn's lawyers had been fighting a battle with American Honda. They sought to obtain, and eventually received, a copy of handwritten notes kept by Sherry Cameron, American Honda's vice president of human resources. Cameron's notes had been made in connection with American Honda's 1992 internal investiga-

tions into rumors of kickbacks. American Honda had appealed Judge DiClerico's decision to order American Honda's release of the notes to the defense, but the First Circuit Court of Appeals refused to reverse the order.

Cameron had testified for the government in March 1995, and Sisti's cross-examination of her had been suspended while the production of her notes was contested. On May 15, 1995, Cameron resumed the witness stand and was faced with poster-sized copies of her notes, one of which revealed that her "point of view" in the investigation was to "try to protect" the company. Cameron further testified that she had limited her investigation to facts, not rumors.

Twomey then called to the stand J. D. Powers, a prominent market research specialist for the automobile industry. Powers testified that in 1983, he sent a letter to Yoshihida Munekujni, then president of American Honda, informing him of widespread rumors of corruption in American Honda. According to Powers, several unindicted top-ranking American Honda executives knew of the kickback schemes in the early 1980s.

This and other evidence allowed Twomey to argue in his closing statement that the conspiracy was so implicit as to constitute one company's policy. Twomey asked the jury whether it could be satisfied that it knew the entire truth in the case. Long contended, in part, that the government had been selective and heavy-handed in its prosecution. The case was submitted to the jury. After five days of deliberations, Billmyer and Josleyn were convicted of all charges. Both vowed to appeal.

Although no Japanese executives were charged in the case, 20 American Honda executives and dealers pleaded guilty, making this the largest conspiracy-based commercial bribery prosecution in the history of the United States.

United States v. Mohamed

Even before the SEPTEMBER 11TH ATTACKS against the United States in 2001, the country and the world were well aware of the activities of Osama bin Laden and the terrorist network known as al Qaeda. In October 2000, 48-year-old Ali A. Mohamed pled guilty in federal court in New York to five counts of conspiracy, including conspiring to kill U.S. nationals; conspiring to murder, kidnap, and maim outside the United States; conspiring to murder in general; and conspiring to destroy U.S. buildings and property. The charges stemmed from the August 7,

An artist's rendition of Ali Mohamed (second from left) as he stands before U.S. District Judge Leonard B. Sand. In October 2000, Mohamed pleaded guilty to five counts of conspiracy related to the 1998 embassy bombings in Kenya and Tanzania.

AP/WIDE WORLD PHOTOS

1998, TERRORISM at U.S. embassies in Nairobi, Kenya, and in Dar es Salaam, Tanzania. More than 200 people, including 12 American citizens, were killed in the attacks, and more than 5,000 were injured.

The case attracted national and international attention because Mohamed was a former U.S. Army officer and because he implicated bin Laden in the bombings. Mohamed, a native Egyptian, served briefly with the CIA in 1984, until the agency determined that Mohamed had revealed his assignment to Middle East terrorists. In 1985, Mohamed moved to the California, seeking to become a U.S. citizen. He enlisted in the U.S. Army and was assigned to the Special Operations Command at Fort Bragg, where the Army trains its Special Forces. Mohamed was trained as a paratrooper and achieved the rank of sergeant before being honorably discharged in 1989. Upon his discharge, he renewed his contacts with the Egyptian "Islamic Jihad," a radical group he had secretly associated with since the early 1980s. In 1991 he was recruited by al Qaeda to serve several missions directly related to bin Laden's terrorist activities.

In 1993, bin Laden asked Mohamed to scout possible sites in Kenya to target for terrorist attacks. Mohamed, then a naturalized U.S. citizen, took photographs and drew diagrams of the U.S. embassy in Nairobi. He personally delivered these to bin Laden, who planned the attack that occurred about five years later. Mohamed became a suspect when one of his aliases turned up at the Nairobi bombing site. After reaching a plea bargain agreement with federal prosecu-

tors, Mohamed implicated bin Laden in the attacks. At the time, prosecutors said it was the first time that a close associate of bin Laden had implicated the reputed terrorist in open court. Mohamed faces a prison term for an unspecified number of years. Less than one year after he gave his testimony, the United States suffered terrorist attacks on its own soil, as al Qaeda operatives destroyed the World Trade Center in New York City and seriously damaged the Pentagon in Washington, D.C.

FURTHER READINGS

Kaplan, John, and Robert Weisberg. 1991. *Criminal Law: Cases and Materials.* 2d ed. Boston: Little, Brown.

Stone, Joseph, and Tim Yohn. 1992. *Prime Time and Misdemeanors.* New Brunswick, N.J.: Rutgers Univ. Press.

CROSS-REFERENCES

Communism.

CONSTABLE

An official of a MUNICIPAL CORPORATION *whose primary duties are to protect and preserve the peace of the community.*

In medieval law, a constable was a high functionary under the French and English kings. The importance and dignity of this position was second only to that of the monarch. The constable led the royal armies and was cognizant of all military matters, exercising both civil and military jurisdiction. It was also his duty to conserve the peace of the nation.

In ENGLISH LAW, a constable was a public civil officer whose general duty was to maintain the peace within his district, although he was frequently charged with additional obligations. "High," "petty," and "special" constables formerly existed. The police have assumed the functions of constables.

State constitutions and laws in the United States generally establish prerequisites for holding the office of constable. In most instances, a constable must be a U.S. citizen, a qualified voter, and a resident in the area of his or her jurisdiction.

The term of office and removal therefrom are usually governed by state constitutions and laws. A basis for removal may reside in neglect of duty.

A constable-elect is generally required to post a bond as security for faithful performance of the duties and obligations of the office. The bond protects those individuals who might otherwise be harmed by any possible neglect of duty.

A constable has the status of peace officer, a person designated by public authority to maintain the peace and arrest persons guilty or suspected of crime. The constable must yield to the superior authority of a sheriff, the chief executive and administrative officer of a county, where a conflict exists concerning jurisdiction.

Service of process—the delivering of a summons which informs a person that he or she is a defendant in a lawsuit—is an important function of a constable. State laws confer the power to serve process. The constable executes the process of magistrates' court and of some other tribunals. The courts do not instruct constables on the manner of serving process. The constable should exercise due diligence to make the service but is not obligated to exert every conceivable effort.

Attachment—the seizure of a debtor's property pursuant to court order—is another function of a constable. It is the constable's duty to assume custody of and carefully preserve the property to be seized. In most instances, the constable is expected to sell the property and collect and distribute the sale proceeds.

Miscellaneous duties assigned to constables by local or state law include the custody of juries, attendance at criminal court sessions, and the service of writs—court orders requiring the performance of a specified act or giving authority to have it done. The powers and duties of constables have, however, been replaced by sheriffs in many jurisdictions.

CONSTITUTE

To comprise or put together. That which is duly constituted *is properly made up and formally correct and valid.*

Constituted authorities are officers who are properly appointed under constitutional provision to govern the people.

CONSTITUTION

The fundamental law, written or unwritten, that establishes the character of a government by defining the basic principles to which a society must conform; by describing the organization of the government and regulation, distribution, and limitations on the functions of different government departments; and by prescribing the extent and manner of the exercise of its sovereign powers.

A legislative charter by which a government or group derives its authority to act.

The concept of a constitution dates to the city-states of ancient Greece. The philosopher ARISTOTLE (384–322 B.C.), in his work *Politics,* analyzed over 150 Greek constitutions. He described a constitution as creating the frame upon which the government and laws of a society are built:

> A constitution may be defined as an organization of offices in a state, by which the method of their distribution is fixed, the sovereign authority is determined, and the nature of the end to be pursued by the association and all its members is prescribed. Laws, as distinct from the frame of the constitution, are the rules by which the magistrates should exercise their powers, and should watch and check transgressors.

In modern Europe, written constitutions came into greater use during the eighteenth and nineteenth centuries. Constitutions such as that of the United States, created in 1787, were influenced by the ancient Greek models. During the twentieth century, an increasing number of countries around the world concluded that constitutions are a necessary part of democratic or republican government. Many thus adopted their own constitutions.

Different forms and levels of government may have constitutions. All 50 states have constitutions, as do many countries including Japan, India, Canada, and Germany. It is also common for nongovernmental organizations and civic groups to have constitutions.

In its ideal form, a constitution emanates from the consent and will of the people whom it governs. Besides establishing the institutions of government and the manner in which they function toward each other and toward the people, a constitution may also set forth the rights of the individual and a government's responsibility to honor those rights.

Constitutions, whether written or unwritten, typically function as an evolving body of legal custom and opinion. Their evolution generally involves changes in judicial interpretation or in themselves, the latter usually through a process called amendment. Amendment of a constitution is usually designed to be a difficult process in order to give the constitution greater stability. On the other hand, if a constitution is extremely difficult to amend, it might be too inflexible to survive over time.

The ongoing evolutionary nature of constitutions explains why England may be described as having a constitution even though it does not have a single written document that is designated as such. England's constitution instead inheres in a body of legal custom and tradition that regulates the relationship among the monarchy, the legislature (Parliament), the judicial system, and COMMON LAW. Although England's constitution is, in a sense, unwritten because it does not originate in a single document, many written laws have been instrumental in its creation, and England in fact has one of the oldest traditions of constitutionalism.

In a truly constitutional form of government, public officials are subject to constitutional rules and provisions and may not violate them without punishment. Such constitutional governments are also called limited governments because the constitution restricts the scope of their power over the people. However, many governments that have constitutions do not practice true constitutionalism. The former Soviet Union, for example, created the 1936 Constitution of the Union of Soviet Socialist Republics, also known as the "Stalin Constitution," but that document did not establish a truly constitutional form of government. JOSEPH STALIN, the ruler of the Soviet Union from 1924 to 1953, could not be formally penalized or called to account for his actions, no matter how heinous, before any other government official, any court, or the people themselves. The Soviet Constitution also claimed to guarantee FREEDOM OF SPEECH, press, and assembly, but in practice the Soviet government continually repressed those who sought to express those freedoms. Constitutions such as that of the former Soviet Union are called nominal constitutions, whereas those that function more truly as prescriptive documents, such as the CONSTITUTION OF THE UNITED STATES, are called normative constitutions.

In the United States, individual state constitutions must conform to the basic principles of the U.S. Constitution—they may not violate rights or standards that it establishes. However, states are free to grant rights that are not defined in the U.S. Constitution, as long as doing so does not interfere with other rights that are drawn from it. For this reason, groups or individuals who seek to file constitutional claims in court are increasingly examining state constitutions for settlement of their grievances. In the issue of SCHOOL DESEGREGATION, for example, groups such as the National Association for the Advancement of Colored People (NAACP) began in the 1990s to shift focus to the state level, with the hope of finding greater protection of rights under state constitutions.

In many states, however, courts have construed their respective state constitutions to provide rights that are equivalent to those provided under the U.S. Constitution. For example, in *Jackson v. Benson*, 578 N.W.2d 602 (Wisc. 1998), the Wisconsin Supreme Court, citing settled precedent, noted that the Wisconsin Constitution's provisions relating to EQUAL PROTECTION provide the same rights as those provisions in the federal counterpart, even though the Wisconsin provisions are phrased quite differently. The NAACP claimed that a school program in Milwaukee, which allowed parents of certain qualifying students of public schools in the city to send their children to any private, nonsectarian school of their choice at no cost, was enacted with discriminatory intent. The court treated the state and federal constitutional claims of the NAACP as alike.

FURTHER READINGS

Barker, Ernest, trans. and ed. 1946. *The Politics of Aristotle.* New York: Oxford Univ. Press.

Hamilton, Alexander, James Madison, and James Jay. Terence Ball, ed. 2003. *The Federalist.* Cambridge, U.K., New York: Cambridge Univ. Press.

CROSS-REFERENCES

Constitution of the United States; "Constitution of the United States" (Appendix, Primary Document).

CONSTITUTION OF THE UNITED STATES

A written document executed by representatives of the people of the United States as the absolute rule of action and decision for all branches and officers of the government, and with which all subsequent laws and ordinances must be in accordance unless it has been changed by a constitutional amendment by the authority that created it.

For over 200 years, the Constitution of the United States has served as the foundation for U.S. government. Created in 1787, the U.S. Constitution establishes and defines the basic outlines of a national government that joins the states in an effective political union. The U.S. Constitution has been and remains one of the most enduring political agreements in the history of the world. Throughout its existence, it has served as an

Constitutional Convention of 1787

The Constitutional Convention of 1787 is a high point in the history of the United States. This remarkable assemblage of men, meeting in Philadelphia between May 23 and September 17, 1787, created the document that has given the United States one of the most stable and admired constitutional democracies in the history of the world.

55 delegates from 12 states attended various parts of the convention. Drawn from the educated and wealthy elite of the country, they included such luminaries as GEORGE WASHINGTON, the commander of American forces in the WAR OF INDEPENDENCE, who presided over the convention, and BENJAMIN FRANKLIN, at 81, the oldest delegate and the country's most famous statesman. A majority of the delegates were lawyers, and many, such as JAMES MADISON, were wealthy landowners. Many notable leaders of the time, however, including THOMAS JEFFERSON, who was in France, and PATRICK HENRY, did not attend.

The meetings of the convention were closed to the public and to the press. Thus, behind closed doors, the delegates hammered out the eventual form of U.S. government. The agreements reached during the convention exemplified the values of constitutional government. In an atmosphere that combined competitive, lively debate with tolerance and respect for differences of opinion, the delegates reached vital compromises on matters that threatened to divide the still loosely connected union of states. Many different factions opposed one another—small states versus large states, farmers versus businesspeople, North versus South, and slave states versus nonslave states.

The Constitutional Convention occurred in three separate phases. The first, from May 23 to July 26, created the basic features of the national government, including its division into legislative, executive, and judicial branches. During this phase, delegates also arrived at one important compromise between the interests of large and small states. That compromise created a bicameral, or two-chamber, legislature, composed of the House of Representatives and the Senate. During the second phase of the convention, from July 27 to August 6, the five-man Committee of Detail created a rough draft of the Constitution. In the third phase, which lasted from August 6 to September 6, the delegates debated remaining sticking points, particularly relating to the EXECUTIVE BRANCH and the means of electing a president. Eventually, they settled on the ELECTORAL COLLEGE suggested by Benjamin Franklin.

On September 17, 39 of the 42 delegates present signed the Constitution. Gouverneur Morris, coauthor of the New York State Constitution and a key delegate, summed up the significance of the Constitution that the convention had created when, after affixing his signature to it, he uttered these words: "The moment this plan goes forth, all other considerations will be laid aside and the great question will be: Shall there be a *national* government or not? And this must take place or a general anarchy will be the alternative."

FURTHER READINGS

Rossiter, Clinton. 1966. *1787: The Grand Convention.* Reprint, New York: Norton, 1987.

Scott, James Brown. 2001. *James Madison's Notes of Debates in the Federal Convention of 1787 and their Relation to a More Perfect Society of Nations.* Union, N.J.: Lawbook Exchange.

---

inspiring example of the potential of constitutional government, causing many other countries and peoples to emulate its provisions.

According to Article VI of the Constitution, the U.S. Constitution is "the supreme Law of the Land." All other laws and judicial decisions are subject to its mandates. The Constitution therefore has higher authority than all other laws in the nation, including statutes and laws passed by Congress and state legislatures. Unlike those other laws, the Constitution may be changed, or amended, only in special ways that reflect its character as a demonstration of the people's will.

The original document of the U.S. Constitution is held at the National Archives, in Washington, D.C.

History of the Constitution

When the United States declared itself a country separate from Great Britain in 1776, it

FEDERALISTS VERSUS ANTI-FEDERALISTS

After the Constitution was signed and approved by delegates of the Constitutional Convention of 1787, it had to be ratified by the states. As determined by Article VII of the Constitution, ratification required the approval of nine special state conventions. States that did not ratify the Constitution would not be considered a part of the Union and would be separate countries.

Passage of the Constitution by the states was by no means certain in 1787. Indeed, many people at that time opposed the creation of a federal, or national, government that would have power over the states. These people were called Anti-Federalists. They included primarily farmers and tradesmen and were less likely to be a part of the wealthy elite than were members of their opposition, who called themselves Federalists. The Anti-Federalists believed that each state should have a sovereign, independent government. Their leaders included some of the most influential figures in the nation, including PATRICK HENRY and GEORGE MASON, leading national figures during the Revolutionary War period. Many Anti-Federalists were local politicians who feared losing power should the Constitution be ratified. As one member of their opposition, EDMUND RANDOLPH, said, these politicians "will not cherish

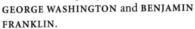

IN FOCUS

the great oak which is to reduce them to paltry shrubs."

The Federalists favored the creation of a strong federal government that would more closely unite the states as one large, continental nation. They tended to come from the wealthier class of merchants and plantation owners. Federalists had been instrumental in the creation of the Constitution, arguing that it was a necessary improvement on the ARTICLES OF CONFEDERATION, the country's first attempt at unifying the states in a national political arrangement. Leaders among the Federalists included two men who helped develop the Constitution, JAMES MADISON and ALEXANDER HAMILTON, and two national heroes whose support would greatly improve the Federalists' prospects for winning, GEORGE WASHINGTON and BENJAMIN FRANKLIN.

Between September 17, 1787, the day the Constitution was signed by the Constitutional Convention, and May 29, 1790, the day Rhode Island became the thirteenth and last state to ratify the Constitution, the Federalists and Anti-Federalists engaged in a fierce national debate on the merits of the Constitution. This debate occurred in meeting halls, on streets, and on the printed page. Both sides in the argument had a considerable following. Many of the questions raised

remain with us today: What is the best form of government? What rights must the government protect? Which government powers should be granted to the states, and which to the federal government?

The Anti-Federalists The Anti-Federalists found many problems in the Constitution. They argued that the document would give the country an entirely new and untested form of government. They saw no sense in throwing out the existing government. Instead, they believed that the Federalists had overstated the current problems of the country. They also maintained that the Framers of the Constitution had met as an elitist group under a veil of secrecy and had violated the provisions of the Articles of Confederation in the means selected for ratification of the Constitution.

In making their arguments, the Anti-Federalists often relied on the rhetoric of the Revolutionary War era, which stressed the virtues of local rule and associated centralized power with a tyrannical monarch. Thus, the Anti-Federalists frequently claimed that the Constitution represented a step away from the democratic goals of the American Revolution and toward the twin evils of monarchy and aristocracy. The Anti-Federalists feared that the Constitution gave the president too much power and that the proposed Congress would be too aristocratic in nature, with too few representa-

did not have a written constitution. Instead, the 13 former colonies each had their own sovereignty and separate bodies of law. How the newly formed United States would act as one nation remained uncertain and undefined. The CONTINENTAL CONGRESS, the first national legislative body of the new nation, attempted to address this state of affairs by drafting the nation's first constitution, the ARTICLES OF CONFEDERATION, which were ratified in 1781, the same year that hostilities in the Revolutionary War against Britain came to an end at Yorktown, Virginia.

The Articles of Confederation proved an ineffective national constitution. That document did not provide for a strong federal, or central, government and allowed each state its own "sovereignty, freedom and independence" (art. II). It also did not provide the federal government power to tax or regulate commerce.

The problems of a weak federal government with insufficient funds for operation became apparent as a number of problems developed in the 1780s: harmful economic warfare between states, inadequate commercial treaties with for-

tives for too many people. They also criticized the Constitution for its lack of a **BILL OF RIGHTS** of the kind that had been passed in England in 1689 to establish and guarantee certain rights of Parliament and of the English people against the king. Moreover, the Anti-Federalists argued that the Constitution would spell an end to all forms of self-rule in the states.

Many Anti-Federalists believed in a type of government that has been described as agrarian republicanism. Such a government is centered on a society of landowning farmers who participate in local politics. **THOMAS JEFFERSON** agreed with this view. He felt that the virtues of democratic freedom were best nurtured in an agrarian, or agricultural, society, and that with increasing urbanization, commercialization, and centralization of power would come a decline in political society and eventual tyranny. Unlike the Anti-Federalists, however, Jefferson supported the Constitution, although rather reluctantly. He was not strongly identified with the Federalist position and would eventually oppose the Federalists as a member of the **DEMOCRATIC-REPUBLICAN PARTY**.

The Anti-Federalists also shared the feeling that so large a country as the United States could not possibly be controlled by one national government. One Pennsylvania Anti-Federalist, who signed his articles "Centinel," declared,

> It is the opinion of the greatest writers, that a very extensive country cannot be governed on democratical principles, on any other plan than a confederation of a number of small republics, possessing all the powers of internal government, but united in the management of their foreign and general concerns.
>
> . . . [A]nything short of despotism could not bind so great a country under one government.

Although the Anti-Federalists were united in their opposition to the Constitution, they did not agree on what form of government made the best alternative to it. Some still believed that the Articles of Confederation could be amended in such a way that they would provide a workable confederation. Some wanted the Union to break up and re-form into three or four different confederacies. Others were even ready to accept the Constitution if it were amended in such a way that the rights of citizens and states would be more fully protected.

The Federalists The Federalists focused their arguments on the inadequacies of national government under the Articles of Confederation and on the benefits of national government as formed by the Constitution. They were also much more favorably disposed toward commerce than were the Anti-Federalists, and they argued that a strong central government would foster the commercial growth of the new country. Moreover, the Federalist vision of society was more pluralistic than the Anti-Federalist vision. That is, the Federalists did not see society as made up principally of farmers, as did the Anti-Federalists, but instead viewed it as comprising many different and competing interests and groups, none of which would be completely dominant in a federalist system of government. For this reason, many later scholars have argued that the Federalists were more aware of the economic and social changes then transforming American society.

The most famous example of Federalist doctrine is *The Federalist Papers,* a collection of 85 essays by Alexander Hamilton, James Madison, and **JOHN JAY**. Published in New York newspapers and in two bound volumes distributed during the ratification debate, these essays were signed with the pseudonym Publius, taken from Publius Valerius Poplicola, a man who reputedly saved the ancient Roman republic. *The Federalist Papers* is an important American contribution to political philosophy and remains a classic today. It is also a great and authoritative commentary on the Constitution.

The Federalist Papers communicates the central ideas of the Federalists: the benefits of a Union between the states; the problems with the confederation as it stood at the time; the importance of an energetic, effective federal government; and a defense of the republicanism of the proposed Constitution. *The Federalist Papers* makes a persuasive case for the necessity of federal government in preserving order and securing the liberty of a large republic. In doing so, it asserts that a weak union of the states will make the

(continued)

eign countries, and the inability to raise an army to oppose British troops in the Northwest Territory. Particularly disturbing for many critics of the Confederation was the lack of a federal response to Shays's Rebellion in 1786–87, an armed uprising by debtor farmers in western Massachusetts directed against courts of law. **GEORGE WASHINGTON** reacted to this lack of response with words that expressed his strong desire for a better union of the states:

> I am mortified beyond expression when I view the clouds that have spread over the brightest morn that ever dawned upon any country. You talk of employing influence to appease the present tumults in Massachusetts. Influence is no government. Let us have a government by which our lives, liberties and properties will be secured; or let us know the worst at once.

Seeking to address the inadequacies of the Articles of Confederation, the Continental Congress called for the Constitutional Convention to create a better basis for union between the states. The convention began in Philadelphia on

FEDERALISTS VERSUS ANTI-FEDERALISTS
(CONTINUED)

country more vulnerable to internal and external dissension, including civil war and invasion from foreign powers.

One of the most famous of its essays is *The Federalist,* number 10, by James Madison. In it, Madison addressed the issue of whether or not the republican government created by the Constitution can protect the liberties of its citizens. The problem that Madison saw as most destructive of popular government is what he called faction. A faction, according to Madison, is "a number of citizens, whether amounting to a majority or minority of the whole, who are united and actuated by some common impulse of passion, or of interest, adverse to the rights of other citizens, or to the permanent and aggregate interests of the community." Factions, Madison added, become especially dangerous when they form a majority of the population.

Madison divided popular government into two types, democratic and republican, and preferred the latter. In a democracy, all citizens participate directly in the decisions of government. In a republic, representatives elected by the people make the decisions of government.

In his intricate argument in *The Federalist,* number 10, Madison contended that a republican government of the kind envisioned by the U.S. Constitution can

best solve the problem of faction not by "removing its causes"—which only tyranny can do—but by "controlling its effects." Madison proposed that elected representatives, as opposed to the people as a whole, will be more disposed to consider the national interest ahead of a particular factional interest. He also argued that the nature of an "extensive," or large, republic such as the United States will naturally frustrate the ability of a single faction to advance its own interests ahead of the interests of other citizens. With the huge variety of parties and interests in an extended republic, it becomes "less probable that a majority of the whole will have a common motive to invade the rights of other citizens." Thus, Madison, in contrast to the Anti-Federalists, saw the large size of the United States as a help rather than a hindrance to the cause of liberty.

This is only one of the many points that *The Federalist Papers* makes in favor of the Constitution. However, as brilliant and carefully reasoned as *The Federalist Papers* may be, it probably did not greatly sway opinion toward ratification of the Constitution. The politics of ratification were instead influenced most by direct, face-to-face contact and negotiation. Nevertheless, *The Federalist Papers* aided the Constitution's cause by giving the Constitution's adherents ideas with which to counter their opposition.

The outcome Ultimately, the ratification provisions of Article VII of the Constitution, created by the Federalists themselves, were one of the best allies the Federalists had in their attempt to ratify the Constitution. After the Constitution had been created at the Constitutional Convention, Federalist leaders quickly returned to their states to elect Federalist delegates to the state conventions. The Anti-Federalists were not able to muster enough votes in response, though in several states, they nearly defeated the Federalists. By 1790, all thirteen states had ratified the document, giving the Federalists and their Constitution a great victory.

The Anti-Federalist outcry was not without its effects, however. By 1791, in response to Anti-Federalist sentiments, state legislatures voted to add the first ten amendments to the Constitution. Those ten amendments are also called the Bill of Rights, and they have become an important part of the Constitution and its heritage of liberty.

FURTHER READINGS

Frohnen, Bruce, ed. 1999. *The Anti-Federalists: Selected Writings and Speeches.* Washington, D.C.: Regnery Pub.

Wills, Garry. 2001. *Explaining America: The Federalist.* New York: Penguin Books.

CROSS-REFERENCES

Federalist Papers.

May 25, 1787, with the original intention of amending the Articles of Confederation. However, the delegates—including BENJAMIN FRANKLIN, ALEXANDER HAMILTON, JAMES MADISON, and George Washington—soon planned an entirely new constitution.

Fifty-five delegates representing 12 states (all but Rhode Island) discussed different plans for a federal government. They agreed to create a government consisting of three separate branches—executive, legislative, and judicial—with checks and balances to keep any one branch from

becoming too powerful. However, they disagreed strongly over particulars.

For example, two plans for representation in a national legislature competed for the loyalty of delegates. The so-called Virginia Plan, presented by EDMUND RANDOLPH and designed by James Madison, called for a bicameral, or two-house, legislature. Representation in the lower house would be proportional to population, and representation in the upper house would be elected by the lower house. Delegates from small states felt that such a plan would give too much power to large states. They favored the New Jersey Plan, which called for a unicameral legislature with equal representation to each state. Delegates settled the issue by voting for a compromise plan—called the Great Compromise, or the Connecticut Compromise—which established a Senate that gave each state two representatives and a House of Representatives that granted each state a number of representatives proportional to its population.

On September 17, 1787, 39 delegates signed the completed Constitution. In subsequent months, the document went before each of the states for ratification. The ratification process was accompanied by a spirited debate on the merits of the Constitution. The Federalists, on one side of the debate, supported ratification. Federalist leaders Alexander Hamilton, JOHN JAY, and James Madison argued eloquently on behalf of the Constitution in a series of newspaper essays that were published as *The Federalist* papers. Those opposed to the Constitution were called Anti-Federalists.

The ratification process, as contained in Article VII of the Constitution, required that nine of the 13 states approve the Constitution in special conventions. Within ten months after the Constitution was completed, ten states had ratified it. Rhode Island was the last of the 13 states to ratify the Constitution, on May 29, 1790, officially making the Constitution the highest law of the land.

Contents of the Constitution

The Constitution is divided into seven articles, or divisions, each addressing a different topic. Each article is divided into sections. The Constitution begins with a preamble that states the purpose of the document and the source of its power:

> We the People of the United States, in Order to form a more perfect Union, establish Justice, insure domestic Tranquility, provide for the common defence, promote the general Welfare, and secure the Blessings of Liberty to ourselves and our Posterity, do ordain and establish this Constitution for the United States of America. The Preamble is not strictly considered a part of the Constitution and is not legally binding on issues relating to either government power or private right (*Jacobson v. Massachusetts*, 197 U.S. 11, 25 S. Ct. 358, 49 L. Ed. 643 [1905]).

Article I Article I of the Constitution deals with the legislative branch of government. It establishes the bicameral Congress, consisting of a Senate and a House of Representatives, and it delineates the means by which Congressional members shall be elected, the length of their terms, and the requirements for membership, including age. It also sets forth guidelines for legislative procedure, including a requirement that bills of revenue, or taxation, must originate in the House; requirements for the process by which bills pass from Congress to the president; and the procedures in case of presidential VETO, or refusal to sign a bill into law.

Article I, Section 2, prescribes for the means of APPORTIONMENT, or the method by which representatives are allocated to the states. Because political power would inevitably flow to the states with the most congressional representatives, this topic was controversial at the time of the framing of the Constitution. Whereas each state receives two votes in the Senate, the number of representatives each state receives in the House is determined by an enumeration, or census, to be conducted every ten years.

According to this same section, a state's population is to "be determined by adding to the whole Number of free Persons, including those bound to Service for a Term of Years, and excluding Indians not taxed, three fifths of all other Persons." Thus, an indentured servant was counted as a whole person, and an African American slave was counted as only three-fifths of a person. This last provision arose out of differences between slave and nonslave states. Counting slaves as equal persons would have given southern states a greater number of representatives and more power in Congress. Northern states vigorously opposed such a scheme, and the resulting compromise was called the Three-fifths Compromise.

Article I, Section 8, gives Congress some of its delegated powers, many of them crucial powers that had been denied to the Congress of the Confederation. These include the powers to "lay and collect Taxes," "borrow Money," "coin Money," "establish Post Offices," "declare War," "raise and support Armies," "provide and maintain a Navy," and "make all Laws which shall be necessary and proper for carrying into Execution" all the other powers. This last clause is called the NECESSARY AND PROPER CLAUSE and has been used to justify later expansion of congressional activity not specifically mentioned in the Constitution. The clause has also been called the elastic clause or implied powers clause.

A depiction of George Washington presiding over the signing of the U.S. Constitution in Philadelphia on September 17, 1787.

LIBRARY OF CONGRESS

Article I, Section 8, also gives Congress the power to "regulate Commerce with foreign nations, and among the several States, and with the Indian Tribes." This is called the COMMERCE CLAUSE. And Article I, Section 8, gives Congress power over a district to "become the Seat of the Government of the United States," later established as the District of Columbia, or Washington, D.C.

Article I, Section 9, limits congressional powers, forbidding the passage of laws prohibiting the "Migration or Importation" of persons before the year 1808. This provision was designed as a concession to slaveholding states, ensuring that the practice of SLAVERY would not be challenged for at least 20 years. Section 9 also prohibits Congress from passing any EX POST FACTO, or retroactive, laws, and from granting any "Title of Nobility."

Article I, Section 10, limits the powers of the states, prohibiting, for example, the states to enter into foreign treaties and coin money.

Article II Article II concerns the EXECUTIVE BRANCH, or the presidency. Section 1 establishes the ELECTORAL COLLEGE as the means of electing the president, identifies the requirements for holding presidential office, and outlines the procedure in case a president is removed from office or dies. It also contains the oath that the president must take before entering the office, which explicitly requires that the president support the Constitution: "I do solemnly swear (or affirm) that I will faithfully execute the Office of President of the United States, and will to the best of my Ability, preserve, protect and defend the Constitution of the United States."

Article II, Section 2, names the president as commander in chief of the armed forces. It also gives the president the power to grant pardons or reprieves; make treaties with foreign powers, subject to approval by the Senate; and appoint ambassadors and Supreme Court justices.

Article II, Section 4, allows for removal and IMPEACHMENT of the president and "all civil Officers of the United States" in cases of conviction for "Treason, BRIBERY, or other High Crimes and Misdemeanors."

Article III Article III establishes the SUPREME COURT OF THE UNITED STATES as the highest judicial power. Section 2 defines the jurisdiction of the federal judiciary. Section 3 defines and limits prosecution for TREASON. The power of JUDICIAL REVIEW, whereby the Supreme Court may declare laws and regulations of government to be unconstitutional, is not explicitly declared in the Constitution and was not established by the Supreme Court until the case of MARBURY V. MADISON, 5 U.S. (1 Cranch) 137, 2 L. Ed. 60 (1803).

Article IV Article IV defines the relations between the states. It requires each state to give "full Faith and Credit" to the laws of the other states; establishes that citizens are entitled to the same "Privileges and Immunities," or liberties and rights, as citizens in every other state; provides for EXTRADITION between states of persons charged with crimes; provides for and limits the admission of new states; gives Congress full power over U.S. territories that are not yet states; and guarantees each state "a Republican Form of Government" and protection against invasion or "domestic Violence."

Article V Article V sets forth a two-step procedure for amending the Constitution: proposal of amendments, followed by ratification. Amendments may be proposed in two ways: by a two-thirds vote of both houses of Congress or by a special convention called by two-thirds of the state legislatures. Amendments are ratified by one of two methods, determined by Congress: approval of three-fourths of the state legislatures or approval of three-fourths of special state conventions.

Article VI Article VI declares the Constitution and the laws and treaties made by the U.S. government under its authority to be "the supreme Law of the Land." This provision is called the SUPREMACY CLAUSE. Article VI also requires that all judges in every state be subject to the provisions of the Constitution, that all state and federal officeholders swear an oath supporting the Constitution, and that "no religious Test shall ever be required as a Qualification to any Office" of the United States.

Amendments The Constitution has been amended 26 times. The first ten amendments were ratified in 1791 and are called the BILL OF RIGHTS.

Principles of the Constitution

The Constitution defined a number of the fundamental and enduring principles of U.S. government, particularly the concepts of SEPARATION OF POWERS, checks and balances, and FEDERALISM.

Separation of powers refers to the division of power between the legislative, executive, and judicial branches of government. Checks and balances refers to a system whereby each branch of government retains some of the powers of the other branches, which it may use to control other branches. Thus, the president may veto bills passed by Congress, the Senate may vote down presidential appointments, and the Supreme Court may strike down laws approved by Congress or regulations put forth by the executive. Such actions keep the separate branches of government in balance and prevent any one of them from becoming too powerful.

The inclusion of the concepts of separation of powers and checks and balances in the Constitution owes much to James Madison, who has been called the Father of the Constitution. The U.S. system of government has often been referred to as the Madisonian Model. According to Madison, a system in which the different elements of government competed against one another, each preventing the other from becoming too powerful, was the best system to prevent the rise of a tyrannical government that would abuse the rights of the people. As he wrote in *The Federalist*, No. 51:

> In framing a government, . . . the great difficulty lies in this: You must first enable the government to control the governed; and in the next place, oblige it to control itself. A dependence on the people is, no doubt, the primary control on the government; but experience has taught the necessity of auxiliary precautions. The Constitution, with its separation of powers and checks and balances, provided just such "auxiliary precautions" to be used in controlling government.

The Constitution is also guided by the concept of federalism in the way that it constructs the U.S. government. Federalism is a system in which smaller political entities—such as states, counties, cities, and localities—are united in a larger political organization. Federalism intends to protect the liberties of people in these smaller political units by providing them with a great degree of freedom in governing themselves. The federal, or larger, government is then a limited government that cedes many decision-making responsibilities—including, for example, the creation of most criminal and civil laws, municipal codes, regulations for administering school districts, and the like—to states and localities, while leaving itself other responsibilities. In short, federalism is a partnership in which a central government shares authority and power with regional or local governments.

The U.S. Constitution gives the federal government—made up of the executive, legislative, and judicial branches—power to make decisions regarding such issues as war, national defense, and trade with foreign countries. The federal government also retains the right to overrule laws or decisions of lower units of government when they are in violation of the Constitution. Thus, for example, the federal government took on responsibilities in the oversight of local school districts after the Supreme Court, in BROWN V. BOARD OF EDUCATION, 347 U.S. 483, 74 S. Ct. 686, 98 L. Ed. 873 (1954), ruled that segregating children in different public schools by race violated the EQUAL PROTECTION CLAUSE of the FOURTEENTH AMENDMENT to the Constitution, which says, "No State shall … deny to any person … the equal protection of the laws."

FURTHER READINGS

Black, Eric. 1988. *Our Constitution: The Myth That Binds Us.* Boulder, Colo.: Westview Press.

Browne, Ray B., and Glenn J. Browne. 1986. *Laws of Our Fathers: Popular Culture and the U.S. Constitution.* Bowling Green, OH: Bowling Green Univ. Press.

Corwin, Edward S. 1978. *The Constitution and What It Means Today.* 14th ed. Rev. Harold W. Chase and Craig R. Ducat. Princeton, N.J.: Princeton Univ. Press.

Hamilton, Alexander, James Madison, and John Jay. 1787–88. *The Federalist Papers.* Ed. Clinton Rossiter. Reprint, New York: New American Library of World Literature, 1961.

Harrigan, John J. 1984. *Politics and the American Future.* Reading, Mass.: Addison-Wesley.

Levy, Michael B. 1982. *Political Thought in America: An Anthology.* Homewood, Ill.: Dorsey Press.

Marshall, Burke, ed. 1987. *A Workable Government?: The Constitution after 200 Years.* New York: Norton.

Maxwell, James A., ed. 1982. *You and Your Rights.* Pleasantville, N.Y.: Reader's Digest.

McGuire, Robert A. 2003. *To Form a More Perfect Union: A New Economic Interpretation of the United States Constitution.* Oxford, New York: Oxford Univ. Press.

Rawle, William. 2003. *A View of the Constitution of the United States of America.* 2d ed. Clark, N.J.: Lawbook Exchange.

Story, Joseph. 2001. *Constitution of the United States: With a Preliminary Review of the Constitutional History of the Colonies and States, Before the Adoption of the Constitution* Union, N.J.: Lawbook Exchange.

CROSS-REFERENCES

Congress of the United States; "Constitution of the United States" (Appendix, Primary Document); Constitutional Amendment; Constitutional Law; Federalist Papers; Full Faith and Credit Clause; Presidential Powers.

CONSTITUTION PARTY

The Constitution Party was founded in 1992 as the U.S. Taxpayers Party. The man who was most responsible for establishing the party was Howard Phillips, a veteran conservative political activist who had left the REPUBLICAN PARTY in 1974 after feeling that the party was insufficiently conservative. Phillips has been the dominant figure in the party since its founding, running as its presidential candidate in 1992, 1996, and 2000.

Phillips had been involved in the Republican Party since his early teens, when he decided to chart a different course. He had served as chairman of the Boston Republican Party, as a staff member at the Republican National Committee in Washington, D.C., and finally as the director of the Office of Economic Opportunity under President RICHARD NIXON, with an explicit mandate to dismantle the program. When, because of political constraints, he was not allowed to do this, he quit the administration and established the Conservative Caucus, a LOBBYING group that became somewhat influential during the presidency of RONALD REAGAN.

Phillips decided that the next step was to form a political party, according to his web site, with "the common goal of limiting the federal government to its Constitutional boundaries and restoring the foundations of civil government back to the fundamental principles our country was founded upon." The party that he formed in 1992 was named the U.S. Taxpayers Party, and befitting its name, it committed itself to stopping all federal expenditures that were not specifically authorized by the U.S. Constitution, and to "restore to the states those powers, programs, and sources of revenue that the federal government has usurped."

Though the original party that Phillips formed had a primarily fiscal purpose, it also took strong conservative stands on social issues, advocating making ABORTION illegal in all instances, supporting a MORATORIUM on immigration into the United States, and calling for the ABOLITION of all WELFARE programs. Taking this platform nationwide, Phillips and his running mate, Albion Knight, managed to get on the presidential ballot in 21 states and garnered approximately 40,000 votes in the 1992 presidential campaign. In 1996, Phillips and running mate, Herb Titus, managed to get on the ballot in 39 states and won 182,000 votes.

In 1999, the U.S. Taxpayer Party renamed itself the Constitution Party. With Phillips once again its presidential candidate, this time running with Dr. J. Curtis Frazier, the party was able to gain access to the ballot in 42 states. However, the totals for Phillips this time were lower than he had received in 1996—approximately 98,000 votes. For the 2004 election, the Constitution Party has as its goal to get its presidential ticket on all 50 states.

The Constitution Party does not only run presidential candidates. For the 2002 election, at least 20 states had candidates affiliated with the Constitution Party running for office, for positions ranging from governor and U.S. Senate down to city council and state house. In Nevada alone, the party had affiliated candidates for 30 offices for the 2002 election. In Wisconsin, the party has two affiliated elected officials: an alderman and a county supervisor.

The Constitution Party takes strongly conservative stands on a variety of issues. The party's preamble to its 2000 National Platform views the American political system with a strongly religious bent. "The U.S. Constitution established a Republic under God, rather than a democracy," it states. "Our Republic is a nation governed by a Constitution that is rooted in Biblical law, administered by representatives who are Constitutionally elected by the citizens."

On abortion, the Constitution Party's 2000 platform stated that "*Roe v. Wade* is illegitimate, contrary to the law of the nation's Charter and Constitution. It must be resisted by all civil government officials, federal, state, and local, and by all branches of the government—legislative, executive, and judicial." It argues that abortion should be illegal nationwide.

Regarding the prevention of AIDS, the Constitution Party states in its platform, "Under no circumstances should the federal government continue to subsidize activities which have the effect of encouraging perverted or promiscuous sexual conduct. Criminal penalties should apply to those whose willful acts of omission or commission place members of the public at risk of contracting AIDS or HIV."

For members of Congress, the Constitution Party suggests abolishing federal pay for members of Congress, and abolishing Congressional pensions. It also advocates abolishing the direct election of Senators and returning that function to the state legislatures. It supports repealing all laws that delegate legislative powers to regulatory agencies, bureaucracies, private organizations, the FEDERAL RESERVE BOARD, international agencies, the president, and the judiciary.

On national defense, the Constitution Party platform advocates "maintenance of a strong, state-of-the-art military on land, sea, in the air,

and in space." It opposes allowing U.S. forces to serve under any foreign flag or command. However, it also opposes "the Presidential assumption of authority to deploy American troops into combat without the consent of Congress."

The Constitution Party would like to see the DEPARTMENT OF EDUCATION abolished, and it also supports the elimination of the FOOD AND DRUG ADMINISTRATION, the Federal Reserve Board, the National Security Administration, and the INTERNAL REVENUE SERVICE. It supports voluntary SOCIAL SECURITY and would change the tax system to offer an apportioned "state-rate tax" in which the responsibility for covering the cost of federal obligations unmet by a tariff on foreign products will be divided among the several states in accordance with their proportion of the total population of the United States, excluding the District of Columbia. Under this system, if a state contains 10 percent of the nation's citizens, it will be responsible for assuming payment of 10 percent of the annual deficit.

On foreign affairs, The Constitution Party would like to see the United States withdraw from all international monetary and financial institutions and agencies, including the INTERNATIONAL MONETARY FUND (IMF), the WORLD BANK, the World Trade Organization (WTO), the NORTH AMERICAN FREE TRADE AGREEMENT (NAFTA), and the GENERAL AGREEMENT ON TARIFFS AND TRADE (GATT). It wants to terminate all programs of foreign aid, whether military or non-military, to any foreign government or to any international organization. It would

Howard Phillips ran as the Constitution Party's candidate in the 1992, 1996, and 2000 presidential elections. He received 98,020 votes in the 2000 election, just under 1 percent of the popular vote.

AP/WIDE WORLD PHOTOS

withdraw the United States from the North Atlantic Treaty Organisation (NATO), and would withdraw recognition of Communist China, which its platform describes as a murderous and tyrannical regime enslaving the Chinese people.

The Constitution Party refuses to take any federal funds for its presidential campaigns. The party made it clear after the 2000 campaign that it planned to be around for a while. On its web site, it stated, "In light of the widespread need across the country, the party is fully dedicated to building party strength and organization at the State, County and local level."

FURTHER READINGS

Constitution Party Website. Available online at <www.constitutionparty.com> (accessed November 20, 2003).

Lucier, James P. 2000. "Phillips Leads the Way for Constitutionalists." *Insight Magazine* (Sept 25).

CROSS-REFERENCES

Democratic Party; Elections; Republican Party; *Roe v. Wade.*

CONSTITUTIONAL

That which is consistent with or dependent upon the fundamental law that defines and establishes government in society and basic principles to which society is to conform.

A law is constitutional when it does not violate any provision of the U.S. Constitution or any state constitution.

CONSTITUTIONAL AMENDMENT

The means by which an alteration to the U.S. Constitution, whether a modification, deletion, or addition, is accomplished.

Article V of the U.S. Constitution establishes the means for amending that document according to a two-step procedure: proposal of amendments, followed by ratification. Amendments may be proposed in two ways: by a two-thirds vote of both houses of Congress or by a special convention summoned by Congress on the petition of two-thirds (34) of the state legislatures.

In the long history of the U.S. Constitution, over 5,000 amendments have been introduced in Congress. Only 33 of these have been formally proposed by Congress, and none has ever been proposed by a special convention.

No matter which method is used for the proposal of a constitutional amendment, Congress retains the power to decide what method will be used for ratification: approval of three-fourths (38) of the state legislatures, or approval of three-fourths (38) of special state conventions. Congress may also place other restrictions, such as a limited time frame, on ratification.

Of the 33 amendments proposed by Congress, 27 were ratified. Of the amendments ratified, only one—the TWENTY-FIRST AMENDMENT, which repealed a PROHIBITION on alcohol—was ratified by the state convention method. The rest have been ratified by three-fourths of the state legislatures.

The process for amending the Constitution is deliberately difficult. Even when an amendment is proposed by Congress, it has taken, on average, two-and-a-half years for it to be ratified. That difficulty creates stability, with its accompanying advantages and disadvantages. The advantages lie in the fact that the Constitution's provisions are not subject to change according to the whims of a particular moment. The disadvantages inhere in the reality that the Constitution must also adapt and be relevant to a changing society. Given the difficulty of amendment, much of the burden of adapting the Constitution to a changing world has fallen on the shoulders of the Supreme Court and its powers of JUDICIAL REVIEW, which have been described as an informal method of changing the Constitution. However, constitutional amendments may in turn modify or overturn judicial opinion, as was the case with the Eleventh, Thirteenth, Fourteenth, Sixteenth, Nineteenth, Twenty-fourth, and Twenty-sixth Amendments.

Commentators have also pointed out that the amendment process is not a very democratic one. As the constitutional scholar EDWARD S. CORWIN wrote: "A proposed amendment can be added to the Constitution by thirty-eight states containing considerably less than half of the population of the country, or can be defeated by thirteen states containing less than one-twentieth of the population of the country."

Brief History of Constitutional Amendments

Before the creation of the U.S. Constitution in 1787, constitutional amendments had already been instituted as part of several early state constitutions. The pioneering framers of these state constitutions recognized the need to incorporate an element of flexibility into CONSTITUTIONAL LAW, and they provided for constitutional amendment through the legislature or through special conventions. However, the first national CONSTITUTION OF THE UNITED STATES, the ARTICLES OF CONFEDERATION, did not have such flexibility. Amendment of that document required a unanimous vote of Congress, nearly impossible to achieve.

The Framers of the U.S. Constitution sought to avoid the inflexibility of the Articles of Confederation. JAMES MADISON, one of the principle architects of the Constitution, argued in *The Federalist Papers* that the new compact's amendment procedures, unlike those of the old Articles, protected "equally against that extreme facility, which would render the Constitution too mutable, and that extreme difficulty, which might perpetuate its discovered faults."

Proving the truth of Madison's contention, the first ten amendments to the Constitution were passed as a package by the first session of Congress in 1791. This group of amendments is called the BILL OF RIGHTS. The Bill of Rights fulfilled a promise that the backers of the Constitution, known as the Federalists, had made during the ratification procedure of the Constitution. It guarantees specific liberties relating to (1) rights of conscience, including the freedoms of speech, press, religion, and peaceable assembly (FIRST AMENDMENT); (2) rights of the accused, including freedom from "unreasonable searches and seizures" (FOURTH AMENDMENT), freedom from compulsory SELF-INCRIMINATION (FIFTH AMENDMENT), the "right to a speedy and public trial, by an impartial jury" and with legal counsel (SIXTH AMENDMENT), and freedom from "excessive bail" and "cruel and unusual punishments" (EIGHTH AMENDMENT); and (3) rights of property, including freedom from seizure of property without "due process of law" (Fifth Amendment).

Subsequent amendments have dealt with many different issues, including the extent of federal judicial jurisdiction (ELEVENTH AMENDMENT [1795]), the method of electing the president (TWELFTH AMENDMENT [1804]), the ABOLITION of SLAVERY (THIRTEENTH AMENDMENT [1865]), legalization of the INCOME TAX (SIXTEENTH AMENDMENT [1913]), granting women the right to vote (NINETEENTH AMENDMENT [1920]), presidential succession (TWENTY-FIFTH AMENDMENT [1967]), and the voting age (TWENTY-SIXTH AMENDMENT [1971]).

The FOURTEENTH AMENDMENT (1868), which holds that no state shall "deprive any person of life, liberty, or property, without DUE PROCESS OF LAW; nor deny to any person ... the EQUAL PROTECTION of the laws," has arguably been the most important and far-reaching of all the amendments, particularly with regard to its Due Process and Equal Protection Clauses. Through the Fourteenth Amendment, most of the provisions of the Bill of Rights were eventually applied to the states.

In 1972, the EQUAL RIGHTS AMENDMENT (ERA) was formally proposed by Congress. The ERA, which would have forbidden discrimination on the basis of sex, failed to gain ratification within the seven-year deadline proposed by Congress, even after a 39-month extension through June 30, 1982.

FURTHER READINGS

Amar, Akhil R. 2000. *The Bill of Rights: Creation and Reconstruction.* New Haven, Conn.: Yale Univ. Press.

Antieau, Chester James. 1995. *A U.S. Constitution for the Year 2000.* Chicago, IL: Loyola.

Chase, Harold W., and Craig R. Ducat, eds. 1978. "Article V." In *The Constitution and What It Means Today,* by Edward S. Corwin. 14th ed. Rev. Harold W. Chase and Craig R. Ducat. Princeton: Princeton Univ. Press.

Gilbert, Robert E., ed. 2000. *Managing Crisis: Presidential Disability and the Twenty-fifth Amendment.* Bronx, N.Y.: Fordham Univ. Press.

Gonzalez, Carlos E. 2002. "Popular Sovereign Generated Versus Government Institution Generated Constitutional Norms: When Does a Constitutional Amendment Not Amend the Constitution?" *Washington University Law Quarterly* 80 (spring): 127–242.

Harrigan, John J. 1984. *Politics and the American Future.* Reading, Mass.: Addison-Wesley.

Kohn, Bernice. 1974. *The Spirit and the Letter: The Struggle for Rights in America.* New York: Viking Penguin.

Palmer, Kris E., ed. 2000. *Constitutional Amendments, 1789 to the Present.* Detroit: Gale Group.

Strauss, David A. 2001. "The Irrelevance of Constitutional Amendments." *Harvard Law Review* 114 (March): 1457–1505.

Vile, John R. 2003. *Encyclopedia of Constitutional Amendments, Proposed Amendments, and Amending Issues, 1789-2002.* 2d ed. Santa Barbara, Calif.: ABC-CLIO.

CROSS-REFERENCES

Constitution of the United States.

CONSTITUTIONAL LAW

The written text of the state and federal constitutions. The body of judicial precedent that has gradually developed through a process in which courts interpret, apply, and explain the meaning of particular constitutional provisions and principles during a legal proceeding. Executive, legislative, and judicial actions that conform with the norms prescribed by a constitutional provision.

The text of the U.S. Constitution is marked by four characteristics: a delegation of power, in which the duties and prerogatives of the executive, legislative, and judicial branches are delineated by express constitutional provisions; a SEPARATION OF POWERS, in which the responsibilities of government are divided and shared among the coordinate branches; a reservation of power, in which the sovereignty of the federal government is qualified by the sovereignty reserved to the state governments; and a limitation of power, in which the prerogatives of the three branches of government are restricted by constitutionally enumerated individual rights, UNENUMERATED RIGHTS derived from sources outside the text of the Constitution, and other constraints inherent in a democratic system where the ultimate source of authority for government action is the consent of the people.

In deciding their cases, courts look to these constitutional provisions and principles for guidance. Once a court has interpreted a constitutional provision in a certain fashion, it becomes a precedent. Under the doctrine of STARE DECISIS, the judicial branch is required to adhere to existing precedent in all future cases presenting analogous factual and legal circumstances, unless it has a compelling reason for deviating from the precedent or overruling it.

A state or federal law is said to be constitutional when it is consistent with the text of a constitutional provision and any relevant judicial interpretations. A law that is inconsistent with either the written text or judicial interpretation of a constitutional provision is unconstitutional.

The Constitution

The U.S. Constitution is the highest law in the land and the foundation on which all U.S. law has been built. By establishing a structure for the federal government and preserving certain areas of sovereignty for the states, the Constitution has created a system of government that has allowed every area of civil, criminal, and ADMINISTRATIVE LAW to evolve with the needs of society. The federal Constitution became binding on the U.S. people in 1788 when New Hampshire, pursuant to Article VII, became the ninth state to vote for ratification.

The federal Constitution comprises seven articles and 26 amendments. Articles I, II, and III set forth the basic structure of the U.S. government. Article I defines congressional law-

making powers, Article II sets forth the presidential executive powers, and Article III establishes federal judicial powers. The first ten amendments to the U.S. Constitution, known as the BILL OF RIGHTS, enumerate certain individual liberties that must be protected against government infringement. The rest of the Constitution contains miscellaneous other provisions, many of which are intended to maintain a federalist system of government in which the federal Constitution is the supreme law of the land and the federal government shares sovereignty with the states.

Article I: The Lawmaking Power Article I of the Constitution allocates the lawmaking power to Congress. Section 1 provides that "[a]ll legislative Powers herein granted shall be vested in a CONGRESS OF THE UNITED STATES, which shall consist of a Senate and a House of Representatives." Article I also requires that candidates running for the House of Representatives be elected directly by the residents of each state. Originally, Article I endowed the state legislatures with the power to choose members of the Senate. However, the SEVENTEENTH AMENDMENT now requires all senators to be elected directly by the people of their home state.

Section 8 enumerates specific lawmaking powers that Congress may exercise. These include the power to declare war; raise and support armies; provide and maintain a navy; regulate commerce; borrow and coin money; establish and collect taxes; pay debts; establish uniform laws for immigration, naturalization, and BANKRUPTCY; and provide for the common defense and GENERAL WELFARE of the United States. Both the Senate and the House must approve all bills before they are submitted to the president. If the president vetoes a bill, Section 7 authorizes Congress to override the VETO by a two-thirds vote in both houses. Because Congress is a public body, this article requires the House and Senate to record and publish its proceedings, including the votes made by any of its members.

Section 8 also grants Congress the power to pass all laws that are "necessary and proper" to the performance of its legislative function. In MCCULLOCH V. MARYLAND, 17 U.S. (4 Wheat.) 316, 4 L. Ed. 579 (1819), the Supreme Court broadly interpreted the NECESSARY AND PROPER CLAUSE to grant Congress the implied powers to enact all laws that are useful, convenient, or essential to fulfilling its lawmaking and fiscal responsibilities. THOMAS JEFFERSON had earlier argued that the Necessary and Proper Clause authorized Congress only to enact measures that are indispensable to the implementation of the enumerated powers.

Congress frequently relies on its authority to regulate commerce as a justification for the legislation it enacts. Section 8 gives Congress the "power to regulate commerce among the several states." In GIBBONS V. OGDEN, 22 U.S. (9 Wheat.) 1, 6 L. Ed. 23 (1824), the Supreme Court ruled that congressional power to regulate commerce is plenary (complete in itself) and extends to all interstate commerce (commercial activity that concerns more than one state). The Court said that intrastate commerce (commercial activity that is conducted exclusively within one state) is beyond the reach of this congressional power.

Congressional commerce power reached its zenith in *Wickard v. Filburn,* 317 U.S. 111, 63 S. Ct. 82, 87 L. Ed. 122 (1942), where the Supreme Court ruled that Congress has authority to regulate a family farm that produces and consumes its own wheat. The Court said that "even if [a farm's] activity be local, and though it may not be regarded as commerce, it may still . . . be reached by Congress, if it exerts a substantial economic effect on interstate commerce . . . irrespective of whether such effect [is] direct or indirect."

This seemingly unfettered power was later limited, in *United States v. Lopez,* 514 U.S. 549, 115 S. Ct. 1624, 131 L. Ed. 2d 626 (1995), where the Supreme Court ruled that mere possession of a gun at or near a school does not substantially affect interstate commerce and may not be regulated at the federal level. Although the interstate commerce power has been given an expansive reading in modern times, the Court said in *Lopez,* the scope of congressional authority in this area

> must be considered in light of our dual system of [state and federal] government and may not be extended so as to embrace effects upon interstate commerce so indirect and remote that to embrace them, in view of our complex society, would effectually obliterate the distinction between what is national and what is local and create a completely centralized government.

Article I of the Constitution not only delegates specific powers to Congress, it also forbids Congress to take certain action. Section 9, for example, prohibits Congress from passing bills of attainder and EX POST FACTO LAWS. (A *bill of attainder* is a legislative act that imposes punish-

ment on a party without the benefit of a judicial proceeding. An *ex post facto* law makes criminal or punishes conduct that was not illegal at the time it occurred.) Section 9 further prohibits Congress from suspending HABEAS CORPUS (a citizen's right to protection against illegal imprisonment) except as may be necessary to preserve national security in time of rebellion or invasion. Although the Constitution delegated this power to Congress, President ABRAHAM LINCOLN suspended habeas corpus during the Civil War without congressional assent. Article I also restricts the power of state legislatures, such as the power to make treaties, alliances, and confederations, are also prohibited by Article I.

Article II: The Executive Power Congressional power is not absolute. The Framers of the Constitution were familiar with the abuses of absolute power. In the century preceding the American Revolution, Parliament acquired unlimited sovereignty. This arrangement replaced an earlier system of government in which the English monarchy ruled with a tyrannical scepter. In the United States, the Framers sought to create a system of checks and balances in which the executive and legislative branches would share power with each other and with the judiciary. In this light, many of the powers delegated to the president must be viewed in conjunction with the powers delegated to the coordinate branches of government.

Article II provides that "[t]he executive Power shall be vested in a President of the United States . . . [who] shall hold . . . Office during the Term of four Years . . . together with the Vice President." The ELECTORAL COLLEGE, which provides the method by which the president and vice president are elected, derives its constitutional authority from Article II as well as from the Twelfth and Twenty-third Amendments. The TWENTY-SECOND AMENDMENT limits the president to two terms in office, and the Twentieth and Twenty-fifth Amendments set forth the order of succession for presidents who are unable to begin their term or continue in office.

Article II, Section 2, makes the president the commander in chief of the armed forces. Yet only Congress has the power to declare war. Between these two powers lies a gray area in which presidents have exercised the prerogative to commit U.S. troops to foreign military excursions without congressional approval. The U.S. involvement in the VIETNAM WAR resulted from one such exercise of power. In response to these executive maneuvers, Congress passed the War Powers Resolution (Pub. L. No. 93-148 [codified at 50 U.S.C.A. §§ 1541 et seq.]), which restricts the president's authority to involve the United States in foreign hostilities for more than 60 days without the approval of Congress.

The president also shares power with Congress in other areas under Article II. Section 2 authorizes the president to make treaties with foreign governments, but only with the advice and consent of the Senate. The president must also seek senatorial approval when appointing ambassadors; federal judges, including Supreme Court justices; and other public ministers.

Section 4 states that the president may be removed from office only through IMPEACHMENT for "Treason, Bribery, or other High Crimes and Misdemeanors." The House is responsible for drafting ARTICLES OF IMPEACHMENT (accusations of misconduct), and the Senate is responsible for holding an impeachment trial. A two-thirds vote in the Senate is required for conviction.

The United States revisited the issue of what constitutes a *High Crime and Misdemeanor* during the impeachment proceedings against President WILLIAM JEFFERSON CLINTON. In 1998 the U.S. House of Representatives approved two articles of impeachment against President Clinton, accusing the president of having committed the crimes of perjury and OBSTRUCTION OF JUSTICE to conceal his relationship with a White-House intern named Monica Lewinsky. The impeachment trial was then held before the Senate from January 7, 1999, through February 12, 1999.

Clinton supporters generally opposed impeachment on grounds that concealing a private, extramarital affair should not constitute an impeachable high crime or misdemeanor. Clinton detractors generally supported impeachment on grounds that perjury and obstruction of justice are felony-level offenses that render a chief executive who is guilty of such offenses incompetent to discharge the duties of his office. Clinton supporters contended that past presidents had concealed their extramarital affairs without it rising to the level of an impeachable offense, while Clinton detractors countered by arguing that the president was not being impeached for having an extramarital affair but for committing crimes to conceal it.

Scholars debated the merits of the Clinton impeachment proceedings as well. However,

constitutional historians on both sides of the debate generally agreed that the phrase *High Crimes and Misdemeanors* had no settled usage at the time the Constitution was ratified by the states, except that the Founding Fathers rejected proposals that would have allowed for impeachment in cases of *maladministration, malpractice,* or *neglect of duty.* The Founding Fathers favored a chief executive who was subject to constitutional checks and balances, but not one who was weak and easy to remove by political opponents. In the end, the Senate voted to acquit President Clinton. Neither article of impeachment was supported by even a majority of votes, far short of the 67 votes required to convict.

Although the president participates in the lawmaking process by preparing budgets for congressional review, recommending legislation on certain subjects, and signing and vetoing bills passed by both houses, no formal lawmaking powers are specifically delegated to the EXECUTIVE BRANCH. The president nonetheless "legislates" by issuing executive orders, decrees, and proclamations. No express provision of the Constitution delineates the parameters of this executive lawmaking power. However, in YOUNGSTOWN SHEET & TUBE CO. V. SAWYER, 343 U.S. 579, 72 S. Ct. 863, 96 L. Ed. 1153 (1952), the Supreme Court set forth some guidelines. Known as the *Steel Seizure* case, *Youngstown* examined the issue of whether the president of the United States could order the government seizure of steel mills that were crippled by a labor strike during the KOREAN WAR. In holding the EXECUTIVE ORDER unconstitutional, the Supreme Court ruled that "the President's power to see that the laws are faithfully executed refutes the idea that [the president] is to be a lawmaker."

Justice ROBERT H. JACKSON, in a concurring opinion, set forth an analysis by which the Supreme Court has subsequently evaluated the constitutionality of presidential action. Jackson opined that PRESIDENTIAL POWERS are not fixed, but fluctuate according to "their disjunction or conjunction with those of Congress." When the president acts pursuant to congressional authorization, the action carries maximum authority. When the executive acts contrary to congressional will, presidential powers are at their lowest ebb. Between these positions, when a president faces an issue on which Congress is silent, the executive acts in "a zone of twilight in which [the president] and Congress may have concurrent authority, or in which the distribution is uncertain." In such instances, Jackson reasoned, courts must balance the interests of the parties and of society to determine if a particular executive action has violated the separation of powers.

Another area that has stirred debate over the appropriate separation of powers involves the delegation of legislative, executive, and judicial authority to federal administrative bodies. Since the mid-1930s, the United States has seen an enormous growth in the administrative state. Administrative agencies have been created to establish, evaluate, and apply rules and policies over a diverse area of law, including taxes, SECURITIES, transportation, antitrust, the environment, and employment relations. Federal administrative bodies are created by statute, and Congress has the authority to prescribe the qualifications for administrative officials who are appointed by the president, courts of law, and heads of government departments.

The NATIONAL LABOR RELATIONS BOARD (NLRB) demonstrates the overlapping powers that may be exercised by an administrative body. The NLRB is empowered by statute to issue regulations that govern union activities. Such regulations are virtually indistinguishable from legislative enactments and are considered no less authoritative. The NLRB also adjudicates disputes between unions and employers, with an administrative law judge presiding over such cases. Finally, the NLRB is endowed with the power to make prosecutorial decisions, a power traditionally exercised by the executive branch. Although successful challenges have been lodged against the delegation of certain powers to federal administrative bodies, by and large, the Supreme Court has permitted administrative officials and agencies to play all three government roles.

Article III: The Judicial Power Article III provides that "[t]he judicial Power of the United States, shall be vested in one supreme Court, and in such inferior Courts as the Congress may from time to time ordain and establish." Pursuant to this constitutional authorization, Congress has created a federal judicial system comprising a lower tier of federal trial courts, known as the U.S. district courts, and an intermediate tier of federal appellate courts, known as the U.S. COURTS OF APPEALS. At least one federal district court is located in each of the 50 states.

The federal appellate courts consist of 11 numbered circuit courts plus the Court of Appeals for the District of Columbia and the Court of Appeals for the Federal Circuit. Each federal appellate court has jurisdiction over a certain geographic area and may only hear appeals from federal district courts within that jurisdiction. Specialized courts of appeals have been created to hear appeals concerning such disputes as international trade (the court of International Trade) and military matters (the Court of Military Appeals). Parties aggrieved by a decision made by any of these federal appellate courts may appeal their case to the Supreme Court, which has the ultimate judicial power. Cases that originate in state court and present a federal question may also be appealed to the U.S. Supreme Court.

The Supreme Court is not required to hear every case that is appealed to it; instead, the Court has broad discretion to accept or decline cases that are appealed by a lower court. Only four justices need to vote in favor of hearing an appeal before a writ of certiorari will be granted. Certiorari is a device that allows the Supreme Court to call up the records of a lower court and review them in order to identify important legal questions that need to be resolved. Granting "cert" has no bearing on the Court's subsequent resolution of a case. The Court is asked to review about 5,000 cases a year and grants certiorari in less than 250 of them.

Federal courts do not have jurisdiction to hear every kind of lawsuit. Article III lists certain types of cases that may be heard by the federal judiciary, including cases arising under the Constitution; under treaties with foreign nations; and under federal laws passed by Congress, the executive, or an administrative body. Federal courts also have jurisdiction to hear lawsuits between two or more states, between citizens of different states, and between a citizen or government of one state and a citizen or government of a foreign country.

The Supreme Court has original jurisdiction over cases involving ambassadors and other public ministers as well as cases in which a state government is a party. Original jurisdiction gives a court the power to hear a lawsuit from the beginning, rather than on appeal. This grant of original jurisdiction does not preclude Congress from giving original jurisdiction to other courts over the same matters. In fact, Congress has granted concurrent original jurisdiction to the federal district courts for all controversies except those between state governments.

Nowhere in Article III, or elsewhere in the Constitution, is the power of the federal judiciary defined. Historically, the role of English and U.S. courts was to interpret and apply the laws passed by the other two branches of government. At the close of the eighteenth century, it was unclear whether that role included the prerogative of JUDICIAL REVIEW, which is the authority of state and federal courts to review and invalidate laws passed by legislatures that violate a constitutional provision or principle.

In MARBURY V. MADISON, 5 U.S. (1 Cranch) 137, 2 L. Ed. 60 (1803), the U.S. Supreme Court clarified this AMBIGUITY by pronouncing that it "is emphatically the duty of the judicial department to say what the law is. Those who apply the rule to particular cases, must of necessity expound and interpret the rule. If two laws conflict with each other, the court must decide on the operation of each." Because the federal Constitution is the supreme law of the land, the Court reasoned, any laws that violate the Constitution must be declared void. It was the essence of judicial duty, the Court intimated, for judges to evaluate the constitutionality of a particular act, because judges are not elected and are therefore independent from the political considerations that may have motivated the popular branches of government to enact that law. The Court reasoned that the executive and legislative branches could not be impartial arbiters of their own laws.

The Bill of Rights

When the U.S. Constitution was ratified by the states in 1789, it contained no bill of rights. During the last days of the Constitutional Convention, one of the delegates proposed that a bill of rights be included, but this proposal was voted down by every state. Many Framers of the Constitution believed that there was no need for a bill of rights because the powers of Congress and of the president were explicitly enumerated and limited, and no provision of the Constitution authorized any branch of government to invade the personal liberties of U.S. citizens.

Other Framers were concerned that any list of rights would be hopelessly incomplete and that the government would deny any liberties left unmentioned. This concern was ultimately expressed by the NINTH AMENDMENT to the U.S. Constitution, which provides that "[t]he enumeration in the Constitution, of certain rights, shall not be construed to deny or disparage oth-

ers retained by the people." The Ninth Amendment was later relied on by the Supreme Court to recognize the unenumerated right of married adults to use BIRTH CONTROL (GRISWOLD V. CONNECTICUT, 381 U.S. 479, 85 S. Ct. 1678, 14 L. Ed. 2d 510 [1965]).

By 1791, the need for a bill of rights was viewed in a different light. The residents of the states soon realized that government by the will of the majority not only achieved democracy, it sometimes achieved majoritarian tyranny. The system of checks and balances created by the original Constitution was insufficient to avoid the pitfalls of absolute power endemic to the English form of government that the American colonists had overthrown. A bill of rights was needed to serve as a bulwark between individual liberty and ARBITRARY government power.

As with each of the 26 amendments to the Constitution, the Bill of Rights was proposed by a two-thirds majority in both houses of Congress and ratified by three-fourths of the states as required by Article V. The Bill of Rights, which comprises the first ten amendments to the Constitution, contains both procedural and substantive protections. In some instances, these protections guarantee the right to do, say, or believe something without government interference. In other instances, these protections guarantee the right to refrain from doing, saying, or believing something without government coercion.

The first three amendments provide substantive protections. The FIRST AMENDMENT guarantees FREEDOM OF SPEECH, press, religion, assembly, and petition. The Free Speech Clause protects "thoughts that we hate" (*United States v. Schwimmer*, 279 U.S. 644, 49 S. Ct. 448, 73 L. Ed. 889 [1929] [Holmes J., dissenting]). Such thoughts can be expressed verbally, as in a racially derogatory remark, or in writing, as in a Marxist-Leninist pamphlet denouncing the U.S. government, and still receive First Amendment protection. The First Amendment also protects certain symbolic expression, such as burning the U.S. flag in protest over government policy (TEXAS V. JOHNSON, 491 U.S. 397, 109 S. Ct. 2533, 105 L. Ed. 2d 342 [1989]). The Supreme Court has ruled that no political speech may be curtailed by the government unless it presents a CLEAR AND PRESENT DANGER of imminent lawless action (*Brandenburg v. Ohio*, 395 U.S. 444, 89 S. Ct. 1827, 23 L. Ed. 2d 430 [1969]).

The Free Press Clause prohibits the government from censoring news stories in the print and electronic media merely because the content is critical of the government. However, the Founding Fathers did not agree on the definition of *censorship*.

A majority of the Founding Fathers adhered to the English COMMON LAW view articulated in the eighteenth century by SIR WILLIAM BLACKSTONE, who equated a free press with the doctrine of no PRIOR RESTRAINT. This doctrine provides that a publication cannot be suppressed by the government before it is released to the public. Nor can publication of something be conditioned upon judicial approval before its release.

While the English common law prohibited prior restraint, it permitted prosecution for libelous and seditious material after publication. Thus, the law protected vituperative political publications only insofar as the author was prepared to serve time in jail or pay a fine for offending the sensibilities of the wrong person.

A minority of Founding Fathers adhered to the view articulated by JAMES MADISON, who said that

> The security of the freedom of the press requires that it should be exempt, not only from previous restraint of the executive, as in Great Britain; but from legislative restraint also; and this exemption, not only from the previous inspection of licensers, but from the subsequent penalty of laws.

Madison was concerned that authors would be deterred from writing articles assailing governmental activity if the government was permitted to prosecute them following release of their works to the public.

In NEAR V. MINNESOTA, 283 U.S. 697, 51 S. Ct 625, 75 L. Ed. 2d 1357 (1931), the Supreme Court incorporated the doctrine of no prior restraint in First Amendment JURISPRUDENCE, when it ruled that under the Free Press Clause there is a constitutional presumption against prior restraint which may not be overcome unless the government can demonstrate that CENSORSHIP is necessary to prevent a *clear and present danger* of a national security breach. In NEW YORK TIMES V. UNITED STATES, 403 U.S. 713 92 S.Ct 2140, 29 L. Ed.2d 822 (1971) the Court applied this presumption against the United States JUSTICE DEPARTMENT which had sought an INJUNCTION to prevent the publication of classified material revealing the secrecy and deception behind American involvement in the Vietnam War. If this classified material, also known as the Pentagon Papers, had threatened American troops by disclosing their location or movement, the Court said, publication would not have been permitted.

The Supreme Court's interpretation of the Free Press Clause has also gone a long way toward adopting Madison's sentiments against subsequent punishments for publishers of materials criticizing public officials. In a series of cases the Supreme Court has held that the First Amendment protects media outlets from being held liable in civil court for money damages merely because a published story contains an inaccuracy or falsehood about a public official. The Supreme Court has ruled that the media are immune from LIBEL actions brought by public officials unless the plaintiff can demonstrate that a particular story was printed or aired with knowledge that it was false or in reckless disregard of its veracity, a principle that has become known as the "actual-malice" standard (NEW YORK TIMES V. SULLIVAN, 376 U.S. 254, 84 S. Ct. 710, 11 L. Ed. 2d 686 [1964]). Finally, the media cannot be punished with civil or criminal sanctions for publishing pornographic material unless that material rises to the level of OBSCENITY (MILLER V. CALIFORNIA, 413 U.S. 15, 93 S. Ct. 2607, 37 L. Ed. 2d 419 [1973]).

The First Amendment contains two religion clauses. One guarantees the free exercise of religion. In most instances, the Free Exercise Clause prohibits the government from compelling a person to act contrary to his or her religious beliefs. For example, in *Wisconsin v. Yoder,* 406 U.S. 205, 92 S. Ct. 1526, 32 L. Ed. 2d 15 (1972), the Supreme Court held that a state cannot compel Amish parents to send their children to school past the eighth grade when doing so would violate their religious faith. However, in *Reynolds v. United States,* 8 U.S. 145, 25 L. Ed. 244 (1879), the Supreme Court refused to exempt Mormons from a federal law against bigamy, reasoning that POLYGAMY was more a religious practice than a religious belief.

The other religion clause in the First Amendment prohibits the government from establishing religion. The Framers drafted the Establishment Clause to prevent the federal government from passing legislation that would create an official national church in the United States as Great Britain had done with the Anglican Church in England. Since the early 1970s, the Supreme Court has applied the Establishment Clause more broadly to strike down certain forms of government assistance to religion, such as financial aid. Such assistance will be invalidated unless the government demonstrates that it has a secular purpose with a primary effect that neither advances nor inhibits religion nor fosters excessive entanglement between government and religion (*Lemon v. Kurtzman,* 403 U.S. 602, 91 S. Ct. 2105, 29 L. Ed. 2d 745 [1971]).

The Second and Third Amendments also provide substantive protections. The SECOND AMENDMENT acknowledges that a "well regulated Militia" is "necessary to the security of a free State," and guarantees "the right of the people to keep and to bear Arms." The right to bear arms is not absolute. It restricts only federal laws regulating the use and possession of firearms and has no applicability to state governments (*Presser v. Illinois,* 116 U.S. 252, 6 S. Ct. 580, 29 L. Ed. 615 [1886]). In addition, Congress may prohibit the possession or use of a firearm that lacks any reasonable relationship to the preservation or efficiency of a well-regulated militia (*United States v. Miller,* 307 U.S. 174, 59 S. Ct. 816, 83 L. Ed. 1206 [1939]). Federal courts have interpreted the term *militia* to include only military groups that are organized by the state governments, such as the NATIONAL GUARD, and to exclude private military groups that are not associated with the government, such as the Kansas POSSE COMITATUS (*United States v. Oakes,* 564 F.2d 384 [10th Cir. 1977]).

The THIRD AMENDMENT, which is an outgrowth of the American Revolution, prohibits the government from compelling homeowners to house soldiers without their consent. Although the Supreme Court has never decided a case that directly involved the forced quartering of soldiers, the Court of Appeals for the Second Circuit ruled that the Third Amendment's protections apply to the National Guard (*Engblom v. Carey,* 724 F.2d 28 [2d Cir. 1982]).

The Fourth, Fifth, Sixth, Seventh, and Eighth Amendments contain a mixture of procedural and substantive rights. Most of the procedural rights pertain to CRIMINAL LAW. As such, these rights offer protection against unconstitutional actions taken by government bodies and officials, such as law enforcement agencies and agents. These rights do not offer protection against action taken by private citizens unaffiliated with the government. For example, the FOURTH AMENDMENT prohibits the government from performing unreasonable SEARCHES AND SEIZURES and from issuing warrants on less than PROBABLE CAUSE. The procedural requirements of the Fourth Amendment protect homes, papers, and other personal belongings in which an individual can demonstrate a "reasonable expectation of privacy" (*Katz v. United States,* 389 U.S. 347, 88 S. Ct. 507, 19 L. Ed. 2d 576 [1967]).

The FIFTH AMENDMENT offers procedural safeguards to criminal defendants and suspects. It provides that no person shall be held to answer for a capital or infamous offense unless first indicted by a GRAND JURY. The Fifth Amendment further safeguards defendants from being "twice put in jeopardy of life or limb" for the "same offence." It also prohibits the government from compelling someone to incriminate himself or herself. The right to be apprised of many of these procedural protections during custodial police interrogations, through what are known as *Miranda* warnings, is derived from the Fifth Amendment (MIRANDA V. ARIZONA, 384 U.S. 436, 86 S. Ct. 1602, 16 L. Ed. 2d 694 [1966]).

The SIXTH AMENDMENT provides a panoply of procedural protections for criminal defendants. Under the Sixth Amendment, defendants are entitled to notice of any criminal accusations against them. The Sixth Amendment guarantees the right to a jury trial for all crimes more serious than a petty offense. The Sixth Amendment guarantees the right to be represented by an attorney during a criminal proceeding and entitles indigent defendants to a state-appointed lawyer when they are charged with a misdemeanor or more serious offense (GIDEON V. WAINWRIGHT, 372 U.S. 355, 83 S. Ct. 792, 9 L. Ed. 2d 799 [1963]). A defendant's right to a speedy and public trial in which she or he can cross-examine adverse witnesses and subpoena favorable witnesses is also protected by the Sixth Amendment.

The protections offered by the EIGHTH AMENDMENT are more substantive. This amendment forbids the government from inflicting a punishment that is "cruel and unusual." The Eighth Amendment also prohibits the government from setting bail in an excessive amount and from imposing a fine that is disproportionate to the seriousness of the crime. Under the CRUEL AND UNUSUAL PUNISHMENTS CLAUSE, the Supreme Court has ruled that it is not necessarily unconstitutional for the government to execute a mentally retarded person (*Penry v. Lynaugh,* 492 U.S. 302, 109 S. Ct. 2934, 106 L. Ed. 2d 256 [1989]) or a juvenile above the age of 15 (*Stanford v. Kentucky,* 492 U.S. 361, 109 S. Ct. 2969, 106 L. Ed. 2d 306 [1989]).

Some of the protections offered by the Bill of Rights apply to civil proceedings. For example, the SEVENTH AMENDMENT guarantees the right to a jury trial in civil "Suits at common law." In condemnation proceedings, the Fifth Amendment recognizes the power of EMINENT DOMAIN, by which the government may appropriate a piece of property owned by a private citizen and convert it to a public use. Concomitantly, the Fifth Amendment guarantees the right to "just compensation" for private landowners when the government exercises its power of eminent domain.

Due Process Clauses

Of all the liberties protected by the Bill of Rights, none has been a greater source of constitutional litigation than DUE PROCESS. The Fifth Amendment provides that no person shall be deprived of "life, liberty, or property, without due process of law." The Supreme Court has interpreted this provision to regulate actions taken by only the federal government, not the state governments (BARRON V. BALTIMORE, 32 U.S. [7 Pet.] 243, 8 L. Ed. 672 [1833]).

Broadly speaking, the Due Process Clause of the Fifth Amendment guarantees litigants the right to be informed of any legal action being taken against them, and the opportunity to be heard during a fair proceeding in which they may assert relevant claims and defenses. Specifically, many procedural protections have been recognized by the Supreme Court as essential to the concept of due process. For example, in criminal cases, the Due Process Clause requires that the prosecution prove its case BEYOND A REASONABLE DOUBT before a conviction may be obtained. In civil cases, the Due Process Clause prohibits a court in one state from asserting jurisdiction over a resident in another state unless that resident has sufficient contacts with the jurisdiction in which that court sits.

The FOURTEENTH AMENDMENT also contains a Due Process Clause. Whereas the Due Process Clause of the Fifth Amendment regulates only the federal government, the Due Process Clause of the Fourteenth Amendment regulates actions taken by state governments. During the twentieth century, the Supreme Court interpreted the Due Process Clause of the Fourteenth Amendment to make most of the liberties enumerated in the Bill of Rights applicable to the states.

Through a series of decisions, the Supreme Court has ruled that certain liberties guaranteed in the Bill of Rights are too fundamental to be denied protection by the state governments. Only the right to bear arms, the right to be indicted by a grand jury, the right to a jury trial in civil cases, the right against excessive bail and fines, and the right against involuntary quartering of soldiers have not been made applicable to the states. Because these constitutional guarantees remain inapplicable to state governments, the Supreme Court is said to have selectively incorporated the Bill of Rights into the Due Process Clause of the Fourteenth Amendment.

The Supreme Court has interpreted the Due Process Clauses to have a substantive content in addition to their procedural content. Procedurally, due process prescribes the manner in which the government may deprive persons of their life, liberty, or property. In short, the procedural guarantees of due process entitle litigants to fair process.

Substantively, the Due Process Clauses of the Fifth and Fourteenth Amendments protect persons from legislation infringing on certain individual rights. Such individual rights may be expressly enumerated in a constitutional provision, as are the liberties that are enumerated in the Bill of Rights and have been incorporated into the Due Process Clause of the Fourteenth Amendment. Since DRED SCOTT V. SANDFORD, 60 U.S. (19 How.) 393, 15 L. Ed. 691 [1856]), where the Supreme Court recognized a slave owner's property interest in his slaves, the Due Process Clauses have been interpreted to protect other liberties that are not expressly enumerated in any provision of the federal Constitution.

These unenumerated rights have been derived from Supreme Court precedent, common law, history, and moral philosophy. Such rights, the Court said, "represent the very essence of ordered liberty" and embody "principles of justice so rooted in the traditions and conscience of our people as to be ranked fundamental" (*Palko v. Connecticut*, 302 U.S. 319, 58 S. Ct. 149, 82 L. Ed. 288 [1937]). Since the mid-1960s, the Supreme Court has relied on the concept of SUBSTANTIVE DUE PROCESS to establish a general right to privacy that protects a woman's decision to terminate her pregnancy under certain circumstances (ROE V. WADE, 410 U.S. 113, 93 S. Ct. 705, 35 L. Ed. 2d 147 [1973]).

Equal Protection Clause

The EQUAL PROTECTION CLAUSE of the Fourteenth Amendment has been another bountiful source of litigation. Ratified during the aftermath of the Civil War along with the THIRTEENTH AMENDMENT, which outlawed SLAVERY, and the FIFTEENTH AMENDMENT, which protected the right to vote from discriminatory infringement, the Fourteenth Amendment was designed to promote racial equality.

Until the middle of the twentieth century, the Supreme Court interpreted the Equal Protection Clause to permit state-implemented racial SEGREGATION. Then, in BROWN V. BOARD OF EDUCATION, 347 U.S. 483, 74 S. Ct. 686, 98 L. Ed. 873 (1954), the Supreme Court declared that the institution of segregation is inherently unequal. Almost immediately after issuing the *Brown* decision, the Court began striking down state-implemented racial segregation at a host of public accommodations, including golf courses, beaches, and public schools. Pursuant to the Fourteenth Amendment, Congress has passed a number of CIVIL RIGHTS statutes that protect African Americans and other racial groups from discrimination in the private sector. Title VII of the Civil Rights Act of 1964 (Pub. L. No. 88-352 [42 U.S.C.A. § 2000e et seq.]), for example, prohibits RACIAL DISCRIMINATION in private employment.

Persons of any race, creed, or ethnic origin may bring a claim against a state government for discriminating against them in violation of the Fourteenth Amendment. The Supreme Court has also relied on the Equal Protection Clause to invalidate state laws that discriminate on the basis of gender, state residency, and national citizenship, among other legislative classifications. In 1996 the U.S. Supreme Court struck down a Colorado constitutional amendment that discriminated against homosexuals, because it served no rational purpose (ROMER V. EVANS, 517 U.S. 620, 116 S. Ct. 1620, 134 L. Ed. 2d 855 [1996]). The CIVIL RIGHTS ACT of 1871 (17 Stat. 13 [42 U.S.C.A. § 1983]) authorizes individuals to enforce the provisions of the Fourteenth Amendment against state governments.

Members of other minority groups, such as persons who are elderly or disabled, are protected from discrimination in both the public and private sectors by federal laws that Congress has passed pursuant to its constitutionally delegated powers. The Americans with Disabilities Act (Pub. L. No. 101-336 [codified at 42 U.S.C.A. §§ 12111 et seq.]) and the Age Discrimination in Employment Act (Pub. L. No. 90-202 [codified at 29 U.S.C.A. § 621 et seq.]) are two such laws.

Supremacy Clause

The SUPREMACY CLAUSE in Article VI makes the Constitution, federal laws, and treaties "the supreme Law of the Land." Under this clause, state courts may not interpret the Bill of Rights, or any other constitutional provision, differently than does the Supreme Court. States may not provide less protection for individual liberties than is provided under the federal Constitution. However, state courts do retain the power to afford their residents greater protection for certain liberties established by their own state constitution than is afforded by the federal Constitution (*Prune Yard Shopping Center v. Robins,* 447 U.S. 74, 100 S. Ct. 2035, 64 L. Ed. 2d 741 [1980]).

Other Constitutional Provisions

The Nineteenth, Twenty-fourth, and Twenty-sixth Amendments provide that the right to vote shall not be denied to a U.S. citizen on account of gender, age (so long as the citizen is at least eighteen years old), or the failure to pay a poll tax. The TWENTY-FIRST AMENDMENT repeals the EIGHTEENTH AMENDMENT, which banned the manufacture, sale, and transportation of intoxicating liquors, otherwise known as PROHIBITION. The SIXTEENTH AMENDMENT establishes the congressional power to lay and collect income taxes.

The Tenth and Eleventh Amendments attempt to preserve the federalist system created by the Constitution, whereby the state and federal governments share sovereignty and jurisdiction. Recognizing the threat presented by an omnipotent federal government, the TENTH AMENDMENT reserves to the states all powers not delegated to the federal government. The text of the ELEVENTH AMENDMENT restricts federal courts from hearing lawsuits against state governments brought by the residents of another state or the citizens of a foreign country. The Supreme Court has also interpreted the Eleventh Amendment to restrict federal courts from hearing lawsuits instituted by residents of the state being sued and lawsuits initiated by the governments of foreign countries.

FURTHER READINGS

Hall, Kermit L. 2002. *Oxford Companion to American Law.* New York: Oxford Univ. Press.

Posner, Richard A. 1999. *An Affair of the State.* Cambridge, Mass.: Harvard Univ. Press.

CROSS-REFERENCES

Abortion; Administrative Law and Procedure; Age Discrimination; Commerce Clause; Congress of the United States;

Constitution of the United States; Criminal Procedure; Custodial Interrogation; Disability Discrimination; Double Jeopardy; Federal Budget; Federalism; Freedom of the Press; Gay and Lesbian Rights; Incorporation Doctrine; Right to Counsel; Sex Discrimination; Speedy Trial.

CONSTRUCTION

The process by which the meaning of an ambiguous provision of a statute, written document, or oral agreement is determined.

A judge usually makes a construction of an unclear term in a document at issue in a case that involves a dispute as to its legal significance. The judge examines the circumstances surrounding the provision, laws, other writings, verbal agreements dealing with the same subject matter, and the probable purpose of the unclear phrase in order to conclude the proper meaning of such words. Once the judge has done so, the court will enforce the words as construed. However, for language that is plain and clear, there cannot be a construction.

When ambiguous language is given its exact and technical meaning, and no other equitable considerations or reasonable implications are made, there has been a strict or literal construction of the unclear term.

A liberal or equitable construction permits a term to be reasonably and fairly evaluated so as to implement the object and purpose for which the document is designed. This does not mean that the words will be strained beyond their natural or customary meanings.

A rule of construction is a principle that either governs the effect of the ascertained intention of a document or agreement containing an ambiguous term or establishes what a court should do if the intention is neither express nor implied. A regular pattern of decisions concerning the application of a particular provision of a statute is a rule of construction that governs how the text is to be applied in similar cases.

The constitutionality of an ambiguous statute is a QUESTION OF LAW and a matter of construction within the province of the court. The meaning of the language of the statute must be determined in light of its objectives, purposes, and practical effect as a whole. If a statute is so ambiguous that a judge cannot make a reasonable construction of its disputed provisions, and a reasonable person could not determine from reading it what the law orders or prohibits, it is VOID FOR VAGUENESS because it violates the guarantee of DUE PROCESS OF LAW.

Some states have codified terms that had in the past been subject to repeated judicial construction. The need for court proceedings to determine the real meaning of some terms has been eliminated by enactment of statutes that give specific meanings—such as specifying that "calendar day" means a twenty-four hour period starting on midnight of one date and ending midnight of the next day.

CROSS-REFERENCES

Canons of Construction; Judicial Action.

CONSTRUCTIVE

That which exists, not in fact, but as a result of the operation of law. That which takes on a character as a consequence of the way it is treated by a rule or policy of law, as opposed to its actual character.

For example, *constructive knowledge* is notice of a fact that a person is presumed by law to have, regardless of whether he or she actually does, since such knowledge is obtainable by the exercise of reasonable care.

For example, possession of the key to a safe-deposit box is *constructive possession* of the contents of the box since the key gives its holder power and control over the contents.

CONSTRUCTIVE DESERTION

The end of marital COHABITATION *brought about when one spouse, by his or her conduct, forces the other to leave home.*

Constructive desertion takes place when a husband or wife intentionally forces the innocent spouse to leave the marital dwelling by acting in an offensive manner. The misconduct must be so extensive as to make marital relations insufferable.

Authority is divided on what constitutes justification for leaving the marital abode. The narrow view is that only conduct that would be grounds for DIVORCE is adequate. In application of this view, cruelty, nonsupport, ADULTERY, or other divorce grounds must be proved before the innocence of the fleeing spouse can be established. Stringent requirements limit the doctrine; in some states a mere unjustified refusal to have sexual relations with one's spouse for a certain length of time constitutes constructive desertion. Similarly, if one spouse communicates venereal disease to the mate, this might constitute constructive desertion. The prolonged nagging or drunkenness of a spouse is not ordinarily viewed as misconduct that would justify marital dissolution based upon constructive desertion.

CONSTRUCTIVE EVICTION

The disturbance, by a landlord, of a tenant's possession of premises that the landlord makes uninhabitable and unsuitable for the purposes for which they were leased, causing the tenant to surrender possession.

Constructive eviction arises when a landlord does not actually evict but does something that renders the premises untenantable. This might occur, for example, where a tenant vacates an apartment because a landlord turns off the heat or water.

The term is also used to mean the breach of a COVENANT of WARRANTY and QUIET ENJOYMENT of real property, which prevents a purchaser from obtaining possession of property due to the existence of a paramount claim of title.

CROSS-REFERENCES

Landlord and Tenant.

CONSTRUCTIVE TRUST

A relationship by which a person who has obtained title to property has an equitable duty to transfer it to another, to whom it rightfully belongs, on the basis that the acquisition or retention of it is wrongful and would unjustly enrich the person if he or she were allowed to retain it.

A constructive trust does not arise because of the expressed intent of a settlor, one who establishes a trust. It is created by a court whenever title to property is held by a person who, in fairness, should not be permitted to retain it. It is frequently based on disloyalty or other breach of trust by an express trustee (the person appointed or required by law to execute a trust), and it is also created where no express trust is created but property is obtained or retained by other UNCONSCIONABLE conduct. The court employs the constructive trust as a remedial device to compel the defendant to convey title to the property to the plaintiff. It treats the defendant as if he or she had been an express trustee from the date of the unlawful holding of the property in question. A constructive trust is not a trust, in the true meaning of the word, in which the trustee is to have duties of administration enduring for a substantial period of time, but rather it is a passive, temporary arrangement, in which the trustee's sole duty is to transfer the title and possession to the beneficiary.

The right to a constructive trust is generally an alternative remedy. The aggrieved party can choose between a trust and other relief at law, such as recovery of money wrongfully taken, but cannot obtain both types of relief.

A constructive trust, as with an express trust, must cover specific property. It cannot be predicated on mere possession of property, or on a breach of contract where no ownership of property is involved.

The court decides what acts are required of the plaintiff as conditions precedent to the securing of a decree (a court order that determines the rights of all the parties to the suit). For example, if the defendant has acquired title to property of the plaintiff by means of FRAUD, the plaintiff will be required to return any consideration (inducement to enter into a contract) received from the defendant. In addition, if the defendant has, during his or her period of wrongful retention of the property, spent money for the preservation or protection of the property, such as by paying taxes or the principal or interest on a mortgage, reimbursement might be required of the plaintiff. If the defendant has made improvements or performed services in managing the property, some courts require the plaintiff to compensate the defendant to the extent of the benefits inuring to the plaintiff through the imposition of a constructive trust, particularly in cases in which the defendant was not an intentional wrongdoer, but rather acted under mistake or ignorance.

The decree establishing the constructive trust requires the defendant to deliver possession and convey title to the property and to pay to the plaintiff profits received or rental value during the period of wrongful holding and otherwise to adjust the equities of the parties after taking an accounting.

Mistake, Undue Influence, or Duress

If by MISTAKE OF FACT the plaintiff conveys title to the wrong person, or the wrong property is conveyed to the intended person, or the plaintiff is otherwise induced to act by reason of mistake, the transfer can be set aside. An alternative is to obtain a decree which reforms the instrument of conveyance so that it expresses the intent of the parties. In these cases, the conveyance is not void (without legal effect). The plaintiff actually intends a transfer, but the circumstances which cause the plaintiff's mind to operate are such that the court considers it unfair for the transferee to retain the property.

The same doctrine applies where the plaintiff is induced to make the conveyance through the exertion of UNDUE INFLUENCE (conduct by a person that dominates and destroys the free will of another). If the conduct of the defendant goes beyond persuading the plaintiff to convey—if it encompasses violence, threats of violence or restraint, or other injury—there is an even stronger case for charging the transferee as a constructive trustee on the ground of duress.

Fraudulent Misrepresentation or Concealment

The courts hold in numerous cases that a transferee who uses fraud to obtain the transfer of property is a constructive trustee. Such situations might involve an affirmative assertion of the truth of a material fact or concealment of the existence of a material fact when there was a duty to speak. The state of the defendant's mind is a material fact and might be a basis for a constructive trust—such as when the defendant promises to use the property for certain purposes beneficial to the plaintiff but intends at the time of the transfer to retain it for himself or herself. The defrauded party can also proceed on the theory of setting aside the transfer, which is substantially equivalent to obtaining a constructive trust, or the defrauded party can sue for damages.

Property Obtained by Homicide

If a person obtains property through a will or intestacy by wrongfully and intentionally killing the owner, a constructive trust can be decreed as to the property obtained. The beneficiaries of the constructive trust imposed on the murderer are those persons who would have taken by intestacy or will or otherwise from the murdered person, as if the murderer had predeceased the victim.

Statutes in many states prevent the murderer from acquiring or retaining the property of the victim. They vary from state to state, but most require that the excluded person must be convicted of wrongfully and intentionally causing the death of the property owner. None applies to negligent killing. It is not necessary for the murderer to have committed the crime for the purpose of acquiring the property. The statutes apply if the murderer commits suicide immediately after killing the property holder. They do not apply, however, to an insane murderer or to one who kills in SELF-DEFENSE.

Gift by Will or Intestacy Based upon Broken Promise

If a property owner is induced to make an absolute gift to the defendant by will due to reliance on an oral promise by the defendant to apply all or part of the property to the use of another designated person and, after the death of the testator, the defendant refuses to do as promised, he or she can be made a constructive trustee. The same result will hold when the property owner is induced to die intestate on the faith of an oral agreement by his or her heir or next of kin.

If the recipient by will or intestacy promises to hold for others to be later described by the property owner and no description is communicated to the recipient until after the death of the property owner, the recipient will hold as a trustee of a RESULTING TRUST for the heirs, next of kin, or residuary legatees or devisees of the property owner. No trust will be established for the intended beneficiaries but such persons might take the property as the recipients of the resulting trust.

If a will provides that a gift is to be made to a recipient as trustee, but no description of the beneficiary appears in the will, and the recipient verbally agrees to hold it for beneficiaries who are orally or otherwise informally described to the recipient, the successors of the decedent can enforce a resulting trust in their favor against the recipient. The courts rely on the argument that a property owner who wishes the property to pass to others than the heirs at his or her death must give it to those others by a formally executed will.

Breach of Express Trust by Disloyalty

If a trustee of an express trust acquires property by a breach of trust—for example, by a violation of an obligation to be loyal to the beneficiary—a constructive trust can be imposed on such property. The constructive trust can be applied not only to the property originally obtained by disloyalty, but also to its products and proceeds. It can be used against persons who succeed the disloyal trustee as the owner of the products of the disloyalty if they are not bona fide purchasers.

It is immaterial that the trustee acted innocently because of ignorance or in the belief that the conduct was not disloyal. It is unnecessary to prove that the acquisition of the property by disloyalty damaged the beneficiary, since it is sufficient to show the receipt by the trustee of property obtained by breach of his or her duty.

In addition, the duty and the remedy exist with respect to persons who are in a confidential relation. This term has no exact definition but entails dominance and superiority of one individual over another because of such elements as a close familiar relationship, an enduring practice of entrusting business matters to the knowledge of a confidant, and differences in age, health, and education.

Breach of Duty in Direct Dealing with Beneficiary

The trustee has a duty to make a complete disclosure and to treat the beneficiary with the utmost fairness when there is a direct conveyance, contract, or other transaction between them. This duty extends to everyone who acts as a fiduciary and to persons in a confidential relation, similar to the duty of loyalty in the administration of a trust. It is a duty arising from the superiority and dominance of the fiduciary and the danger of overreaching or undue influence.

The trustee or other representative can be declared a constructive trustee of any property obtained through a transaction where there was a breach of the duty to make full disclosure and to act fairly. Such clearly inequitable conduct justifies the imposition of a constructive trust. If, therefore, a trustee purchases the interest of one of the beneficiaries under the trust for an inadequate price, without revealing facts that the beneficiary did not know concerning the value of the interest being sold, and later the trustee realizes a profit on the transaction, a constructive trust can be imposed to remove this gain from the trustee.

Statute of Frauds

The STATUTE OF FRAUDS, an old ENGLISH LAW adopted in the United States that requires certain contracts to be in writing, does not apply to constructive trusts. The courts create constructive trusts, whether the evidence on which they are based is oral or written and whether the property involved is real or personal.

However, public policy favors the security of titles to property. Therefore, reluctant to disturb record title or other apparent ownership, courts require the plaintiff to prove his or her case for a constructive trust by clear and convincing evidence. In nearly all suits to establish constructive

trusts, the defendant appears to be the complete owner of the property, by virtue of deeds, wills, records, or otherwise. As a result, the courts reject the plaintiff's claim if the evidence is vague, conflicting, or dubious.

Breach of Unenforceable Contract to Convey Ordinarily the breach of an oral contract to convey realty by deed or will is not a basis for charging the defendant as a constructive trustee, where the defendant employs the statute of frauds as a defense and refuses to perform the contract. The statute provides that contracts to convey interests in land are not enforceable when they are not in writing and no memorandum was signed by the seller. To decree a constructive trust in such a case would usually constitute an evasion of the statute. The plaintiff can be protected adequately by an award of damages that, in effect, mandates a return of any consideration paid for the promise to convey.

With respect to the breach of some contracts, however, the constructive trust is occasionally used to prevent UNJUST ENRICHMENT, as in the case of a contract to leave property by will in return for personal services that have been rendered, the value of which is not computable in money.

Breach of Oral Trust of Realty by Retention of Property When the plaintiff conveys land by absolute deed (a document that transfers real property without restriction) based on an oral promise by the defendant to hold it in trust for the plaintiff or for a third person, and the defendant retains the property for his or her own benefit, refusing to execute the trust because it violates the statute of frauds, the majority of courts refuse to make the defendant a constructive trustee for the plaintiff or for the intended beneficiary of the oral trust. The courts reason that to construct a trust in such a case would circumvent the purpose of the statute of frauds.

A minority of courts grant the decree for a constructive trust for the intended beneficiary of the oral trust because they view it as dishonest for the defendant to withhold the land from the intended beneficiary by employing the statute.

If the defendant obtains the land by MISREPRESENTATION of the state of his or her mind as to intended performance of the oral trust or other false statement and later refuses to perform the trust, the court will enforce a constructive trust against him or her.

If the defendant was in a confidential or fiduciary relation with the plaintiff at the time of the deed and the oral promise to hold in trust, the defendant is usually made a constructive trustee for the intended beneficiary of the oral trust because the wrong entailed a violation of the relationship by repudiation of the promise.

Product of Theft

The remedy of constructive trust applies to PERSONAL PROPERTY that is stolen or misappropriated and used to purchase other property in the name of the perpetrator. A constructive trust in favor of the aggrieved party can be imposed on such property, so long as it remains in the hands of the wrongdoer or any person to whom the wrongdoer transfers it who is not a bona fide purchaser. In order to facilitate the unimpeded flow of commercial transactions, bona fide purchasers are not subject to the application of a constructive trust.

FURTHER READINGS

Condon, Gerald M., and Jeffrey L. Condon. 1996. *Beyond the Grave: The Right Way and the Wrong Way of Leaving Money to Your Children and Others.* New York: Harper-Information.

Daly, Eugene J. 1994. *Thy Will Be Done: A Guide to Wills, Taxation, and Estate Planning for Older Persons.* Amherst, N.Y.: Prometheus Books.

Kull, Andrew. 1998. "Restitution in Bankruptcy: Reclamation and Constructive Trust." *American Bankruptcy Law Journal* 72 (summer): 265–302.

Rapp, Geoffrey. 2000. "Reconsidering Educational Liability: Property-Owners as Litigants, Constructive Trust as Remedy." *Yale Law & Policy Review* 18 (fall): 463–84.

Sitarz, Daniel. 1999. *Wills and Trusts: Laws of the United States.* Carbondale, IL: Nova.

Weinrib, Laura. 2002. "Reconstructing Family: Constructive Trust at Relational Dissolution." *Harvard Civil Rights-Civil Liberties Law Review* 37 (winter): 207–47.

CROSS-REFERENCES

Bona Fide; Clear and Convincing Proof; Fiduciary; Misrepresentation; Personal Property; Unjust Enrichment.

CONSULAR COURT

A tribunal convened by public officials who reside in a foreign country to protect the interests of their country for the settlement of civil cases based upon situations that happened in the foreign nation and which is held pursuant to authority granted by treaty.

A consular court exercises criminal jurisdiction in some instances, but its determinations are reviewable by the courts of the home government. The last of the U.S. consular courts in Morocco was abolished in 1956.

CONSULAR LAW SOCIETY

Founded in 1940, the Consular Law Society is an association of lawyers serving consulates and/or embassies and other attorneys specializing in related international affairs. Its activities include the presentation of awards and the publication of occasional papers. Membership is by invitation.

Committees of the society include Diplomatic and Consular Practice; Governments in Exile; HUMAN RIGHTS; Immigration and Nationality; Immunities; International Companies; International and Comparative Law; International Double Taxation; International Copyright Relations; INTERNATIONAL LAW in U.S. Courts; Neutrality; Private Claims Against Governments; Recognition of States; and Treaties.

The society meets annually.

CONSULS

Public officials stationed in a foreign country who are responsible for developing and securing the economic interests of their government and safeguarding the welfare of their government's citizens who might be traveling or residing within their jurisdiction.

CROSS-REFERENCES

Ambassadors and Consuls.

CONSUMER

An individual who purchases and uses products and services in contradistinction to manufacturers who produce the goods or services and wholesalers or retailers who distribute and sell them. A member of the general category of persons who are protected by state and federal laws regulating price policies, financing practices, quality of goods and services, credit reporting, debt collection, and other trade practices of U.S. commerce. A purchaser of a product or service who has a legal right to enforce any implied or express warranties pertaining to the item against the manufacturer who has introduced the goods or services into the marketplace or the seller who has made them a term of the sale.

CONSUMER CREDIT

Short-term loans made to enable people to purchase goods or services primarily for personal, family, or household purposes.

Consumer credit transactions can be classified into several different classes.

Installment credit involves credit that is repaid by the borrower in several periodic payments; loans repaid in one lump sum are classified as *noninstallment credit.* Installment credit has expanded in popularity, with an increasing number of consumers buying goods on credit in order to spread repayment of the purchase price and the interest owed on the principal borrowed over an extended time.

Originator and Holder

The originator of credit is the person or company who originally extended the credit, while the holder is the individual or business who obtained the debt at a discounted price in order to collect payments at a subsequent time. Auto dealers are credit originators at the time a consumer purchases an auto on credit, but many loans are subsequently assigned by them to banks or sales finance companies, which become credit holders.

Commercial banks buy many consumer installment loans from car dealers and department stores and also participate in all aspects of consumer credit transactions both as originators and holders. The portion of the consumer credit market attributable to banks has greatly increased due in large part to widespread use of bank credit cards.

In addition, two types of finance companies are active in the consumer credit industry. The first type is the *small loan company,* which has contact with consumers as originators and makes loans to them directly. The other type is the *sales finance company,* which does not deal directly with consumers; it purchases and holds consumer installment debts related to the sale of durable goods on time. The distinction between the two decreases in importance as consumer finance companies diversify and engage in business on both levels.

Vendor and Lender

The law might regard credit differently, depending on whether it is offered by a vendor (seller). When an appliance store gives credit to customers who buy such items as washing machines and refrigerators and pay for them over a certain period of time, this action is known as *vendor credit.* When a consumer borrows funds from a finance company to pay for appliances, this action is known as *lender credit,* since the finance company lends but does not sell.

Some states exempt vendor credit transactions from the provisions of state USURY laws. A vendor or a lender can charge the consumer interest (a fee for the use over time of borrowed money). In the past, usury statutes restricting the legal interest rate have ordinarily been applied only to lender credit. The difference in the treatment of lender credit and vendor credit is based upon the assumption made by law that vendors are able to adjust their prices to allow for the period during which they await payment. If, for example, the vendor's *time price* was excessive in that it allowed for a high interest rate, then the consumer could opt for payment of the *cash price.* Courts believe that competitive pricing will prevent vendors from charging too much interest when they extend credit. It is the seller's right to determine how to reduce the time price to encourage consumers to pay cash for goods.

Some courts have found since 1970, however, that these principles have no application to revolving charge accounts because department stores do not charge consumers less for paying for items in cash. There is one uniform purchase price, regardless of whether the sale is a credit or cash transaction. Both finance charges and tax are computed on the basis of the cash price.

In cases where courts have indicated that state usury laws must necessarily be applied in the *vendor credit* extended through revolving charge account customers, state legislatures have enacted statutes to increase the legal rate of interest that may be charged on such accounts. Most consumer credit cannot exist within the usury law limits; therefore, the pattern has been to enact laws that permit special higher finance rates for vendor credit to consumers.

Licensing Creditors

Banks, savings and loan associations, and finance companies ordinarily must be licensed under state or federal statute. Credit companies that purchase retail installment debts from sellers are also subject to governmental licensing regulations.

When the licensing requirement is primarily a revenue-raising device, potential licensees often need only file the appropriate forms and pay the required fee to obtain a license. However, when the licensing provisions require the applicant to be reputable and reliable, the public is protected only if the licensing agency has the energy and resources to investigate the applicant's qualifications.

Credit Reports

When a consumer makes an application for credit, the creditor must decide whether he or she is a good risk. Most creditors regularly order a credit report on an applicant rather than undertake a costly investigation on their own. Files are retained by two types of credit agencies.

Credit Bureaus Credit bureaus publish reports which are primarily used by merchants who are attempting to decide whether to allow consumers to purchase merchandise financed by credit that will be repaid on time. Such reports ordinarily disclose financial information, such as the location and size of an individual's bank accounts, charge accounts, and other debts and the person's bill-paying habits, income, occupation, marital status, and lawsuits.

Credit bureaus supply such information to a group of subscribers who, in exchange, provide them with information for their files. All the information obtained is filed in case it is requested by someone in the future. Nonsubscribers can ordinarily obtain information through the payment of a fee.

A majority of credit bureaus are members of the Associated Credit Bureaus of America, which regulates public information for them. It keeps members apprised of financial transactions that might cause people to be unable to meet their obligations.

Credit Reporting Bureaus Credit reporting bureaus formulate financial reports on individuals for purposes not directly related to the extension of credit. Such reports are used by employers to evaluate job applicants, by insurance companies to assess the risk in relation to a prospective policy buyer, and by landlords to avoid renting to tenants likely to cause damage to the property or disturb other tenants. Bureaus of this type compile data and provide it upon request to interested parties.

These reports contain personal information about the subjects and their families that is obtained from interviews with neighbors, associates, and co-workers. Information is kept for possible future investigation requests.

Problems In the late 1960s, Congress investigated abuses in the collection and dissemination of information by credit bureaus and determined that such bureaus compiled files on more than 50 percent of the people in the United States. These information files, however, frequently contain inaccurate, misleading, or irrelevant facts and were not kept confidential. The most frequent error was to confuse two individuals having the same name or similar names. The possibility of committing this error increased as the area covered by the bureau became larger.

Supervision Many states have enacted statutes to regulate the business practices of credit bureaus. However, the need for national uniformity led to the enactment of federal laws dealing with consumer credit information.

The FAIR CREDIT REPORTING ACT, which is title VI of the CONSUMER CREDIT PROTECTION ACT (15 U.S.C.A. § 1601 et seq.), was enacted in 1970. This congressional enactment affects and regulates businesses that regularly obtain consumer credit information for other businesses, either for payment or in a cooperative exchange.

The law covers any report by an agency if it is related to a consumer's creditworthiness, credit standing or capacity, character, general reputation, personal characteristics, or mode of living. Further, the law applies to any such report when employed or expected to be used for evaluating a consumer for one of four purposes: credit or insurance for personal, family, or household use; employment; licenses to operate particular businesses or practice a profession; and any other legitimate business need.

The requirements of the Fair Credit Reporting Act affect (1) the credit bureau; (2) the businesses that use the credit reports compiled by credit bureaus; (3) the rights of consumers who are the subjects of such reports; and (4) how the consumer can enforce his or her rights when errors are discovered in such reports.

Credit bureaus are required to have *standard procedures* for determining and updating the accuracy of the information in their files. There is a seven-year limit on the information on file, except where the file discloses that the party was bankrupt within a period of ten years. Data relating to an individual's character, reputation, or lifestyle that are obtained through personal interviews with neighbors and friends cannot remain in a file unless it is verified every three months.

While the Fair Credit Reporting Act does not prohibit the collection and compilation of information unrelated to finance—such as appearance, political tenets, and sexual orientation—such information must be accurate and not obsolete. The law does, however, restrict credit bureaus to furnishing reports for reasons of credit, insurance, employment, obtaining a government license or other benefit, or other legitimate business needs related to business transactions with the consumer. Credit bureaus are required to investigate new clients to ascertain that they are using reports solely for one of these five permitted purposes. In addition, prospective clients are required to file a statement with bureaus certifying the purpose for which the reports will be used and agreeing not to use them for any other purposes.

Consumers are legally entitled to ascertain that no inaccurate or obsolete information is kept in files on them and to be notified when a creditor relies upon a report issued by a credit bureau, so the consumer can see the type of information kept on file and correct all mistakes in it.

A consumer, however, has no right to examine the actual file kept on him or her by a credit reporting agency. Anyone who has been refused credit on the basis of a report can discover the nature and substance of all but medical information contained therein, as well as the source of the information, except investigations based on comment from neighbors and associates. The consumer can also find out the identity of anyone who has received the report for employment purposes during the last two years or any other purpose during the last six months.

A consumer who discovers inaccurate or misleading information in his or her file can request that the agency reinvestigate his or her credit background and submit a brief statement which either explains or corrects the information. The agency must include such information in the consumer's file and notify recent users of the changes in the consumer's file upon the consumer's request.

Federal agencies, such as the FEDERAL TRADE COMMISSION (FTC), can issue orders for the enforcement of this law. Officers and employees of the credit bureau who willfully or intentionally violate this law are subject to criminal prosecution. Both a fine and imprisonment for each violation can be imposed upon conviction.

A credit bureau that fails to treat a consumer in the manner required by this law can be sued by the consumer who must prove that the credit bureau or the business that used the report did not properly maintain reasonable procedures to ensure compliance with the law. The consumer must also show that such failure to maintain was negligent or careless and that he or she incurred personal or financial injury from this failure.

Credit Discrimination

Discriminatory practices in the granting of credit led to the enactment of legislation to ensure that all qualified applicants have the same opportunity to receive credit.

Sex In the past, women were systematically denied credit regardless of whether they would be able to repay their loans. It was not uncommon for bankers to refuse to consider a married woman's income when a couple applied for a loan or a mortgage. Banks made the assumption that a woman of childbearing age was an automatic credit risk.

Single women had greater difficulty than single men in obtaining credit, particularly home mortgages. Creditors were also reluctant to extend credit to married women in their own names and refused to count a woman's income when calculating the creditworthiness of a married couple. Women also had a difficult time reestablishing credit upon DIVORCE or widowhood.

In 1974, Congress enacted the Federal Equal Credit Opportunity Act (15 U.S.C.A. § 1691 et seq.), which prohibits credit discrimination based not only upon sex and marital status, but also upon race, religion, and national origin. It has, however, very detailed prohibitions against discrimination based upon sex and marital status. Creditors are not permitted to (1) assign a value to sex or marital status in calculating an applicant's creditworthiness; (2) assign a value to having a telephone in the name of the applicant; (3) question a married couple's childbearing plan; (4) alter the terms of credit or require a reapplication when there is a change in an individual's marital status; (5) refuse to consider the total income of the couple who are making the application; (6) delay action on an application or refuse to consider it; or (7) discourage an individual from making an application for credit.

Federal agencies such as the FTC can guard against violations of this law through the issuance of restraining orders. In addition, consumers can commence an action against creditors who have denied them an equal opportunity to acquire credit. Where credit discrimination is prohibited by a state law also, the consumer can choose whether to pursue the state or the federal remedy.

Other Types of Discrimination Subsequent amendments to the Equal Credit Opportunity Act were concerned with *race* and *age discrimination*. The act provides that a creditor can take an applicant's age into consideration only in a situation where older people are given a preference or where a specific type of credit is allowed someone because that person is elderly. The law also requires that public assistance benefits be counted by creditors as a portion of an applicant's income. The race of an applicant cannot be used as a ground for the denial of credit.

Disclosure of Terms Until the late 1960s, there was considerable variety as to the information given consumers about their credit arrangements. The greatest lack of uniformity was in the statement of the rate of interest charged. Some creditors did not disclose the rate of interest, telling consumers only the number and amount of monthly payments. Those creditors that did state the rate of interest stated it in a variety of ways.

In response, Congress enacted the TRUTH IN LENDING ACT as Title I of the Consumer Credit Protection Act of 1968. The law is essentially a disclosure statute, offering little substantive protection to consumers. A creditor is free to impose any charges for credit permitted by state law. In addition, the statute does not restrict or confine the terms and conditions of the extension of credit. All that the Truth-in-Lending Act requires is that the consumer be informed of the terms and conditions of the credit transaction.

Under the statute and FTC regulations, the creditor must describe the credit terms clearly and conspicuously in a disclosure statement. At the time of disclosure, the creditor must furnish the customer with a copy of the statement. The disclosure requirements of the act are detailed and complex, because they deal with many types of credit transactions. In general, the creditor must disclose the amount financed, the annual percentage rate, and any finance charges associated with the extension of credit to the consumer. Any charges payable in the event of late payment must also be disclosed.

FURTHER READINGS

Bangert, Sharon J., Robert A. Cook, and Joseph D. Looney. 2002. "Unfair and Deceptive Advertising of Consumer Credit." *The Maryland Bar Journal* 35 (March-April): 8–13.

Hammond, Bob. 1996. *Life after Debt: How to Repair Your Credit and Get Out of Debt Once and For All*. Franklin Lakes, NJ: Career.

Hynes, Richard, and Eric A. Posner. 2002. "The Law and Economics of Consumer Finance." *American Law and Economics Review* 4 (spring): 168–207.

Leonard, Robin, and Deanne Loonin. Kathleen Michon, ed. 2002. *Credit Repair*. 6th ed. Berkeley, Calif.: Nolo.

Medoff, James C. 1996. *Indebted Society: Anatomy of an Ongoing Disaster*. New York: Little, Brown.

Paris, James L. 1995. *Living Financially Free*. Eugene, Oreg.: Harvest House.

Suit, Christopher. 2001. *How to Stop Telemarketers, Junk Mail, and Fix Your Credit*. Vancouver, Wash.: Streetlight Pub.

CROSS-REFERENCES

Restraining Order; Truth in Lending Act.

CONSUMER CREDIT PROTECTION ACT

The Consumer Credit Protection Act (15 U.S.C.A. § 1601 et seq. [1972]) is federal statute designed to protect borrowers of money by mandating complete disclosure of the terms and conditions of finance charges in transactions; by limiting the GARNISHMENT of wages; and by regulating the use of charge accounts.

The Consumer Credit Protection Act was the first general federal CONSUMER PROTECTION legislation. Title I of this law, known as the TRUTH-IN-LENDING ACT (15 U.S.C.A. § 1601 et seq. [1968]), requires that the terms in CONSUMER CREDIT transactions be fully explained to the prospective debtors. Title VI of the Consumer Credit Protection Act, known as the FAIR CREDIT REPORTING ACT (15 U.S.C.A. § 1601 et seq. [1978]), applies to businesses that regularly obtain consumer credit information for other businesses. Its purpose is to ensure that consumer reporting activities are conducted in a manner that is fair and equitable to the affected consumer.

Whereas the Consumer Credit Protection Act is federal law, states have also passed many statutes regulating consumer credit. For example, the UNIFORM CONSUMER CREDIT CODE (UCCC) is an initiative that was drafted by the National Conference of Commissioners on Uniform State Laws in 1968 to help provide consistency among the variety of consumer credit laws that exist throughout state jurisdictions. The purpose of the UCCC is threefold: to protect consumers obtaining credit to finance transactions; to ensure that adequate credit is provided; and to generally govern the credit industry. As of 2003, the UCCC had been adopted in only seven states and Guam. Many states, however, continue to enact legislation that would provide consumer debtors similar protections contained in the provisions of the UCCC.

CONSUMER FRAUD

Deceptive practices that result in financial or other losses for consumers in the course of seemingly legitimate business transactions.

Many think that consumer fraud only affects unwitting people who are all too willing to be duped. In truth, even the most savvy customer can fall victim to FRAUD. It may be as simple and seemingly innocuous as getting stuck paying a higher rate for a magazine subscription, or it may be as devastating as having one's identity stolen.

According to the FEDERAL TRADE COMMISSION (FTC), consumers reported $343 million in losses from fraud in 2002. In addition to those who are unwittingly defrauded, there are a number of consumers who share at least a degree of culpability in their losses. People who try to save money on their income taxes by purchasing a new SOCIAL SECURITY number or wage statement may become victims of fraud, but chances are that they understood that their actions were illegal, which makes them guilty of fraud as well.

Consumer fraud can take place in person, by telephone or mail, or over the INTERNET. As technology continues to improve, INTERNET FRAUD has risen faster than other types. With or without technology, however, consumers can protect themselves against fraud by following a few simple, common-sense measures such as not revealing personal information to strangers.

Following are some of the most common types of consumer fraud.

Identity Theft

IDENTITY THEFT accounts for more than 40 percent of all fraud complaints reported to the FTC. All identity theft is serious, but even in its mildest form it can involve the theft of a consumer's long-distance access code. The thief sells the code to individuals who use the code to charge long-distance calls all over the world. In its most serious form, a thief gains access to the victim's Social Security number. With this number, and some other basic information, a thief can create a double of the victim. The victim's information can be used to make purchases, to rent an apartment, or to take out bank loans. Often, victims of identity theft first find out their misfortune when they receive credit card bills totaling thousands of dollars, even though they had neither opened the accounts nor made the purchases.

Identity thieves can gain access to their victim's information by copying it off of forms (for example, if they work in an office where such information is kept), by stealing a wallet or personal papers, or by otherwise exploiting a careless individual. (Fraud experts warn people never to give their Social Security or bank account numbers to someone who has phoned them, even from a seemingly legitimate business.) Often identity thieves work in large rings that span several states, which makes it difficult to track them down. Thus, even when a theft ring is cracked, others quickly crop up to take its place.

Telephone and Mail Solicitations

To most people, junk mail and telemarketer calls are merely a NUISANCE, but unscrupulous companies can use both the mail and the telephone to part innocent (and not merely gullible) people from their money. Applications for credit cards or personal loans promise easy credit, but the fine print promises exorbitant interest rates. Sweepstakes promising millions in winnings await the lucky recipient, who often feels compelled to send an order for several magazines along with the prize receipt. Charities use telemarketing and mass mailings to ask for

Consumer Fraud Complaints, by Consumer Age, in 2002[a]

Age	Percentage
19 and under	3%
20–29	19%
30–39	25%
40–49	25%
50–59	16%
60–69	7%
70 and over	6%

[a]Percentages are based on the total number of fraud complaints where consumers reported their age (140,763). 64% of consumers reported their age.

SOURCE: Federal Trade Commission, *Consumer Sentinel Fraud Complaints.*

donations; while some of those charities are established and legitimate, others are dubious. Many phony charities assume names that sound like better-known organizations in the hope of fooling consumers.

Every day, people are contacted by telephone and mail with phony offers. Despite warnings from consumer-advocacy groups, people continue to provide credit card numbers, bank information, and even Social Security numbers to those whom they do not know. The elderly are a common target, in part because once they find that they have been defrauded they refuse to report the crime because they are embarrassed. Groups such as the Federal Trade Commission, the National Consumers League (NCL), and Consumers Union provide information to the general public in an effort to curtail fraud.

In 2002, several states initiated "do-not-call" programs that allow people to store their telephone numbers in a centralized database that telemarketers are prohibited from calling. A telemarketer who calls a prohibited number faces stiff fines.

Internet Fraud

The growth of the Internet as a communication tool has also meant its growth as an instrument of fraud. Internet fraud has grown so rapidly in recent years that FEDERAL BUREAU OF INVESTIGATION (FBI) and the National White Collar Crime Center launched the Internet Fraud Complaint Center, which compiles data and offers tips on ways to avoid being defrauded. In 2001, Internet fraud accounted for $17.8 million in losses, with a median loss of $435 per victim.

The most common type of fraud, accounting for nearly two thirds of all reported fraud, is Internet-auction fraud. Although there are a number of legitimate online auction houses, there are many that are simply scams. Consumers who purchase items on these sites find that the goods they bid for never existed, or that the goods are stolen, or that the seller has added numerous hidden charges. The seller might even act as a shill by placing false bids. (Some consumers jump on the fraud bandwagon, as well, by using aliases to place multiple phony high bids in order to deter low or moderate bidders.)

The Internet is also home to credit card scams, investment scams, and home-improvement scams. These may appear on web sites or they may be sent in the form of *unsolicited commercial e-mail* (UCE), better known as "spam." One common spam message is the "Nigerian Letter," in which a person who claims to be a former high official, usually from the Nigerian government, seeks help in converting millions of dollars in funds. The consumer is asked to provide bank account information so that the funds can be transferred to that account.

Income Tax Fraud

The INTERNAL REVENUE SERVICE warns taxpayers to be on guard against tax scams that can result in loss of funds and, in some cases, legal difficulties. Some con artists make money at their victims' expense by claiming that they can help to secure tax refunds for their clients. Invariably, the clients must pay a fee up-front. One example of this is a company that claims it can help taxpayers find legal loopholes that will allow them to stop paying taxes. Another is a company that offers to help people submit claims for nonexistent credits. (Some African-Americans have been targeted by a "reparations" scam in which they are told they can apply for a slavery-reparations credit simply by paying a fee. No such credit exists.)

If the taxpayer knowingly engages in a scheme that is illegal (for example, signing up for a new Social Security number), he or she may face fines or imprisonment.

Combating Fraud

Education is key to combating consumer fraud. The FTC, FBI, NCL, Consumers Union, and Direct Marketing Association all work to educate the public and to identify fraudulent businesses. The Better Business Bureau is also a useful tool for consumers who wish to find out information about specific companies.

FURTHER READINGS

Bertrand, Marsha, 2000. *Fraud! How to Protect Yourself from Schemes, Scams, and Swindles.* New York: AMACOM.

U.S. Federal Trade Commission, 1997. *Fighting Consumer Fraud: The Challenge and the Campaign.* Washington, DC: U.S. Federal Trade Commission.

CROSS-REFERENCES

False Advertising; Federal Trade Commission; Internet.

CONSUMER PRICE INDEX

A computation made and issued monthly by the Bureau of Labor Statistics of the federal LABOR DEPARTMENT that attempts to track the price level of designated goods and services purchased by the average consumer.

The consumer price index (CPI) is an indicator of the rate of inflation in the economy because it measures changes in the cost of maintaining a particular standard of living.

CONSUMER PRODUCT SAFETY COMMISSION

The CONSUMER PRODUCT SAFETY COMMISSION was established to protect the public against unreasonable risks of injury from consumer products; to assist consumers in evaluating the comparative safety of consumer products; to develop uniform safety standards for consumer products and to minimize conflicting state and local regulations; and to promote research and investigation into the causes and prevention of product-related deaths, illnesses, and injuries. The commission is an independent federal regulatory agency, established by the act of October 27, 1972 (86 Stat. 1207). It makes information available to the public through its Web site, <http://www.cpsc.gov>.

The commission has primary responsibility for establishing mandatory product-safety standards in order to reduce the unreasonable risk of injury to consumers from consumer products. It also has the authority to ban hazardous consumer products. The Consumer Product Safety Act (15 U.S.C. 2051 et seq. [1972]) authorizes the commission to conduct extensive research on consumer product standards, to engage in broad consumer, industry information, and education programs, and to establish a comprehensive injury-information clearinghouse.

In addition to the authority created by the act, the commission assumes responsibility for the Flammable Fabrics Act (67 Stat. 111; 15 U.S.C. 1191), the Poison Prevention Packaging Act (84 Stat. 1670), the Hazardous Substances Act (74 Stat. 372; 15 U.S.C. 1261), and the act of August 2, 1956 (70 Stat. 953; 15 U.S.C. 1211), which prohibits the transportation of refrigerators without door-safety devices. The act also provides for petitioning of the commission by any interested person, including consumers or consumer organizations, to commence proceedings for the issuance, amendment, or revocation of a consumer product safety rule.

In 1999, the commission introduced a new interactive section for children, on its web site. Geared toward children between the ages of 8 and 12, it features games and puzzles that are designed to test children's knowledge of safety and to teach them safety facts.

CROSS-REFERENCES

Consumer Protection.

CONSUMER PROTECTION

Consumer protection laws are federal and state statutes governing sales and credit practices involving consumer goods. Such statutes prohibit and regulate deceptive or UNCONSCIONABLE advertising and sales practices, product quality, credit financing and reporting, debt collection, leases, and other aspects of consumer transactions.

The goal of consumer protection laws is to place consumers, who are average citizens engaging in business deals such as buying goods or borrowing money, on an even par with companies or citizens who regularly engage in business. Historically, consumer transactions—purchases of goods or services for personal, family, or household use—were presumed fair because it was assumed that buyers and sellers bargained from equal positions. Starting in the 1960s, legislatures began to respond to complaints by consumer advocates that consumers were inherently disadvantaged, particularly when bargaining with large corporations and industries. Several types of agencies and statutes, both state and federal, now work to protect consumers.

Consumer Product Safety Commission

In 1972, Congress established the CONSUMER PRODUCT SAFETY COMMISSION (CPSC). It is the job of the CPSC to protect consumers from faulty or dangerous products by enacting mandatory safety standards for those products. The CPSC has the authority to ban products from the marketplace or to recall products (when a product is recalled, it is removed from the shelves or sales lots, and consumers may be able to return it to the manufacturer or place of purchase for repair, replacement, or a refund). Still, the agency has trouble protecting consumers from hazardous products of which it is unaware.

In recent years, the CPSC has fallen victim to FEDERAL BUDGET cuts. Reductions in the agency's legal staff have prompted the CPSC to rely more and more on manufacturers to voluntarily recall their defective or hazardous products. When manufacturers do not cooperate, the CPSC must commence a legal action that may take years to resolve.

Unfair or Deceptive Trade Practices

The FEDERAL TRADE COMMISSION (FTC), the largest federal agency that handles consumer complaints, regulates unfair or deceptive trade practices. Even local trade practices deemed unfair or deceptive may fall within the jurisdiction of FTC laws and regulations when they have an adverse effect on interstate commerce.

In addition, every state has enacted consumer protection statutes, which are modeled after the Federal Trade Commission Act (15 U.S.C.A. § 45(a)(1)). These acts allow state attorneys, along with general and private consumers, to commence lawsuits over false or deceptive advertisements, or other unfair and injurious consumer practices. Many of the state statutes explicitly provide that courts turn to the federal act and interpretations of the FTC for guidance in construing state laws.

The FTC standard for unfair consumer acts or practices has changed with time. In 1964, the agency instituted criteria for determining unfairness when it enacted its cigarette advertising and labeling rule. A practice was deemed unfair when it (1) offended public policy as defined by statutes, COMMON LAW, or otherwise; (2) was immoral, unethical, oppressive, or unscrupulous; and (3) substantially injured consumers. The FTC changed the standard in 1980. Now, substantial injury of consumers is the most heavily weighed element, and it alone may constitute an unfair practice. Such an unfair practice is illegal pursuant to the Federal Trade Commission Act unless the consumer injury is outweighed by benefits to consumers or competition, or consumers could not reasonably have avoided such injury. The FTC may still consider the public policy criterion, but only in determining whether substantial injury exists. Finally, the FTC no longer considers whether conduct was immoral, unethical, oppressive, or unscrupulous.

The FTC has also developed, over time, its definition of deceptive acts or practices. Historically, an act was deceptive if it had the tendency or capacity to deceive, and the FTC considered the act's effect on the ignorant or credulous consumer. A formal policy statement made by the FTC in 1988 changed this definition: currently, a practice is deceptive if it will likely mislead a consumer, acting reasonably under the circumstances, to that consumer's detriment.

FALSE ADVERTISING is often the cause of consumer complaints. At common law, a consumer had the right to bring an action against a false advertiser for FRAUD, upon proving that the advertiser made false representations about the product, that these representations were made with the advertiser's knowledge of or negligent failure to discover the falsehoods, and that the consumer relied on the false advertisement and was harmed as a result. In 1911, an advertising trade journal called *Printer's Ink* proposed model legislation criminalizing false advertisements. Forty-four states enacted statutes based on this model statute. However, because of the difficulty in proving BEYOND A REASONABLE DOUBT an advertiser's dishonesty, prosecutors seldom use these criminal laws. More frequently, the state attorneys general or the FTC regulates false advertising. For example, the FTC can issue a cease and desist order, forcing a manufacturer to stop advertising, or compelling the advertiser to make corrections or disclosures informing the public of the misrepresentations.

Truth in Lending Act

Consumer credit—home mortgages, student financial aid, and credit cards, for example—is an area fraught with complicated finance terms, and Congress has designed laws requiring lenders to fully disclose and explain those terms to potential borrowers. The CONSUMER CREDIT PROTECTION ACT of 1968 (15 U.S.C.A. § 1601 et seq.), also known as the TRUTH IN LENDING ACT, prohibits lenders from advertising loan terms that are only available to preferred borrowers. In addition, advertisements for CONSUMER CREDIT transactions cannot disclose partial terms; either all the terms of the transaction or none of them must be spelled out. Finally, when the terms of credit provide for repayment in more than four installments, the agreement must conspicuously state that "the cost of credit is included in the price quoted for the goods and services."

The Truth in Lending Act is designed to protect society as a whole, and therefore does not provide the individual consumer with a personal CAUSE OF ACTION when a lender violates the law. Nor are publishers of advertising, such as radio, newspapers, and television, generally held liable for lenders' advertisements that violate the act. Finally, the act does not consider statements made by salespeople in the course of selling products or services to be advertisements, therefore the law does not apply to those statements.

Fair Debt Collection Practices Act

The Consumer Protection Act was amended in 1996 to include the Fair Debt Collection Practices Act (Public Law 104-208, 110 Stat. 3009 [1996]). Congress passed the law to address the

At a November 2002 news conference, Hal Stratton, chairman of the Consumer Products Safety Commission, demonstrates one of the five different brands of collapsing playpens recalled due to the danger of infant strangulation.

AP/WIDE WORLD PHOTOS

abusive, deceptive, and unfair debt collection practices used by many debt collectors. Personal, family, and household debts are covered under the act. This includes money owed for the purchase of an automobile, for medical care, or for charge accounts. A collector may contact a person by mail, telephone, telegram, or fax. However, a debt collector may not contact a debtor at an inconvenient time, such as before 8 A.M. or after 9 P.M., unless the debtor agrees. A debt collector also may not contact a debtor at an inappropriate place. For example, a collector may not contact a debtor at his place of work if the collector knows that the debtor's employer disapproves of such contacts.

Collectors may not contact debtors if the debtors send the collectors a letter asking them to stop. Collectors may not threaten or abuse debtors nor make false statements. Persons may sue collectors for violating the law and can collect up to $1,000 and attorneys' fees for a violation. A group of people also may sue a debt collector and recover money for damages up to $500,000, or one percent of the collector's net worth, whichever is less.

Warranties

Warranties are promises by a manufacturer, made to the consumer purchasing the manufacturer's product, that the product will serve the purpose for which it was designed. The UNIFORM COMMERCIAL CODE is a law, adopted in some form in all states, that regulates sales transactions and specifically the three most common types of consumer warranties: express, merchantability, and fitness.

Express warranties are promises included in the written or oral terms of a sales agreement that assure the quality, description, or performance of the product. Express warranties are usually included in the sales contract, or are written in a separate pamphlet and packaged with the merchandise sold to the consumer. These warranties may be less obvious than are product advertisements. A consumer who relies on a written description of a product in a catalog or on a sample of a product may have a cause of action if the actual product differs. Express warranties can also be verbal, such as promises made by salespeople. However, because oral warranties are extremely difficult to prove, they are rarely litigated.

Merchantability and fitness warranties are both implied warranties, which are promises that arise by operation of law. A warranty of merchantability concerns the basic understanding that the product is fit to be purchased and used in the ordinary way—for instance, a lamp will provide light, a radio will pick up broadcast stations, and a refrigerator will keep food cold. A warranty of fitness concerns the consumer's purpose in purchasing a product, and allows the consumer to rely on the seller to offer goods only if they are suitable for that particular purpose. For example, there may be a breach of the IMPLIED WARRANTY of fitness if a salesperson knowingly sells a consumer software that is not designed for operation on the consumer's computer. For a breach-of-implied-warranty claim to be successful, the consumer must establish that an implied WARRANTY existed and was breached, that the breach harmed the consumer, that the consumer dealt with the party responsible for the implied warranty, and that the consumer notified the seller within a reasonable time. Implied warranties may be disclaimed by the seller if they are denied expressly and specifically at the time of the sale.

The MAGNUSON-MOSS WARRANTY ACT (15 U.S.C.A. § 2301 et seq.) is a federal law that requires sellers to explain, in easy-to-understand language, the terms of warranties that apply to written sales contracts for items costing $5 or more. Under this act, when a product fails to meet the standards promised by the warranty, the seller must repair it, replace it, or refund the purchase price.

Consumer Remedies

Laws protecting consumers vary in the remedies they provide to consumers for violations. Many federal laws merely provide for public agencies to enforce consumer regulations by investigating and resolving consumer complaints. For example, in the case of a false advertisement, a common remedy is the FTC-ordered removal of the offensive advertisements from the media. In other circumstances, consumers may be entitled to money damages, costs, and attorneys' fees; these remedies can be effective in a case involving a breach of warranty. Depending on the amount of damages alleged, consumers may bring such actions in small-claims courts, which tend to be speedier and less expensive than trial courts.

ALTERNATIVE DISPUTE RESOLUTION (ADR) is another option for consumers. Some states pass consumer protection statutes that require some form of ADR—usually ARBITRATION or mediation—before a consumer can seek help from the courts. Finally, when a large number of consumers have been harmed in the same way as a result of the same practice, they may join in a CLASS ACTION, a single lawsuit in which one or more named representatives of the consumer group sue to redress the injuries sustained by all members of the group.

In response to public frustration over telephone solicitations, many states and the FTC began to set up systems to bar unwanted telephone sales calls. The FTC, in 2002, amended the Telemarketing Sales Rule (TSR) to give consumers the option of placing their phone numbers on a national "do not call" registry. It will be illegal for most telemarketers to call a number listed on the registry. The registry was scheduled to go into operation in July 2003, but telephone marketing companies promised a lawsuit to contest the rules, arguing that they violated the FIRST AMENDMENT.

FURTHER READINGS

Craft. 1991. "State Consumer Protection Enforcement: Recent Trends and Developments." *Antitrust Law Journal* 59.

Federal Trade Commission. "The 'Do Not Call' Registry." Available online at <www.ftc.gov/bcp/conline/edcams/donotcall/index.html> (accessed June 3, 2003).

Marsh, Gene A. 1999. *Consumer Protection Law in a Nutshell.* St. Paul, Minn.: West Wadsworth.

Pertschuk, Michael. 1984. *Revolt Against Regulation: The Rise and Pause of the Consumer Movement.* Berkeley: Univ. of California Press.

CROSS-REFERENCES

Consumer Fraud; Product Liability.

CONSUMER SOFTWARE PIRACY

The unauthorized use, possession, downloading, duplication, distribution, or sale of copyrighted computer software.

COPYRIGHT infringement is a serious problem for the computer software industry. Programs can be copied easily on a personal computer, thus making detecting and prosecuting infringements of software copyrights extremely difficult. By estimates of the Software Publisher's Association, nearly 25 percent of all software in use in the United States is pirated (acquired through unlawful copying), and domestic and international losses ran to $10.9 billion in 2001 alone. The growth of computer networks, especially the INTERNET, presents further problems by providing the means for the almost effortless transmission of data. In the 1990s, Congress strengthened protections for software, and aggressive litigation by the computer industry targeted corporations, individuals, and counterfeiters in an effort to clamp down on this massive theft. Yet during the early 2000s, law enforcement remained difficult as software pirates turned to new technologies to share files illegally.

The Copyright Act (17 U.S.C.A. §§ 1 et seq.) gives exclusive rights to the authors of computer software. Their work is a type of INTELLECTUAL PROPERTY, which the law treats differently from tangible property. Software companies own their copyrighted programs even after selling them to consumers. For consumers, buying software is different from buying a car: Purchasers of cars are called owners, whereas purchasers of software are called licensees. Although software buyers own the disc or CD-ROM on which the software is stored, they are entitled to use it in only a specific, limited way. The law provides that manufacturers, as owners of the copyright, retain the *exclusive* right to reproduce and distribute copies of the software. Consumers, as licensees, do not have the same right. They may only copy the software onto a single computer and make another copy for archival purposes.

Consumers break the law when they make unauthorized copies of software. Whether for profit, free distribution, or personal use, such duplication constitutes copyright infringement. Copyright owners can sue infringers for damages that may include profits made by the infringers, or statutory damages of up to $100,000 for each work infringed. The penalties are more severe when software copying is done

Software Publisher's Association

The Software Publisher's Association (SPA) is an 1,100-member trade group representing the legal interests of U.S. software companies. Founded in 1988, SPA fights **COPYRIGHT** infringement from its offices in Washington, D.C., and Paris. SPA is a division of the Software & Information Industry Association (SIIA), which offers rewards of up to $50,000 to individuals who report verifiable corporate end-user **PIRACY** to SIIA through the SIIA hotline or through the SIIA Corporate End-User Piracy Internet Report Form. Its chief goal is to eliminate the unauthorized duplication of computer programs.

On December 16, 1997, President **BILL CLINTON** signed into law the No Electronic Theft (NET) Act of 1997, Pub. L. No. 105-147, 111 Stat.2678. The act was passed to address a loophole in copyright law, which was successfully exploited by a 21-year-old MIT student, David LaMacchia, who escaped federal prosecution for distributing free copyrighted software on the Web. The NET Act punishes software pirates who willfully copy, distribute, and traffic in protected software on the Web whether or not they enjoy a financial gain. David LaMacchia set up a bulletin board on the Internet which he named "Cynosure." LaMacchia then solicited bulletin board correspondents to upload popular software applications such as Excel, WordPerfect, and various computer games such as *Sim City*. He then transferred the uploaded software to a second encrypted address, named "Cynosure II." Users who had access to the Cynosure password could then download the software. The worldwide traffic generated by the offer of free software attracted the notice of university and federal authorities. During the brief six-week life of Cynosure, software copyright holders claim to have lost one million dollars as a result of the free trafficking of their products. Even though a federal **GRAND JURY** returned a one-count indictment charging LaMacchia with conspiring with unknown persons to violate the wire-fraud statute, the government could not prosecute under the criminal copyright statute because there was no evidence that LaMacchia made any profit.

SPA efforts are targeted primarily at the U.S. market, where the industry generates approximately 60 percent of its revenues and where, SPA estimates, nearly 85 percent of losses to software piracy occur.

Successes in cracking down on infringement have made SPA a major player in copyright law. The organization's enforcement actions netted $14 million in recoveries between 1988 and 1995. Among these were a half-million-dollar settlement against a corporation, resulting from an audit, and a $350,000 settlement in May 1991 from a successful lawsuit against Parametrix, an environmental engineering firm. In 2002, in a case originating from SIIA, Yaroslav Suris, 27, of Brooklyn, New York, was convicted of one felony count of Criminal Infringement of a Copyright, in violation of 17 U.S.C. 506(a)(1) and 18 U.S.C. 2319(b)(1). Suris was sentenced to two months incarceration, followed by 14 months of home detention. He was also ordered to pay $290,556 in restitution for computer piracy.

In the area of **LOBBYING**, SPA has asked Congress for tougher legislation designed to stop copyright infringement over computer networks, especially the Internet. SPA anti-piracy department conducts public education campaigns and distributes auditing software that allows businesses and organizations to ensure that they are following the law.

According to SPA, Web framing can be a form of piracy when a viewing window is created for all or a portion of a Web page or a particular piece of content residing on a Web page. Problems with framing typically arise when the manner in which the Web site is framed removes, obscures, or alters navigation tools, links, indicators of source, **TRADEMARKS**, logos, or advertising located on the Website that is framed. Framing of third-party content into another Web page raises many legal issues, including passing off content as one's own, **UNFAIR COMPETITION**, trademark infringement, trademark dilution, misappropriation, and perhaps copyright infringement.

FURTHER READINGS

Albert, G. Peter. 1999. *Intellectual Property Law in Cyberspace.* Edison, NJ: BNA Books.

Zoellick, Bill. 2001. *CyberRegs: A Business Guide to Web Property, Privacy, and Patents.* Boston, MA: Addison-Wesley Longman.

CROSS-REFERENCES

Copyright; Internet; Trademarks.

"willfully and for purposes of commercial advantage or private financial gain" (17 U.S.C.A. § 506). This is a federal crime, carrying fines of up to $250,000 and jail terms of up to five years.

The remote possibility of arrest and prosecution hardly hinders most software thieves. The chances of being caught are slight, and the allure can be difficult to resist. Software packages are often expensive—from around $50 to several hundred dollars—and copying is literally as simple as clicking a mouse.

The rise of computer networking—in which computers are linked within an office or across cities by means of telephone modems—has made illegal copying even easier. Network communication is hard to monitor, especially when it takes place over large geographic distances between or among users who can conceal their identities. Thousands of computer bulletin boards, as well as the Internet, proved fertile ground for young computer enthusiasts who saw copyright law as a minor hurdle in their acquisition of new *warez* (computer hacker slang for "illegally acquired software"). During 1995, the Usenet news group <alt.binaries.warez.ibm-pc> amounted to a bonanza where thousands of dollars worth of copyrighted software was uploaded weekly by anonymous hackers, free for the taking.

Despite gaining ground against infringers, the computer industry's battle is still ongoing. The Software Publisher's Association (SPA), an industry trade group that sues infringers on behalf of its members, claims to have greatly reduced illegal copying in the workplace. However, home copying by individuals and counterfeiters has remained a persistent problem.

In 1994, federal district Judge Richard Stearns dismissed a case against David LaMacchia, a Massachusetts Institute of Technology student who had set up an Internet bulletin board over which users traded more than one million dollars worth of software. The judge ruled that federal copyright law did not cover not-for-profit copying of computer software. Subsequently, the software industry blamed this so-called "LaMacchia loophole" for the proliferation of online PIRACY during the middle and second half of the decade. The industry argued that because federal copyright law defined violations strictly in terms of financial gain, most casual violators fell through the cracks.

During the late 1990s, software manufacturers successfully lobbied Congress to enact stringent, new federal legislation to curb software piracy. The first of two major laws, the No Electronic Theft (NET) Act of 1997, Pub. L. No. 105-147, 111 Stat. 2678, immediately closed the LaMacchia loophole. Under the NET Act, the definition of a violation includes unauthorized reproduction or distribution of copyrighted materials, and financial gain is understood to mean mere possession. The NET Act provides severe penalties for violating the copyright of materials worth more than $1,000 in a six-month period by copying, distributing, or receiving software.

One year later, Congress enacted a second, more sweeping law in the Digital Millennium Copyright Act (DMCA) of 1998. The DMCA broadly revamped U.S. copyright law to keep pace with changing international treaties as well as evolving technologies. One major provision, essentially aimed at hackers, criminalized the use of any device or technology to break anticopying protections on software or other media such as movies and music. But while being embraced by the software and entertainment industries, critics including scientists, scholars, and civil-liberties advocates have argued that the DMCA limits legitimate professional research and stifles technological innovation.

Further complicating antipiracy efforts, new technologies arose following the introduction of Napster in 1999. As a free, online software program used to trade MP3 music files anonymously, Napster proved wildly popular with millions of Internet users before prompting Congressional hearings in 2001 as its parent company came under fierce litigation from the music industry. After the company filed for BANKRUPTCY, file trading moved to other so-called peer-to-peer (or "P2P") networks, such as the popular Gnutella, which similarly allowed users to connect online in order to trade software, music, and movies. Critically, P2P decentralized file trading through the use of programs designed by computer hobbyists, making enforcement efforts all the harder.

As the P2P phenomenon spread, attempts to combat it came from industry, academic administrators, and lawmakers. Industry representatives chiefly targeted colleges where students reportedly were slowing campus computer systems to a crawl with their volume of illegal file trading. Some educational institutions restricted computer use in the face of copyright-infringement lawsuits. Under combined LOBBYING from the software, music and movie industries, a subcommittee of the U.S. House Judiciary Committee held hearings into potential policy solutions in 2003.

Because of the ease with which software piracy may be carried out, and the substantial revenue losses that it causes, software manufacturers continue to call for more stringent legislation and to search for improved methods for detecting and preventing software theft.

FURTHER READINGS

Business Software Alliance. February 26, 2003. "Press Release: BSA Applauds House Subcommittee for Attention to P2P Piracy Problem." *Business Software Alliance.* Available online at <www.bsa.org> (accessed November 20, 2003).

"Congress at 45 RPM." 2001. *The Palm Beach Post.* (April 10): 14A.

Legard, David. February 13, 2003. "IIPA estimates U.S. Global Piracy Losses at $9.2 Billion in 2002." *IDG News Service.* www.nwfusion.com/news/2003/0214iipaestim .html.

Steinberg, Gene. 2002. "Internet File Sharing without Spyware." *Gannett News Service (August 19).*

"Timeline of Events in Napster Case." 2001 *Associated Press* (February 12).

Warren, Mackenzie. 2002. "Online music swapping still rocks on campus: Students Zero in on Peer-to-Peer Sites for Freebies." *Gannett News Service* (July 15).

CROSS-REFERENCES

Computer Crime; Copyright; Intellectual Property.

CONSUMMATE

To carry into completion; to fulfill; to accomplish.

A COMMON-LAW MARRIAGE is consummated when the parties live in a manner intended to bring about public recognition of their relationship as HUSBAND AND WIFE.

To consummate an agreement is to carry it out completely, as in a consummated sale. It is to bring to completion whatever was either intended or undertaken to be done.

CONTEMNER

An individual who intentionally acts to hinder or obstruct the administration of justice by a court, either by refusing to comply with its orders or by disrupting its orderly proceedings, thereby committing CONTEMPT.

CONTEMPLATION OF DEATH

The apprehension of an individual that his or her life will be ended in the immediate future by a par-

ticular illness the person is suffering from or by an imminent known danger which the person faces.

The phrase *in contemplation of death* applies to a gift of property made by its owner who expects to die shortly, the gift being motivated solely by the thought of his or her demise. Such transfers are considered akin to testamentary dispositions since they are ineffective unless the owner dies but differ in that the owner must die within a reasonable time from the making of the gift.

The words *contemplation of death* are synonymous with the Latin phrase *causa mortis.*

CONTEMPT

An act of deliberate disobedience or disregard for the laws, regulations, or decorum of a public authority, such as a court or legislative body.

Individuals may be cited for contempt when they disobey an order, fail to comply with a request, tamper with documents, withhold evidence, interrupt proceedings through their actions or words, or otherwise defy a public authority or hold it up to ridicule and disrespect. The laws and rules governing contempt have developed in a piecemeal fashion over time and give wide discretion to judges and legislative leaders in determining both what constitutes contempt and how it is punished.

Contempt of Court

Contempt of court is behavior that opposes or defies the authority, justice, and dignity of the court. Contempt charges may be brought against parties to proceedings; lawyers or other court officers or personnel; jurors; witnesses; or people who insert themselves in a case, such as protesters outside a courtroom. Courts have great leeway in making contempt charges, and thus confusion sometimes exists about the distinctions between types of contempt. Generally, however, contempt proceedings are categorized as civil or criminal, and direct or indirect.

Civil contempt generally involves the failure to perform an act that is ordered by a court as a means to enforce the rights of individuals or to secure remedies for parties in a civil action. For instance, parents who refuse to pay court-ordered CHILD SUPPORT may be held in contempt of court under civil contempt. *Criminal contempt* involves behavior that assaults the dignity of the court or impairs the ability of the court to conduct its work. Criminal contempt can occur within a civil or criminal case. For example, criminal contempt occurs when a witness or spectator shouts or insults the judge during a trial. A civil contempt usually is a violation of the rights of one person, whereas a criminal contempt is an offense against society. Courts use civil contempt as a coercive power, wielding it only to ask that the contemnor comply with the courts' actions. Criminal contempt is punitive; courts use it to punish parties who have impaired the courts' functioning or bruised their dignity.

A *direct contempt* is an act that occurs in the presence of the court and is intended to embarrass or engender disrespect for the court. Shouting in the courtroom or refusing to answer questions for a judge or attorney under oath is a direct contempt. *Indirect contempt* occurs outside the presence of the court, but its intention is also to belittle, mock, obstruct, interrupt, or degrade the court and its proceedings. Attempting to bribe a district attorney is an example of an indirect contempt. Publishing any material that results in a contempt charge is an indirect contempt. Other kinds of indirect contempt include preventing process service, improperly communicating to or by jurors, and withholding evidence. One man was threatened with contempt charges because he had filed more than 350 lawsuits that the judge considered frivolous. Indirect contempt also may be called constructive or consequential contempt; all three terms mean the same thing.

The essence of contempt of court is that the misconduct impairs the fair and efficient administration of justice. Contempt statutes generally require that the actions present a CLEAR AND PRESENT DANGER that threatens the administration of justice.

The manner in which an act is committed or the tone in which words are spoken can determine whether contempt has occurred. Circumstances, such as the context in which the words were spoken, the tone, the facial expression, the manner, and the emphasis, are also evaluated by the court. Failure to complete an act that, if completed, would tend to bring the court into disrespect does not preclude the act from being contemptuous.

Criticisms of the Contempt-of-Court Power

The discretion permitted to judges in determining what is contempt and how to punish it has led some legal scholars to argue that the contempt power gives too much authority to judges.

Earl C. Dudley, University of Virginia law professor, wrote that in the contempt power, "the roles of victim, prosecutor and judge are dangerously commingled."

Much of the criticism focuses on the lack of restraint or DUE PROCESS in determining punishments for contempt. In criminal contempt, the contempt charges become a separate matter, but they may be heard by the judge who made them. In addition, the same judge may commence punishment immediately, and the punishment may be in effect until the contempt case is settled. Critics have argued that judges—who are the principal offended party—may be too harsh. For instance, in 1994, the U.S. Supreme Court overturned a decision by a Virginia judge who had fined the United Mine Workers of America $52 million in connection with violence that occurred during a 1989 strike. The High Court stated that the fines were excessive and improperly imposed because the union had never had a chance to defend itself in a trial before the fines were imposed.

Similarly, individuals who have refused to provide courts with information have been held in jail—sometimes for years—under contempt charges. In Maryland, a woman involved in a custody battle with her ex-husband refused to reveal the whereabouts of her child. Elizabeth Morgan spent 25 months in jail before her ex-husband dropped the custody case and it was revealed that the child was staying with Morgan's parents in New Zealand. Journalist Myron Farber, of the *New York Times,* spent more than three years in jail for refusing to turn over notes that prosecutors sought for a murder trial.

Judges and scholars have defended the practices of indefinite jail time because the contemnor "carries the keys to his prison in his own pocket" and can be released by complying with the court (*In re Nevitt,* 117 F. 448 [8th Cir. 1902]).

Civil contempt proceedings end when the suit from which they arose is resolved. Criminal contempt continues as a separate matter. Settlements may involve jail time, fines, or other retribution. For instance, when the Cable News Network (CNN) was found guilty of contempt of court for airing audiotapes related to the trial of Manuel Noriega, the deposed president of Panama, the network was given the choice of airing a retraction and an apology for using the tapes or paying a large fine. The network made the apology.

Contempt of Congress

The Constitution does not explicitly grant Congress the power to coerce cooperation from individuals or to punish acts of disobedience or disrespect through contempt proceedings. However, the power was discussed at the Constitutional Convention and was implied in the Constitution. In 1795, Congress used the power of contempt for the first time when it arrested, tried, and punished a man accused of bribing members of the House of Representatives. Then Congress acted on its own authority—subsequently called the SELF-HELP power, which grants Congress the right to compel testimony and punish disobedience without the involvement of a court or other government body if the individual's actions obstruct the legislative process. By 1821, the Supreme Court recognized Congress's power to arrest and punish individuals for contempt. In 1857, Congress created a statute governing prosecution for contempt, which shifted the responsibility for determining contempt from Congress itself to the courts. Until 1945, Congress largely ignored this criminal statute and continued to compel testimony and deal with contemnors through its own power.

In the late twentieth century, the Supreme Court noted, "Congress has practically abandoned its original practice of utilizing the coercive (self-help) sanction of contempt proceedings at the bar of the House" (*Watkins v. United States,* 354 U.S. 178, 77 S. Ct. 1173, 1 L. Ed. 2d 1273[1957]). Under the criminal statute, Congress must petition the U.S. attorney to bring a case of possible contempt before a GRAND JURY. The case is then tried in federal court.

Most contempt citations arise from Congress's investigatory powers. In its decisions since WORLD WAR II, the Supreme Court has outlined requirements that Congress must meet before it can compel testimony. The investigation must have a valid legislative purpose. It must be conducted by a committee or subcommittee of the House of Representatives or Senate, or the authority of the investigating body must be clearly defined in a resolution. The questions asked of witnesses must be pertinent to the subject of inquiry. Contempt proceedings cannot be used to harass an individual or organization. Finally, before individuals can be held in contempt, they must willfully default, either by failing to appear before the investigating body or by refusing to answer pertinent questions.

Congress's contempt power has come into conflict with the FIRST AMENDMENT in several cases. The first of these cases was *Barenblatt v. United States,* 360 U.S. 109, 79 S. Ct. 1081, 3 L. Ed. 2d 1115 (1959), in which Lloyd Barenblatt refused to answer five questions of the House Un-American Activities Committee, regarding Communist infiltration of educational institutions. Barenblatt was convicted of contempt then appealed to the Supreme Court, arguing that the questions violated his First Amendment right to FREEDOM OF ASSOCIATION. The Court, in a 5–4 decision, supported Barenblatt. The Court stated that the questions were too vague to support a contempt citation and that Congress's investigative powers must be balanced against First Amendment rights.

The conflict between Congress's investigative powers and the First Amendment surfaced again in 1992 when Nina Totenberg, a National Public Radio correspondent, refused to answer questions of a Senate special counsel about how she obtained confidential documents related to

In 1957 a federal court found playwright Arthur Miller guilty of contempt of Congress charges for refusing to disclose the names of alleged Communist writers to the House Un-American Activities Committee. The conviction was overturned by an appellate court in 1958.

AP/WIDE WORLD PHOTOS

the nomination of CLARENCE THOMAS to the U.S. Supreme Court. Totenberg had earlier revealed that the SENATE JUDICIARY COMMITTEE was looking into accusations that Thomas had sexually harassed members of his staff. The charges led to public testimony by law professor ANITA HILL. A Senate special counsel asked to have Totenberg held in contempt when she refused to reveal who leaked information about the charges to her. The request was denied by the Senate Rules Committee because of its potential "chilling effect on the media."

Congress also has used the contempt power in conflicts with private parties and the EXECUTIVE BRANCH of government. For instance, business partners of Ferdinand Marcos, former president of the Philippines, produced documents for the House Foreign Affairs Committee only under threat of contempt citations. And James G. Watt, former secretary of the interior, was charged with contempt by a congressional committee in the early 1980s when, citing EXECUTIVE PRIVILEGE, he refused to release INTERIOR DEPARTMENT documents.

Contempt Proceedings against President Clinton

On April 12, 1999, President WILLIAM JEFFERSON CLINTON became the first sitting president in United States history to be held in contempt of court. The contempt charge against President Clinton stemmed from a deposition he gave in connection with a 1994 SEXUAL HARASSMENT lawsuit filed by Paula Jones. *Jones v. Clinton*, 858 F. Supp. 902 (E.D. Ark. 1994). Jones alleged that on May 8, 1991, she was an Arkansas state employee working at a conference held at a hotel in Little Rock. At some point during the conference, Jones claimed she was escorted to a hotel room by one of Clinton's bodyguards, where she was introduced to the then-governor. Shortly after the introduction, Jones alleged that Clinton dropped his trousers and demanded oral sex from her. Jones said that though she refused and was allowed to leave, her career as a state government employee suffered thereafter.

The Jones lawsuit languished in pre-trial discovery for the first three years after it was filed. On January 17, 1998, Jones and her lawyers deposed Clinton, who was now serving his second term as president of the United States. During the deposition, Clinton was asked a series of questions about his relationship with a White House intern named Monica Lewinsky. The president testified that he was never alone with the former White House intern and did not have a sexual relationship with her.

A subsequent probe by independent counsel KENNETH STARR revealed that the president's DNA had been found on Lewinsky's dress, which eventually led Clinton to admit that he had an "inappropriate intimate relationship" with his former intern (*Jones v. Clinton*, 36 F. Supp. 2d 1118 (E.D. Ark. 1999). The discovery of the dress also fueled the House of Representatives to draft ARTICLES OF IMPEACHMENT against the president.

A month after giving the deposition, Clinton filed a motion to dismiss the Jones lawsuit. On April 1, 1998, United States District Judge SUSAN WEBBER WRIGHT granted the motion to dismiss, finding that Jones had "failed to demonstrate that she has a case worthy of submitting to a jury." *Jones v. Clinton*, 990 F. Supp. 657 (E.D. Ark. 1998). While the case was pending on appeal, Clinton and Jones settled the sexual harassment lawsuit for $850,000.

A year later Judge Wright addressed the issue whether President Clinton should be held in contempt for denying his relationship with Lewinsky during the January 1998 deposition. At the time he gave the deposition, there was very little evidence indicating that the president's testimony was false. But in the 14 months that followed, it became clear that the president had not only been alone with Monica Lewinsky but also had some form of sexual relations with her.

Accordingly, Judge Wright found the president in contempt for giving "false, misleading and evasive answers that were designed to obstruct the judicial process" at a deposition over which she personally presided. *Jones v. Clinton*, 36 F. Supp. 2d 1118 (E.D. Ark. 1999). Although Clinton maintained that his "intimate" relationship with Lewinsky did not constitute "sexual" relations, Wright said that it is difficult to construe "the president's sworn statements . . . as anything other than a willful refusal to obey this court's discovery orders." *Jones v. Clinton* 36 F. Supp. 2d 1118 (E.D. Ark. 1999).

In July 1998, Wright leveled a $90,686 fine against the president. Wright said regarding this case that the fine was intended to both punish Clinton for the contempt violation and also "to deter others who might consider emulating the president's misconduct."

Wright then referred the matter to the Arkansas Supreme Court to determine whether the president should lose his license to practice law in that state. In May 1999 the Arkansas Supreme Court Committee on Professional Conduct recommended that Clinton be disbarred. However, on January 19, 2001, his last day in office, President Clinton resolved the case before the state ethics committee by agreeing to surrender his law license for a period of five years and admitting, according to Pete Yost in an AP Online report, that he "knowingly gave evasive and misleading answers" about his relationship with Monica Lewinsky in violation of Arkansas rules governing attorney ethics. Additionally, Clinton agreed to pay a $25,000 fine.

FURTHER READINGS

Alderman, Ellen, and Caroline Kennedy. 1991. *In Our Defense: The Bill of Rights in Action.* New York: Morrow.

Beck, Carl. 1959. *Contempt of Congress: A Study of the Prosecutions Initiated by the Committee on Un-American Activities, 1945–1957.* Hauser Press.

Dudley, Earl C. 1993. "Getting Beyond the Civil/Criminal Distinction: A New Approach to the Regulation of Indirect Contempts." *Virginia Law Review* 79.

Goldfarb, Ronald L. 1963. *The Contempt Power.* New York: Columbia Univ. Press.

Mangan, James J. 1994. "Contempt for the Fourth Estate: No Reporter's Privilege Before a Congressional Investigation." *Georgetown Law Journal* 83.

Yost, Pete. January 20, 2001. "Clinton Admits False Statements." *AP Online.*

CROSS-REFERENCES

Communism; Freedom of the Press.

CONTEST

To defend against an adverse claim made in a court by a plaintiff or a prosecutor; to challenge a position asserted in a judicial proceeding, as to contest the probate of a will.

CONTEXT

The language that precedes and follows a series of words, such as a particular sentence or clause.

The context of a legal document is often scrutinized to shed light upon the intent of an ambiguous or obscure sentence or clause so that it may be interpreted as its drafter intended.

CONTINENTAL CONGRESS

The first national legislative assembly in the United States, existing from 1774 to 1789.

During its fifteen-year existence, the Continental Congress served as the chief legislative and executive body of the federal government. Although hobbled by provisions such as an inability to raise funds directly through taxation, it nevertheless created a viable, if sometimes ineffective, national union during the earliest years of the United States. The Continental Congress passed the DECLARATION OF INDEPENDENCE and other lasting measures, and it set important precedents for the government instituted under the Constitution in 1789. Some of the most important figures of early American history were members of the Continental Congress, including JOHN ADAMS, Samuel Adams, SAMUEL CHASE, BENJAMIN FRANKLIN, ALEXANDER HAMILTON, PATRICK HENRY, JOHN JAY, THOMAS JEFFERSON, JAMES MADISON, and GEORGE WASHINGTON.

The First Continental Congress met in Philadelphia between September 5 and October 26, 1774. Although it was officially called simply the Congress, contemporaries referred to it as the Continental Congress in order to distinguish it from the various state congresses. Fifty-six delegates from twelve colonies (Georgia did not participate) assembled in an attempt to unite the colonies and restore rights and liberties that had been curtailed by Great Britain. The Continental Congress adopted the Declaration of Rights, agreements regarding common policies toward Britain, and a resolution that it would meet again the following year if its grievances were not settled.

When Britain rebuffed their demands, the colonists assembled the Second Continental Congress in May of 1775, again in Philadelphia. Fighting between Britain and Massachusetts at the Battles of Lexington and Concord had already occurred, and the Continental Congress voted to back Massachusetts. It appointed George Washington as commander in chief of colonial armed forces. With this decision, Congress undertook a vital role directing the Revolutionary War.

As the war continued, colonial opinion began to move toward permanent separation from Great Britain. On July 4, 1776, the Continental Congress adopted the Declaration of Independence, which announced the formation of the United States of America as a new nation. In succeeding months, the Congress drafted the ARTICLES OF CONFEDERATION, the new country's first constitution. The Congress approved the Articles on November 15, 1777, but the states did not ratify them until 1781.

The Articles contained provisions for a national legislature designated simply Congress. Although some historians have called this subsequent body the Congress of the Confederation, most group it with its predecessor and call it the Continental Congress. In this Congress, each state had from two to seven delegates but only one vote. Delegates were to serve no more than "three years in any term of six years" (art. V).

During the struggle to approve and then ratify the Articles, the advocates of STATES' RIGHTS greatly weakened its provisions for a strong federal, or national, government. As a result, the Articles did not allow the federal government to raise its own funds directly through taxation. Instead, the central government could only requisition money from the states. The Articles also required a unanimous vote of Congress to approve any amendments, a feature that made it difficult to adapt their provisions to the changing needs of the nation. In addition, Congress as it was constituted under the Articles proved ill suited to tasks that the Constitution later assigned to the EXECUTIVE BRANCH, including the conduct of diplomatic, military, and commercial affairs. For example, Congress fared poorly in negotiating with Britain and France, in paying war debts, and in putting down armed revolts such as SHAYS'S REBELLION.

The problems of the Continental Congress and the Articles of Confederation led to plans for a new federal constitution. During the Constitutional Convention of 1787, leading members of the Continental Congress joined with other politicians and lawmakers to create a framework for a new national government, including a new Congress. Following ratification of the Constitution by the states in 1789, the Continental Congress handed over its legislative powers to the Congress that continues in form to the present day.

Although the Continental Congress had weaknesses, it nevertheless passed crucial legislation and set vital precedents for the framing of the Constitution. Its legislative legacy includes the establishment of the Northwest Territory, provisions for the sale and oversight of western land, and many other laws adopted by the later Congress. According to Edmund C. Burnett, a leading historian on the subject, the

> Continental Congress . . . developed and formulated many of those fundamental princi-

ples of government that have become our national heritage. Indeed it is not too much to say that [a] great part of the materials built into the structure of the Constitution itself were wrought in the forge of the Continental Congress.

FURTHER READINGS

Burnett, Edmund C. 1941. *The Continental Congress.* New York: Macmillan.

Davis, Derek H. 2000. *Religion and the Continental Congress, 1774-1789: Contributions to Original Intent.* New York: Oxford Univ. Press

McCormick, Richard P. 1997. "Ambiguous Authority: The Ordinances of the Confederation Congress, 1781-1789." *American Journal of Legal History* 41 (October): 411–39.

CROSS-REFERENCES

Congress of the United States; Constitution of the United States; "Declaration of the Causes and Necessity of Taking up Arms" (Appendix, Primary Document); Northwest Ordinance.

A depiction of members of the Continental Congress, the first national legislative assembly in the United States, during the signing of the Declaration of Independence. John Hancock, president of the Congress from 1775 to 1777, is shown holding the document.

LIBRARY OF CONGRESS

CONTINGENT

Fortuitous; dependent upon the possible occurrence of a future event, the existence of which is not assured.

The word *contingent* denotes that there is no present interest or right but only a conditional one which will become effective upon the happening of the designated condition. A *contingent remainder* is the right to possess property after the death of a person who holds a life estate in the land provided a specified condition is fulfilled. An owner of land who grants a life estate to a son, with a remainder to a daughter if she marries, has created a contingent remainder, the contingency being the daughter's marriage.

CONTINGENT FEE

Payment to an attorney for legal services that depends, or is contingent, upon there being some recovery or award in the case. The payment is then a percentage of the amount recovered—such as 25 percent if the matter is settled, or 30 percent if it proceeds to trial.

Contingent-fee agreements are valid only in civil cases and are frequently used in personal injury cases. Court rules and statutes often regulate these fees in relation to the type of action and amount of recovery. Such an arrangement is generally used when the party seeking recovery cannot afford to retain an attorney and therefore would not have any effective means of prosecuting a claim.

An attorney is not entitled to a contingent fee in the absence of an express contract. Contingent-fee agreements, although intensively scrutinized by the courts, are valid if equitable and reasonable to the client. The purpose of a contingent fee is to reward attorneys for proficiency and diligence in prosecuting disputed and litigated claims, as opposed to rendering minor services that any inexperienced attorney might perform.

Contingent fees are never permitted in criminal cases, as there is no possibility of a financial recovery that would be the source of the contingent fee. These arrangements are emphatically discouraged in DIVORCE proceedings due to public policy considerations. An attorney may discourage a reconciliation if a fee depends upon the granting of a divorce. Public policy favors the continuation of marriage, which is traditionally viewed as a stabilizing force in society. A contingent-fee contract that prohibits a client from settling a case is also void as against public policy because society views the avoidance of unnecessary litigation as desirable.

When an attorney who was retained on a contingent-fee basis dies, his or her estate will not be entitled to any fee unless the attorney had completely performed the contract prior to death. In some states, the estate cannot recover unless the jury had returned a monetary award in favor of the client before the attorney's death. However, the attorney's personal representatives may collect payment for the reasonable services that were rendered.

An attorney might be entitled to recover his or her share of the proceeds of an action if the contingent-fee contract was substantially per-formed prior to the death of the client. If the case had been submitted to the jury before the client died, and the jury found in favor of the client, the attorney is entitled to his or her fee from the proceeds. If the suit is dismissed or settled by the client's personal representatives, the attorney might have no right to a fee unless the contract so provided. However, the death of a client does not deprive an attorney of the right to recover the reasonable value of his or her services rendered until the time of the client's death.

Jurisdictions are not unanimous as to the question of whether an attorney's contingent fee should be calculated based on the net amount of the recovery that a client actually receives or the gross amount of recovery before any successful counterclaims are factored in. For example, suppose that a personal-injury lawyer agrees to represent the plaintiff for a one-third contingent fee and recovers a $100,000 jury verdict. However, the jury also returned a verdict on the defendant's counterclaim for $10,000. Should the plaintiff's lawyer receive a $33,000 contingent fee or a $30,000 contingent fee?

Section 35 of the Restatement (Third) of the Law Governing Lawyers provides that "when a lawyer has contracted for a contingent fee, the lawyer is entitled to receive the specified fee only when and to the extent the client receives payment." Comment d to section 35 provides that "[i]n the absence of [a] prior agreement to the contrary, the amount of the client's recovery is computed net of any offset, such as a recovery by an opposing party on a counterclaim." To date, Section 35 has been adopted only in Texas. Other states calculate the fee based on the client's full award, regardless of whether the client ever actually recovers the full amount awarded, reasoning that such a calculation better reflects the comprehensive value of the attorney's services and the economic value received by the client.

CONTINUANCE

The adjournment or postponement of an action pending in a court to a later date of the same or another session of the court, granted by a court in response to a motion made by a party to a lawsuit. The entry into the trial record of the adjournment of a case for the purpose of formally evidencing it.

Courts, by virtue of their authority to hear and determine cases, have inherent discretionary power to grant or deny continuances,

Contingent Fee Agreement Form

LEGAL SERVICES AGREEMENT

1. IDENTIFICATION OF PARTIES. This agreement, executed in duplicate with each party receiving an executed original, is made between JOHN SMITH, hereafter referred to as "Attorney," and JANE DOE, hereafter referred to as "Client."

   This agreement is required by Business and Professions Code section 6147 and is intended to fulfill the requirements of that section.

2. LEGAL SERVICES TO BE PROVIDED. The legal services to be provided by Attorney to Client are as follows: Representation of Client with respect to her claim for damages for personal injuries arising out of the automobile accident of September 15, 2002.

3. LEGAL SERVICES SPECIFICALLY EXCLUDED. Legal services that are not to be provided by Attorney under this agreement specifically include, but are not limited to, the following: Representation with respect to (a) any claim for property damage arising out of the accident, (b) any dispute with a medical care provider about amounts owed by Client for services received, or (c) any appeal in which Client is an appellant from a court judgment on Client's personal injury claim (i.e., Attorney's obligation to represent Client under this agreement extends to an appeal only if Client is a respondent).

   If Client wishes that Attorney provide any legal services not to be provided under this agreement, a separate written agreement between Attorney and Client will be required.

4. RESPONSIBILITIES OF ATTORNEY AND CLIENT. Attorney will perform the legal services called for under this agreement, keep Client informed of progress and developments, and respond promptly to Client's inquiries and communications. Client will be truthful and cooperative with Attorney and keep Attorney reasonably informed of developments and of Client's address, telephone number, and whereabouts.

5. ATTORNEY'S FEES. The amount Attorney will receive for attorney's fees for the legal services to be provided under this agreement will be:

   (a) percent of the net recovery if the recovery is obtained before the filing of a lawsuit;

   (b) percent of the net recovery if the recovery is obtained after the filing of a lawsuit but before the arbitration hearing, settlement conference, or trial, whichever occurs first;

   (c) percent of the net recovery if the recovery is obtained at or after the arbitration hearing, settlement conference, or trial, whichever occurs first, but before the filing of Client's brief in an appeal from a court judgment; and

   (d) percent of the net recovery if the recovery is obtained after the filing of Client's brief in an appeal from a court judgment.

   "Net recovery" means the amount remaining after the total amount received (whether by settlement, arbitration award, or court judgment) has been reduced by the sum of all "costs," as defined in Paragraph 7 of this agreement.

   If payment of all or any part of the amount to be received will be deferred (such as in the case of an annuity, a structured settlement, or periodic payments), the "total amount received," for purposes of calculating the attorney's fees, will be the initial lump-sum payment plus the present value, as of the time of the settlement, final arbitration award, or final judgment, of the payments to be received thereafter. The attorney's fees will be paid out of the initial lump-sum payment. If the payment is insufficient to pay the attorney's fees in full, the balance will be paid from subsequent payments of the recovery before any distribution to Client.

   Client is informed that this Attorney's fee is not set by law but rather is negotiable between the Attorney and the Client.

   If there is no net recovery, Attorney will receive no attorney's fees.

6. DIVISION OF ATTORNEY'S FEES. Attorney will divide the attorney's fees received for the legal services provided under this agreement with Margaret Andover. The terms of the division are as follows: Attorney will pay to Margaret Andover one third of all attorney's fees received. Client is informed that, under the Rules of Professional Conduct of the State Bar of California, such a division may be made only with the Client's written consent after a full disclosure to the Client in writing that a division of fees will be made and of the terms of such division. Client hereby expressly consents to the division.

7. COSTS. Attorney will advance all "costs" in connection with Attorney's representation of Client under this agreement. Attorney will be reimbursed out of the recovery before any distribution of fees to Attorney or any distribution to Client. If there is no recovery, or the recovery is insufficient to reimburse Attorney in full for costs advanced, Attorney will bear the loss. Costs include, but are not limited to, court filing fees, deposition costs, expert fees and expenses, investigation costs, long-distance telephone charges, messenger service fees, photocopying expenses, and process server fees. Items that are not to be considered costs, and that must be paid by Client without being either advanced or contributed to by Attorney, include, but are not limited to, Client's medical expenses and other parties' costs, if any, that Client is ultimately required to pay.

8. REPRESENTATION OF ADVERSE INTERESTS. Client is informed that the Rules of Professional Conduct of the State Bar of California require the Client's informed written consent before an Attorney may begin or continue to represent the Client when the attorney has or had a relationship with another party interested in the subject matter of the Attorney's proposed representation of the client.

[continued]

A sample contingent fee agreement between an attorney and a client.

Contingent Fee Agreement Form

Attorney is not aware of any relationship with any other party interested in the subject matter of Attorney's services for Client under this agreement. As long as Attorney's services for Client continue under this agreement, Attorney will not agree to provide legal services for any such party without Client's prior written consent.

9. SETTLEMENT. Attorney will not settle Client's claim without the approval of Client, who will have the absolute right to accept or reject any settlement. Attorney will notify Client promptly of the terms of any settlement offer received by Attorney.

10. ATTORNEY'S LIEN. Attorney will have a lien for Attorney's fees and costs advanced on all claims and causes of action that are the subject of her representation of Client under this agreement and on all proceeds of any recovery obtained (whether by settlement, arbitration award, or court judgment).

11. DISCHARGE OF ATTORNEY. Client may discharge Attorney at any time by written notice effective when received by Attorney. Unless specifically agreed by Attorney and Client, Attorney will provide no further services and advance no further costs on Client's behalf after receipt of the notice. If Attorney is Client's attorney of record in any proceeding, Client will execute and return a substitution-of-attorney form immediately on its receipt from Attorney. Notwithstanding the discharge, Client will be obligated to pay Attorney out of the recovery a reasonable attorney's fee for all services provided and to reimburse Attorney out of the recovery for all costs advanced. If there is no recovery, or the recovery is insufficient to reimburse Attorney in full for costs advanced, Attorney will bear the loss.

12. WITHDRAWAL OF ATTORNEY. Attorney may withdraw at any time as permitted under the Rules of Professional Conduct of the State Bar of California. The circumstances under which the Rules permit such withdrawal include, but are not limited to, the following: (a) The client consents, and (b) the client's conduct renders it unreasonably difficult for the attorney to carry out the employment effectively. Notwithstanding Attorney's withdrawal, Client will be obligated to pay Attorney out of the recovery a reasonable attorney's fee for all services provided, and to reimburse Attorney out of the recovery for all costs advanced, before the withdrawal. If there is no recovery, or the recovery is insufficient to reimburse Attorney in full for costs advanced, Attorney will bear the loss.

13. RELEASE OF CLIENT'S PAPERS AND PROPERTY. At the termination of services under this agreement, Attorney will release promptly to Client on request all of Client's papers and property. "Client's papers and property" include correspondence, deposition transcripts, exhibits, experts' reports, legal documents, physical evidence, and other items reasonably necessary to Client's representation, whether Client has paid for them or not.

14. DISCLAIMER OF GUARANTY. Although Attorney may offer an opinion about possible results regarding the subject matter of this agreement, Attorney cannot guarantee any particular result. Client acknowledges that Attorney has made no promises about the outcome and that any opinion offered by Attorney in the future will not constitute a guaranty.

15. ENTIRE AGREEMENT. This agreement contains the entire agreement of the parties. No other agreement, statement, or promise made on or before the effective date of this agreement will be binding on the parties.

16. SEVERABILITY IN EVENT OF PARTIAL INVALIDITY. If any provision of this agreement is held in whole or in part to be unenforceable for any reason, the remainder of that provision and of the entire agreement will be severable and remain in effect.

17. MODIFICATION BY SUBSEQUENT AGREEMENT. This agreement may be modified by subsequent agreement of the parties only by an instrument in writing signed by both of them or an oral agreement to the extent that the parties carry it out.

18. ARBITRATION OF FEE DISPUTE. If a dispute arises between Attorney and Client regarding attorney's fees under this agreement and Attorney files suit in any court other than small claims court, Client will have the right to stay that suit by timely electing to arbitrate the dispute under Business and Professions Code sections 6200-6206, in which event Attorney must submit the matter to such arbitration.

19. ATTORNEY'S FEES AND COSTS IN ACTION ON AGREEMENT. The prevailing party in any action or proceeding to enforce any provision of this agreement will be awarded reasonable attorney's fees and costs incurred in that action or proceeding or in efforts to negotiate the matter.

20. EFFECTIVE DATE OF AGREEMENT. The effective date of this agreement will be the date when, having been executed by Client, one copy of the agreement is received by Attorney, provided the copy is received on or before February 1, 2002, or Attorney accepts late receipt.

The foregoing is agreed to by:

Date: _____   _____
                                     Client

Date: _____   _____
                                     Attorney

[This agreement is meant to be illustrative only. Counsel should consider what provisions should be included, and what modifications should be made, in a particular fee agreement.]

subject to restrictions imposed by statute. Continuances are granted when necessary to avert a miscarriage of justice but will be denied if sought merely for the purpose of delay. Criminal defendants are entitled to a SPEEDY TRIAL unless good cause justifies a continuance of the action.

In ruling on a motion for a continuance, a court examines all the facts and circumstances of a case—in particular, the applicant's GOOD FAITH, the purpose and necessity for the postponement, the probable advantage that could result from the continuance, and the possibility of prejudice to the rights of other parties. If there are multiple defendants in a case, a continuance granted to one of them postpones the trial of the case against all of them. A continuance is usually granted if requested by a defendant, since the plaintiff should have adequately prepared his or her case before commencing the action.

A court can, sua sponte (on its own motion), order a continuance in certain instances, such as when none of the parties appears on the date of the hearing.

A continuance can occur by operation of law when a case has not been tried or otherwise disposed of during a particular term because of unanticipated problems, such as the death of the presiding judge. The case is automatically postponed until the following term.

Parties in a lawsuit file pleadings (written statements presenting each side of the case before trial to elucidate the issues to be resolved). A plaintiff whose complaint fails to state a CAUSE OF ACTION is not entitled to a continuance to correct this failure, but a defendant can make a motion for a dismissal of the action. Nor can a defendant whose answer to the plaintiff's complaint does not allege a meritorious defense cure this deficiency by seeking a continuance, but the plaintiff might make a motion for a SUMMARY JUDGMENT in his or her favor. A continuance may be granted, however, in a case that was scheduled for trial before the issues were joined or clearly established.

After a trial has begun or while motions are made pending the decision, a court can grant a continuance provided adequate grounds exist.

The trial of a case that has been remanded (sent back) by an appellate court to a lower court for a new trial may be continued at a later date if there is not enough time to prepare for the new trial.

When the parties consent to or stipulate a postponement of a case, a court will grant a continuance only if their agreement meets its approval.

Grounds

Continuances are granted only if valid grounds exist that justify the postponement of the action. For example, a court will continue a case in which all the interested parties have not appeared in order to bring them into the action so that they may present their side of the case. If SERVICE OF PROCESS has not been properly made upon a defendant, a court may grant a continuance to perfect service so that a plaintiff will not be deprived of an opportunity to have the action tried. A delay in filing pleadings, which surprises the opposing party and affects the issues in an action, ordinarily entitles the adverse party to a continuance, since that party must be given time to prepare a response before the trial in order to prevent prejudice to his or her rights. A continuance may be granted for the accidental loss or destruction of papers in an action provided they cannot be readily replaced and the applicant for the continuance was not responsible for their loss.

Lack of Preparation Where the party making the motion is guilty of inexcusable ignorance, delay, or NEGLIGENCE in preparing the case, the court will deny a motion for a continuance. An applicant who can, however, demonstrate some legal or equitable reason or exercise of diligence in trying to prepare for the case may win a continuance.

Change of Counsel Withdrawal of legal counsel or employment of new counsel immediately preceding or during a trial does not necessarily warrant a continuance of the action. For example, if it is clear that a party has changed attorneys a number of times solely as a dilatory tactic for the purpose of delay, that party will be denied a continuance. Only where the circumstances of the case demonstrate that a miscarriage of justice will ensue from a denial of a continuance will a court seriously consider postponing the action.

Pendency of Action A continuance is granted when it is in the interests of justice to await the outcome of another proceeding affecting the same parties or where the interests of the parties are closely related, such as in cases dealing with VICARIOUS LIABILITY.

Illness The illness of a party to a lawsuit justifies a continuance only if injustice would result from proceeding with the case. If an illness is feigned or alleged merely for the purpose of delay, the applicant's motion will be denied and the applicant might be held in CONTEMPT. A party who becomes ill before trial should notify the court and the other parties, as soon as it is reasonably practicable to provide such notice, that his or her condition may jeopardize his or her participation in the proceedings. An AFFIDAVIT or certificate of a physician that a party's illness precludes his or her presence at trial should be filed with the court.

The illness of the judge presiding over the trial operates as a continuance of the action.

Determination

A motion for a continuance is heard by the court which rules upon it after an evaluation of the evidence before it. If a continuance is granted, the trial court will set its duration with regard to the rights of both parties and impose any necessary restrictions. During the time of the adjournment the court may modify or revoke its order if reasonable cause is shown or if the court is satisfied that no injustice will result.

Successive continuances sought by a party are scrutinized closely by a court because there is a likelihood that they are sought for dilatory purposes. Unless the applicant clearly establishes that a postponement is essential to the integrity of the judicial process and a preservation of the rights of the parties, it will be denied. A motion based upon newly discovered evidence will be denied if the applicant could have discovered the evidence sooner by the use of reasonable efforts.

A continuance expires on the date specified in the court order. If the basis for the continuance ceases to exist prior to that date, the court may revoke its order and require that the case proceed to trial.

Waiver

A party relinquishes or waives the right to obtain a continuance if he or she (1) fails to request one; (2) proceeds with the case after the motion for a continuance has been denied without making an exception to the ruling; or (3) voluntarily discontinues the action.

FURTHER READINGS

Yeazell, Stephen C. 1998. *Federal Rules of Civil Procedure: With Selected Statutes and Cases.* Gaithersburg, Md.: Aspen.

CROSS-REFERENCES

Motion; Pleading; Speedy Trial.

CONTINUING LEGAL EDUCATION

The purpose of continuing legal education is to maintain or sharpen the skills of licensed attorneys and judges. Accredited courses examine new areas of the law or review basic practice and trial principles. Programs for continuing legal education are sponsored by state, local, and federal bar associations, law firms, law schools, and groups such as the AMERICAN BAR ASSOCIATION (ABA) and the American Law Institute.

Continuing legal education is mandatory in 40 states; voluntary programs are offered in the remaining 10. Courses are approved by state boards that oversee continuing education. In states with mandatory continuing legal education, attorneys receive credits for attending lectures and seminars taught by respected attorneys, judges, and scholars. The courses cover a variety of topics involving virtually all areas of practice. Written program materials are usually included as part of the tuition fee.

A 1974 informal poll conducted by state and local bar associations revealed widespread support for compulsory continuing legal education. The measure was favored to ensure professional competence and to improve the public image of lawyers. Supporters believed that continuing legal education would reduce the number of LEGAL MALPRACTICE suits, keep lawyers updated on important changes in the law, and improve the representation of clients. A year later, in 1975, Minnesota became the first state to adopt mandatory continuing legal education. The Minnesota Legislature appeared ready to take over the administration of continuing legal education; the Minnesota Supreme Court, however, preferred judicially mandated education, and took appropriate steps to institute it. The court ordered all Minnesota lawyers and judges to complete 45 hours of post-admission legal education every three years.

The Code of Professional Responsibility adopted by every state maintains that lawyers must remain proficient in their work. Continuing legal education is one way to achieve professional competence. Other professions such as medicine, education, and accounting also require continuing education. Beginning in the 1990s, states added specific content requirements. For example, Minnesota requires that in each reporting cycle attorneys must take three hours of ethics-related coursework and two hours of coursework related to the elimination of bias in the legal profession. The state of California requires attorneys to take one hour per reporting cycle of coursework on the prevention and detection of substance abuse.

The delivery of continuing legal education has changed over time. Although most programs are presented at the local level, many providers now videotape sessions and replay them at a variety of sites around a state. This allows attorneys in rural areas and more remote locations to earn their credits locally. In addition, national providers such as the ABA produce seminars that are delivered through satellite transmissions to cities around the United States.

In most states where continuing legal education is required, nonpracticing lawyers may elect to be on restricted status. This means they can maintain their law license but do not have to fulfill continuing education requirements. Sometimes hardship or MITIGATING CIRCUMSTANCES exempt practicing attorneys from a continuing education requirement.

FURTHER READINGS

MacCrate, Robert, ed. 1992. *Legal Education and Professional Development: An Educational Continuum.* St. Paul, Minn.: West.

Sheran, Robert J., and Laurence C. Harmon. 1976. *Minnesota Plan: Mandatory Continuing Legal Education for Lawyers and Judges as a Condition for the Maintaining of Professional Licensing.* Reprinted in *Fordham Law Review* (May).

Tamayo-Calabrese, Macarena, Annette Cook, and Shirley Meyer. August 2002. "Continuing Legal Education in the United States." *Issues of Democracy.* Available online at <usinfo.state.gov/journals/itdhr/0802/ijde/calabrese .htm> (accessed May 22, 2003).

CROSS-REFERENCES

Legal Education.

CONTRA

Against; conflicting; opposite.

A *contra-balance* is the amount in an account of a creditor that is the opposite of the usual balance of such an account. It is an account receivable (a debt owed to the creditor) but with a credit balance (an amount owed to the debtor greater than what is owed to the creditor). The creditor therefore owes the debtor money, the opposite of the normal debtor-creditor relationship.

Marijuana plants, such as these seized by a Miami police officer, are considered contraband because it is illegal to produce or possess them.

AP/WIDE WORLD PHOTOS

CONTRABAND

Any property that it is illegal to produce or possess. Smuggled goods that are imported into or exported from a country in violation of its laws.

Contraband confiscated by law enforcement authorities upon the arrest of a person for the crimes of production or possession of such goods will not be returned, regardless of the outcome of the prosecution.

CONTRACT WITH AMERICA

In the historic 1994 midterm elections, Republicans won a majority in Congress for the first time in forty years, partly on the appeal of a platform called the Contract with America. Put forward by House Republicans, this sweeping ten-point plan promised to reshape government. Its main theme was the decentralization of federal authority: deregulation, tax cuts, reform of social programs, increased power for states, and a balanced FEDERAL BUDGET were its chief ambitions. With unusual speed, all ten items came to a vote in the House of Representatives within one hundred days, and the House passed nine of the ten measures. Yet, even as House Speaker NEWT GINGRICH (R-Ga.) compared the plan to the most important political reforms of the twentieth century, progress on the contract stalled. Senate Republicans were slow to embrace it, Democrats in both chambers denounced it, and President BILL CLINTON threatened to VETO its most radical provisions. Only three of the least controversial measures had become law by the end of 1995 as Congress and the White House battled bitterly over the federal budget.

On the surface, the contract differed little from other modern Republican platforms. It began with a statement of three "core" principles in the form of an argument: the federal government is too big and unresponsive *(accountability)*, and big government programs sap individual and family willpower *(responsibility)*—and thus an overtaxed and overregulated citizenry cannot pursue the American Dream *(opportunity)*. Republicans had been saying as much for at least two decades. Although Democrats had controlled Congress for more than forty years with an almost opposite view of government's duty to its people, Republicans had held the White House from 1980 to 1992. The election of President Clinton in 1992 was a striking setback for REPUBLICAN PARTY strategists. Yet, they took encouragement from voter discontent with the pace of Clinton's legislative plans, two key provisions of which—an economic stimulus package and HEALTH CARE reform—failed to pass even with a Democratic majority in Congress. For the mid-1994 congressional elections, they intended to capitalize on this discontent with a platform that promised quick and dramatic change.

Toward this end, the Contract with America made two promises "to restore the bonds of trust between the people and their elected representatives." First, it promised to change the way Congress works by requiring that lawmakers follow the same workplace laws as the rest of the country—notably, SEXUAL HARASSMENT laws— and by strictly reforming the sluggish committee process in the House of Representatives. Second, it promised that the House would vote on the ten key planks of the contract within the first one hundred days of the new Congress. The contract gave these ten planks names such as the Fiscal Responsibility Act, the Taking Back Our

In September 1994, Newt Gingrich and a group of Republican congressional candidates announced their plans for a platform called Contract with America. The ten-point plan helped the Republican Party win a majority in Congress.

AP/WIDE WORLD PHOTOS

Streets Act, and the Personal Responsibility Act. The contract promised action on the following issues: the federal deficit, crime, WELFARE reform, family values, middle-class tax cuts, national defense, SOCIAL SECURITY, federal deregulation and capital gains tax cuts, legal reform, CIVIL LAW and PRODUCT LIABILITY, and term limits for federal lawmakers.

The actual proposals represented a mixture of old and new ideas. Republicans had long supported deregulation of industry, TORT reform, and middle-class tax cuts. As a deficit reduction solution, the line-item veto was an old idea: ever since the 1980s, Republicans had called for a PRESIDENTIAL POWER to veto specific parts of federal spending bills (rather than the entire bills). More revolutionary was the contract's related proposal: a constitutional amendment requiring a balanced budget. In the same sense, the welfare reform proposals reflected a long-running debate and yet offered ambitiously strict limits on spending, eligibility, and administration, and even sought to transfer authority over traditionally federal programs to the states. Other proposals grew out of more recent concerns. The crime reform measure was a Republican effort to scale back social spending and increase law enforcement spending, in reaction to the Clinton crime bill of 1994; and proposals to curb U.S. military involvement in the United Nations' peacekeeping missions reflected Republican criticism of Clinton's decisions to send troops to Somalia and Haiti.

The contract met with mixed results in 1995. The House Republican leadership did indeed put each item to a vote within the first one hundred days. It divided each item into one or more bills, and thirty-one of the resulting thirty-two measures passed—only one, for congressional term limits, failed. The Senate moved much more slowly. In part, this was because the Senate, as a debating body, customarily proceeds more cautiously. Another reason was that the senators, unlike their first-year counterparts in the House, were far less eager to pass sweeping reforms: the Senate killed the proposal for a constitutional amendment on the budget, for example, and simply delayed action on several other bills. President Clinton's promise to veto any far-ranging welfare and budgetary proposals also crimped Republican plans, and by November 1995 this threat had produced a bitter standoff that resulted in the temporary closing of the federal government.

Three contract proposals became law: the Congressional Accountability Act of 1995 (Pub. L. No. 104-1, 109 Stat. 3), which requires Congress to follow eleven workplace laws; the Unfunded Mandates Reform Act of 1995 (Pub. L. No. 104-4, 109 Stat. 48), which restricts Congress from imposing mandates on states that are not adequately funded; and the Paperwork Reduction Act of 1995 (Pub. L. No. 104-13, 109 Stat. 163), which reduces federal paperwork requirements.

CONTRACTS

Agreements between two entities, creating an enforceable obligation to do, or to refrain from doing, a particular thing.

Nature and Contractual Obligation

The purpose of a contract is to establish the agreement that the parties have made and to fix their rights and duties in accordance with that agreement. The courts must enforce a valid contract as it is made, unless there are grounds that bar its enforcement.

Statutes prescribe and restrict the terms of a contract where the general public is affected. The terms of an insurance contract that protect a common carrier are controlled by statute in order to safeguard the public by guaranteeing that there will be financial resources available in the event of an accident.

The courts may not create a contract for the parties. When the parties have no express or implied agreement on the essential terms of a contract, there is no contract. Courts are only empowered to enforce contracts, not to write them, for the parties. A contract, in order to be enforceable, must be a valid. The function of the court is to enforce agreements only if they exist and not to create them through the imposition of such terms as the court considers reasonable.

It is the policy of the law to encourage the formation of contracts between competent parties for lawful objectives. As a general rule, contracts by competent persons, equitably made, are valid and enforceable. Parties to a contract are bound by the terms to which they have agreed, usually even if the contract appears to be improvident or a bad bargain, as long as it did not result from FRAUD, duress, or UNDUE INFLUENCE.

The binding force of a contract is based on the fact that it evinces a meeting of minds of two parties in GOOD FAITH. A contract, once formed, does not contemplate a right of a party to reject it. Contracts that were mutually entered into between parties with the capacity to contract are binding obligations and may not be set aside due to the caprice of one party or the other unless a statute provides to the contrary.

Types of Contracts

Contracts under Seal Traditionally, a contract was an enforceable legal document only if it was stamped with a seal. The seal represented that the parties intended the agreement to entail legal consequences. No legal benefit or detriment to any party was required, as the seal was a symbol of the solemn acceptance of the legal effect and consequences of the agreement. In the past, all contracts were required to be under seal in order to be valid, but the seal has lost some or all of its effect by statute in many jurisdictions. Recognition by the courts of informal contracts, such as implied contracts, has also diminished the importance and employment of formal contracts under seal.

Express Contracts In an express contract, the parties state the terms, either orally or in writing, at the time of its formation. There is a definite written or oral offer that is accepted by the offeree (i.e., the person to whom the offer is made) in a manner that explicitly demonstrates consent to its terms.

Implied Contracts Although contracts that are *implied in fact* and contracts *implied in law* are both called implied contracts, a true implied contract consists of obligations arising from a mutual agreement and intent to promise, which have not been expressed in words. It is misleading to label as an implied contract one that is implied in law because a contract implied in law lacks the requisites of a true contract. The term quasi-contract is a more accurate designation of contracts implied in law. Implied contracts are as binding as express contracts. An implied contract depends on substance for its existence; therefore, for an implied contract to arise, there must be some act or conduct of a party, in order for them to be bound.

A contract implied in fact is not expressed by the parties but, rather, suggested from facts and circumstances that indicate a mutual intention to contract. Circumstances exist that, according to the ordinary course of dealing and common understanding, demonstrate such an intent that is sufficient to support a finding of an implied contract. Contracts implied in fact do not arise contrary to either the law or the express declaration of the parties. Contracts implied in law (quasi-contracts) are distinguishable in that they are not predicated on the assent of the parties, but, rather, exist regardless of assent.

The implication of a mutual agreement must be a reasonable deduction from all of the circumstances and relations that contemplate parties when they enter into the contract or which are necessary to effectuate their intention. No implied promise will exist where the relations between the parties prevent the inference of a contract.

A contract will not be implied where it would result in inequity or harm. Where doubt and divergence exist in the minds of the parties, the court may not infer a contractual relationship. If, after an agreement expires, the parties continue to perform according to its terms, an implication arises that they have mutually assented to a new contract that contains the same provisions as the old agreement.

A contract implied in fact, which is inferred from the circumstances, is a true contract, whereas a contract implied in law is actually an obligation imposed by law and treated as a contract only for the purposes of a remedy. With respect to contracts implied in fact, the contract defines the duty; in the case of quasi-contracts, the duty defines and imposes the agreement upon the parties.

Executed and Executory Contracts An executed contract is one in which nothing remains to be done by either party. The phrase is, to a certain extent, a misnomer because the completion of performances by the parties signifies that a contract no longer exists. An executory contract is one in which some future act or obligation remains to be performed according to its terms.

Bilateral and Unilateral Contracts The exchange of mutual, reciprocal promises between entities that entails the performance of an act, or forbearance from the performance of an act, with respect to each party, is a BILATERAL CONTRACT. A bilateral contract is sometimes called a two-sided contract because of the two promises that constitute it. The promise that one party makes constitutes sufficient consideration (see discussion below) for the promise made by the other.

A unilateral contract involves a promise that is made by only one party. The offeror (i.e., a person who makes a proposal) promises to do a certain thing if the offeree performs a requested act that he or she knows is the basis of a legally enforceable contract. The performance constitutes an acceptance of the offer, and the contract then becomes executed. Acceptance of the offer may be revoked, however, until the performance has been completed. This is a one-sided type of contract because only the offeror, who makes the promise, will be legally bound. The offeree may act as requested, or may refrain from acting, but may not be sued for failing to perform, or even for abandoning performance once it has begun, because he or she did not make any promises.

Unconscionable Contracts An UNCONSCIONABLE contract is one that is unjust or unduly one-sided in favor of the party who has the superior bargaining power. The adjective *unconscionable* implies an affront to fairness and decency. An unconscionable contract is one that no mentally competent person would accept and that no fair and honest person would enter into. Courts find that unconscionable contracts usually result from the exploitation of consumers who are poorly educated, impoverished, and unable to shop around for the best price available in the competitive marketplace.

The majority of unconscionable contracts occur in consumer transactions. Contractual provisions that indicate gross one-sidedness in favor of the seller include limiting damages or the rights of the purchaser to seek court relief against the seller, or disclaiming a WARRANTY (i.e., a statement of fact concerning the nature or caliber of goods sold the seller, given in order to induce the sale, and relied upon by the purchaser).

Unconscionability is ascertained by examining the circumstances of the parties when the contract was made. This doctrine is applied only where it would be an affront to the integrity of the judicial system to enforce such a contract.

Adhesion Contracts Adhesion contracts are those that are drafted by the party who has the greater bargaining advantage, providing the weaker party with only the opportunity to adhere to (i.e., to accept) the contract or to reject it. (These types of contract are often described by the saying "Take it or leave it.") They are frequently employed because most businesses could not transact business if it were necessary to negotiate all of the terms of every contract. Not all adhesion contracts are unconscionable, as the terms of such contracts do not necessarily exploit the party who assents to the contract.

Courts, however, often refuse to enforce contracts of adhesion on the grounds that a true meeting of the minds never existed, or that there was no acceptance of the offer because the purchaser actually had no choice in the bargain.

Aleatory Contracts An aleatory contract is a mutual agreement the effects of which are triggered by the occurrence of an uncertain event. In this type of contract, one or both parties assume risk. A fire insurance policy is a form of aleatory contract, as an insured will not receive the proceeds of the policy unless a fire occurs, an event that is uncertain to occur.

Void and Voidable Contracts Contracts can be either void or VOIDABLE. A void contract imposes no legal rights or obligations upon the parties and is not enforceable by a court. It is, in effect, no contract at all.

A voidable contract is a legally enforceable agreement, but it may be treated as never having been binding on a party who was suffering from some legal disability or who was a victim of fraud at the time of its execution. The contract is not void unless or until the party chooses to treat it as such by opposing its enforcement. A voidable contract may be ratified either expressly or impliedly by the party who has the right to avoid it. An express ratification occurs when that party who has become legally competent to act declares that he or she accepts the terms and obligations of the contract. An implied ratification occurs when the party, by his or her conduct, manifests an intent to ratify a contract, such as by performing according to its terms. Ratification of a contract entails the same elements as formation of a new contract. There must be intent and complete knowledge of all material facts and circumstances. Oral ACKNOWLEDGMENT of a contract and a promise to perform constitute sufficient ratification. The party who was legally competent at the time that a voidable contract was signed may not, however, assert its voidable nature to escape the enforcement of its terms.

Which Law Governs

Although a general body of contract law exists, some aspects of it, such as construction (i.e., the process of ascertaining the proper explanation of equivocal terms), vary among the different jurisdictions. When courts must select the law to be applied with respect to a contract, they consider what the parties intended as to which law should govern; the place where the contract was entered into; and the place of performance of the contract. Many courts apply the modern doctrine of the "grouping of contracts" or the "center of gravity," in which the law of the jurisdiction that has the closest or most significant relationship with the matter in issue applies.

Courts generally apply the law that the parties expressly or impliedly intend to govern the contract, provided that it bears a reasonable relation to the transaction and the parties acted in good faith. Some jurisdictions follow the law of the place where the contract was performed, unless the intent of the parties is to the contrary. Where foreign law governs, contracts may be recognized and enforced under the doctrine of comity (i.e., the acknowledgment that one nation gives within its territory to the legislative, executive, or judicial acts of another nation).

Elements of a Contract

The requisites for formation of a legal contract are an offer, an acceptance, competent parties who have the legal capacity to contract, lawful subject matter, mutuality of agreement, consideration, mutuality of obligation, and, if required under the STATUTE OF FRAUDS, a writing.

Offer An offer is a promise that is, by its terms, conditional upon an act, forbearance, or return promise being given in exchange for the promise or its performance. It is a demonstration of willingness to enter into a bargain, made so that another party is justified in understanding that his or her assent to the bargain is invited and will conclude it. Any offer must consist of a statement of present intent to enter a contract; a definite proposal that is certain in its terms; and communication of the offer to the identified, prospective offeree. If any of these elements are missing, there is no offer to form the basis of a contract.

Preliminary negotiations, advertisements, invitations to bid Preliminary negotiations are clearly distinguished from offers because they contain no demonstration of present intent to form contractual relations. No contract is formed when prospective purchasers respond to such terms, as they are merely invitations or requests for an offer. Unless this interpretation is employed, any person in a position similar to a seller who advertises goods in any medium would be liable for numerous contracts when there is usually a limited quantity of merchandise for sale.

An advertisement, price quotation, or catalogue is customarily viewed as only an invitation to a customer to make an offer and not as an offer itself. The courts reason that an establishment might not have sufficient stock to satisfy potential demand and that it would not be reasonable for a customer to expect to form a binding contract by responding to advertisements that are intended to make consumers aware of a product for sale. In addition, the courts have held that an advertisement is an offer for a unilateral contract that can be revoked at the will of the offeror, the business enterprise, prior to performance of its terms.

An exception exists, however, to the general rule on advertisements. When the quantity offered for sale is specified and contains words of promise, such as "first come, first served," courts enforce the contract where the store refuses to sell the product when the price is tendered. Where the offer is clear, definite, and explicit, and no matters remain open for negotiation, acceptance of it completes the contract. New conditions may not be imposed on the offer after it has been accepted by the performance of its terms.

An advertisement or request for bids for the sale of particular property or the erection or construction of a particular structure is merely an invitation for offers that cannot be accepted by any particular bid. A submitted bid is, however, an offer, which upon acceptance by the offeree becomes a valid contract.

Mistake in sending offer If an intermediary, such as a telegraph company, errs in the transmission of an offer, most courts hold that the party who selected that method of communication is bound by the terms of the erroneous message. The same rule applies to acceptances. In reaching this result, courts regard the telegraph company as the agent of the party who selected it. Other courts justify the rule on business convenience. A few courts rule that if there is an error in transmission, there is no contract, on the grounds that either the telegraph company is an INDEPENDENT CONTRACTOR and not the sender's agent, or there has been no meeting of the minds of the parties. However, an offeree who knows, or should know, of the mistake in the transmission of an offer may not take advantage of the known mistake by accepting the offer; he or she will be bound by the original terms of the offer.

Termination of an offer An offer remains open until the expiration of its specified time period or, if there is no time limit, until a reasonable time has elapsed. A reasonable time is determined according to what a reasonable person would consider sufficient time to accept the offer.

The death or insanity of either party, before an acceptance is communicated, causes an offer to expire. If the offer has been accepted, the contract is binding, even if one of the parties dies thereafter. The destruction of the subject matter of the contract; conditions that render the contract impossible to perform; or the supervening illegality of the proposed contract results in the termination of the offer.

When the offeror, either verbally or by conduct, clearly demonstrates that the offer is no longer open, the offer is considered revoked when learned by the offeree. Where an offer is made to the general public, it can be revoked by furnishing public notice of its termination in the same way in which the offer was publicized.

Irrevocable offers An option is a right that is purchased by a person in order to have an offer remain open at agreed-upon price and terms, for a specified time, during which it is irrevocable. It constitutes an exception to the general rule that an offer may be withdrawn prior to acceptance. The offeror may not withdraw this offer because that party is bound by the consideration given by the offeree. The offeree is free, however, to decide whether or not to accept the offer.

Most courts hold that an offer for a unilateral contract becomes irrevocable as soon as the offeree starts to perform the requested act, because that action serves as consideration to prevent revocation of the offer. Where it is doubtful whether the offer invites an act (as in the case of a unilateral contract) or a promise (as in the case of a bilateral contract), the presumption is in favor of a promise, and therefore a bilateral contract arises. If an offer to form a unilateral contract requires several acts, it is interpreted as inviting acceptance by completion of the initial act. Performance of the balance constitutes a condition to the offeror's duty of performance. Where such an offer invites only a single act, it includes by implication a subsidiary promise to keep the offer open if the offeree will commence performance. Some courts hold that an offer for a unilateral contract may be revoked at any time prior to completion of the act bargained for, even after the offeree has partially performed it.

Rejection of an offer An offer is rejected when the offeror is justified in understanding from the words or conduct of the offeree that he or she intends not to accept the offer, or to take it under further advisement. Rejection might come in the form of an express refusal to accept an offer by a counteroffer, which is a new proposal that rejects the offer by implication; or by a conditional acceptance that operates as a counteroffer. The offer may continue, however, if the offeree expressly states that the counteroffer shall not constitute a rejection of the offer.

If an offer is rejected, the party who made the original offer no longer has any liability for that offer. The party who rejected the offer may not subsequently, at his or her own option, convert the same offer into a contract by a subsequent acceptance. In such a case, the consent of the offeror must be obtained for a contract to be formed.

Acceptance Acceptance of an offer is an expression of assent to its terms. It must be made by the offeree in a manner requested or authorized by the offeror. An acceptance is valid only if the offeree knows of the offer; the offeree manifests an intention to accept; the acceptance is unequivocal and unconditional; and the acceptance is manifested according to the terms of the offer.

The determination of a valid acceptance is governed by whether a promise or an act by the offeree was the bargained-for response. Since the acceptance of a unilateral contract requires an act rather than a promise, it is unnecessary to furnish notice of intended performance unless the offeror requested it. If, however, the offeree has reason to believe that the offeror will not learn of the acceptance with reasonable promptness, the duty of the offeror is discharged unless the offeree makes a reasonable attempt to give notice; the offeror learns of the performance; or the offer indicates that no notice is required.

In bilateral contracts, the offer is effective when the offeree receives it. The offeree may accept it until the offeree receives notice of revocation from the offeror. Thereafter, an offer is revoked. Under the majority rule, which is known as the "mailbox rule," an acceptance is effective upon dispatch if the offeror explicitly authorizes that method of acceptance to be employed by the offeree, even if the acceptance is lost or destroyed in transit.

The majority rule is inapplicable, however, unless the acceptance is properly addressed and postage prepaid. It has no application to most option contracts, as acceptance of an option contract is effective only when received by the offeror.

If the acceptance mode used by the offeree is implicitly authorized by the offeror, such as the selection by the offeree of the same method used by the offeror, who neglected to designate a method of communication, an acceptance is effective upon dispatch if it is correctly addressed and the expense of its conveyance is prepaid. As with expressly authorized methods, the acceptance need not ever reach the offeror in order to form the contract.

In some jurisdictions, the use of a method not expressly or impliedly authorized by the offeror, even if more rapid in nature, results in a contract only upon receipt of the acceptance. In most jurisdictions, however, if the acceptance mode is inherently faster, it is deemed to be an impliedly authorized means, and acceptance is effective upon dispatch.

If the acceptance is transmitted by an expressly or impliedly authorized method to the wrong address, it is effective only upon receipt by the offeror. A wrong address is any address other than that implicitly authorized, even if the offeror were in a position to receive the acceptance at the substituted address.

An offeror who specifically states that there is no contract until the acceptance is received is entitled to insist upon the condition of receipt or upon any other provision concerning the manner and time of acceptance specified.

Rejection of the offer or revocation of conditional acceptance is effective upon receipt. A late or defective acceptance is treated as a counteroffer, which will not result in a contract unless the offeror accepts it. If offers cross in the mail, there will be no binding contract, as an offer may not be accepted if there is no knowledge of it.

As a general rule, an offer may be accepted only by the offeree or an authorized agent. If, however, the offer is contained in an option contract, it may be the subject of an assignment or transfer without the consent of the offeror, unless the option involves a purchase on credit or expressly prohibits an assignment.

In contracts that do not involve the sale of goods, acceptance must comply exactly with the requirements of the offer (this is known as the "mirror-image rule"), and must omit nothing from the promise or performance requested. An offer of a prize in a contest, for example, becomes a binding contract when a contestant successfully complies with the terms of the offer. If a response to an offer purports to accept it, but adds qualifications or conditions, then it is a counteroffer and not an acceptance.

Acceptance may be inferred from the offeree's acts, conduct, or silence; but as a general rule, silence, without more, can never constitute acceptance. The effect of silence accompanied by AMBIGUITY must be ascertained from all the circumstances in the case.

Prior dealings between the parties may create a duty to act. Silence or the failure to take some action under such circumstances might constitute acceptance. For example, if the parties have engaged in a series of business transactions involving the mailing of goods and payment by the recipient, the recipient will not be permitted to retain an article without paying for it within a reasonable time, due to their prior dealings. A recipient who does not intend to accept the goods is under a duty to inform the sender. Silence, where there is a duty to speak, prevents the offeree from rejecting an offer and the offeror from claiming that there is no acceptance. If ownership rights are exercised over an item, this might be deemed an acceptance.

Unsolicited goods At COMMON LAW, the recipient of unsolicited goods in the mail was not required to accept or to return them, but if the goods were used, a contract and a concomitant obligation to pay for them were created. Today, in order to offer protection against unwanted solicitations, some state statutes have modified the common-law rule by providing that where unsolicited merchandise is received as part of an offer to sell, the goods are an outright gift. The recipient may use the goods and is under no duty to return or pay for them unless he or she knows that they were sent by mistake.

Agreements to agree An "agreement to agree" is not a contract. This type of agreement is frequently employed in industries that require long-term contracts in order to ensure a constant source of supplies and outlet of production. Mutual manifestations of assent that are, in themselves, sufficient to form a binding contract are not deprived of operative effect by the mere fact that the parties agree to prepare a written reproduction of their agreement. In determin-

ing whether, on a given set of facts, there is merely an "agreement to agree" or a sufficiently binding contract, the courts apply certain rules. If the parties express their intention—either to be bound or not bound until a written document is prepared—then that intention controls. If they have not expressed their intention, but they exchange promises of a definite performance and agree upon all essential terms, then the parties have formed a contract even though the written document is never signed. If the expressions of intention are incomplete—as, for example, if a material term such as quantity has been left to further negotiation—the parties do not have a contract. The designation of the material term for further negotiation is interpreted as demonstrating the intention of the parties not to be bound until a complete agreement has been reached.

Competent Parties A natural person who agrees to a transaction has complete legal capacity to become liable for duties under the contract unless he or she is an infant, insane, or intoxicated.

Infants An infant is defined as a person under the age of 18 or 21, depending on the particular jurisdiction. A contract made by an infant is voidable but is valid and enforceable until or unless he or she disaffirms it. He or she may avoid the legal duty to perform the terms of the contract without any liability for breach of contract. INFANTS are treated in such a way because public policy deems it desirable to protect the immature and naive infant from liability for unfair contracts that he or she is too inexperienced to negotiate on equal terms with the other party.

Once an infant attains majority (i.e., the age at which a person is no longer legally considered an infant), he or she must choose either to disaffirm or avoid the contract, or to ratify or accept it. After reaching the age of majority, a person implicitly ratifies and becomes bound to perform the contract if he or she fails to disaffirm it within a reasonable time, which is determined by the circumstances of the particular case. A person who disaffirms a contract must return any benefits or consideration received under it that he or she still possesses. If such benefits have been squandered or destroyed, the person usually has no legal obligation to recompense the other party. The law imposes liability on the infant in certain cases, however. Although the contract of an infant or other person may be voidable, the person still may be liable in quasi-contract in order to prevent UNJUST ENRICHMENT for the reasonable value of goods or services furnished if they are necessaries that are reasonably required for the person's health, comfort, or education.

The majority of courts hold that an infant who willfully misrepresents his or her age may, nevertheless, exercise the power to avoid the contract. As a general rule, however, the infant must place the adult party in the status quo ante (i.e., his or her position prior to the contract). The jurisdictions are in disagreement in regard to whether an infant is liable in TORT (i.e., a civil wrong other than breach of contract) for willful misrepresentation of his or her age. This divergence arises from the rule that a tort action may not be maintained against an infant if it essentially entails the enforcement of a contract. Some courts regard the action for fraud that would be commenced against the infant as being based on the contract. Others rule that the tort is sufficiently independent of the contract so that the granting of relief would not involve indirect enforcement of the contract. The other party, however, is able to avoid a contract entered into on the basis of an infant's fraudulent MISREPRESENTATION with respect to age or other material facts because he or she is the innocent victim of the infant's fraud.

Mental incapacity When a party does not comprehend the nature and consequences of the contract when it is formed, he or she is regarded as having mental incapacity. A distinction must be drawn between those persons who have been adjudicated incompetent by a court and have had a guardian appointed, and those mentally incompetent persons who have not been so adjudicated. A person who has been declared incompetent in a court proceeding lacks the legal capacity to enter into a contract with another. Such a person is unable to consent to the contract, as the court has determined that he or she does not understand the obligations and effects of the contract. A contract made by such a person is void and without any legal effect. Neither party may be legally compelled to perform or comply with the terms of the contract. If there has been no adjudication of insanity, a contract made by a mentally incapacitated individual is voidable by him or her.

Many contract principles that apply to minors also apply to insane persons. There is an obligation to recompense the injured party where a voidable contract is avoided, and to pay for necessaries based upon quasi-contract for the reasonable value of the goods or services. The incompetent, a guardian, or a PERSONAL REPRESENTATIVE after death may avoid the contract. The incompetent may ratify a voidable contract only if they recover the capacity to contract. The right to avoid the contract belongs to the incompetent; the other party may not avoid the contractual obligation. A contract that is ordinarily voidable may not be set aside when it is inherently fair to both parties and has been executed to such an extent that the other party cannot be restored to the position that they occupied prior to the contract.

Intoxicated persons A contract made by an intoxicated person is voidable. When a person is inebriated at the time of entering into a contract with another and subsequently becomes sober and either promises to perform the contract or fails to disaffirm it within a reasonable time after becoming sober, then that person has ratified his or her voidable contract and is legally bound to perform.

Subject Matter Any undertaking may be the subject of a contract, provided that it is not proscribed by law. When a contract is formed in restraint of trade, courts will not enforce it, because it imposes an illegal and unreasonable burden on commerce by hindering competition. Contracts that provide for the commission of a crime or any illegal objective are also void.

Future rights and liabilities—performing or refraining from some designated act, or assuming particular risks or obligations—may constitute the basis of a contract. An idea that never assumes concrete form at the time of disclosure, such as a concept for a short story, even though new and unusual, may not, however, be the subject of a contract.

A person may not legally contract concerning a right that he or she does not have. A seller of a home who does not possess clear title to the property may not promise to convey it without encumbrances. Neither may a seller promise that property will not be appropriated by EMINENT DOMAIN, which is an inherent power of government that is not subject to restrictions imposed by individuals.

Mutual Agreement There must be an agreement between the parties, or mutual assent, for a contract to be formed. In order for an agreement to exist, the parties must have a common intention or a meeting of minds on the terms of the contract and must subscribe to the same bargain. Aside from certain statutory exceptions pertaining to the sale of goods, as prescribed by Article 2 of the UNIFORM COMMERCIAL CODE (UCC), if any of the proposed terms is not settled, or if no method of settlement is provided, then there is no agreement. The parties may settle one term at a time, but their contract becomes complete only when they assent to the final term. An agreement is binding if the parties concur with respect to the essential terms and intend the agreement to be binding, even though all of the details are not definitely fixed. The quantity of goods are usually essential terms of the contract that must be agreed upon if the contract is to be enforced. Exceptions to the rule requiring the terms of an agreement to be definite and certain are contained in article 2 of the UCC, which permits the courts to imply reasonably the missing terms if the essential terms unambiguously demonstrate the mutual agreement of the parties.

Consideration Consideration is a legal detriment that is suffered by the promisee and that is requested by the promisor in exchange for his or her promise. A valid contract requires some exchange of consideration. As a general rule, in a bilateral contract, one promise is valid consideration for the other. In a unilateral contract, the agreed performance by the offeree furnishes the necessary consideration and also operates as an acceptance of the offer.

Consideration may consist of a promise; an act other than a promise; a forbearance from suing on a claim that is the subject of an honest and reasonable dispute; or the creation, modification, or destruction of a legal relationship. It signifies that the promisee will relinquish some legal right in the present, or that he or she will restrict his or her legal freedom of action in the future as an inducement for the promise of the other party. It is not substantially concerned with the benefit that accrues to the promisor.

Love and affection are not permissible forms of consideration. A promise to make a gift contains no consideration because it does not entail a legal benefit received by the promisor or a legal detriment suffered by the promisee. Because a promise to give a gift is freely made by the promisor, who is not subject to any legal duty to do so, the promise is not enforceable unless there is PROMISSORY ESTOPPEL. Promissory estoppel is a doctrine by which a court enforces a promise that the promisor reasonably expects

will induce action or forbearance on the part of a promisee, who justifiably relied on the promise and suffered a substantial detriment as a result. Where a court enforces a promise by applying this doctrine, promissory estoppel serves as a substitute for the required consideration.

At common law, courts refused to inquire into the adequacy or fairness of a bargain, finding that the payment of some price constituted legally sufficient consideration. If one is seeking to prove mistake, misrepresentation, fraud, or duress—or to assert a similar defense—the inadequacy of the price paid for the promise might represent significant evidence for such defenses, but the law does not require adequacy of consideration in order to find an enforceable contract.

Mutuality of Obligation Where promises constitute the consideration in a bilateral contract, they must be mutually binding. This concept is known as mutuality of obligation. If one party's promise does not actually bind him or hers to some performance or forbearance, it is an illusory promise, and there is no enforceable contract.

Where the contract provides one party with the right to cancel, there might be no consideration because of lack of mutuality of obligation. If there is an absolute and unlimited right to cancel the obligation, the promise by the party with the right of cancellation is illusory, and the lack of consideration means that there is no contract. If the power to cancel the contract is restricted in any manner, the contract is usually considered to be binding. Performance of a void promise in a defective bilateral contract may render the other promise legally binding, however. For example, in virtually all states, an oral contract to transfer title to land is not merely unenforceable, it is absolutely void. (See discussion of the statute of frauds, below.) A seller who orally promises to transfer land to a purchaser, for which the purchaser orally promises a designated sum, may sue the purchaser for the price if the purchaser receives title to the land from the seller. The purchaser is not relieved of his or her promise to pay, because of the performance of the void oral promise by the seller.

A promise to perform an act that one is legally bound to do does not qualify as consideration for another promise.

Past consideration consists of actions that occurred prior to the making of the contractual promise, without any purpose of inducing a promise in exchange. It is not valid, because it is not furnished as the bargained-for exchange of the present promise. There are exceptions to this rule, such as a present promise to pay a debt that has been discharged in BANKRUPTCY, which constitutes valid consideration because it renews a former promise to pay a debt that was supported by consideration.

Most states do not recognize moral obligation as consideration, as there is no acceptable method of setting the parameters of moral duty. Some courts will enforce a moral obligation where there has been a benefit conferred on the promisor.

Statute of Frauds The statute of frauds was enacted by the English Parliament in 1677 and has since been the law in both England and in the United States in varying forms. It requires that certain types of contracts be in writing. The principal characteristic of various state laws modeled after the original statute is the provision that no suit or action shall be maintained on a contract unless there is a note or memorandum of its subject matter, terms and conditions, and the identity of the parties, signed by the party to be charged or obligated under it or an authorized agent. The purpose of the statute is to prevent the proof of a nonexistent agreement through fraud or perjury in actions for breach of an alleged contract.

Reality of Consent

The parties must mutually assent to the proposed objectives and terms of a contract in order for it to be enforceable. The manifestation of the common intent of the parties is discerned from their conduct or verbal exchanges.

What one party secretly intended is irrelevant if his or her conduct appears to demonstrate agreement. In a few limited cases, however, where there is no stated expression of the parties' intent, their subjective intentions may establish an enforceable contract if both believe in the same terms of the contract.

There will be no binding contract without the real consent of the parties. Apparent consent may be vitiated because of mistake, fraud, innocent misrepresentation, duress, or undue influence, all of which are defenses to the enforcement of the contract.

Mutual Mistake When there is a mutual MISTAKE OF FACT with respect to the subject of the contract, the subjective intention of the parties is evaluated by the courts to determine whether there had been, in fact, a meeting of the minds of the parties.

If the mutual mistake significantly changed the subject matter of the contract, a court will refuse to enforce the contract. If, however, the difference in the subject matter of the contract concerned some incidental quality that has no (or negligible) effect on the value of the contract, the contract is binding, even though the mistake altered or removed what had been the incentive to one or both parties to enter the contract.

Unilateral Mistake Ordinarily, a unilateral mistake (i.e., an error made by one party) affords no basis for avoiding a contract, but a contract that contains a typographical error may be corrected. A contract may be avoided if the error in value in what is to be exchanged is substantial, or if the mistake is caused by or known to the other party. Unilateral mistakes frequently occur where a contractor submits an erroneous bid for a PUBLIC CONTRACT. Where such a bid is accepted, the contractor will be permitted to avoid the contract only if the agreement has not been executed or if the other party can be placed in the position that they occupied prior to the contract. If the mistake is obvious, the contract will not be enforced, but if it is inconsequential, the contract will be upheld. The mistake must consist of a clerical error or a mistake in computation, as an error in judgment will not permit a contractor to avoid a contract.

Mistake of Law When a party who has full knowledge of the facts reaches an erroneous conclusion as to their legal effect, such a MISTAKE OF LAW will not invalidate a contract or affect its enforceability.

Illiteracy Illiteracy neither excuses a party from the duty of learning the contents of a written contract nor prevents the mutual agreement of the parties. An illiterate person is capable of giving real consent to a contract; the person has a duty to ask someone to read the contract to him or her and to explain it, if necessary. Illiteracy can, however, serve as a basis for invalidating a contract when considered in relation to other factors, such as fraud or overreaching. If the person whom the illiterate designates to read or explain the contract misrepresents it and acts in collusion with the other party to the contract, the contract may be set aside.

Fraud Fraud prevents mutual agreement to a contract because one party intentionally deceives another as to the nature and the consequences of a contract. It is the willful misrepresentation or concealment of a material fact of a contract, and it is designed to persuade another to enter into that contract. If a special relationship exists, such as that of attorney and client, nondisclosure of a material fact is fraud. Many courts have held that mere silence concerning a material fact did not constitute fraud, but the emerging trend is to find a duty to disclose and, therefore, deliberate concealment of a material fact gives rise to an action for fraud.

A contract that is based on fraud is void or voidable, because fraud prevents a meeting of the minds of the parties. If the fraud is in the factum, (i.e., during the execution of the contract) so that the party would not have signed the document if he or she understood its nature, then the contract is void ab initio (i.e., from its inception). The signatory is not bound if a different contract is substituted for the one that he or she had intended to execute. If, however, a party negligently chooses to sign the contract without reading it, then no fraud exists and the contract is enforceable. If the fraud is in the inducement, by which a party is falsely persuaded to sign a contract, the terms of which he or she knows and understands, then the contract is not void but is voidable by the innocent party, as that party executes what is intended to be executed. If, however, due to fraud, a contract fails to express the agreement that the parties intended it to express, then the defrauded party may seek a decree of reformation, by which the court will rewrite a written agreement to conform with the ORIGINAL INTENT of the parties.

Misrepresentation without Fraud A contract may be invalidated if it was based on any innocent misrepresentation pertaining to a material matter on which one party justifiably relied.

Duress Duress is a wrongful act or threat by one party that compels another party to perform some act, such as the signing of a contract, which he or she would not have done voluntarily. As a result, there is no true meeting of minds of the parties and, therefore, there is no legally enforceable contract. Blackmail, threats of physical violence, or threats to institute legal proceedings in an abusive manner can constitute duress. The consensus of most jurisdictions is that the threat to commence legal proceedings, which otherwise might be justifiable, becomes wrongful when done with the corrupt intent to coerce a transaction that bears no relation to the subject of such proceedings and is grossly unjust to the victim.

A contract that is induced by duress is either void or voidable. If the duress consists of one party taking the other's hand as a mechanical instrument by which to sign his or her name to a contract, then the contract is void *ab initio* for lack of any intent on the victim's part to perform the act. The result is the same if the victim is compelled to sign a contract at gunpoint without any knowledge of its contents. These are highly unusual situations. In most cases involving duress, the contract is voidable, and the person who was subjected to the duress may ask the court to declare the contract unenforceable.

Undue Influence Undue influence is unlawful control exercised by one person over another in order to substitute the first person's will for that of the other. It generally occurs in two types of situations. In the first, a person takes advantage of the psychological weakness of another, in order to influence that person to agree to a contract to which, under normal circumstances, he or she would not otherwise consent. The second situation entails undue influence based on a fiduciary relationship that exists between the parties. This occurs where one party occupies a position of trust and confidence in relation to the other, as in familial or professional-client relationships. The question of whether the assent of each party to the contract is real or induced by factors that inhibit the exercise of free choice determines the existence of undue influence. Mere legitimate persuasion and suggestion that do not destroy free will are not considered undue influence and have no effect on the legality of a contract.

Assignments

An assignment of a contract is the transfer to another person of the rights of performance under it. Contracts were not assignable at early common law, but today most contracts are assignable unless the nature of the contract or its provisions demonstrates that the parties intend to make it personal to them and therefore incapable of assignment to others.

Joint and Several Contracts

Joint and several contracts always entail multiple promises for the same performance. Two or more parties to a contract who promise to the same promisee that they will give the same performance are regarded as binding themselves jointly, severally, or jointly and severally.

Promises impose *several liability* only when promisors singly promise to pay or to act. If the three promisors singly promise to pay the party $500, it is as though there are three discrete and individual contracts, except that the promisee is to receive a total of only $500. The three promisors do not promise as a unit, but each individually assumes to pay the entire sum.

Joint liability ensues only when promisors make one promise as a unit. If three promisors promise to pay $500, then the three will owe the debt as a unit, not individually. The party may enforce the contract only against one promisor or against any number of joint promisors. The promisee is entitled, however, to only one award of the amount due.

Promises impose joint and several liability when the promisors promise both as a unit and individually to pay or perform according to the terms of the contract.

If a promisor who is jointly or jointly and severally liable on a contract performs or pays the promisee in full, then the other promisors are thereby discharged from their obligations on the contract to the promisee, as he or she may only collect the amount due to him or her. The promisor who performed, however, has a right to contribution from the co-promisors—that is, the right to receive from the other co-promisors their proportionate share of the debt. The general rule is that a co-obligor who has paid in excess of his or her proportionate share is entitled to contribution, unless there is a particular agreement to the contrary.

Joint and several promises can exist if a promisor promises to pay two promisees a certain sum of money. The promisees are joint and several promisees or obligees, and the promisor has the duty to pay. Both promisees are entitled to performance of the promise jointly and separately, even though there is only one promise made to two people. Any one of the joint obligees in a contract has the power to discharge the promisor from the obligation. If the promisor pays one promisee, this payment operates as a discharge of the promisor's liability under the contract. The promisee who has not been paid may not compel the promisor to pay him or her, as the promisor has been discharged by the payment to the other promisee. The unpaid promisee may seek contribution from the promisee who has been paid, however.

Third-Party Beneficiaries

There are only two principal parties, the offeror and the offeree, to an ordinary contract. The terms of the contract bind one or both parties to render performance to the other in consideration of receiving, or having received, the other's performance. Contracts sometimes specify that the benefits accruing to one party will be conferred upon a third party. The effect of a third-party contract is to provide, to a party who has not assented to it, a legal right to enforce the contract.

A *creditor beneficiary* is a nonparty to a contract who receives the benefit when a promise is made to satisfy a legal duty. For example, suppose that a debtor owed a creditor $500. The debtor lends $500 to a third person, who promises to use the money to pay the debtor's debt. The third person is the promisor, who makes the promise to be enforced. The debtor is the promisee, to whom the promise is made. The contract is between the debtor and the third person, the promisor, and the consideration for the promise is the $500 loan that the promisor received from the debtor. The creditor is the third-party beneficiary. If the promisor refuses to pay the creditor $500, then the creditor may sue the promisor and prevail. Although the creditor is not a party to their contract, both the debtor and the promisor intend that the creditor should be the beneficiary of the contract and have enforceable rights against the promisor, since he or she is to pay the creditor. The debtor or the creditor may sue to enforce the promisor's promise to pay. The creditor's right to enforce the contract between the debtor and the promisor is effective only when he or she learns of, and assents to, the contract. The creditor may also sue the debtor for the $500, as the debtor had a legal duty to pay this loan. The debtor then may sue the promisor for breach of contract for refusing to pay the creditor.

A *donee beneficiary* of the contract is a nonparty who benefits from a promise that is made for the purpose of making a gift to him or her. A donor wishes to give a donee $200 as an anniversary present. The donor plans to sell a television set for $200 to a purchaser, who promises to pay the donee the $200 directly. The donee is a donee beneficiary of the purchaser's promise to pay the money and may enforce this claim against the purchaser. The donee has no claim against the donor, the promisee, as the donor has no legal duty to the donee but is merely giving the donee a gift. However, the donor will be able to sue the purchaser for refusal to pay the donee, because it would be a breach of the terms of their contract of sale.

The difference between a creditor beneficiary and a donee beneficiary becomes significant when the parties to a contract attempt to alter the rights of the third-party beneficiary. The promisor and the promisee have no right or power to alter the accrued rights of the donee beneficiary without consent unless this power was expressly reserved in the contract, regardless of whether the donee knows about the contract. A donee beneficiary's rights become effective when the contract is made for his or her benefit, regardless of whether he or she knows about the contract. In contrast, a creditor beneficiary's rights vest only when the creditor beneficiary learns of, and assents to, the contract.

Conditions and Promises of Performance

The duty of performance under many contracts is contingent upon the occurrence of a designated condition or promise. A condition is an act or event, other than a lapse of time, that affects a duty to render a promised performance that is specified in a contract. A condition may be viewed as a qualification placed upon a promise. A promise or duty is absolute or unconditional when it does not depend on any external events. Nothing but a lapse of time is necessary to make its performance due. When the time for performance of an unconditional promise arrives, immediate performance is due. A dependent or conditional promise is not effective until the occurrence of some external event that the parties have specified. An implied condition is one that the parties should have reasonably comprehended to be part of the contract because of its presence by implication.

Types of Conditions Conditions precedent, conditions concurrent, and conditions subsequent are types of conditions that are commonly found in contracts. A condition precedent is an event that must exist as a fact before the promisor incurs any liability pursuant to it. For example, suppose that an employer informs an employee that if the employee successfully completes an accounting course, he or she will receive $500. The completion of the course must exist as a fact before the employer will be liable to the employee; when that fact occurs, the employer becomes liable.

A condition concurrent must exist as a fact when both parties to a contract are to perform simultaneously. Neither party has a duty to perform until the other has performed or has tendered performance. Practically speaking, however, the party who wants to complete the transaction must perform in order to establish the duty of performance by the other party. The performances are concurrently contingent upon each other. Concurrent conditions are usually found in contracts for the sale of goods and in contracts for the conveyance of land.

A condition subsequent is one that, when it exists, ends the duty of performance or payment under the contract. For example, suppose that an insurance contract provides that suit against it for a loss covered by the policy must be commenced within one year of the insured's loss. If the destruction of the insured's building by fire is a risk that the policy covers, then the insured must file suit against the insurer within the time specified, or the condition subsequent will end the duty of the company pursuant to the policy.

Substantial Performance The failure to comply strictly with the terms of a condition will not prevent recovery if there has been substantial performance of the contractual obligation. Courts created this doctrine in order to prevent forfeitures and to ensure justice. Where recovery is permitted for substantial performance, it is offset by damages for injuries caused by failure to render complete performance. Courts determine whether there has been a breach or a substantial performance of a contract by evaluating the purpose to be served; the excuse for deviation from the letter of the contract; and the cruelty of enforced adherence to the contract. If the deviation from the contract were accidental and resulted in only a trivial difference between what was required by the contract and what was performed, the plaintiff will receive only nominal damages.

Satisfactory Performance A contract may be contingent upon the satisfaction of a person's opinion, taste, or fancy. Most courts apply a good-faith test in determining whether rejection of a performance was reasonable. If a rejection is made in bad faith, the court will enforce the contract.

If satisfaction can be measured with reference to the commercial value or caliber of the subject matter of the contract, the performance must be proved to be deficient in these respects and the dissatisfaction must be proven to be sufficiently reasonable and well-founded to justify non-enforcement of the contract. The test is: What would satisfy a reasonable person? The condition of satisfaction need not be met when the expression of dissatisfaction is made in bad faith and not related to the quality or commercial value of the subject of the contract.

Divisible Contracts The entire performance of a contract can be a condition to the other party's duty to perform. If the contract is legally divisible, the performance of a divisible portion can fulfill the condition precedent to the other party's corresponding divisible performance. A contract is divisible when the performance of each party is divided into two or more parts; each party owes the other a corresponding number of performances; and the performance of each part by one party is the agreed exchange for a corresponding part by the other party. If it is divisible, the contract, for certain purposes, is treated as though it were a number of contracts, as in employment contracts and leases. If an employer hires a prospective employee for one year at a weekly salary, the contract is divisible. Each week's performance is a constructive or implied condition precedent to the employee's right to a week's salary. The right to the salary is not contingent on performance of the obligation to work for one year. In most contracts of employment, the courts allow recovery to the employee for the number of weeks or months of service rendered, on the theory that such contract is divisible. The same is true for a lease of real property or an apartment. If the lease is breached before the entire term has expired, the tenant is liable for the remaining rent as each month occurs, but is not liable prior to that time. In effect, the court treats the lease as a contract for each month, with rent due on the first of each month. In a divisible contract, the performance of a separate unit that is treated as a separate contract entitles the performing party to immediate payment, whereas in an entire contract, the party who is first to perform must render full performance in order to be entitled to performance from the other party.

Breach of Conditions Compliance with a condition can be excused under certain circumstances. As a general rule, if the facts would excuse compliance with a condition, they will also excuse performance of a promise. An excuse for nonperformance of a condition can exist in many forms, such as a waiver (the intentional

relinquishment of a known right) of performance of the condition.

If an unintentional failure to perform a condition would result in a FORFEITURE, a court may excuse compliance in order to prevent injustice. The duty of performance by the other party arises just as though the condition has been fulfilled if compliance with a condition is excused.

Discharge of Contracts

The duties under a contract are discharged when there is a legally binding termination of such duty by a VOLUNTARY ACT of the parties or by operation of law. Among the ways to discharge a contractual duty are impossibility or impracticability to perform personal services because of death or illness; or impossibility caused by the other party.

The two most significant methods of voluntary discharge are ACCORD AND SATISFACTION and novation. An accord is an agreement to accept some performance other than that which was previously owed under a prior contract. Satisfaction is the performance of the terms of that accord. Both elements must occur in order for there to be discharge by these means.

A novation involves the substitution of a new party while discharging one of the original parties to a contract by agreement of all three parties. A new contract is created with the same terms as the original one, but the parties are different.

Contractual liability may be voluntarily discharged by the agreement of the parties, by estoppel, and by the cancellation, intentional destruction, or surrender of a contract under seal with intent to discharge the duty.

The discharge of a contractual duty may also occur by operation of law through illegality, merger, statutory release, such as a discharge in bankruptcy, and objective impossibility. Merger takes place when one contract is extinguished because it is absorbed into another.

There are two types of impossibility of performance that discharge the duty of performance under a contract. *Subjective impossibility* is due to the inability of the individual promisor to perform, such as by illness or death. *Objective impossibility* means that no one can render the performance. The destruction of the subject matter of the contract, the frustration of its purpose, or supervening impossibility after the contract is formed are types of objective impossibility. "Impracticability" because of extreme and unreasonable difficulty, expense, injury, or loss involved is considered part of impossibility.

Breach of Contract

An unjustifiable failure to perform all or some part of a contractual duty constitutes a breach of contract. It ensues when a party who has a duty of immediate performance fails to perform, or when one party hinders or prevents the performance of the other party.

A total, major, material, or substantial breach of contract constitutes a failure to perform properly a material part of the contract. A partial or minor breach of contract is merely a slight deviation from the bargained-for performance. A breach may occur by ANTICIPATORY REPUDIATION, whereby the promisor, without justification and before committing a breach, makes an affirmative statement to the promisee, indicating that he or she will not or cannot perform the contractual duties.

The differences in the types of breach are significant in ascertaining the kinds of remedies and damages available to the aggrieved party.

Remedies

Damages, reformation, RESCISSION, restitution, and SPECIFIC PERFORMANCE are the basic remedies available for breach of contract.

Damages The term *damages* signifies a sum of money awarded as a compensation for injury caused by a breach of contract. The type of breach governs the extent of the damages to be awarded.

Failure to perform The measure of damages in breach-of-contract cases is the sum that would be necessary to recompense the injured party for the amount of losses incurred through breach of contract. The injured party should be placed in the position that he or she would have occupied if the contract had been performed, and they are entitled to receive the *benefit of the bargain,* the net gain that would have accrued to them under the contract. The injured party is not, however, to be put in a better position than he or she would have occupied had performance taken place.

Damages for anticipatory repudiation are ordinarily assessed as of the scheduled performance dates that are fixed by the breached contract. The measure of damages for the breach of an installment contract is determined at the time each installment is due.

When the parties have included a LIQUIDATED DAMAGES clause in a contract, it gener-

ally will be enforced. Such clause is a prior agreement by the parties as to the measure of damages upon breach. Additional damages may not be claimed.

Partial performance When the defendant has failed to complete performance of an agreement according to its terms, the plaintiff may recover such damages as will compensate him or her to the same extent as though the contract had been completely performed. The customary measure of damages is the reasonable expense of completion. Completion refers to a fulfillment of the same work, if possible, which does not involve unreasonable economic waste. The injured party is not automatically entitled to recover the difference between the contract price and the amount it would cost to have the work completed when a contract is breached after partial performance; he or she will be entitled to recover that amount only if completion is actually accomplished at a greater cost.

A provision in a building contract that allows the owner, in the event of a default by the contractor, to complete the job and to deduct the expenses from the contract price does not preclude the owner's recovering damages also where the contractor intentionally leaves the work undone. A plaintiff may also recover the monetary value of materials that are lost through a breach of contract.

A plaintiff contractor who subsequently performs the work upon breach of a contract will ordinarily recover the reasonable value of the labor and materials that he or she has furnished, with the contract price used as a guideline. The award may not properly exceed the benefit that the owner received in the properly completed work, and it will be reduced by the amount of damages that the owner incurs as a result of the contractor's failure to complete performance of the contractual obligation. If the value of the work performed exceeds the contract price, the contractor will not receive the excess.

Where a contract for the performance of services exists with payment to be made in installments, and the obligation to pay for each installment constitutes an independent promise, the individual who is entitled to payment may recover only the installments that are due when the suit is brought.

Defective performance Damages for defective performance of a contractual agreement are measured by calculating the difference in value between what is actually tendered and what is required as performance under the agreement. If the performance tendered is either of no value or unsuitable for the purpose that the contract contemplated, the proper measure of damages is the sum that is necessary to repair the defect. If a defect can be easily remedied through repairs, the measure of damages is the price of the repairs performed.

Generally, the total contract price may not be recovered for substantial performance. If the plaintiff furnished materials for items that were manufactured for the plaintiff in such a manner as to be rendered worthless, the proper measure of damages ordinarily has been held to be the discrepancy between the contract price and the market price of such items if they had been manufactured according to the contract terms.

When a building or construction contract is defectively performed, the proper measure of damages is the difference between the value of the property with the defective work, and its value had there been strict compliance with the contract. Where the contractor deliberately deviates from the contractual agreement, but there has been no substantial performance, damages are determined by the actual expense of reconstructing the building according to the terms of the contract.

Delay in performance The loss precipitated by the wrongful delay of the performance of a contract is calculated by fixing the rental or use of the property or interest as a result of the loss incurred through increased material and labor expenses, as distinguished from what the value would have been had the contract been performed on time.

Reformation Reformation is an equitable remedy that is applied when the written agreement does not correspond to the contract that was actually formed by the parties, as a result of fraud or mutual mistake in drafting the original document. Quasi-contractual relief for the reasonable value of services rendered is also available, although it applies only when there is no enforceable contract.

Rescission Rescission terminates the contract, and the parties are restored to the position of never having entered into the contract in the first place.

Restitution Restitution is a remedy that is designed to restore the injured party to the position that they occupied prior to the formation of the contract.

Specific Performance Specific performance is an equitable remedy by which a contracting party is required to execute, as nearly as practicable, a promised performance when monetary damages would be inadequate to compensate for the breach. A contract to sell land is specifically enforceable because land is considered to be unique and not compensable by money. In addition, property that has sentimental value, as well as antique, heirloom, or one-of-a-kind articles, are viewed as unique, and therefore it would be impossible to estimate damages. A personal-service contract or an employment contract, however, cannot be specifically enforced because the THIRTEENTH AMENDMENT to the U.S. Constitution prohibits SLAVERY. If, however, the contract proscribes a person from performing some act, breach of that negative covenant may be specifically enforced.

Parol Evidence Rule

Tentative terms discussed in preliminary negotiations are subsumed by the provisions of the contract executed by the parties. The PAROL EVIDENCE rule governs the admissibility of evidence other than the actual agreement when a dispute arises over a written contract. When parties memorialize their agreements in writing, all prior oral and written agreements, and all contemporaneous oral agreements, merge in the writing, which is also known as an integration. The written contract may not be modified, altered, or varied by parol or oral evidence, provided that it has been legally executed by a person who intends for it to represent the final and complete expression of his or her understanding of the contract. This is not the case, however, where there has been some mistake or fraud in the drafting of the document.

The parol evidence rule effectuates the presumed intention of the parties; achieves certainty and finality as to the rights and duties of the contracting parties; and prevents fraudulent and perjured claims. It has no application to subsequent oral contracts that modify or discharge the written contract, however.

Ambiguity

Ambiguity in the terms of a contract exists when the court cannot, after applying the rules or tools of interpretation, give a meaning to the language used in an agreement or document. The plain-meaning rule is often applied judicially to ascertain whether a contract is ambiguous. If the contract appears to the trial judge to be clear and unequivocal on its face, then there is no need for parol evidence. However, when a writing is ambiguous, parol evidence is admissable only to elucidate, not to vary, the instrument as written.

Courts have used other rules to resolve ambiguous terms. Where neither party knows, or has reason to know, of the ambiguity, or where both parties know or have reason to know of it, the ambiguous term is given the meaning that each party intended it to convey. As a practical matter, this means that if the parties give the equivocal expression the same meaning, then a contract is formed; but if they give it a different meaning, then there is no contract, at least if the ambiguity pertains to a material term, as there is no meeting of their minds. Where one party knows, or has reason to know, of the ambiguity, and the other does not, it conveys the meaning given to it by the latter—which means, in essence, that there is a contract predicated upon the meaning of the party who is without fault.

Contracts for the Sale of Goods

The nature of a transaction determines the type of contract law that applies. General contract law described above applies to such transactions as service agreements and sales of real property. Contracts for the sale of goods, however, are governed by Article 2 of the UCC, which has been adopted, at least in part, in every state. The UCC defines "goods" as all things that are movable at the time of the sale.

The drafters of the UCC adhered to a more liberal view of contracts, so some of its provisions differ significantly from those that are found in general contract law. A contract for the sale of goods may be made in any manner that is sufficient to show agreement, and courts may consider the conduct of the parties when making this determination. An offer to sell goods may be made in any manner that invites acceptance. Courts also may consider the COURSE OF PERFORMANCE between the parties when determining whether a contract for the sale of goods exists.

The UCC provides for, and recognizes, certain warranties that relate to the goods being sold. For example, an affirmation of fact or a promise made by the seller to the buyer creates an express warranty. Sales also create implied warranties, such as the implied warranties of merchantability and fitness for a particular purpose. Remedies and other damages for breach of a sale-of-goods

contract are also governed by the UCC. In addition to monetary damages, buyers and sellers may take several actions when the other party breaches a sales contract. For example, a seller who has been injured by a breach of contract may withhold delivery of the goods; resell the goods that are subject to the contract; or recover monetary damages. A buyer may seek to "cover" by making a good-faith purchase of substitute goods from a different seller, and then may recover from the original seller any difference between the substitute contract and the original contract.

FURTHER READINGS

Collins, Hugh. 1999. *Regulating Contracts*. New York: Oxford Univ. Press.

DiMatteo, Larry A. 1998. *Contract Theory: The Evolution of Contractual Intent*. East Lansing: Michigan State Univ. Press.

Hare, J. I. Clark. 2003. *The Law of Contracts*. Clark, N.J.: Lawbook Exchange.

Marsh, P.D.V. 2001. *Contract Negotiation Handbook*. Burlington, Vt: Gower.

CONTRAVENTION

A term of French law meaning an act violative of a law, a treaty, or an agreement made between parties; a breach of law punishable by a fine of fifteen francs or less and by an imprisonment of three days or less. In the U.S. legal system, a breach or violation of the provisions of a contract, statute, or treaty.

CONTRIBUTING TO THE DELINQUENCY OF A MINOR

Any action by an adult that allows or encourages illegal behavior by a person under the age of 18, or that places children in situations that expose them to illegal behavior. Contributing to the delinquency of a minor can be as simple as keeping a child home from school and thus, making the child a truant. It also can manifest itself in more serious behavior. For example, an adult who commits a crime in the presence of a child can be charged with contributing to the delinquency of a minor, as can an adult who serves alcoholic beverages to anyone under the legal drinking age. Still more egregious is sexual exploitation, which could include having sexual relations with minors or engaging in the production or trafficking of CHILD PORNOGRAPHY.

CROSS-REFERENCES

Battered Child/Spouse Syndrome; Child Abuse; Child Pornography; Children's Rights; Domestic Violence.

CONTRIBUTION

In maritime law, where the property of one of several parties with interests in a vessel and cargo has been voluntarily sacrificed for the common safety of the vessel—as by casting goods overboard to lighten the vessel—such loss must be made up by the contribution of the others, which is labeled "general average." In CIVIL LAW, *a partition by which the creditors of an insolvent debtor divide among themselves the proceeds of the debtor's property in proportion to the amount of their respective credits. The right of a defendant who has paid an entire debt, or common liability, to recoup a proportionate share of the payment from another defendant who is equally responsible for the payment of that debt or liability.*

Certain principles apply when contribution is sought in contractual situations. Where the parties are severally (individually) liable for a specific portion of a debt, one person who pays in excess of his or her proportionate share has no legal right to contribution from the others for the excess. Where the parties are jointly liable (as a unit) for the payment of a debt, a party who pays in excess of his or her ratable share can seek contribution from the others for the amount of his or her overpayment. If the parties are jointly and severally liable for a debt, both as a unit and as individuals, any party who pays in excess of his or her proportionate share can seek contribution.

To entitle a person to contribution, the payment of the debt or liability must arise from a legal obligation to pay. The payment of the entire debt or liability is unnecessary, but the payment must have exceeded the share of the person seeking contribution.

A plaintiff who procures a judgment (a final court decision that resolves a controversy and determines the rights and obligations of the parties) against two or more joint tortfeasors (those who together commit a civil wrong) can collect that judgment from all, any one, or less than all of them. The English and early U.S. COMMON LAW held that if one such defendant did in fact pay less than a proportionate share of the judgment, that defendant should reimburse the other defendant(s) who paid more, except in cases of intentional TORTS or acts of the defendant that did not justify the court's assistance. During the past century, however, the majority of jurisdictions in this country expanded this exception and denied all common-law contribution among joint tortfeasors regardless of the basis of liability, including cases of NEGLIGENCE and STRICT LIABILITY.

Statutes—some of which are patterned after the Uniform Contribution Among Tortfeasors Act—supersede the common law in more than half the states and provide for contribution in some form. Several jurisdictions continue to permit contribution by judicial decision, never having adhered to the majority rule disallowing it, although some states still generally deny contribution.

Of those states allowing contribution, the majority allocate the damages among the defendants in proportion to their relative fault. In the remainder, which includes almost all those without a statute, the damages are divided equally. Certain defendants, such as an employer and his or her employee, are aggregated and assessed a single share.

Contribution is still generally but not universally denied to willful tortfeasors. If the plaintiff has sued and obtained a judgment against fewer than all joint tortfeasors, some statutes prohibit contribution from one against whom there is no judgment. Other statutes permit contribution in this instance, subject to satisfactory proof of liability.

It is generally held, unless there is a statute requiring otherwise, that a tortfeasor who settles prior to trial—and therefore against whom there is no judgment—can nevertheless obtain contribution from other joint tortfeasors, but must prove the liability to the plaintiff of the other tortfeasors, the amount of the damages, and the reasonableness of the prior settlement.

In an action for contribution, the party seeking it must ordinarily establish that the tortfeasor from whom contribution is sought was subject to liability to the injured plaintiff, if no judgment has been obtained determining that liability. Certain defenses usually bar contribution, such as automobile GUEST STATUTES and the IMMUNITY granted to employers under the WORKERS' COMPENSATION acts, which only the defendant in the action for contribution could have asserted against the injured person. There is some authority to the contrary, however.

CROSS-REFERENCES

Joint and Several Liability.

CONTROLLER

The key financial officer of a state, private, or MUNICIPAL CORPORATION, *who is charged with certain specific responsibilities related to its financial affairs.*

CROSS-REFERENCES

Comptroller.

CONTROVERSY

An actual dispute between individuals who seek judicial resolution of their grievances that have arisen from a conflict of their alleged legal rights.

A controversy describes only civil litigation, which is intended to protect and enforce private rights. In contrast, the term *case* applies to both a civil action and a criminal prosecution, designed to enforce and safeguard the rights of the general public.

The judicial power of a court to provide redress of wrongs exists only when issues arise in a given situation that can be categorized as a case or controversy.

CONTROVERT

To contest, deny, or take issue with.

A claim of reckless driving alleged in a plaintiff's complaint that initiates a lawsuit for NEG-LIGENCE is controverted by the statements made in the defendant's answer that he or she was driving at a speed below the speed limit and was observing the rules of the road.

CONTUMACY

Willful disobedience. The intentional failure of an individual to obey a summons to appear in court to defend against a charge or to obey an order rendered by the court.

Contumacy is a sufficient basis for finding an individual in CONTEMPT of court.

CONVENTION

An agreement or compact, particularly an international agreement, such as the GENEVA CONVENTION. An accord between states or nations, which resembles a treaty: ordinarily applied to agreements prior to an execution of an official treaty or which serve as its foundation; or to international agreements for the regulation of international affairs of common interest not within the ambit of commercial transactions or politics, such as international postage. An agreement between states concerning finance, trade, or other matters considered less significant than those usually governed by a treaty. An assembly or meeting of representatives or members of legislative, political, or fraternal organizations.

A *constitutional convention* is an assembly of representatives or delegates of the people of a state or nation, convened for the purpose of framing, altering, or amending its constitution. Article V of the U.S. Constitution provides that a constitutional convention may be convoked on application of the legislatures of two-thirds of the states.

A *judicial convention* is an assembly of judges of the superior courts (courts of general jurisdiction), empowered in some states to meet during specified periods to adopt uniform rules of practice. The powers of the convention are restricted to making necessary rules that conform to the provisions of the relevant statute. Revision or abrogation of any rule of practice established by statute is prohibited.

A *legislative convention* is a congregation of representatives or delegates selected by the people for extraordinary and special legislative objectives, such as the framing or alteration of a state constitution.

A *political convention* is an assembly of delegates designated by a political party to nominate candidates for a pending election.

CONVENTIONAL

Derived from or contingent upon the mutual agreement of the parties, as opposed to that created by or dependent upon a statute or other act of the law.

A conventional home mortgage is one in which the interest rate is agreed upon by the parties to it: the borrower and the lender.

CONVENTIONAL FORCES IN EUROPE TREATY

The United States, the Soviet Union, and twenty other member countries of the NORTH ATLANTIC TREATY ORGANIZATION (NATO) and the Warsaw Pact signed the Conventional Forces in Europe (CFE) Treaty on November 19, 1990. The most complex and comprehensive conventional ARMS CONTROL treaty in history, the CFE limits levels of conventional—that is, nonnuclear—weapons and equipment with the purpose of creating greater military stability in Europe. The CFE played a crucial stabilizing role during the breakup of the Soviet Union and its satellite states in Eastern Europe during the late 1980s and early 1990s. It also made possible steep reductions in U.S. troop and equipment levels in Europe. In a period of remarkable historical change that transformed the political map of Europe, the treaty's provisions enabled a "velvet" rather than a violent revolution.

The CFE grew out of arms control negotiations between the United States and the Soviet Union during the 1980s. In particular, treaty negotiations were prompted by a 1986 call for conventional arms control by Soviet president Mikhail Gorbachev, and a 1989 proposal by U.S. president GEORGE H. W. BUSH to limit the United States and the Soviet Union to 275,000 troops each in Europe. However, as the Soviet satellites gained independence in the late 1980s and early 1990s and large numbers of U.S. and Soviet troops were transferred out of Europe, the initial level of troops proposed by Bush proved needlessly high, and subsequent negotiations focused on armaments alone.

By November 1990, a treaty had been completed. Meeting in Paris, Bush, Gorbachev, and other leaders signed the CFE that month. The U.S. Senate approved it on November 25, 1991, by a vote of 90–4.

The treaty placed limits on five types of conventional armaments deployed between the Atlantic Ocean and the Ural Mountains: tanks, artillery, armored combat vehicles (such as armored personnel carriers), aircraft, and helicopters. It divided the area covered by the agreement into subzones, each having its own equipment limits. The agreement limited NATO and the Warsaw Pact each to 20,000 tanks, 30,000 armored combat vehicles, 20,000 artillery pieces, 6,800 combat aircraft, and 2,000 attack helicopters. The treaty did not address naval forces.

As originally designed, the CFE was meant to stabilize relations between NATO and the Warsaw Pact. NATO, for its part, sought to relocate Soviet forces eastward from the German border and to prevent their concentration in the Soviet Union west of the Urals. After the dissolution of the Warsaw Pact on July 1, 1991, and the breakup of the Soviet Union into 15 separate nations in December 1991, the CFE began to change its focus from management of the COLD WAR standoff to management of the effects of the Cold War's conclusion.

Later amendments adapted the treaty to the changing European political situation. On May 15, 1992, the Commonwealth of Independent States—the 15 successor states of the Soviet Union—ratified armament limits in their territories as specified by the CFE limits for the Warsaw Pact nations. All adherents to the treaty met

subsequent arms reduction targets, though Russia continued to negotiate changes owing to unrest in Chechnya and other regions within its borders. By September 1994 the CFE had resulted in the destruction of more than 18,000 pieces of military equipment, including 6,000 by the Russian Federation.

The CFE enjoys widespread support in Europe and appears likely to remain in force for some time. CFE supporters argue that its armament limits and inspection requirements prevent an arms race and enhance the exchange of information between European countries, allowing each member nation to easily assess the military capabilities of its neighbors.

German Foreign Minister Hans-Dietrich Genscher looks on as President George H.W. Bush signs the Conventional Forces in Europe Treaty on November 19, 1990. The treaty, which has been amended to reflect changes in the European political system since its original adoption, limits levels of conventional weapons in order to ensure military stability in Europe.

REUTERS NEWMEDIA INC./CORBIS

FURTHER READINGS

Croft, Stuart, ed. 1994. *The Conventional Armed Forces in Europe Treaty: The Cold War Endgame*. Brookfield, Vt.: Dartmouth.

Falkenrath, Richard A. 1995. *Shaping Europe's Military Order: The Origins and Consequences of the CFE Treaty*. Cambridge, Mass.: MIT Press.

McCausland, Jeffrey D. 1995. "The CFE Treaty: Building European Security." *Strategic Forum*, no. 48 (October). National Defense Univ. Press.

Peters, John E., and National Defense Research Institute. 2000. *The Changing Quality of Stability in Europe: The Conventional Forces in Europe Treaty Toward 2001*. Santa Monica, Calif.: Rand.

———. 1997. *CFE and Military Stability in Europe*. Santa Monica, Calif.: Rand.

Treaty on Conventional Armed Forces in Europe (CFE): Briefing of the Commission on Security and Cooperation in Europe. 1997. Washington, D.C.: The Commission.

CROSS-REFERENCES

Arms Control and Disarmament; Intermediate-Range Nuclear Forces Treaty; Strategic Arms Reduction Talks.

CONVERSION

Any unauthorized act that deprives an owner of personal property without his or her consent.

The wrongdoer converts the goods to his or her own use and excludes the owner from use and enjoyment of them. The English COMMON LAW early recognized such an act as wrongful and, by the middle of the fifteenth century, allowed an action in TROVER to compensate the aggrieved owner.

The earliest cases allowing a lawsuit for conversion were based on claims that the plaintiff had possession of certain items of PERSONAL PROPERTY, then casually lost them, and the defendant had found them and had not returned them but instead "converted them to his own use." This phrase was picked up, and it gave a name to a TORT that originally was a kind of ACTION ON THE CASE, a form of TRESPASS. As time passed, the plea that the plaintiff had lost his or her goods and the defendant had found them came to be considered a legal fiction (that is, a decision was made in the case as if the plea were true, and it did not have to be proved). The defendant was not allowed to dispute the allegations but could answer only the claim that the plaintiff had a right to possession of the goods and the defendant had refused to restore them to the plaintiff.

Today the word *conversion* is still applied to the unlawful taking or use of someone else's property. The type of property that can be converted is determined by the original nature of the CAUSE OF ACTION. It must be personal property, because real property cannot be lost and then found. It must be tangible, such as money, an animal, furniture, tools, or receipts. Crops or timber can be subject to conversion after they are severed from the ground. The rights in a paper—such as a life insurance policy, a stock certificate, or a promissory note—can be converted by one who appropriates the paper itself.

A thief, a trespasser, or a bailee may be guilty of conversion because the action may be maintained whether or not the property was lawfully acquired at the outset. For example, a dry cleaner who mistakenly delivers a suit to the wrong customer has converted it. Moving someone's property without his or her permission might constitute a conversion if the inconvenience is substantial: for example, having someone's car towed away in order to take the parking place. Unauthorized use is a conversion—such as a mechanic who, without permission, borrows a sports car that he or she is supposed to repair. Misuse of property can also be a conversion. If a neighbor lends his or her hedge trimmer to a friend, it is a conversion for the friend to use the hedge trimmer to cut down a tree.

CONVEYANCE

The transfer of ownership or interest in real property from one person to another by a document, such as a deed, lease, or mortgage.

CONVICT

To adjudge an accused person guilty of a crime at the conclusion of a criminal prosecution, or after the entry of a plea of guilty or a plea of nolo contendere. *An individual who has been found guilty of a crime and, as a result, is serving a sentence as punishment for the act; a prisoner.*

CONVICTION

The outcome of a criminal prosecution which concludes in a judgment that the defendant is guilty of the crime charged. The juncture of a criminal proceeding during which the question of guilt is ascertained. In a case where the perpetrator has been adjudged guilty and sentenced, a record of the summary proceedings brought pursuant to any penal statute before one or more justices of the peace or other properly authorized persons.

The terms *conviction* and *convicted* refer to the final judgment on a verdict of guilty, a plea of guilty, or a plea of nolo contendere. They do not include a final judgment that has been deleted by a pardon, set aside, reversed, or otherwise rendered inoperative.

The term *summary conviction* refers to the consequence of a trial before a court or magistrate, without a jury, which generally involves a minor misdemeanor.

❖ COOLEY, THOMAS McINTYRE

As a jurist, scholar, and educator in the late nineteenth century, Thomas McIntyre Cooley greatly influenced the development of U.S. CONSTITUTIONAL LAW. In particular, Cooley's writings shaped later interpretation of the DUE PROCESS CLAUSES of the Fifth and Fourteenth Amendments to the Constitution. His ideas were used, and sometimes misused, by others to help define a laissez-faire approach to constitutional law that sought to minimize the power of government over private and commercial life. (*Laissez-*

faire is French for "let [people] do [as they choose].") Cooley's most important books include *A Treatise on the Constitutional Limitations Which Rest upon the Legislative Power of the States of the American Union* (1868) and *A Treatise on the Law of Torts* (1879, 3d ed. 1906), both of which became the leading texts in their respective fields. In his writings, Cooley consistently defended constitutional government and its ability to protect the rights of individuals from ARBITRARY actions by the state.

Cooley had a distinguished career on the Michigan Supreme Court between 1864 and 1885. From the 1870s onward, he was considered a leading candidate for a seat on the U.S. Supreme Court; however, he never received a nomination. Cooley was also a founding member of the University of Michigan's law department in 1859, remaining there as a professor until 1884. As an indication of the complexity of Cooley's brand of conservatism, he served as the first chairman of the INTERSTATE COMMERCE COMMISSION (ICC), the body that regulates interstate transportation. He was instrumental in the establishment of the ICC as the federal government's first regulatory commission.

A descendant of seventeenth-century New England settlers, Cooley was born January 6, 1824, on a farm near Attica, New York, the eighth of his mother's thirteen children. He had a very basic education in local schools and did not attend college. In 1842, he began studying law under Theron R. Strong, a politician and lawyer from Palmyra, New York. After moving to Adrian, Michigan, to explore life on the frontier, Cooley earned ADMISSION TO THE BAR in 1846. In that same year, he married Mary Horton. Cooley's frontier experiences in Michigan had a profound effect on him and shaped much of his

Thomas McIntyre Cooley.

THE GRANGER COLLECTION, NEW YORK

later thought. He learned the benefits of frugality and self-reliance, and he took great pride in being one of the state's pioneers. He later wrote of the way in which Michigan had been transformed before his very eyes: "It was a state almost lost in its woods . . . but the magic touch of industry plied by vigorous hands speedily transformed the scene; the woods opened to the building of many beautiful and prosperous towns."

Cooley was influenced in his youth by the history and traditions of his New England forebears, as well as the values of Jacksonian Democracy, so named for ANDREW JACKSON, president of the United States from 1829 to 1837. The Jacksonians lay claim to the legacy of THOMAS

"THE VALUE OF GOVERNMENT TO ANY MAN IS PROPORTIONED TO THE COMPLETENESS OF THE PROTECTION IT EXTENDS TO ALL MEN."
—THOMAS McINTYRE COOLEY

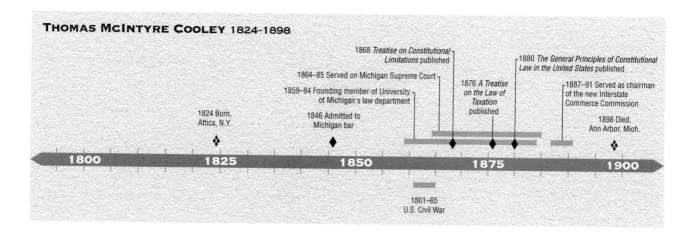

THOMAS McINTYRE COOLEY 1824–1898

1824 Born, Attica, N.Y.

1846 Admitted to Michigan bar

1859–84 Founding member of University of Michigan's law department

1864–85 Served on Michigan Supreme Court

1868 *Treatise on Constitutional Limitations* published

1876 *A Treatise on the Law of Taxation* published

1880 *The General Principles of Constitutional Law in the United States* published

1887–91 Served as chairman of the new Interstate Commerce Commission

1898 Died, Ann Arbor, Mich.

1800   1825   1850   1875   1900

1861–65 U.S. Civil War

JEFFERSON, and, like Jefferson, they had a bias in favor of an agrarian society rather than a commercial one. The Jacksonians were, therefore, suspicious of big government and big business, and saw both as a potential danger to the common individual. Cooley's constitutional philosophy grew out of the Jeffersonian and Jacksonian ideals of self-reliance, free trade, equal rights, limited government, and maximum personal liberties such as FREEDOM OF SPEECH.

During the 1840s and 1850s, Cooley was a member of the radical wing of the DEMOCRATIC PARTY. He was, for example, a Free-Soiler, believing that territories and new states should remain free of SLAVERY. In 1854, he accepted the Democratic nomination to run for district judge of COMMON PLEAS in Toledo, but he lost the election. His views on slavery led him to join the REPUBLICAN PARTY shortly after its inception in 1854, and he remained a member of it for the rest of his life.

After a difficult decade spent moving about and trying to get his legal career underway, in 1855, Cooley formed a law partnership in Adrian with Charles M. Croswell, who later became governor of Michigan. Two years later, the state legislature chose Cooley to compile the state statutes. He performed this task so ably that in 1858 he was appointed the official reporter of the state's supreme court, an office he held through 1865 and in which he edited volumes 5 through 12 of *Michigan Reports*. Cooley became one of the three founding professors of the law department at the University of Michigan in 1859, and later he served as its dean. In 1884, he gave up his position with the law department to serve as professor of U.S. history and constitutional law in the literary department, a position he held until his death on September 12, 1898.

"PERShaps ONE OF THE MOST IMPORTANT ACCOMPLISHMENTS OF MY ADMINISTRATION HAS BEEN MINDING MY OWN BUSINESS."
—CALVIN COOLIDGE

Largely because of his excellent work editing the Michigan Supreme Court's reports, Cooley was elected to the Michigan Supreme Court in 1864. Not long afterward, he began to prepare a book based on his lectures on constitutional law. *A Treatise on Constitutional Limitations* made Cooley a nationally recognized authority on the Constitution.

FURTHER READINGS

Carrington, Paul D. 1997. "The Constitutional Law Scholarship of Thomas McIntyre Cooley." *American Journal of Legal History* 41 (July): 368–99.

Cooley, Thomas M. 1868. *A Treatise on the Constitutional Limitations Which Rest Upon the Legislative Power of the States of the American Union*. Boston: Little, Brown.

Fleener, William J., Jr. 2000. "Thomas McIntyre Cooley: Michigan's Most Influential Lawyer." *Michigan Bar Journal* 79 (February): 208.

Jacobs, Clyde E. 2001. *Law Writers and the Courts: The Influence of Thomas M. Cooley, Christopher G. Tiedeman, and John F. Dillon upon American Constitutional Law*. Union, N.J.: Lawbook Exchange.

Jones, Alan R. 1960. *The Constitutional Conservatism of Thomas McIntyre Cooley: A Study in the History of Ideas*. Ph.D. Thesis. Reprint, New York: Garland, 1987.

❖ COOLIDGE, CALVIN

Born John Calvin Coolidge—after his father—on July 4, 1872, in Plymouth, Vermont, he shortened his name to Calvin Coolidge after leaving college. Coolidge became the thirtieth president of the United States upon the death of President WARREN G. HARDING. He was educated at Amherst College, where he received a bachelor of arts degree in 1895 and a doctor of laws degree in 1919. He also received doctor of laws degrees from several other institutions, including Wesleyan University and Tufts University.

In 1897, Coolidge was admitted to the bar and established his legal firm in Northampton,

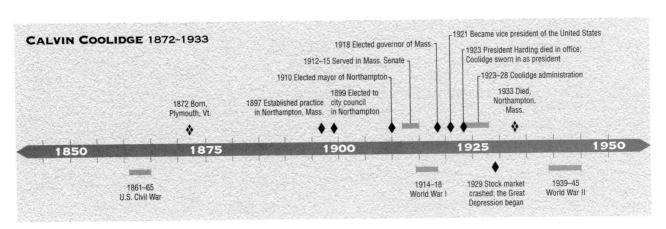

CALVIN COOLIDGE 1872–1933

1921 Became vice president of the United States
1918 Elected governor of Mass.
1923 President Harding died in office; Coolidge sworn in as president
1912–15 Served in Mass. Senate
1910 Elected mayor of Northampton
1923–28 Coolidge administration
1872 Born, Plymouth, Vt.
1897 Established practice in Northampton, Mass.
1899 Elected to city council in Northampton
1933 Died, Northampton, Mass.

1850 1875 1900 1925 1950

1861–65 U.S. Civil War
1914–18 World War I
1929 Stock market crashed; the Great Depression began
1939–45 World War II

Calvin Coolidge. © HARRIS & EWING

Massachusetts, where he practiced until 1919. He became councilman in Northampton in 1899, then city solicitor from 1900 to 1901, clerk of courts in 1904, and member of the General Court of Massachusetts from 1907 to 1908. In 1910, he was elected mayor of Northampton, a post that he held for one year.

Coolidge served in the Massachusetts Senate from 1912 to 1915, acting as president during 1914 and 1915. He was the lieutenant governor of the state from 1916 to 1918 and the following year became governor. As governor, he gained public recognition for his strong policy regarding the Boston police strike of 1919, regarding which he denied the right of any individual or group to strike if the public welfare is jeopardized.

With such extensive experience in state government, Coolidge was a natural choice for a federal position. In 1921, he was elected to the vice presidency of the United States. On August 2, 1923, President Warren G. Harding died suddenly and Coolidge became president. He was sworn in by his father, a NOTARY PUBLIC, on August 3, 1923, at 2:47 A.M. in his hometown of Plymouth, Vermont. In the next presidential election, held in 1924, Coolidge was elected, and so his administration lasted for five years.

As president, Coolidge adopted policies that favored business and discouraged government intervention in the economic system. He influenced the speculative activity of the STOCK MARKET toward the end of the 1920s, which, some believe, precipitated the crash of 1929. When Coolidge left office in that year, the country was on the brink of economic disaster.

Coolidge spent his last years in retirement, writing articles. His *Autobiography* was published in 1929. He died January 5, 1933, in Northampton, Massachusetts.

FURTHER READINGS

Gilbert, Robert E. 2003. *The Tormented President: Calvin Coolidge and the Trauma of Death.* Westport, Conn.: Greenwood.

Sobel, Robert. 2000. *Coolidge: An American Enigma.* Washington, D.C.: Regnery.

CROSS-REFERENCES

Harding, Warren Gamaliel; Hoover, Herbert Clark.

COOLING-OFF PERIOD

An interval of time during which no action of a specific type can be taken by either side in a dispute. An automatic delay in certain jurisdictions, apart from ordinary court delays, between the time when DIVORCE papers are filed and the divorce hearing takes place. An amount of time within which a buyer is permitted to cancel a contract for the purchase of consumer goods—designed to effect CONSUMER PROTECTION. A number of states require that a three-day cancellation period must be allowed purchasers following door-to-door sales.

A cooling-off period is frequently used in labor disputes. There might, for example, be a period of one month following the filing of a grievance by a union or company against the other, during which neither the union nor the company is allowed to take retaliatory actions against each other.

COOPERATIVE

An association or corporation established for the purpose of providing services on a nonprofit basis to its shareholders or members who own and control it.

The nature and functions of cooperatives differ considerably—such as purchasing cooperatives, consumer cooperatives, and marketing cooperatives.

In the context of agriculture, a farmers' cooperative refers to an organization of farmers residing in the same locale that is established for their mutual benefit in regard to the cultivation and harvest of their products, the purchase of farm equipment and supplies at the lowest possible cost, and the sale of their products at the maximum possible price.

The term *cooperative* also signifies the ownership of an apartment building by a nonprofit corporation that holds title to it and the property upon which it is situated. Stock in the corporation is allotted among the apartment units on the basis of their relative value or size. The right of occupancy to a particular apartment is granted to each cooperative member, who purchases the shares assigned to the desired unit. The member subsequently receives a long-term proprietary lease to that unit. The rent payable pursuant to the lease is that member's proportionate share of the expenses the corporation incurs in operating the cooperative—such as insurance, taxes, maintenance, management, and debt service. The cooperative concept evolved in New York City during the early 1900s as a mode of accommodating the public's desire for home ownership; it subsequently expanded to other large urban centers.

In order to finance the purchase or construction of the cooperative building, the cooperative places a blanket mortgage on the property, which is pledged to support the given debt. Lenders usually are hesitant to accept an individual member's stock and proprietary lease as security for a long-term loan. The members' lien (a claim on property to satisfy a debt) on the lease would be subordinate to the blanket mortgage on the property. The purchaser of a cooperative apartment usually must have sufficient cash available to pay for the stock allotted to the unit he or she wishes to obtain. The initial price of the stock generally does not exceed the amount required for a down payment on a single-family residence. As cooperative members accumulate EQUITY (the value of property exceeding the total debts on it) in their stock, subsequent purchasers must either have a substantial amount of cash available or locate a seller who is willing to recoup the equity in installments over several years.

Cooperative members are also financially dependent on each other. The existence of a single blanket mortgage paid by rent receipts means that if several members default in their rent payments, the corporation might not have sufficient funds to pay a mortgage loan installment. Foreclosure will ensue in regard to the entire membership unless it acts to satisfy the default. Although special reserves and assessments are generally employed to cover such a contingency, the available funds might be inadequate to prevent default.

COOPERATIVES

See CONDOMINIUMS AND COOPERATIVES.

COPYRIGHT

A bundle of intangible rights granted by statute to the author or originator of certain literary or artistic productions, whereby, for a limited period, the exclusive privilege is given to that person (or to any party to whom he or she transfers ownership) to make copies of the same for publication and sale.

A copyright is a legal device that gives the creator of a literary, artistic, musical, or other creative work the sole right to publish and sell that work. Copyright owners have the right to control the reproduction of their work, including the right to receive payment for that reproduction. An author may grant or sell those rights to others, including publishers or recording companies. Violation of a copyright is called infringement.

Copyright is distinct from other forms of creator protection such as PATENTS, which give inventors exclusive rights over use of their inventions, and TRADEMARKS, which are legally protected words or symbols or certain other distinguishing features that represent products or services. Similarly, whereas a patent protects the application of an idea, and a trademark protects a device that indicates the provider of particular services or goods, copyright protects the expression of an idea. Whereas the operative notion in patents is novelty, so that a patent represents some invention that is new and has never been made before, the basic concept behind copyright is originality, so that a copyright represents something that has originated from a particular author and not from another. Copyrights, patents, and trademarks are all examples of what is known in the law as INTELLECTUAL PROPERTY.

As the media on which artistic and intellectual works are recorded have changed with time, copyright protection has been extended from the printing of text to many other means of recording original expressions. Besides books, stories, periodicals, poems, and other printed literary works, copyright may protect computer programs; musical compositions; song lyrics; dramas; dramatico-musical compositions; pictorial, graphic, and sculptural works; architectural works; written directions for pantomimes and choreographic works; motion pictures and other audiovisual works; and sound recordings.

History of Copyright Law

U.S. copyright law grew out of English COMMON LAW and statutory law. When the printing press was developed in the fifteenth century, rights for the reproduction of written works extended to printers rather than to authors. In England, a printers' guild, the Stationers' Company, claimed for itself the exclusive right—in effect, a monopoly—on written works. It was not until 1710 that Parliament passed a statute relating to copyright. That law, called the Statute of Anne, established authors' rights to control the reproduction of their work after it was published. It also created a term of protection of 28 years from the date of publication. After that time, an author's work entered the public domain, meaning that anyone could print or distribute it without obtaining the author's permission or paying a royalty, or fee, to the author. Other European countries developed similar laws in the late eighteenth and early nineteenth centuries.

Under the British system, the author retained a common-law right to ownership of his or her work until publication. After publication, copyright was established as a statutory right, protected by the Statute of Anne. U.S. copyright law retained this distinction between prepublication common-law rights and postpublication statutory rights, until 1976.

By the late eighteenth century, the protection of intellectual property as a means of advancing the public interest was considered important enough to receive mention in the U.S. Constitution. The Patent and Copyright Clause—Article I, Section 8, Clause 8—of the U.S. Constitution empowers Congress "To promote the Progress of Science and useful Arts, by securing for limited Times to Authors and Inventors the exclusive Right to their respective Writings and Discoveries." Congress passed its first copyright statute in 1790—and has substantially revised copyright law four times, in 1831, 1870, 1909, and 1976.

Revisions in the copyright law have been driven largely by commercially significant changes in technology. In 1802, for example, graphic prints came under copyright protection, establishing the notion that the Constitution's

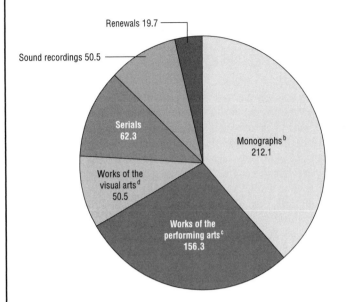

Copyright Registration by Subject Matter, 2001[a] (in thousands)

Renewals 19.7

Sound recordings 50.5

Serials 62.3

Works of the visual arts[d] 50.5

Works of the performing arts[c] 156.3

Monographs[b] 212.1

[a]Includes published and unpublished works.

[b]Includes traditional books, computer software, and machine readable works.

[c]Includes dramatic works, musical works, choreography, pantomimes, motion pictures, and filmstrips.

[d]Two-dimensional works of fine or graphic art, including prints and art reproductions; sculptural works; technical drawings and models; photographs; commercial prints and labels; works of applied arts, cartographic works; and multimedia works.

SOURCE: Library of Congress, U.S. Copyright Office, *Annual Report*, 2001.

language regarding copyright not be interpreted to apply literally to "Writings" alone. In 1831, musical compositions were incorporated into copyright protection, and in 1870, paintings, statues, and other works of fine art were placed under copyright protection.

The distinction between common-law protection for unpublished works and statutory protection of published works received increasing criticism in the twentieth century, particularly as the notion of publication changed greatly with technological innovations in communication. Congress removed this distinction in the landmark Copyright Act of 1976 (17 U.S.C.A. § 102(a)). According to this statute, an author receives copyright protection as soon as a work is recorded in a concrete way—when, for example, it is written on a piece of paper, recorded on an audiotape, or stored on a computer disk. Any unauthorized copying of the work is subject to an infringement suit and criminal charges. The 1976 act also allows copyright protection of works that derive from the original, such as

Copyright Law in Action:
Basic Books v. Kinko's Graphics Corp.

Copyright cases typically involve disputes between competing private interests: an author against someone who has copied the author's work without permission. However, the outcome of such cases often has significant repercussions for the general public as well. One such case with significant public effect was *Basic Books v. Kinko's Graphics Corp.*, 758 F. Supp. 1522 (S.D.N.Y. 1991), which dealt with the question of whether photocopy stores may sell copied excerpts of books to college students without authorization from the books' publishers. The decision in the case ultimately affected the price that the public must pay for access to copyrighted information.

Many college and university students purchase photocopied materials from copy stores in association with courses they are taking. Usually consisting of chapters or sections taken from different books or journals, these photocopied materials enable students to read from a wide variety of sources without having to purchase a large number of books. By the late 1980s, book publishers realized they were losing sales owing to such photocopying. As a result, several publishers, including Basic Books, Inc., filed a lawsuit in federal court against one of the largest photocopy firms in the United States—Kinko's Graphics Corporation, a company that in 1989 had more than two hundred locations and annual sales of $54 million.

At issue in the case was the question of who may profit from the reproduction of an author's work, particularly with regard to the practice that Kinko's called anthologizing, which is the copying of book excerpts into course "packets" sold to college students. The publishers, the plaintiffs in the case, maintained that Kinko's violated the Copyright Act of 1976 (17 U.S.C.A. § 101 et seq.), by failing to secure permission to reprint the excerpts included in course packets and, in turn, pay the necessary fees involved, part of which would be passed on to the authors of the books. Kinko's claimed that its sale of the excerpts was an example of the kind of fair use that is allowed by the Copyright Act.

Citing the commercial interests involved—namely, the fact that Kinko's made a significant amount of money from the sale of course packets, and that packet sales competed with book sales—the court found that Kinko's was guilty of copyright infringement. It ordered the company to pay $500,000 in damages to the publishers and issued an order forbidding it to prepare anthologies without securing permission from and prepaying fees to the appropriate publishers.

Basic Books was a victory for the publishers and authors of books that are excerpted for course anthologies. As for Kinko's, it now has to pay fees to publishers, but it is able to pass on those costs to customers in the form of higher prices. Does this mean that students are the losers in this case? In the short run, yes, because they will pay more for their course materials. But in the long run, students and the rest of society may derive more benefit, even if it is indirect, from a system that rewards authors for their intellectual labor.

motion pictures, CD-ROM multimedia editions, and other adaptations. These subsequent creations are known as derivative works.

Many features of the 1976 act make U.S. copyright law conform more to international copyright standards, particularly with regard to the duration of copyright protection and to the formalities of copyright deposit, registration, and notice. These changes have been greatly influenced by the most important international copyright treaty, the Berne Convention for the Protection of Literary and Artistic Works (828 U.N.T.S. 221, S. Treaty Doc. No. 99-27). In 1988, the United States passed the Berne Convention Implementation Act (102 Stat. 2853), which made the nation an official member of the treaty as of 1989. Section 2(a) of this act holds that provisions of the treaty are not legally binding in the United States without domestic legislation that specifically implements them.

U.S. copyright law has continued to evolve toward greater conformity with international copyright standards. In the 1990s, for example, the Berne Convention added 20 years to the minimum standard for copyright duration, changing it to the length of the author's life plus 70 years. U.S. copyright law followed suit in 1998, with the passage of the Sonny Bono Copyright Term Extension Act.

Copyrightable Works

The 1976 Copyright Act provides that copyright protection "subsists … in original works of authorship fixed in any tangible medium of expression, now known or later developed" (17 U.S.C.A. § 102(a)). Thus, virtually any form of fixed recording is protected, no matter how new the technology.

Originality is the most important quality needed by a work in order for it to receive copyright protection. Originality is not dependent on the work's meeting any standard of aesthetic or artistic quality. Thus, a work need not be fine art to be copyrightable.

Works That Are Not Copyrightable

Copyright protects the *expression* of an idea or vision, not the idea itself. In legal terminology, this concept is called the idea-expression dichotomy, and it has been an important feature of legal reasoning related to copyright. Ideas, procedures, processes, systems, methods of operation, concepts, principles, and discoveries are not within the scope of copyright protection. Other works that are not copyrightable are words and short phrases, including slogans; blank forms for recording information (such as bank checks); and works containing no original authorship (such as standard calendars or simple phone listings).

Some works are not copyrightable because they are not fixed in a tangible medium. These include unrecorded dance choreography, and unrecorded speeches, lectures, and other vocal performances. Although typefaces are tangible, they traditionally have been regarded as lying outside of copyright protection. A dramatic character is not copyrightable.

Holders of a Copyright

A copyright is initially owned by the author or authors of the work, except in the case of a "work for hire." A work for hire can arise in two situations: (1) where an employee creates a work within the scope of his or her employment, in which case the employer owns the copyright to the work upon its creation; (2) where two parties enter a written agreement designating the creation as a work for hire and the work falls within one of nine specific categories of work designated by copyright law. If the work does not fit one of the specified categories, it will not be a work for hire even if the parties have called it one. In such a case, the author or authors retain the copyright, and transfer must be accomplished through a written assignment of copyright. Where there is a valid work for hire, the employer who owns the copyright has the same rights as any copyright holder, including the right to initiate an action for copyright infringement.

The ownership of a copyright, or the ownership of any of the five exclusive rights afforded by a copyright (discussed later in this article), can be transferred to another and is regarded as PERSONAL PROPERTY upon the death of the copyright holder. Copyright ownership and ownership of the material object in which the copyrighted work is embodied are two entirely separate legal entities. Furthermore, transfer of an object and transfer of the copyright to that object are separate, independent transactions, neither of which, by itself, has any effect on the other. Therefore, transfer of a material object, such as an original manuscript, photograph negative, or master tape recording, does not transfer the copyright to that work. Likewise, transfer of the copyright to a work does not require transfer of the original copy of the work.

Exclusive Rights

Copyright affords an author a number of exclusive rights: (1) the exclusive right to reproduce, or copy, the work; (2) the exclusive right to prepare new works that derive from the copyrighted work; (3) the exclusive right to distribute the work to the public by sale or other arrangement; (4) the exclusive right to perform the work publicly; and (5) the exclusive right to display the work publicly. The first two rights, involving reproduction and derivation, are infringed whether violated in public or in private, or whether violated for profit or not. The last three rights are infringed only when violated publicly, that is, before a "substantial number of persons" outside of family and friends (17 U.S.C.A. § 101).

All of the exclusive rights afforded by copyright may have significant economic value. For example, derivative works, which may include translations, dramatizations, films, recordings, and abridgments, can offer substantial rewards to the author. An author may sell, license, or transfer one or all of the exclusive rights.

Duration of Ownership

Under the original provisions of the Copyright Act of 1976, copyright protection of an authored work extended through the life of the author and to fifty years after the author's death. However, in a major piece of legislation, Congress extended copyright terms in 1998 in the Sonny Bono Copyright Term Extension Act, Pub. L. No. 105-298, 112 Stat. 2827 (17 U.S.C.A. §§ 101 et seq.). Title I defines the terms of the copyright extension, while Title II provides a "music licensing exemption for food service or drinking establishments." This portion of the law is also known as the Fairness in Music Licensing Act of 1998.

The duration of copyright law under the 1998 act was extended for all copyrighted materials. Works created on January 1, 1978, or after are protected from the time the work was "fixed in a tangible medium of expression." The term is for life of the creator plus 70 years. If the creator is a corporation, then the term is 95 years from publication or 120 years from the date of creation, whichever is shorter.

Works published between 1923 and 1963 are protected, if they were published with notice, for 28 years and can be renewed for 67 years. If not renewed, they will fall into the public domain. Materials that were published during this period without notice entered the public domain upon publication.

Items published between 1964 and 1977 are protected if they were published with notice. They are protected for 28 years, and the copyright has been automatically extended for 67 years. Works created before January 1, 1978, but not published, are protected for the life of the creator plus 70 years or until December 31, 2002, whichever is later. Materials created before January 1, 1978, but published between then and December 31, 2002, are protected for the life of the creator plus 70 years or until December 31, 2002, whichever is later.

Libraries, archives, museums, and scholars expressed concerns about the 20-year extension. Items created in 1923 would have passed into the public domain on January 1, 1999, if the law had not been changed. At the beginning of 2000, works created in 1924 would have fallen under

the public domain. The act's opponents argued that original scholarly research would be hampered by the extension.

In answer to those concerns, a special clause was included in the Copyright Term Extension Act for libraries, archives, and nonprofit educational institutions. Such institutions are permitted to "reproduce, distribute, display, or perform in facsimile or digital form" a copy of any copyrighted, published work during the last 20 years of its term "for purposes of preservation, scholarship, or research." However, the work must not be used in such a manner if it "can be obtained at a reasonable price."

The changes in the duration of copyrights were made partly to keep pace with the evolution of European copyright laws. In 1995, Europe extended its copyright protection to life of the creator plus 70 years, but in the United States it remained the life of the creator plus 50 years.

Copyright Infringement

Copyright infringement involves any violation of the exclusive rights of the copyright owner. It may be unintentional or intentional. When unintentional, it is called innocent infringement. An example of innocent infringement occurred when former Beatle George Harrison created his song "My Sweet Lord." Harrison was found to have unconsciously copied the tune of another song, "He's So Fine," by the Chiffons, and thus was liable for infringement (*Bright Tunes Music Corp. v. Harrisongs Music*, 420 F. Supp. 177 [S.D.N.Y. 1976]). Vicarious or related infringement refers to those who profit indirectly from the infringement of copyright, as in the case of a theater owner who profits from booking a band that illegally performs copyrighted works.

Since evidence of direct copying or PLAGIARISM of an authored work is difficult to obtain, infringement of copyright is usually established through CIRCUMSTANTIAL EVIDENCE. Such evidence typically must show a *substantial similarity* between the original and the copy, as well as prove that the copier had *access* to the original. This means that where two works are similar or identical, there is nevertheless no infringement if each work was produced through the original and independent work of its creator. An infringer is not relieved of liability by crediting the source or the creator of the infringed work. Although infringement does not require that

Copyright Form

Copyright Office fees are subject to change.
For current fees, check the Copyright Office
website at *www.copyright.gov*, write the Copyright Office, or call (202) 707-3000.

FORM TX
For a Nondramatic Literary Work
UNITED STATES COPYRIGHT OFFICE

REGISTRATION NUMBER

_____
TX _____ TXU _____
EFFECTIVE DATE OF REGISTRATION

Month   Day   Year

DO NOT WRITE ABOVE THIS LINE. IF YOU NEED MORE SPACE, USE A SEPARATE CONTINUATION SHEET.

1

TITLE OF THIS WORK ▼

PREVIOUS OR ALTERNATIVE TITLES ▼

PUBLICATION AS A CONTRIBUTION If this work was published as a contribution to a periodical, serial, or collection, give information about the collective work in which the contribution appeared.   **Title of Collective Work ▼**

If published in a periodical or serial give: **Volume ▼**   **Number ▼**   **Issue Date ▼**   **On Pages ▼**

2

a

NAME OF AUTHOR ▼

DATES OF BIRTH AND DEATH
Year Born ▼   Year Died ▼

NOTE
Under the law, the "author" of a "work made for hire" is generally the employer, not the employee (see instructions). For any part of this work that was "made for hire" check "Yes" in the space provided, give the employer (or other person for whom the work was prepared) as "Author" of that part, and leave the space for dates of birth and death blank.

Was this contribution to the work a "work made for hire"?
☐ Yes
☐ No

AUTHOR'S NATIONALITY OR DOMICILE
Name of Country
OR { Citizen of ▶ _____
{ Domiciled in ▶ _____

WAS THIS AUTHOR'S CONTRIBUTION TO THE WORK
Anonymous?   ☐ Yes ☐ No
Pseudonymous? ☐ Yes ☐ No

If the answer to either of these questions is "Yes," see detailed instructions.

NATURE OF AUTHORSHIP Briefly describe nature of material created by this author in which copyright is claimed. ▼

b

NAME OF AUTHOR ▼

DATES OF BIRTH AND DEATH
Year Born ▼   Year Died ▼

Was this contribution to the work a "work made for hire"?
☐ Yes
☐ No

AUTHOR'S NATIONALITY OR DOMICILE
Name of Country
OR { Citizen of ▶ _____
{ Domiciled in ▶ _____

WAS THIS AUTHOR'S CONTRIBUTION TO THE WORK
Anonymous?   ☐ Yes ☐ No
Pseudonymous? ☐ Yes ☐ No

If the answer to either of these questions is "Yes," see detailed instructions.

NATURE OF AUTHORSHIP Briefly describe nature of material created by this author in which copyright is claimed. ▼

c

NAME OF AUTHOR ▼

DATES OF BIRTH AND DEATH
Year Born ▼   Year Died ▼

Was this contribution to the work a "work made for hire"?
☐ Yes
☐ No

AUTHOR'S NATIONALITY OR DOMICILE
Name of Country
OR { Citizen of ▶ _____
{ Domiciled in ▶ _____

WAS THIS AUTHOR'S CONTRIBUTION TO THE WORK
Anonymous?   ☐ Yes ☐ No
Pseudonymous? ☐ Yes ☐ No

If the answer to either of these questions is "Yes," see detailed instructions.

NATURE OF AUTHORSHIP Briefly describe nature of material created by this author in which copyright is claimed. ▼

3

a
YEAR IN WHICH CREATION OF THIS WORK WAS COMPLETED
_____ ◀ Year
This information must be given in all cases.

b
DATE AND NATION OF FIRST PUBLICATION OF THIS PARTICULAR WORK
Complete this information Month ▶ _____ Day ▶ _____ Year ▶ _____
ONLY if this work has been published. _____ ◀ Nation

4

See instructions before completing this space.

COPYRIGHT CLAIMANT(S) Name and address must be given even if the claimant is the same as the author given in space 2. ▼

TRANSFER If the claimant(s) named here in space 4 is (are) different from the author(s) named in space 2, give a brief statement of how the claimant(s) obtained ownership of the copyright. ▼

DO NOT WRITE HERE OFFICE USE ONLY

APPLICATION RECEIVED

ONE DEPOSIT RECEIVED

TWO DEPOSITS RECEIVED

FUNDS RECEIVED

MORE ON BACK ▶   • Complete all applicable spaces (numbers 5-9) on the reverse side of this page.
• See detailed instructions.   •Sign the form at line 8.

DO NOT WRITE HERE
Page 1 of _____ pages

[continued]

Copyright Form

DO NOT WRITE ABOVE THIS LINE. IF YOU NEED MORE SPACE, USE A SEPARATE CONTINUATION SHEET.

PREVIOUS REGISTRATION Has registration for this work, or for an earlier version of this work, already been made in the Copyright Office?

☐ **Yes** ☐ **No** If your answer is "Yes" why is another registration being sought? (Check appropriate box.) ▼

a. ☐ This is the first published edition of a work previously registered in unpublished form.

b. ☐ This is the first application submitted by this author as copyright claimant.

c. ☐ This is a changed version of the work, as shown by space 6 on this application.

If your answer is "Yes" give: **Previous Registration Number** ▶   **Year of Registration** ▶

5

DERIVATIVE WORK OR COMPILATION

Preexisting Material Identify any preexisting work or works that this work is based on or incorporates. ▼

Material Added to This Work Give a brief, general statement of the material that has been added to this work and in which copyright is claimed. ▼

a **6**

a

See instructions
before completing
this space.

DEPOSIT ACCOUNT If the registration fee is to be charged to a Deposit Account established in the Copyright Office, give name and number of Account.
Name ▼   Account Number ▼

a **7**

CORRESPONDENCE Give name and address to which correspondence about this application should be sent.   Name/Address/Apt/City/State/ZIP ▼

a

Area code and daytime telephone number ▶   Fax number ▶

Email ▶

CERTIFICATION* I, the undersigned, hereby certify that I am the

Check only one ▶ { ☐ author
☐ other copyright claimant
☐ owner of exclusive right(s)
☐ authorized agent of _____

of the work identified in this application and that the statements made by me in this application are correct to the best of my knowledge.

Name of author or other copyright claimant, or owner of exclusive right(s) ▲

8

Typed or printed name and date ▼ If this application gives a date of publication in space 3, do not sign and submit it before that date.

_____   Date ▶ _____

Handwritten signature (X) ▼

X _

Certificate
will be
mailed in
window
envelope
to this
address:

Name ▼

Number/Street/Apt ▼

City/State/ZIP ▼

YOU MUST:
• Complete all necessary spaces
• Sign your application in space 8
**SEND ALL 3 ELEMENTS
IN THE SAME PACKAGE:**
1. Application form
2. Nonrefundable filing fee in check or money order payable to *Register of Copyrights*
3. Deposit material
MAIL TO:
Library of Congress
Copyright Office
101 Independence Avenue, S.E.
Washington, D.C. 20559-6000

9

Fees are subject to
change. For current
fees, check the
Copyright Office
website at
www.copyright.gov,
write the Copyright
Office, or call
(202) 707-3000.

*17 U.S.C. § 506(e): Any person who knowingly makes a false representation of a material fact in the application for copyright registration provided for by section 409, or in any written statement filed in connection with the application, shall be fined not more than $2,500.

Rev: June 2002—20,000   Web Rev: June 2002   ✪ Printed on recycled paper   U.S. Government Printing Office: 2000-461-113/20,021

even a large portion of the work be similar, it does require that a substantial part be similar. It is irrelevant if the copied work is an improvement of the original work.

The Copyright Act of 1976 recognizes a copyright not only in a publisher's collective work, but also a separate copyright for each author's contribution to the work. With the growth in the use of electronic databases and disk to store data, some freelance authors began to object to their articles being sold to companies that produced these databases and disks. The Supreme Court, in *New York Times v. Tasini*, 533 U.S. 483, 121 S. Ct. 2381, 150 L. Ed. 2d 500 (2001), held that the Act protects the copyrights of the writers, rejecting an argument by the publishers that the conversion of the original works to an electronic format constituted a "revision" of the collective work, which would have been permissible under the Copyright Act.

Remedies for Infringement

Because the owner loses the value of a copyright when infringement occurs, relief is often sought through filing a lawsuit in federal court. If infringement is established, the court can grant preliminary and permanent injunctions, or court orders that restrain the offending party from continuing to infringe the copyright. A court may also award monetary damages as a remedy for copyright infringement. The copyright owner can recover for actual financial losses and any additional profits that the infringer earned from the infringement.

The copyright owner may instead choose to receive statutory damages, which range from a minimum of $250 to a maximum of $10,000. The court may adjust these limits based on the innocence or willfulness of the infringer. Innocent infringers may prove their GOOD FAITH and may have damages reduced to as little as $100, whereas willful infringers may be punished by the court with damages as high as $50,000. Courts may also impound and even destroy illicit reproductions of copyrighted works.

Willful copyright infringement can be a federal misdemeanor, punishable by as much as $10,000 or one year's imprisonment. Criminal prosecutions on this basis require that infringement be for the "purposes of commercial advantage or private financial gain" (17 U.S.C.A. § 506(a)). Criminal prosecutions for copyright infringement are generally rare. Nevertheless, PIRACY of music and motion picture recordings

—in which criminals mass-produce such recordings without permission and without paying royalties—has become increasingly common. This fact led to the passage of the Piracy and Counterfeiting Amendments Act of 1982 (18 U.S.C.A. § 2318), which allows punishment of up to $250,000 in fines or five years in prison for pirating 1,000 phonorecords or 65 films within 180 days. The fraudulent use or removal of copyright notices is also a punishable offense.

Fair Use

Fair use is a judicial doctrine that refers to a use of copyrighted material that does not infringe or violate the exclusive rights of the copyright holder. Fair use is an important and well established limitation on the exclusive right of copyright owners. Examples of fair use include the making of braille copies or audio recordings of books for use by blind people, and the making of video recordings of broadcast television programs or films by individuals for certain private, noncommercial use.

Examples of fair use typically involve, according to the Copyright Act of 1976, the reproduction of authored works for the purpose of "criticism, comment, news reporting, teaching . . ., scholarship, or research" (17 U.S.C.A. § 107). The same act also establishes a four-part test to determine fair use according to the following factors: (1) the purpose and character of the use, including whether such use is of a commercial nature or is for nonprofit educational purposes; (2) the nature of the copyrighted work; (3) the amount and substantiality of the portion used in relation to the copyrighted work as a whole; and (4) the effect of the use upon the potential market for, or value of, the copyrighted work (17 U.S.C.A. § 107).

It is usually considered fair use of an authored work to take small quotations or excerpts and to include them in another work, as when quotations are taken from a book and inserted into a book review. However, courts have found that such quotation is not fair use when material is taken from unpublished sources, as happened in the 1985 case *Harper & Row v. Nation Enterprises*, 471 U.S. 539, 105 S. Ct. 2218, 85 L. Ed. 2d 588.

The *Harper* case involved publication by *The Nation* magazine of quotations from Gerald R. Ford's unpublished memoir, *A Time to Heal*. Harper & Row, publisher of the memoir, sued

The Nation, claiming that the magazine's actions had caused it to lose a lucrative contract with *Time Magazine* to publish excerpts from the memoir. The Court ruled in favor of Harper, citing the economic value of first publication to the copyright holder as an important factor in its decision. It found that *The Nation* had infringed Ford's copyright by becoming the first publisher of his original expression, thereby inflicting economic losses on Ford. It rejected *The Nation's* argument that it was simply reporting news. Lower courts have subsequently applied the Court's reasoning to other cases involving quotations from unpublished works. In *Salinger v. Random House,* 811 F.2d 90 (2d Cir. 1987), a federal appeals court blocked publication of a book that used extensive quotations from unpublished letters of the author J. D. Salinger. The court ruled that the author retained copyright ownership of the "expressive content" of the letters, even when the letters themselves were deposited in university library collections.

PARODY often constitutes fair use of copyrighted material. In cases involving parodies of copyrighted works, courts typically assess the purpose and intent involved in taking material from the original expression, and whether or not the author of the parody has borrowed a reasonable amount of material in producing the parody. For example, in the 1994 case of *Campbell v. Acuff-Rose Music,* 501 U.S. 569, 114 S. Ct. 1164, 127 L. Ed. 2d 500— which involved a parody by the rap group 2 Live Crew of the Roy Orbison song "Pretty Woman"—the U.S. Supreme Court ruled that a parody could be fair use under copyright law even if it is created for commercial purposes.

Copyright Registration, Deposit, and Notice

Registration of copyright involves recording the existence of an authored work and the identity of its author with the U.S. Copyright Office, which is a part of the LIBRARY OF CONGRESS. Deposit involves placing the work in its recorded, physical form with the same office. Notice, or notification, involves placing on an authored work the © or the word *Copyright* or the abbreviation *Copr.,* along with the year of first publication and the name of the owner of the copyright.

Many of the major copyright acts in U.S. history have required that works be registered and deposited with a U.S. district court or with the U.S. Copyright Office, in order to be legally enforceable. Over time, however, deposit, registration, and notice of copyright have increasingly become formalities. Under the Copyright Act of 1976, authors automatically receive federal copyright protection when they fix their work in a tangible medium. Even if a copyright is not registered and an authored work is not deposited, the author maintains exclusive rights to the work.

Nevertheless, registration and deposit may have significant legal consequences. Most importantly, owners of copyright cannot sue for copyright infringement until they have registered the copyright (17 U.S.C.A. § § 411, 412). Deposit is not a requirement for copyright protection, but federal law requires that two copies of a published work be deposited within three months of publication. Failure to deposit a copy after it has been demanded by the U.S. Copyright Office is an offense punishable by a fine. Registration of copyright requires the deposit of at least one copy of a work and two copies of a published work. The U.S. Copyright Office has the power to vary these requirements.

Copyright notice serves a number of functions. A lack of copyright notice has traditionally informed users that a particular work is in the public domain, whereas the presence of a notice has warned users that a work is copyrighted and identifies the date and year of the work. Despite these traditions, copyright notice is optional for works distributed after October 31, 1988. Under prior law, an omission of copyright notice resulted in a loss of copyright protection.

Digital Millennium Copyright Act

Copyright laws have had to evolve in order to protect the interests of owners of copyrights from infringement through transfer of digital copies of protected works. INTERNET users may employ a myriad of methods to transmit digital files, and much of the information contained in these files consists of copyrighted works. Given the sheer number of Internet users—estimated by some at more than 500 million in 2002—and trillions of pages on the World Wide Web, protection of electronic publications and media is a global concern.

In 1998, then-President WILLIAM JEFFERSON CLINTON signed the Digital Millennium Copyright Act (DMCA), Pub. L. No. 105-304, 112 Stat. 2860 (17 U.S.C.A. §§ 101 et seq.) into law following a 99-0 vote in the U.S. Senate. This legislation was the focus of intense LOBBYING efforts on the part of a wide range of interest groups. These groups included TELECOMMUNICATIONS companies and online service providers; consumer-electronics manufacturers, library, museum, and university groups; and the publishing, recording, film, and software industries. The primary goal of this legislation was to adapt U.S. copyright laws for the digital age.

Passage of the DMCA was also required for the United States to keep pace with changes in international copyright treaties. In December 1996, the World Intellectual Property Organization (WIPO), an agency of the UNITED NATIONS, negotiated the Copyright Treaty and the Performances and Phonograms Treaty at a meeting in Geneva, Switzerland. WIPO is responsible for the advancement and safeguarding of intellectual property throughout the world, and it has 170 member countries.

The treaties, ratified in 2002, provide increased protection for copyrighted materials in the digital world. By signing, each country agrees to put into place laws, based on their own legal system, in order to enforce the treaties. The DMCA serves that purpose for the United States.

The DMCA consists of five main sections: WIPO Treaties Implementation, Online Copyright Infringement Liability Limitation, Computer Maintenance or Repair Copyright Exemption, Miscellaneous Provisions, and Protection of Certain Original Designs. Title I, WIPO Treaties Implementation, contains an "anti-circumvention" provision, making it illegal to "manufacture, import, offer to the public, provide, or otherwise traffic any technology, product, service, device, component, or part thereof," for the primary purpose of "circumventing a technological measure that effectively controls access to" a copyrighted work. Thus, technologies that are designed to protect digital material are safeguarded.

Moreover, this provision makes the act of circumventing a "technological measure that effectively controls access to a work protected" by copyright illegal. Every three years, the librarian of Congress, the register of copyrights, and the assistant secretary for communications and information of the COMMERCE DEPARTMENT must determine whether people with legitimate noninfringing uses of copyrighted materials are being unfavorably affected by the law. The law

does state that fair use is not affected, but this nevertheless has been a controversial provision. Libraries, museums, and scholars were concerned about digital materials only being available on a pay-per-use basis. An exemption was included for nonprofit libraries, archives, and educational institutions allowing them to circumvent technical protection measures for the purpose of determining whether or not to purchase the copyrighted work.

Title I of the DMCA contains another addition to U.S. copyright law required by the WIPO treaties. This section prohibits the deletion or alteration of information associated with copyrighted material. Organizations will benefit from this provision because it will help protect information and images on their web sites. Furthermore, it prohibits the distribution of false copyright-management information. The DMCA provides for civil and criminal enforcement. However, archives, schools, nonprofit libraries, and public broadcasting stations are exempt from criminal prosecution.

The DCMA also limits the liability for copyright infringement by providing safe harbors for online service providers. The definition of an online service provider is generous. Other organizations may qualify for protection, which could be useful if they provide Internet access, have a company bulletin board or inhouse E-MAIL system, or chat rooms. Prior to the passage of the DMCA, online service providers could have been liable if infringing materials were posted on their sites, even if they were unaware of the problem. The DMCA explains the responsibilities of copyright owners and service providers. Under specific conditions, online service providers are exempt from having to pay monetary damages as long as they are not benefiting financially from infringing activity and as long as they remove the material promptly from the Internet.

Limitations have also been set on exclusive rights for computer programs. A provision allows users to copy programs that are needed in order to maintain and repair a machine. Any such copies must be destroyed as soon as the machine is repaired, however.

One significant exemption for libraries and archives was included in Title IV of the DMCA. Up to three copies may be made of a copyrighted work without the permission of the copyright owner for research use in other libraries or archives through interlibrary loan.

The word "facsimile" has been struck from the former copyright law, thus allowing for digital formats. Libraries and archives can now loan digital copies of works to other libraries and archives by electronic means. Copies for preservation and security purposes are also permitted when the existing format in which the material is stored becomes outdated, or if the work is lost, stolen, damaged, or deteriorating.

Title IV also established guidelines for licensing and ROYALTIES in regard to copyrighted music transmitted over the Internet and in other digital forms. Transmissions are not subject to licensing if transmitted with encoded copyright information and with permission from the copyright owner of the sound recording.

No Electronic Theft Act

The concerns surrounding the protection of the copyrights of electronic data extend to computer software. In 1997, Congress approved the No Electronic Theft (NET) Act, Pub. L. No. 105-147, 111 Stat. 2678, which substantially enhanced existing federal copyright law. Aimed primarily at the rampant theft of computer software, it allows the prosecution of anyone who violates the copyright of materials worth more than $1,000 in a six-month period by copying, distributing, or receiving software.

Congress passed the law in November 1997 after the software and entertainment industries strongly lobbied for it, claiming losses amounting to $2 billion in 1996 in the United States alone. In particular, the law closed a narrow loophole in existing federal law, which made criminal prosecution for copyright violation only possible if the violation resulted in financial gain. Under the NET Act, individuals face fines and jail sentences even if they do not profit financially from the violation. The law was enacted over protests by scientists who feared that it would hinder their research.

Lobbyists pointed to what became known as the "*LaMaccia* loophole." This term refers to an unforeseen weakness in federal law that was exposed by the failed federal prosecution of computer hacker David LaMacchia in 1994 (*United States v. LaMacchia*, 871 F. Supp. 535 [D. Mass. 1994]). LaMacchia, then a 21-year-old student at the Massachusetts Institute of Technology, had used an electronic bulletin board to freely distribute countless commercial software programs. Although he was indicted for wire FRAUD under 18 U.S.C.A. § 1343 for allegedly

causing software companies losses of more than $1 million, the case was dismissed. U.S. District Court Judge Richard Stearns ruled that criminal sanctions did not apply because LaMacchia had not profited from his actions.

According to the software industry, the decision paved the way for piracy of material through web pages and other commonly used Internet sites. Software manufacturers were not only concerned about deliberate piracy by computer hackers; they also wanted to stop the casual lending and copying of computer software between consumers and within offices as well. Joining them in this effort were the music and film industries, which have increasingly become partners of software companies in the production of multimedia CD-ROMs. Additionally, the music industry viewed with alarm the widespread distribution of commercial recordings by fans, which became popular over the Internet in 1997 with the development of new software technology for digitally copying songs.

The NET Act was designed to close the *LaMacchia* loophole. Swiftly passed by the House and subsequently approved by the Senate, the act accomplished this by amending two key parts of federal copyright law: Titles 17 and 18 of the United States Code. These laws previously defined copyright violation strictly in terms of financial gain. The NET Act broadened them to include the reproduction or distribution of one or more copies of copyrighted works and considers financial gain simply to be the possession of copyrighted work. It defines a misdemeanor violation as occurring when the value of the copied material exceeds $1,000 over a 180-day period; a felony occurs if the value exceeds $2,500. Penalties range from a one-year jail sentence and up to $100,000 in fines for first-time offenders, to five years' imprisonment, and up to $250,000 in fines for repeat offenders.

FURTHER READINGS

Electronic Frontier Foundation. 1995. *To Have and to Hold: Can Copyrights Extend to Cyberspace Without Increased Costs and Threats to Privacy?* (June 8).

Goldstein, Paul. 2003. *Copyright's Highway: From Gutenberg to the Celestial Jukebox.* Rev. ed. Stanford, Calif.: Stanford Univ. Press.

Vaidhyanathan, Siva. 2001. *Copyrights and Copywrongs: The Rise of Intellectual Property and How It Threatens Creativity.* New York Univ. Press.

CROSS-REFERENCES

Copyright, International; Intellectual Property.

COPYRIGHT ARBITRATION ROYALTY PANEL

Three-member ad hoc board empowered to make decisions regarding ratemaking and distributions of COPYRIGHT ROYALTIES *collected for compulsory licenses under the Copyright Act of 1976.*

In order for a person to use another's copyrighted work, the person must generally obtain a license from the copyright owner. The terms of the agreement normally depend upon market conditions at the time of the agreement. However, the Copyright Act of 1976, codified in Title 17 of the *United States Code*, creates an exception under some circumstances whereby a prospective user may obtain a compulsory license that allows the individual to use a copyrighted work without the owner's permission. The compulsory license applies so long as the person applying for the license meets statutory requirements and pays the required royalties.

Congress in the 1976 act created the COPYRIGHT ROYALTY TRIBUNAL (CRT), an independent federal agency empowered to distribute royalties collected under the compulsory license provisions, as well as to make periodic adjustments to the royalty rates attached to the compulsory licenses. The original copyright act provided for four compulsory licenses, including those for CABLE TELEVISION, musical mechanical, noncommercial broadcasting, and jukeboxes. In 1992, Congress extended responsibility to the CRT to include distribution of levies collected from manufacturers and importers of digital recording devices.

The Copyright Royalty Tribunal was controversial from its inception. Although the ratemaking provisions were generally clear, the statute was rather ambiguous regarding the methods by which the tribunal should distribute royalties. The tribunal's decisions with respect to its ratemaking powers led to frequent criticism and litigation. Moreover, critics charged that Congress had created a full-time independent agency to perform a part-time job. In 1990, Congress reduced the number of commissioners on the tribunal from five to three, and during hearings in the House of Representatives in 1993, two of the three commissioners testified that they were in favor of abolishing the Copyright Royalty Tribunal.

In 1988, Congress enacted the Satellite Home Viewer Act, Pub. L. No. 100-667, 102 Stat. 3935, which created, at that time, a fifth compulsory license. However, the act required the formation of ad hoc ARBITRATION panels to amend royalty fees for satellite retransmissions, thus bypassing the authority of the CRT. The success of these arbitration panels persuaded Congress to use them for the other forms of compulsory licenses under the Copyright Act. The Copyright Royalty Tribunal Reform Act of 1993, Pub. L. No. 103-198, 107 Stat. 2304, immediately abolished the Copyright Royalty Tribunal and allowed for the formation of ad hoc copyright arbitration royalty panels.

The 1993 act did not change the system of compulsory licenses, but rather it shifted authority from the CRT to the new panels. Arbitrators on these panels are appointed and convened by the librarian of Congress, who acts on the recommendation of the Register of Copyrights. The arbitrators must meet minimum criteria set forth under the statute in order to quality for the position.

At the time of the creation of these arbitration panels, the librarian of Congress was directed to adopt the rules and regulations of the CRT in their entirety, though the CRT no longer existed. These rules and regulations were to remain in force until the librarian decided to supplement or supersede them. The adoption of the tribunal's former rules and regulations presented problems, however, because the 1993 act eliminated a single body—the CRT—and replaced it with a system of ad hoc panels. In December 1993, the librarian of Congress adopted the former CRT rules on an interim basis. One year later, the librarian issued new rules governing the panels, effective January 6, 1995. Additional revisions to the rules governing the panels have also been made since the 1994 revisions.

Like the CRT, the arbitration panels make decisions regarding distribution of royalties and ratemaking for royalties under the compulsory license provisions. Unlike the CRT, the purposes of the copyright arbitration royalty panels are set out clearly in the statute. Among the many purposes of the panels in the statute is the maximization of the availability of creative works to the public; the assurance that copyright owners receive a fair return for their creative works; and the guarantee that the roles of the copyright owner and the copyright user in the product made available to the public were reflected. 18 U.S.C.A. § 801(b) (1998). The statute lists other purposes as well.

The copyright arbitration royalty panels have proven more popular than the former CRT, although disputes still arise regarding ratemaking or distribution decisions by the panels. Convening a panel to make a rate adjustment is more difficult than the procedure that was followed under the CRT, which was a permanent body. The time frame under which a panel decision must be completed is also a concern for those involved in a panel proceeding. All actions by the parties—including discovery, testimony, studies, arguments, motions, and so forth—as well as rulings, orders, and final report issued by the panel, must be completed within 180 days after the librarian of Congress directs the formation of the arbitration panel. Nevertheless, these procedures are generally believed to promote efficiency when these panels make these determinations, and the panels have not been subjected to the same level of criticism as the former tribunals.

FURTHER READINGS

Davis, Mark J. 2003. "Practice Before the Copyright Arbitration Royalty Panel in 17 U.S.C. § 111 Distribution Proceedings." *Vanderbilt Journal of Entertainment Law and Practice* 11.

Goldstein, Paul. 2003. *Copyright.* 2d ed. New York: Aspen.

Nimmer, Melville B., and David Nimmer. 2003. *Nimmer on Copyright.* Newark, NJ: LexisNexis/Matthew Bender.

CROSS-REFERENCES

Copyright; Copyright, International; Copyright Society of the U.S.A.

COPYRIGHT, INTERNATIONAL

The manner in which the exclusive rights to reproduce and distribute copies of various intellectual productions may be obtained in foreign countries.

International copyright protection can be secured in only two ways: (1) by obtaining separate and independent COPYRIGHT protection in each of the countries where such protection is sought, in compliance with the laws of each country; or (2) through international conventions or treaties that provide for the mutual recognition and protection of the literary and INTELLECTUAL PROPERTY of the citizens of the nations that are parties to such treaties or conventions. Citizens of the United States who seek copyright protection in foreign countries may sometimes avail themselves of the first method, sometimes the second, and sometimes neither, depending upon the laws of the countries in which the foreign copyrights issue.

In 1989, the United States for the first time became a signatory to the oldest and most widely approved international copyright treaty, the Berne Convention for the Protection of Literary and Artistic Works (828 U.N.T.S. 221, S. Treaty Doc. No. 99-27). In doing so, the United States ended a long history of noncompliance with the Berne Convention, finally joining the vast majority of developed countries. As of the mid 1990s, 96 countries had signed the Berne Convention.

Among the works protected by the Berne Convention are books, pamphlets, and other printed materials; dramatic and dramatico-musical works and musical compositions; drawings and paintings; works of architecture, sculpture, engraving, and lithography; illustrations and geographic charts, plans, and sketches; translations, adaptations, arrangements of music, and collections of various works; and cinematographic and photographic works.

History of the Berne Convention

The Berne Convention was first adopted on September 9, 1886, in Berne, Switzerland, and was later revised at several conferences: Paris, 1896; Berlin, 1908; Berne, 1914; Rome, 1928; Brussels, 1948; Stockholm, 1967; and Paris, 1971. The agreement grew out of a perceived need in the late nineteenth century to protect authored works from international PIRACY, or unauthorized copying. A growing demand for new printed materials during this era was motivating many publishers to reprint unauthorized versions of foreign works. Authors whose works were pirated had little recourse against those publishers because copyright laws were typically enacted on a national basis. Such laws gave copyright protection only to authors who were nationals of the country in which the laws were enacted.

A few countries negotiated bilateral treaties—two-party contracts termed reciprocal agreements—that protected the nationals of both countries, but such arrangements were rare. In the mid nineteenth century, a nongovernment organization, the Association Littéraire et Artistique International, was formed in Paris and led the movement for international copyright protection. This organization created the draft of what eventually became the Berne Convention. Among the first countries adhering to the Berne Convention were France, Germany, and the United Kingdom.

The Berne Convention established several principles of international copyright that have remained through all of the treaty's versions. First, rather than operating on a system of reciprocity (under which a country protects foreign authors only to the extent that its own authors are protected in return), the convention works on the principle of national treatment (under which a country extends the same protection to foreigners that it accords to its own authors). Second, rather than trying to impose the same standards on all nations, the convention solved the problem of national differences in copyright protection by establishing minimum standards of protection that all signatories must meet. Thus, member countries may treat the copyrighted work of their own nationals in any way they choose, but they must treat works from nationals of other treaty members according to minimum treaty standards. Third, the convention provides for automatic protection of copyrighted works as soon as they are created, without any required formalities, such as notice or registration.

The United States and the Berne Convention

Influenced greatly by its early status as a net importer of copyrighted materials, the United States resisted joining the Berne Convention for over a century. Adherence to the treaty's conventions would have required U.S. publishers of foreign works—many of whom produced pirated copies—to pay ROYALTIES and fees to foreign copyright holders, thus causing a significant amount of money to flow overseas. However, by the end of WORLD WAR II, the United States had become a major exporter of copyrighted materials, and it became clear that it would be to the country's economic advantage if its own authors and copyright holders could be assured of receiving royalties from overseas publishing.

At that point, rather than joining the Berne Convention, the United States lobbied for a different international treaty, the Universal Copyright Convention (UCC) (25 U.S.T. 1341, T.I.A.S. No. 7868), established in 1952 under the auspices of the U.N. Educational, Scientific, and Cultural Organization (UNESCO). The United States became a member of the UCC in 1955. Many countries that already belonged to the Berne Convention—including France, West Germany, and Japan—also joined the UCC. The UCC generally operated on the national-treatment principle, thus allowing U.S. authors to receive the same copyright protection in a specific country that the country afforded its own authors, and not requiring the United States to reciprocate that treatment for foreign authors.

The United States experienced still more international pressure to join the Berne Convention after passage of the Copyright Act of 1976 (17 U.S.C.A. §§ 101 et seq.). This statute brought several important features of the Berne Convention into U.S. law, including relaxed standards on the formalities of copyright registration, deposit, and notice, and new provisions that extended the duration of copyright protection to the Berne minimum of the author's life plus 50 years (which has since been extended to life plus 70 years). The act also phased out a protectionist manufacturing clause that had required foreign works to be set in type in the United States in order to receive U.S. copyright protection—a clause that had benefited U.S. printers for decades. (In fact, LOBBYING by printers had long stymied attempts to make the United States part of the Berne Convention.)

By the 1980s, the United States was still one of the few major developed countries not abiding by the Berne Convention. When it became clear that the United States' role as a pariah in international copyright circles had begun to erode its position in reaching other trade agreements concerning intellectual property, Congress finally passed the Berne Convention Implementation Act of 1988 (Pub. L. No. 100-568, 102 Stat. 2853). That act made the United States a party to the Berne Convention beginning in 1989, officially ending U.S. copyright isolationism.

Protection of Copyright in the Digital Age

Protection of the interests of copyright owners and enforcement of their rights has become more difficult since the rise of INTERNET around the world. The World Wide Web, a component of the Internet, now consists of trillions of individual web pages, and according to some estimates, the number of Internet users has increased to more than 500 million.

The Internet has created a new avenue for copyright infringement on a global scale. Although virtually all types of works that are subject to copyright law can be transferred through digital networks, transfers of music recordings have received the most attention. A web-based company, Napster, during the 1990s became the most well-known and heavily used portal for transferring electronic files containing copies of music. Users of this system were capable of transferring copyrighted works in a format called MP3 (MPEG-1 Audio Layer 3) to their home computers, with a sound quality that was comparable to that of a compact disc. The musical compositions in most of these files were copyrighted, and owners of those copyrighted materials complained that the file transfers infringed their copyrights. The Recording Industry Association of America sued Napster, eventually prevailing and causing Napster to close down. Napster was not merely a phenomenon in the United States and North America. The company had an estimated 16.9 million worldwide users, and the system accommodated about 65 million downloads.

Domestic copyright law is limited in its protection of some of these works because the Copyright Act generally has no application outside of the United States. For example, in *Subafilms, Inc. v. MGM—Pathe Communications Co.*, 24 F.3d 1088 (9th Cir. 1994), U.S. Court of Appeals for the Ninth Circuit noted as much in holding that a copyright holder could not sue individuals who distributed the plaintiff's movies abroad, because the infringement occurred outside of U.S. soil. Although the Berne Convention, as well as such international intellectual property treaties as the Geneva Phonograms Convention and the Rome Convention, protect such copyrights, additional protection was needed.

In 1996, the World Trade Organization approved the Agreement on Trade-Related Aspects of Intellectual Property Rights (TRIPS), which requires member countries to provide certain levels of protection for copyright holders in their countries. Additional protection came in the form of so-called "digital treaties" approved by the World Intellectual Property Organization, including the Copyright Treaty and the Performance and Phonograms Treaty. Both of these treaties, which became effective in 2002, clarified and extended the Berne and TRIPS provisions by allowing copyright holders to encrypt their works in order to protect their rights.

COPYRIGHT ROYALTY TRIBUNAL

The Copyright Royalty Tribunal was established by an act of October 19, 1976 (90 Stat. 2594; 17 U.S.C. 801).

The tribunal made determinations concerning the adjustment of COPYRIGHT royalty rates for records, jukeboxes, and certain CABLE TELEVISION transmissions. After compulsory cable television and jukebox ROYALTIES were deposited with the register of copyrights, the tribunal distributed the fees and, in cases of controversy among claimants, determined their distribution.

The tribunal established and made determinations concerning terms and rates of royalty payments for the use by public broadcasting stations of published nondramatic compositions and pictorial, graphic, and sculptural works. Cost-of-living adjustments were made to noncommercial broadcasting rates in August of each year.

Tribunal decisions factor in the existence of economic conditions, the impact on copyright owners and users and the industry involved, and the maximization of public availability of creative works. Recognizing copyright owners' right to receive a fair return, the tribunal ensured them access to information about the use of their works.

It was supplanted by COPYRIGHT ARBITRATION ROYALTY PANELS.

COPYRIGHT SOCIETY OF THE U.S.A.

The Copyright Society of the U.S.A. was founded in 1953 to promote the protection and study of intellectual property rights in areas such as art, literature, motion pictures, and music. Its primary function is gathering, disseminating, and interchanging information concerning protection and use of copyrighted materials. The organization undertakes and engages in research in the field of COPYRIGHT law in cooperation with universities, law schools, libraries, governmental agencies, lawyers, and industry representatives in the United States and foreign countries. It also seeks to promote better understanding of copyright and the vital importance of legal and economic protection of INTELLECTUAL PROPERTY in general, and copyright in particular, among the general public, in industry, and in the academic world. It also provides information to the public through its web site, http://www.csusa.org.

To accomplish its goals, the society has undertaken a wide-ranging program including symposia on copyright subjects; workshops for people in such fields as music, motion pictures, and publishing, stressing the practical aspects and mechanics of copyright administration; and publication of materials relating to copyright that otherwise would not be available. Its members are lawyers, laypersons, firms, libraries, universities, and publishers. The society publishes a journal and holds annual meetings. In 2001, it launched its Copyright Kids web site (www .copyrightkids.org), a comprehensive resource for school-age children that explains copyright facts and regulations and answers questions about the importance of copyright protection.

CORAM

[Latin, Before; in the presence of.]

The term *coram* is used in phrases that refer to the appearance of a person before another individual or a group. *Coram non judice,* "in the presence of a person not a judge," is a phrase that describes a proceeding brought before a court that lacks the jurisdiction to hear such a matter. Any judgment rendered by the court in such a case is void.

CORAM NOBIS

[Latin, In our presence; before us.] The designation of a remedy for setting aside an erroneous judgment in a civil or criminal action that resulted from an error of fact in the proceeding.

In civil actions, a petition for a writ of *coram nobis* was addressed to the court in which the judgment was made, unlike an appeal, which is made to a superior court. The petition asserted that the court had made an erroneous judgment due to the defendant's excusable failure to make a valid defense as a result of FRAUD, duress, or excusable neglect, such as illness. *Coram nobis* could not be used where a party caused an error because of NEGLIGENCE.

The writ of *coram nobis* has been abolished in civil actions by the rules of federal CIVIL PROCEDURE and similar provisions of state codes of civil procedure that, instead, establish different methods for setting aside judgments.

In CRIMINAL PROCEDURE, *coram nobis* serves the same purpose as it did in civil actions and is a recognized procedure in federal criminal prosecutions. Traditionally, it was available to direct the court's attention to information that did appear in the trial record and was not admitted into evidence because of fraud, duress, or excusable mistake. A defendant could not use *coram nobis* to relitigate the same charges if, through his or her own fault, such facts were not introduced as evidence.

Modern statutes have expanded the grounds for relief based upon the principles derived from the ancient writ of *coram nobis.* It is no longer a common-law remedy, but statutes provide for the vacation of a conviction and usually order a new trial if there is insufficient evidence to sustain the conviction, newly discovered evidence, erroneous instruction to the jury, or prejudicial comments or conduct by the prosecutor during the trial.

CORAM REGE

[Latin, In the presence of the king himself.]

After the Norman Conquest of England in 1066, court was held before the king himself— *coram rege*—whenever matters affecting the royal interest were in issue. When the king began to appoint a tribunal to hear cases for him, it was called the Curia Regis, or the King's Court. From the Curia Regis developed the royal common-law courts.

❖ CORBIN, ARTHUR LINTON

Arthur Linton Corbin was a leading legal scholar and professor who made significant and influential contributions to the development of U.S. contract law.

Corbin was born October 17, 1874, in Cripple Creek, a small mining town near Colorado Springs. He was raised in Cripple Creek and then left Colorado to attend the University of Kansas, from which he graduated in 1894. He went on to the Yale Law School, graduating magna cum laude in 1899. After several years of practicing law and teaching high school back in Cripple Creek, he returned to Yale in 1903 to accept a position as an instructor in contracts. He became a full professor in 1909 and remained at Yale until his retirement in 1943 at the age of 68.

During his tenure at Yale, Corbin played a major role in establishing the institution as a major national law school and center for legal scholarship. He was instrumental in recruiting more highly qualified students to the school by convincing the administration to tighten admission standards. He also drew praise for his efforts to persuade the school to hire and maintain a full-time faculty that would be committed to teaching and writing, instead of relying on judges and practicing lawyers who taught only part-time and thus were not always available to students. In addition, Corbin helped to imple-

"WHERE NEITHER CUSTOM NOR AGREEMENT DETERMINES THE ALLOCATION OF RISK, THE COURT MUST EXERCISE ITS EQUITY POWERS AND PRAY FOR THE WISDOM OF SOLOMON."
—ARTHUR LINTON CORBIN

ment the CASE METHOD of teaching at Yale, in which students glean the principles of law through the study of cases rather than simply by rote without reference to COMMON LAW as developed by the courts. Corbin was a popular and committed teacher, even filling in as a writer and editor for the *Yale Law Journal* when the First World War left a serious shortage of student editors and contributors.

Corbin made his greatest contribution to contemporary legal thought through his extensive and widely studied writings on the law of contracts. He authored many books and articles on the subject and served as adviser to the reporters of the first and second Restatement of Contracts, treatises designed to set forth and analyze the relevant principles governing contract law. Corbin is best known for his own eight-volume treatise on contracts, *Corbin on Contracts: A Comprehensive Treatise on the Working Rules of Contracts Law*, which was first published in 1950, 17 years after his retirement from Yale Law School. Corbin kept his work up-to-date until his death, through his own revisions and by adding new material to "pocket parts" at the back of each volume. *Corbin on Contracts* quickly became a classic in the field for practicing attorneys and is still considered essential reading for students of contract law.

Corbin subscribed to a "realist" philosophy in his legal writings and thought. He believed that the law is a critical part of everyday life and that resulting rules governing conduct had to reflect a changing social context. He wrote,

> Law does not consist of a series of unchangeable rules or principles. . . . Every system of justice and of right is of human development, and the necessary corollary is that no known system is eternal. In the long history of the law, one can observe the birth and death of

legal principles. . . . The law is merely part of our changing civilization.

In 1954, on his eightieth birthday, Corbin reiterated his belief that law is inextricably tied to human experience, stating that the "development of our law—common, statutory, and constitutional—is part of the continuing evolutionary development of life in society."

Corbin's legal realist views are strongly evident in his approach to contract law. The main purpose of a contract, he stated in his treatise, is "the realization of reasonable expectations that have been induced by the making of a promise." Reasonableness, he maintained, is an expression of customs and mores, which in turn could be discerned from what he called the operative facts of judicial decisions. To solve a contractual dispute, Corbin believed, a judge should first determine the intention of the parties, and thus the terms of the promise or agreement; then analyze the intention in terms of reasonableness; and finally apply rules, doctrines, or other principles to determine what remedy should be offered. Above all, Corbin believed that the reasonable expectations of the parties should be protected. Thus, according to Corbin, even if the price term were left open in an agreement that otherwise had been concluded, the court should consider whether the parties had intended to be bound by the contract. The court, he maintained, should make every effort to fill in the gaps of an agreement by looking to reasonable terms consistent with what the parties had previously agreed upon. The contract should fail only if it appears that the parties did not intend to be bound, or if reasonable terms cannot be ascertained.

Corbin further believed that in resolving contractual disputes, courts should not be lim-

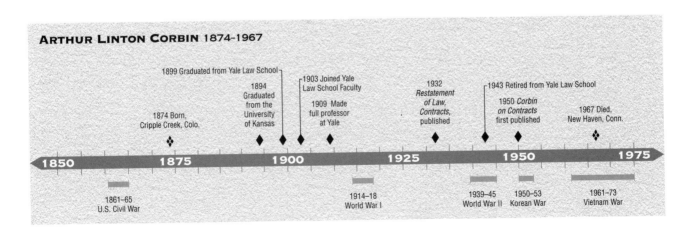

ARTHUR LINTON CORBIN 1874–1967

1899 Graduated from Yale Law School

1894 Graduated from the University of Kansas

1903 Joined Yale Law School Faculty

1909 Made full professor at Yale

1932 *Restatement of Law, Contracts,* published

1943 Retired from Yale Law School

1950 *Corbin on Contracts* first published

1874 Born, Cripple Creek, Colo.

1967 Died, New Haven, Conn.

1850   1875   1900   1925   1950   1975

1861–65 U.S. Civil War

1914–18 World War I

1939–45 World War II

1950–53 Korean War

1961–73 Vietnam War

ited to a contract's "four corners" (the explicit terms of the agreement) or to the "plain meaning" of those terms. The parties' intent should be gleaned from what they stated and from their conduct; their prior course of dealing, trade practices, or any other pertinent circumstances also should be considered. Corbin's views are evident in the UNIFORM COMMERCIAL CODE, adopted in 49 states, and in the law of contracts as developed by the courts since the mid 1900s.

Corbin's views often stand in contrast to those of another leading American scholar in contracts, SAMUEL WILLISTON. Williston subscribed to the theory of legal formalism, which views the law as a body of scientific rules from which legal decisions can be readily deduced. Legal formalism dominated legal thought in the early twentieth century, and those who advocated its application viewed law as essentially conservative. Williston applied many of his theories in the first *Restatement of Contracts*, which the American Law Institute completed in 1932. *Williston on Contracts* has been a leading treatise in American contract law since the early 1900s and is still a competitor of Corbin's treatise.

In addition to the Uniform Commercial Code, Corbin also contributed to the second *Restatement of Contracts*, the provisions of which represented a considerable shift from the conservative views in the first *Restatement*. Corbin continued his study and writing well into his later life, stopping work on the second *Restatement* when he was nearly 90, and only because of failing eyesight. Corbin died in 1967, at the age of 93. The second *Restatement* was first published in 1981, 14 years after Corbin's death. To a significant extent, the second *Restatement* advocates changes in the law of contracts, many of which are based upon Corbin's views.

FURTHER READINGS

Gilmore, Grant. 1977. *The Ages of American Law*. New Haven, Conn.: Yale Univ. Press.

Kessler, Friedrich. 1969. "Arthur Linton Corbin." *Yale Law Journal* 78.

CROSS-REFERENCES

Legal Realism; Restatement of Law.

CORESPONDENT

One of two or more parties against whom a lawsuit is commenced. A person named with others who must answer claims alleged in a bill, petition, or LIBEL in a judicial proceeding. An individual who is accused of ADULTERY with another's spouse being sued for DIVORCE on that ground and who thereby becomes a defendant in the action.

CORNER

For surveying purposes, the designation given to a particular location formed by the intersection of two boundary lines of real property.

The process by which a group of investors or dealers in a particular commodity exploit its market by purchasing it in large quantities and removing it from general sale for a time, thereby dramatically increasing its market price because its limited supply is greatly exceeded by the demand for it. The condition created when a commitment is made to sell at a special time of delivery in the future, a much greater quantity of a commodity than is available in the present market.

This type of commitment is known as a futures contract. Frequently, neither buyer nor seller expects actual delivery of the goods. They are solely speculating on the difference between the contract price and market price on a particular date. The market price is affected by various economic factors. When a corner is created, the demand for the commodity far exceeds its supply, thereby driving up market prices. On the date of delivery, therefore, the market price will exceed the contract price if no additional quantities can be delivered by persons other than the seller who has "cornered" the market. The buyer must then pay the seller, who had a corner on the specified commodity, the amount by which the market price exceeds the contract price. If, however, additional quantities of the commodity are available in the market, the seller incurs financial losses because the market price will be less than the contract price at which the market was "cornered."

The COMMODITY FUTURES TRADING COMMISSION is the federal regulatory agency charged with the administration of the Commodity Exchange Act (7 U.S.C.A. § 1 et seq.), which is designed to protect all commodity investors from manipulative practices that hinder the free flow of commerce. Anyone who deliberately exploits the commodities market to create a corner may be prosecuted under federal law for commission of a felony, punishable by a fine of not more than $500,000 or imprisonment of not more than five years, or both, plus the costs of prosecution.

COROLLARY

A consequence or result that can be logically drawn from the existence of a set of facts by the exercise of common sense and reason.

CORONER

An official of a MUNICIPAL CORPORATION *whose designated functions include the investigation of the cause of any violent or suspicious death that takes place within the geographical boundaries of his or her municipality.*

The office of the coroner was established at COMMON LAW and was one of great dignity since coroners dealt primarily with pleas concerning the crown. In the early 2000s, statutes establish the terms and procedure of the coroner's office, which has been replaced in some states with the office of medical examiner.

The main function of a coroner is to conduct inquests, but other powers and duties may include the duty of acting as sheriff, in the event of the sheriff's incapacity, as conservator of the peace, or as magistrate. The duties are considered to be either judicial, ministerial, or both.

Holding Inquests

The purpose of an inquest is to gather evidence that may be used by the police in their exploration of a violent or suspicious death and the subsequent prosecution of a person if death ensued from a criminal act.

An inquest is not a trial but rather a criminal proceeding of a preliminary, investigatory nature. It is not a criminal prosecution but may result in the discovery of facts justifying one.

Statutes mandate that whenever there exists reasonable ground to believe that a death resulted from violence, unlawful means, or other mysterious or unknown causes, an inquest must be held. Death by disease, natural causes, NEGLIGENCE of the deceased, accident, or suicide does not warrant the commencement of an inquest, unless statute so requires.

A coroner should not arbitrarily or capriciously hold an inquest. The presumption is that when a coroner decides to hold an inquest it is made in exercise of his or her sound discretion, in GOOD FAITH, and for sufficient cause. Most statutes require that a coroner make a preliminary inquiry into the cause of death before summoning a jury.

Time and Place The general requirement is that an inquest be held immediately upon the notice to the coroner of the death or discovery of the dead body. The inquest may either take place in the territory of the coroner in whose jurisdiction the body was found or where the death itself took place.

Summoning and Swearing the Jury If it is public knowledge that the decedent was killed by someone who is already in police custody, then it is not necessary to summon a jury to hold an inquest. A coroner's jury is usually summoned by warrant but may be summoned personally by the coroner. A juror who refuses to attend an inquest may be subject to a fine and a CONTEMPT citation. The general practice is that the jury should be sworn in in the presence of the body.

Autopsy Incident to the coroner's duties is the power to order an autopsy when appropriate and essential to ascertain the circumstances and the nature of death. The reasons underlying this power are numerous—the primary one being that a thorough examination of a body is necessary since an accused person may be acquitted if there is some doubt as to the cause of death. Similarly, a proper examination of the cause of death should exclude all other possible causes that would not support a criminal investigation and subsequent prosecution.

Some statutes provide that a coroner is not authorized to hold an autopsy where no suspicion of foul play exists or where no inquest is being held. A needless autopsy may be considered unreasonable interference with a dead body. If authorized, however, a coroner may hold an autopsy without the consent of the decedent's next of kin. Civil liability may be imposed upon coroners and their physicians who perform improper or unauthorized autopsies.

To examine the body during an autopsy, a coroner may hire an expert physician, the selection of whom is within the coroner's discretion. This power must be exercised with great caution. During the autopsy, the coroner has the discretionary power to decide who, if anyone, should be present aside from the surgeon or surgeons. Neither a person accused of criminally causing the death nor the jurors have a right to witness the actual dissection of the cadaver.

View of Body Statutes require that the coroner and jury together must have a view of the body except in cases where the body cannot be found or is too decomposed for view. The purpose of this inspection is to ascertain from the appearance of the body how the death was caused. The jury also hears the summaries of various medical reports regarding the condition of the body to help it reach its determinations concerning the cause of death.

Verdict and Inquisition It is the duty of the coroner to accept from the jury the verdict, which should identify the deceased, if possible, or state that the deceased is unknown and should include how, when, and where the decedent died. The coroner submits a return of inquest, also known as an inquisition, which is a record of the jury's finding, that must be executed in accordance with statutory requirements.

The effect of the verdict at common law is that it is a sufficient basis for prosecution for murder or MANSLAUGHTER so long as the jury finds evidence supporting prosecution. Under some statutes, its effect is not as strong as a finding by a GRAND JURY but has merely been held to render a person accused of illegally causing the death liable to arrest.

Many jurisdictions require that the coroner complete a certificate of death showing the cause and probable manner of death subsequent to the termination of the inquest.

Arrest

It is the power and the duty of the coroner to have anyone implicated by an inquest in murder or manslaughter to be arrested and held for trial. If a statute gives a coroner magisterial jurisdiction in HOMICIDE cases, he or she may issue warrants for the arrest of the person probably chargeable with the crime and hold the person to answer or discharge the charges.

Record of Inquest as Evidence

Civil Actions In general, evidence given at an inquest has not been permitted to be used against either party in a civil action. There are, however, exceptions to this rule. Some authorities hold the testimony of a witness before a coroner to be admissible if used to contradict other testimony given when the person is a witness or party in such an action. Other jurisdictions hold that such evidence by a party is admissible as an admission against interest. For example, a defendant's admission at an inquest of driving at an unlawful speed was admissible as an admission against interest in a civil action for negligence.

Some jurisdictions allow the coroner's findings to be used in a civil action to show the cause of death. The general practice in most jurisdic-

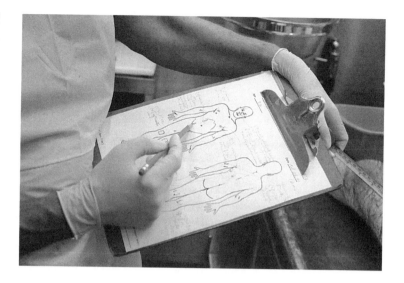

A coroner's office worker prepares an autopsy report at the Harris County Medical Examiner Office's morgue in Houston, Texas. Coroners have the right to order autopsies to determine the causes of violent or suspicious deaths.
SHEPARD SHERBELL/CORBIS SABA

tions, however, is to allow the verdict to show that the deceased is dead but not to show the cause of death. The rationale underlying this rule is that a person is not entitled to be represented by counsel at an inquest since it is merely a preliminary investigation. The practical consequences of allowing the coroner's verdict to be used as evidence of the cause of death is that it could easily become the key piece of evidence in the action. If this were to occur, the judgment awarded in the case would probably end up being a ratification or formal adoption of the coroner's verdict, thereby depriving the party to the action of his or her rights. That person is entitled to a formal judicial hearing or a "day in court," with all procedural safeguards, so that an opportunity to dispute the evidence will be given.

Criminal Prosecutions The main purpose of a coroner's inquest is to provide information and evidence for use by the police in their investigation and detection of a crime; therefore, the proceedings of an inquest are generally inadmissible at a trial for homicide.

When a person is either under arrest or accused of a crime at a coroner's inquest, any testimony that he or she gives cannot subsequently be used against him or her at a trial that stems from the inquest, unless such testimony was given voluntarily after the party was advised of his or her constitutional rights. If an individual testifies as a witness at an inquest but is subsequently prosecuted, that testimony is admissible in his or her prosecution since it was voluntarily given at the inquest. Generally, the testimony of witnesses at an inquest cannot be used in a trial for homicide unless the witness has died or is otherwise unavailable at the time of the criminal prosecution.

Ordinarily, on an indictment for homicide, neither the verdict of the coroner's jury nor the finding of the coroner can be used as evidence for any purpose.

Liabilities of a Coroner

A coroner who is acting pursuant to his or her statutory authority is immune for error, mistake, or misconduct in the exercise of judicial functions. A coroner, acting in a ministerial capacity, is answerable for any abuse of those powers. Some statutes make it a criminal offense for a coroner to deliberately hold an inquest when to do so clearly exceeds the scope of his or her powers.

FURTHER READINGS

Cornwell, Patricia. 1999. *Body of Evidence.* New York: Pocket Books.

Noguchi, Thomas T. 1985. *Coroner at Large.* New York: Simon & Schuster.

———. 1984. *Coroner.* New York: Pocket Books.

CROSS-REFERENCES

Autopsy; Jury; Presumption.

CORPORAL PUNISHMENT

Physical punishment, as distinguished from pecuniary punishment or a fine; any kind of punishment inflicted on the body.

Corporal punishment arises in two main contexts: as a method of discipline in schools and as a form of punishment for committing a crime.

Corporal punishment, usually in the form of paddling, though practiced in U.S. schools since the American Revolution, was only sanctioned by the U.S. Supreme Court in the late 1970s. In *Ingraham v. Wright,* 430 U.S. 651, 97 S. Ct. 1401, 51 L. Ed. 2d 711 (1977), students from a Florida junior high school had received physical punishment, including paddling so severe that one student had required medical treatment. The plaintiffs, parents of students who had been disciplined, brought suit against the school district, alleging that corporal punishment in public schools constituted CRUEL AND UNUSUAL PUNISHMENT in violation of the EIGHTH AMENDMENT to the U.S. Constitution. The plaintiffs also maintained that the FOURTEENTH AMENDMENT required DUE PROCESS before corporal punishment could be administered.

The Court rejected the Eighth Amendment claim, holding that the prohibition against cruel and unusual punishment was designed to protect persons who were convicted of crimes, not students who were paddled as a form of discipline. The Court also held that although corporal punishment did implicate a constitutionally protected liberty interest, traditional COMMON LAW remedies, such as filing an action in TORT, were "fully adequate to afford due process." Thus, the Court concluded, teachers could use "reasonable but not excessive" corporal punishment to discipline students.

Since the Court's decision in *Ingraham,* corporal punishment in the schools has been challenged on other constitutional grounds. In *Hall v. Tawney,* 621 F.2d 607 (4th Cir. 1980), a grade-school student from West Virginia alleged that she had been severely injured after she had been struck repeatedly with a hard, rubber paddle by her teacher while the school principal had looked on. She filed suit against the school, claiming that her Eighth Amendment rights had been violated and that she had been deprived of her procedural due process rights. She further alleged that she had been denied SUBSTANTIVE DUE PROCESS under 42 U.S.C.A. § 1983, which provides that a civil action may be brought for a deprivation of constitutional rights. While the case was pending, the U.S. Supreme Court handed down its decision in *Ingraham,* thus foreclosing the plaintiff's Eighth Amendment and procedural due process claims.

Addressing the remaining constitutional claim, the U.S. Court of Appeals for the Fourth Circuit held that excessive corporal punishment in public schools could violate a student's constitutional right to substantive due process and thus subject school officials to liability under § 1983. The standard to be applied, the court ruled, was whether the force applied were to cause injury so severe and disproportionate to the need for it and were " so inspired by malice or sadism rather than a merely careless or unwise excess of zeal that it amounted to a brutal and inhuman abuse of official power literally shocking to the conscience." The case was remanded to the lower court so that the plaintiff's § 1983 claim could be tried in light of the Fourth Circuit's ruling. Other federal appeals courts have since followed *Hall* in corporal punishment cases involving schools, although the high standard has proved very difficult for plaintiffs to meet.

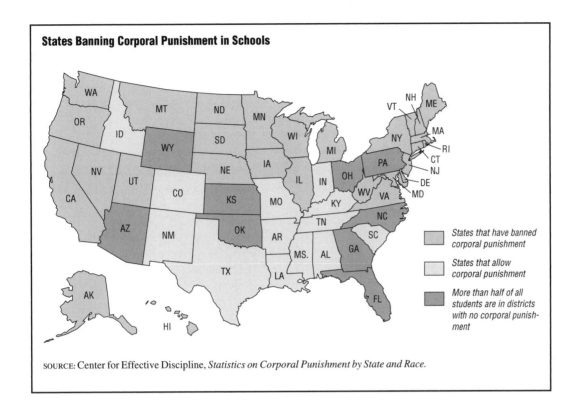

States Banning Corporal Punishment in Schools

States that have banned corporal punishment

States that allow corporal punishment

More than half of all students are in districts with no corporal punishment

SOURCE: Center for Effective Discipline, *Statistics on Corporal Punishment by State and Race.*

In cases where plaintiffs have been successful, the conduct of the educator is often rather extreme. In *Neal ex rel. Neal v. Fulton County Board of Education*, 229 F.3d 1069 (11th Cir. 2000), a high-school teacher and football coach, while breaking up a fight, struck one of the fighting students with a metal weight lock. The blow to the student was so severe that it knocked his eyeball out of its socket. The Eleventh Circuit Court of Appeals found that because the punishment inflicted by the coach had been intentional, and obviously excessive, and that it had created a foreseeable risk of serious injury, the student had stated a claim upon which he could recover. Many other cases, on the other hand, have held in favor of educators and school districts because the students who brought suit could not prove the elements necessary to hold the defendants liable.

As a result of limited success in the courts, opponents of corporal punishment have turned to the political process and have worked to persuade state legislatures to outlaw the use of corporal punishment in schools. Scientific studies over the past decade have demonstrated that corporal punishment contributes to such behavioral problems as increased anger, aggression, tolerance for violence, and lower self-esteem. Partially as a result of these studies, a growing

number of groups, including the NATIONAL EDUCATION ASSOCIATION, the American Academy of Pediatrics, the American Academy of Child & Adolescent Psychiatry, and the AMERICAN BAR ASSOCIATION, disfavor corporal punishment and have sought to ban it in public schools. These LOBBYING efforts have proven successful: Only about half of the states continue to practice corporal punishment, whereas the other half specifically prohibit it by state statute or regulation.

In California, for example, state law provides that "[]no person employed by . . . a public school shall inflict, or cause to be inflicted corporal punishment upon a pupil" (Cal. Educ. Code § 49001 [West 1996]). But despite the trend against permitting corporal punishment in schools, public opinion is split on the issue: In a 1995 Scripps Howard News Service Poll, 49 percent of those surveyed favored corporal punishment, and 46 percent opposed it.

Like corporal punishment in schools, physical punishment for committing a crime also dates back to the American Revolution. The CONTINENTAL CONGRESS allowed floggings on U.S. warships, and confinement in stocks and public hangings were common. Gradually, imprisonment and other forms of rehabilitation began to replace corporal punishment, largely

This 1907 photograph taken in a Delaware prison shows two inmates in a pillory with another receiving a whipping. Such forms of punishment have been outlawed.

LIBRARY OF CONGRESS

because of the work of reformers who campaigned against its use on convicts and advocated for improved prison conditions. Most states eventually abolished public floggings and other forms of physical punishment for crimes, but in some jurisdictions "whipping laws" remained in effect until the early 1970s. In addition, courts have held that corporal punishment in prisons can take a variety of forms (e.g., whipping, deprivation of food, and placement in restraints) and is prohibited by the Eighth Amendment.

The mid-1990s case of a U.S. teenager convicted of VANDALISM in a foreign country revived a long-dormant debate over whether criminals should be corporally punished. In May 1994, Michael Fay was sentenced to six strokes with a rattan cane and four months in jail for painting graffiti on parked cars and for other acts of vandalism he had committed while living in Singapore. The case drew immediate international attention. Many U.S. citizens—including President BILL CLINTON, who appealed to the government of Singapore for clemency—were outraged by the sentence. Despite the intervention of the U.S. government and HUMAN RIGHTS groups, the punishment was eventually carried out, although the number of strokes was reduced to four.

In the wake of the publicity surrounding the Fay matter, polls indicated that a surprising number of U.S. citizens supported the sentence. Unconvinced that current penalties provide a sufficient deterrent, many believed that the long-standing prohibition against physical punishment should be reconsidered, at least with respect to juvenile offenders. In some states, lawmakers introduced legislation to provide for corporal punishment of juveniles who were convicted of certain crimes. In California, for example, a bill requiring paddling of juvenile graffiti vandals was proposed (1995 California Assembly Bill No. 7, California 1995–96 Regular Session).

Proposed measures in other states have not limited the use of corporal punishment to juveniles. In Tennessee, for instance, a bill was introduced in 1995 providing for floggings for property crimes such as BURGLARY, vandalism, and trespassing. The measure would further provide for the punishment to be administered by the county sheriff on the courthouse steps of the county where the crime was committed. According to the bill's sponsor, "People that follow a life of crime generally get started in the area of property crimes ... if you knew they were going to ... whale the living daylights out of you, you might think twice about it." This bill, like other measures proposed for physically punishing juveniles, failed to pass the state legislature.

In response to renewed calls for physical punishment for criminals, critics have argued that such measures may meet a "revenge" need on the part of the public but that they do nothing in the long term to address the deeper issue of why crime occurs. Groups such as the AMERICAN CIVIL LIBERTIES UNION, in lobbying against corporal punishment, maintain that state legislators, law enforcement personnel, criminologists, and social scientists should instead direct their efforts to what can be done to prevent crime in the first place.

FURTHER READINGS

Bloom, Scott. 1995. "Spare the Rod, Spoil the Child? A Legal Framework for Recent Corporal Punishment Proposals." *Golden Gate University Law Review* 25.

Dayton, John. 1994. "Corporal Punishment in Public Schools: The Legal and Political Battle Continues." *Education Law Reporter* 89.

Parkinson, Jerry R. 1994. "Federal Court Treatment of Corporal Punishment in Public Schools: Jurisprudence That Is Literally Shocking to the Conscience." *South Dakota Law Review* 39.

CROSS-REFERENCES

Juvenile Law.

CORPORATE

Pertaining to or possessing the qualities of a corporation, a legal entity created—pursuant to state law—to serve the purposes set out in its certificate of incorporation.

A *corporate officer* is an individual who is charged with the management of a corporation by virtue of a position as its president, vice president, treasurer, or secretary.

CORPORATE FRAUD

On October 16, 2001, Enron, the seventh largest corporation in the U.S., announced a $638 million loss in third-quarter earnings. On November 8, 2001, the company publicly admitted to having overstated earnings for four years by $586 million and to having created limited partnerships to hide $3 billion in debt. As investors lost confidence in the company, Enron stock, which had been worth as much as $90 per share in 2000, plummeted to less than $1 per share. Thousands of Enron employees lost their jobs and retirement savings, which had been invested in corporate stock through a 401(k) retirement plan. Banks and lenders lost millions of dollars in loans made to Enron based on the fraudulent earnings reports.

Enron Corporation started as a pipeline company in Houston, Texas, that delivered gas at market price. Over the next 15 years, Enron expanded into an energy power broker that traded electricity and other commodities, such as water and broadband INTERNET services. Enron became one of the nation's most successful companies, employing 21,000 people in more than 40 countries. The senior executives at Enron attributed their success to their corporate strategy, which was to be light in assets but heavy in innovation.

The innovative business practices of overstating profits and concealing debt increased the company's stock value, thus allowing the company to borrow more money and to expand. It also led to some top executives selling their stock and making over one billion dollars. Those former executives were later indicted for FRAUD, MONEY LAUNDERING, and conspiracy, and they also face dozens of civil lawsuits filed by PENSION funds and former employees. The company's accounting firm, Arthur Andersen, admitted to having shredded Enron documents after it had learned that the SECURITIES AND EXCHANGE COMMISSION (SEC) was conducting an investigation of the corporation. The accounting firm was convicted of OBSTRUCTION OF JUSTICE, lost hundreds of clients and employees, and went out of business.

After the Enron scandal became public knowledge, many wondered how such an overstatement could have escaped notice. What the public soon would learn was that Enron was only one among many such stories.

In March 2002, the world learned that WorldCom, the second largest long-distance phone company in the U.S., had overstated profits by listing $3.8 billion in normal operating expenses (which were basically routine maintenance costs) as capital expenses. This move allowed them to spread the expenses out over several years, thereby making profits look much larger and artificially inflating the company's value in order to meet Wall Street's expected earnings. WorldCom stock, which was valued as high as $60 per share in 1999, dropped to 20 cents per share in response to the news. Seventeen thousand WorldCom employees lost their jobs. The JUSTICE DEPARTMENT has secured indictments against the former Chief Financial Officer, Richard Breeden, for bank fraud, SECURITIES fraud, conspiracy and false statements in SEC filings. Four other former WorldCom executives have pled guilty to securities fraud and agreed to cooperate with the prosecution. The SEC has filed a civil suit against the company. As of 2003, the SEC has uncovered over $9 billion in bogus accounting. In July 2002, WorldCom filed the world's largest BANKRUPTCY.

After Enron's and WorldCom's fraudulent accounting practices became public knowledge, news of more corporate accounting scandals came flooding in. In February 2002, Global Crossing was caught inflating revenue and shredding documents that contained accounting information. In April 2002, Adelphia Communications made headlines amidst the discovery that $3.1 billion worth of secret loans had been made to the company's founding family—some of whom were later arrested—and earnings were overstated. In May 2002, Tyco International, Ltd. accused three former senior executives of having fraudulently taken out loans from the company without permission and without paying them back. The men also allegedly issued bonuses to themselves and other employees without approval from the company's board of directors. The SEC has since charged the three for fraud and theft and is investigating whether the company had knowl-

ENRON: AN INVESTIGATION INTO CORPORATE FRAUD

The collapse of Enron Corporation in 2001 led to massive investigations involving allegations of a range of criminal activities perpetrated by some of the company's top executives. In January 2002, the U.S. JUSTICE DEPARTMENT announced that it had formed an Enron Task Force consisting of a team of federal prosecutors and under the supervision of the department, agents of the FEDERAL BUREAU OF INVESTIGATION, and agents of the criminal division of the INTERNAL REVENUE SERVICE. The scandal developed into a case study of corporate fraud, poor management decisions, and faulty accounting practices.

Enron had built itself into the seventh largest company in the United States, with annual revenues of $100 billion. In December 2000, the company's stock sold for as much as $84.87 per share. However, stock prices fell throughout much of 2001. In October, the company announced that it had overstated its revenues, claiming losses of $638 million during the third quarter of 2001 alone.

Stock prices then plunged, hurting investors and employees with retirement plans that were tied into company stock. By the beginning of December, Enron's stock prices had fallen to below $1 per share. Enron filed for Chapter 11 BANKRUPTCY protection on December 2, 2001. To date, the event constituted the largest bankruptcy in U.S. history.

Much of the early investigation into the Enron fiasco focused on the company's financial reporting practices. Though the company followed generally accepted accounting principles (GAAP), these practices gave the false impression that the company was more profitable and more secure than it really was. The company reported revenues that were actually funds flowing through transitional transactions with related companies. Moreover, the company hid its losses and debts in partnerships that did not appear on Enron's financial statements.

The first criminal charges were filed against Enron's accounting firm, Arthur Andersen, L.L.P. The Justice Department brought charges that the accounting firm had destroyed thousands of documents, including computer files, related to its dealings with Enron. Anderson was also convicted for doctoring a memo and misstating a news release related to Enron. The company was found guilty of OBSTRUCTION OF JUSTICE in June 2002—an appeal is still pending as of September 2003. It was placed on PROBATION for five years and required to pay a fine of $500,000. Analysts questioned whether the accounting firm would survive after the conviction. In addition to its role as accountant, Arthur Andersen had served as a consultant to Enron for a number of years, thus raising conflicts of interest questions.

Because the Justice Department had not moved forward with criminal indictments against Enron officials, several critics charged that the federal government under President GEORGE W. BUSH was protecting top Enron executives. Several of these executives were questioned by the Senate Commerce Committee in February 2002, but no charges were filed. Several of Enron's senior executives

edge of this conduct. In July 2002, it was revealed that AOL Time Warner had inflated sales figures. Amid further investigations, the company admitted to having possibly overstated revenue by $49 million. Other companies in the spotlight for corporate accounting scandal allegations include Bristol-Myers Squibb, Kmart, Qwest Communications International, and Xerox. In addition to corporate scandal, television personality and home decorating maven Martha Stewart was indicted for allegedly selling 3,928 shares of stock in ImClone Systems, thus making about $227,824, based on an insider trading tip that she had received from the company's founder, Samuel Waksal.

Many fraudulent accounting practices came about over the past decade when energy, telecommunication, and other industries were expanding rapidly, and competition was especially fierce. The STOCK MARKET indices were reaching all-time records, and investors were looking for short-term earnings targets. Many corporate executives did whatever was necessary to meet the quarterly expectations of the analysts on Wall Street, thereby increasing the price of their stock. This often allowed their companies to borrow more money to grow and compete. Since most top executives also enjoyed stock options that rose in value with their companies' stock prices, they had the added incentive of making significant profits by selling their stocks at the higher prices. This resulted in a considerable transfer of money from individual shareholders to corporate managers. However, the individual investors were still making profits and therefore not paying attention to conflicts of interest and reportedly had personal interests in certain risky transactions. These executives even sold Enron stock while at the same time convincing employees to hold their stock. The board of directors of the company also allegedly failed to provide significant oversight regarding the auditing and reporting by the company.

The first major criminal charges involving an Enron executive were brought against Michael Kopper, who had served as an aide to chief financial officer Andrew Fastow. Kopper pleaded guilty to charges of MONEY LAUNDERING and conspiracy to commit FRAUD in August 2002. Kopper implicated Fastow, claiming that Fastow had conducted transactions on behalf of Enron for the benefit of third-party partnerships owned by Fastow.

The Justice Department then focused its attention on Fastow, who allegedly had $12.8 million in funds and was constructing a $2.6 million house. The government alleged that Fastow and Kopper had accumulated $22 million from illegal Enron deals. In November 2002, the Justice Department indicted Fastow on 78 counts, including fraud, money laundering, and obstruction of justice. The criminal indictment did not include former CEO Kenneth Lay, former CEO Jeffrey Skilling, or any other top executives. The

Justice Department also announced that it could file a superseding indictment with additional charges. This superseding indictment might name additional defendants as well.

Fastow appeared before the SECURITIES AND EXCHANGE COMMISSION in December 2002 but invoked his FIFTH AMENDMENT PRIVILEGE AGAINST SELF-INCRIMINATION. In several trade publications in the late 1990s, Fastow had discussed his accounting practices at Enron, including methods for keeping funds off of Enron's books. According to several commentators, Fastow could represent a "fall guy" for the Enron fiasco, as it was probable that other executives and members of the board were aware of these reporting practices.

Others involved in Enron transactions were also brought up on criminal charges. In July 2002, three British bankers were charged with wire fraud for their dealings with Enron. The Justice Department subsequently focused its attention on Enron Broadband Services, an INTERNET division of the company. The *Houston Chronicle* reported in April 2003 that executives of that branch were likely to be indicted for insider trading, fraud, and money laundering.

As of the end of April 2003, twelve charges had been filed relating to the

Enron fiasco, though only seven were filed against company insiders.

FURTHER READINGS

Ackman, Dan. 2002. "Andrew Fastow, Fall Guy." *Forbes* (October 3). Available online at <www.forbes.com/2002/10/03/1003top news_print.html> (accessed July 11, 2003).

Baird, Douglas G., and Robert K. Rasmussen. 2002. "Four (or Five) Easy Lessons from Enron." *Vanderbilt Law Review* 55 (November): 1787–812.

Flood, Mary, and Tom Fowler. 2003. "Five Men Could Be Charged." *Houston Chronicle* (April 26).

Fox, Loren. 2003. *Enron: The Rise and Fall.* Hoboken, N.J.: Wiley.

"Key Enron Figure Strikes a Deal." 2002. CBS News.com (August 21). Available online at <www.cbsnews.com/stories/2002/08/22/national/printable519479.shtml> (accessed July 11, 2003).

Salem, Christina R.. 2003. "The New Mandate of the Corporate Lawyer After the Fall of Enron and the Enactment of the Sarbanes-Oxley Act." *Fordham Journal of Corporate & Financial Law* 8 (summer): 765–87.

Swartz, Mimi, with Sherron Watkins. 2003. *Power Failure: The Inside Story of the Collapse of Enron.* New York: Doubleday.

CROSS-REFERENCES

Accounting; Bankruptcy; Embezzlement; Fraud.

---

fraudulent practices, thus allowing the executives to go almost unchecked in their actions.

Since the collapse of Enron and WorldCom, some corrective actions have been taken. The New York Stock Exchange has made improvements in its accounting, auditing, and corporate governance rules for corporations that want to list their stock on the exchange. Congress approved the SARBANES-OXLEY ACT, Pub. L. No. 107-204, 116 Stat. 745, which created the Public Accounting Oversight Board to monitor public accountants, made changes in auditing rules, and authorized an increase in criminal penalties for more WHITE-COLLAR CRIMES. The declining economy and bear market has also changed the attitude of corporate managers who had to downsize and apply more caution in making new investments and deciding executive salaries

and bonuses. Most importantly, corporate employees and individual investors are paying more attention to the actions of the executives who control their investments.

FURTHER READINGS

Arnold, James. "WorldCom's Star Falls to Earth." July 22, 2002. Available online at <news.bbc.co.uk/l/hi/business/2066885.stm> (accessed Novmber 20, 2003).

"Cato Handbook for Congress, 108 Congress, Chapter 22: Enron, WorldCom and Other Disasters." Available online at <www.cato.org/pubs/handbook/hb108/hb108-22.pdf> (accessed November 20, 2003).

"Enron Scandal At-a-Glance." Available online at <news.bbc.co.uk/l/hi/business/1780075.stm> (accessed November 20, 2003).

Patsuris, Penelope. "The Corporate Scandal Sheet." August 26, 2002. Available online at <www.forbes.com/2002/07/25/accountingtracker_print.html> (accessed November 20, 2003).

CORPORATE PERSONALITY

The distinct status of a business organization that has complied with law for its recognition as a legal entity and that has an independent legal existence from that of its officers, directors, and shareholders.

Corporate personality encompasses the capacity of a corporation to have a name of its own, to sue and be sued, and to have the right to purchase, sell, lease, and mortgage its property in its own name. In addition, property cannot be taken away from a corporation without DUE PROCESS OF LAW.

CORPORATIONS

Artificial entities that are created by state statute, and that are treated much like individuals under the law, having legally enforceable rights, the ability to acquire debt and to pay out profits, the ability to hold and transfer property, the ability to enter into contracts, the requirement to pay taxes, and the ability to sue and be sued.

The rights and responsibilities of a corporation are independent and distinct from the people who own or invest in them. A corporation simply provides a way for individuals to run a business and to share in profits and losses.

History

The concept of a corporate personality traces its roots to ROMAN LAW and found its way to the American colonies through the British. After gaining independence, the states, not the federal government, assumed authority over corporations.

Although corporations initially served only limited purposes, the Industrial Revolution spurred their development. The corporation became the ideal way to run a large enterprise, combining centralized control and direction with moderate investments by a potentially unlimited number of people.

The corporation today remains the most common form of business organization because, theoretically, a corporation can exist forever and because a corporation, not its owners or investors, is liable for its contracts. But these benefits do not come free. A corporation must follow many formalities, is subject to publicity, and is governed by state and federal regulations.

Many states have drafted their statutes governing corporations based upon the Model Business Corporation Act. This document, prepared by the American Bar Association Section of Business Law, Committee on Corporate Laws, and approved by the AMERICAN LAW INSTITUTE, provides a framework for all aspects of corporate governance as well as other aspects of corporations. Like other MODEL ACTS, the Model Business Corporation Act is not necessarily designed to be adopted wholesale by the various states, but rather is designed to provide guidance to states when they adopt their own acts.

Types of Corporations

Corporations can be private, nonprofit, municipal, or quasi-public. Private corporations are in business to make money, whereas nonprofit corporations generally are designed to benefit the general public. Municipal corporations are typically cities and towns that help the state to function at the local level. Quasi-public corporations would be considered private, but their business serves the public's needs, such as by offering utilities or telephone service.

There are two types of private corporations. One is the public corporation, which has a large number of investors, called shareholders. Corporations that trade their shares, or investment stakes, on SECURITIES exchanges or that regularly publish share prices are typical publicly held corporations.

The other type of private corporation is the closely held corporation. Closely held corporations have relatively few shareholders (usually 15 to 35 or fewer), often all in a single family; little or no outside market exists for sale of the shares; all or most of the shareholders help run the business; and the sale or transfer of shares is restricted. The vast majority of corporations are closely held.

Getting a Corporation Started

Many corporations get their start through the efforts of a person called a promoter, who goes about developing and organizing a business venture. A promoter's efforts typically involve arranging the needed capital, or financing, using loans, money from investors, or the promoter's own money; assembling the people and assets (such as land, buildings, and leases) necessary to run the corporation; and fulfilling the legal requirements for forming the corporation.

A corporation cannot be automatically liable for obligations that a promoter incurred on its behalf. Technically, a corporation does not exist during a promoter's pre-incorporation activities. A promoter therefore cannot serve as a legal agent, who could bind a corporation to a con-

Delaware: The Mighty Mite of Corporations

Delaware may be among the United States' smallest states, but it is the biggest when it comes to corporations: more than a third of all corporations listed by the New York Stock Exchange are incorporated in Delaware.

Delaware's allure is explained through a combination of history and law. Although today the state's corporations law is not necessarily less restrictive and less rigid than other states' corporation laws, Delaware could boast more corporation friendly statutes before model corporation laws came into vogue. As a result, corporate lawyers nationwide are more familiar with Delaware's law, and its statutes and case law provide certainty and easy access.

Delaware, more than any other state, relies on franchise tax revenues; thus, Delaware, more than any other state, is committed to remaining a responsive and desirable incorporation site. In addition, Delaware offers a level of certainty and stability: the state's constitution requires a two-thirds vote of both legislative houses to change its corporations statutes.

Delaware also has a specialized court that is staffed by lawyers from the corporate bar, and its highest court has similar expertise. Lawyers in the state continually work to keep Delaware's corporate law current, effective, and flexible. All combine to make Delaware the first state for incorporation.

tract. After formation, a corporation must somehow assent before it can be bound by an obligation that a promoter has made on its behalf. Usually, if a corporation gets the benefits of a promoter's contract, it will be treated as though it has assented to, and accepted, the contract.

The first question facing incorporators (those forming a corporation) is where to incorporate. The answer often depends on the type of corporation. Theoretically, both closely held and large public corporations may incorporate in any state. Small businesses operating in a single state usually incorporate in that state. Most large corporations select Delaware as their state of incorporation because of its sophistication in dealing with corporation law.

Incorporators then must follow the mechanics that are set forth in the state's statutes. Corporation statutes vary from state to state, but most require basically the same essentials in forming a corporation. Every statute requires incorporators to file a document, usually called the articles of incorporation, and pay a filing fee to the secretary of state's office, which reviews the filing. If the filing receives approval, the corporation is considered to have started existing on the date of the first filing.

The articles of incorporation typically must contain (1) the name of the corporation, which often must include an element like *Company, Corporation, Incorporated, or Limited*," and may not resemble too closely the names of other corporations in the state; (2) the length of time the corporation will exist, which can be perpetual or renewable; (3) the corporation's purpose, usually described as "any lawful business purpose"; (4) the number and types of shares that the corporation may issue and the rights and preferences of those shares; (5) the address of the corporation's registered office, which need not be the corporation's business office, and the registered agent at that office who can accept legal SERVICE OF PROCESS; (6) the number of directors and the names and addresses of the first directors; and (7) each incorporator's name and address.

A corporation's bylaws usually contain the rules for the actual running of the corporation. Bylaws normally are not filed with the SECRETARY OF STATE and are easier to amend than are the articles of incorporation. The bylaws should be complete enough so that corporate officers can rely on them to manage the corporation's affairs. The bylaws regulate the conduct of direc-

Proctor and Gamble president and CEO A.G. Lafley addresses shareholders at the company's annual meeting in 2002. A corporation's officers are responsible for running day-to-day business affairs and carrying out policies established by the directors.
AP/WIDE WORLD PHOTOS

tors, officers, and shareholders and set forth rules governing internal affairs. They can include definitions of management's duties, as well as times, locations, and voting procedures for meetings that affect the corporation.

People Behind a Corporation: Rights and Responsibilities

The primary players in a corporation are the shareholders, directors, and officers. Shareholders are the investors in, and owners of, a corporation. They elect, and sometimes remove, the directors, and occasionally they must vote on specific corporate transactions or operations. The board of directors is the top governing body. Directors establish corporate policy and hire officers, to whom they usually delegate their obligations to administer and manage the corporation's affairs. Officers run the day-to-day business affairs and carry out the policies the directors establish.

Shareholders Shareholders' financial interests in the corporation is determined by the percentage of the total outstanding shares of stock that they own. Along with their financial stakes, shareholders generally receive a number of rights, all designed to protect their investments. Foremost among these rights is the power to vote. Shareholders vote to elect and remove

directors, to change or add to the bylaws, to ratify (i.e., approve after the fact) directors' actions where the bylaws require shareholder approval, and to accept or reject changes that are not part of the regular course of business, such as mergers or dissolution. This power to vote, although limited, gives the shareholders some role in running a corporation.

Shareholders typically exercise their VOTING RIGHTS at annual or special meetings. Most statutes provide for an annual meeting, with requirements for some advance notice, and any shareholder can get a court order to hold an annual meeting when one has not been held within a specified period of time. Although the main purpose of the annual meeting is to elect directors, the meeting may address any relevant matter, even one that has not been mentioned specifically in the advance notice. Almost all states allow shareholders to conduct business by unanimous written consent, without a meeting.

Shareholders elect directors each year at the annual meeting. Most statutes provide that directors be elected by a majority of the voting shares that are present at the meeting. The same number of shares needed to elect a director normally is required to remove a director, usually without proof of cause, such as FRAUD or abuse of authority.

A special meeting is any meeting other than an annual meeting. The bylaws govern the persons who may call a special meeting; typically, the directors, certain officers, or the holders of a specified percentage of outstanding shares may do so. The only subjects that a special meeting may address are those that are specifically listed in an advance notice.

Statutes require that a quorum exist at any corporation meeting. A quorum exists when a specified number of a corporation's outstanding shares are represented. Statutes determine what level of representation constitutes a quorum; most require one-third. Once a quorum exists, most statutes require an affirmative vote of the majority of the shares present before a vote can bind a corporation. Generally, once a quorum is present, it continues, and the withdrawal of a faction of voters does not prevent the others from acting.

A corporation determines who may vote based on its records. Corporations issue share certificates in the name of a person, who becomes the record owner (i.e., the owner according to company records) and is treated as the sole owner of the shares. The company records of these transactions are called stock-transfer books or share registers. A shareholder who does not receive a new certificate is called the beneficial owner and cannot vote, but the beneficial owner is the real owner and can compel the record owner to act as the beneficial owner desires.

Those who hold shares by a specified date before a meeting, called the record date, may vote at the meeting. Before each meeting, a corporation must prepare a list of shareholders who are eligible to vote, and each shareholder has an unqualified right to inspect this voting list.

Shareholders typically have two ways of voting: straight voting or cumulative voting. Under straight voting, a shareholder may vote his or her shares once for each position on the board. For example, if a shareholder owns 50 shares and there are three director positions, the shareholder may cast 50 votes for each position. Under cumulative voting, the same shareholder has the option of casting all 150 votes for a single candidate. Cumulative voting increases the participation of minority shareholders by boosting the power of their votes.

Shareholders also may vote as a group or block. A shareholder voting agreement is a contract among a group of shareholders to vote in a specified manner on certain issues; this is also called a pooling agreement. Such an agreement is designed to maintain control or to maximize voting power. Another arrangement is a voting trust. This has the same objectives as a pooling agreement, but in a voting trust, shareholders assign their voting rights to a trustee who votes on behalf of all the shares in the trust.

Shareholders need not attend meetings in order to vote; they may authorize a person, called a proxy, to vote their shares. Proxy appointment often is solicited by parties who are interested in gaining control of the board of directors or in passing a particular proposal; their request is called a proxy solicitation. Proxy appointment must be in writing. It usually may last no longer than a year, and it can be revoked.

Federal law generates most proxy regulation, and the Securities and Exchange Commission (SEC) has comprehensive and detailed regulations. These rules define the form of proxy-solicitation documents and require the distribution of substantial information about director candidates and other issues that are up for shareholder vote. Not all corporations are subject to federal proxy law; generally, the law covers only large corporations with many shareholders and with shares that are traded on a national securities exchange. These regulations aim to protect investors from promiscuous proxy solicitation by irresponsible outsiders who seek to gain control of a corporation, and from unscrupulous officers who seek to retain control of management by hiding or distorting facts.

In addition to voting rights, shareholders also have a right to inspect a corporation's books and records. A corporation almost always views the invocation of this right as hostile. Shareholders may only inspect records if they do so for a "proper purpose"; that is, is a purpose that is reasonably relevant to the shareholder's financial interest, such as determining the worth of his or her holdings. Shareholders can be required to own a specified amount of shares or to have held the shares for a specified period of time before inspection is allowed. Shareholders generally may review all relevant records that are needed, in order to gather information in which they have a legitimate interest. Shareholders also may examine a corporation's record of shareholders, including names and addresses and classes of shares.

Directors Statutes contemplate that a corporation's business and affairs will be managed by the board of directors or under the board's authority or direction. Directors often delegate to corporate officers their authority to formulate policy and to manage the business. In closely held corporations, directors normally involve themselves more in management than do their counterparts in large corporations. Statutes empower directors to decide whether to declare dividends; to formulate proposed important corporate changes, such as mergers or amendments to the articles of incorporation; and to submit proposed changes to shareholders. Many boards appoint committees to handle technical matters, such as litigation, but the board itself must address important matters. Directors customarily are paid a salary and often receive incentive plans that can supplement that salary.

A corporation's articles or bylaws typically control the number of directors, the terms of the directors' service, and the directors' ability to change their number and terms. The shareholders' power of removal functions as a check on directors who may wish to act in a way that is contrary to the majority shareholders' wishes. The directors' own fiduciary duties, or obligations to act for the benefit of the corporation, also serve as checks on directors.

The bylaws usually regulate the frequency of regular board meetings. Directors also may hold special board meetings, which are any meetings other than regular board meetings. Special meetings require some advance notice, but the agenda of special directors' meetings is not limited to what is set forth in the notice, as it is with shareholders' special meetings. In most states, directors may hold board meetings by phone and may act by unanimous written consent without a meeting.

A quorum for board meetings usually exists if a majority of the directors in office immediately before the meeting are present. The quorum number may be increased or decreased by amending the bylaws, although it may not be decreased below any statutory minimum. A quorum must be present for directors to act, except when the board is filling a vacancy. Most statutes allow either the board itself or shareholders to fill vacancies.

Directors' fiduciary duties fall under three broad categories: the duty of care, the duty of loyalty, and duties imposed by statute. Generally, a fiduciary duty is the duty to act for the benefit of another—here, the corporation— while subordinating personal interests. A fiduciary occupies a position of trust for another and owes the other a high degree of fidelity and loyalty.

A director owes the corporation the duty to manage the entity's business with due care. Statutes typically define using due care as acting in GOOD FAITH, using the care that an ordinarily prudent person would use in a similar position and situation, and acting in a manner that the director reasonably thinks is in the corporation's best interests. Courts seldom second-guess directors, but they usually find personal liability for corporate losses where there is self-dealing or NEGLIGENCE.

Self-dealing transactions raise questions about directors' duty of loyalty. A self-dealing transaction occurs when a director is on both sides of the same transaction, representing both the corporation and another person or entity who is involved in the transaction. Self-dealing may endanger a corporation because the corporation may be treated unfairly. If a transaction is questioned, the director bears the burden of proving that it was in fact satisfactory.

Self-dealing usually occurs in one of four types of situations: transactions between a director and the corporation; transactions between corporations where the same director serves on both corporations' boards; by a director who takes advantage of an opportunity for business that arguably may belong to the corporation; and by a director who competes with the corporation.

The usurping of a corporate opportunity poses the most significant challenge to a director's duty of loyalty. A director cannot exploit the position of director by taking for himself or herself a business opportunity that rightly belongs to the corporation. Most courts facing this question compare how closely related the opportunity is to the corporation's current or potential business. Part of this analysis involves assessing the fairness of taking the opportunity. Simply taking a corporation's opportunity does not automatically violate the duty of loyalty. A corporation may relinquish the opportunity, or the corporation may be incapable of taking the opportunity for itself.

Directors who are charged with violating their duty of care usually are protected by what courts call the BUSINESS JUDGMENT RULE. Essentially, the rule states that even if the directors' decisions turn out badly for the corporation, the directors themselves will not be personally liable for losses if those decisions were based on reasonable information and if the directors acted rationally. Unless the directors commit fraud, a breach of good faith, or an illegal act, courts presume that their judgment was formed to promote the best interests of the corporation. In other words, courts focus on the process of reaching a decision, not on the decision itself, and require directors to make informed, not passive, decisions.

State statutes often impose additional duties and liabilities on directors as fiduciaries to a corporation. These laws may govern conduct such as paying dividends when a statute or the articles prohibit doing so; buying shares when a statute or the articles prohibit doing so; giving assets to shareholders during liquidation without resolving a corporation's debts, liabilities, or obligations; and making a prohibited loan to another director, an officer, or a shareholder.

If a court finds that a director has violated a duty, the director still might not face personal liability. Some statutes require or permit corporations to indemnify a director who violated a duty but acted in good faith, who received no improper personal benefit, and who reasonably thought that the action was lawful and in the corporation's best interests. Indemnification means that the corporation reimburses the director for expenses incurred defending himself or herself and for amounts he or she paid after losing or settling a claim.

Officers The duties and powers of corporate officers can be found in statutes, articles of incorporation, bylaws, or corporate resolutions. Some statutes require a corporation to have specific officers; others merely require that the bylaws contain a description of the officers. Officers usually serve at the will of those who appointed them, and they generally can be fired with or without cause, although some officers sign employment contracts.

Corporations typically have as officers a president, one or more vice presidents, a secretary, and a treasurer. The president is the primary officer and supervises the corporation's business affairs. This officer sometimes is referred to as the chief executive officer, but the ultimate authority lies with the directors. The vice president fills in for the president when the latter cannot or will not act. The secretary keeps minutes of meetings, oversees notices, and manages the corporation's records. The treasurer manages and is responsible for the corporation's finances.

Officers act as a corporation's agents and can bind the corporation to contracts and agreements. Many parties who deal with corporations require that the board pass a resolution approving any contract negotiated by an officer, as a sure way to bind the corporation to the contract. In the absence of a specific resolution, the corporation still may be bound if it ratified the contract by accepting its benefits or if the officer appeared to have the authority to bind the corporation. Courts treat corporations as having knowledge of information if a corporate officer or employee has that knowledge.

Like directors, officers owe fiduciary duties to the corporation: good faith, diligence, and a high degree of honesty. But most litigation about fiduciary duties involves directors, not officers.

An officer does not face personal liability for a transaction if he or she merely acts as the corporation's agent. Nevertheless, the officer may be personally liable for a transaction where the officer intends to be bound personally or creates the impression that he or she will be so bound; where the officer exceeds his or her authority; where the officer exceeds his or her authority;

and where a statute imposes liability on the officer, such as for failure to pay taxes.

Finances

Shares A corporation divides its ownership units into shares, and can issue more than one type or class of shares. The articles of incorporation must state the type or types and the number of shares that can be issued. A corporation may offer additional shares once it has begun operating, sometimes subject to current shareholders' preemptive rights to buy new shares in proportion to their current ownership.

Directors usually determine the price of shares. Some states require corporations to assign a nominal or minimum value to shares, called a par value, although many states are eliminating this practice. Many states allow some types of non-cash property to be exchanged for shares. Corporations also raise money through debt financing—also called debt securities—which gives the creditor an interest in the corporation that ultimately must be paid back by the corporation, much like a loan.

If a corporation issues only one type of share, its shares are called common stock or common shares. Holders of common stock typically have the power to vote and a right to their share of the corporation's net assets. Statutes allow corporations to create different classes of common stock, with varying voting power and dividend rights.

A corporation also may issue preferred shares. These are typically nonvoting shares, and their holders receive a preference over holders of common shares for payment of dividends or liquidations. Some preferred dividends may be carried over into another year, either in whole or in part.

Dividends A dividend is a payment to shareholders, in proportion to their holdings, of current or past earnings or profits, usually on a regular and periodic basis. Directors determine whether to issue dividends. A dividend can take the form of cash, property, or additional shares. Shareholders have the right to force payment of a dividend, but they usually succeed only if the directors abused their discretion.

Restrictions on the distribution of dividends can be found in the articles of incorporation and in statutes, which seek to ensure that the dividends come out of current and past earnings. Directors who vote for illegal dividends can be held personally liable to the corporation. In

PIERCING THE CORPORATE VEIL

When a corporation is a sham, engages in FRAUD or other wrongful acts, or is used solely for the personal benefit of its directors, officers, or shareholders, courts may disregard the separate corporate existence and impose personal liability on the directors, officers, or shareholders. In other words, courts may pierce the "veil" that the law uses to divide the corporation (and its liabilities and assets) from the people behind the corporation. The veil creates a separate, legally recognized corporate entity and shields the people behind the corporation from personal liability.

In these cases, courts look beyond the form to the substance of the corporation's actions. The facts of a particular case must show some misuse of the corporate privilege or show a reason to cut back or limit the corporate privilege to prevent fraud, MISREPRESENTATION, or illegality or to achieve EQUITY or fairness.

Courts traditionally require fraud, illegality, or misrepresentation before they will pierce the corporate veil. Courts also may ignore the corporate existence where the controlling shareholder or shareholders use the corporation as merely their instrumentality or alter ego, where the corporation is undercapitalized, and where the corporation ignores the formalities required by law or commingles its assets with those of a controlling shareholder or shareholders. In addition,

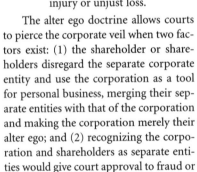

IN FOCUS

courts may refuse to recognize a separate corporate existence when doing so would violate a clearly defined statutory policy.

Courts may pierce the corporate veil in taxation or BANKRUPTCY cases, in addition to cases involving plaintiffs with contract or TORT claims. Federal law in this area is usually similar to state law.

The instrumentality and alter ego doctrines used by courts are practically indistinguishable. Courts following the instrumentality doctrine concentrate on finding three factors: (1) the people behind the corporation dominate the corporation's finances and business practices so much that the corporate entity has no separate will or existence; (2) the control has resulted in a fraud or wrong, or a dishonest or unjust act; and (3) the control and harm directly caused the plaintiff's injury or unjust loss.

The alter ego doctrine allows courts to pierce the corporate veil when two factors exist: (1) the shareholder or shareholders disregard the separate corporate entity and use the corporation as a tool for personal business, merging their separate entities with that of the corporation and making the corporation merely their alter ego; and (2) recognizing the corporation and shareholders as separate entities would give court approval to fraud or cause an unfair result.

It may appear that a corporation owned by one or two persons or a single family would almost automatically lose

its separate legal existence under these doctrines, but this is not necessarily so. A sole owner of a business, for example, can incorporate herself or himself, or the business; issue all shares to herself or himself; and set up dummy directors to follow the necessary corporate formalities. However, the sole shareholder may lose the protection of limited liability—just as any other corporation would—if the corporate affairs and assets are confused or commingled with personal affairs and assets, if the sole shareholder abuses her or his control, or if the sole shareholder ignores the necessary corporate formalities.

When courts ponder piercing the corporate veil, they consider undercapitalization to exist when a corporation's assets or the value it receives for issuing shares or bonds is disproportionately small considering the nature of the business and the risks of engaging in that business. Courts assess undercapitalization by examining the capitalization at the time the corporation was formed or entered a new business. For example, if a corporation that faces or may face obligations to creditors and potential lawsuits has received only a token or minimal amount for its shares, or has siphoned off its assets through dividends or salaries, courts may find undercapitalization. Such corporations are called shells or shams designed to take advantage of limited liability protections while not exposing to a risk of loss any of the profits or assets they gained by incorporating.

addition, a corporation's creditors often will contractually restrict the corporation's power to make distributions.

Changes and Challenges Faced by Corporations

Amendments The most straightforward and common changes faced by corporations are amendments to their bylaws and articles. The directors or incorporators initially adopt the bylaws. After that, the shareholders or directors,

or both, hold the power to repeal or amend the bylaws, usually at shareholders' meetings and subject to a corporation's voting regulations. Those who hold this power can adopt or change quorum requirements; prescribe procedures for the removal or replacement of directors; or fix the qualifications, terms, and numbers of directors. Most modern statutes limit the authority to amend articles only by requiring that an amendment would have been legal to include in the

The undercapitalization doctrine especially comes into play when courts must determine who should bear a loss— a corporation's shareholders or a third person. This determination usually depends on whether the claim involves a contract or a tort (civil wrong or injury). In contract cases, the third party usually has had some earlier dealings with the corporation and should know that the corporation is a shell. So, unless there has been deception, courts typically find that the third party assumes the risk and should suffer the loss. In tort cases, the third party normally has not dealt voluntarily with the corporation. Courts thus must decide whether the owners of the business can shift the risk of loss or injury off themselves and onto the innocent general public simply by creating a marginally financed corporation to conduct their business.

Courts may disregard the separate corporate existence when a corporation fails to follow the formalities required by corporation statutes. Courts often cite the lack of corporate formalities in finding that a corporation has become the alter ego or instrumentality of the controlling shareholder or shareholders. For example, a court may justify piercing the corporate veil if a corporation began to conduct business before its incorporation was completed; failed to hold shareholders' and directors' meetings; failed to file an **ANNUAL REPORT** or tax return; or directed the corporation's business receipts straight to the controlling shareholder's or shareholders' personal accounts.

Courts also may ignore the corporate existence when a corporation's funds or assets are commingled with the controlling shareholder's or shareholders' funds or assets. For example, they may pierce the corporate veil when no sharp distinction is drawn between corporate and **PERSONAL PROPERTY**; corporate money has been used to pay personal debts without the appropriate accounting, and vice versa; the controlling shareholder's or shareholders' personal assets have been depreciated along with corporate assets; or the controlling shareholder or shareholders have endorsed company checks in their own name.

Many times, a controlling shareholder is itself a corporation: the controlling shareholder is the parent corporation, and the controlled corporation is a subsidiary. In some circumstances courts may pierce the corporate veil protecting the parent and hold the parent liable for the subsidiary's obligations. This happens where the subsidiary loses its independent existence because the parent dominates the subsidiary's affairs by participating in day-to-day operations, resolving important policy decisions, making business decisions without consulting the subsidiary's directors or officers, and issuing instructions directly to the subsidiary's employees or instructing its own employees to conduct the subsidiary's business.

Courts also hold the parent liable where the parent runs the subsidiary in an unfair manner by allocating profits to the parent and losses to the subsidiary; the parent represents the subsidiary as a division or branch rather than as a subsidiary; the subsidiary does not follow its own corporate formalities; or the parent and subsidiary are engaged in essentially the same business, and the subsidiary is undercapitalized.

A final scenario in which courts may pierce the corporate veil involves an enterprise entity, which is a single business enterprise divided into separate corporations. For example, a taxicab enterprise may consist of five corporations with two taxis each, a corporation for the dispatching unit, and a corporation for the parking garage. All the corporations, though separate, essentially engage in a single business—providing taxi service.

Courts often harbor suspicions that such arrangements are made in an attempt to minimize each corporation's assets that would be subject to claims by creditors or injured persons. Courts often will, in essence, put the corporations together as a single entity and make that entity liable to a creditor or injured person, perhaps because treating them as separate entities is unfair to those who believe they really form a single unit.

FURTHER READINGS

Bainbridge, Stephen M. 2001. "Abolishing Veil Piercing." *The Journal of Corporation Law* 26 (spring): 479–535.

Huss, Rebecca J. 2001. "Revamping Veil Piercing for All Limited Liability Entities: Forcing the Common Law Doctrine into the Statutory Age." *University of Cincinnati Law Review* 70 (fall): 93–135.

Roche, Vincent M. 2003. "Bashing the Corporate Shield: The Untenable Evisceration of Freedom of Contract in the Corporate Context." *The Journal of Corporation Law* 28 (winter): 289–312.

original articles. Some statutes shield minority shareholders from harmful majority-approved amendments.

Mergers and Acquisitions A merger or acquisition generally is a transaction or device that allows one corporation to merge into or to take over another corporation. **MERGERS AND ACQUISITIONS** are complicated processes that require the involvement and approval of the directors and the shareholders.

In a merger or consolidation, two corporations become one by either maintaining one of the original corporations or creating a new corporation consisting of the prior corporations. Where statutes authorize these combinations, these changes are called statutory mergers. The statutes allow the surviving or new corporation to automatically assume ownership of the assets and liabilities of the disappearing corporation or corporations.

Statutes protect shareholder interests during mergers, and state courts assess these combinations using the fiduciary principles that are applied in self-dealing transactions. Most statutes require a majority of the shareholders in order to approve a merger; some require two-thirds. Statutes also allow shareholders to dissent from such transactions, to have a court appraise the value of their stake, and to force payment at a judicially determined price.

Mergers can involve sophisticated transactions that are designed simply to combine corporations or to create a new corporation or to eliminate minority shareholder interests. In some mergers, an acquiring corporation creates a subsidiary as the form for the merged or acquired entity. A subsidiary is a corporation that is majority-owned or wholly owned by another corporation. Creating a subsidiary allows an acquiring corporation to avoid responsibility for an acquired corporation's liabilities, while providing shareholders in the acquired corporation with an interest in the acquiring corporation.

Mergers also can involve parent corporations and their subsidiaries. A similar, though distinct, transaction is the sale, lease, or exchange of all or practically all of a corporation's property and assets. The purchaser in such a transaction typically continues operating the business, although its scope may be narrowed or broadened. In most states, shareholders have a statutory right of dissent and appraisal in these transactions, unless the sale is part of ordinary business dealings, such as issuing a mortgage or deed of trust covering all of a corporation's assets.

Not all business combinations are consensual. Often, an aggressor corporation will use takeover techniques to acquire a target corporation. Aggressor corporations primarily use the cash tender offer in a takeover: The aggressor attempts to persuade the target corporation's shareholders to sell, or tender, their shares at a price that the aggressor will pay in cash. The aggressor sets the purchase price above the current market price, usually 25 to 50 percent higher, to make the offer attractive. This practice often requires the aggressor to assume significant debts in the takeover, and these debts often are paid for by selling off parts of the target corporation's business.

Restraints and protections exist for these situations. In takeovers of registered or large, publicly held corporations, federal law requires the disclosure of certain information, such as the source of the money in the tender offer. In smaller corporations, a controlling shareholder, who holds a majority of a corporation's shares, may not transfer control to someone outside the corporation without a reasonable investigation of the potential buyer. A controlling shareholder also may not transfer control where there is a suspicion that the buyer will use the corporation's assets to pay the purchase price or otherwise wrongfully take the corporation's assets.

Corporations can employ defensive tactics to fend off a takeover. They can find a more compatible buyer (a "white knight"); issue additional shares to make the takeover less attractive (a "lock-up"); create new classes of stock whose rights increase if any person obtains more than a prescribed percentage (a "poison pill"); or boost share prices to make the takeover price less appealing.

Dissolution A corporation can terminate its legal existence by engaging in the dissolution process. Most statutes allow corporations to dissolve before they begin to operate as well as after they get started. The normal process requires the directors to adopt a resolution for dissolution, and the shareholders to approve it, by either a simple majority or, in some states, a two-thirds majority. After approval, the corporation engages in a "winding-up" period, during which it fulfills its obligations for taxes and debts, before making final, liquidation distributions to shareholders.

Derivative Suits Shareholders can bring suit on behalf of a corporation to enforce a right or to remedy a wrong that has been done to the corporation. Shareholders "derive" their right to bring suit from a corporation's right. One common claim in a derivative suit would allege misappropriation of corporate assets or other breaches of duty by the directors or officers. Shareholders most often bring derivative suits in federal courts.

Shareholders must maneuver through several procedural hoops before actually filing suit. Many statutes require them to put up security, often in the form of a bond, for the corporation's expenses and attorneys' fees from the suit, to be paid if the suit fails; this requirement often kills a suit before it even begins. The shareholders must have held stock at the time of the contested action and must have owned it continuously ever since. The shareholders first must demand that the directors enforce the right or remedy the wrong; if they fail to make a demand, they must offer sufficient proof of the futility of such a demand. Normally, a committee formed by the directors handles—and dismisses—the demand, and informed decisions are protected by the business judgment rule.

Proxy Contests A proxy contest is a struggle for control of a public corporation. In a typical proxy contest, a nonmanagement group vies with management to gain enough proxy votes to elect a majority of the board and to gain control of the corporation. A proxy contest may be a part of a takeover attempt.

Management holds most of the cards in such disputes: It has the current list of shareholders; shareholders normally are biased in its favor; and the nonmanagement group must finance its part of the proxy contest, but if management acts in good faith, it can use corporate money for its solicitation of proxy votes. In proxy contests over large, publicly held corporations, federal regulations prohibit, among other things, false or misleading statements in solicitations for proxy votes.

Insider Trading Federal, and often state, laws prohibit a corporate insider from using nonpublic information to buy or sell stock. Most cases involving violations of these laws are brought before federal courts because the federal law governing this conduct is extensive. The federal law, which is essentially an antifraud statute, states that anyone who knowingly or recklessly misrepresents, omits, or fails to correct a material or important fact that causes reliance in a sale or purchase, is liable to the buyer or seller. Those with inside information must either disclose the information or abstain from buying or selling.

Permutations

Corporations do not represent the only, or necessarily the best, type of business. Several other forms of business offer varying degrees of organizational, financial, and tax benefits and drawbacks. The selection of a particular form depends upon the investors' or owners' objectives and preferences, and upon the type of business to be conducted.

A partnership is the simplest business organization involving more than one person. It is an association of two or more people to carry on business as co-owners, with shared rights to manage and to gain profits and with shared personal liability for business debts. A sole proprietorship is more or less a one-person partnership. It is a business owned by one person, who alone manages its operation and takes its profits and is personally liable for all of its debts. A limited partnership is a partnership with two or more general partners, who manage the business and have personal and unlimited liability for its debts, and one or more limited partners, who have almost no management powers and whose liability is limited to the amount of their investment. In a LIMITED LIABILITY COMPANY, the limited liability of a limited partnership is combined with the tax treatment of a partnership, and all partners have limited liability and the authority to manage. This is a relatively new business form.

A corporation thus provides limited liability for shareholders, unlike a partnership, a sole proprietorship, or a limited partnership, each of which exposes owners to unlimited liability. A corporation is taxed like a separate entity on earnings, out of which the corporation pays dividends, which are then taxed (again) to the shareholders; this is considered double taxation. Partnerships and limited partnerships are not taxed as separate entities, and income or losses are allocated to the partners, who are directly taxed; this "flow-through" or "pass-through" taxation allocates income or losses only once. Corporations centralize management in the directors and officers, whereas partnerships divide management among all partners or general partners. Corporations can continue indefinitely despite the death or withdrawal of a shareholder; partnerships and limited partnerships, however, dissolve with the death or withdrawal of a partner. Shareholders in a publicly held corporation generally can sell or transfer their stock without limitation. Holders of interest in a partnership or limited partnership, however, can convey their interest only if the other partners approve. Corporations must abide by significant formalities and must cope with a great volume of paperwork; partnerships and limited partnerships face few formalities and few limitations in operating their business.

New Issues Faced by Corporations

Corporations in the United States have suffered a series of major fiascos in recent years that have cost investors and employees billions of dollars and have eroded public confidence in the governance of major corporations. During the mid to late 1990s, the U.S. economy grew in record numbers, much to the delight of investors and the public in general. Adding to this elation

throughout 2001. In the third quarter of 2001 alone, Enron reported losses of $638 million, leading to an announcement that the company was reducing shareholder EQUITY by $1.2 billion. The SEC began an inquiry into possible conflicts of interest within the company regarding outside partnerships. The SEC investigation became formal in October 2001, and initial reports focused on problems with Enron's dealings with partnerships run by the company's chief financial offer.

Many additional allegations continued to surface throughout November 2001, including rumors suggesting that company officials sought the assistance of top-level White House officials, including Treasury Secretary Paul O'Neill. In December 2001, Enron's stock prices fell below $1 per share in the largest single-day trading volume on either the New York Stock Exchange or the NASDAQ. Because the company's employees' 401(k) plans were tied into company stock, these employees lost their retirement plans.

Concerns over corporate governance continued to dominate business news in 2002, as WorldCom, Inc., the second-largest long-distance provider in the United States, filed for bankruptcy. Like Enron employees, WorldCom's employee 401(k) plans held company stock, and by 2003, the value of these plans had decreased by 98 percent from their value in 1999. Moreover, similar to the Enron fiasco, many allegations focused upon the accounting methods that WorldCom's accountants employed. The company's board of directors and chief executive officer expressed "shock" that the company had misstated $38 billion in capital expenses and that the company may have lost money in 2001 and 2002 when, instead, it had claimed a profit.

The SEC has responded to these problems by requiring greater oversight of the accounting profession in the United States. New regulations have also modified the accounting methods that by these companies employed. Nevertheless, public confidence in U.S. corporations and the capital markets remains shaken, and much of the criticism has focused upon the lack of oversight regarding corporate directors and officers. Many have called for reforms that will hold these directors and officers responsible in instances of malfeasance.

was the success of Internet-based companies, known generally as "dot-coms." Business commentators and the general press referred to this collective success as the "dot-com bubble."

The "bubble" burst during the early part of 2000. Marketing analysts in 1999 predicted that the enormous flow of capital, coupled with a limited range of business models that tended to copy from one another, would lead to a severe downturn or shakedown. Early in 2000, stock in several of these companies sank rapidly, leading to hundreds of BANKRUPTCY filings and thousands of employees losing their jobs. Although not all of the companies shut down, entrepreneurs and investors have been weary to follow this model since the collapse.

Confidence in American corporations decreased further with a series of corporate failure based largely upon mismanagement by directors and officers. In 2001, Enron Corporation, a large energy, commodities, and service company, suffered an enormous collapse that led to the largest bankruptcy in U.S. history. Many of the company's employees lost their 401(k) retirements plans that held company stock. The controversy also extended to the company's auditor, Arthur Andersen, L.L.P., which was accused of destroying thousands of Enron documents.

Enron reported annual revenues of $101 billion in 2000, but stock prices began to fall

FURTHER READINGS

Cox, James D., Thomas L. Hazen, and F. Hodge O'Neal. 1995. *Corporations I, II, III.* Boston: Little, Brown.

CROSS-REFERENCES

Bonds "Michael R. Milken: Genius, Villain, or Scapegoat?" (Sidebar); Golden Parachute; Greenmail; Instrumentality Rule; Preferred Stock; Stockholder's Derivative Suit; Transnational Corporation.

CORPOREAL

Possessing a physical nature; having an objective, tangible existence; being capable of perception by touch and sight.

Under COMMON LAW, corporeal hereditaments are physical objects encompassed in land, including the land itself and any tangible object on it, that can be inherited.

Corporeal is the opposite of incorporeal, that which exists but is incapable of physical manifestation, as in the right to bring a lawsuit.

CORPSE

The physical remains of an expired human being prior to complete decomposition.

Property and Possession Rights

In the ordinary use of the term, a property right does not exist in a corpse. For the purpose of burial, however, the corpse of a human being is considered to be property or quasi-property, the rights to which are held by the surviving spouse or next of kin. This right cannot be conveyed and does not exist while the decedent is living. Following burial, the body is considered part of the ground in which it is placed. Articles of PERSONAL PROPERTY that have been buried with the body, such as jewelry, may be taken by their rightful owner as determined by traditional property rules or laws relating to DESCENT AND DISTRIBUTION or wills, as they are material objects independent of the body.

A corpse may not be retained by an undertaker as security for unpaid funeral expenses, particularly if a body was kept without authorization and payment was demanded as a condition precedent to its release.

At times, the need to perform an autopsy or postmortem examination gives the local CORONER a superior right to possess the corpse until such an examination is performed. The general rule is that such examinations should be performed with discretion and not routinely. Some state statutes regulate the times when an autopsy may be performed, which may require the procurement of a court order and written permission of a designated person, usually the one with property rights in the corpse.

Burial Rights

The right to a decent burial has long been recognized as COMMON LAW, but no universal rule exists as to whom the right of burial is granted. Generally, unless otherwise provided before death by the deceased, the right will go to the surviving spouse; if there is none, it will go to the next of kin. When a controversy arises concerning the right of burial, each case will be considered on its own merits. The burial right per se is a sacred trust for those who have an interest in the remains.

Although the surviving spouse usually has the principal right to custody of the remains and to burial, special circumstances undermine this right, such as the absence or neglect of the surviving spouse or the separation of the parties at the time of death.

When there is no surviving spouse, the next of kin, in order of age, have the burial rights, unless a friend or remote relative is found by the court to have a superior right. The caretaker of an elderly, childless decedent who lived with the decedent for years prior to his or her death and to whom the estate was bequeathed might have a burial right that is superior to that of relatives.

In the case of the death of a child of divorced parents, the paramount privilege of burial is awarded to the parent who had custody.

The preference of the deceased concerning the disposition of his or her body is a right that should be strictly enforced. Some states confer this right, considering a decedent's wishes of foremost importance.

In most instances, the courts will honor the wishes of the decedent, even in the face of opposition by the surviving spouse or next of kin. If for some reason a decedent's wishes cannot be carried out, direction should be sought by the court. The court will decide how the body should be disposed of and will most likely do so according to the wishes of the surviving spouse or next of kin, provided those wishes are reasonable and not contrary to public policy.

When an individual wishes to direct the disposition of his or her remains, no formality is required. Oral directions are considered to be sufficient, and an individual's last wish will ordinarily be the controlling factor, provided it is within the limits of reason and decency.

Occasionally, a decision by the person who holds the right to burial can cause controversy beyond the deceased's family. One of the more

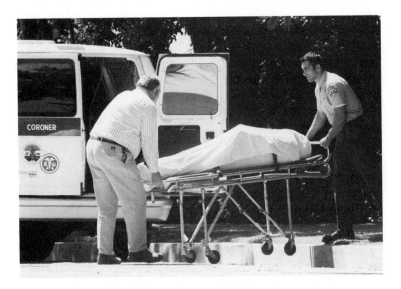

In some cases, the need to perform an autopsy or postmortem examination gives the local coroner a superior right to retain possession of a corpse until the examination is performed.

unusual cases involves the body of Ted Williams, one of the greatest baseball players in the history of the game, as well as a military hero in WORLD WAR II and the KOREAN WAR. John Henry Williams, Ted's son, decided when his father died in July 2002 to freeze the body in liquid nitrogen in a process called cryonics. The body is stored in a warehouse in Arizona. Friends and family have suggested that Ted Williams wanted to be cremated, but his body remains in a frozen state. John Henry's decision has been a major controversy, not only among close friends and family, but among former teammates, baseball fans, and commentators.

Duties as to Burial

Public policy favors the concept of what is colloquially referred to as a "decent burial." There is a strong societal interest in the proper disposition of the bodies of deceased persons. It is universally recognized that a duty is owed to both society and the deceased that the body be buried without any unnecessary delay. This duty rests upon whoever has the right to bury the decedent. At common law, the duty was imposed upon the person under whose roof the deceased died.

Some state statutes specifically name those people who are charged with the duty of having a decedent buried. Statutes of this kind have been enacted for various policy reasons, such as the general interests of public health and the protection of public welfare, as well as the relief of anxiety that some people might experience concerning the proper disposition of their remains.

Rights to Disinterment

After a body has been buried, it is considered to be in the custody of the law; therefore, disinterment is not a matter of right. The disturbance or removal of an interred body is subject to the control and direction of the court.

The law does not favor disinterment, based on the public policy that the sanctity of the grave should be maintained. Once buried, a body should not be disturbed. A court will not ordinarily order or permit a body to be disinterred unless there is a strong showing of necessity that disinterment is within the interests of justice. Each case is individually decided, based on its own particular facts and circumstances.

The courts frequently allow a change of burial place in order to enable people who were together during life to be buried together, such as husbands and wives, or family members. Disinterment for the purposes of reburial in a family plot acquired at a later date is generally authorized by law, particularly if the request is made by the surviving members of the decedent's family.

Disinterment may be allowed under certain circumstances, such as when a cemetery has been abandoned as a burial place or when it is condemned by the state by virtue of its EMINENT DOMAIN power for public improvement.

Consideration of the deceased's wishes as to his or her burial place is instrumental in a decision of a court as to whether or not a body should be disinterred. Such wishes are of paramount importance but are not necessarily controlling in all cases, such as when subsequent circumstances require a change of burial.

In states that have statutes regulating the exhumation or removal of the dead, such statutes are controlling.

Purchasing a lot in a cemetery entails a contract that obligates the purchaser and his or her survivors to abide by and observe the laws, rules, and regulations of the cemetery as well as those of the religious group that maintains it. When a dispute over the right to disinter a corpse arises, the court must make a finding of fact as to whether or not the rules or regulations of the cemetery forbid it.

Rights of Particular Persons to Disinterment The surviving spouse or next of kin of a deceased person has the right to let the body remain undisturbed. This right, however, is not absolute and can be violated when it conflicts with the public good or when the demands of justice require it.

Also, the right to change the place of burial is not absolute, and the courts take various factors into consideration when deciding whether a body should be removed for burial elsewhere, such as the occurrence of unforeseen events. If an elderly woman's husband died and was buried in New York and she subsequently moved to California, she might be allowed to have his remains removed to a different location to facilitate her visits to his grave.

The consent of the surviving spouse of a decedent to the decedent's original resting place is another factor that the court will consider in determining whether a body may be disinterred, particularly if it is against the wishes of the next of kin. Once consent has been shown, the burial will usually not be disturbed in the absence of strong and convincing evidence of new and unforeseen events.

If a body is improperly buried—that is, buried in a grave belonging to someone else who has not consented to the burial—the court will order the body removed for reburial.

A landowner who allows the burial of a deceased person on his or her property cannot later remove the body against the will of the surviving spouse or next of kin. On the other hand, the landowner is entitled to object to the removal of the remains from his or her land. A landowner may not assert that a burial was made without his or her consent if he or she fails to raise any objections within a reasonable time after the interment of the decedent.

Disinterment for Autopsies The disinterment of a body may be ordered by the courts for the purpose of an autopsy. Courts may permit a body to be exhumed and an autopsy to be performed under certain circumstances in order to discover truth and promote justice. If disinterment for the purpose of examination is to be allowed, good cause and exigent circumstances must exist to make such action necessary, such as controversy over the cause of death, or to determine in an heirship proceeding whether or not a decedent ever gave birth to a child.

Disinterment for an autopsy should not be granted arbitrarily. The law will only search for facts by this method in the rarest of cases and when there is a reasonable probability that answers will be found through disturbing interment.

Civil Liabilities

A civil action for breach of contract as to the care and burial of a corpse may be brought under certain circumstances. An individual who makes an agreement to properly bury a corpse may be subject to a lawsuit if he or she gives the body an improper burial, negligently allows the body to be taken from his or her custody, or allows the body to suffer indignities while in his or her possession.

General rules that govern damages for breach of contract have been applied in these actions.

In one case, an undertaker was sued for failure to embalm a body in such a manner that it would be preserved for a reasonably long time. The plaintiff recovered damages for illness and disability suffered when he found out that the body had disintegrated and become infested with insects as a result of the undertaker's breach of contract. However, exemplary or PUNITIVE DAMAGES are not recoverable in such cases.

Funeral or Burial Expenses Even in the absence of a contract or statute, a person may be liable for funeral or burial expenses based on his or her relationship to the decedent, such as a HUSBAND AND WIFE, or a PARENT AND CHILD. Statutes may also dictate liability. Some statutes designate the persons charged with the duty of burial but do not impose financial responsibility for burial or funeral expenses. Others impose financial liability on designated people in the order in which they are named in the statute.

Liability for burial expenses is not ordinarily imposed on someone merely because that person received a financial benefit as a result of the decedent's death. A joint tenant will not be charged with funeral expenses merely as a result of the joint ownership of property with the deceased.

Contractual Liability An individual who would not ordinarily be obligated to pay for burial or funeral expenses may accept responsibility to do so by contract. The terms of such an agreement must be very clear. The mere direction to furnish funeral services does not automatically create a contract for their payment. Liability for funeral services cannot be imposed arbitrarily. The obligation to pay the costs of a decent burial will be enforced by the law on those who should properly pay.

Although there is a lack of authority on the question of who should bear the costs of disinterment and reburial, it has generally been held as the responsibility of the person who caused it to be done.

Torts In the law of TORTS, there are a large number of cases involving the mishandling of corpses. These cases are concerned with mutilation, unauthorized disinterment, interference with proper burial, and other types of intentional disturbance. The breach of any duty as well as the unlawful invasion of any right existing with regard to a corpse is a tort for which an action may be commenced. For example, if the wrong body is delivered to a funeral home and the family discovers this when they attend the wake, they may be able to recover damages for mental suffering. Thus, the right of recovery is not necessarily based directly on injury to the corpse per se. Exemplary damages may be awarded in cases where the injury to plaintiffs was either malicious or resulting from gross negligence.

The award of damages is subject to appellate court review, and the adequacy or excessiveness of the amount awarded is dependent upon the particular circumstances of each case.

A tort action for damages in such cases may be maintained to protect the personal feelings of the survivors and, mainly, to compensate for the mental distress that has been caused.

Mutilation, Embalmment, and Autopsy An important component of the right to decent burial is the right to possession of the body in the same condition in which it is left by death. There is no additional basis for recovery where mutilation is caused simultaneously with death, as in the case of a person who dies in a train crash or who is fatally stabbed.

Some statutes authorize the delivery of corpses to medical colleges for dissection under certain conditions. It is mandatory, however, that the consent of relatives be obtained if such relatives can be found. Only a reasonable inquiry is necessary, the duty of which is on the school and on those delivering the body.

The unauthorized embalming of a body alone does not necessarily support a CAUSE OF ACTION for damages based upon mutilation or mishandling. When such unauthorized embalming occurs, combined with the resulting mental suffering of the next of kin and other such factors, a legal action may be brought. If, for example, an unauthorized embalming contrary to the decedent's religious beliefs is performed, an actionable wrong occurs for which damages may be granted.

Generally, an unauthorized autopsy is a tort. No liability exists, however, when an autopsy is performed in accordance with the consent of the individual having burial rights or pursuant to statute or the proper execution of the duties of the coroner.

Offenses and Prosecutions

Several varied offenses with respect to corpses are recognized both at common law and under statute. At common law, it is an offense to treat a corpse indecently by keeping, handling, and exposing it to view in order to create the impression that the deceased is still alive. The attempt to dispose of a corpse for gain and profit is a misdemeanor punishable at common law. Ordinarily, it is a misdemeanor for the individual possessing the duty of having a body buried to refuse or neglect to do so, or to dispose of the corpse indecently. The burning of a corpse in such a way as to incite the feelings of the public is a common-law offense.

At common law and often under statute, interfering with another person's right of burial or neglecting to bury or cremate a body within a reasonable time after death is an offense. It is also a crime to detain a body as security for the payment of a debt.

The mutilation of a corpse is an offense at common law, and under some statutes, the unauthorized dissection of a corpse is a specific criminal offense. Someone who receives a corpse for the purpose of dissection with the knowledge that it has been unlawfully removed is subject to prosecution.

The unauthorized disturbance of a grave is indictable at common law and by statute as highly contrary to acceptable community conduct. Similarly, the unauthorized disinterment of a body is a criminal offense under some statutes and at common law.

Some statutes make disinterment for specified purposes an offense; therefore, an offense is not committed unless disinterment was done for such purposes. A case where a body was exhumed and a portion of the body was removed by the next of kin for use as evidence in a MALPRACTICE trial, however, did not warrant prosecution for removal of the body because of mere wantonness, as set forth in a statute.

Under laws that proscribe opening a grave to remove anything interred, the act is forbidden per se and is conclusive as to the intent with which it is done. In such cases, no SPECIFIC

INTENT, whether felonious or otherwise, needs to be shown.

Statutes that make make disinterment an offense do not apply to exhumations made by public officials attempting to ascertain whether a crime has been committed. Similarly, statutes are not directed against cemetery authorities who wish to change the place of burial and who are authorized to do so; nor are they directed against people who had obtained the permission of those having burial rights or against those who, under necessary permit, remove the corpse of a relative for reinterment.

CORPUS

[Latin, Body, aggregate, or mass.]

Corpus might be used to mean a human body, or a body or group of laws. The term is used often in CIVIL LAW to denote a substantial or positive fact, as opposed to one that is ambiguous. The corpus of a trust is the sum of money or property that is set aside to produce income for a named beneficiary. In the law of estates, the corpus of an estate is the amount of property left when an individual dies. Corpus juris means a body of law or a body of the law. Corpus Juris Secundum (C.J.S.®) is an all-inclusive, multivolume legal encyclopedia.

CORPUS DELICTI

[Latin, The body of the crime.] The foundation or material substance of a crime.

The phrase *corpus delicti* might be used to mean the physical object upon which the crime was committed, such as a dead body or the charred remains of a house, or it might signify the act itself, that is, the murder or ARSON.

The *corpus delicti* is also used to describe the evidence that proves that a crime has been committed.

CORPUS JURIS

[Latin, A body of law.] A phrase used to designate a volume encompassing several collections of law, such as the Corpus Juris Civilis. The name of an American legal encyclopedia, the most recent edition of which is known as Corpus Juris Secundum (C.J.S.®).

CORPUS JURIS CIVILIS

[Latin, The body of the civil law.] The name given in the early seventeenth century to the col- *lection of* CIVIL LAW *based upon the compilation and* CODIFICATION *of the Roman system of* JURISPRUDENCE *directed by the Emperor* JUSTIN-IAN I *during the years from 528 to 534* A.D.

CORRELATIVE

Having a reciprocal relationship in that the existence of one relationship normally implies the existence of the other.

Mother and *child,* and *duty* and *claim,* are correlative terms.

In the law governing gas and oil transactions, a *correlative right* is the opportunity of each owner of land making up part of a common source of supply of oil and gas to produce an equitable share of such products.

In the law governing WATER RIGHTS, the correlative rights doctrine gives the individual owners of land overlying a strata of percolating waters limited rights to use the water reasonably when there is not enough water to meet the needs of everyone in the area.

CORRESPONDENCE AUDIT

An examination of the accuracy of a taxpayer's income tax return conducted through the mail by the INTERNAL REVENUE SERVICE, *which sends the taxpayer a request for proof of a particular deduction or exemption taken by either completing a special form or sending photocopies of relevant financial records.*

A correspondence audit is distinguishable from a field audit and an office audit in the manner in which it is conducted.

CORRESPONDENT

A bank, SECURITIES *firm, or other financial institution that regularly renders services for another in an area or market to which the other party lacks direct access. A bank that functions as an agent for another bank and carries a deposit balance for a bank in another city.*

Securities firms may have correspondents in foreign countries or on exchanges—organizations that provide facilities for convening purchasers and sellers of securities—of which the firms are not members.

The term *correspondent* is distinct from corespondent—a person summoned to respond to litigation, together with another person, particularly, a paramour in a DIVORCE action based on ADULTERY.

CORROBORATE

To support or enhance the believability of a fact or assertion by the presentation of additional information that confirms the truthfulness of the item.

The testimony of a witness is corroborated if subsequent evidence, such as a coroner's report or the testimony of other witnesses, substantiates it.

CORRUPTION OF BLOOD

In ENGLISH LAW, *the result of attainder, in that the attainted person lost all rights to inherit land or other hereditaments from an ancestor, to retain possession of such property and to transfer any property rights to anyone, including heirs, by virtue of his or her conviction for* TREASON *or a felony punishable by death, because the law considered the person's blood tainted by the crime.*

Attainder and the consequent corruption of the blood were abolished by English statutes and are virtually unknown in the United States.

❖ CORWIN, EDWARD SAMUEL

Edward Samuel Corwin was a noted historian, political scientist, and CONSTITUTIONAL LAW scholar.

Born January 19, 1878, on a farm in rural Plymouth, Michigan, Corwin graduated Phi Beta Kappa from the University of Michigan in 1900, where he was president of his class. He entered graduate school at the University of Pennsylvania, earning his doctor's degree in 1905. Corwin then took a teaching position at Princeton University, where he began a long association with WOODROW WILSON, then president of Princeton. Wilson had recruited Corwin to be one of the first faculty at the university to teach undergraduates in small seminars called

> "WHAT THE PRESIDENCY IS AT ANY PARTICULAR MOMENT DEPENDS IN IMPORTANT MEASURE ON WHO IS PRESIDENT."
> —EDWARD CORWIN

precepts, one of Wilson's many educational innovations. Wilson and Corwin quickly became friends, though Corwin often disagreed with Wilson's more conservative views. Corwin was selected by Wilson to update his book *Division and Reunion,* and Corwin wrote part 6 of the text, which was published in 1909.

In 1911, Corwin was promoted to full professor. Seven years later, he was appointed to a chair first occupied by Wilson, the McCormick Professor of Jurisprudence, which Corwin held until his retirement from Princeton in 1946. In 1924, he also became chair of the newly formed Department of Politics. Corwin was known at Princeton as a demanding yet popular professor; students regularly voted his courses on constitutional interpretation as the most difficult but also the most valuable.

While pursuing his teaching career, Corwin authored an impressive number of books and articles. In his first book, *National Supremacy— Treaty Power vs. State Power* (1913), Corwin explored the complex relationship between federal and state powers in foreign affairs. His later books, including *The President: Office and Powers* (1940, 3d ed. 1948), *The Twilight of the Supreme Court* (1934), *Court over the Constitution* (1938), *Constitutional Revolution, Ltd.* (1941), *The Constitution and World Organization* (1944), *Total War and the Constitution* (1947), and *Liberty against Government* (1948) established him as a preeminent authority on the Constitution. Some of his books—including *The Constitution and What It Means Today* (first published in 1920 and now called *Edward S. Corwin's Constitution and What It Means Today*) and *The Constitution of the United States of America: Analysis and Interpretation* (1949)—

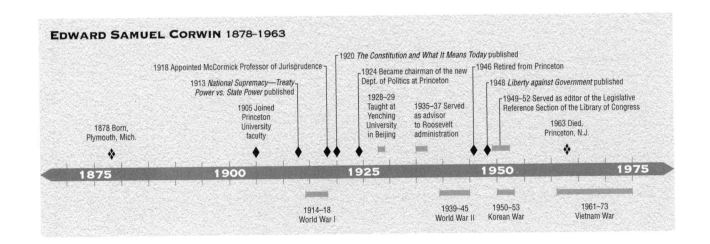

EDWARD SAMUEL CORWIN 1878–1963

1918 Appointed McCormick Professor of Jurisprudence

1920 *The Constitution and What It Means Today* published

1913 *National Supremacy—Treaty Power vs. State Power* published

1924 Became chairman of the new Dept. of Politics at Princeton

1946 Retired from Princeton

1948 *Liberty against Government* published

1905 Joined Princeton University faculty

1928–29 Taught at Yenching University in Beijing

1935–37 Served as advisor to Roosevelt administration

1949–52 Served as editor of the Legislative Reference Section of the Library of Congress

1878 Born, Plymouth, Mich.

1963 Died, Princeton, N.J.

1875   1900   1925   1950   1975

1914–18 World War I

1939–45 World War II

1950–53 Korean War

1961–73 Vietnam War

are considered standard texts in the field of constitutional law and are still kept current.

In addition to his work at Princeton, Corwin served as a visiting professor and lecturer at major universities, including Johns Hopkins University, New York University, Boston University, and Yale University. From 1928 to 1929, he was visiting professor at Yenching University, in Beijing. He was also the recipient of a number of major awards, including the American Philosophical Society's Franklin Medal in 1940 and the Henry M. Phillips Prize in the Science and Philosophy of Jurisprudence in 1942.

Corwin's expertise eventually led him to federal government service. In 1935, he became adviser to the Public Works Administration, and from 1936 to 1937, he acted as special assistant and consultant to the attorney general, on constitutional issues. He publicly supported President FRANKLIN D. ROOSEVELT's COURT-PACKING PLAN—a bill proposed by Roosevelt to expand the U.S. Supreme Court so that he could nominate justices who would uphold NEW DEAL legislation—but opposed Roosevelt's run for a third term as a breach of tradition.

Corwin maintained an active career following his retirement from Princeton in 1946. During the 1947–48 academic year, he served as a visiting professor at Columbia University, and from 1949 to 1952, he was an editor for the Legislative Reference Section, LIBRARY OF CONGRESS, where he directed a major research project that resulted in the multivolume *Constitution Annotated: Analysis and Interpretation* (1952). In 1954, he became chairman of a national committee opposed to the Bricker Amendment, S.J. Res. 1, 83d Cong., 1st Sess. (1953), which had been proposed to restrict the president's treaty-making power.

Corwin, who died in 1963 at the age of 85, carries the distinction of being the only non-lawyer among the ten legal scholars and writers most frequently cited by the Supreme Court of the United States. Corwin was acutely aware of his important role, noting that "if judges make law, so do commentators."

FURTHER READINGS

Loss, Richard. 1981. *Corwin on the Constitution.* Ithaca, N.Y.: Cornell Univ. Press.

COSIGNER

An obligor—a person who becomes obligated, under a COMMERCIAL PAPER, *such as a promis-* *sory note or check—by signing the instrument in conjunction with the original obligor, thereby promising to pay it in full.*

The cosigner may be held equally responsible for the payment of the debt or may be required to pay only upon the failure of the original obligor to do so, depending upon state law and the terms of the agreement that also determine the rights of the cosigner.

Cosigner is synonymous with the term comaker.

COSTS

Fees and charges required by law to be paid to the courts or their officers, the amount of which is specified by court rule or statute. A monetary allowance, granted by the court to a prevailing party and recoverable from the unsuccessful party, for expenses incurred in instituting or defending an action or a separate proceeding within an action.

A *bill of costs* is a certified, itemized statement of the amount of the expenses incurred in bringing or defending a lawsuit.

A *cost bond,* or bond for costs, is a promise to pay litigation expenses; it is provided by a party to an action as a guarantee of payment of any costs awarded against him or her. A cost bond also might be required of an appealing party in a civil case, in order to cover the appellee's expenses if the judgment is affirmed.

Final costs are paid at the conclusion of an action, the liability for which depends upon its final outcome.

Interlocutory costs ACCRUE during the intermediate stages of a proceeding, as distinguished from final costs.

Security for costs refers to an assurance of payment that a defendant may demand of a plaintiff who does not reside within the jurisdiction of the court, for the payment of such costs as might be awarded to the defendant.

Statutory costs are amounts specified by law to be awarded for various phases of litigation.

The award of costs is not a penalty but is a method used to reimburse an innocent party for the expenses of litigation. Costs include the payment of court fees for the commencement of the litigation; the submission of pleadings or other documents; or the SERVICE OF PROCESS or other papers by a public officer. The appointment by a court of a referee to hear extremely technical testimony, or a receiver to retain and preserve the defendant's funds or property during litigation, is included in costs. Costs entail expenditures made in interviewing parties or witnesses prior to trial and the fees that are properly paid to witnesses who testify. Printing expenses for maps or necessary documents are also included.

Costs do not include the compensation of an attorney. Expenditures in terms of the adversary nature of the proceedings, however, are included. Only when specifically authorized by law may attorney's fees be awarded in addition to costs.

Prevailing Party

A party must request the court to award costs. The court generally defers its decision until judgment is rendered, then determines whether the prevailing party is entitled to costs. The successful party is not required to prevail on every issue or to obtain the entire amount of damages sought. Costs are also awarded to a party prevailing on appeal, even though the case was lost in the trial court.

Under the Federal Rules of Civil Procedure, after which most states have patterned their own procedural rules, "costs shall be allowed as of course to the prevailing party unless the court otherwise directs." Since state laws vary on this subject, however, the applicable state law must be consulted to determine the exact rules.

Costs cannot be assessed against a party merely because of tenacity in pursuing the claim. In *Delta Air Lines, Inc. v. August*, 450 U.S. 346, 101 S. Ct. 1146, 67 L. Ed. 2d 287 (1981), the justices held that plaintiffs who lose their lawsuits in federal court after rejecting a settlement offer (a proposal to avoid litigation by compromising a disputed claim that does not admit liability) are not required to pay the defendant's costs and attorney fees.

Parties may determine the imposition of costs pursuant to an agreement. The court will enforce a contractual provision or a stipulation provided neither is UNCONSCIONABLE or the result of FRAUD.

When cases involve multiple parties—more than one plaintiff or more than one defendant—a court may allocate costs among the losing parties.

If one party is a stakeholder—a person who is or might be exposed to multiple liability from adverse claims—the stakeholder's costs are generally obtained from all the other parties to an INTERPLEADER action or from the stake: funds or property deposited by two persons with a third person, the stakeholder, for delivery to the person entitled to it upon the occurrence of a particular event.

Amount

In some instances, the amount of costs is specified by law, which restricts a party who is awarded costs to the figure permitted by law for each component of the total costs.

Security

A court may order a party to post a bond to guarantee that costs will be paid if he or she is unsuccessful. Three other alternatives provide sufficient security: a signed statement by the party that he or she will pay determined costs; the deposit of sufficient funds with the court; or the promise of a person who accepts the obligation to pay in full if the party who would normally be responsible fails to do so.

Denial of Costs

A court may deny costs, although they are ordinarily awarded to the prevailing party. Misconduct, such as the concealment of a party's actual financial circumstances, when relevant to the action, justifies the denial of costs. A court that incurs additional, unnecessary expenses as a result of inadequate preparation of the case by the counsel of the prevailing party is entitled to reject a request for costs. In such an instance, the court has the discretion to order the attorney to pay a client's costs, particularly where his or her actions were grossly negligent.

Criminal Proceedings

Costs in criminal proceedings are those expenses specified by law that have been necessarily incurred in a criminal prosecution. The concept of costs was unknown at COMMON LAW. The allowance of costs, therefore, is based on the applicable statutory provisions.

COUNCIL

A legislative body of local government. A group of persons who, whether elected or appointed, serve as representatives of the public to establish state or municipal policies and to assist the chief executive of the government unit in the performance of duties.

COUNSEL

An attorney or lawyer. The rendition of advice and guidance concerning a legal matter, contemplated form of argument, claim, or action.

The terms *counsel* and *advise* are frequently employed as synonyms for the term aid and abet to describe a person who, while not actually performing a criminal act, induced its performance or contributed to it.

The term *junior counsel* refers to the younger member of the team of attorneys retained on the same side of a case, or the one lower in the hierarchy of the firm, or one who is assigned to the preparation or trial of less significant aspects of the case.

The term of counsel refers to the description given to an attorney who is not the principal lawyer in charge of a case but who merely contributes his advice on the way it should be handled.

Where *of counsel* follows an attorney's name on a letterhead or office sign, this designation indicates that the person is employed by the firm primarily as a consultant on specialized matters, not as a full-time partner or associate.

COUNSELLOR

One engaged in the PRACTICE OF LAW; *lawyer; advocate.*

The term *counsellor* is commonly used interchangeably with attorney, except in a few states where the terms refer to lawyers of different ranks. In such states, an attorney may become a counsellor only after practicing law for a certain designated period of time and passing an additional examination.

Formerly, the Supreme Court of the United States made a distinction between a counsellor and an attorney. A counsellor was a lawyer who litigated on a party's behalf whereas an attorney at law did not do any trial work. This distinction is no longer made by the Court.

COUNT

In COMMON-LAW PLEADING *or* CODE PLEADING, *the initial statements made by a plaintiff that set forth a* CAUSE OF ACTION *to commence a civil lawsuit; the different points of a plaintiff's declaration, each of which constitute a basis for relief. In* CRIMINAL PROCEDURE, *one of several parts or charges of an indictment, each accusing the defendant of a different offense.*

The term *count* has been replaced by the word complaint in the Federal Rules of Civil Procedure and many state codes of civil procedure. Sometimes *count* is used to denote the numbered paragraphs of a complaint, each of which sets out an essential element of the claim.

Federal and state rules of criminal procedure govern the standards that a criminal count must satisfy in federal and state criminal matters.

COUNTERCLAIM

A claim by a defendant opposing the claim of the plaintiff and seeking some relief from the plaintiff for the defendant.

A counterclaim contains assertions that the defendant could have made by starting a lawsuit if the plaintiff had not already begun the action. It is governed by many of the same rules that regulate the claims made by a plaintiff except that it is a part of the answer that the defendant produces in response to the plaintiff's complaint. In general a counterclaim must contain facts sufficient to support the granting of relief to the defendant if the facts are proved to be true. These facts may refer to the same event that gave rise to the plaintiff's CAUSE OF ACTION or they may refer to an entirely different claim that the defendant has against the plaintiff. Where there is more than one party on a side, a counterclaim may be made by any defendant against any plaintiff or plaintiffs.

According to the rules governing federal CIVIL PROCEDURE, a defendant usually is required to make a counterclaim in an answer if the counterclaim arises from the same transaction or occurrence on which the plaintiff is suing. This is called a compulsory counterclaim because the claim must be made in response to the plaintiff's complaint and cannot be made later or in a separate lawsuit. There are also permissive counterclaims that may be made in the defendant's answer at a later time. A claim against the plaintiff that is based on an entirely different event is one kind of PERMISSIVE COUNTERCLAIM. For example, a man may sue a woman for money damages because of a minor injury and some property damage after their cars collided. Under the rules governing PLEADING in most courts, the woman would be required to assert a demand for money damages for the same accident in her answer to the man's complaint or she would lose the right to sue on that claim. If the man also happens to be a neighbor who borrowed the woman's chain saw and never returned it, the woman could demand return of the saw as a counterclaim or she could wait and sue the man for that at some other time. She might decide to wait in order to sue in a different court or because she does not want to argue the different circumstances of both claims before the same jury.

A defendant usually cannot make a counterclaim if it is not possible to make the same claim by starting a lawsuit. For example, a lawsuit to collect on a claim cannot be started after the period of time allowed by a STATUTE OF LIMITATIONS has run out. In certain situations, however, a defendant may assert an expired cause of action as a counterclaim. This procedure, allowed for reasons of fairness and justice, is called equitable recoupment. The court may reduce the plaintiff's money damages up to the amount of the defendant's counterclaim, but the defendant will not be allowed an affirmative recovery of money over and above the amount to which the plaintiff may be entitled.

CROSS-REFERENCES

Set-off.

COUNTERCLAIMS AND SET-OFFS AGAINST SOVEREIGNS

A comprehensive term for the vulnerability of a foreign government to retaliatory suits against it arising out of a lawsuit that it commences against a party.

The Federal Foreign Sovereign Immunities Act (28 U.S.C.A. § 1602 et seq. [1976]) provides that, in any action initiated by a foreign state or in which a foreign state intervenes, such a state is not afforded IMMUNITY regarding any counterclaim for which no immunity would have been granted if such a claim had been brought in a separate action against the foreign state. In addition, a foreign state is not entitled to immunity in cases involving counterclaims that arise out of the transaction that is the subject matter of the foreign state's claim, or to the extent that the counterclaim does not seek relief that is in excess of, or different from, the type sought by the foreign state.

The Foreign Sovereign Immunities Act codified the general rule that when a foreign government brings suit, it is deemed to have submitted to the court's jurisdiction and waives its immunity to the extent that a counterclaim arising out of the same transaction or to the extent that the counterclaim, when used defensively in the form of a SET-OFF, is not in excess of the amount of the foreign state's claims.

A foreign nation that is a plaintiff in an action brought before a court of another nation is not barred in appropriate cases from invoking the act of state doctrine to preclude a counterclaim against it. This doctrine provides that, as a general rule, the acts of one foreign state committed within its own boundaries or territories are not reviewable by the courts of another nation.

CROSS-REFERENCES

International Law; Set-off.

COUNTERFEIT

To falsify, deceive, or defraud. A copy or imitation of something that is intended to be taken as authentic and genuine in order to deceive another.

A counterfeit coin is one that may pass for a genuine coin and may include a lower denomination coin altered so that it may pass as a higher denomination coin.

COUNTERFEITING

The process of fraudulently manufacturing, altering, or distributing a product that is of lesser value than the genuine product.

Counterfeiting is a criminal offense when it involves an intent to defraud in passing off the counterfeit item. The law contains exemptions for collector's items and items that are so obviously dissimilar from the original that a reasonable person would not consider them real. However, making a poor copy is no defense if the intent to defraud exists.

Counterfeiting most commonly applies to currency and coins. It is illegal to manufacture, possess, or sell equipment or materials for use in producing counterfeit coins and currency. Federal law also prohibits producing counterfeit postmarks, postage stamps, military papers, or government SECURITIES. Counterfeiting also applies to the fraudulent manufacture and sale of other items, such as computer software, CDs, consumer products, airplane parts, and even designer dresses. An increase in this type of counterfeiting has led to a strengthening of intellectual property laws worldwide. Counterfeiting or conspiracy to distribute counterfeit goods can lead to state or federal criminal charges. Civil lawsuits also can result from allegations of counterfeiting.

Coins and Currency

Counterfeit coins appeared within a century of the first legitimate coins, which appeared in about the seventh century B.C. The severity of the punishment for counterfeiting (death, in many cultures) and the difficulty of creating counterfeit coins that did not include some metal of value (and therefore cost a significant amount to produce) kept the practice in check. However, counterfeiting flourished after the development of paper money in about A.D. 1650, especially in American colonies where counterfeit bills and even coins were sometimes more common than genuine ones. Counterfeiters had honed their skills so much that when the United States issued its first federal coins in the 1780s, the government hired an ex-counterfeiter to cut the dies. Counterfeiting boomed again during the Civil War, when the United States issued its first paper money.

For many decades, the skills and equipment that are needed to create counterfeit money confined the practice to a few professionals, and the SECRET SERVICE, the branch of the TREASURY DEPARTMENT that is charged with enforcing counterfeiting laws, discovered most counterfeiters before the money leaked into circulation. But in the late twentieth century, with the availability of new technologies, such as color copying and electronic reprographics, more counterfeit schemes emerged. The Department of the Treasury estimated that $25 million worth

of counterfeit bills were passed off in fiscal year 1994. Further damaging U.S. currency was a flood of fraudulent $100 bills on the world market. The Secret Service believes that from the early to mid 1990s, as much as $10 billion worth of nearly perfect counterfeit $100 bills were circulating internationally. It believes that the bills were printed on a press that is similar to those used by the U.S. Treasury and that had been sold to Iran in the 1970s. In 2002, authorities seized $130 million in fraudulent U.S. notes worldwide before they were circulated, and detected $44.3 million in spurious U.S. currency after it had passed into unwitting hands. But according to the Secret Service, the amount of fake money circulating has been fairly constant over recent decades, and only one or two notes in every 10,000 are counterfeit.

The increase in counterfeiting prompted Congress to pass the Counterfeit Deterrence Act of 1992 (18 U.S.C.A. § 471 note) to increase penalties. Prior to the enactment of new law, it was not a criminal act to manufacture counterfeit U.S. currency abroad. The law also instructed the Department of the Treasury to redesign paper money in order to make it more difficult to reproduce. In 1996, the first new currency was released. The bills' portraits were increased in size and moved to the left, to make

A fan displays both a counterfeit (top) and an actual ticket to the opening game of the 1996 World Series. Counterfeiting laws apply to a wide variety of products, not just currency.

room for watermark miniatures of them. Treasury officials believe that the watermark and the use of color-shifting inks make the currency nearly impossible to reproduce with current technologies.

Other Items

Counterfeiting also applies to reproductions of packaging when the intent is to defraud or to violate protections under TRADEMARK, COPYRIGHT, or patent laws. It is estimated that U.S. companies lose $8.1 billion annually in overseas business owing to violations of INTELLECTUAL PROPERTY laws. Increasing the enforcement of trademark and copyright law to discourage counterfeiting has been a focus of U.S. trade negotiations, both with individual countries and during the Uruguay Round of the international GENERAL AGREEMENT ON TARIFFS AND TRADE, Pub. L. No. 103-465, 108 Stat. 4809 (1994).

Disputes over counterfeit CDs and computer software have been at the center of U.S. trade conflicts with China for several years. Software manufacturers claim that 98 percent of the software used in China, including that used by the government, was illegally copied. Other goods that are distributed under false trademarks include cereal, razor blades, and soap. Under pressure from the United States, China strengthened its copyright and trademark laws in 1993. Lax enforcement resulted in a new trade agreement in 1995, which was designed to give U.S. manufacturers greater access to Chinese markets. Nevertheless, counterfeiting in China remains rampant.

Although most counterfeiting allegations are brought through the criminal courts, counterfeiting that violates patent, trademark, or copyright laws has resulted in civil lawsuits. For example, in 1994, a Paris court found that designer Ralph Lauren had copied a tuxedo dress pattern from Yves Saint Laurent's collection and ordered Lauren to pay his competitor $386,000 in damages.

Punishment

Under federal law, counterfeiting is a class C felony, punishable by up to 12 years in prison and/or a fine of as much as $250,000. State laws also establish penalties for counterfeiting.

FURTHER READINGS

Glaser, Lynn. 1968. *Counterfeiting in America: The History of an American Way to Wealth.* New York: Potter.

COUNTEROFFER

In contract law, a proposal made in response to an original offer modifying its terms, but which has the legal effect of rejecting it.

A counteroffer normally terminates the original offer, but the original offer remains open for acceptance if the counteroffer expressly provides that the counteroffer shall not constitute a rejection of the offer.

The UNIFORM COMMERCIAL CODE (UCC)—a body of law adopted by the states that governs commercial transactions—modifies this principle of contract law with respect to the sale of goods by providing that the "additional terms are to be construed as proposals for addition to the contract."

COUNTERSIGN

The inscription of one's name at the end of a writing, done by a secretary or a subordinate, to attest to the fact that such a writing has been signed by a principal or a superior, thereby vouching for the genuineness of the signature. To write one's name at the end of a document—in addition to the inscription of a name by another—to attest to the authenticity of the signature.

COUNTY

A political subdivision of a state, the power and importance of which varies from one state to another.

A county is distinguishable from a city or MUNICIPAL CORPORATION, since a municipal corporation has a dual character, both public and private, while a county is established by the state and is considered to be an agency thereof. Through home rule, a municipality may make certain decisions on matters of local concern, while a county is controlled by the state and does the work of state administration.

In the state of Louisiana, a state political subdivision is known as a parish. Comparable to counties, parishes have no independent existence apart from the state but possess only such authority as the state grants them.

Status

The state constitution determines the procedures for the formation of a county. Certain states require a specific minimum size population or property value before a county is created. A county government that is too small can be either completely abolished or subject to a consolidation plan designed to merge urban and rural areas. Conversely, a county that becomes too large or diverse following an extended period of development can be divided by the state to form a new county.

The principle of SOVEREIGN IMMUNITY permits states to refuse to allow anyone to sue them. This doctrine protects counties from legal action to the same extent that the states they exist in are so protected. States and counties can only be sued where state law specifically permits it.

Boundaries

Ordinarily, the boundaries of a county are set by the state legislature. If a boundary is marked by a stream or river, the county extends to the center and remains there from the time of the county's creation, even if the stream subsequently changes course. When a lake is the boundary, the county line ordinarily extends to the bank or the low water mark. A boundary that is on the ocean extends to the three-mile limit offshore.

State law provides for the revision of the boundaries of counties. Certain state statutes proscribe the creation of a new county line too close to an already existing county seat. Ordinarily voters can petition for the expansion or division of a county where population and commercial growth justify it. Although citizens have no absolute right to prevent the alteration of county lines by state legislatures, the legislature cannot change boundaries for the purpose of diluting the voting power of some of the citizens in an election.

The state retains power to designate special districts for purposes of irrigation, flood control, fire protection, or library services, which do not affect the makeup of existing counties.

Government

The government of a county is located at the county seat, a city or town where court sessions are held and duties are performed by county officers. The county board, comprised of public officials who are elected or appointed to serve on it, is the body that manages the government of the county. Other county officials include sheriffs, clerks, surveyors, and commissioners responsible for certain areas such as highways and HUMAN RIGHTS.

The state gives counties express authority to purchase and sell property and to raise funds from taxes, licenses, or bond issues. Counties have state-granted authority to make provisions for public health, safety, welfare, and morals of its residents through the enactment and enforcement of ordinances and regulations. The state, however, has the authority to make the decision whether to create courts on the county level or to use counties to designate intrastate judicial districts.

COUPON

A certificate evidencing the obligation to pay an installment of interest or a dividend that must be cut and presented to its issuer for payment when it is due.

Coupons are usually attached to a document, such as a promissory note, bond, share of stock, or a bearer instrument. A coupon is a written contract for the payment of a definite amount on a specified date according to the terms of the main document from which it must be separated for presentation for payment. Each coupon represents a separate promise by its issuer to pay its holder on the due date. Failure to do so will support a CAUSE OF ACTION for breach of contract.

COURSE OF DEALING

A clearly recognizable pattern of previous conduct between parties to a business transaction.

The course of dealing between parties to an action is examined by a court in ascertaining what the parties intended when they entered into a contract. The supposition is that the parties drew up the contract in view of the customary manner in which business had been transacted prior to the signing of the contract.

In a breach-of-contract action, evidence of the course of dealing is admissible in order to interpret ambiguities in the contract, but not to effectuate an alteration or contradiction of the contract's provisions. A term that was seemingly unambiguous when the contract was entered into might subsequently prove to be problematic.

Course of dealing is distinguishable from both COURSE OF PERFORMANCE and TRADE USAGE. Course of performance refers to a pattern of conduct that occurs subsequent to approval of the contract terms. Trade usage entails behavior that is the standard of conformity for a majority of businesses engaged in a particular business or commercial venture.

Course of dealing safeguards the expectations of the parties and augments the certainty of their transactions, based upon their prior experiences with each other.

The concepts of course of dealing, course of performance, and trade usage in the context of contract law are derived largely from the work of LINTON CORBIN, who did not believe that courts should be bound by the so-called four corners of a contract or to the "plain meaning" to those terms. Corbin was instrumental in the drafting of the UNIFORM COMMERCIAL CODE (UCC), which governs commercial agreements and transactions in most states. The UCC defines course of dealing in its general provisions (U.C.C. § 1-205). The term applies, for example, to the laws governing contracts for the sale of goods, negotiable instruments, and SECURED TRANSACTIONS.

COURSE OF EMPLOYMENT

As set forth in WORKERS' COMPENSATION *acts, the time, place, and conditions under which an on-the-job accident occurs. The performance of an act that an employee might prudently do while in the appropriate area during working hours.*

In the event that an employee causes an injury to another or another's property, it is necessary to ascertain whether the employee was acting within the course of employment. The employer is legally responsible for the damages if the employee caused them while performing a job. If a driver for a transportation firm is involved in an accident with a pedestrian, for example, the pedestrian can sue both the driver and the firm. Under the doctrine of RESPONDEAT SUPERIOR, an employer can be held liable for a TORT, a civil wrong other than breach of contract, committed by an employee operating within the scope of the employee's employment.

Workers' compensation laws require the payment of compensation from the employer to the employee in conformity with a schedule for a particular category of injury, provided that the employee is injured during the course of employment. The course of employment encompasses the actual period of employment and the period during which the employee, while on the employer's premises, prepares to commence or to depart from work, such as by changing clothes. Employer-sponsored recreational activities are also considered part of the course of employment when organized, encouraged, or supported by the employer for business purposes, such as the promotion of efficiency. The test is whether the recreation inured to the employee's exclusive benefit or whether the employer had some interest in the activity. Injuries suffered by an employee while observing, participating, or traveling to or from recreational activities sponsored in whole or in part by the employer but conducted on the employee's time and off the employer's premises are not compensable.

Where the recreational activity is part of the employee's compensation, an injury is compensable. If an employer, for business reasons, arranges and pays for an employee to join and participate in a social or athletic club, the employee's activities are an incident of the course of employment and an injury is, therefore, compensable.

The periods during which an employee prepares for work while at home or commutes to his or her place of business are not within the course of employment, and, therefore, are not covered by workers' compensation laws.

COURSE OF PERFORMANCE

Evidence of the conduct of parties concerning the execution of obligations under a contract requiring more than one performance that is used for the purpose of interpreting the contract's provisions.

Course of performance refers to the systematic and uniform conduct in which parties engage after they enter into a contract. The intent of the parties in regard to the meaning of the agreement is reliably ascertainable through the application of course of performance only when a contract requires a repetitive series of performances. There must be more than one performance, but no particular number is required. The fewer the performances, the more probable it is that such performances cannot constitute a course of performance.

If a party accepts a course of performance without objection, his or her ACQUIESCENCE is relevant to determining the meaning of the contract. The recipient of the performance need not expressly assent to the performance; the lack of an objection is sufficient. Unless there has been acceptance without objection, a party who performs cannot benefit from the application of course of performance.

Sometimes the acts of the parties may be inconsistent with the pertinent contractual language. A party may argue that the meaning of the agreement is unequivocal—that the course of performance is inconsistent with the contract provisions—and, therefore, that the express terms of the contract should predominate over the course of performance.

The prevailing view is that no contractual term is so clearly defined that a party cannot demonstrate the way in which the parties actually applied it. Pursuant to the admissibility of the course of performance, and assuming that this evidence is credible, the language selected by the parties has the meaning that they had ascribed to it, and, therefore, no inconsistency exists between the contract provisions and the course of performance.

A minority of jurisdictions hold that some words have a PLAIN MEANING and, consequently, that course of performance is inadmissible to show their meaning when they are not ambiguous. Other courts reason that it is relevant to show that there has been either a waiver, an intentional relinquishment of a known right, or a modification of the contract before the application of course of performance.

The concept of course of performance in the context of contract law, along with such concepts as course of dealing and TRADE USAGE, is derived largely from the work of ARTHUR LINTON CORBIN. One of the leading theorists in the field of contract law in the twentieth century, Corbin did not believe that courts should be bound by a formal reading of the "four corners" of the contract. Corbin was instrumental in the drafting of the UNIFORM COMMERCIAL CODE (UCC), which governs commercial agreements and transactions in most states. Under the UCC, courts may consider course of performance of the parties in order to determine, for example, whether the parties have formed a contract for the sale or lease of goods (U.C.C. §§ 2-208, 2A-207).

CROSS-REFERENCES

Plain-Meaning Rule.

COURT

A judicial tribunal established to administer justice. An entity in the government to which the administration of justice is delegated. In a broader sense, the term may also refer to a legislative assembly; a deliberative body, such as the General Court of Massachusetts, which is its legislature. The words court, judge, *or* judges, *when used in laws, are often synonymous. A kangaroo court is a mock legal proceeding that disregards law and justice by issuing a biased, predetermined judgment regardless of the evidence presented before it.*

Judicial courts are created by the government through the enactment of statutes or by constitutional provisions for the purpose of enforcing the law for the public good. They are impartial forums for the resolution of controversies between parties who seek redress from a violation of a legal right. Both civil and criminal matters may be heard in the same court, with different court rules and procedures for each.

The public has a right to attend judicial proceedings. This right ensures that the proceedings will be conducted in a fair and unbiased manner. Anyone who wants may attend trials as a spectator unless a judge has closed a courtroom for particular proceedings in order to maintain order, to assure DUE PROCESS OF LAW, or to protect a witness's identity.

The U.S. Judicial System consists of 52 separate court systems, plus territorial courts, in the United States. Each state and the District of Columbia has its own independent system, and the United States government maintains federal courts throughout the country. The federal courts and state courts are independent of each other. The federal courts are authorized by Article III, Section 2, of the Constitution to hear controversies that especially affect federal interests. Sometimes the existence of two parallel court systems in every state creates a strain and raises important issues concerning FEDERALISM, the relationship between the states and the United States. For some of these questions, the SUPREME COURT OF THE UNITED STATES makes the final determination that is binding on everyone.

Most courts have a multilevel structure. A few states have a two-tiered system, but the federal government and most states use a three-tiered model. All litigants have an opportunity to argue their cases before a trial-level court, and subsequently they may be able to pursue the matter further up through two levels of appeals courts.

In the federal court system the trial-level court is the district court. Each state contains at least one district court, and most of these courts have more than one judge available to try cases. Litigants may file an appeal with the U.S. Court of Appeals that has jurisdiction over that district if they are unhappy with the lower court's decision, and the decision is the type that may be appealed. The United States is divided into 13 judicial circuits, and one court of appeals sits in

The First Virtual State Court

U.S. courts have adopted various new technologies that can assist in the administration of justice, but the state of Michigan took the most radical step in 2002 when it authorized the creation of the first fully functioning cybercourt in the country. This virtual court, once fully operational, would allow attorneys to file court appearances, briefs, and other court documents online. Specially trained district and circuit judges would serve three-year assignments on this court.

The cybercourt in its first incarnation is to be limited in jurisdiction to business disputes with an amount in controversy exceeding $25,000. The court would not use juries, as it was designed to assist businesses that need quick resolutions of disputes, such as those involving trade secrets. Critics have pointed out that the system would not allow judges to examine evidence physically or even to view evidence with any certainty, given the limitations in viewing screen resolution in many video or real-time communications. In addition, critics contend that many business disputes involve issues of federal law and diversity jurisdiction, thereby denying this court the opportunity to hear many cases.

The Michigan Supreme Court proposed new rules to govern the operation of the cybercourt. These rules addressed: the filing of pleadings and other documents via the **INTERNET**; the prevention of tampering with electronic documents; how testimony would be given via the Internet, videoconferencing, or interactive video; how serving notice on parties to a lawsuit via **E-MAIL** will work; and how court proceedings will be made accessible to the public.

The Michigan cybercourt was supposed to be operational by late 2002 but by mid-2003 it was still on the drawing board. In June 2003 the state legislature debated whether to provide $2 million to establish it in three locations.

FURTHER READINGS

Issenberg, Doug. 2001. "See You in Cybercourt?" *Internet World* (April 1).

"Michigan Bill Will Create Cybercourt." 2002. *Associated Press* (January 9). Available online at <www.ap.org/> (accessed September 1, 2003).

"Michigan House Battles Over Cybercourt Funding." *Michigan Technology News.* Available online at <www.mitechnews .com/registry/technews/breakingnews.htm> (accessed July 1, 2003).

"Michigan Wants to Speed Business Dispute Resolution with Cybercourt." 2001. *Associated Press* (February 23). Available online at <www.ap.org/> (accessed September 1, 2003).

Stephens, Gene. 2001. "Trial Run for Virtual Court." *Futurist* (November-December).

"Website of the Week." 2002. *National Law Journal* (February 11).

"Wired Future for Courtrooms." 2001. *Associated Press* (March 1). Available online at <www.ap.org/> (accessed September 1, 2003).

CROSS-REFERENCES

Courtroom Television Network; Internet.

each of twelve geographical circuits. The Court of Appeals for the Federal District sits in the thirteenth district to hear cases formerly entertained in the Court of Claims and the Court of Customs and Patents Appeals, which were abolished by the enactment of the Federal Courts Improvement Act of 1982 (28 U.S.C.A. § 1 note). Each court of appeals has four or more judges who sit either as panels of three or as a whole to review the decisions of district courts and to review or enforce the orders of many federal. administrative agencies. If a court sits as a whole, it is called an *en banc* court. Litigants who lose a cause in a court of appeals may be able to carry the appeal to the U.S. Supreme Court.

Cases in state courts may also proceed from the trial-level court up through appeals in an appellate court and then to a state supreme court. Different systems assign different functions to the state supreme court, which is usually the court of last resort, but this is not the case in every state. When an issue based on the federal Constitution, a treaty, or a federal statute is involved, the U.S. Supreme Court may agree to hear an appeal from the state supreme court.

The organization of a court and its personnel is determined by the law that created that court and by the court's own rules. Generally, the papers for each lawsuit must be filed with the clerk of the court. The clerk and his or her staff organize all of the records for the judges assigned to the court. Each judge may have a law secretary or law clerk, or there may be several clerks who perform legal research and assist in the drafting of decisions, orders, and memoranda. Court officers, court attendants, or bailiffs are available to give information and to maintain order and peace around the courthouse. Interpreters may be kept on call to translate for witnesses and parties who do not speak English well. A county sheriff or federal marshal has the responsibility for enforcement of various judicial orders. PROBATION officers are usually civilian employees who assist the court by administering the probation system for criminal offenders and supervise court-ordered custody or payments of money, especially CHILD SUPPORT. A court stenographer, or court reporter creates a written record of proceedings word for word.

Attorneys are called officers of the court because they have a dual responsibility to protect the integrity of the legal system and pursue their clients' claims. An attorney who has been admitted to the bar in one state is entitled to practice in the courts of that state but that does not entitle him or her to practice in the courts of another state, in a federal court, or in the Supreme Court. In order to do so, he or she must qualify and be sworn in separately.

A term is the time during which a court is authorized to hear cases, and a session is one of those periods in a term when a judge is actually hearing cases. A regular term is one called for by law, and a special term may be called by a judge or other official when the circumstances warrant it. A jury may hear a case during the jury term while a motion for relief may be made to the court during the motion term. A general term sometimes means the time that all of the judges of a court sit together, or en banc, but occasionally it refers to a single judge's hearing all of the cases on a particular subject.

Laws or court rules fix the particular terms or sessions when a court is open for judicial business. If none is fixed, a court is open at all times. Any judicial action taken by a judge of the court is not invalid in such circumstances because of the time when it was taken, but it

does not necessarily mean that the courthouse doors are unlocked 24 hours a day.

Rules of CIVIL PROCEDURE and of CRIMINAL PROCEDURE regulate practice in the courts. The rules spell out rights and the manner of proceeding in regard to a court's jurisdiction and venue, the commencement of an action, parties, motions, subpoenas, pretrial discovery, juries, evidence, the order of a trial, provisional remedies, judgments, and appeals.

COURT ADMINISTRATOR

An officer of the judicial system who performs administrative and clerical duties essential to the proper operation of the business of a court, such as tracking trial dates, keeping records, entering judgments, and issuing process.

A go-between for judges, attorneys, and clients, the court administrator essentially runs the court's business. The behind-the-scenes work of this position ranges from scheduling trial dates to handling all official correspondence. Courts produce volumes of paper; the administrator's office processes them, accepting lawsuit filings, authenticating court documents, and issuing writs and summonses. Formerly known as the clerk, the post has evolved since the mid-1980s as technology has streamlined some elements of the justice system.

State and county administrators do essentially the same job. Unlike those in past decades, nearly all administrators today are appointed by judges. Judicial appointment has helped take politics out of this powerful position, and by the mid-1990s, only the state of Montana still preserved an elected post for its court administrator. State administrators operate under statutory authority that entitles them to execute court affairs and provides an annual staff budget. County-level administrators are generally chosen by committee, with funding for their offices commonly generated by court fees.

Contemporary trends in court management have reshaped this traditional office. Technology has led the change: where once courts relied entirely on paper records, computer databases are fast becoming the norm. For example, using computer software to track trial dates has begun to replace the ancient practice of relying on the court docket. Beyond allowing for greater flexibility, this new method also turns the tables on lawyers who have customarily controlled the pace of cases. A related trend in the mid-1990s, introduced by Minnesota, is toward uniformity:

the state's General Rules of Practice place all jurisdictions under the same uniform rules, aiming to save time in scheduling as well as ensuring that local attorneys have no advantage over out-of-state attorneys.

COURT COMMISSIONERS

Persons appointed by a judge to find facts, to hear testimony, or to perform a specific function connected with certain types of cases.

An attorney, a judge, a retired judge, or any person with the background necessary to comprehend complex legal matters may be a court commissioner, although a court commissioner is not a judge. The court that the court commissioner serves ordinarily reviews his or her decisions.

Commissioners may take testimony in hearings to determine the validity of a will; proceedings concerning the entry of default judgments or stipulations; pretrial conferences in criminal cases; or proceedings involving family court petitions to modify ALIMONY or CHILD SUPPORT.

State law governs the powers of court commissioners.

COURT HAND

In old English practice, the peculiar style and form of writing in which court records were transcribed from the earliest period to the reign of George II, circa 1760.

This form of Latin shorthand was characteristically concise, strong, and absolutely uniform even though it was handwritten. Due to the numerous and unusual abbreviations and contractions, proficiency in the art of court hand was an important step in entering the "clerkship" profession. Court hand imported to the ancient record the essential quality of durability.

COURT-MARTIAL

A tribunal that tries violations of military CRIMINAL LAW. It often refers to the entire military justice process, from actual court proceedings to punishment.

First established in eighteenth-century U.S. law, the court-martial is today the result of tremendous modernization that has made it similar to a trial in federal district court. Defendants are presumed innocent until proven guilty, accorded considerable legal protections, and guaranteed the right to appeal. The court-

martial is governed by the UNIFORM CODE OF MILITARY JUSTICE (10 U.S.C.A. §§ 801–940), a federal law that Congress originally passed in 1950, but that legislators, presidents, and the U.S. Supreme Court have since changed several times. Significant reforms of the court-martial now grant military defendants essentially the same DUE PROCESS rights that are afforded defendants in civilian courts.

The Uniform Code of Military Justice vests in the president of the United States the authority to draft and to amend the Manual for Courts-Martial, United States (10 U.S.C.A. §§ 801-946). This document includes a number of procedural rules in the military justice system, including the Rules for Courts-Martial and Military Rules of Evidence. These rules are practiced by judge advocates, who serve as the attorneys in the military justice system. While many of the rules are similar or analogous to procedural rules in the civil justice system, such as the Federal Rules of Criminal Procedure and the FEDERAL RULES OF EVIDENCE, the military rules provide specific rights and procedures that do not have civil counterparts. In 1998, President WILLIAM JEFFERSON CLINTON approved several amendments to the Manual, including those related to pre- and post-trial confinement, trials, sentencing, substantive criminal offenses and defenses, post-trial procedures, and the authority of the Judge Advocate General.

Three levels of courts exist in the military justice system: military trial courts, courts of military review, and the U.S. Court of Military Appeals. Courts-martial are handled by the lowest courts, which are presided over by military trial judges who are quite similar to U.S. district court judges. These judges are commissioned officers selected by judge advocates according to rules established by Congress, and their responsibility for individual cases begins and ends with the court-martial process. The military trial courts are organized by the type of courts-martial that they address—summary, special, and general, which reflect increasingly serious charges and punishments.

Just as trials in civilian criminal courts are the result of work by police officers and prosecutors, courts-martial are preceded by a formal investigation. During questioning, military suspects have the same FIFTH AMENDMENT right to remain silent, as do civilians, as well as some additional rights. Civilian police officers must read a suspect the *Miranda* rights at the time of arrest. Article 31 of the Uniform Code of Military Justice requires military investigators to go even further: As soon as suspicion focuses on a suspect during interrogation, they must advise him or her of the right to remain silent. This stringent requirement places a higher burden on military investigators to protect suspects' rights, and later it can become grounds for the dismissal of charges if it is not followed.

Military laws provide generous protections to defendants before a case goes to trial. These include complete pretrial discovery, allowing defendants free access to witnesses and evidence, as well as a requirement that prosecutors reveal the names of witnesses who will be called during all stages of the trial. In addition, the government must provide defendants with expert witnesses at its own expense; judges may delay or dismiss trials if prosecutors fail to do so. The military judge is empowered to hear pretrial motions on a broad range of issues, ranging from alleged violations of the defendant's constitutional rights to the admissibility of evidence. Before the case is heard, defendants have the choice of trial by judge or jury, and enlisted members can request that at least one-third of the court be enlistees. Defendants may also elect to be provided with military counsel or to hire a civilian attorney.

The court-martial closely resembles a trial in federal court. Military judges have the same authority as federal judges to rule on all matters of law and to give orders to the prosecution and the defense on such procedural matters as arguments, motions, and challenges. Two differences are particularly significant. First, whereas few civilian courts allow jurors to pose questions to witnesses, military courts have long permitted the practice. Jurors may submit written questions, which both the prosecution and the defense read in order to prepare any possible objections, which also must be in writing. The judge then decides which questions to allow. Second, military judges have a greater duty than do federal judges to review a defendant's entry of a guilty plea. This duty is designed to protect defendants from PLEADING guilty because of coercion, which could be more likely in the military because of its strict code of discipline and obedience to authority. MILITARY LAW requires judges to reject the plea at any stage of a proceeding if any hint of coercion is found.

The right to appeal convictions in military courts is different from that in civilian courts. Options for appeal are determined by the type of court-martial: Summary court-martial convictions, which are for lesser offenses, offer only the right to appeal to the commander who convened the court, and to make a further petition for review to the judge advocate general. Convictions in special and general courts-martial can be appealed to higher authorities, but the type of sentence handed down also governs a convicted party's rights. If the sentence is less than six months' confinement or a bad-conduct discharge, the case is reviewed by a legal officer in the convening authority's staff judge advocate's office, with no further appeals other than a right to petition the judge advocate general.

Greater convictions are automatically appealed to a court of military review, which considers matters of fact and law. Consisting largely of higher-ranking military judges, these courts exist for each branch of the military and have a total of 31 appellate military judges. The Uniform Code of Military Justice requires them to review serious sentences such as confinement of one year or more, dishonorable discharge, or dismissal of officers or cadets. Sentences to general officers and flag officers are also reviewed automatically. In all cases, defendants are granted free counsel for their appeals.

At the next level, the Court of Military Appeals—composed of five civilian judges who are appointed by the president of the United States—may decide to hear any petition from an unsuccessful appeal to a court of military review.

Finally, once military remedies have been exhausted, federal courts, including the U.S. Supreme Court, will review a court-martial conviction for claims of denial of constitutional rights.

FURTHER READINGS

Ferris, Andrew M. 1994. "Military Justice: Removing the Probability of Unfairness." *University of Cincinnati Law Review* (fall).

Fuger, Stanley T. 1992. "Military Justice: Variation on a Theme." *Connecticut Bar Journal* (June).

Konecke, Eric J. 1995. "The Appointments Clause and Military Judges." *Seton Hall Constitutional Law Journal* (spring).

Wiener, Frederick B. 1990. "American Military Law in the Light of the First Mutiny Act's Tricentennial." *Military Law Review* (fall).

ANY LAST WORDS? THE EVOLUTION OF THE COURT-MARTIAL

Throughout most of its two-hundred-year history, the court-martial was the ogre of U.S. law. Modeled on sixteenth-century European ideas about discipline and punishment, courts-martial worked smoothly. Commanders ran them, defendants had few rights, and punishments were **ARBITRARY**: disobedient soldiers were fined, jailed, or discharged, and deserters flogged or hanged. **CONSTITUTIONAL LAW** rarely got in the way. Between 1775 and 1950, the U.S. military scarcely altered its methods. It was not until the **VIETNAM WAR** era that reform came at the hands of federal lawmakers and judges. Today, the military tribunal resembles the average federal court.

Historically, the military justice system has always been distinct from the civilian court system. It formally began in 1775 when the **CONTINENTAL CONGRESS** enacted the first American Articles of War, closely modeled on the British Articles of War, which had their roots in sixteenth-century Europe. Under the articles, military justice had a simple two-sided goal: to promote good behavior and punish bad behavior. It specified civilian offenses such as murder and **LARCENY**, and military offenses such as disobedience, disrespect to officers, and desertion. To try defendants for violations, it established a simple tribunal made up of officers under the control of their commander. Accused parties had few if any of the **DUE PROCESS** and appeal rights enjoyed by

defendants in civilian courts. No standard rules for punishment existed; as with all matters in a court-martial, punishment was decided completely at the discretion of the commander.

Free from the constraints of civilian courts, early courts-martial produced stark results. General **GEORGE WASHINGTON**, like other commanders, understood the court-martial's potential for keeping order in the ranks. During the Revolutionary War, he ordered his troops to watch the execution of fellow soldiers who had been convicted of desertion. Discipline—often severe—remained the hallmark of the court-martial for the next century. Few citizens or politicians objected because military culture was highly esteemed. Soldiers who brought shame on the service were thought to deserve whatever they got.

IN FOCUS

Despite earnest efforts, few early critics of the court-martial achieved much. By the mid-1800s, scholarly calls for reform began with the work of John O'Brien, an Army lieutenant who wrote *A Treatise on American Military Laws, and the Practice of Courts Martial: with Suggestions for Their Improvements* in 1846. O'Brien argued for lessening the influence of commanders, enacting more uniform rules, and clearly establishing specific punishments. But neither lawmakers nor the courts were very impressed. Congress had always accepted the distinction between civilian and military justice, and

in a number of decisions, the U.S. Supreme Court consistently upheld the constitutionality of the court-martial system.

The onset of **WORLD WAR** I brought changes in the form of new Articles of War (Act of August 29, 1916, ch. 418, §§ 3–4, 39 Stat. 619, 650). Defense counsel was guaranteed "if such counsel be reasonably available," but there was no provision for appealing convictions. The author of the revision, Judge Advocate General Enoch H. Crowder, had scoffed at the latter idea in testimony before the U.S. Senate:

> In a military code there can be, of course, no provision for courts of appeal. Military discipline and the purposes which it is expected to [serve] will not permit of the vexatious delays. . . . However, we safeguard the rights of an accused, and I think we effectively safeguard them, by requiring every case to be appealed in [the] sense [that commanding generals must approve every sentence, and sentences of death or dismissal require additional confirmation by the president] (S. Rep. No. 130, 64th Cong., 1st Sess. 34–35).

As a startling example soon showed, these protections had little if any value. In November 1917, a court-martial tried sixty-three members of the all-black Twenty-fourth Infantry Division of the U.S. Army who were charged with a vari-

---

COURT OF APPEAL

An intermediate federal judicial tribunal of review that is found in thirteen judicial districts, called circuits, in the United States.

A state judicial tribunal that reviews a decision rendered by an inferior tribunal to determine whether it made errors that warrant the reversal of its judgment.

U.S. COURTS OF APPEALS were created by Congress in 1891 and were known until 1948 as U.S. Circuit Courts of Appeals. Such courts have appellate jurisdiction over the majority of cases decided by U.S. District Courts except those cases in which the court has made an **INTERLOCUTORY** order regarding an **INJUNCTION**; such cases are directly reviewable by the

ety of offenses, including mutiny and murder, stemming from a race riot in Houston in which over a dozen people had died. The court-martial convicted fifty-eight men. Thirteen were sentenced to death and hanged the following morning. Despite General Crowder's assurances, neither the president nor even the military authorities in Washington, D.C., had been informed. According to regulations, the authority of a department commander was sufficient in time of war to confirm death sentences and the commander's order needed no further confirmation because he was the convening authority who had started the court-martial.

The Houston hangings prompted an immediate tightening of the rules for death sentences, but the experience of drafted men in World War I and WORLD WAR II brought about greater change. Called up to fight in the millions—and also court-martialed in the millions—civilians disliked their taste of military justice. As a result of public outcry, Senate hearings in 1917 led to a 1920 revision of the Articles of War. This revision provided for preliminary investigations, defense counsel, the presence of a legally trained member at every court-martial, and higher review of all sentences of death, dismissal, or dishonorable discharge. The right to defense counsel for soldiers was ahead of its time; civilians would not have this right universally recognized by the U.S. Supreme Court for several more decades. The new Articles of War also provided for automatic appellate review of convictions.

In practice, not all the provisions of the new articles were followed. Resources for carrying them out were limited, and commanders could not always be counted on to depart from tradition. The aftermath of World War II, in which some 2 million soldiers faced court-martial, brought even greater calls for reform.

Major reform began in 1950. Congress passed the UNIFORM CODE OF MILITARY JUSTICE (10 U.S.C.A. §§ 801–940), a sweeping reform of the military justice system applying to all branches of the service. This code created the Court of Military Appeals, a three-judge civilian body designed to review certain convictions. The code also extended greater protections to defendants: lawyers had to be assigned to defend them, and they now enjoyed significant due process rights. On the other hand, the military retained all other authority over the administration of military justice. The code kept the traditional hierarchy of three courts convened by commanders at increasingly higher command levels with escalating punishments—summary, special, and general courts-martial. It established "law officers" who functioned like judges, but it retained much of the traditional model of command control, which gave to commanders the power to appoint the investigating officer, counsel, and court members (with the enlisted accused having the right to request that one-third be enlisted members). And it extended court-martial jurisdiction over both service members and certain classes of civilians.

Further reform came through the courts and Congress. In 1955, the U.S. Supreme Court held that discharged service members could not be court-martialed for crimes committed while they were on active duty (United States ex rel. Toth v. Quarles, 350 U.S. 11, 76 S. Ct. 1, 100 L. Ed. 8). In 1969 the Court held that a case could be tried at court-martial only if the offense was connected to the defendant's military service in O'Callahan v. Parker, 395 U.S. 258, 89 S. Ct. 1683, 23 L. Ed. 2d 291. In 1970, the Court of Military Appeals held that civilian employees of the military overseas could not be subjected to court-martial (United States v. Averette, 19 U.S.C.M.A 363).

Congress brought reform with the Military Justice Act of 1968 (Pub. L. 90-632, Oct. 24, 1968, 82 Stat. 1335), which revamped the Uniform Code of Military Justice. It accomplished several key changes: (1) court-martial procedures were made to resemble more closely those of U.S. district courts; (2) the law officer was changed to a military judge, with functions and powers like those of a federal district judge; (3) the military judge was protected from influence by military authorities; (4) new intermediate appellate courts of military review were created in each service; and (5) defendants were given the choice of trial by judge or by jury. Additional reform came in the Military Justice Act of 1983 (Pub. L. 98-209, Dec. 6, 1983, 97 Stat. 1393), which specifically provided for review of Court of Military Appeals decisions by the U.S. Supreme Court. By 1987, military justice had improved to the point that the U.S. Supreme Court overturned O'Callahan and returned to the military greater authority to conduct courts-martial (Solorio v. United States, 483 U.S. 435, 107 S. Ct. 2924, 97 L. Ed. 2d 364).

Today the court-martial functions smoothly as a system governed by law. In every significant way, the modern court-martial is at least the equivalent of a federal criminal trial.

SUPREME COURT OF THE UNITED STATES. Federal courts of appeals are also empowered to review orders of many federal administrative agencies, such as the NATIONAL LABOR RELATIONS BOARD.

Cases before the court of appeals are usually heard by a panel of three judges, but in some circuit cases, actions involving significant constitutional questions are heard en banc, with all the judges serving on the court present to decide the case by a majority vote. In 1982 Congress enacted the Federal Courts Improvement Act (96 Stat. 25; 28 U.S.C.A. § 1 note) creating the Court of Appeals for the Federal Circuit which commenced hearing cases on October 1, 1982, and constitutes the thirteenth circuit in the United States. The Court of Appeals for the Federal Circuit provides a national forum for the uniform application and enforcement of law in cases involving similar issues, particularly those involving patent and public contracts law, which in the past were often decided differently from circuit to circuit, necessitating appeal to the Supreme Court for a definitive answer. This court was established from the merger of the Federal Court of Claims and the Court of Customs and Patent Appeals. Although structurally similar to the 12 other courts of appeals, it differs from them in that its intermediate appellate jurisdiction is based upon subject matter, not geography, and it hears appeals from all federal circuits. This topical approach toward adjudication results from the new court assuming appellate jurisdiction from cases formerly brought before the Court of Claims and the Court of Patent Appeals. The court also entertains appeals from the Court of International Trade, the PATENT AND TRADEMARK OFFICE, the MERIT SYSTEMS PROTECTION BOARD, and other agencies.

In some states, the court of appeals is an intermediate appellate tribunal that reviews the decisions of lower courts on appeal. Its decisions are, however, subject to review by the highest appellate tribunal in the state if the unsuccessful party files an appeal and the justices agree to hear the case. When the state court of appeals is the intermediate level of appellate review, it possesses mandatory jurisdiction; litigants have a statutory right to appeal their cases to it.

State courts of appeals are frequently courts of last resort when their decisions are final and are not subject to review by any other state tribunal. When it is the highest appellate court in the state, the court of appeals has discretionary jurisdiction; it selects the decisions it will review. If a case presents questions involving federal statutes or the Constitution, the U.S. Supreme Court might accept the case for review of the judgment rendered by the state courts of appeals.

There might be two separate systems of state courts of appeals: one for the review of civil cases and one for the appeal of criminal matters.

CROSS-REFERENCES

Appellate Court; Federal Courts.

COURT OF CLAIMS

A state judicial tribunal established as the forum in which to bring certain types of lawsuits against the state or its political subdivisions, such as a county. The former designation given to a federal tribunal created in 1855 by Congress with original

jurisdiction—initial authority—to decide an action brought against the United States that is based upon the Constitution, federal law, any regulation of the executive department, or any express or implied contracts with the federal government.

Such courts are created by statute or constitution and can entertain only actions specified by law, such as those involving violations of provisions of the state constitution or law or based upon breach of government contracts.

The Federal Courts Improvement Act of 1982 (28 U.S.C.A. § 1 et seq.) abolished the U.S. Court of Claims and established the Court of Appeals for the Federal Circuit and the U.S. Claims Court to share various aspects of the jurisdiction of the former court.

COURT OF PROBATE

A judicial body that exercises jurisdiction over the acceptance of wills as valid documents and over the management and settlement of the estates of minors or of spendthrifts, of mentally incompetent persons, and of habitual drunkards.

Such courts possess a limited jurisdiction in civil and criminal cases in some states. In some jurisdictions, they are also called ORPHANS' COURTS and surrogate courts.

COURT OPINION

A statement that is prepared by a judge or court announcing the decision after a case is tried; includes a summary of the facts, a recitation of the applicable law and how it relates to the facts, the rationale supporting the decision, and a judgment; and is usually presented in writing, though occasionally an oral opinion is rendered.

Court opinions are the pronouncements of judges on the legal controversies that come before them. In a common-law system, court opinions constitute the law by which all controversies are settled. Attorneys analyze prior opinions on similar legal issues, attempting to draw parallels between their case and favorable court opinions and to distinguish unfavorable opinions. Judges study relevant opinions in rendering their decisions.

The majority of court opinions are not released for publication. Those that are released by the courts are collected in law books called reporters. Each state has at least one reporter that contains the opinions of its courts, and the nation has several reporters that contain the opinions of the federal courts.

Who's Suing Whom? Terms and Abbreviations in Case Titles

The titles of court cases frequently contain terms and abbreviations that help to indicate the nature of the dispute. The accompanying chart iden- tifies and explains many of the terms that may appear in case titles.

Term	Definition	Example
ad hoc	For this; for this purpose	*Capital City Press v. Mouton, Judge ad Hoc*
ad litem	For the suit; for the litigation	*Estate of Langhorn v. Laws, Administrator Ad Litem*
adm'r	Administrator	*Grievance Adm'r v. Lange*
adm'r de bonis non	Administrator of the remainder of a partially settled estate.	*Vogel, Adm'r De Bonis Non v. Wells*
ad valorem	According to value; a tax imposed on value of property	*Aerospace Workers Inc. v. Dept. of Revenue, Division of ad Valorem Taxes*
a.k.a., a/k/a	Also known as	*Luis Barras, a.k.a. Luis Ramos v. State of Texas*
alter ego	The other self (*Alter ego* asserts that the defendants are one for purposes of liability)	*Ledford v. Mining Specialists, Inc., and Its Alter Ego, Point Mining, Inc.*
amicus curiae	Friend of the court; one with an interest in the case, but not a party	*Livingston v. Guice. United States of America, Amicus Curiae*
appellant	Party appealing a court's decision to a higher court	*Moore, Appellant v. Derwinski, Appellee*
appellee	Party against whom an appeal is taken	*Moore, Appellant v. Derwinski, Appellee*
certiorari, cert.	Writ requiring a certified record of a case from a court	*In re Petition of Johnson for a Writ of Certiorari*
complainant	One who applies to a court for legal redress	*Florida Bar, Complainant v. Clement, Respondent*
d.b.a., d/b/a	Doing business as	*M./t/L. Rendleman d.b.a. Commercial Insulators, Inc. v. Clarke*
de facto	In fact; in deed; actually	*McMullen, a De Facto Guardian v. Muir*
defendant	Party defending against or denying allegations	*Gretencord, Plaintiff v. Ford Motor Co., Defendant*
defendant in error	Appellee	*May v. State of Wisconsin, Defendant in Error*
duces tecum	A command to produce certain evidence	*In re Grand Jury Subpoena Duces Tecum*
et alius, et allii, et al.	And another; and others	*City of Lubbock et alius v. Knox*

Term	Definition	Example
et uxor; et ux.	And wife	*Kostohryz et ux. v. McGuire*
et vir	And husband	*Broadwater v. Dorsey et vir*
ex officio	By virtue of the office	*Tenneco Oil Co. v. Stephens, Ex Officio Tax Collector*
ex parte	By or for one party	*Ex parte Johnson*
ex'r	Executor	*Marilyn Haudrich as Ex'r v. Howmedica*
ex relatione, ex rel.	On information or on behalf of an interested party	*State ex rel. Miller v. Miller*
feme sole	A single woman	*Holman, Feme Sole v. Stephen F. Austin Hotel*
guardian ad litem	Guardian for the suit or litigation (concerning an incompetent or minor)	*Grace M., as Guardian ad Litem for Laurie M., a Minor v. Oakland Unified School District*
habeas corpus	Writ commanding that a person be released from unlawful detention	*In re Writ of Habeas Corpus for Martinez*
in personam	Against the person	*Claudio v. United States and Ken's Marine Service, Inc., in personam*
in re	In the matter of	*In re Estate of Lange*
in rem	Against the thing; against the property	*Scindia Steam Navigation Co., Ltd. v. 3,952.536 Metric Tons Peerless Eagle Coal, in rem, et al.*
inter alia	Among others	*Kot v. Inter alia, North East Detective Division*
inter vivos	Between the living	*Rudd v. Ruth inter vivos Family Trust*
mandamus	Writ commanding the performance of an act or the restoration of illegally deprived rights	*Ex parte Sierra Club Petition for Writ of Mandamus v. Alabama Environmental Management Commission*
n.k.a., n/k/a	Now known as	*Bernasek n.k.a. Staron v. Bernasek*
nunc pro tunc	After a deadline and given retroactive effect	*Application of West for Admission to the Bar nunc pro tunc*
pendente lite	Pending the suit; during the litigation	*Parsley, Administrator Pendente Lite v. Harlan*
petitioner	Party filing a petition	*Walton, Petitioner v. Walton, etc., et al., Respondents*
plaintiff	Party bringing a civil action by filing a complaint	*Oetting, Plaintiff v. United States, Defendant*
plaintiff in error	Appellant	*Miles, Plaintiff in Error v. Justice of the Peace Court #13*
pro forma	As a matter of form	*Pentecostal Church of God of America, a Pro Forma Corporation v. Hughlett*
pro hac vice	For this occasion	*Mohawk Assoc. and Furlough, Inc., as Owner Pro Hac Vice of the Tug Mohawk for exoneration from liability*

Term	Definition	Example
pro se	For one's own behalf; appearing for oneself	*Loftin, Individually, pro se v. United States*
quasi	As if; analogous to	*Mount Carbon Metropolitan District, a Quasi-Municipal Corporation, v. Lake George Co.*
respondent	Appellee	*Forehand, Petitioner v. Fogg, Respondent*
sub nom	Under the name	*Jones v. Lujan, sub nom. Hodel*
versus, vs., v.	Against	*Roe v. Wade*

All published opinions are similar in format. At the top of each reporter page appears the name of the reporter preceded by the volume number. In the upper outside corner of the page is the page number. The volume, reporter name, and page number constitute the citation, which is used to locate the opinion or to refer to it. This citation may be abbreviated; for example, the citation "100 Cal. Rptr. 600" is a shorthand reference to the opinion that appears in volume 100 of the California Reporter at page 600. Many opinions are published in more than one reporter. In that situation, the additional citations are called parallel citations.

The first segment of the court opinion itself is the title of the action. It identifies the parties to the case and their roles in the action, such as plaintiff or defendant. If the opinion is from an appellate court, the party who appealed the lower court's decision is identified as appellant, and the party who is defending the lower court's decision is identified as respondent. In a criminal case, the plaintiff is usually the state prosecuting the crime—or the United States, if the federal government is prosecuting. After the title, a docket or calendar number assigned by the court appears, followed by the name of the court delivering the opinion and the date of the decision.

After this identifying information, most reporters insert a summary of the facts and the decision. In addition, some reporters classify the points of law applied by the court into individual paragraphs, called headnotes, that help the reader extract and analyze each legal concept discussed. The summary and headnotes are written by the publisher of the reporter for the convenience of the reader and are not part of the court's opinion.

The court's discussion of the case is often preceded by a syllabus, written by the court reporter, which briefly summarizes the case. After the syllabus, the court identifies the attorneys representing the parties.

Finally, the text of the opinion is presented. It usually opens with the name of the judge who wrote it. If the words *per curiam* or *by the court* appear at this point, they mean that the court chose not to identify any individual judge as the author. If the opinion is designated a memorandum opinion, it is usually a concise opinion of the entire court.

At the beginning of the opinion, the court briefly recounts the facts and issues involved in the case. Then, it delineates the applicable RULES OF LAW and explains how they relate to the facts of the case. In determining what the applicable law is, the court first looks for any relevant statutes. If no statute governs the action, the court relies on past decisions in similar cases, or precedent. If it is a case of first impression—that is, no existing statute or precedent governs the case—the court bases its opinion on similar decisions and on its own reasoning.

A court opinion may be as brief as a few sentences or as long as several hundred pages. In its course, the judge or the court may make observations or express convictions that do not contribute to the final holding in the case. These statements are called dicta and have no binding or precedential force. After the discussion of the facts and the applicable law, the opinion announces the holding, which is the legal principle or principles derived from the opinion. Only the holding is binding precedent in subsequent cases.

Each reported decision may comprise one opinion written by one judge on behalf of the entire court, or several opinions written by individuals or groups of judges. Not all the opinions in a case have the same legal force. The most significant is a majority opinion, in which a majority of the members of the court agree both with the reasoning and with the holding. A majority opinion has the most conclusive precedential value of any opinion. An opinion agreed upon by the largest number of judges but fewer than a majority of those on the court is a plurality opinion. A plurality may occur where, for example, four of nine justices join one opinion, two others write concurrences, and three write dissents. A plurality opinion constitutes the holding of the court, since it is joined by the largest number of justices, but it carries less precedential value than a majority opinion because it is not agreed upon by a majority of the court. If a judge or judges agree with the outcome of the case but not with the majority's reasoning, they may write a separate concurring opinion. Conversely, a dissenting opinion may be written by a judge or judges who disagree with the decision of the court. Neither a concurrence nor a dissent has precedential value.

The last segment of a majority or plurality opinion sets forth the judgment of the court. The judgment is the official decision of the court on the rights and claims of the parties and resolves the controversy between them. It may be a final determination, or it may remand the case (send it back) to a lower court for further action. A judgment may be completely in favor of one party, or partly in favor of one and partly in favor of another. It may be a straightforward affirmance or reversal of a lower court's decision, or it may affirm on some questions, reverse on others, and remand on still others.

FURTHER READINGS

Ochs, Linnea L. 1983. *Legal Word Finder.* Englewood Cliffs, N.J.: Prentice-Hall.

Statsky, William P. 2003. *Introduction to Paralegalism: Perspectives, Problems, and Skills.* 6th ed. Clifton Park, N.J.: Thomson/Delmar Learning.

Wren, Christopher G., and Jill R. Wren. 1999. *The Legal Research Manual: A Game Plan for Legal Research and Analysis.* Madison, Wis.: Legal Education.

CROSS-REFERENCES

Canons of Construction; Stare Decisis.

COURTROOM TELEVISION NETWORK

The Courtroom Television Network (Court TV) is a cable network devoted to explaining law to the layperson. Founded in 1991, this novel venture in television programming was a long shot: few thought a twenty-four-hour-a-day, seven-day-a-week diet of live trials and legal analysis would succeed. Within two years, though, the network ranked fourth in the Nielsen Company's daytime cable ratings. It built this record with gavel-to-gavel coverage of civil and criminal trials, including a string of highly publicized cases in the early 1990s, as well as with a mixture of regular programs that examine in simple language how the legal system works. This nuts-and-bolts approach coincided with—and, to an extent, helped influence—controversial changes in legal journalism. Lawyers, judges, and the media are divided over whether the public is served or misled by the Court TV approach, and this debate only intensified after comprehensive coverage of the O. J. Simpson murder trial in 1995.

Changes in the media and the law paved the way for Court TV. From the 1960s to the 1980s, reporting on legal affairs was largely the business of two markets: specialized publications for lawyers and daily newspapers. The former was highly detailed; the latter took a broad, general approach. Television took the most sparing look at the law, usually in small slices of news broadcasts. But as state laws increasingly permitted television cameras in state courtrooms, the role of television increased. At the same time, another trend shook up television itself: the public's appetite for so-called reality programming, a format popularized by shows such as the National Broadcasting Company's *Unsolved Mysteries* and the Fox Network's *Cops* and *America's Most Wanted.* Cheaper to make than dramas and sitcoms, this programming subsequently glutted the airwaves in the form of cops-and-criminals shows, tabloid journalism, and "infotainment" (the combination of information and entertainment).

Court TV was created by legal publisher Steven Brill. Known as an innovator, Brill had founded *American Lawyer* magazine in 1978. Neither as technical as law journals nor as cursory as the mainstream press, the trade magazine critically profiled attorneys and law firms, dealt with matters such as how juries reach decisions, and generally modeled its methods on investigative journalism. It emphasized the inner workings of the law—taking an approach that, ten years later, television was avidly pursuing with law enforcement. In July 1991, with the financial backing of Time Warner, Brill launched Court TV. The network initially broadcast an obscure Florida murder trial but soon had high profile cases to cover, including the prosecution of murderer-cannibal Jeffrey Dahmer and the trials of accused parent murderers Erik and Lyle Menendez. Court TV's viewership slowly increased.

In addition to essentially live trial broadcasts—delayed by ten seconds to preserve confidential information about jurors, witnesses, and attorney-client privilege—Court TV developed legal affairs programs. *In Context,* an analysis show hosted by Arthur Miller, a Harvard Law School professor, was an intellectual look at legal and social issues. *Instant Justice,* in contrast, turned its cameras on the often emotional scenes played out in night courts by problem drinkers and traffic violators. Other programs condensed entire trials into two-hour highlights (*Prime Time Justice*) or followed accused persons from jail to court (*The System*) in what the network called "the ultimate lesson on how the judicial process works, outlining legal failures and successes through the lives of those who are players in the system." Its also featured a weekly debate program, *Washington Watch,* which featured guests such as U.S. attorneys general JANET RENO and EDWIN MEESE III.

Steven Brill's decision in 1997 to sell his stake in Court TV to his partners, Time Warner and Liberty Media, changed the direction of the channel. CEO Henry Schleiff decided to expand into new areas, worried that the network's reliance on trials was turning it into a niche network like C-SPAN or the Golf Channel. He also disliked that ratings were dependent on the availability of a "hot" trial. For example, ratings dropped dramatically after the O.J. SIMPSON TRIAL ended—down 80 percent by 1997.

Court TV moved to purchase programming from the broadcast networks to syndicate to its viewers. *Homicide: Life on the Street* and *NYPD Blue* were two of its early acquisitions. Schleiff also hired Catherine Crier away from Fox News Channel to host her own news and talk show.

Court TV also decided to get more into original programming. In 2000, the network introduced *Forensic Files,* which profiled actual

criminal cases and the scientific sleuthing done by the coroners, medical examiners, and physicians who solve them. The launch of *Forensic Files* occurred at the same time that CBS television premiered its fictional forensics-based hit *CSI: Crime Scene Investigation.* The resulting public interest in all things forensic made *Forensic Files* a smash hit by CABLE TELEVISION standards. The series became so popular that NBC "borrowed" it for its own network schedule.

Buoyed by its success with *Forensic Files,* Court TV expanded its original programming. Among the new shows it introduced was *Dominick Dunne's Power, Privilege and Justice,* a look at cases involving people from high society hosted by the noted author, and *From the Case Files of Dayle Hinman,* a real life criminal profiler. It also began to show original movies, based on one of the many crime documentaries Court TV produces each year.

As a result of all this, five years after Brill's departure, Court TV's ratings had increased 10-fold. It had moved from being available in 30 million homes to being available in 70 million homes. And advertising revenue grew to $64 million, from $15 million in 1998.

Despite this success, Court TV did not completely abandon televising court trials. In 2002 it went to court in a failed effort to televise the trial of terrorist suspect Zacarias Moussaoui. Trial broadcasts and analysis still make up a substantial part of its programming for the 2002–03 season, including its entire schedule from 9 A.M. to 5 P.M. on weekdays. Schleiff has promised this will continue. Trial analysis is "what distinguishes Court TV," he says. "The combination is what makes us different."

In 2001 the Court TV Network marked its tenth anniversary. Henry Schleiff, the network's chairman and CEO, stands beside Fred Graham, Court TV's first employee and chief anchor.

AP/WIDE WORLD PHOTOS

Although Court TV continues to broadcast programming around the clock, many local cable affiliates only air its programming during particular times of the day, such as during prime time, day time, or early morning hours.

FURTHER READINGS

Court Television Network. Available online at <www.courtv.com> (accessed November 20, 2003).

Johnson, Steve. 2002. "Even as It Seeks Terror Trial, Court TV Looks Beyond the Gavel." *Chicago Tribune* (January 7).

Larson, Megan. 2002. "Out-of-Court Settlement: Ratings, Sales Improving as Court TV Moves away from Trials, Acquired Shows." *Mediaweek* (July 29).

CROSS-REFERENCES

Broadcasting; Cameras in Court; Simpson, O. J.

COURTS OF REQUEST

Inferior judicial tribunals in England, created by special enactments of Parliament, that possessed local jurisdiction to determine actions involving claims for small debts. These courts were abolished in 1846 and replaced by county courts.

COVENANT

An agreement, contract, or written promise between two individuals that frequently constitutes a pledge to do or refrain from doing something.

The individual making the promise or agreement is known as the *covenantor,* and the individual to whom such promise is made is called the *covenantee.*

Covenants are really a type of contractual arrangement that, if validly reached, is enforceable by a court. They can be phrased so as to prohibit certain actions and in such cases are sometimes called negative covenants.

There are two major categories of covenants in the law governing real property transactions: *covenants running with the land* and *covenants for title.*

Covenants Running with the Land

A covenant is said to run with the land in the event that the covenant is annexed to the estate and cannot be separated from the land or the land transferred without it. Such a covenant exists if the original owner as well as each successive owner of the property is either subject to its *burden* or entitled to its *benefit.* A covenant running with the land is said to touch and con-

cern the property. For example, an individual might own property subject to the restriction that it is only to be used for church purposes. When selling the land, the person can only do so upon an agreement by the buyer that he or she, too, will only use the land for church purposes. The land is thereby burdened or encumbered by a RESTRICTIVE COVENANT, since the covenant specifically limits the use to which the land can be put. In addition, the covenant runs with the land because it remains attached to it despite subsequent changes in its ownership. This type of covenant is also called a *covenant appurtenant.*

Certain EASEMENTS also run with the land. An easement, for example, that permits one landowner to walk across a particular portion of the property of an adjoining landowner in order to gain access to the street would run with the land. Subsequent owners of both plots would take the land subject to such easement.

A *covenant in gross* is unlike a covenant running with the land in that it is personal, binding only the particular owner and not the land itself. A subsequent owner is not required to keep the promise as one would with a covenant appurtenant.

Covenants for Title

When an individual obtains title to, or possession and ownership of, real property, six covenants are ordinarily afforded to him or her. They are (1) covenant for seisin; (2) covenant of the right to convey; (3) covenant against encumbrances; (4) covenant for QUIET ENJOYMENT; (5) covenant of general WARRANTY; and (6) covenant for further assurances.

A deed to real property that provides for *usual covenants* generally includes the first five of these covenants. When a deed provides for *full covenants,* it is regarded as giving such protection as is extended pursuant to all six covenants.

Covenants for seisin and of the right to convey are ordinarily regarded as being the same thing. Essentially, they make a guarantee to the grantee that the grantor is actually the owner of the estate that he or she is transferring.

The covenant against encumbrances promises to the grantee that the property being conveyed is not subject to any outstanding rights or interests by other parties, such as mortgages, liens, easements, profits, or restrictions on its

Covenant Not to Sue

A sample covenant
not to sue.

COVENANT NOT TO SUE

For good and valuable consideration the receipt of which is hereby acknowledged, _____ ,

the undersigned being the holder of an actual, asserted or potential claim against _____ arising from:

do hereby covenant that I shall not commence or maintain any suit thereon against said party whether at law or in equity provided nothing in this agreement constitutes a release of this or any other party thereto.

This covenant shall be binding upon, and inure to, the benefit of the parties, their successors, assigns and executors, administrators, personal representatives and heirs.

_____
Signature

_____
Witness

STATE OF)

COUNTY OF)

Subscribed and sworn to me by _____ , on this _____ day of _____ , 20_____.

WITNESS my hand and official seal.

_____

My commission expires:

Notary Public

---

use that would diminish its value. The existence of ZONING restrictions do not constitute breach of this covenant; however, the existence of a violation of some type of zoning or building restriction might be regarded as a breach thereof.

The covenants of quiet enjoyment and general warranty both have the legal effect of protecting the grantee against all unlawful claims of others, including the grantor and third parties, who might attempt to effect an actual or constructive eviction of the grantee.

The sixth covenant, which is the covenant for further assurances, is not widely used in the United States. It is an agreement by the grantor to perform any further necessary acts within his or her ability to perfect the grantee's title.

The first three covenants of title ordinarily do not run with the land, since they become personal choses in action—rights to initiate a lawsuit—if breached upon delivery of the deed. The others are covenants appurtenant or run with the land and are enforceable by all grantees of the land.

In order to recover on the basis of a breach of a covenant of title, financial loss must actually be sustained by the covenantee, since such covenants are contracts of indemnity. In most jurisdictions, the maximum amount of damages recoverable for such a breach is the purchase price of the land plus interest.

Purposes

Land use planning is often effected through the use of covenants. Covenants facilitate the creation of particular types of neighborhoods as part of a *neighborhood plan*. A housing developer might, for example, buy up vacant land to divide into building lots. A low price is paid for the undeveloped land, which the developer subsequently sells burdened with a number of restrictive covenants. The developer might stipulate in the contract of sale that the owner must retain the original size of a lot. Developers can also make owners agree that houses to be constructed upon the lots must be larger than a certain size and include other specifications to ensure that such property will more than likely sell for premium prices because of the desirability of the neighborhood. Courts enforce such covenants provided they benefit and burden all the property owners in a neighborhood equally.

Covenants will not, however, be enforced if they are intended to accomplish an illegal purpose. The Supreme Court ruled in *Shelley v. Kraemer,* 334 U.S. 1, 68 S. Ct. 836, 92 L. Ed. 1161 (1948), that no court or state officials have the power under law to take any action toward the enforcement of a *racial covenant*. In this case, a group of neighbors were bringing suit to prohibit a property owner from selling his home to blacks, based on the argument that the owner had purchased the home subject to the restrictive covenant not to sell to blacks. The covenant was found to be unenforceable based on equal housing laws. To enforce it would constitute a CIVIL RIGHTS violation.

FURTHER READINGS

Bell, Cedric D. 2000. *The Law of Real Property.* London: Old Bailey.

Brinig, Margaret F., and Steven Nock. 1999. "Covenant and Contract." *Regent University Law Review* 12 (spring): 9–26.

Kraut, Jayson, et al. 1983. *American Jurisprudence.* Rochester, N.Y.: Lawyers Cooperative.

CROSS-REFERENCES

Chose in Action; Easement; Encumbrance; Estate.

COVENANT, ACTION OF

One of the old common-law FORMS OF ACTION *by which the plaintiff claimed damages for breach of a* COVENANT, *that is, a contract under seal.*

When the common-law system was first developing in England after the Norman Conquest of 1066, the king's courts were little concerned with the personal disputes of private parties. When the royal courts began assuming more authority the procedure for asserting a legal claim became more technical. A dispute would not be heard unless the plaintiff could make out a claim in an established form, or form of action. The courts initially refused to hear cases involving private agreements because parties could not testify in their own cases, and there often was no other way to prove the existence of a contract or its terms. Gradually, judges came to the conclusion that a contract could be proved by introducing a written agreement bearing a seal—an impression in wax or in the paper itself—and by offering evidence that the agreement had been properly delivered to the party who held it. Such a sealed writing was known as a covenant, and it was legally sufficient to give the plaintiff grounds to sue on the rights embodied in it.

The action of covenant gained recognition in the thirteenth century and remained important for centuries, as long as agreements were enforceable only if they were under seal. It was not until the end of the fourteenth century that the law began to recognize as legally enforceable a contract that was supported by consideration but not under seal.

In very early times an action of covenant could be used by a tenant who had been wrongfully ousted from his or her premises before the term of the lease had expired. If it were the landlord who ejected the tenant, the tenant could seek damages as well as recovery of tenancy, but the only remedy against anyone else was money damages. As time went by, the action was not allowed for agreements involving real property.

Originally, the action of covenant was intended to force the defendant to perform his or her part of the bargain. Where that performance could not be forced and the defendant remained adamant, the plaintiff was entitled to damages in proportion to losses. The COMMON LAW first collected amercements, or fines, from the defendant and later ordered the defendant to pay money damages to the plaintiff as well.

Today, the common-law forms of action have been supplanted in U.S. law by modern rules of CIVIL PROCEDURE, and the action of covenant no longer exists. Even so, some states have preserved certain legal consequences for contracts under seal.

CROSS-REFERENCES
Assumpsit.

COVENANT MARRIAGE

A legal union of HUSBAND AND WIFE *that requires premarital counseling, marital counseling if problems occur, and limited grounds for* DIVORCE.

The declining stability of U.S. marriages has been dramatic. In 2002, the CENSUS BUREAU issued a study that concluded almost half of all first marriages will end in divorce. The rise in the divorce rate began in the 1960s and accelerated in the 1970s, after most states enacted no-fault divorce laws, which made it much easier for married couples to dissolve their marriage contracts. By the 1990s, a small but vocal number of people argued that it was too easy to divorce. Prior generations of husbands and wives had worked out their problems and preserved their marriages. Current divorce laws allowed couples to quit a marriage at the first sign of trouble.

These concerns led Louisiana, in 1997, to enact the first covenant marriage law in the United States (L.S.A.-R.S. 9:272 et seq. [1997]). The law created two forms of marriage in the state: the traditional *marriage contract,* with minimal formalities of formation and dissolution, and a *covenant marriage,* which imposes heightened requirements for entering and leaving a marriage. Supporters of the covenant marriage law saw it as a way to strengthen marriages and families. Opponents expressed doubts. They were troubled over the creation of a marriage contract that had religious connotations—the word *covenant* is associated in Christianity with a contract between man and God. Critics also pointed out that there would be additional costs associated with the additional requirements.

The law mandates three significant requirements for couples who choose to enter into a covenant marriage: (1) the couple must legally agree to seek marital counseling if problems develop during the marriage; and (2) the couple can only seek a divorce or legal separation for limited reasons. In addition, before obtaining a covenant marriage license, the couple must receive premarital counseling from a priest, minister, rabbi, clergyman of any religious sect, or a professional marriage counselor.

For the premarital counseling to be accepted by the state the couple must sign a notarized AFFIDAVIT, which is attested to by the counselor, that (1) the counselor has discussed the seriousness of a covenant marriage; (2) the commitment to the marriage is one for life; (3) the couple will fulfill the obligation of seeking marital counseling if problems arise in the marriage; and (4) they received an informational pamphlet on the legal requirements of covenant marriage prepared by the Louisiana attorney general. The state grants a marriage license when the couple furnishes both the affidavit and a signed declaration of intent to enter into a covenant marriage. In addition, couples who have been married under the traditional marriage contract have the option of converting to a covenant marriage by filing a declaration of intent and participating in marital counseling.

Once married, a husband and wife are expected to commit to a lifetime partnership. However, the law recognizes that some couples will want to separate or divorce. The covenant marriage provisions require a spouse to first obtain counseling and then prove one or more grounds for separation or divorce as listed in the statute. This is the key difference between the two types of marriage: in essence, a spouse has to prove fault by the other spouse. The grounds for legal separation are: ADULTERY by the other spouse; commission of a felony by the other spouse and a sentence of imprisonment at hard labor, or death; ABANDONMENT by the other spouse for one year; physical or SEXUAL ABUSE of the spouse or of a child of either spouse; the spouses have lived separate and apart for two years; or habitual intemperance (for example, alcohol or drug abuse), cruel treatment, or severe ill treatment by the other spouse. The reasons for divorce exclude this last ground but include the other four.

The enactment of the Louisiana law did not signal a swift change in marriage law preferences. In the first year only one percent of couples elected covenant marriage; the rate remains less than five percent. Advocates of covenant marriage introduced similar legislation in other states but the results have not been overwhelming. Arizona passed a covenant marriage law in 1998 (A.R.S. § 25-901 et seq. [1998]), but it is less restrictive in setting grounds for divorce and does not have a two-year waiting period. Arkansas passed its covenant marriage law in 2001 (Covenant Marriage Act of 2001, § 9-11-801 et seq.). At least 16 other state legislatures considered laws between 1999 and 2002, but failed to enact them.

It is too early to tell whether covenant marriage will gain in popularity or whether other states will enact similar measures. In addition, it will take many years for researchers to assess the effectiveness of this type of marriage contract and to determine whether it helps couples avoid divorce. The small number of couples who seek covenant marriage may be the very ones who would have succeeded with a traditional marriage, as they have demonstrated a serious commitment to making their marriages last.

FURTHER READINGS

Hager, Susan. 1998. "Nostalgic Attempts to Recapture What Never Was: Louisiana's Covenant Marriage Act." *Nebraska Law Review* 77.

Scott, Elizabeth S. 2000. "Social Norms and the Legal Regulation of Marriage." *Virginia Law Review* 86.

Spaht, Katherine Shaw. 1998. "Louisiana's Covenant Marriage: Social Analysis and Legal Implications." *Louisiana Law Review* 59.

CROSS-REFERENCES

Common-Law Marriage; Defense of Marriage Act of 1996.

COVER

To protect or shelter; to make good; to insure. To cover a check means to deposit sufficient funds in a bank account to pay the amount written on a check or checks.

The right of a purchaser to buy goods other than those that were originally contracted for as a remedy in the event of a breach of contract by the seller.

In contract law concerning sales transactions, the UNIFORM COMMERCIAL CODE provides that a buyer may use cover for protection in an action for breach of a sales contract. The person may, in GOOD FAITH, purchase substitute goods when a seller violates their contract by failure to deliver goods. The buyer may then recover the difference between the original goods or contract price and the cost of cover.

COVERAGE

The risks that are included in the terms of an insurance contract for protection under the policy; the amount and type of insurance.

An insurance policy provides coverage for particular losses, such as theft, fire, or accidents. The provisions of each individual policy determine the duration, extent, and nature of the coverage.

COVERTURE

An archaic term that refers to the legal status of a married woman.

At COMMON LAW, coverture was the protection and control of a woman by her husband that gave rise to various rights and obligations. Upon marriage, a HUSBAND AND WIFE were said to have acquired unity of person that resulted in the husband having numerous rights over the property of his wife and in the wife being deprived of her power to enter into contracts or to bring lawsuits as an independent person. These restrictions were abolished by various statutes.

During coverture means within the duration of the marriage.

❖ COX, ARCHIBALD

Archibald Cox, a former Harvard Law School professor, came to national attention in the 1950s as a federal labor official. From 1961 to 1965, he served as SOLICITOR GENERAL. He is best known for his appointment in 1973 as the Department of Justice's special prosecutor in charge of investigating President RICHARD M. NIXON during the WATERGATE scandal. Cox's tenacious pursuit of Nixon's secret tape recordings precipitated a constitutional crisis, led to Cox's firing, and ultimately set the stage for Nixon's resignation from office in 1974.

Born on May 17, 1912, in Plainfield, New Jersey, Cox was one of six children of Archibald Cox and Francis Bruen Cox. He studied American history and economics before entering Harvard Law School, from which he graduated magna cum laude in 1937. After serving a law clerkship for the celebrated federal appellate judge LEARNED HAND, Cox entered private practice. In 1946, he became a full professor of law at Harvard. He held various federal positions in the area of LABOR LAW during the 1940s and 1950s, including that of head of the Korean War–era Wage Stabilization Board following an appointment in 1952 by President HARRY S. TRUMAN. Throughout those decades, he also arbitrated national labor disputes.

By the 1960s, Cox had established a reputation as a specialist in labor law. President JOHN F. KENNEDY sought him out as a campaign adviser in the 1960 election. After winning office, the president rewarded Cox by appointing him U.S. solicitor general, the attorney who argues government cases before the U.S. Supreme Court. Cox held the post until 1965, and then returned

"THROUGH THE CENTURIES, MEN OF LAW HAVE BEEN PERSISTENTLY CONCERNED WITH THE RESOLUTION OF DISPUTES ... IN WAYS THAT ENABLE SOCIETY TO ACHIEVE ITS GOALS WITH A MINIMUM OF FORCE AND A MAXIMUM OF REASON."
—ARCHIBALD COX

to teaching law. He remained a highly sought-after negotiator and mediator. He was chosen by the New York City school system to help settle a teacher strike in 1967, and by Columbia University to investigate riots on its campus in 1968. He served as a special investigator for the Massachusetts state legislature in 1972.

For Cox, the pivotal appointment came in May 1973, when attorney general designate ELLIOT RICHARDSON appointed him to investigate President Nixon's role in the Watergate affair. The scandal had been simmering since the arrest, in June 1972, of five Republican political operatives for breaking into the Democratic party's national headquarters in the Watergate office complex in Washington, D.C. Nixon denied any involvement. But after evidence suggested a connection to White House aides, he promised to appoint a special prosecutor to investigate. When Cox took the appointment, Watergate was chiefly an embarrassment to Nixon; partly through Cox's efforts, it would become Nixon's undoing.

Since 1971, the president had been surreptitiously recording conversations in the White House, and Cox believed that the tapes contained key evidence. Cox put pressure on Nixon to release the recordings. Nixon refused, claiming that he had a constitutional right to keep presidential documents confidential. Cox warned that the refusal would precipitate a constitutional crisis. The Senate Select Committee on Presidential Campaign Activities was also conducting an investigation and was then holding public hearings. The two investigations resulted in a lawsuit that sought to force Nixon to release the tapes, and U.S. district court judge

Archibald Cox.
LIBRARY OF CONGRESS

John J. Sirica ultimately ordered the president to do so. The president stonewalled.

By October 1973, Nixon had had enough. He wanted Cox gone. But rather than compromise the integrity of the DEPARTMENT OF JUSTICE by firing the special prosecutor, Attorney General Richardson and Deputy Attorney General William D. Ruckelshaus resigned. Nixon ultimately found someone who was willing to do the job. He promoted Solicitor General ROBERT H. BORK to acting attorney general, and Bork fired Cox. Cox told the press, "Whether ours shall continue to be a government of laws and

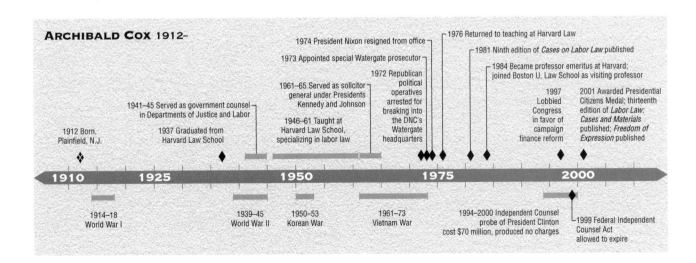

ARCHIBALD COX 1912–

1974 President Nixon resigned from office
1973 Appointed special Watergate prosecutor

1976 Returned to teaching at Harvard Law
1981 Ninth edition of *Cases on Labor Law* published
1984 Became professor emeritus at Harvard; joined Boston U. Law School as visiting professor

1972 Republican political operatives arrested for breaking into the DNC's Watergate headquarters

1961–65 Served as solicitor general under Presidents Kennedy and Johnson

1941–45 Served as government counsel in Departments of Justice and Labor

1946–61 Taught at Harvard Law School, specializing in labor law

1912 Born, Plainfield, N.J.

1937 Graduated from Harvard Law School

1997 Lobbied Congress in favor of campaign finance reform

2001 Awarded Presidential Citizens Medal; thirteenth edition of *Labor Law: Cases and Materials* published; *Freedom of Expression* published

1910   1925   1950   1975   2000

1914–18 World War I

1939–45 World War II

1950–53 Korean War

1961–73 Vietnam War

1994–2000 Independent Counsel probe of President Clinton cost $70 million, produced no charges

1999 Federal Independent Counsel Act allowed to expire

not of men is now for Congress and ultimately the American people to decide."

The public uproar following Cox's firing—including 3 million messages of protest sent to Congress—further destabilized the president, who was increasingly viewed as covering up his role in Watergate. Resolutions urging IMPEACHMENT were quickly introduced in the House of Representatives. Nine months later, the U.S. Supreme Court, in UNITED STATES V. NIXON, 418 U.S. 683, 94 S. Ct. 3090, 41 L. Ed. 2d 1039 (1974), ordered Nixon to surrender materials that he had withheld from the Senate. On August 9, 1974, with impeachment almost certain, he resigned from office.

Cox returned to teaching at Harvard in 1976, pronouncing himself satisfied with the outcome of the Watergate affair. He remained at Harvard until 1984 and then served as a visiting professor of law at Boston University from 1984 to 1996. In his later years, he has advocated reform of campaign finance laws, delivering several speeches about the ethics of campaign financing in presidential elections. In 2000, he joined a lawsuit against the FEDERAL ELECTION COMMISSION, claiming that political party-financed advertisements in support of presidential candidates were illegal. The case was eventually dismissed by the U.S. Court of Appeals for the District of Columbia Circuit. *Wertheimer v. Federal Election Comm'n,* 268 F.3d 1070 (D.C. Cir. 2001).

Besides writings in the legal and popular press, Cox's prodigious output of scholarship includes *Cases on Labor Law* (1948, 8th edition 1976), *Civil Rights, the Constitution, and the Courts* (1967), *The Role of the Supreme Court in American Government* (1976), and *The Court and the Constitution* (1987). Cox is a member of the American Academy of Arts and Sciences and the recipient of eight honorary law degrees from U.S. universities.

In 1997, Cox was the subject of a biography entitled *Archibald Cox: Conscience of a Nation* by Ken Gormley. The book focuses on Cox's long and distinguished career as a public servant. In 2001, Cox was honored with the Presidential Citizens Medal for exemplary public service.

CPA

An abbreviation for certified public accountant. A CPA is a trained accountant who has been examined and licensed by the state. He or she is permitted to perform all the tasks of an ordinary accountant in addition to examining the books and records of various business organizations, such as corporations.

CRAFT UNION

An association of laborers wherein all the members do the same type of work.

In a craft union, the members all perform an occupation, or trade, that relies on the use of the hands. They practice a particular trade and perform their work in different industries for a variety of employers. Carpenters and tool and die makers are types of employees who may belong to a craft union.

CROSS-REFERENCES

Labor Union.

❖ CRANCH, WILLIAM

William Cranch served as a federal judge for more than five decades, and was also reporter of decisions for the SUPREME COURT OF THE UNITED STATES from 1801 to 1815.

Cranch was born July 17, 1769, in Weymouth, Massachusetts. His father, Richard Cranch, was a member of the Massachusetts Legislature and judge of the court of COMMON PLEAS, and his mother, Mary Cranch, was the sister of Abigail Adams, wife of the future president JOHN ADAMS. Educated privately in his early life, Cranch entered Harvard in 1784 and graduated with honors in 1787. He then studied law in Boston and was admitted to the Massachusetts bar in 1790. He subsequently practiced law briefly, first in Braintree, Massachusetts, and then in Haverhill, Massachusetts.

In 1791, Cranch moved to Washington, D.C., to become a legal agent for a real estate firm that made large and speculative investments in the city based on the municipality's recent selection to be the nation's capital. The venture later proved to be financially disastrous, and Cranch was financially ruined as a result of its collapse. In 1800, John Adams, by then president, came to Cranch's rescue by appointing him a commissioner of public buildings for the District of Columbia. In early 1801, the District of Columbia Circuit Court was established, and Adams appointed Cranch an assistant judge of the court. Cranch was elevated to chief judge in 1805 and served on the court for fifty-four years.

About the same time Cranch became a judge, the Supreme Court of the United States moved from Philadelphia to Washington, D.C.

"IT OFTEN HAPPENS THAT THE PRISONER SEEKS TO PALLIATE HIS CRIME BY THE PLEAS OF INTOXICATION; AS IF THE VOLUNTARY ABANDONMENT OF REASON . . . WERE NOT, OF ITSELF, AN OFFENSE SUFFICIENT TO MAKE HIM RESPONSIBLE FOR ALL ITS CONSEQUENCES."
—WILLIAM CRANCH

ALEXANDER J. DALLAS, who had reported some of the Court's decisions on an unofficial and fairly informal basis during its terms in Philadelphia, left the position after the Court relocated, and Cranch, while serving on the circuit court, became reporter of the Supreme Court's decisions in 1802. As reporter, Cranch assembled and published the Court's decisions and then sold them to the public and the practicing bar. Cranch was not appointed to the position but took it strictly on his own initiative. Cranch's first volume of published opinions contained the Court's decisions from 1801 to 1804. Before 1804, the Court's opinions had not been readily available to the practicing bar and were known even less by the general public.

In his preface to his first volume, Cranch stated that he hoped the publication of the Court's decisions would eliminate the "uncertainty of the law" while also ensuring its consistency. "Every case decided is a check upon the judge," he wrote. "He cannot decide a similar case differently, without strong reasons, which, for his own justification, he will wish to make public. The avenues to corruption are thus obstructed, and the sources of litigation closed." Cranch went on to publish nine volumes in all, which contained many of the important CONSTITUTIONAL LAW decisions of the Court when it was headed by Chief Justice JOHN MARSHALL. As was the practice during the early days of the Court, the volumes published by Cranch bear his name on the spine.

In addition to his duties as Supreme Court reporter, Cranch enjoyed a distinguished career as a federal circuit court judge. He decided *United States v. Bollman & Swartwout*, 1 Cranch 379, later upheld on appeal to the Supreme

William Cranch.
LIBRARY OF CONGRESS

Court (80 S. (4 Cranch) 75 [1807]). *Bollman* was a TREASON case tried against Dr. Justus E. Bollman, Samuel Swartwout, and AARON BURR, who were accused of conspiring to create a new nation in the western United States. In *Bollman*, Cranch found that, despite popular opinion to the contrary, the arrest of Aaron Burr's accomplices was not justified because of insufficient evidence. Cranch also wrote a number of papers and articles on legal topics, and in 1817, delivered a series of lectures about his uncle, the president, that was later published as *Memoir of the Life, Character, and Writings of John Adams* (1827).

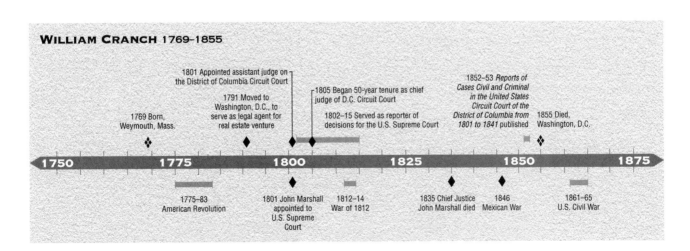

WILLIAM CRANCH 1769–1855

1801 Appointed assistant judge on the District of Columbia Circuit Court

1791 Moved to Washington, D.C., to serve as legal agent for real estate venture

1769 Born, Weymouth, Mass.

1805 Began 50-year tenure as chief judge of D.C. Circuit Court

1802–15 Served as reporter of decisions for the U.S. Supreme Court

1852–53 *Reports of Cases Civil and Criminal in the United States Circuit Court of the District of Columbia from 1801 to 1841* published

1855 Died, Washington, D.C.

1750   1775   1800   1825   1850   1875

1775–83 American Revolution

1801 John Marshall appointed to U.S. Supreme Court

1812–14 War of 1812

1835 Chief Justice John Marshall died

1846 Mexican War

1861–65 U.S. Civil War

Cranch continued as reporter through the WAR OF 1812. By that time, his own judicial workload as well as the increasing number of opinions issued by the Marshall Court caused him to fall steadily behind schedule, so that opinions often did not appear in print until long after they had first been issued by the Court. Furthermore, though Cranch was credited for providing the text of lawyers' arguments and introducing summaries of the principal points decided in a case, he was also widely criticized by members of the bar for his inaccurate and sometimes obscure notes and annotations. Under pressure from some members of the Court, Cranch resigned the reporter's post, which had not been financially lucrative for him, and was replaced in 1815 by HENRY WHEATON, the Court's first officially appointed reporter and the first to be paid a yearly salary.

Cranch continued to serve as judge on the District of Columbia Circuit Court for another forty years after leaving the Supreme Court. He remained active in publishing, assembling and publishing in 1853 the decisions of his own court in six volumes. He also wrote other scholarly and political works, sometimes published under pseudonyms, until his death in 1855 at the age of eighty-seven.

FURTHER READINGS

White, Edward G. 1988. *The Marshall Court and Cultural Change, 1815–1835.* Vols. 3 and 4, *History of the Supreme Court of the United States, 1815–1835.* New York: Macmillan.

Witt, Elder. 1990. *Guide to the U.S. Supreme Court.* 2d ed. Washington, D.C.: Congressional Quarterly.

CROSS-REFERENCES

Legal Publishing.

CREDIBILITY

Believability. The major legal application of the term credibility *relates to the testimony of a witness or party during a trial. Testimony must be both competent and credible if it is to be accepted by the trier of fact as proof of an issue being litigated.*

The credibility of a witness or party is based upon the ability of the jury to trust and believe what he or she says, and relates to the accuracy of his or her testimony as well as to its logic, truthfulness, and sincerity. *Personal credibility* depends upon the qualities of a person that would lead a jury to believe or disbelieve what the person said.

CREDIT

A term used in accounting to describe either an entry on the righthand side of an account or the process of making such an entry. A credit records the increases in liabilities, owners' EQUITY, *and revenues as well as the decreases in assets and expenses.*

A sum in taxation that is subtracted from the computed tax, as opposed to a deduction that is ordinarily subtracted from gross income to determine adjusted gross income or taxable income. A claim for a particular sum of money.

The ability of an individual or a company to borrow money or procure goods on time, as a result of a positive opinion by the particular lender concerning such borrower's solvency and reliability. The right granted by a creditor to a debtor to delay satisfaction of a debt, or to incur a debt and defer the payment thereof.

CONSUMER CREDIT consists of short-term loans made to people so that they can purchase consumer goods and services for personal or household purposes.

The term *credit* has various applications to transactions that involve borrowing. Credit can be used in reference to the ability to postpone payment, as in the case of an individual who has credit with a local store that allows purchase of items on a weekly basis and settlement of account due once a month. An individual might also be extended a credit line, the maximum amount of money that a lender will put at a borrower's disposal. In such case, an individual enters into an agreement for the taking out of a series of loans. Since there is a fixed limitation on the amount to be borrowed, payments must be made to reduce the debt incurred when the maximum is reached.

A letter of credit, sometimes called a creditor's bill, is a written instrument from a bank or merchant in one location requesting that anyone, or some specifically named individual, advance money or items on credit to the individual holding, or named in, the letter. Repayment of the debt is guaranteed by the bank or merchant issuing the letter. Letters of credit are popular in international commercial transactions because they enable parties to transact business without the need to exchange large amounts of cash. This type of instrument was also popular prior to the common usage of credit cards and travelers' checks.

Personal credit is granted based upon an individual's character, reputation, and business standing regarding his or her financial reliability.

Plain-language Cardholder Agreement

A sample plain-language cardholder agreement for a bank credit card.

Erie Shores Credit Union, Inc.
VISA CARDHOLDER AGREEMENT

Effective: February 2002

This Agreement covers your credit card account with us, Erie Shores Credit Union, Inc.. The person ("Account Holder" or "You") whose name is embossed on the face of the Visa credit card ("Card") provided to Account Holder and issued by us and each Account Holder, by signing or using the Card, agrees with Issuer to the following terms:

1. Your Account. If you have a joint account, each Account Holder has the right to use the account up to the extended credit limit as described below. Each Account Holder is bound by these terms and each, individually, will be liable for all charges, even if only one of you uses the account. For joint accounts, each individual separately, and both individuals together, are referred to in this Agreement as "You".

2. Credit Card Account Services. These services are available through your Card account, up to the amount of your credit limit.

    a. Credit Purchases. You can use your account to purchase goods and services wherever Visa credit cards are accepted (referred to in this Agreement as "Credit Purchases").

    b. Cash Advances. You can get a Cash Advance (referred to in this Agreement as a "Cash Advance") from your account by presenting your Card at a financial institution that accepts Visa. You can also use your Card to obtain up to $1005 per day in cash from any authorized Erie Shores Credit Union, Inc. Automated Teller Machine ("ATM"). You may not obtain a Cash Advance if your account is delinquent, closed or the amount of the advance would cause your balance to go over your credit limit.

3. Your promise to pay.

    3.1 You promise to pay us, when due, the total of all Credit Purchases and Cash Advances you make on your account. You also promise to pay the total of any Finance Charge and other charges due on the account. You also promise to pay all costs and expenses, including reasonable attorneys' fees that we incur in enforcing this Agreement.

    3.2 You may pay your entire balance at any time.

4. Additional Card Holders or Others Using Your Account. You may authorize others to use your account. You may add up to 3 additional card holder(s) to your account at no extra charge. Each additional card holder will receive a credit card with his or her individual name embossed. You promise to pay for all Credit Purchases and Cash Advances made by anyone you authorize to use your account, with or without a card, and whether or not you notify us that he or she will be using it. If another person has use of your account and you want to end that person's privilege, you must recover and return that person's credit card, if any. If you are unable to recover and return the card, you will continue to be liable for any charges made unless you tell us to cancel all cards and establish a new account for you, which will be done automatically if you notify us of unauthorized use under Paragraph 22 of this Agreement. We may request written verification from you regarding any change or cancellation to your account.

5. U.S. Currency. If you make a purchase or cash advance in foreign currency the transaction will be converted into U.S. Dollars by Visa.

    For Visa Accounts: To the extent that you have used your Visa card to purchase goods or services, or obtain cash in another country, your statement may reflect the conversion into U.S. dollars of transactions which occurred, initially, in a different currency. The exchange rate applied to such transactions is a (I) wholesale market rate or (ii) government-mandated rate in effect one day prior to the processing date, increased by one percent.

6. Your Credit Limit; Overlimit Fees. Your credit limit is shown on each of your billing statements. You agree not to use your account in any way that will cause your balance to go over your limit. If you do, we may at our option, close your account, and/or exercise any of our other remedies under this Agreement or at law. You must pay the full amount of your balance which is over the credit limit. The fact that we do not ask you for that amount as part of the Minimum Periodic Payment shown on your billing statement does not relieve you of your obligation to pay it immediately. We will charge you a fee each time your balance exceeds your credit limit by $1.00 or more. We will not authorize any new Credit Purchases or Cash Advances if your records show that doing so will cause your balance to go over your limit. If we do authorize any such Credit Purchase or Cash Advance, such authorization will not result in any waiver of our rights under this section. If we increase your credit limit, we will notify you.

7. Law Governing This Agreement. TO THE EXTENT NOT EXPRESSLY PROHIBITED BY APPLICABLE LAW, THIS AGREEMENT AND YOUR ACCOUNT, AS WELL AS OUR RIGHTS AND DUTIES AND YOUR RIGHTS AND DUTIES REGARDING THIS AGREEMENT AND YOUR ACCOUNT, WILL BE GOVERNED BY AND INTERPRETED IN ACCORDANCE WITH THE LAWS OF THE STATE OF OHIO, (EXCLUDING THE CONFLICTS LAW OF OHIO AND THE UNITED STATES, REGARDLESS OF WHERE YOU MAY RESIDE OR USE YOUR ACCOUNT AT ANY TIME. This choice of law is made because of a strong relationship between this Agreement and your account to Erie Shores Credit Union, Inc., because Issuer is located in Ohio, and to insure uniform procedures and interpretation for all of our customers, no matter where they reside or use their accounts. If any term or provision of this Agreement is found to be unenforceable, this will not make any other terms or provision unenforceable.

8. Limitation on Lawsuits. You agree that any lawsuit based on any cause of action which you may have against us must be filed within one year from the date that it arises or you will be barred from filing a lawsuit. This limitation is intended to include tort, contract, and all other causes of action for which you and we may lawfully contract to set limitations for bringing suit.

9. Honoring Your Card. We will not have any responsibility to you if anyone refuses to honor a Card issued on your account. Any refund, adjustment or credit allowed by a Seller shall not be by cash but rather by a credit advice to us which shall be shown as a credit on your account statement.

10. Security for This Account. If I am in default, I authorize the Credit Union to exercise its right of offset, to use any funds in its possession which are titled in my name or joint name, except funds in an Individual Retirement Account to pay the balance due on this VISA account.

    If you have other loans or credit extensions from Issuer, or take out other loans or credit extensions with Issuer in the future, collateral securing those loans or credit extensions will also secure your obligations under this Agreement. However,

[continued]

A sample plain-language cardholder agreement for a bank credit card (continued).

Plain-language Cardholder Agreement

unless you expressly agree otherwise, your household goods and dwelling will not secure your obligations under this Agreement even if Issuer has or later acquires a security interest in the household goods or a mortgage on the dwelling. If you have executed a written agreement granting a security interest in any deposit accounts (checking, savings, or share accounts) or other funds held by Issuer to secure your obligations under this credit card plan, such accounts and/or funds are additional security for your obligations to Issuer arising from the use of your Card.

11. Payment Period. You will receive monthly billing statements from us. The New Balance shown on your statement is the total of unpaid obligations, which have been posted to your account as of the statement date. You can either pay the entire New Balance or you can pay in installments, but we must receive at least the Minimum Periodic Payment shown on your billing statement by the payment due date. The Minimum Periodic Payment is figured as follows:

If Your New Balance is:	Your Minimum Periodic Payment is:
$10.00 or less	The amount of your New Balance.
Over $10.00	2.5% of that portion of the New Balance which does not exceed your credit limit, plus the entire portion of the New Balance in excess of your credit limit, plus any amount past due, or $10.00 whichever is greater.

12. Payment Applications. Payments made to your account will be applied in the following order: Fees and Finance Charges; previously billed purchases; cash advances; and new purchases. We may accept checks marked "Payment in Full" or with words of similar effect without losing any of our rights to collect the full balance of your account.

13. Immediate Repayment of Your Full Balance. You will be in default, and we may, without notifying you, temporarily suspend your credit, close your account, cancel all credit cards issued on it and require immediate payment of your entire balance if any of the following occurs:

    a.   You fail to make a payment when it is due;
    b.   You do not follow the terms of this Agreement in any way;
    c.   You have made any false or misleading statement on the application for your account;
    d.   You fail to pay any other loans you owe us;
    e.   You become insolvent or die;
    f.   There is an attachment, execution or levy against your property or you make an assignment for the benefit of creditors;
    g.   A bankruptcy petition is filed by or against you or your spouse;
    h.   A guardian, conservator, receiver, custodian or trustee is appointed for you;
    i.   You are generally not paying your debts as they become due; or
    j.   There has been a material adverse change in your financial standing.

14. Reevaluation of Credit. We can reinvestigate and reevaluate any information you provided on your credit application at any time, and in the course of doing so, we may ask you for additional information, request credit bureau reports and/or otherwise verify your current credit standing.

15. Periodic FINANCE CHARGE. Your account will be subject to the Monthly Periodic FINANCE CHARGE Rate and corresponding Annual Percentage Rate applicable to the Erie Shores Credit Union, Inc. accounts, set forth in the Initial Disclosure provided to you by us.

The Periodic Finance charge on Cash Advances is calculated as follows:

A Finance Charge will be imposed on Cash Advances from the date of the Cash Advance, or from the first day of the billing cycle in which the Cash Advance is posted to your account, whichever is later, and will otherwise be calculated in the same manner as explained for Credit Purchases.

The Periodic Finance Charge on Credit Purchases is calculated as follows:

A Finance Charge will be imposed on Credit Purchases only if you elect not to pay the entire New Balance shown on your monthly statement for the previous billing cycle within 25 days from the closing date of that statement. If you elect not to pay the entire New Balance shown on your previous monthly statement within that 25-day period, a Finance Charge will be imposed on the unpaid average daily balance of such Credit Purchases from the previous statement closing date and on new Credit Purchases from the date of posting to your account during the current billing cycle, and will continue to accrue until the closing date of the billing cycle preceding the date on which the entire New Balance is paid in full or until the date of payment if more than 25 days from the closing date.

The Finance Charge for a billing cycle is computed by applying the monthly Periodic Rate to the average daily balance of Credit Purchases, which is determined by dividing the sum of the daily balances during the billing cycle by the number of days in the cycle. Each daily balance of Credit Purchases is determined by adding to the outstanding unpaid balance of Credit Purchases at the beginning of the billing cycle any new Credit Purchases posted to your account, and subtracting any payments as received and credits as posted to your account, but excluding any unpaid Finance Charges.

16. Transaction Finance Charge. The Transaction Finance Charge is a one-time charge made each time a new Cash Advance is posted to your account. The charge for each Cash Advance obtained through any ATM is $2.00. The charge of each Cash Advance obtained through any other source is $2.00.

Since Transaction Finance charges are one-time charges that must be included in calculating the Annual Percentage Rate, the actual Annual Percentage Rate shown on your periodic statement may exceed the corresponding Annual Percentage Rate (which is based on Periodic Finance Charge) in any month for which a new Cash Advance is posted to your account.

17. When Finance Charge Begins. The Transaction Finance Charge is assessed on the date the new Cash Advance is posted to your account. The Periodic Finance Charge for Credit Purchases and Cash Advances begins on the dates as described in paragraph 15 of this document.

[continued]

A sample plain-language cardholder agreement for a bank credit card (continued).

Plain-language Cardholder Agreement

18.   Other Charges. The Total Other Charges is the sum of:

a.   Membership Fee. We charge a membership fee of $0 per year, which will be billed to your account during the same "renewal month" each year. If we assign your account a renewal month other than the month of your first billing statement, we may assess a partial Membership Fee prorated for the period until the first renewal month. All Membership Fees are payable when posted to your account and are non-refundable except as otherwise provided for by law. This annual fee shall be treated as a credit purchase for purposes of calculating Finance Charges unless prohibited by law.

b.   Late Charge. If we do not receive at least your minimum required payment within 10 days after the closing date subsequent to the payment due date indicated on your billing statement, we will impose a late or delinquency charge of $25.00.

c.   Overlimit Charge. Each time your New Balance exceeds your maximum authorized credit we will impose an Overlimit Charge of $25.00.

d.   Replacement Card. We reserve the right to charge you $15.00 to replace a card.

e.   Non-Sufficient Funds. We reserve the right to charge $25.00 for non-sufficient funds.

19.   If You Change Your Name or Address. You agree to notify us in writing within twenty days if you change your name, your home or mailing address, or home or business telephone number.

20.   Our Right to Cancel Your Account. We can cancel your account at any time, or reduce the amount of your credit line, without notice to you, except in those situations where notice is required by law. If we cancel your account, you agree to destroy all Cards issued on your account by cutting them in half and returning them to us. You will continue to be responsible for full payment of the balance on your account and all charges to your account, including those not yet received by us, as well as subsequent Finance Charge and other charges. Each Card is our property, and you agree that the Cards are not transferable and to surrender any Card upon demand.

21.   Change in Terms of Your Account. We can change any terms of your account at any time. We will provide you with such notice as is required by law by mailing a notice to you at the latest address shown in our records. Subject to applicable law, any change will apply to the current balance of your account, as well as to future balances.

22.   If Your Card is Lost or Stolen or if an Unauthorized Use May Occur. You agree to notify us immediately if your card is ever lost or stolen or if an unauthorized use may have occurred. The telephone number to call is (800) 325-3678, and you agree to follow up your call with notice in writing to us at: Credit Card Security Department, P.O. Box 30035, Tampa, Florida 33630. You also agree to assist us in determining the facts, circumstances and other pertinent information relating to any loss, theft or possible unauthorized use of your credit card and comply with such procedures as we may require in connection with our investigation, including assisting in the prosecution of any unauthorized user.

23.   Liability for Unauthorized Use of Credit Card. We may hold you liable for the unauthorized use of your credit card. You will not be liable for unauthorized use that occurs after you notify us orally or in writing of the loss, theft, or possible unauthorized use. In any case, your liability will not exceed $50.00.

24.   Credit Information. You agree that we may release information to others, such as credit bureaus, regarding the status and history of your account. However, we are not obligated to release any such information to anyone unless we are required by law to do so.

25.   Waivers. If, for any reason, we do not make use of any of our rights under this Agreement on a particular occasion, that will not limit our rights in the future in any way.

26.   Our Address. To send payment: Payments must be sent to the address listed on the front of the billing statement after the phrase "make check payable to." To inquire or send correspondence: Write us at the address indicated on the front of the billing statement after the phrase "send inquiries to."

27.   Important Notice to Our Customer Who Contacts Us by Phone. Cardholder agrees that Issuer, its agents and service companies may, without the need to seek additional confirmation from Cardholder, monitor and/or record any telephone communications with Cardholder to insure that inquiries from you are handled promptly, courteously, and accurately.

28.   Visa Rules and Regulations. The services being provided to you under this Agreement are made possible by Issuer's status as a licensee of Visa U.S.A. You recognize Issuer's responsibility to comply with the current Visa U.S.A. rules and regulations and changes to them in order to continue to provide these services. Visa cards may not be used for any illegal transaction.

29.   Regulation Z Initial Disclosures. By using your card, you acknowledge receipt from us of the Initial Disclosures required by Regulation Z of the Truth-In-Lending Act and that the terms contained in the Initial Disclosures apply to you and your use of the card and are incorporated in full into this Agreement. The information about the terms and costs of the Card described in this Customer Agreement is accurate as of the Effective Date. This information may have changed after that date. To find out what may have changed, call us or write to us.

Write to:	Erie Shores Credit Union, Inc. P.O. Box 9037 1688 Woodlands Drive Maumee, OH 43537
Call at:	(800) 248-8110 or (419) 897-8110

Printed Nov-01

Development of the Law of Credit

Traditionally, the law has sought to protect borrowers since they are easily exploitable by lenders. Often the two parties do not have equal bargaining opportunities to negotiate all the terms of the agreement, and, therefore, the stronger is able to take advantage of the more vulnerable. The established legal viewpoint is that a lender can properly charge a fee for use of the funds he or she lends, but the rate of interest should be neither unfair nor UNCONSCIONABLE.

USURY traditionally meant charging interest or a fee in exchange for a loan, but it has come to mean charging an illegal rate of interest. Certain credit transactions, such as the loan of money pursuant to a mortgage, are exempt from the provisions of usury statutes.

Amortization Amortization—a system that allows a borrower to discharge a debt in regular, equal installments—was developed in the nineteenth century by savings and loan associations. To amortize a loan, the lender must calculate the total interest due over the term of repayment, add that figure to the total sum borrowed, and divide the total by the number of payments to determine the size of regular, periodically scheduled payments to be made by a debtor.

Morris Plans The establishment of Morris plan companies, still found in some states, was a significant development in the consumer credit business. These industrial banks accept deposits from the general public and issue investment certificates in the amount of each deposit. The certificates entitle the holder to obtain interest on a deposit at regularly scheduled intervals. The bank utilizes the funds primarily to make small loans to wage earners who are steadily employed. It is necessary for borrowers to secure two other salaried individuals to endorse the agreement. The loan is repaid in installments during the course of a one-year period.

State Consumer Laws Originally the fact that consumer loans were difficult to obtain created loan sharking—the practice of lending money at usurious interest rates—coupled with the threat or use of extortionate methods of enforcing repayment. The Russell Sage Foundation analyzed the loan shark problem in 1916 and suggested that credit should be made available to consumers. It proposed a Uniform Small Loan Law for enactment by the states that defined small loans as those under $300. A maximum interest rate of three and one-half percent monthly on small loans was suggested. The interest rate was stated as a per-month charge in order to encourage legislators to adopt the act and to prevent consumers from going to loan sharks who make a practice of concealing their true rates of interest.

The Uniform Small Loan Law was subsequently revised but was important since it made way for legal lending to consumers. It was created as an exception to state usury laws and furnished the pattern for the subsequent creation of consumer credit legislation.

Legal Rate of Interest

Interest can be computed in a number of ways, and creditors generally attempt to use the most profitable way that is within legal limits. In figuring the legal rate of interest, it is essential to determine which expenses are a part of the finance or interest charges. Not customarily considered components of finance charges are fees for filing or recording a document, for payment of an individual who does an appraisal, and for the expense of preparing documents; closing costs; and prepayment penalties.

CREDIT BUREAU

A privately owned, profit-making establishment that—as a regular business—collects and compiles data regarding the solvency, character, responsibility, and reputation of a particular individual or business in order to furnish such information to subscribers, in the form of a report allowing them to evaluate the financial stability of the subject of the report.

Credit bureaus ordinarily prepare and issue reports for lending institutions and stores that investigate the financial reliability of an applicant for credit prior to the execution of the credit agreement.

Credit bureaus are regulated by the federal FAIR CREDIT REPORTING ACT (15 U.S.C.A. § 1681 et seq. [1970]) and by state statute to safeguard against abusive and damaging practices.

CRÉDIT MOBILIER SCANDAL

The Reconstruction era after the Civil War was a time of chaos, reorganization, and corruption that affected not only lesser state officials but also federal government agents. The Crédit Mobilier affair, which had its early beginnings in 1864 but was not publicly investigated until 1873, is an example of the corrupt practices that characterized the period.

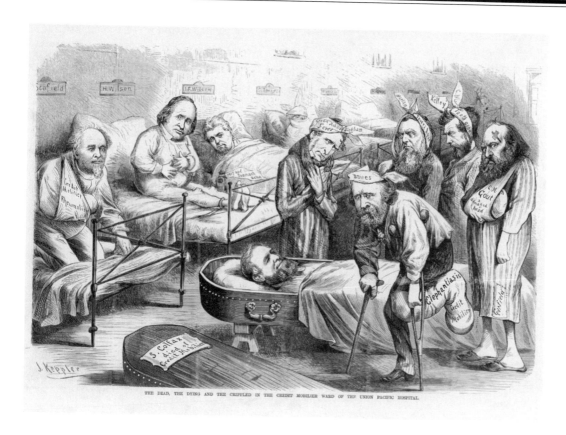

Cartoonist Joseph Keppler offered a satirical portrayal of the Crédit Mobilier Scandal by depicting politicians involved in the affair as residents in a hospital ward. In actuality, punishment was lenient: Representatives James Brooks and Oakes Ames were merely censured.

CORBIS

THE DEAD, THE DYING AND THE CRIPPLED IN THE CREDIT MOBILIER WARD OF THE UNION PACIFIC HOSPITAL.

In 1864, Thomas C. Durant, an administrator of the Union Pacific Railroad, bought the Pennsylvania Fiscal Agency, which was chartered in 1859. The agency was renamed Crédit Mobilier of America and its proposed purpose as a construction company was the building of the Union Pacific Railroad. The federal government had granted the railroad generous loans and contracts for its construction, and the administrators of the railroad planned to divert this money into the Crédit Mobilier Company, allowing the stockholders of the company to enjoy huge profits. Government officials first became involved in 1865 when Oakes Ames, congressional representative from Massachusetts, and his brother Oliver bought shares of stock in the Crédit Mobilier and, indirectly, in the Union Pacific Railroad. The Ames brothers soon became the power behind the Union Pacific, and, in 1866, Durant was replaced by Oliver Ames.

The building of the railroad was fraudulently financed for approximately $50 million more than was necessary. In addition, Oakes Ames sold a large number of shares of stock in Crédit Mobilier at a reduced rate to several of his fellow congressmen. This move on the part of Ames was to allay any suspicious interest in the under-takings of the two companies and to encourage legislation beneficial to the railroad. This maneuver occurred in 1867, and for the next five years rumors surrounding the activities of Ames and other government officials circulated.

The scandal erupted in 1872 when the details of the Crédit Mobilier Company became an issue of the presidential campaign of that year. Several important officials were involved including vice presidential candidate Henry Wilson, incumbent vice president Schyler Colfax, future president and member of the House of Representatives JAMES A. GARFIELD, and Speaker of the House James G. Blaine. An investigation began in 1873. The punishments for such behavior were surprisingly lenient, however, and the Crédit Mobilier Company and Congressman Ames were merely publicly censured.

CREDIT UNION

A corporation formed under special statutory provisions to further thrift among its members while providing credit for them at more favorable rates of interest than those offered by other lending institutions. A credit union is a cooperative association that utilizes funds deposited by a small group of people who are its sole borrowers and beneficiaries. It is ordinarily subject to regulation by state banking boards or commissions. When formed pursuant to the Federal Credit Union Act (12 U.S.C.A. § 1751 et seq. [1934]), credit unions are chartered and regulated by the NATIONAL CREDIT UNION ADMINISTRATION.

A credit union can be distinguished from other financial institutions by the fact that membership is ordinarily restricted to individuals who meet certain residential or occupational criteria. In addition, it can make loans of a more diversified nature than certain institutions, such as building and loan associations.

CREDITOR

An individual to whom an obligation is owed because he or she has given something of value in exchange. One who may legally demand and receive money, either through the fulfillment of a contract or due to injury sustained as a result of another's NEGLIGENCE *or intentionally wrongful act. The term* creditor *is also used to describe an individual who is engaged in the business of lending money or selling items for which immediate payment is not demanded but an obligation of repayment exists as of a future date.*

An attachment *creditor* is an individual who has obtained an order of attachment from a court to command a sheriff to seize the property of a debtor who has defaulted in the repayment of an outstanding obligation so that the property may be used to satisfy the creditor's claim.

A JUDGMENT CREDITOR is a party who has gone to court and obtained a judgment against the person who owes him or her money. If that judgment creditor obtains an order of attachment, he or she becomes an attachment creditor.

A general creditor or *creditor at large* is an individual who has neither a lien nor a security interest in the property of the debtor.

A *junior creditor* is one whose right to collect money from a debtor is subordinate to that of another individual who also has a right to collect payment of a different debt from the same debtor. The person with the primary right to payment is known as a *senior creditor.*

A *principal creditor* is the party who has a claim against the debtor that is far greater than the debt owed to any other creditor, and in some instances, to all other creditors combined.

A secured creditor holds a special legal right in particular property of the debtor to assure him or her of repayment of the debt. A creditor who has the protection of a lien or mortgage is secured.

A *single creditor* has a lien on only one of the debtor's funds or accounts.

Petitioning creditors are those parties to whom one debtor owes money and who apply to the court of BANKRUPTCY in order to secure the debtor's property and distribute it equitably among them.

CREDITOR'S BILL

An equitable proceeding initiated by a person who has obtained—and is entitled to enforce—a money judgment against a debtor to collect the payment of a debt that cannot be reached through normal legal procedures.

A plaintiff might, for example, win a lawsuit against a defendant whereupon the defendant might be ordered to pay damages. In the event that the defendant does not pay promptly, the usual way for the plaintiff to obtain payment is to pay a certain designated fee to the sheriff who would seize the defendant's property, sell it, and pay the plaintiff with the proceeds. If, for example, the defendant only has property that is worth less than the plaintiff's judgment, the plaintiff creditor might pursue the defendant's rights to collect money from others. The person can then initiate a creditor's bill, also known as *creditor's suit,* requesting that the court authorize a way to obtain the money affected by such rights. Such funds as those that come from corporate stock, ANNUITY checks, growing crops, and money owed to the debtor from another person can all be subjected to creditors' suits. A creditor's bill cannot, however, be used to obtain a liquor license, property in another state, or future unearned wages or salary.

CRIME CONTROL ACTS

The vast majority of substantive criminal statutes may be characterized, in one way or another, as "crime control acts." The term "crime control act" is often used in the titles of comprehensive bills that can be hundreds of pages long. These acts can identify a broad array of new crimes, revise existing criminal laws, enhance sentencing and other penalties attached to those crimes, and finance the provisions of these bills. Congress enacted a series of crime control statutes, especially during the late twentieth century, that has introduced a myriad of new forms of CRIMINAL LAW at the federal level, including provisions prohibiting MONEY LAUNDERING, CARJACKING, drug enforcement, criminal forfeiture, and offenses under the RACKETEER INFLUENCED AND CORRUPT ORGANIZATIONS ACT.

According to the Task Force on Federalization of Criminal Law of the AMERICAN BAR ASSOCIATION, only an "initial handful" of federal statutes existed at the turn of the nineteenth century, as federal criminal law consisted of a total of 17 statutes. Throughout the nineteenth century, federal criminal statutes were fairly narrow, generally protecting only federal interests and interests where the states held limited power to address a particular form of crime. The number of federal crimes, however, grew considerably toward the latter part of the nineteenth century and into the early twentieth century. By the 1930s, Congress sought to address concerns that crime had become rampant across the United States, and that states had difficulty handling the increase of crime effectively.

Many of the federal criminal statutes in the 1930s addressed specific forms of criminal activity, such as KIDNAPPING, RACKETEERING, SECURITIES FRAUD, and the illegal use and sale of firearms. In 1934, Congress enacted a series of statutes known as the Crime Control Acts, chs. 299-304, 48 Stat. 780-83 (codified as amended in scattered sections of 18 U.S.C.A.). These acts included provisions for punishment for killing and assaulting federal officers, EXTORTION, transportation of kidnapped persons, and interstate flight, as well as provisions defining crimes in connection with the administration of federal prisons and crimes committed against banks operating under the laws of the United States.

Although the number of federal crimes continued to grow throughout the twentieth century, the perception persisted that crime was rampant throughout the United States, particularly during the turbulent times of the 1960s. Faced with the high incidence of crime throughout the country, Congress enacted the Omnibus Crime Control and Safe Streets Act of 1968, Pub. L. No. 90-351, 82 Stat. 197 (codified as amended in scattered sections of 18 U.S.C.A.). When enacting this legislation, Congress acknowledged that crime is fundamentally a state and local problem, and that it requires the efforts of state and local law enforcement in order to control crime effectively. The 1968 statute encouraged states and units of local government to prepare and adopt comprehensive plans to address crime in those particular states or localities. Under the statute, Congress also authorized grants to the states and local entities to strengthen and improve law enforcement, and encouraged research and development that would be aimed at the improvement of law enforcement methods, the reduction of crime, and the detection and apprehension of criminals.

Included within the original Omnibus Crime Control and Safe Streets Act were a number of controversial provisions regarding wire intercepting and interception of oral communications, as well as measures to allow states and local agencies to control firearms at the local level. The provisions contained in this act have been amended and revised dozens of times since the initial 1968 enactment.

The federalization of criminal law continued during the 1970s. The Crime Control Act of 1973, 93-83, 87 Stat. 197 (codified as amended in scattered sections of 18 U.S.C.A.) serviced the same general purpose as the Omnibus Crime Control and Safe Streets Act. Its primary purpose was to provide grants and other funding to law enforcement agencies in their fights against crime at the state and local levels. Three years later, Congress approved the Crime Control Act of 1976, Pub. L. No. 94-503, 90 Stat. 2407 (codified as amended in scattered sections of 18 U.S.C.A.). The 1976 act established the Office of Community Crime Programs and other measures that were designed to enhance the ability of local law enforcement agencies.

Although federal criminal law had undergone a metamorphosis in the 1960s and 1970s, the federal criminal code had not undergone a comprehensive revision since the early 1900s. In 1984, Congress wrangled with a major bill that would provide this comprehensive revision, eventually enacting the Comprehensive Crime Control Act of 1984, Pub. L. No. 98-473, 98 Stat. 1976. Although controversial sections of the original bill related to CAPITAL PUNISHMENT, an exception to the EXCLUSIONARY RULE in CRIMINAL PROCEDURE, restrictions on HABEAS CORPUS proceedings in federal courts, and liability of the government for CIVIL RIGHTS violations were removed before the bill was passed, the final draft of the legislation was not satisfactory to several members of Congress. Within days of the passage of the Comprehensive Crime Control Act, Congress enacted the Criminal Fine Enforcement Act, Pub. L. No. 98-596, 98 Stat. 3134, which repealed some of the provisions of the Comprehensive Crime Control Act soon after they became effective. Nevertheless, the provisions that remained intact were significant in federal criminal law.

Among the new provisions in the Comprehensive Crime Control Act were those addressing violent offenses, federal anti-terrorism provisions, certain economic offenses, controlled substances, and a number of other miscellaneous crimes. One of the more important measures in the act included a new system governing sentencing for federal crimes. Chapter 2 of the act, the Sentencing Reform Act of 1984, established the UNITED STATES SENTENCING COMMISSION, which is responsible for drafting and revising the Federal Sentencing Guidelines. The first of these sentencing guidelines went into effect in 1987, although they have been amended significantly since then. The Federal Sentencing Guidelines not only have changed the sentencing procedures in federal courts, but also have affected the ways in which state courts approach sentencing.

Comprehensive crime control legislation continued into the 1990s. The Crime Control Act of 1990, Pub. L. No. 101-647, 104 Stat. 4789 further revised provisions of previous crime control statutes. Four years later, Congress addressed problems associated with violent crimes with the enactment of the VIOLENT CRIME CONTROL AND LAW ENFORCEMENT ACT OF 1994, Pub. L. No. 103-322, 108 Stat. 1796. That statute increased and enhanced punishment for violent offenders, including punishment of young offenders. The statute included numerous provisions regarding crime prevention. Some of the more controversial provisions of this act were contained in title IV of the statute, known as the VIOLENCE AGAINST WOMEN ACT. Although the statute has increased funds for research and education to enhance knowledge and awareness for judges and judicial staff in matters involving DOMESTIC VIOLENCE and sexual assault, the original statute also contained a measure that would make gender-motivated crimes a violation of federal civil rights law. The U.S. Supreme Court, in *United States v. Morrison*, 529 U.S. 598, 120 S. Ct. 1740, 146 L. Ed. 2d 658 (2000), struck down the latter provision as unconstitutional.

Other crime control acts have addressed specific areas of concern with respect to crime. The Organized Crime Control Act of 1970, Pub. L. No. 91-452, 84 Stat. 922, for instance, addressed specific problems relating to ORGANIZED CRIME,

including the establishment of protected facilities to house government witnesses. The ongoing war against drugs has similarly led to the enactment of comprehensive legislation, including the Anti-Drug Abuse Act of 1986, Pub. L. No. 99-570, 100 Stat. 3207 and the Anti-Drug Abuse Act of 1988, Pub. L. No. 100-690, 102 Stat. 4181.

Scholars have criticized the continued growth of the federalization of criminal law, as Congress continues to enact these comprehensive crime control bills. Federal criminal law now consists of more than 3,000 individual criminal offenses, many times more than the number that existed a century ago. Supporters of these bills note, however, that state and local officials have not shown the ability to address many of the criminal problems that are addressed under the new federal laws, and that federal law enforcement is in a better position to conduct the type of investigation that is necessary to curb incidents of crime throughout the country.

FURTHER READINGS

Abrams, Norman, and Sara Sun Beale. 2000. *Federal Criminal Law and Its Enforcement*. St. Paul, Minn.: West Group.

George, B. James, Jr. 1986. *The Comprehensive Crime Control Act of 1984*. New York: Law & Business.

Partridge, Anthony. 1985. *The Crime Control and Fine Enforcement Acts of 1984: A Synopsis*. Washington, D.C.: Federal Judicial Center.

Strazzella, James A. 1996. *The Federal Role in Criminal Law*. Thousand Oaks, Calif.: Sage Periodicals Press.

CROSS-REFERENCES

Criminal Law; Criminal Procedure; Sentencing.

CRIMES

Acts or omissions that are in violation of law.

Each state in the United States, as well as the federal government, maintains a body of criminal laws. As populations have increased and personal interactions and business transactions have grown more complicated, criminal laws have likewise grown in number and complexity. Most jurisdictions codify criminal statutes in a separate section in their laws. However, some crimes are placed in chapters or titles outside the designated criminal code. Generally, criminal laws are divided into several broad categories: offenses affecting public order, health, and morals; offenses involving trade, business, and professions; and offenses against the family. These categories often overlap. Juveniles and minors generally receive special treatment under criminal statutes.

Offenses Affecting Public Order, Health, and Morals

A number of acts are made criminal to preserve public order, health, and morals. Some of these laws are based in the COMMON LAW but have undergone significant changes over the years. Prostitution, if discreet and practiced indoors, was generally tolerated in colonial America, but streetwalkers were charged under lewdness, VAGRANCY, or similar laws. In the late nineteenth century, states began to identify and prohibit all prostitution, in criminal statutes, where it was defined as engaging in sex for hire. Prostitution is now illegal in all states except Nevada, where it is strictly regulated.

Pandering, or inducing another into prostitution, is illegal in all states, including Nevada. The solicitation of prostitution is illegal in all states except Nevada, where it is allowed only in licensed brothels.

Public OBSCENITY laws find their roots in the religious prohibitions of blasphemy and heresy, or defiance of the church. Laws prohibiting blasphemy and heresy were passed in colonial America, but after the passage of the FIRST AMENDMENT in 1791, states began to focus obscenity statutes on material with a sexual content. In 1996, the U.S. Congress passed the Telecommunications Act of 1996, Pub. L. 104-104, Feb. 8, 1996, 110 Stat. 56, which included criminal punishment for the transmission of obscenity through cyberspace.

The definition of obscenity is generally a matter of contemporary community standards. In New York, for example, any material or performance is obscene if "the average person, applying contemporary community standards," would find that the predominant effect of the work as a whole appeals "to the prurient interest in sex" (N.Y. Penal Law § 235.00 [McKinney 1995]). To be defined as obscene, the material or performance must also depict or describe "in an offensive manner, actual or simulated: sexual intercourse, sexual bestiality, masturbation, sadism, masochism, excretion or lewd exhibition of the genitals." Finally, the material or performance must lack "serious literary, artistic, political and scientific value" before its creator can be punished for obscenity.

Obscenity laws include the prohibition of public profanity. The federal government, for example, outlaws visible written profanity in the mails and profanity on radio and television. The FEDERAL COMMUNICATIONS COMMISSION makes some exceptions for certain words during nighttime hours. Profanity, like obscenity, is a fluid concept, and its treatment is frequently the subject of legislation.

Gambling is illegal in some states. Other states allow only certain forms of gambling. Even where gambling is legal, it is strictly regulated, and the regulations are enforced by criminal statutes. For example, persons who maintain an unlicensed gambling operation in New Jersey may be charged with a crime of the fourth degree. Fourth-degree crimes in New Jersey normally carry a penalty of a $7,500 fine or eighteen months' imprisonment, or both; when the crime is unlicensed gambling, fines may reach $25,000 for individuals and $100,000 for organizations.

The U.S. Congress and state legislatures prohibit the manufacture, possession, and sale of certain mood-altering substances, such as marijuana, cocaine, heroin, and hallucinogens. Many manufactured drugs yielding psychotropic effects are legal, but only under the administration of a physician.

All states maintain laws that prohibit the driving of motorized vehicles while under the influence of alcohol or other mood-altering substances. These driving-under-the-influence (DUI) and driving-while-intoxicated (DWI) statutes outlaw or prohibit the drunken driving of boats and snowmobiles in addition to passenger vehicles and motorcycles. The range of vehicles subject to these laws is ever expanding: in 1996, a Texas man was charged with riding a bicycle while intoxicated. Intoxication is defined by statute at a specified blood-alcohol ratio.

Some criminal statutes are mainly designed to preserve public order. For example, many states criminalize loitering or prowling. In New Hampshire, no person is allowed to appear "at a place, or at a time, under circumstances that warrant alarm for the safety of persons or property in the vicinity" (N.H. Rev. Stat. Ann. § 644:6). When challenged, however, many loitering statutes are held by courts to be unconstitutionally vague.

Breach of the peace is a generic description for a range of DISORDERLY CONDUCT. Generally, breach-of-the-peace crimes consist of acts that disturb public tranquility and order. STALKING, or menacing, is the related crime of continually following or forcing unwanted contact on another.

The federal Racketeer Influenced and Corrupt Organizations Act (RICO) (18 U.S.C.A. §§ 1961 et seq.) is designed to investigate, control, and prosecute ORGANIZED CRIME. Many states have enacted their own RACKETEERING laws to mirror RICO. Essentially, RICO punishes a pattern of racketeering activity that is accomplished through an organized enterprise. Prosecutors have broadened the use of RICO to support an additional criminal charge for even the most loosely organized crimes. For example, a person who conspires with another to commit FRAUD may be charged with fraud and violation of RICO, if the conspiracy was the product of an organized enterprise. Youth GANGS are among the organizations subject to RICO laws.

State and federal statutes criminalize the unlicensed possession of firearms. Firearm statutes prevent convicted felons from owning a gun. State and federal laws also place an outright ban on some models of automatic firearms.

Other criminal laws respecting public order, health, and morals are many and varied. State and federal election laws have burgeoned since the nineteenth century to prohibit a wide range of acts in connection with the public vote, such as campaigning on election day, coercing voters, and engaging in fraud. Immigration laws provide criminal penalties for immigrating illegally and for hiring illegal immigrants. All states maintain statutes to punish littering and the unauthorized dumping or storage of toxic waste. In Mississippi, DUELING is outlawed (Miss. Code Ann. § 97-39-1), as is cruelty to animals (§ 97-41-1). In New Hampshire, desecration of the U.S. flag is punishable as a misdemeanor (N.H. Rev. Stat. Ann. § 646-A:4).

Offenses Involving Trade, Business, and Professions

Fraud, theft, and MISREPRESENTATION are extensively covered in state and federal statutes concerning virtually every occupation. These laws prohibit a wide variety of acts ranging from simulating gemstones and rigging weight scales to impersonating a doctor or a police officer, breaching confidentiality, and engaging in insider trading (the buying or selling of publicly held corporate shares by persons with inside or advance information regarding the corporation). The fraudulent use of credit cards is also the subject of criminal statutes. And CABLE TELEVISION and computers have inspired a number of criminal statutes punishing their abuse; state statutes, for example, punish the theft of cable television services.

Offenses Against the Family

State legislatures enact numerous statutes to protect people against members of their own family. CHILD ABUSE laws make criminal the physical or mental abuse of a child. Spousal abuse is also punished under state statutes.

The failure of a parent to pay court-ordered CHILD SUPPORT is made criminal in state statutes. States work together in apprehending so-called deadbeat parents through a uniform statute called the Uniform Interstate Family Support Act (U.L.A. Unif. Interstate Family Support Act [1995]). A divorced parent who flees with a child may be criminally charged under state and federal KIDNAPPING statutes as well as CHILD CUSTODY statutes.

Juveniles and Minors

Persons under the age of eighteen, known as juveniles, are presumed incapable of forming the criminal intent to commit criminal acts. They are, then, generally immune from prosecution for their crimes. They can still be held responsible in juvenile court for committing "delinquent acts," which, if they were committed as an adult, would be considered crimes. However, a juvenile may be tried for a crime if the prosecution is able to convince the court to certify the juvenile as an adult. A prosecutor generally reserves certification of a juvenile for serious crimes, such as murder or rape. In the 1990s, some state legislatures passed statutes allowing prosecutors to certify for criminal trial juveniles as young as age 14.

Minors also warrant special protection from society. Criminal statutes punish adults for contributing to the delinquency of a minor. This crime can be any act that tends to make a child delinquent. For example, giving a minor illegal drugs or PORNOGRAPHY is criminal under these statutes. State statutes also criminalize the sale of other adult materials, such as tobacco and alcohol, to minors.

FURTHER READINGS

Douglas, John E., and Mark Olshaker. 1996. *Mindhunters: Inside the FBI's Elite Serial Crime Unit.* New York: Pocket Books.

Richardson, Jeb J. 1998. *The Ten Worst Frauds Against America's Seniors.* Fairfax, Va: Seniors Coalition.

CROSS-REFERENCES

Computer Crime; Domestic Violence; Drugs and Narcotics; Gaming; Juvenile Law.

CRIMINAL

Pertaining to, or involving, crimes or the administration of penal justice. An individual who has been found guilty of the commission of conduct that causes social harm and that is punishable by law; a person who has committed a crime.

CRIMINAL ACTION

The procedure by which a person accused of committing a crime is charged, brought to trial, and judged.

The main part of a criminal action is the trial in which the innocence or guilt of the accused is determined. If the defendant is not found guilty, he or she will be acquitted of the charges. If the defendant is found to be guilty, a suitable punishment, such as a fine, imprisonment, or even a death sentence, will be imposed depending upon the punishment provided in the statute under which he or she was prosecuted.

CRIMINAL CONVERSATION

A TORT under COMMON LAW that involves the seduction of another person's spouse.

A few states still permit a lawsuit for damages by the injured spouse against the wrongdoer. Many states have abolished this action.

Criminal conversation is not the same as alienation of affection, which does not necessarily involve the commission of ADULTERY.

CRIMINAL FORFEITURE

The loss of a criminal defendant's rights to property which is confiscated by the government when the property was used in the commission of a crime. The seizure by law enforcement officers of an automobile used in the transportation of illegal narcotics is a criminal forfeiture.

Property that is subject to criminal FORFEITURE is taken from its owner without any compensation being made because of its use in illegal conduct. The taking of such property by the government is an exception to the principles of condemnation provided that the item is seized and retained as a result of the valid exercise of the POLICE POWER of the state or pursuant to constitutional federal statutes.

CRIMINAL LAW

A body of rules and statutes that defines conduct prohibited by the government because it threatens and harms public safety and welfare and that

establishes punishment to be imposed for the commission of such acts.

The term *criminal law* generally refers to substantive criminal laws. Substantive criminal laws define crimes and may establish punishments. In contrast, CRIMINAL PROCEDURE describes the process through which the criminal laws are enforced. For example, the law prohibiting murder is a substantive criminal law. The manner in which government enforces this substantive law—through the gathering of evidence and prosecution—is generally considered a procedural matter.

Crimes are usually categorized as felonies or misdemeanors based on their nature and the maximum punishment that can be imposed. A felony involves serious misconduct that is punishable by death or by imprisonment for more than one year. Most state criminal laws subdivide felonies into different classes with varying degrees of punishment. Crimes that do not amount to felonies are misdemeanors or violations. A misdemeanor is misconduct for which the law prescribes punishment of no more than one year in prison. Lesser offenses, such as traffic and parking infractions, are often called violations and are considered a part of criminal law.

The power to make certain conduct illegal is granted to Congress by virtue of the NECESSARY AND PROPER CLAUSE of the Constitution (art. I, § 8, cl. 18). Congress has the power to define and punish crimes whenever it is necessary and proper to do so, in order to accomplish and safeguard the goals of government and of society in general. Congress has wide discretion in classifying crimes as felonies or misdemeanors, and it may revise the classification of crimes.

State legislatures have the exclusive and inherent power to pass a law prohibiting and punishing any act, provided that the law does not contravene the provisions of the U.S. or state constitution. When classifying conduct as criminal, state legislatures must ensure that the classification bears some reasonable relation to the welfare and safety of society. Municipalities may make designated behavior illegal insofar as the power to do so has been delegated to them by the state legislature.

Laws passed by Congress or a state must define crimes with certainty. A citizen and the courts must have a clear understanding of a criminal law's requirements and prohibitions. The elements of a criminal law must be stated explicitly, and the statute must embody some reasonably discoverable standards of guilt. If the language of a statute does not plainly show what the legislature intended to prohibit and punish, the statute may be declared VOID FOR VAGUENESS.

In deciding whether a statute is sufficiently certain and plain, the court must evaluate it from the standpoint of a person of ordinary intelligence who might be subject to its terms. A statute that fails to give such a person fair notice that the particular conduct is forbidden is indefinite and therefore void. Courts will not hold a person criminally responsible for conduct that could not reasonably be understood to be illegal. However, mere difficulty in understanding the meaning of the words used, or the AMBIGUITY of certain language, will not nullify a statute for vagueness.

A criminal statute does not lapse by failure of authorities to prosecute violations of it. If a statute is expressly repealed by the legislature, but some of its provisions are at the same time re-enacted, the re-enacted provisions continue in force without interruption. If a penal statute is repealed without a saving clause, which would provide that the statute continues in effect for crimes that were committed prior to its repeal, violations committed prior to its repeal cannot be prosecuted or punished after its repeal.

The same principles govern pending criminal proceedings. The punishment that is provided under a repealed statute without a saving clause cannot be enforced, nor can the proceeding be prosecuted further, even if the accused pleads guilty. A court cannot inflict punishment under a statute that no longer exists. If a relevant statute is repealed while an appeal of a conviction is pending, the conviction must be set aside if there is no saving clause. However, once a final judgment of conviction is handed down on appeal, a subsequent repeal of the statute upon which the conviction is based does not require reversal of the judgment.

Generally, two elements are required in order to find a person guilty of a crime: an overt criminal act and criminal intent. The requirement of an OVERT ACT is fulfilled when the defendant purposely, knowingly, or recklessly does something prohibited by law. An act is purposeful when a person holds a conscious objective to engage in certain conduct or to cause a particular result. To act knowingly means to do so voluntarily and deliberately, and not owing to mistake or some other innocent reason. An act is reckless when a person knows of an unjustifiable risk and consciously disregards it.

An omission, or failure to act, may constitute a criminal act if there is a duty to act. For example, a parent has a duty to protect his or her child from harm. A parent's failure to take reasonable steps to protect a child could result in criminal charges if the omission were considered to be at least reckless.

Ordinarily, a person cannot be convicted of a crime unless he or she is aware of all the facts that make his or her conduct criminal. However, if a person fails to be aware of a substantial and unjustifiable risk, an act or omission involving that risk may constitute negligent conduct that leads to criminal charges. NEGLIGENCE gives rise to criminal charges only if the defendant took a very unreasonable risk by acting or failing to act.

Intent

Criminal intent must be formed before the act, and it must unite with the act. It need not exist for any given length of time before the act; the intent and the act can be as instantaneous as simultaneous or successive thoughts.

A jury may be permitted to infer criminal intent from facts that would lead a reasonable person to believe that it existed. For example, the intent to commit BURGLARY may be inferred from the accused's possession of tools for picking locks.

Criminal intent may also be presumed from the commission of the act. That is, the prosecution may rely on the presumption that a person intends the NATURAL AND PROBABLE CONSEQUENCES of his or her voluntary acts. For example, the intent to commit murder may be demonstrated by the particular voluntary movement that caused the death, such as the pointing and shooting of a firearm. A defendant may rebut this presumption by introducing evidence showing a lack of criminal intent. In the preceding example, if the murder defendant reasonably believed that the firearm was actually a toy, evidence showing that belief might rebut the presumption that death was intended.

Proof of general criminal intent is required for the conviction of most crimes. The intent element is usually fulfilled if the defendant was generally aware that he or she was very likely committing a crime. This means that the prosecution need not prove that the defendant was aware of all of the elements constituting the crime. For example, in a prosecution for the possession of more than a certain amount of a controlled substance, it is not necessary to prove that the defendant knew the precise quantity. Other examples of general-intent crimes are BATTERY, rape, KIDNAPPING, and FALSE IMPRISONMENT.

Some crimes require a SPECIFIC INTENT. Where specific intent is an element of a crime, it must be proved by the prosecution as an independent fact. For example, ROBBERY is the taking of property from another's presence by force or threat of force. The intent element is fulfilled only by evidence showing that the defendant specifically intended to steal the property. Unlike general intent, specific intent may not be inferred from the commission of the unlawful act. Examples of specific-intent crimes are solicitation, attempt, conspiracy, first-degree premeditated murder, assault, LARCENY, robbery, burglary, forgery, false pretense, and EMBEZZLEMENT.

Most criminal laws require that the specified crime be committed with knowledge of the act's criminality and with criminal intent. However, some statutes make an act criminal regardless of intent. When a statute is silent as to intent, knowledge of criminality and criminal intent need not be proved. Such statutes are called STRICT LIABILITY laws. Examples are laws forbidding the sale of alcohol to minors, and STATUTORY RAPE laws.

The doctrine of transferred intent is another nuance of criminal intent. Transferred intent occurs where one intends the harm that is actually caused, but the injury occurs to a different victim or object. To illustrate, the law allows prosecution where the defendant intends to burn one house but actually burns another instead. The concept of transferred intent applies to HOMICIDE, battery, and ARSON.

Felony-murder statutes evince a special brand of transferred intent. Under a felony-murder statute, any death caused in the commission of, or in an attempt to commit, a predicate felony is murder. It is not necessary to prove that the defendant intended to kill the victim. For example, a death resulting from arson will give rise to a murder charge even though the defendant intentionally set the structure on fire without intending to kill a human being. Furthermore, the underlying crime need not have been the direct cause of the death. In the arson example, the victim need not die of burns; a fatal heart attack will trigger a charge of felony murder. In most jurisdictions, a death resulting from the perpetration of certain felonies will consti-

tute first-degree murder. Such felonies usually include arson, robbery, burglary, rape, and kidnapping.

Malice

Malice is a state of mind that compels a person to deliberately cause unjustifiable injury to another person. At COMMON LAW, murder was the unlawful killing of one human being by another with malice aforethought, or a predetermination to kill without legal justification or excuse. Most jurisdictions have omitted malice from statutes, in favor of less-nebulous terms to describe intent, such as *purpose* and *knowing*.

Massachusetts, for example, has retained malice as an element in criminal prosecutions. Under the General Laws of the Commonwealth of Massachusetts, Chapter 265, Section 1, malice is an essential element of first- and second-degree murder. According to the Supreme Judicial Court of Massachusetts malice is a mental state that "includes any unexcused intent to kill, to do grievous bodily harm, or to do an act creating a plain and strong likelihood that death or grievous harm will follow" (*Commonwealth v. Huot*, 403 N.E.2d 411 [1980]).

Motives

Motives are the causes or reasons that induce a person to form the intent to commit a crime. They are not the same as intent. Rather, they explains why the person acted to violate the law. For example, knowledge that one will receive insurance funds upon the death of another may be a motive for murder, and sudden financial difficulty may be motive for embezzlement or burglary.

Proof of a motive is not required for the conviction of a crime. The existence of a motive is immaterial to the matter of guilt when that guilt is clearly established. However, when guilt is not clearly established, the presence of a motive might help to establish it. If a prosecution is based entirely on CIRCUMSTANTIAL EVIDENCE, the presence of a motive might be persuasive in establishing guilt; likewise, the absence of a motive might support a finding of innocence.

Defenses

Defenses Negating Criminal Capacity To be held responsible for a crime, a person must understand the nature and consequences of his or her unlawful conduct. Under certain circumstances, a person who commits a crime lacks the legal capacity to be held responsible for the act.

SHOULD MORE CRIMES BE MADE FEDERAL OFFENSES?

Enforcement of criminal laws in the United States has traditionally been a matter handled by the states. The federal government, conversely, has typically limited itself to policing only crimes against the federal government and interstate crime. This is just one expression of the U.S. system of FEDERALISM, the notion that the federal government exists in tandem with the states and does not, without necessity, deprive states of their powers. The TENTH AMENDMENT to the U.S. Constitution is an example of federalism at work. That amendment states, "The powers not delegated to the United States by the Constitution, nor prohibited by it to the States, are reserved to the States respectively, or to the people."

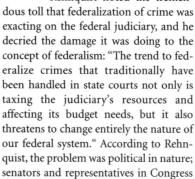

IN FOCUS

Near the end of the twentieth century, however, Congress passed a host of federal laws that directly overlap with existing state criminal laws. Such laws include the Anti-Car Theft Act of 1992, the Child Support Recovery Act of 1992, the Animal Enterprise Protection Act of 1992, and new criminal laws on ARSON, narcotics and dangerous drugs, guns, MONEY LAUNDERING and reporting, DOMESTIC VIOLENCE, environmental

transgressions, career criminals, and repeat offenders. As a result, in 1998, the number of criminal prosecutions in federal courts increased by 15 percent. The increase was nearly three times the increase in federal criminal prosecutions in 1997.

In a Report of the Federal Judiciary issued at the end of 1998, U.S. Supreme Court Chief Justice WILLIAM H. REHNQUIST criticized the congressional movement toward federalizing the criminal justice system. "Federal courts were not created to adjudicate local crimes," Rehnquist instructed, "no matter how sensational or heinous the crimes may be." Rehnquist noted the tremendous toll that federalization of crime was exacting on the federal judiciary, and he decried the damage it was doing to the concept of federalism: "The trend to federalize crimes that traditionally have been handled in state courts not only is taxing the judiciary's resources and affecting its budget needs, but it also threatens to change entirely the nature of our federal system." According to Rehnquist, the problem was political in nature; senators and representatives in Congress

were using the act of lawmaking to win or keep their seats: "The pressure in Congress to appear responsive to every highly publicized societal ill or sensational crime needs to be balanced with an inquiry into whether states are doing an adequate job in this particular area and, ultimately, whether we want most of our legal relationships decided at the national rather than local level."

In his 1998 report, Rehnquist cited a report on federal courts issued by the 1995 JUDICIAL CONFERENCE OF THE UNITED STATES. The Judicial Conference recommended that federal courts be used for only five types of cases: 1) offenses against the government or its inherent interests; 2) criminal activity with substantial multi-state or international aspects; 3) criminal activity involving complex commercial or institutional enterprises most effectively prosecuted under federal resources or expertise; 4) serious high level or widespread state or local government corruption; and 5) criminal cases raising highly sensitive local issues. "Although Congress need not follow the recommendations of the Judicial Conference," Rehnquist wrote, "this Long-Range Plan is based not simply on the preference of federal judges, but on

---

Examples of legal incapacity are infancy, incompetence,and intoxication.

Children are not criminally responsible for their actions until they are old enough to understand the difference between right and wrong and the nature of their actions. Children under the age of seven are conclusively presumed to lack the capacity to commit a crime. Between the ages of seven and 14, children are presumed to be incapable of committing a crime. However, this presumption is not conclusive; it can be rebutted by the prosecution through the admission of evidence that the child knew that what he or she was doing was wrong. Anyone over the age of 14 is presumed to be capable of committing a crime,

but this presumption can be rebutted by proof of either mental or physical incapacity.

All states have juvenile courts, which are separate from criminal courts. Juveniles who are accused of a crime are tried in these courts as delinquent children, rather than as criminal defendants. This alternative prevents children from invoking the defense of infancy. In juvenile courts, criminal charges lead to an adjudication rather than prosecution, because the aim of juvenile courts is to rehabilitate, rather than to punish. In the 1990s, some state legislatures passed laws to make it easier to prosecute juveniles in adult courts, especially in cases involving violent crimes.

the traditional principle of federalism that has guided the country throughout its existence."

Concern over the federalization trend spread during the late 1990s. The Criminal Justice Section of the **AMERICAN BAR ASSOCIATION** (ABA) organized a task force—the Task Force on the Federalization of Criminal Law—to look into the matter. In 1998, the task force issued a report in which it criticized the trend. Victor S. (Torry) Johnson, a representative of the National District Attorneys Association (NDAA) on the task force, declared in *Prosecutor,* "By trying to fight street crime through federal legislation, Congress misleads the public into believing that a national response will be effective and that the problem will be solved with federal intervention." Congress then fails to provide enough federal funding to prosecute all the new laws, creating a situation in which the efforts of local law enforcement "are undermined by the unrealistic expectations created by Congress' well-publicized enactments."

In his 1999 article for *Corrections Today,* James A. Gondles Jr., executive director of the American Correctional Association, lamented the introduction of low-level, local criminals into the federal system. According to Gondles, mixing such prisoners with big-time federal criminals blurs the jurisdictional line and makes it "more difficult for those at the state and local levels to do their jobs."

Not everyone is troubled by the federalization of criminal law enforcement. Proponents of federal criminal laws argue that they are necessary in an increasingly mobile society. Crime tends to span more than one state and even local crime can have effects which cross state boundaries. In his article for the *Hastings Law Journal,* Rory K. Little, a professor of law at the University of California, Hastings College of Law, defended the increase in federal crimes as a protection against the inability of states to catch and prosecute all criminals. If the quality of justice is better in the federal courts, Little opines, "then problems of crime cannot be ignored federally while state criminal justice systems slowly sink and justice fails."

A U.S. Supreme Court decision in March 1999 constituted an approval of increased federal authority over crime. In *United States v. Rodriguez-Moreno,* 526 U.S. 275, 119 S.Ct. 1239, 143 L.Ed.2d 388 (1999), Jacinto Rodriguez-Moreno **KIDNAPPED** a drug associate and took him from Texas to New Jersey, then to New York, and finally to Maryland. Rodriguez-Moreno was charged with, among other crimes, kidnapping and using and carrying a firearm in relation to a kidnapping, an act that violated 18 U.S.C.A. § 924(c)(1). Section 924(c)(1) makes it a crime to use or carry a firearm during, and in relation to, any crime of violence. Rodriguez-Moreno was tried in

New Jersey on the charges, even though he did not have a gun in New Jersey.

Rodriguez-Moreno, who did not want to be tried in New Jersey, argued that the statute did not allow the federal government to prosecute him for the § 924 crime in New Jersey because he did not commit the crime in that state. The Court rejected the argument, holding that because the crime of violence (kidnapping) continued through several states, prosecution was proper in any district where the crime of violence was committed, even if the firearm was used or carried in only one state. The decision made it easier for federal prosecutors to pick and choose the venues for their cases.

FURTHER READINGS

"Federalization of Crimes: Chief Justice Rehnquist on Federalization of Crimes." 1999. *Prosecutor* (March/April).

"Federalization of Crimes: NDAA's Representative Reports on ABA's Federalization Task Force." 1999. *Prosecutor* (March/April).

Gondles, James A. 1999. "The Federalization of Criminal Justice." *Corrections Today* (April).

Little, Rory K. 1995. "Myths and Principles of Federalization." *Hastings Law Journal* (April).

CROSS-REFERENCES

Federal Courts; State Courts; States' Rights.

Insane persons cannot, in a legal sense, form the intent necessary to commit a crime. They are not, therefore, criminally responsible for their actions. Courts have applied a variety of legal tests to determine the mental state of a criminal defendant who claims that he or she was insane at the time of the alleged crime. One test is the **M'NAGHTEN RULE,** which was originally used by an English court in the criminal prosecution of Daniel M'Naghten.

M'Naghten had an insane delusion that the prime minister of England, Sir Robert Peel, was trying to kill him. Mistaking the prime minister's secretary, Edward Drummond, for the prime minister, M'Naghten killed the sec-

retary. At his trial, M'Naghten asserted that he had been insane when he committed the crime. The jury accepted his argument and acquitted him. From that decision evolved the *M'Naghten* test, under which, in order to disclaim criminal responsibility, a defendant must be affected by a disease of the mind at the time he or she commits the act. The disease must cause the ability to reason to become so defective that the person does not know the nature and quality of the act or else does not know that the act is wrong. A successful invocation of the *M'Naghten* defense results in commitment to a mental institution for treatment, rather than imprisonment.

A number of states prefer the "irresistible impulse" test as the standard for determining the sanity of a criminal defendant. If the defendant is suffering from a mental disease that prevents control of personal conduct, he or she may be adjudged not guilty by reason of insanity, even if he or she knows the difference between right and wrong.

The MODEL PENAL CODE of the American Law Institute established another test of insanity that has been adopted by almost all of the federal courts and by numerous state legislatures. Under the Model Penal Code test, a person is not responsible for criminal conduct if, at the time of such conduct, he or she lacks the capacity either to appreciate the criminality or the wrongfulness of the conduct, or to conform his or her conduct to the requirement of law. This lack-of-capacity excuse does not apply to abnormalities demonstrated by a repetitive pattern of illegal or violent acts.

Some states employ the "lack-of-substantial-capacity" test. The phrase "lacks substantial capacity" is a qualification of the *M'Naghten* rule and the irresistible-impulse test, both of which require the total absence of capacity. This test also requires a showing of causality. The defense is not established merely by a showing of a mental disease; rather, it is established only if, as a result of the disease, the defendant lacks the substantial capacity that is required in order to hold him or her criminally responsible. For example, pyromania may be a defense to a charge of arson, but it is no defense to a charge of larceny. An IRRESISTIBLE IMPULSE arising from anger, jealousy, or a desire for revenge does not excuse a defendant from criminal responsibility unless such emotions are part of the mental disease that caused the crime.

Generally, voluntary intoxication from drugs or alcohol does not excuse a criminal act. Involuntary intoxication is, however, a valid defense. It occurs when a person is forced to take an intoxicating substance against his or her will, or does so by mistake. If a defendant's involuntary intoxicated condition causes a criminal act, the defendant will not be convicted if, because of the intoxication, he or she is unable to appreciate the criminality of the conduct.

Fair Warning Defense The DUE PROCESS Clauses contained in the Fifth and Fourteenth Amendments to the U.S. Constitution require that before a defendant may be prosecuted for criminal conduct, the law must make clear which conduct is criminal. Justice OLIVER WENDELL HOLMES articulated the standard when he wrote that a criminal statute must give "fair warning . . . in language that the common world will understand, of what the law intends to do if a certain line is passed. To make the warning fair, so far as possible the line should be clear." *McBoyle v. United States,* 283 U.S. 25, 27, 51 S.Ct. 340, 341, 75 L. Ed. 816 (1931)."

The U.S. Supreme Court had the opportunity to revisit the fair-warning requirement in *United States. v. Lanier,* 520 U.S. 259, 117 S. Ct. 1219, 137 L. Ed. 2d 432 (1997). Lanier was a case involving a prosecution under 18 U.S.C.A. § 242, a Reconstruction-era CIVIL RIGHTS law that makes it a federal crime to deprive another of "any rights, privileges, or immunities secured or protected by the constitution or laws of the United States" while acting "under color of any law."

Congress originally passed the law to afford a federal right in federal courts for situations when, by reason of prejudice, passion, neglect, intolerance, or otherwise, state courts might not be as vigilant as federal courts in protecting the rights that are guaranteed by the FOURTEENTH AMENDMENT to the U.S. Constitution.

Traditionally, Section 242 had been primarily invoked against police officers and prison guards. The Lanier case arose from allegations of sexual misconduct against the sole state Chancery Court judge for two rural counties in western Tennessee, David Lanier. The trial record shows that from 1989 to 1991, while Lanier was in office, he sexually assaulted several women in his judicial chambers.

Lanier's most serious assault involved a woman whose DIVORCE proceedings had come before his chancery court and whose daughter's custody remained subject to his jurisdiction. When the woman applied for a secretarial job at Lanier's courthouse, Lanier interviewed her. As the woman got up to leave, Lanier grabbed her, sexually assaulted her, and finally committed oral rape.

On five other occasions Lanier sexually assaulted four other women: two of his secretaries, a Youth Services officer, and a local coordinator for a federal program who had been in Lanier's chambers to discuss a matter affecting the same court.

Lanier was later charged with 11 violations of Section 242. Each count of the indictment alleged that Lanier, acting willfully and under color of Tennessee law, had deprived the victims of the right to be free from willful sexual assault. Before trial, Lanier moved to dismiss the indictment on the ground that Section 242 is void for vagueness. The district court denied the motion.

The jury returned verdicts of guilty on seven counts, and not guilty on three (one count having been dismissed at the close of the prosecution's case). Lanier was then sentenced to consecutive maximum terms totaling 25 years.

A panel of the U.S. Court of Appeals for the Sixth Circuit affirmed the convictions and sentence, *United States v. Lanier*, 33 F.3d 639 (6th Cir. 1994), but the full court vacated that decision and granted a rehearing en banc. *United States. v. Lanier*, 43 F.3d 1033 (1995). On rehearing, the full court set aside Lanier's convictions for "lack of any notice . . . that this ambiguous criminal statute [i.e., Section 242] includes simple or sexual assault crimes within its coverage." *United States v. Lanier*, 73 F.3d 1380 (6th Cir. 1996).

Specifically, the Sixth Circuit held that criminal liability may be imposed under Section 242 only if the constitutional right said to have been violated is first identified in a decision of the U.S. Supreme Court (not any other federal or state court), and only when that right has been held to apply in "a factual situation fundamentally similar to the one at bar."

The Sixth Circuit then said it could not find any decision of the U.S. Supreme Court that recognized, under Section 242, a right to be free from unjustified assault or invasions of bodily integrity in a situation "fundamentally similar" to those circumstances under which Lanier was charged.

In the absence of such a decision, the Sixth Circuit said that Tennessee had violated Lanier's due process right to be fairly warned that particular conduct is prohibited and carries with it the possibility for criminal punishment. Accordingly, the Sixth Circuit reversed the judgment of conviction and instructed the trial court to dismiss the indictment.

The state of Tennessee appealed, and the U.S. Supreme Court reversed the Sixth Circuit, observing that there are three manifestations of the "fair warning requirement." First, the "vagueness doctrine" bars enforcement of statutes that either forbid or require an act in terms that are so vague that men of common intelligence must necessarily guess at their meaning and differ as to their application. Sec-

ond, the Court wrote that the "canon of STRICT CONSTRUCTION of criminal statutes" ensures fair warning by limiting application of ambiguous criminal statutes to conduct that is clearly covered. Third, due process bars courts from applying a novel construction of a criminal statute to conduct that neither the statute nor any prior judicial decision has fairly disclosed to be within its scope. In other words, a trial court cannot "clarify" a statute by supplying terms through its own interpretation of the law, when those terms were not clearly contemplated by the statutory language chosen by the legislature.

However, the Court emphasized that the due process fair-warning requirement does not require that prohibited criminal conduct be previously identified by one of its own decisions and held to apply in a factual situation "fundamentally similar" to the defendant's case at bar. Instead, the Court wrote, "all that can usefully be said about criminal liability under [Section 242] is that [liability] may be imposed for deprivation of constitutional right if, but only if, in light of preexisting law, unlawfulness under the constitution is apparent."

The Court then remanded the case to the Sixth Circuit for further proceedings in light of its opinion. After reading the high court's opinion, the Sixth Circuit vacated its earlier decision and ordered Lanier to begin serving his sentence. One Sixth Circuit judge dissented, criticizing the U.S. Supreme Court for not writing a clearer opinion that articulated what constituted "apparent" unlawful conduct.

Exculpatory Defenses Exculpatory defenses are factors that excuse a competent person from liability for a criminal act. Duress is an exculpatory defense. One who commits a crime as a result of the pressure of an unlawful threat of harm from another person is under duress and may be excused from criminal liability. At trial, whether the defendant was under duress is a QUESTION OF FACT for the judge or jury. The defense of duress was invoked in the 1976 trial of Patricia Campbell Hearst, the young daughter of wealthy newspaper owners Randolph A. Hearst and Catherine C. Hearst. On February 4, 1974, Patricia Hearst was kidnapped by the Symbionese Liberation Army (SLA) and held for the unusual ransom of food distribution to the poor. Shortly after the abduction, Hearst sent a recorded message to her parents, in which she announced that she had become a social revolutionary.

On April 15, Hearst participated in a bank robbery with members of the SLA. She was arrested in September 1975 and tried for armed bank robbery. At trial, Hearst's lawyers argued, in part, that Hearst's participation in the robbery had been caused by duress. Hearst testified that she had feared for her life as she had stood inside the Hibernia Bank. On cross-examination, Hearst invoked her FIFTH AMENDMENT privilege against SELF-INCRIMINATION 42 times. The refusal to answer so many prosecution questions might have damaged Hearst's credibility, and the jury did not accept her argument of duress. Hearst was convicted and sentenced to seven years in prison. (President JIMMY CARTER commuted her sentence on February 1, 1979, and ordered her release from prison.)

ENTRAPMENT is another exculpatory defense to criminal charges. Entrapment exists if a law enforcement officer induces a person to commit a crime, for the purpose of instituting a criminal prosecution against that person. It is not available if law enforcement merely provides material for the crime.

Mistakes of law or fact are seldom successful defenses. Generally, a MISTAKE OF LAW is applicable only if the criminal statute was not published or made reasonably available prior to the act; the accused reasonably relied on the contrary teaching of another statute or judicial decision; or, in some jurisdictions, the accused reasonably relied on contrary official advice or a contrary official interpretation. A MISTAKE OF FACT may excuse a defendant if the mistake shows that the defendant lacked the state of mind required for the crime. For example, in a specific-intent crime such as embezzlement, evidence that the accused was unaware of transfers into his or her own bank account would negate the specific criminal intent required for conviction.

Justification defenses include necessity, SELF-DEFENSE, defense of others, and defense of property. If a person acts to protect the life or health of another in a reasonable manner and with no other reasonable choice, that person may invoke the defense of necessity. According to the Model Penal Code, self-defense and defense of others are permissible when it reasonably appears necessary that force is required to defend against an aggressor's imminent use of unlawful force. Nondeadly force may be used in order to retain property, and DEADLY FORCE may be used only to prevent serious bodily harm.

Merger

Under common law, when a person committed a major crime that included a lesser offense, the latter merged with the former. This meant that the accused could not be charged with both crimes. The modern law of merger applies only to solicitation and attempt. One who solicits another to commit a crime may not be convicted of both the solicitation and the completed crime. Likewise, a person who attempts and completes a crime may not be convicted of both the attempt and the completed crime.

Attempt

An attempt to commit a crime is conduct intended to lead to the commission of the crime. It is more than mere preparation, but it falls short of actual commission of the intended offense. An intent to commit a crime is not the same as an attempt to commit a crime. Intent is a mental quality that implies a purpose, whereas attempt implies an effort to carry that purpose or intent into execution. An attempt goes beyond preliminary planning and involves a move toward commission of the crime.

As a general rule, an attempt to commit a crime is a misdemeanor, whether the crime itself is a felony or a misdemeanor. However, in a case of violent crime, an attempt may be classified as a felony. Attempted murder and attempted rape are examples of felonious attempts. In an attempt case, the prosecution must prove that the defendant specifically intended to commit the attempted crime that has been charged. General intent will not suffice. For example, in an attempted-murder case, evidence must show a specific intent to kill, independent from the actual act, such as a note or words conveying the intent. In a murder case, intent may be inferred from the killing itself.

Conspiracy

When two or more persons act together to break the law, conspiracy is an additional charge to the intended crime. For example, if two persons conspire to commit robbery, and they commit the robbery, both face two charges: conspiracy to commit robbery and robbery.

FURTHER READINGS

Jonathan Clough, and Carmel Mulhern. 1999. *Criminal Law.* Sydney: Butterworths.

Kaplan, John, and Robert Weisberg. 1991. *Criminal Law: Cases and Materials.* 2d ed. Boston: Little, Brown.

McMahon, Katherine E. 1993. "Murder, Malice, and Mental State: A Review of Recent Precedent Recognizing Diminished Capacity, from *Commonwealth v. Grey* to *Commonwealth v. Sama.*" *Massachusetts Law Review* (June).

CROSS-REFERENCES

Juvenile Law.

CRIMINAL NEGLIGENCE

The failure to use reasonable care to avoid consequences that threaten or harm the safety of the public and that are the foreseeable outcome of acting in a particular manner.

Criminal negligence is a statutory offense that arises primarily in situations involving the death of an innocent party as a result of the operation of a motor vehicle by a person who is under the influence of DRUGS AND NARCOTICS or alcohol. Most statutes define such conduct as criminally negligent HOMICIDE. Unlike the TORT of NEGLIGENCE, in which the party who acted wrongfully is liable for damages to the injured party, a person who is convicted of criminal negligence is subject to a fine, imprisonment, or both, because of the status of the conduct as a crime.

CRIMINAL PROCEDURE

The framework of laws and rules that govern the administration of justice in cases involving an individual who has been accused of a crime, beginning with the initial investigation of the crime and concluding either with the unconditional release of the accused by virtue of acquittal (a judgment of not guilty) or by the imposition of a term of punishment pursuant to a conviction for the crime.

Introduction

Criminal procedures are safeguards against the indiscriminate application of criminal laws and the wanton treatment of suspected criminals. Specifically, they are designed to enforce the constitutional rights of criminal suspects and defendants, beginning with initial police contact and continuing through arrest, investigation, trial, sentencing, and appeals.

The main constitutional provisions regarding criminal procedure can be found in Amendments IV, V, VI, and VIII to the U.S. Constitution. The FOURTH AMENDMENT covers the right to be free from unreasonable searches and arrests:

The right of the people to be secure in their persons, houses, papers, and effects, against unreasonable searches and seizures, shall not be violated, and no Warrants shall issue, but upon probable cause, supported by Oath or affirmation, and particularly describing the place to be searched, and the persons or things to be seized. A warrant is a paper that shows judicial approval of a search or arrest. The U.S. Supreme Court has held that the Fourth Amendment does not require a warrant for all searches; rather, it prohibits unreasonable searches. All warrantless searches are unreasonable unless they are executed pursuant to one of several exceptions carved out by the Court.

The FIFTH AMENDMENT covers an array of procedural concerns, including the death penalty, multiple trials for the same criminal offense (DOUBLE JEOPARDY), SELF-INCRIMINATION, and the general right to DUE PROCESS. It reads, in relevant part,

No person shall be held to answer for a capital, or otherwise infamous crime, unless on a presentment or indictment of a Grand Jury . . . nor shall any person be subject for the same offence to be twice put in jeopardy of life or limb; nor shall be compelled in any criminal case to be a witness against himself, nor be deprived of life, liberty, or property, without due process of law.

The SIXTH AMENDMENT addresses the procedures required at trial. It provides,

In all criminal prosecutions, the accused shall enjoy the right to a speedy and public trial, by an impartial jury of the State and district wherein the crime shall have been committed, which district shall have been previously ascertained by law, and to be informed of the nature and cause of the accusation; to be confronted with the witnesses against him; to have compulsory process for obtaining witnesses in his favor, and to have the Assistance of Counsel for his defence.

Finally, the EIGHTH AMENDMENT states, "Excessive bail shall not be required, nor excessive fines imposed, nor cruel and unusual punishments inflicted."

At first, these amendments were construed as applying only to federal prosecutions. The states were free to enact criminal procedures contrary to them until the passage of the FOURTEENTH AMENDMENT in 1868. The Fourteenth Amendment forbids the states to "deprive any person of life, liberty, or property, without due process of law" (§ 1). Under the Fourteenth Amendment, states must provide most of the criminal safeguards found in the Fourth, Fifth, Sixth, and Eighth Amendments.

Federal courts must comply with all the criminal procedures listed in the amendments to the Constitution. For state courts, the U.S. Supreme Court has adopted a "selective incorporation" approach to determine precisely what process is due a criminal defendant. Under this approach, only fundamental rights are protected.

According to the Court, fundamental rights in criminal procedure include freedom from unreasonable SEARCHES AND SEIZURES; freedom from CRUEL AND UNUSUAL PUNISHMENT; assistance of counsel; PROTECTION AGAINST SELF-INCRIMINATION; confrontation of opposing witnesses; a SPEEDY TRIAL; compulsory process for obtaining witnesses; a jury trial for prosecutions for cases in which the defendant could be incarcerated; and protection against double jeopardy. The only protections that are not specifically required of states are the Eighth Amendment prohibition against excessive bail and the Fifth Amendment requirement that infamous crimes be prosecuted by grand jury.

The judicial interpretation of fundamental rights has allowed states considerable leeway in shaping their own criminal procedures. Although their procedural rules and statutes are similar in many respects, federal and state legislatures are responsible for their own criminal procedures, and procedures vary from state to state. State and federal governments may not limit the protections guaranteed by the Constitution, but they may expand them.

Automobile Exception to the Warrant Requirement

An example of this principle may be seen with the so-called automobile exception to the Constitution's search-warrant requirement. Under the automobile exception, states may allow the warrantless search of an automobile, except for the trunk, if the police officer reasonably believes that the vehicle holds evidence of a crime. The U.S. Supreme Court has determined that this exception is not a violation of the Fourth Amendment because drivers have a "reduced expectation of privacy" and because a vehicle is inherently mobile. This reduced expectation of privacy also allows police officers with PROBABLE CAUSE to search a car to inspect drivers' and passengers' belongings that are capable of concealing the object of the search, even if there is no proof that the driver and passenger

were engaged in a common enterprise. *Wyoming v. Houghton*, 526 U.S. 295, 119 S. Ct. 1297, 143 L. Ed. 2d 408 (1999).

However, states are not required to adopt the automobile exception. The New Hampshire Supreme Court, for example, ruled that all warrantless searches are unreasonable except for a group of well-defined such searches, and this group does not include warrantless AUTOMOBILE SEARCHES (*State v. Sterndale,* 139 N.H. 445, 656 A.2d 409 [1995]). Thus, in New Hampshire, a police officer may not base the warrantless search of a vehicle on the mere fact that the place to be searched is a vehicle. New Hampshire, therefore, provides expanded protections under the Fourth Amendment.

Conversely, a state may not allow the search of any vehicle without reasonable suspicion. A vehicle search that is conducted in the absence of reasonable suspicion would be an infringement of guaranteed Fourth Amendment protection, and a court would strike down such an infringement as unconstitutional. A state law may not diminish the scope of the automobile exception by authorizing a warrantless search of an entire vehicle following a traffic stop in which the driver is issued a citation for speeding. Although law enforcement may conduct a full vehicle search if the defendant is formally arrested, the issuance of a traffic citation does not justify the considerably greater intrusion of a full-fledged search. *Knowles v. Iowa*, 525 U.S. 113, 119 S. Ct. 484, 142 L. Ed. 2d 492 (1998)

Investigation

Criminal prosecutions officially begin with an arrest. However, even before the arrest, the law protects the defendant against unconstitutional police tactics. The Fourth Amendment protects persons against unreasonable searches and seizures by law enforcement officers. Generally, a SEARCH WARRANT is required before an officer may search a person or place, although police officers may lawfully prevent a criminal suspect from entering his or her home while they obtain a search warrant. *Illinois v. McArthur*, U.S. 326, 121 S. Ct. 946, 148 L. Ed. 2d 838 (2001).

Police officers need no justification under the Fourth Amendment to stop persons on the street and ask questions, and persons who are stopped for questioning are completely free to refuse to answer any such questions and to go about their business. But the Fourth Amendment does prohibit police officers from detaining pedestrians and conducting any kind of search of their clothing without first having a reasonable and articulable suspicion that the pedestrians are engaged in criminal activity. The U.S. Supreme Court has held that reasonable suspicion is provided for a stop-and-frisk type of search when a pedestrian who, upon seeing police officers patrolling the streets in an area known for heavy narcotics trafficking, flees from the officers on foot. *Illinois v. Wardlow*, 528 U.S. 119, 120 S. Ct. 673, 145 L. Ed. 2d 570 (2000)

The warrant requirement is waived for many other searches and seizures as well, including a search incident to a lawful arrest; a seizure of items in plain view; a search to which the suspect consents; a search after a HOT PURSUIT; and a search under exigent or emergency circumstances. Nor does the Fourth Amendment require the police to obtain a warrant before seizing an automobile from a public place when they have probable cause to believe that the vehicle is forfeitable contraband. *Florida v. White*, 526 U.S. 559, 119 S. Ct. 1555, 143 L. Ed. 2d 748 (1999).

However, the Fourth Amendment does prohibit police use of a thermal-imaging device aimed at a private home from a public street to detect relative amounts of heat within the home. Such devices are typically employed to determine whether a suspect is using a high-intensity lamp to grow marijuana in his or her home. The U.S. Supreme Court has ruled that the use of thermal-imaging devices constitutes a "search" within the meaning of the Fourth Amendment, and thus their use is presumptively unreasonable without a warrant. *Kyllo v. United States*, 533 U.S. 27, 121 S. Ct. 2038, 150 L. Ed. 2d 94 (2001).

The Supreme Court also ruled that a state hospital conducted an unreasonable search when it undertook warrantless and nonconsensual urine testing of pregnant women who had manifested symptoms of possible cocaine use. The governmental interest in using the threat of criminal sanctions to deter pregnant women from using cocaine did not justify a departure from the general rule that an official nonconsensual search is unconstitutional if not authorized by a valid search warrant. *Ferguson v. City of Charleston*, 532 U.S. 67, 121 S. Ct. 1281, 149 L. Ed. 2d 205 (2001).

The U.S. Supreme Court's Fourth Amendment JURISPRUDENCE is splintered over the constitutionality of using fixed checkpoints or roadblocks to conduct warrantless and suspicionless vehicle seizures. The Court has held that the Fourth Amendment allows law enforcement to perform warrantless vehicle seizures at a fixed checkpoint along the nation's border to intercept illegal ALIENS, so long as the search is reasonable in light of the "totality of the circumstances". *United States v. Arvizu*, 534 U.S. 266, 122 S. Ct. 744, 151 L. Ed. 2d 740 (2002). The Court also ruled that roadblocks may be used to intercept drunk drivers. However, the Court rejected on Fourth Amendment grounds the use of a roadblock to perform warrantless and suspicionless searches of automobiles for the purpose of drug interdiction. *Indianapolis v. Edmond*, 531 U.S. 32, 121 S. Ct. 447, 148 L. Ed. 2d 333 (2000).

When an officer seeks a search warrant, he or she must present evidence to a judge or magistrate. The evidence must be sufficient to establish probable cause that evidence of a crime will be found at the place to be searched. Probable cause is a level of belief beyond mere suspicion but short of full certainty. Whether an officer can establish probable cause to obtain a search warrant depends on the facts of the case. For example, if an arrested person is discovered with a small amount of marijuana, this alone will not justify a search of the person's home. However, if the person is discovered with a large amount of marijuana, the quantity may support the suspicion that more marijuana may be found in the person's home, and the large amount may be used as the basis for obtaining a search warrant.

Police officers seeking a search warrant must state, under oath and with particularity, the facts supporting probable cause. If the search warrant is later found to be lacking in probable cause, or if important statements made by the officers are found to have been intentionally misleading, the evidence seized pursuant to the warrant might not be admissible at trial. Moreover, if the search goes beyond the scope granted in the warrant, the evidence seized as a result of that encroachment might not be admissible at trial. For example, if the warrant states that the officers may search only the suspect's apartment, they may not expand the search to a storage closet outside the apartment.

In executing a search warrant pursuant to the Fourth Amendment, law enforcement officers may enter private property without knocking or announcing their presence if the officers have reasonable suspicion that knocking and

THE STAGES OF A CRIMINAL PROSECUTION

A criminal prosecution usually begins with an arrest. In some cases, the arrest is the culmination of a police investigation; in other cases, it may occur with minimal police investigation. Either way, the manner in which the police investigate suspects and collect evidence is almost always an issue in a criminal case.

During an arrest, a criminal suspect is advised of his or her *Miranda* rights. These include the right to remain silent and the right to an attorney. After arrest, the defendant is subjected to a cursory search for weapons and contraband. The defendant is then driven to the nearest jail, police station, or detention center for booking. During booking, the defendant is photographed and fingerprinted, and the arrest is entered into the police log, or blotter. The defendant is informed of the charge or charges if she or he has not already been so informed. The defendant is also allowed to make one telephone call. After being stripped of all personal items, belts, and shoelaces, the defendant may be placed in a holding cell to await presentation before a magistrate. For misdemeanors, which are less serious than felonies, the defendant may be released with the posting of a cash bond and a promise to appear before a magistrate.

While the person waits for this first appearance before the court, a police officer prepares a complaint against the suspect. The complaint is a document that describes the alleged crime. It is screened by prosecutors and then submitted to the court. The court reviews the complaint to determine whether there is sufficient legal basis to hold the person in custody. If the magistrate finds that the facts alleged do not establish **PROBABLE CAUSE** to believe that the suspect committed the crime, the magistrate must dismiss the complaint and order the release of the person from custody.

IN FOCUS

The first appearance must be held without unnecessary delay. Many jurisdictions impose a twenty-four-hour limit on initial detention before a hearing, but this limit may extend to seventy-two hours if the arrest is made on a Friday.

In the first appearance, the magistrate informs the defendant of the charge or charges as set forth in the complaint. The magistrate also informs the defendant of his or her rights, such as the right to remain silent and the right to an attorney. If the defendant in a felony case is not already represented by private counsel and is unable to afford private counsel, the court appoints an attorney. This is usually a public defender, but it may be a private defense attorney paid by the court or working free of charge. In most states, the attorney meets with and represents the defendant in the first appearance. The defendant in a misdemeanor case does not always qualify for a free attorney.

If the magistrate finds probable cause, the magistrate sets bail in the first appearance. Bail consists of the conditions the defendant will have to meet to gain release from custody pending trial. Acceptable bail is usually cash or other liquid assets. Bail is intended to guarantee the defendant's appearance at trial. In some jurisdictions, if the magistrate determines that the defendant presents a danger to the community or may attempt to flee, the magistrate may refuse to set bail. In such a case, the defendant is forced to remain in jail until the case is resolved.

If the charge is a misdemeanor, the first appearance serves as an **ARRAIGNMENT**, where the defendant enters a plea of guilty or not guilty. The magistrate then allows the defendant to post bail or leave on her or his own recognizance, with the understanding that the defendant will reappear for trial.

Following the first appearance, a felony case proceeds to a **PRELIMINARY HEARING**. Before this hearing is held, the prosecutor and the defense attorney communicate to see if there is any possibility of a plea bargain, or a mutually acceptable disposition of the case. If a deal can be reached, and it is acceptable to the defendant, it is presented to the court for approval at the preliminary hearing.

announcing would be dangerous, futile, or would inhibit an effective criminal investigation by allowing the destruction of evidence. While the lawfulness of a "no-knock" entry does not depend on whether property is subsequently damaged during the search, excessive or unnecessary destruction of property in the course of the search might violate Fourth Amendment rights, even though the entry itself is lawful and the fruits of search are not subject to suppression. *United States v. Ramirez*, 523 U.S. 65, 118 S. Ct. 992, 140 L. Ed. 2d 191 (1998).

The Exclusionary Rule

The **EXCLUSIONARY RULE** protects the right to be free from unreasonable searches. This rule holds that otherwise incriminating subject matter that police officers have obtained illegally must be excluded from evidence. Along with the right of appeal, the exclusionary rule is a defendant's chief remedy for a violation of his or her rights in a criminal procedure.

The exclusionary rule deters **POLICE MISCONDUCT** in searches. Without the admission of the evidence at trial, the case against the alleged

The preliminary hearing is conducted by the magistrate to determine whether the prosecution has sufficient evidence to continue the prosecution. Unlike the first appearance, the preliminary hearing is adversarial. The prosecutor relies on witnesses to present the prosecution's evidence, and the defendant may do the same. Both sides are allowed to question, or cross-examine, the opposing side's witnesses. After this hearing, the court may dismiss the charges if they are not supported by probable cause.

In some states, review by a **GRAND JURY** is also required before a felony prosecution may continue; this review is not required for a misdemeanor prosecution. A grand jury is a group of private citizens summoned to review, in private, the prosecution's evidence. Generally, a grand jury consists of more jurors than a trial jury, which usually numbers twelve. In a grand jury proceeding, the prosecutor presents the evidence against the defendant to the grand jurors, and the grand jurors may ask questions of the prosecutor. The prosecutor then presents a proposed indictment, or a written accusation sworn to by the prosecutor. If a majority of the grand jury finds no probable cause for the prosecution, it returns a no bill, or a refusal of the indictment. If a majority finds probable cause, the grand jury returns a true bill, and prosecution continues.

Following a true-bill finding by a grand jury, the prosecution files the indictment with the trial court. Where no grand jury was required and only a preliminary hearing was held, the prosecution files an information, which is similar in form to an indictment but written and approved by the prosecutor alone.

After the indictment or information courts review criminal convictions for trial court errors. They rarely overturn verdicts on evidentiary bases. Even if an appeals court finds a trial court error, it will affirm the conviction if it feels the error did not affect the outcome of the case.

Generally, state court defendants appeal to a first court of appeals, then to the highest state court (usually the state supreme court), and then to the U.S. Supreme Court. In federal cases, defendants appeal to a U.S. court of appeals and then to the U.S. Supreme Court. The review of appeals after the first appeal is discretionary; that is, the court may decline to hear the case.

After exhausting all appeals, a defendant sentenced to incarceration may collaterally attack the conviction and sentence. This means the defendant attacks the conviction in an action other than an appeal. The most common method of collateral attack is submission of a petition for a writ of **HABEAS CORPUS**. This is a civil action against the warden of a prison, challenging the legality of the imprisonment. If the court approves the writ, the inmate must be set free.

A habeas corpus petition is not an appeal; courts will grant a writ of habeas corpus only if the defendant can prove that the court that sent the petitioner to prison was actually powerless to do so or that such detention violated the petitioner's constitutional rights. Generally, an inmate will ask for the writ in state court before filing in federal court.

All states also have a procedure in place to hear claims of newly discovered evidence. However, no relief is granted if the new evidence would not have made a difference in the verdict.

Some inmates are given early release from prison, or **PAROLE**. Parole is granted by the state or federal parole board or correctional board. It allows the inmate to finish the prison sentence in the community. The court requires a paroled defendant, or parolee, to meet certain conditions on release and to meet regularly with a parole officer for the duration of the sentence.

In some states, if the conviction was for first-degree murder, the defendant may be sentenced to death. Where the sentence is death and the defendant has lost all appeals and collateral attacks, the defendant may ask the governor of the state for clemency. For federal crimes, the president retains the power of clemency. Clemency is forgiveness and mercy, and it usually comes in the form of a pardon or of a commutation of a sentence. A pardon releases the inmate from custody and restores his or her legal rights and privileges, such as voting and gun ownership. A commutation decreases or suspends an inmate's sentence. A commutation is a lesser form of clemency because it does not restore the legal rights of the inmate.

CROSS-REFERENCES

Criminal Procedure; Double Jeopardy.

criminal may be dismissed, and the officer's actions in gathering that evidence will have been wasted effort. The exclusionary rule also prohibits the use of evidence obtained in violation of other constitutional rights, such as statements of the accused that are elicited in violation of the right against self-incrimination.

The most important exception to the exclusionary rule is the good-faith exception. Essentially, the good-faith exception allows the use of evidence obtained in violation of a person's constitutional rights if the officer who obtained the evidence acted in a reasonable manner. If evidence is illegally seized and does not fall under an exception but is erroneously admitted at trial by the judge, a guilty verdict will be reversed on appeal if the prosecution cannot show **BEYOND A REASONABLE DOUBT** that the evidence did not contribute to the conviction.

When officers have collected evidence pursuant to a search warrant, the burden is on the defendant to show that the warrant lacked probable cause or that other problems tainted the collection process. For a warrantless search, the prosecution bears the burden of proving that the search was reasonable. However, before evidence seized during a warrantless search will be excluded from trial, the defendant must prove that he or she had a reasonable expectation of privacy in the place that was searched. Homeowners, for example, enjoy a reasonable expectation of privacy in items that they keep inside their homes. However, houseguests might not have a similar expectation of privacy in the homes they are visiting, especially when they do not stay overnight and their sole purpose for being inside the house is to participate in criminal activity such as a drug transaction. *Minnesota v. Carter*, 525 U.S. 83, 119 S. Ct. 469, 142 L. Ed. 2d 373 (1998). Disputes over the application of the exclusionary rule are usually resolved at a pretrial proceeding called a "suppression hearing."

Arrest

The general rule is that to make an arrest, the police must obtain an arrest warrant. However, if an officer has probable cause to believe that a crime has been committed, and there is no time to obtain a warrant, the officer may make a warrantless arrest. An officer also may make a warrantless arrest of persons who commit a crime in the officer's presence.

An invalid arrest is not generally a defense to prosecution. However, if an arrest is unsupported by probable cause, evidence obtained pursuant to the invalid arrest can be excluded from trial.

When an arrest is made, the arresting officer must read the *Miranda* warnings to the arrestee. These warnings apprise an arrestee of the right to obtain counsel and the right to remain silent. If these warnings are not read to an arrestee as soon as he or she is taken into custody, any statements that the arrestee makes after the arrest may be excluded from trial.

After the arrest, the police must follow certain guidelines during their investigations. For example, if the arrestee requests an attorney or expresses a wish to remain silent, the officers must honor the request and refrain from questioning the arrestee. However, the police may attempt to confirm that they have arrested the right person. They may do so by showing a victim a photo array that includes a picture of the suspect; by arranging a lineup of live persons at the police station, with the suspect included in the lineup; or by organizing a show-up, which is a personal showing of the arrestee to the victim shortly after commission of the crime.

Where photo arrays or lineups are used, the police must refrain from highlighting the arrestee. For example, if an arrestee is white, an officer may not show a witness a series of photographs in which all of the other subjects are black. If an identification procedure is too suggestive, any identification by the victim may be excluded from trial.

Trial

At trial, a criminal defendant has a number of constitutional rights, including the RIGHT TO COUNSEL, the right to a public trial, the right to a trial by jury, the right to a fair and impartial trial, the right to confront witnesses in court, the right to compulsory process to obtain witnesses, and the PRIVILEGE AGAINST SELF-INCRIMINATION. Violation of any of these rights may result in the reversal or vacation of a conviction on appeal.

There are exceptions and nuances to most of the procedural trial rights. Under the Sixth Amendment, if a defendant is indigent, or unable to afford an attorney, the court will appoint an attorney. This right applies only for felony charges and cases in which actual imprisonment may be imposed. Accordingly, an indigent who is not represented by counsel at trial may not be sentenced to incarceration, regardless of whether conviction of the offense warrants incarceration (*Scott v. Illinois*, 440 U.S. 367, 99 S. Ct. 1158, 59 L. Ed. 2d 383 [1979]). However, a defendant will not be appointed an attorney if the he or she is able to pay for a private one.

A criminal defendant has the right to an attorney from the first critical stage of the criminal process through the end. An attorney must be present at the request of the defendant during such events as interrogation, lineup identifications after charges have been filed, preliminary hearings before the court, trial, and sentencing.

The Sixth Amendment right to counsel includes the mandate that a defendant's counsel must be effective and not incompetent. Attorneys must generally consult with their clients about trial strategy and tactics, in order to be effective and competent. However, a criminal defense attorney's failure to consult with a client before deciding against filing a post-conviction appeal does not necessarily render his or her assistance ineffective or incompetent. While the better practice would be for attorneys to always consult with their clients regarding the possibility of appeal, the Sixth Amendment only requires such consultation when there is reason to believe either (1) that any rational defendant would want to appeal; or (2) that this particular defendant reasonably demonstrated to counsel that he was interested in appealing. *Roe v. Flores-Ortega*, 528 U.S. 470, 120 S. Ct. 1029, 145 L. Ed. 2d 985 (2000).

A defendant is free to reject counsel and to proceed pro se, or by self-representation. However, a judge may disregard the defendant's request and appoint an attorney if the pro se defendant engages in dilatory or disruptive tactics. Additionally, state courts of appeal may disregard a defendant's request to represent himself or herself on appeal without violating Sixth Amendment rights. *Martinez v. Court of Appeals of California, Fourth Appellate Dist.,* , 528 U.S. 152, 120 S. Ct. 684, 145 L. Ed. 2d 597 (2000)

The Sixth Amendment right to a trial by jury does not guarantee a jury in all cases. The right generally applies only in "serious cases"—which are generally considered to be those in which conviction can result in incarceration for more than six months. When a jury trial is not guaranteed, the trial court judge will hear the case and make a decision.

In federal court, a jury verdict must be unanimous. This directive is not applicable to the states. In some states, a vote of nine out of twelve jurors is sufficient to convict or to acquit. States may even provide as few as six jurors. Six is the minimum, because juries should represent a cross section of the community. If a jury of six is used, the verdict must be unanimous.

Under the Confrontation Clause of the Sixth Amendment, a defendant has the right to cross-examine all prosecution witnesses at trial. In limited circumstances, the out-of-court statements made by a witness who is absent from court may be offered through the testimony of a third party. Known as HEARSAY statements, this type of evidence may be admitted if the statements were made under oath and subject to cross-examination by the defendant's attorney, and if the witness is unavailable to testify at trial despite the best efforts of the prosecution. However, a defendant's Sixth Amendment right to confront and to cross-examine the accuser in open court is violated when the prosecution introduces the incriminating hearsay statements of a non-testifying co-defendant in a joint trial, even if the defendant's name is redacted from the incriminating statements, because juries will often realize that the redacted portions are referring to the defendant. *Gray v. Maryland*, 523 U.S. 185, 118 S. Ct. 1151, 140 L. Ed. 2d 294 (1998)

The Fifth Amendment privilege against self-incrimination extends from the moment of custody. A defendant need not make statements or testify at trial, and that right is absolute. However, with a sufficient showing of need by the prosecution, self-incrimination may come from sources other than the defendant's statements or testimony. For example, a court may force a defendant to appear before witnesses for identification; to provide handwriting or blood or voice or fingerprint samples; or to repeat certain words or gestures.

However, the mere fact that a defendant has pled guilty to a criminal act does not waive the privilege against self-incrimination during the sentencing phase. As a result, a defendant has the right to remain silent, during sentencing, about facts that bear upon the severity of the sentence, and the sentencing court may not draw an adverse inference from the defendant's silence. *Mitchell v. United States*, 526 U.S. 314, 119 S. Ct. 1307, 143 L. Ed. 2d 424 (1999).

If the defendant does testify, he or she may be questioned by the prosecutor about previously inadmissible statements that contradict that testimony. Thus, the Fifth Amendment privilege against self-incrimination will not apply if the defendant has made statements that are contrary to testimony given on the witness stand. Nor does the Fifth Amendment prohibit a prosecutor from calling the jury's attention during closing arguments to the fact that the defendant had the opportunity to hear all other witnesses testify and to tailor his testimony accordingly. The Fifth Amendment prohibits the prosecution from commenting to the jury about the defendant's failure to testify at trial, but it does not prohibit the prosecution from making comments that impeach the defendant's credibility after her or she has testified. *Portuondo v. Agard*, 529 U.S. 61, 120 S. Ct. 1119, 146 L. Ed. 2d 47 294 (2000).

The Compulsory Process Clause of the Sixth Amendment gives a defendant the right to obtain favorable witnesses. This means that the defendant has the same power as the prosecutor to subpoena witnesses. However, if the government, acting in GOOD FAITH, deports a potential defense witness (i.e., makes the witness leave the jurisdiction), it does not violate compulsory process rights.

The Sixth Amendment grants the right to "an impartial jury of the State and district wherein the crime shall have been committed." This clause gives a defendant the right to question jurors for bias and prejudice. The right belongs to both the defense and the prosecution, and it is exercised in a proceeding called VOIR DIRE. In voir dire, both sides are allowed to question jurors and to reject a certain number of jurors, until the jury pool is complete. The rejection of jurors may not be based on race, sex, or national origin.

At trial, the prosecution has the burden of proving the defendant's guilt beyond a REASONABLE DOUBT. This level of belief is abstract and has been described in a number of ways. The best definition is that any doubt regarding the defendant's guilt should not be fanciful or conjured up to avoid delivering a verdict of guilty. This standard is reserved for criminal trials; it is a higher standard than "a preponderance of the evidence" and "clear and convincing evidence," the burdens of proof used in civil trials.

The vast majority of criminal cases are resolved with a plea of guilty before, or sometimes during, trial. Prosecutors may use their discretion to reduce charges in exchange for a guilty plea, in an arrangement known as a plea-bargain. A plea of guilty cannot be revoked after a court has accepted it. Generally, it is appealable only if the right to a trial was not knowingly, intelligently, and voluntarily waived.

Prosecutors are often content with a plea-bargain because it satisfies the criminal justice system's goal of encouraging people to accept responsibility for their actions, and because plea-bargains avoid costly, time-consuming trials. A prosecutor also may agree to defer prosecution and to drop charges after a specified period if the defendant fulfills certain conditions. A defense attorney may seek a plea-bargain if the evidence against the defendant is overwhelming. Both sides are free to reject any plea-bargains and to proceed to trial.

If a defendant is acquitted of all criminal charges, the prosecution may not subsequently prosecute the defendant for the same act that produced those charges. This right is derived from the prohibition of double jeopardy that is found in the Fifth Amendment. In a jury trial, double jeopardy protection attaches when the jury is impaneled and sworn in. For bench trials, or cases presented to a judge only, double jeopardy protection begins when the first witness is

sworn in. Under double jeopardy protection, the prosecution may not deliberately cause a mistrial if the trial is going poorly for the prosecution. However, if the jury cannot reach a verdict, and the court declares a mistrial, the defendant may be retried for the same offense.

Generally, a defendant may not face both federal and state prosecutions for the same offense. One exception to this general rule is that a defendant in state court may face charges in federal court for the same act with the permission of the attorney general, but only if the offense is within the jurisdiction of the federal court. For example, a conviction for driving while intoxicated raises no federal concerns; federal laws do not address that offense. Thus, the attorney general may not authorize the federal prosecution of a defendant who has been acquitted in state court of driving while intoxicated. The acquitted defendant may, however, face a civil lawsuit for damages, because civil actions do not put a person "in jeopardy of life or limb," and therefore double jeopardy does not apply to them (U.S. Const. amend. V, cl. 2). Similarly, the Double Jeopardy Clause is not violated when a defendant faces both criminal and administrative proceedings arising out of a single wrongful act. *Hudson v. United States*, 522 U.S. 93, 118 S. Ct. 488, 139 L. Ed. 2d 450 (1997).

Postconviction

Sentencing After conviction, a defendant may be allowed to remain free until sentencing. The decision on this issue is made by the court, and it depends on the nature of the conviction and the nature of the defendant's perceived character. For example, a court will not allow a convicted murderer or rapist to remain free until sentencing. A court may, however, allow a nonviolent convict to post a bond and to remain free pending sentencing.

Sentencing for a felony conviction is usually heard by the court in a separate hearing held several days or weeks after the verdict. At a felony sentencing hearing, the prosecution makes a recommendation of punishment, and the defendant usually argues for leniency. For lesser offenses, such as misdemeanors and violations, sentencing may immediately follow the verdict.

Judges generally have wide discretion to craft individualized sentences within statutory guidelines. However, states violate defendants' Sixth Amendment right to trial by jury in capital cases when they authorize the sentencing judge alone to determine the presence or absence of aggravating factors required for the imposition of the death penalty. *Ring v. Arizona,* 536 U.S. 584, 122 S. Ct. 2428, 153 L. Ed. 2d 556 (2002). And where a capital defendant's future dangerousness is at issue and the only sentencing alternative to death available to the jury is life imprisonment without the possibility of PAROLE, due process requires the court to allow the defendant to inform the jury of his or her parole ineligibility, either by a jury instruction or in arguments by counsel. *Shafer v. South Carolina,* 532 U.S. 36, 121 S. Ct. 1263, 149 L. Ed. 2d 178 (2001).

Sentencing can include any combination of community service, FORFEITURE of property, fines, and incarceration. Courts may also exercise their sentencing discretion and order a term of PROBATION.

Under state and federal forfeiture laws, law enforcement authorities are authorized to confiscate property of certain criminal defendants. Under federal law, persons who have been convicted of controlled-substance violations or RACKETEERING schemes may be forced to relinquish much of their PERSONAL PROPERTY, including real estate, stocks, cash savings, and vehicles. States also authorize forfeitures for the violation of certain state laws, such as those regarding controlled substances and the solicitation of prostitution.

Probation releases a convicted defendant into the community under the supervision of a probation officer. This type of sentence is generally reserved for first-time offenders, to give them an opportunity to reform and rehabilitate.

A probationer will be called back into court and sentenced to serve a term of incarceration if he or she breaks the terms of the probation. For example, suppose that a person who has been convicted of marijuana possession and sentenced to probation has been ordered to complete treatment for chemical dependency and to report to a probation officer twice a week. If the probationer fails to complete these requirements, the court may order the defendant to serve a period of incarceration for the marijuana offense.

If probation is revoked, the probationer is entitled to counsel. However, an indigent probationer is not automatically entitled to a court-appointed attorney. Whether a probationer receives free counsel depends on a number of factors. Generally, the court will appoint an attorney if an indigent probationer denies committing the alleged act and faces lengthy imprisonment.

Under the Eighth Amendment prohibition of cruel and unusual punishment, sentencing and confinement in jail or prison may not involve torture or barbarity. The Eighth Amendment is also construed as meaning that the punishment should fit the crime. For example, it would be cruel and unusual punishment to sentence a person who has been convicted of trespassing to the same punishment as a person who has been convicted of HOMICIDE.

With regard to the amount of punishment that may be inflicted, the prohibition against cruel and unusual punishment also bars punishment that is clearly out of proportion to the offense committed. The U.S. Supreme Court has considered the issue of proportionality, particularly in the context of the death penalty. In *Coker v. Georgia,* 433 U.S. 584, 97 S. Ct. 2861, 53 L. Ed. 2d 982 (1977), the Court held that death was a disproportionate penalty for the crime of raping an adult woman.

But the high court has held that the death penalty itself is not inherently cruel, instead describing it as "an extreme sanction, suitable to the most extreme of crimes" (GREGG V. GEORGIA, 428 U.S. 153, 96 S. Ct. 2909, 49 L. Ed. 2d 859 [1976]). Modern methods of administering CAPITAL PUNISHMENT, such as shooting, hanging, electrocution, and lethal injection, have been upheld as constitutional by federal and state courts. The U.S. Supreme Court has held that statutes providing a mandatory death sentence for certain degrees or categories of murder are unconstitutional because they preclude sentencing authorities from considering aspects of a particular defendant's character or record, or from considering circumstances that might mitigate a particular crime (see *Lockett v. Ohio,* 438 U.S. 586, 98 S. Ct. 2954, 57 L. Ed. 2d 973 [1978]). In *Ford v. Wainwright,* 477 U.S. 399, 106 S. Ct. 2595, 91 L. Ed. 2d 335 (1986), the Court held that the Eighth Amendment prohibits states from inflicting the penalty of death upon a prisoner who is insane.

The U.S. Supreme Court has also ruled that the execution of mentally retarded criminals violates the Eighth Amendment's guarantee against cruel and unusual punishment. ATKINS V. VIRGINIA, 536 U.S. 304, 122 S. Ct. 2242, 153 L. Ed. 2d 335 (2002). Citing "evolving standards of decency," the Court stated that its decision was informed by a national consensus reflected in deliberations of the American public, legislators, scholars, and judges. *Atkins* overruled *Penry v. Lynaugh*, 492 U.S. 302, 109 S. Ct. 2934, 106 L. Ed. 2d 256 (1989), a decision rendered just 13 years earlier. However, in *Stanford v. Kentucky*, 492 U.S. 361, 109 S. Ct. 2969, 106 L. Ed. 2d 306 (1989), the Court found that there was no national consensus prohibiting the execution of juvenile offenders over age 15.

Appeal Contrary to popular belief, the U.S. Constitution does not guarantee the right to appeal a criminal conviction. Most states do provide the right to an appellate review of criminal convictions, to protect against trial court errors. However, many states limit their review of state court convictions by hearing only short oral arguments and issuing decisions without explanation.

Federal statutes grant criminal defendants in federal court the right to appeal. Only one review is granted as a matter of right, and this is to a U.S. court of appeals. Review of state and federal convictions in the U.S. Supreme Court is discretionary.

Where a criminal appeal is granted by state law as a matter of right, the court is required to appoint an attorney to represent indigent defendants on appeal. An indigent defendant is also entitled to a free trial transcript or other means of affording appellate review; this applies to any indigent defendant, including one who is punished only with a fine.

On appeal, the burden is on the defendant to prove that an error occurred in the trial or that the evidence was insufficient to convict. Appellate courts reviewing a defendant's challenge to the appropriateness of a particular sentence must generally apply a deferential standard of review. Sentencing courts are in a better position than are appellate courts to decide whether a particular set of individual circumstances justifies the imposition of a given sentence under the sentencing guidelines, the U.S. Supreme Court has observed. *Burford v. United States*, 532 U.S. 59, 121 S. Ct. 1276, 149 L. Ed. 2d 197 (2001). Defendants must raise all claims of trial error in their first appeal in order to preserve the claims for future appeals.

Habeas Corpus Petitions After an incarcerated defendant has exhausted all appeals without success, he or she may file a writ of HABEAS CORPUS. This is a civil suit against the warden of the prison (in his or her professional capacity), challenging the constitutionality of the incarceration. There is no right to the assistance of an attorney for habeas corpus petitions.

A habeas corpus petition is not another appeal. The only basis for a writ of habeas corpus is the deprivation of a constitutional right. For example, an inmate may claim that he or she was denied the assistance of counsel guaranteed by the Sixth Amendment, because the defense attorney was incompetent. But defendants generally may not rely on habeas corpus proceedings to challenge a federal sentence on the ground that the prior state convictions upon which the federal sentence was based had been unconstitutionally obtained. *Daniels v. United States*, 5532 U.S. 394, 121 S.Ct. 1567, 149 L. Ed. 2d 608 (2001).

Parole If an inmate is released on parole and then violates the terms of the parole, he or she must attend a hearing to determine whether parole will be revoked. The parolee may be entitled to the assistance of counsel at the revocation hearing. This entitlement will depend on a number of factors, including whether the parolee denies committing the alleged acts, as well as the rules of the parole board. If the parolee can afford a private attorney, he or she is free to hire one; there is no bar to representation in parole-revocation hearings.

Inmates who seek parole often cite mitigating factors that existed either before, after, or at the time the crime was committed. However, parole boards and related EXECUTIVE BRANCH departments are under no obligation to give mitigating evidence any weight, and may typically reject an inmate's request for parole without providing any reason for doing so. Accordingly, the federal Bureau of Prisons has the authority to adopt regulations that categorically deny early-release incentive to prisoners whose current offense was a felony attended by "the carrying, possession, or use of a firearm." *Lopez v. Davis*, 531 U.S. 230, 121 S.Ct. 714, 148 L. Ed. 2d 635 (2001).

FURTHER READINGS

Arkin, Marc M. 1992. "Rethinking the Constitutional Right to a Criminal Appeal." *University of California at Los Angeles Law Review* 39.

Israel, Jerold H., Yale Kamisar, and Wayne R. LaFave. 1993. *Criminal Procedure and the Constitution: Leading Supreme Court Cases and Introductory Text.* St. Paul, Minn.: West.

PMBR. 1993. "Criminal Procedure." *Multistate Workbook.* vol. 2. Multistate Legal Studies.

Automobile Searches "Is the Fourth Amendment in Jeopardy?" (In Focus); Custodial Interrogation; Incorporation Doctrine; Prisoners' Rights; Public Defender; Right to Counsel.

CRIMINOLOGY

The scientific study of the causation, correction, and prevention of crime.

As a subdivision of the larger field of sociology, criminology draws on psychology, economics, anthropology, psychiatry, biology, statistics, and other disciplines to explain the causes and prevention of criminal behavior. Subdivisions of criminology include penology, the study of prisons and prison systems; biocriminology, the study of the biological basis of criminal behavior; feminist criminology, the study of women and crime; and criminalistics, the study of crime detection, which is related to the field of FORENSIC SCIENCE.

Criminology has historically played a reforming role in relation to CRIMINAL LAW and the criminal justice system. As an applied discipline, it has produced findings that have influenced legislators, judges, prosecutors, lawyers, PROBATION officers, and prison officials, prompting them to better understand crime and criminals and to develop better and more humane sentences and treatments for criminal behavior.

History

The origins of criminology are usually located in the late-eighteenth-century writings of those who sought to reform criminal justice and penal systems that they perceived as cruel, inhumane, and ARBITRARY. These old systems applied the law unequally, were subject to great corruption, and often used torture and the death penalty indiscriminately.

The leading theorist of this classical school of criminology, the Italian Cesare BONESANO BECCARIA (1738–94), argued that the law must apply equally to all, and that punishments for specific crimes should be standardized by legislatures, thus avoiding judicial abuses of power. Both Beccaria and another classical theorist, the Englishman JEREMY BENTHAM (1748–1832), argued that people are rational beings who exercise free will in making choices. Beccaria and Bentham understood the dominant motive in making choices to be the seeking of pleasure and the avoidance of pain. Thus, they argued that a punishment should fit the crime in such a way that the pain involved in potential punishment would be greater than any pleasure derived from committing the crime. The writings of these theorists led to greater CODIFICATION and standardization of European and U.S. laws.

Criminologists of the early nineteenth century argued that legal punishments that had been created under the guidance of the classical school did not sufficiently consider the widely varying circumstances of those who found themselves in the gears of the criminal justice system. Accordingly, they proposed that those who could not distinguish right from wrong, particularly children and mentally ill persons, should be exempted from the punishments that were normally meted out to mentally capable adults who had committed the same crimes. Along with the contributions of a later generation of criminologists, known as the positivists, such writers argued that the punishment should fit the criminal, not the crime.

Later in the nineteenth century, the positivist school of criminology brought a scientific approach to criminology, including findings from biology and medicine. The leading figure of this school was the Italian Cesare Lombroso (1836–1909). Influenced by Charles R. Darwin's theory of evolution, Lombroso measured the physical features of prison inmates and concluded that criminal behavior correlated with specific bodily characteristics, particularly cranial, skeletal, and neurological malformations. According to Lombroso, biology created a criminal class among the human population. Subsequent generations of criminologists have disagreed harshly with Lombroso's conclusions on this matter. However, Lombroso had a more lasting effect on criminology with other findings that emphasized the multiple causes of crime, including environmental causes that were not biologically determined. He was also a pioneer of the case-study approach to criminology.

Other late-nineteenth-century developments in criminology included the work of statisticians of the cartographic school, who analyzed data on population and crime. These included Lambert Adolphe Quetelet, (1796–1874) of France and André Michel Guerry, of Belgium. Both of these researchers compiled detailed, statistical information relating to crime and also attempted to identify the circumstances that predisposed people to commit crimes.

The writings of French sociologist Emile Durkheim (1858–1917) also exerted a great influence on criminology. Durkheim advanced the hypothesis that criminal behavior is a normal part of all societies. No society, he argued, can ever have complete uniformity of moral consciousness. All societies must permit some deviancy, including criminal deviancy, or they will stagnate. He saw the criminal as an acceptable human being and one of the prices that a society pays for freedom.

Durkheim also theorized about the ways in which modern, industrial societies differ from nonindustrial ones. Industrial societies are not as effective at producing what Durkheim called a collective conscience that effectively controls the behavior of individuals. Individuals in industrial societies are more likely to exhibit what Durkheim called *anomie*—a Greek word meaning "without norms." Consequently, modern societies have had to develop specialized laws and criminal justice systems that were not necessary in early societies to control behavior.

Early efforts to organize criminologists in the United States attracted law enforcement officials and others who were interested in the criminal justice system. In 1941, a group of individuals in California organized for the purpose of improving police training and the standardization of police-training curricula. In 1946, this movement developed into the establishment of the Society for the Advancement of Criminology, which changed its name to the American Society of Criminology in 1957. Initial efforts of this organization focused upon scientific crime detection, investigation, and identification; crime prevention, public safety, and security; law enforcement administration; administration of criminal justice; traffic administration; and probation.

The American Society of Criminology has since attracted thousands of members, including academics, practitioners, and students of the criminal justice system. Studies of criminology include both the theoretical and the pragmatic, and some combine elements of both. Although some aspects of criminology as a science are still considered radical, others have developed as standards in the study of crime and criminal justice.

Sociology and Criminology

During the twentieth century, the sociological approach to criminology became the most influential approach. Sociology is the study of social behavior, systems, and structures. In rela-

tion to criminology, it may be divided into social-structural and social-process approaches.

Social-Structural Criminology Social-structural approaches to criminology examine the way in which social situations and structures influence or relate to criminal behavior. An early example of this approach, the ecological school of criminology, was developed in the 1920s and 1930s at the University of Chicago. It seeks to explain crime's relationship to social and environmental change. For example, it attempts to describe why certain areas of a city will have a tendency to attract crime and also have less-vigorous police enforcement. Researchers have found that urban areas in transition from residential to business uses are most often targeted by criminals. Such communities often have disorganized social networks that foster a weaker sense of social standards.

Another social-structural approach is the conflict school of criminology. It traces its roots to Marxist theories that saw crime as ultimately a product of conflict between different classes under the system of capitalism. Criminology conflict theory suggests that the laws of society emerge out of conflict rather than out of consensus. It holds that laws are made by the group that is in power, to control those who are not in power. Conflict theorists propose, as do other theorists, that those who commit crimes are not fundamentally different from the rest of the population. They call the idea that society may be clearly divided into criminals and noncriminals a dualistic fallacy, or a misguided notion. These theorists maintain, instead, that the determination of whether someone is a criminal or not often depends on the way society reacts to those who deviate from accepted norms. Many conflict theorists and others argue that minorities and poor people are more quickly labeled as criminals than are members of the majority and wealthy individuals.

Critical criminology, also called radical criminology, shares with conflict criminology a debt to Marxism. It came into prominence in the early 1970s and attempted to explain contemporary social upheavals. Critical criminology relies on economic explanations of behavior and argues that economic and social inequalities cause criminal behavior. It focuses less on the study of individual criminals, and advances the belief that existing crime cannot be eliminated within the capitalist system. It also asserts, like the conflict school, that law has an inherent bias in favor of the upper or ruling class, and that the state and its legal system exist to advance the interests of the ruling class. Critical criminologists argue that corporate, political, and environmental crime are underreported and inadequately addressed in the current criminal justice system.

Feminist criminology emphasizes the subordinate position of women in society. According to feminist criminologists, women remain in a position of inferiority that has not been fully rectified by changes in the law during the late twentieth century. Feminist criminology also explores the ways in which women's criminal behavior is related to their objectification as commodities in the sex industry.

Others using the social-structural approach have studied GANGS, juvenile delinquency, and the relationship between family structure and criminal behavior.

Social-Process Criminology Social-process criminology theories attempt to explain how people become criminals. These theories developed through recognition of the fact that not all people who are exposed to the same social-structural conditions become criminals. They focus on criminal behavior as learned behavior.

Edwin H. Sutherland (1883–1950), a U.S. sociologist and criminologist who first presented his ideas in the 1920s and 1930s, advanced the theory of differential association to explain criminal behavior. He emphasized that criminal behavior is learned in interaction with others, usually in small groups, and that criminals learn to favor criminal behavior over noncriminal behavior through association with both forms of behavior in different degrees. As Sutherland wrote, "When persons become criminal, they do so because of contacts with criminal patterns and also because of isolation from anticriminal patterns." Although his theory has been greatly influential, Sutherland himself admitted that it did not satisfactorily explain all criminal behavior. Later theorists have modified his approach in an attempt to correct its shortcomings.

Control theory, developed in the 1960s and 1970s, attempts to explain ways to train people to engage in law-abiding behavior. Although there are different approaches within control theory, they share the view that humans require nurturing in order to develop attachments or bonds to people and that personal bonds are key in producing internal controls such as con-

science and guilt and external controls such as shame. According to this view, crime is the result of insufficient attachment and commitment to others.

Walter C. Reckless developed one version of control theory, called *containment*. He argued that a combination of internal psychological containments and external social containments prevents people from deviating from social norms. In simple communities, social pressure to conform to community standards, usually enforced by social ostracism, was sufficient to control behavior. As societies became more complex, internal containments played a more crucial role in determining whether people behaved according to public laws. Furthermore, containment theorists have found that internal containments require a positive self-image. All too often, a sense of alienation from society and its norms forms in modern individuals, who, as a result, do not develop internal containment mechanisms.

The sociologist Travis Hirschi has developed his own control theory that attempts to explain conforming, or lawful, rather than deviant, or unlawful, behavior. He stresses the importance of the individual's bond to society in determining conforming behavior. His research has found that socioeconomic class has little to do with determining delinquent behavior, and that young people who are not very attached to their parents or to school are more likely to be delinquent than those who are strongly attached. He also found that youths who have a strongly positive view of their own accomplishments are more likely to view society's laws as valid constraints on their behavior.

Political Criminology

Political criminology is similar to the other camps in this area. It involves study into the forces that determine how, why, and with what consequences societies chose to address criminals and crime in general. Those who are involved with political criminology focus on the causes of crime, the nature of crime, the social and political meanings that attach to crime, and crime-control policies, including the study of the bases upon which crime and punishment is committed and the choices made by the principals in criminal justice.

Although the theories of political criminology and conflict criminology overlap to some extent, political criminologists deny that the terms are interchangeable. The primary focus points in the new movement of political criminology similarly overlap with other theories, including the concerns and ramifications of street crime and the distribution of power in crime-control strategies. This movement has largely been a loose, academic effort.

Other Issues

Criminologists also study a host of other issues related to crime and the law. These include studies of the VICTIMS OF CRIME, focusing upon their relations to the criminal, and their role as potential causal agents in crime; juvenile delinquency and its correction; and the media and their relation to crime, including the influence of PORNOGRAPHY. Much research related to criminology has focused on the biological basis of criminal behavior. In fact, a field of study called biocriminology, which attempts to explore the biological basis of criminal behavior, has emerged. Research in this area has focused on chromosomal abnormalities, hormonal and brain chemical imbalances, diet, neurological conditions, drugs, and alcohol as variables that contribute to criminal behavior.

The true effect of criminology upon practices in the criminal justice system is still subject to question. Although a number of commentators have noted that studies in criminology have led to significant changes among criminal laws in the various states, other critics have suggested that studies in criminology have not directly led to a reduction of crime.

In *McCleskey v. Kemp*, 481 U.S. 279, 107 S. Ct. 1756, 95 L. Ed. 2d 262 (1987), an individual who had been sentenced to death for a murder in Georgia demonstrated to the U.S. Supreme Court that a criminologist's study showed that the race of individuals in that state impacted whether the defendant was sentenced to life or to death. The study demonstrated that a black defendant who had killed a white victim was four times more likely to be sentenced to death than was a defendant who had killed a black victim. The defendant claimed that the study demonstrated that the state of Georgia had violated his rights under the EQUAL PROTECTION CLAUSE of the FOURTEENTH AMENDMENT, as well as under the Eighth Amendment's protection against CRUEL AND UNUSUAL PUNISHMENT.

The high court disagreed. Although the majority did question the validity of the study's findings, it held that the study did not establish that officials in Georgia had acted with discriminatory purpose, and that it did not establish

that racial bias had affected the officials' decisions with respect to the death sentence. Accordingly, the death sentence violated neither the Fourteenth Amendment nor the EIGHTH AMENDMENT.

Criminology has had more of an effect when states and the federal government consider new criminal laws and sentencing provisions. Criminologists' theories are also often debated in the context of the death penalty and crime control acts among legislators and policymakers. In this light, criminology is perhaps not at the forefront of the development of the criminal justice system, but it most certainly works in the background in the determination of criminal justice policies.

FURTHER READINGS

Carrington, Kerry, and Russell Hogg, eds. 2002. *Critical Criminology: Issues, Debates, Challenges.* Portland, Ore.: Willan Publishing.

Cullen, Francis T., and Velmer S. Burton, Jr. 1994. *Contemporary Criminological Theory.* New York: New York Univ. Press.

Reid, Sue T. 1994. *Crime and Criminology.* 7th ed. Madison, Wis.: Times Mirror Higher Education Group, Brown & Benchmark.

White, Rob. 2001. "Criminology for Sale: Institutional Change and Intellectual Field." *Current Issues in Criminal Justice* 13 (November).

CROSS-REFERENCES

Critical Legal Studies; Forensic Science; Marx, Karl Heinrich.

CRITICAL LEGAL STUDIES

An intellectual movement whose members argue that law is neither neutral nor value free but is in fact inseparable from politics.

Critical legal studies (CLS) is a sometimes revolutionary movement that challenges and seeks to overturn accepted norms and standards in legal theory and practice. CLS seeks to fundamentally alter JURISPRUDENCE, exposing it as not a rational system of accumulated wisdom but an ideology that supports and makes possible an unjust political system. CLS scholars attempt to debunk the law's pretensions to determinacy, neutrality, and objectivity. The law, in CLS scholarship, is a tool used by the establishment to maintain its power and domination over an unequal status quo. Openly a movement of leftist politics, CLS seeks to subvert the philosophical and political authority of what it sees as an unjust social system. CLS advances a theoretical and practical project of reconstruction of the law and of society itself. CLS is also a membership organization that seeks to advance its own cause and that of its members.

CLS was officially started in the spring of 1977 at a conference at the University of Wisconsin in Madison. However, the roots of the organization extend back to LEGAL REALISM, a movement in U.S. legal scholarship that flourished in the 1920s and 1930s. OLIVER WENDELL HOLMES is credited with being the grandfather of CLS with his various observations in *The Common Law* (1881). The legal realists rebelled against the accepted legal theories of the day, including most of the accepted wisdom of nineteenth-century legal thought. Like CLS, legal realism emphasized that judicial decisions depend largely on the predilections and social situation of the judge. Thus, the legal realists urged that much more attention be paid to the social context of the law. The legal realists eventually influenced the development of the NEW DEAL under President FRANKLIN D. ROOSEVELT in the 1930s, and many served in positions where they affected government policy.

In the 1960s, many of the founding members of CLS participated in social activism connected to the CIVIL RIGHTS MOVEMENT and the VIETNAM WAR. Many future CLS scholars entered law school in those years or shortly thereafter, and they quickly became unhappy with what they saw as a lack of philosophical depth and rigor in the teaching and theory of law. Roberto Mangabeira Unger, a leading CLS theorist, has described the law faculty of those days as "a priesthood that had lost their faith and kept their jobs." These young students began to apply the ideas, theories, and philosophies of postmodernity (intellectual movements of the last half of the twentieth century) to the study of law, borrowing from fields as diverse as social theory, political philosophy, economics, and literary theory. Since then, CLS has steadily grown in influence. By 1989, over 700 articles and books had been published expounding the ideas of this movement. Besides Unger, noted CLS theorists include Robert W. Gordon, Morton J. Horwitz, Duncan Kennedy, and CATHARINE A. MACKINNON.

CLS has been largely a U.S. movement, though it has borrowed heavily from European philosophers, including nineteenth-century German social theorists such as KARL MARX, Friedrich Engels, and MAX WEBER; Max Horkheimer and Herbert Marcuse of the Frankfurt school of German social philosophy; the

Italian Marxist Antonio Gramsci; and poststructuralist French thinkers such as Michel Foucault and Jacques Derrida, representing, respectively, the fields of history and literary theory.

Several subcategories exist within the CLS movement: feminist legal criticism, which examines the role of gender in the law; critical race theory (CRT), which is concerned with the role of race in the law; postmodernism, a critique of the law influenced by developments in literary theory; and a subcategory that emphasizes political economy and the economic context of legal decisions and issues. Scholars disagree about the extent to which CLS is a coherent intellectual movement. Some see it simply as a political position adopted by a disparate group of legal theorists who have fundamentally different, even contradictory, views. Others emphasize that CLS theorists share a number of important ideas and approaches that together constitute a new approach to legal scholarship.

First among the basic ideas that CLS scholars tend to share is the notion that law is politics—in other words, that law and politics are indistinguishable from one another. Liberalism, according to CLS theorists, has traditionally viewed the law as an objective, rational process of precise decision-making and politics as a realm of imprecise, often irrational opinions and competing interests. According to CLS theorists, however, the law is not separate from the political realm and its disputes. Legal reasoning, rather than being a strong fortress of objective rationality, is a fragile structure fraught with contradictory and ARBITRARY categorizations that are endlessly redefined and reworked.

In this view, the law is only an elaborate political ideology, which, like other political ideologies, exists to support the interests of the party or class that forms it. The legal system, according to CLS, supports the status quo, perpetuating the established power relations of society. The law does have logic and structure, but these grow out of the power relationships of society. CLS therefore sees the law as a collection of beliefs and prejudices that covers the injustices of society with a mask of legitimacy. Law is an instrument for oppression used by the wealthy and the powerful to maintain their place in the hierarchy.

As part of its project, CLS exposes what it sees as the flaws in various aspects of liberal legal theory and practice. It argues, for example, that judicial objectivity is impossible because political neutrality or philosophical objectivity cannot exist. CLS thus strips the judiciary of its supposedly disinterested role in society. As Allan C. Hutchinson, a CLS theorist, wrote: "The judicial emperor, clothed and coifed in appropriately legitimate and voguish garb by the scholarly rag trade, chooses and acts to protect and preserve the propertied interest of vested white and male power." In this way, CLS seeks to "delegitimate" and "demystify" the law—that is, it seeks to undermine the law's acceptance and to remove the cloak of mystery and awe surrounding its functioning.

CLS theorists also share the related view that the law is indeterminate. They have shown that using standard legal arguments, it is possible to reach sharply contrasting conclusions in individual cases. The conclusions reached in any case will have more to do with the social context in which they are argued and decided than with any overarching scheme of legal reasoning. Moreover, CLS scholars argue that the esoteric and convoluted nature of legal reasoning actually screens the law's indeterminacy. They have used the ideas of deconstruction to explore the ways in which legal texts are open to multiple interpretations. (Deconstruction is a movement in literary theory that is connected to the work of French philosopher Derrida and that emphasizes the fundamental indeterminacy of language.)

Consistent with their position on the political left, CLS scholars have a common dissatisfaction with the established legal and political order and particularly for the liberalism that they see as the dominant political ideology. CLS demonstrates how liberalism describes the world according to categories that exist as dualities: subjective-objective, male-female, public-private, self-other, individual-community, and so forth. These dualities are sometimes called paired opposites by CLS theorists. CLS then breaks down the dualities and shows how they create an ideology that furthers the interests of the ruling class. CLS theorists also decry the individualism that liberal society fosters, and they call for a renewed emphasis on communal rather than individual values. They particularly object to capitalism as an economic system, and they see liberalism as capitalism's greatest apologist.

Feminist Legal Criticism

Catharine A. MacKinnon is a leading figure in radical feminist criticism (sometimes called fem-crit). Throughout her career, MacKinnon

has attempted to show the ways in which the established legal system reflects the sexism of the society that created it. The law, according to MacKinnon, is only one extension of a male-dominated society that is characterized by inequality between the genders and by the sexual objectification of women. As the product of a male-oriented view of the world and a male-dominated state, the law systematically victimizes and discriminates against women. "The law," MacKinnon wrote, "sees and treats women the way men see and treat women." It ensures male control over female sexuality. The feminist project to counter this negative aspect of the legal tradition, MacKinnon wrote, is "to uncover and claim as valid the experience of women, the major content of which is the devalidation of women's experience."

One topic that MacKinnon has examined in detail is the legal doctrine regarding rape. Citing the difficulty that women have proving legally that they have been raped, MacKinnon interprets rape doctrine as the product of male ideology. She argues that rape and the laws surrounding it, which are often ineffective in securing convictions of male rapists, are used by men to keep women in a position of submission and inferiority. The law's standards of objectivity and neutrality, according to MacKinnon, actually hide a male bias that makes it very difficult for a woman to win a rape case in the legal system. The state thus perpetuates rape in a way that promotes the dominance of men.

MacKinnon also uses rape as an example of the way in which the conventional liberal distinction between public and private spheres actually enhances male power. For women, according to MacKinnon, the private sphere cannot be separated from the public. The private sphere as it is usually understood—that is, the home—is actually a place where the law defines men's right to dominate women through domestic abuse, marital rape, and exploitive work conditions. The law, according to MacKinnon, overlooks such injustices, and legal doctrines regarding the private sphere of the home perpetuate rather than resolve them.

Critical Race Theory (CRT)

CRT began in the mid-1970s when many intellectuals perceived that the civil rights movement of the 1960s had ended and that in fact many of its gains were being turned back. As a result, they began to develop new theories and concepts that would allow them to understand the causes and implications of these new developments. Like CLS, CRT gathers disparate scholars and theorists under a common heading. However, CRT is a less formally organized school of thought than CLS. Leading critical race theorists include DERRICK ALBERT BELL JR., Alan D. Freeman, and Patricia J. Williams. The first annotated bibliography of CRT writings, published in 1993, listed over 200 books and articles.

Critical race theorists share a number of themes. Like CLS, CRT finds major faults in liberalism and particular features of liberal jurisprudence that bear on race, including AFFIRMATIVE ACTION, neutrality, and "color blindness." Many CRT writers, for example, dispute that the Constitution is or ever can be "color-blind." They also assert that supposed breakthroughs in the area of racial rights by the Supreme Court serve only to validate an unjust political system by creating the illusion that racial inequalities are being ended when in fact they are not. CRT scholars generally seek a greater understanding of the social origins of race and racism, and, like CLS theorists, they employ social theory and science in that cause. Many in the CRT movement examine how the structure of legal thought or culture influences its content, usually in a way that maintains the status quo. Some in the movement make a case for cultural separatism or nationalism for people of color, arguing that preserving the diversity and separateness of different racial groups will benefit everyone. CRT also attempts to understand the cyclical nature of U.S. race relations—characterized by periods of racial progress and relative harmony followed by periods of racial retrenchment and discord. CRT writers also make frequent use of historical and social theories regarding colonialism and SLAVERY.

Many CRT writers employ unconventional narrative methods—sometimes called legal storytelling—in their legal writing, including fiction, myth, parable, anecdote, and autobiography. These approaches often demonstrate the way in which the majoritarian mind-set (in this case, the outlook of the white majority, including its prejudices and presuppositions) impedes the cause of racial reform. Bell, for example, published in a legal journal a science fiction story with implications for race relations in the United States. In it, an extraterrestrial race comes to earth and offers to solve the United States' economic and environmental problems

in exchange for possession of all black U.S. citizens. In describing what happens after this event, the story shows how a majority group (here, white U.S. citizens) must always put some other group on the bottom of the socioeconomic ladder as a scapegoat for the country's social ills.

CLS and Its Alternative View of the Law and Society

Consistent with their leftist heritage, CLS theorists call for radical changes in the law and in the structure of society itself. Unger has called this radical project "institutional reconstruction." Many in the CLS movement want to overturn the hierarchical structures of domination in modern society, and many of them have focused on the law as a tool in achieving this goal. The law, CLS claims, has played a key role in maintaining that hierarchy by impeding efforts at social change. In general, CLS argues that there is no natural or inevitable form of social organization, and there is by no means agreement between CLS scholars as to what form society and its laws should take. CLS thus avoids the kind of blueprint for social revolution that radical leftist movements such as Marxism-Leninism supplied in the past. Instead, leading CLS devotees envision a potential emancipation of individuals from the structures of power that restrict and victimize them. For these reasons, the political philosophy of many in the CLS movement has been described as utopian, a characterization that many do not completely deny.

Unger provides the most well-known example of the utopian tendencies in CLS. In his writings, he has attempted to outline a "cultural-revolutionary practice" that will lead to nothing less than "the systematic remaking of all direct personal connections ... through their progressive emancipation from a background plan of social division and hierarchy." Unger envisions a future in which the categories that currently divide and separate people—including sexual, racial, political, and class categories—are broken down, allowing people to share more values and to create a more harmonious society. He calls for an "empowered democracy" with a government and economy that are largely decentralized. In terms of the economy, he proposes that capital be controlled by the government, which would establish a "rotating capital fund" that would pass to "teams of workers or technicians" who would decide how to use it. Many conditions of the economy, such as income disparity between individuals, would be addressed by "central agencies of government."

Such innovations would require major changes in the law, particularly as regards an understanding of rights, including property rights. In his call for a radical restructuring of rights, Unger proposes creating four categories: IMMUNITY rights, which protect the individual from the state, organizations, and other individuals; destabilization rights, which make it possible to dismantle institutions and practices that create social hierarchy and division; market rights, which constitute claims to social capital and replace conventional property rights; and solidarity rights, which are "the legal entitlements of communal life." Despite his criticism of liberalism, Unger calls his philosophy "superliberalism":

> It pushes the liberal premises about state and society, about freedom from dependence and governance of social relations by the will, to the point at which they merge into a larger ambition: the building of a social world less alien to a self that can always violate the generative rules of its own mental or social constructs and put other rules and other constructs in their place.Unger therefore seeks to reform the law and society in such a way as to liberate and empower every individual.

CLS has many critics. Some see it as lacking coherence, fraught with the very contradictions that it identifies in liberalism. Others accuse the movement of being nihilistic, of destroying the foundations of legal reasoning without putting anything in its place or without even making positive recommendations for change. They find CLS prescriptions for the future to be too vague and utopian for practical application. Another widespread complaint is that the writings of CLS scholars are unnecessarily obscure, opaque, and turgid.

Despite these criticisms, CLS has greatly influenced the study and theory of the law. After some early battles to gain acceptance in the 1970s and 1980s, it earned an accepted position in law schools across the United States. However, some legal scholars, both inside and outside the CLS movement, argue that as many of the original CLS adherents age and reach positions of power in established law schools, their original radical impetus will fade and moderate. Others argue that the call for justice and equality will always require an untempered radicalism that will be fueled by CLS. Whatever the outcome,

CLS has permanently changed the landscape of legal theory.

FURTHER READINGS

Boyle, James. 1992. *Critical Legal Studies.* New York: New York Univ. Press.

Delgado, Richard. 1993. "Critical Race Theory: An Annotated Bibliography." *Virginia Law Review* 79.

Hutchinson, Allan C., ed. 1989. *Critical Legal Studies.* Totowa, N.J.: Rowman & Littlefield.

———1987. *Critical Legal Studies.* Lanham, Md.: Rowman & Littlefield.

Unger, Roberto M. 1986. *The Critical Legal Studies Movement.* Cambridge, Mass.: Harvard Univ. Press.

Oetken, J. Paul. 1991. "Form and Substance in Critical Legal Studies." *Yale Law Journal* 100.

Tushnet, Mark. 1991. "Critical Legal Studies: A Political History." *Yale Law Journal* 100.

Unger, Roberto M. 1986. *The Critical Legal Studies Movement.* Cambridge, Mass.: Harvard Univ. Press.

CROSS-REFERENCES

Legal Education.

❖ CRITTENDEN, JOHN JORDAN

John Jordan Crittenden served as attorney general of the United States in 1841 under President WILLIAM H. HARRISON, and again in 1850 under President MILLARD FILLMORE. He is also known for his efforts to keep Kentucky in the Union during the Civil War.

Crittenden was born September 10, 1787, near Versailles, Woodford County, Kentucky. His father was a Revolutionary War soldier and an early Kentucky settler. Crittenden was schooled near his home in Jessamine County, Kentucky. He showed a great aptitude for learning and was encouraged to pursue a career in the law. He attended William and Mary College, and graduated in 1807. His first law practice was established in Logan County, Kentucky.

After two years as a struggling country lawyer, Crittenden was appointed attorney general for the Illinois Territory by Governor Vinian Edwards, of Kentucky, in 1809. His first experience as a public servant was cut short by the WAR OF 1812. Crittenden returned to Kentucky and enlisted as a volunteer; he served for three years and experienced firsthand the tragedy of war.

In 1816 Crittenden was elected to a term in the Kentucky state legislature. The following year, he was elected to a seat in the U.S. Senate, but he did not complete the term. Finding local politics more to his liking, he resigned in 1819 and returned to Frankfort, Kentucky, to reclaim his old seat in the statehouse.

"I HOPE TO FIND MY COUNTRY IN THE RIGHT; HOWEVER, I WILL STAND BY HER, RIGHT OR WRONG."
—JOHN J. CRITTENDEN

Though he had little affection for national politics, Crittenden did support fellow Kentuckian HENRY CLAY in his unsuccessful 1824 bid for the presidency. Crittenden respected Clay's views on a number of issues, and they became political allies and lifelong friends. It was because of his association with Clay that Crittenden lost his next job. In 1827 Crittenden was appointed U.S. district attorney for Kentucky by President JOHN QUINCY ADAMS. He held the post until 1829, when he was removed by President Andrew Jackson—after Crittenden and Clay had voiced their opposition to the financial policies of the Jackson administration.

In 1835 Crittenden decided to give politics another chance. Again, he sought and won a seat in the U.S. Senate. Crittenden was beginning his second Senate term when he was offered the position of attorney general by President Harrison. He accepted.

Crittenden had been an ardent Harrison supporter and had campaigned for him in 1840. When Harrison died of pneumonia shortly after his inauguration and was succeeded by Vice President JOHN TYLER, Crittenden was unable to support the new president. Along with other Whigs in the cabinet, Crittenden resigned in September 1841. In 1842 Crittenden found himself back in the U.S. Senate, appointed to fill the seat left vacant by the retirement of Clay. He finished Clay's term and was subsequently reelected in his own right.

Throughout his five separate terms in the Senate, Crittenden was affiliated with the Whigs. With the WHIG PARTY, he opposed the annexation of Texas, discouraged animosity toward Great Britain over the Oregon boundary, and refused to give enthusiastic support to the Mexican War.

John J. Crittenden.
LIBRARY OF CONGRESS

In 1848 while still a U.S. senator, Crittenden was elected governor of Kentucky; he resigned his Senate seat to accept the job. His return to Kentucky brought renewed contact with Clay, who was again running for the presidency. Crittenden, convinced that Clay was not a viable candidate, threw his support to ZACHARY TAYLOR, and caused a permanent rift between himself and Clay.

Following the death of President Taylor and the succession of Vice President Fillmore, Crittenden was offered his old cabinet post as attorney general. He again accepted, and through this office he authored an opinion upholding the

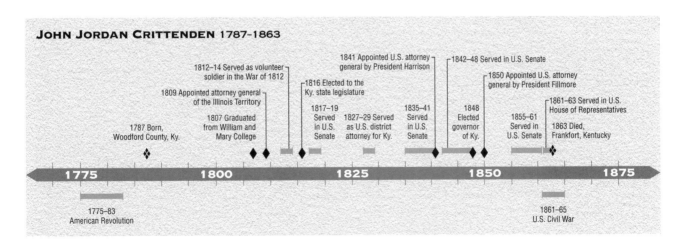

JOHN JORDAN CRITTENDEN 1787–1863

1787 Born, Woodford County, Ky.

1807 Graduated from William and Mary College

1809 Appointed attorney general of the Illinois Territory

1812–14 Served as volunteer soldier in the War of 1812

1816 Elected to the Ky. state legislature

1817–19 Served in U.S. Senate

1827–29 Served as U.S. district attorney for Ky.

1835–41 Served in U.S. Senate

1841 Appointed U.S. attorney general by President Harrison

1842–48 Served in U.S. Senate

1848 Elected governor of Ky.

1850 Appointed U.S. attorney general by President Fillmore

1855–61 Served in U.S. Senate

1861–63 Served in U.S. House of Representatives

1863 Died, Frankfort, Kentucky

1775 1800 1825 1850 1875

1775–83 American Revolution

1861–65 U.S. Civil War

constitutionality of fugitive slave laws. Though many of Crittenden's writings were controversial, he agreed with the view that attorney general opinions were only advisory and could be ignored by the president.

In 1855 Crittenden was elected to another term in the U.S. Senate. There, he vigorously opposed the KANSAS-NEBRASKA ACT of 1854. When the issue led to the breakup of the Whig party, he joined the KNOW-NOTHING PARTY in 1856. Two years later, he joined the Constitutional Union party, and campaigned on behalf of JOHN BELL and Edward Everett in the 1860 presidential election that brought ABRAHAM LINCOLN to the White House.

Although Crittenden did not agree with Lincoln on all matters of policy, he did oppose secession of the Southern states and he did support Lincoln's efforts to preserve the Union. As a prominent political figure in both the North and the South, Crittenden worked hard to effect a compromise that would avert a civil war.

In December 1860, he proposed an amendment to the Constitution that has come to be known as the Crittenden Resolution. To bring the Union together, he suggested that the Missouri Compromise line be restored and continued to California, that SLAVERY be guaranteed indefinitely in the District of Columbia, and that slaveholders be reimbursed for runaway slaves.

Crittenden's compromise effort was defeated by Lincoln's strong stand against any extension of slavery into the territories, and by opposition from strong Republican leaders in Congress. Nevertheless, Crittenden stood with the government and continued to support Lincoln's position that it was the right and duty of the government to maintain the Union.

Returning to Kentucky in early 1861, Crittenden traveled the state urging citizens to support the Union cause and to remain neutral in the escalating conflict. On May 27, 1861, he acted as chairman of the Frankfort Convention and successfully argued against leaders who encouraged Kentucky to join the Southern secessionists. For his efforts, Crittenden was returned to Congress, but this time to the U.S. House of Representatives.

As a representative, he opposed the confiscation acts, the EMANCIPATION PROCLAMATION, the military regime in Kentucky, the employment of slaves as soldiers, and the war in general.

> "NO OTHER PROFESSIONAL GROUP BEARS A RESPONSIBILITY AS GREAT AS THAT OF THE LEGAL PROFESSION FOR RIDDING OUR LAW AND OUR BODY POLITIC OF THIS CANCEROUS GROWTH OF RACISM."
> —GEORGE W. CROCKETT

On July 19, 1861, he offered a resolution that was adopted with only two dissenting votes:

Resolved by the house of representatives of the CONGRESS OF THE UNITED STATES, That the present deplorable civil war has been forced upon the country by the disunionists of the southern states, now in arms against the constitutional government, and in arms around the capital; that in this national emergency congress, banishing all feelings of mere passion or resentment, will recollect its only duty to the whole country; this war is not waged on their part in any spirit of oppression, or for any purpose of conquest or subjugation, or purpose of overthrowing or interfering with the rights of established institutions of those states, but to defend and maintain the supremacy of the constitution, and to preserve the Union with all the dignity, equality, and rights of the several states unimpaired; and that as soon as these objects are accomplished the war ought to cease.

By 1863 Crittenden had held political office for almost forty-five years. He had served two presidents as attorney general, completed five terms as a U.S. senator, and finished a single term as a U.S. representative. He was preparing to run for another term in the House when he died. He was remembered at his funeral as a man with fine personal qualities, a gift for public speaking, and a firm commitment to the Union.

Crittenden's efforts to preserve the Union were personal as well as political: two of his sons were on opposite sides of the issues and the battle lines. His youngest son, Thomas L. Crittenden, was a commissioned officer in the Union army; another son, George Bibb Crittenden, held similar rank in the army of the Confederacy.

❖ CROCKETT, GEORGE WILLIAM, JR.

George William Crockett Jr.'s political career spanned almost six decades. He was an attorney, a judge, and a leading CIVIL RIGHTS and LABOR UNION activist. At the age of 71, he was tapped to represent Michigan's 13th district in the U.S. House of Representatives. His ten-year stint in Congress was marked by many milestones and much controversy.

Crockett was born August 10, 1909, in Jacksonville, Florida. He grew up in the South when racial SEGREGATION was a fact of everyday life, an experience that fueled his commitment to correct injustices. He attended public schools and graduated with a bachelor of arts degree from Morehouse College in Atlanta in 1931. He studied law at the University of Michigan, graduating in 1934. He was admitted to the Florida bar in the same year and began his legal career in Jacksonville.

In 1939, Crockett became the first African American lawyer in the U.S. DEPARTMENT OF LABOR. He was one of the first hearing examiners in the Fair Employment Practices Commission. Crockett's early involvement in LABOR LAW led to his founding and directing the Fair Employment Practices Department of the International United Auto Workers (UAW) Union in 1944. He also served as treasurer and associate general counsel to the UAW and as assistant to the union's secretary-treasurer.

After leaving the UAW, Crockett returned to private practice with the law firm of Goodman, Crockett, Eden, and Rob, where he was a partner from 1946 to 1966. He remained active in the civil rights and labor movements throughout his career. In the 1949 Foley Square trial, he defended several members of the U.S. Communist Party against charges of un-American activities. (*United States v. Foster*, 9 F.R.D. 367 [S.D.N.Y.]). Crockett's clients, along with many codefendants, were charged with conspiracy to advocate the overthrow or destruction of the government by force or violence and conspiracy to organize the Communist Party as a society advocating such overthrow or destruction. During the trial, he railed against what he thought were the judge's abuses of his clients' rights. His refusal to back down earned him a CONTEMPT citation (*United States v. Sacher*, 9 F.R.D. 394 [S.D.N.Y.]). His conviction and sentence for contempt were upheld on appeal, 182 F.2d 416 (2nd Cir.), and he spent four months in the penitentiary at Ashland, Kentucky, in 1952.

George W. Crockett.
AP/WIDE WORLD PHOTOS

While serving his prison term, Crockett wrote to his son that prison is a good place to learn patience because the relentless passage of time teaches the value of persistence. Crockett's patience was severely tested after his return from prison when he was ostracized and forced to fight a move to disbar him. Because of his involvement in the Foley Square trial, the labor movement, and the CIVIL RIGHTS MOVEMENT, he was labeled a communist sympathizer. However, in 1963, when President JOHN F. KENNEDY planned a meeting of civil rights lawyers at the White House, Crockett's name was on the list of those the president wanted to attend. To be allowed into the White House, Crockett had to

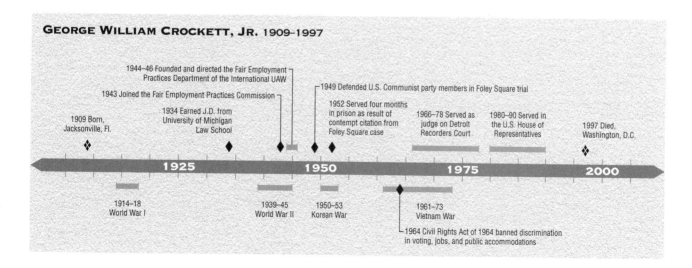

GEORGE WILLIAM CROCKETT, JR. 1909–1997

1944–46 Founded and directed the Fair Employment Practices Department of the International UAW

1943 Joined the Fair Employment Practices Commission

1949 Defended U.S. Communist party members in Foley Square trial

1934 Earned J.D. from University of Michigan Law School

1952 Served four months in prison as result of contempt citation from Foley Square case

1966–78 Served as judge on Detroit Recorders Court

1980–90 Served in the U.S. House of Representatives

1909 Born, Jacksonville, Fl.

1997 Died, Washington, D.C.

1925   1950   1975   2000

1914–18 World War I

1939–45 World War II

1950–53 Korean War

1961–73 Vietnam War

1964 Civil Rights Act of 1964 banned discrimination in voting, jobs, and public accommodations

be investigated by the FEDERAL BUREAU OF INVESTIGATION, which finally granted him a security clearance.

Crockett served as a judge of the Detroit Recorder's (Criminal) Court from 1966 to 1978. His years on the bench included a term as presiding judge in 1974. He retired from the recorder's court in 1978, but soon returned to public service. In 1980, Representative Charles C. Diggs Jr. (D-Mich.), one of the few people who had befriended Crockett upon his return from prison in 1952, was himself sentenced to three years in prison, for accepting kickbacks from his congressional staff. Diggs endorsed Crockett to replace him, and, in a special election to fill the vacancy, Crockett was elected to the post.

At the age of 71, Crockett launched into his new career in Congress. He continued to take controversial positions on issues ranging from African Americans in the foreign service to decriminalization of drugs. He was arrested in 1984 at a demonstration protesting South Africa's policy of apartheid. In 1985, when tensions between Arabs and Jews in the Middle East were high and the United States officially supported Israel, Crockett invited a representative of the Palestine Liberation Organization (PLO) to brief members of Congress on the PLO's views about conditions in the Middle East. The invitation was denounced by some members of the House, and, after intervention by the SECRETARY OF STATE, the visit was canceled.

In 1986, Crockett criticized President Ronald Reagan's administration for not appointing more African American ambassadors. He noted that the number of African Americans in the foreign service had declined during the years Reagan had been president. He used his position as chair of the House Subcommittee on Western Hemisphere Activities to initiate a hearing on racism in appointments to the foreign service. The result was a promise from the secretary of state that the STATE DEPARTMENT would pursue a goal of appointing more members of minority groups to foreign service positions. In 1987, President Reagan appointed Crockett to the position of public delegate to the UNITED NATIONS.

In addition to chairing the House Subcommittee on Western Hemisphere Activities, Crockett served on the Committee on Foreign Affairs, the Committee on the Judiciary, and the Select Committee on Aging. His final controversial act as a representative came in 1989 when he became the first member of Congress to recommend publicly the decriminalization of drug possession. Stating, "Our courts are burdened down with these drug cases and there is nothing they can do about it," Crockett called for decriminalization as "the only solution." He was sharply criticized by many members of the administration, including William J. Bennett, who was the director of federal drug policy.

Crockett retired from public life at the end of his fifth term in the House, which ended January 3, 1991, but remained one of Detroit's best-known civil rights leaders. In 1992, he surprised many when he openly backed Dennis Archer in the Detroit mayoral race, and encouraged long-time friend Coleman Young to step down. In 1995, Crockett's story was recounted in a chapter of *Black Judges on Justice*. Crockett died on September 7, 1997, in Washington, D.C, after suffering a stroke. He had been battling bone cancer.

FURTHER READINGS

Gordon Press. 1991. *Black Americans in Congress, 1870–1989*. Bowling Green Station, N.Y.: Gordon Press.

McGraw, Bill. 1997. "George Crockett is Dead at 88: Activist and Judge Stood for the Underdog." *Detroit Free Press* (September 8). Available online at <www.freep.com/news/obituaries/qcrock8.htm> (accessed June 29, 2003).

U.S. Government Printing Office. 1988. *Biographical Directory of the U.S. Congress, 1774–1989*. Washington, D.C.: U.S. Government Printing Office.

Washington, Linn. 1995. *Black Judges on Justice: Perspectives from the Bench*. New York: New Press.

CROP INSURANCE

A contract of indemnity by which, for a specified premium, one party promises to compensate another for the financial loss incurred by the destruction of agricultural products from the forces of nature, such as rain, hail, frost, or insect infestation.

The federal government, acting through the Federal Crop Insurance Corporation, an agency of the DEPARTMENT OF AGRICULTURE, sponsors such insurance. By improving the economic stability of agriculture, crop insurance promotes the welfare of the nation.

CROSS-REFERENCES

Agricultural Law.

CROPS

Commodities produced from the earth which are planted, raised, and gathered within the course of a single season.

Crops might be produced either naturally or under cultivation. This distinction becomes important when determining whether a crop is to be sold as PERSONAL PROPERTY or as real estate, and also in terms of how crops are to be devised.

Fructus naturales are crops that are produced by the powers of nature alone, without any harvesting methods. They include fruit trees, berries growing on bushes, and hay growing spontaneously from perennial roots. They are considered real property when they are not severed from the land, but personal property when severed.

Fructus industriales, or emblements, are annual crops that are raised by yearly labor and owe their existence to human intervention and cultivation. Such crops include wheat, corn, and vegetables. Authorities differ as to whether they constitute real or personal property.

The ownership of crops is generally held to be in the owner of the land, whether the crops are natural or cultivated. The owner may voluntarily choose to sever and sell the crops, without being obligated to sell the land upon which they are grown. The situation often arises in which the land belongs to one person and the crops belong to another, such as in the case of one person leasing land from another person. In such a case, whoever is in possession of the land subject to the consent of the owner may take and carry away the products of land resulting from his or her own care and labor.

Ordinarily, crops that are attached to land at the time of a sale pass automatically to the buyer, except where the owner has provided to the contrary. Someone disposing of land may, therefore, stipulate the retention of the title to the crops.

It has been widely held that a trespasser who enters another person's land and cultivates crops does not acquire title to them, since the owner is lawfully entitled to full possession and enjoyment of his or her property. Some authorities have held that as long as crops planted by an intruder remain unsevered, they are the property of the owner of the land upon which they are planted, whereas severed crops belong to the trespasser if he or she possesses the land when the crops are ready to be harvested.

CROSS-REFERENCES

Agricultural Law.

Crops, such as these green peppers, are commodities that are planted and gathered within a single season.

AP/WIDE WORLD PHOTOS

CROSS-ACTION

A separate and independent lawsuit brought by the defendant against a plaintiff for some reason arising from the same transaction or event that is the basis for the plaintiff's lawsuit.

Under some circumstances, the court may order a consolidation of the actions.

CROSS-CLAIM

A demand made in a PLEADING *against another party on the same side of the lawsuit.*

For example, a manufacturer of desks shipped thirty desks to a buyer by truck. When the buyer refused to pay because the desks arrived in a damaged condition, the manufacturer sued both the buyer and the trucking company. The buyer did not know whether the manufacturer or the trucking company was responsible for the damage, so the buyer served an answer containing a denial that he owed money to the manufacturer for unusable desks and a cross-claim demanding that the trucking company compensate him for the damage to the desks.

A counterclaim is comparable to a cross-claim except that it is a claim against an adverse party in the lawsuit, not a party on the same side of the lawsuit.

CROSS-COMPLAINT

A type of PLEADING *that asserts a claim against any of the parties suing the person making the complaint, or against anyone else involved in the same controversy or having an interest in the same property that is the subject of the lawsuit.*

The rules in many states permit or require a defendant to make claims for recovery from another party using a counterclaim or a cross-claim within the answer rather than using a different kind of pleading, but some jurisdictions permit a cross-complaint to be used instead of an answer for this purpose.

CROSS-DEMAND

A claim made against someone who has already made a demand of the person asserting that claim.

These mutual claims are called cross-demands. A counterclaim is a kind of cross-demand.

CROSS-EXAMINATION

The questioning of a witness or party during a trial, hearing, or deposition by the party opposing the one who asked the person to testify in order to evaluate the truth of that person's testimony, to develop the testimony further, or to accomplish any other objective. The interrogation of a witness or party by the party opposed to the one who called the witness or party, upon a subject raised during direct examination—the initial questioning of a witness or party—on the merits of that testimony.

The scope of cross-examination is generally restricted to matters covered during direct examination.

CRUEL AND INHUMAN TREATMENT

Another name for cruelty, or for the intentional, hostile infliction of physical or mental suffering upon another individual, which is a ground for DIVORCE *in many states.*

Cruel and inhuman treatment ordinarily encompasses mental and physical cruelty of any kind and is also known as *cruel and abusive treatment* and as *cruel and barbarous treatment.*

CRUEL AND UNUSUAL PUNISHMENT

Such punishment as would amount to torture or barbarity, any cruel and degrading punishment not known to the COMMON LAW, *or any fine, penalty, confinement, or treatment that is so disproportionate to the offense as to shock the moral sense of the community.*

The EIGHTH AMENDMENT to the U.S. Constitution prohibits the federal government from imposing cruel and unusual punishment for federal crimes. The amendment states, "Excessive bail shall not be required, nor excessive fines imposed, nor cruel and unusual punishment inflicted." The DUE PROCESS CLAUSE of the FOURTEENTH AMENDMENT to the U.S. Constitution bars the states from inflicting such punishment for state crimes, and most state constitutions also prohibit the infliction of cruel and unusual punishment.

In attempting to define cruel and unusual punishment, federal and state courts have generally analyzed two aspects of punishment: the method and the amount. As to the method of punishment, the Eighth Amendment clearly bars punishments that were considered cruel at the time of its ADOPTION, such as burning at the stake, crucifixion, or breaking on the wheel (see *In re Kemmler,* 136 U.S. 436, 10 S. Ct. 930, 34 L. Ed. 519 [1890]). In *Hudson v. McMillian,* 503 U.S. 1, 112 S. Ct. 995, 117 L. Ed. 2d 156 (1992), the U.S. Supreme Court held that the use of excessive physical force against a prisoner may constitute cruel and unusual punishment even if the prisoner does not suffer serious injury. When an inmate does suffer serious injury from the excessive use of force by prison officials, a violation of the Cruel and Unusual Punishment Clause is clear. In *Hope v. Pelzer,* 536 U.S. 730, 122 S.Ct. 2508, 153 L. Ed. 2d 666 (2002), the U.S. Supreme Court held that the Eighth Amendment had been contravened when prison officials had disciplined an inmate for disruptive behavior by handcuffing him to a "hitching post", once for two hours and once for seven hours, depriving the inmate of his shirt, exposing him to the sun, denying his requests for hydration, and refusing to allow him the opportunity to use the bathroom.

However, a defendant need not suffer actual physical injury or pain before a punishment will be declared cruel and unusual. In *Trop v. Dulles,* 356 U.S. 86, 78 S. Ct. 590, 2 L. Ed. 2d 630 (1958), the U.S. Supreme Court held that the use of denationalization (the deprivation of citizenship) as a punishment is barred by the Eighth Amendment. The Court reasoned that when someone is denationalized, "[t]here may be involved no physical mistreatment, no primitive torture. There is instead the total destruction of the individual's status in organized society. It is a form of punishment more primitive than torture, for it destroys for the individual the political existence that was centuries in the development." The Court also opined that the Eighth Amendment must "draw its meaning from the evolving standards of decency that mark the progress of a maturing society."

The U.S. Supreme Court has held that the death penalty itself is not inherently cruel, but has described it as "an extreme sanction, suitable to the most extreme of crimes" (GREGG V. GEORGIA, 428 U.S. 153, 96 S. Ct. 2909, 49 L. Ed. 2d 859 [1976]). Federal and state courts have upheld modern methods of carrying out the death penalty, such as shooting, hanging, electrocution, and lethal injection, as constitutional. The U.S. Supreme Court has held that statutes providing a mandatory death sentence for certain degrees or categories of murder are unconstitutional because they preclude sentencing authorities from considering aspects of a particular defendant's character or record, or from considering circumstances that might mitigate a particular crime (see *Lockett v. Ohio,* 438 U.S. 586, 98 S. Ct. 2954, 57 L. Ed. 2d 973 [1978]). In *Ford v. Wainwright,* 477 U.S. 399, 106 S. Ct. 2595, 91 L. Ed. 2d 335 (1986), the Court held that the Eighth Amendment prohibits states from inflicting the death penalty upon a prisoner who is insane.

The Court has also ruled that execution of mentally retarded criminals violates the Eighth Amendment's guarantee against cruel and unusual punishment. ATKINS V. VIRGINIA, 536 U.S. 304, 122 S. Ct. 2242, 153 L. Ed. 2d 335 (2002). Citing "evolving standards of decency," the Court in *Atkins* stated that its decision was informed by a national consensus reflected in deliberations of the American public, legislators, scholars, and judges. *Atkins* overruled *Penry v. Lynaugh,* 492 U.S. 302, 109 S.Ct. 2934, 106 L. Ed. 2d 256 (1989), a decision rendered just 13 years earlier. However, in *Stanford v. Kentucky,* 492 U.S. 361, 109 S. Ct. 2969, 106 L. Ed. 2d 306 (1989), the Court found that there was no national consensus prohibiting the execution of juvenile offenders over age 15.

With regard to the amount of punishment that may be inflicted, the prohibition against cruel and unusual punishment also bars punishment that is clearly out of proportion to the offense committed. The U.S. Supreme Court has considered the issue of proportionality, particularly in the context of the death penalty. In *Coker v. Georgia,* 433 U.S. 584, 97 S. Ct. 2861, 53 L. Ed. 2d 982 (1977), the Court held that death was a

The "hitching post" at Alabama's Limestone Correctional facility was the subject of former inmate Larry Hope's (not pictured) lawsuit, Hope v. Pelzer, *alleging cruel and unusual punishment.*

AP/WIDE WORLD PHOTOS

disproportionate penalty for the crime of raping an adult woman. In *Enmund v. Florida,* 458 U.S. 782, 102 S. Ct. 3368, 73 L. Ed. 2d 1140 (1982), the Court held that the Eighth Amendment does not permit the imposition of the death penalty upon a defendant who aids and abets a felony during which murder is committed by someone else, when the defendant does not kill or attempt to kill, or does not intend that murder take place or that lethal force be used.

In *Solem v. Helm,* 463 U.S. 277, 103 S. Ct. 3001, 77 L. Ed. 2d 637 (1983), the Court applied its proportionality analysis to felony prison sentences. In *Solem,* the defendant had passed a bad check in the amount of $100. Although this crime ordinarily would be punishable by a maximum five-year sentence, the defendant had been sentenced to life imprisonment without PAROLE because of six prior felony convictions. The Court held that the sentence was significantly disproportionate to the defendant's crime and that it was thus prohibited by the Eighth Amendment.

The U.S. Court of Appeals for the Ninth Circuit applied the proportionality analysis in overturning the life sentence of a defendant who had been convicted under California's "three-strikes" law, which requires that courts impose harsh sentences upon defendants who have been convicted of three felonies. Cal. Penal Code Section 667. In *Brown v. Mayle,* 283 F.3d 1019 (9th Cir. 2002), the defendants were charged with

IS DEATH BY ELECTROCUTION CRUEL AND UNUSUAL UNDER EVOLVING STANDARDS?

Convicted killer Kenneth Spivey's attorneys argued that Spivey's impending death in Georgia's electric chair constituted cruel and unusual punishment under the EIGHTH AMENDMENT and the FOURTEENTH AMENDMENT to the Constitution of the United States. In a March 2001 opinion that initially stayed s punishment, Justice Leah J. Sears wrote, "Electrocution offends the evolving standards of decency that characterize a mature, civilized society." *Spivey v. State of Georgia*, 544 S.E. 2d 136 (Ga. 2001). Georgia's attorney general and a county prosecutor asked the court for reconsideration. In October of the same year, the Georgia Supreme Court outlawed electrocution as a means of execution in the state because it was deemed cruel and unusual punishment under the *state* constitution and because of the implications of the state's year 2000 revised CAPITAL PUNISHMENT statute (*Dawson v. State of Georgia*, 554 S.E. 2d 137 [Ga. 2001]). The 4–3 ruling gave momentum to the movement against death by electrocution elsewhere, but the U.S. Supreme Court continued to refuse appeals of this nature, leaving the decision in the hands of state courts and legislatures.

In early May 2001, several radio stations, including WYNC in New York, aired audiotapes of electrocutions in Georgia's prisons spanning a period from 1983 to 1998. The recordings were made by state officials to protect themselves from litigation over the manner in which they followed policies to ensure smooth executions. The tapes were devoid of emotion and merely recorded the voices of the executing officials during the process. There were no shouts or cries of pain, but several tapes contained the final words of the inmates. The tapes might support the argument that electrocution, when properly conducted, is as humane as other alternatives.

Dr. Chris Sparry, Georgia's chief medical examiner, who has testified on the matter, stated:

> The best evidence that exists to indicate that people who are judicially executed never feel any conscious pain or suffering rests in the tens of thousands of people who have sustained accidental electrocutions and have survived. None of those people can even remember the event if the current goes through their head . . . consciousness is obliterated instantly when the current is passed through the body because the amount of the current is so very, very great.

Georgia was one of four states still employing the use of electric chairs for execution of condemned criminals, although both Georgia and Florida changed their *primary* means of execution to lethal injection for the newly-convicted starting in 2000. Nebraska and Alabama continue to use their electric chairs as the sole means of execution although both states have considered legislation to allow lethal injection as well.

In an April 2001 Gallup poll, roughly two of every three surveyed Americans said they favored the death penalty. Despite some of the media's characterization of declining support, the percentage remained consistently above 60 percent for at least the preceding five years. The all-time high for supporting capital punishment was in 1994 at 80 percent; the

IN FOCUS

---

misdemeanor petty theft for stealing three videotapes and a steering wheel alarm, together worth less than $400.00. However, because both defendants had two prior felony convictions involving violent crimes, the misdemeanor petty theft charges were enhanced and prosecuted as felonies. The Ninth Circuit ruled that the defendants' sentences constituted cruel and unusual punishment, for the trial court was effectively imposing life sentences for what was the legislature classified as a misdemeanor under any other circumstances.

The U.S. Supreme Court granted certiorari, reversed, and remanded the case with instructions for the Ninth Circuit to reconsider its decision in light of *Lockyer v. Andrade*, 538 U.S. 63,

123 S. Ct. 1166, 155 L. Ed. 144 (2003), where the Court ruled that the Eighth Amendment's proportionality principle was not violated by the imposition of two 25-years-to-life sentences under the California Three Strikes law, on a conviction of two counts of petty theft with a prior conviction. The defendant in *Andrade* had been convicted of stealing videotapes worth $153.54.

The prohibition on cruel and unusual punishment also bans all penal sanctions in certain situations. For example, in ROBINSON V. CALIFORNIA, 370 U.S. 660, 82 S. Ct. 1417, 8 L. Ed. 2d 758 (1962), the Court ruled that punishment may not be inflicted simply because a person is in a certain condition or has a particular illness. *Robinson* concerned a California statute (Cal.

low of 42 percent was in 1966. The manner by which execution is accomplished is a different matter toward which there is growing sensitivity.

In many states, condemned persons are given the opportunity to elect the method by which they will die. Some Americans bristle at the thought that "humane consideration" should be given to those who have wreaked heinous inhumanity upon others. There remains a palpable undercurrent of opinion/attitude that execution should hurt, not only because it may serve to deter future wrongdoers but also because of the belief that death is intended as a punishment, not an escape.

Still, as of spring 2001, 36 of the 38 states with death penalty laws employed lethal injection as the preferred method. With lethal injection, the victim is first put to sleep with sodium pentothal, after which other drugs are administered to paralyze the body and stop the heart. The person never regains consciousness.

The U.S. Supreme Court has provided guidance as to what should constitute cruel and unusual punishment under the Eighth Amendment, but made it clear that the standards must be evolving and dynamic. "Difficulty would attend the effort to define with exactness the extent of the constitutional provision which provides that cruel and unusual punishments shall not be inflicted; but it is safe to affirm that punishments of torture [such as drawing and quartering, emboweling alive, beheading, public dissecting, and burning alive], and all others in the same line of unnecessary cruelty, are forbidden by that amendment to the Constitution," the Court said, more than 100 years ago, in *Wilkerson v. Utah*, 99 U.S. 130, 25 L. Ed. 345 (1878), which upheld an execution by firing squad. Twelve years later, in *In re Kemmler*, 136 U.S. 436, 10 S. Ct. 930, 34 L. Ed. 519 (1890), the Court, under the Fourteenth Amendment's DUE PROCESS CLAUSE, found electrocution to be a permissible method of execution. Moreover, in assuming the applicability of the Eighth Amendment to the States, the Court, many years later, held that a second electrocution, resulting from the failure of the first one, did not violate the proscription. "The cruelty against which the Constitution protects a convicted man is cruelty inherent in the method of punishment, not the necessary suffering involved in any method employed to extinguish life humanely," the majority opinion stated. *Louisiana ex rel. Francis v. Resweber*, 329 U.S. 459, 67 S. Ct. 374, 916 L. Ed. 422 (1947).

In *Trop v. Dulles* 356 U.S. 86, 78 S. Ct. 590, 2 L. Ed. 2d 630 (1958), the Supreme Court, in referring to the United States as "an enlightened democracy," held that "The [Eighth] Amendment must draw its meaning from the evolving standards of decency that mark the progress of a maturing society." That language was repeated again in GREGG V. GEORGIA 428 U.S. 153, 96 S. Ct. 2909, 49 L. Ed. 2d 859 (1978), wherein the Court noted that the Eighth Amendment was to be interpreted "in a flexible and dynamic manner to accord with evolving standards of decency." Most likely, this is the language from which the Georgia Supreme Court formed their ultimate *Spivey* ruling. The U.S. Supreme Court, on the other hand, denied certiorari to an appeal challenging Alabama's use of the electric chair and had not ruled against electrocution as of the end of the 2003 term.

FURTHER READINGS

Harry, Jennifer L. 2000. "Death Penalty Disquiet Stirs Nation." *Corrections Today* (December).

Macready, Dawn. 2000. "The 'Shocking' Truth about the Electric Chair: An Analysis of the Unconstitutionality of Electrocution." *Ohio Northern University Law Review* 26 (summer).

Roy, Patricia. 2002. "Not So Shocking: The Death of the Electric Chair in Georgia at the Hands of the Georgia Supreme Court." *Mercer Law Review* 53 (summer).

Weinstein, Bob, and Jim Bessant. 1996. *Death Row Confidential*. New York: HarperPaperbacks.

CROSS-REFERENCES

Capital Punishment; Eighth Amendment; Fourteenth Amendment.

Health & Safety Code § 11721 [West]) that criminalized addiction to narcotics, rather than the possession, use, or sale of them. The Court struck down the statute, stating,

We hold that a state law which imprisons a person thus afflicted as a criminal, even though he has never touched any narcotic drug within the State or been guilty of any irregular behavior there, inflicts a cruel and unusual punishment.... To be sure, imprisonment for ninety days [the sentence imposed in this case] is not, in the abstract, a punishment which is either cruel or unusual. But the question cannot be considered in the abstract. Even one day in prison would be a cruel and unusual punishment for the "crime" of having a common cold.

FURTHER READINGS

Denno, Deborah W. 2000. "Adieu to Electrocution." *Ohio Northern University Law Review* 26 (summer): 665–88.

Harding, Roberta M. 1994. "'Endgame': Competency and the Execution of Condemned Inmates—A Proposal to Satisfy the Eighth Amendment's Prohibition against the Infliction of Cruel and Unusual Punishment." *St. Louis University Public Law Review* 14.

LaFave, Wayne R., and Austin W. Scott Jr. 1986. *Substantive Criminal Law*. St. Paul, Minn.: West.

Macready, Dawn. 2000. "The 'Shocking' Truth About the Electric Chair: An Analysis of the Unconstitutionality of Electrocution." *Ohio Northern University Law Review* 26 (summer): 781–800.

Nelson, Diane A. 1993. "*Hudson v. McMillian*: The Evolving Standard of Eighth Amendment Application to the Use of Excessive Force Against Prison Inmates." *North Carolina Law Review* 71 (June).

Capital Punishment; Determinate Sentence; Juvenile Law; Sentencing.

CRUELTY

The deliberate and malicious infliction of mental or physical pain upon persons or animals.

As applied to people, cruelty encompasses abusive, outrageous, and inhumane treatment that results in the wanton and unnecessary infliction of suffering upon the body or mind.

Legal cruelty involves conduct that warrants the granting of a DIVORCE to the injured spouse. Phrases such as "cruel and inhuman treatment," "cruel and abusive treatment," or "cruel and barbarous treatment" are commonly employed in matrimonial law. The term comprehends mental and physical harm, but a single act of cruelty is usually insufficient for divorce; a pattern of cruel conduct must occur over a period of time. This ground of divorce is of diminished significance due to the enactment of no-fault legislation by most jurisdictions.

Cruelty to children, also known as CHILD ABUSE, encompasses mental and physical battering and abuse, as defined by statutes in a majority of jurisdictions.

Cruelty to animals involves the infliction of physical pain or death upon an animal, when unnecessary for disciplinary, instructional, or humanitarian purposes, such as the release of the animal from incurable illness.

A person commits a misdemeanor if he or she intentionally or recklessly neglects any animal in his or her custody, mistreats any animal, or kills or injures any animal without legal privilege or the consent of its owner.

CROSS-REFERENCES
Animal Rights.

C-SPAN

The Cable-Satellite Public Affairs Network (C-SPAN) broadcasts proceedings of the U.S. Congress, as well as other public events and programs, on CABLE TELEVISION. It is funded entirely by the U.S. cable television industry and receives no government support.

C-SPAN was established by Brian P. Lamb as a nonprofit venture in 1977. On March 19, 1979, C-SPAN began live and unedited television broadcasts of proceedings in the U.S. House of Representatives. On June 2, 1986, C-SPAN II broadcast, for the first time, proceedings on the floor of the U.S. Senate.

C-SPAN also broadcasts congressional hearings; call-in programs with elected officials, policy makers, and journalists; coverage of Democratic and Republican conventions and presidential campaigns; programs reviewing the activities of the U.S. Supreme Court and developments in the law; coverage of such events as the annual meetings of the National Governors Association and the U.S. Conference of Mayors; speeches at the National Press Club; proceedings of foreign legislatures such as Canada's House of Commons and the United Kingdom's House of Commons; and many other public-affairs programs.

As part of its mission, C-SPAN seeks to provide direct access to proceedings of government in the United States, free of the editing, commentary, and analysis that are typical in most other media. In 1989, ten years after C-SPAN's first broadcast, the network was available in 40 million homes. On this tenth anniversary, Congress issued a resolution honoring the cable television industry for funding the public affairs channel and for 'the invaluable contribution it has made and continues to make toward informing and educating the citizenry of this Nation and thereby enhancing the quality of its government of, by and for the people" (S. Con. Res. 22, 101st Cong., 1st Sess., 135 Cong. Rec. S2732-02 [1989]).

C-SPAN has expanded its programming since the mid-1990s. Like many other cable television networks, it has added such sister stations as C-SPAN2 and C-SPAN3, both of which are available to millions of cable subscribers. C-SPAN has also expanded to radio and has added content developed for INTERNET users with broadband access. Regular programming on the C-SPAN stations includes *American Writers*, *American Presidents*, and *Book TV*. According to a survey conducted by the network in December 2000, about 28.5 million people watch C-SPAN's programming each week. More than 90 percent of those who watch the network are registered voters. More than half are in the 18- to 49-year-old demographic. About 48 percent of the viewers are women.

C-SPAN is increasingly used in school classrooms as a teaching tool. The network offers a program called C-SPAN in the Classroom, which included free membership and resources to educators who use the network's resources in the classroom. For classrooms that do not have cable access, C-SPAN offers videotapes and web access so students can view the content. The network also offers a Teacher Fellowship Program through the C-SPAN Education Foundation to honor educators who have demonstrated creative use of the programming in the classroom.

FURTHER READINGS

Frantzich, Stephen E., and John Sullivan. 1996. *The C-SPAN Revolution.* Norman, Okla.: Univ. of Oklahoma Press.

CROSS-REFERENCES

Broadcasting.

CTA

An abbreviation for cum testamento annexo, Latin for "with the will annexed."

CUBAN MISSILE CRISIS

The 1962 Cuban Missile Crisis was a dangerous moment in the COLD WAR between the United States and the Soviet Union. The actions taken by President John F. Kennedy's administration prevented the installation of Soviet nuclear missiles in Cuba, just 90 miles from Florida. The crisis also illustrated the limitations of international law,as the United States relied on military actions and threats to accomplish its goal.

The crisis grew out of political changes in Cuba. In the 1950s, Fidel Castro, a young lawyer, led a guerrilla movement against Cuban dictator Fulgencio Batista. Batista lost the confidence of the Cuban people and on January 1, 1959, fled the country. Castro became premier of the new government.

At first, the United States supported the Castro government. This changed when Castro seized U.S.-owned sugar estates and cattle ranches in Cuba. The United States subsequently embargoed trade with Cuba, and the CENTRAL INTELLIGENCE AGENCY (CIA) began covert operations to topple Castro. In 1960, Castro openly embraced COMMUNISM and signed Cuba's first trade agreement with the Soviet Union.

Many Cubans had left the island of Cuba for the United States following the Castro revolution. Aided by the United States, a Cuban exile army was trained for an invasion. Although most of the planning took place in 1960, when President DWIGHT D. EISENHOWER was finishing his second term, the final decision to invade came during the first months of the Kennedy

administration. In April 1961, Cuban exiles invaded Cuba at the Bay of Pigs. The invasion was a debacle, in part because U.S. air support that had been promised was not provided. The exile army was captured.

Convinced that the United States would attempt another invasion, Castro asked Premier Nikita Khrushchev, of the Soviet Union, for nuclear missiles. Khrushchev agreed to what would be the first deployment of NUCLEAR WEAPONS outside the Soviet Union. President Kennedy at first did not believe the Soviets would follow through on their promise. On October 14, 1962, however, photographs taken by reconnaissance planes showed that missile sites were being built in Cuba. The president convened a small group of trusted advisers, called the Executive Committee of the NATIONAL SECURITY COUNCIL (Ex Com). Attorney General ROBERT F. KENNEDY served on Ex Com and became the key adviser to President Kennedy during the crisis.

Military officials advocated bombing the missile sites or invading Cuba. Others argued for a nuclear strike on Cuba. These ideas were rejected in favor of a naval blockade of Cuba. All ships attempting to enter Cuba were to be stopped and searched for missiles and related military material. President Kennedy, believing that the Soviets were using the missiles to test his will, resolved to make the crisis public. Bypassing private, diplomatic procedures, Kennedy went on national television on October 22 and

U.S. Ambassador Adlai Stevenson (seated, far right) addresses members of the U.N. Security Council on October 25, 1962. On display are aerial photographs of missile sites in Cuba—proof that the Soviet Union had indeed been building missile sites on the island.

AP/WIDE WORLD PHOTOS

informed the United States of the missile sites, the naval blockade, and his resolve to take any action necessary to prevent the missile deployment.

Tension built during the last days of October as the world awaited the approach of Soviet missile-bearing ships at the blockade line. If Soviet ships refused to turn back, it was likely that U.S. ships would either stop them or sink them. If that happened, nuclear war seemed probable.

During the crisis, the UNITED NATIONS was not used as a vehicle for negotiation or mediation. The United States and the Soviet Union ignored an appeal by Secretary General U Thant, of the United Nations, that they reduce tensions for a few weeks. Instead, the Security Council of the United Nations became a stage for both sides to trade accusations. Ambassador ADLAI STEVENSON, from the United States, presented photographs of the missile sites to back up U.S. claims.

On October 24, the crisis began to ease, as 12 Soviet ships on their way to Cuba were, on orders from Moscow, diverted or halted. However, construction on the missile sites continued. On October 26, Premier Khrushchev sent a long, emotional letter to President Kennedy, claiming that the missiles were defensive. He implied that a pledge by the United States not to invade Cuba would allow him to remove the missiles. President Kennedy replied, accepting the proposal to exchange withdrawal of the missiles for the promise not to invade. He also stated that if the Soviet Union did not answer his reply in two or three days, Cuba would be bombed. On October 28, the Soviets announced on Radio Moscow that the missile sites were being dismantled.

Some historians maintain that President Kennedy acted heroically to meet a threat to the security of the United States. Others claim that the missiles at issue were of limited range and were purely defensive, and that Kennedy was reckless in brandishing the threat of nuclear war. Most agree that the crisis was probably the closest the Soviet Union and the United States ever got to nuclear war.

The significance of the crisis to INTERNATIONAL LAW and the management of international crises has led to many books, articles, and scholarly conferences. In October 2002, a conference hosted by Fidel Castro was held in Havana. It was a rare event because participants from the United States, Soviet, and Cuban governments attended the gathering, sharing their impressions of what had happened during the crisis. Participants included former U.S. defense secretary Robert McNamara, Kennedy presidential aides Arthur Schlesinger, Ted Sorensen, and Richard Goodwin, as well as Ethel Kennedy, the widow of ROBERT KENNEDY.

The Cuban government declassified documents relating to the crisis and Castro took center stage, arguing that Khrushchev had inflamed the situation by lying to Kennedy that there were no nuclear weapons in Cuba. McNamara confirmed that most of Kennedy's advisers, both military and civilian, had recommended he attack Cuba. The conference ended with a trip to a former missile silo on the western side of Cuba.

FURTHER READINGS

Blight, James G., et al. 2002. *Cuba on the Brink: Castro, the Missile Crisis, and the Soviet Collapse.* Lanham, Md.: Rowman & Littlefield.

Diez Acosta, Tomás. 2002. *October 1962: The "Missile" Crisis as Seen from Cuba.* New York: Pathfinder.

Garthoff, Raymond. 2002. "The Havana Conference on the Cuban Missile Crisis." Cold War International History Project, Woodrow Wilson International Center for Scholars. Available online at <www.gwu.edu/~nsarchiv/CWIHP/BULLETINS/b1a1.htm> (accessed May 30, 2003).

O'Neill, William L. 1971. *Coming Apart: An Informal History of America in the 1960s.* New York: Quadrangle Books.

CROSS-REFERENCES

Embargo.

CULPA

[Latin, Fault, blame, or neglect.] A CIVIL LAW *term that implies that certain conduct is actionable.*

The word *culpa* is applied to acts of commission and omission in both TORT and contract cases. It implies the failure to perform a legally imposed duty, or NEGLIGENCE.

Lata culpa means gross or wanton fault, or neglect. *Levis culpa* is common or ordinary negligence, or the absence of reasonable care. *Levissima culpa* is slight neglect or fault.

CULPABLE

Blameworthy; involving the commission of a fault or the breach of a duty imposed by law.

Culpability generally implies that an act performed is wrong but does not involve any evil intent by the wrongdoer. The connotation of the term is fault rather than malice or a guilty purpose. It has limited significance in CRIMINAL

LAW except in cases of reckless HOMICIDE in which a person acts negligently or demonstrates a reckless disregard for life, which results in another person's death. In general, however, culpability has milder connotations. It is used to mean reprehensible rather than wantonly or grossly negligent behavior. Culpable conduct may be wrong but it is not necessarily criminal.

Culpable ignorance is the lack of knowledge or understanding that results from the omission of ordinary care to acquire such knowledge or understanding.

CULPRIT

An individual who has been formally charged with a criminal offense but who has not yet been tried and convicted.

Culprit is a colloquial rather than a legal term and is commonly applied to someone who is guilty of a minor degree of moral reprehensibility. According to SIR WILLIAM BLACKSTONE, the term is most likely a derivative of the archaic mode of ARRAIGNMENT during which upon a prisoner's plea of not guilty the cleric would say *culpabilis prit,* meaning "he is guilty and the crown is ready." The more common derivation is from culpa, meaning "fault or blame."

CUM TESTAMENTO ANNEXO

[Latin, With the will annexed.] A phrase that describes an administrator named by a probate or surrogate court to settle and distribute an estate according to the terms of a will in which the testator, its maker, has failed to name an executor, or in which the one named refuses to act or is legally incapable of acting.

The term is often applied to the administration conducted by such a person.

❖ CUMMINGS, HOMER STILLE

Homer Stille Cummings was the 55th attorney general of the United States, serving from 1933 to 1939 in the administration of President FRANKLIN D. ROOSEVELT. Cummings was a DEMOCRATIC PARTY leader and an advocate for reform of prisons in the United States. He was instrumental in establishing the Alcatraz Island Prison, which was envisioned as a model for housing maximum security-level inmates in the federal prison system.

Cummings was born in Chicago, Illinois, on April 30, 1870. He attended Yale University where he received his undergraduate degree in 1891 and two years later, his law degree. Cummings was admitted to the Connecticut bar in 1893 and began a private practice in Stamford. He rose in prominence as a litigator, becoming a member of the New York bar. He also was admitted to practice before a number of federal district courts and the U.S. Supreme Court.

Cummings became involved with the Democratic Party and was elected mayor of Stamford for three terms. He also served, from 1908 to 1912, as the city's corporation counsel. In 1902, Cummings ran for a seat as congressman at large from Connecticut and lost; he also ran unsuccessfully for a U.S. Senate seat in 1916. Cummings's entry on the national scene began when he served seven terms as a delegate at large to the Democratic National Convention. From 1919 to 1920, he was chairman of the Democratic National Committee.

Beginning in 1914, Cummings served for a decade as the state's attorney for Fairfield County, Connecticut. His interest in the topic of prison reform paid off in 1930 when he was appointed chairman of Connecticut's Committee on State Prison Conditions. Cummings's

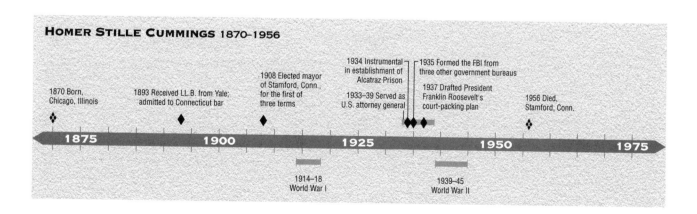

HOMER STILLE CUMMINGS 1870–1956

1870 Born, Chicago, Illinois

1893 Received LL.B. from Yale; admitted to Connecticut bar

1908 Elected mayor of Stamford, Conn., for the first of three terms

1934 Instrumental in establishment of Alcatraz Prison

1933–39 Served as U.S. attorney general

1935 Formed the FBI from three other government bureaus

1937 Drafted President Franklin Roosevelt's court-packing plan

1956 Died, Stamford, Conn.

1875　1900　1925　1950　1975

1914–18 World War I

1939–45 World War II

Homer S. Cummings.
LIBRARY OF CONGRESS

long years of labor on behalf of the Democratic Party and his work on the successful 1932 presidential campaign of Franklin D. Roosevelt were rewarded. In 1933, President Roosevelt appointed Senator Thomas J. Walsh of Montana to be his attorney general, but Walsh died suddenly of a heart attack on a train trip to Washington, D.C., to attend the presidential inauguration. Roosevelt then appointed Cummings as U.S. attorney general. Cummings turned out to be the first of four attorneys general appointed by Roosevelt, the nation's longest-serving president.

The 63-year-old Cummings's interest in and experience concerning prison reform proved to be significant in his work as attorney general. Cummings proposed and oversaw improvements in various prison conditions and in the general operation of the Federal Bureau of Prisons that had been established in 1930 to oversee the 11 federal prisons that then existed.

With public fear escalating over the 1932 KIDNAPPING of the baby son of national hero Charles Lindbergh, an expanding list of "public enemies," and mob violence at a peak, Cummings also advocated for the establishment of a maximum security prison for the nation's most dangerous criminals. He chose Alcatraz Island, located in the San Francisco Bay, to house the country's most dangerous criminals. Nick-

named "Uncle Sam's Devil's Island," the prison opened in 1934 and quickly entered the public imagination as a symbol of the tough punishment to be dealt out to the worst offenders.

In 1935, Cummings merged the Justice Department's Bureau of Investigation (BI), the Prohibition Bureau, and the Bureau of Identification into the newly renamed FEDERAL BUREAU OF INVESTIGATION (FBI), all under the control of FBI Director J. EDGAR HOOVER.

In 1937, after the conservative U.S. Supreme Court had overturned much of Roosevelt's NEW DEAL legislative reforms that focused on moving the country back on the road to economic prosperity, Cummings drafted a proposal that came to be known as the court-packing plan. Enthusiastically endorsed by Roosevelt, the plan would have given the president the power to appoint a new judge for each incumbent judge who was 70 or older. Because six of the nine justices were over the age of 70, the new law would have meant a Supreme Court with 15 members. While the president and his attorney general saw the proposal as a way to get around the fact that Supreme Court justices have lifetime tenure, such a drastic change in the composition of the court was too much even for the Democratic Congress, and the bill failed. Chief Justice CHARLES EVANS HUGHES and Associate Justice OWEN ROBERTS began to vote more often with the more liberal justices, however, thus allowing Roosevelt to proceed with many of his economic reform measures. Many saw the failed proposal as having been the stimulus for Justice Hughes's changed voting pattern. Cummings remained as attorney general until his retirement in 1939. He died on September 10, 1956, in Stamford, Connecticut.

FURTHER READINGS

Attorneys General of the United States, 1789–1985. 1985. Justice Department. Washington, D.C.: Government Printing Office.

CUMULATIVE EVIDENCE

Facts or information that proves what has previously been established by other information concerning the same issue.

Cumulative evidence is synonymous with corroborative evidence.

CUMULATIVE SENTENCE

Separate consecutive terms of imprisonment imposed upon a defendant who has been convicted of two or more distinct offenses; any term of imprisonment that becomes effective subsequent to the expiration of a prior one.

A cumulative sentence is also known as a *from and after* sentence.

CUMULATIVE VOTING

A method of election of the board of directors used by corporations whereby a stockholder may cast as many votes for directors as he or she has shares of stock, multiplied by the number of directors to be elected.

A plan used for the election of members to the lower house of the Illinois legislature by which voters, each of whom is given three votes, may cast all of the votes for one candidate or allocate them among two or three candidates.

The purpose of cumulative voting is to facilitate the representation of minority stockholders on the board. The stockholder may cast all of his or her votes for one or more, but not all, of the directors on the ballot, which therefore promotes representation of small shareholders. Cumulative voting is mandatory under the corporate laws of some states and is allowed in most states.

CUNNILINGUS

An act in which the female sexual organ is orally stimulated.

At COMMON LAW, cunnilingus was not a crime. It is presently a crime in some jurisdictions and is usually treated as SODOMY.

CURE

The act of restoring health after injury or illness. Care, including medical and nursing services rendered to a sailor throughout a period of duty, pursuant to the principle that the owner of a vessel must furnish maintenance and cure to a sailor who becomes ill or is injured during service.

The right of a seller, under the UNIFORM COMMERCIAL CODE (UCC), a body of law governing commercial transactions, to correct a delivery of goods that do not conform to contractual terms made to a buyer within the period specified by the contract in order to avoid a breach of contract action.

The actual payment of all amounts that are past due in regard to a default in such payments.

CURFEW

A curfew is a law, regulation, or ordinance that forbids particular people or particular classes of people from being outdoors in public places at certain specified times of the day.

Juvenile Curfews

Local ordinances and state statutes may make it unlawful for minors below a certain age to be on public streets, unless they are accompanied by a parent or an adult or on lawful and necessary business on behalf of their parents or guardians. For example, a Michigan state law provides that "[n]o minor under the age of 12 years shall loiter, idle or congregate in or on any public street, highway, alley or park between the hours of 10 o'clock P.M. and 6 o'clock A.M., unless the minor is accompanied by a parent or guardian, or some adult delegated by the parent or guardian to accompany the child." MCLA § 722.751; MSA § 28.342(1). Curfew laws in other states and cities typically set forth different curfews for minors of different ages.

Curfew laws and ordinances have been sustained as necessary to control the presence of juveniles in public places at nighttime with the attendant risk of mischief. *In re Osman*, 109 Ohio App. 3d 731, 672 N.E.2d 1114 (1996). Courts have found that curfew ordinances promote the safety and good order of the community by reducing the incidence of juvenile criminal activity. *Schleifer v. City of Charlottesville*, 159 F.3d 843 (4th Cir. 1998).

Curfew laws have generally been upheld against constitutional challenges on FIRST AMENDMENT and DUE PROCESS grounds. Hodgkins ex rel. Hodgkins v. Peterson, 175 F. Supp. 2d 1132 (S.D. Ind. 2001). One federal court held that minors have no fundamental right to freedom of movement or travel that protects them from restrictions imposed by curfew laws. *Hutchins v. District of Columbia*, 188 F.3d 531,(D.C. Cir. 1999). However, a juvenile curfew ordinance that exempted minors who had graduated from high school was found to violate the EQUAL PROTECTION CLAUSE of the FOURTEENTH AMENDMENT to the U.S. Constitution. *In re Mosier*, 59 Ohio Misc. 83, 394 N.E.2d 368, 13 O.O.3d 290 (Ohio Com. Pl. 1978).

In some instances, courts will find particular language in a juvenile curfew law to be impermissibly vague under the "void for vagueness" doctrine (a FIFTH AMENDMENT doctrine that requires all laws to be sufficiently clear that persons of average intelligence will understand in advance which conduct is prohibited). If possible, courts will simply delete offending language from the law so that what remains passes constitutional muster. For example, one curfew law allowed the city's mayor to issue permits for minors to use public streets during prohibited times if the mayor found that such use was "consistent with the public interest." A California state court held that that language failed to provide any standards by which the mayor could lawfully exercise the discretion to grant permits. The court deleted the language but said the mayor could still grant permits when to do so would be consistent with the purposes of ordinance as expressly set forth therein. *Bykofsky v. Borough of Middletown*, 401 F. Supp. 1242 (M.D. Pa. 1975).

Curfew as a Condition of Probation

State laws typically allow courts to impose curfews on criminal defendants as a condition of pre-trial release, and on probationers as a condition for successful discharge from PROBATION. Defendants and probationers who are subject to curfews can be ordered to pay the cost of monitoring their compliance with the terms of the order. Curfew violations can result in the revocation of probation or termination of the pre-trial release bond.

However, curfew orders themselves must be reasonable, and courts must be careful to explain the rationale underlying them. Orders imposing curfews that are harsh or excessive, for example, have been invalidated. *People v. Braun*, 177 A.D. 2d 981, 578 N.Y.S.2d (1991). Similarly, orders that cite no justification for a curfew have also been overturned. *People v Sztuk*, 126 A.D. 2d 950, 511 N.Y.S.2d 720 (1987).

Adult Curfews & Strict Scrutiny

Curfews directed at adults touch upon fundamental constitutional rights and thus are subject to strict judicial scrutiny. The U. S. Supreme Court has ruled that "[t]he right to walk the streets, or to meet publicly with one's friends for a noble purpose or for no purpose at all—and to do so whenever one pleases—is an integral component of life in a free and ordered society." *Papachristou v. City of Jacksonville*, 405 US 156, 164, 31 L. Ed. 2d 110, 92 S. Ct 839 (1972).

To satisfy strict-scrutiny analysis, a government-imposed curfew on adults must be supported by a compelling state interest that is narrowly tailored to serve the curfew's objective. Court's are loath to find that an interest advanced by the government is compelling. The more justifications that courts find to uphold a curfew on adults, the more watered-down becomes the fundamental right to travel and to associate with others in public places at all times of the day.

The U.S. Supreme Court has ruled that this right may be legitimately curtailed when a community has been ravaged by flood, fire, or disease, or when its safety and WELFARE are otherwise threatened. *Zemel v. Rusk*, 381 U.S. 1, 85 S. Ct. 1271, 14 L. Ed. 2d 179 (1965). The California Court of Appeals cited this ruling in a case that reviewed an order issued by the city of Long Beach, California, which declared a state of emergency and imposed curfews on all adults (and minors) within the city's confines after widespread civil disorder broke out following the Rodney G. King beating trial, in which four white Los Angeles police officers were acquitted of using excessive force in subduing an African-American motorist following a high-speed traffic chase. In re Juan C., 28 Cal. App. 4th 1093, 33 Cal. Rptr. 2d 919 (Cal. App. 1994).

"Rioting, looting and burning," the California court wrote, "pose a similar threat to the safety and welfare of a community, and provide a compelling reason to impose a curfew." "The right to travel is a hollow promise when members of the community face the possibility of being beaten or shot by an unruly mob if they attempt to exercise this right,"the court continued, and "[t]emporary restrictions on the right. . .are a reasonable means of reclaiming order from ANARCHY so that all might exercise their constitutional rights freely and safely."

CURIA

[Latin, Court.] A judicial tribunal or court convened in the sovereign's palace to dispense justice. A court that exercised jurisdiction over civil matters, as distinguished from religious matters, which were determined by ecclesiastical courts, a system of courts in England that were held by authority of the sovereign and had jurisdiction over matters concerning the religion and ritual of the established church.

In England the tribunal of the king's justice was the curia regis, so named because the king originally presided over its proceedings.

CURIA REGIS

[Latin, The King's Court.]

The Anglo-Saxon kings of England regularly summoned the bishops and great men of the kingdom to a council (Witenagemot), which advised the king and occasionally served as a court of justice. Building upon this foundation, the Norman kings after the Conquest in 1066 developed more effective ways of centralizing royal government. By the end of the eleventh century the king was entrusting business to his Curia, a body of officials appointed from the ranks of the highest noblemen, church leaders, and officers of the royal court. With the king, the *Curia Regis* administered all of the king's business—financial, legislative, and judicial. From the *Curia Regis* developed the common-law courts, the Chancery, and even the Parliament.

CURRENT ACCOUNT

A detailed financial statement representing the debit and credit relationship between two parties that has not been finally settled or paid because of the continuous, ongoing dealings of the parties.

CURTESY

An estate to which a man is entitled by common-law right on the death of his wife, in all the lands that his wife owned at any time during their marriage, provided a child is born of the marriage who could inherit the land.

COMMON LAW provided that upon marriage a husband acquired a right, sometimes called a freehold estate, to the use and profits of his wife's lands. His estate *jure uxoris* (Latin for "in the right of the wife") continued only during the marriage and terminated upon the death of either spouse or upon theirdivorce. At early common law in England, an absolute DIVORCE could be obtained only by an Act of Parliament. Consequently, for practical purposes, the husband acquired a right to the use and profit of the land during the joint lives of the parties. This estate was subject to sale or mortgage by the husband and could be reached to satisfy the claims of his creditors. The estate *jure uxoris* virtually disappeared with the enactment of Married Women's Acts, which gave married women a right to manage their own separate estates.

Pursuant to common law, upon the birth of a child capable of inheriting the land, a husband acquires a life estate, or property interest, the duration of which is limited to the life of the party holding it or to that of some other person, in the lands his wife owns. This estate is desig-

nated as *curtesy initiate*, which replaces the husband's estate *jure uxoris* under early common law. The husband can sell or mortgage the land, and it can be reached to satisfy the claims of his creditors. Upon the death of the wife, it becomes *curtesy consummate*.

In some states, due to the Married Women's Acts, the birth of a child does not give the husband a vested interest in his wife's property. Until the death of the wife, the husband has a right of curtesy, which is not a present right, but which might develop into a legally enforceable right if not barred, extinguished, or divested. This interest cannot be subjected to the claims of the husband's creditors.

The right of curtesy rests upon proof of a legally recognized marriage, as distinguished from a GOOD FAITH marriage or a de facto marriage, one in which the parties live together as HUSBAND AND WIFE, but the union has no legal effect due to defects in form, such as an invalid license. A VOIDABLE marriage, one that is valid when entered into and that remains valid until either party obtains a lawful court order dissolving the marital relationship, suffices for purposes of curtesy if the marriage is not rendered null before the right to the estate arises.

Curtesy has gradually lost much of its previous significance in the law. In some jurisdictions, curtesy attaches only to the real estate that the wife owns at death, rather than to the real estate owned by the wife during the marriage. In others, curtesy has been abolished and replaced by a statutory elective share in the wife's estate. A few jurisdictions have enacted statutes that embody the basic principles of common-law curtesy but with some modification.

Common law provides that an absolute divorce bars a claim of curtesy. A legal separation—sometimes called a divorce, or a mensa et thoro "from bed and board"—does not terminate the marital relationship. In the absence of an express statute, such a divorce will not bar curtesy. This is also true in regard to an interlocutory decree of divorce, a temporary, interim order of the court.

Statutes in some states provide that curtesy can be denied upon proof of certain types of misconduct, such as ADULTERY, voluntary sexual intercourse of a married person with a person other than one's spouse. Several states have statutes preserving curtesy if a divorce or legal separation was obtained because of the fault of the wife.

Statutes in many states provide that a murderer is not entitled to property rights in the estate of the victim. Some decisions apply these statutes to cases involving curtesy. In other states, these interests are barred upon the principle that a person must not be permitted to profit from his or her own wrong. In accordance with this theory, a CONSTRUCTIVE TRUST will be declared in favor of the heirs or devisees of the deceased wife who is murdered by her husband.

CROSS-REFERENCES

Husband and Wife.

CURTILAGE

The area, usually enclosed, encompassing the grounds and buildings immediately surrounding a home that is used in the daily activities of domestic life.

A garage, barn, smokehouse, chicken house, and garden are curtilage if their locations are reasonably near to the home. The determination of what constitutes curtilage is important for purposes of the FOURTH AMENDMENT to the Constitution, which prohibits unreasonable SEARCHES AND SEIZURES of a person and of his or her home or property. Courts have construed the word *home* to include curtilage so that a person is protected against unlawful searches and seizures of his or her curtilage.

◈ CURTIS, BENJAMIN ROBBINS

Benjamin Robbins Curtis served as an associate justice of the U.S. Supreme Court from 1851 to 1857. A native of Massachusetts, Curtis wrote a famous dissent in DRED SCOTT V. SANDFORD, 60 U.S. 393, 15 L. Ed. 691 (1857), a case that upheld the legitimacy of SLAVERY and denied free African Americans U.S. citizenship.

Curtis was born in Watertown, Massachusetts, on November 4, 1809. He graduated from

Harvard College in 1829 and Harvard Law School in 1832. Curtis established a law practice and became active in the WHIG PARTY. In 1851, he was elected to the Massachusetts House of Representatives and later that year was nominated to the U.S. Supreme Court by President MILLARD FILLMORE.

During his brief tenure on the U.S. Supreme Court, Curtis made a lasting impact with his dissent in *Dred Scott* and his majority opinion in *Cooley v. Board of Wardens*, 53 U.S. 299, 13 L. Ed. 996 (1851). Curtis was one of two dissenters in *Dred Scott*, which the majority opinion viewed as the final word on the legal merits of slavery and the issue of citizenship for African Americans. Chief Justice Roger Taney's majority opinion concluded that at the time of the ratification of the Constitution, there were no African-American citizens in the United States. Therefore, the Framers never contemplated that African Americans could be U.S. citizens. Curtis refuted this conclusion, pointing out that there were African-American citizens in both northern and southern states at the time of ratification. They were part of the "people of the United States" that the Constitution described. In addition, Curtis stated that "every free person born on the soil of a State, who is a citizen of that State by force of its Constitution or laws, is also a citizen of the United States."

The majority opinion also held that the Missouri Compromise was unconstitutional because Congress did not have the power to legislate policies on slavery in the federal territories. Curtis countered this finding by noting 14 instances where Congress had legislated on slavery prior to the Missouri Compromise. He concluded that this demonstrated that Congress had the power to regulate slavery in the territories.

In *Cooley v. Board of Wardens*, Curtis enunciated an enduring principle concerning the COMMERCE CLAUSE of the Constitution. Prior to

"AT THE TIME OF THE RATIFICATION OF THE ARTICLES OF CONFEDERATION, ALL FREE NATIVE-BORN INHABITANTS OF . . . [FIVE STATES], THOUGH DESCENDED FROM AFRICAN SLAVES, WERE NOT ONLY CITIZENS OF THOSE STATES, BUT . . . POSSESSED THE FRANCHISE OF ELECTORS . . ."
—BENJAMIN ROBBINS CURTIS

BENJAMIN ROBBINS CURTIS 1809–1874

1809 Born, Watertown, Mass.

1829 Graduated from Harvard College; began attending Harvard Law School

1834 Joined law partnership with cousin Charles Curtis in Boston

1851 Elected to Mass. Legislature; nominated to U.S. Supreme Court by President Fillmore

1854 *Reports of Cases in the Circuit Courts of the United States* published

1857 Wrote dissenting opinion in *Dred Scott v. Sandford*; resigned from the Court

1868 Served as lead defense counsel at President Andrew Johnson's impeachment trial

1874 Died, Newport, R.I.

1800   1825   1850   1875

1861–65 U.S. Civil War

Benjamin Robbins Curtis. LIBRARY OF CONGRESS

Cooley, the Supreme Court had failed to resolve the issue of state power to regulate interstate commerce. In his majority opinion, Curtis held that the Commerce Clause did not automatically bar all state regulation in this field. At issue in this case was the constitutionality of a Pennsylvania law requiring ships entering or leaving the port of Philadelphia to hire local harbor pilots. Although this was a regulation of interstate commerce, Curtis upheld the law. He reasoned that the term *commerce* covered many topics, some requiring national uniformity, others calling for diversity of local control. The distinction between local and national aspects of interstate commerce was a major contribution to constitutional interpretation. *Cooley* is regarded as one of the most significant Commerce Clause cases of the nineteenth century.

Curtis left the Supreme Court shortly after the *Dred Scott* decision. The decision so polarized the Court that Curtis did not feel comfortable serving with the other members. He returned to Boston and resumed his law practice.

Curtis was pulled back into the national arena in 1868, when he served as defense counsel at the IMPEACHMENT trial of President ANDREW JOHNSON. He made a lasting contribution to the theory of impeachment by convincing the Senate that impeachment is a judicial trial, not a political proceeding. This meant that impeachment required evidence of misconduct rather than a finding of no-confidence in the president.

As an author, Curtis gained prominence for his publications *Reports of Cases in the Circuit Courts of the United States* (1854), *Digest of the Decisions of the Supreme Court* (1856), and his posthumously published *Memoirs* (1879).

Curtis died on September 15, 1874.

FURTHER READINGS

Curtis, Benjamin R., ed. 2002. *A Memoir of Benjamin Robbins Curtis, LL.D.: With Some of His Professional and Miscellaneous Writing.* Union, N.J: Lawbook Exchange.

Maltz, Earl M. 1996. "The Unlikely Hero of Dred Scott: Benjamin Robbins Curtis and the Constitutional Law of Slavery." *Cardozo Law Review* 17 (May).

❖ CUSHING, CALEB

Caleb Cushing was a lawyer, politician, diplomat, and statesman who served as attorney general of the United States under President FRANKLIN PIERCE. Cushing was the nation's first full-time attorney general; he is credited with institutionalizing and expanding the office.

Cushing was born January 17, 1800, in Salisbury, Massachusetts, descending from a family with roots in colonial Massachusetts. A gifted student, he tutored classmates in mathematics and philosophy, and he graduated from Harvard at the age of seventeen. He studied law in Boston and was admitted to the Massachusetts bar in 1821. The same year, he moved to Newburyport, Massachusetts, and established his first practice. Although he represented a number of clients and interests as a young lawyer, he spent most of his time in public service. Cushing also had a long-standing love of literature and devoted his free time to a variety of literary pursuits.

His political career began in 1825 when he was elected, as a Republican candidate, to the lower house of the Massachusetts Legislature; in 1826, he was elected to the state senate.

His formal writing career also began in 1826 with the publication of his first two books, *History of the Town of Newburyport* and *The Practical Principles of Political Economy*. Encouraged by interest in these texts and eager to develop his talent, Cushing resigned his state senate office and moved to Europe in 1829. He devoted the next two years to writing. His two-volume *Historical and Political Review of the Late Revolution in France* and his *Reminiscences of Spain* were published in 1833.

Returning to the United States, Cushing ran for Congress in 1832. In his first effort, he was defeated—largely because of divisions within the REPUBLICAN PARTY. In 1834 he was elected as a

"THE SPIRIT OF THE CONSTITUTION, THE SENTIMENT OF NATIONALITY, THE FEELING OF EMOTION AND AMERICANISM, IS THE TRUE UNION, THE ONLY UNION WORTH HAVING, THE ONLY UNION POSSIBLE TO KEEP."
—CALEB CUSHING

Caleb Cushing.

Whig candidate from the Essex North District of Massachusetts. He served the district in Congress for four consecutive terms. He also continued to write. His *Growth and Territorial Progress in the United States* was published in 1839.

In 1840 Cushing supported the successful candidacy of WILLIAM H. HARRISON for president. To aid the campaign, he authored a biographical booklet called *The Life of William H. Harrison.* When Vice President JOHN TYLER succeeded to the presidency after Harrison's death in 1841, Cushing was one of the few northern Whigs to support him. During the Tyler administration, a break in the WHIG PARTY occurred, and Cushing became allied with the Democrats—making his third change of party affiliation in a decade.

Cushing's support of Tyler was rewarded in 1843 with a nomination as secretary of the treasury. But, suspicious of his party hopping, the Senate would not confirm him. Nevertheless, several months later, he was confirmed by the Senate as the new U.S. commissioner to China.

During the early 1840s, U.S. traders had asked the U.S. government for help in easing the restrictive trade conditions in China. Congress responded by setting up a commission to negotiate a trade agreement with China's representatives; Cushing was selected to head the commission. His work in China, known as the Cushing Mission, resulted in the first trade treaty between China and the United States—the Treaty of Wanghia (Wangxia, Wangsia, Wang-Hsia), signed in 1844.

After completing his mission in China, Cushing returned to serve in the Massachusetts state legislature until the outbreak of the Mexican War. In 1847, he raised a volunteer regiment at his own expense and traveled to Mexico to participate in the conflict. He attained the rank of brigadier general.

While still in Mexico, Cushing was drafted as a gubernatorial candidate by Massachusetts's DEMOCRATIC PARTY. He lost the election, and subsequent bids for the governor's seat in 1847 and 1848. He served a term in the Massachusetts state legislature from 1850 to 1852, and was then appointed an associate justice of the Massachusetts Supreme Court.

One year later, Cushing was named attorney general of the United States by President Pierce. Cushing had been a personal friend of the new president's for more than twenty years, and he was one of the most influential members of the Pierce cabinet. According to biographer Claude M. Fuess, "Cushing had a part in nearly every

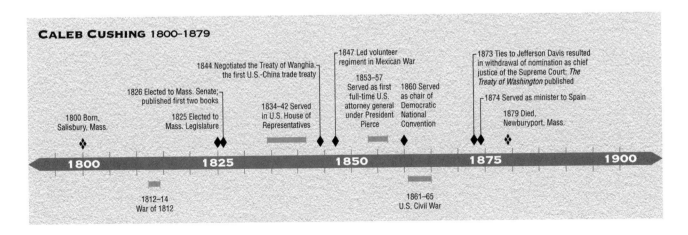

CALEB CUSHING 1800–1879

1847 Led volunteer regiment in Mexican War

1844 Negotiated the Treaty of Wanghia, the first U.S.-China trade treaty

1873 Ties to Jefferson Davis resulted in withdrawal of nomination as chief justice of the Supreme Court; *The Treaty of Washington* published

1826 Elected to Mass. Senate; published first two books

1853–57 Served as first full-time U.S. attorney general under President Pierce

1860 Served as chair of Democratic National Convention

1874 Served as minister to Spain

1800 Born, Salisbury, Mass.

1825 Elected to Mass. Legislature

1834–42 Served in U.S. House of Representatives

1879 Died, Newburyport, Mass.

1800 1825 1850 1875 1900

1812–14 War of 1812

1861–65 U.S. Civil War

matter of significance arising during the next four years in Washington."

When Cushing accepted the job of attorney general, it was a part-time position with a substantially smaller salary than those of other cabinet positions. Cushing's appointment coincided with a move by Congress to increase the attorney general's salary, and to enforce a residency requirement that had been routinely ignored by previous appointees.

Cushing interpreted Congress's actions as a mandate to relinquish his private practice and serve as attorney general full-time. His decision to abandon his practice was controversial. The old tradition of continuing a private practice while in office was thought by many to be essential in maintaining sharp legal skills and keeping abreast of current law. In defense of his action, Cushing wrote,

> Within the last few years . . . the condition of the country has undergone changes, occasioning a vast augmentation in the amount of administrative business . . . and it would not be possible now . . . for the Attorney General . . . to be frequently absent from the seat of government, attending to private professional pursuits, nor could he find much leisure to prepare and argue private causes even before the Supreme Court.

With the barriers of low pay and part-time status removed, the attorney general became an equal member of the cabinet, and the office became more visible and more constant than in previous administrations. The changes had the cumulative effect of stabilizing and institutionalizing the office.

As a full-time cabinet officer, Cushing had both the time and the personal inclination to be active in a broad range of government activities. He assumed responsibility for several functions previously overseen by the SECRETARY OF STATE, such as pardons, legal and judicial appointments, and EXTRADITION cases.

In keeping with his lifelong love of writing, Cushing wrote frequently about the office of attorney general and his duties and responsibilities. In an 1856 treatise on the office, Cushing described his role as the administrative head of the government's legal business. He also took his opinion-writing function seriously. An opinion, he wrote, "is in practice final and conclusive,—not only as respects the action of public officers in administrative matters . . . but also in questions of private right, inasmuch as parties, having concerns with the government, possess in

general no means of bringing a controverted matter before the courts of law."

Following his term as attorney general, Cushing continued to play a conspicuous role in both local and national politics until the end of his life. He returned to the Massachusetts state legislature from 1857 to 1859. In 1860 he served as chairman of the Democratic National Convention in Charleston, South Carolina, but he gave loyal support to Republican President ABRAHAM LINCOLN and the Union during the Civil War.

In 1866 he was named to a commission charged with revising and codifying the laws of Congress. In 1868, he served on a diplomatic mission to Bogota, Colombia. And in 1872, he was appointed counsel for the United States at the Geneva conference for the settlement of the *Alabama* claims, where arbitrators determined the amount of the award in a dispute concerning the construction and release of confederate cruisers by Great Britain.

In 1873 he was nominated by President ULYSSES S. GRANT as chief justice of the Supreme Court. With the memory of the Civil War still fresh, Cushing's opponents questioned his cordial relations with Jefferson Davis (based upon his Democratic connections) and forced the withdrawal of his nomination. *The Treaty of Washington*, Cushing's last work—and said to be his most important—was published in 1873. In 1874, he was nominated and confirmed as minister to Spain; he finished his term abroad in 1877.

Cushing died at his Newburyport home on January 2, 1879, just two weeks short of his eightieth birthday.

FURTHER READINGS

Baker, Nancy V. 1992. *Conflicting Loyalties: Law and Politics in the Attorney General's Office, 1789–1990.* Lawrence: Univ. Press of Kansas.

Donahue, William J. 1982. *The Caleb Cushing Mission.*

Fuess, Claude Moore. 1965. *The Life of Caleb Cushing.* Reprint. Hamden, Conn.: Archon.

Hodgson, Sister Michael Catherine. 1955. *Caleb Cushing, Attorney General of the United States, 1853–1957.* Washington, D.C.: Catholic Univ. of America Press.

Welch, Richard E., Jr. 1957. "Caleb Cushing's Chinese Mission and the Treaty of Wanghia: A Review." *Oregon Historical Quarterly* 58 (December).

❖ CUSHING, LUTHER STEARNS

Luther Stearns Cushing achieved prominence as a legal educator, author, and jurist. He was born June 22, 1803, in Lunenberg, Massachusetts.

"ALL LANGUAGE, NOT ADDRESSED TO THE HOUSE, IN A PARLIAMENTARY COURSE, MUST BE CONSIDERED NOISE AND DISTURBITIVE."
—LUTHER CUSHING

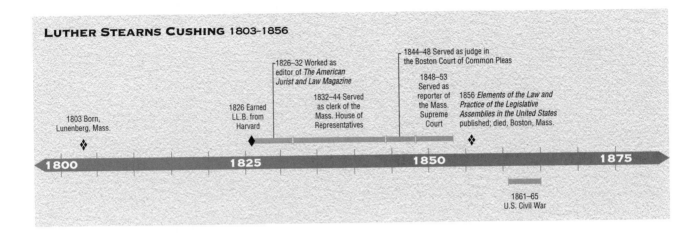

LUTHER STEARNS CUSHING 1803–1856

1803 Born, Lunenberg, Mass.

1826 Earned LL.B. from Harvard

1826–32 Worked as editor of *The American Jurist and Law Magazine*

1832–44 Served as clerk of the Mass. House of Representatives

1844–48 Served as judge in the Boston Court of Common Pleas

1848–53 Served as reporter of the Mass. Supreme Court

1856 *Elements of the Law and Practice of the Legislative Assemblies in the United States* published; died, Boston, Mass.

1800   1825   1850   1875

1861–65 U.S. Civil War

Cushing graduated from Harvard University with a bachelor of laws degree in 1826.

From 1826 to 1832, Cushing was an editor for *The American Jurist and Law Magazine.* For the next twelve years, he served in the state government system as clerk of the Massachusetts House of Representatives.

Cushing entered the judicial phase of his career in 1844, presiding as judge of the Boston Court of Common Pleas for a four-year period. In 1848, he became a reporter for the Massachusetts Supreme Court, performing these duties until 1853.

In 1848 Cushing returned to his alma mater, Harvard University, and presented a series of lectures on ROMAN LAW at the Harvard Law School until 1851.

As an author, Cushing is famous for several publications, including *A Manual of Parliamentary Practice,* also known as *Cushing's Manual,* published in 1844, and *Elements of the Law and Practice of the Legislative Assemblies in the United States,* published in 1856.

> "WHERE [STATES' RIGHTS HAVE] BEEN ABRIDGED, IT WAS THOUGHT NECESSARY FOR THE GREATER, INDISPENSABLE GOOD OF THE WHOLE."
> —WILLIAM CUSHING

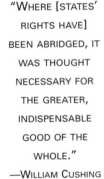

Cushing died June 22, 1856, in Boston, Massachusetts.

❖ CUSHING, WILLIAM

William Cushing was born March 1, 1732. He graduated from Harvard College in 1751, and received an honorary master of arts degree from Yale University in 1753 and an honorary doctor of laws degree from Harvard University in 1785.

After his ADMISSION TO THE BAR in 1755, Cushing began his judicial career in Lincoln County, Massachusetts (now a part of Maine), as judge for the Probate Court of that county during 1760 and 1761. In 1772, he served as a justice for the Massachusetts Superior Court, followed by a term as chief justice of that court from 1777 to 1789.

In 1779, Cushing was a member of the first Massachusetts Constitutional Convention. In 1788, he acted as vice president at the Massachusetts Convention, a convention that endorsed the U.S. Constitution.

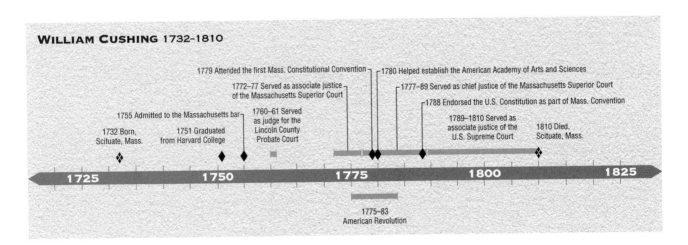

WILLIAM CUSHING 1732–1810

1732 Born, Scituate, Mass.

1751 Graduated from Harvard College

1755 Admitted to the Massachusetts bar

1760–61 Served as judge for the Lincoln County Probate Court

1772–77 Served as associate justice of the Massachusetts Superior Court

1779 Attended the first Mass. Constitutional Convention

1780 Helped establish the American Academy of Arts and Sciences

1777–89 Served as chief justice of the Massachusetts Superior Court

1788 Endorsed the U.S. Constitution as part of Mass. Convention

1789–1810 Served as associate justice of the U.S. Supreme Court

1810 Died, Scituate, Mass.

1725   1750   1775   1800   1825

1775–83 American Revolution

William Cushing. U.S. SUPREME COURT

Cushing returned to the bench in 1789 as associate justice of the U.S. Supreme Court, rendering decisions until 1810.

In addition to his legal and judicial career, Cushing was active in the establishment of the American Academy of Arts and Sciences and was a fellow of that institution from 1780 to 1810.

Cushing died September 13, 1810, in Scituate, Massachusetts.

CUSTODIAL INTERROGATION

Questioning initiated by law enforcement officers after a person is taken into custody or otherwise deprived of his or her freedom in any significant way, thus requiring that the person be advised of his or her applicable constitutional rights.

In the landmark decision MIRANDA V. ARIZONA, 384 U.S. 436, 86 S. Ct. 1602, 16 L. Ed. 2d 694 (1966), the U.S. Supreme Court set standards for law enforcement officers to follow when attempting to interrogate suspects whom they hold in custody. Suspects who are subject to custodial interrogation must be warned that they have the right to remain silent; that any statements that they make may be used as evidence against them; that they have the right to

an attorney; and that if they cannot afford an attorney, one will be appointed for them prior to any questioning, if they so desire. Under *Miranda,* unless those warnings are given, no evidence obtained during the interrogation may be used against the accused.

Since *Miranda* was decided, state and federal courts have struggled with a number of issues with regard to its application, including: when a suspect is deemed to be in custody and thus entitled to the warnings required by *Miranda;* and when a suspect will be deemed to have waived the right to have an attorney present during questioning. Some recent decisions by the U.S. Supreme Court have attempted to answer these difficult questions.

In *Stansbury v. California,* 511 U.S. 318, 114 S. Ct. 1526, 128 L. Ed. 2d 293 (1994), the Court considered whether a police officer's subjective and undisclosed opinion concerning whether a person who had been questioned had been a suspect was relevant in determining whether that person had been in custody and thus entitled to the *Miranda* warnings. In 1982, Robert Stansbury was convicted of first-degree murder, rape, KIDNAPPING, and a lewd act on a child under the age of 14. The morning after ten-year-old Robyn Jackson had disappeared from a Baldwin Park, California, playground, a witness in Pasadena, California, had observed a large man leaving a turquoise car and throwing something into a nearby flood-control channel. The witness called the police, who discovered Jackson's body in the channel. She had been raped, strangled, and struck on the head with a blunt instrument. The police later learned that Jackson had talked to two ice-cream truck drivers, one of whom was Stansbury, shortly before she disappeared. Officers went to Stansbury's home and asked Stansbury to go to the police station to answer some questions concerning their investigation into Jackson's murder. Stansbury agreed and accepted a ride to the station in a police car.

At the police station, Stansbury was questioned about his whereabouts and activities on the day Jackson's body was discovered. The police did not read him the *Miranda* warnings at the time. Stansbury told the police that he had talked to the girl, that he had returned to his trailer a few hours later, and that he had left around midnight in his roommate's turquoise car. The car matched the description given by the witness. Stansbury also admitted that he pre-

After a person has been taken into custody by law enforcement officials, he must be advised of his constitutional rights before the officials begin an interrogation. Pictured is Jose Canseco in 2003.

AP/WIDE WORLD PHOTOS

viously had been convicted of rape, kidnapping, and CHILD MOLESTATION. The detective interviewing Stansbury then terminated the conversation and read Stansbury the *Miranda* warnings. Stansbury was later charged with first-degree murder and other crimes.

At a PRETRIAL CONFERENCE, Stansbury moved to suppress all of the statements that he had made at the station, as well as the evidence that had been discovered as a result of those statements. The trial court denied his motion, ruling that Stansbury had not been in custody—and thus that he had not been entitled to the *Miranda* warnings—until he had mentioned the turquoise car. Before that point in the interview, the court reasoned, Stansbury had not been considered a suspect. Based on that conclusion, the trial court permitted introduction of the statements that Stansbury had made before he had mentioned the car. Stansbury was convicted on all charges and was sentenced to death for first-degree murder.

On appeal, the California Supreme Court affirmed Stansbury's conviction, rejecting the "in-custody" claim that he had raised in the trial court. The state supreme court, applying an in-custody legal standard based on whether the investigation has focused on the subject, agreed with the trial court's conclusion that suspicion had focused on Stansbury only after he mentioned driving the turquoise car on the night of the crime. Therefore, the court held, Stansbury had not been subject to custodial interrogation

before that time, and in turn *Miranda* warnings had not been required, and his statements were admissible.

The U.S. Supreme Court reversed and remanded the case. In a per curiam decision (a brief, unanimous, and unsigned opinion), the Court held that "an officer's subjective and undisclosed view concerning whether the person being interrogated is a suspect is irrelevant to the assessment [of] whether the person is in custody." Instead, according to the Court, the key inquiry should be whether the individual had been placed under formal arrest, or whether the restraint placed on the individual's freedom of movement rose to the level of a formal arrest. The Court further noted that the "initial determination of custody depends on the objective circumstances of the interrogation, not on the subjective views harbored by either the interrogation officers or the person being questioned." So long as an officer's subjective view that an individual being questioned is a suspect is not disclosed to the individual, the officer's view has no bearing on the in-custody issue. If the officer's knowledge or beliefs are communicated to the individual being questioned, the Court stated, that knowledge or those beliefs are relevant only to the extent that the individual "would gauge the breadth of his or her 'freedom of action.'" But a statement from the officer that the individual is the prime suspect, in and of itself, is not "dispositive of the custody issue."

In *Stansbury,* the California Supreme Court had not analyzed the in-custody issue based on these principles. Thus, the U.S. Supreme Court remanded the case to the trial court to determine whether the objective facts surrounding Stansbury's interrogation supported the trial court's original conclusion that Stansbury had not been in custody before he mentioned the turquoise car.

The high court tackled another difficult *Miranda* issue in *Davis v. United States,* 512 U.S. 452, 114 S. Ct. 2350, 129 L. Ed. 2d (1994), when it considered the circumstances under which a suspect who was subject to custodial interrogation has validly waived the right to have an attorney present during questioning. In an earlier decision, *Edwards v. Arizona,* 451 U.S. 477, 101 S. Ct. 1880, 68 L. Ed. 2d 378 (1981), the Court had held that such a waiver must be "knowing and intelligent." Furthermore, the Court had made clear in *Edwards* that police officers must immediately stop questioning a suspect who clearly asserts the right to have legal counsel present during the interrogation.

Edwards applied only when a suspect clearly asserted the right to have counsel present; it did not provide guidance to officers when a suspect made an ambiguous or equivocal request for counsel. Addressing that situation, some jurisdictions had held that any mention of counsel, no matter how ambiguous, required that questioning cease. Other courts had attempted to define a threshold standard of clarity, under which comments that fell below the required clarity did not invoke the RIGHT TO COUNSEL. Still other jurisdictions had ruled that questioning must cease upon any mention of counsel, but officers were permitted to ask further, narrow questions to clarify whether the suspect desired an attorney. In *Davis,* the U.S. Supreme Court settled the issue, holding that officers are not required to cease questioning if a suspect makes an ambiguous request for counsel. Questioning may continue until the suspect makes an "unambiguous" request for an attorney. Furthermore, the Court held, police officers have no duty to seek clarification of an ambiguous request.

The case began when Robert Davis, a member of the U.S. Navy, became a suspect in the murder of another sailor at the Charleston, South Carolina, naval base. Davis was interviewed by the authorities and informed of his *Miranda* rights. He waived, orally and in writing, his right to remain silent and his right to counsel. But after talking with agents for 90 minutes, he stated, "Maybe I should talk to a lawyer." One of the agents asked Davis whether he wanted an attorney, or whether he was just making a comment. Davis replied, "No, I'm not asking for a lawyer." After a short break, the agents reminded him of his right to remain silent and then resumed the questioning. An hour later, Davis said, "I think I want a lawyer before I say anything else." The agents then stopped the interview.

At his general COURT-MARTIAL, Davis maintained that the statements made during the interview after his ambiguous statement concerning the need to talk with a lawyer should not be admitted. The court ruled that the ambiguous statement had not been in the form of a request for an attorney, and thus the statements made after it were admissible. Davis was found guilty of unpremeditated murder and sentenced to life imprisonment. His conviction was affirmed by the military appellate court.

The U.S. Supreme Court also affirmed the conviction. Writing for the majority, Justice SANDRA DAY O'CONNOR noted that none of the Court's previous decisions addressing *Miranda* issues required that questioning of a suspect be terminated if the suspect makes an ambiguous or equivocal request for counsel. To gain *Miranda* protection, she maintained, a suspect must "unambiguously request counsel," and the request must "articulate [the suspect's] desire to have counsel present sufficiently clearly that a reasonable police officer in the circumstances would understand the statement to be a request for an attorney." She further stated that requiring questioning to stop when a suspect makes ambiguous references to requesting an attorney would transform the *Miranda* protections into "wholly irrational obstacles to legitimate police investigative activity." Police officers, she maintained, would be forced to end questioning even if the suspect does not want an attorney, thus hampering effective law enforcement. Permitting a mere reference to an attorney to end an interrogation would require police officers to "make difficult judgment calls whether the suspect in fact wants a lawyer even though he hasn't said so, with the threat of suppression if they guess wrong."

In a separate opinion, Justice DAVID H. SOUTER, joined by Justices HARRY A. BLACKMUN, JOHN PAUL STEVENS, and RUTH BADER GINSBURG, concurred in the judgment affirming Davis's conviction. In Souter's view, officers could constitutionally pose questions to clarify a suspect's ambiguous reference for counsel, as was done in *Davis.* Souter believed that the statements given by Davis, after the counsel issue was clarified, indicated that Davis did not want an attorney. Nevertheless, Souter disagreed with the Court's ruling that the agents could entirely disregard Davis's references to wanting one. He argued that, like the agents in *Davis,* the Court should adopt a rule barring officers from further questioning until they have determined whether a suspect's ambiguous statement was meant as a request for an attorney. According to Souter, a "timid or verbally inept subject" might not understand what is required in order for him or her to stop the interrogation and to consult with an attorney. If the suspect understands that a request has been ignored, he or she may not object further and may see "confession (true or not) as the only way to end [the] interrogation."

The Future of Miranda

Miranda and its progeny have long served as a whipping post for politicians, legal commentators, and others who perceive the decision as "coddling criminals." They argue that the *Miranda* warnings impede police officers from efficiently and effectively doing their jobs by adding additional layers of unnecessary procedure to the law enforcement process. *Miranda* critics also maintain that the police are punished, and that society is harmed, when defendants are set free, because key evidence is suppressed after being obtained in violation of the Fifth Amendment's prohibition against un-Mirandized confessions. Moreover, *Miranda* critics contend that criminal suspects seldom fully understand the meaning or importance of the rights recited to them. Finally, critics cite studies indicating that the *Miranda* decision has had little effect in reducing the number of confessions and requests for lawyers made by suspects in custody.

In 1999, the U.S. Court of Appeals for the Fourth Circuit fueled long-standing speculation that *Miranda* would be overruled when it held that the admissibility of confessions in federal court is governed not by *Miranda*, but by a federal statute enacted two years after *Miranda*. The statute, 18 U.S.C.A. § 3501, provides that a confession is admissible if voluntarily given, with the voluntariness of each confession being evaluated by the "totality of the circumstances" on a cases-by-case basis, without any requirement that the defendant be Mirandized. Congress enacted the statute to overturn *Miranda*, the Fourth Circuit wrote, and Congress had the authority to do so pursuant to its authority to overrule judicially created RULES OF EVIDENCE that are not mandated by the Constitution. *United States v. Dickerson*, 166 F.3d 667 (4th Cir. 1999).

The U.S. Supreme Court reversed. In a 7-2 opinion authored by Chief Justice WILLIAM REHNQUIST, the Court wrote that whether or not it agreed with *Miranda*, the principles of STARE DECISIS weigh heavily against overruling it then. While the Court has overruled other precedents when subsequent cases have undermined their doctrinal underpinnings, that has not happened to the *Miranda* decision, which the Court said "has become embedded in routine police practice to the point where the warnings have become part of our national culture." Although a few guilty defendants may some-times go free as the result of the application of the *Miranda* rule, the Court observed, experience shows that the totality-of-the-circumstances test set forth in Section 3501 is more difficult than *Miranda* for law enforcement officers and courts to apply in a consistent manner. *Dickerson v. United States*, 530 U.S. 428, 120 S. Ct. 2326, 147 L. Ed. 2d 405 (2000).

The Court said that a contrary conclusion is not required by the fact that it has subsequently made exceptions to the Miranda rule. No constitutional rule is immutable, much less immune from the sort of refinements *Miranda* has undergone to adapt to the needs and realities of law enforcement. Moreover, the Court emphasized, these exceptions have reduced some of the law enforcement inefficiencies that *Miranda* critics were predicting would undermine the efficiency of criminal investigations, as the *Miranda* warnings are now often provided in a rote and perfunctory manner during arrest and custodial interrogation. "If anything," Rehnquist wrote, "subsequent cases have reduced the impact of the Miranda rule on legitimate law enforcement while reaffirming the decision's core ruling that unwarned statements may not be used as evidence in the prosecution's case in chief."

Dickerson surprised many observers, not only because the Court declined to overrule *Miranda*, but also because Chief Justice William Rehnquist authored the opinion upholding *Miranda*, even suggesting that *Miranda* had become so "embedded" in the nation's JURISPRUDENCE as to be unlikely to be overturned in the foreseeable future. Most observers consider Rehnquist to be one of the Court's more conservative members. His opinions are frequently joined by fellow conservatives, Justices ANTONIN SCALIA and CLARENCE THOMAS, both of whom dissented in *Dickerson*. On any number of other issues, civil libertarians have assailed the chief justice for what they regard as his narrow reading of the BILL OF RIGHTS. *Dickerson* both tempered that criticism and quieted speculation about the future of *Miranda*.

FURTHER READINGS

Clymer, Steven D. 2002. "Are Police Free to Disregard *Miranda*?" *Yale Law Journal* 112 (December).

Kenney, Jack. 1998. "Custodial Interrogation, Invocation of Right to Counsel." *Res Gestae* 42 (November–December).

Pearce, Gene A. 2001. "Constitutional Law—Criminal Law: The United States Supreme Court Affirms the Use of

Miranda Rights by Police to Determine the Admissibility of Statements Made During Custodial Interrogation." *North Dakota Law Review* 77 (winter).

CROSS-REFERENCES

Criminal Procedure; Privilege Against Self-Incrimination; Right to Counsel; Self-Incrimination.

CUSTODY

The care, possession, and control of a thing or person. The retention, inspection, guarding, maintenance, or security of a thing within the immediate care and control of the person to whom it is committed. The detention of a person by lawful authority or process.

For example, in a BAILMENT, the bailee has custody of goods delivered to him or her in trust for the execution of a special object upon such goods.

The term is flexible and may mean actual imprisonment or the mere power—legal or physical—of imprisoning or assuming manual possession. A petitioner must be "in custody" to be entitled to HABEAS CORPUS relief, which provides for release from unlawful confinement in violation of constitutional rights. Custody in this context is synonymous with restraint of liberty and does not necessarily mean actual physical imprisonment. Persons who are on PROBATION or who are released on their own recognizance are "in custody" for purposes of habeas corpus proceedings.

CHILD CUSTODY, which encompasses the care, control, guardianship, and maintenance of a child, may be awarded to one of the parents in a DIVORCE or separation proceeding. Joint custody is an emerging concept that involves the apportionment of custody between the parents during specified periods of time. For example, a child may reside with each parent for six months each year.

Jurisdiction of courts over custody disputes has been heavily litigated, especially in child-custody cases. In the past, some parents sought to obtain custody over their children by removing them from one state, then seeking to obtain custody through a decree in another state. The federal and state governments have sought to prevent this occurrence through the enactment of a series of statutes. In 1967, the COMMISSIONERS ON UNIFORM LAWS approved the Uniform Child Custody Jurisdiction Act, which was eventually adopted in every state. The act provides that a state court will not accept a custody case unless it has original jurisdiction or unless the state with original jurisdiction relinquishes it. The Commissioners on Uniform Laws updated the law in 1997 with the approval of the Uniform Child Custody Jurisdiction and Enforcement Act, which more than 30 states have adopted. Congress has enacted similar legislation, including the Parental KIDNAPPING Prevention Act (28 U.S.C.A. § 1738A [Supp. 2003]). That statute requires that a state give FULL FAITH AND CREDIT to another state's custody order.

The jurisdiction of federal courts over custody of ALIENS has also become a significant issue with the enactment of several anti-TERRORISM statutes since the late 1990s. In 1996, Congress enacted the Antiterrorism and Effective Death Penalty Act, Pub. L. No. 104-132, 110 Stat. 1214 (1996), and the Illegal Immigration Reform and Immigrant Responsibility Act, Pub. L. No. 104-208, 110 Stat. 3009 (1996), both of which removed much of the power from federal courts to review cases involving immigrants who are held in custody for certain crimes. Several legal commentators criticized the application of these statutes due to their limitation of the habeas corpus rights that traditionally are extended to aliens. Commentators have similarly raised questions with respect to orders issued by President GEORGE W. BUSH, which limit the ability of federal courts to review cases of suspected terrorists who are held in custody.

CUSTOMS DUTIES

Tariffs or taxes payable on merchandise imported or exported from one country to another.

Customs laws seek to equalize the charges imposed by other countries, furnish income for the federal government, and preserve the financial stability of domestic industries.

Congress has the exclusive authority to determine the imposition and enforcement of such duties and federal courts have exclusive jurisdiction to resolve controversies involving customs duties.

Customs Service

The U.S. Customs Service has these responsibilities: the proper assessment and collection of customs duties, excise taxes, fees, and penalties owing on imported items; the prohibition and seizure of contraband, including narcotics and illegal drugs; the processing of people, car-

Customs duties are taxes paid on merchandise brought into the United States, including, for example, gifts brought home to another person.

MARTHA TABOR/WORKING IMAGES PHOTOGRAPHS

riers, cargo, and mail into and out of the country; the administration of certain navigation laws; the detection and apprehension of individuals engaged in fraudulent activities who intend to circumvent customs; the protection of U.S. business and labor through the enforcement of statutes, regulations, and countervailing duty; the enforcement of COPYRIGHT, patent, and TRADEMARK provisions and quotas; and the setting of requirements for imported merchandise.

Goods and Merchandise Subject to Duties

Federal tariff schedules set forth terms that prescribe those goods that are to be subject to duties. Such schedules specify the items upon which a duty is to be imposed when imported into the United States and the rates at which the items will be taxed based upon the monetary value of each item.

Exemptions Any U.S. resident, including an infant, who returns from a foreign trip is permitted an exemption from being charged duty on specific items that would otherwise be subject to duty, provided the individual was out of the United States for a minimum of 48 hours. The size of the exemption depends upon the reasonable retail value of each item, which is determined by the place of purchase, not by what it would sell for in the United States. Articles must be for personal or household purposes or for use as gifts. Included within the exemption are limited amounts of alcoholic beverages, cigars, and cigarettes.

Household goods—including rugs, draperies, and furniture—obtained abroad and used there for a period of one year can be imported

without the imposition of a duty, provided these goods are not brought into the country for sale or for use by some other individual. Cameras, stereo equipment, and watches do not fall under the classification of household goods; therefore, a duty must be paid on such items. Household goods transported abroad from the United States are, upon their return, exempt from duty. In addition, personal articles, such as cameras and jewelry, that were originally manufactured in a foreign country can also be returned without the imposition of a duty, provided they were purchased in the United States and identified and registered with the Customs Service prior to being brought to a foreign country.

Vehicles, including automobiles, that are taken abroad for nonbusiness purposes can be sent back to the United States duty free upon proof that such vehicles were shipped from the United States. Such proof can be in the form of either a state motor vehicle certificate or customs registration certificate upon the registration of the automobile prior to shipment. If an automobile is repaired while abroad, the value of the repairs must be stated and a duty must be discharged on their value.

Gifts The established exemption applies to both gifts received abroad and those brought home for others. Gifts that do not exceed a value of $50 in the country of shipment can be accepted by the recipient in the United States free from any duty charges and, therefore, have no effect on the exemption. However, no one person can receive gifts exceeding $50 on any one day. If this occurs, a duty and, if applicable, a tax will be imposed on all articles. The $50 limit does not include gifts of liquor or tobacco, nor does it include gifts that an individual sends to himself or herself or to any person with whom he or she is traveling. The common practice is to have gifts wrapped and labeled separately so as to avoid having them included in the sum total of purchases by the customs officer.

Other Purchases In the event that the total dollar value of the imported items is greater than the set exemption amount, the purchaser must complete a written declaration itemizing all articles. A duty of 10 percent on the first $1,000 in the excess amount must be paid, but the duties on goods above that amount vary, based on their wholesale, rather than on their fair retail, value. Those articles assessed at the maximum duty rates are included within the exemption, whereas those assessed at lower rates are put in the excess category. Discharge of the duty on the excess items can be made with American money, a personal check, a government check, a traveler's check, or a money order. Personal checks cannot be drawn on foreign banks; rather, they must be drawn on a national or state bank or trust company of the United States. In the event that a government check, traveler's check, or money order is used, it must not be for an amount higher than $50 in excess of the duty charge.

Restricted Articles Various items such as plants that shelter harmful insects are subject to restrictions because they are hazardous to the GENERAL WELFARE of the United States as a whole or to a particular segment of society. Restricted plants cannot be brought into the United States unless the Customs Service issues special permits. Livestock—including horses, goats, sheep, and zoo animals—are also restricted and require permits for their importation. Pets must pass inspection by veterinarians employed by the U.S. DEPARTMENT OF AGRICULTURE and are frequently subject to a quarantine period prior to entry into the United States.

Importation of firearms and ammunition requires a permit. Weapons taken abroad to be used on a hunting expedition can be brought back by the individual who removed them without a permit. The owners of firearms customarily register them with the Customs Service before their departure; however, no more than three firearms and one thousand cartridges can be registered.

Prohibited Articles A wide range of items cannot be brought back to the United States from a foreign country. Included in this category are plants in soil, citrus peels, fresh dairy products, and seeds from a number of plants. Narcotic drugs are strictly prohibited; however, medication containing narcotic substances can be brought in provided the substances are properly identified and the traveler has a doctor's prescription or a statement relating to the drug. The importation of various articles from certain countries, including Cuba and Vietnam, are prohibited without a license obtained from the Office of Foreign Assets Control of the DEPARTMENT OF THE TREASURY.

Penalties Failure to declare articles that must be declared makes the items subject to seizure and FORFEITURE. An individual who fails to declare an article is held liable for a penalty equivalent to its value, which is its worth in the place where it was acquired. An individual who fails to declare an item can also be subject to a criminal action.

Seizure and forfeiture provisions are also applicable in the event that the value of an item is understated or misrepresented and the individual who is guilty of such understatement or MISREPRESENTATION must pay the duty on the forfeited item.

FURTHER READINGS

Korb, Lawrence J. 2003. *A New National Security Strategy in an Age of Terrorists, Tyrants, and Weapons of Mass Destruction.* New York: Council on Foreign Relations.

Oldham, Charles, ed. 2002. *United States Coast Guard: The Americas' Lifesaver and Guardian of the Seas.* Tampa, Fla.: Government Services Group.

CROSS-REFERENCES

Contraband; Tariff.

CY PRES

Abbreviated form of cy pres comme possible, *French for "as near as possible." The name of a rule employed in the construction of such instruments as trusts and wills, by which the intention of the person who executes the instrument is effectuated as nearly as possible when circumstances make it impossible or illegal to give literal effect to the document.*

Cy pres is applied in cases where the court concludes that, under the circumstances, the intent of the settlor who creates a trust or the testator who makes a will will not be contradicted by employing a flexible approach toward the application of the provisions of the document. Without cy pres, the intent of the settlor or testator will never be implemented because the document will be without any legal effect and not subject to enforcement by the court. In one case a settlor directed that his property be used as a home for retired clergymen, but the clergymen's wives were prohibited from residing there with them. This trust provision substantially reduced the number of applicants to the home. A court ordered the trustee, a person either appointed by the settlor or required by law to execute a trust, to ignore this provision under the doctrine of cy pres. However, a court does not have the power to alter a settlor's dispositive provisions. For example, a trustee who is in charge of two charitable trusts cannot be authorized by a court to transfer funds from one charity to the other.

A court also has the power under the cy pres doctrine to order trust funds to be applied to a charitable purpose other than the one specifically named by a settlor when it was the settlor's intention to benefit charity in general and it has become impossible, inexpedient, or impractical to accomplish his or her specific purpose. Since a CHARITABLE TRUST can be perpetual, many become obsolete due to changing social, political, economic, or other conditions. A trust established in 1790 to combat yellow fever would, for example, be of little or no practical value now, since that disease has been virtually eradicated as a result of advances in medicine. When cy pres is applied, the court reasons that the settlor would have wanted his or her general charitable purposes implemented despite the changing conditions. In one case a testator provided for two trusts: the first to facilitate the end of SLAVERY, and the second to assist runaway slaves. Shortly after the testator died, slavery was abolished, so the purposes of both trusts were completely outdated. A court reasoned that the testator intended the broad purpose of aiding African Americans, so the changes in the structure of society justified the court's application of funds of the trusts to purposes similar to those chosen by the testator. The first trust fund was applied to the education of former slaves in the South, and the second was used to assist impoverished blacks in the city where the testator had lived and granted preference to those who had previously escaped from slavery.

The cy pres doctrine can be applied only by a court, never by the trustees of a trust who must execute the terms of the trust. Trustees can, however, apply to the court for cy pres instructions when they believe the trust arrangement warrants it. A cy pres action is instituted by the trustees with the state attorney general as a party to the action, or the attorney general can initiate the suit. Once conditions are deemed suitable for the employment of cy pres, the court has broad discretion in the framing of a scheme for the application of the charitable fund to a purpose "as near as possible" to the one designated by the settlor. Some states authorize the living settlor to VETO the application of cy pres to an irrevocable trust that he or she created.

The doctrine of cy pres is not employed where a settlor was concerned with only one specific charitable objective and it fails, or when the settlor provides that a gift be made to another upon failure of the charitable gift. When cy pres is not applied and the trust fails without any provision for the property to be given to another, there is a RESULTING TRUST for the settlor or his successors.

FURTHER READINGS

Menocal, Armando M. 1998. "Proposed Guidelines for Cy Pres Distribution." *Judges Journal* 37 (winter): 22.

Rudko, Frances Howell. 1998. "The Cy Pres Doctrine in the United States: From Extreme Reluctance to Affirmative Action." *Cleveland State Law Review* 46 (summer): 471–88.

❖ DALLAS, ALEXANDER JAMES

Alexander James Dallas achieved prominence as a jurist, statesman, and author. Dallas was born June 21, 1759, in Jamaica, British West Indies. He relocated to the United States, becoming a citizen in 1783.

In 1785, Dallas was admitted to the Pennsylvania bar and began his judicial career as counselor of the Pennsylvania Supreme Court. Six years later he acted as secretary of the Commonwealth of Pennsylvania. He also performed editorial duties on the first series of the U.S. Supreme Court Reports and served as U.S. district attorney from 1801 to 1814, before entering the federal government system.

Dallas became secretary of the treasury in 1814 and remained in the cabinet of President JAMES MADISON for two years. He gained recognition during his tenure for his policies advocating protective tariffs, public credit, and the formation of the Second Bank of the United States. His programs were responsible for restoring the United States to a strong financial position after several years of depression. In addition to these duties, he served concurrently as acting secretary of war from 1815 to 1816.

As an author, Dallas wrote many noteworthy publications, including *Features of Mr. Jay's Treaty* (1795); *Laws of the Commonwealth of Pennsylvania,* four volumes (1793 to 1801); *Reports of Cases Ruled and Adjudged in the Several Courts of the United States and Pennsylvania,* four volumes (1790 to 1807); and *Treasury Reports: An Exposition of the Causes and Character of the War* (1815).

Dallas died January 16, 1817, in Trenton, New Jersey.

> "OVER THEIR REPRESENTATIVES THE PEOPLE HAVE A COMPLETE CONTROL, AND IF ONE SET TRANSGRESS THEY CAN APPOINT ANOTHER SET, WHO CAN RESCIND AND ANNUL ALL PREVIOUS BAD LAWS."
> —ALEXANDER J. DALLAS

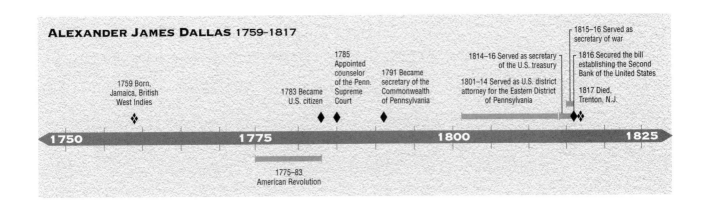

ALEXANDER JAMES DALLAS 1759–1817

1759 Born, Jamaica, British West Indies

1783 Became U.S. citizen

1785 Appointed counselor of the Penn. Supreme Court

1791 Became secretary of the Commonwealth of Pennsylvania

1801–14 Served as U.S. district attorney for the Eastern District of Pennsylvania

1814–16 Served as secretary of the U.S. treasury

1815–16 Served as secretary of war

1816 Secured the bill establishing the Second Bank of the United States

1817 Died, Trenton, N.J.

1750 　 1775 　 1800 　 1825

1775–83 American Revolution

Alexander J. Dallas.

CROSS-REFERENCES

Bank of the United States.

George M. Dallas.

❖ DALLAS, GEORGE MIFFLIN

George Mifflin Dallas was born July 10, 1792, to statesman ALEXANDER JAMES DALLAS. He graduated from Princeton University in 1810 and was admitted to the bar three years later.

In 1813, statesman Albert Gallatin was dispatched to Russia for the purpose of securing Russian aid in negotiating an end to the WAR OF 1812 between the United States and Great Britain. Dallas performed the duties of secretary to Gallatin and was commissioned in 1814 by the American delegates at the Ghent Peace Conference to relay the terms of peace to the British.

Dallas returned to Philadelphia and served as deputy attorney general before becoming mayor in 1829 for a three-year period. He also acted as U.S. district attorney, and in 1831, he entered the federal government.

Dallas filled a vacancy in the U.S. Senate and represented Pennsylvania until 1833; in that same year, he also performed the duties of attorney general of Pennsylvania and continued in this capacity until 1835.

In 1837, Dallas again acted as a diplomat, serving as emissary to Russia. Eight years later, he was elected as U.S. vice president during the

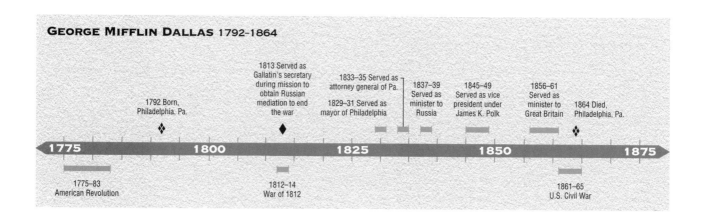

GEORGE MIFFLIN DALLAS 1792–1864

1792 Born, Philadelphia, Pa.

1813 Served as Gallatin's secretary during mission to obtain Russian mediation to end the war

1829–31 Served as mayor of Philadelphia

1833–35 Served as attorney general of Pa.

1837–39 Served as minister to Russia

1845–49 Served as vice president under James K. Polk

1856–61 Served as minister to Great Britain

1864 Died, Philadelphia, Pa.

1775 1800 1825 1850 1875

1775–83 American Revolution

1812–14 War of 1812

1861–65 U.S. Civil War

administration of JAMES K. POLK. His term lasted until 1849, and in 1856, he returned to foreign service, acting as minister to Great Britain until 1861. During his tenure Dallas was instrumental in the negotiations that resulted in the formation of the Dallas-Clarendon Convention of 1856, for the purpose of arbitrating disputes concerning Central America between the United States and Great Britain.

Dallas died December 31, 1864, in Philadelphia, Pennsylvania.

DAMAGES

Monetary compensation that is awarded by a court in a civil action to an individual who has been injured through the wrongful conduct of another party.

Damages attempt to measure in financial terms the extent of harm a plaintiff has suffered because of a defendant's actions. Damages are distinguishable from costs, which are the expenses incurred as a result of bringing a lawsuit and which the court may order the losing party to pay. Damages also differ from the verdict, which is the final decision issued by a jury.

The purpose of damages is to restore an injured party to the position the party was in before being harmed. As a result, damages are generally regarded as remedial rather than preventive or punitive. However, PUNITIVE DAMAGES may be awarded for particular types of wrongful conduct. Before an individual can recover damages, the injury suffered must be one recognized by law as warranting redress, and must have actually been sustained by the individual.

The law recognizes three major categories of damages: COMPENSATORY DAMAGES, which are intended to restore what a plaintiff has lost as a result of a defendant's wrongful conduct; nominal damages, which consist of a small sum awarded to a plaintiff who has suffered no substantial loss or injury but has nevertheless experienced an invasion of rights; and punitive damages, which are awarded not to compensate a plaintiff for injury suffered but to penalize a defendant for particularly egregious, wrongful conduct. In specific situations, two other forms of damages may be awarded: treble and liquidated.

Compensatory Damages

With respect to compensatory damages, a defendant is liable to a plaintiff for all the natural and direct consequences of the defendant's wrongful act. Remote consequences of a defendant's act or omission cannot form the basis for an award of compensatory damages.

Consequential damages, a type of compensatory damages, may be awarded when the loss suffered by a plaintiff is not caused directly or immediately by the wrongful conduct of a defendant, but results from the defendant's action instead. For example, if a defendant carried a ladder and negligently walked into a plaintiff who was a professional model, injuring the plaintiff's face, the plaintiff could recover consequential damages for the loss of income resulting from the injury. These consequential damages are based on the resulting harm to the plaintiff's career. They are not based on the injury itself, which was the direct result of the defendant's conduct.

The measure of compensatory damages must be real and tangible, although it can be difficult to fix the amount with certainty, especially in cases involving claims such as pain and suffering or emotional distress. In assessing the amount of compensatory damages to be awarded, a trier of fact (the jury or, if no jury exists, the judge) must exercise good judgment and common sense, based on general experience and knowledge of economics and social affairs. Within these broad guidelines, the jury or judge has wide discretion to award damages in whatever amount is deemed appropriate, so long as the amount is supported by the evidence in the case.

A plaintiff can recover damages for a number of different injuries suffered as a result of another person's wrongful conduct. The plaintiff can recover for a physical impairment if it results directly from a harm caused by the defendant. The jury, in determining damages, considers the present as well as long-range effects of the disease or injury on the physical well-being of the plaintiff, who must demonstrate the disability with reasonable certainty.

Compensatory damages can be awarded for mental impairment, such as a loss of memory or a reduction in intellectual capacity suffered as a result of a defendant's wrongful conduct.

A plaintiff may recover compensatory damages for both present and future physical pain and suffering. Compensation for future pain is permitted when there is a reasonable likelihood that the plaintiff will experience it; the plaintiff is not permitted to recover for future pain and suffering that is speculative. The jury has broad discretion to award damages for pain and suffering, and its judgment will be overturned only if it appears that the jury abused its discretion in reaching the decision.

Mental pain and suffering can be considered in assessing compensatory damages. Mental pain and suffering includes fright, nervousness, grief, emotional trauma, anxiety, humiliation, and indignity. Historically, a plaintiff could not recover damages for mental pain and suffering without an accompanying physical injury. Today, most jurisdictions have modified this rule, allowing recovery for mental anguish alone where the act precipitating the anguish was willful or intentional, or done with extreme carelessness or recklessness. Ordinarily, mental distress brought on by sympathy for the injury of another will not warrant an award of damages, although some jurisdictions may allow recovery if the injury was caused by the willful or malicious conduct of the defendant. For instance, if an individual wrongfully and intentionally injures a child in the presence of the child's mother, and the mother suffers psychological trauma as a result, the defendant can be liable for the mother's mental suffering. In some jurisdictions, a bystander can recover damages for mental distress caused by observing an event in which another person negligently, but not intentionally, causes harm to a family member.

Compensatory damages of an economic nature may also be recovered by an injured party. A plaintiff may recover for loss of earnings resulting from an injury. The measure of lost earnings is the amount of money that the plaintiff might reasonably have earned by working in her or his profession during the time the plaintiff was incapacitated because of the injury. In the case of a permanent disability, this amount can be determined by calculating the earnings that the injured party actually lost and multiplying that figure out to the age of retirement—with adjustments. If the amount of earnings actually lost cannot be determined with certainty, as in the case of a salesperson paid by commission, the plaintiff's average earnings or general qualities and qualifications for the occupation in which she or he has been employed are considered. Evidence of past earnings can also be used to determine loss of future earnings. As a general rule, lost earnings that are speculative are not recoverable, although each case must be examined individually to determine whether damages can be established with reasonable certainty. For example, a plaintiff who bought a restaurant immediately before suffering an injury could not recover damages for the profits he might have made running it, because such profits would be speculative. A plaintiff who is unable to accept a promotion to another job because of an injury would stand a better chance of recovering damages for loss of earnings, because the amount lost could be established with more certainty.

Individuals injured by the wrongful conduct of another may also recover damages for impairment of earning capacity, so long as that impairment is a direct and foreseeable consequence of a disabling injury of a permanent or lingering nature. The amount of damages is determined by calculating the difference between the amount of money the injured person had the capacity to earn prior to the injury and the amount he or she is capable of earning after the injury, in view of his or her life expectancy.

Loss of profit is another element of compensatory damages, allowing an individual to recover if such a loss can be established with sufficient certainty and is a direct and probable result of the defendant's wrongful actions. Expected profits that are uncertain or contingent upon fluctuating conditions would not be recoverable, nor would they be awarded if no evidence existed from which they could be reasonably determined.

A plaintiff can recover all reasonable and necessary expenses brought about by an injury caused by the wrongful acts of a defendant. In a contract action, for example, the party who has been injured by another's breach can recover compensatory damages that include the reasonable expenses that result from reliance on the contract, such as the cost of transporting perishable goods wrongfully refused by the other contracting party. In other actions, expenses awarded as part of compensatory damages may include medical, nursing, and prescription drug costs; the costs of future medical treatment, if necessary; or the costs of restoring a damaged vehicle and of renting another vehicle while repairs are performed.

Interest can be awarded to compensate an injured party for money wrongfully withheld from her or him, as when an individual defaults on an obligation to pay money owed under a contract. Interest is ordinarily awarded from the date of default, which is set by the time stated in the contract for payment, the date a demand for payment is made, or the date the lawsuit alleging the breach of the contract is initiated.

Nominal Damages

Nominal damages are generally recoverable by a plaintiff who successfully establishes that he or she has suffered an injury caused by the wrongful conduct of a defendant, but cannot offer proof of a loss that can be compensated. For example, an injured plaintiff who proves that a defendant's actions caused the injury but fails to submit medical records to show the extent of the injury may be awarded only nominal damages. The amount awarded is generally a small, symbolic sum, such as one dollar, although in some jurisdictions it may equal the costs of bringing the lawsuit.

Punitive Damages

Punitive damages, also known as exemplary damages, may be awarded to a plaintiff in addition to compensatory damages when a defendant's conduct is particularly willful, wanton, malicious, vindictive, or oppressive. Punitive damages are awarded not as compensation, but to punish the wrongdoer and to act as a deterrent to others who might engage in similar conduct.

The amount of punitive damages to be awarded lies within the discretion of the trier of fact, which must consider the nature of the wrongdoer's behavior, the extent of the plaintiff's loss or injury, and the degree to which the defendant's conduct is repugnant to a societal sense of justice and decency. An award of punitive damages will usually not be disturbed on the grounds that it is excessive, unless it can be shown that the jury or judge was influenced by prejudice, bias, passion, partiality, or corruption.

In the late twentieth century, the constitutionality of punitive damages has been considered in several U.S. Supreme Court decisions. In 1989, the Court held that large punitive damages awards did not violate the EIGHTH AMENDMENT prohibition against the imposition of excessive fines (*Browning-Ferris Industries of Vermont v. Kelco Disposal,* 492 U.S. 257, 109 S. Ct. 2909, 106 L. Ed. 2d 219). Later, in *Pacific Mutual Life Insurance Co. v. Haslip,* 499 U.S. 1, 111 S. Ct. 1032, 113 L. Ed. 2d 1 (1991), the Court held that unlimited jury discretion in awarding punitive damages is not "so inherently unfair" as to be unconstitutional under the DUE PROCESS CLAUSE of the FOURTEENTH AMENDMENT to the U.S. Constitution. And in *TXO Production Corp. v. Alliance Resources Corp.,* 509 U.S. 443, 113 S. Ct. 2711, 125 L. Ed. 2d 366 (1993), the Court ruled that a punitive damages award that was 526 times the compensatory award did not violate due process. Both *Haslip* and *TXO Production* disappointed observers who hoped that the Court would place limits on large and increasingly common punitive damages awards. In a 1994 decision, the Court did strike down an amendment to the Oregon Constitution that prohibited JUDICIAL REVIEW of punitive damages awards, on the ground that it violated due process (*Honda Motor Co. v. Oberg,* 512 U.S. 415, 114 S. Ct. 2331, 129 L. Ed. 2d 336).

In a jury proceeding, the court may review the award, although the amount of damages to be awarded is an issue for the jury. If the court determines that the verdict is excessive in view of the particular circumstances of the case, it can order REMITTITUR, which is a procedural process in which the jury verdict is reduced. The opposite process, known as ADDITUR, occurs when the court deems the jury's award of damages to be inadequate and orders the defendant to pay a greater sum. Both *remittitur* and *additur* are used at the discretion of the trial judge, and are designed to remedy a blatantly inaccurate damages award by the jury without the necessity of a new trial or an appeal.

Treble Damages

In some situations, where provided by statute, treble damages may be awarded. In such situations, a statute will authorize a judge to multiply the amount of monetary damages awarded by a jury by three, and to order that a plaintiff receive the tripled amount. The CLAYTON ACT of 1914 (15 U.S.C.A. §§ 12 et seq.), for example, directs that treble damages be awarded for violations of federal ANTITRUST LAWS.

Liquidated Damages

LIQUIDATED DAMAGES constitute compensation agreed upon by the parties entering into a contract, to be paid by a party who breaches the contract to a nonbreaching party. Liquidated damages may be used when it would be difficult to prove the actual harm or loss caused by a breach. The amount of liquidated damages must represent a reasonable estimate of the actual damages that a breach would cause. A contract term fixing unreasonably large or disproportionate liquidated damages may be void because it constitutes a penalty, or punishment for default. Furthermore, if it appears that the parties have made no attempt to calculate the amount of actual damages that might be sustained in the event of a breach, a liquidated damages provision will be deemed unenforceable. In determining whether a particular contract provision constitutes liquidated damages or an unenforceable penalty, a court will look to the intention of the parties, even if the terms *liquidated damages* and *penalty* are specifically used and defined in the contract.

Appellate Review of Damages

When reviewing a trial court's award of damages, an appellate court generally examines all of the evidence from the trial to determine whether the evidence supports the award. When reviewing awards for compensatory damages, an appellate court determines from the lower court's record whether the trial judge abused his or her discretion in allowing a jury's damage award to stand or in making his or her own damage award, called a *bench award*. A bench award by a judge is typically subject to closer scrutiny than an award by a jury.

An appellate court may determine that a damage award is excessive or inadequate. If the court of appeals determines that the damages are excessive or inadequate, and can determine the proper amount with reasonable certainty, the court may adjust the award so that it corresponds with the evidence. One common method for altering an award is through the use of remittitur, whereby the judge directs the plaintiff either to accept a lower award or face a new trial. On the other hand, if the appellate court cannot determine the proper amount of the award based upon the evidence, the court may order a new trial. A court of appeals will also review a trial court's decision whether to admit or to exclude evidence that supports the damage award, such as the decision whether to admit or exclude testimony regarding SCIENTIFIC EVIDENCE. Appellate courts typically review the trial court's decision with respect to admission or exclusion of evidence under the ABUSE OF DISCRETION standard.

Courts review awards of punitive damages differently than other types of damage awards. Several federal courts of appeals are engaged in an ongoing struggle over what standard of review should be applied to punitive damages at the appellate court level. In *Cooper Industries, Inc. v. Leatherman Tool Group, Inc.*, 532 U.S. 424, 121 S. Ct. 1678, 149 L. Ed. 2d 674 (2001), the U.S. Supreme Court ruled that appellate courts must conduct de novo review rather than apply an abuse of discretion standards. This ruling means that federal appellate courts have great freedom to review and reduce punitive damages based on previous U.S. Supreme Court standards. The decision is one more example of the Court expressing its desire to control excessive punitive damage awards.

Cooper Industries, Inc. involved a suit for TRADEMARK infringement, where Cooper Industries was accused of using photographs of a knife manufactured by Leatherman Tool Group. A jury awarded Leatherman $50,000 in general damages and $4.5 million in punitive damages. On appeal, the U.S. Court of Appeals for the Ninth Circuit upheld the trial court, basing its analysis on the abuse of discretion standard. This standard is very deferential to the trial court's actions, allowing the appeals courts to overturn a decision only if the trial judge clearly abused his or her authority. By comparison, de novo review empowers the appeals court to review all of the evidence on punitive damages without regard to the trial court's decision.

The U.S. Supreme Court agreed to hear Cooper's appeal to resolve the division among the federal circuits over the appropriate standard of review for punitive damages. The Court, in an 8–1 decision, determined that the federal courts should apply de novo review. Justice JOHN PAUL STEVENS, writing for the majority, concluded that the nature of punitive damages demanded that appeals courts conduct a fresh inquiry. He noted the similarities of punitive damages to criminal fines and cited various criminal cases that addressed the proportionality of sentences that relied on de novo review. Moreover, Stevens rejected the idea that when a jury awards punitive damages, it makes a finding of fact that could not be disturbed by an appeals court unless it was clearly erroneous.

FURTHER READINGS

Gibeaut, John. 2003. "Pruning Punitives: High Court Stresses Guidelines for Deciding Damages." *ABA Journal* 89 (June).

Kagehiro, Dorothy K., and Robert D. Minick. 2002. "How Juries Determine Damages Awards." *For the Defense* 44 (July).

Reis, John W. 2002. "Measure of Damages in Property Loss Cases." *Florida Bar Journal* 76 (October).

Shaw, Robert Ward. 2003. "Punitive Damages in Medical Malpractice: an Economic Evaluation." *North Carolina Law Review* 81 (September).

DAMNUM

[Latin, Damage.] The loss or reduction in the value of property, life, or health of an individual as a consequence of FRAUD, *carelessness, or accident.*

The phrase *ad damnum*, "to the damage," is the name of a clause in a complaint that states the damages for which the individual seeks judicial relief.

❖ DANA, RICHARD HENRY

Richard Henry Dana achieved prominence as a lawyer and author, and for his knowledge of the sea.

Dana was born August 1, 1815, in Cambridge, Massachusetts. A student at Harvard University, he interrupted his studies in 1834 and spent two years as a sailor. In 1836, he returned to Harvard, graduating in 1837. He subsequently received an honorary doctor of laws degree in 1866.

Before entering a legal career, Dana taught elocution at Harvard from 1839 to 1840. He was admitted to the bar in 1840 and established a successful legal practice, demonstrating his expertise in ADMIRALTY cases.

Dana entered politics in 1848 as an organizer of the FREE SOIL PARTY, which opposed the principles of SLAVERY. He attended the party's convention of that same year, held in Buffalo, New York.

In 1861, Dana performed the duties of U.S. attorney for the district of Massachusetts, serving in this capacity until 1866. From 1867 to 1868, he participated in the TREASON trial against confederate President Jefferson Davis,

Richard H. Dana.
PHOTOGRAPH BY J.W. BLACK & COMPANY. LIBRARY OF CONGRESS/CORBIS

acting as attorney for the United States. During 1866 and 1868, he also returned to Harvard as a lecturer at the law school. In 1877, Dana was selected to represent the United States as senior counsel at the fisheries commission held at Halifax, Nova Scotia.

Dana is regarded as an eminent writer, as is evidenced by the enduring popularity of *Two Years Before the Mast*, published in 1840. In this book, Dana described his experiences as a sailor, recounting his voyage from Boston around Cape Horn to California from 1834 to 1836. He also authored *The Seaman's Friend* (1841) and *To Cuba and Back* (1859), and he edited *Wheaton's Elements of International Law* (1866).

He died January 6, 1882, in Rome, Italy.

"IN ORDER THAT JUSTICE MAY BE DONE TO THE WEAKEST, AND THAT IN ANY HOUR OF FRENZY OR MISTAKE, WE MAY NOT TOUCH THE HAIR OF [HIS] HEAD, WE WILL GIVE HIM A TRIBUNAL WHICH SHALL BE INDEPENDENT OF THE FLUCTUATIONS OF OUR OPINIONS OR PASSIONS."
—RICHARD H. DANA

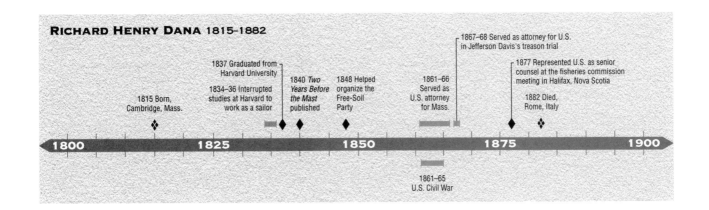

RICHARD HENRY DANA 1815–1882

1867–68 Served as attorney for U.S. in Jefferson Davis's treason trial

1837 Graduated from Harvard University

1877 Represented U.S. as senior counsel at the fisheries commission meeting in Halifax, Nova Scotia

1834–36 Interrupted studies at Harvard to work as a sailor

1840 *Two Years Before the Mast* published

1848 Helped organize the Free-Soil Party

1861–66 Served as U.S. attorney for Mass.

1882 Died, Rome, Italy

1815 Born, Cambridge, Mass.

1800   1825   1850   1875   1900

1861–65 U.S. Civil War

DANELAGE

A system of law introduced into England as a result of its invasion and conquest by the Danes during the eighth and ninth centuries, which occurred primarily in some of the midland counties and on the eastern coast.

Danelage provided basic values and customs to which the later Norman conquerors of England added their customs to provide the foundation of ENGLISH LAW.

DANGEROUS INSTRUMENTALITY

Any article that is inherently hazardous or has the potential for harming people through its careless use.

Examples of a dangerous instrumentality include explosives and electrically charged wires. Statutes and case law must be consulted to determine what items are regarded as dangerous instrumentalities.

When dealing with dangerous instrumentalities, some jurisdictions require that due care be exercised to prevent harm to those who are reasonably expected to be in proximity with them. Others impose STRICT LIABILITY for injuries and losses caused by them.

❖ DANIEL, PETER VIVIAN

Peter Vivian Daniel served as an associate justice of the U.S. Supreme Court from 1841 to 1860. A prominent lawyer and Democratic politician from Virginia, Daniel adhered to a Jeffersonian political philosophy that favored STATES' RIGHTS and disfavored large economic institutions. A minor figure in the history of the Supreme Court, Daniel joined the majority in DRED SCOTT V. SANDFORD, 60 U.S. (19 How.) 393, 15 L. Ed. 691 (1857), which held that freed black slaves could not be citizens under the Constitution because they had originally been property, not citizens.

Daniel was born in Stafford County, Virginia, on April 24, 1784. He came from a wealthy family and was educated at Princeton University, graduating in 1805. He read the law in the Richmond offices of EDMUND RANDOLPH, who helped draft the Constitution. He was admitted to the Virginia bar in 1808.

Although Daniel maintained a law practice, his focus was on politics and government. He was elected to the Virginia House of Delegates in 1809. In 1812 he was appointed by the house to serve on the PRIVY COUNCIL, which acted as an advisory board for the state governor. Daniel remained on the council for twenty-three years, serving as lieutenant governor for much of his term.

Daniel was active in the DEMOCRATIC PARTY and was a strong supporter of President ANDREW JACKSON. In 1836 Jackson appointed Daniel as a judge to the U.S. District Court for Eastern Virginia. Five years later President MARTIN VAN BUREN appointed Daniel to the U.S. Supreme Court. This move sparked controversy because it occurred at the end of Van Buren's term of office. The WHIG PARTY's presidential candidate, WILLIAM HENRY HARRISON, was elected president. Whigs in Congress tried to block the appointment of Daniel so Harrison could choose a justice. Daniel was confirmed by the Senate on March 3, 1841, in the last moments of the Van Buren administration.

Throughout his years on the Supreme Court, Daniel maintained his commitment to Jeffersonian government. THOMAS JEFFERSON's view of republican government valued an agricultural economy and a limited role for government. Daniel also adopted the Jacksonian

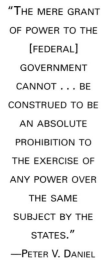

"THE MERE GRANT OF POWER TO THE [FEDERAL] GOVERNMENT CANNOT . . . BE CONSTRUED TO BE AN ABSOLUTE PROHIBITION TO THE EXERCISE OF ANY POWER OVER THE SAME SUBJECT BY THE STATES."
—PETER V. DANIEL

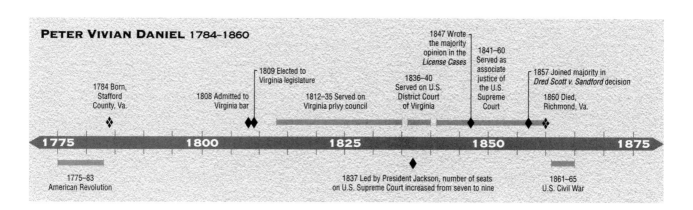

PETER VIVIAN DANIEL 1784–1860

1784 Born, Stafford County, Va.

1808 Admitted to Virginia bar

1809 Elected to Virginia legislature

1812–35 Served on Virginia privy council

1836–40 Served on U.S. District Court of Virginia

1847 Wrote the majority opinion in the *License Cases*

1841–60 Served as associate justice of the U.S. Supreme Court

1857 Joined majority in *Dred Scott v. Sandford* decision

1860 Died, Richmond, Va.

1775   1800   1825   1850   1875

1775–83 American Revolution

1837 Led by President Jackson, number of seats on U.S. Supreme Court increased from seven to nine

1861–65 U.S. Civil War

variation, which included hostility to banks, corporations, and the federal government. A southerner and a believer in states' rights, he supported the right of states to maintain the institution of SLAVERY.

Daniel was known more for his dissents than for crafting majority opinions. He did, however, join the majority in the *Dred Scott* case. Dred Scott was a slave owned by an army surgeon, John Emerson, who resided in Missouri. In 1836 Emerson took Scott to Fort Snelling, in what is now Minnesota but was then a territory where slavery had been expressly forbidden by the MISSOURI COMPROMISE legislation of 1820. In 1846 Scott sued for his freedom in Missouri state court, arguing that his residence in a free territory released him from slavery. The Missouri Supreme Court rejected his argument, and Scott appealed to the U.S. Supreme Court.

The Court heard arguments on *Dred Scott* in 1855 and 1856. A key issue was whether African Americans could be citizens of the United States, even if they were not slaves. Daniel was a loyal southerner, holding in his concurring opinion that African Americans who had been freed since the enactment of the Constitution could never be citizens. The Framers had not contemplated the prospect of granting citizenship to persons who were legally recognized as property when the Constitution was drafted.

During his term on the Supreme Court, Daniel's adherence to his principles led him to drift further from the mainstream. As the national economy expanded, and with it both big business and the federal government, Daniel's Jeffersonian beliefs lost relevance.

Daniel died May 31, 1860, in Richmond, Virginia.

❖ DARROW, CLARENCE SEWARD

Lawyer and social reformer Clarence Seward Darrow was the most famous and controversial defense attorney of the early twentieth century. He won unprecedented fame in momentous courtroom battles in which he championed the causes of labor, liberal social thought, and the use of scientific CRIMINOLOGY. His aggressive legal tactics, as well as his outspoken denunciations of industrial capitalism, political corruption, and popular religion, aroused animosities throughout his life. But in the end, his compassion for oppressed persons, as well as his winsome personality, compelled friends and foes

Peter V. Daniel.
CORBIS

alike to honor his unparalleled legal career as attorney for the damned.

Darrow was the master of the courtroom drama. One striking and effective aspect of his legal style was his physical appearance in the courtroom. He wore rumpled suits—often bared to shirtsleeves and suspenders—and let his tousled hair hang into his face. He had a halting walk and slouching stance, and his habits of smoking long cigars slowly during the proceedings and even reading and writing during the prosecution's presentation were endlessly arresting for juries and distracting for opponents.

Darrow was born poor, on April 18, 1857, near Kinsman, Ohio. His mother died when he was fourteen, and his father, an embittered seminary student–turned–undertaker, bore the stigma of the village atheist in an intensely religious rural community. As a child, Darrow hated formal schooling, but with his father's encouragement, he read widely from the extensive family library to educate himself. As his father's intellectual companion, Darrow grew to love reading, to hate being poor, and to willingly embrace unpopular causes. Once, Darrow's father went to observe a public hanging to see what it was like, but left before the moment of execution and reported to Darrow how he felt a terrible shame and guilt for being any part of such a "barbaric practice." This report was not lost on Darrow, who would become a fierce public opponent of the popular practice of capital

"I DO NOT CONSIDER IT AN INSULT, BUT RATHER A COMPLIMENT TO BE CALLED AN AGNOSTIC. I DO NOT PRETEND TO KNOW WHERE MANY IGNORANT MEN ARE SURE— THAT IS ALL AGNOSTICISM MEANS."
—CLARENCE DARROW

Clarence Darrow.

punishment, defending fifty murderers in his legal career, with only one being sentenced to death and executed.

Darrow's entrance into the PRACTICE OF LAW was strained by poverty. He left his studies at Allegheny College after one year for lack of money. After three years teaching in a rural one-room schoolhouse and one year at the Michigan University Law School, where he again withdrew for lack of tuition, Darrow gained an apprenticeship with a law firm in Youngstown, Ohio. There, he read the law and passed the bar exam in 1878 at the age of 21. Returning home, he married his childhood sweetheart, Jessie Ohl, began his own practice in the rural Ohio towns of Andover and Ashtabula, and fathered his only child, a son. In search of a better income for his family and eager for opportunity, Darrow accepted an invitation from his brother Everett Darrow to move to Chicago—then the commercial and cultural center of the Midwest—in 1887.

Darrow's path from the country to the city was well-worn by millions of others at the end of the nineteenth century. The lure of jobs and opportunities following the Civil War combined with mass migrations from Europe added 31 million residents to U.S. cities between 1860 and 1930. Chicago, which had barely existed in 1830, had grown by 1900 to 3 million inhabitants. Along with other large U.S. cities such as New York and Boston, Chicago was unprepared for this overwhelming influx of urban immigrants. The results were poverty, crime, and corruption spawning human misery on a grand scale.

When Darrow moved his hopes and his family to Chicago, the city was in the midst of both a population and an industrial boom. With its being the railroad center of the nation, the meat-packing, lumber, steel, and agricultural industries were rapidly expanding. A devastating fire in 1871 had leveled much of the city and helped to inspire new building programs and fresh commercial initiatives. The city had also become a magnet for social reformers, artists, and intellectuals, including JANE ADDAMS, Lincoln Steffens, UPTON SINCLAIR, Edgar Lee Masters, and Theodore Dreiser, who viewed the human suffering of the great city with outrage.

Darrow found Chicago both fascinating and troubling. While he saw opportunity for himself to advance, he was moved by the evident suffering of laboring families, poor people, and those who were imprisoned. His passion for the lower class only increased as he witnessed the economic contrasts of industry and labor. Throughout the city, industrial tycoons were striking it rich off the backs of laborers—often uneducated and poor—who earned poverty wages under hazardous conditions. Similarly, the prisons were filled with poor and broken people who had little means of defending themselves.

Having read the prison reform writings of Judge John P. Altgeld of Illinois, Darrow shortly introduced himself to this social reformer who would one day become governor. He began a mentorship in the law and politics of reform under Altgeld that would last until Altgeld's death. When Darrow became outraged by the heavy sentences laid upon four anarchist defendants in the Haymarket Square bombing of 1887, Altgeld urged him to join the alliance for their AMNESTY. In turn, Darrow later successfully implored Altgeld as governor to commute their sentences.

In 1888, after being impressed by Darrow's public speaking ability, Mayor DeWitt Cregier, of Chicago, offered him an appointment as a special assessment attorney. Within a year, Darrow rose to chief corporation counsel—becoming the head of the legal department for the entire city of Chicago at age thirty-three. From this vantage point, he observed firsthand the plight of the city's working class in industries where labor had little power to organize, and government had little power to regulate.

After four years, with his city appointment about to be terminated, Darrow accepted an offer to become chief counsel for the Chicago and Northwestern Railway (CNR), which he had recently defeated in court. He imposed one condition: that he be allowed to continue his outside legal assistance work as long as it did not conflict with his loyalty to the company. Within two years, a decisive conflict was staring Darrow in the face: the PULLMAN STRIKE of 1894. This bitter dispute pitted the workers of the newly formed American Railway Union (ARU) against the powerful Pullman Company and its railroad industry allies. The conflict was so violent that President GROVER CLEVELAND sent in army troops to protect the trains.

Darrow resigned his corporate position with CNR despite enticing offers of higher pay. Instead, he took the case of the ARU's national leader EUGENE V. DEBS, who was charged with violating a strike INJUNCTION. Darrow's defense strategy was not to quibble about the violation of an injunction order but to expose the working conditions imposed upon railroad workers by the industry—in this case, the enormously wealthy Pullman Company. To do this, Darrow boldly subpoenaed company president George M. Pullman to testify, but the tycoon went into hiding rather than appear. So, after describing the abysmal working conditions of Pullman's railroad workers and their families, he argued fervently that people had a right to strike for just causes, and that adequate wages and safe working conditions were such causes.

Darrow defended Debs in two trials—taking an appeal to the U.S. Supreme Court before finally losing and seeing his client sentenced to six months in prison. In this defense of the underdog against the powerful, Darrow had found his calling. In just six years, Darrow had moved from positions of political power and financial security to that of gladiator in the nation's emerging class struggle.

In 1894 Darrow handled his first criminal case in Chicago, defending Eugene Prendergast. Prendergast was a mentally ill drifter who had murdered Mayor Carter H. Harrison Sr. of Chicago, then walked to a police station and confessed to the crime. Darrow attempted an INSANITY DEFENSE and failed, and Prendergast was executed. Of the fifty murder defendants Darrow represented in his lifetime, this was the first and last one he lost to execution.

In 1897, Darrow divorced his wife of 17 years. In 1903, he married Ruby Hamerstrom, a Chicago newspaper journalist. This second marriage for Darrow lasted for the rest of his lifetime but produced no children.

In 1907, the former governor of Idaho Frank Steunenberg was killed by a booby trap bomb on his front gate. Steunenberg had been a powerful supporter of the mining industry. WILLIAM ("BIG BILL") HAYWOOD, leader of the Western Federation of Miners union, and several others were abducted by PINKERTON AGENTS from other states and brought to Boise, where they were charged with conspiracy to murder. The miners' union hired Darrow for the defense, and he traveled with Ruby to Idaho and assembled a defense team.

The prominence of the individuals involved and the violent nature of the crime drew national attention to the trial. Darrow was able to crack the government's case with painstaking

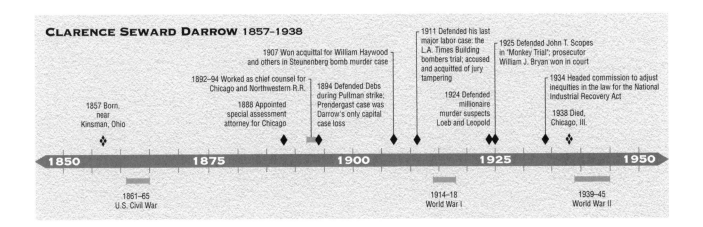

Clarence Seward Darrow 1857–1938

1857 Born, near Kinsman, Ohio

1861–65 U.S. Civil War

1888 Appointed special assessment attorney for Chicago

1892–94 Worked as chief counsel for Chicago and Northwestern R.R.

1894 Defended Debs during Pullman strike; Prendergast case was Darrow's only capital case loss

1907 Won acquittal for William Haywood and others in Steunenberg bomb murder case

1911 Defended his last major labor case: the L.A. Times Building bombers trial; accused and acquitted of jury tampering

1914–18 World War I

1924 Defended millionaire murder suspects Loeb and Leopold

1925 Defended John T. Scopes in "Monkey Trial"; prosecutor William J. Bryan won in court

1934 Headed commission to adjust inequities in the law for the National Industrial Recovery Act

1938 Died, Chicago, Ill.

1939–45 World War II

cross-examination of its star witness, the self-confessed perpetrator of the crime, Harry Orchard. Darrow exposed Orchard to be a man bent on personal revenge who had implicated the labor leaders only after being prompted to do so by the prosecutors. Darrow's moving summation in defense of the labor movement—"for the poor, for the weak, for the weary—who, in darkness and despair, have borne the labors of the human race"—drew tears in the courtroom, and Haywood and the others were acquitted.

Thanks to Darrow, labor was again vindicated over opponents in government and industry. But the cost to Darrow was considerable. After the trial, he was broke and in poor health. His legal fees from the union had already been spent, and he suffered from an acute ear infection. When he returned to Chicago, the financial crash of 1907 had wiped out all of his savings, and he returned to his law practice.

Darrow reluctantly entered the limelight again in 1911, when he agreed to defend the accused in what newspapers called the crime of the century. At one o'clock in the morning on October 10, 1910, Los Angeles was rocked by two explosions that blew apart the Los Angeles Times Building with over one hundred people inside. Twenty-one people were killed and 40 injured in the concussion and the fire that followed. The *Times*'s prominent and antiunion editor, Harrison Gray Otis, managed to get out an edition with the headline "Unionist Bombs Wreck Times."

Under pressure from Otis, the mayor of Los Angeles hired a private detective agency to investigate and abduct labor movement suspects living in Indiana and Michigan and return them to Los Angeles to stand trial. Labor movement members appealed to Darrow, but he resisted, still drained and wary from the Haywood defense. Renowned labor leader SAMUEL GOMPERS, then president of the AMERICAN FEDERATION OF LABOR (AFL), visited Darrow in Chicago and appealed to him to defend labor, the innocent, and DUE PROCESS. In return, Gompers promised that a nationwide AFL union war chest would generously compensate him for his services. Darrow agreed.

By the time Darrow arrived in Los Angeles, the three defendants had already confessed to the crime. Darrow entered guilty pleas on their behalf in an attempt to save them from execution. The shock and outrage from labor supporters were devastating. Darrow was jeered by

a waiting crowd and shunned by Gompers and other labor leaders. The promised legal fees evaporated.

Within days, Darrow was charged with attempting to bribe the jury and was brought to trial. Away from home, and without funds or allies to make a strong defense, Darrow fell into a depression that lasted through most of the proceedings. But in the closing arguments, he arose to defend himself to the jury with such force and poignancy that he again brought the jury, the audience, the press, and even the judge to tears. When the verdict came, and Darrow was acquitted, the courtroom burst into sustained cheers and embraces. Darrow never again took a major labor case.

Darrow continued to take the unpopular route in his court cases. When the United States entered WORLD WAR I despite a strong pacifist movement, Darrow managed to offend people on both sides of the war issue by personally supporting the war while professionally defending pacifists who refused to serve.

Darrow's choice of clients in a notorious murder case further outraged popular sentiments. In 1924, two Chicago teens from millionaire families—Richard Loeb, age 18, and Nathan Leopold Jr., age 19—decided to commit a murder for the thrill of it. Loeb had graduated with honors from the University of Michigan and was on his way to Harvard Law School. Leopold was a Phi Beta Kappa member, already attending law school. They thought they were clever enough that they would not get caught. Luring a 14-year-old friend named Bobby Franks into their car, Loeb killed Franks with a chisel. The two then stuffed his body into the trunk before sending ransom notes to the boy's millionaire family. Two days after the boys had been caught, had been charged, and had confessed, three members of the Loeb family came to Darrow's home in the early morning before he had yet awakened and insisted on making their way to his bedside to beg him to take the case. As a friend of the family, and because of their desperation, Darrow accepted.

Hoping to save the boys from execution, Darrow had his clients plead guilty and then presented expert scientific testimony from 14 psychiatrists and psychologists. These witnesses contended that the boys suffered from a mental illness that caused them to commit the crime. Loeb and Leopold received life sentences. This verdict was extremely unpopular with the public, for many had called for the death penalty for this unusually grisly murder. Darrow was attacked in the press and threatened in the mail, and the millionaire families who had begged him to save their children balked at paying the agreed legal fees. Darrow, by then age 67, spoke of retiring from legal work unless he could really "have some fun" doing it. The following year, he got his chance.

Intent on stemming the influence of modernist thinking in the schools, in 1925, the Tennessee legislature passed a law making it illegal to teach anything that contradicted the account of the Creation portrayed in the Bible's book of Genesis. With the help of local citizens and the support of the AMERICAN CIVIL LIBERTIES UNION (ACLU), a 24-year-old biology teacher in rural Dayton (TN), a Tennessee native named John T. Scopes, challenged the law by teaching the evolutionary theories of Charles R. Darwin in his high-school classroom. When Scopes was arrested and charged with violating the law, WILLIAM JENNINGS BRYAN, a well-known former member of the U.S. House, offered his services. At Scopes's insistence, the ACLU recruited the most controversial defense attorney and atheist in the country, Darrow.

For nearly a century, European scholars in linguistics and geology, as well as in Darwin's biology, had contested certain beliefs about the Bible, which left many of the faithful anxious. The fundamentalists in the Tennessee legislature had attempted one solution to this problem: forbid the teaching of anything in conflict with creationism in the public schools. Since Darrow passionately opposed this in principle and was no friend of religion, he happily took the case.

The trial drew enormous media attention in the form of international newspaper coverage and live nationwide radio broadcasts. The popular Henry L. Mencken covered the story and joined other major newspaper reporters in calling it the "Monkey Trial." Since the weather was hot and muggy, and the trial had drawn more than 2,000 visitors, the judge moved the proceedings outside the courthouse onto a platform built for the occasion. There, the two masters of law and rhetoric sparred before a stirred crowd and an international audience. The trial was ostensibly intended to determine whether Scopes had violated the law, which clearly he had purposely done. But the exchanges between Bryan and Darrow quickly revealed deeper issues, such as the constitutional

guarantee of free speech and the struggle between fundamentalist and modernist interpretations of the Bible.

This time, Darrow's favorite strategies of elevating the crime to a context of higher issues and presenting expert SCIENTIFIC EVIDENCE did not work. The presiding judge repeatedly upheld objections to these defense tactics. So, knowing that the local folk were overwhelmingly fundamentalist and that they saw Bryan as their champion, Darrow took a masterful gamble and put Bryan himself on the stand as a Bible expert for the defense. In a series of deft and probing questions about the Bible, Darrow managed to so befuddle the champion of fundamentalism that the crowds were finally laughing with Darrow and at Bryan. To many observers, Bryan and his cause were humiliated.

Although the jury voted to convict, the judge imposed only a nominal fine of $100 on Scopes, who was immediately rehired by the school board. Five days later, after eating a characteristically heavy meal, Bryan died in his sleep. Many believed that the devastating cross-examination by Darrow and the court's decision against imposing a larger fine upon Scopes were the cause of Bryan's death.

After the Scopes trial, Darrow became a public celebrity once again. He received many invitations to speak and to debate the issue of religion. As he had in the Pullman case, Darrow lost in the courts but seemingly won before a wider audience.

A year later, the National Association for the Advancement of Colored People (NAACP) asked Darrow to defend 11 blacks in Detroit who were being charged in the death of a single white during an ugly racial incident. Darrow again, at age 69, called upon his powerful defense skills to prove that none of the accused had fired the fatal bullet but that all were instead the target of racial prejudice. All charges were dismissed.

In 1934, President FRANKLIN D. ROOSEVELT appointed Darrow, at age 77, to head a commission to adjust inequities in the law for the NATIONAL INDUSTRIAL RECOVERY ACT, a program intended to relieve the Depression. Darrow's work proved successful when the Supreme Court declared the law unconstitutional, and the necessary revisions were made. The same year, Darrow was asked to chair the opening session of the American Inquiry Commission, a citizens' committee to study the darkening events in Germany. He emerged to tell Mayor Fiorello La

Guardia, of New York, at lunch that "Herr Hitler is a very dangerous man and should be destroyed."

Darrow died in Chicago in 1938, at the age of 81. He had asked his friend Judge William H. Holly to deliver his eulogy because, as Darrow put it, "he knows everything about me, and has the sense not to tell it." As Darrow's body lay in state in Chicago for two days, thousands from every sector of humanity lined up in a driving rain to say good-bye. The tributes to Darrow were bountiful. He was commended for his courage and compassion; his public service and his private practice; his support for labor, minority groups, poor people, and criminals; and, always, his defense of freedom. Although his popularity rose and fell during his lifetime, Darrow's memory has received the highest accolades. Popular and scholarly biographies, as well as theater, cinema, and television dramatizations of his impassioned career and complex life, have won for Darrow a legendary stature in U.S. law and history.

Despite wavering public opinion, fickle allies, and powerful opponents, he was an uncommonly skillful and courageous warrior for justice in the courts and in public life. The secret of his courage was revealed in a memorial comment by the eminent attorney JOSEPH N. WELCH: Darrow was "so brave and fearless that he never seemed to realize he was either."

FURTHER READINGS

Cowan, Geoffrey. 1999. "A Man for Some Seasons: The Darrow Legend Once Inspired Generations of Young Idealists; Stripped of His Mythic Stature, Clarence Darrow Is Now a Man We Worship Less but Identify with More." *American Lawyer* 21 (December): 56.

———. 1993. *The People v. Clarence Darrow.* New York: Times Books.

Darrow, Clarence. 1996. *The Story of My Life.* New York: Da Capo Press.

Driemen, John E. 1992. *Clarence Darrow.* New York: Chelsea House.

Tierney, Kevin. 1979. *Darrow: A Biography.* New York: Crowell.

Uelmen, Gerald F. 2000. "Who Is the Lawyer of the Century?" *Loyola of Los Angeles Law Review* 33 (January): 613–53.

Vine, Phyllis. 2004. *One Man's Castle: Clarence Darrow in Defense of the American Dream.* New York: Amistad.

Weinberg, Arthur, and Lila Weinberg. 1987. *Clarence Darrow: A Sentimental Rebel.* New York: Atheneum.

CROSS-REFERENCES

Haymarket Riot; Labor Union; Leopold and Loeb Trial; Scopes Monkey Trial.

DARTMOUTH COLLEGE CASE

See TRUSTEES OF DARTMOUTH COLLEGE V. WOODWARD.

DAUBERT TEST

In 1993, the U.S. Supreme Court handed down the seminal decision of *Daubert v. Merrell Dow Pharmaceuticals,* 509 U.S. 579, 113 S.Ct. 2786, 125 L.Ed.2d 469, (U.S. Jun 28, 1993) (NO. 92-102). The case involved the admissibility of novel SCIENTIFIC EVIDENCE. But to begin to understand the significance of *Daubert,* one needs to view the case in its wider context, going back 70 years to *Frye v. United States,* 293 F. 1013 (D.C. Cir. 1923).

Frye involved the admissibility of opinion evidence based upon the use of an early version of the POLYGRAPH. The D.C. Circuit Court held that scientific evidence was admissible if it was based on a scientific technique generally accepted as reliable in the scientific community. Thus, EXPERT TESTIMONY was admitted based on the expert's credentials, experience, skill, and reputation. The theory was that deficiencies or flaws in the expert's conclusions would be exposed through cross-examination. This decision became known as the *Frye* test or the *general-acceptance test.* By the 1990s, the *Frye* test had become the majority view in federal and state courts for the admissibility of new or unusual scientific evidence, even in view of Federal Rule of Evidence 702, passed in 1975, which some courts believed to provide a more flexible test for admissibility of opinion testimony by expert witnesses.

Then, in *Daubert v. Merrell Dow Pharmaceuticals, Inc.,* the U.S. Supreme Court changed the standard for admissibility of expert testimony. Under *Daubert,* a trial judge has a duty to scrutinize evidence more rigorously to determine whether it meets the requirements of Federal Rule of Evidence 702. This rule states, "If scientific, technical, or other specialized knowledge will assist the trier of fact to understand the evidence or to determine a fact in issue, a witness qualified as an expert by knowledge, skill, experience, training, or education, may testify thereto in the form of an opinion or otherwise, if (1) the testimony is based upon sufficient facts or data, (2) the testimony is the product of reliable principles and methods, and (3) the witness has applied the principles and methods reliably to the facts of the case."

In *Daubert,* the Court stated that evidence based on innovative or unusual scientific knowledge may be admitted only after it has been established that the evidence is reliable and scientifically valid. The Court also imposed a gatekeeping function on trial judges by charging them with preventing "junk science" from entering the courtroom as evidence. To that end, *Daubert* outlined four considerations: testing, peer review, error rates, and acceptability in the relevant scientific community. These four tests for reliability are known as the *Daubert* factors or the *Daubert* test.

In 1999, the U.S. Supreme Court significantly broadened that test and the trial court's gatekeeping role to include expert testimony based on technical and other specialized knowledge. *Kumho Tire Co., Ltd. v. Carmichael,* 526 U.S. 137, 119 S.Ct. 1167, 143 L.Ed.2d 238 (U.S. Mar 23, 1999) (NO. 97-1709). In *Kumho,* the Court held that the gatekeeping obligation imposed upon trial judges by *Daubert* applies to scientific testimony as well as to expert opinion testimony. In order to meet its gatekeeping obligation, a trial court may use the criteria identified in *Daubert* only when they can be applied to determine the reliability of either the underlying scientific technique or the expert's conclusions. But inasmuch as the *Daubert* gatekeeping function is meant to be a flexible one, it must necessarily be tied to the particular facts of a case. Thus, the factors identified in *Daubert* do not constitute an exhaustive checklist or a definitive litmus test.

In *Kumho,* the Court continued to grant trial judges a great deal of discretion. The Court generally permits trial judges to apply any useful factors that will assist the trial court in making a determination of reliability of proffered evidence as deemed appropriate in the particular case. The trial judge may use these factors whether they are identified in *Daubert* or elsewhere.

Despite *Daubert* and the cases that have followed in its aftermath, several issues involving expert testimony remain unresolved, and courts have reached various conclusions on these questions. One such question arises from the U.S. Supreme Court's language defining scientific knowledge. A related issue involves identifying four specific factors by which reliability of such knowledge was to be determined. In forming this definition, the Court drew almost exclusively from the physical sciences. But critics have argued that the *Daubert* factors are not easily applied to many other types of expert testimony, particularly those that depended on unique skills, generalized knowledge and experience, technical prowess, or even on applied science or clinical judgment. Another unresolved issue is whether a *Daubert* inquiry would even be required at all when a court is considering nonscientific expert opinion evidence, or when a particular technique already had gained widespread judicial acceptance.

FURTHER READINGS

Dixon, Lloyd, and Brian Gill. 2001. *Changes in the Standards for Admitting Expert Evidence in Federal Civil Cases Since the Daubert Decision.* Santa Monica, Calif.: Rand Corporation.

Florida Bar Continuing Legal Education Committee and the Business Law Section. 1999. *Daubert and Kumho Tire: The Law, Science and Economics of Expert Testimony in Business Litigation.* Tallahassee, Fla.: Florida Bar.

Kramer, Larry, ed. 1996. *Reforming the Civil Justice System.* New York: New York Univ. Press.

Smith, Frederick T. 2000. *Daubert and Its Progeny: Scientific Evidence in Product Liability Litigation.* Washington, D.C.: Washington Legal Foundation.

❖ DAUGHERTY, HARRY MICAJAH

Harry Micajah Daugherty served as the 51st attorney general of the United States, under Presidents WARREN G. HARDING and CALVIN COOLIDGE, but left office with his reputation forever tainted by accusations of political corruption and scandal.

Daugherty was born in Ohio on January 26, 1860, in a town called Washington Court House. He received his law degree in 1881 from the University of Michigan. He moved back to Ohio and was admitted to the state bar. Daugherty began practicing law in his hometown before entering politics. Daugherty became township clerk and, in 1890, was elected to the Ohio General Assembly. The ambitious Daugherty served two terms in the assembly before moving to Columbus in 1894. In Columbus he established a lucrative corporate law practice and continued to build his connections within the REPUBLICAN PARTY. Daugherty ran for state attorney general in 1895 and lost. In 1897, he failed in his attempt to become governor of Ohio.

In 1902, Daugherty established the law firm of Daugherty, Todd & Rarey; he remained a senior member of the firm until his appointment as U.S. attorney general in 1921. Daugherty had become acquainted with rising Republican star

Harry M. Daugherty.

Warren G. Harding, who served as lieutenant governor of Ohio from 1904 to 1905. Daugherty became involved in Harding's campaigns, which included an unsuccessful run for governor in 1910. Daugherty managed Harding's successful campaign for the U.S. Senate in 1914.

At the 1920 Republican Convention, a standoff developed between supporters of the presidential candidacies of former Army Chief of Staff General Leonard Wood and Illinois Governor Frank O. Lowden. Although Harding had introduced no significant national legislation and was not known for his leadership abilities, Daugherty and a group of Harding's political supporters managed to position him as the ideal compromise candidate to break the deadlock. Harding was elected as the Republican party nominee on the 10th ballot and went on to become the 29th president of the United States.

In return for his help and support, Harding appointed Daugherty U.S. attorney general in 1921.

U.S. Supreme Court Chief Justice WILLIAM HOWARD TAFT, faced with a backlog of cases in the federal courts and efforts by some congressmen to end lifetime tenure for federal judges, had sought judicial reform by proposing the creation of a conference of judges to assess lower court needs. He also suggested the appointment of at-large judges who could be assigned as needed to various courts. Daugherty joined with Taft to urge Congress to pass the proposed legislation. In 1922, Congress established what ultimately became the JUDICIAL CONFERENCE OF THE UNITED STATES.

Daugherty and many of the Ohio Republicans who had helped Harding achieve the presidency moved to Washington with him, and became mired in allegations of corrupt self-enrichment schemes. Harding's sudden death in August 1923 and the succession of Calvin Coolidge as president happened just as the public was beginning to become aware of the machinations of those the press dubbed the "Ohio Gang."

Daugherty was acquitted of charges that he was directly involved in the most famous of these scandals, the TEAPOT DOME SCANDAL, where the secretary of the interior was accused of arranging for the private development of federally-owned oil fields in return for a bribe of $100,000. However, Daugherty's failure to aggressively prosecute those involved and further allegations that he obstructed justice by trying to block a congressional investigation resulted in a loss of confidence in the attorney general. An investigation led by Democratic Senator Burton K. Wheeler of Montana resulted in Daugherty's resignation in March 1924.

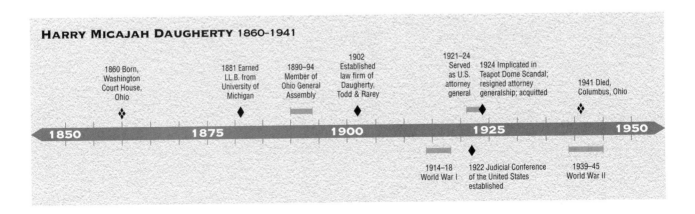

HARRY MICAJAH DAUGHERTY 1860–1941

1860 Born, Washington Court House, Ohio	
1881 Earned LL.B. from University of Michigan	
1890–94 Member of Ohio General Assembly	
1902 Established law firm of Daugherty, Todd & Rarey	
1921–24 Served as U.S. attorney general	
1924 Implicated in Teapot Dome Scandal; resigned attorney generalship; acquitted	
1941 Died, Columbus, Ohio	

1850   1875   1900   1925   1950

1914–18 World War I

1922 Judicial Conference of the United States established

1939–45 World War II

In 1927, Daugherty was tried twice on charges of engaging in graft and FRAUD while serving as attorney general. Both cases ended in a hung jury. Daugherty spent the rest of his life practicing law in Ohio and attempting to rehabilitate both his own reputation and that of Harding. In 1932, he coauthored a book with Thomas Dixon called *The Inside Story of the Harding Tragedy.* Daugherty died of a heart attack in Columbus, Ohio, on October 12, 1941, at the age of 81.

FURTHER READINGS

Daugherty, Harry M., and Thomas Dixon. 1932. *The Inside Story of the Harding Tragedy.* New York: Churchill.

U.S. Justice Department. 1985. *Attorneys General of the United States, 1789–1985.* Washington, D.C.: Government Printing Office.

CROSS-REFERENCES

Teapot Dome Scandal.

DAVIS-BACON ACT

The Davis-Bacon Act (40 U.S.C.A. §§ 276a to 276a-5) is federal law that governs the MINIMUM WAGE rate to be paid to laborers and mechanics employed on federal public works projects. It was enacted on March 3, 1931, and has been amended. Its purpose is to preserve local wage standards and promote local employment by preventing contractors who bid on public contracts from basing their bids on the use of cheap labor recruited from foreign sources.

When controversies arise under the Davis-Bacon Act, they are first submitted to the federal agency that is in charge of the project. Thereafter, if the dispute is not satisfactorily resolved, the matter is submitted to the secretary of labor. The Wage Appeals Board of the LABOR DEPARTMENT acts on behalf of the secretary in reviewing QUESTIONS OF LAW and fact made in wage determinations issued under the act and its related prevailing wage statutes. The board has discretion in selecting the controversies that it will review. Following these administrative procedures, a dissatisfied party may seek relief in the federal courts. The courts, however, will only review whether there has been compliance with the constitutional, statutory, and procedural requirements of the practices and procedures of the agencies involved in the dispute.

CROSS-REFERENCES

Labor Law.

❖ DAVIS, ANGELA YVONNE

Angela Yvonne Davis, political activist, author, professor, and Communist party member, was an international symbol of the black liberation movement of the 1960s and 1970s.

Davis was born in Birmingham, Alabama, on January 26, 1944, the eldest of four children. Her family was relatively well-off among the blacks in the city. Her father and mother were teachers in the Birmingham school system, and her father later purchased and operated a service station.

When Davis was four years old, the family moved out of the Birmingham projects and bought a large wooden house in a nearby neighborhood. Other black families soon followed. Incensed white neighbors drew a dividing line between the white and black sections and began trying to drive the black families out by bombing their homes. The area soon was nicknamed Dynamite Hill. Davis's mother had in college been involved in antiracism movements that had brought her into contact with sympathetic whites. She and Davis's father tried to teach their daughter that this hostility between blacks and whites was not preordained.

All of Birmingham was segregated during Davis's childhood. She attended blacks-only schools and theaters and was relegated to the back of city buses and the back doors of shops, which rankled her. On one occasion, as teenagers, Davis and her sister Fania entered a Birmingham shoe store and pretended to be non-English-speaking French visitors. After receiving deferential treatment by the salesmen and other customers, Davis announced in English that black people only had to pretend to be from another country to be treated like dignitaries.

Davis later wrote that although the black schools she attended were much poorer than the white schools in Birmingham, her studies of black historical and contemporary figures such as FREDERICK DOUGLASS, SOJOURNER TRUTH, and Harriet Tubman helped her develop a strong positive identification with black history.

The CIVIL RIGHTS MOVEMENT was beginning to touch Birmingham at the time Davis entered high school. Her parents were members of the National Association for the Advancement of Colored People (NAACP). In her junior year of high school, Davis decided to leave what she considered to be the provincialism of Birm-

> "WE HAVE ACCUMULATED A WEALTH OF HISTORICAL EXPERIENCE WHICH CONFIRMS OUR BELIEF THAT THE SCALES OF JUSTICE ARE OUT OF BALANCE."
> —ANGELA DAVIS

Angela Davis.
AP/WIDE WORLD
PHOTOS

ingham. She applied for an early entrance program at Fisk University, in Nashville, Tennessee, and an experimental program developed by the American Friends Service Committee (AFSC) through which black students from the South could attend integrated high schools in the North. Although Davis was admitted to Fisk—which she viewed as a stepping-stone to medical school, where she could pursue a childhood dream of becoming a pediatrician—she chose the AFSC program.

At age 15, she boarded a train for New York City. There, she lived with a white family headed by an Episcopalian minister who had been forced from his church after speaking out against Senator JOSEPH R. MCCARTHY's anti-Communist witch-hunts. Davis attended Elisabeth Irwin High School, located on the edge of Greenwich Village. The school originally had been a public school experiment in progressive education; when funding was cut off, the teachers turned it into a private school. Here, Davis learned about SOCIALISM and avidly studied the *Communist Manifesto.* She also joined a Marxist-Leninist youth organization called Advance, which had ties to the Communist Party.

In September 1961, Davis entered Brandeis University, in Waltham, Massachusetts, on a full scholarship. One of only three black first-year students, she felt alienated and alone. The fol-

lowing summer, eager to meet revolutionary young people from other countries, Davis attended a gathering of communist youth from around the world in Helsinki, Finland. Here, she was particularly struck by the cultural presentations put on by the Cuban delegation. She also found that the U.S. CENTRAL INTELLIGENCE AGENCY had stationed agents and informers throughout the festival. Upon her return to the United States, Davis was met by an investigator from the FEDERAL BUREAU OF INVESTIGATION (FBI), who questioned her about her participation in a communist event.

Meeting people from around the world convinced Davis of the importance of tearing down cultural barriers like language, and she decided to major in French at Brandeis. She was accepted in the Hamilton College Junior Year in France Program, and studied contemporary French literature at the Sorbonne, in Paris. Upon her return to Brandeis, Davis, who had always had an interest in philosophy, studied with the German philosopher Herbert Marcuse. The following year, she received a scholarship to study philosophy in Frankfurt, Germany, where she focused on the works of the Germans IMMANUEL KANT, GEORG HEGEL, and KARL MARX.

During the two years Davis spent in Germany, the black liberation and BLACK POWER MOVEMENTS were emerging in the United States. The BLACK PANTHER PARTY FOR SELF-DEFENSE had been formed in Oakland to protect the black community from police brutality. In the summer of 1967, Davis decided to return home to join these movements.

Back in Los Angeles, Davis worked with various academic and community organizations to build a coalition to address issues of concern to the African American community. Among these groups was the Black Panther Political Party (unrelated to HUEY NEWTON and Bobby Seale's Black Panther Party for Self-Defense). During this period, Davis was heavily criticized by black male activists for doing what they considered to be men's work. Women should not assume leadership roles, they claimed, but should educate children and should support men so that they could direct the struggle for black liberation. Davis was to encounter this attitude in many of her political activities.

By 1968, Davis had decided to join a collective organization in order to achieve her goal of organizing people for political action. She first considered joining the Communist Party. But because she related more to Marxist groups, she decided instead to join the Black Panther Political Party, which later became the Los Angeles branch of the STUDENT NONVIOLENT COORDINATING COMMITTEE (SNCC). SNCC was soon embroiled in internal disputes. After her long-time friend Franklin Kenard was expelled from his leadership position in the group because of his Communist Party membership, Davis resigned from the organization. In July 1968, she joined the Che-Lumumba Club, the black cell of the Communist Party in Los Angeles.

In 1969, Davis was hired as an assistant professor of philosophy at the University of California, Los Angeles. In July 1969, Davis joined a delegation of Communist Party members who had been invited to spend a month in Cuba. There, she worked in coffee and sugarcane fields, and visited schools, hospitals, and historical sites. Davis remarked that everywhere she went in Cuba, she was immensely impressed with the gains that had been made against racism. She saw blacks in leadership positions throughout the country, and she concluded that only under a socialist system such as that established by Cuban leader Fidel Castro could the fight against racism have been so successful.

When she returned to the United States, she discovered that several newspaper articles had been published detailing her membership in the Communist Party and accusing her of activities such as gunrunning for the Black Panther party. Governor RONALD REAGAN, of California, invoked a regulation in the handbook of the regents of the University of California that pro-hibited the hiring of communists. Davis responded by affirming her membership in the Communist Party, and she began to receive hate mail and threatening phone calls. After she obtained an INJUNCTION prohibiting the regents from firing her, the threats multiplied. Soon, she was receiving so many bomb threats that the campus police stopped checking her car for explosives, forcing her to learn the procedure for doing so herself. By the end of the year, the courts had ruled that the regulation prohibiting the hiring of communists was unconstitutional. However, in June 1970, the regents announced that Davis would not be rehired the following year, on the grounds that her political speeches outside the classroom were unbefitting a university professor.

During this time, Davis became involved with the movement to free three black inmates of Soledad Prison in California: George Jackson, John Clutchette, and Fleeta Drumgo. The men, known as the Soledad Brothers, had been indicted for the murder of a prison guard. The guard had been pushed over a prison railing when he inadvertently stumbled into a rebellion among black prisoners caused by the killing of three black prisoners by another prison guard. Although Jackson, Clutchette, and Drumgo claimed there was no evidence that they had killed the guard, they were charged with his murder. Davis began corresponding with Jackson and soon developed a personal relationship with him. She attended all the court hearings relating to the Soledad Brothers' indictment, along with many other supporters, including Jackson's younger brother, Jonathon Jackson,

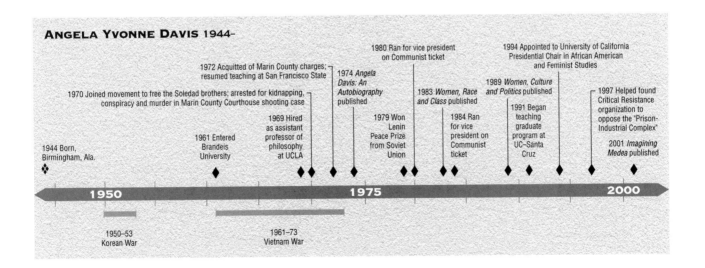

ANGELA YVONNE DAVIS 1944–

1944 Born, Birmingham, Ala.

1961 Entered Brandeis University

1969 Hired as assistant professor of philosophy at UCLA

1970 Joined movement to free the Soledad brothers; arrested for kidnapping, conspiracy and murder in Marin County Courthouse shooting case

1972 Acquitted of Marin County charges; resumed teaching at San Francisco State

1974 Angela Davis: An Autobiography published

1979 Won Lenin Peace Prize from Soviet Union

1980 Ran for vice president on Communist ticket

1983 Women, Race and Class published

1984 Ran for vice president on Communist ticket

1989 Women, Culture and Politics published

1991 Began teaching graduate program at UC–Santa Cruz

1994 Appointed to University of California Presidential Chair in African American and Feminist Studies

1997 Helped found Critical Resistance organization to oppose the "Prison-Industrial Complex"

2001 Imagining Medea published

1950   1975   2000

1950–53 Korean War

1961–73 Vietnam War

who was committed to freeing his brother and the other inmates. On August 7, 1970, using guns registered to Davis, Jonathon attempted to free his brother in a shoot-out at the Marin County Courthouse. Four people were killed, including Jonathon and superior court judge Harold Haley.

Davis was charged with KIDNAPPING, conspiracy, and murder, which was punishable in California by death. She fled, traveling in disguise from Los Angeles to Las Vegas, Chicago, Detroit, New York, Miami, and finally back to New York. In October 1970, she was arrested by the FBI, which had placed her on its most wanted list. In December, after two months in jail, Davis was extradited to California, where she spent the next 14 months in jail. She later said that this period was pivotal to her understanding of the black political struggle in the United States. Having worked to organize people in communities and on campuses against political repression, Davis now found herself a victim of that repression. In August 1971, while incarcerated in the Marin County Jail, she was devastated to learn that George Jackson had been killed by a guard in San Quentin Prison, allegedly while trying to escape.

In February 1972, Davis was released on bail following the California Supreme Court's decision to abolish the death penalty (*People v. Anderson,* 6 Cal. 3d 628, 100 Cal. Rptr. 152, 493 P.2d 880). Previously, bail had not been available to persons accused of crimes punishable by death. Her trial began a few days later, and lasted until early June 1972, when a jury acquitted her of all charges.

After her acquittal, Davis resumed her teaching career, at San Francisco State University. She continued her affiliation with the Communist Party, receiving the Lenin Peace Prize from the Soviet Union in 1979 and running for vice president of the United States on the Communist Party ticket in 1980 and 1984. Davis is also a founder and cochair of the National Alliance against Racist and Political Repression, and is on the national board of the National Political Congress of Black Women and on the board of the Atlanta-based National Black Women's Health Project. She has authored several books, including *Angela Davis: An Autobiography* (1974), *Women, Race, and Class* (1983), *Women, Culture, and Politics* (1989), and *Blues Legacies and Black Feminism* (1998). In 1980, she married Hilton Braithwaite, a photographer and fac-

ulty colleague at San Francisco State. The marriage ended in DIVORCE several years later.

In 1991, Davis began teaching an interdisciplinary graduate program titled the History of Consciousness at the University of California, Santa Cruz. In 1994, she found herself again surrounded by controversy when she was awarded a prestigious University of California President's Chair by university president Jack Peltason. The appointment provides $75,000 over several years to develop new ethnic studies courses. Some state lawmakers were outraged over the award and unsuccessfully demanded that Peltason rescind the appointment. Davis held the position until 1997.

In the late 1990s and early 2000s, Davis was still speaking out against and writing about the plight of persons she considered to be political prisoners, such as Indian activist Leonard Pelletier and ex-Black Panther Mumia Abu-Jamal, both convicted of killing law enforcement officers. She has continued to call for the decriminalization of prostitution on the basis that it would greatly reduce the number of women in prison. And she has lectured on what she calls the Prison Industrial Complex (PIC), positing that imprisonment has become the most common answer to societal problems and that corporations are profiting from prison labor thereby weakening the chances of prison reform. In 1997, Davis helped found Critical Resistance, an organization that seeks to build an international movement dedicated to dismantling the PIC.

Since the late 1970s, Davis has lectured throughout the United States and in countries in Africa, Europe, and Asia. She also remains a prolific author, producing numerous articles and essays. In 2003, in addition to writing and traveling for speaking engagements, Davis continued her work as tenured professor at the University of California at Santa Cruz.

FURTHER READINGS

Davis, Angela. 1974. *Angela Davis: An Autobiography.* New York: International Publishers.

James, Joy, ed. 1998. *The Angela Y. Davis Reader.* Malden, Mass.: Blackwell.

"The Two Nations of Black America: Interview with Angela Davis." 1998. PBS: Frontline. Available online at <www .pbs.org/wgbh/pages/frontline/shows/race/interviews/ davis.html> (accessed June 30, 2003).

CROSS-REFERENCES

Carmichael, Stokely; Cleaver, LeRoy Eldridge; Communism.

❖ DAVIS, DAVID

David Davis served as an associate justice of the U.S. Supreme Court from 1862 to 1877. An Illinois attorney and judge, Davis acted as Abraham Lincoln's campaign manager in the 1860 election, working tirelessly to win the REPUBLICAN PARTY nomination and the general election for Lincoln.

Davis was born in Sassafras Neck, Maryland, on March 9, 1815. He attended Kenyon College at the age of thirteen. Following graduation he read the law in a Massachusetts law firm, before attending New Haven Law School for less than a year. In 1835 he moved to Illinois and was admitted to the bar, and opened a law firm in Pekin. In 1836 he purchased a law practice in Bloomington, Illinois, where he remained a resident the rest of his life.

He was soon drawn into politics. After losing a bid for a seat in the Illinois Senate in 1840, he was elected to the Illinois House of Representatives in 1844. He participated in the Illinois Constitutional Convention, which convened in 1847. A force for judicial reform, Davis was elected to Illinois's Eighth Judicial Circuit, where he served as presiding judge until 1862.

During his years as a practicing attorney and judge, Davis became a close friend and adviser to ABRAHAM LINCOLN. Ignoring the traditional concept of judicial neutrality concerning politics, Davis acted as Lincoln's campaign manager during the 1860 election. His actions have been credited with securing the Republican party nomination for Lincoln.

In 1862 Lincoln rewarded his friend with an appointment to the U.S. Supreme Court. Davis's tenure encompassed both the Civil War and Reconstruction. He is best remembered for his 1866 majority opinion in EX PARTE MILLIGAN, 71 U.S. 2, 18 L. Ed. 281. In 1864 Lamdin Milligan

David Davis.
CORBIS

was arrested and tried for TREASON by a military commission established by order of President Lincoln. He was convicted and sentenced to death, but the sentence was not carried out.

In his majority opinion, Davis noted that the civilian courts were open and operating in Indiana when Milligan was arrested and tried by the military. In ordering Milligan's release, Davis condemned Lincoln's directive establishing military jurisdiction over civilians outside of the immediate war area. He strongly affirmed the fundamental right of a civilian to be tried in a regular court of law, with all the required procedural safeguards.

In 1872 Davis was nominated for president by the National Labor Reform party, but he turned down the opportunity. However, political ambition led him to resign from the Supreme

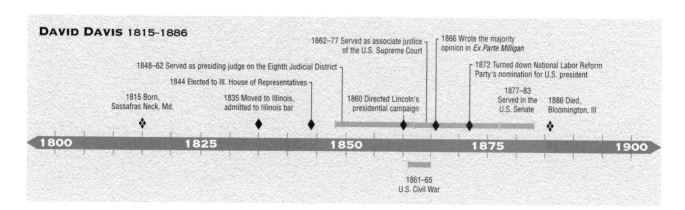

DAVID DAVIS 1815–1886

- 1815 Born, Sassafras Neck, Md.
- 1835 Moved to Illinois, admitted to Illinois bar
- 1844 Elected to Ill. House of Representatives
- 1848–62 Served as presiding judge on the Eighth Judicial District
- 1860 Directed Lincoln's presidential campaign
- 1861–65 U.S. Civil War
- 1862–77 Served as associate justice of the U.S. Supreme Court
- 1866 Wrote the majority opinion in *Ex Parte Milligan*
- 1872 Turned down National Labor Reform Party's nomination for U.S. president
- 1877–83 Served in the U.S. Senate
- 1886 Died, Bloomington, Ill

1800   1825   1850   1875   1900

Court in 1877 and run for the Senate, representing Illinois. He was elected as an independent and served one six-year term. From 1881 to 1883, he served as president pro tempore of the Senate.

Davis died June 26, 1886, in Bloomington, Illinois.

DAVIS, GEORGE

See CONFEDERATE ATTORNEYS GENERAL.

❖ DAVIS, JOHN CHANDLER BANCROFT

John Chandler Bancroft Davis enjoyed a long and prolific career as a diplomat, jurist, and legal historian.

The son of John Davis, a Massachusetts governor and U.S. senator, Davis was born December 29, 1822, in Worcester, Massachusetts. He entered Harvard College in 1840, but was suspended (unjustly, by some accounts) during his senior year. He then studied law and was admitted to the Massachusetts bar in 1844. Three years later, he received his law degree from Harvard.

Davis practiced law in New York City until August 1849, when he was appointed secretary of the U.S. legation in Great Britain. He was also acting chargé d'affaires of the embassy for a brief time. Davis left his diplomatic post in November 1852 to resume his law practice and to become U.S. correspondent for the London *Times*. Illness forced him to give up his law practice, and in 1862 he and his wife settled on a farm in rural New York State.

Six years later, after regaining his health, Davis was elected to the New York State Assembly. In 1869, he left the legislature to accept an

John C. Davis.

appointment as assistant SECRETARY OF STATE under President ULYSSES S. GRANT. As the assistant secretary, Davis arbitrated a dispute between Portugal and Great Britain over their African possessions. In 1871, a joint high commission was created to settle a dispute between the United States and Great Britain over damages sustained by Confederate vessels during the Civil War. Davis resigned his position with the STATE DEPARTMENT to become U.S. secretary to the commission. He prepared the case for the United States and wrote a 500-page book, *The*

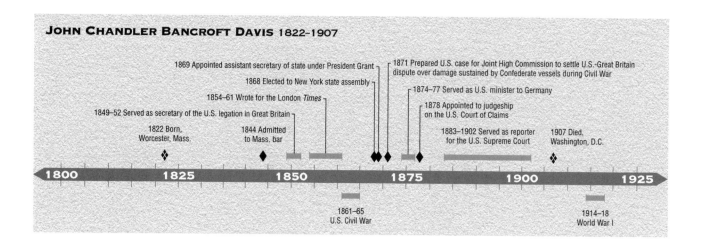

JOHN CHANDLER BANCROFT DAVIS 1822–1907

1869 Appointed assistant secretary of state under President Grant

1868 Elected to New York state assembly

1854–61 Wrote for the London *Times*

1849–52 Served as secretary of the U.S. legation in Great Britain

1871 Prepared U.S. case for Joint High Commission to settle U.S.-Great Britain dispute over damage sustained by Confederate vessels during Civil War

1874–77 Served as U.S. minister to Germany

1878 Appointed to judgeship on the U.S. Court of Claims

1822 Born, Worcester, Mass.

1844 Admitted to Mass. bar

1883–1902 Served as reporter for the U.S. Supreme Court

1907 Died, Washington, D.C.

1800 1825 1850 1875 1900 1925

1861–65 U.S. Civil War

1914–18 World War I

Case of the United States, in which the government demanded compensation for losses sustained by Confederate cruisers and for injuries to commerce. The Tribunal of Arbitration at Geneva later awarded the United States over $15 million in gold for damages.

Davis was reappointed assistant secretary of state in January 1873 but resigned in July 1874 to succeed his uncle, George Bancroft, as minister to Germany.

After three years in Berlin, Davis gave up his diplomatic career to become a judge on the U.S. Court of Claims. He sat on the court for five years and then served for nearly twenty years as reporter of decisions for the U.S. Supreme Court. As reporter for the Court, he edited over 75 volumes of the *United States Reports,* the official publication of the Court's opinions. Davis also classified important historical data on the federal judiciary. At the time of his death in 1907, at age 85, he had authored significant works on diplomacy, religion, and history, including *The Massachusetts Justice* (1847), *Mr. Fish and the Alabama Claims* (1893), and *Origin of the Book of Common Prayer of the Protestant Episcopal Church in the United States of America* (1897).

❖ DAVIS, JOHN WILLIAM

John William Davis was born April 13, 1873, in Clarksburg, West Virginia. Davis earned a bachelor of arts degree from Washington and Lee University in 1892, a bachelor of laws degree in 1895, and a doctor of laws degree in 1915. He also received doctor of laws degrees from numerous other institutions, including the University of Birmingham, England, 1919; Yale, 1921; Dartmouth, 1923; Princeton, 1924; and

Oberlin College, 1947. Three doctor of CIVIL LAW degrees were bestowed upon Davis, by Oxford University in England, 1950; Columbia, 1953; and Hofstra College, 1953.

After his ADMISSION TO THE BAR in 1895, Davis returned to his alma mater, Washington and Lee University, as an assistant professor of law, teaching from 1896 to 1897. In the latter year, he established his law practice in Clarksburg, West Virginia, serving as counselor until 1913.

Davis entered politics in 1899 by participating in the West Virginia House of Delegates. He was a member of the Democratic National Conventions from 1904 to 1932.

In 1911, he served the federal government as a congressman, representing West Virginia until 1915. Davis left this post to perform the duties of SOLICITOR GENERAL from 1913 to 1918.

The next phase of Davis's career encompassed foreign service. He was appointed ambassador to Great Britain in 1918 and acted in this capacity until 1921. Also in 1918, Davis was chosen as an American delegate to Berne, Switzerland, to the conference with Germany regarding prisoners of war captured during WORLD WAR I.

In 1924, Davis was the Democratic candidate for president of the United States; he was defeated by CALVIN COOLIDGE.

Davis died March 24, 1955, in Charleston, South Carolina.

DAY CERTAIN

A specified date. A term used in the rules of civil and CRIMINAL PROCEDURE *to designate a particular time by which all motions for a new trial must be submitted to the court.*

> "THERE IS NOTHING I RESENT MORE THAN THE IDEA THAT A LAWYER SELLS HIMSELF BODY AND SOUL TO HIS CLIENTS."
> —JOHN WILLIAM DAVIS

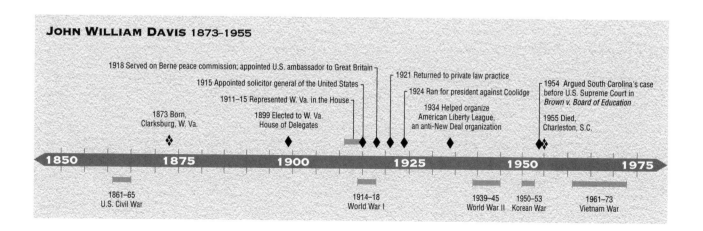

JOHN WILLIAM DAVIS 1873–1955

1918 Served on Berne peace commission; appointed U.S. ambassador to Great Britain

1915 Appointed solicitor general of the United States

1911–15 Represented W. Va. in the House

1873 Born, Clarksburg, W. Va.

1899 Elected to W. Va. House of Delegates

1921 Returned to private law practice

1924 Ran for president against Coolidge

1934 Helped organize American Liberty League, an anti-New Deal organization

1954 Argued South Carolina's case before U.S. Supreme Court in *Brown v. Board of Education*

1955 Died, Charleston, S.C.

1850   1875   1900   1925   1950   1975

1861–65 U.S. Civil War

1914–18 World War I

1939–45 World War II

1950–53 Korean War

1961–73 Vietnam War

DAY IN COURT

The opportunity afforded an individual to have a claim litigated in a judicial setting.

A person is said to have his or her day in court when he or she is given notice to appear and has the opportunity to defend his or her rights, seek relief, or set forth his or her claims. When someone has had his or her day in court with reference to a particular matter, that individual will generally be prevented from relitigating the claim in a subsequent action unless grounds exist that warrant an appeal of the matter.

❖ DAY, WILLIAM RUFUS

William Rufus Day served as an associate justice of the U.S. Supreme Court from 1903 to 1922. Day served on a Court dominated by Justice OLIVER WENDELL HOLMES JR., yet Day played a key role during a period when the federal government began to extend its police and regulatory powers.

Day was born April 17, 1849, in Ravenna, Ohio. He graduated from the University of Michigan in 1870 and attended its law school for one year. He was admitted to the Ohio bar in 1872 and entered practice in Canton, Ohio.

Ohio was a hotbed of REPUBLICAN PARTY politics in the late nineteenth century. Day became active in the party and, more important, became a trusted friend and adviser to WILLIAM MCKINLEY, who was elected president in 1896. McKinley appointed Day SECRETARY OF STATE in April 1898. Five months later Day was chosen to head the U.S. Peace Commission to negotiate an end to the SPANISH-AMERICAN WAR with Spain. He left his cabinet post to fulfill this duty.

McKinley rewarded Day for his friendship, political counsel, and service as secretary of state

with an appointment in 1899 to the U.S. Sixth Circuit Court of Appeals. With McKinley's assassination in 1901, Vice President THEODORE ROOSEVELT assumed the presidency. In 1903 Roosevelt appointed Day to the Supreme Court, in part because Roosevelt needed to strengthen his ties with Ohio Republicans.

Day held a centrist position on the Supreme Court. More liberal justices such as Holmes and LOUIS D. BRANDEIS sought to allow more active government involvement in the national economy. Conservative justices continued to restrict government regulation of business and the growth of federal power. Day took a middle course, though some commentators believe he tilted more to supporting STATES' RIGHTS.

His most famous opinion, HAMMER V. DAGENHART, 247 U.S. 251, 38 S. Ct. 529, 62 L. Ed. 1101 (1918), illustrates his more conservative tendencies. In the early 1900s, Congress sought to regulate the use of child labor, passing a child labor act in 1916 (39 Stat. 675, c. 432, formally known as the Keating-Owen Act). The act prohibited the movement in interstate commerce of goods that were made by children. In *Hammer*, a manufacturer was charged with violating the act. Under the Constitution's COMMERCE CLAUSE, Congress has the right to regulate interstate commerce. Day gave the clause a restrictive reading, ruling that commerce did not include manufactured goods that were themselves harmless. In addition, he said, Congress had intruded into an area of regulation that was reserved to the states. To allow Congress to regulate industry would destroy FEDERALISM and the system of government set out in the Constitution.

Despite this hostility to the Child Labor Act, Day upheld the federal government's power to regulate interstate commerce in other cases that

"PROPERTY IS MORE THAN THE MERE THING WHICH A PERSON OWNS. IT IS ELEMENTARY THAT IT INCLUDES THE RIGHT TO ACQUIRE, USE, AND DISPOSE OF IT. THE CONSTITUTION PROTECTS THESE ESSENTIAL ATTRIBUTES OF PROPERTY."
—WILLIAM DAY

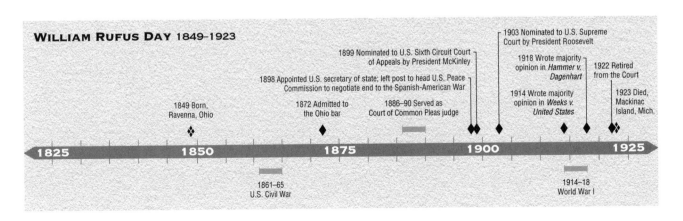

WILLIAM RUFUS DAY 1849–1923

1903 Nominated to U.S. Supreme Court by President Roosevelt

1899 Nominated to U.S. Sixth Circuit Court of Appeals by President McKinley

1918 Wrote majority opinion in *Hammer v. Dagenhart*

1922 Retired from the Court

1898 Appointed U.S. secretary of state; left post to head U.S. Peace Commission to negotiate end to the Spanish-American War

1849 Born, Ravenna, Ohio

1872 Admitted to the Ohio bar

1886–90 Served as Court of Common Pleas judge

1914 Wrote majority opinion in *Weeks v. United States*

1923 Died, Mackinac Island, Mich.

1825 1850 1875 1900 1925

1861–65 U.S. Civil War

1914–18 World War I

involved the shipment of impure food, drugs, and liquor. He was also supportive of federal antitrust prosecutions that involved restraint of trade.

However, Day's opposition to federal regulation of the workplace did not carry over to state regulation of industry. This is revealed in his dissent in LOCHNER V. NEW YORK, 198 U.S. 45, 25 S. Ct. 539, 49 L. Ed. 937 (1905). In *Lochner* the Court, on a 5–4 vote, struck down a New York state law that specified a maximum sixty-hour week for bakery employees. The Court ruled that the law was a "meddlesome interference" with business, concluding that the regulation of work hours was an unjustified infringement on "the right to labor, and with the right of free contract on the part of the individual, either as employer or employee." Although Holmes's dissent has received more attention, Day's made clear that the state had the right to promote public welfare, even if it came in conflict with the concept of liberty of contract.

Finally, Day authored the opinion in *Weeks v. United States*, 232 U.S. 383, 34 S. Ct. 341, 58 L. Ed. 652 (1914), which established the federal EXCLUSIONARY RULE for criminal evidence seized in violation of the FOURTH AMENDMENT. Day's opinion suggested that exclusion of tainted evidence was implicit in the requirement of the Fourth Amendment. If illegally seized evidence could be admitted in a criminal trial, he said, "the protection of the 4th Amendment . . . is of no value . . . and might as well be stricken from the Constitution."

Day retired from the Court in 1922. He died on Mackinac Island, Michigan, on July 9, 1923.

CROSS-REFERENCES

Child Labor Laws; Labor Law.

DAYS OF GRACE

An extension of the time originally scheduled for the performance of an act, such as payment for a debt, granted merely as a gratuitous favor by the person to whom the performance is owed.

In old English practice, days of grace allowed a person an extra three days beyond the date specified in a writ summoning him or her before a court in which to make an appearance without being subject to punishment for failure to appear. This allowance of time was granted in consideration of the far distances that had to be traveled to court.

William R. Day.
THE GRANGER
COLLECTION, NEW
YORK

The laws and customs that regulate the commercial affairs of merchants have recognized days of grace as a means of facilitating various transactions. Three days of grace were originally allowed to give a maker or acceptor of a note, bill, or draft, in which the person is ordered to make payment according to its terms, a longer time to pay than specified by the date in the document. This practice was begun merely as a favor to those who regularly engaged in business with each other, but it soon became a custom between merchants. Eventually, the courts recognized this right, often as a result of statute; in some cases, it has become a right that must be demanded.

The phrase *days of grace* is sometimes used interchangeably with grace period, a term used in insurance law to denote an extension of time within which to pay a premium due on a policy, but the terms do not have identical meanings.

DE BONIS NON ADMINISTRATIS

[Latin, Of the goods not administered.] When an administrator is appointed to succeed another who has left the estate partially unsettled, the administrator is said to be granted "administration de bonis non," that is, of the goods not already administered.

DE FACTO

[Latin, In fact.] In fact, in deed, actually.

This phrase is used to characterize an officer, a government, a past action, or a state of affairs that must be accepted for all practical purposes, but is illegal or illegitimate. Thus, an office, position, or status existing under a claim or color of right, such as a de facto corporation. In this sense it is the contrary of *de jure,* which means rightful, legitimate, just, or constitutional. Thus, an officer, king, or government *de facto* is one that is in actual possession of the office or supreme power, but by usurpation, or without lawful title; while an officer, king, or governor *de jure* is one who has just claim and rightful title to the office or power, but has never had plenary possession of it, or is not in actual possession. A wife *de facto* is one whose marriage is VOIDABLE by decree, as distinguished from a wife *de jure,* or lawful wife. But the term is also frequently used independently of any distinction from *de jure;* thus a blockade *de facto* is a blockade that is actually maintained, as distinguished from a mere paper blockade.

A de facto corporation is one that has been given legal status despite the fact that it has not complied with all the statutory formalities required for corporate existence. Only the state may challenge the validity of the existence of a de facto corporation.

De facto SEGREGATION is the separation of members of different races by various social and economic factors, not by virtue of any government action or statute.

DE JURE

[Latin, In law.] Legitimate; lawful, as a MATTER OF LAW. Having complied with all the requirements imposed by law.

De jure is commonly paired with *de facto,* which means "in fact." In the course of ordinary events, the term *de jure* is superfluous. For example, in everyday discourse, when one speaks of a corporation or a government, the understood meaning is a de jure corporation or a de jure government.

A de jure corporation is one that has completely fulfilled the statutory formalities imposed by state corporation law in order to be granted corporate existence. In comparison, a de facto corporation is one that has acted in GOOD FAITH and would be an ordinary corporation but for failure to comply with some technical requirements.

A de jure government is the legal, legitimate government of a state and is so recognized by other states. In contrast, a de facto government is in actual possession of authority and control of the state. For example, a government that has been overthrown and has moved to another state will attain de jure status if other nations refuse to accept the legitimacy of the revolutionary government.

De jure SEGREGATION refers to intentional actions by the state to enforce racial segregation. The JIM CROW LAWS of the southern states, which endured until the 1960s, are examples of de jure segregation. In contrast, de facto racial segregation, which occurred in other states, was accomplished by factors apart from conscious government activity.

DE MINIMIS

An abbreviated form of the Latin MAXIM *de minimis non curat lex, "the law cares not for small things." A legal doctrine by which a court refuses to consider trifling matters.*

In a lawsuit, a court applies the *de minimis* doctrine to avoid the resolution of trivial matters that are not worthy of judicial scrutiny. Its application sometimes results in the dismissal of an action, particularly when the only redress sought is for a nominal sum, such as one dollar. Appellate courts also use the *de minimis* doctrine when appropriate.

DE NOVO

[Latin, Anew.] A second time; afresh. A trial or a hearing that is ordered by an appellate court that has reviewed the record of a hearing in a lower court and sent the matter back to the original court for a new trial, as if it had not been previously heard nor decided.

DEAD MAN'S STATUTES

State RULES OF EVIDENCE *that make the oral statements of a decedent inadmissible in a civil lawsuit against the executor or administrator of the decedent's estate when presented by persons to bolster their claims against the estate.*

Dead man's statutes are designed to protect the estate of a deceased person from fraudulent claims made by a person who had engaged in transactions with the decedent. These laws do not permit the claimant to testify as to what terms a decedent verbally accepted, since the decedent is unable to testify and give his or her version of the transaction.

Such statutes are derived from common-law principles that disqualified witnesses from testifying in an action if they would be affected by the outcome of the case. Many states admit such testimony as evidence under specific statutory conditions, such as if the decedent's statements can be corroborated by the testimony of other disinterested witnesses.

The FEDERAL RULES OF EVIDENCE govern the use of oral statements made by decedents in federal cases.

DEADLY FORCE

An amount of force that is likely to cause either serious bodily injury or death to another person.

Police officers may use deadly force in specific circumstances when they are trying to enforce the law. Private citizens may use deadly force in certain circumstances in SELF-DEFENSE. The rules governing the use of deadly force for police officers are different from those for citizens.

During the twelfth century, the COMMON LAW allowed the police to use deadly force if they needed it to capture a felony suspect, regardless of the circumstances. At that time, felonies were not as common as they are now and were usually punishable by death. Also, law officers had a more difficult time capturing suspects because they did not have the technology and weaponry that are present in today's world. In modern times, the courts have restricted the use of deadly force to certain, dangerous situations.

In police jargon, deadly force is also referred to as shoot to kill. The Supreme Court has ruled that, depending on the circumstances, if an offender resists arrest, police officers may use as much force as is reasonably required to overcome the resistance. Whether the force is reasonable is determined by the judgment of a reasonable officer at the scene, rather than by hindsight. Because police officers can find themselves in dangerous or rapidly changing situations where split second decisions are necessary, the judgment of someone at the scene is vital when looking back at the actions of a police officer.

The Supreme Court has defined the "objective reasonableness" standard as a balance between the rights of the person being arrested and the government interests that allow the use

In specific circumstances, police officers may use deadly force when attempting to enforce the law. These SWAT team members resorted to the use of deadly force after attempting to arrest a suspect in a November 1995 hijacking in Miami, Florida.

AP/WIDE WORLD PHOTOS

of force. The FOURTH AMENDMENT protects U.S. citizens from unreasonable searches and seizures, the category into which an arrest falls. The Supreme Court has said that a SEARCH AND SEIZURE is reasonable if it is based on PROBABLE CAUSE and if it does not unreasonably intrude on the rights and privacy of the individual. This standard does not question a police officer's intent or motivation for using deadly force during an arrest; it only looks at the situation as it has happened.

For deadly force to be constitutional when an arrest is taking place, it must be the reasonable choice under all the circumstances at the time. Therefore, deadly force should be looked at as an option that is used when it is believed that no other action will succeed. The MODEL PENAL CODE, although not adopted in all states, restricts police action regarding deadly force. According to the code, officers should not use deadly force unless the action will not endanger innocent bystanders, the suspect used deadly force in committing the crime, or the officers believe a delay in arrest may result in injury or death to other people.

Circumstances that are taken into consideration are the severity of the offense, how much of a threat the suspect poses, and the suspect's attempts to resist or flee the police officer. When arresting someone for a misdemeanor, the police have the right to shoot the alleged offender only in self-defense. If an officer shoots a suspect accused of a misdemeanor for a reason other than self-defense, the officer can be held liable for criminal charges and damages for injuries to the suspect. This standard was demonstrated in the Iowa case of *Klinkel v. Saddler,* 211 Iowa 368, 233 N.W. 538 (1930), where a sheriff faced a WRONGFUL DEATH lawsuit because he had killed a misdemeanor suspect during an arrest. The sheriff said he had used deadly force to defend himself, and the court ruled in his favor.

When police officers are arresting someone for a felony, the courts have given them a little more leeway. The police may use all the force that is necessary to overcome resistance, even if that means killing the person they are trying to arrest. However, if it is proved that an officer used more force than was necessary, the officer can be held criminally and civilly liable. In *Tennessee v. Garner,* 471 U.S. 1, 105 S. Ct. 1694, 85 L. Ed. 2d 1 (1985), the Supreme Court ruled that it is a violation of the Fourth Amendment for police officers to use deadly force to stop fleeing felony suspects who are nonviolent and unarmed. The decision, with an opinion written by Justice BYRON R. WHITE, said, in part, "We conclude that such force may not be used unless it is necessary to prevent the escape and the officer has probable cause to believe that the suspect poses a significant threat of death or serious physical injury to the officer or others."

When deadly force is used by a private citizen, the reasonableness rule does not apply. The citizen must be able to prove that a felony occurred or was being attempted, and that the felony threatened death or bodily harm. Mere suspicion of a felony is considered an insufficient ground for a private citizen to use deadly force.

This was demonstrated in the Michigan case of *People v. Couch,* 436 Mich. 414, 461 N.W.2d 683 (1990), where the defendant shot and killed a suspected felon who was fleeing the scene of the crime. The Michigan supreme court ruled that Archie L. Couch did not have the right to use deadly force against the suspected felon because the suspect did not pose a threat of injury or death to Couch.

FURTHER READINGS

Griffin, Thomas J. 1971. "Private Person's Authority, in Making Arrest for Felony, to Shoot or Kill Alleged Felon." *American Law Reports 3d* 32:1078.

Hatch, David E. 2003. *Officer-Involved Shootings and Use of Force: Practical Investigative Techniques.* Boca Raton, Fla.: CRC Press.

McGuinness, J. Michael. 2000. "Shootings by Police Officers Are Analyzed Under Standards Based on Objective Reasonableness." *New York State Bar Association Journal* 72 (September): 17.

Owens, Michael Douglas. 2001. "The Inherent Constitutionality of the Police Use of Deadly Force to Stop Dangerous Pursuits." *Mercer Law Review* 52 (summer): 1599–1643.

Pearson, James O., Jr. 1978. "Modern Status: Right of Peace Officer to Use Deadly Force in Attempting to Arrest Fleeing Felon." *American Law Reports 3d* 83:174.

———. 1978. "Peace Officer's Civil Liability for Death or Personal Injuries Caused by Intentional Force in Arresting Misdemeanant." *American Law Reports 3d* 83:238.

Sullivan, G. Russell. 1985. "Constitutional Law—Deadly Force and the Fourth Amendment: *Tennessee v. Garner.*" *Suffolk Univ. Law Review* 20.

DEATH AND DYING

Death *is the end of life.* Dying *is the process of approaching death, including the choices and actions involved in that process.*

Death has always been a central concern of the law. The many legal issues related to death include laws that determine whether a death has actually occurred, as well as when and how it occurred, and whether or not another individual will be charged for having caused it. With the development of increasingly complex and powerful medical procedures and devices in the middle and late twentieth century, the U.S. legal system has had to establish rules and standards for the removal of life-sustaining medical care. This would include, for example, withdrawing an artificial respirator or a feeding tube from a comatose person, or withholding chemotherapy from a terminally ill cancer patient. Such laws and judicial decisions involve the right of individuals to refuse medical treatment—sometimes called the right to die—as well as the boundaries of that right, particularly in regard to the state's interest in protecting life and the medical profession's right to protect its standards. The issues involved in death and dying have often pitted PATIENTS' RIGHTS groups against physicians' professional organizations as each vies for control over the decision of how and when people die.

Defining Death in the Law

The law recognizes different forms of death, not all of them meaning the end of physical life. The term *civil death* is used in some states to describe the circumstance of an individual who has been convicted of a serious crime or sentenced to life imprisonment. Such an individual forfeits his or her CIVIL RIGHTS, including the ability to marry, the capacity to own property, and the right to contract. *Legal death* is a presumption by law that a person has died. It arises following a prolonged absence, generally for a prescribed number of years, during which no one has seen or heard from the person and there is no known reason for the person's disappearance that would be incompatible with a finding that the individual is dead (e.g., the individual had not planned to move to another place). *Natural death* is death by action of natural causes without the aid or inducement of any intervening instrumentality. *Violent death* is death caused or accelerated by the application of extreme or excessive force. *Brain death,* a medical term first used in the late 1960s, is the cessation of all functions of the whole brain. *Wrongful death* is the end of life through a willful or negligent act.

In the eyes of the law, death is not a continuing event but something that takes place at a precise moment in time. The courts will not wield authority concerning a death. The determination of whether an individual has died, and the way in which this is proved by the person's vital signs, is not a legal decision but rather a medical judgment. The opinion of qualified medical personnel will be taken into consideration by judges when a controversy exists as to whether an individual is still alive or has died.

Legal Death and Missing Persons

There is a legal presumption that an individual is alive until proved dead. In attempting to determine whether a person has died after having been missing for a certain period of time, the law assumes that the person is alive until a reason exists to believe otherwise.

The common-law rule is that where evidence indicates that the absent person was subject to a particular peril, he or she will be legally presumed dead after seven years unless the disappearance can be otherwise explained. The seven-year interval may be shortened if the state decides to enact legislation to change it. Some states may permit the dissolution of a marriage or the administration of an estate based on a mysterious disappearance that endures for less than seven years. A majority of states will not make the assumption that a missing person is dead unless it is reasonable to assume that the person would return if still alive.

A special problem emerges in a situation where a person disappears following a threat made on his or her life. Such an individual would have a valid reason for voluntarily leaving and concealing his or her identity. Conversely, however, the person would in fact be dead if the plot succeeded. A court would have to examine carefully the facts of a particular case of this nature.

In some states, the court will not hold that an individual has died without proof that an earnest search was made for him or her. During such a search, public records must be consulted, wherever the person might have resided, for information regarding marriage, death, payment of taxes, or application for government benefits. The investigation must also include questioning of the missing person's friends or relatives as to his or her whereabouts.

Death Certificates

The laws of each state require that the manner in which an individual has died be determined and recorded on a death certificate. Coroners or medical examiners must deal with issues establishing whether someone can be legally blamed for causing the death. Such issues are subsequently determined by CRIMINAL LAW in the event that someone is charged with HOMICIDE, and by TORT LAW in the event of a civil suit for WRONGFUL DEATH.

The Nature of Dying

Because of the many advances in modern medicine, the nature of death and dying has changed greatly in the past several centuries. A majority of people in industrial societies such as the United States no longer perish, as they once did, from infectious or parasitic diseases. Instead, life expectancies range above 70 years and the major causes of mortality are illnesses such as cancer and heart disease. Medicine is able to prolong life by many means, including artificial circulatory and respiratory systems, intravenous feeding and hydration, chemotherapy, and antibiotics.

The cultural circumstances of death have changed as well. A study published by the American Lung Association in the late 1990s, indicated that 90 percent of patients who are in intensive care units of hospitals die as a result of surrogates and physicians deciding together to withhold life-sustaining medical care. This rate doubled from earlier in the decade.

Brain Death

In traditional Western medical practice, death was defined as the cessation of the body's circulatory and respiratory (blood pumping and breathing) functions. With the invention of machines that provide artificial circulation and respiration that definition has ceased to be practical and has been modified to include another category of death called brain death. People can now be kept alive using such machines even when their brains have effectively died and are no longer able to control their bodily functions. Moreover, in certain medical procedures, such as open-heart surgery, individuals do not breathe or pump blood on their own. Since it would be wrong to declare as dead all persons whose circulatory or respiratory systems are temporarily maintained by artificial means (a category that includes many patients undergoing surgery), the medical community has determined that an individual may be declared dead if brain death has occurred—that is, if the whole brain has ceased to function, or has entered what is sometimes called a persistent vegetative state. An individual whose brain stem (lower brain) has died is not able to maintain the vegetative functions of life, including respiration, circulation, and swallowing. According to the Uniform Determination of Death Act (§ 1, U.L.A. [1980]), from which most states have developed their brain death statutes, "An individual who has sustained either (1) irreversible cessation of circulatory and respiratory function, or (2) irreversible cessation of all functions of the entire brain, including the brain stem, is dead."

Brain death becomes a crucial issue in part because of the importance of organ transplants. A brain-dead person may have organs—a heart, a liver, and lungs, for example—that could save other people's lives. And for an individual to be an acceptable organ donor, he or she must be dead but still breathing and circulating blood. If a brain-dead person is maintained on artificial respiration until his or her heart fails, then these usable organs would perish. Thus, the medical category of brain death makes it possible to accomplish another goal: saving lives with organ transplants.

The Right to Die: Individual Autonomy and State Interests

The first significant legal case to deal with the issue of termination of life-sustaining medical care was IN RE QUINLAN, 70 N.J. 10, 355 A.2d 647. This 1976 case helped resolve the question of whether a person could be held liable for withdrawing a life-support system even if the patient's condition is irreversible. In 1975, Karen Ann Quinlan inexplainably became comatose and was put on a mechanical respirator. Her parents authorized physicians to use every possible means to revive her, but no treatment improved her condition. Although doctors agreed that the possibility of her recovering consciousness was remote, they would not pronounce her case hopeless. When her parents themselves lost all hope of Quinlan's recovery, they presented the hospital with an authorization for the removal of the respirator and an exemption of the hospital and doctors from responsibility for the result. However, the attending doctor refused to turn off the respirator on the grounds that doing so would violate his professional oath. Quinlan's parents then initiated a lawsuit asking the court to keep the doctors and the hospital from interfering with their decision to remove Quinlan's respirator.

In a unanimous decision, the New Jersey Supreme Court ruled that Quinlan had a constitutional right of privacy that could be safeguarded by her legal guardian; that the private decision of Quinlan's guardian and family should be honored; and that the hospital could be exempted from criminal liability for turning off a respirator if a hospital ethics committee agreed that the chance for recovery is remote. Quinlan was removed from the respirator, and she continued to live in a coma for ten years, nourished through a nasal feeding tube.

In cases following *Quinlan,* courts have ruled that life-sustaining procedures such as artificial feeding and hydration are the legal equivalent of mechanical respirators and may be removed using the same standards (*Gray v. Romeo,* 697 F. Supp. 580 [D.R.I. 1988]). Courts have also defined the right to die according to standards other than that of a constitutional right to privacy. The patient's legal right to refuse medical treatment has been grounded as well on the common-law right of bodily integrity, also called bodily self-determination, and on the liberty interest under the DUE PROCESS CLAUSE of the FOURTEENTH AMENDMENT. These concepts are often collected under the term *individual autonomy,* or *patient autonomy.*

Subsequent cases have also defined the limits of the right to die, particularly the state's interest in those limits. The state's interests in

cases concerning the termination of medical care are the preservation of life (including the prevention of suicide), the protection of dependent third parties such as children, and the protection of the standards of the medical profession. The interests of the state may, in some cases, outweigh those of the patient.

In 1990, the U.S. Supreme Court issued its first decision on the right-to-die issue, *Cruzan v. Director of Missouri Department of Health,* 497 U.S. 261, 110 S. Ct. 2841, 111 L. Ed. 2d 224. *Cruzan* illustrates the way in which individual and state interests are construed on this issue, but leaves many of the legal questions on the issue still unresolved. Nancy Cruzan was in a persistent vegetative state as a result of severe brain injuries suffered in an automobile accident in 1983. She had no chance of recovery, although with artificial nutrition and hydration could have lived another 30 years. Her parents' attempts to authorize removal of Cruzan's medical support were first approved by a trial court and then denied by the Missouri Supreme Court. Her parents then appealed the case to the U.S. Supreme Court.

The Court held that the guarantee of liberty contained in the Fourteenth Amendment to the Constitution does not prohibit Missouri from insisting that "evidence of the incompetent [patient's] wishes as to the withdrawal of treatment be proved by clear and convincing evidence." The Court left other states free to adopt this "clear-and-convincing evidence" standard but did not compel them to do so. Thus, existing state laws remained the same after the *Cruzan* decision. Although the Court affirmed that a competent patient has a constitutionally protected freedom to refuse unwanted medical treatment, it emphasized that an incompetent person is unable to make an informed choice to exercise that freedom.

The Court explained that the state has an interest in the preservation of human life and in safeguarding against potential abuses by surrogates and is therefore not required to accept the "substituted judgment" of the patient's family. The Court agreed with the Missouri Supreme Court ruling that statements made by Cruzan to a housemate a year before her accident did not amount to clear-and-convincing proof that she desired to have hydration and nutrition withdrawn. Cruzan had allegedly made statements to the effect that she would not want to live should she face life as a "vegetable." There was no testimony that she had actually discussed withdrawal of medical treatment, hydration, or nutrition.

After the Court's decision, Cruzan's parents went back to the Missouri probate court with new evidence regarding their daughter's wishes. On December 14, 1990, a Missouri judge ruled that clear evidence of Cruzan's wishes existed, and permitted her parents to authorize withdrawing artificial nutrition and hydration. Cruzan died on December 27, 12 days after feeding tubes were removed.

Advance Directives

A court must consider many factors and standards in right-to-die cases. It must determine, for example, whether a patient is *competent* or *incompetent*. A competent patient is deemed by the court to be able to give informed consent or refusal relative to the treatment under consideration, whereas an incompetent patient (e.g., a patient in a coma) lacks the decision-making capacity to do so. According to the principle of individual autonomy, the court must honor the informed consent of competent patients regarding their medical care.

For incompetent patients who cannot make informed decisions regarding their care, an *advance directive* may provide a means of decision making for the termination of life-supporting treatment. An advance directive is a document, prepared in advance of incompetence, which gives patients some control over their HEALTH CARE after they have lost the ability to make decisions owing to a medical condition. It may consist of detailed instructions about medical treatment, as in a LIVING WILL; or the appointment of a proxy, or substitute, who will make the difficult choices regarding medical care with the patient's earlier directions in mind. The appointment of a proxy is sometimes called a *proxy directive* or *durable power of attorney*. The patient names a proxy decision maker when he or she is competent. In other cases, the physician may appoint a proxy, or the court may appoint a legal guardian who acts on behalf of an incompetent person. Usually, a relative such as a spouse, adult child, or sibling is chosen as a proxy. If an advance directive provides adequate evidence of a patient's wishes, a decision about the termination of life support can often be made without involving a court of law.

For an incompetent patient whose preferences regarding medical care are known from prior oral statements, the patient's proxy may make a *substituted judgment*—that is, a judgment consistent with what the patient would have chosen for himself. If no preference regarding medical treatment is known, the standard for the proxy's decision is the "best interests of the patient." According to that standard, the proxy's decision should approximate what most reasonable individuals in the same circumstances as the patient would choose. Individual states have statutes governing the requirements for living wills and advance directives.

FURTHER READINGS

Callahan, Daniel. 1990. "Current Trends in Biomedical Ethics in the United States." *Bioethics: Issues and Perspectives.* Washington, D.C.: Pan American Health Organization.

Cohen-Almagor, Raphael. 2001. *The Right to Die With Dignity: An Argument in Ethics, Medicine, and Law.* New Brunswick, N.J.: Rutgers Univ. Press.

Council on Ethical and Judicial Affairs, American Medical Association. 1994. *Code of Medical Ethics.* Chicago: American Medical Association.

Ditto, Peter H., Joseph H. Danks, William D. Smucker, et al. 2001. "Advanced Directives as Acts of Communication." *Archives of Internal Medicine* 161.

Howarth, Glennys, and Oliver Leaman, eds. 2001. *Encyclopedia of Death and Dying.* New York: Routledge.

Humphry, Derek. 1993. *Lawful Exit: The Limits of Freedom for Help in Dying.* Junction City, Ore.: Norris Lane Press.

———. 1991. *Final Exit.* Eugene, Ore.: Hemlock Society.

Monagle, John F., and David C. Thomasma. 1994. *Health Care Ethics: Critical Issues.* Gaithersburg, Md.: Aspen.

Schneider, Carl E., ed. 2000. *Law at the End of Life: The Supreme Court and Assisted Suicide.* Ann Arbor: Univ. of Michigan Press.

Urofsky, Melvin. 1994. *Letting Go: Death, Dying, and the Law.* Norman: Univ. of Oklahoma Press.

CROSS-REFERENCES

Euthanasia; Physicians and Surgeons; Power of Attorney.

DEATH PENALTY

See CAPITAL PUNISHMENT.

DEATH WARRANT

An order from the executive, the governor of a state, or the president directing the warden of a prison or a sheriff or other appropriate officer to carry into execution a sentence of death; an order commanding that a named person be put to death in a specified manner at a specific time.

CROSS-REFERENCES

Capital Punishment.

Debenture

A sample debenture.

I.D. Control # _____

License # _____

DEBENTURE

$ _____ (the "Original Principal Amount")

_____ (the "Maturity Date")

_____ (the "Company")

_____

| (Street) | (City) | (State) | (Zip) |

PART I – PERIOD SPECIFIC TERMS

  A. Applicable for the Scheduled Interim Period (and New Interim Periods, as applicable)

Interest rate per annum for the Scheduled Interim Period: _____%
Annual Charge applicable to the Scheduled Interim Period: 1% per annum

Date of Issuance: _____

Scheduled Pooling Date: _____
Scheduled Interim Period: from and including the Date of Issuance to but excluding the Scheduled Pooling Date

The following italicized terms will apply if the Interim Period is extended by SBA:

New interest rate(s) per annum	(a)	%	(b)	%	(c)	%	
New Annual Charge per annum	(a)	1%	(b)	1%	(c)	1%	
New Pooling Date(s):	(a) _____		(b) _____		(c) _____		
New Interim Period(s): from and including:	(a) _____		(b) _____		(c) _____		
to but excluding:	(a) _____		(b) _____		(c) _____		

The Company, for value received, promises to pay to The Chase Manhattan Bank, as Custodian (the "Custodian") for the U.S. Small Business Administration ("SBA") and SBIC Funding Corporation (the "Funding Corporation"), pursuant to the Custody and Administration Agreement (the "Custody Agreement") dated as of April 27, 1998 among SBA, the Funding Corporation, the Federal Home Loan Bank of Chicago, as Interim Funding Provider (the "Interim Funding Provider"), and the Custodian: (i) interest on the Original Principal Amount listed above at the applicable rate per annum listed above, and (ii) an Annual Charge on the Original Principal Amount listed above at the applicable rate per annum listed above, each at such location on SBA, as guarantor of this Debenture, may direct and each at the related rate per annum identified for the Scheduled Interim Period (and each New Interim Period, if any). This Debenture will bear interest for, and the Annual Charge will apply to, the Scheduled interim Period (and each New Interim Period, if any) at the rate(s) and for the applicable period(s) indicated above, to be paid in arrears by 1:00 p.m. (New York City time) on the Business Day prior to the Scheduled Pooling Date (and each New Pooling Date, if any) listed above. As used throughout this Debenture, "Business Day" means any day other than: (i) a Saturday or Sunday; (ii) a legal holiday in Washington, D.C.; and (iii) a day on which banking institutions in New York City are authorized or obligated by law or executive order to be closed. Interest on this Debenture and the Annual Charge for the Scheduled Interim Period (and each New Interim Period, if any) will each be computed on the basis of the actual number of days in the applicable Interest Period divided by 360. The Company may not prepay this Debenture, in whole or in part, during the Scheduled Interim Period or any New Interim Period.

  B. This Section B. is effective only after (i) the Scheduled Interim Period and any New Interim Period(s) expire and (ii) the Custodian receives this Debenture for pooling.

The Company, for value received, promises to pay to the order of The Chase Manhattan Bank, acting as Trustee (the "Trustee") under that certain Amended and Restated Trust Agreement dated as of February 1, 1997, as the same may be amended from time to time, by and among the Trustee, the SBA and SBIC Funding Corporation, and as the Holder hereof, interest semiannually on March 1st and September 1st (the "{Payment Dates}") of each year, at such location as SBA, as guarantor of this Debenture, may direct at the rate of _____% per annum (the "Stated Interest Rate"), and to pay a 1% per annum fee to SBA on each Payment Date, each calculated on the basis of a year of 365 days, for the actual number of days elapsed (including the first day but excluding the last day), on the principal sum from the last day of the Interim Period until payment of such principal sum has been made or duly provided for. The Company shall deposit all payments with respect to this Debenture not later than 12:00 noon (New York City time) on the applicable Payment Date or the next Business Day if the Payment Date is not a Business Day, all as directed by SBA.

The Company may elect to prepay this Debenture, in whole and not in part, on any Payment Date, in the manner and at the price as next described. The prepayment price (the "Prepayment Price") must be an amount equal to the outstanding principal balance of this Debenture, plus interest accrued and unpaid thereon to the Payment Date selected for prepayment, plus a prepayment premium (the "Prepayment Premium"). The Prepayment Premium amount is calculated as a declining percentage (the "Applicable Percentage") multiplied by the Original Principal Amount of this Debenture in accordance with the following table:

Consecutive Payment Dates	Applicable Percentage
1st or 2nd	5%
3rd or 4th	4%
5th or 6th	3%
7th or 8th	2%
9th or (10th - If not also Maturity Date)	1%

[continued]

A sample debenture (continued).

Debenture

No Prepayment Premium is required to repay this Debenture on its Maturity Date. No Prepayment Premium is required when the prepayment occurs on a Payment Date that is on or after the 11th consecutive Payment Date of this Debenture, if this debenture has a 20 consecutive Payment Date term.

The amount of the Prepayment price must be sent to SBA or such agent as SBA may direct, by wire payment in immediately available funds, not less than three Business Days prior to the regular Payment Date. Until the Company is notified otherwise in writing by SBA, any Prepayment Price must be paid to the account maintained by the Trustee, entitled the SBA Prepayment Subaccount and must include an identification of the Company by name and SBA-assigned license number, the loan number appearing on the face of this Debenture, and such other information as SBA or its agent may specify.

II. –GENERAL TERMS

For value received, the Company promises to pay to the order of the Trustee the Original Principal Amount on the Maturity Date at such location as SBA, as guarantor of this Debenture, may direct.

This Debenture is issued by the Company and guaranteed by SBA, pursuant and subject to Section 303 of the Small Business Investment Act of 1958, as amended (the "Act") (15 U.S.C. Section 683). This Debenture is subject to all of the regulations promulgated under the Act, as amended from time to time, provided, however, that 13 C.F.R. Sections 107.1810 and 107.1830 through 107.1850 as in effect on the date of this Debenture are incorporated in this Debenture as if fully set forth. If this Debenture is accelerated, then the Company promises to pay an amount equal to the outstanding principal balance of this Debenture, plus interest accrued and unpaid on such balance to but excluding the next Payment Date following such acceleration.

This Debenture is deemed issued in the District of Columbia as of the day, month, and year first stated above. The terms and conditions of this Debenture must be construed in accordance with, and its validity and enforcement governed by, federal law.

The warranties, representations, or certification made to SBA on any SBA Form 1022 or any application letter of the Company for an SBA commitment related to this Debenture, and any documents submitted in connection with the issuance of this Debenture, are incorporated in this Debenture as if fully set forth.

Should any provision of this Debenture or any of the documents incorporated by reference in this Debenture be declared illegal or unenforceable by a court of competent jurisdiction, the remaining provisions will remain in full force and effect and this Debenture must be construed as if such provisions were not contained in this Debenture.

All notices to the Company which are required or may be given under this Debenture shall be sufficient in all respects if sent to the above-noted address of the Company. For the purposes of this Debenture, the Company may change this address only upon written approval of SBA.

COMPANY ORGANIZED AS CORPORATION

IN WITNESS WHEREOF, the Company has caused this debenture to be signed by its duly authorized officer and its corporate seal to be hereunto affixed and attested by its Secretary or Assistant Secretary as of the date of issuance stated above.

CORPORATE SEAL

_____
(Name of Licensee)

By: _____

_____
(Typed Name and Title)

ATTEST:

_____
Secretary or Assistant Secretary (Strike One)

SBA FORM 444C (Revised 6/98)

DEBENTURE

[Latin, Are due.] A promissory note or bond offered by a corporation to a creditor in exchange for a loan, the repayment of which is backed only by the general creditworthiness of the corporation and not by a mortgage or a lien on any specific property.

Debentures are usually offered in issues under an INDENTURE, a document that sets the terms of the exchange. A debenture is usually a bearer instrument. When it is presented for payment, the person in possession of it will be paid, even if the person is not the original creditor. Coupons representing annual or semi-annual payments of interest on the debt are attached, to be clipped and presented for payment on their due dates. They may be deposited in, and collected by, the banks of holders of the debentures, the creditors of the corporation.

A *convertible debenture* is one that can be changed or converted, at the option of its holder, into shares of stock, usually common stock, at a fixed ratio as stated in the indenture. The ratio can be adjusted in light of stock dividends; otherwise the value of converting the debt into SECURITIES would be worth less than retaining the debenture until its date of maturity.

A *subordinate debenture* is one that will be repaid only after other corporate debts have been satisfied.

A *convertible subordinate debenture* is one that is subject or subordinate to the prior repayment of other debts of the corporation but which can be converted into another form of security.

A *sinking fund debenture* is one whereby repayment is secured by periodic payments by the corporation into a sinking fund, an amount of money made up of corporate assets and earnings that are set aside for the repayment of designated debentures and long-term debts.

DEBIT

A sum charged as due or owing. An entry made on the asset side of a ledger or account. The term is used in bookkeeping to denote the left side of the ledger, or the charging of a person or an account with all that is supplied to or paid out for that person or for the subject of the account. Also, the balance of an account where it is shown that something remains due to the party keeping the account.

As a noun, an entry on the left-hand side of an account. As a verb, to make an entry on the left-hand side of an account. A term used in accounting or bookkeeping that results in an increase to an asset and an expense account and a decrease to a liability, revenue, or owner's EQUITY *account.*

❖ DEBS, EUGENE

Labor leader, presidential candidate, author, and radical, social, and political agitator, Eugene Debs employed a combination of self-determination, grit, defiance, and risk-taking to play a sometimes pivotal role in American law from the late 1890s through the early twentieth century.

The son of Alsatian immigrants, Eugene Victor Debs was born in Terre Haute, Indiana, on November 5, 1855. As a young teenager growing up in Terre Haute, Debs took a job as a railway fireman, where he became active in the Brotherhood of Locomotive Firemen (BLF). Although Debs left his job as a railway fireman four years later, he remained active in the BLF, undertaking increased leadership responsibilities. Debs then was elected to serve two terms as the city clerk for Terre Haute and one term in the Indiana House of Representatives. In winning all three elections, Debs leveraged his role as grand secretary and treasurer in the BLF to garner votes from working class laborers.

In 1893, Debs broke with the tradition of limiting membership in craft unions to skilled artisans by helping found the American Railway Union, which organized both skilled and unskilled workers. Debs believed that labor's greatest strength lay more in its sheer numbers and less in the individual skills of its members.

The following year Debs, now president of the American Railway Union, led a strike against the Pullman Palace Car Company, which was owned by George Pullman and located in Pullman, Illinois, a company town in which nearly all residents worked for Pullman. Pullman also provided housing units for his workers to rent. In 1894, Pullman began laying off workers, cutting wages, and withholding their paychecks as payment for unpaid rent.

The Debs-led strike, known as the Pullman Boycott, turned violent when workers began pillaging, rioting, and burning railway cars. Railway strikes erupted across the Midwest, forcing much of the nation's railroad system to shut down. President GROVER CLEVELAND deployed 12,000 troops to quell the strike in Pullman.

"WHILE THERE IS A LOWER CLASS, I AM IN IT; WHILE THERE IS A CRIMINAL ELEMENT, I AM OF IT; AND WHILE THERE IS A SOUL IN PRISON, I AM NOT FREE."
—EUGENE DEBS

Eugene Debs.
LIBRARY OF CONGRESS

that he had been denied the SIXTH AMENDMENT right to a jury trial.

The U.S. Supreme Court rejected Debs's argument, finding that he and the other union leaders had formed an unlawful conspiracy in restraint of trade (*In re Debs*, 158 U.S. 564, 15 S.Ct. 900, 39 L.Ed. 1092 [U.S. 1895]). The injunction obtained by the federal government was an equitable remedy, the Supreme Court said, and the Sixth Amendment right to a jury trial does not apply in equitable proceedings. To preserve their power in equitable proceedings, judges must have the authority to punish violations through the power of contempt, the Court concluded. Debs was forced to serve out the full six months of his jail sentence.

The Supreme Court's decision in *Debs* served to legitimize Cleveland's deployment of the strike-breaking troops, even though the Court did not expressly weigh in on that issue. Almost 40 years would pass before industrial unions would receive increased recognition and protection from U.S. law.

Nonetheless, Debs continued advocating unions as the best means to advance labor's interests. The same year that Debs led the PULL-MAN STRIKE, President Cleveland signed into law an act that declared the first Monday in September as a holiday to honor the American laborer. Despite the concession from the White House, Debs forged his own brand of politics by organizing the Social Democratic Party of America in 1897. As its candidate for president in 1900, he received 96,116 votes. Thereafter he spent most of his time as a lecturer and organizer in the socialist movement, although he purported to be less interested in the political underpinnings of the movement and instead,

After two workers were killed in clashes with the troops, President Cleveland declared the strike over. Workers were allowed to return to work only if they promised not to unionize again.

A few weeks before Cleveland deployed the troops, a federal court had issued an INJUNCTION ordering Debs and the other union leaders to cease and desist their concerted activities against Pullman. Debs ignored the injunction, and was eventually arrested and cited for CONTEMPT of court. Tried before a judge without a jury and defended by CLARENCE DARROW, Debs lost and was sentenced to six months in jail. Debs challenged his conviction on the ground

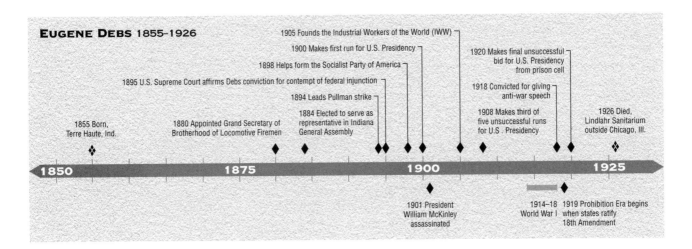

EUGENE DEBS 1855–1926

1905 Founds the Industrial Workers of the World (IWW)
1900 Makes first run for U.S. Presidency
1898 Helps form the Socialist Party of America
1895 U.S. Supreme Court affirms Debs conviction for contempt of federal injunction
1894 Leads Pullman strike
1884 Elected to serve as representative in Indiana General Assembly
1855 Born, Terre Haute, Ind.
1880 Appointed Grand Secretary of Brotherhood of Locomotive Firemen
1920 Makes final unsuccessful bid for U.S. Presidency from prison cell
1918 Convicted for giving anti-war speech
1908 Makes third of five unsuccessful runs for U.S. Presidency
1926 Died, Lindlahr Sanitarium outside Chicago, Ill.

1850   1875   1900   1925

1901 President William McKinley assassinated
1914–18 World War I
1919 Prohibition Era begins when states ratify 18th Amendment

viewed SOCIALISM as a means to guarantee dignity and equality for the average worker. He was the presidential candidate of the SOCIALIST PARTY in 1904, 1908, and 1912.

In 1905, Debs's politics moved further to the left when he helped form the INDUSTRIAL WORKERS OF THE WORLD (IWW), also known as the Wobblies. The IWW was an inclusive organization that sought to create "One Big Union," by welcoming African Americans, immigrants, and women. The IWW promoted a rigorous standard of racial equality, and attempted to educate workers about the ways in which capitalists used race to undermine labor interests. Debs marketed IWW to workers as a radical alternative to the AMERICAN FEDERATION OF LABOR led by SAMUEL GOMPERS.

In 1907, Debs was named associate editor for the progressive magazine *Appeal to Reason*, published in Girard, Kansas. For the next five years he received a salary of $100 per week. The weekly magazine achieved a circulation of several hundred thousand due in part to the powerful writing of Debs.

In 1918, during WORLD WAR I, Debs was convicted of violating the ESPIONAGE ACT OF 1917, after he gave a speech in Canton, Ohio, encouraging listeners to obstruct the draft. The Supreme Court upheld the conviction, notwithstanding Debs's argument that the federal law violated his rights to free speech guaranteed by the FIRST AMENDMENT to the U.S. Constitution (*Debs v. United States*, 39 S.Ct. 252, 249 U.S. 211, 63 L.Ed. 566 [U.S. 1919]). Debs served two years in prison, from 1919 to 1921. While in prison he again ran for president on the Socialist ticket in 1920 and received almost one million votes.

Debs died on October 20, 1926, in Elmhurst, Illinois. He was survived by his wife of 41 years, Kate Metzel. They had no children. In 1962, the Debs Foundation was established in Terre Haute, as a memorial to Eugene Debs, and as an archive and research center for the study of the social sciences, and labor and political history. Each year the foundation bestows the Eugene V. Debs Award on an individual "who has contributed to the advancement of the causes of industrial unionism, social justice, or world peace."

FURTHER READINGS

Debs, Eugene V. 1918. "The Canton, Ohio, Anti-War Speech." Available online at <www.marxists.org/archive/debs/works/1918/canton.htm> (accessed July 3, 2003).

Eugene V. Debs Foundation. Available online at <www.eugenevdebs.com/index.htm> (accessed June 30, 2003).

Ginger, Ray. 1992. *The Bending Cross: A Biography of Eugene Debs*. Kirksville, Mo.: Thomas Jefferson Univ. Press.

Papke, David Ray. 1999. *The Pullman Case: The Clash of Labor and Capital in Industrial America*. Lawrence: Univ. Press of Kansas.

DEBT

A sum of money that is owed or due to be paid because of an express agreement; a specified sum of money that one person is obligated to pay and that another has the legal right to collect or receive.

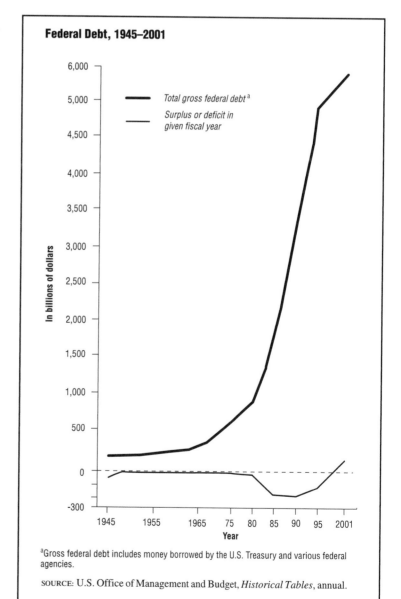

Federal Debt, 1945–2001

In billions of dollars

— Total gross federal debt[a]
— Surplus or deficit in given fiscal year

[a]Gross federal debt includes money borrowed by the U.S. Treasury and various federal agencies.

SOURCE: U.S. Office of Management and Budget, *Historical Tables*, annual.

A fixed and certain obligation to pay money or some other valuable thing or things, either in the present or in the future. In a still more general sense, that which is due from one person to another, whether money, goods, or services. In a broad sense, any duty to respond to another in money, labor, or service; it may even mean a moral or honorary obligation, unenforceable by legal action. Also, sometimes an aggregate of separate debts, or the total sum of the existing claims against a person or company. Thus we speak of the "national debt," the "bonded debt" of a corporation, and so on.

DEBT, ACTION OF

One of the oldest common-law FORMS OF ACTION *available to private litigants seeking to collect what is owed to them because of a harm done to them by another.*

Originally, the action was allowed for any plaintiff who claimed an obligation owed by another person, but the courts gradually began to recognize two forms of action: DETINUE, an action to collect a specific item of property, and a debt for a sum of money. The distinction had become clear in England by the early thirteenth century. In debt, as in detinue, a defendant who lost the case had the option of either paying a sum of money for the judgment or giving back the property that gave rise to the debt. Later in the thirteenth century, courts began to permit REPLEVIN, an action for the return of goods wrongfully taken or withheld, and COVENANT, an action for damages from someone who broke an agreement. Gradually, judges began to demand firm proof of the agreement, and finally they would accept nothing less than a contract made under seal. Later the action in ASSUMPSIT enlarged the rights of a disappointed party to a contract by allowing monetary damages for any breach. This action enjoyed growing popularity and supplanted the action of debt for a time because it permitted the defendant to prove his or her case by swearing in open court and by bringing along eleven neighbors who would proclaim their belief in their neighbor's truthfulness. When this procedure, called the WAGER OF LAW, was abolished during the reign of King William IV (1830–1837), the action of debt again became important as an action to enforce a simple contract.

As long as common-law forms of action were the required modes for PLEADING civil actions, the action of debt continued to be use-ful. Relief was available only for those whose claims fit exactly into its form, however, and there was criticism of its rigidity and technicalities. By the end of the nineteenth century most states had passed laws to replace the old forms of action with CODE PLEADING. Today, the law of CIVIL PROCEDURE recognizes only one form for a lawsuit, the civil action. An individual can still sue to collect what is due on a debt, but no longer is it necessary to draw the complaint in the form of the ancient action of debt.

DEBT POOLERS

Individuals or organizations who receive and apply monthly funds from a person owing money to several creditors and who make arrangements to pay these creditors less than what is actually owed.

Debt poolers, also known as *debt adjusters* or *consolidators,* are helpful to consumers, particularly when they are nonprofit organizations that provide their services free or for a reasonable fee. In other cases, however, their usefulness to consumers is lessened when they charge fees that would make it less costly for consumers to make similar arrangements with creditors on their own.

DEBTOR

One who owes a debt or the performance of an obligation to another, who is called the creditor; one who may be compelled to pay a claim or demand; anyone liable on a claim, whether due or to become due. In BANKRUPTCY *law, a person who files a voluntary petition or person against whom an involuntary petition is filed. A person or municipality concerning which a bankruptcy case has been commenced.*

DECALOGUE SOCIETY OF LAWYERS

Founded in 1934, the Decalogue Society of Lawyers is an association of attorneys of the Jewish faith who seek to advance and improve the law, the legal profession, and the administration of justice; to foster friendly relations among its members, and between its members and other members of the bar, the courts, and the public; to cooperate as lawyers and citizens in worthy movements for the public welfare; to maintain vigilance against public practices that are antisocial or discriminatory; and to cooperate with other bar associations for the attainment of those objectives. Activities include a forum on legal topics of general and Jewish interest, lectures and seminars on recent decisions and legislation, and the presentation of awards. The society provides a placement service for members and maintains a welfare fund. Meetings are held annually in June.

The society has several active committees including those on ARBITRATION, civic affairs, CIVIL RIGHTS, FAMILY LAW, lawyer counseling, LEGAL EDUCATION, legislation, and professional relations.

The society publishes *The Decalogue Journal* (quarterly) and a membership directory (annually).

DECEDENT

An individual who has died. The term literally means "one who is dying," but it is commonly used in the law to denote one who has died, particularly someone who has recently passed away.

A decedent's estate is the real and PERSONAL PROPERTY that an individual owns upon his or her death.

DECEIT

A MISREPRESENTATION *made with the express intention of defrauding someone, which subsequently causes injury to that person.*

In order for a statement to be deceit, it must be untrue, made with knowledge of its falsity, or made in reckless disregard of the truth. The misrepresentation must be such that it causes harm to another individual.

DECENNIAL DIGEST®

One of the titles of the American Digest System that classifies by topic the summaries of court decisions that were reported chronologically in the various units of the National Reporter System.

Each of the more than 400 subject classifications corresponds to a general legal concept—torts, for example—and all cases found under a specific topic discuss similar points of law. The digest contains summaries of cases decided during the period from 1897 to 1905 and for every ten-year period until 1976, and every five years thereafter.

DECISION

A conclusion reached after an evaluation of facts and law.

As a generic term, *decision* refers to both administrative and judicial determinations. It includes final judgments, rulings, and INTERLOCUTORY or provisional orders made by the court pending the outcome of the case. Frequently, a decision is considered the initial step in a rendition by a court of a judgment in an action.

When referring to judicial matters, a decision is not the same as an opinion, although the terms are sometimes used interchangeably. A decision is the pronouncement of the solution of the court or judgment in a case, while an opinion is a statement of the reasons for its determination made by the court.

DECISION ON THE MERITS

An ultimate determination rendered by a court in an action that concludes the status of legal rights contested in a controversy and precludes a later lawsuit on the same CAUSE OF ACTION *by the parties to the original lawsuit.*

A decision on the merits is made by the application of SUBSTANTIVE LAW to the essential facts of the case, not solely upon technical or procedural grounds.

DECLARATION

The first PLEADING *in a lawsuit governed by the rule of* COMMON-LAW PLEADING. *In the law of evidence, a statement or narration made not under oath but simply in the middle of things, as a part of what is happening. Also, a proclamation.*

A declaration is the plaintiff's statement of a claim against the defendant, formally and specifically setting out the facts and circumstances that make up the case. It generally is broken into several sections, which describe the different counts of the CAUSE OF ACTION. The declaration should give the title of the action, the court and place of trial, the basis for the claim, and the relief demanded. The defendant then answers with a plea. Common-law pleading has been abolished in the United States, and modern systems of CODE PLEADING and rules based on federal CIVIL PROCEDURE now provide for a complaint to accomplish the same purpose as did the declaration in former times.

Under some circumstances, statements made out of court by one person may be repeated in court by someone else even though the HEARSAY rule ordinarily forbids secondhand testimony. For example, a DYING DECLARATION

On December 8, 1941, President Franklin Delano Roosevelt signs the Congressional Declaration of War on Japan.
NATIONAL ARCHIVES AND RECORDS ADMINISTRATION

is a statement in which a HOMICIDE victim names his or her killer on his or her deathbed. If the victim had known who had attacked him or her, had abandoned all hope of recovery, and had in fact died of the wounds, a person who heard the dying declaration can repeat it in court at the time the killer is brought to trial. The theory is that a deceased person would not have lied just before dying.

A *declaration against interest* is another type of statement received into evidence even though it is being repeated by someone who heard it out of court. It is any comment that admits something harmful to the rights of the person who made the statement. For example, a driver says to his or her passenger just before the car misses a curve and ends up in a ditch, "I know the brakes are bad, but don't worry." Later when suing to recover compensation for injuries, the passenger can testify that he or she heard the driver make a declaration against his or her interest even though that testimony is hearsay.

Customs law requires all persons entering the United States to provide officers with a list of merchandise they are bringing into the country. This list is also called a declaration.

Real property laws in various states require the filing of statements to disclose plans that establish certain rights in particular buildings or parcels. For example, a homeowners' association formed by neighbors to maintain a recreation center owned by all of them together may file a declaration of covenants. A builder may be required to file a declaration of condominium before beginning to sell new units.

As a preliminary step before becoming naturalized U.S. citizens, ALIENS must file a declaration of intention which states that they are honestly trying to become citizens and that they formally renounce all allegiance to any other nation where they were ever citizens or subjects.

The Declaration of Independence was a formal announcement on July 4, 1776, by which the Continental Congress of the United States of America proclaimed the independence of the people of the colonies from the rule of Great Britain. It explained the reasons for their assertion of political autonomy and announced to the world that the United States was a free and independent nation.

INTERNATIONAL LAW recognized that nations may formally and publicly proclaim a condition of armed conflict by a declaration of war, which in effect forbids all persons to aid or assist the enemy. In the United States, the Congress has the authority to declare war, and a declaration fixes a beginning date for the war.

A *declaration of a dividend* is an act of a corporation in setting aside a portion of net or surplus income for proportional distribution as a dividend to those who hold shares of stock.

DECLARATION OF INDEPENDENCE

Since its creation in 1776, the Declaration of Independence has been considered the single most important expression of the ideals of U.S. democracy. As a statement of the fundamental principles of the United States, the Declaration is an enduring reminder of the country's commitment to popular government and equal rights for all.

The Declaration of Independence is a product of the early days of the Revolutionary War. On July 2, 1776, the Second Continental Congress—the legislature of the American colonies—voted for independence from Great Britain. It then appointed a committee of five—JOHN ADAMS, BENJAMIN FRANKLIN, THOMAS JEFFERSON, ROGER SHERMAN, and Robert R. Livingston—to draft a formal statement of independence designed to influence public opinion at home and abroad. Because of his reputation as an eloquent and forceful writer, Jefferson was assigned the task of creating the document, and the final product is almost entirely his own work. The Congress did not approve all of Jefferson's original draft, however, rejecting most notably his denunciation of the slave trade. Delegates from South Carolina and Georgia were not yet ready to extend the notion of inalienable rights to African Americans.

On July 4, 1776, the day of birth for the new country, the CONTINENTAL CONGRESS approved the Declaration of Independence on behalf of the people living in the American colonies. The Declaration served a number of purposes for the newly formed United States. With regard to the power politics of the day, it functioned as a propaganda statement intended to build support for American independence abroad, particularly in France, from which the Americans hoped to have support in their struggle for independence. Similarly, it served as a clear message of intention to the British. Even more important for the later Republic of the United States, it functioned as a statement of governmental ideals.

In keeping with its immediate diplomatic purposes, most of the Declaration consists of a list of 30 grievances against acts of the British monarch George III. Many of these were traditional and legitimate grievances under British CONSTITUTIONAL LAW. The Declaration firmly announces that British actions had established "an absolute Tyranny over these States." Britain's acts of despotism, according to the Declaration's list, included taxation of Americans without representation in Parliament; imposition of standing armies on American communities; establishment of the military above the civil power; obstruction of the right to trial by jury; interference with the operation of colonial legislatures; and cutting off of trade with the rest of the world. The Declaration ends with the decisive resolution that "these United Colonies are, and of Right ought to be Free and Independent States; that they are Absolved from all Allegiance to the British Crown, and that all political connection between them and the State of Great Britain, is and ought to be totally dissolved."

The first sentences of the document and their statement of political ideals have remained the Declaration's most memorable and influential section. Among these sentences are the following:

> We hold these truths to be self-evident, that all men are created equal, that they are endowed by their Creator with certain inalienable Rights, that among these are Life, Liberty and the pursuit of Happiness.—That

to secure these rights, Governments are instituted among Men, deriving their just powers from the consent of the governed,—That whenever any Form of Government becomes destructive of these ends, it is the Right of the People to alter or to abolish it, and to institute new Government.

Ever since their creation, these ideas have guided the development of U.S. government, including the creation of the U.S. Constitution in 1787. The concepts of equal and inalienable rights for all, limited government, popular consent, and freedom to rebel have had a lasting effect on U.S. law and politics.

Scholars have long debated the relative importance of the different sources Jefferson used for his ideas in the Declaration. Most agree that the natural rights philosophy of English philosopher JOHN LOCKE greatly influenced Jefferson's composition of the Declaration. In par-

The Declaration of Independence was signed July 4, 1776. This work, assembled by John Binns in 1819, surrounds a facsimile of the document's text with portraits of George Washington, John Hancock, and Thomas Jefferson, along with the seals of the 13 original states.

LIBRARY OF CONGRESS

ticular, Locke advanced the ideas that a just government derives its legitimacy and power from the consent of the governed, that people possess inalienable rights that no legitimate government may take away, and that the people have the right and duty to overthrow a government that violates their rights. Jefferson also paralleled Locke in his identification of three major rights—the rights to "Life, Liberty and the pursuit of Happiness"—though the last of his three is a change from Locke's right to "property."

Jefferson himself minimized the Declaration's contribution to political philosophy. In a letter that he wrote in 1825, 50 years after the Declaration was signed, he described the document as "an appeal to the tribunal of the world." Its object, he wrote, was

> [n]ot to find out new principles or new arguments, never before thought of, not merely to say things which had never been said before; but to place before mankind the common sense of the subject, in terms so plain and firm as to command their assent, and to justify ourselves in the independent stand we are compelled to take. Neither aiming at originality of principle or sentiment, nor yet copied from any particular and previous writing, it was intended to be an expression of the American mind, and to give to that expression the proper tone and spirit called for by the occasion.

Although the Declaration of Independence stands with the Constitution as a founding document of the United States of America, its position in U.S. law is much less certain than that of the Constitution. The Declaration has been recognized as the founding act of law establishing the United States as a sovereign and independent nation, and Congress has placed it at the beginning of the U.S. Code, under the heading "The Organic Laws of the United States of America." The Supreme Court, however, has generally not considered it a part of the organic law of the country. For example, although the Declaration mentions a right to rebellion, this right, particularly with regard to violent rebellion, has not been recognized by the Supreme Court and other branches of the federal government. The most notable failure to uphold this right occurred when the Union put down the rebellion by the Southern Confederacy in the Civil War.

Despite its secondary authority, many later reform movements have quoted the Declaration in support of their cause, including movements for universal suffrage, ABOLITION of SLAVERY, women's rights, and CIVIL RIGHTS for African Americans. Many have argued that this document influenced the passage and wording of such important developments in U.S. law and government as the Thirteenth and Fourteenth Amendments, which banned slavery and sought to make African Americans equal citizens. In this way, the Declaration of Independence remains the most outstanding example of the spirit, as opposed to the letter, of U.S. law.

FURTHER READINGS

Cunningham, Noble E., Jr. 1987. *In Pursuit of Reason: The Life of Thomas Jefferson.* Baton Rouge, La.: Louisiana State Univ. Press.

Gerber, Scott Douglas, ed. 2002. *The Declaration of Independence: Origins and Impact.* Washington, D.C.: CQ Press.

Levy, Michael B. 1982. *Political Thought in America.* Homewood, Ill.: Dorsey Press.

Machan, Tibor R., ed. 2001. *Individual Rights Reconsidered: Are the Truths of the U.S. Declaration of Independence Lasting?* Stanford, Calif.: Hoover Institution.

Murray, Charles. 1988. *In Pursuit of Happiness and Good Government.* New York: Simon & Schuster.

CROSS-REFERENCES

"Declaration of Independence" (Appendix, Primary Document); Fourteenth Amendment; Thirteenth Amendment.

DECLARATION OF TRUST

An assertion by a property owner that he or she holds the property or estate for the benefit of another person, or for particular designated objectives.

The term also signifies the deed or other instrument that contains the statement—which may be either written or oral, depending upon the applicable state law.

DECLARATORY JUDGMENT

Statutory remedy for the determination of a JUSTICIABLE controversy where the plaintiff is in doubt as to his or her legal rights. A binding adjudication of the rights and status of litigants even though no consequential relief is awarded.

Individuals may seek a declaratory judgment after a legal controversy has arisen but before any damages have occurred or any laws have been violated. A declaratory judgment differs from other judicial rulings in that it does not require that any action be taken. Instead, the judge, after analyzing the controversy, simply issues an opinion declaring the rights of each of the parties involved. A declaratory judgment may only be granted in justiciable controversies—that is, in actual, rather than hypothetical, controversies that fall within a court's jurisdiction.

A declaratory judgment, sometimes called declaratory relief, is conclusive and legally binding as to the present and future rights of the parties involved. The parties involved in a declaratory judgment may not later seek another court resolution of the same legal issue unless they appeal the judgment.

Declaratory judgments are often sought in situations involving contracts, deeds, leases, and wills. An insurance company, for example, might seek a declaratory judgment as to whether a policy applies to a certain person or event. Declaratory judgments also commonly involve individuals or parties who seek to determine their rights under specific regulatory or criminal laws.

Declaratory judgments are considered a type of preventive justice because, by informing parties of their rights, they help them to avoid violating specific laws or the terms of a contract. In 1934 Congress enacted the Declaratory Judgment Act (28 U.S.C.A. § 2201 et seq.), which allows for declaratory judgments concerning issues of federal law. At the state level, the National Conference of Commissioners on Uniform State Laws passed the Uniform Declaratory Judgments Act (12 U.L.A. 109) in 1922. Between 1922 and 1993, this act was adopted in forty-one states, the Virgin Islands, and the Commonwealth of Puerto Rico. Most other states have varying laws that provide for declaratory judgments. Most declaratory judgment laws grant judges discretion to decide whether or not to issue a declaratory judgment.

FURTHER READINGS

Howard, Davis J. 1994. "Declaratory Judgment Coverage Actions." *Ohio Northern University Law Review* 13.

DECREE

A judgment of a court that announces the legal consequences of the facts found in a case and orders that the court's decision be carried out. A decree in EQUITY *is a sentence or order of the court, pronounced on hearing and understanding all the points in issue, and determining the rights of all the parties to the suit, according to equity and good conscience. It is a declaration of the court announcing the legal consequences of the facts found. With the procedural merger of law and equity in the federal and most state courts under*
the Rules of Civil Procedure, the term *judgment has generally replaced* decree.

A *divorce decree* sets out the conclusions of the court relating to the facts asserted as grounds for the DIVORCE, and it subsequently dissolves the marriage.

Decree is sometimes used interchangeably with determination and order.

DEDICATION

In COPYRIGHT *law the first publication of a work that does not comply with the requirements relating to copyright notice and which therefore permits anyone to legally republish it. The gift of land—or an* EASEMENT*, that is, a right of use of the property of another—by the owner to the government for public use, and accepted for such use by or on behalf of the public.*

The owner of the land does not retain any rights that are inconsistent with the complete exercise and enjoyment of the public uses to which the property has been committed.

A dedication is express where the gift is formally declared, but it can also be implied by operation of law from the owner's actions and the facts and circumstances of the case.

A dedication may be made under COMMON LAW or pursuant to the requirements of statute. A common-law dedication is not subject to the STATUTE OF FRAUDS, an ENGLISH LAW adopted in the United States, which provides that certain agreements must be in writing. Therefore, a common-law dedication does not have to be expressed in writing to be effective; it is based on ESTOPPEL. If the landowner indicates that his or her land is to be used for a public purpose and public use then occurs, the landowner is estopped, or prevented, from refuting the existence of the public right.

An *express common-law dedication* is one in which the intent is explicitly indicated—such as by ordinary deeds or recorded plats, which are maps showing the locations and boundaries of individual land parcels subdivided into lots—but the execution of the dedication has not been in accordance with law or certification of it has been defective so as not to constitute a statutory dedication.

A *statutory dedication* is necessarily express, since it is executed pursuant to, and in conformity with, the provisions of a statute regulating the subject. It cannot be implied from the circumstances of the case.

A dedication can result from the contrary exclusive use of land by the public pursuant to a claim of right with the knowledge, actual or attributed, and the acceptance of the owner. This method is known as *dedication by adverse user.*

DEDUCTIBLE

That which may be taken away or subtracted. In taxation, an item that may be subtracted from gross income or adjusted gross income in determining taxable income (e.g., interest expenses, charitable contributions, certain taxes).

The portion of an insured loss to be borne by the insured before he or she is entitled to recovery from the insurer.

Automotive insurance policies frequently include a deductible, such as $250 or $500, which the insured must pay before receiving reimbursement under the policy. Usually, the insured motorist chooses among several levels of deductible, with the policy payment being somewhat lower when the insured chooses a higher deductible.

Many types of insurance policies include a deductible amount.

DEDUCTION

That which is deducted; the part taken away; abatement; as in deductions from gross income in arriving at net income for tax purposes.

In CIVIL LAW, a portion or thing that an heir has a right to take from the mass of the succession before any partition takes place.

A contribution to a charity can be used as a deduction to reduce income for INCOME TAX purposes if the taxpayer meets the requirements imposed by law.

DEED

A written instrument, which has been signed and delivered, by which one individual, the grantor, conveys title to real property to another individual, the grantee; a conveyance of land, tenements, or hereditaments, from one individual to another.

At COMMON LAW, a deed was an instrument under seal that contained a COVENANT or contract delivered by the individual who was to be bound by it to the party to whom it was granted. It is no longer required that such an instrument be sealed.

Transfer of Land

Land can only be transferred from one individual to another in the legally prescribed manner. Historically speaking, a written deed is the instrument used to convey ownership of real property.

A deed is labeled an instrument of conveyance. Under Spanish law, which was in effect at an early date in areas of the western United States, a written deed was not necessary to convey title to land. A verbal grant was sufficient to complete the transaction, provided that it was accompanied by a transfer of possession. Verbal grants of land in Texas have, therefore, been given recognition in U.S. courts.

A deed must describe with reasonable certainty the land that is being conveyed. The conveyance must include operative words of grant; however, technical terms do not need to be used. The grantor must be adequately identified by the conveyance, although it is not required that the grantor's name be specifically mentioned. State laws sometimes require that the deed indicate the residence of the grantor by town, city, county, and state.

In order for title to property to pass, a deed must specify the grantee with sufficient certainty to distinguish that individual from the rest of the world. Some statutes mandate that the deed list the grantee's residence by town, city, county, and state.

Execution

In order for a deed to be properly executed, certain acts must be performed to create a valid conveyance. Ordinarily, an essential element of execution is the signature of the grantor in the proper place. It is not necessary, however, that the grantee sign the deed in order for it to take effect as a conveyance. Generally state statutes require that the deed be signed in the presence of witnesses, attesting to the grantor's request.

Delivery

Proper delivery of a deed from the grantor to the grantee is an essential element of its effectiveness. In addition, the grantor must make some statement or perform some act that implies his or her intention to transfer title. It is insufficient for a grantor to have the mere intention to transfer title, in the absence of further conduct that consummates the purpose.

There is no particular prescribed act, method, or ceremony required for delivery, and it is unnecessary that express words be employed or used in a specified manner. The deed need not be physically delivered to the grantee. It is sufficient to mail it to the grantee. Delivery of the deed by the attorney who has written the instrument for the grantor is also adequate. Unless otherwise provided by statute, a deed becomes effective upon its delivery date. The mere fact that the grantee has physical possession of the deed does not constitute delivery unless it was so intended by the grantor.

Acceptance

A deed must be accepted by the grantee in order for proper transfer of title to land to be accomplished. There are no fixed principles regarding what acts are sufficient to effect acceptance, since the issue is largely dependent upon the party's intent.

Acceptance of a deed need not be made by express words or in writing, absent a contrary statutory provision. A deed is ordinarily accepted when the grantee retains it or obtains a mortgage on the property at issue.

Recording

Legal policy mandates that a deed to real property be a matter of public record; therefore, subsequent to delivery and acceptance, a deed must be properly recorded.

The recording process begins when the deed is presented to the clerk's or recorder's office in the county where the property is located. The entire instrument is duplicated, ordinarily by photocopying. The copy is inserted into the current book of official records, which consists exclusively of copies of documents that are maintained and labeled in numerical order.

A properly recorded deed provides constructive notice of its contents, which means that all parties concerned are considered to have notice of the deed whether or not they actually saw it. A majority of jurisdictions place the burden upon home buyers to investigate any suspicious facts concerning the property of which they have actual or constructive notice. If, for example, there is a reference to the property for sale in the records to other deeds, the purchaser might be required to determine whether such instruments give rights in the property to other individuals.

A map referred to in a recorded deed that describes the property conveyed becomes part of the document for identification purposes.

The original copy of a deed is returned to the owner once it has been duplicated, recorded, and filed in the office of the recorder.

A records or clerk's office maintains a set of indexes, in addition to official records, in which information about each deed is recorded, so that upon a search for a document such information can be disclosed. A majority of states have a grantor-grantee index, a set of volumes containing a reference to all documents recorded alphabetically according to the grantor's name. The index lists the name of the grantor first, followed by the name of the grantee, then ordinarily a description of the instrument and sometimes of the property, and ultimately a reference to the volume and page number in the official record where the document has been copied. A grantee-grantor index has the identical information, but it is listed alphabetically according to the grantees' names. A *tract index* arranges all of the entries based upon the location of the property.

Indexes are frequently classified according to time periods. Therefore separate sets of indexes covering various periods of time may be available.

A significant problem can result in the event that a deed cannot be located through the indexes. This situation could result from a mistake in the recording process, such as indexing the deed under the wrong name. In a number of states, the courts will hold that such a deed was never recorded inasmuch as it was not indexed in such a manner as to provide notice to someone properly conducting a check on the title. In these jurisdictions, all grantees have the duty to return to the recorder's office after filing to protect themselves by checking on the indexing of their deeds. A purchaser who lives in a state with such laws should protect himself or herself either by consulting an attorney or returning to the recorder's office to ascertain that the deed is properly recorded and indexed. Other state statutes provide that a document is considered recorded when it is deposited in the proper office even if it is improperly recorded such that it cannot be located. In these states, there are no practical steps for subsequent buyers to take to circumvent this problem.

Types of Deeds

Three basic types of deeds commonly used are the grant deed, the quitclaim deed, and the warranty deed.

Grant Deed By use of a grant deed, the conveyor says, "I grant (convey, bargain, or sell) the property to you." In a number of jurisdictions a representation that the conveyor actually owns

A sample grant deed.

GRANT DEED

RECORDING REQUESTED BY

_____

AND WHEN RECORDED MAIL THIS DEED AND,
UNLESS OTHERWISE SHOWN BELOW, MAIL
TAX STATEMENT TO:

NAME_____

STREET
ADDRESS_____

CITY, STATE &
ZIP CODE _____

TITLE ORDER NO. _____ ESCROW NO. _____

———— SPACE ABOVE THIS LINE FOR RECORDER'S USE ————

GRANT DEED

DOCUMENTARY TRANSFER TAX $ _____
☐ computed on full value of property conveyed, or
☐ computed on full value less liens and
   encumbrances remaining at time of sale.

_____
Signature of Declarant or Agent Determining Tax   Firm Name

FOR VALUABLE CONSIDERATION, receipt of which is acknowledged, I (We), _____

_____

grant to _____
(NAME OF GRANTOR(S))

all that real property situated in the City of _____ (or in an unincorporated area of)
(NAME OF GRANTEE(S))

_____County, _____ described as follows (insert legal description):
(NAME OF COUNTY)   (STATE)

_____

_____

_____

_____

_____

_____

_____

Accessor's parcel No. _____

Executed on _____ _____, at _____
(CITY AND STATE)

_____

STATE OF _____

COUNTY OF _____

On _____ before me, _____
(NAME/TITLE i.e. "JANE DOE, NOTARY PUBLIC")

personally appeared _____ personally known to me
or proved to me on the basis of satisfactory evidence to be the person(s) whose name(s) is/are subscribed to
the within instrument and acknowledged to me that he/she/they executed the same in his/her/their authorized
capacity(ies), and that by his/her/their signature(s) on the instrument the person(s), or the entity upon behalf
of which the person(s) acted, executed the instrument.

WITNESS my hand and official seal.

_____   (SEAL)
(SIGNATURE OF NOTARY)

MAIL TAX
STATEMENTS TO: _____

_____

RIGHT THUMBPRINT (Optional)

CAPACITY CLAIMED BY SIGNER(S)
☐ INDIVIDUAL(S)
☐ CORPORATE _____
   OFFICER(S) _____
      (TITLES)
☐ PARTNER(S) ☐ LIMITED
      ☐ GENERAL
☐ ATTORNEY IN FACT
☐ TRUSTEE(S)
☐ GUARDIAN/CONSERVATOR
☐ OTHER _____

SIGNER IS REPRESENTING:
Name of Person(s) or Executive(s)

_____

_____

SBR98

the property he or she is transferring is implied from such language.

Quitclaim Deed A *quitclaim deed* is intended to pass any title, interest, or claim that the grantor has in the property but makes no representation that such title is valid. In effect, this type of deed states that if the grantor actually owns the premises described or any interest therein, it is to be conveyed to the grantee. For this type of deed, some state statutes require a WARRANTY by the grantor, stating that neither the grantor nor anyone associated with him or her has encumbered the property, and that the grantor will defend the title against any defects that arise under and through him or her, but as to no others.

Warranty Deed In a *warranty deed* the grantor inserts covenants for title, promising that such title is good and clear. The customary covenants of title include warranty of seisin, QUIET ENJOYMENT, the right to convey, freedom from encumbrances, and a defense of the title as to all claims.

Validity

If a deed is to have any validity, it must be made voluntarily. The test of the capacity of an individual to execute a valid deed is based upon that person's ability to comprehend the consequences of his or her act. If a deed is not made through the conscious act of the grantor, it can be set aside in court. Relevant factors for the determination of whether a particular individual is capable of executing a valid deed are his or her age, and mental and physical condition. Extreme physical weakness resulting from old age or disease is a proper element for consideration in establishing capacity. Mental capacity, however, is the most important factor. If an individual is deemed to be mentally capable of disposing of his or her own property, the deed is ordinarily valid and would withstand objections made to it.

If FRAUD is committed by either the grantor or grantee, a deed can be declared invalid. For example, a deed that is a forgery is completely ineffective.

The exercise of UNDUE INFLUENCE also ordinarily serves to invalidate a deed. The test of whether such influence has been exerted turns upon the issue of whether the grantor executed the deed voluntarily. Undue influence is wrongful and serves to confuse the judgment and to control the will of the grantor. Ordinary influence is insufficient to invalidate a deed. Deeds between parties who share a confidential relationship are frequently examined by the courts for undue influence. For example, the courts might place a deed under close scrutiny if the grantor's attorney or physician is named grantee. In addition, if the grantor is a drunkard or uses DRUGS AND NARCOTICS to excess, such would be circumstances for consideration when a court determines whether undue influence was exercised upon the grantor.

Defects

In a number of jurisdictions, an individual selling a house is required to disclose any material defect known to him or her but not to the purchaser. A failure to disclose gives the buyer the right to cancel the deed, sue for damages, and in some instances, recover for personal injuries incurred as a result of such defect.

FURTHER READINGS

Dasso, Jerome J., et al. 1995. *Real Estate.* 12th ed. Englewood Cliffs, N.J.: Prentice-Hall.

Karvel, George, and Maurice Unger. 1991. *Real Estate: Principles and Practices.* 9th ed. Cincinnati: South-Western.

CROSS-REFERENCES

Quitclaim Deed; Records; Recording of Land Titles.

DEED OF TRUST

A document that embodies the agreement between a lender and a borrower to transfer an interest in the borrower's land to a neutral third party, a trustee, to secure the payment of a debt by the borrower.

A deed of trust, also called a trust deed or a Potomac Mortgage, is used in some states in place of a mortgage, a transfer of interest in land by a mortgagor-borrower to a mortgagee-lender to secure the payment of the borrower's debt. Although a deed of trust serves the same purpose as a type of security, it differs from a mortgage. A deed of trust is an arrangement among three parties: the borrower, the lender, and an impartial trustee. In exchange for a loan of money from the lender, the borrower places legal title to real property in the hands of the trustee who holds it for the benefit of the lender, named in the deed as the beneficiary. The borrower retains equitable title to, and possession of, the property.

The terms of the deed provide that the transfer of legal title to the trustee will be void on the timely payment of the debt. If the borrower defaults in the payment of the debt, the trustee is empowered by the deed to sell the property

A sample deed of trust.

DEED OF TRUST

GENERAL FORM

Deed of trust made on _____ (*date*), between _____, of
_____ (*address*), referred to as trustor,
_____, of
_____ (*address*),
referred to as trustee, and _____, of
_____ (*address*), referred to as beneficiary.

Trustor, in consideration of the indebtedness recited below, irrevocably grants, bargains, sells, assigns, and conveys to trustee in trust, with power of sale, the property in _____
(*location and address*) described as _____
_____ (*description of property*), together with all the tenements, hereditaments, and appurtenances now or hereafter belonging or in any wise appertaining. To have and to hold the same, with the appurtenances, unto trustee.

For the purpose of securing performance of each agreement of trustor and of securing payment of the sum of _____ (*amount*) ($_____) with interest thereon according to the terms of a _____ (*Note or Bond*), dated _____ (*month & day*), _____ (*year*) payable to beneficiary or order and made or executed by trustor, the final payment of principal and interest, if not paid sooner, to be due and payable on _____ (*month & day*), _____ (*year*) at the office of _____, at _____ (*address*), or at such other place as beneficiary may designate in writing delivered or mailed to trustor. The terms of the _____ (*Note or Bond*) are incorporated by reference.

Trustor covenants and agrees as follows:

1. PAYMENT OF INDEBTEDNESS

1.1 Trustor shall pay the indebtedness, as provided above. Trustor reserves the right and privilege to prepay at any time, without premium or fee, the entire indebtedness or any part of it not less than the amount of one installment, or _____ (*amount*) ($_____), whichever is less. Any prepayment made on other than an installment due date will not be credited until the next following installment due date.

2. OWNERSHIP OF PROPERTY

2.1 Trustor is lawfully seized (in possession) of _____
_____ (*description of estate*) and, except as otherwise stated, the premises are free from any encumbrances. Trustor hereby warrants the usual covenants to the same extent as a statutory _____ (*warranty*) deed under the laws of _____ (*state*), and all covenants herein made, and trustor will defend against any breach of any such covenant.

3. CONTINUED EFFECTIVENESS

3.1 The provisions of this instrument shall remain in full force and effect during any postponement or extension of the time of payment of the indebtedness or any part of it.

4. TAXES AND ASSESSMENTS

4.1 Trustor shall pay all taxes, assessments, water rates, and other governmental or municipal charges, fines, or impositions; and, in default thereof, beneficiary may pay the same.

5. WASTE; REPAIR OR REMOVAL OF STRUCTURES

5.1 Trustor shall not commit waste or authorize the repair or the removal of any structures on the premises, and shall not do or permit any act that may lawfully result in the creation of a lien or claim on the land or the improvements of equal or prior rank to the claim of this trust deed without prior written consent of beneficiary; but shall maintain the property in as good condition as at present, reasonable wear and tear excepted. On any failure to so maintain, beneficiary, at its option, may cause reasonable maintenance work to be performed at trustor's cost.

6. INSURANCE

6.1 Trustor shall maintain continuously hazard insurance of such type or types and amounts as beneficiary may from time to time require on the improvements now or hereafter on the premises, and shall pay promptly when due any premiums for such insurance. All insurance

[continued]

DEED OF TRUST

shall be carried with companies approved by beneficiary, and the policies and renewals shall be held by beneficiary and provide that loss be payable solely and in form acceptable to beneficiary. In event of loss, trustor shall give immediate notice by mail to beneficiary, who may make proof of loss if not made promptly by trustor, and each insurance company concerned is hereby authorized and directed to make payment of the loss directly to beneficiary, rather than to trustor and beneficiary jointly. The insurance proceeds, or any part of them, may be applied by beneficiary, at its option, either to the reduction of the indebtedness hereby secured or to the restoration or repair of the property damaged. In the event of a conveyance to beneficiary, or other transfer of title to the premises in extinguishment of the indebtedness secured hereby, all right, title, and interest of trustor in and to any insurance policies then in force shall pass to the purchaser or grantee.

7. BENEFICIARY PAYMENT IN EVENT OF DEFAULT

7.1 If trustor defaults in any of the covenants or agreements contained in this trust deed, or in the _____ (*Note or Bond*) secured by it, then beneficiary, at its option, may perform the same. All expenditures made by beneficiary in so doing shall draw interest at the rate provided for in the principal indebtedness, and shall be repayable by trustor to beneficiary, and, together with interest and costs accruing thereon, shall be secured by this trust deed.

8. SUPPLEMENTAL NOTES

8.1 On beneficiary's request, trustor shall execute and deliver a supplemental note or notes for the sum or sums advanced by beneficiary for the alteration, modernization, improvement, maintenance, or repair of such premises, for taxes or assessments against the same, and for any other purpose authorized under this trust deed. The note or notes shall be secured by this trust deed with equal priority and as fully as if the advance evidenced thereby were included in the _____ (*Note or Bond*) first described above. The supplemental note or notes shall bear interest at the rate provided for in the principal indebtedness and shall be payable in approximately equal _____ (*monthly*) payments for such period as may be agreed on by trustor and beneficiary. On the failure to agree on the maturity, the whole of the sum or sums so advanced shall be due and payable _____ days after beneficiary's demand. In no event, shall the maturity extend beyond the ultimate maturity of the _____ (*Note or Bond*) first described above.

9. RIGHT OF BENEFICIARY TO APPEAR

9.1 Beneficiary may appear in and defend any action or proceeding purporting to affect the security of this trust deed, and trustor shall pay all costs and expenses, including the costs of evidence of title and reasonable attorney fees, in any such action or proceeding in which beneficiary may appear.

10. WAIVER OF NOTICE

10.1 Trustor waives notice of the exercise of any option granted to beneficiary in this trust deed or in such _____ (*Note or Bond*).

11. CONDEMNATION

11.1 Any award of compensation or damages in connection with any condemnation for public use of or injury to the premises or any part of them is hereby assigned and shall be paid to beneficiary, who may apply or release such moneys received in the same manner and with the same effect as provided above for the disposition of fire or other insurance proceeds.

12. NONWAIVER OF RIGHTS

12.1 Beneficiary's accepting payment of any sum secured by this trust deed after its due date shall not constitute a waiver of its right either to require prompt payment when due of all other sums so secured or to declare default for failure so to pay.

13. RIGHTS OF TRUSTEE

13.1 At any time or from time to time, without liability therefor and without notice, on beneficiary's written request and presentation of this trust deed and such _____ (*Note or Bond*) for Endorsement, and without affecting the personal liability of any person for payment of the indebtedness secured by this trust deed, trustee may: reconvey all or any part of the premises; consent to the making of any map or plat thereof; join in granting any easement thereon; or join in any extension agreement or any agreement subordinating this trust deed to subsequent liens or charges.

14. RECONVEYANCE

14.1 On beneficiary's written request stating that all sums secured by this trust deed have been paid, and on surrender of this trust deed and such _____ (*Note or Bond*) to trustee for cancellation and retention, and on payment of trustee's fees, trustee shall reconvey, without warranty, the property then held under this trust deed. The recitals in any reconveyance accepted under this trust deed of any matters or facts shall be conclusive proof of their truthfulness. The grantee in such reconveyance may be described as "the person or persons legally entitled thereto."

15. RENTS, ISSUES, AND PROFITS

15.1 As additional security, trustor hereby gives to and confers on beneficiary the right, power, and authority during the continuance of the interests created by this trust deed to collect the rents, issues, and profits of the premises, reserving to trustor the right, prior to any

[continued]

A sample deed of trust (continued).

DEED OF TRUST

default by trustor in payment of any indebtedness secured by this trust deed or in the performance of any agreement under this trust deed, to collect and retain such rents, issues, and profits as they become due and payable. On any such default, beneficiary may at any time without notice, either in person, by agent, or by a court-appointed receiver, and without regard to the adequacy of any security for the indebtedness secured by this trust deed, enter on and take possession of the premises or any part of them, in its own name sue for or otherwise collect such rents, issues, and profits, including those past due and unpaid, and apply the same, less costs and expenses of operation and collection, including reasonable attorney fees, on any indebtedness secured by this trust deed, and in such order as beneficiary may determine. The entering on and taking possession of the premises, the collection of the rents, issues, and profits, and the application thereof as stated above shall not cure or waive any default or notice of default under this trust deed or invalidate any act done pursuant to such notice.

16. DEFAULT; BANKRUPTCY

16.1 On default by trustor in payment of any indebtedness secured by this trust deed, or in performance of any agreement herein contained, or if trustor is adjudicated bankrupt or made defendant in a bankruptcy or receivership proceeding, all sums secured by this trust deed shall, at beneficiary's option, immediately become due and payable. In the event of default, beneficiary shall execute or cause trustee to execute a written notice of such default and of beneficiary's election to cause the above-described property to be sold to satisfy the obligation hereof, and shall cause such notice to be recorded as then required by law.

16.2 On notice of sale as then required by law and elapse of the then-required time period after recordation of notice of default, trustee, without demand on trustor, shall sell the property at the time and place of sale fixed by it in the notice of sale, either as a whole or in separate parcels and in such order as it may determine, at public auction to the highest and best bidder for cash, payable at the time of sale. Trustee may postpone the sale of all or any part of the property by public announcement at the time and place of sale, and from time to time thereafter may postpone the sale by public announcement at the time fixed by the preceding postponement. Trustee shall deliver to the purchaser its deed conveying the property so sold, but without any covenant or warranty, express or implied. The recitals in the deed of any matters or facts shall be conclusive proof of the truthfulness thereof. Any person, including trustor, trustee, or beneficiary, as defined under this trust deed, may purchase at such sale.

16.3 After deducting all costs, fees, and expenses of trustee and of this trust, including the cost of evidence of title and reasonable counsel fees in connection with the sale, trustee shall apply the proceeds of the sale to the payment of all sums expended under the trust terms, not then repaid with accrued interest at the rate provided on the principal debt, all other sums then secured by this trust deed, and the remainder, if any, to the person or persons legally entitled to receive them.

17. APPLICATION OF TRUST DEED

17.1 This trust deed applies to, inures to the benefit of, and binds all parties to this agreement, their heirs, legatees, devisees, administrators, executors, successors, and assigns. The term "beneficiary" shall mean the holder and owner, including pledgee, of the

_____ (*Note or Bond*) secured by this trust deed, whether or not named as a beneficiary herein. Whenever the context of this trust deed so requires, the masculine gender includes the feminine and/or neuter, and the singular number includes the plural.

18. ACCEPTANCE OF TRUST

18.1 Trustee accepts this trust when this trust deed, duly executed and acknowledged, is made a public record as provided by law. Trustee is not obligated to notify any party to this trust deed of any pending sale under any other trust deed or of any action or proceeding in which trustor, beneficiary, or trustee shall be a party, unless brought by trustee.

19. SUCCESSOR TRUSTEE

19.1 Beneficiary may, from time to time, as provided by statute, appoint another trustee in place of trustee herein named, and on such appointment, trustee herein named shall be discharged and the trustee so appointed shall be substituted as trustee with the same effect as if originally named trustee.

20. MULTIPLE TRUSTEES

20.1 If two or more persons are designated as trustee, all powers granted to trustee may be exercised by any of such persons, if the other person or persons are unable, for any reason, to act; and any recital of such inability in any instrument executed by any of such persons shall be conclusive against trustor, or trustor's heirs and assigns.

_____ (If appropriate, add: _____, the _____ (*wife or husband*) of trustor, for the above-stated consideration, hereby relinquishes _____ (*her or his*) right of _____ (*dower or curtesy*) _____ (*and homestead*) in and to the above-described premises.)

20.2 The undersigned trustor requests that a copy of any notice of default and of any notice of sale under this trust deed be mailed to trustor's address set forth above.

In witness whereof, trustor has executed this trust deed the day and year first written above.

_____   _____
Signature   Date

_____   _____
Signature   Date

and pay the lender the proceeds to satisfy the debt. Any surplus will be returned to the borrower.

The right of the trustee to sell the premises is called foreclosure by power of sale. It differs in several respects from the power of a mortgagee to sell mortgaged property upon default, which is called a judicial foreclosure. A foreclosure by power of sale is neither supervised nor confirmed by a court, unlike a judicial foreclosure. While the rights received by a purchaser at a foreclosure by power of sale are the same as those obtained at a judicial foreclosure, there is a practical difference. Since the sale has not been judicially approved, there is a greater possibility of litigation over title, thereby making title to the purchased premises less secure than one purchased at a judicial foreclosure. In addition, the lender may purchase the property for sale under the provisions of a deed of trust, since the neutral trustee conducts the sale. This is not the case in a foreclosure, unless contract or statute provides otherwise, since the mortgagee must act impartially in selling the property to satisfy the debt. Some mortgages may, however, provide for foreclosure by power of sale.

The procedure for a foreclosure by power of sale is regulated by statute, a characteristic shared by a judicial foreclosure. All interested parties must be given notice of the sale, which must be published in local newspapers, usually in the public notice columns, for a certain period of time as required by statute. The sale is usually open to the public to ensure that the property will be sold at its fair market value.

DEEM

To hold; consider; adjudge; believe; condemn; determine; treat as if; construe.

To deem is to consider something as having certain characteristics. If an act is deemed a crime by law, then it is held to be a crime. If someone is deemed liable for damages, then he or she will have to pay them.

DEFALCATION

The misappropriation or EMBEZZLEMENT of money.

Defalcation implies that funds have in some way been mishandled, particularly where an officer or agent has breached his or her fiduciary duty. It is commonly applied to public officers who fail to account for money received by them in their official capacity, or to officers of corporations who misappropriate company funds for their own private use.

Colloquially, the term is used to mean any type of bad faith, deceit, misconduct, or dishonesty.

DEFAMATION

Any intentional false communication, either written or spoken, that harms a person's reputation; decreases the respect, regard, or confidence in which a person is held; or induces disparaging, hostile, or disagreeable opinions or feelings against a person.

Defamation may be a criminal or civil charge. It encompasses both written statements, known as LIBEL, and spoken statements, called slander.

The probability that a plaintiff will recover damages in a defamation suit depends largely on whether the plaintiff is a public or private figure in the eyes of the law. The public figure law of defamation was first delineated in NEW YORK TIMES V. SULLIVAN, 376 U.S. 254, 84 S. Ct. 710, 11 L. Ed. 2d 686 (1964). In *Sullivan*, the plaintiff, a police official, claimed that false allegations about him appeared in the *New York Times,* and sued the newspaper for libel. The Supreme Court balanced the plaintiff's interest in preserving his reputation against the public's interest in freedom of expression in the area of political debate. It held that a public official alleging libel must prove actual malice in order to recover damages. The Court declared that the FIRST AMENDMENT protects open and robust debate on public issues even when such debate includes "vehement, caustic, unpleasantly sharp attacks on government and public officials." A public official or other plaintiff who has voluntarily assumed a position in the public eye must prove that defamatory statements were made with knowledge that they were false or with reckless disregard of whether they were false.

Where the plaintiff in a defamation action is a private citizen who is not in the public eye, the law extends a lesser degree of constitutional protection to defamatory statements. Public figures voluntarily place themselves in a position that invites close scrutiny, whereas private citizens who have not entered public life do not relinquish their interest in protecting their reputation. In addition, public figures have greater access to the means to publicly counteract false statements about them. For these reasons, a private citizen's reputation and privacy interests tend to outweigh free speech considerations and deserve greater protection from the courts. (See *Gertz v. Robert Welch, Inc.*, 418 U.S. 323, 94 S. Ct. 2997, 41 L. Ed. 2d 789 [1974]).

Distinguishing between public and private figures for the purposes of defamation law is sometimes difficult. For an individual to be considered a public figure in all situations, the person's name must be so familiar as to be a household word—for example, Michael Jordan. Because most people do not fit into that category of notoriety, the Court recognized the limited-purpose public figure, who is voluntarily injected into a public controversy and becomes a public figure for a limited range of issues. Limited-purpose public figures, like public figures, have at least temporary access to the means to counteract false statements about them. They also voluntarily place themselves in the public eye and consequently relinquish some of their privacy rights. For these reasons, false statements about limited-purpose public figures that relate to the public controversies in which those figures are involved are not considered defamatory unless they meet the actual-malice test set forth in *Sullivan*.

Determining who is a limited-purpose public figure can also be problematic. In *Time, Inc. v. Firestone*, 424 U.S. 448, 96 S. Ct. 958, 47 L. Ed. 2d 154 (1976), the Court held that the plaintiff, a prominent socialite involved in a scandalous DIVORCE, was not a public figure because her divorce was not a public controversy and because she had not voluntarily involved herself in a public controversy. The Court recognized that the divorce was newsworthy, but drew a distinction between matters of public interest and matters of public controversy. In *Hutchinson v. Proxmire*, 443 U.S. 111, 99 S. Ct. 2675, 61 L. Ed. 2d 411 (1979), the Court determined that a scientist whose federally supported research was ridiculed as wasteful by Senator William Proxmire was not a limited-purpose public figure because he had not sought public scrutiny in order to influence others on a matter of public controversy, and was not otherwise well-known.

FURTHER READINGS

Collins, Matthew. 2001. *The Law of Defamation and the Internet.* New York: Oxford Univ. Press.

Friedman, Jessica R. 1995. "Defamation." *Fordham Law Review* 64 (December).

Jones, William K. 2003. *Insult to Injury: Libel, Slander, and Invasions of Privacy.* Boulder, Colo.: Univ. Press of Colorado.

Smolla, Rodney A. 1999. *Law of Defamation.* 2d ed. St. Paul, Minn.: West Group.

CROSS-REFERENCES

Freedom of the Press; Libel and Slander.

DEFAULT

An omission; a failure to do that which is anticipated, expected, or required in a given situation.

Default is distinguishable from NEGLIGENCE in that it does not involve carelessness or imprudence with respect to the discharge of a duty or obligation but rather the intentional omission or nonperformance of a duty.

To default on a debt is to fail to pay it upon its due date. Default in contract law implies failure to perform a contractual obligation.

A *default* judgment is one that may be entered against a party in a lawsuit for failure to comply with a procedural step in the suit, such as failure to file an answer to a complaint or failure to file a paper on time. A default judgment is not one that goes to the merits of a lawsuit but is procedural in nature.

DEFAULT JUDGMENT

Judgment entered against a party who has failed to defend against a claim that has been brought by another party. Under rules of CIVIL PROCEDURE, when a party against whom a judgment for affirmative relief is sought has failed to plead (i.e., answer) or otherwise defend, the party is in default and a judgment by default may be entered either by the clerk or the court.

DEFEASANCE CLAUSE

A provision of a mortgage—an interest in land given to a mortgagee-lender to secure the payment of a debt—which promises that the mortgagor-borrower will regain title to the mortgaged property when all the terms of the mortgage have been met.

Defeasance clauses are found in mortgages in the few states that still follow the common-law theory of mortgages. At early English COMMON LAW, a mortgagee who lent money to a mortgagor received in exchange a deed of defeasible fee to the property, offered as security for the payment of the debt. Such title was subject to defeat or cancellation upon payment of the debt on the law day, that is, at its maturity, and

A sample default judgment.

Default Judgment

UNITED STATES DISTRICT COURT
SOUTHERN DISTRICT OF NEW YORK

_____X

                          Plaintiff,   _____ Civ. _____ (   )

— against —   **DEFAULT JUDGMENT**

                          Defendant.

_____X

    This action having been commenced on _____ by
                                             (date)

the filing of the Summons and Complaint, and a copy of the Summons and Complaint having been personally served on the defendant,

_____ , on _____
               (name)   *(date)*

by _____ *(STATE SPECIFICALLY HOW SERVICE WAS MADE ON DEFENDANT)*

personal service on _____ , and a proof of service
                                      (name)

having been filed on _____ and the defendant not having answered the Complaint, and the time for
                       (date)

answering the Complaint having expired, it is

    ORDERED, ADJUDGED AND DECREED: That the plaintiff have judgment against defendant in the liquidated amount of $ _____

with interest at _____ % from _____ amounting to $ _____ plus costs
                              (date)

and disbursements of this action in the amount of $ _____ amounting in all to $ _____ .

Dated: New York, New York

_____

                                _____
                                            U.S.D.J.

                    This document was entered on the docket on

                                _____ .

SDNY Web 5/99

---

the mortgagor would at that time regain title to the property. If the mortgagor failed to pay the debt, even by only one day, the mortgagee's title became an estate in fee simple absolute, which gave the mortgagee absolute ownership of the property. A defeasance clause embodies these common-law principles that govern this type of mortgage agreement.

Defeasance clauses are not found in mortgages based upon the lien theory, observed in most states. The mortgage creates a lien for the mortgagee on the mortgaged property, which gives the mortgagee the right to its possession only after the mortgage has been foreclosed. Since the mortgage has not been given defeasible title, there is no need for a defeasance clause.

DEFEASIBLE

Potentially subject to defeat, termination, or ANNULMENT *upon the occurrence of a future action or event, or the performance of a condition subsequent.*

The most common legal application of the term is with respect to estates as interest in land, such as in the case of a conveyance or a life estate, which is defeasible upon the happening of a certain specified event, for example, the death of the person holding such an interest.

DEFECT

Imperfection, flaw, or deficiency.

That which is subject to a defect is missing a requisite element and, therefore, is not legally binding. Defective SERVICE OF PROCESS, for example, is service that does not comply with a procedural or jurisdictional requirement. A defective will is one that has not been properly drawn up, has been obtained by unlawful means, or does not comply with a particular law. In some cases, however, defects can be cured; for example, defective service of process can be cured by the service of an amended complaint.

In PRODUCT LIABILITY, a defective product is one that cannot be used for the purposes intended or is made dangerous as a result of a flaw or imperfection. Such a defect might exist in the entire design of a product or in the production of a particular individual product. A *latent defect* is one that is not readily observable by the buyer of an item, whereas a *patent defect* is obvious or immediately apparent upon observation.

A *fatal defect* is one that, due to its serious nature, serves to nullify a contract.

Product Defect Notice

Date:_____

To:_____

Dear_____:

Notice is hereby provided that we have purchased a product manufactured, distributed, or sold by you and described as:

You are advised of a product defect or warranty claim. In support of same we provide the following information:

1. Date of Purchase:

2. Nature of Defect:

3. Injuries or Damage:

4. Item Purchased From:

This is provided to give you earliest notice of said claim. I request that you or your representative contact me as soon as possible.

Very truly,

_____
Name

_____
Address

_____
City, State, Zip

_____
Telephone Number

CERTIFIED MAIL, Return Receipt Requested

A sample form letter providing notice to manufacturer for a product defect.

DEFENDANT

The person defending or denying; the party against whom relief or recovery is sought in an action or suit, or the accused in a criminal case.

In every legal action, whether civil or criminal, there are two sides. The person suing is the plaintiff and the person against whom the suit is brought is the defendant. In some instances, there may be more than one plaintiff or defendant.

If an individual is being sued by his or her neighbor for TRESPASS, then he or she is the defendant in a civil suit. The person being accused of murder by the state in a HOMICIDE case is the defendant in a criminal action.

DEFENSE

The forcible repulsion of an unlawful and violent attack, such as the defense of one's person, property, or country in time of war.

The totality of the facts, law, and contentions presented by the party against whom a civil action or ciminal prosecution is instituted in order to defeat or diminish the plaintiff's CAUSE OF ACTION or the prosecutor's case. A reply to the claims of the other party, which asserts reasons why the claims should be disallowed. The defense may involve an absolute denial of the other party's factual allegations or may entail an AFFIRMATIVE DEFENSE, which sets forth completely new factual allegations. Pursuant to the rules of federal CIVIL PROCEDURE, numerous defenses may be asserted by motion as well as by answer, while other defenses must be pleaded affirmatively.

A *frivolous defense* is one that entails a vacuous assertion, which is not supported by argument or evidence. The rules of federal procedure provide that on motion such defense may be ordered stricken from the pleadings.

A *meritorious defense* is one that involves the essence or substance of the case, as distinguished from technical objections or delaying tactics.

With respect to a criminal charge, defenses such as alibi, consent, duress, ENTRAPMENT, ignorance or mistake, infancy, insanity, intoxication, and SELF-DEFENSE can result in a party's acquittal.

DEFENSE DEPARTMENT

The Department of Defense (DOD) is the executive department in the federal government that is responsible for providing the military forces needed to deter war and to protect the security of the United States. The major elements of the military forces under its control are the Army, Navy, Air Force, and Marine Corps, consisting of about 1.5 million men and women on active duty. They are backed, in case of emergency, by 1 million members of reserve units. In addition, the DOD employs approximately nine hundred thousand civilians.

Although every state has some defense activities, the central headquarters of the DOD is in northern Virginia at the Pentagon, the "world's largest office building."

The National Security Act of 1947 (50 U.S.C.A. § 401) created the National Military Establishment, which replaced the War Department and was later renamed the Department of Defence. It was established as an executive department of the government by the National Security Act Amendments of 1949, with the secretary of defense as its head (5 U.S.C.A. § 101). Since 1949, many legislative and administrative changes have occurred, evolving the department into the structure under which it currently operates.

Structure

The DOD includes the Office of the Secretary of Defense, the military departments and the military services within those departments, the chair of the Joint Chiefs of Staff and the Joint Staff, the unified combatant commands, the DOD agencies, the DOD field activities, and such other offices, agencies, activities, and commands as may be established or designated by law or by the president or the secretary of defense.

Office of the Secretary

The secretary of defense is the principal adviser on defense policy to the president. The secretary is responsible for the formulation of general defense policy and DOD policy and for the execution of approved policy. Under the direction of the president, the secretary exercises authority, direction, and control over the DOD. The deputy secretary of defense has full power and authority to act for the secretary of defense.

Three positions are designated as undersecretary of defense. The undersecretary of defense for acquisition and technology chairs the Defense Acquisition Board and advises the secretary of defense on all matters relating to the acquisition system, research and development, test and evaluation, production, logistics, military construction, procurement, and economic affairs.

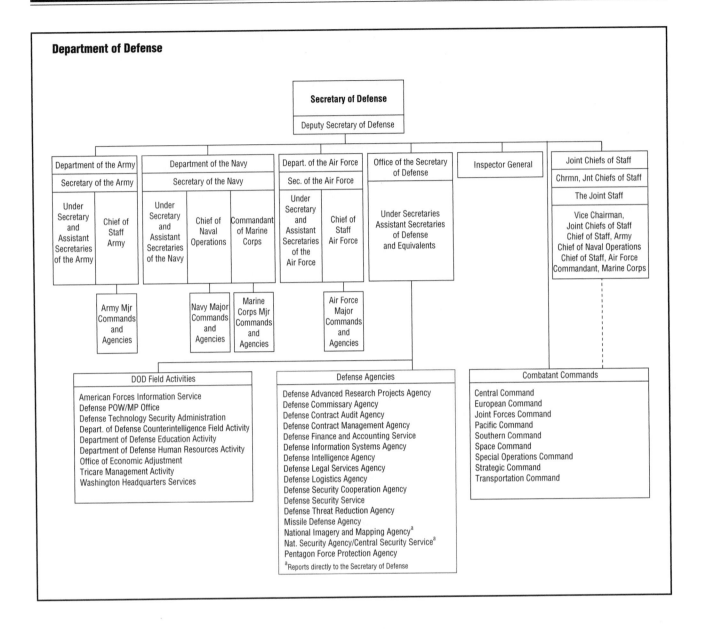

Department of Defense

Secretary of Defense

Deputy Secretary of Defense

Department of the Army
Secretary of the Army

Under Secretary and Assistant Secretaries of the Army | Chief of Staff Army

Army Mjr Commands and Agencies

Department of the Navy
Secretary of the Navy

Under Secretary and Assistant Secretaries of the Navy | Chief of Naval Operations | Commandant of Marine Corps

Navy Major Commands and Agencies | Marine Corps Mjr Commands and Agencies

Depart. of the Air Force
Sec. of the Air Force

Under Secretary and Assistant Secretaries of the Air Force | Chief of Staff Air Force

Air Force Major Commands and Agencies

Office of the Secretary of Defense

Under Secretaries Assistant Secretaries of Defense and Equivalents

Inspector General

Joint Chiefs of Staff
Chrmn, Jnt Chiefs of Staff

The Joint Staff

Vice Chairman, Joint Chiefs of Staff
Chief of Staff, Army
Chief of Naval Operations
Chief of Staff, Air Force
Commandant, Marine Corps

DOD Field Activities
American Forces Information Service
Defense POW/MP Office
Defense Technology Security Administration
Depart. of Defense Counterintelligence Field Activity
Department of Defense Education Activity
Department of Defense Human Resources Activity
Office of Economic Adjustment
Tricare Management Activity
Washington Headquarters Services

Defense Agencies
Defense Advanced Research Projects Agency
Defense Commissary Agency
Defense Contract Audit Agency
Defense Contract Management Agency
Defense Finance and Accounting Service
Defense Information Systems Agency
Defense Intelligence Agency
Defense Legal Services Agency
Defense Logistics Agency
Defense Security Cooperation Agency
Defense Security Service
Defense Threat Reduction Agency
Missile Defense Agency
National Imagery and Mapping Agency[a]
Nat. Security Agency/Central Security Service[a]
Pentagon Force Protection Agency
[a]Reports directly to the Secretary of Defense

Combatant Commands
Central Command
European Command
Joint Forces Command
Pacific Command
Southern Command
Space Command
Special Operations Command
Strategic Command
Transportation Command

The undersecretary of defense for policy advises the secretary of defense on policy matters relating to overall international security and political-military affairs, including NORTH ATLANTIC TREATY ORGANIZATION affairs, arms limitations agreements, and international trade and technology.

The undersecretary of defense for personnel and readiness develops policies and administrative processes to ensure that the military forces have sufficient readiness to execute the National Military Strategy; develops civilian and military personnel policies including health and drug policies, equal opportunity programs, and family issues and support; and oversees matters concerning the reserve components.

The comptroller and chief financial officer of the DOD is the principal adviser and assistant to the secretary of defense for budgetary and fiscal matters, including financial management, accounting policy, and systems and budget formulation and execution.

The director of operational test and evaluation serves as a staff assistant and adviser to the secretary of defense, prescribing policies and procedures for the conduct of operational test and evaluation within the department, including assessments of operational effectiveness and of the suitability of major defense acquisition programs.

The assistant secretary of defense for command, control, communications, and intelligence (C3I) is the principal staff assistant and adviser to the secretary of defense for C3I, information management, counterintelligence, and security countermeasures.

The assistant secretary of defense for legislative affairs is responsible for maintaining a direct liaison with Congress, coordinating departmental actions relating to congressional consideration of the legislative program of the department, coordinating responses to requests for information by members of Congress, and arranging for witnesses from the DOD and the various military departments at congressional hearings on defense matters.

The general counsel is the chief legal officer of the DOD and is responsible for the preparation and processing of legislation, executive orders, and proclamations, and reports and comments thereon. The general counsel also serves as director of the Defense Legal Services Agency, providing legal advice and services for the Office of the Secretary of Defense, its field activities, and the defense agencies. The general counsel also administers the Defense Industrial Security Clearance Review Program and the Standards of Conduct Ethics Program.

The inspector general serves as an independent and objective official in the DOD. The inspector general is responsible for conducting, supervising, monitoring, and initiating audits, investigations, and inspections relating to programs and operations of the department. The inspector general coordinates activities designed to promote economy, efficiency, and effectiveness in the administration of such programs and operations, and to prevent and detect FRAUD and abuse in them.

The assistant secretary of defense for public affairs is responsible for the functional areas of the DOD, which include public and internal information, audiovisual activities, community relations, and security clearance. The assistant secretary also reviews information intended for public release, and implements programs under the FREEDOM OF INFORMATION ACT (5 U.S.C.A. § 552) and Federal Privacy Act (5 U.S.C.A. § 552a) within the DOD.

The assistant secretary of defense for intelligence oversight conducts independent oversight inspections of DOD intelligence and counterintelligence operations to ensure compliance with legal requirements, and reviews all allegations that raise questions of legality or propriety involving intelligence and counterintelligence activities.

The director of administration and management serves as the principal staff assistant to the secretary and deputy secretary of defense on matters concerning department-wide organizational and administrative management, and also serves as the director of the Washington Headquarters Service.

Joint Chiefs of Staff

The Joint Chiefs of Staff consists of a chair and vice chair, the chief of staff of the U.S. Army, the chief of naval operations, the chief of staff of the U.S. Air Force, and the commandant of the Marine Corps.

The chair of the Joint Chiefs of Staff is the principal military adviser to the president, the NATIONAL SECURITY COUNCIL, and the secretary of defense. While serving, the chair holds the grade of general or admiral and outranks all other officers of the armed forces.

The chair of the Joint Chiefs of Staff helps the president and the secretary of defense to provide for the strategic direction and planning of the armed forces, including resource allocation, the assessment of the military strength of potential adversaries, and the preparation of both contingency plans and joint logistic and mobility plans. In addition, the chair coordinates military education and training, represents the United States on the Military Staff Committee of the UNITED NATIONS, and convenes and presides over regular meetings of the Joint Chiefs of Staff.

The Department of Defense in the Response to Terrorism

Recent acts of TERRORISM have required the Department of Defense to reconsider some of its methods for protecting the United States from

In March 2002, (l-r) Gen. Eric Shinseki, Adm. Vernon Clark, Gen. James Jones, and Gen. John Jumper, members of the Joint Chiefs of Staff, appear before the Senate Armed Services Committee to discuss the Defense Department's 2003 budget.

AP/WIDE WORLD PHOTOS

foreign threats. The SEPTEMBER 11TH ATTACKS perpetrated by the terrorist organization al Qaeda not only destroyed the World Trade Center towers in New York City but also severely damaged the Pentagon building in Virginia. In the months following these attacks, the U.S. military engaged in operations in Afghanistan, which had harbored suspected al Qaeda leader Osama bin Laden. Since the campaign against Afghanistan, the secretary of defense under President GEORGE W. BUSH, Donald Rumsfeld, has become a central figure in the American media.

The WAR ON TERRORISM, dubbed Operation Enduring Freedom by President Bush, has required the Department of Defense to work closely with other nations. The department has assisted in rebuilding Afghanistan after the former regime, known as the Taliban, was toppled. Since that time, the department has focused much of its attention on nations that have been suspected of assisting and harboring terrorist organizations—especially Iraq. In 2002 and 2003, the United States maintained a campaign calling for the disarmament of Iraq, a campaign that led to the second armed conflict between the two countries in twelve years when the United States attacked Iraq on March 19, 2003.

The Department of Defense also restructured other operations and developed new defense strategies in light of new threats against the United States. In 2002, the department redrafted the Unified Command Plan as part the largest restructuring of the military since WORLD WAR II. The revised structure places more emphasis on terrorism and other threats, with considerable focus on the development of technologies to assist in fighting these threats. Homeland security has also been a primary focus for the department. In 2002, more than 10,000 members of the NATIONAL GUARD provided security at the nation's airports and borders.

Field Activities

The American Forces Information Service, established in 1977 under the supervision of the assistant secretary of defense for public affairs, is responsible for the department's internal information program and visual information policy. The Armed Forces Radio and Television Service and Broadcast Center and the American Forces Press and Publications Service (which includes among its many products the *Current News*

Early Bird) function under the director of the American Forces Information Service. *Current News Early Bird* is a Pentagon-produced newspaper that contains clippings and analysis of defense-related articles from newspapers around the country. The American Forces Information Service provides policy guidance and oversight for departmental periodicals and pamphlets, the *Stars and Stripes* newspapers, military command newspapers, and the Defense Information School, among other projects.

The Department of Defense Civilian Personnel Management Service was established on August 30, 1993, and functions under the authority, direction, and control of the undersecretary of defense for personnel and readiness. It provides services in civilian personnel policy, support, functional information management, and civilian personnel administration to DOD components and their activities.

The Department of Defense Education Activity (DODEA) was established in 1992, and also functions under the authority, direction, and control of the undersecretary of defense for personnel and readiness. It consists of three subordinate entities: the DOD dependents schools, the DOD section 6 schools, and the Continuing Adult and Post-Secondary Education Office. The DODEA formulates, develops, and implements policies, technical guidance plans, and standards for the effective management of defense activities and programs both stateside and overseas.

The Office of Civilian Health and Medical Program of the Uniformed Services (OCHAMPUS) was established as a field activity in 1974. The office administers a civilian health and medical care program for retired service members and the spouses and dependent children of active duty, retired, disabled, and deceased service members, and also administers a program for payment of emergency medical and dental services provided to active duty service members by civilian medical personnel.

The Defense Medical Programs Activity develops and maintains the department's Unified Medical Program to provide resources for all medical activities, including planning, programming, and budgeting construction projects for medical facilities. It also provides information systems and related communications and automated systems in support of the activities of the DOD Military Health Services System (MHSS), the Defense Enrollment Eligibility and

Reporting System, the Tri-Service Medical Information System, the Reportable Disease Database, and other department-wide automated MHSS information systems.

The Defense Prisoner of War/Missing in Action Office was established on July 16, 1993, under the authority, direction, and control of the assistant secretary of defense for international security affairs. It provides centralized management of prisoner of war–missing in action (POW-MIA) affairs with the DOD. The office provides DOD personnel to negotiate with officials of foreign governments to achieve the fullest possible accounting of missing U.S. military personnel and also assembles and administrates information and databases on U.S. military and civilian personnel who are, or were, prisoners of war or missing in action. The office declassifies DOD documents and maintains open channels of communication between the department and Congress, POW-MIA families, and veterans' organizations.

The Defense Technology Security Administration was established on May 10, 1985 and functions under the control, direction, and authority of the undersecretary of defense for policy. This office is responsible for reviewing the international transfer of defense technology, goods, services, and munitions, consistent with U.S. foreign policy and national security objectives.

The Office of Economic Adjustment is responsible for planning and managing the DOD's economic adjustment programs and for assisting federal, state, and local officials in cooperative efforts to alleviate any serious social and economic side effects resulting from major departmental realignments or other actions. The office supports the secretary of defense in his or her capacity as chair of the Economic Adjustment Committee, an interagency group established to coordinate federal economic adjustment activities.

The Washington Headquarters Service is headed by the director of administration and management. It provides administrative and operational support to certain DOD activities in the Washington, D.C., area. This support includes budgeting and accounting, personnel management, office services, security, travel aid, information and data systems, and other services as required.

Web site: http://www.defenselink.mil/.

FURTHER READINGS

DefenseLINK - Official Web Site of the US Department of Defense. Available online at <www.defenselink.mil> (accessed November 20, 2003).

U.S. Government Manual Website. Available online at <www.gpoaccess.gov/gmanual> (accessed November 10, 2003).

CROSS-REFERENCES

Armed Services; Arms Control and Disarmament; Military Law.

DEFENSE OF MARRIAGE ACT OF 1996

The Defense of Marriage Act (DOMA) (Pub.L. 104-199, Sept. 21, 1996, 110 Stat. 2419) is a federal law that denies federal recognition of same-sex marriages and authorizes states to refuse to recognize same-sex marriages licensed in other states. DOMA was passed out of the fear that a lawsuit in Hawaii would force that state to recognize same-sex marriages. Under the U.S. Constitution's FULL FAITH AND CREDIT CLAUSE (Article IV, Section 1), states are expected to recognize the public acts, records, and judicial proceedings of every other state. Therefore, Congress was alarmed at the prospect of a gay or lesbian couple being married in Hawaii and then going to another state and expecting that state to recognize them as legally married. In addition, Congress did not want to grant same-sex couples the same federal benefits that are given to heterosexual couples who are legally married.

The apparent need for DOMA began after the Hawaii Supreme Court issued a ruling in *Baehr v. Lewin*, 852 P,2d 44 (1993). In this case three same-gender couples filed a lawsuit after being denied marriage licenses. The couples alleged the state had acted unconstitutionally because Hawaii's state constitution contains an equal rights provision, which mandates that all persons, regardless of gender, should be given EQUAL PROTECTION of the law. The state marriage law did not state that licenses should be issued only to male-female couples. The supreme court agreed that the state marriage law should guarantee same-gender couples equal protection but did not order the state to grant the couples licenses. Instead, the court sent the case back to the lower court of appeals and directed the state to prove that the inequality of marriage rights (in this case, involving same-sex marriages) was justified.

In 1994, the Hawaii legislature changed the marriage law to explicitly state that the contract of marriage applied only to marriages between a man and a woman. Despite this change and the reluctance of the state supreme court to address the issue again, supporters of traditional marriage around the United States voiced concern that same-sex marriage could be legitimized. If this happened in Hawaii it would generate lawsuits in other states from same-gender couples married in Hawaii seeking recognition of their new legal status. These fears intensified when the Hawaii legislature failed in 1996 to pass a proposed constitutional amendment that would overrule the court decision.

In 1996, DOMA was introduced in the House of Representatives by Representative Bob Barr (R-Ga.) and in the Senate by Senator Don Nickles (R-Okla.). It passed the House by a vote of 342–67 and the Senate by a vote of 85–14. President BILL CLINTON signed the act into law on September 21, 1996. Supporters of GAY AND LESBIAN RIGHTS had no success in stopping DOMA, in part because the vote became a REFERENDUM on the idea of "gay marriage." Even liberal Democrats who were staunch supporters of gay and lesbian rights voted for DOMA, arguing that it would be better to give same-gender couples some form of legal recognition short of traditional marriage.

The text of DOMA is very brief and contains only two provisions. The first provision states that no state, territory, or Indian tribe shall be required to legally recognize a "relationship between persons of the same sex that is treated as a marriage under the laws of another state, territory, or Indian tribe." This language tells these jurisdictions that the Full Faith and Credit Clause has no application to same sex marriages.

The second provision directs the federal government to follow a definition of the word *marriage* that means "only a legal union between one man and one woman as husband and wife." Likewise, the word *spouse* is defined as a "person of the opposite sex who is a husband or a wife." These definitions are meant to preclude a same-sex couple that has been married in a state from being eligible for federal benefits such as married INCOME TAX status and SOCIAL SECURITY survivor benefits. In effect, DOMA bars federal recognition of same-sex marriages through the use of these definitions.

Although opponents of DOMA argued that it violates both the DUE PROCESS CLAUSE of the FIFTH AMENDMENT and the Full Faith and Credit Clause they did not file a lawsuit challenging its constitutionality. By 2002, 36 states had passed laws that bar same-sex marriages or the recognition of same-sex marriages formed in other states. Hawaii, the state that started the debate, passed a constitutional amendment in 1998 that gave the legislature the right to decide on the legality of same-sex marriages. In 1999, the Hawaii Supreme Court ruled that the 1998 amendment and the act of the legislature barring same-sex marriages ended the litigation that had been pending since 1993.

Gay and lesbian organizations have shifted their political agenda since DOMA, seeking some lesser form of civil recognition for same-sex couples. Vermont became the first state to enact a law recognizing "civil unions" between same-sex couples (23 V.S.A. § 1201 et seq. [2000]). The 2000 law came in response to a 1999 Vermont Supreme Court ruling that its state constitution required same-sex couples to receive the same benefits and protections given to opposite-sex couples. The court, in *Baker v. Vermont*, 170 Vt. 194, 744 A.2d 864 (1999), rejected the plaintiffs' claim that as same-sex couples they were eligible for marriage licenses under the marriage statutes. Vermont laws reflected the common understanding that marriage consists of a union between a man and a woman.

However, the court was persuaded by the plaintiffs' constitutional claims. The plaintiffs contended that their ineligibility for a marriage license violated their rights to the common benefit and protection of the law guaranteed by Chapter I, Article 7 of the Vermont constitution. By denying them access to a civil marriage license, the law effectively excluded them from a wide array of benefits and protections, including access to a spouse's medical, life, and disability insurance; hospital visitation, and other medical decision-making privileges; spousal support; the ability to inherit property from the deceased spouse without a will; homestead protections; and over two hundred other statutory items. The court stopped short of legalizing gay marriage, stating that it was up to the legislature to modify the marriage laws, create a parallel domestic partnership system, or create some "equivalent statutory alternative." The legislature responded with the civil union statute.

Some commentators have speculated that couples from other states that are granted a civil union in Vermont may file a lawsuit in their home states challenging the constitutionality of DOMA and state laws barring same-sex marriages.

FURTHER READINGS

Fruehwald, Scott. 1999. "Choice of Law and Same-Sex Marriage." *Florida Law Review* 51.

Goldberg-Hiller, Jonathan. 2002. *The Limits to Union: Same-Sex Marriage and the Politics of Civil Rights.* Ann Arbor: Univ. of Michigan Press.

"Same-Sex Marriages and Civil Unions: On Meaning, Free Exercise, and Constitutional Guarantees." 2002. *Loyola Law Journal* 33.

CROSS-REFERENCES

Covenant Marriage; Gay and Lesbian Rights; Marriage.

DEFENSE RESEARCH INSTITUTE

The Defense Research Institute (DRI) was founded in 1960 to limit the abuse of legal processes for personal injury compensation through a program of education and information. The institute seeks to improve the knowledge and ability of defense attorneys and the fairness of the ADVERSARY SYSTEM of justice. It is intended to be a counterpart to the American Trial Lawyers Association (ATLA), which is plaintiff-oriented. The institute provides research facilities such as files of speeches, briefs, and names of expert witnesses, plus a small library. Activities include institutes and programs for lawyers, law students, the general public, and special interest groups. Its members include attorneys, claims investigators, adjusters, insurance companies, trade associations, corporations, and groups of frequently targeted defendants such as doctors, pharmacists, engineers, and manufacturers.

The institute is organized into three divisions: the Arbitration Program, the Individual Research Service, and Transcripts of Economists' Testimony. DRI also has various committees including those with the following titles: ADMIRALTY LAW, Congressional Liaison, ENVIRONMENTAL LAW, Manufacturers' Corporate Counsel, Medical-Legal, PRODUCT LIABILITY, Professional Liability, Property and Liability Insurance, and Workers' Compensation.

The institute publishes *For the Defense* (monthly), *Brief Bank Index* (annually), and a membership directory. It also maintains a database of expert witnesses for defense litigation purposes.

FURTHER READINGS

Defense Research Institute. Available online at <www.dri.org> (accessed June 2, 2003).

CROSS-REFERENCES

Defendant; Defense.

DEFICIENCY

A shortage or insufficiency. The amount by which federal INCOME TAX due exceeds the amount reported by the taxpayer on his or her return; also, the amount owed by a taxpayer who has not filed a return. The outstanding balance of a debt secured by a mortgage after the mortgaged property has been sold to satisfy the obligation at a price less than the debt.

DEFICIENCY JUDGMENT

An assessment of personal liability against a mortgagor, a person who pledges title to property to secure a debt, for the unpaid balance of the mortgage debt when the proceeds of a foreclosure sale are insufficient to satisfy the debt.

Legislation enacted during the Depression still restricts the availability of deficiency judgments in several states. In some jurisdictions, deficiency judgments are proscribed in certain situations, while in other states, they are limited to the amount by which the debt exceeds the fair market value of the property. Waiver, the intentional relinquishment of a known right, of the benefits conferred by antideficiency legislation contravenes public policy and is ineffective.

DEFICIT

A deficiency, misappropriation, or defalcation; a minus balance; something wanting.

Deficit is commonly used to mean any kind of shortage, as in an account, a number, or a balance due. Deficit spending or financing involves taking in less money than the amount that is paid out.

CROSS-REFERENCES

Federal Budget.

DEFINITIVE

Conclusive; ending all controversy and discussion in a lawsuit.

That which is definitive is capable of finally and completely settling a legal question or action.

A *definitive judgment* is final and not provisional; a *definitive sentence* mandates imprisonment for a certain specified period of time.

A sample deficiency judgment.

Deficiency Judgment

**IN THE UNITED STATES DISTRICT COURT
FOR THE NORTHERN DISTRICT OF TEXAS**

ORDER STRIKING/UNFILING PLEADING

The Clerk, having identified a defect in the form of the document indicated below, and the Court, having independently determined that the document should be stricken, it is ordered that the document be stricken from the record of this case. The Clerk is hereby directed to unfile and return this document to the party who filed it.

_____   _____
DATE   JUDICIAL OFFICER

NOTICE OF DEFICIENCY

Judge: _____   Date: _____

Case Number: _____   Plaintiff: _____

Deputy Clerk: _____   Telephone Number: _____

* * * * * * * * * * * * * *

A(n) _____

has been filed by_____ and is considered deficient in the areas(s) noted below:

_____ 1.   A civil cover sheet must be filed with the complaint. See LR 3.1(c).

_____ 2.   The document(s) must be in proper form. See LR 10.1.

_____ 3.   The signature of the attorney of record or the party proceeding *pro se* is required on each document filed. See F.R.C.P. 11.

_____ 4.   A completed certificate of service as defined in F.R.C.P. 5(d) is required.

_____ 5.   Each separate document contained therein must be identified. See LR 5.1(c).

_____ 6.   The motion must include:

a. ____   certificate of conference or inability to confer. See LR 7.1(b).

b. ____   brief in support of motion. See LR 7.1(d) or LR 56.5(a).

c. ____   proposed order. See LR 7.1(c).

d. ____   documentary or non-documentary evidence in a separate appendix. See LR 7.1(i) or LR 56.6(a).

_____ 7.   A motion for leave to amend must be accompanied by a copy of the proposed amended pleading attached as an exhibit and an original and second copy of the proposed pleading that is neither attached to the motion nor made an exhibit to the motion. See LR 15.1.

_____ 8.   A motion for continuance of a trial setting must be signed by the party as well as by the attorney of record. See LR 40.1.

_____ 9.   An attorney seeking *pro hac vice* admission must apply for admission on an approved form and pay a $25.00 fee. See LR 83.9(b).

_____10.   Additional copies are required. See LR 5.1(b).

_____11.   The attorney filing the pleading is not admitted to practice in this district. See LR 83.7.

_____12.   The document requires a separately signed certificate of interested persons. See LR 3.1(f), LR 7.4, or LR 81.1 (a)(3)(D).

_____13.   Other _____

DEFORCEMENT

The common-law name given to the wrongful possession of land to which another person is rightfully entitled; the detention of DOWER *from a widow.*

Although the term includes disseisin, abatement, discontinuance, and intrusion, deforcement especially applies to situations in which a person is entitled to a life estate or absolute ownership of land but has never taken possession.

DEFRAUD

To make a MISREPRESENTATION of an existing material fact, knowing it to be false or making it recklessly without regard to whether it is true or false, intending for someone to rely on the misrepresentation and under circumstances in which such person does rely on it to his or her damage. To practice FRAUD; to cheat or trick. To deprive a person of property or any interest, estate, or right by fraud, deceit, or artifice.

Intent to defraud means an intention to deceive another person, and to induce such other person, in reliance upon such deception, to assume, create, transfer, alter, or terminate a right, obligation, or power with reference to property.

DEGREE

Extent, measure, or scope of an action, condition, or relation. Legal extent of guilt or NEGLIGENCE. Title conferred on graduates of school, college, or university. The state or civil condition of a person. The grade or distance one thing may be removed from another; i.e., the distance, or number of removes that separate two persons who are related by consanguinity. Thus, a sibling is in the second degree of kinship but a parent is in the first degree of kinship.

DEL CREDERE

[Italian, Of belief or trust.] An arrangement in which an agent or factor—an individual who takes possession and agrees to sell goods for another—consents for an additional fee to guarantee that the purchaser, to whom credit has been extended, is financially solvent and will perform the contract.

As the result of a del credere agency, the del credere agent becomes a surety of the purchaser. If the purchaser defaults, the agent is responsible to the principal for the outstanding amount. A del credere commission is the extra fee paid to the agent for such promises.

DELECTUS PERSONAE

[Latin, Choice of the person.] By this term is understood the right of partners to exercise their choice and preference as to the admission of any new members to the partnership, and as to the persons to be so admitted, if any. The doctrine is equally applicable to close and family corporations and is exemplified in the use of restrictions for the transfer of shares of stock.

DELEGATE

A person who is appointed, authorized, delegated, or commissioned to act in the place of another. Transfer of authority from one to another. A person to whom affairs are committed by another.

A person elected or appointed to be a member of a representative assembly. Usually spoken of one sent to a special or occasional assembly or convention. Person selected by a constituency and authorized to act for it at a party or state political convention.

As a verb, it means to transfer authority from one person to another; to empower one to perform a task in behalf of another, e.g., a landlord may delegate an agent to collect rents.

DELEGATION

A sending away; a putting into commission; the assignment of a debt to another; the entrusting of another with a general power to act for the good of those who depute him or her; a body of delegates. The transfer of authority by one person to another.

The body of delegates from a state to a national nominating convention or from a county to a state or other party convention. The whole body of delegates or representatives sent to a convention or assembly from one district, place, or political unit is collectively spoken of as a delegation.

Delegation of powers, for example, occurs when a government branch in which authority is placed imparts such authority to another branch or to an ADMINISTRATIVE AGENCY. The U.S. Constitution delegates different powers to the three branches of government: the executive, legislative, and judicial. However, certain powers may not be transferred from one branch of government to another, such as the congressional power to declare war.

Congress has wide latitude in delegating powers to administrative agencies, and the breadth of the powers given to these agencies has led to a perception that administrative bodies are a "fourth branch" of the U.S. government. On a few occasions, mostly in the early twentieth century, the U.S. Supreme Court has applied the "non-delegation doctrine," which restricts the ability of Congress to delegate responsibilities reserved for one of the three branches of government established in the Constitution. However, the Court has seldom invoked this doctrine and rarely finds that Congress has exceeded its authority in delegating powers to agencies. Legal scholars nevertheless continue to debate what the proper limits of congressional delegation should be.

CROSS-REFERENCES

Administrative Law and Procedure.

DELIBERATE

Willful; purposeful; determined after thoughtful evaluation of all relevant factors; dispassionate. To act with a particular intent, which is derived from a careful consideration of factors that influence the choice to be made.

When used to describe a crime, deliberate denotes that the perpetrator has weighed the motives for the conduct against its consequences and the criminal character of the conduct before deciding to act in such a manner. A deliberate person does not act rashly or suddenly but with a preconceived intention.

Deliberate is synonymous with premeditated.

DELICTUM

[Latin, A fault.] An injury, an offense, or a tort—a wrong done to the property or person of another that does not involve breach of contract. Culpability; blameworthiness of a criminal nature, as in the Latin phrase in pari delicto—*in equal fault or equally criminal—used to describe accomplices to a crime.*

An *actio ex delicto* is a lawsuit based upon the commission of a TORT, as opposed to an *actio ex contractu*, an action for breach of contract.

DELIVERY

The transfer of possession of real property or PERSONAL PROPERTY from one person to another.

Two elements of a valid gift are delivery and donative intent. Delivery is not restricted to the actual physical transfer of an item—in some cases delivery may be symbolic. Such is the case where one person gives land to another person. Land cannot be physically delivered, but delivery of the deed constitutes the transfer if coupled with the requisite intent to pass the land on to another.

Similarly, delivery can take place in a situation where goods are set apart and notice is given to whoever is scheduled to receive them. This is known as constructive delivery.

DEMAND

Peremptory allegation or assertion of a legal right.

A demand is an emphatic claim, which presumes that no doubt exists regarding its legal force and effect. It is a request made with authority.

A *money demand* is a demand for a fixed sum of money that arises out of an agreement or contract. COMMERCIAL PAPER is frequently payable on demand or immediately upon request.

A *legal demand* is one that is made by a lawfully authorized individual and is proper as to form, time, and place.

DEMEANOR

The outward physical behavior and appearance of a person.

Demeanor is not merely what someone says but the manner in which it is said. Factors that contribute to an individual's demeanor include tone of voice, facial expressions, gestures, and carriage.

The term *demeanor* is most often applied to a witness during a trial. Demeanor evidence is quite valuable in shedding light on the credibility of a witness, which is one of the reasons why personal presence at trial is considered to be of paramount importance and has great significance concerning the HEARSAY rule. To aid a jury in its determination of whether or not it should believe or disbelieve particular testimony, it should be provided with the opportunity to hear statements directly from a witness in court whenever possible.

DEMISE

Death. A conveyance of property, usually of an interest in land. Originally meant a posthumous grant but has come to be applied commonly to a conveyance that is made for a definitive term, such as an estate for a term of years. A lease is a common example, and demise is sometimes used synonymously with "lease" or "let."

DEMOCRATIC PARTY

The modern Democratic Party is the descendant of the DEMOCRATIC-REPUBLICAN PARTY, an early-nineteenth-century political organization led by THOMAS JEFFERSON and JAMES MADISON. Also known as the Jeffersonian Republican Party, the Democratic-Republican Party began as an antifederalist group, opposed to strong, centralized government. The party was officially established at a national nominating convention in 1832. It dropped the Republican portion of its name in 1840.

Despite destructive struggles and philosophical shifts, the Democratic Party remains a dominant political force in the United States. The Democrats compete for office with the Republicans, their counterparts in the United States's de facto two-party system though third-party candidates and independents have experienced increasing success at both the state and federal levels, with Minnesota Governor Jesse Ventura, a former professional wrestler and Navy Seal, being the most visible example. He won the gubernatorial race as a member of the state's REFORM PARTY.

The Democratic Party of the late 1990s supports liberal government policies in social and economic matters. The early party disapproved of federal involvement. Jefferson, Madison, and James Monroe—Virginians who were each elected president of the United States—favored limited powers for the national government.

The fundamental change in Democratic philosophy was the result of fluid coalitions and historical circumstance. The master coalition builder and founder of the modern Democratic Party was ANDREW JACKSON, a populist president who was portrayed as a donkey by political satirists. Jackson transformed presidential politics by expanding party involvement. (The donkey later became the symbol for the Democratic Party.)

The transformation began after Jackson's first unsuccessful bid for the White House. In the 1824 presidential election, Jackson won the popular vote but failed to win a majority in the ELECTORAL COLLEGE. The U.S. Constitution requires the House of Representatives to select the president under these circumstances. When the House chose JOHN QUINCY ADAMS, Jackson was incensed—and began a four-year campaign to win the next presidential election.

With help from political adviser and future president MARTIN VAN BUREN, Jackson won the presidency in 1828.

Jackson had benefited from growth in the nation's population and from laws that increased the number of U.S. citizens eligible to vote. In the 1824 presidential election, about 365,000 votes had been counted. In the 1828 election, over 1 million votes were cast, an

Democratic National Convention Sites, 1832 to 2004	
Year	**Site**
1832	Baltimore
1836	Baltimore
1840	Baltimore
1844	Baltimore
1848	Baltimore
1852	Baltimore
1856	Cincinnati
1860	Baltimore[a]
1864	Chicago
1868	New York City
1872	Baltimore
1876	St. Louis
1880	Cincinnati
1884	Chicago
1888	St. Louis
1892	Chicago
1896	Chicago
1900	Kansas City, MO
1904	St. Louis
1908	Denver
1912	Baltimore
1916	St. Louis
1920	San Francisco
1924	New York City
1928	Houston
1932	Chicago
1936	Philadelphia
1940	Chicago
1944	Chicago
1948	Philadelphia
1952	Chicago
1956	Chicago
1960	Los Angeles
1964	Atlantic City
1968	Chicago
1972	Miami Beach
1976	New York City
1980	New York City
1984	San Francisco
1988	Atlanta
1992	New York City
1996	Chicago
2000	Los Angeles
2004	Boston

[a]An earlier convention, held in Charleston, South Carolina, had resulted in a split ticket in the party. The official nomination was made at the Baltimore convention.

SOURCE: *Democratic Nation Convention* website.

increase that clearly helped Jackson, the so-called people's president.

In reaching his goal, Jackson laid the groundwork for a strong party system. He set up an efficient Democratic political organization by forming committees at the local, district, and state levels; holding rallies and conventions; generating publicity; registering new voters; and getting people to the polls.

Jackson also backed the newly created convention system for nominating presidential candidates and was himself nominated for reelection at the 1832 Democratic convention. The original purpose of conventions was to allow local input in the political process. In Jackson's time, conventions were forums for debate and deal making.

As the Democratic Party changed in form and purpose, alliances became more difficult. Relations between southern and northern Democrats were increasingly strained. Southern states sought the reduction of tariffs, or taxes on imports, whereas northern states favored tariffs to safeguard their manufactured goods. Some southern Democrats suggested that individual states could nullify federal tariff laws.

Even more troublesome was the issue of STATES' RIGHTS and SLAVERY. The regional split within the party widened over the designation of new territories as free or slave states. The breaking point was the 1860 national convention. The Democrats were divided—the southern faction favored John C. Breckinridge, and the northerners selected STEPHEN A. DOUGLAS. Although Douglas advocated limited national control, or popular sovereignty, the southern delegates were not appeased. Republican nominee ABRAHAM LINCOLN capitalized on the dissension in the Democratic Party and won the election.

Following Lincoln's election came a twenty-four-year spell with no Democrat in the White House. After the Civil War, Democrats were denounced in the North because they had not supported legislation to finance the war or to enlist new soldiers. Meanwhile, the South became solidly Democratic in response to the Republicans' unpopular Reconstruction policies.

During the nineteenth century, the Democrats also created powerful urban political machines such as New York City's TAMMANY HALL. In these systems, people were offered political jobs or money in exchange for voter loyalty. Immigrants tended to support the Democratic Party and machine politics as a way to gain a foothold in their new country. Unfortunately, the machines became sources of corruption and graft.

In 1884, Democratic nominee GROVER CLEVELAND, of New York, was elected president with a pledge to end political patronage and support for the gold standard. Again, factional-

ism undermined Democratic strength. WILLIAM JENNINGS BRYAN, a powerful Democratic orator, supported free coinage of silver currency. He tapped into the discontent of southern and western farmers who sought government assistance. He also drew support from the labor movement. With Bryan as the unsuccessful Democratic presidential nominee in 1896, 1900, and 1908, the party's original position on limited government was all but abandoned.

Factionalism was the party's strength as well as its weakness. On the one hand, it gave minority interests a chance to be heard. However, successful coalitions among the different interests were difficult to achieve. The traditional Democratic alliance consisted of labor supporters, immigrants, farmers, urban interests, and southern populists. Later, African Americans and northern liberals joined the coalition.

After Bryan's losses, the Democrats were determined to regain the White House. In 1912, former Princeton University President WOODROW WILSON won the nomination on the forty-sixth ballot of the Democratic convention. A liberal reformer, Wilson defeated Republican WILLIAM HOWARD TAFT and third-party candidate THEODORE ROOSEVELT. Wilson's accomplishments as president included lowering tariffs, establishing the FEDERAL TRADE COMMISSION, backing antitrust legislation, and leading the country during WORLD WAR I. However, the Republicans regained the presidency in 1920 with a huge victory by WARREN G. HARDING.

The Republicans prevailed for the next decade. Finally, in 1932, the Democratic Party triumphed at the polls with the election of New York's FRANKLIN D. ROOSEVELT. Roosevelt introduced his sweeping NEW DEAL to pull the nation out of the Great Depression. Ambitious government programs helped put many businesses and millions of people back on their feet. The Roosevelt administration openly embraced social WELFARE programs and economic regulation. Elected president in 1932, 1936, 1940, and 1944, Roosevelt was the only president in U.S. history to win four terms in office, before the constitutional limitation of two consecutive terms was put in place in 1951 with the ratification of the TWENTY-SECOND AMENDMENT to the U.S. Constitution. He also steered the nation through most of WORLD WAR II.

After Roosevelt's death in 1945, Vice President HARRY S. TRUMAN assumed office. In 1948, after Truman had supported key CIVIL RIGHTS legislation, a cadre of southern Democrats rebelled by joining the Dixiecrat Party, a group advocating states' rights and SEGREGATION. The Dixiecrats eventually disbanded, and some southern Democrats switched to the REPUBLICAN PARTY. This shift began in earnest with the election of DWIGHT D. EISENHOWER in 1952 and peaked with the election of RONALD REAGAN in 1980 and 1984.

In 1960, Democratic nominee JOHN F. KENNEDY became the first Roman Catholic to hold the Oval Office. Kennedy's administration, called the New Frontier, established the Peace Corps; weathered the CUBAN MISSILE CRISIS, in which it convinced the Soviet Union to dismantle long-range nuclear missile sites in Cuba and return the missiles to Russia; and lent support to INTEGRATION efforts in the South. After Kennedy's assassination in 1963, Vice President LYNDON B. JOHNSON was sworn in as president. He later defeated Republican BARRY M. GOLDWATER for the chief executive position in the 1964 general election.

Johnson strongly supported civil rights, a position that further eroded the Democrats' base of southern whites and northern labor and ethnic voters. Johnson's policies for U.S. military involvement in Southeast Asia made him unpopular at home and abroad. In 1968, after Johnson declined a reelection bid, the Democrats held a tumultuous convention in Chicago that tarnished the image of party leaders and Chicago police. As protesters and police officers clashed on the streets, convention delegates nominated Minnesota's HUBERT H. HUMPHREY, despite a groundswell of support for VIETNAM WAR critic EUGENE MCCARTHY. Humphrey lost the general election to Republican RICHARD M. NIXON.

In 1976, Governor JIMMY CARTER, of Georgia, reclaimed the White House and the South for Democrats. Carter served one term, losing the 1980 election to Republican Reagan. Another southern Democrat, Governor BILL CLINTON, of Arkansas, won the presidency in 1992 and again in 1996, becoming the first Democratic president to win reelection since Franklin D. Roosevelt.

Under Bill Clinton, the Democratic Party was led to what many believed to be a centrist position. After the failure of his HEALTH CARE plan in the early part of his term, Clinton backed welfare reform and ran a budget surplus through most of his presidency. At the same

Al Gore and Joe Lieberman, the Democratic Party's candidates for president and vice president in the 2000 election, at the Democratic National Convention in Los Angeles.

AP/WIDE WORLD PHOTOS

time, Clinton did not shrink from all liberal positions, vetoing Republican efforts to ban partial-birth ABORTION and to reform BANKRUPTCY laws to help creditors, among other things, and allowing the government to be shut down for a long period rather than give in to Republican spending cuts.

The IMPEACHMENT of Clinton in 1999 furthered the partisan divide in the country. Led by a Republican Congress, the impeachment was backed by a majority of Republicans and opposed by a majority of Democrats. Despite the embarrassment to Clinton, the impeachment did not seem to hurt the Democrats in the same way WATERGATE hurt the Republicans— the Democrats actually picked up seats in the House and the Senate in both the 1998 and 2000 elections.

Just how evenly the country was split between the Republicans and Democrats was illustrated by the 2000 election. Democratic presidential candidate AL GORE won the popular vote by over 500,000 votes; however, the Electoral College was another story. A disputed ballot count in Florida kept the election from being officially decided for over a month after Election Day. When it was over, GEORGE W. BUSH had become president of the United States by a mere 537 votes, according to the Florida statewide official tally. Bush beat Al Gore in the Electoral College 271-266, one of the closest results in U.S. history.

Ironically, considering that they won the popular vote for president and picked up seats in both the House and Senate, the 2000 election paradoxically left the Democrats in their weakest position since the Eisenhower administration. In addition to the presidency, the Republicans controlled the House and the Senate by slim majorities. In the Senate, that majority consisted of one seat.

However, the decision by Republican Senator Jim Jeffords, of Vermont, to become an independent in 2001 gave the Senate majority to the Democrats for the first time since 1994. Using their majority, the Democrats were able to frustrate President Bush on some of his proposed policies, though they were too weak to pass legislation on their own. The Republicans strengthened their position after the 2002 election, regaining control of the Senate and increasing the number of seats they controlled in the House. But they still did not have enough votes to stop a Democratic filibuster in the Senate, thus giving the Democrats a measure of power.

Some party activists felt at the end of the 2002 campaign that the Democratic Party had lost its way with the centrist policies advocated by former President Clinton and others—they saw the way back to power to take the party in a more liberal direction and to delineate more strongly their differences with Republicans. Others saw this as political suicide, pointing out that Clinton was the only successful Democratic candidate in the past quarter century. Whom the Democrats nominate for the 2004 presidential election was seen as an important determinant of what direction the Democratic Party goes from here, in an era when much of Middle America appears politically ambivalent, fluctuating across party lines.

FURTHER READINGS

Judis, John B., and Teixeira, Ruy. 2002. *The Emerging Democratic Majority.* New York: Scribner.

Wilson, James Q. 2004. *American Government: Institutions and Policies.* 9th ed. Boston: Houghton Mifflin.

CROSS-REFERENCES

Elections; Republican Party.

DEMOCRATIC-REPUBLICAN PARTY

The Jeffersonian Republican party, better known as the Democratic-Republican Party, is an ancestor of the modern DEMOCRATIC PARTY. It evolved in the 1790s during the early days of GEORGE WASHINGTON's presidency. Washington had been unanimously chosen president in 1789 and had a broad base of support. THOMAS JEFFERSON served as Washington's SECRETARY OF STATE, while ALEXANDER HAMILTON served as

secretary of the treasury. Jefferson and his followers favored states' rights and a strict interpretation of the Constitution. They believed that a powerful central government posed a threat to individual liberties. They viewed the United States more as a confederation of sovereign entities woven together by a common interest. Hamilton and his followers argued that a strong central government was essential to the unity of the new nation. They favored a broad interpretation of the Constitution, which they saw as a document that should evolve with the country as it grew.

Virtually all the leading political figures of the new country, starting with Washington, believed that political parties would polarize citizens and paralyze government. Hamilton and Jefferson agreed with this notion, but by 1793 the two groups that they represented had broken off into separate factions. Hamilton's group became the Federalists, while Jefferson's faction adopted the name "Democratic Republicans."

One early and divisive difference between the Federalists and the Democratic-Republicans was how they approached Britain and France. The Federalists believed that American foreign policy should favor British interests, while the Democratic-Republicans wanted to strengthen ties with the French. The Democratic-Republicans supported the government that had taken over France after the revolution of 1789.

On economic matters, the Jeffersonians differed strongly with the Federalists. The Democratic-Republicans believed in protecting the interests of the working classes—merchants, farmers, and laborers. They believed that an agrarian economy would best serve these citizens. They saw the establishment of a national BANK OF THE UNITED STATES (which Hamilton strongly favored) as a means of usurping power that belonged to individual states, and they also believed that it would be tied too closely to the rich. The Federalists saw industry and manufacturing as the best means of domestic growth and economic self-sufficiency. They favored the existence of protective tariffs on imports (which had Congress had adopted in 1789) both as a means of protecting domestic production and as a source of revenue.

The ratification in 1795 of Jay's Treaty (named after JOHN JAY) sparked anger at the Federalists from a wide array of citizens. The British were still in control of fur-trading posts in the Northwest Territories, and they were accused of encouraging Indians to rise up against the Americans. British ships were seizing American ships and impressing American sailors; they were also prohibiting American ships from engaging in trade with the West Indies. Jay, the chief justice of the U.S. Supreme Court, was sent to England as an envoy and returned with a treaty that gave the British a deadline for leaving the fur posts. Almost none of the other issues was addressed. A particularly unpopular provision of the treaty called for the U.S. to settle pre-Revolution debts to the British, totaling $2.6 million.

Jeffersonians, and even many Federalists, felt that the treaty had been too generous to the British, although Hamilton saw it as a necessary action because Britain generated tariff revenues through its exports. In 1796, JOHN ADAMS (a Federalist) was elected the nation's second president with 71 electoral votes, defeating Jefferson by three votes. Jefferson became vice president.

Meanwhile, relations with France were deteriorating rapidly. The notorious "XYZ Affair" in 1796 was typical of what Jeffersonians saw as the weakness of FEDERALISM. The XYZ AFFAIR involved an unsuccessful attempt by a French agent to exact bribes in exchange for France's cooperation in negotiating an international trade treaty. France, angered by the pro-British Jay's Treaty, began to interfere with American ships. An American delegation was sent to France, and the French demanded a loan to the French government as well as a $240,000 bribe.

Although American public opinion hardened against the French, President Adams tried to repair the situation diplomatically, which angered many Federalists who thought that declaring war on France was the best course of action. This split within the FEDERALIST PARTY helped to ensure Jefferson's victory in the 1800 presidential election. Democratic-Republicans also won a majority of the seats in Congress.

Jefferson's party dominated American politics for the next two decades. One reason was that the Jeffersonians proved themselves to be willing to adapt to change. An example was the LOUISIANA PURCHASE of 1803. As a Republican, Jefferson initially felt that the president did not have the power to make such a large purchase (828,000 square miles). He recognized, however, that the price of $15 million (about three cents per acre) was a significant bargain, and that the purchase would double the size of the U.S. and also eliminate the danger of having an imperial-

ist French colony on its border. He went against his partisan instinct and made what he believed was the right decision for the country.

During the WAR OF 1812, Jefferson's successor, JAMES MADISON, battled the British overseas and the Federalists at home. Many Federalists, especially in the New England states, felt that the war would irreparably damage their ability to trade by sea with Europe. This anti-war stance proved unpopular, however, since the war ended in what most Americans perceived as a victory over Great Britain. Thus the Federalists were soundly defeated in the 1816 presidential election. The new president, JAMES MONROE, presided over a time of relative political calm during which many Federalists came to support the Republicans. This period was known as the "Era of Good Feeling," and although Monroe enjoyed wide support during his two terms in office, various factions were developing within his own party.

In the election of 1824, JOHN QUINCY ADAMS was elected president, narrowly defeating War of 1812 military hero ANDREW JACKSON. Although both were Democratic-Republicans, Adams's political philosophy was closer to that of the Federalists, and during his term in office the party split into two main factions. When Jackson ran for president in 1828, he ran as a Democrat—and won handily. Adams's wing of the party became known as the National Republicans, many of whom later formed the WHIG PARTY.

FURTHER READINGS

Bell, Rudolph M., 1973. *Party and Faction in American Politics: The House of Representatives 1789–1801*. Westport, Conn.: Greenwood Press.

Cunningham, Noble E., 1963. *The Jeffersonian Republicans in Power: Party Operations, 1801–1809*. Chapel Hill, N.C.: Univ. of North Carolina Press.

DEMONSTRATIVE EVIDENCE

Evidence other than testimony that is presented during the course of a civil or criminal trial. Demonstrative evidence includes actual evidence (e.g., a set of bloody gloves from a murder scene) and illustrative evidence (e.g., photographs and charts).

Many trial attorneys view the presentation of evidence to the jury as analogous to the presentation of information by a teacher to students. As in the classroom, the involvement of more than one of a juror's senses in the courtroom increases the amount of information retained by that juror. For example, combining verbal testimony from witnesses with before and after X rays, or introducing a defective machine part that jurors can hold in their hands for inspection, makes for compelling courtroom activity. In a modern, "show-me" society, the ability of a trial lawyer to use demonstrative evidence effectively can make the difference between winning and losing a case.

One common and effective example of demonstrative evidence is the still photograph. Photographs of a plaintiff's bruises taken immediately after an accident can help a jury understand those injuries in a trial that occurs months or even years after the accident, when the injuries may have healed. Aerial photographs of the scene of a vehicular accident can show how a particular intersection is laid out, and can make more clear an ambiguous description of a blind intersection given by a witness.

X rays and medical models and illustrations can be very helpful to a jury in physical injury cases. These examples of demonstrative evidence help the jury "see inside" the victim to understand the nature and extent of the injuries. X rays can show not only fractures but also permanent metal pins and plates. Accurate models of a plaintiff's head and neck can show the interaction between the cervical area of the spine and the surrounding muscle and tissues in a soft-tissue injury case. Sometimes, partial or full skeletons are brought into courtrooms to demonstrate losses or restrictions of movement due to injuries. Modern computer-generated illustrations can show the exact injury to a specific plaintiff, as opposed to the generic injury represented in a stock medical illustration.

Graphs and charts are perhaps the most useful forms of demonstrative evidence. These tools can vividly illustrate a loss of earnings, a decrease in life expectancy, and past and future medical bills. Clear and concise charts can help a jury to arrange a complex set of events in a chronological fashion. These time lines can be crucial in organizing evidence, whether in a criminal trial or in a complex SECURITIES litigation. Often, maps and other geographic charts are used to show water flow, elevation, and other physical characteristics of real property (land).

Graphs and charts can be presented to a jury in a variety of ways. In addition to offering the standard large prepared poster board on an easel, some attorneys prefer to create charts as they speak to the jury, using large blank pieces of poster board and colored marker pens. Other attorneys like the dramatic effect of dimming the courtroom lights and using an overhead projector or computer screen to focus visual attention on their illuminated charts and graphs. Whatever the style of presentation, well-constructed charts and graphs that make good use of color and are clear and easy to understand are appreciated by jurors and can have a big effect during deliberations.

Articles and objects are also forms of demonstrative evidence. In addition to actual evidence that is introduced at trial (like the knife from a murder scene), other physical articles and objects can be used to help the jury understand the testimony. For example, in a PRODUCT LIABILITY action based on a defective artificial hip, giving the jury models of ball-and-socket joints to manipulate and examine with their own hands can clarify testimony regarding the replacement joint that is still inside the plaintiff. Three-dimensional models and mock-ups of roadways, accident sites, or proposed buildings can simulate the outside world inside the courtroom to give proportion and scale to a witness's testimony.

With the permission of the judge, attorneys may be allowed to take the jurors to the scene of the crime or accident. Here, all a juror's senses are at work, and testimony presented in court can be compared to and contrasted with the physical scene. A list prepared by both attorneys of items to "notice" may be read by the bailiff at the scene. Many juries appreciate not only the chance to get outside the courtroom but also the opportunity to see for themselves the place where it all happened.

With the advent of low-cost videocassette players and recorders, it has become more and more common to see videotape in the courtroom. A "day in the life of . . ." video can graphically demonstrate the activities of a plaintiff living with debilitating injuries. For example, a plaintiff witness may say, "I can't pick up my children," whereas a video can actually show the plaintiff's young children milling about with the plaintiff able only to sit by and watch them. Videotapes can also show the traffic volume at a busy intersection or provide a driver's-eye view of a road sign obstructed by brush and leaves. If a jury is unable to leave the courtroom to visit the scene of a fire, a video camera can provide a tour through the burned-out remains of the family's residence. Some attorneys have actually begun hiring stuntpersons to re-create vehicular accidents, driving comparable vehicles at the speeds they were going when the accidents occurred, and filming the results. Unlike a controlled dramatic re-creation, this kind of actual re-creation, with its inherent danger yet accurate representation of accident conditions, can be an effective tool at trial.

Though waning in popularity owing to the greater availability and lower cost of computers, slide projectors and human-created animation are still used by some attorneys. By taking two slide projectors, superimposing their projections, and connecting them with a sophisticated mechanical device, an attorney can make a before picture fade into an after picture with dramatic results. As with a presentation using an overhead projector, the dark courtroom and brightly-lit screen of a slide presentation focus the jury's visual attention. Animated cartoon shorts, hand inked by artists, are eye-catching and can portray exactly what the attorney wants to emphasize to the jury: for example, a cutaway "operating" engine might show how a defective part can cause the engine to break down.

Computers and computer-generated displays are at the cutting edge of demonstrative evidence. Computer-enhanced graphics can demonstrate anything from the speed of a vehicle to the loss of range of motion on an injured portion of the body. Computers also provide high storage capacity. One CD-ROM disc can store thousands of still photos, graphs, charts, digitized video clips, and even three-dimensional computer animations. An attorney who uses a computer to coordinate a presentation can combine many different forms of demonstrative evidence into a cohesive and dramatic whole. Still photos of an injury might be followed by a digitized video showing limited physical abilities after the injury. X-ray images can fade into graphs showing a loss of earning capacity. All these exhibits can be stored in a laptop computer and presented with minimal setup and distraction to the jurors. And the attorney making the presentation can instantly return to a particular demonstrative exhibit when making a point during closing arguments.

Another significant development in courtroom technology is the use of bar codes. This technology is helpful in organizing evidence in cases with numerous exhibits. Bar codes function in court much as they do in the department or grocery store. Exhibits, be they photographs or documents, are stored on CD-ROM accord-

ing to bar code. By entering or scanning the number, the item is immediately retrieved and can be displayed on the computer screen.

Many newer courtrooms are now equipped with individual computer terminals, so that jurors may view computer displays by attorneys on individual screens in the jury box. A future development may be the use of virtual reality—where individuals see and hear computer-generated images and sounds, and through body sensors "see" their hands and body within the simulation.

No matter the technology, demonstrative evidence must still conform to standard evidentiary rules. The trial court may disallow any item of demonstrative evidence that is inaccurate or incomplete. Courts can also strike evidence if it is unnecessarily cumulative: for example, 30 photographs of one bruise that can be seen clearly in one or two photographs constitute evidence that is unnecessarily cumulative.

An attorney must keep in mind that demonstrative evidence is not real evidence: it merely illustrates the points being argued to the jury and court. Computer-generated animation may only portray evidence that has been properly presented to the jury through testimony or as physical evidence. A chart or graph may only present numbers and amounts that have been properly calculated and proved. No matter how exciting the "show," the attorney must remember that items of demonstrative evidence are merely props, and that the witnesses and their testimony are still the primary method of presenting evidence to a jury.

A common and effective type of demonstrative evidence is the still photograph. A police technician points to an area on an interior photograph of a defendant's home where fiber evidence (actual evidence) submitted in a San Diego, California, murder trial was discovered.

AP/WIDE WORLD PHOTOS

FURTHER READINGS

Brain, Robert D., and Daniel J. Broderick. 1992. "The Derivative Relevance of Demonstrative Evidence: Charting

Its Proper Evidentiary Status." *University of California at Davis Law Review* 25.

Branson, Frank L. 1989. "Innovative Techniques in Demonstrative Evidence." *American Law Institute-American Bar Association* C396 (January 19).

Heffernan, Thomas A. 1987. "Effective Use of Demonstrative Evidence—'Seeing Is Believing.'" *American Jury Trial Advocate* 10.

Lilly, Graham C. 1996. *An Introduction to the Law of Evidence.* 3d ed. St. Paul, Minn.: West.

Mauet, Thomas A., and Warren D. Wolfson. 2001. *Trial Evidence.* 2d ed. Gaithersburg, Md.: Aspen Law & Business.

O'Callaghan, Richard M. 1988. "Introduction and Use of Demonstrative Evidence." *Practising Law Institute/Litigation* 360 (October 1).

Reuben, Richard. 1995. "Stuntpersons Add Drama to Cases." *American Bar Association Journal* (November).

Taub, Theodore C. "Demonstrative Evidence." *American Law Institute-American Bar Association* C432 (August 14).

DEMONSTRATIVE LEGACY

A gift by will of money or other PERSONAL PROPERTY *that is to be paid to an heir from a fund designated in the provisions of the will but, in any event, is to be paid if there are sufficient available assets in the estate.*

A demonstrative legacy differs from a specific legacy, a gift of particular personal property by will. A demonstrative legacy is payable from the general assets of the estate that have not been specifically devised or bequeathed if its designated source has been adeemed or no longer exists or if it is inadequate to satisfy the gift. In the case of a specific legacy the ADEMPTION of property revokes the gift completely so that the heir receives nothing. However, if the value of the gift has only been reduced, the heir receives the decreased value.

Courts often interpret provisions of a will that appear to grant specific legacies of money or shares of stock as demonstrative legacies to avoid the consequences of ademption where it is clear that the testator intended the gift to be made in any event.

DEMUR

To dispute a legal PLEADING *or a statement of the facts being alleged through the use of a demurrer.*

DEMURRAGE

A separate freight charge, in addition to ordinary shipping costs, which is imposed according to the terms of a carriage contract upon the person responsible for unreasonable delays in loading or unloading cargo. In maritime law, demurrage is the amount identified in a charter contract as damages payable to a shipowner as compensation for the detention of a ship beyond the time specified by a charter party for loading and unloading or for sailing.

Demurrage is intended to serve the public interest by facilitating the flow of commerce through the prompt loading and unloading of cargo. In general, the person liable for demurrage is the one who assumed the duty to unload or load the cargo but failed to fulfill it. A consignee who agrees to unload a shipment but unreasonably delays in doing so is liable for the charge.

Payment of demurrage is excused only if the delay was unavoidable, such as a delay caused by a natural disaster or the fault of the carrier. *Reciprocal demurrage* may be imposed upon a carrier who unreasonably delays in providing transportation to customers. The practical effect of reciprocal demurrage is a reduction in the customer's shipping charges unless the contractual amount exceeds that figure. If a person against whom demurrage is imposed fails to pay, the carrier might have a right to keep the goods until payment is made. This is known as demurrage lien, enforceable only if authorized by statute, contract, or custom.

CROSS-REFERENCES

Shipping Law.

DEMURRER

An assertion by the defendant that although the facts alleged by the plaintiff in the complaint may be true, they do not entitle the plaintiff to prevail in the lawsuit.

The pleadings of the parties to a lawsuit describe the dispute to be resolved. The plaintiff sets out the facts that support the claim made in the complaint, and the defendant then has an opportunity to respond in an answer.

A demurrer is a type of answer used in systems of CODE PLEADING, established by statute to replace the earlier common-law FORMS OF ACTION. While a demurrer admits the truth of the plaintiff's set of facts, it contends that those facts are insufficient to grant the complaint in favor of the plaintiff. A demurrer may further contend that the complaint does not set forth enough facts to justify legal relief or it may introduce additional facts that defeat the legal effectiveness of the plaintiff's complaint. A demurrer asserts that, even if the plaintiff's facts are correct, the defendant should not have to answer them or proceed with the case.

Under the modern rules of PLEADING established by the rules of federal CIVIL PROCEDURE and followed in a number of states, the demurrer has been abolished as a formal type of answer. The same argument against the plaintiff's CAUSE OF ACTION can be, however, made by motion to dismiss the plaintiff's action on the ground that he or she has failed to state a claim on which relief can be granted. Even where the formal demurrer is no longer used, lawyers and judges often use the old term for an argument of the same type.

DENY

To refuse to acknowledge something; to disclaim connection with or responsibility for an action or statement. To deny someone of a legal right is to deprive him or her of that right.

A *denial* is a part of a legal PLEADING that refutes the facts set forth by the opposing side. A *general denial* takes exception to all the material elements of the complaint or petition, and a specific denial addresses a particular allegation in issue.

DEPARTMENT OF . . .

See specific department; e.g., EDUCATION DEPARTMENT.

DEPENDENT

A person whose support and maintenance is contingent upon the aid of another. Conditional.

A dependent is someone who is sustained by another person, such as a child supported by his or her parents.

In an insurance policy, the term *legal dependent* generally includes all of those people whom the insured person is under a legal duty to support, such as a spouse and minor children. A *lawful dependent* includes someone whom an insured person is permitted, but not required, to support.

That which is dependent is conditional upon the occurrence of another event. A *dependent contract* is an agreement between two parties that is conditional upon another agreement. For example, one person agrees to deliver goods to another person only after that person contracts to purchase such goods from the first person only for a certain designated period.

DEPENDENT RELATIVE REVOCATION

The doctrine that regards as mutually interrelated the acts of a testator destroying a will and executing a second will. In such cases, if the second will is either never made or improperly executed, there is a rebuttable presumption that the testator would have preferred the former will to no will at all, which allows the possibility of probate of the destroyed will.

Some jurisdictions decline to apply the doctrine of dependent relative revocation to cases to eliminate a written revocation of a will, but apply it to declare the ineffectiveness of a physical act of revocation. The justification for the distinction is that the physical act is inherently equivocal. The court has the power to interpret the ambiguous act to ascertain what the testator did but not to disregard an express statement of the testator and substitute its own conception of what the testator should have done.

The doctrine of dependent relative revocation contravenes the strict interpretation of and demand for rigid adherence to the specific language of the statutes concerning the execution and revocation of wills and the theory of the PAROL EVIDENCE rule. In deciding whether to apply the doctrine, the court considers the testamentary pattern of the decedent, the terms of the prior wills, the respective identities and shares of the beneficiaries under the previous will and the new will in question, the nature of the defect that prevents the new will from taking effect, and the trustworthiness of the proof of the reasons for the testator's desire to make the desired objective to the former testamentary plans as contrasted to the application of the laws of DESCENT AND DISTRIBUTION. The court will not execute a new will, but it will eradicate revocations to infuse new life into a prior will that achieves the same objective.

DEPENDENT STATES

States can be classified into two general categories: dependent and independent. A dependent state does not exercise the full range of power over external affairs that an independent state possesses under INTERNATIONAL LAW. The controlling or protecting state may also regulate some of the internal affairs of the dependent state. Formal treaties and the conditions under which the status of dependency has been recognized by other states govern the balance of sovereign powers exercised by the protecting state and the dependent state. Various terms have

Federal law allows the owners of mining operations, such as this copper mine in southeastern Arizona, to claim a tax deduction upon the depletion of the mine's natural deposits.

AP/WIDE WORLD PHOTOS

been used to describe different types of dependent states, such as condominium, mandate, protectorate, and vassal state. Since 1945 there has been strong international pressure to eliminate forms of dependency associated with colonialism.

DEPLETION ALLOWANCE

A tax deduction authorized by federal law for the exhaustion of oil and gas wells, mines, timber, mineral deposits or reserves, and other natural deposits.

Frequently, the ownership of such resources is split so that the depletion deduction is allotted among the various owners. Rights to royalty payments, leases, and subleases are not the same as ownership but the holders of such rights may be entitled to depletion deductions under the theory of "economic interest" formulated by the courts to ascertain the right to depletion allowances. Such economic interest, which signifies an investment interest in the minerals that furnish the sole resource for recouping the investment, is usually determined by the parties according to the provisions of their contract.

The cost method and the percentage, or statutory, method represent the two ways of calculating the DEPLETION ALLOWANCE.

Cost depletion, like depreciation, bases the allowance on the original cost of the income-generating property. For example, a taxpayer who purchases rights to extricate oil for $2 million should be permitted to regain the capital tax-free when he or she extracts and markets the oil. The earnings from the depletable property

should be viewed as encompassing a return of the taxpayer's capital investment. A proportionate segment of such receipts each year should be exempt from taxation as income. When oil is viewed as a "wasting asset," cost depletion permits yearly deductions for the receipt of $2 million tax-free over the duration of the pumping operations. The tax law permits the taxpayer to divide the cost of the investment by the estimated total of recoverable units in the natural deposit. This cost per unit is subsequently multiplied by the number of units sold annually, which results in the depletion deduction permitted for that year.

The percentage, or statutory, method does not employ recovery of cost in the computation of the deduction. A percentage of annual income, rather than cost, is deductible each year, even if the owner has recovered all cost or discovery value of the depletable asset. The federal tax laws vary from year to year in regard to the percentage depletion allowable for oil and some other deposits, and the categories of producers entitled to such allowances.

Percentage depletion, which applies to other mineral deposits or energy sources such as geothermal steam, provides an extremely profitable allowance as an alternative to cost depletion. The taxpayer calculates a fixed percentage of his or her gross income and deducts that amount from gross income annually for as long as the property generates income, even after he or she has completely recovered the actual cost. Some taxpayers employ cost depletion at the outset of operations, when a large number of units of the deposit are extracted and sold, and then convert to percentage depletion upon recoupment of cost in other circumstances—when percentage depletion yields a more sizable deduction.

Percentage depletion furnishes an additional tax subsidy to detection, development, and dissipation of qualified reserves. The subsidy approach began during WORLD WAR I to induce exploration for minerals. Cost depletion had been expanded to permit discovery value rather than cost to serve as the gauge of tax-exempt recovery. A problem in estimating the quantity of depletable units prior to extraction existed, however, and percentage depletion was enacted in 1924 as the solution. This method was subsequently extended to include additional minerals and other deposits and to raise rates of depletion in some instances. It was eventually diminished due to excessive profits and tax benefits obtained by some companies. Only depletion, rather than percentage depletion, may be used for gas, water, soil, timber, and oil.

For percentage depletion, gross income must be restricted to income from extracting and selling the deposit, not from refining, processing, or manufacturing it.

The option to deduct present exploration and development expenditures rather than capitalizing them represents an additional tax advantage for the industries entitled to depletion allowances. A more substantial tax benefit ensues if such expenses are deducted immediately, since they would never be recovered through the application of percentage depletion, which is based on gross income and not the cost of the capital invested in the enterprise.

CROSS-REFERENCES

Income Tax; Mine and Mineral Law.

DEPONENT

An individual who, under oath or affirmation, gives out-of-court testimony in a deposition. A deponent is someone who gives evidence or acts as a witness. The testimony of a deponent is written and carries the deponent's signature.

DEPORTATION

Banishment to a foreign country, attended with confiscation of property and deprivation of CIVIL RIGHTS.

The transfer of an alien, by exclusion or expulsion, from the United States to a foreign country. The removal or sending back of an alien to the country from which he or she came because his or her presence is deemed inconsistent with the public welfare, and without any punishment being imposed or contemplated. The grounds for deportation are set forth at 8 U.S.C.A. § 1251, and the procedures are provided for in §§ 1252–1254.

To further clarify deportation, the U.S. Supreme Court, in *Zadvydas v. Davis,* 533 U.S. 678, 121 S.Ct.2491, 150 L.Ed.2d 653 (2001), ruled that ALIENS who are under investigation cannot be held indefinitely. This would be in violation of the DUE PROCESS CLAUSE of the FIFTH AMENDMENT of the federal Constitution. Moreover, the Court established a maximum six-month detention period. At that point the alien must provide information as to why removal to the country of origin is not likely in the foreseeable future. For example, in this case,

Kestutis Zadvydas was born to Lithuanian parents who were held in a German displaced persons camp; both Lithuania and Germany refused to accept him into their countries because he was not a citizen. If the government cannot rebut this information, the alien must be released from confinement. Finally, the Court declared that the federal courts are the proper place to review issues of deportation, rejecting the government's claim that immigration is strictly the province of the EXECUTIVE BRANCH.

Following the September 11, 2001, terrorist attacks on the United States, Congress created the USA PATRIOT ACT, Pub.L. No. 107-56, 115 Stat. 272 (2001). The law deals with various means of combating TERRORISM and includes provisions that authorize the deportation of individuals who provide lawful assistance to any group that provides assistance to terrorists. Accused persons must convince the government that they did not know their contributions were being used for terrorist activities.

FURTHER READINGS

Cole, David, Jack X. Dempsey, and Carol E. Goldberg. 2002. *Terrorism and the Constitution: Sacrificing Civil Liberties in the Name of National Security.* New York: New Press.

Ngai, Mae M. 2003. "The Strange Career of the Illegal Alien: Immigration Restriction and Deportation Policy in the United States. *Law and History Review* 21 (spring): 69–107.

DEPOSE

To make a deposition; to give evidence in the shape of a deposition; to make statements that are written down and sworn to; to give testimony that is reduced to writing by a duly qualified officer and sworn to by the deponent.

To deprive an individual of a public employment or office against his or her will. The term is usually applied to the deprivation of all authority of a sovereign.

In ancient usage, to testify as a witness; to give evidence under oath.

DEPOSITION

The testimony of a party or witness in a civil or criminal proceeding taken before trial, usually in an attorney's office.

Deposition testimony is taken orally, with an attorney asking questions and the deponent (the individual being questioned) answering while a court reporter or tape recorder (or sometimes both) records the testimony. Deposition testi-

Depositions, the pretrial testimonies of parties or witnesses in civil or criminal proceedings, are often recorded by a court reporter on a stenographic machine.

AP/WIDE WORLD PHOTOS

mony is generally taken under oath, and the court reporter and the deponent often sign affidavits attesting to the accuracy of the subsequent printed transcript.

Depositions are a discovery tool. (Discovery is the process of assembling the testimonial and documentary evidence in a case before trial.) Other forms of discovery include interrogatories (written questions that are provided to a party and require written answers) and requests for production of documents.

Depositions are commonly used in civil litigation (suits for money damages or equitable relief); they are not commonly used in criminal proceedings (actions by a government entity seeking fines or imprisonment). A minority of states provide for depositions in criminal matters under special circumstances, such as to compel statements from an uncooperative witness and a few provide for depositions in criminal matters generally.

Before a deposition takes place, the deponent must be given adequate notice as to its time and place. Five days' notice is usually sufficient, but local rules may vary. Persons who are witnesses but not parties to the lawsuit must also be served with a subpoena (a command to appear and give testimony, backed by the authority of the court).

Depositions commonly take place after the exchange of interrogatories and requests for production of documents, because the evidence obtained from the latter often provides foundation for the questions posed to the deponent. Any documents, photographs, or other evidence referred to during the deposition is marked and numbered as exhibits for the deposition, and the court reporter attaches copies of these exhibits to the subsequent deposition transcript. Generally, at the outset of the deposition, the court reporter, who is often also a NOTARY PUBLIC, leads the deponent through an oath that the testimony that will be given will be true and correct.

The examining attorney begins the deposition and may ask the deponent a wide variety of questions. Questions that could not be asked of a witness in court because of doubts about their relevance or concerns about HEARSAY (statements of a third party) are usually allowed in the deposition setting, because they might reasonably lead to admissible statements or evidence. A party who refuses to answer a reasonable question can be subject to a court order and sanctions. However, a party may refuse to answer questions on the basis of privilege (a legal right not to testify). For example, statements made to an attorney, psychiatrist, or physician by a client seeking professional services can remain confidential, and a client may assert a privilege against being required to disclose these statements.

After the examining attorney's questions are completed, the attorney representing the adverse party in the litigation is permitted to ask follow-up questions to clarify or emphasize the deponent's testimony. In litigation involving a number of represented parties, any other attorney present may also ask questions.

The court reporter often records the proceedings in a deposition on a stenographic machine, which creates a phonetic and coded paper record as the parties speak. Occasionally, an attorney or witness may ask the court reporter to read back a portion of previous testimony during the deposition.

Most modern stenographic machines also write a text file directly to a computer diskette during the deposition. In the past, arduous manual labor was required to turn the phonetic and coded paper copy into a complete handtyped transcript. This is now rarely necessary because sophisticated computer programs can create a transcript automatically from the text file on the diskette. When the transcription is complete, copies are provided to the attorneys, and the deponent is given the opportunity to review the testimony and correct any typographic errors.

The deposition, because it is taken with counsel present and under oath, becomes a significant evidentiary document. Based upon the deposition testimony, motions for SUMMARY JUDGMENT or partial summary judgment as to some claims in the lawsuit may be brought. (Summary judgment allows a judge to find that one party to the lawsuit prevails without trial, if there are no disputed material facts and judgment must be rendered as a matter of law.) If motions for summary judgment are denied and the case goes to trial, the deposition can be used to impeach (challenge) a party or witness who gives contradictory testimony on the witness stand.

The advent of sophisticated and low-cost video technology has resulted in increased videotaping of depositions. Both sides must agree to the videotaping, through a signed agreement called a stipulation, and in some jurisdictions, the parties must also seek a court order.

A videotaped record of a deposition offers several advantages. First, a videotape shows clearly the facial expressions and posture of the witnesses, which can clarify otherwise ambiguous statements. Second, physical injuries such as burns, scars, or limitations can easily be demonstrated. Third, a videotape may have a greater effect on a jury if portions of the deposition are introduced at trial as evidence. Finally, a videotape can serve as a more effective substitute for a party who cannot testify at trial, like an expert witness from another state or a witness who is too ill to be brought to the courtroom. If a witness dies unexpectedly before trial, a videotaped deposition can be admitted in lieu of live testimony because the deposition was taken under oath and the opposing attorney had the opportunity to cross-examine the witness.

Another advance in technology is the ability to take depositions by telephone. Telephonic depositions are allowed under the federal rules and are acceptable in most states. The procedures for a telephonic deposition are the same as for a regular deposition, although it is preferable (and sometimes required) that the examining attorney state for the record that the deposition is being taken over the telephone. A telephonic deposition can occur with the attorneys and the deponent in three different sites; in any case, federal and state rules stipulate that the judicial district within which the deponent is located is the official site of the deposition.

Another technology used for depositions is videoconferencing, where sound transmitters and receivers are combined with video cameras and monitors, allowing the attorneys and deponents to see each other as a deposition proceeds. Videoconferencing makes the examination of exhibits easier and also helps reduce confusion among the participants that may result from ambiguous or unclear verbal responses.

FURTHER READINGS

Balabanian, David M. 1987. "Medium v. Tedium: Video Depositions Come of Age." *Practising Law Institute/ Litigation* 328.

Collins, Maureen B. 2002. "Taking the Deposition (and Getting It Right)." *Illinois Bar Journal* 90 (June): 323.

Malone, David M., and Peter T. Hoffman. 2001. *The Effective Deposition: Techniques and Strategies That Work.* rev. 2d ed. Notre Dame, Ind.: National Institute for Trial Advocacy.

Martiniak, Chris. 2002. *How to Take and Defend Depositions.* 3d ed. New York: Aspen Law & Business.

McElhaney, James W. 2003. "Deposition Goals: Develop a Plan to Get What You're After from Witnesses in Discovery." *ABA Journal* 89 (August): 30.

Montoya, Jean. 1995. "A Theory of Compulsory Process Clause Discovery Rights." *Indiana Law Journal* 70.

Zweifach, Lawrence J., and Gerson Zweifach. 1994. "Preparing to Take and Taking the Deposition." *Practising Law Institute/Litigation* 507.

DEPOSITORY

The place where a deposit is placed and kept, e.g., a bank, savings and loan institution, credit union, or trust company. A place where something is deposited or stored as for safekeeping or convenience, e.g., a safety deposit box.

This term should not be confused with *depositary,* which is the person or institution taking responsibility for the deposit, rather than the place itself.

U. S. depositories are banks selected and designated to receive deposits of the public funds (e.g., taxes) of the United States.

DEPOSITS IN COURT

The payments of funds or property to an officer of the court as a precautionary measure during the pendency of litigation.

The amount placed with the court constitutes the acknowledged liability of a person who is uncertain as to whom he or she is liable. The ascertainment of the court as to who is entitled to the property is binding.

This term also encompasses payment into court pursuant to court order.

DEPRECIATION

The gradual decline in the financial value of property used to produce income due to its increasing age and eventual obsolescence, which is measured by a formula that takes into account these factors in addition to the cost of the property and its estimated useful life.

Depreciation is a concept used in accounting to measure the decline in an asset's value spread over the asset's economic life. Depreciation allows for future investment that is required to replace used-up assets. In addition, the U.S. INTERNAL REVENUE SERVICE allows a reasonable deduction for depreciation as a business expense in determining taxable net income. This deduction is used only for property that generates income. For example, a building used for rent income can be depreciated, but a building used as a residence cannot be depreciated.

Depreciation arises from a strong public policy in favor of investment. Income-producing assets such as machines, trucks, tools, and structures have a limited useful life—that is, they wear out and grow obsolete while generating income. In effect, a taxpayer using such assets in business is gradually selling those assets. To encourage continued investment, part of the gross income should be seen as a return on a capital expenditure, and not as profit. Accordingly, tax law has developed to separate the return of capital amounts from net income.

Generally, depreciation covers deterioration from use, age, and exposure to the elements. An asset likely to become obsolete, such as a computer system, can also be depreciated. An asset that is damaged or destroyed by fire, accident, or disaster cannot be depreciated. An asset that is used in one year cannot be depreciated; instead, the loss on such an asset may be written off as a business expense.

Several methods are used for depreciating income-producing business assets. The most common and simplest is the straight-line method. Straight-line depreciation is figured by first taking the original cost of an asset and sub-tracting the estimated value of the asset at the end of its useful life, to arrive at the depreciable basis. Then, to determine the annual depreciation for the asset, the depreciable basis is divided by the estimated life span of the asset. For example, if a manufacturing machine costs $1,200 and is expected to be worth $200 at the end of its useful life, its depreciable basis is $1,000. If the useful life span of the machine is 10 years, the depreciation each year is $100 ($1,000 divided by 10 years). Thus, $100 can be deducted from the business's taxable net income each year for 10 years.

Accelerated depreciation provides a larger tax write-off for the early years of an asset. Various methods are used to accelerate depreciation. One method, called declining-balance depreciation, is calculated by deducting a percentage up to two times higher than that recognized by the straight-line method, and applying that percentage to the undepreciated balance at the start of each tax period. For the manufacturing machine example, the business could deduct up to $200 (20 percent of $1,000) in the first year, $160 (20 percent of the balance, $800) the second year, and so on. As soon as the amount of depreciation under the declining-balance method would be less than that under the straight-line method (in our example, $100), the straight-line method is used to finish depreciating the asset.

Another method of accelerating depreciation is the sum-of-the-years method. This is calculated by multiplying an asset's depreciable basis by a particular fraction. The fraction used to determine the deductible amount is figured by adding the number of years of the asset's useful life. For example, for a 10-year useful life span, one would add 1, 2, 3, 4, 5, 6, 7, 8, 9, and 10, to arrive at 55. This is the denominator of the fraction. The numerator is the actual number of useful years for the machine, 10. The fraction is thus 10/55. This fraction is multiplied by the depreciable basis ($1,000) to arrive at the depreciation deduction for the first year. For the second year, the fraction 9/55 is multiplied against the depreciable basis, and so on until the end of the asset's useful life. Sum-of-years is a more gradual form of accelerated depreciation than declining-balance depreciation.

Depreciation is allowed by the government as a reward to those investing in business. In 1981, the Accelerated Cost Recovery System (ACRS) (I.R.C. § 168) was authorized by Congress for use as a tax accounting method to recover capital costs for most tangible depreciable property. ACRS uses accelerated methods applied over predetermined recovery periods shorter than, and unrelated to, the useful life of assets. ACRS covers depreciation for most depreciable property, and more quickly than prior law permitted. Not all property has a predetermined rate of depreciation under ACRS. The INTERNAL REVENUE CODE indicates which assets are covered by ACRS.

FURTHER READINGS

Brestoff, Nelson E. 1985. *How to Write Off Your Down Payment*. New York: Putnam.

Hudson, David M., and Stephen A. Lind. 1994. *Federal Income Taxation*. 5th ed. St. Paul, Minn.: West.

CROSS-REFERENCES

Income Tax; Taxable Income.

DEPUTY

A person duly authorized by an officer to serve as his or her substitute by performing some or all of the officer's functions.

A *deputy* sheriff is designated to act on behalf of the sheriff in regard to official business.

A *general deputy* or undersheriff, pursuant to an appointment, has authority to execute all of the regular duties of the office of sheriff and serves process without any special authority from the sheriff.

A *special deputy,* who is an officer *pro hac vice* (Latin for "for this turn"), is appointed to render a special service. A special deputy acts under a specific, rather than a general, appointment and authority.

CROSS-REFERENCES

Service of Process.

DERIVATIVE ACTION

A lawsuit brought by a shareholder of a corporation on its behalf to enforce or defend a legal right or claim, which the corporation has failed to do.

A derivative action, more popularly known as a STOCKHOLDER'S DERIVATIVE SUIT, is derived from the primary right of the corporation to seek redress of legal grievances through the courts. The procedure to be followed in such an action is governed by the rules of federal CIVIL PROCEDURE and state provisions, where applicable.

DERIVATIVE EVIDENCE

Facts, information, or physical objects that tend to prove an issue in a criminal prosecution but which are excluded from consideration by the trier of fact because they were learned directly from information illegally obtained in violation of the constitutional guarantee against unreasonable SEARCHES AND SEIZURES.

Derivative evidence is inadmissible as proof because of the application of the FRUIT OF THE POISONOUS TREE doctrine, which treats the original evidence and any evidence derived from it as tainted because of the illegal way in which it was obtained by agents of the government.

DEROGATION

The partial repeal of a law, usually by a subsequent act that in some way diminishes its ORIGINAL INTENT or scope.

Derogation is distinguishable from abrogation, which is the total ANNULMENT of a law.

❖ DERSHOWITZ, ALAN MORTON

Scholar and constitutional authority Alan Morton Dershowitz is a well-known, controversial, and successful U.S. appellate attorney. A professor at the Harvard School of Law, he has a reputation for taking on the cases of little-loved criminal defendants. His list of clients is a who's who of notoriety, ranging from wealthy socialites to a pornographic film star and a convicted spy. Dershowitz has captured attention both in the courtroom and out, as much for his sometimes brilliant legal strategies as for his ubiquitous books, articles, and TV appearances. A staunch defender of FIRST AMENDMENT freedoms, civil and HUMAN RIGHTS, and Jewish issues, he has earned praise and enmity for his influence on U.S. law.

Dershowitz, born September 1, 1938, in Brooklyn, was raised in the orthodox Jewish area of Boro Park, New York. He attended Yeshiva University High School, where a principal advised the unexceptional but talkative student to seek a career "where you use your mouth, not your brains" (Keegan 1992). He apparently ignored that advice, graduating magna cum laude from Brooklyn College and gaining admittance to Yale Law School. As a law student, he quickly distinguished himself: he was named editor of the *Yale Law Journal* in his second year, and his research on the relationship of psychiatry to the law was such that Harvard offered

"IN POKER IT IS IMPOSSIBLE TO BLUFF WITH ALL YOUR CARDS SHOWING. IN LAW IT IS DIFFICULT, BUT NOT IMPOSSIBLE."
—ALAN DERSHOWITZ

Alan Dershowitz.
AP/WIDE WORLD PHOTOS

Dershowitz a teaching position upon his graduation. Finishing at the top of his class in 1962, he postponed the Harvard offer to clerk for Chief Judge David L. Bazelon, of the U.S. Court of Appeals. This clerkship was followed by another with U.S. Supreme Court Justice ARTHUR J. GOLDBERG.

Appointed associate professor at Harvard Law School in 1964, Dershowitz went on to become, three years later, the youngest tenured professor in the school's history at 28. His specialty, CRIMINAL LAW, did not prevent him from continuing the academic research he had begun at Yale, and he coauthored the standard casebook *Psychoanalysis, Psychiatry, and the Law* (1967). He also began a lifelong immersion in liberal political issues. As protest over the VIETNAM WAR galvanized campuses around the United States, Dershowitz created a course on legal concerns raised by the war, which inspired similar courses at numerous law schools. He worked privately on behalf of several antiwar protesters, including Harvard students facing disciplinary proceedings and the antiwar leader Dr. Benjamin M. Spock. In 1972, he drafted a successful appeal for WILLIAM M. KUNSTLER, a radical lawyer convicted of CONTEMPT of court for his defense of the CHICAGO EIGHT antiwar activists at the 1968 Democratic convention.

Free speech concerns animated Dershowitz to fight CENSORSHIP of PORNOGRAPHY. In his view, "There is simply no justification for government censorship of offensive material of any kind." Even if pornography can be shown to lead to violence against women, Dershowitz opposes any controls on it. His position is that of a classic First Amendment absolutist: fight bad speech with good speech, but do not limit speech.

Dershowitz made his first U.S. Supreme Court argument in 1969, attempting to remove a Boston ban on screenings of the internationally acclaimed Swedish film *I am Curious (Yellow)*. Championed by intellectuals such as Norman Mailer, the sexually explicit film was the first of its kind to be distributed commercially in the United States. Dershowitz successfully argued before a three-judge Court that the First Amendment protected the rights of consenting adults to view whatever they chose in a discreet setting. After the Supreme Court remanded the case, the prosecution was dismissed and the ban was lifted.

In 1976, Dershowitz handled the appeal of Harry Reems, a star in the pornographic film *Deep Throat*. Several years after acting in the film, Reems had been convicted on federal charges of taking part in an ongoing conspiracy to transport it across state lines. Dershowitz won a new trial for Reems, and the JUSTICE DEPARTMENT later dropped the indictment.

The attorney took his first criminal case in 1972. His defense of Sheldon Seigel, accused of making a bomb used by the terrorist Jewish Defense League (JDL), established a pattern that Dershowitz would follow throughout his career: a commitment to civil liberties and constitutional rights regardless of the notoriety or apparent immorality of his clients. The bomb Seigel was said to have made had exploded in the Manhattan office of arts impresario Sol Hurok, killing a young woman. While associated with the JDL, Seigel had also been a government informer. When the case came to trial, the government denied making a deal protecting him from testifying against his associates. Using secret tape recordings of his client and government agents, Dershowitz destroyed the prosecution's claims. An appellate court ruled against forcing Seigel to testify, and the case against the JDL suspects was dismissed for lack of evidence. Dershowitz later said he cried upon realizing that he had gotten Seigel acquitted, thinking about the woman killed by the bomb. Yet the case had allowed him to challenge what he saw as systematic unconstitutionality in the government's handling of informers.

Defending other unpopular clients has sometimes earned Dershowitz the criticism of his peers. The attorney nonetheless accepts cases few other lawyers will touch, making him, in the words of *Time* magazine, the "patron saint of hopeless cases." In 1975, he was widely criticized for agreeing to represent Bernard Bergman, a New York City nursing home operator, on appeal of his conviction for MEDICARE FRAUD and attempted BRIBERY. The press and the public had vilified Bergman for running a chain of nursing homes in which elderly patients were abused. Dershowitz tried, unsuccessfully, to have Bergman's one-year sentence reduced to four months, arguing that the special prosecutor in the case had violated a plea bargain.

In 1980, Dershowitz represented two brothers, Ricky Tison and Raymond Tison, who were convicted and sentenced to die for the crime of felony murder. The brothers had helped their father, Gary Tison, escape from prison; the father subsequently took part in a murder. Dershowitz raised the question of whether the brothers could be executed for a murder they did not plan or commit. In 1987, he argued for their lives before the Supreme Court, which remanded the case and ordered a new hearing.

A 1982 appeal for socialite Claus von Bulow catapulted Dershowitz to greater public attention than had any of his previous endeavors. Closely watched by the press, von Bulow's trial seemed the stuff of best-selling fiction. He had been convicted of attempting to murder his wife, heiress Martha (Sunny) Crawford von Bulow, by injecting her with insulin—presumably, to lay hands on her millions. On appeal, Dershowitz made multiple arguments for reversal or retrial. He contended that his client had been the victim of an unconstitutional search, that evidence had

been withheld from the defense, and that new medical evidence raised doubts about the insulin found in Crawford's blood. The appeals court reversed von Bulow's conviction in April 1984, and at a subsequent trial, with Dershowitz directing the defense strategy, a second jury acquitted him in 1985. The attorney wrote an account of the trial, *Reversal of Fortune* (1986), which later became an Academy Award-winning film.

Throughout the 1980s and 1990s, Dershowitz seldom escaped public notice for his work on behalf of a string of controversial clients. He represented, among others, Leona Helmsley, a hotel magnate convicted of TAX EVASION; Michael R. Milken, a Wall Street junk-bond financier who pleaded guilty to six felonies; Jonathan Pollard, a U.S. intelligence analyst who pleaded guilty to spying for Israel; and Mike Tyson, a former heavyweight champion who was convicted of rape. Dershowitz lost these appeals, but not for want of trying. His tactics routinely include a vociferous use of the media, on the assumption that judges and juries are influenced by what they see and read. Besides numerous interviews, he also has taken out full-page ads in the *New York Times* on behalf of clients, for example, Milken.

Dershowitz was in the limelight as a member of the "Dream Team," assembled to defend O.J. SIMPSON, who was acquitted of murder charges in October 1995. Like many others involved in the case, Dershowitz published a book, *Reasonable Doubts: The Criminal Justice System and the O.J. Simpson Case* (1997). Not all Dershowitz's clients, however, are celebrities. He conducts PRO BONO work for those unable to afford a lawyer, let alone his reputed $400-an-hour fee.

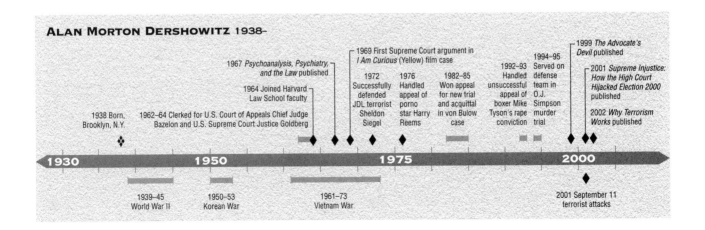

ALAN MORTON DERSHOWITZ 1938–

1938 Born, Brooklyn, N.Y.

1962–64 Clerked for U.S. Court of Appeals Chief Judge Bazelon and U.S. Supreme Court Justice Goldberg

1964 Joined Harvard Law School faculty

1967 *Psychoanalysis, Psychiatry, and the Law* published

1969 First Supreme Court argument in *I Am Curious* (Yellow) film case

1972 Successfully defended JDL terrorist Sheldon Siegel

1976 Handled appeal of porno star Harry Reems

1982–85 Won appeal for new trial and acquittal in von Bulow case

1992–93 Handled unsuccessful appeal of boxer Mike Tyson's rape conviction

1994–95 Served on defense team in O.J. Simpson murder trial

1999 *The Advocate's Devil* published

2001 *Supreme Injustice: How the High Court Hijacked Election 2000* published

2002 *Why Terrorism Works* published

1930   1950   1975   2000

1939–45 World War II

1950–53 Korean War

1961–73 Vietnam War

2001 September 11 terrorist attacks

As an appellate lawyer, Dershowitz estimates his chance of losing a client's appeal at 95 percent, saying, "I'm like a brain surgeon brought in after the tumor's been discovered." He cites constitutional concerns as his justification for his choice of clients. Others have accused him of greed and grandstanding. His one-time ally, the late Kunstler, was one such critic, bemoaning what he considered a former idealist's selling out. No stranger to criticism, Dershowitz gives as well as he gets. He frequently addresses audiences, writes articles, gives press conferences, and conducts debates with his critics and those with whom he disagrees. In the mid-1980s, he attacked the Justice Department under President RONALD REAGAN as "dangerous for our constitutional health." A major area of battle for him in the early 1990s was the trend on university and college campuses toward "political correctness," which he views as stifling to free speech and detrimental to education. Denouncing the trend, Dershowitz said, "We are tolerating and teaching intolerance and hypocrisy."

Committed to working on behalf of Jewish rights, Dershowitz traveled to the Soviet Union in 1974 as part of the Soviet Jewry Defense Project. This U.S. group submitted appeals on behalf of 14 Russian Jews and two non-Jews sentenced to prison terms for conspiracy after their emigration visas were refused. The effort helped to bring about the early release of several prisoners, who immigrated to Israel. Dershowitz also attempted to represent Russian dissident Anatoly Scharansky, but was blocked by Soviet authorities. A tireless foe of anti-Semitism whose office door is decorated with hate mail, Dershowitz argued in his best-selling 1991 book *Chutzpah* that U.S. Jews have too long accepted being second-class citizens. Named for the Yiddish expression for brashness, *Chutzpah* made an impassioned plea for greater pride: "We need not be apologetic or defensive about our power in America." The book won high praise from Nobel laureate Saul Bellow and others, although some Jewish intellectuals regarded it as overzealous.

Dershowitz continues to be a prolific and highly topical writer. In 2001, Dershowitz, a strong supporter of Al Gore's presidential bid, published *Supreme Injustice: How the High Court Hijacked Election 2000*. In 2002, he published books on two subjects that were in the forefront of national attention: *Why Terrorism Works: Understanding the Threat, Responding to the Challenge* and *Shouting Fire: Civil Liberties in a Turbulent Age*.

After the September 11, 2001, attack on the World Trade Center, Dershowitz garnered a great deal of attention and controversy when he wrote a column in the *Los Angeles Times* in which he posited that if United States authorities were to engage in torture to extract information from prisoners, judges should have to issue "torture warrants."

In addition to his numerous writings (including over one thousand op ed articles), Dershowitz continues to lecture in the United States and around the world. He also delivers legal commentary on TV and radio shows, as well as INTERNET broadcasts. Dershowitz maintains his ties with Harvard Law School where he has been the FELIX FRANKFURTER Professor of Law since 1993.

Dershowitz has received many awards honoring his work for civil and human rights. These include a Guggenheim Fellowship in 1979, a commendation from the New York Criminal Bar Association in 1981, and the WILLIAM O. DOUGLAS First Amendment Award from the ANTI-DEFAMATION LEAGUE of the B'nai Brith in 1983. He has also received honorary degrees and awards from Yeshiva University, Syracuse University, Hebrew Union College, the University of Haifa, Monmouth College, Fitchburg College, and Brooklyn College. In 1996, he received the FREEDOM OF SPEECH Award from the National Association of Radio Talk Show Hosts.

FURTHER READINGS

Dershowitz, Alan M. 2001. "Is There a Torturous Road to Justice?" *The Los Angeles Times* (November 8).

DESCENT

Hereditary succession. Succession to the ownership of an estate by inheritance, or by any act of law, as distinguished from purchase. Title by descent is the title by which one person, upon the death of another, acquires the real estate of the latter as an heir at law. The title by inheritance is in all cases called descent, although by statute law the title is sometimes made to ascend. The division among those legally entitled thereto of the real property of intestates.

DESCENT AND DISTRIBUTION

The area of law that pertains to the transfer of real property or PERSONAL PROPERTY of a decedent who failed to leave a will or make a valid will and the rights and liabilities of heirs, next of kin, and distributees who are entitled to a share of the property.

Origin of the Law

The passage of property from ancestors to children has been recognized and enforced since biblical times. As a general rule, the law, and not the deceased person, confers the right of succession—the passing of title to a decedent's property—and determines who shall take intestate property. In the United States, such law is derived from the CIVIL LAW and English statutes of distributions, rather than from the COMMON LAW, which preferred the eldest male, under the doctrine of primogeniture, and males over females. Statutes in every state prescribe the order in which persons succeed to a decedent's property if he or she dies intestate, which means without a lawfully executed will. These statutes provide for an orderly administration by identifying successors to a decedent's, also called an intestate's, estate. They seek to implement the distribution that most intestates would have provided had they made wills, on the theory that most persons prefer that their property pass to their nearest relatives rather than to more remote ones. An order of preference among certain relatives of the deceased is established by the statute. If there are no relatives who can inherit the property, the estate escheats, or reverts, to the state.

Persons Entitled

The terms *heirs, next of kin,* and *distributees* usually refer to the persons who by operation of law—the application of the established rules of law—inherit or succeed to the property of a person intestate on his or her death. Statutes generally confer rights of inheritance only on blood relatives, adopted children, adoptive parents, and the surviving spouse. *Line of descent* is the order or series of persons who have descended one from the other or all from a common ancestor, placed in a line in the order of their birth showing the connection of all blood relatives. The direct line of descent involves persons who are directly descended from the same ancestor, such as father and son, or grandfather and grandson. Whether an adopted child can be regarded as in the direct line of descent depends upon the law in the particular jurisdiction. The collateral line of descent involves persons who are descended from a common ancestor, such as brothers who share the same father or cousins

who have the same grandfather. Title by descent differs from title by purchase because descent involves the operation of law, while purchase involves the act or agreement of the parties. Usually direct descendants have first preference in the order of succession, followed by ascendants (persons in the collateral line of ascent), and finally, collateral heirs. Each generation is called a degree in determining the consanguinity, or blood relationship, of one or more persons to an intestate. Where the next of kin of the intestate who are entitled to share in the estate are in equal degree to the deceased, such as children, they share equally in the estate. For example, consider a mother who has two daughters, her only living relations, and dies intestate, leaving an estate of $100,000. Since the two daughters occupy the same proximity of blood relationship to their mother, they share her estate equally, each inheriting $50,000.

Issue has been defined as all persons in the line of descent without regard to the degree of nearness or remoteness from the original source.

Law Governing

If at the time of death, the intestate's estate is located in the state of his or her domicile or permanent residence, the law of that state will govern its descent and distribution. Local laws that govern the area where the property is located generally determine the descent of real property, such as land, houses, and farms, regardless of the domicile of the deceased owner. The succession to and the disposition and distribution of personal or movable property, wherever situated, are governed by the law of the domicile of the owner or intestate at the time of death, unless a statute in the state where the property is located provides otherwise.

Since the privilege of receiving property by inheritance is not a natural right but a creation of law, the legislature of a state has plenary power, or complete authority, over the descent and distribution of property within the borders of the state subject to restrictions found in constitutions and treaties. The disposition of the property of an intestate is governed by the statutes in force at the time of death.

Property Subject to Descent and Distribution

As a general rule, property subject to descent and distribution includes all vested rights and interests owned by the deceased at the time of

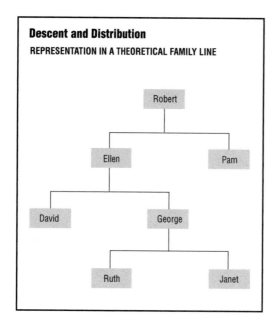

Descent and Distribution

REPRESENTATION IN A THEORETICAL FAMILY LINE

Robert

Ellen

Pam

David

George

Ruth

Janet

death. However, rights or interests that are personal to the deceased, and not of an inheritable nature, ordinarily are not subject to descent and distribution. Examples are a personal right to use land or a statutory right to contest a will.

If a seller dies prior to the completion of the sale of real property, the legal title to land that the seller contracted to sell vests in the heirs at law on the owner's death, subject to their obligation to convey the land to the purchaser according to the contract. A few states authorize the distribution of property among different persons according to whether it is real or personal, but this is not the general rule.

Representation, Per Stirpes, Per Capita

Representation is the principle of law by which the children, or their descendants, of an heir to an estate, who dies without leaving a will, have a collective interest in the intestate's share of the property. Taking by representation means taking per stirpes. For example, Robert, who only has two daughters, Ellen and Pam, dies intestate, leaving an estate of $200,000 after the payment of debts and charges. Under a typical statute, Robert's daughters are his distributees, each receiving $100,000. However, Ellen predeceases her father and leaves two sons, David and George. Since Ellen is not alive to take her share, there would be a per stirpes division of Robert's estate, which means that Ellen's share of $100,000 would be divided equally between David and George, and each would receive $50,000. Pam's $100,000 share of her father's

estate remains unaffected. Since they are brothers, the degree of blood relationship between David and George is equal; therefore, they take per capita, or equal, parts of Ellen's share. However, they have taken per stirpes shares of Robert's estate. Assume that George also died before his grandfather and left two daughters, Ruth and Janet, but his brother David was still alive. David would take $50,000, but Ruth and Janet would have $25,000 apiece. Pam, who is still alive, would still be entitled to $100,000, her share of Robert's estate. The degrees of consanguinity among David and Ruth and Janet are unequal, since David is Robert's grandchild, while Ruth and Janet are his great-grandchildren. David and Ruth and Janet share Ellen's portion of Robert's estate per stirpes. David takes 50 percent, or $50,000, whereas Ruth and Janet each take 25 percent, or $25,000, because of the unequal degrees of blood relationship to Ellen. David is one generation removed from Ellen, while Ruth and Janet are two generations removed from her.

Kindred of the Half Blood

The term *kindred of the half blood* refers to persons who share a half blood relationship with the intestate because they have only one parent in common with each other. As a general rule, kindred of the half blood inherit equally with kindred of the whole blood who have the same parents, unless expressly prohibited by statute. For example, A and B shared the same father with C and D but had a different mother. If A dies, leaving no surviving spouse, children, or parents, C and D share equally with B in A's estate, even though C and D were of the half blood in relation to A, since they had only one parent in common. C and D inherit as if they had both the same parents as A and B.

Necessary or Forced Heirs

The law of forced heirship gave certain relatives, besides the spouse, an absolute legal right, of which they could not be deprived by will or gift, to inherit a certain portion of the decedent's estate. Ordinarily, a person has no right to prevent another from disposing of his or her property by gift or will to someone else. The law of forced heirship in effect in only Louisiana limits the disposition of a decedent's property if his or her parents or legitimate children or their descendants are alive at his or her death. Such persons are expressly declared by law to be forced heirs, and a decedent cannot deprive them of the portion of an estate reserved to them by law unless there is JUST CAUSE to disinherit them. Anyone else who received the property can be legally obligated to return it or to make up the portion of which the forced heirs have been deprived out of his or her own property.

Designated Heirs

In some jurisdictions, statutes permit a person, the designator, to name another to stand in his or her place as an heir at law in the event of his or her death. Anyone can be a designated heir, even a stranger to the designator. The statute does not grant a designated heir any status until the designation becomes effective on the death of the designator. The designator can revoke the designation until the time of his or her death and then designate another. After the death of the designator, a designated heir has the status of an heir at law, and under the statute, the status of a legitimate child of the designator. For example, H designates his wife W as his heir at law. H and W are childless. H is the only child of F. F dies intestate after H's death. The applicable statute of descent and distribution gives all of F's property to his lineal descendants. W will inherit all of F's property since she was H's designated heir at law and is, for inheritance purposes, considered a child of H. She is, therefore, a lineal descendant of F. If the designated heir dies before the designator, his or her heirs generally will not have a right of inheritance in the designator's intestate estate.

Descendants

Subject to the rights of the surviving spouse, children have superior inheritance rights compared to those of other blood relatives. In many jurisdictions, the same principle applies to adopted children of the intestate. Once the debts of the estate have been paid and the surviving spouse has taken his or her legal share, the remainder of the estate is apportioned in equal distributive shares, the portions specified by the law of descent and distribution, among the number of children of the decedent. The rights of the decedent's child or children are greater than not only those of the deceased's brothers and sisters, nephews and nieces, and other collateral kindred but also of the deceased's parents.

Posthumous Children A posthumous child is one born after the death of its father or mother (as, for example, by Caesarean section).

Both at common law and under various state statutes, a posthumous child takes as an heir and a distributee as long as it is born alive after a period of fetal existence that indicates that it was conceived before the death of the intestate father, usually a period of nine months. Some statutes require that a child be born within ten months after the death of the intestate in order to be regarded as a posthumous child. The technique of ARTIFICIAL INSEMINATION, through which a woman can be impregnated with frozen sperm months or even years after the death of the father, poses problems for courts interpreting posthumous child statutes.

Children of Successive Marriages On the death of an intestate who had children by different marriages, all of his or her children take equal shares of the estate once the estate debts have been paid off and the surviving spouse has taken the legal portion. This method of distribution applies unless barred by statute, such as in cases where the property of an intestate was received from a deceased spouse of a former marriage. In that instance, only children of that particular marriage would inherit that property to the exclusion of children of other marriages. In a few states, a slightly different distribution is made of COMMUNITY PROPERTY of the first marriage—one half of that property belonging to the deceased spouse going to the children of that marriage in equal shares, and those children together with the children of the second marriage dividing equally the other half, subject to any rights of the surviving spouse.

Issues of Children who Predecease Intestate The share that a child who dies before the intestate would have inherited if he or she had survived the intestate parent is inherited by his or her children or descendants by the right of representation in per stirpes shares. Grandchildren have better inheritance rights than brothers and sisters of the intestate and their children. However, they do not inherit unless their parent, the child of the intestate, is dead.

Illegitimate Children At common law, an illegitimate child was a filius nullius (Latin for "child of no one") and had no right to inherit. Only legitimate children and issue could inherit an estate upon the death of an intestate parent. This is no longer the case as a result of statutes that vary from state to state. As a general rule, an illegitimate child is treated as the child of the mother and can inherit from her and her relatives and they from the child. In some jurisdictions, the illegitimate child is usually not regarded as a child of the father unless legitimated by the subsequent marriage of the parents or acknowledged by the father as his child, such as in affiliation proceedings. A legitimated child has the same inheritance rights as any other child of the parent. Many statutes permit a child to inherit from his or her father if the PATERNITY is judicially established before the father's death. In the case of *Trimble v. Gordon*, 430 U.S. 762, 97 S. Ct. 1459, 52 L. Ed. 2d 31 (1977), the SUPREME COURT OF THE UNITED STATES decided that it is unconstitutional for states to deprive an illegitimate child of the right to inherit from his or her father when he dies without leaving a will, especially in cases where paternity is already established in state court proceedings prior to the father's death.

Parents

Some statutes permit one or both parents of the intestate to inherit, to some extent, the property of a child leaving no issue or descendants subject to the rights of a surviving spouse. Provisions differ as to whether one or both parents take, whether they take exclusively or share with brothers and sisters, and as to the extent of the share taken. Frequently, if one parent is dead, the surviving parent takes the entire estate, both real and personal, of a deceased child who dies without issue. Some statutes provide that a surviving parent shares with the brothers and sisters.

Stepchildren, Stepparents

Ordinarily, a stepparent does not inherit from the estate of a deceased stepchild. Similarly, stepchildren do not inherit from their stepparent unless the terms of a statute grant them this right.

Brothers, Sisters, and Their Descendants

Brothers and Sisters If an intestate dies without a surviving spouse, issue, or parents, the decedent's brothers and sisters and the children of deceased brothers and sisters will inherit the estate. Brothers and sisters inherit when and only when there are no other surviving persons having priority by virtue of statute. Their inheritance rights are subordinate to children and grandchildren and the parents of the intestate in a number of jurisdictions.

Nephews and Nieces Nephews and nieces usually inherit only if their parent is deceased and would have inherited if he or she had survived the intestate.

Grandparents and Remote Ascendants

Generally, where paternal and maternal grandparents are next of kin to the decedent, they share equally in the estate of an intestate. Some statutes provide that where the estate descended to the intestate from his or her father, it will go to a paternal grandparent to the exclusion of a maternal grandparent. State statutes vary as to whether the grandparents all inherit, or where there are surviving aunts and uncles, as to whether they are excluded by the grandparents. There is a similar division of authority as to whether great-grandparents share with surviving great-uncles and great-aunts.

Remote Collaterals

A collateral heir is one who is not of the direct line of the deceased but comes from a collateral line, such as a brother, a sister, an uncle, an aunt, a nephew, a niece, or a cousin of the deceased. People are related collaterally when they have a common ancestor, such as a parent or grandparent. Where the property in question is within a statute directing the course of descent of property that came to the intestate by gift, devise, or descent from an ancestor, as long as they are the nearest heirs, the remote collateral heirs (for example, cousins) who share that common ancestor are entitled to inherit to the exclusion of collateral heirs who do not.

Operation and Effect of a Will

Rights under intestacy laws are only taken away by a properly executed will disposing of the testator's entire property. These laws can, however, operate in case of partial intestacy where part of the decedent's property is not disposed of by will.

Surviving Spouse

The right of a surviving spouse to share in the estate of a deceased spouse arises automatically from the marital status and not from any contract, conveyance, or other act of the spouse. Statutes conferring such rights on a surviving spouse make the spouse a statutory heir. Some statutes regulating the rights of inheritance of a surviving spouse treat property acquired by the decedent prior to the marriage differently than that acquired during the course of the marriage. Others relating to the descent of ancestral estates and property acquired by gifts do not, ordinarily, exclude a surviving spouse.

Right of Surviving Wife As a general rule, modern statutes confer rights of inheritance on a widow. At common law, the wife was entitled to DOWER, which was a fixed interest in all the land owned by her husband during the marriage. This interest in the lands of her husband was inchoate during his life. She had to survive her husband before she could take possession of her interest in the property. Most states have abolished common-law dower and have replaced it with statutes allowing the surviving widow to take an elective share prescribed by statute, usually one-third or what would have gone to her by intestacy or the provision made in her spouse's will. The extent of and the method for computing the inheritance depends on the terms of the statute applicable to the facts in the particular case. Her rights attach only to property that her husband owned at the time of death. The right of a wife to share in the estate of her husband is qualified by his right to make a valid will. The widow, however, will be given a RIGHT OF ELECTION to choose between the elective share, which is usually her share under the laws of intestacy, or the provision in the will, whichever is larger.

Right of Surviving Husband At common law, a surviving husband had an estate by curtesy in his wife's real property to which he was absolutely entitled upon her death. Curtesy has been abolished by many jurisdictions. As of the early 2000s, a husband's rights of inheritance are regulated by statute applicable to the facts in the particular case. As a general rule, a widower's rights of inheritance attach only to property that his wife owned and possessed at the time she died.

Rights in Case of Remarriage

Unless a statute provides otherwise, a surviving spouse's rights of inheritance are not affected by a later marriage after the death of the decedent. The rights of a survivor of a second or subsequent marriage of the decedent are the same as though he or she were the survivor of the first marriage. In a number of states, the rights of a survivor of a second or subsequent marriage of the deceased or of a surviving spouse who subsequently remarries are, or have been, governed by statutes specifically regulating descent in cases of remarriage.

Waiver or Release of Right

A spouse can waive the right of inheritance to the estate of the other spouse by an antenuptial agreement, which is fairly entered into by both parties with knowledge of all the relevant facts, such as the extent of the spouse's wealth.

This is frequently done by couples who remarry late in life, in order to protect the inheritance rights of their children by previous marriages. For example, an affluent couple executes an antenuptial agreement by which they both agree to surrender their inheritance rights in each other's estate. This insures the inheritance rights of their children from prior marriages in their respective estates, without having the estate reduced by the share given to the surviving spouse under the laws of intestacy. To be effective as a bar, the agreement must, in clear terms or by necessary implication, relinquish the surviving spouse's right of inheritance. It must affirmatively appear that neither spouse took advantage of the confidential relation existing between the parties at the time of its execution.

Unless there are statutory provisions to the contrary, a husband or wife can waive, release, or be estopped (prevented) from asserting rights of inheritance in the estate of the other by certain acts or conduct on his or her part during marriage. As a general rule, a spouse can waive his or her rights in the estate of the other by an express postnuptial agreement. Such an agreement is effective only if it manifests a clear and unmistakable intention to trade away such rights, and it must be supported by a valid and valuable consideration, freely and fairly made; be just and equitable in its provisions; and free from FRAUD and deceit. In one case, the assent of a wife to cohabit with her husband only upon his execution of a release of any claim on her property did not constitute sufficient consideration for his agreement, since she was under a legal duty as his wife to live with him.

A separation agreement can provide for the mutual release of the rights of each spouse in the other's property, including an inchoate or potential right of inheritance that will not vest until the death of one spouse. The rights of inheritance in the property of the husband or wife are not to be denied the surviving spouse unless the purpose to exclude him or her is expressed or can be clearly inferred. A PROPERTY SETTLEMENT agreement conditioned upon a DIVORCE cannot bar a spouse's statutory share in the other's estate where the divorce was never finalized because of the death of the spouse. A mere agreement between HUSBAND AND WIFE in contemplation of divorce, by which specific articles of property are to be held by each separately, is no bar to the rights of the surviving spouse, if no divorce has in fact been granted.

The surviving spouse, however, is not prevented from asserting his or her rights in the estate of the deceased spouse by an agreement entered into as a result of ignorance or mistake as to his or her legal rights.

Forfeiture of Rights

As a general rule, a surviving spouse's misconduct, whether criminal or otherwise, does not bar his or her rights to succeed to the deceased person's estate where the statute of descent and distribution confers certain rights on the surviving spouse and makes no exception on account of misconduct.

Abandonment, Adultery, and Nonsupport Unless there are statutes to the contrary, the fact that one spouse abandoned or deserted the other, or even the fact that he or she abandoned the other and lived in ADULTERY, does not bar that spouse's rights of inheritance in the other's estate. However, in a number of jurisdictions express statutory provisions do not permit a surviving wife to succeed to her husband's estate if she has abandoned him or left him to live in adultery. A surviving husband similarly loses his statutory right to inherit from his wife's estate where he abandoned or willfully and maliciously deserted her or neglected or refused to support her. In order to constitute a FORFEITURE of inheritance rights, such conduct must be deliberate and unjustified and continue for a period of time specified by statute. Mere separation is not necessarily ABANDONMENT or desertion if the parties have consented to the separation or there is reasonable and justifiable cause for the action. The fact of one spouse's subsequent meretricious conduct is not abandonment if a separation agreement does not provide for forfeiture of that spouse's right to share in the decedent's estate.

Murder of Spouse There is no uniform rule as to whether a person who murders his or her spouse can succeed to the decedent's estate as the surviving spouse. Some jurisdictions refuse to recognize the murderer as a surviving spouse. In others, a statute that confers certain rights on the surviving spouse does not strip the spouse of that right because he or she caused the death of the intestate spouse by criminal conduct. Different states have enacted statutes that preclude any person who has caused or procured the death of another from inheriting the decedent's property under certain circumstances. An intentional killing will bar an inheritance, but a death that occurs as a result of NEGLIGENCE, accidental

means, or insanity will not have this effect. For example, where conviction is essential to create a forfeiture under the statute, a surviving spouse who is not convicted but is committed to a state hospital for the legally insane is not excluded from the rights of inheritance. A conviction of MANSLAUGHTER might be sufficient to satisfy the statutory requirement of conviction, but it is insufficient if the statute requires actual conviction of murder.

Bigamous Marriage In some jurisdictions, a spouse who commits bigamy, marrying while still legally married to another, can be denied any rights of inheritance in the estate of his or her lawful spouse. This is true even if the bigamous marriage had been terminated long before the death of the lawful spouse. In a few jurisdictions, the fact that one who was legally married to the decedent contracted a bigamous marriage does not bar his or her rights of inheritance in the decedent's estate.

Divorce Generally, a person who has been divorced can claim no share in the estate of the former spouse. Under some statutes, a divorce a mensa et thoro (Latin for "from bed or board"), which is a legal separation, can abrogate any right of intestate inheritance in the spouse's estate, even though the decedent and spouse remained lawfully married until the death of the decedent.

Rights and Liabilities of Heirs

No one is an heir to a living person. Before the death of the ancestor, an expectant heir or distributee has no vested interest but only a mere expectancy or possibility of inheritance. Such an individual cannot on the basis of his or her prospective right maintain an action during the life of the ancestor to cancel a transfer of property made by the ancestor.

Advancements An advancement is similar to an absolute or irrevocable gift of money or real or personal property. It is made in the present by a parent to a child in anticipation of what the child's intestate share will be when the parent dies. An advancement differs from an ordinary gift in that it reduces only the child's distributive share of the parent's estate by the stated amount, while a gift diminishes the entire estate. The doctrine of advancements is based on the theory that a parent is presumed to intend that all his or her children have equal rights not only in what may remain at the parent's death but in all property owned by the parent. Statutes of descent and distribution can provide for consideration of advancements made by a deceased during his or her lifetime to achieve equality in the distribution of the estate among the children.

An advancement can also be made by grandparents and, where statutes permit, by spouses and collateral relatives. A parent's gifts to a child cannot be deemed advancements while the donor is alive, since they are significant only in relation to a decedent's estate. Several statutes provide that no gift or grant of realty can be deemed to have been made as an advancement unless expressed in writing by the donor or acknowledged in writing by the donee. A transfer based on love and affection or a nominal consideration can constitute an advancement, while a transfer for a valuable consideration cannot, since as a gift, an advancement is made without consideration.

Release, Renunciation, or Acceptance of Rights An heir can relinquish his or her rights to an estate by an express waiver, release, or ESTOPPEL. Generally, the release of an expected share, fairly and freely made to an ancestor in consideration of an advancement or for other valuable consideration, excludes the heir from sharing in the ancestor's estate at the time of death. It is necessary that the person executing the release be competent to contract at the time, that the release not be obtained by means of fraud or UNDUE INFLUENCE, and that the instrument or transaction in question be sufficient to constitute a release or renunciation of rights. In one case, a daughter gave her father a receipt acknowledging payment of money that she accepted as her "partial" share of all real estate left by him. The court held that she was not barred from sharing in the remainder of the real estate left upon her father's death, since the word *partial* indicated that the money received was merely an advancement.

At common law, a person could not renounce an intestate share, but modern statutes permit renunciation. A renunciation or a waiver sometimes requires the execution and delivery of a formal document. Renunciation is frequently employed by those who would incur an increased tax burden if the gift were to be accepted.

A simple acceptance can be either express or implied. A person can be barred from accepting his or her rights to an estate by a lapse of time, as specified by statute. Once a person accepts an intestate share, he or she cannot subsequently renounce the share under most statutes. A person who renounces the succession cannot revoke the renunciation after the other heirs have accepted the property that constitutes his or her share. However, that person can accept his or her share if the other heirs have not yet done so.

Gifts and Conveyances in Fraud of Heirs

A person ordinarily has the right to dispose of his or her property as he or she sees fit, so that heirs and distributees cannot attack transfers or distributions made during the decedent's lifetime as being without consideration or in fraud of their rights. For example, a parent during his or her life can distribute property among his or her children any way he or she wants with or without reason, and those adversely affected have no standing to challenge the distribution.

One spouse can deprive the other of rights of inheritance given by statute through absolute transfers of property during his or her life. In some jurisdictions, however, transfers made by a spouse for the mere purpose of depriving the other of a distributive share are invalid. Whether a transfer made by a spouse was real or made merely to deprive the other spouse of the statutory share is determined by whether the person actually surrenders complete ownership and possession of the property. For example, a husband's transfer of all his property to a trustee is void and illusory as to the rights of his surviving wife if he reserves to himself the income of the property for life, the power to revoke and modify the trust, and a significant amount of control over the management of the trust. There is no intent to part with ownership of his property until his death. Such a trust is a device created to deprive the wife of her distributive share. Advancements or gifts to children, including children by a former marriage, which are reasonable in relation to the amount of property owned and are made in GOOD FAITH without any intent to defraud a spouse, afford that spouse no grounds of complaint. Good faith is shown where the other spouse knew of the advancements. If a spouse gives all or most of his or her property to the children without the other spouse's knowledge, a rebuttable presumption of fraud arises that might be explained by the children.

Title of Heirs and Distributees

Inheritance rights vest immediately on the death of an intestate, and the heirs are usually determined as of that time. The title to realty ordinarily vests in an intestate's heirs immediately upon his or her death, subject, under varying circumstances, to certain burdens, such as the rights of the surviving spouse or the debts of the intestate. The title obtained by the heirs on the death of their ancestor is subject to funeral expenses, the expenses, debts, or charges of the administration, and the charges for which the real property is liable, such as liens and encumbrances attached to the land during the lifetime of the intestate.

At common law and under the statutes of most states, the title to personal property of a deceased person does not ordinarily vest in his or her heirs, next of kin, or distributees on his or her death. Their title and rights, therefore, must generally be obtained or enforced by virtue of administration or distribution. Legal title to personal property is suspended between the time of the intestate's death and the granting of the LETTERS OF ADMINISTRATION. On distribution, the title of the distributees relates back to the date of the intestate's death. While the title to personal property does not immediately vest in the heirs, their interest in the estate does. The heirs have a vested equitable right, title, or estate in the personal property, subject to the rights of creditors and to charges and expenses of the administration. The personal estate of an intestate goes ultimately to those who are next of kin at the time of the intestate's death as opposed to those who are next of kin at the time that the estate is to be distributed. If a person who is entitled as a distributee dies after the death of the intestate and before distribution, his or her share does not go to the other persons entitled as distributees, but instead passes to his or her own heirs.

Debts of Intestate Estate

Heirs and distributees generally receive property of their ancestor subject to his or her debts. The obligation of an heir or distributee to pay an ancestor's debt is based upon his or her possession of the ancestor's property. All property of an intestate ordinarily can be applied to pay his or her debts, but, generally, the personal property must be exhausted first before realty can be used.

Rights and Remedies of Creditors, Heirs, and Distributees

The interest of an heir or distributee in the estate of an ancestor can be taken by his or her creditors for the payment of debts, depending upon the applicable law. Advancements received by an heir or distributee must be deducted first from his or her share before the rights of creditors of the heir or distributee can be enforced against the share.

FURTHER READINGS

Akright, Carol. 2001. *Funding your Dreams Generation to Generation: Intergenerational Financial Planning to Ensure your Family's Health, Wealth, and Personal Values.* Chicago: Dearborn Trade.

Brashier, Ralph C. 2004. *Inheritance Law and the Evolving Family.* Philadelphia, Pa.: Temple Univ. Press.

Condon, Gerald M., and Jeffrey L. Condon. 1994. *Beyond the Grave: The Right Way and the Wrong Way of Leaving Money to Your Children.* New York: HarperInformation.

Daly, Eugene J. 1994. *Thy Will Be Done: A Guide to Wills, Taxation, and Estate Planning for Older Persons.* Amherst, N.Y.: Prometheus.

CROSS-REFERENCES

Consanguinity; Decedent; Escheat; Premarital Agreement.

DESCRIPTIVE WORD INDEX

An alphabetically arranged aid used in legal research used to locate cases that have discussed a particular topic.

The descriptive word index contains key WORDS AND PHRASES that lead researchers to the information they are seeking. For example, in preparing a brief on behalf of a client who slipped and fell in a supermarket, an attorney might look in the descriptive word index under the heading "slip and fall" to find legal precedent for the case.

Descriptive word indices are generally part of all case digests.

DESEGREGATION

See SCHOOL DESEGREGATION.

DESERTION

The act by which a person abandons and forsakes, without justification, a condition of public, social, or family life, renouncing its responsibilities and evading its duties. A willful ABANDONMENT of an employment or duty in violation of a legal or moral obligation.

Criminal desertion is a husband's or wife's abandonment or willful failure without JUST CAUSE to provide for the care, protection, or support of a spouse who is in ill health or necessitous circumstances.

Desertion, which is called abandonment in some statutes, is a DIVORCE ground in a majority of states. Most statutes mandate that the abandonment continue for a certain period of time before a divorce action may be commenced. The length of this period varies between one and five years; it is most commonly one year. The period of separation must be continuous and uninterrupted. In addition, proof that the departed spouse left without the consent of the other spouse is required in most states.

Ordinarily, proof of desertion is a clear-cut factual matter. Courts generally require evidence that the departure was voluntary and that the deserted husband or wife in no way provoked or agreed to the abandonment. Constructive desertion occurs when one party makes life so intolerable for his or her spouse that the spouse has no real choice but to leave the marital home. For an individual to have legal justification for departing, it is often required that the spouse act so wrongfully as to constitute grounds for divorce. For example, a wife might leave her husband if she finds that he is guilty of ADULTERY.

In desertion cases, it is not necessary to prove the emotional state of the abandoning spouse, but only the intent to break off matrimonial ties with no animus revertendi, the intention to return.

Mere separation does not constitute desertion if a HUSBAND AND WIFE agree that they cannot cohabit harmoniously. Sexual relations between the parties must be totally severed during the period of separation. If two people live apart from one another but meet on a regular basis for sex, this does not constitute desertion. State law dictates whether or not an infrequent meeting for sexual relations amounts to an interruption of the period required for desertion. Some statutes provide that an occasional act of sexual intercourse terminates the period only if the husband and wife are attempting reconciliation.

Unintentional abandonment is not desertion. For example, if a man is missing in action while serving in the ARMED SERVICES, his wife may not obtain a divorce on desertion grounds since her spouse did not intend to leave his family and flee the marital relationship. The COMMON LAW allows an individual to presume that a spouse is dead if the spouse is unexplainably absent for a seven-year period. If the spouse returns at any time, the marriage remains intact under common law.

Laws that embody the ENOCH ARDEN DOCTRINE grant a divorce if evidence establishes that an individual's spouse has vanished and cannot be found through diligent efforts. A particular period of time must elapse. Sometimes, if conditions evidencing death can be exhibited, a divorce may be granted prior to the expiration of the time specified by law.

In some jurisdictions, the law is stringent regarding divorce grounds. In such instances, an Enoch Arden decree might be labeled a dissolution of the marriage rather than a divorce.

Upon the granting of an Enoch Arden decree, the marriage is terminated regardless of whether or not the absent spouse returns. Generally, the court provides that the plaintiff must show precisely what has been done to locate the missing person. Efforts to find the absent spouse might include inquiries made to friends or relatives to determine if they have had contact with the missing spouse, or checking public records for such documents as a marriage license, death certificate, tax returns, or application for SOCIAL SECURITY in locations where the individual is known to have resided.

Desertion is frequently coupled with nonsupport, which is a failure to provide monetary resources for those to whom such an obligation is due. Nonsupport is a crime in a majority of states but prosecutions are uncommon.

DESK AUDIT

An evaluation of a particular civil service position to determine whether its duties and responsibilities correspond to its job classification and salary grade.

DESTROY

In general, to ruin completely; may include a taking. To ruin the structure, organic existence, or condition of a thing; to demolish; to injure or mutilate beyond possibility of use; to nullify.

As used in policies of insurance, in leases, and in maritime law, and under various statutes, this term is often applied to an act that renders the subject useless for its intended purpose, though it does not literally demolish or annihilate it.

In relation to wills, contracts, and other documents, the term *destroy* does not mean the annihilation of the instrument or its resolution into other forms of matter, but a destruction of its legal efficacy, which may be by cancellation, obliterating, tearing into fragments, and so on.

DESUETUDE

The state of being unused; legally, the doctrine by which a law or treaty is rendered obsolete because of disuse. The concept encompasses situations in which a court refuses to enforce an unused law even if the law has not been repealed.

Desuetude saw use as a defense during the U.S. Supreme Court's landmark 2003 decision in LAWRENCE V. TEXAS, which dealt with Texas' SODOMY law. Lawrence successfully argued that since statutes prohibiting sodomy had either fallen into obscurity or been overturned in most states, Texas' statute was similarly invalid.

DETAINER

The act (or the juridical fact) of withholding from a lawfully entitled person the possession of land or goods, or the restraint of a person's personal liberty against his or her will; detention. The wrongful keeping of a person's goods is called an UNLAWFUL DETAINER although the original taking may have been lawful.

A request filed by a criminal justice agency with the institution in which a prisoner is incarcerated asking the institution either to hold the prisoner for the agency or to notify the agency when release of the prisoner is imminent.

DETECTIVES

Individuals whose business it is to observe and provide information about alleged criminals or to discover matters of secrecy for the protection of the public.

Private detectives are those who are hired by individuals for private protection or to obtain information. A private detective is licensed but is not ordinarily considered to be a public officer. In cases where private detectives perform the duties and exercise the powers of public officers, the constitutional provisions governing such officers can be applied to them.

Public detectives are employed by the general community for the protection of society and, as members of public law enforcement agencies and police departments, are considered peace officers.

The incorporation of private detective companies or associations may be subject to statutory requirements. Detectives are regulated by legislation as well as the rules of the municipality where they are employed. In the absence of contrary statutory provision, private detectives do not have the same powers as public peace officers.

A private detective can be held liable for *rough shadowing*—the open and public surveillance of an individual done in an unreasonable manner that constitutes an invasion of privacy.

DETENTION

The act of keeping back, restraining, or withholding, either accidentally or by design, a person or thing.

Detention occurs whenever a police officer accosts an individual and restrains his or her freedom to walk away, or approaches and questions an individual, or stops an individual suspected of being personally involved in criminal activity. Such a detention is not a formal arrest. Physical restraint is not an essential element of detention.

Detention is also an element of the TORT of FALSE IMPRISONMENT.

DETERMINABLE

Liable to come to an end upon the happening of a certain contingency. Susceptible of being determined, found out, definitely decided upon, or settled.

DETERMINATE SENTENCE

A sentence to confinement for a fixed or minimum period that is specified by statute.

Determinate sentencing encompasses sentencing guidelines, mandatory minimum sentences, and enhanced sentences for certain

The approach and questioning of an individual by law enforcement officials is considered an act of detention. Police officers in Norfolk, Virginia, question a man following the September 2002 robbery of a U.S. bank branch.

AP/WIDE WORLD PHOTOS

crimes. Sentencing guidelines allow judges to consider the individual circumstances of the case when determining a sentence, whereas mandatory minimum and enhanced-sentence statutes leave little or no discretion to judges in setting the terms of a sentence.

Determinate sentencing statutes have existed at various times throughout the history of the United States. They became popular in the 1980s, when public concern over crime increased dramatically and the public demanded stringent laws to address the crime problem. Operating under the belief that certainty of punishment deters crime, Congress and the states responded by passing laws that dictate specific sentences for certain crimes or for repeat offenders. These laws have been a source of considerable controversy.

Many of the determinate sentencing measures adopted during the 1980s and 1990s were by-products of the war on drugs. They require strict, harsh, and non-negotiable sentences for the possession of narcotics. These stringent laws have led to some unintended and inconsistent results. For example, repeat offenders who have information that is useful to the police sometimes receive lighter sentences than do nonviolent, first-time offenders, in return for their testimony.

Another type of determinate sentence that has been popular since the 1990s is the "three-strikes-and-you're-out" law, which mandates a heavy sentence for anyone who is convicted of a third felony. For example, California Penal Code, section 667, requires a minimum sentence of 25 years to life for a third conviction for a serious felony, and it doubles the usual sentence imposed for a crime when it is a second offense. The purposes of the law are to incapacitate repeat offenders and to deter others from committing crimes.

The constitutionality of the three-strikes laws has come into question in a number of decisions. In 2003, the U.S. Supreme Court, in *Lockyer v. Andrade*, 538 U.S. 63, 123 S. Ct. 1166, 155 L. Ed. 2d 144 (2003), held that these laws do not violate the Eighth Amendment's prohibition against CRUEL AND UNUSUAL PUNISHMENT, thus reversing a decision by the Ninth Circuit Court of Appeals. The decision resolved a dispute between state and federal courts in California.

Leandro Andrade received a life sentence with no possibility for PAROLE for 50 years for stealing nine videotapes worth a total of $153.54. The California trial court applied the three-strikes provision and elevated the crimes to felonies. These felony convictions for petty theft counted as "strikes" three and four against Andrade. Andrade appealed his sentence to a California appellate court, which upheld the trial court's ruling and rejected, among other claims, that the sentence violated Andrade's EIGHTH AMENDMENT rights.

Andrade then filed a petition for a writ of HABEAS CORPUS with a federal district court in California, which denied the petition. He then appealed to the Ninth Circuit, which reversed the denial of the petition in *Andrade v. Lockyer*, 270 F.3d 743 (9th Cir. 2001). The appeals court noted that, while all other states enhance sentences for repeat offenders, California's law is unusually strict. It held that the sentence was so grossly disproportionate to Andrade's crime that it violated the Eighth Amendment's prohibition against cruel and unusual punishment. Andrade would not be eligible for parole until age 87.

The Ninth Circuit's opinion relied in part on the U.S. Supreme Court's decision in *Solem v. Helm*, 463 U.S. 277, 103 S. Ct. 3001, 77 L. Ed. 2d 637 (1983), which held that the Eighth Amendment prohibits sentences that are disproportionate to the crime committed. The Ninth Circuit panel disapproved the ruling by the California appellate court that had heard Andrade's original appeal, because the state court had disregarded *Solem* in making its decision. In the months that followed the Ninth Circuit's decision, two California courts of appeals affirmed trial-court sentences of 25 years to life for petty theft convictions. According to the California court, the Ninth Circuit's majority opinion in *Andrade* was flawed. More than a dozen additional California courts refused to follow *Andrade* because the facts in those cases could be distinguished from those in *Andrade*.

The Supreme Court in *Lockyer v. Andrade* analyzed the Ninth Circuit's decision in light of the Antiterrorism and Effective Death Penalty Act, 28 U.S.C.A. § 2254(d)(1) (2003). Under that statute, a federal court may grant a writ of habeas corpus if a state court correctly identifies a legal principle from U.S. Supreme Court decisions, but incorrectly applies the principle to the facts of the case under review. The Ninth Circuit had determined that the California appellate court had improperly applied "clearly established" U.S. Supreme Court precedent to Andrade's case.

Determinate Sentence

AVERAGE PRISON SENTENCES FOR SELECTED OFFENSES, IN 2001[a]

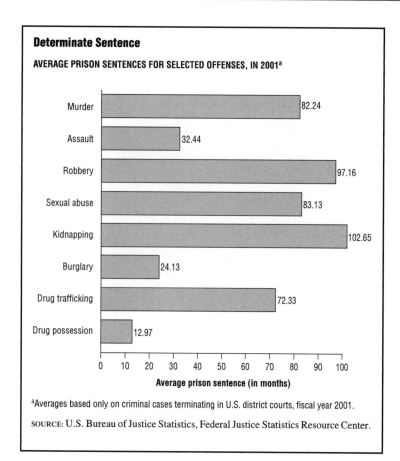

Murder 82.24
Assault 32.44
Robbery 97.16
Sexual abuse 83.13
Kidnapping 102.65
Burglary 24.13
Drug trafficking 72.33
Drug possession 12.97

Average prison sentence (in months)

[a]Averages based only on criminal cases terminating in U.S. district courts, fiscal year 2001.

SOURCE: U.S. Bureau of Justice Statistics, Federal Justice Statistics Resource Center.

The Court found that prior decisions by the Court had not provided sufficient clarity on the issue, and that the California appellate court had not misapplied "clearly established" precedent. The fact that the 50-year sentence was essentially a life sentence because of the age of the defendant did not change the outcome, a point that Justice DAVID SOUTER raised in a dissent. Justice SANDRA DAY O'CONNOR, who wrote the majority opinion, disagreed, stating that Justice Souter's argument "misses the point." According to the analysis by the Court, because the state court had not violated a "clearly established" principle, the federal court should not have granted the writ of habeas corpus.

Although the Court focused on the standard for a federal court granting habeas corpus, the effect of the decision is that the three-strikes law does not violate the Eighth Amendment. Accordingly, the several states are generally free to enact such sentencing provisions, and the debate for and against such laws has been left to the various state legislatures.

Supporters of three-strikes laws maintain that the severity of the third crime is not impor-

tant. Rather, the pattern of violations indicates a life of lawlessness deserving severe penalty. Critics contend that the punishment is sometimes out of proportion to the crime. They point to the example of Jerry Williams, who, in January 1995, was convicted of felony petty theft for stealing a slice of pizza from a group of children in Redondo Beach. Usually, petty theft is a misdemeanor; prosecutors were allowed to charge Williams with felony petty theft because he had previous felony convictions. Williams's 1995 conviction triggered the three-strikes law and brought him an automatic sentence of 25 years to life. A similar case involved Steve Gordon, who had turned to petty crime to support his drug habit after he was fired from his job in 1985. Gordon was convicted of stealing $200 from the cash register at a fast-food restaurant and of snatching a purse, and then, in March 1994, of attempting to steal a wallet. His third conviction triggered the mandatory minimum sentence of 25 years to life.

Many judges oppose determinate sentencing when it prescribes mandatory minimum terms. A 1994 survey of federal judges conducted by the AMERICAN BAR ASSOCIATION found that a majority strongly supported repealing most or all mandatory minimum sentences. In March 1994, during a hearing before the House Appropriations Committee on the U.S. Supreme Court's budget, Justice ANTHONY M. KENNEDY, of the Supreme Court, called mandatory sentence legislation imprudent, unwise, and potentially unjust. Most judges feel that sentencing guidelines, which prescribe sentences that may be altered in accord with aggravating or MITIGATING CIRCUMSTANCES, are preferable to mandatory minimums.

Some judges have attempted to circumvent determinate sentences, but their efforts have failed. In July 1994, Judge Lawrence Antolini, of the Sonoma County, California, Superior Court, challenged California's three-strikes law by sentencing Jeffrey Missamore, a three-time offender, to PROBATION and drug treatment instead of the 25 years to life that the statute mandated. The state petitioned the appellate court to overturn Antolini's probation order. The Superior Court of Sonoma County granted the writ, stating that it is not the role of the judiciary to question the appropriateness of the public policy decisions embodied in the three-strikes law. The court held, "If people (including judges) feel those provisions . . . lead to unfair results, the law can be changed" (*People v. Superior Court*, 45 Cal. Rptr. 2d 392 [Cal. App. 1995]).

Another divisive issue in the determinate sentencing debate is the disparate effects of new laws concerning cocaine. The penalties for the possession of crack cocaine are substantially higher than those for powder cocaine. Crack is a less expensive form of cocaine that is smoked rather than snorted. Because crack is less expensive than powder, it is used more widely by young people, poor people, and members of minority groups—who constitute a disproportionate number of those incarcerated on drug charges. Critics have attacked the enhanced and mandatory penalties for possession of crack as discriminatory.

Whether determinate sentences work to deter crime is an open question. Both sides of the debate summon statistical evidence to support their positions. Opponents claim that from 1986 to 1991, when determinate sentencing was used extensively, violent crime continued to increase, even as the rate of incarceration rose dramatically. Supporters counter that the FBI's Uniform Crime Index shows a four percent drop in serious crime between 1989 and 1993, suggesting that perhaps stringent sentencing is beginning to affect the crime rate. Supporters also cite statistics indicating that the number of federal drug convictions doubled from 1985 to 1993. Opponents counter that most of those who were convicted were first-time offenders or low-level drug dealers, not the powerful drug kingpins whom the laws were designed to ensnare.

FURTHER READINGS

Forer, Lois G. 1994. *A Rage to Punish*. New York: Norton.

"Mandatory Sentencing: Do Tough Sentencing Laws Reduce Crime?" 1995. *CQ Researcher* (May 26).

O'Connell, John P. 1995. "Throwing Away the Key (and State Money)." *Spectrum: the Journal of State Government* (winter).

Reske, Henry J. 1994. "Judges Irked by Tough-on-Crime Laws." *American Bar Association Journal* (October).

Sauer, Kristen K. 1995. "Informed Conviction: Instructing the Jury about Mandatory Sentencing Consequences." *Columbia Law Review* 95: 1232.

Sklansky, David A. 1995. "Cocaine, Race, and Equal Protection." *Stanford Law Review* 47: 1283.

DETERMINATION

The final resolution or conclusion of a controversy.

In legal use, determination usually implies the conclusion of a dispute or lawsuit by the rendering of a final decision. After consideration of the facts, a determination is generally set forth by a court of justice or other type of formal decision maker, such as the head of an ADMINISTRATIVE AGENCY.

Determination has been used synonymously with adjudication, award, decree, and judgment. A ruling is a judicial determination concerning matters, such as the admissibility of evidence or a judicial or an administrative interpretation of a statute or regulation.

DETERRENCE

A theory that criminal laws are passed with well-defined punishments to discourage individual criminal defendants from becoming repeat offenders and to discourage others in society from engaging in similar criminal activity

Deterrence is one of the primary objects of the CRIMINAL LAW. Its primary goal is to discourage members of society from committing criminal acts out of fear of punishment. The most powerful deterrent would be a criminal justice system that guaranteed with certainty that all persons who broke the law would be apprehended, convicted, and punished, and would receive no personal benefit from their wrongdoing. However, it is unrealistic to believe that any criminal justice system could ever accomplish this goal, no matter how many law enforcement resources were dedicated to achieving it.

As a result, philosophers, criminologists, judges, lawyers, and others have debated whether and to what extent any criminal justice system actually serves as a deterrent. Deterrence requires the would-be criminal to possess some degree of reflective capacity before the crime is committed, at least enough reflection to consider the possible consequences of violating the law if caught.

Since many crimes are committed during "the heat of the moment" when an individual's reflective capacities are severely compromised, most observers agree that some crimes simply cannot be deterred. Individuals who commit crimes for the thrill of "getting away with it" and outwitting law enforcement officials probably cannot be deterred either. In fact, such individuals may only be tempted and encouraged by law enforcement claims of superior crime-prevention and crime-solving skills.

CROSS-REFERENCES

Criminology; Justification; Motive.

DETINUE

One of the old common-law FORMS OF ACTION *used to recover* PERSONAL PROPERTY *from a person who refuses to give it up. Also used to collect money damages for losses caused by the wrongful detention.*

Dating back to the twelfth century, detinue is one of the oldest forms of action in common law, along with the action of debt—a lawsuit for a specific sum of money owed. In detinue a favorable judgment awarded the plaintiff the actual chattels—items of personal property— or their value in money. For example, an action of detinue was available against someone who wrongfully refused to return goods that were held subject to a BAILMENT, such as a deposit for safekeeping or repair. It could be used against an executor who refused to turn over a deed for the deceased person's property to the proper heir. Since the plaintiff did not have to show wrongful detention to prove his or her case, the action was appropriate for recovering goods from a thief as well as from someone who first acquired the property lawfully.

There were several drawbacks in an action of detinue. The defendant could prove his or her case by WAGER OF LAW, for example. That meant that the defendant could swear in open court and bring along eleven neighbors who would take an oath that they, in good conscience, believed the defendant was telling the truth. If the plaintiff won the case, the defendant was required only to give up the items in question. This was small comfort when the goods were damaged or spoiled, since there was no remedy at detinue for harm done to the property while it was in the hands of the defendant. By the fifteenth century, plaintiffs were able to use the more satisfactory form of action on the case, and in the sixteenth century a special kind of action on the case, called TROVER, was intro-

duced. After that, these forms were used much more often than detinue to recover personal property.

Today the action of detinue has been almost entirely superseded by statutes that streamline CIVIL PROCEDURE, but the principles underlying the ancient COMMON LAW form of action are still the foundation of modern actions for the recovery of personal property.

DETRIMENT

Any loss or harm to a person or property; relinquishment of a legal right, benefit, or something of value.

Detriment is most frequently applied to contract formation, since it is an essential element of consideration, which is a prerequisite of a legally enforceable contract. To incur detriment means to cement a promise by either refraining from doing something that one has a legal right to do or by doing something that one is not under any legal obligation to do.

❖ DEVENS, CHARLES

Charles Devens was born April 4, 1820, in Charlestown, Massachusetts. He graduated from Harvard University in 1838 and received a doctor of laws degree in 1877. He was admitted to the Massachusetts bar in 1840 and began a career that encompassed military and legal achievements.

Devens participated in the Massachusetts Senate during 1848 and 1849, followed by service as U.S. marshal from 1849 to 1853. He acted as solicitor for the city of Worcester, Massachusetts, from 1856 to 1858 and then left government service to pursue a military career in 1861.

The Civil War provided Devens with many opportunities to display his military expertise. He fought for the Union in three major Virginia

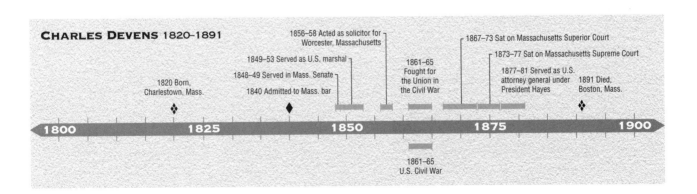

CHARLES DEVENS 1820–1891

1820 Born, Charlestown, Mass.

1840 Admitted to Mass. bar

1848–49 Served in Mass. Senate

1849–53 Served as U.S. marshal

1856–58 Acted as solicitor for Worcester, Massachusetts

1861–65 Fought for the Union in the Civil War

1867–73 Sat on Massachusetts Superior Court

1873–77 Sat on Massachusetts Supreme Court

1877–81 Served as U.S. attorney general under President Hayes

1891 Died, Boston, Mass.

1800   1825   1850   1875   1900

1861–65 U.S. Civil War

battles fought at Fredericksburg, Chancellorville, and Cold Harbor, earning the rank of major general.

In 1867, he began his judicial career and served as judge of the Massachusetts Superior Court. In 1873, he was appointed to the bench of the Massachusetts Supreme Court.

He began service to the federal government in 1877 as attorney general under President RUTHERFORD B. HAYES, a post he held until 1881.

An army post, Camp Devens, in Ayer, Massachusetts, was named for Charles Devens in recognition of his military accomplishments.

Devens died January 7, 1891, in Boston.

DEVIANCE

Conspicuous dissimilarity with, or variation from, customarily acceptable behavior.

Deviance implies a lack of compliance to societal norms, such as by engaging in activities that are frowned upon by society and frequently have legal sanctions as well, for example, the illegal use of drugs.

DEVISE

A testamentary disposition of land or realty; a gift of real property by the last will and testament of the donor. When used as a noun, it means a testamentary disposition of real or PERSONAL PROPERTY, and when used as a verb, it means to dispose of real or personal property by will. To contrive; plan; scheme; invent; prepare.

DEWEY DECIMAL SYSTEM

A numerical classification system of books employed by libraries.

Thomas E. Dewey.
LIBRARY OF CONGRESS

The Dewey Decimal System, created by Melvil Dewey, is a reference system that classifies all subjects by number. The numbers in a particular grouping all refer to a designated general topic. For example, the numbers in the 340s concern topics of law. Each new number after the decimal point further subdivides the previous number and the subject it covers.

❖ DEWEY, THOMAS EDMUND

Thomas Edmund Dewey was born March 24, 1902, in Owosso, Michigan. He received a bachelor of arts degree in 1923 from the University of Michigan and a bachelor of laws degree from Columbia University in 1925.

After his admission to the bar in 1925, Dewey established his legal practice before becoming U. S. Attorney for the Southern Dis-

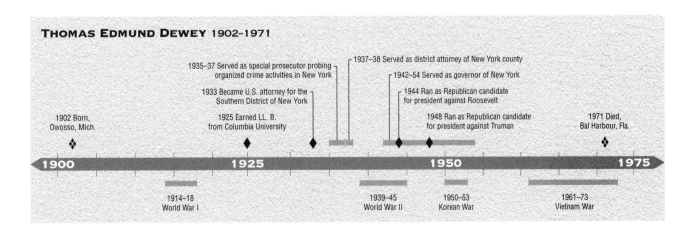

THOMAS EDMUND DEWEY 1902–1971

1935–37 Served as special prosecutor probing organized crime activities in New York

1937–38 Served as district attorney of New York county

1933 Became U.S. attorney for the Southern District of New York

1942–54 Served as governor of New York

1944 Ran as Republican candidate for president against Roosevelt

1948 Ran as Republican candidate for president against Truman

1902 Born, Owosso, Mich.

1925 Earned LL. B. from Columbia University

1971 Died, Bal Harbour, Fla.

1900   1925   1950   1975

1914–18 World War I

1939–45 World War II

1950–53 Korean War

1961–73 Vietnam War

trict of New York in 1933. During the next three years, Dewey achieved prominence for his campaign against crime in New York City, serving as special prosecutor to probe the activities of ORGANIZED CRIME from 1935 to 1937 and as district attorney of New York county from 1937 to 1938.

Dewey's public service to the state of New York culminated in his election as governor in 1942; he remained in this post until 1954.

Twice during his years as governor, Dewey unsuccessfully sought election to the U. S. presidency. He was the Republican candidate in 1944 but was defeated by FRANKLIN DELANO ROOSEVELT; he ran again in 1948 but lost by a small percentage of votes to HARRY S. TRUMAN.

As an author, Dewey is famous for several publications, including *Journey to the Far Pacific* (1952), which is a chronicle of his trip to the Far East.

Dewey died March 16, 1971, in Bal Harbour, Florida.

❖ DICKINSON, JOHN

John Dickinson was born November 8, 1732, in Talbot County, Maryland. He was educated at the College of New Jersey (today known as Princeton University), where he earned a doctor of laws degree in 1768. He also pursued legal studies at the Middle Temple, Inn of the Court, England.

After his admission to the Philadelphia bar in 1757, Dickinson established a prestigious legal practice in that city and subsequently entered politics on the state level.

> "IT IS INSEPARABLY ESSENTIAL TO THE FREEDOM OF A PEOPLE THAT NO TAXES BE IMPOSED ON THEM BUT WITH THEIR OWN CONSENT, GIVEN PERSONALLY OR BY THEIR REPRESENTATIVES."
> —JOHN DICKINSON

In 1760, Dickinson served in the Assembly of Lower Counties, Delaware, and performed the duties of speaker. Two years later, he participated in the Pennsylvania legislature, representing Philadelphia until 1764, and again, from 1770 to 1776. In 1765, Dickinson wrote a pamphlet titled *The Late Regulations Respecting the British Colonies on the Continent of America Considered,* which protested the passage of two unjust acts of taxation, the STAMP ACT and the Sugar Act, by England. In the same year, he also served at the Stamp Act Congress and drafted a series of requests to King George III. Although he opposed many of the policies enforced by England, Dickinson favored conciliatory action over violence.

England passed the unpopular TOWNSHEND ACTS in 1767, which levied tariffs on colonial imports of certain items. Dickinson composed another publication in protest, known as "Letters from a Farmer in Pennsylvania"; these letters advocated nonimportation of the taxed materials, rather than a violent reaction to the passage of the act.

Dickinson continued to serve in pre-Revolutionary War activities, including the Committee of Correspondence in 1774 and the CONTINENTAL CONGRESS from 1774 to 1776 and from 1779 to 1781. He still hoped for reconciliation with England and, as a result of this sentiment, opposed the Declaration of Independence. However, with the outbreak of the Revolutionary War, Dickinson served a tour of military duty.

From 1781 to 1785, Dickinson was a participant in state government activities, acting as

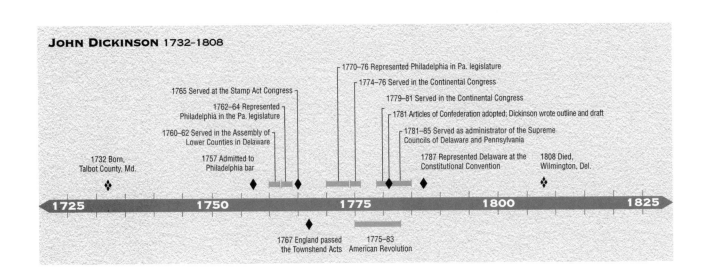

JOHN DICKINSON 1732–1808

1770–76 Represented Philadelphia in Pa. legislature
1774–76 Served in the Continental Congress
1765 Served at the Stamp Act Congress
1779–81 Served in the Continental Congress
1762–64 Represented Philadelphia in the Pa. legislature
1781 Articles of Confederation adopted; Dickinson wrote outline and draft
1760–62 Served in the Assembly of Lower Counties in Delaware
1781–85 Served as administrator of the Supreme Councils of Delaware and Pennsylvania
1732 Born, Talbot County, Md.
1757 Admitted to Philadelphia bar
1787 Represented Delaware at the Constitutional Convention
1808 Died, Wilmington, Del.

1725   1750   1775   1800   1825

1767 England passed the Townshend Acts
1775–83 American Revolution

administrator of the Supreme Council of Delaware in 1781 and performing the same duty for the Supreme Council of Pennsylvania from 1782 to 1785.

Dickinson was instrumental in the formation of the ARTICLES OF CONFEDERATION, adopted in 1781, by serving as presiding officer of the committee appointed to compose the document and creating the outline that became the foundation of the articles. In 1787, he represented Delaware at the Constitutional Convention and advocated the ratification of the Constitution through a series of letters published under the name of Fabius.

In addition to his achievements as a statesman, Dickinson also contributed to the field of education as a founder of Dickinson College, located at Carlisle, Pennsylvania.

Dickinson died February 14, 1808, in Wilmington, Delaware.

John Dickinson.
LIBRARY OF CONGRESS

DICTA

Opinions of a judge that do not embody the resolution or determination of the specific case before the court. Expressions in a court's opinion that go beyond the facts before the court and therefore are individual views of the author of the opinion and not binding in subsequent cases as legal precedent. The plural of dictum.

DICTUM

[Latin, A remark.] A statement, comment, or opinion. An abbreviated version of obiter dictum, "a remark by the way," which is a collateral opinion stated by a judge in the decision of a case concerning legal matters that do not directly involve the facts or affect the outcome of the case, such as a legal principle that is introduced by way of illustration, argument, analogy, or suggestion.

Dictum has no binding authority and, therefore, cannot be cited as precedent in subsequent lawsuits. Dictum is the singular form of *dicta.*

DIGEST

A collection or compilation that embodies the chief matter of numerous books, articles, court decisions, and so on, disposed under proper heads or titles, and usually by an alphabetical arrangement, for facility in reference.

An index to reported cases, providing brief statements of court holdings or facts of cases, which is arranged by subject and subdivided by jurisdiction and courts.

As a legal term, *digest* is to be distinguished from *abridgment*. The latter is a summary of the contents of a single work, in which, as a rule, the original order or sequence of parts is preserved, and in which the principal labor of the compiler is in the matter of consolidation. A digest is wider in its scope, is made up of quotations or paraphrased passages, and has its own system of classification and arrangement. An *index* merely points out the places where particular matters may be found, without purporting to give such matters *in extenso*. A treatise or *commentary* is not a compilation, but an original composition, though it may include quotations and excerpts.

DILATORY

Tending to cause a delay in judicial proceedings.

Dilatory tactics are methods by which the rules of procedure are used by a party to a lawsuit in an abusive manner to delay the progress of the proceedings. For example, when numerous motions brought before a court for postponement are baseless, time is wasted because the court must stop the course of ongoing proceedings to examine whether there is any merit to the motions. The party in whose interests the motion is brought uses this tactic to gain time to enhance his or her position, or to postpone an action by a court as long as possible to minimize the impact of a decree rendered against him or her. A party found to engage in dilatory tactics may be held in CONTEMPT of court.

DILATORY PLEA

In common-law-pleading, any of several types of defenses that could be asserted against a plaintiff's CAUSE OF ACTION, *delaying the time when the court would begin consideration of the actual facts in the case.*

Under COMMON LAW, a plaintiff began the lawsuit and drew up a paper reciting the events that supported his or her claim to relief. The defendant was entitled to enter a plea responding to the plaintiff's allegations. If the defendant's plea required the court to decide some threshold question not related to the merits of the plaintiff's case, it was called a dilatory plea. For example, a plea to the jurisdiction challenged the authority of the court to hear the kind of matters described by the plaintiff. A *plea in suspension* presented facts to justify a temporary halt to the proceedings, such as when a guardian was needed for one of the parties. A plea in abatement objected to the place, manner, or time of the lawsuit; it did not defeat the plaintiff's claim entirely but, if successful, forced the plaintiff to renew the suit in another form, place, or time.

Federal courts and states that follow the pattern of PLEADING permitted by the rules of federal CIVIL PROCEDURE no longer specifically allow dilatory pleas. The same assertions can be made by motion, but the motions may sometimes be called dilatory pleas by persons complaining that they unnecessarily delay proceedings.

DILIGENCE

Vigilant activity; attentiveness; or care, of which there are infinite shades, from the slightest momentary thought to the most vigilant anxiety. Attentive and persistent in doing a thing; steadily applied; active; sedulous; laborious; unremitting; untiring. The attention and care required of a person in a given situation; the opposite of NEGLIGENCE.

There may be a high degree of diligence, a common degree of diligence, and a slight degree of diligence, with their corresponding degrees of negligence. Common or ordinary diligence is that degree of diligence which persons generally exercise in respect to their own concerns; high or

great diligence is, of course, extraordinary diligence, or that which very prudent persons take of their own concerns; and low or slight diligence is that which persons of less than common prudence, or indeed of any prudence at all, take of their own concerns.

Special diligence is the skill that a good businessperson exercises in his or her specialty. It is more highly regarded than ordinary diligence or the diligence of a nonspecialist in a given set of circumstances.

DIMINISHED CAPACITY

This doctrine recognizes that although, at the time the offense was committed, an accused was not suffering from a mental disease or defect sufficient to exonerate him or her from all criminal responsibility, the accused's mental capacity may have been diminished by intoxication, trauma, or mental disease so that he or she did not possess the specific mental state or intent essential to the particular offense charged.

DIMINUTION

Taking away; reduction; lessening; incompleteness.

The term *diminution* is used in law to signify that a record submitted by an inferior court to a superior court for review is not complete or not fully certified.

Diminution in market value is a rule of damages, within which the proper measure of damages for permanent injury to real property is the reduction of market value for any use to which the property might be appropriated. It is a rule providing for the before-and-after value of stolen or damaged property.

DIPLOMATIC AGENTS

Government representatives who are sent by one country to live and work in another, to serve as intermediaries between the two countries.

The concept of diplomatic agents residing in another country dates to the fifteenth century, but the role of diplomats has evolved with the passage of time. Originally, agents were asked to help to work out specific negotiations between countries. Nowadays, their duties include cultivating a relationship between their native country and the host country; serving as intermediaries by relaying each country's positions to the other; and trying to ensure the best possible treatment for their home countries.

The Vienna Convention on Diplomatic Relations (Apr. 18, 1961, 23 U.S.T. 3227, 500 U.N.T.S. 95) contains the most widely accepted description of the INTERNATIONAL LAW on diplomacy. The convention splits the functions of diplomatic agents into six categories: representing the sending state; protecting the sending state's nationals within the receiving state; negotiating with the receiving state; notifying the sending state of conditions and developments within the receiving state; promoting friendly relations between the two states; and developing economic, cultural, and scientific relations between the two states.

Historically, the nomination of U.S. ambassadors to foreign countries is based on the recommendation of the president and is subject to approval by the Senate. It has also been a U.S. tradition that nominations are often given to acquaintances of the president or to those who have contributed heavily to political campaigns. The United States is the only major country that assigns ambassadorships as political rewards.

Despite legislation passed by Congress in 1980 stating that "contributions to political campaigns should not be a factor in the appointment" of an ambassador (22 U.S.C.A. § 3944), this practice of political spoils continues. Former president GEORGE H. W. BUSH nominated six Republicans as U.S. ambassadors in 1989. Each was a member of Bush's Team 100, contributors who had given more than $100,000 to the GOP.

The practice did not change when Democrat BILL CLINTON first won the presidency in 1992. According to an Associated Press review, by the end of Clinton's first year in office, he had nominated five $100,000-plus donors as foreign ambassadors. However, Clinton was able to deflect some of the criticism following these appointments by shifting the focus to the qualifications of his appointees. He stressed that his recommendations extended beyond campaign participation and that they required some real expertise that suited the demands of the appointments. For example, the Japanese regarded Clinton's pick for ambassador to Japan, Walter F. Mondale, as a well-qualified diplomat who would help to steady U.S.-Japanese partnership. Investment banker Nicholas A. Rey was chosen as ambassador to Warsaw on the basis that he spoke fluent Polish and that he had previously led an effort to stimulate private investments in Poland.

Howard Baker is sworn in as ambassador to Japan by Secretary of State Colin Powell on June 26, 2001.

AP/WIDE WORLD PHOTOS

President GEORGE W. BUSH similarly rewarded contributors with ambassador positions, but he came under heavier criticism due to the number of contributors who had received these appointments. Bush set a fundraising record during the 2000 presidential election, receiving more than $100 million from individual donors. He later appointed 43 "elite" fundraisers—those who donated at least $100,000 to the campaign.

Another topic involving diplomatic agents that has come under scrutiny in the 1990s involves a shift toward commercialism. Promoting exports and assisting U.S. businesses with their foreign dealings has become a top priority for the U.S. embassies. Since Deputy SECRETARY OF STATE Lawrence Eagleburger took office in 1989, all new foreign service officers and ambassadors have studied commerce as part of their basic training. Eagleburger has emphasized a necessity for diplomats to understand the needs of U.S. businesses and ways to help them to make the right connections abroad. This transition toward trade diplomacy is not new: Diplomats have always tried, in one way or another, to increase U.S. exports. The trend now is for diplomats to help specific companies to obtain specific contracts overseas and to help to find buyers for U.S. exports.

U.S. ambassadors direct, supervise, and coordinate a body of representatives in the country to which they have been assigned. This body of representatives from the sending government is referred to as a diplomatic mission. Under the Vienna Convention, both the property and the employees of a diplomatic mission are considered inviolable. However, the convention leaves to the receiving state the decision of how to protect a resident diplomatic agent from assault.

In the United States, specific legislation outlines the penalties that will be imposed if someone attacks a diplomatic officer residing in the United States. The penalties apply to anyone who "assaults, strikes, wounds, imprisons, or offers violence to a foreign official, official guest, or internationally protected person, his official premises, private accommodation, or means of transport or attempts to commit any of the foregoing" (Act of Oct. 24, 1972, Pub. L. No. 92-539, 18 U.S.C.A. § 112(a)). This statute criminalizes acts or attempts to "intimidate, coerce, threaten or harass a foreign official" (18 U.S.C.A. § 112). This section applies to any conduct outside the District of Columbia, which has somewhat different laws that penalize certain conduct directed at foreign embassies (see *Boos v. Barry,* 485 U.S. 312, 108 S. Ct. 1157, 99 L. Ed. 2d 333 (1988) [striking down part of the D.C. law as violating freedom of speech]).

The United States is among a number of signatories to two separate conventions that are intended to protect visiting dignitaries. These include the Organization of American States Convention to Prevent and Punish the Acts of Terrorism Taking the Form of Crimes against Persons and Related EXTORTION That Are of International Significance, and the UNITED NATIONS Convention on the Prevention and Punishment of Crimes against Internationally Protected Persons, Including Diplomatic Agents. Both conventions require host countries to take measures to prevent terrorist acts, and to make efforts to arrest and to punish the offenders should an attack occur.

The Vienna Convention grants special PRIVILEGES AND IMMUNITIES to diplomats, on the grounds that these are necessary to allow performance of official duties without outside interference or constraint. Some examples of privileges are exemption from customs on goods that diplomats import for their own or their family's use, from property taxes on mission property, from income taxes for pay received for their diplomatic duties, and from military obligations. Diplomatic agents and their families are also immune from civil or criminal prosecution. If a diplomat is accused of committing a crime, the STATE DEPARTMENT takes specific steps,

including notifying the diplomat's home country and asking to have the diplomat's IMMUNITY waived so that the case can advance to the U.S. judicial system. Diplomatic agents are also exempt from serving as witnesses in civil or criminal proceedings, unless their country waives their immunity if the agents feel their testimony is essential to the case. For example, in 1881, Venezuela asked its minister to the United States to testify in the trial of Charles J. Guiteau for the assassination of U.S. president JAMES GARFIELD.

CROSS-REFERENCES

Ambassadors and Consuls; Diplomatic Immunity.

DIPLOMATIC IMMUNITY

A principle of INTERNATIONAL LAW *that provides foreign diplomats with protection from legal action in the country in which they work.*

Established in large part by the Vienna conventions, diplomatic immunity is granted to individuals depending on their rank and the amount of immunity they need to carry out their duties without legal harassment. Diplomatic immunity allows foreign representatives to work in host countries without fully understanding all the customs of that country. However, diplomats are still expected to respect and follow the laws and regulations of their host countries; immunity is not a license to commit crimes.

In the United States, several levels of immunity are granted: the higher the rank, the greater the immunity. DIPLOMATIC AGENTS and their immediate families have the most protection and are immune from criminal prosecution and civil lawsuits. The lowest level of protection is granted to embassy and consular employees, who receive immunity only for acts that are part of their official duties—for example, they cannot be forced to testify in court about the actions of the people they work with. The Diplomatic Relations Act of 1978 [22 U.S.C.A. § 254a et seq.] follows the principles introduced by the Vienna conventions. The United States has had a tendency to be generous when granting diplomatic immunity to visiting diplomats because a large number of U.S. diplomats work in host countries less protective of individual rights. If the United States were to punish a visiting diplomat without sufficient grounds, U.S. representatives in other countries could receive harsher treatment.

In the United States, if a person with immunity is alleged to have committed a crime or faces a civil lawsuit, the DEPARTMENT OF STATE alerts the government that the diplomat works for. The Department of State also asks the home country to waive immunity of the alleged offender so that the complaint can be moved to the courts. If immunity is not waived, prosecution cannot be undertaken. However, the Department of State still has the discretion to ask the diplomat to withdraw from her or his duties in the United States. In addition, the diplomat's visas are often canceled, and the diplomat and her or his family are barred from returning to the United States. Crimes committed by members of a diplomat's family can also result in dismissal.

Abuse of diplomatic immunity was made more visible by media coverage in the early 1990s. The abuse spans a variety of activities, ranging from parking violations to more serious criminal behavior such as domestic abuse and rape. In February 1995 Mayor Rudolph Giuliani of New York City forgave $800,000 in parking tickets accumulated by foreign diplomats. Although no clear reason was given, the action, which was perhaps meant as a show of goodwill, sent a message to visiting diplomats that the U.S. government may be willing to allow diplomats greater leniency than its own private citizens. This is a good example of how some diplomatic debts have either been erased or not collected. However, outstanding debts may not be the worst illustration of how diplomatic immunity can be abused.

Diplomats and their families have also been known to use diplomatic immunity to avoid prosecution for criminal behavior. For example, in a 1983 case the New York City Police Department suspected a diplomat's son of 15 different rapes. The son was allowed to leave the United States without ever being taken to court because he claimed diplomatic immunity. If diplomatic immunity is used as a shield, the police cannot prosecute, no matter how serious the crime may be.

U.S. citizens and businesses are often at a disadvantage when filing civil claims against a diplomat, especially in cases of unpaid debts, such as rent, ALIMONY, and CHILD SUPPORT. In the summer of 1994 U.S. diplomat Victor Marrero reportedly complained to the UNITED NATIONS secretariat that foreign diplomats' debts in the United States were $5.3 million. The *New Yorker*

later reported that a well-informed source had said the figure had risen "closer to $7 million."

The bulk of diplomatic debt lies in the rental of office space and living quarters. Individual debts can range from a few thousand dollars to $1 million in back rent. A group of diplomats and the office space in which they work are referred to as a *mission*. Creditors cannot sue missions individually to collect money they owe. Landlords and creditors have found that the only thing they can do is contact a city agency to see if they can try to get some money back. They cannot enter the offices or apartments of diplomats to evict them because the Foreign Sovereign Immunities Act says that "the property in the United States of a foreign state shall be immune from attachment, arrest and execution" (28 U.S.C.A. § 1609). This has led creditors who are owed money by diplomats to become more cautious about their renters and to change their rental or payment policies. For example, Milford Management, a New York-based company that rents deluxe apartments, is owed more than $20,000 in back rent from diplomats from five different countries. Milford and other creditors have created their own "insurance" policies by refusing to rent to foreign missions unless there is a way of guaranteeing payment, such as collecting money in advance.

The issue of abusing diplomatic immunity in family relations, especially alimony and child support, has become enough of a widespread problem that it prompted discussion at the 1995 United Nations Fourth World Conference on Women, in Beijing. Historically, the United Nations has not gotten involved with family disputes and has refused to garnishee the wages of diplomats who owe money for child support, citing SOVEREIGN IMMUNITY. However, in September 1995, the incumbent head of legal affairs for the United Nations acknowledged there was a moral and legal obligation to take at least a partial responsibility in family disputes. Deadbeat "diplodads" were increasing in numbers in the United Nations: several men who had left their wives and children were still claiming U.N. dependency, travel, and education allowances for their families even though they are no longer supporting those families. One U.S. woman, Barbara Elzohairy, and her daughter were threatened with eviction from their New Jersey apartment because they did not pay their rent. Their reason? Elzohairy's husband, a U.N. representative from Egypt, refused to pay her $16,000 in court-ordered support. The United Nations told diplomats they must meet their moral obligations, but there were no consequences if they did not.

DIVORCE is difficult for the spouses of foreign diplomats, as illustrated in the case of *Fernandez v. Fernandez*, 208 Conn. 329, 545 A.2d 1036, 57 USLW 2115 (Conn., Jul 19, 1988) (NO. 13283). This case involved a U.S. citizen, Barbara Fernandez, who wanted a divorce from her husband, Antonio Diende Fernandez, a U.N. representative from the Republic of Mozambique. Along with the divorce, Fernandez wanted a monetary settlement and property rights to the home the couple owned in a New York suburb. Her husband asked that the courts dismiss her claim on the grounds that he had diplomatic immunity. Under the trial court's interpretation of the Vienna Convention, a U.S. citizen who marries a foreign diplomat is married until either the diplomat dies or the diplomat's country grants permission for divorce proceedings. The Republic of Mozambique gave the court permission to grant the divorce but would not allow the court to make a decision on Fernandez's property or monetary claims. The case went on to the Connecticut Supreme Court, which dissolved the marriage and allowed Fernandez to claim property rights under article 31 of the Vienna Convention.

Article 31 gives diplomats immunity from all civil cases except for those that involve "private immovable property." The Connecticut Supreme Court interpreted that exception to apply to Fernandez's claim on the home, which was valued at more than $8 million. Article 31 of the Vienna Convention does not allow the "private residence of a diplomatic agent" to be included in a civil suit. However, the Connecticut Supreme Court declined to consider this article as a form of defense for Fernandez's husband. The Vienna Convention specifically does not allow exceptions for spouses to seek monetary compensation in divorce proceedings, so Fernandez was not granted any money by the Connecticut court.

The *Fernandez* decision did not settle all the issues revolving around dissolution of diplomats' marriages, such as whether U.S. courts can grant a divorce without the permission of the diplomat's country. Critics of *Fernandez* say it might cause foreign countries to think twice before granting permission to dissolve marriages because property claims can then also be brought against the diplomats.

FURTHER READINGS

Ashman, Chuck, and Pamela Trescott. 1987. *Diplomatic Crime*. Washington, D.C.: Acropolis.

———. 1986. *Outrage: The Abuse of Diplomatic Immunity*. London: W. H. Allen.

Barker, J. Craig. 1998. "State Immunity, Diplomatic Immunity and Act of State: A Triple Protection Against Legal Action?" *International and Comparative Law Quarterly* 47 (October): 950–8.

Denza, Eileen. 1998. *Diplomatic Law: A Commentary on the Vienna Convention on Diplomatic Relations*. 2d ed. Oxford: Clarendon Press, New York: Oxford Univ. Press.

Felice, Phil. 1998. "Diplomatic Immunity: Time for a Change? *Touro Law Review* 15 (fall): 327–46.

Opara, Victor Nnamdi. "Sovereign & Diplomatic Immunity as Customary International Law: Beyond *R. v. Bow Street Stipendiary Magistrate & Others, ex parte Pinochet Ugarte*." *Wisconsin International Law Journal* 21 (spring): 255–297 .

United States Department of State. 1998. *Consular Notification and Access: Instructions for Federal, State, and Local Law Enforcement and Other Officials Regarding Foreign Nationals in the United States and the Rights of Consular Officials to Assist Them*. Washington, D.C.: U.S. Department of State.

CROSS-REFERENCES

Ambassadors and Consuls.

DIRECT

As a verb, to point to; guide; order; command; instruct. To advise; suggest; request. As an adjective, immediate; proximate; by the shortest course; without circuity; operating by an immediate connection or relation, instead of operating through an intermediary; the opposite of indirect. *In the usual or regular course or order, as distinguished from that which diverts, interrupts, or opposes. The opposite of cross, contrary, collateral, or remote. Without any intervening medium, agency, or influence; unconditional.*

DIRECT EVIDENCE

Evidence in the form of testimony from a witness who actually saw, heard, or touched the subject of questioning. Evidence that, if believed, proves existence of the fact in issue without inference or presumption. That means of proof which tends to show the existence of a fact in question, without the intervention of the proof of any other fact, and which is distinguished from CIRCUMSTANTIAL EVIDENCE, *often called* indirect.

Evidence that directly proves a fact, without an inference or presumption, and which in itself, if true, conclusively establishes that fact.

DIRECT EXAMINATION

The primary questioning of a witness during a trial that is conducted by the side for which that person is acting as a witness.

During the course of a direct examination, the attorney who is conducting the interrogation generally asks specific questions that provide the foundation of the case. After a witness is directly examined, the opposing side conducts a cross-examination, the purpose of which is to impeach or test the validity of the testimony.

DIRECT TAX

A charge levied by the government upon property, which is determined by its financial worth.

A direct tax is usually a property tax or ad valorem tax, as opposed to an indirect tax imposed upon some right or privilege, such as a franchise tax.

DIRECTED VERDICT

A procedural device whereby the decision in a case is taken out of the hands of the jury by the judge.

A verdict is generally directed in a jury trial where there is no other possible conclusion because the side with the BURDEN OF PROOF has not offered sufficient evidence to establish a PRIMA FACIE case.

A directed verdict is provided for by federal and state rules of CIVIL PROCEDURE. In a criminal action, an acquittal may be directed in favor of a defendant, based upon rules of CRIMINAL PROCEDURE.

DIRECTOR

One who supervises, regulates, or controls.

A director is the head of an organization, either elected or appointed, who generally has certain powers and duties relating to management or administration. A corporation's board of directors is composed of a group of people who are elected by the shareholders to make important company policy decisions.

Director has been used synonymously with manager.

DIRECTORY

A provision in a statute, rule of procedure, or the like, that is a mere direction or instruction of no obligatory force and involves no invalidating consequence for its disregard, as opposed to an imperative or mandatory provision, which must be followed. The general rule is that the prescriptions of a statute relating to the performance of a public duty are so far directory that, though neglect of them may be punishable, it does not affect the validity of the acts done under them, as in the case of a statute requiring an officer to prepare and deliver a document to another officer on or before a certain day.

Generally, statutory provisions that do not relate to the essence of a thing to be done, and as to which compliance is a matter of convenience rather than of substance, are *directory*, while provisions that relate to the essence of a thing to be done, that is, matters of substance, are mandatory.

DISABILITY

The lack of competent physical and mental faculties; the absence of legal capability to perform an act.

Directed Verdict

After hearing a motion at the close of the evidence. I have determined that the plaintiff has failed to present the proof that the law requires

to prevail on his/her claim [or: to prevail on some of the claims, namely, _____].
Since I have made this legal determination, I am directing you that the law requires that you render a verdict in favor of the defendant. [or:

in favor of the defendant on Counts _____ and _____].

The verdict form which you will use for this purpose is headed "Defendant's Verdict" [describe finding for defendant on particular counts on the verdict form]. You should elect a foreperson, who should sign this verdict form on behalf of the jury at the direction of the court.

REVISED TO DECEMBER 31, 1998

A sample judgment on directed verdict, for the defendant.

The term disability *usually signifies an incapacity to exercise all the legal rights ordinarily possessed by an average person. Convicts, minors, and incompetents are regarded to be under a disability. The term is also used in a more restricted sense when it indicates a hindrance to marriage or a deficiency in legal qualifications to hold office.*

The impairment of earning capacity; the loss of physical function resulting in diminished efficiency; the inability to work.

In the context of WORKERS' COMPENSATION statutes, disability consists of an actual incapacity to perform tasks within the course of employment, with resulting wage loss, in addition to physical impairment that might, or might not, be incapacitating.

Under federal law, the definition of a disability, for SOCIAL SECURITY benefits purposes, requires the existence of a medically ascertainable physical or mental impairment that can be expected to result in death or endures for a stated period, and an inability to engage in any substantial gainful activity due to the impairment.

DISABILITY DISCRIMINATION

Approximately 43 million people in the United States are physically or mentally disabled. Like individuals of various races, religions, genders, and national origins, individuals with physical or mental limitations historically have faced discrimination in the forms of exclusion from mainstream society; intentional and unintentional SEGREGATION; unequal or inferior services, benefits, or activities; and screening criteria that do not correlate with actual ability. Legal commentators have noted that the discrimination against DISABLED PERSONS differs from other forms of discrimination in that a rational basis for treating members of other excluded groups differently rarely exists, whereas a person's disability might hinder his or her abilities and might provide a rational basis for different treatment. Thus, the mere fact that an individual with a disability is treated differently is insufficient for a finding of illegal discrimination.

Another frequently noted difference between discrimination based on disability and discrimination based on race, color, religion, gender, and national origin is the attitude behind the discrimination. For example, discrimination based on race tends to be rooted in hostility toward a different race. On the other

hand, discrimination based on disability is often caused by discomfort and pity, or misguided compassion that materializes as paternalistic and patronizing behavior. Other times, discrimination against disabled persons is the result of "benign neglect" and is "primarily the result of apathetic attitudes rather than affirmative animus" (*Alexander v. Choate*, 469 U.S. 287, 105 S. Ct. 712, 83 L. Ed. 2d 661 [1985]). For example, a restaurant owner who fails to provide a wheelchair ramp to the restaurant's entrance is more likely to be guilty of failing to consider the needs of patrons than of expressing a specific dislike of wheelchair users.

Whatever its roots, discrimination impedes those with disabilities from obtaining jobs that they are qualified to perform; access to some buildings and modes of transportation; and the independence and dignity that nondisabled people take for granted. The U.S. Constitution provides little relief. Courts have held that mentally and physically disabled persons do not fall within a suspect or quasi-suspect class (i.e., classes subjected to a history of purposeful unequal treatment or political powerlessness). This means that under the Constitution's EQUAL PROTECTION CLAUSE, courts review government action affecting disabled people without the heightened or STRICT SCRUTINY afforded suspect or quasi-suspect classes formed by race or religion.

This lack of distinct constitutional protection has resulted in legislative action. Following a concerted LOBBYING effort by and on behalf of individuals with disabilities, Congress in the late 1960s and early 1970s passed the first federal laws designed to protect disabled persons. Lobbying continued when these laws proved to be inadequate owing to their limited coverage. Then, in 1990, Congress passed the much-heralded Americans with Disabilities Act (ADA) (42 U.S.C.A. §§ 12101–12213), legislation with a much broader application and a fair amount of controversy over the relative cost of its effectiveness.

Rehabilitation Act of 1973

The Rehabilitation Act of 1973 (19 U.S.C.A. §§ 791, 793, 794) prohibits disability discrimination by federal agencies, federal contractors, and other recipients of federal financial assistance. Types of prohibited discrimination include employment; education; building accessibility; and health, welfare, and social services. Courts have held that private individuals may file actions under the Rehabilitation Act against federal employers or against recipients of federal financial assistance; the action need not be brought by a government entity. A plaintiff who proves that a federal employer discriminated intentionally in violation of the Rehabilitation Act may receive compensatory and PUNITIVE DAMAGES.

What constitutes a disability under the Rehabilitation Act is often the source of controversy. Blindness, deafness, diabetes, cardiac problems, mobility impairments, and chronic fatigue syndrome have been recognized as physical impairments. The U.S. Supreme Court has held that tuberculosis, a contagious disease, is a physical impairment (*School Board v. Arline,* 480 U.S. 273, 107 S. Ct. 1123, 94 L. Ed. 2d 307 [1987]). Numerous courts have followed the logic in *Arline* in holding that individuals who have AIDS or who have tested positive for HIV, the virus that causes AIDS, are physically impaired. Courts also have held that alcoholism, anxiety panic disorder, and post-traumatic stress disorder are impairments under the Rehabilitation Act.

Prior to the enactment of the Americans with Disabilities Act, section 504 of the Rehabilitation Act was the principal federal prohibition of discrimination on the basis of disability. Even with the ADA, the Rehabilitation Act remains an important protection for those with disabilities. The ADA expressly excludes from its coverage protection against discriminatory acts by the federal government, so the Rehabilitation Act provides the only private CAUSE OF ACTION for disability discrimination by federal employers and agencies. The Rehabilitation Act also remains an alternative means of remedying discrimination even when a plaintiff concurrently invokes ADA protection.

Individuals with Disabilities Education Act

The Individuals with Disabilities Education Act (IDEA) (20 U.S.C.A. §§ 1400–1485) requires states to provide a free, appropriate public education to children who are disabled. Formerly known as the Education of the Handicapped Act or the Education for All Handicapped Children Act, the law was established in 1975 in response to studies showing that more than half of all disabled children were receiving an inappropriate public education, and about one-eighth of those children were simply excluded from public education altogether.

The Individuals with Disabilities Education Act requires that states provide a free and appropriate public education to children who are disabled.

AP/WIDE WORLD PHOTOS

IDEA requires states seeking federal financial assistance for education to develop plans ensuring disabled children a free education that meets their needs. IDEA covers children ages three to 21 who have educational disabilities—in other words, mental retardation; hearing, speech, or language impairments; visual impairments; serious emotional disturbances; orthopedic impairments; autism; traumatic brain injuries; and specific learning disabilities—and as a result of such conditions require special education and related services such as transportation to and from school. The act does not, under normal circumstances, cover a child who is nearsighted and needs glasses, or a child who walks with a leg brace; many children with minor disabilities can be educated without special attention.

Each child covered by IDEA is entitled to have an individualized educational program, or IEP, developed jointly by the child's parents and school personnel. The IEP describes the child's abilities and needs, and outlines educational placement and services that will address the listed needs. IDEA contains procedural safeguards designed to ensure that parents can participate in the IEP process and have methods of recourse if they disagree with educators about their child's education.

Finally, IDEA supports the INTEGRATION of disabled children by requiring that they receive their education in the least restrictive environment. The goal of this requirement is to keep children with disabilities in regular public school classrooms to the extent possible. Only when a satisfactory education cannot be achieved in regular classes, even with the use of supplementary aids and services, may a disabled child be removed from regular classes. In many cases, children with disabilities are mainstreamed—placed in a regular educational setting—for part of their school day, and removed to a special-needs setting for the other part. Depending on the disability, children may be mainstreamed into certain academic classes or simply during lunch, during study hall, or on the school bus.

Architectural Barriers Act

The Architectural Barriers Act (ABA) (42 U.S.C.A. §§ 4151–4157) requires that federally owned, leased, or financed buildings be accessible to disabled persons. Originally enacted in 1968, this law requires each of four federal agencies—the DEPARTMENT OF HOUSING AND URBAN DEVELOPMENT, the DEPARTMENT OF DEFENSE, the GENERAL SERVICES ADMINISTRATION, and the Postal Service—to promulgate design, construction, and alteration standards for buildings within its jurisdiction.

The coverage, and thus the effectiveness, of the ABA is limited. The act encompasses the subway system in Washington, D.C., as well as (1) structures that the federal government constructs or alters; (2) structures that the federal government leases; and (3) structures that depend on federal grants or loans for their design, construction, or alteration. If a federal agency is housed in a building that was constructed by the federal government prior to the ABA's original enactment date in 1968, and that building is not altered, it need not be accessible to disabled individuals under the ABA. Further, when structures covered by the ABA are altered, only the altered portion need be made accessible. Thus, an altered wing of a building may have elevators, wheelchair ramps, and accessible rest rooms, whereas stairs in front of the building's entrance render the building inaccessible to wheelchair users. Perhaps the most obvious shortcoming of the ABA's effectiveness is that it covers only buildings that are owned, leased, or financed by the U.S. government. Even after the ABA's enactment, individuals with disabilities remained challenged by the many inaccessible buildings not covered under it.

Americans with Disabilities Act

Despite the efforts of Congress, until 1990, no federal law outlawed most of the disability discrimination by employers, owners of places of public accommodation, and program administrators. During the late 1980s, two-thirds of employable, working-age, disabled persons in the United States had a job, and many of those who were employed held a job far below their actual capabilities. In the United States in 1990, more than 8 million persons with disabilities who wanted to work were unable to find jobs and were forced to live on welfare and other government subsidies funded by taxpayers.

Disabled individuals faced more obstacles when it came to transportation. Because disabilities often prevent people from driving cars, many with disabilities must rely on buses, trains, and subways. As of 1990, very few public modes of transportation were accessible to those with disabilities. That same year, Congress passed the Americans with Disabilities Act in the hopes of alleviating day-to-day problems faced by those with disabilities.

Employment Discrimination and the ADA
Titles I and II of the ADA prohibit employers, employment agencies, labor organizations, and joint labor-management committees, in the private sector and in state and local governments, from discriminating on the basis of disability. At the ADA's effective date in July 1992, the act covered private employers with 25 or more employees; since July 1994, the act has covered private employers with 15 or more employees. All state and local government employers are covered, regardless of their number of employees.

The EQUAL EMPLOYMENT OPPORTUNITY COMMISSION (EEOC) is the federal agency charged with overseeing the employment-discrimination provisions of the ADA. That agency administers complaints and enforces the ADA. The act also provides that its powers, remedies, and procedures may be invoked by the EEOC, the U.S. attorney general, and any person alleging illegal discrimination pursuant to the ADA or its underlying regulations. Any party seeking redress for ADA-prohibited discrimination must exhaust certain administrative remedies before instituting a lawsuit.

The employment discrimination outlawed by the ADA may take one of several forms explicitly defined by the act: (1) limiting, segregating, or classifying job applicants or employees in a way that adversely affects the status or opportunities of a disabled individual; (2) entering into a contract or business arrangement that has the effect of discriminating against a disabled individual; (3) implementing administrative procedures or criteria that have the effect of discriminating against a disabled individual; (4) denying a disabled person equal jobs or benefits; (5) failing to make reasonable accommodations to allow those with disabilities to perform their job in the workplace; (6) using criteria that screen, or tend to screen, disabled individuals from the workplace; and (7) administering employment tests for the purpose, or partial purpose, of measuring a job applicant's disabilities. In determining whether illegal discrimination has occurred under the ADA, it is irrelevant that the employer did not intend to discriminate. But discriminatory actions are permissible if they are job related and necessary for the business, and if the required job performance cannot be accomplished with reasonable accommodation.

Reasonable accommodation can be modifications or adjustments to the job application process, to the work environment, or to the manner or circumstances under which the job is performed. The ADA does not require an employer to reasonably accommodate an employee who does not make his or her disability known to the employer, and unless it is obvious, the employer may legally require documented proof of a disability before accommodating it. Examples of reasonable accommodation include making work areas, and nonwork areas such as lunch rooms and rest rooms, accessible; modifying work schedules; modifying equipment such as computers and desks; and providing interpreters for blind or deaf workers. An accommodation that imposes an undue hardship, causing the employer significant difficulty or expense, is not a reasonable accommodation. An accommodation that fundamentally alters the business is also not reasonable. For example, a nightclub would not be forced to provide bright lighting for a visually impaired employee, because bright lighting would significantly alter the nightclub's business. An employer is not responsible for providing personal items of accommodation such as eyeglasses, leg braces, and prostheses, nor is an employer responsible for accommodating current users of illegal drugs. But the ADA does protect rehabilitated drug users and rehabilitated and nonrehabilitated alcoholics,

Title II of the Americans with Disabilities Act requires state and local governments to ensure that modes of public transportation—such as this Oklahoma City Metro Transit bus—are accessible to those with disabilities.

AP/WIDE WORLD PHOTOS

provided that the employees do not threaten the employer's property or the health and safety of others in the workplace. Whether an accommodation is reasonable is, under the ADA, determined on a case-by-case basis, considering all relevant factors including hardship and cost to the employer.

The ADA does not require employers to accommodate every individual with a disability. Only qualified individuals with disabilities—disabled individuals who can perform, with or without reasonable accommodation, the job's essential functions—are protected from discrimination. Two factors are involved in the determination of whether a disabled individual is qualified. First, the employer must determine whether the individual satisfies the job prerequisites at the time of the hiring decision. This determination should not be based on speculative fears that the employee will not be able to function on the job, or that the employer's insurance premiums will rise. Second, the employer must determine whether the individual can perform the job's essential functions with or without reasonable accommodation. The essential functions of a job are tasks that are fundamental as opposed to marginal. Written job descriptions are frequently considered relevant evidence of essential functions.

To ensure that employers do not consider a person's disability at the time of hiring, the ADA prohibits employers from inquiring about disabilities or conducting medical examinations of prospective employees before hiring them. It is illegal to ask questions about medical history, prior WORKERS' COMPENSATION claims, and overall health before a hiring decision is made. The employer is permitted to inquire about the applicant's abilities as they relate to essential or nonessential job functions—although refusing to hire an applicant because of his or her inability to perform a nonessential job function is prohibited. Upon extending a job offer, the employer may require the prospective worker to submit to a medical examination, provided that all prospective workers face the same requirement. In fact, a job offer may be conditioned upon the results of the examination, and the employer may rescind the offer if the examination indicates that the prospective worker would pose a direct threat to health or safety in the workplace, or that he or she would not be able to perform the job's essential functions even with reasonable accommodation. The ADA does not consider tests for illegal drugs to be within its definition of a medical examination; therefore, before extending a job offer, employers may test applicants for illegal drugs—but not prescription drugs or alcohol. An employer may legally test for HIV only after an employment offer has been extended. Even then, the employer may not fire or refuse to hire an individual because of that person's HIV status, unless such discrimination is both related to the job and necessary for the business.

When an employer violates the ADA, the aggrieved party usually is entitled only to equitable relief, such as a court order requiring the construction of wheelchair ramps or the provision of voice-activated computers. Only when the employee shows intentional discrimination may compensatory or punitive damages be awarded. Where the dispute involves the provision of a reasonable accommodation, and the employer made GOOD FAITH efforts to make reasonable accommodation, the court may not award money damages; it may award only equitable relief.

Public Accessibility and the ADA Title II of the ADA requires that state and local government programs and activities be accessible to those with disabilities. Title III of the ADA applies the same requirement to certain private entities that own, lease, or operate places of public accommodation: (1) hotels, motels, and certain other places of lodging; (2) restaurants, bars, and other establishments that serve food or drink; (3) theaters, stadiums, concert halls, and other places of

exhibition or entertainment; (4) auditoriums, convention centers, and lecture halls; (5) retail or rental establishments such as grocery stores, bakeries, shopping centers, and hardware stores; (6) self-service laundries, dry cleaners, banks, hair salons, travel services, shoe repair services, gas stations, law offices, accounting offices, pharmacies, doctors' offices, hospitals, and other service establishments; (7) public transit stations and depots; (8) museums, libraries, and galleries; (9) parks, zoos, and other places of recreation; (10) private schools; (11) day care centers, homeless shelters, food banks, and other social-service establishments; and (12) health clubs, gymnasiums, bowling alleys, golf courses, and other places of exercise or recreation. The ADA does not limit its coverage to the size of the public accommodation; if a private entity fits into one of the twelve descriptive categories, it must comply with the ADA accessibility requirements. The ADA does exempt from its coverage some private clubs and religious entities.

When a private entity falls within a class of public accommodation, it must provide reasonable modifications in its practices, policies, or procedures, or auxiliary aids and services, for those with disabilities, unless such modifications would fundamentally alter the nature of the entity or would result in an undue burden of significant difficulty or expense. Title III requires only that those with disabilities be given equal opportunities to achieve the same results as nondisabled individuals. For example, a clothing store need not print price tags in braille so long as a sales clerk is available to read the price tags to a blind shopper. Auxiliary aids, such as closed-captioned televisions for hearing-impaired hotel guests, are required, but this provision is often flexible. Thus, the owner or operator of a public accommodation may often determine the type of auxiliary aid to assist the disabled individual, provided that the chosen aid is effective.

Title III also requires the owners and operators of public accommodation in existing facilities to remove structural, architectural, and communication barriers when such removal is "easily accomplishable and able to be carried out without much difficulty and expense" (42 U.S.C.A. § 12181(9)). To determine whether barrier removal is readily achievable, courts look at the nature and cost of the action needed; the number of people employed at the facility and its financial resources; the action's effect on the facility; and the size, nature, type, and financial resources of the covered entity. Under Title II, state and local governments must remove barriers unless the removal would cause a fundamental alteration to the program or activity, or unless it would cause the government entity an undue financial and administrative burden.

A private individual may enforce the provisions of Title III, as may the U.S. attorney general. To enforce the provisions of Title II, a private individual may file an administrative complaint with the appropriate federal agency (usually the agency that provides federal funding to the public entity that is the subject of the complaint) or the U.S. DEPARTMENT OF JUSTICE, or the individual may file a federal lawsuit.

On May 29, 2001, the U.S. Supreme Court ruled 7-2 that federal disability rights law entitled professional golfer Casey Martin to ride a golf cart among shots while competing in PGA Tour events, *PGA Tour, Inc. v. Martin,* 532 U.S. 661, 121 S.Ct. 1879, 149 L.Ed.2d 904 (U.S.Or., May 29, 2001) (NO. 00-24). In reaching its decision, the Court addressed two distinct legal issues, ruling that the PGA tour is a "public accommodation" subject to ADA requirements, and that under those requirements Martin's use of a cart was a "reasonable modification." The decision was the first high court case to interpret the non-discrimination mandate of Title III of the ADA.

The ADA and Public Perception Many individuals with disabilities credit the ADA with helping them to overcome the special challenges that they face from day to day. From the visually impaired social worker who is able to take his licensing test in braille, to the wheelchair user who is able to park her car just a few yards from her office's entrance, the ADA has helped many disabled people to become fully functioning members of society. But not everyone heralds the act, particularly when the price of compliance outweighs the legislation's effectiveness. Business owners complain that they have to make their buildings accessible even when those buildings are never used by disabled individuals. Between 1990 and 1995, local governments within Orange County, Florida, spent more than $2 million on architectural changes to make buildings accessible. The city of Winter Park, Florida, spent approximately $35,000 to make a new tennis facility that would be accessible to the disabled, yet the facility's manager reported that only one disabled person used the building in the first year after it opened.

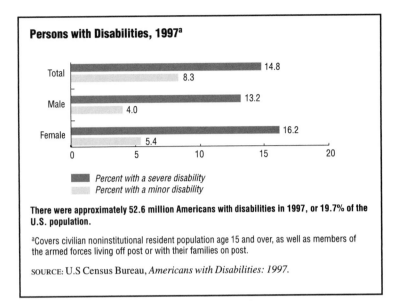

Persons with Disabilities, 1997[a]

There were approximately 52.6 million Americans with disabilities in 1997, or 19.7% of the U.S. population.

[a]Covers civilian noninstitutional resident population age 15 and over, as well as members of the armed forces living off post or with their families on post.

SOURCE: U.S Census Bureau, *Americans with Disabilities: 1997.*

Other critics of the ADA contend that the law is draining administrative and legal resources. During the first three years following the effective date of the ADA's employment provisions, the EEOC reported a 25 percent increase in its workload owing to ADA-related complaints. About 20 percent of those complaints were found to be without merit. By the early 1990s, the act had done little to improve the employment rate for those with disabilities. According to figures by the National Organization on Disability, a private group, as of December 1993, 31 percent of working-age disabled people were employed, whereas in 1986, prior to the ADA's enactment, 33 percent were employed. More recent figures indicate that employment and opportunities for disabled persons are on the rise.

Some legal commentators argue that the act is new and evolving. As courts interpret the law and Congress fine-tunes it, the ADA's benefits will become clearer. Peter David Blanck, a fellow at the Annenberg Washington Program, has stated that people with disabilities are not the only beneficiaries of the ADA. Businesses have found a new market, and new technology developed to help those with disabilities often helps the nondisabled as well.

Restrictions on ADA Application

Defining Disability In *Sutton v. United Airlines,* 527 U.S. 471, 119 S.Ct 2139, 144 L.Ed.2d 450 (1999), the U.S. Supreme Court held that for the purposes of the Americans with Disabilities Act, whether a person has a disability is to be determined based on the person's condition when that person uses corrective measures. The case concerned two women who had been denied positions as airline pilots because they each had extremely poor vision when they were not wearing glasses. The Court held that because the women had perfect vision when wearing glasses, they were not disabled and thus not protected by the ADA. It stated that "if a person is taking measures to correct for, or mitigate, a physical or mental impairment, the effects of those measures, both positive and negative, must be taken into account when judging whether that person is substantially limited in a major life activity and thus disabled under the [ADA]." That is, to determine whether someone is disabled, ask whether her physical or mental impairment, when mitigated by medication or other corrective devices, substantially limits her ability to perform major life activities.

In *Toyota Motor Manufacturing v. Williams*, 534 U.S. 184, 122 S.Ct. 681, 151 L.Ed.2d 615 (U.S., Jan 8, 2002) (NO. 00-1089), the high court further narrowed the standard for establishing that one has a disability covered under the ADA. In that case, Ella Williams, an assembly line worker in a Toyota automobile-manufacturing plant, developed severe carpal tunnel syndrome from her job. Her physician imposed limitations on her manual activities, disqualifying her from most of the assembly jobs in the plant. Toyota eventually accommodated her by assigning her to a lighter-duty unit but later required her to rotate to an additional job station, where she had to work at regular intervals with her hands and arms above shoulder height. Her disabling symptoms reappeared and worsened, but her request to be returned to her original accommodation was denied. She became unable to work and lost her job soon afterward. The court ruled that under the ADA, the inability to perform occupation-specific tasks does not necessarily mean that employee is substantially limited in performing a major life activity.

Damage Limitations In *Barnes v. Gorman*, 536 U.S. 181, 122 S.Ct. 2097, 153 L.Ed.2d 230 (U.S., Jun 17, 2002) (NO. 01-682), the U.S. Supreme Court declared that persons excluded by local governments from programs funded with federal dollars may not receive punitive damages, no matter how egregious the discrimination that they have suffered. In that case, Jeffrey Gorman, who was confined to a wheelchair, was arrested one night in Kansas City, Missouri,

and transported in a city police van that did not have the right equipment to take him safely. He sustained serious injuries, which prevented him from further gainful employment. At trial, the jury learned that the police department had failed to comply with the Rehabilitation Act since its passage in 1973, and even worse, it had done nothing after Gorman was hurt to prevent further injuries. A federal appeals court upheld the jury's damages award of more than $2 million. Local officials appealed the punitive damages portion, about half the total award, to the U.S. Supreme Court, arguing that punitive damages for disability discrimination could bankrupt city governments. Several groups, including AARP, pointed out that in Gorman's case, and other instances of egregious, intentional discrimination, punitive damages serve the worthy goals of deterring illegal conduct and compensating victims for their unneeded suffering. The U.S. Supreme Court reversed in a decision reflecting that neither the Rehabilitation Act nor the ADA permits an award of punitive damages in cases of access to public services.

Eleventh Amendment Issues In *University of Alabama v. Garrett*, 531 U.S. 356, 121 S.Ct. 955, 148 L.Ed.2d 866 (U.S.Ala., Feb 21, 2001) (NO. 99-1240), Respondents Garrett and Ash filed separate lawsuits against petitioners, Alabama state employers, seeking money damages under Title I of the ADA. In an opinion disposing of both cases, the District Court found that the ADA exceeds Congress's authority to abrogate the State's ELEVENTH AMENDMENT IMMUNITY. The Eleventh Circuit reversed on the ground that the ADA validly abrogates such immunity. The U.S. Supreme Court held that suits in federal court by state employees to recover money damages by reason of the state's failure to comply with Title I of the ADA are barred by the Eleventh Amendment.

FURTHER READINGS

Jones, Nancy Lee. 2003. *The Americans with Disabilities Act (ADA): Overview, Regulations, and Interpretations.* New York: Novinka Books.

Gaskill, Ricca. 1994. *Americans with Disabilities Act: An Analysis of Developments Relating to Disability Law.* New York: Practising Law Institute.

Poston, Sarah. 1994. "Developments in Federal Disability Discrimination Law: An Emerging Resolution to the Section 504 Damages Issue." *1992/1993 Annual Survey of American Law* 419.

CROSS-REFERENCES

Acquired Immune Deficiency Syndrome; Equity.

DISABILITY INSURANCE

See OLD-AGE, SURVIVORS, AND DISABILITY INSURANCE.

DISAFFIRM

Repudiate; revoke consent; refuse to support former acts or agreements.

Disaffirm is commonly applied in situations where an individual has made an agreement and opts to cancel it, which he or she may do by right—such as a minor who disaffirms a contract.

A disaffirmance is a denial or nullification of the existence of something, as opposed to a revocation, which is the breaking of an existing agreement.

DISALLOW

To exclude; reject; deny the force or validity of.

The term *disallow* is applied to such things as an insurance company's refusal to pay a claim.

DISARMAMENT

See ARMS CONTROL AND DISARMAMENT.

DISASTER RELIEF

Monies or services made available to individuals and communities that have experienced losses due to disasters such as floods, hurricanes, earthquakes, drought, tornadoes, and riots.

The term *disaster* has been applied in U.S. law in a broad sense to mean both human-made and natural catastrophes. Human-made catastrophes include civil disturbances such as riots and demonstrations; warfare-related upheavals, including those created by guerrilla activity and TERRORISM; refugee crises involving the forced movements of people across borders; and many possible accidents, including transportation, mining, POLLUTION, chemical, and nuclear incidents.

Natural disasters may be divided into three categories: meteorological disasters, such as hur-

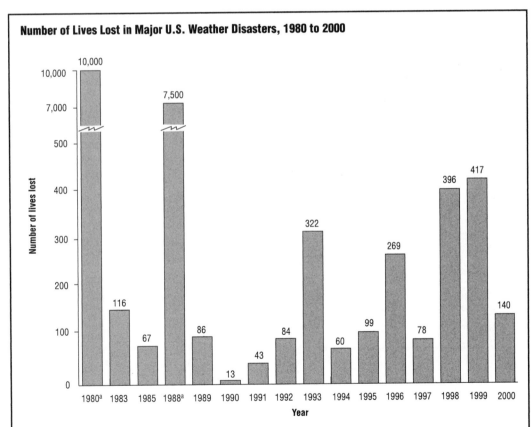

Number of Lives Lost in Major U.S. Weather Disasters, 1980 to 2000

Number of lives lost

Year	Lives lost
1980a	10,000
1983	116
1985	67
1988a	7,500
1989	86
1990	13
1991	43
1992	84
1993	322
1994	60
1995	99
1996	269
1997	78
1998	396
1999	417
2000	140

aA drought/heat wave occurred across the central and eastern United States during the summer months.

SOURCE: U.S. National Oceanic and Atmospheric Administration, *Billion Dollar U.S. Weather Disasters Since 1980*, and U.S. Census Bureau, *Statistical Abstract of the United States*, 2000.

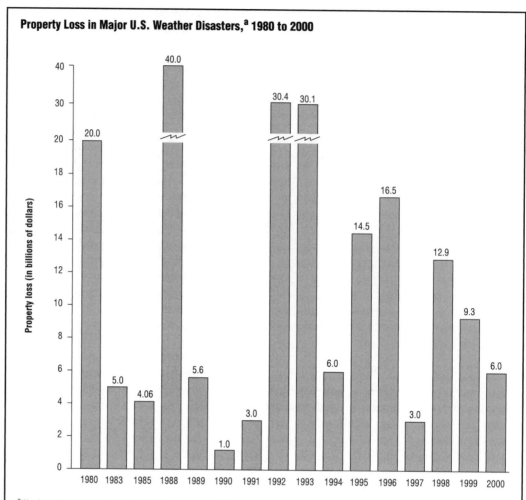

Property Loss in Major U.S. Weather Disasters,[a] **1980 to 2000**

Property loss (in billions of dollars)

Year	Loss
1980	20.0
1983	5.0
1985	4.06
1988	40.0
1989	5.6
1990	1.0
1991	3.0
1992	30.4
1993	30.1
1994	6.0
1995	14.5
1996	16.5
1997	3.0
1998	12.9
1999	9.3
2000	6.0

[a]Weather related disasters costing $1 billion or more, including hurricanes, tropical storms, floods, droughts, blizzards, severe freezes, ice storms, and wildfires.

SOURCE: U.S. National Oceanic and Atmospheric Administration, *Billion Dollar U.S. Weather Disasters Since 1980*, and U.S. Census Bureau, *Statistical Abstract of the United States*, 2000.

ricanes, hailstorms, tornadoes, typhoons, snowstorms, droughts, cold spells, and heat waves; topological catastrophes, such as earthquakes, avalanches, landslides, and floods; and biological disasters, including insect swarms and disease epidemics.

A disaster may also be defined in sociological terms as a major disruption of the social pattern of individuals and groups.

Disaster relief efforts are typically an example of FEDERALISM at work, as local, state, and national governments take on varied responsibilities. However, disaster relief has historically been considered a local responsibility, with the federal government providing assistance when local and state relief capacities are exhausted.

Most states have agencies that coordinate disaster relief and planning. A majority of states have statutes that define appropriate procedures for disaster declarations and emergency orders. Such statutes also empower relief agencies to utilize state and local resources, commandeer private property, and arrange for temporary housing during an emergency.

The federal government has played an increasingly influential role in disaster response and preparedness. In fact, as federal disaster assistance grew in the late twentieth century, it became a unique form of aid to states and localities. Often, significant amounts of money are made available to a disaster area for years after the disaster has occurred.

At all levels of government, disaster relief is carried out under the authority of an executive official: a city mayor, a state governor, or the nation's president. In the last instance, federal disaster legislation gives the president wide powers. The president decides what situations may be declared disasters and dictates the extent of federal assistance.

Under the Robert T. Stafford Disaster Relief and Emergency Assistance Act (Stafford Act) (Pub. L. No. 93-288, 42 U.S.C.A. § 5121 et seq.), the president may declare a catastrophe either an emergency or a major disaster. This classification is not necessarily indicative of the severity of the event. Instead, the designation determines the extent of federal aid available for the particular calamity. In general, more federal funds are available for major disasters than for emergencies. For the president to declare either an emergency or a major disaster, the governor of the affected state must announce that the catastrophe is of such severity that state resources cannot effectively cope with it.

After a formal declaration has been made at the federal level, all authority for disaster relief operations descends from the president, through the FEDERAL EMERGENCY MANAGEMENT AGENCY (FEMA), and down to other agencies engaged in relief operations. First established in 1979, FEMA coordinates federal efforts related to natural disaster planning, preparedness, response, and recovery. FEMA funds emergency programs and works closely with state and local governments.

After the president declares an emergency or major disaster, FEMA implements the Federal Response Plan. This plan identifies 12 emergency support functions (ESFs), each of which entails a particular aspect of the relief operation, and assigns specific federal agencies to each function. For example, under the Stafford Act, the DEPARTMENT OF DEFENSE (DOD) is the primary agency responsible for ESF 3 (public works and engineering), and ESF 9 (urban search and rescue). The DOD may provide secondary support for all other ESFs.

FEMA administers the President's Disaster Assistance Program, which provides supplemental federal assistance in declared disasters and emergencies. FEMA also operates the Emergency Food and Shelter Program, which provides grants to private, nonprofit organizations for temporary food and shelter for HOMELESS PERSONS. In addition, FEMA controls the Federal Insurance Administration, which oversees the National Flood Insurance Program, a self-supporting program that provides flood insurance to communities that adopt its floodplain management regulations to reduce the effect of future floods.

Although the Stafford Act authorizes the president to call on the DOD to assist state and local governments in times of disaster, the use of the federal armed forces in such situations is limited by law. For example, the POSSE COMITATUS Act (18 U.S.C.A. § 1385) prohibits the military from performing the duties of CIVIL LAW enforcement. The DOD has no independent authority to undertake disaster relief operations, though according to the Stafford Act, it may do so for an emergency ten-day period before the president declares an emergency or disaster. In times of civil disturbance such as the 1992 Los Angeles riots, the president may issue a proclamation that permits federal armed forces to take on law enforcement duties in order to put down a civil disturbance (10 U.S.C.A. §§ 331–334).

Congress and state legislatures may also make assistance available in times of disaster. For example, the Disaster Assistance Act of 1988 (7 U.S.C.A. §§ 1421, 1471; 26 U.S.C.A. § 451) made $5 billion available to farmers during a severe drought. Farmers who had lost more than 35 percent of their crops could receive up to $100,000 to cover 65 percent of their losses over an initial threshold. When Hurricane Hugo hit the southeastern coastal states in 1989, Congress approved $1.1 billion in aid only six days later.

Congress has also authorized other agencies to provide disaster assistance. The Small Business Administration's Office of Disaster Assistance supplies loans to businesses that suffer economic losses owing to natural disasters. The AGRICULTURE DEPARTMENT provides emergency loans to eligible farmers and ranchers for losses owing to natural disasters. It may also give farmers cost-sharing assistance as well as the use of land that was previously set aside for conservation purposes. The U.S. government's Agency for International Development makes disaster relief and planning available to foreign countries.

Private organizations, including the Red Cross and the Salvation Army, play a significant role in disaster relief as well. In 1905, Congress officially recognized the Red Cross and its role in responding to significant crises (36 U.S.C.A. § 1), and all subsequent federal disaster laws

A member of the American Red Cross Disaster Relief Team admits displaced persons to a shelter following a chemical spill near Knoxville, Tennessee. The role the Red Cross has traditionally played in disaster relief was first recognized by Congress in 1905.

AP/WIDE WORLD PHOTOS

after a disaster had occurred. Critics often complained that the federal response to disasters was dilatory, insufficient, and inconsistent.

During the 1930s, the expansion of the federal government under the New Deal—including greater federal participation in public works projects—led to a greater federal role in disaster assistance. NEW DEAL agencies such as the Reconstruction Finance Corporation, Federal Emergency Relief Administration, Federal Civilian Works Administration, Works Progress Administration, and Civilian Conservation Corps all participated in disaster control and recovery. The Army Corps of Engineers helped communities to prevent and recover from flood damage, and the DEPARTMENT OF AGRICULTURE offered aid to farmers who sustained economic losses in disasters. The 1930s marked the federal government's first use of low-interest loans and outright grants for disaster relief—both features of subsequent disaster laws. During this same decade, Congress considered making the American Red Cross a government agency, but Red Cross officials chose to keep their organization private.

With the passage of the Disaster Relief Act of 1950 (Pub. L. No. 81-875, 64 Stat. 1109), Congress for the first time authorized a coordinated federal response to major disasters. The act, which was repealed in 1970, defined a disaster as "[a]ny flood, drought, fire, hurricane, earthquake, storm, or other catastrophe in any part of the U.S. which in the determination of the President, is or threatens to be of sufficient severity and magnitude to warrant disaster assistance by the Federal government." Significantly, this definition gave the president broad powers to respond to a crisis, powers that are related to the president's role as commander in chief of the nation's military and that have remained in all subsequent federal disaster legislation.

Later laws gradually increased the scope of federal disaster assistance. In the 1950s and 1960s, Congress authorized the provision of temporary shelter, surplus federal supplies, loans, and unemployment assistance for disaster victims. Many of these features were later incorporated into the comprehensive Disaster Relief Act of 1970 (84 Stat. 1744 [42 U.S.C.A. § 4401 et seq.]). This act also offered generous assistance for the reconstruction of public facilities, authorizing 100 percent federal financing for such projects even when reconstruction went beyond damage caused by a particular disaster.

have renewed this recognition. The Red Cross makes a careful distinction between its humanitarian relief activities, including the provision of food and shelter, and activities that it believes are best handled by government.

Experts on disaster relief have increasingly called for a greater emphasis on prevention as opposed to relief. Plans for improved disaster preparedness often call for a greater use of new technologies, including satellite and radar technologies that would aid in the early detection of potential disasters.

Before 1950, disaster response was characterized by an ad hoc, or case by case, approach. Relief involved a reaction to specific crises with little planning or preparation for future disasters. Then, as now, it was initially activated by local or state officials, and, if necessary, appeals were made to the federal government. Such an approach was often so disorganized that it frustrated effective disaster relief. Federal aid was rarely immediate and instead came some time

The Stafford Act expanded further the role of the federal government in disaster relief. Under this legislation, the federal government may provide grants to fund a number of additional forms of assistance: the full cost for the reconstruction of certain private, nonprofit facilities and owner-occupied private residential structures; loans to local governments to cover operating expenses; free temporary housing for up to 12 months; the installation of essential utilities; mortgage or rental payments to individuals for up to one year; and food stamps, legal services, and counseling services for low-income citizens. The act also includes an unprecedented authorization of long-range community economic recovery programs for disaster areas. Under these provisions, recovery planning councils develop five-year recovery investment plans, which are eligible to receive up to 90 percent of their funding from the federal government.

In 1979, concerns about overly bureaucratic procedures and a lack of coordination in government efforts to respond to disasters, as well as the need for improved programs for disaster prevention and preparedness, led to the creation of FEMA. A poor federal response to disasters such as Hurricane Hugo and the Loma Prieta earthquake, both occurring in 1989, prompted calls for a greater use of the military in disaster relief. In 1993, amendments to the Stafford Act empowered the president to more readily call on the federal armed forces to assist in disaster relief.

Disaster Relief for September 11 Victims

The SEPTEMBER 11, 2001, TERRORIST ATTACKS against the United States triggered what became an unprecedented level of federal disaster relief. The twin towers at the World Trade Center complex in New York City collapsed after being targeted by two hijacked commercial airliners, and four other buildings partially collapsed shortly thereafter. Several nearby buildings also suffered extensive collateral damage. After the World Trade Center attacks, another hijacked plane was deliberately crashed into the Pentagon and a fourth hijacked plane crashed in Somerset County, Pennsylvania.

In response to the attacks, President GEORGE W. BUSH immediately signed a major disaster declaration for 5 counties in New York. The disaster declaration was amended on September 27 and again on October 2, 2001, making all coun-ties in the state of New York eligible for some form of federal disaster assistance in the wake of the terrorist attack. The president also promptly declared a federal emergency in Virginia under subsection 501(b) of the Stafford Act, and a short time later declared a major disaster in Virginia to trigger a broader range of Stafford-Act responses.

In addition, the president declared an emergency for all 21 counties in New Jersey. These declarations made available federal programs that provide assistance for families and individuals victimized by the attacks. Normally, the federal government provides 75 percent of the disaster response costs with the remaining 25 percent of the costs undertaken by non-federal entities. However, FEMA reimbursed the states and affected local governments for 100 percent of the eligible costs for debris removal, emergency protective measures, and public infrastructure rebuilding costs in response to the September 11 terrorist attacks.

Minutes after the first hijacked airplane hit the World Trade Center, FEMA activated a full Emergency Support Team at its National Interagency Emergency Operations Center in Washington, D.C. Federal officials immediately began arriving at the center to coordinate the nationwide response and recovery effort. Some 1,800 federal workers were deployed to New York to support the disaster response, about 800 from FEMA and almost 1,000 from other federal departments and agencies.

FEMA'S top priorities throughout its entire disaster response effort included: (1) providing urban search and rescue support; (2) assisting in life saving operations; (3) meeting individual and public assistance needs; (4) implementing human services and victims assistance programs; and (5) assisting in debris removal (FEMA helped remove close to 1.4 million tons of debris from the disaster areas, then transported the debris to the sorting and disposal site at the Staten Island landfill).

The New York City Office of Emergency Management's US&R Task Force was among the first responders at the World Trade Center. The New York Force is part of FEMA's 28 Task Forces that make up the National US&R Response System. Its Task Force leader, Chief Raymond Downey, was one of the first responders on the scene, where he ultimately died during search and rescue operations. The DEPARTMENT OF HEALTH AND HUMAN SERVICES and PUBLIC

HEALTH SERVICE played an important role in the health and medical response. One hundred and sixty-seven persons were assigned to Disaster Medical Assistance Teams and a Medical Support Team to support the response in New York and remain in the City. Thirty-three Centers for Disease Control epidemiologists were assigned to track illness trends. A Veterinary Medical Assistance Team was deployed to treat the rescue dogs.

Since the Stafford Act prohibits FEMA from duplicating disaster assistance, FEMA had to be very careful in coordinating its activities with all of the organizations providing disaster relief. For example, FEMA worked with the Department of Justice's Office for Victims of Crime to maximize the investigative resources deployed at Ground Zero, which was not only a disaster area but a crime scene as well. FEMA also deployed resources to non-governmental organizations that were having difficulty managing the flood of charitable donations made by people around the world. Finally, FEMA worked with the NATIONAL TRANSPORTATION SAFETY BOARD (NTSB) to provide assistance from United and American Airlines to the families of the victims.

FURTHER READINGS

Copelan, John J., Jr. 1995. "Disaster Law and Hurricane Andrew: Government Lawyers Leading the Way to Recovery." *Urban Lawyer* 27 (winter).

Ferris, Elizabeth G. 1998. *Uprooted!: Refugees and Forced Migrants.* New York: Friendship.

Junger, Sebastian. 2001. *Fire.* New York: Norton.

Landis, Michele L. 1998. "Let Me Next Time Be 'Tried by Fire': Disaster Relief and the Origins of the American Welfare State 1789–1874. *Northwestern University Law Review* 92 (spring): 967–1034.

Moss, David A. 2002. *When All Else Fails: Government as the Ultimate Risk Manager.* Cambridge, Mass.: Harvard Univ. Press.

Reitman, Judith. 1996. *Bad Blood: Crisis in the American Red Cross.* New York: Kensington.

Stratton, Ruth M. 1989. *Disaster Relief: The Politics of Intergovernmental Relations.* Lanham, Md.: Univ. Press of America.

Swanson, Howard D. 2000. "The Delicate Art of Practicing Municipal Law Under Conditions of Hell and High Water. *North Dakota Law Review* 76 (summer): 487–509.

Tierney, Kathleen J., Michael K. Lindell, and Ronald W. Perry. 2001. *Facing the Unexpected: Disaster Preparedness and Response in the United States.* Washington, D.C.: Joseph Henry Press.

U.S. Government Manual Website. Available online at <www.gpoaccess.gov/gmanual> (accessed November 10, 2003).

CROSS-REFERENCES

Refugees.

DISBAR

To revoke an attorney's license to practice law.

A disbarment proceeding is the investigation into the conduct of a member of the bar in order to determine whether or not that person should be disbarred or disciplined. The state bar association normally takes such action based on allegations of a lawyer's unethical conduct. For example, the bar association might initiate an action for disbarment against a lawyer who has revealed information obtained from the PRIVILEGED COMMUNICATION between the lawyer and a client.

In one of the more high-profile cases of disbarment in recent history, the U.S. Supreme Court in 2001 moved to disbar former President WILLIAM JEFFERSON CLINTON, thus preventing him from practicing before the high court. The Court's action came after a similar move by the Arkansas Supreme Court's Committee on Professional Conduct, which recommended disbarment of the former president in that state. The actions stemmed from charges of CONTEMPT, OBSTRUCTION OF JUSTICE, and perjury based on misleading statements made by Clinton about his relationship with White House intern Monica Lewinsky. Those charges led to Clinton's IMPEACHMENT by the U.S. House of Representatives in 1998. Clinton agreed to a fine and suspension imposed by the Arkansas Supreme Court disbarment committee and later asked to resign from the U.S. Supreme Court bar.

DISCHARGE

To liberate or free; to terminate or extinguish. A discharge is the act or instrument by which a contract or agreement is ended. A mortgage is discharged if it has been carried out to the full extent originally contemplated or terminated prior to total execution.

Discharge also means to release, as from legal confinement in prison or the military service, or from some legal obligation such as jury duty, or the payment of debts by a person who is bankrupt. The document that indicates that an individual has been legally released from the military service is called a discharge.

The performance of a duty discharges it. An attorney may speak of discharging a legal obligation.

DISCIPLINARY RULES

Precepts, such as the Code of Professional Responsibility, that proscribe an attorney from taking certain actions in the PRACTICE OF LAW.

Proceedings can be instituted to disbar an attorney who violates the disciplinary rules.

DISCLAIMER

The denial, refusal, or rejection of a right, power, or responsibility.

A disclaimer is a defensive measure, used generally with the purpose of protection from unwanted claims or liability. A restaurant may disclaim responsibility for loss or damage to a customer's PERSONAL PROPERTY, or a disclaimer clause in a contract might set forth certain promises and deny all other promises or responsibilities.

A disclaimer of WARRANTY, which is provided for in the UNIFORM COMMERCIAL CODE, limits a warranty in the sale of goods. It may be general or specific in its terms.

DISCONTINUANCE

Cessation; ending; giving up. The discontinuance of a lawsuit, also known as a dismissal or a nonsuit, is the voluntary or involuntary termination of an action.

DISCOVERY

A category of procedural devices employed by a party to a civil or criminal action, prior to trial, to require the adverse party to disclose information that is essential for the preparation of the requesting party's case and that the other party alone knows or possesses.

Civil Procedure

Discovery devices used in civil lawsuits are derived from the practice rules of EQUITY, which gave a party the right to compel an adverse party to disclose material facts and documents that established a CAUSE OF ACTION. The federal rules of CIVIL PROCEDURE have supplanted the traditional equity rules by regulating discovery in federal court proceedings. State laws governing the procedure for civil lawsuits, many of which are based upon the federal rules, have also replaced the equity practices.

Discovery is generally obtained either by the service of an adverse party with a notice to examine prepared by the applicant's attorney or by a court order pursuant to statutory provisions.

Discovery devices narrow the issues of a lawsuit, obtain evidence not readily accessible to the applicant for use at trial, and ascertain the existence of information that might be introduced as evidence at trial. Public policy considers it desirable to give litigants access to all material facts not protected by privilege to facilitate the fair and speedy administration of justice. Discovery procedures promote the settlement of a lawsuit prior to trial by providing the parties with opportunities to realistically evaluate the facts before them.

Discovery is contingent upon a party's reasonable belief that he or she has a good cause of action or defense. A court will deny discovery if the party is using it as a fishing expedition to ascertain information for the purpose of starting an action or developing a defense. A court is responsible for protecting against the unreasonable investigation into a party's affairs and must deny discovery if it is intended to annoy, embarrass, oppress, or injure the parties or the witnesses who will be subject to it. A court will stop discovery when used in bad faith.

Information Discovered Pretrial discovery is used for the disclosure of the identities of persons who know facts relevant to the commencement of an action but not for the disclosure of the identities of additional parties to the case. In a few jurisdictions, however, the identity of the proper party to sue can be obtained through discovery. Discovery pursuant to state and federal procedural rules may require a party to reveal the names and addresses of witnesses to be used in the development of the case.

Discovery is not automatically denied if an applicant already knows the matters for which he or she is seeking discovery since one of its purposes is to frame a PLEADING in a lawsuit. On the other hand, discovery is permitted only when the desired information is material to the preparation of the applicant's case or defense. Discovery is denied if the matter is irrelevant or if it comes within the protection of a privilege.

Privileged Information Privileged matters are not a proper subject for discovery. For example, a person cannot be forced to disclose confidential communications regarding matters that come within the ATTORNEY-CLIENT PRIVILEGE. Discovery cannot be obtained to compel a person to reveal information that would violate his or her constitutional guarantee against SELF-INCRIMINATION. However, if a party or witness has been granted IMMUNITY regarding the matters that are the basis of the asserted privilege, that party can be required to disclose such information on pretrial examination.

A person who refuses to comply with discovery on the basis of an asserted privilege must claim the privilege for each particular question at the time of the pretrial examination. An attorney or the court itself cannot claim the privilege for that person. However, a person may waive the privilege and answer the questions put to him or her during discovery.

Objections A party may challenge the validity of a pretrial examination if asserted prior to trial. The merits of such an objection will be evaluated by the court during the trial when it rules on the admissibility of the evidence. If the questions to be asked during a discovery, such as the identity and location of a particular witness, pose a threat to anyone's life or safety, a party can make a motion to a court for a protective order to deny discovery of such information.

Refusal to Respond Failing to appear or answer questions at an examination before trial might result in a CONTEMPT citation, particularly if the person has disobeyed the command of a subpoena to attend. If discovery is pursuant to a court order, the court will require that the party's refusal to answer questions be treated as if the party admitted them in favor of the requesting party. Such an order is called a preclusion order since the uncooperative party is precluded from denying or contradicting the matters admitted due to his or her intentional failure to comply with a discovery order.

Costs

A party who makes a motion for a court to order discovery may be required to pay or make provision for payment of costs—expenses incurred in obtaining discovery when it is granted. If the party eventually wins the lawsuit, the court may demand that the costs be paid by the adversary in the proceedings.

Types of Discovery Devices

Discovery of material information is obtainable by use of DEPOSITIONS, interrogatories, requests for the production and inspection of writings and other materials, requests for admission of facts, and physical examinations.

Depositions A party to a lawsuit may obtain an oral pretrial examination of an adverse party or witness—the deponent—who is under oath to respond truthfully to the ques-

tions. This interrogation is known as a deposition or an examination before trial (EBT). The notice or order of examination must specify the particular matters to be discovered, and the line of questioning is usually restricted to such matters. However, the scope and extent of the examination is within the discretion of the court.

In some jurisdictions, a deponent may bring along documents to refresh his or her memory and facilitate testimony. Such materials can be used only when relevant to the line of questioning to which the deponent is subject and only by the designated deponent.

Interrogatories Interrogatories are specific written questions submitted by a person, pursuant to a discovery order, to an adversary who must respond under oath and in writing. Interrogatories must state questions in a precise manner so as to elicit an answer that is pertinent to the issues being litigated.

Production and Inspection A litigant is generally entitled to the production and inspection of relevant documents in the possession or control of an adversary pursuant to discovery. The applicant must have a reasonable belief that such evidence is necessary to the lawsuit if discovery is to be granted.

Requests for Admissions of Facts A party may ask an adversary to admit any material fact or the authenticity of a document that is to be presented as evidence during the trial. This procedure, called a request for an admission of fact, facilitates the fair and efficient administration of justice by minimizing the time and expense incurred in proving issues that are not in dispute.

Only facts, not matters or conclusions of law or opinions, can be admitted when there is no disagreement between the parties. The requesting party does not have to make a motion before a court prior to making such a demand but must comply with any statutory requirements. The matters or documents to be admitted must be particularly described and there must be a time limit for a reply. The response should admit or deny the request or explain in detail the reason for refusing to do so—for example, if the request calls for admission of a MATTER OF LAW. Failure to make a response within the specified time results in the matter being admitted, precluding the noncomplying party from challenging its admission during the trial.

Physical Examination A mental or physical examination of a party whose condition is an issue in litigation may be authorized by a court in the exercise of its discretion.

Criminal Procedure

Under COMMON LAW, there was no discovery in criminal cases. As of the early 2000s, in federal and many state criminal prosecutions, only limited discovery is permissible, unlike the full disclosure of information available in civil actions. Limited discovery prevents the possible intimidation of prosecution witnesses and the increased likelihood of perjury that might result from unabridged disclosure. The obligation of the prosecutor to prove the case BEYOND A REASONABLE DOUBT, the possibility of an unconstitutional infringement upon a defendant's right against self-incrimination, and violations of the attorney-client privilege pursuant to a client's RIGHT TO COUNSEL also hinder complete discovery. A defendant who requests particular documents from the government may be required to submit items of a similar nature to the government upon its request for discovery. The disclosure of false evidence or the failure of the prosecution to disclose documents that are beneficial to the defense can result in a denial of DUE PROCESS OF LAW.

The federal Jencks Act (18 U.S.C.A. § 3500 [1957]) entitles a defendant to obtain access to prosecution documents necessary to impeach the testimony of a prosecution witness by showing that the witness had made earlier statements that contradict present testimony. Theoretically, the defense cannot receive the statements until the witness has finished testimony on direct examination, but, in practice, such statements are usually available before then. Many states have similar disclosure rules.

FURTHER READINGS

Grenig, Jay E. 2002. *Handbook of Federal Civil Discovery and Disclosure.* 2d ed. St. Paul, Minn. West group.

Haydock, Roger S. 2002. *Discovery Practice.* 4th ed. New York: Aspen Law & Business.

CROSS-REFERENCES

Deposition; Immunity; Interrogatories; Self-Incrimination.

DISCRETION IN DECISION MAKING

Discretion *is the power or right to make official decisions using reason and judgment to choose from among acceptable alternatives.*

Legislatures, the president and the governors of the various states, trial and appellate judges, and administrative agencies are among the public officers and offices charged with making discretionary decisions in the discharge of public duties. All discretionary decisions made are subject to some kind of review and are also subject to reversal or modification if there has been an ABUSE OF DISCRETION.

An abuse of discretion occurs when a decision is not an acceptable alternative. The decision may be unacceptable because it is logically unsound, because it is ARBITRARY and clearly not supported by the facts at hand, or because it is explicitly prohibited by a statute or RULE OF LAW.

Discretion in decision making can be viewed from the perspective of the flexibility and choices granted to the decision maker based on the decision being made. Only the Constitution, through judicial enforcement, can limit discretionary decision making by legislative bodies to pass laws. Great flexibility is granted to the EXECUTIVE BRANCH in the area of foreign relations decision making. Statutes and prior judicial decisions limit the flexibility and discretion of a judge in a court of law. Moreover, Congress has granted broad decision-making authority to administrative agencies and their administrators, giving them great flexibility to make decisions within their area of concern.

Legislative Discretion

Legislatures have very broad discretion to create and pass laws that prohibit, regulate, and encourage a wide variety of activities. In Article I, Section 8, of the U.S. Constitution, Congress is empowered to "make all Laws which shall be necessary and proper" for carrying out its enumerated powers. Most state legislatures are empowered by similar language from their state constitution. An example of a proper exercise of legislative discretion is to make STALKING a crime and to make that crime punishable by fines or imprisonment.

The discretion of legislatures is also limited by the U.S. and state constitutions. A state may not pass a statute that allows the police to search any person's residence at any time for any reason, because that statute would clearly violate the U.S. Constitution's FOURTH AMENDMENT protection against unreasonable SEARCHES AND SEIZURES.

Executive Discretion

Executive discretion, like that vested in the president by Article II of the U.S. Constitution, is most evident in the area of foreign affairs: the

Judges' discretion in decision making has been reduced by federal sentencing guidelines, but they still enjoy some latitude as they sentence those found guilty of crimes.

AP/WIDE WORLD PHOTOS

president is the commander in chief of all the military forces and also has the power to make treaties with other countries. If Congress is silent on a particular issue—that is, if Congress has not passed a specific statute or resolution concerning that issue—then the president has broad discretion to act. This arrangement is particularly relevant in the area of foreign policy during war or other military action, when decisions must be made quickly in response to rapidly changing circumstances.

One improper exercise of executive discretion that is almost always reversed by reviewing courts is IMPOUNDMENT, whereby a president places in reserve a sum of money appropriated by Congress for a particular purpose, effectively blocking that appropriation. Courts have routinely held that the president has no implied power to take such action. Implied powers are those held by the president but not granted expressly by statute, regulation, or constitution. The act of impoundment, then, constitutes an abuse of discretion by the executive branch.

Judicial Discretion

Judicial discretion is a very broad concept because of the different kinds of decisions made by judges and because of the different limits placed on those decisions. Article III, Section 2, of the U.S. Constitution grants the judiciary broad power, which extends "to all Cases, in Law and Equity, arising under this Constitution, the Laws of the United States, and Treaties made." Judges' decisions must be made based on the "rule of law," which, in the United States, derives not only from statutes passed by Congress but also from the tenets of the Constitution. In addition, COMMON LAW, or judge-made law, pro-

vides limits based on the principle of STARE DECISIS, which holds that a court's decision in a particular case must comport with the RULES OF LAW as they have been determined by that court or by other, higher-level courts, in previous cases. Legal conclusions that do not fit within the prescribed limits of both statutory and common law may be overturned by a reviewing court if that court determines that the conclusions were an abuse of judicial discretion.

At one time, the sentencing of those convicted of crimes was almost entirely within the discretion of judges. Judges could take into account various mitigating factors (circumstances reducing the degree of blame or fault attributed to the offender) and craft a punishment that most appropriately fit the crime. For example, a first-time petty offender convicted of shoplifting might be sentenced to PAROLE and community service.

With the implementation of Federal Sentencing Guidelines and with mandatory minimum sentencing legislation, which passed in both Congress and the states, judges no longer had the broad latitude to make the sentence fit the crime and the defendant. In some states, first-time offenders have been sent to jail for life for the possession of large amounts of controlled substances. Many federal judges must incarcerate parole violators for minor parole violations because the guidelines specifically direct them to and severely limit their sentencing choices. A judge's failure to abide by the sentencing guidelines in issuing a sentence would constitute an abuse of judicial discretion.

Administrative Agency Discretion

Legislative, executive, and judicial discretion in decision making is limited within the structure of the three branches of the U.S. government as established in the Constitution. Each branch is subject to the influence, review, and even rejection of certain decisions. Administrative agencies, granted authority by Congress to administer specific government programs and areas of concern, operate outside this tripartite system, and many decisions made by administrative agencies are protected from review. For this reason, the administrative branches of federal and state governments have often been referred to as the headless fourth branch of government.

The U.S. Constitution does not expressly grant administrative authority. However, Congress may create administrative agencies as an extension of its authority to make laws that are necessary and proper, to help it execute its powers (U.S. Const. art. I). The president may appoint the heads of these agencies under a general grant of authority to appoint "public Ministers and Consuls" and "all other Officers of the United States, whose Appointments are not herein otherwise provided for" (U.S. Const. art. II). The judiciary, under its very broad grant of authority to hear all cases in law and equity, has a right, in some circumstances, to review and overturn administrative decisions (U.S. Const. art. III).

Administrative agencies, like the SOCIAL SECURITY ADMINISTRATION and the EQUAL EMPLOYMENT OPPORTUNITY COMMISSION (EEOC), and the Bureau of Citizen and Immigration Services (BCIS), formerly the Immigration and Naturalization Service (INS), make both rules and adjudicative decisions, which means that they not only promulgate regulations but also decide conflicts dealing with their area of concern.

For example, the Social Security Administration promulgates regulations concerning the provision of income for totally disabled people and also decides who is or is not disabled. The EEOC promulgates regulations and guidance dealing with SEXUAL HARASSMENT and also decides whether PROBABLE CAUSE exists to pursue a particular claim of harassment. (Probable cause, which is a reasonable basis to believe the facts alleged, must be established before litigation can commence.) The BCIS not only helps to set immigration quotas but also makes individual decisions regarding deportation.

To review an agency decision under the standard of abuse of discretion, courts must follow a three-part analysis. First, courts must look to the legislation passed by Congress that gave the decision-making authority to the particular agency and determine if the administrator acted within the limits of that authority. Second, courts must determine if a clear error of judgment has occurred. Without clear error, a court cannot substitute its own judgment; if it did so, the court would itself commit an abuse of discretion. Third, courts must determine whether the administrator followed the procedural requirements.

Courts reviewing administrative decisions for abuse of discretion give great deference to the administrator or agency, who not only is an expert in the area of concern but also had access to all the facts that influenced the decision. This "hands-off" approach gives administrative agencies the opportunity to execute the authority granted them by Congress efficiently and effectively.

An administrative decision that is difficult to reverse or challenge is that made by the Board of Immigration Appeals to uphold an immigration judge's decision to deport an ALIEN. Once a deportation decision is made and upheld, the alien can seek to have the attorney general reverse it. Should the attorney general uphold the deportation, a court reviewing this discretionary decision will have limited opportunity to challenge it, because the Board of Immigration Appeals clearly has authority to make the decision in the first place. The alien must show either failure to follow procedure or clear error of judgment on the part of the board. Deportation challenges are common, but successful challenges are rare because the great discretion afforded to the BCIS makes an abuse of discretion extremely difficult to prove.

FURTHER READINGS

Davis, Kenneth C. 1971. *Discretionary Justice: A Preliminary Inquiry.* Champaign, Ill.: Univ. of Illinois.

Feinstein, Mary S. 1986. "*American Cetacean Society v. Baldrige*: Executive Agreements and the Constitutional Limits of Executive Branch Discretion in American Foreign Policy." *Brooklyn Journal of International Law* 12.

Goldstein, Abraham S. 1981. *The Passive Judiciary: Prosecutorial Discretion and the Guilty Plea.* Baton Rouge, La.: Louisiana State Univ. Press.

Heyman, Michael G. 1994. "Judicial Review of Discretionary Immigration Decisionmaking." *San Diego Law Review* 31.

Koch, Charles H. 1986. "Judicial Review of Administrative Discretion." *George Washington Law Review* 54.

Maranville, Deborah. 1986. "Nonacquiescence: Outlaw Agencies, Imperial Courts, and the Perils of Pluralism." *Vanderbilt Law Review* 39.

Mills, Linda G. 1999. *A Penchant for Prejudice: Unraveling Bias in Judicial Decision Making.* Ann Arbor: Univ. of Michigan Press.

Neuren, Cathy S. 1984. "Addressing the Resurgence of Presidential Budgetmaking Initiative: A Proposal to Reform the Impoundment Control Act of 1974." *Texas Law Review* 63.

Paquette, J., and D. Allison. 1997. "Decision-Making and Discretion: The Agony and Ecstasy of Law and Administration." *Education & Law Journal* 8 (September): 161–81.

Shapiro, Sidney A., and Robert L. Glicksman. 1988. "Congress, the Supreme Court, and the Quiet Revolution in Administrative Law." *Duke Law Journal.*

Vila, Marisa Iglesias. 2001. *Facing Judicial Discretion: Legal Knowledge and Right Answers Revisited.* Dordrecht, Netherlands, Boston: Kluwer Academic.

CROSS-REFERENCES

Abuse of Discretion; Discovery.

DISCRETIONARY TRUST

An arrangement whereby property is set aside with directions that it be used for the benefit of another, the beneficiary, and which provides that the trustee (one appointed or required by law to administer the property) has the right to accumulate, rather than pay out to the beneficiary, the annual income generated by the property or a portion of the property itself.

Depending on the terms of the instrument that creates the trust, such income can be accumulated for future distributions to the income beneficiaries or added to the corpus, the main body or principal of a trust, for the benefit of the remainderman, one who is entitled to the balance of the estate after a particular estate carved out of it has expired. This is a discretionary trust since the trustee has the latitude or discretion to give or deny the beneficiary some benefits under the trust. The beneficiary cannot compel the trustee to use any of the trust property for the beneficiary's advantage.

In this type of trust the beneficiary has no interest that can be transferred or reached by creditors unless the trustee decides to pay or apply some of the trust property for the benefit of the beneficiary. At that time, the beneficiary's creditors can reach it unless it is protected by a SPENDTHRIFT TRUST clause. An assignee, a person who has received an interest in the trust from the beneficiary by assignment (a transfer of property), can hold the trustee liable for any future payment to the beneficiary by giving notice of the assignment. As an illustration, the settlor, one who creates a trust, delivers $10,000 to the trustee in trust for the beneficiary, and the trustee has the discretion to make any and every payment, or no payment at all, to the beneficiary from the corpus or income. Before the trustee has decided to make any payment to the beneficiary, the beneficiary assigns a right to $50 of any payment the trustee elects to make to him or her. The assignee notifies the trustee of the assignment and demands that if the trustee decides to pay the beneficiary any amount up to $50, the trustee must pay the assignee and not the beneficiary. If the trustee decides not to pay the beneficiary, the assignee has no right to payment. If the trustee subsequently decides to pay the beneficiary $50, the trustee will be liable to the assignee for it.

A person can create a discretionary trust for his or her own benefit, but creditors can reach the maximum amount that the trust can apply for or pay to the beneficiary under the trust terms, regardless of whether he or she actually received payment.

DISCRIMINATION

In CONSTITUTIONAL LAW, *the grant by statute of particular privileges to a class arbitrarily designated from a sizable number of persons, where no reasonable distinction exists between the favored and disfavored classes. Federal laws, supplemented by court decisions, prohibit discrimination in such areas as employment, housing,* VOTING RIGHTS, *education, and access to public facilities. They also proscribe discrimination on the basis of race, age, sex, nationality, disability, or religion. In addition, state and local laws can prohibit discrimination in these areas and in others not covered by federal laws.*

In the 1960s, in response to the CIVIL RIGHTS MOVEMENT and an increasing awareness of discrimination against minorities, several pieces of landmark legislation were signed into law. Title VII of the CIVIL RIGHTS ACT OF 1964 (42 U.S.C.A. § 2000e et seq.), the most comprehensive CIVIL RIGHTS legislation in U.S. history, prohibits discrimination on the basis of sex, race, religion, nationality, or color. Title VII was designed to provide for parity in the use and enjoyment of public accommodations, facilities, and education as well as in federally assisted programs and employment. It further allows an injured party to bring suit and obtain damages from any individual who illegally infringes upon the party's civil rights. The VOTING RIGHTS ACT OF 1965 (42 U.S.C.A. § 1973 et seq.) prohibits the states and their political subdivisions from imposing voting qualifications or prerequisites to voting or standards, practices, or procedures that deny or curtail the right of citizens to vote, because of race, color, or membership in a language minority group. The FAIR HOUSING ACT OF 1968 (42 U.S.C.A. § 3601 et seq.) prohibits discrimination based on race, color, religion, sex, and national origin, in connection with the sale or rental of residential housing. In 1988, Congress passed the Fair Housing Amendments Act, which extends the same protections to handicapped people.

Other important federal laws have been aimed at remedying discrimination against other groups, including older U.S. citizens and individuals with disabilities. The Age Discrimination in Employment Act of 1967 (ADEA) (29 U.S.C.A. § 621 et seq.) prohibits employers with 20 or more employees from discriminating because of age against employees over age 40. Industries affecting commerce as well as state and local governments are covered by the ADEA. Disabled individuals received federal protection against discrimination with the passage of the Rehabilitation Act of 1973 (29 U.S.C.A. § 701 et seq.), which prohibits any program activity receiving federal funds from denying access to a handicapped person. In 1990, Congress enacted the Americans with Disabilities Act (ADA) (codified in scattered sections of 42, 29, 47 U.S.C.A.). The ADA was widely hailed as the most significant piece of civil rights legislation since the Civil Rights Act of 1964. It provides even broader protection, prohibiting discrimination against disabled individuals, in employment, public accommodations, transportation, and TELECOMMUNICATIONS.

Although discrimination on the basis of gender is included in title VII of the Civil Rights Act of 1964, a number of other federal laws also prohibit SEX DISCRIMINATION. The EQUAL PAY ACT OF 1963 (29 U.S.C.A. § 206 [d]) amended the FAIR LABOR STANDARDS ACT of 1938 (29 U.S.C.A. §§ 201–219). It prohibits discrimination through different forms of compensation for jobs with equal skill, effort, and responsibility. The Pregnancy Discrimination Act of 1978 (42 U.S.C.A. § 2000e[k]) prohibits discrimination against employees on the basis of pregnancy and childbirth, in employment and benefits. Title IX of the Education Amendments of 1972 (20 U.S.C.A. §§ 1681–1686) prohibits sex discrimination in educational institutions that receive federal funds, including exclusions from noncontact team sports on the basis of sex. In addition, the Equal Credit Opportunity Act (15 U.S.C.A. § 1691 et seq.) prohibits discrimination in the extension of credit, on the basis of sex or marital status.

State and local laws can also protect individuals from discrimination. For example, GAYS AND LESBIANS, although not yet included under federal civil rights laws, are protected in many cities by local ordinances outlawing discrimination against individuals on the basis of sexual orientation. Minnesota, New Jersey, Rhode Island, Vermont, Wisconsin, and other states have passed such legislation—although some voters have sought to repeal it, with mixed results.

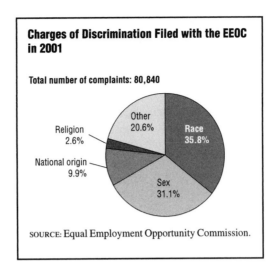

Charges of Discrimination Filed with the EEOC in 2001

Total number of complaints: 80,840

Other 20.6%
Religion 2.6%
National origin 9.9%
Race 35.8%
Sex 31.1%

SOURCE: Equal Employment Opportunity Commission.

Local antidiscrimination laws have been used to deny funding to groups that bar members because of their sexual orientation. This was the case after the Supreme Court issued its ruling in *Boys Scouts of America v. Dale*, 530 U.S. 640, 120 S.Ct. 2446, 147 L.Ed.2d 554 (2000). The Court held that the Boy Scouts of America (BSA), as a private organization, had the constitutional right to bar homosexual troop leaders and members from its ranks. The Boy Scouts hailed this as an important victory, but many corporations and local governments were angered by the decision.

Major corporate sponsors withdrew their support, and school districts and city councils reviewed their relationships with the BSA. The one million Boy Scouts are organized into 19,000 local troops. Many of the troops use public schools or community centers for their meetings. In light of the court decision, a number of cities around the United States either barred the Boy Scouts from using public space or required them to pay, citing antidiscrimination ordinances and policies. In at least 39 cities, the local United Way charitable organizations withdrew funding to the BSA, again citing antidiscrimination policies. The BSA estimated in 2002 that these decisions cut local troop income by 10 to 15 percent, totaling millions of dollars.

FURTHER READINGS

Cokorinos, Lee. 2003. *The Assault on Diversity: An Organized Challenge to Racial and Gender Justice.* New York: Rowman & Littlefield.

Price, Joyce Howard. 2002. "Scouts Lose United Way Funds Over Gay Ban." *Washington Times* (March 15).

Richards, David A. J. 1999. *Identity and the Case for Gay Rights: Race, Gender, Religion as Analogies.* Chicago: Univ. of Chicago Press.

CROSS-REFERENCES

Affirmative Action; Age Discrimination; Club; Colleges and Universities; Disability Discrimination; Equal Employment Opportunity Commission; Gay and Lesbian Rights; Women's Rights.

DISFRANCHISEMENT

The removal of the rights and privileges inherent in an association with a group; the taking away of the rights of a free citizen, especially the right to vote. Sometimes called disenfranchisement.

The relinquishment of a person's right to membership in a corporation is distinguishable from a motion, which is the act of removing an officer from an office without depriving him or her of membership in the corporate body.

In U.S. law, disfranchisement most commonly refers to the removal of the right to vote, which is also called the franchise or suffrage. Historically, states passed a variety of laws disfranchising poor people, insane people, and criminals. Most conspicuously, the JIM CROW LAWS passed by Southern states effectively disfranchised African-Americans from the late nineteenth century until well into the 20th century.

During Reconstruction, following the Civil War, African-Americans in the South briefly enjoyed voting privileges that were nearly equal to those of whites. However, beginning around 1890, legally sanctioned disfranchisement occurred on a huge scale. For example, during the years directly following the Civil War, African-Americans made up as much as 44 percent of the registered electorate in Louisiana, but by 1920, they constituted only 1 percent of the electorate. In Mississippi, almost 70 percent of eligible African-Americans were registered to vote in 1867; after 1890, fewer than 6 percent were eligible to vote. There were similar decreases in the percentages of elected black officials in all Southern states.

Although the FIFTEENTH AMENDMENT to the Constitution, passed in 1870, asserts that "the right of citizens of the United States to vote shall not be denied or abridged by the United States or by any State on account of race, color, or previous condition of servitude," Southern states established laws and practices that circumvented these provisions. They employed disfranchisement devices such as POLL TAXES, property tests, literacy tests, and all-white primaries to prevent African-Americans from voting. On the surface, such laws discriminated on the basis of education and property ownership

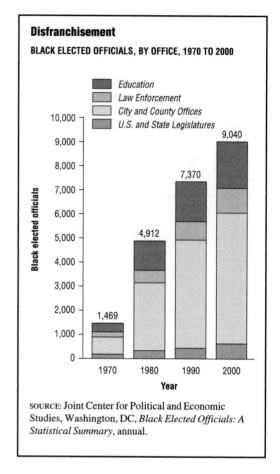

Disfranchisement

BLACK ELECTED OFFICIALS, BY OFFICE, 1970 TO 2000

Legend:
- Education
- Law Enforcement
- City and County Offices
- U.S. and State Legislatures

(Y-axis: Black elected officials, 0 to 10,000; X-axis: Year)

1970: 1,469
1980: 4,912
1990: 7,370
2000: 9,040

SOURCE: Joint Center for Political and Economic Studies, Washington, DC, *Black Elected Officials: A Statistical Summary*, annual.

rather than race, but their practical and intended effect was to block African-Americans from the polls. Legal devices called grandfather clauses allowed poor and illiterate whites to avoid discriminatory tests on the grounds that they or their ancestors had previously had the franchise. When discriminatory laws were combined with the violence and intimidation directed at potential black voters by white hate groups such as the KU KLUX KLAN, the silencing of the African-American political voice was almost complete.

Despite Supreme Court rulings striking down discriminatory measures as early as 1915 (see, e.g., *Guinn v. United States,* 238 U.S. 347, 35 S. Ct. 926, 59 L. Ed. 1340 [1915]), Southern states continued to bar African-Americans from voting for most of the twentieth century. Only with the passage of the VOTING RIGHTS ACT OF 1965 (42 U.S.C.A. § 1973 et seq.) did twentieth-century African-Americans in the South finally reach the polls in significant numbers. For example, in 1965, only 19 percent of non-whites in Alabama and 7 percent of non-whites in Mississippi were registered to vote. Four years later, after passage of the VOTING RIGHTS ACT, the percentages of non-white registrants in Alabama and Mississippi had jumped to 57 percent and 59 percent, respectively.

Although blatant disfranchisement is somewhat rare in current elections, claims of racism still occur. During the 2000 presidential election, which was one of the most heavily contested and highly controversial in history, thousands of minority voters claimed that their votes were not counted due to minor errors on their ballots. Federal election law leaves the particular voting procedures in presidential elections to the states, so the states use a variety of techniques to count the ballots. Many states used a hole-punch method, where machines count ballots based upon holes punched in ballot cards. If the machine could not read the card, which may occur if the hole punch is incomplete or if more than one hole is punched, the vote was not counted. This was particularly problematic in the state of Florida, which was the subject of a national controversy surrounding the proper vote count. During the initial election on November 7, 2000, and during subsequent recounts during the weeks following the election, many votes were not counted due to errors, and many minority voters claimed that they cast many of the discounted votes. Minority groups have pressured Congress to enact stricter standards in order to prevent this occurrence in future elections.

Other forms of disfranchisement, including the disfranchisement of criminals, remain controversial. Since the early 1990s, all but three states prohibited imprisoned offenders from voting. Thirty-five states disfranchise offenders on PROBATION or PAROLE, and fourteen disfranchise ex-offenders for life. Because a disproportionate share of convicted criminals are non-white, some have argued that such laws constitute a racially discriminatory voting barrier that is as pernicious as poll taxes and literacy tests. Many state criminal disfranchisement laws date back to the Reconstruction era, and such laws were often targeted at offenses for which African-Americans were disproportionately convicted. For this reason, some groups have called for the reform or removal of criminal disfranchisement laws.

FURTHER READINGS

Belknap, Michael, ed. 1991. *Civil Rights, the White House, and the Justice Department.* New York: Garland.

Reitman, Alan, and Robert B. Davidson. 1972. *The Election Process: Voting Laws and Procedures.* Dobbs Ferry, N.Y.: Oceana.

Schmidt, Benno C., Jr. 1982. "Black Disfranchisement from the KKK to the Grandfather Clause." *Columbia Law Review* 82 (June).

Shapiro, Andrew L. 1993. "Challenging Criminal Disenfranchisement under the Voting Rights Act." *Yale Law Journal* 103 (November).

DISHONOR

To refuse to accept or pay a draft or to pay a promissory note when duly presented. An instrument is dishonored when a necessary or optional presentment is made and due acceptance or payment is refused, or cannot be obtained within the prescribed time, or in case of bank collections, the instrument is seasonably returned by the midnight deadline; or presentment is excused and the instrument is not duly accepted or paid. Includes the insurer of a letter of credit refusing to pay or accept a draft or demand for payment.

As respects the flag, to deface or defile, imputing a lively sense of shaming or an equivalent acquiescent callousness.

DISINHERIT

To cut off from an inheritance. To deprive someone, who would otherwise be an heir to property or another right, of his or her right to inherit.

A parent who wishes to disinherit a child may specifically state so in a will.

DISINTERESTED

Free from bias, prejudice, or partiality.

A *disinterested witness* is one who has no interest in the case at bar, or matter in issue, and is legally competent to give testimony.

DISMISSAL

A discharge of an individual or corporation from employment. The disposition of a civil or criminal proceeding or a claim or charge made therein by a court order without a trial or prior to its completion which, in effect, is a denial of the relief sought by the commencement of the action.

The legal effect of a dismissal varies depending upon its type. A dismissal, granted by a court that has exercised its discretion in evaluating the particular case before it, operates similarly in civil and criminal actions.

Civil Proceedings

Rules embodied in state codes of CIVIL PROCEDURE and the Federal Rules of Civil Procedure govern the granting of dismissals in civil actions brought in state and federal courts. The primary function of a dismissal is to promote the speedy and efficient administration of justice by removing from the consideration of a court any matters that have been unnecessarily delayed to the disadvantage of the defendant.

Dismissal with Prejudice A dismissal with prejudice is a judgment rendered in a lawsuit on its merits that prevents the plaintiff from bringing the same lawsuit against the same defendant in the future. It is a harsh remedy that has the effect of canceling the action so that it can never again be commenced. A dismissal with prejudice is RES JUDICATA as to every issue litigated in the action.

The possibility of such a dismissal acts as a deterrent to the use of dilatory tactics by a plaintiff who wants to prejudice a defendant's case by unreasonably hindering the disposition of the action from the time of the filing of the action to the actual trial of the issues. It is also designed to minimize, if not eliminate, the congestion of court calendars caused by unnecessary delays in pending cases. Because it is regarded as a drastic remedy, courts grant dismissals with prejudice only in the most egregious cases in response to a motion brought by a defendant or by a court sua sponte or on its own will.

Motion by a Defendant A defendant may make a motion to a court to dismiss the CAUSE OF ACTION if the plaintiff has failed to appear to prosecute his or her case. A plaintiff is obligated to prosecute the action with due diligence within a reasonable time of commencing the action. If the passage of time hurts the defendant in the preparation of his or her case or if it substantially affects the defendant's rights, then the defendant may seek a dismissal with prejudice. A dismissal will not be granted if the failure to prosecute resulted from unavoidable circumstances, such as the death of the plaintiff, and there is a delay in the appointment of a PERSONAL REPRESENTATIVE to continue the action. When the parties attempt to negotiate a settlement of the controversy, consequent delays in reaching an agreement will not provide a basis for dismissal with prejudice. If, however, a plaintiff delays prosecution based on the mere possibility of a settlement without demonstrating concrete efforts to achieve an agreement, a court may grant a dismissal upon the defendant's motion.

The defendant must be free of any responsibility for delay when he or she seeks a dismissal for failure to prosecute. A lawsuit will not be dismissed if the defendant caused or contributed to the delay, such as if the individual leaves the state to avoid the trial.

Sua sponte power of court A court has inherent power to dismiss an action with prejudice if it is vexatious, brought in bad faith, or when there has been a failure to prosecute it within a reasonable time. If a plaintiff who has commenced an action fails to comply with discovery devices, a court, which has issued the order of compliance, may *sua sponte* dismiss the case with prejudice.

Dismissal without Prejudice A plaintiff is not subsequently barred from suing the same defendant on the same cause of action when a court grants a dismissal WITHOUT PREJUDICE of his or her case. Such a dismissal operates to terminate the case. It is not, however, an ultimate disposition of the controversy on the merits, but rather it is usually based upon procedural errors that do not substantially harm the defendant's rights. It effectively treats the matter as if the lawsuit had never been commenced, but it does not relieve a plaintiff of the duty of complying with the STATUTE OF LIMITATIONS, the time limit within which his or her action must be commenced. A dismissal without prejudice is granted in response to a notice of dismissal, stipulations, or a court order.

Notice of Dismissal A plaintiff may serve a notice of dismissal upon a defendant only if the defendant has not yet submitted an answer in response to the plaintiff's complaint. A notice of dismissal preserves the right of the plaintiff to commence a lawsuit at a later date. While not commonly employed, such a notice is useful when exigent circumstances—such as the sudden unavailability of witnesses—warrant the termination of the action. The clerk of the court in which the lawsuit was commenced must receive a copy of the notice of dismissal served upon the defendant to adjust the record of the action accordingly.

Stipulation Once a defendant has served an answer to the plaintiff's complaint, the plaintiff may obtain a dismissal without prejudice by entering a formal agreement, a stipulation, with the defendant. The parties agree to the terms of the dismissal, which must be filed with the court clerk and put into effect by the action of the clerk. A dismissal agreement is a court order that enforces the stipulation of the parties. A dismissal by stipulation is a dismissal without prejudice unless the parties otherwise agree and record their agreement in the text of the stipulation.

Court Order A plaintiff may make a motion to dismiss his or her action without prejudice if the plaintiff cannot serve a notice of dismissal or obtain a stipulation. A dismissal will not be granted to a plaintiff, however, if it would prejudice the rights of any other individual who has a legal interest in the subject matter of a lawsuit. If a joint tenant fails to agree with his or her co-tenant to dismiss an action against a landlord for breach of the WARRANTY of habitability without prejudice, then there will not be a dismissal.

Criminal Prosecutions

A dismissal in a criminal prosecution is a decision of a court, which has exercised its discretion prior to trial or before a verdict is reached, that terminates the proceedings against the defendant. The procedure by which dismissals in state and federal criminal actions are obtained are governed, respectively, by the state and federal rules of CRIMINAL PROCEDURE. In criminal prosecutions, delay often prejudices the defendant's rights because of the greater likelihood that evidence would be lost or memories or events would not be recalled easily. The possibility of dismissal ensures the prompt government prosecution of individuals accused of criminal activity.

The legal effect of a dismissal in a criminal prosecution is dependent upon the type that is granted by the court.

Dismissal with Prejudice A dismissal with prejudice bars the government from prosecuting the accused on the same charge at a later date. The defendant cannot subsequently be reindicted because of the constitutional guarantee against DOUBLE JEOPARDY. A dismissal with prejudice is made in response to a motion to the court by the defendant or by the court *sua sponte*.

Motion by a Defendant A defendant may make a motion to the court to have the charges against him or her—whether embodied in an indictment, information, or complaint—dismissed with prejudice because the delay has violated the individual's constitutional right to a SPEEDY TRIAL or there is no sufficient evidence to support the charges. In deciding whether a delay is unreasonable, the court evaluates the extent of the delay, the reasons for it, the prejudice to the defendant, and the defendant's contribution to the delay.

Sua Sponte Power of Court A court with jurisdiction to decide criminal matters can *sua sponte* dismiss a criminal prosecution with prejudice if the facts of the case clearly established that an accused has been deprived of his or her constitutional right to a speedy trial.

Dismissal without Prejudice A dismissal without prejudice that permits the reindictment or retrial of a defendant on the same charge at a subsequent date may be granted by a court acting *sua sponte* or after the prosecuting attorney has made a motion to do so. Only nonconstitutional grounds that do not adversely affect the rights of the defendant, such as the crowding of court calendars, might be sufficient to warrant the dismissal of a criminal action without prejudice.

FURTHER READINGS

Cohen, Alan G., ed., et al. 1992. *The Living Law: A Guide to Modern Legal Research.* Rochester, N.Y.: Lawyers Cooperative.

Kraut, Jayson, et al. 1983. *American Jurisprudence.* Rochester, N.Y.: Lawyers Cooperative.

CROSS-REFERENCES

Civil Action; Criminal Procedure; Discovery; Double Jeopardy.

DISORDERLY CONDUCT

A broad term describing conduct that disturbs the peace or endangers the morals, health, or safety of a community.

Unlike the offense of breach of the peace, which originated under COMMON LAW, disorderly conduct is strictly a statutory crime. It is commonly considered a broader term than breach of the peace and, under some statutes, breach of the peace is an element of disorderly conduct.

The elements of disorderly conduct vary from one jurisdiction to another. Most statutes specify the misconduct that constitutes the offense. Acts such as the use of vulgar and obscene language in a public place, VAGRANCY, loitering, causing a crowd to gather in a public place, or annoying passengers on a mode of public transportation have been regarded as disorderly conduct by statute or ordinance. The offense is not committed unless the act complained of clearly falls within the statute.

In most jurisdictions, the decision of whether or not the act complained of is disorderly conduct is made by a judge. Following this determination, a jury decides whether or not the accused is guilty of the offense, provided there is a QUESTION OF FACT to be decided.

The punishment for disorderly conduct is usually fixed by statute. Under most statutes the penalty consists of a fine, imprisonment, or both. Some statutes provide that an accused cannot be imprisoned for disorderly conduct unless he or she has been given an opportunity to pay a fine and has defaulted on the payment.

CROSS-REFERENCES

Disturbance of the Peace.

DISORDERLY HOUSE

A place where individuals reside or which they frequent for purposes that pose a threat to public health, morals, convenience, or safety, and that may create a public NUISANCE. *A disorderly house is an all-inclusive term that may be used to describe such places as a house of prostitution, an illegal gambling casino, or a site where drugs are constantly bought and sold. It is any place where unlawful practices are habitually carried on by the public.*

Various offenses concerning disorderly houses exist at COMMON LAW and under criminal statutes. The maintenance of a disorderly house is considered to be an ongoing offense and, at times, the offense involves a specific type of place, such as a bordello or GAMING house. The offenses are divided into four classes, which encompass keeping or maintaining a disorderly house, letting a house to be used as a disorderly house, frequenting or abiding permanently in a disorderly house, and disguising a disorderly house by displaying a sign of an honest occupation—such as disguising a house of prostitution as a dress shop.

Statutes

In most jurisdictions, the maintenance of a disorderly house is an offense and, in order to be valid, each statute must clearly state the nature of the offense. Ordinarily, most statutes merely define the common-law offense rather than create a new statute. In states with statutes that provide for the punishment of an offense but do not define what a disorderly house is, the common law is examined to determine what the definition should be. In contrast, where the statute embodies a characterization of the house as well as prohibited conduct therein, the statute itself determines what constitutes the offense.

The prohibition against disorderly houses and the offenses they encompass are valid exercises of the POLICE POWER of the state.

Elements

The elements of the offense of maintaining a disorderly house depend on statutory provisions that vary from state to state. A place may be named a disorderly house if alcohol is sold on the premises and if the law in that jurisdiction prohibits such sale. Essential to all offenses involving disorderly houses is the character of the house.

House or Other Building or Place The commission of the offense is dependent upon the presence of a house or place of public resort, the physical characteristics of which are immaterial. A disorderly house may be any place, including a room in a building or a steamship, an apartment, a garden, or a space under the grandstand at the racetrack.

The character of the place as a public resort is important. The general rule is that a disorderly house must be a place to which the general public or a segment of the public retreats for immoral purposes without prior invitation. A disorderly house may be used for other purposes that are not prohibited by law in addition to immoral purposes, but this in no way affects its classification as a disorderly house.

Annoyance or Injury to the Public The annoyance to the general public, as opposed to anyone in particular, is an essential element of the definition of a disorderly house. This annoyance or injury is based on the fact that activities being conducted are considered detrimental to public morals, welfare, and safety. They need not disturb the peace and quiet of a neighborhood to be construed as disorderly. A house where drugs are sold quietly or where a bordello is discreetly operated would be considered an endangerment to the public peace.

Persons Liable

The liability of those concerned in offenses in connection with disorderly houses is not based upon their civil or contractual status. Some statutes specify who may be liable and in such cases, only those designated may be prosecuted. Partners, servants, and agents as well as the officers of a corporation have all been held liable for the operation of disorderly houses and the various offenses committed on the premises.

DISPARAGEMENT

In old ENGLISH LAW, *an injury resulting from the comparison of a person or thing with an individual or thing of inferior quality; to discredit oneself by marriage below one's class. A statement made by one person that casts aspersions on another person's goods, property, or intangible things.*

In TORTS, a considerable body of law has come about concerning interference with business or economic relations. The TORT of injurious falsehood, or disparagement, is concerned with the publication of derogatory information about a person's title to his or her property, to his or her business in general, or anything else made for the purpose of discouraging people from dealing with the individual. Generally, if the aspersions are cast upon the quality of what the person has to sell, or the person's business itself, proof of damages is essential.

Disparagement of goods is a false or misleading statement by an entrepreneur about a competitor's goods. It is made with the intention of influencing people adversely so they will not buy the goods.

Disparagement of title is a false or malicious statement made about an individual's title to real or PERSONAL PROPERTY. Such disparagement may result in a pecuniary loss due to impairment of vendibility that the defamatory statements might cause.

CROSS-REFERENCES

Defamation.

DISPARATE IMPACT

A theory of liability that prohibits an employer from using a facially neutral employment practice that has an unjustified adverse impact on members of a protected class. A facially neutral employment practice is one that does not appear to be discriminatory on its face; rather it is one that is discriminatory in its application or effect.

Under Title VII of the CIVIL RIGHTS ACT OF 1964, plaintiffs may sue employers who discriminate on the basis of race, color, gender, religion, or national origin. Employers who intentionally discriminate are obvious candidates for a lawsuit, but the courts also allow plaintiffs to prove liability if the employer has treated classes of people differently using apparently neutral employment policies. The *disparate impact* theory of liability will succeed if the plaintiff can prove that these employment policies had the effect of excluding persons who are members of Title VII's protected classes. Once disparate impact is established, the employer must justify the continued use of the procedure or procedures causing the adverse impact as a "business necessity."

Proof of discriminatory motive is not required, because in these types of cases Congress is concerned with the consequences of employment practices, not simply the motivation. If the employer proves that the requirement being challenged is job related, the plaintiff must then show that other selection devices without a similar discriminatory effect would also serve the employer's legitimate interest in efficient workmanship.

The Supreme Court, in *Griggs v. Duke Power Co.*, 401 U.S. 424, 91 S.Ct. 849, 28 L.Ed.2d 158 (1971), articulated the disparate impact theory and constructed a model of proof that the plaintiff and defendant must use in presenting their cases. In *Griggs*, the employer required a high school diploma and a passing score on two professionally developed tests. Although the lower courts found no liability because the plaintiff failed to prove that the employer had a discriminatory motive for the requirements, the Supreme Court reversed the decision. The Court stated that Title VII "proscribes not only overt discrimination but also practices that are fair in form, but discriminatory in operation." In a famous quote, the Court said that the "absence of discriminatory intent does not redeem employment procedures or testing mechanisms that operate as 'built in headwinds' for minority groups and are unrelated to measuring job capacity."

In the three-step model defined by the *Griggs* Court, the plaintiff must first prove that a specific employment practice adversely affects employment opportunities of Title VII protected classes. If the plaintiff can establish a disparate impact, the employer must demonstrate that the challenged practice is justified by "business necessity" or that the practice is "manifestly related" to job duties. The courts, between 1971 and 1989, used these two phrases interchangeably. If the employer does not meet the burdens of production and persuasion in proving business necessity, the plaintiff prevails. If the employer does meet these burdens, the third step requires the plaintiff to demonstrate that alternative practices exist that would meet the business needs of the employer yet would not have a discriminatory effect.

The plaintiff has the burden of persuading the fact finder that the employment practice used by the employer adversely affects the employment opportunities of a Title VII protected class. If the plaintiff fails to meet this burden, the court will dismiss the action under Rule 41(b) of the Federal Rules of Civil Procedure.

Demonstrating that the employer's workforce does not reflect the racial, ethnic, or gender percentage of the population of the area does not prove disparate impact. Such an imbalance may be the product of legitimate factors, such as geography, cultural differences, or the lack of unchallenged qualifications for the job. Therefore, it is incumbent upon the plaintiff to show that the imbalance is *because of* the challenged practice. The most compelling evidence of disparate impact is proof that an employment practice selects members of a protected class in a proportion smaller than their percentage in the pool of actual applicants, or, in promotion and benefit cases, in a proportion smaller than in the actual pool of eligible employees.

If the plaintiff proves that the employer's practice had a disproportionate impact on a protected class, the burden shifts to the defendant to justify its use of the challenged practice. *Griggs* labeled this burden as business necessity, but suggested that exclusionary practices would be justified if they were manifestly related to job duties.

Business necessity is the only known defense against the accusation that a personnel practice denies protected classes equal opportunity for hire, promotion, training, earnings and any other term or condition of employment. Three conditions must exist before business necessity can be asserted: (1) The standard used as the basis for the employment practice must be apparently neutral; (2) the standard must be uniformly applied by the employer; and (3) the standard must have a disparate impact on a protected class.

The term *business necessity* is a fluid concept rather than a bright-line rule (a firm legal standard that courts are required to honor without regard to the particular circumstances of the case being heard). In some cases, courts conclude that business necessity is established by showing a reasonable relationship between the practice in question and the employer's business needs. However, the majority of courts hold that an employment practice having a discriminatory impact can be justified on business necessity grounds only if it is "essential" to the safety and efficiency of the employer's operations. These courts contend that the mere fact that the employment practice serves legitimate management functions will not justify discrimination.

The Supreme Court, in *Wards Cove Packing v. Atonio*, 490 U.S. 642, 109 S.Ct. 2115, 104 L.Ed.2d 733 (1989), revisited the concept of business necessity and realigned the burdens of proof and persuasion. The Wards Cove Packing Company employed low-paid cannery workers in its salmon canning facility in Alaska and higher-paid non-cannery workers at the company offices in Washington and Oregon. Non-white workers filled a high percentage of the cannery worker positions; primarily white workers held the non-cannery worker jobs. The court of appeals found this statistical disparity sufficient to establish a PRIMA FACIE case of disparate impact.

The Supreme Court reversed and remanded because the statistical proof the plaintiffs offered was not adequate. As to the defendant's BURDEN OF PROOF, the Court stated that the employer "carries the burden of producing evidence of a business justification for his employment practice. The BURDEN OF PERSUASION, however, remains with the disparate-impact plaintiff." This meant that although the employer had to show a legitimate business reason for using a test or certain job requirements, the plaintiff had to prove that he or she was denied a desired employment opportunity based on race, color, religion, gender, or national origin. This pushed the burden closer to that of *disparate treatment,* where the plaintiff has to show intentional discrimination by the employer. This is often difficult to prove. In addition, the Court held that just because the plaintiff could offer nondiscriminatory alternatives did not prove that the employer had improper motivations for the use of the employment practice.

The *Wards Cove* decision was severely criticized by CIVIL RIGHTS leaders, who believed the Supreme Court had made disparate impact cases almost impossible to win. Congress responded by passing the CIVIL RIGHTS ACT of 1991, which overturned *Wards Cove*. In effect, Congress reversed the Court's holding that the burden of proof must remain with the employee at all times. Therefore, once the plaintiff has carried the burden of proving that the challenged employment practice causes a disparate impact, the employer must not only articulate a business justification for the practice but must also prove the validity of the asserted justification.

The Supreme Court has put limits on the disparate impact theory. For example, the Court has made it clear that it is not unlawful for an employer to apply different standards of compensation or different terms or conditions of employment to employees, if the employer acts according to a legitimate seniority system. This is true even if the seniority system has a discriminatory effect, as long as the system was not intended to be discriminatory. In addition, it has ruled that disparate impact theory cannot be applied in AGE DISCRIMINATION cases under the Age Discrimination in Employment Act of 1967.

FURTHER READINGS

Fick, Barbara. 1997. *The American Bar Association Guide to Workplace Law: Everything You Need to Know About Your Rights As an Employee or Employer.* New York: Times Books.

CROSS-REFERENCES

Employment Law.

DISPOSABLE EARNINGS

That portion of one's income that a person is free to spend or invest as he or she sees fit, after payment of taxes and other obligations.

Legally mandated deductions are those for the payment of taxes and SOCIAL SECURITY. Any deductions for medical insurance, PENSION plans, life insurance, or employee savings plans do not qualify and must be included in the disposable earnings. Take-home pay is, therefore, not necessarily synonymous with disposable earnings because of this distinction between the deductions.

The federal CONSUMER CREDIT PROTECTION ACT (15 U.S.C.A. § 1601 et seq. [1968]) establishes a minimum amount of disposable earnings that can be garnished by a debtor's creditors. The lesser figure of 25 percent of a worker's weekly disposable earnings or the amount by which his or her disposable earnings exceed thirty times the maximum hourly wage is subject to GARNISHMENT.

State laws also impose restrictions on the garnishment of debtor's wages.

DISPOSITION

Act of disposing; transferring to the care or possession of another. The parting with, alienation of, or giving up of property. The final settlement of a matter and, with reference to decisions announced by a court, a judge's ruling is commonly referred to as disposition, regardless of level of resolution. In CRIMINAL PROCEDURE, *the sentencing or other final settlement of a criminal case. With respect to a mental state, means an attitude, prevailing tendency, or inclination.*

DISPOSITIVE FACT

Information or evidence that unqualifiedly brings a conclusion to a legal controversy.

Dispositive facts clearly settle an issue. The fact that the defendant in a personal injury case ran a red light and hit the plaintiff with his or her car settles the question of the defendant's NEGLIGENCE and is, therefore, a dispositive fact.

DISPOSSESSION

The wrongful, nonconsensual ouster or removal of a person from his or her property by trick, compulsion, or misuse of the law, whereby the violator obtains actual occupation of the land. Dispossession encompasses intrusion, disseisin, or deforcement.

DISPUTE

A conflict or controversy; a conflict of claims or rights; an assertion of a right, claim, or demand on one side, met by contrary claims or allegations on the other. The subject of litigation; the matter for which a suit is brought and upon which issue is joined, and in relation to which jurors are called and witnesses examined.

International Longshore and Warehouse Union members rally in August 2002 in an attempt to keep the Bush administration out of their labor dispute with the Pacific Maritime Association.

AP/WIDE WORLD PHOTOS

A *labor dispute* is any disagreement between an employer and his or her employees concerning anything job-related, such as tenure, hours, wages, fringe benefits, and employment conditions.

DISQUALIFY

To deprive of eligibility or render unfit; to disable or incapacitate.

To be disqualified is to be stripped of legal capacity. A wife would be disqualified as a juror in her husband's trial for murder due to the nature of their relationship. A person may be disqualified for employment at a certain job because of a physical disability.

DISSENT

An explicit disagreement by one or more judges with the decision of the majority on a case before them.

A dissent is often accompanied by a written dissenting opinion, and the terms *dissent* and *dissenting opinion* are used interchangeably.

Dissents have several functions. In some cases, they are a simple declaration of disagreement with the majority. In others, they instruct, prod, scold, or otherwise urge the majority to consider the dissenter's point of view.

Dissents carry no precedential weight and are not relied on as authority in subsequent cases. However, attorneys and judges sometimes consult them to understand the dissenter's analysis of the majority opinion. Attorneys and judges may also cite a dissent if they agree with its reasoning and conclusion and seek support for a change in the law.

Although the majority opinion constitutes the judgment of the court, its legal weight can be diminished if a sufficient number of judges dissent. On issues that divide the courts and the country, there can be sharply divergent opinions on what the law is or should be. During the 1990s, for example, one divisive question before the U.S. Supreme Court was whether AFFIRMATIVE ACTION programs to redress the effects of past discrimination were constitutional. In *Miller v. Johnson,* 515 U.S. 900, 115 S. Ct. 2475, 132 L. Ed. 2d 762 (1995), the U.S. Supreme Court held that Georgia's congressional redistricting plan, implemented to give minorities a strong voting block, constituted racial gerrymandering and violated the EQUAL PROTECTION CLAUSE. However, the case was not an unqualified success for those urging the rejection of affirmative action. Five justices joined in the majority block (plurality) in the case, and four justices filed dissents. With such a large minority, the dissents gained significance. Legal analysts monitor close cases such as *Miller* because a shift by one justice would signal a change in the law.

Dissents are a relatively recent phenomenon. Chief Justice JOHN MARSHALL, who served on the Supreme Court from 1801 to 1835, urged unanimity on the Court to demonstrate that its opinions were the last word on an issue. Others believed that individual conscience should dictate a justice's opinions, without regard to unanimity. In its early years, most of the Supreme Court's decisions showed little or no dissent. During the late nineteenth century and early twentieth century, as the Court became firmly established as the law of the land, more dissents appeared. Yet, even those who dissented during this period often recognized the importance of consensus opinions. For instance, Justice OLIVER WENDELL HOLMES JR., a frequent and famous dissenter, wrote a scathing dissent in LOCHNER V. NEW YORK, 198 U.S. 45, 25 S. Ct. 539, 49 L. Ed. 937 (1905), but not before he expressed his reluctance to do so: "I regret sincerely that I am unable to agree with the judgment in this case, and that I think it is my duty to express my dissent."

By the 1960s and 1970s, dissents were an accepted part of the Court's business, perhaps reflecting the fractious political and social climate of those years. One frequent dissenter during the mid-twentieth century was Justice WILLIAM O. DOUGLAS. During his thirty-six years on the Court, from 1939 to 1975, Douglas wrote 524 opinions of the Court, 154 concurring opinions, and an astounding 486 dissenting opinions. In addition, he dissented without opinion in 309 cases.

Justice BENJAMIN N. CARDOZO, of the Supreme Court, defended those who disagree with the majority, writing that the dissenter is "the gladiator making a last stand against the lions." A few justices raised their roles as dissenters to an art form. Justices WILLIAM J. BRENNAN JR. and THURGOOD MARSHALL displayed particular courage in opposition to the majority. During their long tenure on the Court, Brennan and Marshall were unwavering in their conviction that the death penalty violates the Constitution. By doggedly and relentlessly repeating their dissent, they sought to win others to their view that the law on CAPITAL PUNISHMENT should be changed.

Together as well as separately, Brennan and Marshall wrote scores of dissents in death penalty cases. In so doing, they opposed clear precedent that supported the legality of capital punishment. However, both were convinced that they were justified in their continued opposition. Brennan felt that the intrinsic morality of the EIGHTH AMENDMENT superseded any right of individual states to impose capital punishment. He wrote, "It would effectively write the [CRUEL AND UNUSUAL PUNISHMENT] clause out of the BILL OF RIGHTS were we to permit legislatures to police themselves by having the last word on the scope of the protection that the clause is intended to secure against their own overreaching." Marshall's opposition was less philosophical and more practical. He repeatedly pointed out that the application of the death penalty was ARBITRARY and unfair, and affected minorities disproportionately. He felt a responsibility to continue bringing this issue before the public and believed that most people, if sufficiently informed about all its ramifications, would find capital punishment "shocking, unjust, and unacceptable" (FURMAN V. GEORGIA, 408 U.S. 238, 92 S. Ct. 2726, 33 L. Ed. 2d 346 [1972] [Marshall, J., dissenting]).

Some legal analysts believe that dissents are an important part of the system of checks and balances. Justice CHARLES E. HUGHES—who served on the Court from 1910 to 1916, left the bench to run for president, and then returned to the Court as chief justice from 1930 to 1941—wrote, "A dissent . . . is an appeal to the brooding spirit of the law, to the intelligence of a future day, when a later decision may possibly correct the error into which the dissenting judge believes the court to have been betrayed."

FURTHER READINGS

Mello, Michael. 1995. "Adhering to Our Views: Justices Brennan and Marshall and the Relentless Dissent to Death as a Punishment." *Florida State University Law Review* 22 (winter).

CROSS-REFERENCES

Court Opinion.

DISSOLUTION

Act or process of dissolving; termination; winding up. In this sense it is frequently used in the phrase dissolution of a partnership.

The dissolution of a contract is its RESCISSION by the parties themselves or by a court that nullifies its binding force and reinstates each party to his or her original position prior to the contract.

The dissolution of a corporation is the termination of its existence as a legal entity. This might occur pursuant to a statute, the surrender or expiration of its charter, legal proceedings, or BANKRUPTCY.

In domestic relations law, the term *dissolution* refers to the ending of a marriage through DIVORCE.

The dissolution of a partnership is the end of the relationship that exists among the partners as a result of any partner discontinuing his or her involvement in the partnership, as distinguished from the winding up of the outstanding obligations of the business.

DISSOLVE

To terminate; abrogate; cancel; annul; disintegrate. To release or unloose the binding force of anything.

The dissolution of something is the act of disorganizing or disuniting it, as in marriage, contracts, or corporations.

DISTINGUISH

To set apart as being separate or different; to point out an essential disparity.

To distinguish one case from another case means to show the dissimilarities between the two. It means to prove a case that is cited as applicable to the case currently in dispute is really inapplicable because the two cases are different.

DISTRAIN

To seize the property of an individual and retain it until an obligation is performed. The taking of the goods and chattels of a tenant by a landlord in order to satisfy an unpaid debt.

Distrain is a comprehensive term that may be used in reference to any detention of PERSONAL PROPERTY, lawful or unlawful.

DISTRESS

The seizure of PERSONAL PROPERTY for the satisfaction of a demand.

The process of distress, sometimes called distrain, began at COMMON LAW wherein a landlord had the right to confiscate the chattels of a tenant who had defaulted on a rent payment. Today, it is regulated by statute, and is used to mean the taking of property to enforce the performance of some obligation.

A *warrant of distress* is a writ that authorizes an officer to seize a person's goods. It is usually used in situations where a landlord has the right to obtain a lien on a tenant's goods for nonpayment of rent.

If personal property is seized to enforce the payment of taxes and then publicly sold if the taxes are not subsequently paid, the sale is called a *distress sale*. *Distressed goods* are chattels sold at a distress sale.

DISTRIBUTEE

An heir; a person entitled to share in the distribution of an estate. This term is used to denote one of the persons who is entitled, under the statute of distributions, to the personal estate of one who is dead intestate.

DISTRIBUTOR

A wholesaler; an individual, corporation, or partnership buying goods in bulk quantities from a manufacturer at a price close to the cost of manufacturing them and reselling them at a higher price to other dealers, or to various retailers, but not directly to the general public.

DISTRICT

One of the territorial areas into which an entire state or country, county, municipality, or other political subdivision is divided, for judicial, political, electoral, or administrative purposes.

The circuit or territory within which a person may be compelled to appear. Circuit of authority; province.

A *judicial district* is a designated area of a state over which a court has been empowered to hear lawsuits that arise within it or that involve its inhabitants. A *federal judicial district* is an area of a state in which a federal district court sits to determine matters involving federal questions or DIVERSITY OF CITIZENSHIP of the parties.

A *congressional district* is a geographical subdivision of a state that elects a representative to Congress.

A *legislative district* is a specific section of a state that elects a representative to the state legislature.

DISTRICT AND PROSECUTING ATTORNEYS

The elected or appointed public officers of each state, county, or other political subdivision who institute criminal proceedings on behalf of the government.

Federal attorneys who represent the United States in prosecuting federal offenses are U.S. attorneys.

A district or prosecuting attorney is the legal representative of the state, county, or municipality, whose primary function resides in instituting criminal proceedings against violators of state or municipal penal laws. The law of the particular jurisdiction determines whether they are appointed or elected to office and their term of office.

The legislature may, within the restrictions imposed by constitution or statute, prescribe the qualifications of the prosecuting attorney. He or she may be required to reside in the district or satisfy a particular minimum-age requisite. District attorneys usually must be attorneys-at-law who are licensed to practice in the state and, depending upon the jurisdiction, must have spent a specified number of years practicing law.

The duty of the district attorney is to ensure that offenses committed against the public are rectified pursuant to the commencement of criminal prosecutions. He or she may exercise considerable discretion in ascertaining the manner in which the duty of district attorney should be performed. The prosecuting attorney, however, must be fair and unbiased, and refrain from conduct that would deprive the defendant of any constitutional or statutory right. The legislature may regulate his or her functions within statutory or constitutional limitations.

A district attorney determines when to initiate a particular prosecution and must exercise due diligence in conducting the prosecution. The individual may neither restrain the GRAND JURY from considering charges by asserting that the government will not prosecute nor dismiss a criminal charge pending before it. He or she does, however, maintain control of criminal proceedings in the trial court. Statutes define the duties of the prosecuting attorney with respect to civil litigation.

The respective powers of the district attorney and of the ATTORNEY GENERAL, the principal law officer of the state, are ordinarily disparate. Neither the district attorney nor the attorney general may impinge upon powers reserved exclusively to the other.

A district attorney is immune from liability for damages incurred as a result of his or her acts or omissions that occur within the scope of official duties, although the person may be held liable for conduct in excess of such scope.

Statutes prescribe the compensation of prosecuting attorneys.

A prosecuting attorney whose term is regulated by law cannot be removed or suspended from office, other than pursuant to the manner authorized by constitution or statute. The grounds specified by law govern removal. Mere misconduct committed in office, such as habitual intoxication, is usually an insufficient basis for removal. In some jurisdictions, however, conduct that is entirely extraneous to official duties may reveal flaws in personal character that render the individual unfit to hold the office and subject him or her to removal.

Suspension or removal may ensue from official misconduct or neglect of duty, such as the improper refusal to initiate criminal investigations or prosecutions, or inept execution of such proceedings.

Removal may also be justified on the basis of the prosecuting attorney's failure to comply with the constitutional duties of disclosure imposed by *Brady v. Maryland,* 373 U.S. 83, 83 S. Ct. 1194, 10 L. Ed. 2d 215 (1963). The Supreme Court held that "the suppression by the prosecution of evidence favorable to an accused upon request violates DUE PROCESS where the evidence is material either to guilt or to punishment, irrespective of the GOOD FAITH or bad faith of the prosecution."

Removal of a prosecuting attorney may also be predicated on his or her conferral of positions in the office to friends or relatives regardless of their qualifications.

The removal process must comply with constitutional or statutory requirements. In some jurisdictions, the district attorney may be removed by the court in proceedings commenced by the interested parties or by IMPEACHMENT. The legislature, within constitutional limitations, may designate the nature of the removal proceeding.

Statutes provide for the appointment of assistant district attorneys to render supplementary services to the district attorney. Independent of statute, however, the courts frequently exercise discretionary power to appoint attor-

neys to assist the prosecuting attorney in criminal cases. Statutes primarily govern the qualifications, salary, tenure, powers, and removal of such attorneys.

Special prosecutors are attorneys appointed by the government to investigate criminal offenses involving officials of the EXECUTIVE BRANCH, since the government cannot effectively investigate itself.

DISTRICT COURT

A designation of an inferior state court that exercises general jurisdiction that it has been granted by the constitution or statute which created it. A U.S. judicial tribunal with original jurisdiction to try cases or controversies that fall within its limited jurisdiction.

A state district might, for example, determine civil actions between state residents based upon contract violations or tortious conduct that occurred within the state.

Federal district courts are located in places designated by federal law, hearing cases in at least one place in every state. Most federal cases, whether civil actions or criminal prosecutions for violations of federal law, commence in district court. Cases arising under the Constitution, federal law, or treaty, or cases between citizens of different states, must also involve an interest worth more than $75,000 before the district court can exercise its jurisdiction.

The federal district courts also have original and exclusive jurisdiction of BANKRUPTCY cases, and ADMIRALTY, maritime, and prize cases, which determine rights in ships and cargo captured at sea. State courts are powerless to hear these kinds of controversies.

A party can appeal a decision made in district court in the Court of Appeal.

DISTRICT OF COLUMBIA

"To exercise exclusive Legislation in all Cases whatsoever, over such District (not exceeding ten miles square) as may, by Cession of particular States, and the acceptance of Congress, become the Seat of the Government of the United States" (U.S. Const. Art. I, § 8). The U.S.

Constitution, with this proclamation, left the legal formation of a national capital up to the U.S. Congress. To this day, the District of Columbia is neither a state nor a territory and remains under congressional jurisdiction.

History

The location of the national capital was born out of a political compromise between the northern and southern states after the United States had achieved its independence. The South feared that the North would have too much influence if the capital were placed in a northern city. The North demanded federal assistance in paying its Revolutionary War debt, something the South was strongly against. ALEXANDER HAMILTON initiated a compromise whereby the federal government would pay off the war debt in return for locating the capital between the states of Maryland and Virginia on the Potomac River.

In 1800, Virginia and Maryland ceded portions of land to the federal government. The citizens living in the new capital were required to give up all the political rights they had enjoyed as inhabitants of Maryland and Virginia. In return, Congress, which had exclusive power over the district, would allow them some form of self-government. In 1802, Congress called for an appointed mayor and an elected council in the district. By 1820, the election of the mayor was also permitted.

This form of representative government lasted in the district until 1874, when Congress abolished the citizens' right to vote for their local officials and established a three-person board of commissioners appointed by the president. For over one hundred years, the residents of the District of Columbia were denied the democratic right to elected local representation.

Although residents of the district had always been required to pay federal INCOME TAX and serve in the military, their right to vote in presidential elections was denied until the 1961 passage of the TWENTY-THIRD AMENDMENT to the Constitution. This amendment granted the district a number of votes in the ELECTORAL COLLEGE, not to exceed the number given to the least populous state.

Home Rule

In 1967, through an EXECUTIVE ORDER (Exec. Order No. 11379, 32 FR 15625, 1967 WL 7776 [Pres.]), President LYNDON B. JOHNSON

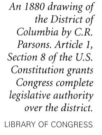

An 1880 drawing of the District of Columbia by C.R. Parsons. Article 1, Section 8 of the U.S. Constitution grants Congress complete legislative authority over the district.

LIBRARY OF CONGRESS

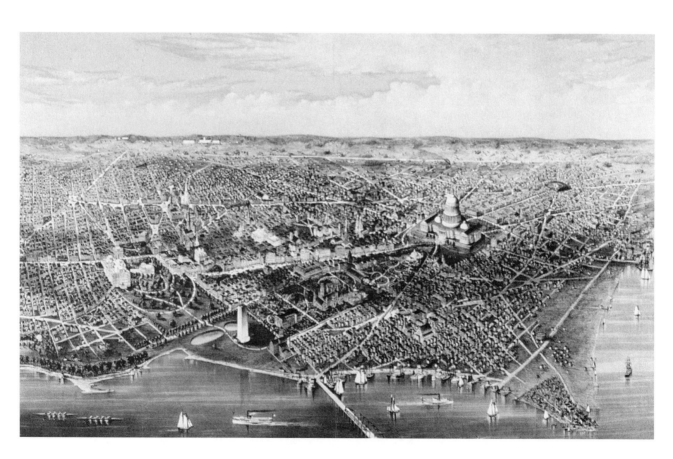

did away with the three-member board of commissioners and appointed a mayor and a council for the district. In 1970, the district was given back its nonvoting delegate in Congress. But this still did not satisfy residents who demanded full self-determination. Congress then passed the District Home Rule Act of 1973 (Pub. L. 93-198, Dec. 24, 1973, 87 Stat. 774), and restored to the citizens their right to vote for a local government. For the first time in exactly a hundred years, the residents of the District of Columbia were able to vote for a mayor and a 13-member council.

The Constitution granted Congress complete legislative authority over the District of Columbia. Congress alone has the jurisdiction to expand the district's powers over local government affairs. It also has the jurisdiction to contract those same powers. Congress, through the Home Rule Act, dictated the legislative powers to the district council and the executive powers to the mayor. Advisory neighborhood commissions, which are groups elected by the residents, advise the council on matters of public policy. Congress still retains ultimate legislative authority through its power to VETO any of the district's legislation.

Statehood

Besides the citizens of U.S. territories, district residents are the only U.S. citizens without full representation in Congress and with federal limitations on their own local government. Advocates of statehood rebel against such restrictions. They argue that because the district's congressional delegate is not allowed to vote, residents are subject to a fundamental democratic wrong, taxation without representation. They add that because Congress retains control over the city's purse strings, city officials are powerless in raising more revenue. Federal restrictions on taxation have prevented the district from taxing commuters as have some other U.S. cities, which could have given the district a huge tax windfall.

Opponents of statehood argue that the District of Columbia belongs to all U.S. citizens, and therefore all citizens should have a say in how it is managed. Constitutionally, Congress has complete authority over the district, and to have it otherwise would require a constitutional amendment (supporters dismiss this argument, pointing out that 37 states were allowed into the Union through only a simple majority vote in Congress). If the district were to become an independent state, some opponents argue, the federal government would have to abide by the laws of this new state. Opponents of statehood also maintain that the district's power needs to be checked by Congress because of the district's financial difficulties.

The push toward statehood has become a partisan issue, with the DEMOCRATIC PARTY generally in favor of it and the REPUBLICAN PARTY generally opposed. One reason for this division is the political makeup of the city, which is predominantly Democratic. Statehood would add more Democratic members to the House and the Senate. When the Democrats won the White House in 1992, the stage was set for the statehood issue to move forward through the 103d Congress.

On November 21, 1993, the House considered Bill 51, calling for the creation of New Columbia, the nation's fifty-first state. Democrats spoke in favor of statehood, saying it would give D.C. residents the same benefits of citizenship that are enjoyed by other U.S. citizens. Republicans spoke out against it, saying the city was unable to govern itself. Republican sentiments carried the day, defeating the bill by a vote of 277–153.

Legal Challenge to Voting Rights

After Congress rejected the idea of statehood for the district, D.C. residents felt they had exhausted their legislative options for change. They explored other ways of increasing their influence in Congress, but again the fact that their representative could not vote in Congress posed a major roadblock. A group of residents sought to overcome this limitation by filing a federal lawsuit that challenged the status quo.

Lois Adams and 75 other D.C. residents filed the lawsuit against the president and Congress, arguing that it was unjust that they pay taxes and defend the country in times of war, yet they could not send elected representatives to vote on taxes and war. They claimed that this deprived them of EQUAL PROTECTION of the law and denied them a republican form of government. They also argued that this deprivation violated their DUE PROCESS rights and abridged their PRIVILEGES AND IMMUNITIES as citizens of the United States.

A special three-judge panel heard the case but in the end rejected these arguments. In *Adams v. Clinton,* 90 F.Supp.2d 35 (D.C. 2000), the court addressed both jurisdictional and constitutional issues. Regarding jurisdiction, the executive and legislative branches contended that the court had no right to even hear the case because the plaintiffs raised issues that were not subject to review by the judicial branch. However, the court rejected the idea that the issues were POLITICAL QUESTIONS beyond its reach and reviewed the merits of the case.

The court looked at the language of the Constitution, as well as history and legal precedent, in making is decisions. It first held that Article I of the Constitution repeatedly refers to "each state," thereby demonstrating that the term did not refer generally to all the people of the United States but to citizens of individual states. Tying the right to Congressional representation to statehood was reinforced by the fact that residents of U.S. territories cannot elect voting representatives to Congress. In addition, history and precedent revealed that the District of Columbia had never been considered a "state" for constitutional purposes. Therefore, the direct constitutional challenge had no merit.

The court rejected an even more novel theory advanced by the plaintiffs that they were entitled to vote in Maryland elections because of their "residual citizenship." This theory relies on the fact that residents of the land ceded by Maryland to form the district continued to vote in Maryland elections between 1790 and 1801, when Congress assumed jurisdiction and provided for the district's government. The court dismissed this claim, noting that a 1964 court decision had rejected the concept of residual citizenship based on the fact that former residents of Maryland lost their state citizenship when the District of Columbia separated from it.

Finally, the court concluded that the EQUAL PROTECTION CLAUSE of the FOURTEENTH AMENDMENT could not be used to strike down another constitutional provision. Though the court found that Congress and the EXECUTIVE BRANCH had failed to give a compelling reason for denying D.C. residents voting representatives, the denial was based on a provision of Article I. Unlike a statute that contains illegal classifications, the constitution cannot be ruled unconstitutional. Therefore, D.C. residents had to convince Congress to either grant it statehood or pass a constitutional amendment that would allow voting representatives from the district.

The Courts

The courts of the District of Columbia were established by an act of Congress. Originally, federal courts heard controversies that arose in the District of Columbia. Disputes over federal or district law came under the jurisdiction of the federal district courts. Appeals went from the district courts to the Court of Appeals for the District of Columbia Circuit, and then to the U.S. Supreme Court.

Just as the legislative branch of the district government became less dependent on the federal system in the 1970s, so too did the courts. The district court system was completely reorganized under the District of Columbia Court Reform and Criminal Procedure Act of 1970 (Pub. L. 91-358, July 29, 1970, 84 Stat. 473; Pub. L. 99-573, § 17, Oct. 28, 1973, 100 Stat. 3234, 3235). The U.S. District court no longer has jurisdiction over criminal or civil actions occurring under D.C. law. These cases are now heard by the district's new trial court, the Superior Court. The District of Columbia Court of Appeals has jurisdiction to review decisions of the Superior Court.

FURTHER READINGS

Harris, Charles Wesley. 1995. *The Conflict of Federal and Local Interests.* Washington D.C.: Georgetown Univ. Press.

Kofie, Nelson. 1999. *Race, Class, and the Struggle for Neighborhood in Washington, D.C.* New York: Garland Press.

Markham, Steven. 1998. *Statehood for the District of Columbia.* Washington, D.C.: National Legal Center for the Public Interest.

Schrag, Philip G. 1985. *Behind the Scenes: The Politics of a Constitutional Convention.* Washington D.C.: Georgetown Univ. Press.

CROSS-REFERENCES

States' Rights.

DISTURBANCE OF PUBLIC MEETINGS

It was a misdemeanor at COMMON LAW to be guilty of conduct that tended to disturb a public assembly, though the prosecution, in most instances, was required to prove that the disturbance was caused wantonly or willfully. In most jurisdictions there is statutory crime for such conduct and the disturbance need not be so turbulent as to constitute a RIOT.

DISTURBANCE OF THE PEACE

An offense constituting a malicious and willful intrusion upon the peace and quiet of a community or neighborhood.

The crime is usually committed by an offensive or tumultuous act, such as the making of loud or unusual noises, or quarreling in public.

The term is similar in meaning to breach of the peace, however, the latter is generally a broader term, encompassing all violations of public peace and order. It can also be a form of DISORDERLY CONDUCT and is similarly punishable upon conviction by a fine, imprisonment, or both.

DIVERS

Several; any number more than two; different.

Divers is a collective term used to group a number of unspecified people, objects, or acts. It is used frequently to describe property, as in divers parcels of land.

DIVERSION

A turning aside or altering of the natural course or route of a thing. The term is chiefly applied to the unauthorized change or alteration of a water course to the prejudice of a lower riparian, or to the unauthorized use of funds.

A program for the disposition of a criminal charge without a criminal trial; sometimes called operation de nova, intervention, or deferred prosecution.

The disposition is conditional on the defendant's performing certain tasks or participating in a treatment program. If the conditions are successfully completed, the charge is dismissed. But if the accused does not meet his or her obligations, prosecution may be instituted.

CROSS-REFERENCES

Riparian Rights.

DIVERSITY OF CITIZENSHIP

A phrase used with reference to the jurisdiction of the federal courts which, under the U.S. Constitution, Art. III, § 2, extends to cases between citizens of different states designating the condition existing when the party on one side of a lawsuit is a citizen of one state and the party on the other side is a citizen of another state, or between a citizen of a state and an ALIEN. The requisite jurisdictional amount must, in addition, be met.

Diversity of citizenship is one of the factors that will allow a federal district court to exercise its authority to hear a lawsuit. This authority is called diversity jurisdiction. It means that a case involving questions that must be answered according to state laws may be heard in federal court if the parties on the two sides of the case are from different states. No matter how many parties are involved in a lawsuit, there must be complete diversity in order for the federal court to exercise this type of authority. If a single plaintiff is a citizen of the same state as any defendant, there is no diversity and the case must be pursued in a state court.

Being a citizen of a state is something more than simply owning property or being physically present within the state. Citizenship means that the individual has a residence in the state and intends to have that residence as his or her present home. Residence plus this intent makes that place the individual's domicile, and a party can have only one domicile at a time. Citizenship does not mean that the individual must swear that he or she never intends to move, but the residence and the intent to consider it home are essential. Students, prisoners, and service personnel can establish a domicile in a state even though they are living in it involuntarily or temporarily.

Corporations are citizens of the state in which they are incorporated and also of the state where they maintain their principal place of business. This citizenship in two places has the effect of narrowing the number of cases that qualify for a federal court's diversity jurisdiction because a corporation's citizenship is not diverse from the citizenship of anyone else in either of those two states.

The citizenship of each party must be determined as of the time the lawsuit is commenced. A party's domicile at the time of the events that give rise to the CAUSE OF ACTION or a change of domicile during the course of proceedings does not affect the court's jurisdiction. This rule, of course, gives a person contemplating a lawsuit the opportunity to change his or her domicile just before serving legal papers that start an action. This tactic has been challenged on a few occasions on the ground that it violates another federal law that prohibits collusion to create federal jurisdiction. Generally, the courts have ruled that a plaintiff's motives in moving to a new state are not determinative, and the only question is whether in fact the plaintiff's domicile is different from that of the defendants at the time the lawsuit begins.

The right of an individual to take his or her case into a federal court is assured by Article III, § 2 of the U.S. Constitution. This provision extends the federal judicial power to controversies between the citizen of a state and the government of a different state, citizens of a different state, or between a state or its citizens and a foreign government or its citizens. It is put into effect by a statute that limits federal diversity jurisdiction to cases involving a dispute worth more than $10,000. This minimum is intended to keep small cases from clogging the calendars of federal courts. Cases worth less than $10,000 must be brought in a state court even though diversity of the parties' citizenship otherwise would entitle them to be brought in federal court.

The origin and purposes of federal diversity jurisdiction have long been debated. It was created when the Constitution was first adopted, a time when loyalty to one's state was usually stronger than feelings for the United States. It was undoubtedly intended to balance national purposes with the independence of the states. Chief Justice JOHN MARSHALL of the Supreme Court wrote in *Bank of United States v. Deveaux*, 9 U.S. (5 Cranch) 61, 87, 3 L. Ed. 38 (1809):

> However true the fact may be, that the tribunals of the states will administer justice as impartially as those of the nation, ... it is not less true that the constitution itself either entertains apprehensions on this subject, or views with such indulgence the possible fears and apprehensions of suitors, that it has established national tribunals for the decision of controversies ... between citizens of different states.

Some scholars believe that the opportunity to take business and commercial disputes into an impartial federal court helped to encourage investment in the developing South and West. People from the industrialized Northeast felt more secure when their financial transactions in other states were not necessarily at the mercy of local prejudices.

Even if diversity jurisdiction did help the economic growth of the United States, many people question whether it continues to be useful. Because these cases require substantial investments of time and energy by the federal judiciary in cases that arise under state law, proposals to curtail or abolish diversity jurisdiction have been introduced repeatedly in Congress since the 1920s. None of the proposals have been adopted, however.

FURTHER READINGS

Freer, Richard D. 1998. "Toward a Principled Statutory Approach to Supplemental Jurisdiction in Diversity of Citizenship Cases." *Indiana Law Journal* 74 (winter): 5–23.

Jacobsohn, Gary Jeffrey, and Susan Dunn, ed. 1996. *Diversity and Citizenship: Rediscovering American Nationhood.* Lanham, Md.: Rowman & Littlefield.

Pickus, Noah M.J. 1998. *Immigration and Citizenship in the Twenty-First Century.* Lanham, Md.: Rowman & Littlefield.

DIVEST

To deprive or take away.

Divest is usually used in reference to the relinquishment of authority, power, property, or title. If, for example, an individual is disinherited, he or she is divested of the right to inherit money. Similarly, an individual may be divested of his or her citizenship for TREASON.

Divest is also spelled *devest.*

DIVIDEND

The distribution of current or accumulated earnings to the shareholders of a corporation pro rata based on the number of shares owned. Dividends are usually issued in cash. However, they may be issued in the form of stock or property. The dividend on preferred shares is generally a fixed amount; however, on common shares the dividend varies depending on such things as the earnings and available cash of the corporation as well as future plans for the acquisition of property and equipment by the corporation.

DIVINE RIGHT OF KINGS

The authority of a monarch to rule a realm by virtue of birth.

The concept of the divine right of kings, as postulated by the patriarchal theory of government, was based upon the laws of God and nature. The king's power to rule was derived from his ancestors who, as monarchs, were appointed to serve by God. Regardless of misconduct, a king or his heir could not be forced to forfeit the right to the obedience of subjects or the right to succeed to the throne. This concept was formulated to dispel any possibility of papal and ecclesiastical claims to supremacy in secular as well as spiritual matters.

DIVORCE

A court decree that terminates a marriage; also known as marital dissolution.

A divorce decree establishes the new relations between the parties, including their duties and obligations relating to property that they own, support responsibilities of either or both of them, and provisions for any children.

When a marriage breaks up, divorce law provides legal solutions for issues that the HUSBAND AND WIFE are unable to resolve through mutual cooperation. Historically, the most important question in a divorce case was whether the court should grant a divorce. When a divorce was granted, the resolution of continuing obligations was simple: The wife was awarded custody of any children, and the husband was required to support the wife and children.

Modern divorce laws have inverted the involvement of courts. The issue of whether a divorce should be granted is now generally decided by one or both of the spouses. Contemporary courts are more involved in determining the legal ramifications of the marriage breakup, such as spousal maintenance, CHILD SUPPORT, and CHILD CUSTODY. Other legal issues relating to divorce include court jurisdiction, antenuptial and postnuptial agreements, and the right to obtain a divorce. State laws govern a wide range of divorce issues, but district, county, and family courts are given broad discretion in fixing legal obligations between the parties.

In early civilizations, marriage and marriage dissolution were considered private matters. Marriage and divorce were first placed under comprehensive state regulation in Rome during the reign of Augustus (27 B.C.–A.D. 14). As Christianity spread, governments came under religious control, and the Roman Catholic Church strictly forbade divorce. The only exception to this ban was if one of the parties had not converted to Christianity before the marriage.

During the 1500s, the Protestant Reformation movement in Europe rejected religious control over marriage and helped to move the matter of divorce from the church to the state. European courts granted divorces upon a showing of fault, such as ADULTERY, cruelty, or desertion.

England struggled with the matter of divorce. From 1669 to 1850, only 229 divorces were granted in that country. Marriage and divorce were controlled by the Anglican Church, which, like the Roman Catholic Church, strictly forbade divorce. The Anglican Church allowed separations, but neither spouse was allowed to remarry while the other was still living.

The law of divorce in the American colonies varied according to the religious and social mores of the founding colonists. England insisted that its American colonies refrain from enacting legislation that contradicted the restrictive English laws, and a colonial divorce was not considered final until it had been approved by the English monarch. Despite these deterrents, a few northern colonies adopted laws allowing divorce in the 1650s.

Divorce law in the middle and northern colonies was often curious. Under one late-seventeenth-century Pennsylvania law, divorce seemed a mere afterthought: If a married man committed SODOMY or bestiality, his punishment was castration, and "the injured wife shall have a divorce if required." In Connecticut, divorce was allowed on the grounds of adultery, desertion, and the husband's failure in his conjugal duties. In the Massachusetts Bay Colony, a woman was allowed to divorce her husband if the husband had committed adultery and another offense. A man could divorce if his wife committed adultery or the "cruel usage of the husband."

After the Revolutionary War, divorce law in the United States continued to develop regionally. The U.S. Constitution was silent as to divorce, leaving the matter to the states for regulation. For the next 150 years, state legislatures passed and maintained laws that granted divorce only upon a showing of fault on the part of a spouse. If a divorce were contested, the divorcing spouse would be required to establish, before a court, specific grounds for the action. If the court felt that the divorcing spouse had not proved the grounds alleged, it would be free to deny the petition for divorce.

The most common traditional grounds for divorce were cruelty, desertion, and adultery. Other grounds included nonsupport or neglect, alcoholism, drug addiction, insanity, criminal conviction, and voluntary separation. Fault-based divorce laws proliferated, but not without protest. In 1901, author JAMES BRYCE was moved to remark that U.S. divorce laws were "the largest and the strangest, and perhaps the saddest, body of legislative experiments in the sphere of FAMILY LAW which free, self-governing communities have ever tried."

In 1933, New Mexico became the first state to allow divorce on the ground of incompatibility. This new ground reduced the need for divorcing spouses to show fault. In 1969, California became the first state to completely revise its divorce laws. The California Family Law Act of 1969 provided, in part, that only one of two grounds was necessary to obtain a divorce: irreconcilable differences that have caused the irremediable breakdown of the marriage, or incurable insanity (Cal. Civ. Code § D. 4, pt. 5 [West], *repealed by* Stat. 1992, ch. 162 [A.B. 2650], § 3 [operative Jan. 1, 1994]). In divorce proceedings, testimony or other evidence of specific acts of misconduct were excluded. The one exception to this rule was where the court was required to award child custody. In such a case, serious misconduct on the part of one parent would be relevant.

California's was the first comprehensive "no-fault" divorce law, and it inspired a nationwide debate over divorce reform. Supporters of no-fault divorce noted that there were numerous problems with fault-based divorce. Fault-based divorce was an odious event that destroyed friendships. It also encouraged spouses to fabricate one of the grounds for divorce required under statute. No-fault divorce, conversely, recognized that a marriage breakdown might not be the result of one spouse's misconduct. No-fault divorce laws avoided much of the acrimony that plagued fault-based divorce laws. They also simplified the divorce process and made it more consistent nationwide, thus obviating the need for desperate couples to cross state lines in search of simpler divorce laws.

In 1970, the Commissioners on Uniform State Laws prepared a Uniform Marriage and Divorce Act, which provides for no-fault divorce if a court finds that the marriage is "irretrievably broken" (U.L.A., Uniform Marriage and Divorce Act §§ 101 et seq.). Such a finding requires little more than the desire of one spouse to end the marriage. Many state legislatures adopted the law, and by the end of the 1970s, nearly every state legislature had enacted laws allowing no-fault divorce, or divorce after a specified period of separation. Some states replaced all traditional grounds with a single no-fault provision. Other states added the ground of irreconcilable differences to existing statutes. In such states, a divorce petitioner remains free to file for divorce under traditional grounds.

Most states allow the filing of a divorce petition at any time, unless the petitioner has not been a resident of the state for a specified period of time. Some states require a waiting period for their residents. The waiting period can range from six weeks to two or three years.

Illinois and South Dakota maintain the strictest divorce laws. In Illinois, a marriage may be dissolved without regard to fault where three conditions exist: the parties have lived apart for a continuous period of two years; irreconcilable differences have caused the irretrievable breakdown of the marriage; and efforts at reconciliation would be impracticable and not in the best interests of the family (Ill. Rev. Stat. ch. 750 I.L.C.S. § 5/401(a)(2)). In South Dakota, irreconcilable differences are a valid ground for divorce, which suggests some measure of fault blindness (S.D. Codified Laws Ann. § 25:4-2). However, irreconcilable differences exist only when the court determines that there are "substantial reasons for not continuing the marriage and which make it appear that the marriage should be dissolved" (§ 25:4-17.1).

In Minnesota, the statute covering dissolution of marriage reads like a primer on no-fault divorce. Minnesota Statutes Annotated, Section 518.05, defines dissolution as "the termination of the marital relationship between a husband and wife" and concludes that a divorce "shall be granted by a county or district court when the court finds there has been an irretrievable breakdown of the marriage relationship." "Irretrievable breakdown" is left undefined in the statute. In Texas, the no-fault statute is titled "Insupportability." This law provides that on petition by either party, "a divorce may be decreed without regard to fault if the marriage has become insupportable because of discord or conflict of personalities" that destroys the purpose of marriage and renders reconciliation improbable (Tex. Fam. Code Ann. § 3.01 [West]).

No-fault is not without its detractors. Some critics argue that strict, no-fault divorce can provide a cover for serious marital misconduct. By refusing to examine the marital conduct of parties in setting future obligations, some states prevent spouses, usually impoverished wives, from exposing and receiving redress for tortious or criminal conduct. In response to this problem, the vast majority of states have abolished statutes that prevent one spouse from suing the other. However, TORT claims for marital misconduct are often treated with suspicion, and juries are seldom eager to settle marital discord. A marital tort claim is also subject to business judgment: If the case does not appear cost-effective, an attorney might be reluctant to accept it.

Fault has survived in some aspects of divorce proceedings. It was once relevant to a decree of divorce and irrelevant to such matters as child custody and property divisions. Under current trends, marital misconduct is irrelevant to the divorce itself, but it may be relevant to related matters such as child custody, child support and VISITATION RIGHTS, spousal maintenance, and property distribution.

A recent movement in a small number of states has sought to reintroduce fault as an element in divorce proceedings. In 1997, Louisiana approved a COVENANT MARRIAGE law that is designed to provide an alternative to the traditional method for obtaining a marriage license. La. Rev. Stat. Ann. §§ 9:272-75, 9:307-09 (West Supp. 2003). Under the covenant marriage law, couples who wish to obtain a marriage license must first enter pre-marriage counseling, and then must provide an AFFIDAVIT from a marriage counselor stating that they have completed this counseling. Once the couple is married, the covenant marriage does not differ from a traditional marriage until the potential dissolution of the marriage. Before partners to a covenant marriage may divorce, they must complete pre-divorce counseling and must provide an affidavit stating that the counseling has taken place. The statute is designed to make it more difficult to obtain a so-called "quickie" divorce.

The introduction of covenant marriage as an alternative to the traditional marriage agreement comes in the wake of several studies regarding the implications of divorce on children. Studies have shown that the economic standard of living for divorced women and children of a marriage decrease significantly after the divorce, while the standard of living for men increases. Likewise, other studies have shown that children of divorced parents are less likely to marry, have less education, and are more likely to abuse drugs and alcohol later in life.

In response to these and similar statistics, legislatures considered several means by which they could curb the climbing rate of divorce. Highly restrictive provisions on divorce, including the elimination of no-fault divorce, failed to pass any state legislature. Louisiana's covenant marriage law represents a compromise in that it leaves the decision to enter into such a marriage up to the couples. Several states in 1997 and 1998 considered enacting similar laws, but only Arizona and Arkansas have done so.

Covenant marriage laws also do not appear popular with couples in the three states that have adopted such laws. According to an article in the *New York Times*, only three percent of couples in Louisiana and Arizona have chosen to pursue this type of marital agreement, and stud-ies show that tougher divorce laws have failed to gain popularity in those states. Moreover, several commentators have noted that the divorce rate in Louisiana and Arizona is not likely to decrease even with these laws in place.

Other states that have not enacted covenant marriage laws have considered other methods to discourage divorce. Several states have included provisions that encourage couples to seek pre-marital counseling before entering into the marriage. Unlike the covenant marriage laws, these provisions do not mandate such counseling, and they leave the decision to pursue counseling to the individual couples. The various statutes provide a number of incentives for seeking counseling, including, for example, reduction in the cost for a marriage license upon completion of counseling.

Historically, custody of the children of divorcing parents was awarded to the mother. Today, courts exercise their discretion in awarding custody, considering all relevant factors, including marital misconduct, to determine the children's best interests. Many parents are able to reach settlements on custody and visitation through mediation. Joint custody is a popular option among conciliatory spouses. Child custody is, however, a frequent battleground for less-than-conciliatory spouses.

In determining child-support obligations, courts generally hold that each parent should contribute in accordance with his or her means. Child support is a mutual duty. However, for pre-school children, the primary caretaker may not be obligated to obtain employment; in such cases, caretaking may be regarded as being in lieu of financial contribution.

All states have enacted some form of the Reciprocal Enforcement of Support Act, a uniform law designed to facilitate the interstate enforcement of support obligations by spouses and parents (U.L.A., Uniform Interstate Family Support Act of 1992). Such statutes prevent a nonsupporting spouse or parent from escaping obligations by moving to a different state. State laws also make nonsupport of a spouse or child a criminal offense, and uniform laws now give states the power to detain and surrender individuals who are wanted for criminal nonsupport in another state.

Property distribution is frequently contested in modern divorce proceedings. Commonly disputed property includes real estate, PERSONAL PROPERTY, cash savings, stocks, bonds, savings

A sample finding of fact and conclusions of law, which are part of a judgment and decree of divorce.

Finding of Fact and Conclusions of Law

At the *Matrimonial/IAS* Part _____

of New York State Supreme Court at

the Courthouse, _____

County, on _____

Present:

Hon. _____ *Justice/Referee* X

_____ Plaintiff,

-against-

Index No.:

Calendar No.:

FINDINGS OF FACT
AND
CONCLUSIONS OF LAW

Defendant.

_____ X

_____

The issues of this action having ☐ *been submitted to* **OR** ☐ *been heard* before me as one of the *Justices/Referees* of this Court at Part _____ hereof, held in and for the County of _____ on _____ , and having considered the allegations and proofs of the respective parties, and due deliberation having been had thereon.

NOW, after ☐ *reading and considering the papers submitted* ☐ *hearing the testimony,* I do hereby make the following findings of essential facts which I deem established by the evidence and reach the following conclusions of law.

FINDINGS OF FACT

FIRST: Plaintiff and Defendant were both eighteen (18) years of age or over when this action was commenced.

SECOND:

☐ The Plaintiff has resided in New York State for a continuous period in excess of two years immediately preceding the commencement of this action.

OR

☐ The Defendant has resided in New York State for a continuous period in excess of two years immediately preceding the commencement of this action

OR

☐ The Plaintiff has resided in New York State for a continuous period in excess of one year immediately preceding the commencement of this action, and:

a. ☐ the parties were married in New York State.

b. ☐ the Plaintiff has lived as husband or wife in New York State with the Defendant.

c. ☐ the cause of action occurred in New York State.

OR

☐ The Defendant has resided in New York State for a continuous period in excess of one year immediately preceding the commencement of this action; and:

a. ☐ the parties were married in New York State.

b. ☐ the Defendant has lived as husband or wife in New York State with the Plaintiff.

c. ☐ the cause of action occurred in New York State.

OR

☐ The cause of action occurred in New York State and both parties were residents thereof at the time of the commencement of this action.

THIRD: The Plaintiff and the Defendant were married on the date of _____ in the City, Town or Village of _____ , County of _____ , State or Country of _____ ; in a ☐ *civil* **OR** ☐ *religious* ceremony.

FOURTH: That no decree, judgment or order of divorce, annulment or dissolution of marriage has been granted to either party against the other in any Court of competent jurisdiction of this state or any other state, territory or country, and that there is no other action pending for divorce by either party against the other in any Court.

FIFTH: That this action was commenced by filing the ☐ *Summons With Notice* **OR** ☐ *Summons and Verified Complaint* with the County Clerk on _____ . Defendant was served ☐ *personally* **OR** ☐ *pursuant to Court order* dated _____ with the above stated pleadings. Defendant ☐ *defaulted in appearance* **OR** ☐ *appeared and waived his/her right to answer* **OR** ☐ *filed an answer/amended answer withdrawing any previous pleading, and neither admitting nor denying the allegations in plaintiff's complaint, and consenting to entry of judgment.*

[continued]

Finding of Fact and Conclusions of Law

A sample finding of
fact and conclusions
of law, which are part
of a judgment and
decree of divorce
(continued).

SIXTH: ☐ That Defendant is not in the military service of the United States of America, the State of New York, or any other state. **OR**
☐ Defendant is a member of the military service of the _____ and ☐ has appeared by affidavit and does not oppose the
action **OR** ☐ is in default.

SEVENTH: ☐ There are no children of the marriage. **OR** ☐ There *is/are* _____ child(ren) of the marriage. Their name(s), social
security number(s), address(es) and date(s) of birth are:

Name & Social Security Number	Date of Birth	Address
_____	_____	_____
_____	_____	_____
_____	_____	_____
_____	_____	_____
_____	_____	_____

EIGHTH: The grounds for divorce that are alleged in the Verified Complaint were proved as follows:

Cruel and Inhuman Treatment (DRL §170(1)):

☐ At the following times, none of which are earlier than (5) years prior to commencement of this action, the Defendant engaged in
conduct that so endangered the mental and physical well being of the Plaintiff, so as to render it unsafe and improper for the
parties to cohabit (live together) as husband and wife.

(State the facts that demonstrate cruel and inhuman conduct giving dates, places and specific acts. Conduct may include physical,
verbal, sexual or emotional behavior).

_____
_____
_____
_____
_____
_____
_____
_____
_____
_____
_____
_____

(Attach an additional sheet, if necessary).

Abandonment (DRL §170(2)):

☐ That commencing on or about _____ , and continuing for a period of more than one (1) year
immediately prior to commencement of this action, the Defendant left the marital residence of the parties located at _____
_____ , and did not return. Such absence was without cause or justification,
and was without Plaintiff's consent.

☐ That commencing on or about _____ , and continuing for a period of more than
one (1) year immediately prior to commencement of this action, the Defendant refused to have sexual relations with the Plaintiff
despite Plaintiff's repeated requests to resume such relations. Defendant does not suffer from any disability which would prevent
her/him from engaging in such sexual relations with Plaintiff. The refusal to engage in sexual relations was without good cause or
justification and occurred at the marital residence located at _____ .

☐ That commencing on or about _____ , and continuing for a period of more than one(1) year
immediately prior to commencement of this action, the Defendant willfully and without cause or justification abandoned the
the Plaintiff, who had been a faithful and dutiful *husband/wife*, by depriving Plaintiff of access to the marital residence located at
_____ . This deprivation was without the consent of the
Plaintiff and continued for a period of greater than one year.

Confinement to Prison (DRL §170(3)):

☐ a. That after the marriage of Plaintiff and Defendant, Defendant was confined in prison for a period of three or more consecutive
years, to wit: that Defendant was confined in _____ prison on _____ ,
and has remained confined to this date; and

[continued]

A sample finding of fact and conclusions of law, which are part of a judgment and decree of divorce (continued).

Finding of Fact and Conclusions of Law

b. not more that five (5) years elapsed between the end of the third year of imprisonment and the date of commencement of this action.

Adultery (DRL §170(4)):

☐ a. That on _____ , at the premises located at _____

_____ , the Defendant engaged in sexual intercourse with _____ , without the procurement nor the connivance of the Plaintiff and the Plaintiff ceased to cohabit (live) with the Defendant upon the discovery of the adultery.

b. not more than five (5) years elapsed between the date of said adultery and the date of commencement of this action.

(Attach a corroborating affidavit of a third party witness or other additional proof).

Living Separate and Apart Pursuant to a Separation Decree or Judgment of Separation (DRL §170(5)):

☐ a. That the _____ Court, _____ County, (Country

or State) rendered a decree or judgment of separation on _____ under Index Number

_____ ; and

b. that the parties have lived separate and apart for a period of one year or longer after the granting of such decree; and

c. that the Plaintiff has substantially complied with all the terms and conditions of such decree or judgment.

Living Separate and Apart Pursuant to a Separation Agreement (DRL §170(6)):

☐ a. That the Plaintiff and Defendant entered into a written agreement of separation, which they subscribed and acknowledged on

_____ , in the form required to entitle a deed to be recorded; and

b. that the *agreement/memorandum of said agreement* was filed _____ in the Office of the

Clerk of the County of _____ , wherein *Plaintiff/Defendant* resided; and

c. that the parties have lived separate and apart for a period of one year or longer after the execution of said agreement; and

d. that the Plaintiff has substantially complied with all terms and conditions of such agreement.

NINTH:

☐ A sworn statement pursuant to DRL §253 that Plaintiff has taken all steps within his or her power to remove all barriers to Defendant's remarriage following the divorce was served on the Defendant.

☐ A sworn statement as to the removal of barriers to remarriage is not required because the parties were married in a civil ceremony.

☐ A sworn statement as to the removal of barriers to remarriage is not required because Defendant waived the need for the statement in his or her affidavit.

TENTH: ☐ *The parties have agreed* **OR** ☐ *the court has determined* that ☐ *Plaintiff* **OR** ☐ *Defendant* will receive maintenance of

$ _____ ☐ *per week* **OR** ☐ bi-weekly **OR** ☐ *per month* commencing on _____ pursuant to DRL §236(B)(6)(C).

ELEVENTH: The children of the marriage now reside with ☐ *Plaintiff* **OR** ☐ *Defendant* **OR** ☐ *third party*, namely _____

_____ . The ☐ *Plaintiff* **OR** ☐ *Defendant* is entitled to visitation away from the custodial residence.

The ☐ *Plaintiff* **OR** ☐ *Defendant* **OR** ☐ *Third Party*, namely _____ is entitled to custody. **OR** ☐ No award of custody due to the child(ren) of the marriage not residing in New York State, **OR** ☐ Other custody arrangement (specify): _____

TWELFTH: Equitable Distribution and ancillary issues shall be ☐ *in accordance with the settlement agreement* **OR** ☐ *pursuant to the decision of the court* **OR** ☐ *Equitable Distribution is not an issue.* _____

THIRTEENTH: ☐ There *is/are* no unemancipated child(ren). **OR** ☐ The award of child support is based upon the following:
(A) The children of the marriage entitled to receive support are:

Name	Date of Birth
_____	_____
_____	_____
_____	_____
_____	_____
_____	_____
_____	_____

(B) (1) By order of _____ Court, _____ County, *Index/Docket No.* _____

dated _____ the *Plaintiff/Defendant* was directed to pay the sum of _____ per _____ for child support. Said Order shall continue.

[continued]

Finding of Fact and Conclusions of Law

A sample finding of fact and conclusions of law, which are part of a judgment and decree of divorce (continued).

OR

(2) The adjusted gross income of the Plaintiff who is the ☐ *custodial* **OR** ☐ *non-custodial* parent is _____ per year and the adjusted gross income of the Defendant who is the ☐ *custodial* **OR** ☐ *non-custodial* parent is _____ per year and the combined parental annual income is _____ . The applicable child support percentage is *17/25/29/31/35%*. The combined basic child support obligation attributable to both parents is _____ per year on income to $80,000 and _____ per year on income over $80,000. The Plaintiff's pro rata share of the combined parental income is _____ % and the Defendant's pro rata share of the combined parental income is _____ %. The non-custodial parent's pro rata share of the child support obligation on combined income to $80,000 is _____ per year or ☐ *per week* ☐ *bi-weekly* ☐ *per month*. The non-custodial parent's pro rata share of the child support obligation on combined income over $80,000 is _____ per year or _____ ☐ *per week* ☐ *bi-weekly* ☐ *per month*. The non-custodial parent's pro rata share of future health care expenses not covered by insurance, child care expenses, educational or other extraordinary expenses is _____ %.

OR

(3) The parties entered into a *stipulation/agreement* on _____ wherein the ☐ *Plantiff* **OR** ☐ *Defendant* agrees to pay _____ ☐ *per week* **OR** ☐ *bi-weekly* **OR** ☐ *per month* child support ☐ *directly* **OR** ☐ *through* the Support Collection Unit to ☐ *Plaintiff* **OR** ☐ *Defendant* **OR** ☐ *Third Party, namely* _____ . The parties agree to ☐ *waive* **OR** ☐ *apply* the Child Support Standards Act to Combined income over $80,000. The parties have agreed that health care expenses not covered by insurance shall be paid by ☐ *Plaintiff* **OR** ☐ *Defendant* in the amount of _____ ☐ *per week* **OR** ☐ *bi-weekly* **OR** ☐ *per month* **OR** _____ % of the uncovered expenses. The parties have agreed that child care expenses shall be paid by ☐ *Plaintiff* **OR** ☐ *Defendant* to ☐ *Plaintiff* **OR** ☐ *Defendant* in the amount of _____ ☐ *per week* **OR** ☐ *bi-weekly* **OR** ☐ *per month* **OR** ☐ _____ % of said child care expenses. The parties have agreed that educational and extraordinary expenses shall be paid by ☐ *Plaintiff* **OR** ☐ *Defendant* to ☐ *Plaintiff* **OR** ☐ *Defendant* in the amount of _____ ☐ *per week* **OR** ☐ *bi-weekly* **OR** ☐ *per month* **OR** ☐ _____ % of said educational and extraordinary expenses. Said agreement reciting in compliance with DRL §2401-b(h): The parties have been advised of the Child Support Standards Act. The basic child support obligation presumptively results in the correct amount of child support. The unrepresented party, if any, has received a copy of the Child Support Standards Chart promulgated by Commissioner of Social Services Law Section 111-1. The presumptive amount of child support attributable to the non-custodial parent is _____ ☐ *per week* **OR** ☐ *bi-weekly* **OR** ☐ *per month*. The amount of child support agreed to ☐ *conforms with the non-custodial parent's basic child support obligation* **OR** ☐ *deviates from the non-custodial parent's basic child support obligation for the following reasons:*

_____

_____

_____

_____

FOURTEENTH: The Plaintiff's address is _____ and social security number is _____ . The Defendant's address is _____ , and social security number is _____ .

☐   There are no unemancipated children. **OR**

☐   There are no health plans available to the parties through their employment. **OR**

☐   The parties are covered by the following group health plans through their employment:

Plaintiff	**Defendant**
Group Health Plan: _____	Group Health Plan: _____
Address: _____	Address: _____
Identification Number: _____	Identification Number: _____
Plan Administrator: _____	Plan Administrator: _____
Type of Coverage: _____	Type of Coverage: _____

☐ *The parties have agreed or stipulated* **OR** ☐ *the court has determined* that the ☐ *Plaintiff* **OR** ☐ *Defendant* shall be the legally responsible relative and that the unemancipated child(ren) shall be enrolled in *his/her* group health plan as specified above *until the age of 21 years* **OR** *until the child(ren) is/are sooner emancipated.*

[continued]

A sample finding of fact and conclusions of law, which are part of a judgment and decree of divorce (continued).

Finding of Fact and Conclusions of Law

FIFTEENTH: The _____ Court entered the following order(s) under Index No(s)./Docket No(s).: _____

_____

SIXTEENTH: ☐ *Plaintiff* **OR** ☐ *Defendant* may resume use of the prior surname: _____

CONCLUSIONS OF LAW

FIRST: Residency as required by DRL §230 has been satisfied.

SECOND: ☐ *Plaintiff* **OR** ☐ *Defendant* is entitled to a judgment of divorce on the grounds of DRL §170 subd. _____ and granting the incidental relief awarded.

Dated: _____   _____
                                                                                        J.S.C./Referee

(Form UD-10 - Rev. 5/99)

plans, and retirement benefits. The statutes that govern property division vary by state, but they generally can be grouped into two types: equitable distribution and COMMUNITY PROPERTY. Most states follow the equitable-distribution method. Generally, this method provides that courts divide a divorcing couple's assets in a fair and equitable manner, given the particular circumstances of the case.

Some equitable-distribution states look to the conduct of the parties and permit findings of marital fault to affect property distribution. New Hampshire, Rhode Island, South Carolina, and Vermont have statutes that explicitly include both economic and marital misconduct as factors in the disposition of property. Connecticut, Florida, Maryland, Massachusetts, Missouri, Virginia, and Wyoming all consider marital conduct in property distribution. In Florida and Virginia, only fault relating to economic WELFARE is relevant in property distribution. Alaska, Kentucky, Minnesota, Montana, and Wisconsin expressly exclude marital misconduct from consideration in the disposition of marital property.

Equitable-distribution states generally give the court considerable discretion as to the division of property between the parties. The courts consider not only the joint assets held by the parties, but also separate assets that the parties either brought with them into the marriage or that they inherited or received as gifts during the marriage. Generally, if the separate property is kept separate during the marriage, and not commingled with joint assets like a joint bank account, then the court will recognize that it belongs separately to the individual spouse, and they will not divide it along with the marital assets. A minority of states, however, support the idea that all separate property of the parties becomes joint marital property upon marriage.

As for the division of marital assets, equitable-distribution states look to the monetary and nonmonetary contributions that each spouse made to the marriage. If one party made a greater contribution, the court may grant that party a greater share of the joint assets. Some states do not consider a professional degree earned by one spouse during the marriage to be a joint asset, but do acknowledge any financial support contributed by the other spouse, and they let that be reflected in the property distribution. Other states do consider a professional degree or license to be a joint marital asset and have devised various ways to distribute it or its benefits.

States that follow community-property laws provide that nearly all of the property that has been acquired during the marriage belongs to the marital "community," such that the husband and wife each have a one-half interest in it upon death or divorce. It is presumed that all property that has been acquired during the marriage by either spouse, including earned income, belongs to the community unless proved otherwise. Exceptions are made for property received as a gift or through inheritance, and for the property that each party brought into the marriage. Those types of property are considered separate and not part of the community. Upon divorce, each party keeps his or her own separate property, as well as half of the community property. True community property systems exist in Arizona, California, Idaho, Louisiana, Nevada, New Mexico, Texas, and Washington. Other states, such as Wisconsin, have adopted variations of the community-property laws.

ALIMONY, or spousal maintenance, is the financial support that one spouse provides to the other after divorce. It is separate from, and in addition to, the division of marital property. It can be either temporary or permanent. Its use originally arose from the common-law right of a wife to receive support from her husband. Under contemporary law, men and women are eligible for spousal maintenance. Factors that are relevant to an order of maintenance include the age and marketable skills of the intended recipient, the length of the marriage, and the income of both spouses.

Maintenance is most often used to provide temporary support to a spouse who was financially dependent on the other during the marriage. Temporary maintenance is designed to provide the necessary support for a spouse until he or she either remarries or becomes self-supporting. Many states allow courts to consider marital fault in determining whether, and how much, maintenance should be granted. These states include Connecticut, Georgia, Hawaii, Iowa, Kansas, Kentucky, Maine, Massachusetts, Missouri, Nebraska, North Carolina, Ohio, Oklahoma, Pennsylvania, Rhode Island, South Carolina, South Dakota, Tennessee, Virginia, West Virginia, and Wisconsin.

Like the entire body of divorce law, the issue of maintenance differs from state to state. If a spouse is found to have caused the breakup of the marriage, Georgia, North Carolina, Virginia, and West Virginia allow a court to refuse maintenance, even if that spouse was financially dependent on the other. North Carolina requires a showing of the supporting spouse's fault before awarding maintenance. Illinois allows fault grounds for divorce but excludes consideration of fault in maintenance and property settlements. Florida offers only no-fault grounds for divorce but admits evidence of adultery in maintenance determinations.

An antenuptial agreement, or PREMARITAL AGREEMENT, is a contract between persons who plan to marry, concerning property rights upon divorce. A postnuptial agreement is a contract entered into by divorcing parties before they reach court. Traditionally, antenuptial agreements were discouraged by state legislatures and courts as being contrary to the public policy in favor of lifetime marriage. An antenuptial agreement is made under the assumption that the marriage may not last forever, which suggests that it facilitates divorce. No state expressly prohibits antenuptial agreements, but, as in any contract case, courts reserve the right to void any that it finds UNCONSCIONABLE or to have been made under duress.

State statutes that authorize antenuptial and postnuptial agreements usually require that the parties fulfill certain conditions. In Delaware, for example, a man and a woman may execute an antenuptial agreement in the presence of two witnesses at least ten days before their marriage. Such an agreement, if notarized, may be filed as a deed with the office of the recorder in any county of the state (Del. Code Ann. tit. 13, § 301). Both antenuptial and postnuptial contracts concerning real estate must be recorded in the registry of deeds where the land is situated (§ 302).

Jurisdiction over a divorce case is usually determined by residency. That is, a divorcing spouse is required to bring the divorce action in the state where he or she maintains a permanent home. States are obligated to acknowledge a divorce that was obtained in another state. This rule derives from the FULL FAITH AND CREDIT CLAUSE of the U.S. Constitution (art. IV, § 1), which requires states to recognize the valid laws and court orders of other states. However, if the divorce was originally granted by a court with no jurisdictional authority, a state is free to disregard it.

In a divorce proceeding where one spouse is not present (an ex parte proceeding), the divorce is given full recognition if the spouse received proper notice and the original divorce forum was the bona fide domicile of the divorcing spouse. However, a second state may reject the divorce decree if it finds that the divorce forum was improper.

State courts are not constitutionally required to recognize divorce judgments granted in foreign countries. A U.S. citizen who leaves the country to evade divorce laws will not be protected if the foreign divorce is subsequently challenged. However, where the foreign divorce court had valid jurisdiction over both parties, most U.S. courts will recognize the foreign court's decree.

The only way that an individual may obtain a divorce is through the state. Therefore, under the DUE PROCESS CLAUSE of the FOURTEENTH AMENDMENT to the U.S. Constitution, a state must make divorce available to everyone. If a party seeking divorce cannot afford the court expenses, filing fees, and costs associated with the serving or publication of legal papers, the party may file for divorce free of charge. Most states offer mediation as an alternative to court appearance. Mediation is less expensive and less adversarial than appearing in public court.

In January 1994, the American Bar Association Standing Committee on the Delivery of Legal Services published a report entitled *Responding to the Needs of the Self-Represented Divorce Litigant*. The committee recognized that a growing number of persons are divorcing pro se, or without the benefit of an attorney. Some of these persons are pro se litigants by choice, but many want the assistance of an attorney and are unable to afford one. In response to this trend, the committee offered several ideas to the state bar associations and state legislatures, including the formation of simplified divorce pleadings and the passage of plainly worded statutes. The committee also endorsed the creation of courthouse day care for children of divorcing spouses, night-court divorce sessions, and workshop clinics that give instruction to pro se divorce litigants. Many such programs are currently operating at district, county, and family courts around the United States.

In the United States, divorce law consists of 51 different sets of conditions—one for each state and the District of Columbia. Each state holds dear its power to regulate domestic relations, and peculiar divorce laws abound. Nevertheless, divorce law in most states has evolved to recognize the difference between regulating the actual decision to divorce and regulating the practical ramifications of such a decision, such as property distribution, support obligations, and child custody. Most courts ignore marital fault in determining whether to grant a divorce, but many still consider it in setting future obligations between the parties. To determine the exact nature of the rights and duties relating to a divorce, one must consult the relevant statutes for the state in which the divorce is filed.

FURTHER READINGS

American Bar Association Standing Committee on the Delivery of Legal Services. 1994. "Responding to the Needs of the Self-Represented Divorce Litigant." Chicago: American Bar Association.

Boumil, Marcia M., et al. 1994. *Law and Gender Bias*. Littleton, Colo.: Rothman.

Mather, Lynn. 2003. "Changing Patterns of Legal Representation in Divorce: From Lawyers to Pro Se." *Journal of Law and Society* 30 (March).

Phillips, Roderick. 1991. *Untying the Knot*. Cambridge, England: Cambridge Univ. Press.

Wadlington, Walter. 1990. *Domestic Relations: Cases and Materials*. 2d ed. Westbury, N.Y.: Foundation Press.

Warle, Lynn D. 1994. "Divorce Violence and the No-Fault Divorce Culture." *Utah Law Review* (spring).

Woodhouse, Barbara Bennet. 1994. "Sex, Lies, and Dissipation: The Discourse of Fault in a No-Fault Era." *Georgetown Law Journal* 82.

CROSS-REFERENCES

Annulment; Family Law; Premarital Agreement.

❖ DIX, DOROTHEA LYNDE

Dorothea Lynde Dix was a remarkably foresighted educator and social reformer who made major contributions to the welfare of persons with mental illness, prisoners, and injured Civil War soldiers. Dix was born on April 4, 1802, in Hampden, Maine. Her father, Joseph Dix, was an alcoholic and circuit-riding Methodist preacher who required young Dorothea to spend her time laboriously stitching and pasting the thick religious tracts he wrote and sold during his travels. Although considered a strict and sometimes abusive father, Joseph Dix taught his daughter to read and write at an early age. Dix, in turn, taught reading and writing to her two younger brothers. Her mother, Mary (Bigelow) Dix, suffered from depression that made it difficult for her to care for her three children.

At age 12, Dix lived briefly with her father's mother in Boston and then moved in with an aunt in Worcester, Massachusetts. Although her grandmother helped with her education, Dix

Dorothea Dix.

had little formal training. Gifted with strong beliefs and intellectual abilities, Dix, at age 14, began teaching young girls a rigorous curriculum that she had created with emphasis on the natural sciences and ethical responsibilities. In 1821, Dix moved back to Boston and opened a private school on property belonging to her grandmother.

Dix combined teaching with a prolific schedule of writing books and religious tracts, including *Meditations for Private Hours* (1828), *The Garland of Flora* (1829), and *American Moral Tales for Young Persons* (1832). One of her best known and most-often reprinted publications was *Conversations on Common Things,* which was published in 1824 as a guide to help parents answer everyday questions, such as "Why do we call this day Monday?" and "What is tin?"

After her father's death in 1821, Dix used her income to support her mother and her two younger brothers who had come to live with her in Boston. In addition to the private school she ran, Dix also conducted free evening classes for indigent children. She read prodigiously, continued to study the natural sciences as well as history and literature, attended public lectures, and met the leading members of Boston's intellectual and religious communities. She made the acquaintance of many Unitarians and became friends with William Ellery Channing,

"MAN IS NOT MADE BETTER BY BEING DEGRADED; HE IS SELDOM RESTRAINED FROM CRIME BY HARSH MEASURES, EXCEPT THE PRINCIPLE OF FEAR PREDOMINATES IN HIS CHARACTER; AND THEN HE IS NEVER MADE RADICALLY BETTER FOR ITS INFLUENCE."
—DOROTHEA DIX

the famed pastor of Unitarian Federal Street Church in Boston and his wife Julia Allen Channing.

Never robust, Dix suffered intermittently from depression and chronic upper respiratory infections variously attributed to tuberculosis and malaria. Her illnesses would flare up from time to time, exacerbated by the demanding schedule she kept and she developed a pattern of cutting back briefly on her work until she was able to resume her tasks. In 1836, Dix broke down while trying to care for her ill grandmother in addition to all her other duties and it became clear that she would need to take an extended period of rest.

She closed her school and sailed to Europe where she stayed in Liverpool, England, with William Rathbone and his wife who were friends of the Channings. Rathbone was a prominent humanitarian and philanthropist who introduced Dix to a number of social welfare advocates including prison reformer Elizabeth Fry and William Tuke, a Quaker who had opened the York Retreat for the Mentally Disordered and who pioneered the theory of humane treatment for persons with mental illness.

While Dix was in England, both her mother and her grandmother died, the latter leaving Dix a large inheritance. The income from the inheritance and ROYALTIES from her books were sufficient to give Dix a comfortable living for the rest of her life. Dix returned to Boston in 1838 and spent several years visiting friends and family members and traveling to various points of interest.

In 1841, a ministerial student asked Dix to teach a Sunday school class to a group of women incarcerated in the East Cambridge Jail in Massachusetts. Her first visit to the jail marked a turning point in her life. After teaching the class, Dix toured the jail. On the lower level she found the "dungeon cells" that housed inmates considered to be insane. Dix was horrified to find men, women, and children, half-naked and underfed, chained to walls, and forced to sleep on the floors of the filthy unlit cells.

Dix immediately took action. She surveyed every jail, poorhouse, and prison in Massachusetts. In 1843, she delivered a report to the Massachusetts state legislature. Legislators and others at first criticized the report and denied the charges. When Dix's charges were sustained by independent observations, the legislature allocated funds to expand the State Mental Hospital at Worcester.

Dix continued her investigations in other states, first in New England and eventually nationwide. Dix traveled the country systematically collecting data that she would then present in reports (called "memorials") to various state legislatures. Seeking the establishment of state-supported institutions, Dix would lobby state officials and influential persons and attempt to raise a public outcry over the dreadful conditions she had found.

Until Dix began her campaign to better the lives of persons with mental illness, the popular assumption was that persons who were insane were incurable and did not feel deprivation in the same way as ordinary persons. Dix was among the first to espouse the theory that insanity was treatable and that better living conditions could do much to help persons with mental illness.

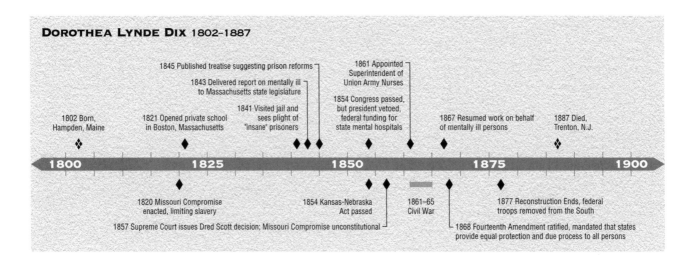

DOROTHEA LYNDE DIX 1802–1887

1845 Published treatise suggesting prison reforms

1843 Delivered report on mentally ill to Massachusetts state legislature

1841 Visited jail and sees plight of "insane" prisoners

1861 Appointed Superintendent of Union Army Nurses

1854 Congress passed, but president vetoed, federal funding for state mental hospitals

1802 Born, Hampden, Maine

1821 Opened private school in Boston, Massachusetts

1867 Resumed work on behalf of mentally ill persons

1887 Died, Trenton, N.J.

1800   1825   1850   1875   1900

1820 Missouri Compromise enacted, limiting slavery

1854 Kansas-Nebraska Act passed

1861–65 Civil War

1877 Reconstruction Ends, federal troops removed from the South

1857 Supreme Court issues Dred Scott decision; Missouri Compromise unconstitutional

1868 Fourteenth Amendment ratified, mandated that states provide equal protection and due process to all persons

In three years, the indefatigable Dix traveled over 30,000 miles crusading for her cause. Her labors proved highly successful. In 1843, when she delivered her first memorial, there were 13 mental institutions in the United States. Several decades later, that number had grown to 123 with Dix helping to found 32 of them. In addition, Dix's efforts played a major part in the founding of 15 schools for what were then called the "feeble-minded," a school for blind persons, and a number of training schools for nurses.

Buoyed by her success, Dix next set out to accomplish her goal of persuading Congress to set aside five million acres in federal land grants; the idea was that income from the land trusts would be used to endow state mental hospitals. In 1854, Congress passed the legislation she sought. Although President MILLARD FILLMORE favored the bill, it did not reach his desk before the end of his term. The bill was vetoed by Fillmore's successor, President FRANKLIN PIERCE, thus dashing the hopes of Dix and her supporters of establishing federal funding for mentally ill persons. Eventually, in 1855, Congress provided funds for the founding of St. Elizabeth's Hospital in Washington, D.C., which remains the oldest large mental hospital that is federally funded.

Worn out and discouraged, Dix traveled to Europe to rest. Instead, she found herself investigating the same deplorable conditions in prisons and poorhouses in numerous European countries and once again began campaigning for, and achieving, many reforms. Throughout the 1850s, Dix worked for humanitarian reform in the United States and Europe as well in Canada, Russia, and Japan.

In 1845, Dix published a treatise entitled *Remarks on Prisons and Prison Discipline in the United States,* in which she advocated for progressive reforms for ordinary prisoners including the separation of prisoners according to the type of offense committed and the need for education of prisoners.

In 1861, at the beginning of the Civil War, the 59-year-old Dix volunteered her services and was made superintendent of women nurses for the Union Army. Although she worked until 1866 helping to organize women volunteers, establish hospitals, and raise funds, her capabilities as an administrator were questioned and her tenure was viewed as only partially successful.

Dix resumed her work with persons with mental illness in 1867. She found many problems including rising immigration rates, state treasuries depleted by the war, a growing population of indigent persons with mental illness, and state legislatures that had new priorities. She continued her fight until ill health forced her to stop. In 1881, Dix took up residence in the guest quarters of the Trenton, New Jersey, state hospital she had helped found. She lived there until her death on July 17, 1887.

FURTHER READINGS

Brown, Thomas J. 1998. *Dorothea Dix: New England Reformer.* Cambridge, Mass.: Harvard Univ. Press.

Dix, Dorothea. 1999. *Asylum, Prison, and Poorhouse: The Writings and Reform Work of Dorothea Dix in Illinois.* Edited by David L. Lightner. Carbondale: Southern Illinois Univ. Press.

———. 1845. Remarks on Prisons and Prison Discipline in the United States. Edited by Leonard D. Savitz. Reprint, Montclair, N.J.: Patterson Smith, 1984.

❖ DIXON, JULIAN CAREY

Representative Julian C. Dixon, who served the West Los Angeles District for twenty-two years in Congress, left a legacy as a supporting legislator on CIVIL RIGHTS and national security matters. He is also remembered for the differences he made in California and in the District of Columbia in his various roles serving in the U.S. House of Representatives.

Julian Carey Dixon was born in Washington, D.C., in 1934. He moved to Los Angeles, California, with his family at the age of ten. He grew up and attended public school in Los Angeles. In 1957 he left to serve in the Army, returning in 1960 to receive his degree from California State University in 1962. Dixon then went on to earn his law degree from Southwestern State University in Los Angeles in 1967.

Dixon spent only a few years in the private PRACTICE OF LAW before entering a life devoted to politics and public service. In 1972 he was elected to the California State Assembly, where he served for six years. In 1978 he was elected to serve in the U.S. House of Representatives. He served his constituents in the 32nd District of California for twenty-two more years in the House.

Throughout his career, Julian Dixon was a strong advocate for civil rights causes. During the 1980s he was chairman of the Congressional Black Caucus. He also created a MARTIN LUTHER KING JR. memorial in Washington, D.C. The

Human Rights Campaign, this nation's largest lesbian and gay political organization, views Dixon as an advocate for their cause, citing his introduction of the $8.6 billion relief bill after the 1994 earthquake in Los Angeles. The bill, for the first time ever in a federal law, specifically outlawed discrimination of disaster victims on the grounds of sexual orientation. Dixon was also co-sponsor of bills which sought to reduce discrimination against minority groups, including the Employment Non-Discrimination Act and Hate Crimes Prevention Act.

From the beginning of his career on Capitol Hill, Dixon earned the respect of his peers and served as chairman of several committees. In 1984 he was Rules Committee chairman of the Democratic Convention. He also served as chairman of the Committee on Standards of Official Conduct, better known as the Ethics Committee. This position proved to be Dixon's most challenging position, particularly in 1989 when then-House Speaker JIM WRIGHT a Democrat from Texas, was being investigated for ethics violations. Georgia Republican NEWT GINGRICH backed the Republicans in their attacks against the speaker, which predictably sparked a defensive tone from Democrats. As chairman of the Ethics Committee, Dixon emerged as a bi-partisan leader who focused on the facts and the true issues presented. In June 1989, Wright resigned. As a result of his leadership in this episode, Dixon was commended by members of both sides of the House for his fairness and judgment.

More recently, Dixon was ranking Democrat on the House Permanent Select Committee on Intelligence. Additionally, he served on a panel to determine defense spending. Here, he fought on behalf of his constituents for the appropriation of funds to aid southern California communities hurt by base closings and defense budget cuts.

Dixon was also a senior member of the Appropriations Committee and, during the mid-1990s, chaired the Washington, D.C., subcommittee where he was able to make a difference in the city of his birth by focusing on public safety and education. During his leadership of the subcommittee, Congress began a crackdown on the scandal-ridden administration of Mayor Marion Barry, leading the way for a federal takeover of the finances for Washington, D.C. Because of his efforts in Washington, Dixon is still heralded by the leadership of Capitol Hill and the citizens of the city.

Dixon is, of course, highly regarded and remembered by his own constituents in western Los Angeles. He always came through with aid in times of emergency. In 1992 the streets of Los Angeles were rocked as buildings were broken into, looted, and burned after a verdict of "not guilty" was issued in the trial of two white police officers who beat motorist RODNEY KING in a highly-broadcast, videotaped incident. Dixon acquired emergency funds for the businesses of Los Angeles that suffered in the riots. He also came to the aid of his city after the 1994 Northridge earthquake.

Perhaps his most lasting contribution to the Los Angeles community, however, was the effort he put into establishing the MTA, the commuter rail system in Los Angeles. Dixon was well aware that the city needed a solution to its major traffic problems, and high-speed public transportation seemed to be a good answer. The city and MTA recognized his efforts; they renamed one of the busiest rail stations the "Julian Dixon Metro Rail Station." Dixon was so highly revered by his constituents that he won re-election in the November 2000 election with 84 percent of the vote. He died one month later, on December 8, 2000, at the age of 66 in Inglewood, California.

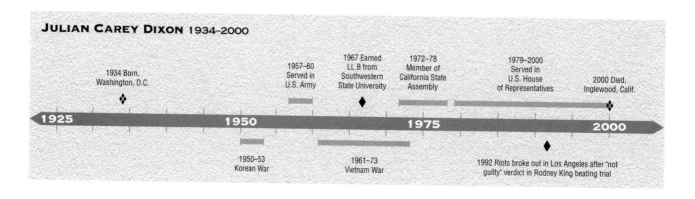

JULIAN CAREY DIXON 1934–2000

1934 Born, Washington, D.C.

1957–60 Served in U.S. Army

1967 Earned LL.B from Southwestern State University

1972–78 Member of California State Assembly

1979–2000 Served in U.S. House of Representatives

2000 Died, Inglewood, Calif.

1925   1950   1975   2000

1950–53 Korean War

1961–73 Vietnam War

1992 Riots broke out in Los Angeles after "not guilty" verdict in Rodney King beating trial

DNA EVIDENCE

Among the many new tools that science has provided for the analysis of forensic evidence is the powerful and controversial analysis of deoxyribonucleic acid, or DNA, the material that makes up the genetic code of most organisms. DNA analysis, also called DNA typing or DNA profiling, examines DNA found in physical evidence such as blood, hair, and semen, and determines whether it can be matched to DNA taken from specific individuals. DNA analysis has become a common form of evidence in criminal trials. It is also used in civil litigation, particularly in cases involving the determination of PATERNITY or identity.

History and Process of DNA Analysis

DNA, sometimes called the building block or genetic blueprint of life, was first described by the scientists Francis H. C. Crick and James D. Watson in 1953. Crick and Watson identified the double-helix structure of DNA, which resembles a twisted ladder, and established the role of DNA as the material that makes up the genetic code of living organisms. The pattern of the compounds that constitute the DNA of an individual lifeform determines the development of that lifeform. DNA is the same in every cell throughout an individual's body, whether it is a skin cell, sperm cell, or blood cell. With the exception of identical twins, no two individuals have the same DNA blueprint.

DNA analysis was first proposed in 1985 by the English scientist Alec J. Jeffreys. By the late 1980s, it was being performed by law enforcement agencies, including the FEDERAL BUREAU OF INVESTIGATION (FBI), and by commercial laboratories. It consists of comparing selected segments of DNA molecules from different individuals. Because a DNA molecule is made up of billions of segments, only a small proportion of an individual's entire genetic code is analyzed.

In DNA analysis for a criminal investigation, using highly sophisticated scientific equipment, first a DNA molecule from the suspect is disassembled, and selected segments are isolated and measured. Then the suspect's DNA profile is compared with one derived from a sample of physical evidence to see whether the two match. If a conclusive nonmatch occurs, the suspect may be eliminated from consideration. If a match occurs, a statistical analysis is performed to determine the probability that the sample of physical evidence came from another person with the same DNA profile as the suspect's.

Juries use this statistical result in determining whether a suspect is guilty or innocent.

Although DNA analysis is sometimes called DNA fingerprinting, this term is a misnomer. Because the entire DNA structure of billions of compounds cannot be evaluated in the same way that an entire fingerprint can, a "match" resulting from DNA typing represents only a statistical likelihood. Thus, the results of DNA typing are not considered absolute proof of identity. A DNA nonmatch is considered conclusive, however, because any variation in DNA structure means that the DNA samples have been drawn from different sources.

An example from the early 1990s illustrates the way in which DNA evidence is used in the criminal justice system. After a Vermont woman was KIDNAPPED and raped in a semi-trailer truck, police identified Randolph Jakobetz, a truck driver, as a suspect in the crime. Officers searched the trailer that Jakobetz had hauled on the night of the crime and found hairs matching those of the victim. After arresting Jakobetz, law enforcement officials sent a sample of his blood to the FBI laboratory in Washington, D.C., for DNA analysis and for comparison with DNA taken from semen found in the victim shortly after the crime.

At Jakobetz's trial, an FBI expert testified that the blood and semen samples were a "match," concluding that there was one chance in 300 million that the semen samples could have come from someone other than Jakobetz. Based on this and other strong evidence, Jakobetz was convicted and sentenced to almost 30 years in prison.

Jakobetz appealed the decision, claiming that DNA profiling was unreliable and that it should not be admitted as evidence. In the first major federal decision on DNA profiling, the U.S. Court of Appeals for the Second Circuit upheld the lower court's decision to admit the DNA evidence (*United States v. Jakobetz*, 955 F.2d 786 [2d Cir. 1992]). The U.S. Supreme Court later declined to hear an appeal.

The *Jakobetz* case illustrates the way in which the probabilities generated by DNA analysis can be used as devastating evidence against a criminal suspect. Juries have tended to view the statistical results of this analysis as highly incriminating, which has caused many defense attorneys to challenge the validity of the results, and many prosecuting attorneys to defend them. At the same time, defense lawyers have used DNA

DNA EVIDENCE: BOON OR BOONDOGGLE FOR CRIMINAL JUSTICE?

Since its first use in the late 1980s, DNA evidence has been a subject of controversy in the U.S. criminal justice system. Although courts have increasingly allowed DNA analysis to be admitted as evidence, doubts about the propriety of such evidence remain. In general, the debate over DNA evidence pits those, such as prosecutors and law enforcement officials, who are eager to use it as a tool to fight crime, against those, particularly defense attorneys, who claim that it is unreliable and will lead to the wrongful conviction of innocent people.

Law enforcement officials and prosecuting attorneys are quick to identify the benefits of DNA evidence for the criminal justice system. DNA evidence, they argue, is even more useful than fingerprinting, with several advantages over that more traditional tool of investigation. DNA evidence is more readily available in criminal investigations than are legible fingerprints because body fluids and hair are more likely to be left at the scene of a crime. DNA evidence is also "robust"; that is, it does not decay or disappear over time. The DNA in a piece of physical evidence such as a hair may be examined years after a crime.

Law enforcement officials have confidence in the reliability of DNA analysis performed by commercial and government forensic laboratories. They main-tain that innocent people have no need to worry about the use of DNA evidence in the legal system. In fact, they argue, DNA evidence will help to ensure that innocent suspects are not convicted because the DNA of such suspects will not match that taken from crime-related samples.

Proponents of DNA evidence fear that successful courtroom attacks on its reliability will erode public confidence in its use, giving the state less power in bringing criminals to justice. But most remain confident that it will be a permanent part of criminal investigation.

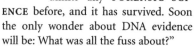

IN FOCUS

According to Eric E. Wright, an assistant attorney general for Maine, "[T]he history of forensic DNA evidence consistently and ever increasingly demonstrates its reliability. It has been subjected to savage scrutiny unlike any FORENSIC SCIENCE before, and it has survived. Soon the only wonder about DNA evidence will be: What was all the fuss about?"

Defense attorneys and others who are skeptical about DNA evidence strongly disagree with many of these claims. While generally accepting the scientific theory behind DNA evidence, including its ability to exculpate the innocent suspect, they assert that it is not nearly as reliable in practice as its proponents claim. They argue that DNA evidence may be unreliable for any number of reasons, including contamination owing to improper police procedures and faulty laboratory work that may produce incorrect results.

Barry C. Scheck is a leading critic of DNA evidence. A professor at the Benjamin N. Cardozo School of Law, a defense attorney in several notable cases involving DNA evidence, and an expert for the defense in the celebrated 1995 murder trial of O. J. SIMPSON, Scheck has led the movement for increased scrutiny of DNA evidence. Conceding that "there is no scientific dispute about the validity of the general principles underlying DNA evidence," he nevertheless argued that serious problems with DNA evidence remained. He found particular fault in the work of forensic laboratories and pointed to research that showed that as many as one to four percent of the DNA matches produced by laboratories were in error. Laboratories denied such claims.

Scheck also criticized the procedures used by laboratories to estimate the likelihood of a DNA match. Because juries consider the probabilities generated by the labs—figures such as one in 300 million or one in 5 million—when assessing the validity of DNA results, it is important to ensure that they are accurate.

DNA critics assert that statistical estimates of a match may be skewed by incorrect assumptions about the genetic variation across a population. In some population subgroups, they claim, individuals may be so genetically similar that a DNA match is more likely to occur when comparing samples drawn from

analysis as evidence to reverse the convictions of their clients.

Legal History of DNA Evidence

In general, state and federal courts have increasingly accepted DNA evidence as admissible. The first state appellate court decision to uphold the admission of DNA evidence was in 1988 (*Andrews v. Florida*, 533 So. 2d 841 [Fla. App.]), and the first major federal court decision to uphold its admission occurred in *Jakobetz*. By the mid-1990s, most states' courts admitted DNA test results into evidence.

No court has rejected DNA evidence on the grounds that the underlying scientific theory is invalid. However, some courts have excluded it from evidence because of problems with the possible contamination of samples, questions surrounding the significance of its statistical probabilities, and laboratory errors. Several states have passed laws that recognize DNA evi-

within that subgroup. Examples of such subgroups are geographically isolated populations or tightly knit immigrant or religious communities. Other problems may occur in cases where suspects are closely related to one another. Critics call for more research on population substructures and DNA similarities within them, in order to get a better understanding of statistical properties.

In response to these arguments, proponents of DNA analysis maintain that the importance of frequency calculations has been overrated. They claim that such calculations are, if anything, conservative. Furthermore, they argue that a match itself is more important than a frequency calculation and that questions of how to calculate frequency should not mean that DNA evidence is inaccurate.

DNA critics call for a number of other procedures to make DNA testing more accurate. They advocate sample splitting, a procedure by which samples of physical evidence are sent to two forensic laboratories in order to better guard against mistaken matches. They also ask that all DNA laboratories be required to undergo proficiency testing through blind trials. Such trials would have laboratories analyze DNA samples without knowing whether the analysis was being done for an actual investigation or for evaluation purposes only. Blind trials would yield error rates for each laboratory that could be given to a jury to help it weigh the significance of DNA evidence. Blind trials would also provide incentives for laboratories to lower their error rates.

Criminal defense lawyers have also called for state-funded access to the services of experts who can evaluate the handling and analysis of DNA evidence. These "counter experts" would give the defense a chance to scrutinize DNA evidence more closely. Defense attorneys also assert the need for access to laboratory records and physical samples for retesting. Providing this access would require the state to preserve samples.

Prosecutors and attorneys have continued to identify new uses for DNA in law enforcement and in the legal system. In July 2001, a Milwaukee, Wisconsin, appeals court judge upheld the validity of a criminal warrant for the arrest of "John Doe 12," issued for a 1994 rape case just days before the STATUTE OF LIMITATIONS was to expire. What made the warrant noteworthy was that the suspect was identified only by his DNA profile. This was the first known case in which prosecutors sought arrest warrants based solely on a DNA description. When a DNA evaluation matched the DNA of "John Doe 12" with Bobby Richard Dabney Jr., the state replaced "John Doe" with Dabney's name. Dabney's attorney sought to dismiss the claim because Dabney was not named in the original complaint until after a six-year statute of limitations had expired. A Milwaukee County Circuit Court Judge denied the motion to dismiss the case.

In September 2001, the Wisconsin state legislature effected new changes to the statute of limitations. This legislation expressly addresses DNA evidence and extends the time limits for such cases. The amendments permit prosecution any time within 12 months of the time a DNA match results in a probable identification of a person.

In another legal "first," attorneys for plaintiff Nanette Sexton Bailey of West Palm Beach, Florida, used DNA evidence found on bed sheets to allege ADULTERY on the part of her husband in a pending DIVORCE matter. Five years into their marriage, the couple mutually agreed to amend their prenuptial agreement to include a "bad boy clause," guaranteeing Sexton $20,000 per month for her husband's infidelity. When she found a nightgown and stained bed sheets in their home, she wrapped them in a plastic bag. When the sheets and nightgown were examined by a Denver laboratory, it confirmed that the DNA on the items belonged to another woman. Although the husband eventually challenged the "bad boy" clause, the judge ruled that the DNA evidence was admissible as evidence of the adultery.

Science may eventually solve many of the problems regarding DNA evidence. In the meantime, debate over its use has already led to changes that will allow courts and juries to better assess the guilt or innocence of criminal suspects.

FURTHER READINGS

Committee on DNA Forensic Science. 1996. *The Evaluation of Forensic DNA Evidence.* Washington, D.C.: National Academy Press.

Federal Judicial Center. 2000. *Reference Manual on Scientific Evidence.* New York: Lexis Publishing.

National Institute for Justice. 2001. *Understanding DNA Evidence: A Guide for Victim Service Providers.* Washington, D.C.: National Institute for Justice.

CROSS-REFERENCES

Forensic Science.

dence as admissible in criminal cases, and others have enacted laws that specifically admit DNA evidence to help resolve civil paternity cases.

The admissibility of novel SCIENTIFIC EVIDENCE such as DNA profiling is governed by two different judicial tests or standards: the *Frye,* or general acceptance, standard, and the *Daubert,* or relevancy-reliability, standard. The *Frye* test, which comes from the 1923 case *Frye v. United States* 293 F. 1013 (D.C. Cir.), holds that the admissibility of evidence gathered by a specific technique (such as DNA analysis) is determined by whether that technique has been "sufficiently established to have gained general acceptance in the particular field in which it belongs." In *Frye,* the Court of Appeals for the District of Columbia Circuit ruled that a lie-detector test using a blood-pressure reading was not admissible as evidence. By the 1970s, 45 states had adopted this common-law standard for the admission of novel scientific evidence.

The U.S. Supreme Court overruled use of the *Frye* test in federal courts in its 1993 decision *Daubert v. Merrell Dow,* 509 U.S. 579, 113 S. Ct. 2786, 125 L. Ed. 2d 469. In *Daubert,* the Court held that the FEDERAL RULES OF EVIDENCE, enacted in 1975, govern the admission of novel scientific evidence in federal courts. It found that *Frye* provides too stringent a test and that it is incompatible with the federal rules, which allow the admission of all evidence that has "any tendency to make the existence of any fact that is of consequence to the determination of the action more probable or less probable than it would be without the evidence" (Fed. R. Evid. 401). The Court found that judges have a responsibility to "ensure that any and all scientific testimony or evidence admitted is not only relevant, but reliable."

In general, courts that have used the *Daubert* standard have been more likely to admit DNA evidence, although many jurisdictions that have relied on *Frye* have permitted it as well. Nearly all cases in which DNA evidence has been ruled inadmissible have been in jurisdictions that have used *Frye.*

States are free to adopt their own standards for the admission of evidence, and have increasingly adopted the *Daubert* standard. By 1995, the number of states using the *Frye* standard had dropped to 23, while 21 had adopted the *Daubert* standard.

Current Issues Surrounding Use of DNA Evidence

A report issued by the JUSTICE DEPARTMENT in 2002 indicated that two-thirds of chief prosecutors in the United States rely on DNA testing during investigations and trials. The use of DNA evidence has exonerated at least ten individuals who were wrongly convicted of murder and faced the death penalty, while the sentences of more than 100 others convicted of lesser crimes were overturned based upon DNA evidence. The FBI maintains a database that may be used to compare DNA samples from unsolved state and federal crimes. Since its inception in 1992, the FBI's database has made more than 5,000 matches, thus allowing law enforcement officials to solve crimes that might not have been solved without the use of DNA.

The FBI crime laboratory dominated research in forensic sciences for much of the 1980s and 1990s. However, allegations surfaced in 1995 that suggested scientists at the crime lab had tainted evidence related to the 1993 bombing of the World Trade Center in New York City. A former chemist in the lab, Frederic Whitehurst, testified before the House Committee on the Judiciary that the FBI had knowingly drafted misleading scientific reports and pressured FBI scientists to commit perjury by backing up the false reports. These allegations injured the FBI's reputation and led to speculation in the late 1990s that prosecutors could not rely on the FBI's analysis of DNA evidence.

Even as the FBI rebuilt its reputation, other questions surrounding the use of DNA evidence have arisen since the late 1990s. In 1999, the DEPARTMENT OF JUSTICE issued a report stating that evidence from at least 180,000 unsolved rape cases had not been submitted for testing. A 2002 report by *USA Today* suggested that several thousand pieces of evidence from rape and HOMICIDE cases had not been submitted for DNA testing, so they do not appear in the FBI's database. In 2000, Congress allocated $125 million to support the national DNA database system, including $45 million designated to allow states to test evidence from unsolved crimes. However, several states claim that their law enforcement officials are so swamped with current cases that they cannot test older, unsolved cases. Moreover, a small number of states—primarily New York, Florida, Virginia, and Illinois—have aggressively developed their own DNA databases and have contributed heavily to the FBI's system. These states accounted for more than half of the FBI's DNA matches between 1992 and 2002.

Use of DNA evidence to overturn criminal convictions remains a common topic of discussion among legal and criminal justice experts, as well as the popular media. One of the most closely followed cases involved the convictions of five young men for the rape of a jogger in Central Park in New York City in 1989. The five men in the case, dubbed the "Central Park Jogger Case," served sentences ranging from seven to eleven years for the incident. However, another man, Matias Reyes, who was convicted for murder in 1989, confessed to the rape. Testing confirmed that the semen found in the victim and on the victim's sock matched Reyes's DNA.

Upon receiving the new evidence, the New York County district attorney's office asked the New York State Supreme Court to overturn the convictions of the five men. Several groups, including WOMEN'S RIGHTS groups, cited this case as an example of why law enforcement should be more proactive in pursuing unsolved rape cases through the use of DNA testing.

FURTHER READINGS

Bennett, Margann. 1995. "Admissibility Issues of Forensic DNA Evidence." *University of Kansas Law Review* 44 (November).

"Confronting the New Challenges of Scientific Evidence: DNA Evidence and the Criminal Defense." 1995. *Harvard Law Review* 108 (May).

Federal Bureau of Investigation. 1994. *Handbook of Forensic Science.* Washington, D.C.: U.S. Government Printing Office.

National Research Council. 1992. *DNA Technology in Forensic Science.* Washington, D.C.: National Academy Press.

Wright, Eric E. 1995. "DNA Evidence: Where We've Been, Where We Are, and Where We Are Going." *Maine Bar Journal* 10 (July).

CROSS-REFERENCES

Forensic Science.

DOCK

To curtail or diminish, as, for example, to dock a person's wages for lateness or poor work. The cage or enclosed space in a criminal court where prisoners stand when brought in for trial.

DOCKET

A written list of judicial proceedings set down for trial in a court.

To enter the dates of judicial proceedings scheduled for trial in a book kept by a court.

In practice, a docket is a roster that the clerk of the court prepares, listing the cases pending trial.

An *appearance docket* contains a list of the appearances in actions and a brief abstract of the successive steps in each case.

A *judgment docket* is a listing of the judgments entered in a particular court that is available to the public for examination. Its purpose is to give official notice of the existence of liens or judgments to interested parties.

A *docket fee* is a sum of money charged for the docketing of a case or a judgment or a set amount chargeable as part of the costs of the action.

DOCTRINE

A legal rule, tenet, theory, or principle. A political policy.

Examples of common legal doctrines include the clean hands doctrine, the doctrine of false demonstration, and the doctrine of merger.

The MONROE DOCTRINE, enunciated by President JAMES MONROE on December 2, 1823, was an American policy to consider any aggression by a European country against any western hemisphere country to be a hostile act toward the United States.

DOCTRINE OF EQUALITY OF STATES

One of the fundamental rights of a state is equality with all other states. This right is inherent in the concept of a state as a subject of INTERNATIONAL LAW and is given general recognition by long-standing state practice. Precise definition of the principle of equality of states is difficult, however, since many factors affect its application in any particular situation. Thus, it is best to differentiate between *legal equality,* that is, the concept of state equality as it applies to the legal relations that states maintain with each other, and *political equality,* which reflects the relative distribution of economic and military power between states.

In its legal effects the principle of state equality has several important consequences. Probably the most important manifestation of the doctrine is the right of every state to have one vote in matters requiring the consent of states. A natural consequence of this is that the vote of every state, no matter how large or small the state, counts the same as the individual votes of all other states. Legal equality also means that no state can claim jurisdiction over other states, and as corollary, a state is independent of the political will of all other states. From this also flows the concept of SOVEREIGN IMMUNITY, which prevents one state from being sued in the courts of another state without the consent of the first state. Likewise, equality of states means that no other state can question the legality of official acts of another state, a rule known in U.S. law as the act of state doctrine.

The doctrine of equality of states means one thing in legal effect, but it also must be reflected against the realities imposed by differences in political power. Political equality is in some sense a fiction, because in political terms few states are equals. More powerful states can establish arrangements that less powerful states assent to informally, even though under a strict legal regime, they would not be bound by the agreement.

A sample docketing statement.

Docketing Statements (Civil)

Appellate Docket Number: _____

Appellate Case Style:

DOCKETING STATEMENT (CIVIL)
Tenth Court of Appeals
P.O. Box 1606, Waco, Texas 76703-1606
(254) 757-5200

[to be filed in the court of appeals upon perfection of appeal

under TRAP 32]

I. Parties (TRAP 32.1(a), (e)):	
Appellant(s):	Appellee(s):
(*See* note at bottom of page)	(*See* note at bottom of page)
Attorney (lead appellate counsel):	Attorney (lead appellate counsel, if known; if not, then trial counsel):
Address (lead counsel):	Address (lead appellate counsel, if known; if not, then trial counsel):
Telephone: (include area code)	Telephone: (include area code)
Telecopy: (include area code)	Telecopy: (include area code)
SBN (lead counsel):	SBN (lead counsel):

[continued]

Docketing Statements (Civil)

A sample docketing statement (continued).

If not represented by counsel, provide appellant's/appellee's address, telephone number, and telecopy number.

On Attachment 1, or a separate attachment if needed, list the same information stated above for any additional parties to the trial court's judgment.

II. Perfection Of Appeal And Jurisdiction (TRAP 32.1(b), (c), (g), (j)):

Date order or judgment signed:	Date notice of appeal filed in trial court:
(Attach a signed copy, if possible)	(Attach file-stamped copy; if mailed to the trial court clerk, also give the date of mailing)
What type of judgment? (e.g., jury trial, bench trial, summary judgment, directed verdict, other (specify))	Interlocutory appeal of appealable order: ☐ Yes ☐ No (Please specify statutory or other basis on which interlocutory order is appealable) (See TRAP 28)
If money judgment, what was the amount? Actual damages:	Accelerated appeal (See TRAP 28): ☐ Yes ☐ No
Punitive (or similar) damages:	(Please specify statutory or other basis on which appeal is accelerated)
Attorneys' fees (trial):	
Attorneys' fees (appellate):	

[continued]

A sample docketing statement (continued).

Docketing Statements (Civil)

Other (specify):

Appeal that receives precedence, preference, or priority under statute or rule?

☐ Yes ☐ No

(Please specify statutory or other basis for such status)

Appeal from final judgment? Yes ☐ No ☐

Does judgment dispose of all parties and issues:

Yes ☐ No ☐

Does judgment have a Mother Hubbard clause?

(E.g.: "All relief not expressly granted is denied"):

Yes ☐ No ☐

Does judgment have language that one or more parties "take nothing"?

Yes ☐ No ☐

Other basis for finality?

Will you challenge this Court's jurisdiction? If yes, explain.

III. Actions Extending Time To Perfect Appeal (TRAP 32.1(d)):

Action	Filed Check as appropriate		Date Filed
Motion for New Trial	No	Yes	
Motion to Modify Judgment	No	Yes	
Request for Findings of Fact and Conclusions of Law	No	Yes	
Motion to Reinstate	No	Yes	
Motion under TRCP 306a	No	Yes	
Other (specify):	No	Yes	

IV. Indigency Of Party (TRAP 32.1(k)): (Attach file-stamped copy of affidavit)

Event	Filed Check as appropriate		Date	N/A
Affidavit filed	No	Yes		
Contest filed	No	Yes		
Date ruling on contest due:				
Ruling on contest: Sustained Overruled				

[continued]

Docketing Statements (Civil)

A sample docketing statement (continued).

V. Bankruptcy (TRAP 8):

Will the appeal be stayed by bankruptcy? Date bankruptcy filed?

Name of bankruptcy court: Bankruptcy Case No.:

Style of bankruptcy case:

VI. Trial Court And Record (TRAP 32.1(c), (h), (i)):

Court:	County:	Trial Court Docket Number (Cause No.):

Trial Judge (who tried or disposed of case):	Court Clerk (district clerk):
Telephone Number:	Telephone Number:
(include area code)	(include area code)
Telecopy Number:	Telecopy Number:
(include area code)	(include area code)
Address:	Address:

Clerk's Record	Sworn copy for accelerated appeal	Will request	Was requested on:
Yes	Yes (*See* TRAP 28.3)	(Note: No request required under TRAP 34.5(a), (b))	

Court Reporter or Court Recorder:	Court Reporter or Court Recorder:
Telephone Number:	Telephone Number:
(include area code)	(include area code)
Telecopy Number:	Telecopy Number:
(include area code)	(include area code)

[continued]

A sample docketing statement (continued).

Docketing Statements (Civil)

Address: Address:

(Attach additional sheet if necessary for additional court reporters/recorders)

Length of trial (approximate):   State arrangements made for payment of court reporter/recorder:

Reporter's or Recorder's Record   None   Will request   Was requested on:
(check if electronic recording)

VII. Nature Of The Case (TRAP 32.1(f)) (Subject matter or type of case: E.g., personal injury, breach of contract, workers' compensation, or temporary injunction) (see list below):

Administrative/agency _____	Malpractice
	Legal _____
	Medical _____
Banking _____	Other _____
Business _____	Motor Vehicle _____
Condemnation _____	Municipal _____
Consumer/DTPA _____	Oil & Gas _____
Construction _____	Personal Injury _____
Contract _____	Premises Liability _____
Employment/Labor _____	Probate _____
Family _____	Products Liability _____
Custody _____	Real Property _____
Property Division _____	Securities _____
Termination _____	Tax _____
Other _____	U.C.C./Tex. Bus. & Com. Code _____
Fraud _____	Venue _____
Insurance _____	Workers' compensation _____
Juvenile _____	Other (specify): _____
Landlord/Tenant _____	

VIII. Supersedeas Bond   None   Will file   Was filed on:

(TRAP 32.1(1)):

IX. Extraordinary Relief: Will you request extraordinary relief (e.g., temporary or ancillary relief) from this Court? Yes ☐ No ☐
If yes, briefly state the basis for your request.

[continued]

A sample docketing statement (continued).

Docketing Statements (Civil)

X. Alternative Dispute Resolution/Mediation (if applicable) (As of 8/19/97, these programs exist in the 1st (Houston), 3rd (Austin), 4th (San Antonio), 5th (Dallas), 9th (Beaumont), 13th (Corpus Christi), and 14th (Houston)). (Use additional sheets, if necessary)

1. Should this appeal be referred to mediation? If not, why not.

2. Has the case been through an ADR procedure in the trial court?

If yes, answer the following:

a. Who was the mediator?

b. What type of ADR procedure?

c. At what stage did the case go through ADR? (Specify pre-trial, trial, post-trial, other)

d. Rate the case for complexity. Use 1 for the least complex and 5 for the most complex. Circle one.
   1 2 3 4 5

e. Can the parties agree on an appellate mediator? If yes, give name, address, and telephone and telecopy numbers (with area codes).

f. Languages other than English in which the mediator should be proficient:

3. Give a brief description of the issues to be raised on appeal, the relief sought, and the applicable standard of review, **if known** (without prejudice to the right to raise additional issues or request additional relief; use a separate attachment, if necessary).

[continued]

A sample docketing statement (continued).

Docketing Statements (Civil)

XI. Related Matters: List any pending or past related **appeals or original proceedings** (e.g., mandamus, injunction, habeas corpus) before this or any other Texas appellate court by court, docket number, and style.

XII. Any other information requested by the court (see attachments, if any).

XIII. Signature:

_____ Date:
Signature of counsel

(or pro se party) State Bar No.:_____

Printed Name: _____

XIV. Certificate of Service: The undersigned counsel certifies that this docketing statement has been served on the following lead counsel for all parties to the trial court's order or judgment as follows on _____, 19____.

_____
Signature

(TRAP 9.5(e) requirements stated below; use additional sheets, if necessary)

Note: Certificate of Service Requirements (TRAP 9.5(e)): A certificate of service must be signed by the person who made the service and must state:

(1) the date and manner of service;

(2) the name and address of each person served; and

(3) if the person served is a party's attorney, the name of the party represented by that attorney.

The differences between legal and political equality are also recognized in the organization of the UNITED NATIONS. Although the Charter of the United Nations expressly recognizes the sovereign equality of states, and the General Assembly formally operates according to that principle, the five permanent members of the Security Council retain express VETO power over several important aspects of U.N. functions, such as use of enforcement measures, admission to membership, amendments to the Charter, and election of the Secretary-General. Notwithstanding the fact that nations recognize limits on the principle of state equality in instances where political power is crucial, the principle of legal equality is basic to the operation of international law and a symbolic concept incorporated into the formal structure of most international institutions.

DOCUMENT

A written or printed instrument that conveys information.

The term *document* generally refers to a particular writing or instrument that has a bearing upon specific transactions. A deed, a marriage license, and a record of account are all considered to be documents.

When a document is signed and the signature is authentic, the law accurately expresses the state of mind of the individual who signed it. A *false document* is one of which a material portion is purported to have been made or authorized by someone who did not do so. It can also be a document that is falsely dated or which has allegedly been made by or on behalf of someone who did not in fact exist.

An ancient document is a writing presumed by the court to be genuine due to its antiquity, because it has been produced from a reliable source where it would be logically found, and because it has been carefully kept.

A *private document* is any instrument executed by a private citizen. A *public document* is one that is or should legally be readily available for inspection by the public, as a document issued by Congress or a governmental department.

Judicial documents include inquisitions, depositions, examinations, and affidavits.

CROSS-REFERENCES

Ancient Writing.

DOCUMENT OF TITLE

Any written instrument, such as a bill of lading, a warehouse receipt, or an order for the delivery of goods, that in the usual course of business or financing is considered sufficient proof that the person who possesses it is entitled to receive, hold, and dispose of the instrument and the goods that it covers.

A document of title is usually either issued or addressed by a bailee—an individual who has custody of the goods of another—to a bailor—the person who has entrusted the goods to him or her. Its terms must describe the goods covered by it so that they are identifiable as well as set forth the conditions of the contractual agreement. Possession of a document of title is symbolic of ownership of the goods that are described within it.

Documents of title are an integral part of the business world since they facilitate commercial transactions by serving as security for loans sought by their possessors and by promoting the free flow of goods without unduly burdening the channels of commerce.

A person who possesses a document of title can legally transfer ownership of the goods covered by it by delivering or endorsing it over to another without physically moving the goods. In such a situation, a document of title is a negotiable instrument because it transfers legal rights of ownership from one person to another merely by its delivery or endorsement. It is negotiable only if its terms state that the goods are to be delivered to the bearer, the holder of the document, to the order of the named party, or, where recognized in overseas trade, to a named person or his or her assigns. The UNIFORM COMMERCIAL CODE and various federal and state regulatory laws define the legal rights and obligations of the parties to a document of title.

DOCUMENTARY EVIDENCE

A type of written proof that is offered at a trial to establish the existence or nonexistence of a fact that is in dispute.

Letters, contracts, deeds, licenses, certificates, tickets, or other writings are documentary evidence.

❖ DOE, CHARLES

Charles Doe was a prominent nineteenth-century jurist, serving as chief justice of the New Hampshire Supreme Court from 1876 until his death in 1896. Doe has been regarded by legal historians as one of the greatest judges in U.S. history but he remains an obscure figure. He is best remembered for his procedural reforms, which sought to overcome burdensome COMMON LAW practices that filled the legal landscape with many pitfalls.

Doe was born in 1830 in Derry, New Hampshire. He came from a wealthy and prominent family, and thus it was not surprising that he would matriculate at Dartmouth College. After graduating in 1849 he studied law with a New Hampshire lawyer for several years. At this time in the United States most aspiring lawyers "read the law" as Doe did, apprenticing themselves until they were ready to take the state bar exam. Doe passed the New Hampshire bar exam in 1852 and began a private law practice in Dover. During the 1850s, he also served as the county solicitor and assistant clerk to the New Hampshire State Senate.

In 1859, at the age of 29, Doe was appointed an associate justice to the New Hampshire Supreme Judicial Court. At this point in the state's history the Supreme Judicial Court functioned as both a trial and appellate court. Doe spent much of his time riding circuit and hearing cases. Before the Civil War he left the DEMOCRATIC PARTY over the party's pro-slavery position and joined the REPUBLICAN PARTY. This action temporarily hurt his judicial career when the court was dissolved in 1874 by the Democratic state legislature. He spent two years in private practice before the 1876 state constitutional convention created a new Supreme Court and a Republican administration named him chief justice. He would serve for the next 20 years in this capacity.

Though personally eccentric (he dressed in the clothes of a farmer instead of judicial garb and insisted that the courtroom window be removed during frigid winter weather), Doe distinguished himself as a jurist. He was primarily concerned with simplifying and codifying court procedures and the RULES OF EVIDENCE. He did not develop a judicial philosophy but subscribed to New England Yankee "practicality." Doe ignored court precedents, which are the bedrock of the common law, to adopt simplified procedures. In addition, he was the first judge to abandon the common law rule that required a new criminal trial if any prejudicial error was found. Instead, Doe stated that a new trial should be limited to only the issues in which the error had occurred. In the realm of evidence rules, Doe dispensed with many exclusionary rules and placed as much information before the jury as possible. He did so out of respect for the wisdom of the jury.

Doe died in 1896 in Rollinsford, New Hampshire, having spent 35 years on the state's highest court.

FURTHER READINGS

"Doe of New Hampshire: Reflections on a Nineteenth Century Judge." 1950. *Harvard Law Review.*

DOING BUSINESS

A qualification imposed in state LONG-ARM STATUTES governing the SERVICE OF PROCESS, the method by which a lawsuit is commenced, which requires nonresident corporations to engage in commercial transactions within state borders in order to be subject to the PERSONAL JURISDICTION of state courts.

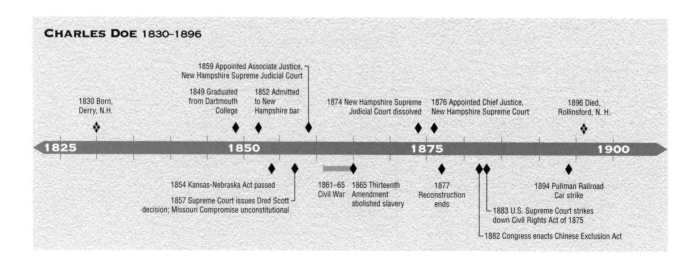

CHARLES DOE 1830–1896

1830 Born, Derry, N.H.

1849 Graduated from Dartmouth College

1852 Admitted to New Hampshire bar

1859 Appointed Associate Justice, New Hampshire Supreme Judicial Court

1874 New Hampshire Supreme Judicial Court dissolved

1876 Appointed Chief Justice, New Hampshire Supreme Court

1896 Died, Rollinsford, N. H.

1825   1850   1875   1900

1854 Kansas-Nebraska Act passed

1857 Supreme Court issues Dred Scott decision; Missouri Compromise unconstitutional

1861–65 Civil War

1865 Thirteenth Amendment abolished slavery

1877 Reconstruction ends

1894 Pullman Railroad Car strike

1883 U.S. Supreme Court strikes down Civil Rights Act of 1875

1882 Congress enacts Chinese Exclusion Act

The DUE PROCESS CLAUSE of the U.S. Constitution, and similar provisions found in state constitutions, guarantees the fair and orderly administration of justice by the courts by providing that any individual, including corporations, must receive notice of the charges against him or her or it and an opportunity to present a defense prior to the rendition of judgment. This clause has been interpreted by courts to require a state to have some tie or relationship to a defendant before its courts acquire the power to bind the individual personally. Employing this reasoning, state legislatures enacted statutory provisions requiring nonresident or foreign corporations to do or transact business within the state if they are to be amenable to the personal jurisdiction of its courts. Doing business is one kind of minimum contact that brings such a corporation within the jurisdiction of the court.

The nature and extent of business to be done within a state varies according to the jurisdiction. It must be an exercise of some of the functions for which the enterprise is incorporated and it must be of a sufficient nature to justify an inference that the corporation is present within the state. If so, the corporation is viewed as having received some benefit of the laws of the state and, therefore, should also be liable for its actions therein. In the past, there had to be a substantial tie to the state, such as the operation of an office or the presence of a resident employee. Today, courts consider this requirement fulfilled by a single commercial transaction, if the cause of action—facts providing a right to a judicial remedy—arises from it. If the CAUSE OF ACTION does not, however, a nonresident corporation is not amenable to service of process unless it has a substantial and regular relationship with the state comparable to the residency of an individual, such as having its corporate headquarters in the forum state. In cases involving subsidiary corporations, the intrastate business engaged in by a subsidiary is sufficient to make its parent corporation amenable to process in the state because the parent corporation is deemed to be doing business in the state.

The laws of each state must be consulted to determine whether a foreign corporation is doing business within a state to make it amenable to process therein.

The phrase *doing business* is sometimes used in the assessment of local taxes upon a nonresident corporation in jurisdictions other than the place of its incorporation in which it engages in business.

❖ DOLE, ROBERT JOSEPH

Robert Joseph "Bob" Dole overcame childhood poverty and a wartime injury that left him partially paralyzed to become one of the most powerful players in national politics. The Republican majority leader from Kansas often won praise from Republicans and Democrats alike for finding a middle course through difficult issues. His long career in national politics put him at the center of major legislative debates; and whether in budgetary, social, or foreign policy matters, he often bridged party differences. These battles made him not only a skilled negotiator but, by the 1990s, the most powerful leader in his party. His politics were generally characterized by economic conservatism, support for CIVIL RIGHTS, and moderation on social issues. In addition to being a vice presidential candidate in 1976, Dole mounted three presidential campaigns, in 1980, 1988, and 1996.

The values of Dole's working-class family informed his upbringing. He was born on July 22, 1923, in Russell, Kansas, the son of an egg and cream station owner, Doran Ray Dole, and a traveling sewing machine saleswoman, Bina Talbot Dole. An athletic young man, Dole excelled in football, basketball, and track. He worked at several jobs and wanted to be a doctor. At age 18, he enrolled in the pre-med program at the University of Kansas. Drafted two years later, in 1943, he found himself fighting in Italy. WORLD WAR II had almost ended in April 1945 when a shell hit him on the battlefield, smashing his neck, shoulder, and spine. Doctors thought he would be crippled. But Dole's persistence through three years of operations and therapy brought an amazing recovery. His only permanent disabilities are a lack of control of his right arm and hand, and partial loss of control of his left.

The 25-year-old survivor was transformed. With new earnestness, he finished his undergraduate studies at the University of Arizona and earned a law degree with honors from Washburn University of Topeka.

Law quickly led to politics. Dole served one term in the Kansas Legislature in 1951, and for the remainder of the decade worked as a prosecutor in his local county. He entered national politics in 1960 with election to the U.S. House of Representatives, where he won reelection

"THE GOVERNMENT CANNOT DIRECT THE PEOPLE, THE PEOPLE MUST DIRECT THE GOVERNMENT."
—BOB DOLE

Bob Dole.
LIBRARY OF CONGRESS

a vociferous supporter, and earned Dole the post of Republican National Committee (RNC) chairman in 1971.

The 1970s and 1980s brought Dole prominence in national politics. One reason for this was his marriage in 1975 to Elizabeth Hanford, an accomplished Harvard graduate who later held the posts of secretary of transportation and secretary of labor. Dole's chairmanship of the RNC also brought dividends. In 1976, President GERALD R. FORD chose Dole as his vice presidential running mate in an unsuccessful bid for reelection. The 1976 race whetted Dole's appetite for more, and he mounted his own campaign for president in 1980, losing out to RONALD REAGAN.

In 1984, Dole was elevated to Senate majority leader. Although his function in this role was to deliver party loyalty on votes in the Senate, he also became a strong supporter of President Reagan. During the IRAN-CONTRA scandal, Dole took a leading role in damage control. He made public reassurances and traveled the United States to rally support for the president.

Dole made another bid for president after Reagan's departure in 1988. This unsuccessful struggle for the Republican nomination against Vice President GEORGE H. W. BUSH revealed what many critics had long seen as a mixed blessing in Dole: his acerbic tongue. This had appeared as an issue as early as 1976, when, while campaigning as Gerald Ford's running mate, Dole had ridiculed Democratic candidate JIMMY CARTER as "Southern Fried McGovern." In 1988, again while campaigning, he lashed out at George H. W. Bush on national TV, saying

every two years through 1968. Dole advocated fiscal conservatism while supporting limited WELFARE spending. He voted against the GREAT SOCIETY programs of President LYNDON B. JOHNSON, but he supported aid to hungry and DISABLED PERSONS and to farmers. He strongly backed civil rights legislation, a position from which he never wavered throughout his career. His model in politics—and the figure who ultimately became his mentor—was RICHARD M. NIXON, a friend since the 1950s. Dole's election to the U.S. Senate in 1968 gave President Nixon

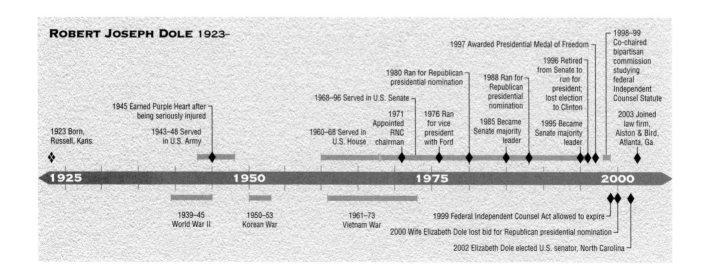

ROBERT JOSEPH DOLE 1923–

1923 Born, Russell, Kans.

1945 Earned Purple Heart after being seriously injured

1943–48 Served in U.S. Army

1960–68 Served in U.S. House

1968–96 Served in U.S. Senate

1971 Appointed RNC chairman

1976 Ran for vice president with Ford

1980 Ran for Republican presidential nomination

1985 Became Senate majority leader

1988 Ran for Republican presidential nomination

1995 Became Senate majority leader

1996 Retired from Senate to run for president; lost election to Clinton

1997 Awarded Presidential Medal of Freedom

1998–99 Co-chaired bipartisan commission studying federal Independent Counsel Statute

2003 Joined law firm, Alston & Bird, Atlanta, Ga.

1925   1950   1975   2000

1939–45 World War II

1950–53 Korean War

1961–73 Vietnam War

1999 Federal Independent Counsel Act allowed to expire

2000 Wife Elizabeth Dole lost bid for Republican presidential nomination

2002 Elizabeth Dole elected U.S. senator, North Carolina

Bush had lied about him. The attack on Bush raised some speculation about whether Dole could control his temper.

In 1996, Dole's third run for the White House was characterized by a rightward shift. Soon after declaring his candidacy, he attacked Hollywood for making movies that "revel in mindless violence and loveless sex." Dole called for making English the nation's official language, returned the campaign contribution of a gay Republican organization (later calling the move a mistake), and quit attending a United Methodist church that conservative critics had denounced as excessively liberal.

More crucially, perhaps, Dole's ideas on economics now resembled those that he had found untenable in President Reagan. The senator who had won bipartisan praise for a 1982 tax compromise now told voters, "We can cut taxes and balance the budget at the same time." And less apparent was his trademark willingness to compromise: throughout late 1995 and early 1996, Dole and House Majority Leader NEWT GINGRICH (R-Ga.) engaged in a budget deadlock with President BILL CLINTON that forced a shutdown of the federal government. He lost the 1996 election to Clinton.

Although he retired from elective politics in 1996, Dole remained active. In 1997, President Clinton awarded Dole the Presidential Medal of Freedom, the nation's highest civilian award. That same year, Dole was appointed chair of the International Commission on Missing Persons, an organization established to help find information on the fates of thousands of persons missing in the former Yugoslavia; and chair of the National World War II Memorial, the first

national memorial dedicated to those who served in World War II. He also helped establish the Robert J. Dole Institute of Politics at the University of Kansas. In 1998, he campaigned in 37 states for Republican candidates; in 2000, he was active in GEORGE W. BUSH's campaign for the presidency; and in 2002, he worked on the successful senatorial campaign of his wife Elizabeth.

After the September 11, 2001, attack on the World Trade Center, Dole joined with Clinton, his former political rival, as co-chair of a scholarship fund that raised money to provide education assistance to the families of persons killed or wounded in the terrorist attacks. In 2003, Dole began a series of appearances with Clinton on the CBS news show *Sixty Minutes*. The format of the segment, two-minute debates on highly topical subjects, was based on the show's highly popular *Point/Counterpoint* segments that aired in the 1970s. Noting that both his wife and President Clinton's wife were freshman senators, Dole quipped that they had permission to do the show, "We both cleared it with our wives so we won't get into trouble."

FURTHER READINGS

Bob Dole website. Available online at <www.bobdole.org> (accessed July 1, 2003).

Moraes, Lisa. 2003. "Clinton and Dole Agree to Disagree Weekly on 'Sixty Minutes'." *Washington Post* (March 6).

The Robert J. Dole Institute of Politics. Available online at <www.ku.edu/~dole> (accessed July 1, 2003).

❖ DOLE, SANFORD BALLARD

Sanford Ballard Dole was a prominent figure in the creation of Hawaii as a republic and its annexation to the United States. Dole was born

"THE UPRISING OF A SMALL PEOPLE MAY BE AS INSPIRING AS THE UPRISING OF A GREAT NATION."
—SANFORD B. DOLE

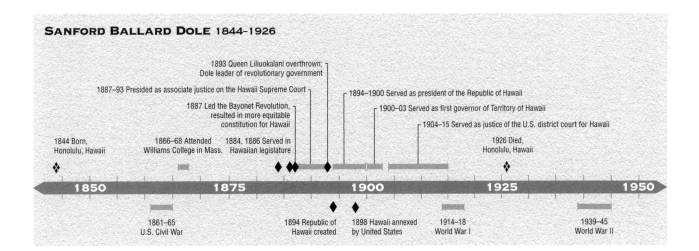

SANFORD BALLARD DOLE 1844–1926

1893 Queen Liliuokalani overthrown; Dole leader of revolutionary government

1887–93 Presided as associate justice on the Hawaii Supreme Court

1894–1900 Served as president of the Republic of Hawaii

1887 Led the Bayonet Revolution, resulted in more equitable constitution for Hawaii

1900–03 Served as first governor of Territory of Hawaii

1904–15 Served as justice of the U.S. district court for Hawaii

1844 Born, Honolulu, Hawaii

1866–68 Attended Williams College in Mass.

1884, 1886 Served in Hawaiian legislature

1926 Died, Honolulu, Hawaii

1850   1875   1900   1925   1950

1861–65 U.S. Civil War

1894 Republic of Hawaii created

1898 Hawaii annexed by United States

1914–18 World War I

1939–45 World War II

Sanford B. Dole.
LIBRARY OF CONGRESS

in 1844. His parents were American missionaries assigned to Hawaii, and Dole was raised and educated there. After attending Williams College and his admission to the Massachusetts bar in 1868, he settled in Hawaii and began his law practice.

In 1884 and 1886, he served in the Hawaiian legislature. His first act of dissension against the existing monarchy was as a leader of the Bayonet Revolution in 1887. As a result, the power of the monarchy was reduced and a more equitable constitution was adopted.

Also in 1887, Dole sat on the bench of the Hawaii Supreme Court as an associate justice.

In 1893, Queen Liliuokalani refused to recognize the limitations imposed upon her by the 1887 constitution. An insurrection occurred and the queen was overthrown. Dole left his post as justice to become the leader of the revolutionary provisional government that replaced the monarchy.

The republic of Hawaii was created in 1894, and Dole acted as its president. He began his efforts for the U.S. annexation of Hawaii, but his first attempts were thwarted by President GROVER CLEVELAND, who opposed the deposition of the monarchy. Dole wrote a treatise defending the revolution and its results but to no avail. He was finally able to achieve annexation under the administration of President WILLIAM MCKINLEY in 1898. Dole continued to serve as president throughout these years.

With the annexation of Hawaii completed, Dole became the first governor of the newly formed Territory of Hawaii. He performed these duties from 1900 to 1903.

In 1904, Dole returned to the judiciary and served as justice of the U.S. district court for Hawaii until 1915. He died in Hawaii in 1926.

DOMAIN

The complete and absolute ownership of land. Also the real estate so owned. The inherent sovereign power claimed by the legislature of a state, of controlling private property for public uses, is termed the right of *eminent domain.*

National domain is sometimes applied to the aggregate of the property owned directly by a nation. Public domain embraces all lands, the title to which is in the United States, including land occupied for the purposes of federal buildings, arsenals, dock-yards, and so on, and land of an agricultural or mineral character not yet granted to private owners.

Sphere of influence. Range of control or rule; realm.

DOMBEC

[Saxon, Judgment book.] The name given by the Saxons to the code of laws by which they lived.

Several Saxon kings published dombecs, also spelled dombocs. Dombecs were also known as dome-books or doom-books. The dombec compiled during the ninth-century reign of Alfred the Great was among the most important because it contained the law for the entire kingdom of England, encompassing the principal maxims of COMMON LAW, the penalties for crimes, and the forms of judicial proceedings.

A dombec is not the same as the Domesday Book, although the two are often confused.

DOMESDAY BOOK

An ancient record of land ownership in England.

Commissioned by William the Conqueror in the year 1085 and finished in 1086, the book is a superb example of thorough and speedy administration, unequaled by any other project undertaken during the Middle Ages. Minute and accurate surveys of all of England were done for the purpose of compiling information essential for levying taxes and enforcing the land tenure system.

The work was done by five justices in each county who took a census and listed all the feudal landowners, their PERSONAL PROPERTY, and other information. The judges gathered their information by summoning each man and having him give testimony under oath. This is perhaps the earliest use of the inquest procedure in England, and it established the right of the king to require citizens to give information, a foundation of the jury trial.

Domesday was a Saxon word meaning Judgment Day, at the end of time when God will pronounce judgment against all of mankind. The name given to this record may have come from the popular opinion that the inquiry was as thorough as that promised for Judgment Day.

Two volumes of the Domesday Book are still in existence, and they continue to be valuable for historical information about social and economic conditions. They are kept in the Public Record Office in England.

DOMESTIC

Pertaining to the house or home. A person employed by a household to perform various servient duties. Any household servant, such as a maid or butler. Relating to a place of birth, origin, or domicile.

That which is domestic is related to household uses. A *domestic animal* is one that is sufficiently tame to live with a family, such as a dog or cat, or one that can be used to contribute to a family's support, such as a cow, chicken, or horse. When something is *domesticated,* it is converted to domestic use, as in the case of a wild animal that is tamed.

Domestic relations are relationships between various family members, such as a HUSBAND AND WIFE, that are regulated by FAMILY LAW.

A domestic corporation of a particular state is one that has been organized and chartered in that state as opposed to a foreign corporation, which has been incorporated in another state or territory. In tax law, a domestic corporation is one that has originated in any U.S. state or territory.

Domestic products are goods that are manufactured within a particular territory rather than imported from outside that territory.

DOMESTIC PARTNERSHIP LAW

The area of law that deals with the rights of unmarried adults who choose to live together in the same manner as a married couple but who are not married.

Domestic partnership law is evolving rapidly, in part because more individuals are choosing to identify themselves as domestic partners. Although any two adults living together in a loving relationship may be called partners, the term is most frequently used to describe same-sex couples.

In the last decade of the twentieth century and continuing into the twenty-first, a number of city and county governments enacted domestic partnership laws, including Seattle, New York City, and Broward County, Florida. In 1999, California passed a state domestic partnership law that provided a number of protections that formerly had been offered only to married couples. These protections include the right to inherit from a partner's estate; the right to make medical decisions for an incapacitated partner; the right to use sick leave to care for a partner; the right to obtain HEALTH INSURANCE through a partner; and the right to adopt a partner's child as a stepparent. Domestic partners in California may obtain these benefits by registering with the state.

Although domestic partnership law is intended to provide benefits to partners, it still represents uncharted territory and is far from comprehensive or complete. Using the California law as an example, a domestic partner is defined as a committed member of a same-sex couple; heterosexual couples who cohabit may not register as domestic partners. The rationale is that heterosexual couples in a committed relationship have the option of marriage, an option that is not open to same-sex couples. The only exception for heterosexual couples is when one partner is age 62 or older, because frequently SENIOR CITIZENS who cohabit run the risk of losing part of their SOCIAL SECURITY benefits if they marry.

A more problematic issue for domestic partners is the fact that their partnership is generally not recognized outside of their jurisdiction. Thus, their domestic partnership rights are not binding if they should move to a community that has no such laws of its own. In fact, domestic partners who relocate to a new community that does have protective laws are advised to re-register in their new home in order to eliminate any AMBIGUITY.

CROSS-REFERENCES

Adoption; Gay and Lesbian Rights; Family Law.

DOMESTIC VIOLENCE

Any abusive, violent, coercive, forceful, or threatening act or word inflicted by one member of a family or household on another can constitute domestic violence.

Domestic violence, once considered one of the most underreported crimes, became more widely recognized during the 1980s and 1990s.

Various individuals and groups have defined domestic violence to include everything from saying unkind or demeaning words, to grabbing a person's arm, to hitting, kicking, choking, or even murdering. Domestic violence most often refers to violence between married or cohabiting couples, although it sometimes refers to violence against other members of a household, such as children or elderly relatives. It occurs in every racial, socioeconomic, ethnic, and religious group, although conditions such as poverty, drug or alcohol abuse, and mental illness increase its likelihood. Studies indicate that the incidence of domestic violence among homosexual couples is approximately equivalent to that found among heterosexual couples.

Domestic violence involving married or cohabiting couples received vast media attention during the 1990s. The highly publicized 1995 trial of former professional football player and movie actor O.J. (Orenthal James) Simpson for the murders of his ex-wife Nicole Brown Simpson and her friend Ronald Lyle Goldman thrust it onto the front pages of newspapers for many months. Simpson was acquitted of the murder charges, but evidence produced at his trial showed that he had been arrested in 1989 for spousal BATTERY and that he had threatened to kill his ex-wife. The disclosure that a prominent sports figure and movie star had abused his wife prompted a national discussion on the causes of domestic violence, its prevalence, and effective means of eliminating it.

Despite the attention that domestic violence issues have received, publicized instances of domestic violence continue to occur. Like the case of O.J. SIMPSON, several of these cases involved current or former athletes. Jim Brown, who, like Simpson, was both a famous football player and actor, received a six-month sentence in 2000 for vandalizing his wife's car during an argument. Also like Simpson, Brown had a history of alleged domestic-violence incidents, though he had not been convicted in the previous allegations.

Although thousands of cases involving domestic violence occur each year, those that involve celebrities continue to attract the most attention. In 1999, movie director John Singleton pled no-contest to charges of battering his girlfriend. Singleton is best known for such movies as *Boyz 'n the Hood* and *Poetic Justice*. In 2001, Rae Carruth, a player for the National Football League's Carolina Panthers, was found guilty of conspiracy to commit the murder of his former girlfriend, who had been carrying Carruth's child at the time of her death. Although he avoided the death penalty, Carruth was sentenced to up to 25 years in prison. Also in 2001, former heavyweight boxing champion Riddick Bowe was charged with third-degree assault for a fight with his wife.

Those who have studied domestic violence believe that it usually occurs in a cycle with three general stages. First, the abuser uses words or threats, perhaps humiliation or ridicule. Next, the abuser explodes at some perceived infraction by the other person, and the abuser's rage is manifested in physical violence. Finally, the abuser "cools off," asks forgiveness, and promises that the violence will never occur again. At that point, the victim often abandons any attempt to leave the situation or to have charges brought against the abuser, although some prosecutors will go forward with charges even if the victim is unwilling to do so. Typically, the abuser's rage begins to build again after the reconciliation, and the violent cycle is repeated.

In some cases of repeated domestic violence, the victim eventually strikes back and harms or kills the abuser. People who are repeatedly victimized by spouses or other partners often suffer from low self-esteem, feelings of shame and guilt, and a sense that they are trapped in a situation from which there is no escape. Some who feel that they have no outside protection from their batterer may turn to self-protection. During the 1980s, in a number of cases in which a victim of repeated domestic abuse struck back, the battered spouse defense was used to exonerate the victim. However, in order to rely on the battered-spouse defense, victims must prove that they genuinely and reasonably believed that they were in immediate danger of death or great bodily injury and that they used only such force as they believed was reasonably necessary to protect themselves. Because this is a very difficult standard to meet, it is estimated that fewer than one-third of victims who invoke the battered-spouse defense are acquitted.

Heightened awareness and an increase in reports of domestic violence has led to a widespread legal response since the 1980s. Once thought to be a problem that was best handled without legal intervention, domestic violence is now treated as a criminal offense. Many states and municipalities have instituted measures designed to deal swiftly and harshly with domestic abusers. In addition, governments have attempted to protect the victims of domestic violence from further danger and have launched programs designed to address the root causes of this abuse. One example is Alexandria, Virginia, which, in 1994, began prosecuting repeat abusers under a Virginia law (Va. St. § 18.2–57.2 Code 1950, § 18.2–57.2) that makes the third conviction for ASSAULT AND BATTERY a felony punishable by up to five years in prison. In addition, the city established a shelter for battered women, a victims' task force, and a domestic-violence intervention program that includes a mandatory arrest policy and court-ordered counseling. As a result, domestic homicides in Alexandria declined from 40 percent of all homicides in 1987, to 16 percent of those between 1988 and 1994. Other states have adopted similar measures. States that already had specific laws directed toward domestic violence toughened the penalties during the 1990s. For example, a 1995 amendment to California's domestic-abuse law (West's Ann. Cal. Penal Code §§ 14140–14143) revoked a provision that allowed first-time abusers to have their criminal record expunged if they attended counseling.

Public outrage over domestic violence also led to the inclusion of the VIOLENCE AGAINST WOMEN ACT as title IV of the VIOLENT CRIME CONTROL AND LAW ENFORCEMENT ACT OF 1994 (Pub. L. No. 103-322, 108 Stat. 1796 [codified as amended in scattered sections of 18 and 42 U.S.C.A.]). The act authorized research and education programs for judges and judicial staff to enhance knowledge and awareness of domestic violence and sexual assault. It also provided funding for police training and for shelters, increased penalties for domestic violence and rape, and provided for enhanced privacy protection for victims, although the U.S. Supreme Court struck it down as unconstitutional in 2000.

One of the more controversial portions of the original act made gender-motivated crimes a

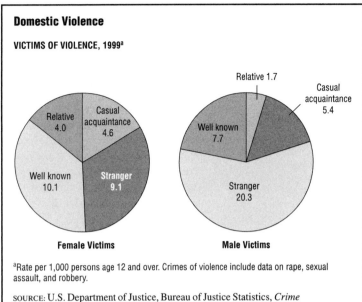

Domestic Violence

VICTIMS OF VIOLENCE, 1999[a]

Female Victims

Relative 4.0
Casual acquaintance 4.6
Well known 10.1
Stranger 9.1

Male Victims

Relative 1.7
Casual acquaintance 5.4
Well known 7.7
Stranger 20.3

[a]Rate per 1,000 persons age 12 and over. Crimes of violence include data on rape, sexual assault, and robbery.

SOURCE: U.S. Department of Justice, Bureau of Justice Statistics, *Crime Victimization in the United States*, 1999.

violation of federal CIVIL RIGHTS law. In 2000, the U.S. Supreme Court considered the application of this portion in *United States v. Morrison*, 529 U.S. 598, 120 S. Ct. 1740, 146 L. Ed. 2d 658 (2000). In that case, a woman brought suit against a group of University of Virginia students who allegedly had raped her. Although the district court found that the woman had stated a claim against the respondents, it held that Congress did not have authority to enact the provision under the COMMERCE CLAUSE or § 5 of the FOURTEENTH AMENDMENT to the U.S. Constitution. The U.S. Court of Appeals for the Fourth Circuit affirmed the decision, and the United States, which had intervened to defend the statute, appealed to the U.S. Supreme Court. The Court, per an opinion by Chief Justice WILLIAM H. REHNQUIST, agreed with the lower courts, holding the Congress had exceeded its constitutional power. The result of the case is that the civil-remedy provisions in the original statute should fall under the purview of the states, rather than the federal government.

Studies on the incidence of domestic violence vary a great deal. Research conducted by Murray A. Straus of the University of New Hampshire and Richard J. Gelles of the University of Rhode Island, both veterans of extensive research into family violence, found that approximately four million people each year are victims of some form of domestic assault, ranging from minor threats and thrown objects to severe beatings. This number represents women and men who report suffering attacks by partners. In a 1995 survey conducted by Dr. Jeanne McCauley of Johns Hopkins University School of Medicine, one in three women responding to a confidential questionnaire indicated that she had been physically or sexually attacked, and half of these incidents had occurred before the age of 18. The National Coalition against Domestic Violence reported in 1993 that 50 percent of all married women will experience some form of violence from their spouse, and that more than one-third are battered repeatedly each year.

The JUSTICE DEPARTMENT suggests that incidents of rape and assault against women at the hands of intimates dropped between 1993 and 2001. According to these statistics, 588,490 women were victims of rape and assault by intimates in 2001, down from 1.1 million in 1993. The same report noted that men were victims of 103,220 violent crimes by intimate partners, down from about 160,000 in 1993. Statistics regarding domestic violence against men have been in dispute for several years. Straus and Gelles reported that men were as likely to endure domestic assault as women, but that women were far more likely to be injured. Domestic-violence activists dispute the notion that men suffer domestic assault at approximately the same rate as women, and other statistical reports, including those issued by the DEPARTMENT OF JUSTICE, tend to support these claims.

FURTHER READINGS

Douglas, Heather, and Lee Godden. 2003. "The Decriminalisation of Domestic Violence: Examining the Interaction between the Criminal Law and Domestic Violence." *Criminal Law Journal* 27 (February): 32-43.

Rohr, Janelle, ed. 1990. *Violence in America: Opposing Viewpoints.* San Diego: Greenhaven Press.

Sommers, Christina Hoff. 1994. *Who Stole Feminism?* New York: Simon & Schuster.

Straus, Murray, and Richard Gelles. 1988. *Intimate Violence.* New York: Simon & Schuster.

CROSS-REFERENCES

Child Abuse; Family Law.

DOMICILIARY ADMINISTRATION

The settlement and distribution of a decedent's estate in the state of his or her permanent residence, the place to which the decedent intended to return even though he or she might actually have resided elsewhere.

Domiciliary administration is deemed principal or primary administration and is distinguishable from ancillary administration, which is the management of a decedent's property in the state where it is situated, which is other than the state in which the decedent permanently resided.

DOMINANT

Prevalent; paramount in force or effect; of primary importance or consideration. That which is dominant possesses rights that prevail over those of others.

In PROPERTY LAW, the estate to which an EASEMENT, or right of use, is given is called the *dominant tenement* or *estate,* and the one upon which the easement is imposed is called the *servient tenement* or *estate.*

DOMINANT CAUSE

The essential or most direct source of an accident or injury, regardless of when it occurred.

In TORT LAW, the dominant cause of an injury is the proximate cause, or the primary or moving cause, without which the injury would not have occurred.

DOMINION

Perfect control in right of ownership. The word implies both title and possession and appears to require a complete retention of control over disposition. Title to an article of property, which arises from the power of disposition and the right of claiming it. Sovereignty; as in the dominion of the seas or over a territory.

In CIVIL LAW, *with reference to the title to property that is transferred by a sale of it, dominion is said to be either* proximate *or* remote, *the former being the kind of title vesting in the purchaser when he or she has acquired both the ownership and the possession of the article, the latter describing the nature of the title when he or she has legitimately acquired the ownership of the property but there has been no delivery.*

DONATIVE

Relating to the gratuitous transfer of something as in the nature of a gift.

A *donative* trust is the conveyance of property in trust set up as a gift from one person to another.

Donative intent is the intent to give something as a gift.

DONEE

The recipient of a gift. An individual to whom a power of appointment is conveyed.

DONOR

The party conferring a power. One who makes a gift. One who creates a trust.

DOOM

An archaic term for a court's judgment. For example, some criminal sentences still end with the phrase "... which is pronounced for doom."

DORMANT

Latent; inactive; silent. That which is dormant is not used, asserted, or enforced.

A *dormant* partner is a member of a partnership who has a financial interest yet is silent, in that he or she takes no control over the business. The partner's identity is secret because the individual is unknown to the public.

◆ DORR, THOMAS WILSON

Known for his central role in Rhode Island's 1842 Dorr's Rebellion, Thomas Wilson Dorr fought for changes in the voting laws of his native state. Until the tumultuous 1842 election of Dorr as governor, long-standing laws, based on the state's initial charter from England, had limited VOTING RIGHTS to men who owned at least $134 in land. Dorr helped to initiate a new state constitution that granted more liberal voting rights to white males. Once he was governor, some of Rhode Island's other authorities treated him as a traitor to the aristocracy. However,

Dorr's extension of voting rights to a larger section of the populace stands as a cornerstone in the democratization of the United States.

The changes in voting rights that Dorr proposed flew in the face of Rhode Island's staunch political conservatism. Although the example of newer, noncolonial states had changed the way in which some older, seaboard states practiced government, Rhode Island adhered to the charter it had received from the English monarchy in 1663. This document's property requirement for voting excluded more than half of the white males in the state. By 1840 even though only one other state retained a possession-of-property requirement, Rhode Island's leaders claimed that their constitution served as a standard of law and order. The Rhode Island charter, they said, had spared the state from one unwelcome effect of industrialization: political turmoil. Changes in government, however, were inevitable, even in Rhode Island. An increase in industry led to an increase in crime, unemployment, and poverty. Such changes brought a demand for a populist voice in the workings of government.

During this time of change, Dorr emerged as a legal spokesman. Born November 5, 1805, the son of a wealthy Providence merchant, Dorr graduated from Harvard in 1823. He then pursued legal studies, and was admitted to the Rhode Island bar in 1827. In 1834 he participated in the Rhode Island legislature, where he led a campaign to secure extended voting rights. When the movement gained momentum, the Rhode Island Suffrage Association was founded, which Dorr headed in 1840. As support for Dorr grew, he formed the People's party. In 1841 the party organized a convention and drafted a

> "THE SERVANTS OF A RIGHTEOUS CAUSE MAY FAIL OR FALL IN THE DEFENSE OF IT. BUT ALL THE TRUTH THAT IT CONTAINS IS INDESTRUCTIBLE."
> —THOMAS DORR

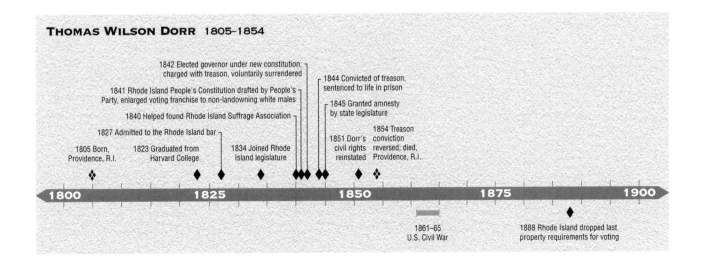

THOMAS WILSON DORR 1805–1854

1842 Elected governor under new constitution; charged with treason, voluntarily surrendered

1841 Rhode Island People's Constitution drafted by People's Party, enlarged voting franchise to non-landowning white males

1840 Helped found Rhode Island Suffrage Association

1827 Admitted to the Rhode Island bar

1805 Born, Providence, R.I.

1823 Graduated from Harvard College

1834 Joined Rhode Island legislature

1844 Convicted of treason, sentenced to life in prison

1845 Granted amnesty by state legislature

1851 Dorr's civil rights reinstated

1854 Treason conviction reversed; died, Providence, R.I.

1800   1825   1850   1875   1900

1861–65 U.S. Civil War

1888 Rhode Island dropped last property requirements for voting

more liberal state constitution, the People's Constitution. It appealed to voteless urban workers by issuing the vote to all white adult males.

To counteract Dorr's movement, the Rhode Island state legislature called for a convention in Newport in November 1841. Conservatives saw this as their chance to derail the newly drafted constitution. Many others, however, supported Dorr's constitution, and two rival positions emerged. In 1842 Dorr's supporters elected him governor of the state. For a while, Rhode Island had to juggle two state governments. Samuel H. King, representing opponents of Dorr's efforts, also served as governor, under the guides of the old charter. Both sides wooed the federal government for recognition. President JOHN TYLER wrote to King and warned him that any attempt to overthrow Dorr's government would result in the presence of federal troops in Rhode Island.

Dorr sought to establish an entirely new state government in Providence. King declared that Dorr's party had initiated an insurrection. The sides of the dual government clashed, and, under King's authority, many of Dorr's supporters were imprisoned. On May 17, 1842, Dorr countered King's efforts to crush the People's "treason" and attacked the Providence arsenal. But the state militia held back the attack, and Dorr subsequently fled the state. King declared MARTIAL LAW and offered a reward for Dorr's capture.

A compromise came about when the state drafted a new constitution that extended voting rights. When the state adopted the new constitution, Dorr surrendered to authorities. Convicted of TREASON in 1844, Dorr faced a life sentence of solitary confinement and hard labor. Protests followed the severe sentence. One year later, the state legislature granted him AMNESTY and Dorr was set free.

Meanwhile, a suit arose from the competing state governments (*Luther v. Borden,* 48 U.S. (7 How.) 1, 12 L. Ed. 581 [1849]). In response to one of the "political questions" in the case, the Supreme Court declared that Congress, under Article IV, Section 4, of the Constitution, held the power to ensure a republican state government while simultaneously recognizing the lawful government of that state. The court ruled that the president had the authority to support a lawful state government with federal troops if an armed conflict occurred. The federal courts could not disturb these rights of Congress and the president. As President Tyler had not taken the opportunity to act on his power, the Court was left with much to decide regarding the balance between Rhode Island's new constitution and the federal executive and legislative powers.

The reform movement set forth by Dorr, later known as Dorrism, had helped to solidify a greater trend in U.S. government. As more and more people were granted the right to vote, the United States strayed further and further from the original English monarchical rule. Although the rebellion of Dorr and his followers consisted of only a few skirmishes, its influence extended through a long period of time. For conservatives, Dorrism represented bloody class conflict. For many others, Dorr appeared to be less a traitor than a representative for the common person. In 1851, Dorr's CIVIL RIGHTS were reinstated, and in 1854, the verdict against him was reversed. Later that year, on December 27, Dorr died in Providence, in his native Rhode Island.

A.	Atlantic Reporter	ACT	American College Test
A. 2d	Atlantic Reporter, Second Series	Act'g Legal Adv.	Acting Legal Advisor
AA	Alcoholics Anonymous	ACUS	Administrative Conference of the United States
AAA	American Arbitration Association; Agricultural Adjustment Act of 1933	ACYF	Administration on Children, Youth, and Families
AALS	Association of American Law Schools	A.D. 2d	Appellate Division, Second Series, N.Y.
AAPRP	All African People's Revolutionary Party	ADA	Americans with Disabilities Act of 1990
AARP	American Association of Retired Persons	ADAMHA	Alcohol, Drug Abuse, and Mental Health Administration
AAS	American Anti-Slavery Society	ADC	Aid to Dependent Children
ABA	American Bar Association; Architectural Barriers Act of 1968; American Bankers Association	ADD	Administration on Developmental Disabilities
		ADEA	Age Discrimination in Employment Act of 1967
ABC	American Broadcasting Companies, Inc. (formerly American Broadcasting Corporation)	ADL	Anti-Defamation League
		ADR	Alternative dispute resolution
		AEC	Atomic Energy Commission
ABM	Antiballistic missile	AECB	Arms Export Control Board
ABM Treaty	Anti-Ballistic Missile Treaty of 1972	AEDPA	Antiterrorism and Effective Death Penalty Act
ABVP	Anti-Biased Violence Project	A.E.R.	All England Law Reports
A/C	Account	AFA	American Family Association; Alabama Freethought Association
A.C.	Appeal cases		
ACAA	Air Carrier Access Act		
ACCA	Armed Career Criminal Act of 1984	AFB	American Farm Bureau
		AFBF	American Farm Bureau Federation
ACF	Administration for Children and Families	AFDC	Aid to Families with Dependent Children
ACLU	American Civil Liberties Union	aff'd per cur.	Affirmed by the court
ACRS	Accelerated Cost Recovery System	AFIS	Automated fingerprint identification system
ACS	Agricultural Cooperative Service	AFL	American Federation of Labor

AFL-CIO	American Federation of Labor and Congress of Industrial Organizations	ANA	Administration for Native Americans
AFRes	Air Force Reserve	Ann. Dig.	Annual Digest of Public International Law Cases
AFSC	American Friends Service Committee	ANPA	American Newspaper Publishers Association
AFSCME	American Federation of State, County, and Municipal Employees	ANSCA	Alaska Native Claims Act
		ANZUS	Australia-New Zealand-United States Security Treaty Organization
AGRICOLA	Agricultural Online Access		
AIA	Association of Insurance Attorneys	AOA	Administration on Aging
		AOE	Arizonans for Official English
AIB	American Institute for Banking	AOL	America Online
AID	Artificial insemination using a third-party donor's sperm; Agency for International Development	AP	Associated Press
		APA	Administrative Procedure Act of 1946
		APHIS	Animal and Plant Health Inspection Service
AIDS	Acquired immune deficiency syndrome	App. Div.	Appellate Division Reports, N.Y. Supreme Court
AIH	Artificial insemination using the husband's sperm	Arb. Trib., U.S.-British	Arbitration Tribunal, Claim Convention of 1853, United States and Great Britain Convention of 1853
AIM	American Indian Movement		
AIPAC	American Israel Public Affairs Committee		
		Ardcor	American Roller Die Corporation
AIUSA	Amnesty International, U.S.A. Affiliate	ARPA	Advanced Research Projects Agency
AJS	American Judicature Society		
ALA	American Library Association	ARPANET	Advanced Research Projects Agency Network
Alcoa	Aluminum Company of America	ARS	Advanced Record System
		Art.	Article
ALEC	American Legislative Exchange Council	ARU	American Railway Union
		ASCME	American Federation of State, County, and Municipal Employees
ALF	Animal Liberation Front		
ALI	American Law Institute		
ALJ	Administrative law judge	ASCS	Agriculture Stabilization and Conservation Service
All E.R.	All England Law Reports		
ALO	Agency Liaison	ASM	Available Seatmile
A.L.R.	American Law Reports	ASPCA	American Society for the Prevention of Cruelty to Animals
ALY	*American Law Yearbook*		
AMA	American Medical Association		
		Asst. Att. Gen.	Assistant Attorney General
AMAA	Agricultural Marketing Agreement Act	AT&T	American Telephone and Telegraph
Am. Dec.	American Decisions	ATFD	Alcohol, Tobacco and Firearms Division
amdt.	Amendment		
Amer. St. Papers, For. Rels.	American State Papers, Legislative and Executive Documents of the Congress of the U.S., Class I, Foreign Relations, 1832–1859	ATLA	Association of Trial Lawyers of America
		ATO	Alpha Tau Omega
		ATTD	Alcohol and Tobacco Tax Division
		ATU	Alcohol Tax Unit
AMS	Agricultural Marketing Service	AUAM	American Union against Militarism
AMVETS	American Veterans (of World War II)	AUM	Animal Unit Month
		AZT	Azidothymidine

BAC	Blood alcohol concentration	CAA	Clean Air Act
BALSA	Black-American Law Student Association	CAB	Civil Aeronautics Board; Corporation for American Banking
BATF	Bureau of Alcohol, Tobacco and Firearms	CAFE	Corporate average fuel economy
BBS	Bulletin Board System	Cal. 2d	California Reports, Second Series
BCCI	Bank of Credit and Commerce International	Cal. 3d	California Reports, Third Series
BEA	Bureau of Economic Analysis	CALR	Computer-assisted legal research
Bell's Cr. C.	Bell's English Crown Cases		
Bevans	United States Treaties, etc. *Treaties and Other International Agreements of the United States of America, 1776–1949* (compiled under the direction of Charles I. Bevans, 1968–76)	Cal. Rptr.	California Reporter
		CAP	Common Agricultural Policy
		CARA	Classification and Ratings Administration
		CATV	Community antenna television
BFOQ	Bona fide occupational qualification	CBO	Congressional Budget Office
		CBS	Columbia Broadcasting System
BI	Bureau of Investigation		
BIA	Bureau of Indian Affairs; Board of Immigration Appeals	CBOEC	Chicago Board of Election Commissioners
		CCC	Commodity Credit Corporation
BID	Business improvement district	CCDBG	Child Care and Development Block Grant of 1990
BJS	Bureau of Justice Statistics	C.C.D. Pa.	Circuit Court Decisions, Pennsylvania
Black.	Black's United States Supreme Court Reports	C.C.D. Va.	Circuit Court Decisions, Virginia
Blatchf.	Blatchford's United States Circuit Court Reports		
BLM	Bureau of Land Management	CCEA	Cabinet Council on Economic Affairs
BLS	Bureau of Labor Statistics	CCP	Chinese Communist Party
BMD	Ballistic missile defense	CCR	Center for Constitutional Rights
BNA	Bureau of National Affairs		
BOCA	Building Officials and Code Administrators International	C.C.R.I.	Circuit Court, Rhode Island
		CD	Certificate of deposit; compact disc
BOP	Bureau of Prisons	CDA	Communications Decency Act
BPP	Black Panther Party for Self-defense		
		CDBG	Community Development Block Grant Program
Brit. and For.	British and Foreign State Papers	CDC	Centers for Disease Control and Prevention; Community Development Corporation
BSA	Boy Scouts of America		
BTP	Beta Theta Pi		
Burr.	James Burrows, *Report of Cases Argued and Determined in the Court of King's Bench during the Time of Lord Mansfield* (1766–1780)	CDF	Children's Defense Fund
		CDL	Citizens for Decency through Law
		CD-ROM	Compact disc read-only memory
BVA	Board of Veterans Appeals	CDS	Community Dispute Services
c.	Chapter	CDW	Collision damage waiver
C³I	Command, Control, Communications, and Intelligence	CENTO	Central Treaty Organization
		CEO	Chief executive officer
		CEQ	Council on Environmental Quality
C.A.	Court of Appeals		

CERCLA	Comprehensive Environmental Response, Compensation, and Liability Act of 1980	CLASP	Center for Law and Social Policy
cert.	*Certiorari*	CLE	Center for Law and Education; Continuing Legal Education
CETA	Comprehensive Employment and Training Act	CLEO	Council on Legal Education Opportunity; Chief Law Enforcement Officer
C & F	Cost and freight		
CFC	Chlorofluorocarbon	CLP	Communist Labor Party of America
CFE Treaty	Conventional Forces in Europe Treaty of 1990	CLS	Christian Legal Society; critical legal studies (movement); Critical Legal Studies (membership organization)
C.F. & I.	Cost, freight, and insurance		
C.F.R	Code of Federal Regulations		
CFNP	Community Food and Nutrition Program		
CFTA	Canadian Free Trade Agreement		
CFTC	Commodity Futures Trading Commission	C.M.A.	Court of Military Appeals
		CMEA	Council for Mutual Economic Assistance
Ch.	Chancery Division, English Law Reports	CMHS	Center for Mental Health Services
CHAMPVA	Civilian Health and Medical Program at the Veterans Administration	C.M.R.	Court of Military Review
		CNN	Cable News Network
		CNO	Chief of Naval Operations
CHEP	Cuban/Haitian Entrant Program	CNOL	Consolidated net operating loss
CHINS	Children in need of supervision	CNR	Chicago and Northwestern Railway
CHIPS	Child in need of protective services	CO	Conscientious Objector
		C.O.D.	Cash on delivery
Ch.N.Y.	Chancery Reports, New York	COGP	Commission on Government Procurement
Chr. Rob.	Christopher Robinson, *Reports of Cases Argued and Determined in the High Court of Admiralty* (1801–1808)	COINTELPRO	Counterintelligence Program
		Coke Rep.	Coke's English King's Bench Reports
		COLA	Cost-of-living adjustment
CIA	Central Intelligence Agency	COMCEN	Federal Communications Center
CID	Commercial Item Descriptions		
C.I.F.	Cost, insurance, and freight	Comp.	Compilation
CINCNORAD	Commander in Chief, North American Air Defense Command	Conn.	Connecticut Reports
		CONTU	National Commission on New Technological Uses of Copyrighted Works
C.I.O.	Congress of Industrial Organizations		
		Conv.	Convention
CIPE	Center for International Private Enterprise	COPA	Child Online Protection Act (1998)
C.J.	Chief justice	COPS	Community Oriented Policing Services
CJIS	Criminal Justice Information Services	Corbin	Arthur L. Corbin, *Corbin on Contracts: A Comprehensive Treatise on the Rules of Contract Law* (1950)
C.J.S.	Corpus Juris Secundum		
Claims Arb. under Spec. Conv., Nielsen's Rept.	Frederick Kenelm Nielsen, *American and British Claims Arbitration under the Special Agreement Concluded between the United States and Great Britain, August 18, 1910* (1926)		
		CORE	Congress on Racial Equality
		Cox's Crim. Cases	Cox's Criminal Cases (England)
		COYOTE	Call Off Your Old Tired Ethics

CPA	Certified public accountant	DACORB	Department of the Army Conscientious Objector Review Board
CPB	Corporation for Public Broadcasting, the		
CPI	Consumer Price Index	Dall.	Dallas's Pennsylvania and United States Reports
CPPA	Child Pornography Prevention Act	DAR	Daughters of the American Revolution
CPSC	Consumer Product Safety Commission	DARPA	Defense Advanced Research Projects Agency
Cranch	Cranch's United States Supreme Court Reports	DAVA	Defense Audiovisual Agency
CRF	Constitutional Rights Foundation	D.C.	United States District Court; District of Columbia
CRR	Center for Constitutional Rights	D.C. Del.	United States District Court, Delaware
CRS	Congressional Research Service; Community Relations Service	D.C. Mass.	United States District Court, Massachusetts
		D.C. Md.	United States District Court, Maryland
CRT	Critical race theory	D.C.N.D.Cal.	United States District Court, Northern District, California
CSA	Community Services Administration		
CSAP	Center for Substance Abuse Prevention	D.C.N.Y.	United States District Court, New York
CSAT	Center for Substance Abuse Treatment	D.C.Pa.	United States District Court, Pennsylvania
CSC	Civil Service Commission	DCS	Deputy Chiefs of Staff
CSCE	Conference on Security and Cooperation in Europe	DCZ	District of the Canal Zone
		DDT	Dichlorodiphenyltricloro-ethane
CSG	Council of State Governments	DEA	Drug Enforcement Administration
CSO	Community Service Organization	Decl. Lond.	Declaration of London, February 26, 1909
CSP	Center for the Study of the Presidency	Dev. & B.	Devereux & Battle's North Carolina Reports
C-SPAN	Cable-Satellite Public Affairs Network	DFL	Minnesota Democratic-Farmer-Labor
CSRS	Cooperative State Research Service	DFTA	Department for the Aging
CSWPL	Center on Social Welfare Policy and Law	Dig. U.S. Practice in Intl. Law	Digest of U.S. Practice in International Law
CTA	Cum testamento annexo (with the will attached)	Dist. Ct.	D.C. United States District Court, District of Columbia
Ct. Ap. D.C.	Court of Appeals, District of Columbia		
Ct. App. No. Ireland	Court of Appeals, Northern Ireland	D.L.R.	Dominion Law Reports (Canada)
Ct. Cl.	Court of Claims, United States	DMCA	Digital Millennium Copyright Act
Ct. Crim. Apps.	Court of Criminal Appeals (England)	DNA	Deoxyribonucleic acid
		Dnase	Deoxyribonuclease
CTI	Consolidated taxable income	DNC	Democratic National Committee
Ct. of Sess., Scot.	Court of Sessions, Scotland	DOC	Department of Commerce
CU	Credit union	DOD	Department of Defense
CUNY	City University of New York	DODEA	Department of Defense Education Activity
Cush.	Cushing's Massachusetts Reports	Dodson	Dodson's Reports, English Admiralty Courts
CWA	Civil Works Administration; Clean Water Act	DOE	Department of Energy

DOER	Department of Employee Relations	ERA	Equal Rights Amendment
DOJ	Department of Justice	ERDC	Energy Research and Development Commission
DOL	Department of Labor	ERISA	Employee Retirement Income
DOMA	Defense of Marriage Act of 1996		Security Act of 1974
DOS	Disk operating system	ERS	Economic Research Service
DOT	Department of Transportation	ERTA	Economic Recovery Tax Act of 1981
DPT	Diphtheria, pertussis, and tetanus	ESA	Endangered Species Act of 1973
DRI	Defense Research Institute	ESF	Emergency support function; Economic Support Fund
DSAA	Defense Security Assistance Agency	ESRD	End-Stage Renal Disease Program
DUI	Driving under the influence; driving under intoxication	ETA	Employment and Training Administration
DVD	Digital versatile disc	ETS	Environmental tobacco smoke
DWI	Driving while intoxicated	et seq.	*Et sequentes* or *et sequentia*
EAHCA	Education for All Handicapped Children Act of 1975	EU	("and the following") European Union
EBT	Examination before trial	Euratom	European Atomic Energy
E.coli	Escherichia coli		Community
ECPA	Electronic Communications Privacy Act of 1986	Eur. Ct. H.R.	European Court of Human Rights
ECSC	Treaty of the European Coal and Steel Community	Ex.	English Exchequer Reports, Welsby, Hurlstone &
EDA	Economic Development Administration		Gordon
EDF	Environmental Defense Fund	Exch.	Exchequer Reports (Welsby, Hurlstone & Gordon)
E.D.N.Y.	Eastern District, New York	Ex Com	Executive Committee of the
EDP	Electronic data processing		National Security Council
E.D. Pa.	Eastern-District, Pennsylvania	Eximbank	Export-Import Bank of the United States
EDSC	Eastern District, South Carolina	F.	Federal Reporter
EDT	Eastern daylight time	F. 2d	Federal Reporter, Second Series
E.D. Va.	Eastern District, Virginia	FAA	Federal Aviation
EEC	European Economic Community; European Economic Community Treaty	FAAA	Administration; Federal Arbitration Act Federal Alcohol Administration Act
EEOC	Equal Employment Opportunity Commission	FACE	Freedom of Access to Clinic Entrances Act of 1994
EFF	Electronic Frontier Foundation	FACT	Feminist Anti-Censorship Task Force
EFT	Electronic funds transfer	FAIRA	Federal Agriculture
Eliz.	Queen Elizabeth (Great Britain)		Improvement and Reform Act of 1996
Em. App.	Temporary Emergency Court of Appeals	FAMLA	Family and Medical Leave Act of 1993
ENE	Early neutral evaluation	Fannie Mae	Federal National Mortgage
Eng. Rep.	English Reports		Association
EOP	Executive Office of the President	FAO	Food and Agriculture Organization of the
EPA	Environmental Protection Agency; Equal Pay Act of 1963	FAR	United Nations Federal Acquisition Regulations

FAS	Foreign Agricultural Service	FIP	Forestry Incentives Program
FBA	Federal Bar Association	FIRREA	Financial Institutions Reform, Recovery, and Enforcement Act of 1989
FBI	Federal Bureau of Investigation		
FCA	Farm Credit Administration	FISA	Foreign Intelligence Surveillance Act of 1978
F. Cas.	Federal Cases		
FCC	Federal Communications Commission	FISC	Foreign Intelligence Surveillance Court of Review
FCIA	Foreign Credit Insurance Association		
		FJC	Federal Judicial Center
FCIC	Federal Crop Insurance Corporation	FLSA	Fair Labor Standards Act
		FMC	Federal Maritime Commission
FCLAA	Federal Cigarette Labeling and Advertising Act	FMCS	Federal Mediation and Conciliation Service
FCRA	Fair Credit Reporting Act		
FCU	Federal credit unions	FmHA	Farmers Home Administration
FCUA	Federal Credit Union Act		
FCZ	Fishery Conservation Zone	FMLA	Family and Medical Leave Act of 1993
FDA	Food and Drug Administration	FNMA	Federal National Mortgage Association, "Fannie Mae"
FDIC	Federal Deposit Insurance Corporation		
		F.O.B.	Free on board
FDPC	Federal Data Processing Center	FOIA	Freedom of Information Act
		FOMC	Federal Open Market Committee
FEC	Federal Election Commission		
		FPA	Federal Power Act of 1935
FECA	Federal Election Campaign Act of 1971	FPC	Federal Power Commission
		FPMR	Federal Property Management Regulations
Fed. Cas.	Federal Cases		
FEHA	Fair Employment and Housing Act	FPRS	Federal Property Resources Service
FEHBA	Federal Employees Health Benefit Act	FR	Federal Register
		FRA	Federal Railroad Administration
FEMA	Federal Emergency Management Agency	FRB	Federal Reserve Board
FERC	Federal Energy Regulatory Commission	FRC	Federal Radio Commission
		F.R.D.	Federal Rules Decisions
FFB	Federal Financing Bank	FSA	Family Support Act
FFDC	Federal Food, Drug, and Cosmetics Act	FSB	Federal'naya Sluzhba Bezopasnosti (the Federal Security Service of Russia)
FGIS	Federal Grain Inspection Service		
		FSLIC	Federal Savings and Loan Insurance Corporation
FHA	Federal Housing Administration		
		FSQS	Food Safety and Quality Service
FHAA	Fair Housing Amendments Act of 1998		
		FSS	Federal Supply Service
FHWA	Federal Highway Administration	F. Supp.	Federal Supplement
		FTA	U.S.-Canada Free Trade Agreement of 1988
FIA	Federal Insurance Administration		
		FTC	Federal Trade Commission
FIC	Federal Information Centers; Federation of Insurance Counsel	FTCA	Federal Tort Claims Act
		FTS	Federal Telecommunications System
FICA	Federal Insurance Contributions Act	FTS2000	Federal Telecommunications System 2000
FIFRA	Federal Insecticide, Fungicide, and Rodenticide Act	FUCA	Federal Unemployment Compensation Act of 1988

FUTA	Federal Unemployment Tax Act	HBO	Home Box Office
FWPCA	Federal Water Pollution Control Act of 1948	HCFA	Health Care Financing Administration
FWS	Fish and Wildlife Service	H.Ct.	High Court
GAL	Guardian ad litem	HDS	Office of Human Development Services
GAO	General Accounting Office; Governmental Affairs Office	Hen. & M.	Hening & Munford's Virginia Reports
GAOR	General Assembly Official Records, United Nations	HEW	Department of Health, Education, and Welfare
GAAP	Generally accepted accounting principles	HFCA	Health Care Financing Administration
GA Res.	General Assembly Resolution (United Nations)	HGI	Handgun Control, Incorporated
GATT	General Agreement on Tariffs and Trade	HHS	Department of Health and Human Services
GCA	Gun Control Act	Hill	Hill's New York Reports
Gen. Cls. Comm.	General Claims Commission, United States and Panama; General Claims United States and Mexico	HIRE	Help through Industry Retraining and Employment
Geo. II	King George II (Great Britain)	HIV	Human immunodeficiency virus
Geo. III	King George III (Great Britain)	H.L.	House of Lords Cases (England)
GHB	Gamma-hydroxybutrate	H. Lords	House of Lords (England)
GI	Government Issue	HMO	Health Maintenance Organization
GID	General Intelligence Division	HNIS	Human Nutrition Information Service
GM	General Motors	Hong Kong L.R.	Hong Kong Law Reports
GNMA	Government National Mortgage Association, "Ginnie Mae"	How.	Howard's United States Supreme Court Reports
GNP	Gross national product	How. St. Trials	Howell's English State Trials
GOP	Grand Old Party (Republican Party)	HUAC	House Un-American Activities Committee
GOPAC	Grand Old Party Action Committee	HUD	Department of Housing and Urban Development
GPA	Office of Governmental and Public Affairs	Hudson, Internatl. Legis.	Manley Ottmer Hudson, ed., *International Legislation: A Collection of the Texts of Multipartite International Instruments of General Interest Beginning with the Covenant of the League of Nations* (1931)
GPO	Government Printing Office		
GRAS	Generally recognized as safe		
Gr. Br., Crim. Ct. App.	Great Britain, Court of Criminal Appeals		
GRNL	Gay Rights-National Lobby		
GSA	General Services Administration	Hudson, World Court Reps.	Manley Ottmer Hudson, ea., *World Court Reports* (1934–)
Hackworth	Green Haywood Hackworth, *Digest of International Law* (1940–1944)	Hun	Hun's New York Supreme Court Reports
Hay and Marriott	Great Britain. High Court of Admiralty, *Decisions in the High Court of Admiralty during the Time of Sir George Hay and of Sir James Marriott, Late Judges of That Court* (1801)	Hunt's Rept.	Bert L. Hunt, *Report of the American and Panamanian General Claims Arbitration* (1934)
		IAEA	International Atomic Energy Agency
		IALL	International Association of Law Libraries

IBA	International Bar Association	IRA	Individual retirement account; Irish Republican Army
IBM	International Business Machines	IRC	Internal Revenue Code
ICA	Interstate Commerce Act	IRCA	Immigration Reform and Control Act of 1986
ICBM	Intercontinental ballistic missile	IRS	Internal Revenue Service
ICC	Interstate Commerce Commission; International Criminal Court	ISO	Independent service organization
		ISP	Internet service provider
ICJ	International Court of Justice	ISSN	International Standard Serial Numbers
ICM	Institute for Court Management	ITA	International Trade Administration
IDEA	Individuals with Disabilities Education Act of 1975	ITI	Information Technology Integration
IDOP	International Dolphin Conservation Program	ITO	International Trade Organization
IEP	Individualized educational program	ITS	Information Technology Service
IFC	International Finance Corporation	ITT	International Telephone and Telegraph Corporation
IGRA	Indian Gaming Regulatory Act of 1988	ITU	International Telecommunication Union
IJA	Institute of Judicial Administration	IUD	Intrauterine device
IJC	International Joint Commission	IWC	International Whaling Commission
ILC	International Law Commission	IWW	Industrial Workers of the World
ILD	International Labor Defense	JAGC	Judge Advocate General's Corps
Ill. Dec.	Illinois Decisions		
ILO	International Labor Organization	JCS	Joint Chiefs of Staff
		JDL	Jewish Defense League
IMF	International Monetary Fund	JNOV	Judgment *non obstante veredicto* ("judgment nothing to recommend it" or "judgment notwithstanding the verdict")
INA	Immigration and Nationality Act		
IND	Investigational new drug		
INF Treaty	Intermediate-Range Nuclear Forces Treaty of 1987	JOBS	Jobs Opportunity and Basic Skills
INS	Immigration and Naturalization Service	John. Ch.	Johnson's New York Chancery Reports
INTELSAT	International Telecommunications Satellite Organization	Johns.	Johnson's Reports (New York)
Interpol	International Criminal Police Organization	JP	Justice of the peace
		K.B.	King's Bench Reports (England)
Int'l. Law Reps.	International Law Reports		
Intl. Legal Mats.	International Legal Materials	KFC	Kentucky Fried Chicken
IOC	International Olympic Committee	KGB	Komitet Gosudarstvennoi Bezopasnosti (the State Security Committee for countries in the former Soviet Union)
IPDC	International Program for the Development of Communication		
IPO	Intellectual Property Owners	KKK	Ku Klux Klan
IPP	Independent power producer	KMT	Kuomintang (Chinese, "national people's party")
IQ	Intelligence quotient		
I.R.	Irish Reports	LAD	Law Against Discrimination

LAPD	Los Angeles Police Department		II, 35 vols. [1876–1908]; Series III [1909–])
LC	Library of Congress	Mass.	Massachusetts Reports
LCHA	Longshoremen's and Harbor Workers Compensation Act of 1927	MCC	Metropolitan Correctional Center
LD50	Lethal dose 50	MCCA	Medicare Catastrophic Coverage Act of 1988
LDEF	Legal Defense and Education Fund (NOW)	MCH	Maternal and Child Health Bureau
LDF	Legal Defense Fund, Legal Defense and Educational Fund of the NAACP	MCRA	Medical Care Recovery Act of 1962
LEAA	Law Enforcement Assistance Administration	MDA	Medical Devices Amendments of 1976
L.Ed.	Lawyers' Edition Supreme Court Reports	Md. App.	Maryland, Appeal Cases
LI	Letter of interpretation	M.D. Ga.	Middle District, Georgia
LLC	Limited Liability Company	Mercy	Movement Ensuring the Right to Choose for Yourself
LLP	Limited Liability Partnership	Metc.	Metcalf's Massachusetts Reports
LMSA	Labor-Management Services Administration	MFDP	Mississippi Freedom Democratic party
LNTS	League of Nations Treaty Series	MGT	Management
Lofft's Rep.	Lofft's English King's Bench Reports	MHSS	Military Health Services System
L.R.	Law Reports (English)	Miller	David Hunter Miller, ea., *Treaties and Other International Acts of the United States of America* (1931–1948)
LSAC	Law School Admission Council		
LSAS	Law School Admission Service		
LSAT	Law School Aptitude Test	Minn.	Minnesota Reports
LSC	Legal Services Corporation; Legal Services for Children	MINS	Minors in need of supervision
		MIRV	Multiple independently targetable reentry vehicle
LSD	Lysergic acid diethylamide		
LSDAS	Law School Data Assembly Service	MIRVed ICBM	Multiple independently targetable reentry vehicled intercontinental ballistic missile
LTBT	Limited Test Ban Treaty		
LTC	Long Term Care		
MAD	Mutual assured destruction	Misc.	Miscellaneous Reports, New York
MADD	Mothers against Drunk Driving	Mixed Claims Comm., Report of Decs	Mixed Claims Commission, United States and Germany, Report of Decisions
MALDEF	Mexican American Legal Defense and Educational Fund		
Malloy	William M. Malloy, ed., *Treaties, Conventions International Acts, Protocols, and Agreements between the United States of America and Other Powers* (1910–1938)	M.J.	Military Justice Reporter
		MLAP	Migrant Legal Action Program
		MLB	Major League Baseball
		MLDP	Mississippi Loyalist Democratic Party
		MMI	Moslem Mosque, Incorporated
Martens	Georg Friedrich von Martens, ea., *Noveau recueil général de traités et autres actes relatifs aux rapports de droit international* (Series I, 20 vols. [1843–1875]; Series	MMPA	Marine Mammal Protection Act of 1972
		Mo.	Missouri Reports
		MOD	Masters of Deception
		Mod.	Modern Reports, English King's Bench, etc.

Moore, Dig. Intl. Law	John Bassett Moore, *A Digest of International Law,* 8 vols. (1906)	NARAL	National Abortion and Reproductive Rights Action League
Moore, Intl. Arbs.	John Bassett Moore, *History and Digest of the International Arbitrations to Which United States Has Been a Party,* 6 vols. (1898)	NARF	Native American Rights Fund
		NARS	National Archives and Record Service
		NASA	National Aeronautics and Space Administration
Morison	William Maxwell Morison, *The Scots Revised Report: Morison's Dictionary of Decisions* (1908–09)	NASD	National Association of Securities Dealers
		NATO	North Atlantic Treaty Organization
M.P.	Member of Parliament	NAVINFO	Navy Information Offices
MP3	MPEG Audio Layer 3	NAWSA	National American Woman's Suffrage Association
MPAA	Motion Picture Association of America	NBA	National Bar Association; National Basketball Association
MPAS	Michigan Protection and Advocacy Service		
MPEG	Motion Picture Experts Group	NBC	National Broadcasting Company
mpg	Miles per gallon	NBLSA	National Black Law Student Association
MPPDA	Motion Picture Producers and Distributors of America	NBS	National Bureau of Standards
MPRSA	Marine Protection, Research, and Sanctuaries Act of 1972	NCA	Noise Control Act; National Command Authorities
		NCAA	National Collegiate Athletic Association
M.R.	Master of the Rolls		
MS-DOS	Microsoft Disk Operating System	NCAC	National Coalition against Censorship
MSHA	Mine Safety and Health Administration	NCCB	National Consumer Cooperative Bank
MSPB	Merit Systems Protection Board	NCE	Northwest Community Exchange
MSSA	Military Selective Service Act	NCF	National Chamber Foundation
N/A	Not Available		
NAACP	National Association for the Advancement of Colored People	NCIP	National Crime Insurance Program
		NCJA	National Criminal Justice Association
NAAQS	National Ambient Air Quality Standards	NCLB	National Civil Liberties Bureau
NAB	National Association of Broadcasters	NCP	National contingency plan
NABSW	National Association of Black Social Workers	NCSC	National Center for State Courts
NACDL	National Association of Criminal Defense Lawyers	NCUA	National Credit Union Administration
NAFTA	North American Free Trade Agreement of 1993	NDA	New drug application
		N.D. Ill.	Northern District, Illinois
NAGHSR	National Association of Governors' Highway Safety Representatives	NDU	National Defense University
		N.D. Wash.	Northern District, Washington
NALA	National Association of Legal Assistants	N.E.	North Eastern Reporter
		N.E. 2d	North Eastern Reporter, Second Series
NAM	National Association of Manufacturers	NEA	National Endowment for the Arts; National Education Association
NAR	National Association of Realtors		

NEH	National Endowment for the Humanities	NORML	National Organization for the Reform of Marijuana Laws
NEPA	National Environmental Protection Act; National Endowment Policy Act	NOW	National Organization for Women
NET Act	No Electronic Theft Act	NOW LDEF	National Organization for Women Legal Defense and Education Fund
NFIB	National Federation of Independent Businesses		
NFIP	National Flood Insurance Program	NOW/PAC	National Organization for Women Political Action Committee
NFL	National Football League		
NFPA	National Federation of Paralegal Associations	NPDES	National Pollutant Discharge Elimination System
NGLTF	National Gay and Lesbian Task Force	NPL	National priorities list
		NPR	National Public Radio
NHL	National Hockey League	NPT	Nuclear Non-Proliferation Treaty of 1970
NHRA	Nursing Home Reform Act of 1987		
NHTSA	National Highway Traffic Safety Administration	NRA	National Rifle Association; National Recovery Act
Nielsen's Rept.	Frederick Kenelm Nielsen, *American and British Claims Arbitration under the Special Agreement Concluded between the United States and Great Britain, August 18, 1910* (1926)	NRC	Nuclear Regulatory Commission
		NRLC	National Right to Life Committee
		NRTA	National Retired Teachers Association
		NSA	National Security Agency
		NSC	National Security Council
NIEO	New International Economic Order	NSCLC	National Senior Citizens Law Center
NIGC	National Indian Gaming Commission	NSF	National Science Foundation
		NSFNET	National Science Foundation Network
NIH	National Institutes of Health	NSI	Network Solutions, Inc.
NIJ	National Institute of Justice	NTIA	National Telecommunications and Information Administration
NIRA	National Industrial Recovery Act of 1933; National Industrial Recovery Administration		
NIST	National Institute of Standards and Technology	NTID	National Technical Institute for the Deaf
N.J.	New Jersey Reports	NTIS	National Technical Information Service
N.J. Super.	New Jersey Superior Court Reports	NTS	Naval Telecommunications System
NLEA	Nutrition Labeling and Education Act of 1990	NTSB	National Transportation Safety Board
NLRA	National Labor Relations Act	NVRA	National Voter Registration Act
NLRB	National Labor Relations Board		
NMFS	National Marine Fisheries Service	N.W.	North Western Reporter
		N.W. 2d	North Western Reporter, Second Series
No.	Number	NWSA	National Woman Suffrage Association
NOAA	National Oceanic and Atmospheric Administration	N.Y.	New York Court of Appeals Reports
NOC	National Olympic Committee	N.Y. 2d	New York Court of Appeals Reports, Second Series
NOI	Nation of Islam	N.Y.S.	New York Supplement Reporter
NOL	Net operating loss		

N.Y.S. 2d	New York Supplement Reporter, Second Series	OPIC	Overseas Private Investment Corporation
NYSE	New York Stock Exchange	Ops. Atts. Gen.	Opinions of the Attorneys-General of the United States
NYSLA	New York State Liquor Authority	Ops. Comms.	Opinions of the Commissioners
N.Y. Sup.	New York Supreme Court Reports	OPSP	Office of Product Standards Policy
NYU	New York University	O.R.	Ontario Reports
OAAU	Organization of Afro American Unity	OR	Official Records
OAP	Office of Administrative Procedure	OSHA	Occupational Safety and Health Act
OAS	Organization of American States	OSHRC	Occupational Safety and Health Review Commission
OASDI	Old-age, Survivors, and Disability Insurance Benefits	OSM	Office of Surface Mining
		OSS	Office of Strategic Services
OASHDS	Office of the Assistant Secretary for Human Development Services	OST	Office of the Secretary
		OT	Office of Transportation
		OTA	Office of Technology Assessment
OCC	Office of Comptroller of the Currency	OTC	Over-the-counter
OCED	Office of Comprehensive Employment Development	OTS	Office of Thrift Supervisors
OCHAMPUS	Office of Civilian Health and Medical Program of the Uniformed Services	OUI	Operating under the influence
		OVCI	Offshore Voluntary Compliance Initiative
OCSE	Office of Child Support Enforcement	OWBPA	Older Workers Benefit Protection Act
OEA	Organización de los Estados Americanos	OWRT	Office of Water Research and Technology
OEM	Original Equipment Manufacturer	P.	Pacific Reporter
		P. 2d	Pacific Reporter, Second Series
OFCCP	Office of Federal Contract Compliance Programs	PAC	Political action committee
OFPP	Office of Federal Procurement Policy	Pa. Oyer and Terminer	Pennsylvania Oyer and Terminer Reports
OIC	Office of the Independent Counsel	PATCO	Professional Air Traffic Controllers Organization
OICD	Office of International Cooperation and Development	PBGC	Pension Benefit Guaranty Corporation
OIG	Office of the Inspector General	PBS	Public Broadcasting Service; Public Buildings Service
OJARS	Office of Justice Assistance, Research, and Statistics	P.C.	Privy Council (English Law Reports)
OMB	Office of Management and Budget	PC	Personal computer; politically correct
OMPC	Office of Management, Planning, and Communications	PCBs	Polychlorinated biphenyls
		PCIJ	Permanent Court of International Justice Series A-Judgments and Orders (1922–30)
ONP	Office of National Programs		Series B-Advisory Opinions (1922–30)
OPD	Office of Policy Development		Series A/B-Judgments, Orders, and Advisory Opinions (1931–40)
OPEC	Organization of Petroleum Exporting Countries		

PCIJ (cont'd.)	Series C-Pleadings, Oral Statements, and Documents relating to Judgments and Advisory Opinions (1923–42)	PNET	Peaceful Nuclear Explosions Treaty
		PONY	Prostitutes of New York
		POW-MIA	Prisoner of war-missing in action
	Series D-Acts and Documents concerning the Organization of the World Court (1922 –47)	Pratt	Frederic Thomas Pratt, *Law of Contraband of War, with a Selection of Cases from Papers of the Right Honourable Sir George Lee* (1856)
	Series E-Annual Reports (1925–45)		
PCP	Phencyclidine	PRIDE	Prostitution to Independence, Dignity, and Equality
P.D.	Probate Division, English Law Reports (1876–1890)	Proc.	Proceedings
PDA	Pregnancy Discrimination Act of 1978	PRP	Potentially responsible party
		PSRO	Professional Standards Review Organization
PD & R	Policy Development and Research	PTO	Patents and Trademark Office
Pepco	Potomac Electric Power Company	PURPA	Public Utilities Regulatory Policies Act
Perm. Ct. of Arb.	Permanent Court of Arbitration	PUSH	People United to Serve Humanity
PES	Post-Enumeration Survey		
Pet.	Peters' United States Supreme Court Reports	PUSH-Excel	PUSH for Excellence
		PWA	Public Works Administration
PETA	People for the Ethical Treatment of Animals	PWSA	Ports and Waterways Safety Act of 1972
PGA	Professional Golfers Association	Q.B.	Queen's Bench (England)
PGM	Program	QTIP	Qualified Terminable Interest Property
PHA	Public Housing Agency		
Phila. Ct. of Oyer and Terminer	Philadelphia Court of Oyer and Terminer	Ralston's Rept.	Jackson Harvey Ralston, ed., *Venezuelan Arbitrations of 1903* (1904)
PhRMA	Pharmaceutical Research and Manufacturers of America	RC	Regional Commissioner
PHS	Public Health Service	RCRA	Resource Conservation and Recovery Act
PIC	Private Industry Council	RCWP	Rural Clean Water Program
PICJ	Permanent International Court of Justice	RDA	Rural Development Administration
Pick.	Pickering's Massachusetts Reports	REA	Rural Electrification Administration
PIK	Payment in Kind		
PINS	Persons in need of supervision	Rec. des Decs. des Trib. Arb. Mixtes	G. Gidel, ed., *Recueil des décisions des tribunaux arbitraux mixtes, institués par les traités de paix* (1922–30)
PIRG	Public Interest Research Group		
P.L.	Public Laws		
PLAN	Pro-Life Action Network	Redmond	Vol. 3 of Charles I. Bevans, *Treaties and Other International Agreements of the United States of America, 1776–1949* (compiled by C. F. Redmond) (1969)
PLC	Plaintiffs' Legal Committee		
PLE	Product liability expenses		
PLI	Practicing Law Institute		
PLL	Product liability loss		
PLLP	Professional Limited Liability Partnership		
PLO	Palestine Liberation Organization	RESPA	Real Estate Settlement Procedure Act of 1974
PLRA	Prison Litigation Reform Act of 1995	RFC	Reconstruction Finance Corporation

RFRA	Religious Freedom Restoration Act of 1993	SCCC	South Central Correctional Center
RIAA	Recording Industry Association of America	SCLC	Southern Christian Leadership Conference
RICO	Racketeer Influenced and Corrupt Organizations	Scott's Repts.	James Brown Scott, ed., *The Hague Court Reports*, 2 vols. (1916–32)
RLUIPA	Religious Land Use and Institutionalized Persons Act	SCS	Soil Conservation Service; Social Conservative Service
RNC	Republican National Committee	SCSEP	Senior Community Service Employment Program
Roscoe	Edward Stanley Roscoe, ed., *Reports of Prize Cases Determined in the High Court Admiralty before the Lords Commissioners of Appeals in Prize Causes and before the judicial Committee of the Privy Council from 1745 to 1859* (1905)	S.Ct.	Supreme Court Reporter
		S.D. Cal.	Southern District, California
		S.D. Fla.	Southern District, Florida
		S.D. Ga.	Southern District, Georgia
		SDI	Strategic Defense Initiative
		S.D. Me.	Southern District, Maine
		S.D.N.Y.	Southern District, New York
		SDS	Students for a Democratic Society
ROTC	Reserve Officers' Training Corps	S.E.	South Eastern Reporter
RPP	Representative Payee Program	S.E. 2d	South Eastern Reporter, Second Series
R.S.	Revised Statutes	SEA	Science and Education Administration
RTC	Resolution Trust Corp.		
RUDs	Reservations, understandings, and declarations	SEATO	Southeast Asia Treaty Organization
		SEC	Securities and Exchange Commission
Ryan White CARE Act	Ryan White Comprehensive AIDS Research Emergency Act of 1990	Sec.	Section
		SEEK	Search for Elevation, Education and Knowledge
SAC	Strategic Air Command		
SACB	Subversive Activities Control Board	SEOO	State Economic Opportunity Office
SADD	Students against Drunk Driving	SEP	Simplified employee pension plan
SAF	Student Activities Fund	Ser.	Series
SAIF	Savings Association Insurance Fund	Sess.	Session
		SGLI	Servicemen's Group Life Insurance
SALT	Strategic Arms Limitation Talks	SIP	State implementation plan
SALT I	Strategic Arms Limitation Talks of 1969–72	SLA	Symbionese Liberation Army
		SLAPPs	Strategic Lawsuits Against Public Participation
SAMHSA	Substance Abuse and Mental Health Services Administration	SLBM	Submarine-launched ballistic missile
Sandf.	Sandford's New York Superior Court Reports	SNCC	Student Nonviolent Coordinating Committee
S and L	Savings and loan	So.	Southern Reporter
SARA	Superfund Amendment and Reauthorization Act	So. 2d	Southern Reporter, Second Series
SAT	Scholastic Aptitude Test	SPA	Software Publisher's Association
Sawy.	Sawyer's United States Circuit Court Reports	Spec. Sess.	Special Session
		SPLC	Southern Poverty Law Center
SBA	Small Business Administration	SRA	Sentencing Reform Act of 1984
SBI	Small Business Institute		

SS	*Schutzstaffel* (German, "Protection Echelon")	TVA	Tennessee Valley Authority
		TWA	Trans World Airlines
SSA	Social Security Administration	UAW	United Auto Workers; United Automobile, Aerospace, and Agricultural Implements Workers of America
SSI	Supplemental Security Income		
START I	Strategic Arms Reduction Treaty of 1991		
START II	Strategic Arms Reduction Treaty of 1993	U.C.C.	Uniform Commercial Code; Universal Copyright Convention
Stat.	United States Statutes at Large	U.C.C.C.	Uniform Consumer Credit Code
STS	Space Transportation Systems	UCCJA	Uniform Child Custody Jurisdiction Act
St. Tr.	State Trials, English	UCMJ	Uniform Code of Military Justice
STURAA	Surface Transportation and Uniform Relocation Assistance Act of 1987	UCPP	Urban Crime Prevention Program
Sup. Ct. of Justice, Mexico	Supreme Court of Justice, Mexico	UCS	United Counseling Service
		UDC	United Daughters of the Confederacy
Supp.	Supplement		
S.W.	South Western Reporter	UFW	United Farm Workers
S.W. 2d	South Western Reporter, Second Series	UHF	Ultrahigh frequency
		UIFSA	Uniform Interstate Family Support Act
SWAPO	South-West Africa People's Organization	UIS	Unemployment Insurance Service
SWAT	Special Weapons and Tactics		
SWP	Socialist Workers Party	UMDA	Uniform Marriage and Divorce Act
TDP	Trade and Development Program	UMTA	Urban Mass Transportation Administration
Tex. Sup.	Texas Supreme Court Reports		
THAAD	Theater High-Altitude Area Defense System	U.N.	United Nations
		UNCITRAL	United Nations Commission on International Trade Law
THC	Tetrahydrocannabinol		
TI	Tobacco Institute		
TIA	Trust Indenture Act of 1939	UNCTAD	United Nations Conference on Trade and Development
TIAS	Treaties and Other International Acts Series (United States)		
		UN Doc.	United Nations Documents
TNT	Trinitrotoluene	UNDP	United Nations Development Program
TOP	Targeted Outreach Program		
TPUS	Transportation and Public Utilities Service	UNEF	United Nations Emergency Force
TQM	Total Quality Management	UNESCO	United Nations Educational, Scientific, and Cultural Organization
Tripartite Claims Comm., Decs. and Ops.	Tripartite Claims Commission (United States, Austria, and Hungary), Decisions and Opinions		
		UNICEF	United Nations Children's Fund (formerly United Nations International Children's Emergency Fund)
TRI-TAC	Joint Tactical Communications		
TRO	Temporary restraining order		
TS	Treaty Series, United States	UNIDO	United Nations Industrial and Development Organization
TSCA	Toxic Substance Control Act		
TSDs	Transporters, storers, and disposers		
		Unif. L. Ann.	Uniform Laws Annotated
TSU	Texas Southern University	UN Repts. Intl. Arb. Awards	United Nations Reports of International Arbitral Awards
TTBT	Threshold Test Ban Treaty		
TV	Television		

UNTS	United Nations Treaty Series	VIN	Vehicle identification number
UPI	United Press International		
URESA	Uniform Reciprocal Enforcement of Support Act	VISTA	Volunteers in Service to America
		VJRA	Veterans Judicial Review Act of 1988
U.S.	United States Reports		
U.S.A.	United States of America	V.L.A.	Volunteer Lawyers for the Arts
USAF	United States Air Force		
USA PATRIOT Act	Uniting and Strengthening America by Providing Appropriate Tools Required to Intercept and Obstruct Terrorism Act	VMI	Virginia Military Institute
		VMLI	Veterans Mortgage Life Insurance
		VOCAL	Victims of Child Abuse Laws
		VRA	Voting Rights Act
U.S. App. D.C.	United States Court of Appeals for the District of Columbia	WAC	Women's Army Corps
		Wall.	Wallace's United States Supreme Court Reports
U.S.C.	United States Code; University of Southern California	Wash. 2d	Washington Reports, Second Series
		WAVES	Women Accepted for Volunteer Service
U.S.C.A.	United States Code Annotated		
		WCTU	Women's Christian Temperance Union
U.S.C.C.A.N.	United States Code Congressional and Administrative News	W.D. Wash.	Western District, Washington
		W.D. Wis.	Western District, Wisconsin
USCMA	United States Court of Military Appeals	WEAL	*West's Encyclopedia of American Law*, Women's Equity Action League
USDA	U.S. Department of Agriculture		
USES	United States Employment Service	Wend.	Wendell's New York Reports
		WFSE	Washington Federation of State Employees
USF	U.S. Forestry Service		
USFA	United States Fire Administration	Wheat.	Wheaton's United States Supreme Court Reports
USGA	United States Golf Association	Wheel. Cr. Cases	Wheeler's New York Criminal Cases
USICA	International Communication Agency, United States	WHISPER	Women Hurt in Systems of Prostitution Engaged in Revolt
USMS	U.S. Marshals Service	Whiteman	Marjorie Millace Whiteman, *Digest of International Law*, 15 vols. (1963–73)
USOC	U.S. Olympic Committee		
USSC	U.S. Sentencing Commission		
USSG	United States Sentencing Guidelines	WHO	World Health Organization
		WIC	Women, Infants, and Children program
U.S.S.R.	Union of Soviet Socialist Republics	Will. and Mar.	King William and Queen Mary (Great Britain)
UST	United States Treaties		
USTS	United States Travel Service	WIN	WESTLAW Is Natural; Whip Inflation Now; Work Incentive Program
v.	*Versus*		
VA	Veterans Administration		
VAR	Veterans Affairs and Rehabilitation Commission	WIPO	World Intellectual Property Organization
		WIU	Workers' Industrial Union
VAWA	Violence against Women Act	W.L.R.	Weekly Law Reports, England
VFW	Veterans of Foreign Wars		
VGLI	Veterans Group Life Insurance	WPA	Works Progress Administration
Vict.	Queen Victoria (Great Britain)	WPPDA	Welfare and Pension Plans Disclosure Act

WTO	World Trade Organization	YMCA	Young Men's Christian Association
WWI	World War I		
WWII	World War II	YWCA	Young Women's Christian Association
Yates Sel. Cas.	Yates's New York Select Cases		